CREDIT RISK FRONTIERS

CREDIT RISK FRONTIERS

Subprime Crisis, Pricing and Hedging, CVA, MBS, Ratings, and Liquidity

Tomasz R. Bielecki, Damiano Brigo, and Frédéric Patras

BLOOMBERG PRESS

An Imprint of

⟨W⟩WILEY

Library of Congress Cataloging-in-Publication Data:

Bielecki, Tomasz R., 1955–
    Credit risk frontiers : subprime crisis, pricing and hedging, CVA, MBS, ratings, and liquidity / Tomasz R. Bielecki, Damiano Brigo, and Frédéric Patras.
        p. cm.
    Includes index.
    ISBN 978-1-57660-358-1 (hardback); ISBN 978-0-47087-923 (ebk); ISBN 978-1-11800-382-4 (ebk);
    ISBN 978-1-11800-383-1 (ebk)
    1. Credit derivatives—United States.   2. Global financial crisis, 2008–2009.   I. Brigo, Damiano, 1966–
II. Patras, Frédéric.   III. Title.
    HG6024.U6B54 2011
    332.64'57—dc22

                                                                                                    2010045236

10 9 8 7 6 5 4 3 2 1

Contents

Foreword

The current economic environment, with its unprecedented global financial crisis and slow resolution, has stimulated a wealth of innovative and constructive solutions in credit risk modeling and credit derivatives in particular. While it is true that this volume includes some of the more important research of the past year, significantly, I credit the editors for having facilitated a heightened quality within the individual contributions.

Importantly, chapters are split with a good balance of the theoretical versus the practical. Especially since 2007, credit markets have extraordinarily stressed both theoretical frameworks and empirical calibrations.

Similarly, and refreshingly, contributing authors are evenly split between academic versus practitioners from industry. For example, different contributions on collateralized debt obligations (CDOs) illustrate the diversity.

Parenthetically, I have been continually amazed these past two years to see that new CDO research has been the fastest growing category of research posted on DefaultRisk.com. This is quite ironic because the new issuance of CDOs has collapsed to a small fraction of 2007 levels.

I feel this volume of research is explained by not only the existing/troubling inventory of CDOs that must be managed, but also because CDOs—as a structure— offer a defined microcosm of the larger/general credit portfolio.

There are gratifyingly few redundancies across the contributing authors. Of course, it is beneficial to have a good diversity of views brought from different perspectives. For example, the different collateralized loan obligation (CLO) and residential mortgage-backed security (RMBS) chapters offer complementary discussions.

By contrast, it is not at all surprising that several contributions address the ever more liquid credit default swap (CDS) market, their options, and their liquidity. Other important and very timely contributions concern counterparty risk and credit valuation adjustment (CVA), which are here addressed in five chapters, and hybrid modeling of credit and equity, which is addressed in a novel way.

These are just a few examples of the innovation and originality in a single volume that has, among other merits, the courage to deal in a single source with several urgent topics such as the subprime crisis, pricing and hedging of credit risk, CVA, CDO, CLO, MBS, ratings, and liquidity.

Finally, this volume would not have been possible without the diligent work this past year from many people too numerous to list. Beyond the editors and contributing authors, we are grateful to all the conference attendees and panel members in September 2009 at the Université de Nice Sophia Antipolis. The interaction was spirited and the comments were invaluable. Enjoy.

GREG M. GUPTON
May 2010
DefaultRisk.com
Author of the CreditMetrics Technical Document

CREDIT RISK FRONTIERS

Introduction

The recent decade has witnessed a rapid development of more and more advanced quantitative methodologies for modeling, valuation, and risk management of credit risk, with focus on credit derivatives that constitute the vast majority of credit markets. In part, this rapid development was a response of academics and practitioners to the demands of trading and risk managing in the rapidly growing market of more and more complex credit derivative products. Even basic credit derivatives such as credit default swaps (CDSs) have witnessed considerable growth, reaching a notional value of US$45 trillion by the end of 2007, although notional amounts fell during 2008 to $38.6 trillion.[1] More complex credit derivatives, such as collateralized debt obligations (CDOs), featured a global issuance of $157.8 billion in 2004, reaching $481 billion in 2007, although in 2009 this has gone down to $4.3 billion.[2]

The size and complexity of credit markets in general, and credit derivatives markets in particular, undoubtedly posed a challenge for (quantitative) modelers and for market practitioners. The recent turmoil in the credit markets can be attributed to many factors, but one of the factors is probably the fact that in many respects the challenge has not been properly addressed.

This volume studies aspects of modeling and analysis of credit risk that, in our opinion, have not been adequately understood in the past. This is immediately evident also from the book subtitle, in that counterparty risk, mortgage-backed securities (MBSs), liquidity modeling, ratings, and in general pricing and hedging of complex credit derivatives are all among the areas that have not been fully or adequately addressed.

An important and original feature of this book is that it gathers contributions from practitioners and academics in an equilibrated way. Whereas the practitioners' contributions are deeply grounded in concrete experience of markets and products, the contributing academics are often involved in consulting and similar activities and have therefore a real empirical knowledge of financial products as well.

We indeed found it essential, when conceiving the volume, to keep in mind two guiding principles that, according to us, have to structure the research and practice in credit risk and, more generally, in modern finance. First, research has to be rooted in experience and rely on the knowledge of the empirical behavior of markets. Losing sight of experience or disconnecting the sophisticated mathematics of modern financial theories from the day-to-day practice may be dangerous for obvious reasons, besides compromising the necessary dialogue between decision makers and

1

quantitative analysts. Second, a high level of technicality is required to deal with current credit markets. A naive approach that would not rely on cutting-edge research would simply be condemned to fail, at least as far as derivatives or tail distributions involved in risk management are concerned. We hope the present volume will contribute to making the difficult synthesis of these two requirements (rooting in experience, technical complexity) effective.

The volume contains expert opinion articles, survey articles, as well as articles featuring the cutting-edge research regarding these aspects. This is important, as we believe that once the dust settles after the recent credit crisis, the credit markets will be facing challenges that this research addresses, so the volume may contribute to improvement of the health of the postcrisis credit universe.

The volume is directed to senior management and quants in financial institutions, such as banks and hedge funds, but also to traders and academics. In particular, academics and students in need of strengthening their understanding of how complex mathematics can be effectively used in realistic financial settings can benefit from its reading.

The volume provides a coherent presentation of the recent advancements in theory and practice of credit risk analysis and management with emphasis on some specific topics that are relevant to the current state and to the future of credit markets. The presented research is high-level on all the involved sides: financial, mathematical, and computational. This is the only way, we believe, that modeling should be presented and discussed so as to be meaningful, constructive, and useful. In addition, readers will also benefit from quality survey articles regarding selected topics.

The present collection of articles is one of several analytical texts that have appeared in recent months as a reaction by the quantitative community to the financial crisis that exploded in 2008. We refer, for example, to Lipton and Rennie (2007), which appeared before the crisis, and Brigo, Pallavicini, and Torresetti (2010), reporting both pre- and postcrisis research. These two books are just two examples of the necessity for the quantitative community to assess its status quo vis-à-vis financial markets in general, and credit markets in particular.

The volume opens with two expert opinion articles reflecting on the role of quantitative modeling in the past and in the future, on how it did or how it did not contribute to the current credit crisis, on what lessons modeling should incorporate from the credit crunch crisis, and on whether modeling should still be relevant.

These opening chapters form the first part of the book and are followed by articles focusing on some specific issues and areas reaching toward the frontiers of credit risk modeling, valuation, and hedging.

The second and third parts are closely related, although we found it convenient to divide their contents into two separate groups. They both deal with credit derivatives. Part II focuses on general methods in multiname credit derivatives, namely derivative products that depend on more than one credit entity at the same time. This part is meant to deal with the usual key issues of multiname credit derivatives but using revisited approaches and analysis. The topics covered include a survey of multiname credit derivatives methods and approaches, methods to deal with heterogeneity and dynamic features, analysis of hedging behavior of models, filtering and information, and the modeling of options on credit derivatives.

The focus of the third part is more oriented toward products and more specifically toward asset-backed securities (ABSs) in which the analysis of cash flows presents specific difficulties that are not present in the familiar synthetic CDO framework— although we should point out that these contributions involve general ideas and techniques that are relevant for all asset classes in the field of credit. The first chapter of this part introduces the factor models, with a particular emphasis on the ABX indexes. Topics included in the other chapters are a modeling and analysis framework for collateralized loan obligations (CLOs), a valuation and risk analysis framework for residential mortgage-backed securities (RMBSs), together with a survey of postcrisis solutions to various issues such as interest rate modeling and the handling of numerical complexity.

The fourth part is devoted to the valuation of credit valuation adjustment (CVA) and counterparty risk in the current environment. It is well-known that counterparty risk was underestimated before the subprime crisis. This contributed heavily to the crisis when many financial institutions discovered billions of dollars' worth of counterparty exposures were at risk, either directly in case the counterparty would default, or indirectly through downgrades (the downgrades of monoline insurers come to mind). Since then, counterparty risk measurement has become a key issue and has attracted a lot of attention, both from the financial industry and from academia. The first chapter of this part settles the general framework of CVA valuation, including subtle mathematical features. Topics in this part include: models and mathematical tools for CVA on credit derivatives, from both the intensity and the structural points of view; CVA for bonds and swaps; accounting issues; and advanced features related to netted positions and margin agreements.

The fifth part is devoted to equity-to-credit modeling. The idea of unifying the universes of credit and equity into a single mathematical framework is an old dream of mathematical finance. The so-called Merton model, predicting defaults by viewing the stock market value of a listed firm as a call option on its assets with a threshold computed from its debt, offers a general strategy, but the corresponding numerical results are known to be unsatisfactory: hence the need for new models incorporating advanced features such as jumps or random volatility. The two chapters introduce such models and discuss the application domain of equity-to-credit modeling that runs from joint pricing of credit and equity to relative value analysis. One of the papers in the CVA part also deals with equity-to-credit modeling but with a focus on counterparty risk for equity payoffs.

The last "Miscellanea" part gathers various contributions on important topics. They include: liquidity risk (offering a detailed survey of the existing methodologies for liquidity modeling in credit default swaps), ratings (with the case study of constant proportion debt obligations [CPDOs]), modern Monte Carlo methods (with an emphasis on interacting particle systems), and a survey of the theory of risk contributions in credit risk management.

Notes

1. International Swap and Derivatives Association, "Market Survey Year-End 2008."
2. Securities Industry and Financial Markets Association, 2010. "Global CDO data" press release 2010-07-02.

References

Brigo, D., A. Pallavicini, and R. Torresetti. 2010. *Credit models and the crisis: A journey into CDOs, copulas, correlations and dynamic models.* Hoboken, NJ: John Wiley & Sons.

Lipton, A., and A. Rennie, eds. 2007. *Credit correlation—Life after copulas.* Singapore: World Scientific.

PART I

Expert Views

CHAPTER 1

Origins of the Crisis and Suggestions for Further Research

Jean-Pierre Lardy

JPLC

We review several of the factual failures that the 2008 subprime crisis has revealed and analyze the root causes for these. Credit rating, regulation, models, accounting, leverage, risk management, and other aspects are reviewed. In each case, we survey solutions proposed as well as suggest directions for further research.

1.1 Introduction

The many roots of the 2008 financial crisis have been well covered in several publications. The aim of this review is to provide a short list of the ones most frequently raised and in each case try to distill one important aspect of the problem, the current proposals, and, possibly, what could be a direction of research to better understand the issue. A lesson from past decades is certainly that crises are not easy to forecast in terms of timing and magnitude, and when they occur (we can only forecast that they *will* occur), it is not always easy to separate, to paraphrase a famous quote from financier J.P. Morgan,[1] what was wrong as a matter of judgment from what was wrong as a matter of principle. These same questions apply in today's modern finance of sophisticated markets, products, and models, with the additional complexity of separating, when something went wrong, a technical failure of the "machine" (or of the principles on which it is built) from a failure of the "user" (or its judgment). To use an analogy (I find it useful)—investing is like riding a bicycle, and there is always a trade-off between performance and risk and improvements from better machines or better driving.

After working 20 years in the financial markets, including roles at two investment banks in equity and credit derivatives,[2] I have witnessed several stages of their development. I was lucky enough to reach levels of responsibility giving me a view on how decisions are made, good and bad, individually or collectively. Being mostly in the "engines room" kept me in the front lines of crises and allowed me to see how things work in practice on investment banks' trading floors. Last, having been present at early stages of the developments of these markets helped me to keep a healthy sense of pragmatism about them: The following paragraphs are personal reflections on the drivers of the crisis.[3]

In the remainder of this article, the various topics are organized into three sections: actors and markets, methods and products, and finally a last section on global risk management. To use an analogy with transportation, the first section would be about geography and population preferences; the second section about engineering of roads, airplanes, railways, and so on; and the third section about the rules of the road, safety procedures, and so forth. The choice of these three sections helps to distinguish the different natures of the topics, but the topics are greatly interrelated and overlap the sections in several ways.

1.2 The Real Economy: Actors and Markets

In this section, I review the issues in the 2008 financial crisis that are more closely related to the natural needs and organization of the real economy. This may be where the most important roots of the crisis lie, but also where alternatives are not easy to propose or to achieve quickly, or even possible to do so, especially when it comes to human behavior.

1.2.1 Loan Origination

With regard to the subprime crisis, it's legitimate to start with loan origination. Although no one yet knows what the full extent of the damage will be, the gradual deterioration of U.S. retail loan quality standards over the years is a fact. The negative incentives of securitization markets (originate to distribute), the flaws (and fraud) on documentation and appraisal values, the political environment supportive to increase home ownership, the lack of intervention by federal regulatory authorities despite several local whistle-blower cases all played a role (Berner and Grow 2008). The irony is that the United States was by far the most advanced country in terms of retail credit scoring (FICO scores, etc.).

The new regulatory proposals will force loan originators to keep more "skin in the game," with a vertical slice of any securitization (not cherry-picking a part of the origination).[4] Further research could also explore what is the right balance between statistical credit scoring and proximity and human judgment, with all its diversity, and for which there is no substitute, in credit decisions.

1.2.2 Macroeconomic Imbalance

The increased Asian savings following the 1997 crisis, compounded with the surplus of China and oil-exporting countries, created a large supply of liquidity and a formidable demand for (apparently) high-quality fixed-income assets. Despite the large supply of notes and bonds from Western government deficits, the low-interest-rate environment fueled a demand for higher-yielding fixed-income assets. Wall Street engineered the products that met such demand, which was broadly characterized by a risk aversion for idiosyncratic risk (first-loss or nonrated products), but generally complacent for systemic risk, favoring highly rated products (especially AAA), albeit from complex structures and rating techniques.

Low interest rates also favored the emergence of the financial bubble in real estate prices, construction, and infrastructure, boosting growth and job creation—all welcomed by politicians and their communities.

The new regulatory proposals favor the creation of a systemic regulator[5] to monitor these imbalances, and to raise concerns with persuasive (yet nonbinding) powers.

Further research could now explore what anticyclical macro policies can be global, targeting all countries at once, to avoid diplomatic crises.[6]

1.2.3 Rating Agencies

Rating agencies regularly and successfully improved their methodologies to take advantage of the increase in computing power and the increased availability of financial and market data. The wider availability of external ratings became a key component of regulation with Basel II, increasing furthermore the need for ratings. The irony is that the rating agencies' worst failures relate to credit products that were, by design, built on credit ratings, such as collateralized debt obligations (CDOs) of mezzanine asset-backed securities (ABSs).

In fact, the rating agencies have been hurt by the consequences of the weak parts of their business models: Who pays obviously makes a difference, sophisticated quantitative methodologies should not be pushed beyond their limits, and critical human judgment must always remain (McCreevy 2009).

As concerns further research, one wonders whether perhaps ratings should incorporate some external or open-source elements (academics' and practitioners' contributions, etc.) to their methodologies or reports to keep pace with innovation and information (in particular for complex or new structures).

1.2.4 Hedge Funds

After the precedent of Long-Term Capital Management (LTCM) in 1998, there had been growing fears in the years before 2007 about the growth of the hedge fund industry, but hedge funds were not at the origin of the 2008 crisis (High-Level Group on Financial Supervision in the EU 2009). A few hedge funds failed (Amaranth, etc.), and many had to trigger gates, causing damage to their investors, but all of these were idiosyncratic events. Obviously, withdrawing excess liquidity from Bear Stearns or Lehman Brothers added to the runs on these banks, but hedge funds were no different in this respect than corporations or mutual funds, and they also withdrew excess liquidity from Goldman Sachs, Morgan Stanley, and others. The irony is that prime brokerage contracts are all about haircuts, independent amounts, stress tests, daily margining, and so on, designed to protect the banks from the hedge fund risk, and suddenly these contracts backfired against the banks' liquidity, as hedge funds were scared about the risk of their prime brokers and were left little choice (their deposits are not guaranteed like retail depositors' are). The other irony from the Lehman bankruptcy is that hedge funds active in derivatives ended up better than funds invested in cash securities (in particular in jurisdictions with no segregations of securities).

Regulators should enforce that hedge funds' play by the technical rules of the markets. Beyond that, encouraging through regulatory best practices for collateral handling seems the best direction in order to limit the systemic impact of hedge fund failure.[7]

1.2.5 Remunerations

For many thinkers, the remuneration of human capital is the main engine of progress.[8] It is also a source of excess and injustice. However, the irony is that Wall Street, in the language of economists, is one of a very few examples of Marxist industries, where the greatest share of added value is kept by workers, instead of the capitalists' "surplus-value." In this field, a delicate balance must be found: a better alignment of remuneration horizons in order not to give up-front rewards for long-term risks, while the virtue of division-level cash compensation budgets necessarily moderates payoffs and therefore the moral hazard that can be associated with corporate-wide stock options plans.

Further research should explore whether the remuneration problem is an extension of the shareholder versus bondholder governance issue (Billet, Mauer, and Zheng 2006). For example, should bondholders of highly levered entities have a vote in the top remunerations schemes?

1.2.6 Leverage

The social benefit of the financial system is to transform information into liquidity for the rest of the world: Assets that are illiquid but good risks are transformed by banks and markets into liquid liabilities (that are liquid assets for the rest of the world). Yet the 2008 crisis is also a consequence of an excessive leverage from banks and from the shadow banking system of banks' vehicles, money market funds, and hedge fund financing: Basel I created an incentive for banks to use off-balance-sheet vehicles for certain (apparently) low-risk assets; money market funds were also competing for the same assets with lower regulatory and capital constraints; and providing leverage to hedge funds is a highly collateralized lending and fee-generating business.

As banks' regulatory capital ratios are risk weighted and do not directly control leverage, the current discussions revolve around the accounting of a universally accepted leverage ratio (as is currently the case in the United States and Switzerland).

Further research could be conducted as to whether, for that purpose, full debt consolidation would be desirable, with the necessary accounting precaution to differentiate the part of consolidated debt that is associated with the minority interests in the equity (or minority debt).

1.3　The Financial Techniques: Products and Methods

In this section, I review the issues in the subprime crisis that are more related to the technical choices that have been made historically or more recently by the financial world to provide or facilitate its business. This may be the part where correcting mistakes is more a matter of time and experience. In financial markets, like everywhere else, progress is not linear, and knowledge is built on both successes and mistakes of prior periods.

1.3.1　Mathematics

Whether the representation of the real world by mathematics is adequate must partly involve the mathematicians' responsibility, especially as they indirectly expect to get a higher demand for their services. Initially, there is a virtuous circle where practitioners' rules of thumb can be rebuilt by more formal approaches that confirm one other and allow further innovations. After a while, innovations can go too far; naive assumptions taken for granted are no longer valid but no longer questioned; teachers and students place theory before practice; and so on. The irony is the parallel with rating agencies: a possible excess of sophistication that is not counterbalanced by experience.

There is ground for further research on what assumptions in financial mathematics should not be made by convenience. Shouldn't there be more academic refutations, counter-examples according to their consequences if they aren't verified?

1.3.2　Models

Models generally do not take well enough into account the potential for markets to deviate far from equilibrium, especially illiquid assets. In this case, third-party models based on reasonable assumptions (such as rating agency models) usually underestimated tail risks, which were envisioned only by internal stress tests, and the later ones were often judged as lacking plausibility. Proprietary models used for their own accounts generally performed better as long as they were nimble enough to allow the user's critical eye and the ability to continually correct deficiencies. It can be preferable to have several (albeit simpler) competing models that can bring different inputs to the same risk, instead of an ultrasophisticated monolithic approach that might miss the point. The irony is again a possible excess of sophistication, crowding out caution.

Further research: From the past experiences of macroeconomic and financial models, what is the right level of complexity not to be fooled by equations?[9]

1.3.3   Derivative Products

The social benefit of a derivative product should be the same as that of any other financial market instrument: allowing the transfer of risk and reward from a willing seller to a willing buyer, and providing information to the rest of the world about such transfer to help further decisions to invest, produce, consume, and so on. Even with turbulence, market risks are preferable to Knightian uncertainty (Knight 1921). The successful product innovation of derivatives growth is twofold: more customized products to fit transfer preferences, more vanilla products to build liquidity and market information. The industry must balance both aspects for success.

Derivative structures are also part of the tool kit used by services offered by the financial industry. It is in such services that possible conflicts of interest are more likely.[10] Last, although the management of counterparty and legal risks in derivative transactions has made tremendous progress, it is still an area of concern due to the size of these markets.

Further research: Exchanges and central clearing can improve liquid derivatives. What about public initiatives in favor of third-party collateral schemes[11] to address the broader needs of bilateral contracts?

1.3.4   Funding

Historically, funding was somewhat an exception to the risk management trend to push the responsibilities of all risks as closely as possible to their originators. Trading desks have usually few options in their funding policy. The bank or institution treasury takes care of long-term cash provided by certain activities on the bid, while funding the debits of other desks at the offer: Term funding is typically not the problem of trading desks.

Moreover, financial models are doing the same by discounting risk-free future cash flows at short-term interbank "XIBOR" rates and using swap rates for medium and long-term maturities.

The global crisis of 2008 demonstrated how funding risk can derail the normal arbitrage relationship between cash and related unfunded products: The short-term London Interbank Offered Rate (LIBOR) is a real loan (and can incorporate a funding risk premium), while swap rates, which are unfunded, can significantly miss the point of prices driven by fire sales or unwinds of riskless but cash-funded products.

Further research should quantify how a global systemic short-term funding squeeze translates not only into temporary negative interest margins, but also fire-sale transactions on the basis of cash capital as term funding of last resort, prompting negative long-term swap spreads, large negative basis on cash bonds versus credit default swaps (CDSs), and so on.

1.3.5 Short Sales

In the 1990s crises (both Latin America 1994 and Asia 1997), short sales were blamed for declining markets, and authorities hastily changed the rules of equity lending and borrowing and short sales (Malaysia, Taiwan, etc.). Even though G-7 countries' markets have constant surveillance against price manipulation (as they should), similar moves happened in G-7 countries in the autumn of 2008: This is more surprising but obviously understandable. At the same time, the worst daily market moves (such as limit down days) occur when the panic of long investors finds no bid from a lack of short interest. Only the shorts are buying during crashes. Also, markets with no ability to sell short are more prone to the creation of bubbles and subsequent disasters (real estate being a prime example). In summary, the irony is that past short sales are the most natural financial market contracyclical mechanism.

In the future, we could see an interesting duality from regulators toward short sales: While market regulators continue to actively regulate the appropriate execution and reporting of short sales, shouldn't newly established systemic regulators want to encourage more efficient frameworks for term borrowing? And why not encourage a sufficient amount of long-term short interest?

1.3.6 Accounting

Accrual accounting was at the root of many disasters where banks had negative economic net worth while remaining liquid in the 1980s: Accrual accounting can allow poor management for too long. Fair value accounting was brought in to provide investors (and management) financial results where the flexibility of accrual accounting is replaced by binding market levels (directly or indirectly through predefined valuation models). Bank managers should have known that markets can be brutal; the rules applying to individual traders were suddenly applied at an entirely different scale, leading to severe systemic consequences. In particular, illiquid markets with granular positions are inefficient, and the unwinding of one losing position creates further losses and further forced sales.

Proposals seem to go in the direction of a middle ground: a simplification of doubtful refinements around available for sale (AFS), held to maturity (HTM), and so on, with the possibility of some management judgment to overrule aberrant market prices (either too high or too low), whenever necessary to reflect a reality based on prudent accounting, and not misleading automatic rules (IASB Exposure Draft 2009).

Further research could explore whether taxes can also play a role to promote prudent accounting, and also potentially reduce the volatility of tax revenues.

1.3.7 Legal

The proper handling of legal risks is critical for the financial industry where so much of the business relates to promises of future performance. To limit the temptation to walk away from wrong past decisions requires a strong legal framework. The capital markets are also very technical, and precise rules of compliance must be followed in order to prevent manipulations, trading on inside information, false rumors, and so on. The markets' legal environment has made great progress on all of this. The crisis pointed out a few important problems: strictly national bankruptcy laws where assets can be frozen in one country against the legitimate rights of alien owners (collateral transfers and rehypothecation) (King 2009). Also, certain derivatives terminations or interpretations by the nondefaulting counterparts of Lehman Brothers are controversial and being disputed (Ng and Spector 2009).

Immediate proposals call for broader use of transaction documents where the legalities are closer to the economic intent, and based on electronic format (FpML) instead of paper.

However, further research should review whether an international bankruptcy standard could be enforceable for asset conveyance—for example, by transferring the disputed asset in a third-party jurisdiction.

1.4 The Global Risk Management Challenge

In this last section are grouped issues that relate to the organization and control of the interactions or the communication of information between all the moving parts. Although they do not belong—strictly speaking—to the previous two sections, they participate directly or have great influence indirectly on the real world itself and the corresponding financial techniques.

1.4.1 Regulation

Basel I allowed a better capitalization of the banking systems following the crisis of the 1980s. Basel II was designed to correct Basel I undifferentiated risk weights, which created incentives for banks to take assets off balance sheets. Basel II greatly reduced these regulatory arbitrages but potentially increased systemic risks with the reliance on external ratings and models. The irony is that the subprime crisis—and the collapse of many off-balance-sheet structures[12] inspired by Basel I—struck at the time Basel II was coming into effect.

It is critical that regulations anticipate and be aware of unintended consequences: Many of the toxic off-balance-sheet vehicles were a consequence of Basel I, and much of the demand for toxic highly rated fixed-income products was a consequence of Basel II.

Further research could explore how to address quickly regulatory weaknesses, which otherwise are systemic and procyclical by nature. A practical solution could be through fast-track specific additional disclosures required under Basel II's Pillar 3.

1.4.2 Diversification

If first-loss risk is the fear of the individual credit analyst, concentration risk is the fear for the portfolio manager. The search for diversification benefits, the avoidance of measurable concentration risks, and the continued innovation in the securitization and derivative markets were indirectly responsible for the globalization of certain risks. The last-named, combined with the increase of correlations, probably outweighed the diversification benefits. Yet many studies had previously shown how quickly adverse selection could cancel out diversification (Acharya, Hasan, and Saunders 2002). More simply, whatever the subordination, the most senior positions of a securitization will remain affected by the troubles of the vehicle, or of the entire asset class, and command a discount.

Further research should look into what share of any asset class corresponds to systemic, truly undiversifiable risk, which one way or another will remain in the global economy, and more systematically how this aggregate exposure compares with the net worth and leverage of the global economy.

1.4.3 Counterpart Risk

Certain institutions were weak in the management of counterpart risk, and in particular lacked judgment on the realization of wrong-way risks from monoline insurers. Counterpart risk management, from the internal governance of credit authorities, risk assessments, limits, collateral, and so on down to the stop-payment instructions, is operationally hugely complex. From there, counterpart credit valuation adjustment (CVA) is naturally a challenge.

It is also entangled with disputable accounting rules for the credit risk on your own liabilities—or debit valuation adjustment (DVA): Your liabilities are assets for others; if their losses are your gain, should poor investments be globally a zero-sum game? More importantly, isn't what matters to one's balance sheet the fair value of the liabilities (and assets) independently of the host (e.g., if they were the liabilities of any acceptable replacement party)?

The debate is not closed on the DVA (Dimon 2008), and current proposals go in the direction of central clearing for standardized products as a way to reduce circular counterparty risk from multiple entities with large portfolios among them (Duffie 2009).

Further research should be dedicated to the level and nature of interbank and regulatory communication channels that are needed to avoid the potential failure of a central counterpart (Tett 2009).

1.4.4 Risk Policy

Being overly restrictive in the risk tolerance of visible factors of risk can translate into more invisible risks being built into the system. Many institutions involuntarily replaced market risks with even more toxic credit, counterpart, or legal risks. In effect, the risk management policy has shifted some quarterly volatility to potentially more disastrous consequences. The lessons are very clear: Risk management must consider all risks, not only vanilla or easily measurable ones; and owners and managers must have tolerance for a level of acceptable profit and loss (P&L) volatility, fully understanding that under a certain level, it is simply unrealistic to be in the business.

Further research: Banks are not all the same, and have subtle differences of risk attitude, aversion, and tolerance, which depend on their internal culture, their history, the background of their managers, and so on. Shouldn't bank regulators' focus be directed to finding such weaknesses in relation to the previous items, which by definition are difficult to know from the inside?

1.4.5   Disclosure

The disclosure of financial data has generally kept pace with the possibility offered by information technology. The quantitative amount of text and data does not necessarily increase the information and its usefulness if standards are different, and with the difficulty to process it due to formats, access costs, lack of standards, extensive list of fields with missing or incorrect data, and so on. Pillar 3 of Basel II officially mandates the standards of quantity and quality of risk information that must be provided by banks. In practice, it is, however, still quite difficult to reconcile many of the data. Is more data always better?

Alternatively, more efforts should take place to determine the simplest and minimum data that could be reported by all firms (and possibly governments and public entities), with universal interpretation (and minimal possibility of manipulation), and yet capture the biggest density of information about risks and rewards.

1.5   Conclusion

Credit risk is at the core of the 2008 crisis: first, because of its retail U.S. subprime origins, and also more importantly in all the dimensions that allowed the contagion: lack of depth of secondary markets, interbank market freeze, credit crunch, and so on. Banks have clearly suffered from liquidity risk, overleverage, and possibly also lack of capital; regulations will be revised accordingly. The lessons are that models insufficiently took into account the potential for market prices to deviate far from equilibrium due to a simultaneous increase of risk premium and lack of cash-funded risk capital. At the same time, management and control of the visible main risk factors—which are quantified—must not indirectly favor more toxic risks that are less visible. Ultimately, the crisis demonstrated that sophistication can give a false illusion of risk management ability; extremely smart techniques can fail where commonsense caution may not.

Research must take up the challenge: The equations are not an end in themselves but merely tools for improving the merits of investing. Experience and judgment matter; otherwise, too much talent (young and old) is being wasted.

Notes

1. "Since we have not more power of knowing the future than any other men, we have made many mistakes (who has not during the past five years?), but our mistakes have been errors of judgment and not of principle."—J. P. Morgan Jr., excerpt from statement made before the U.S. Senate, 1933.

2. Managing Director, JPMorgan and Société Générale.
3. These are not reflective of views of former colleagues, clients of JPLC, or partners of the CRIS consortium.
4. The 5 percent rule of Article 122 of the EU Capital Requirement Directive (2009).
5. European Systemic Risk Board (ERSB) of the European Union.
6. It is legitimate to assume that systemic regulation is subordinated to diplomacy.
7. Such rules could also apply to limit the systemic risk of central clearing in periods of crisis.
8. Jean Bodin: *Il n'est de richesses que d'hommes.*
9. Improving bikes takes as much from driving experience as from pure engineering.
10. Derivative structures—with a dedicated derivative contractual setup—are opposed here to derivative products whose contractual setup is standardized.
11. Collateral of counterparts is held by an appropriate third party.
12. Structured investment vehicles (SIVs), conduits, and so on.

References

Acharya V., I. Hasan, and A. Saunders. 2002. Should banks be diversified? Evidence from individual bank loan portfolios. BIS Working Papers, September.

Berner, R., and B. Grow. 2008. They warned us about the mortgage crisis. *BusinessWeek*, October.

Billet, M., D. Mauer, and Y. Zhang. 2006. Stockholder and bondholder wealth effect of CEO incentives grants. University of Iowa, August.

Dimon, J. 2008. III—Fundamental causes and contributions to the financial crisis. JPMorgan Chase Annual Report, 14.

Duffie, D., and H. Zhu. 2009. Does a central clearing counterparty reduce counterparty risk? Stanford University, March.

The High-Level Group on Financial Supervision in the EU. 2009. Chaired by Jacques de Larosière. Report (February): 24.

International Accounting Standards Board (IASB) Exposure Draft. 2009. Financial instruments: Classification and measurement (July).

King, M. 2009. Global banks are global in life, but national in death, [by] Mervyn King, Governor of the Bank of England. *Financial Stability Report* (June).

Knight, F. H. 1921. *Risk, uncertainty and profit.* Boston: Houghton Mifflin.

McCreevy, C. 2009. The credit crisis—Looking ahead. Institute of European Affairs, February.

Ng, S., and M. Spector. 2009. The specter of Lehman shadows trade partners. *Wall Street Journal*, September 17.

Tett, G. 2009. Insight: The clearing house rules. *Financial Times*, November 5.

CHAPTER 2

Quantitative Finance: Friend or Foe?

Benjamin Herzog

Société Générale

Julien Turc

Société Générale

The subprime crisis of 2007 and the global recession that followed have gotten financial analysts thinking. Given the systemic nature of the crisis, the tools financial institutions used to develop their lending and investment banking units have been examined for weaknesses. Flaws attributed to financial engineering have been singled out on several occasions. This article starts by introducing a simple risk model that takes extreme risks into account and then runs an out-of-sample analysis of the years 2007–2008. We continue with an analysis of modern pricing models and lessons learned from the crisis.

Models do not accurately render the real behavior of financial markets. However, they do provide a common language that enables market players to interact. The simplicity of this language has allowed derivative markets to grow quickly across asset classes. When the assumptions underlying a model break down, the consequences are proportional to the model's success. It is therefore crucial to analyze the risks of using quantitative models both for pricing and hedging financial securities and for risk management.

- *Pricing and hedging.* Models can be used to evaluate the price of a security and the sensitivity of that price to market parameters, using both observable and nonobservable inputs. The nonobservable inputs are typically used to calibrate the model to market prices, while the observable ones can be used to find an optimal replication of a security's payoff using tradable assets. We discuss these models in the second part of this article.

- *Risk management.* Models are also used to analyze the impact of various market scenarios on the mark-to-market and risk profiles of single securities or portfolios of securities. The market scenarios are weighted by their probabilities in order to provide a synthetic view of a trading book's risks. Risk management models provide mark-to-market valuations and risk profiles, as well as frameworks to estimate the probability of the market scenarios. The first part of this article is dedicated to such value at risk (VaR) models and illustrated with the use of extreme value theory to analyze the first two years of the crisis (2007–2008) in and out of sample.

2.1   What Future for VaR Models?

Value at risk (VaR) models are popularly used to estimate regulatory capital for financial institutions. In a nutshell, they estimate the amount at risk on a given portfolio in worst-case scenarios. This is achieved in two steps:

1. Marginal and joint distributions are estimated for a series of observable and hidden parameters that determine the portfolio's dynamics.
2. A worst-case scenario is then simulated based on the previous joint distribution.

In the following we focus on the estimation of probability distributions for observable parameters, which has been at the center of recent criticism of VaR models. This chapter does not examine VaR from a portfolio standpoint, so we do not discuss netting effects and correlation models.

2.1.1   Introducing Extreme Value Distributions

Quantitative finance is sometimes criticized for an alleged excessive use of Gaussian distributions. Gaussian distributions are useful to describe business-as-usual situations, but perform poorly in cases of deviations—large or even moderate ones—from usual market equilibriums. Fortunately, one major field of quantitative finance is dedicated to modeling extreme risks. Extreme value theory provides tools to model financial risks for all types of deviations.

In particular, the extremal types theorem (see Fisher and Tippett 1928 and von Mises 1936) states that the maximum of a large pool of independent and identically distributed (i.i.d.) variables follows a specific well-known probability law, the generalized extreme value (GEV) law. This makes GEV the tool of choice to model extreme movements in financial markets.

The extreme value distribution provides one parameter to locate the peak of the distribution and another to measure the size of possible deviations from this peak. GEV differs from Gaussian distribution thanks to its third parameter, which generates

FIGURE 2.1 Generalized Extreme Value Distribution Allows Modeling of Extreme Scenarios

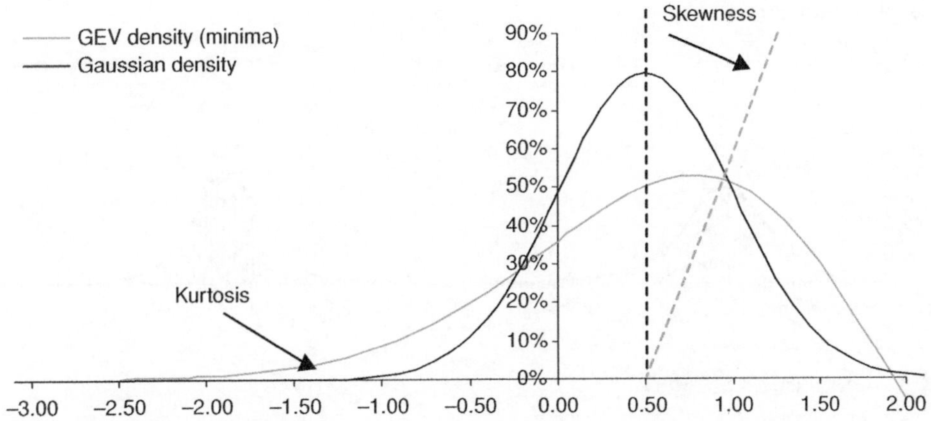

Source: SG Cross Asset Research.

asymmetry or skewness in the distribution and kurtosis, which measures the fatness of the tails (see Figure 2.1).

$$\mathrm{GEV}(x) = \exp\left\{-\left[1+\xi\left(\frac{x-\mu}{\sigma}\right)\right]^{-\frac{1}{\xi}}\right\}$$

GEV parameters are:

- μ—locates the peak of the distribution.
- σ—is proportional to the standard deviation.
- ξ—generates some skewness and kurtosis.

2.1.2 Extreme Value Theory in Practice

We begin this section with a few examples of GEV distributions. We show that it can adapt efficiently to various empirical observations thanks to simple adjustments to its three parameters.

We start our analysis with one of the most liquid credit indexes, the iTraxx Main (see Figure 2.2). As credit indexes began to trade only in 2004, we have reconstructed the time series back to 2001 using principal component analysis (PCA) on a basket of 300 single-name credit default swaps (CDSs).

The 30-day density is clearly skewed toward widening scenarios. This is consistent with the observed behavior of credit spreads, which tend to jump wider more often and more abruptly than they jump tighter. Using a weekly sampling frequency, the density becomes more symmetrical, although still skewed toward negative scenarios.

Moving on to equity indexes, we find fairly similar results (see Figure 2.3). The 30-day distribution is skewed toward the negative scenarios, but in a slightly different

FIGURE 2.2   iTraxx Main Density

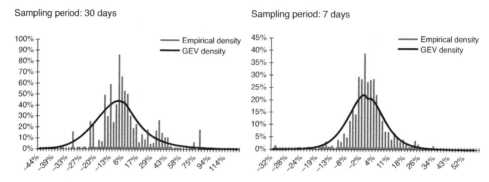

Source: SG Cross Asset Research.

way. In credit, the amplitude of the biggest observed widening move is almost three times that of the biggest tightening move. The difference is much less for the EuroStoxx 50 index, although the downward scenarios still clearly exhibit a much fatter tail. This highlights the jumpy nature of credit spreads compared to stock prices.

Finally, we calibrate our GEV model to 10-year EUR swap rates (see Figure 2.4). At first sight, the 30-day density of 10-year EUR swap rates seems relatively symmetrical. However, the empirical density of the maximum increase in 30 days is centered at 2 percent in relative terms, while the density of the maximum decrease is centered at –4 percent. This shows that on average, 10-year rates tend to decrease more rapidly than they increase. Moreover, the GEV density provides an excellent fit to seven-day empirical density.

So far, we have provided theoretical justification for using the GEV distribution for VaR calculations and we have illustrated the explanatory power of GEV through a series of examples.

FIGURE 2.3   EuroStoxx 50 Density

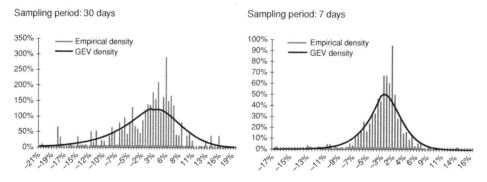

Source: SG Cross Asset Research.

FIGURE 2.4   EUR 10-Year Density

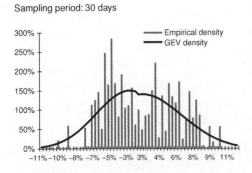

Sampling period: 30 days

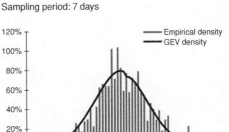

Sampling period: 7 days

Source: SG Cross Asset Research.

2.1.3   Calculating Value at Risk

GEV distributions can be used by risk managers to compute value at risk by extracting extreme quantiles conditional on some chosen GEV parameters. For example, the 1 percent quantile is a tail event that has a 1 percent probability of occurring according to a given probability law. For example, using the GEV law, the 1 percent quantile $x_{1\%}$ is such that $P^{\text{GEV}}[X < x_{1\%}] = 1\%$.

Geometrically speaking, the quantile measures the size of the tails of our distribution as shown in Figure 2.5.

Risk managers express quantiles in terms of frequency: A 1 percent quantile when looking at monthly variations corresponds to an event that should occur every eight years on average.

FIGURE 2.5   Quantiles Measure the Size of Distributions' Tails

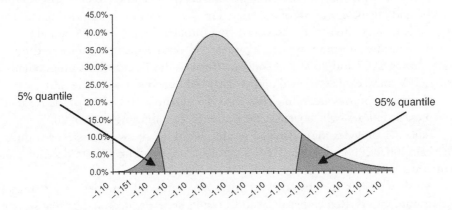

Source: SG Cross Asset Research.

FIGURE 2.6   Comparing GEV Quantiles to the Worst Moves of the Crisis

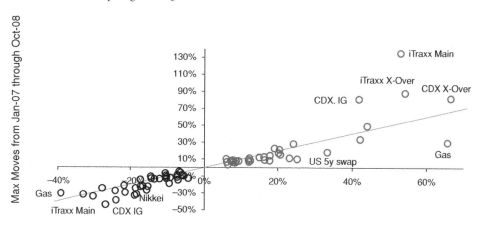

Source: SG Cross Asset Research.

2.1.4   Impact of a Crisis on VaR Calculations

Critics of quantitative risk management argue that extreme events by their very nature escape attempts to model them. They consider that by blindly using risk models, market players would wrongly assume that risks are under control, and suffer unexpected losses in case of a real crisis. We now challenge that assumption.

The previous section has shown that not all distributions used in quantitative finance ignore extreme risks. We now turn to concrete applications in term of risk management. We assume that at the end of 2006, a portfolio manager measures the VaR using GEV distributions. We will compare GEV estimates to the losses suffered during the years 2007–2008 on directional trades in various markets.

Concretely, we calibrate the GEV parameters (μ, σ, and ξ) to data series ending in 2006 and calculate the VaR of directional trades for various securities. We compare these VaR estimates to actual losses occurring through the 2007–2008 period.

We consider the most extreme upward and downward moves observed on 30 assets during 2007 and 2008 and compare them to the 1 percent quantiles obtained using GEV on weekly data based on the 2001–2006 period (see Figure 2.6).

Most of the moves are in line with the GEV quantiles. The biggest discrepancies are on credit indexes, which were at the center of the subprime crisis of 2007.

Table 2.1 provides more detailed results. We show the worst losses seen during the years 2007–2008, as well as GEV quantiles corresponding to both decennial and centennial VaR.

We show results for both downward moves (rates, oil, equities, credit spreads) and upward moves. Remember that model results are estimated on data that stopped before the crisis actually started.

TABLE 2.1 Comparing VaR Estimates to Worst Moves of Current Crisis

	Downward Moves			Upward Moves		
	2007–2008 Worst Losses	Decennial VaR	Centennial VaR	2007–2008 Worst Losses	Decennial VaR	Centennial VaR
EUR interest rates	−13.08%	−13.35%	−16.88%	12.83%	15.52%	19.70%
USD interest rates	−20.31%	−18.09%	−23.31%	21.54%	30.92%	49.96%
Oil prices	−27.78%	−24.14%	−31.53%	17.00%	20.20%	21.07%
Equity indexes	−26.32%	−18.22%	−25.39%	11.98%	15.16%	17.96%
FX rates vs. USD	−10.97%	−6.94%	−9.04%	6.91%	7.39%	8.73%
Credit indexes (spread)	−35.52%	−27.12%	−32.82%	96.57%	53.90%	112.65%

Source: SG Cross Asset Research.

- *2007–2008 worst loss.* Maximum loss due to an upward or a downward move from January 2007 through October 2008.
- *Decennial/centennial VaR.* Estimated value at risk using available data prior to 2006.

The capital estimated as necessary for a decennial crisis covers more than 85 percent of actual losses on long positions in interest rates or oil. It covers 76 percent of losses on long credit spread (i.e., short risk) positions and 70 percent of losses on long equity positions. It is quite interesting to note that only 30 percent of losses would have been incurred on equity positions, despite the unprecedented volatility we saw during that period. On short positions, losses would have been overhedged in most asset classes—except on credit spreads (i.e., long risk), where barely 55 percent of losses would have been covered.

However, losses from the current crisis remain well below those from the centennial crisis simulated by our model (even on credit). This shows that quant models are well able to consider extreme scenarios. In the credit market, losses were roughly in line with the estimated centennial crisis. This result highlights the severity of the credit crisis, but it is also due to the lack of long-term historical data for credit spreads at the frequency required for our analysis. That said, even with arguably little representative historical data, this simple model proves to be a good guide for the crisis.

2.1.5 Proper Use of a Risk Model

The previous results show that some asset classes were not sufficiently hedged by the GEV-based VaR model (short credit protection positions, for example) while others were overhedged and therefore too expensive to put on. This brings us to the question of how we want to use the model following its initial calibration to historical prices. Playing on ξ to increase the size of the tails would make some positions safer and more costly to implement. On the contrary, reducing tail size would allow more aggressive positions and more leverage.

TABLE 2.2 Percentage Change in GEV Parameters and 1 Percent Quantiles Following 2007–2008 Crisis

Asset	Minimum				Maximum			
	Mu	Sigma	Ksi	1% Quantile	Mu	Sigma	Ksi	1% Quantile
EUR interest rates	−0.98%	−0.46%	−3.59%	−1.50%	19.11%	−1.38%	12.86%	−2.31%
USD interest rates	−0.66%	5.43%	−3.20%	1.85%	−6.23%	−1.75%	−70.05%	−3.82%
Oil prices	3.84%	−3.04%	−5.64%	−2.76%	3.87%	−7.78%	−5.99%	−0.56%
Equity indexes	1.65%	0.16%	−0.94%	0.06%	−3.00%	−2.26%	−14.96%	−2.91%
FX rates vs. USD	−0.53%	3.44%	3.67%	2.72%	2.14%	6.89%	9.72%	1.53%
Credit indexes	9.74%	26.82%	23.89%	19.66%	68.83%	26.21%	11.79%	87.41%

Source: SG Cross Asset Research.

Clearly, the choice of the quantile and of the stress test we apply to the GEV distribution will result in a trade-off between leverage and risk. There are several parameters available to the risk manager to design a policy:

- *VaR quantile.* A 1 percent quantile for monthly distributions corresponds to a frequency of once every eight years. This means that the value at risk is calculated as the loss due to an event occurring once every eight years.
- *GEV parameters.* GEV parameters are a sound way of stress-testing the model. Instead of adding some arbitrary extreme simulations to a VaR framework, we can play with the GEV parameters to impact quantiles. For example, ξ will directly impact tail size and therefore modify the 1 percent quantile.

Table 2.2 shows the impact of the crisis on the GEV parameters and the corresponding 1 percent quantiles. This gives an idea of the kind of stress test that would have improved the efficiency of the GEV method over the current crisis.

Looking at the distributions of minima, the crisis mainly impacted long-term rates, some currencies against the U.S. dollar, and credit indexes. Interestingly, the parameters for equity indexes were left mostly unchanged, meaning that capital requirements for a long position on stocks would not have been affected by the crisis if the GEV-based VaR model had been used.

On the distributions of maxima, the fat tail parameter ξ has suffered more ups and downs. The most significant changes in terms of the corresponding quantile are on some foreign exchange (FX) and on credit indexes in general. The most extreme changes are on the investment-grade (IG) indexes: They contain a significant proportion of financial names and have therefore been at the center of the recent crisis. The tail parameter of their GEV distributions moved by more than 250 percent, and the corresponding quantile increased by more than 100 percent on the CDX IG and more than 150 percent on the iTraxx Main.

The GEV-based VaR model we have presented is obviously very simplistic, as it solely addresses the single-factor case. Yet it is an interesting building block for risk management tools and it shows how the language provided by quantitative finance can help risk managers adapt to new environments.

2.2 What Future for Pricing Models?

We now move on to models designed for pricing and hedging. Pricing models are used to estimate the price of a security using both observable and nonobservable inputs. The nonobservable inputs are typically used to calibrate the model to market prices, while the observable ones can be used to find optimal replication of a security's payoff using tradable assets. The validity of that replication is one of the crucial assumptions made by most complete market pricing theories. In practice, however, the unobservable parameters can become extremely volatile, making any previous replication virtually useless (see Figure 2.7).

2.2.1 Market Making: A Partial Solution for Incomplete Markets

When pricing a popular financial product requires the use of unobservable parameters and those unobservable parameters become volatile, dealers try to pull them into the observable world by creating dedicated market-making activities. As the newly born market takes off, the replication of the product's payoff can be extended in order to improve the model's hedging power.

FIGURE 2.7 Use of Models for Pricing and Hedging

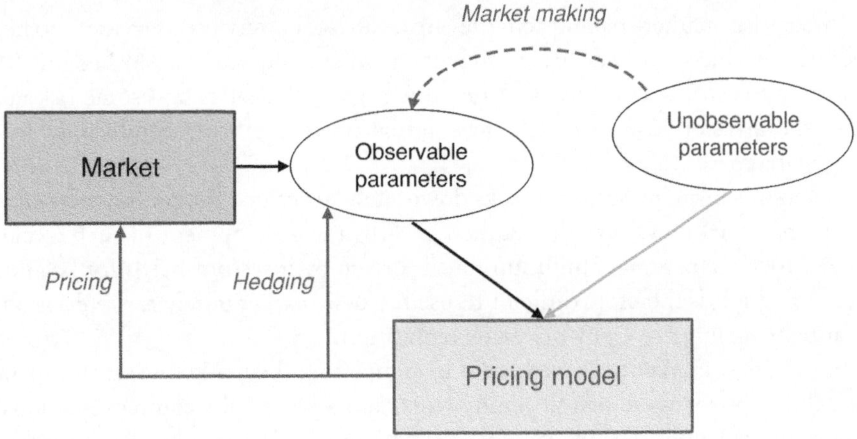

Source: SG Cross Asset Research.

Let's take a few concrete examples of such markets:

- *Equity correlation.* In order to hedge calls and puts on baskets of stocks, a market was created to allow dealers to hedge their exposures to stock correlation.
- *Swap rate correlation.* Constant maturity swap (CMS) spread (swap rate differential) options started trading because dealers needed to replicate the payoffs of range accruals (products that pay a coupon proportional to the number of days some CMS spreads spend within a given range).
- *Default correlation.* A standard correlation market was created in credit to help dealers hedge the exposure gained from CDO issuance. Default correlation is a particularly good example, as not only is it not observable in the market, but it is not even measurable, as past default data is scarce.

These markets were successful in adding several unobservable asset correlations to the set of observable parameters. It therefore became possible to use them in replication portfolios to improve hedging power. Yet these new replications are more risky, for two main reasons:

1. *Complexity.* As a market becomes complete, it also becomes more complex to model. We now need to properly render the relationship between the initial observable variables and the new ones. For example, in the credit market we need to model the relationship between credit spreads and default correlation. Since the new parameters were initially unobservable, this relationship will be purely model-based. So there is a strong model risk, which increases rapidly with the volumes traded on the corresponding market.
2. *Reflexivity.* We borrow billionaire investor George Soros's theory of reflexivity (see Soros 2003), which says that market changes influence players' decisions as much as players' decisions influence market changes. In other words, financial markets are equally influenced by a natural equilibrium and by the players involved in the markets.

In our case, market-making activities are created for a very precise reason: to hedge structured products. So a newly created market will initially see one-way hedging flows supporting the structured activity. When things go well, dealers find some risk takers within the investor base to match these initial flows and bring equilibrium to the young market.

When this first equilibrium breaks down, new structured products can be created to bring balanced flows into the market. Clearly, the development of such a market does not follow a natural equilibrium but is driven by investors' needs for balance in hedging flows. It is therefore difficult to use the new market purely for replication, as it is initially mainly driven by this same replication.

For the new market to be successful in completing the market, we therefore need a model that provides enough flexibility to explain a potentially complex relationship between the newly observable variable and the others. We also need the market to attract new players that are not involved with the originating structured market. Such players would help diversify the flows, decreasing the reflexivity problem.

FIGURE 2.8   Creating a Complete Equity-Credit Universe: The Smile to Credit (S2C) Model

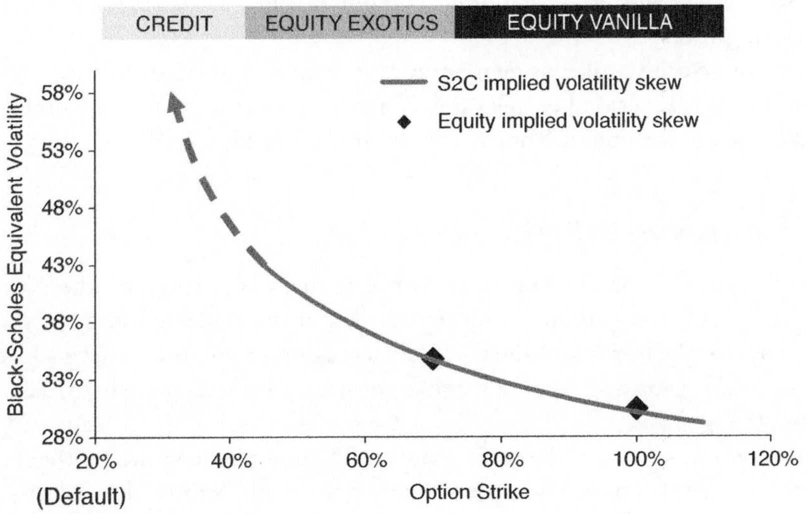

Source: SG Cross Asset Research.

2.2.2   Using Models to Complete Markets

Another way to proceed is to use a model to bring together existing liquid markets which are traditionally treated separately. The most obvious example is equity-credit models as shown in Figure 2.8.

In Chapter 17 of this book, Herzog and Turc (2011) describe a model that provides a common framework for equity and credit derivatives pricing. They start by considering both stock price and volatility as random variables. This framework is easily completed by adding vanilla options to our hedging portfolio. However, vanilla options cannot be used to hedge abrupt jumps in stock price. The model allows for this by adding jumps to the stock diffusion.

If we want to complete the market, we need to add a new instrument to the portfolio, and most of all to make the unrealistic assumption that the jump size is known in advance. To get around that problem, Herzog and Turc assume that small jumps can be hedged using out-of-the-money options (taken into account via stochastic volatility) and that the actual jump parameter in the model represents a jump to zero—in other words, that it merely provides the timing of default for the reference entity. The market is then completed by adding short-term credit default swaps (CDSs) to the hedging portfolio.

This example shows how models can be used to create a sound pricing environment by bringing markets together and therefore reducing incompleteness. However, this approach has its pitfalls:

- Completeness is never achieved. For example, in the smile to credit (S2C) model in Chapter 17, even though the jump is considered as a default indicator, in case of default the stock will not necessarily jump to zero, as the company might remain solvent. More generally, the loss given default (LGD) is not known in advance and should be considered as another random variable, adding a further source of incompleteness.

- As we complete the market using more advanced models and more instruments, both modeling and execution become more complex. This clearly raises the problems of model risk and the liquidity of the various instruments involved.

2.2.3   Pricing in Incomplete Markets

As explained earlier, pricing theory in complete markets is based on the possibility of perfectly replicating the price of any security using tradable assets. In order to compensate for the fragility of the completeness assumption, dealers have added new assets via market-making activities and have used advanced models to design the hedging strategies.

In incomplete markets, the price of a security cannot be replicated, either because an asset is missing from the replicating portfolio or simply because the replication can be performed only at discrete times in the real world. Moreover, the missing asset may be either observable or nonobservable.

When the perfect replication assumption is waived, pricing and hedging are no longer carried out by estimating the value of the replicating portfolio Π, but by minimizing the expected squared error between the best replicating portfolio Π^* and the actual value of the security Σ under the real-world measure:

$$\Pi^* = \arg\min_{\Pi} E_P \left[(\Pi - \Sigma)^2 \right]$$

In a way, this optimization is performed by derivatives traders as they estimate the optimal rebalancing frequency and delta hedge ratios in order to minimize execution costs and replication risks. From an option seller's point of view, we can also see this optimization in terms of utility function U:

$$(p, \Pi)^* = \arg\max_{p, \Pi} E_P \left[U(p, \Pi) \right]$$

where p is the price at which the trader is willing to sell the option. From a buyer's standpoint, the option should trade at the lowest price at which the seller would be willing to trade, given an optimal hedging strategy:

$$p^* = \inf \left\{ p; U(p, \Pi^*) > U(0, \Pi^*) \right\}$$

The price p of the option is determined as the equilibrium price at which both buyers and sellers are willing to trade (i.e., the expected utility of trading is higher than that of not trading).

Another way to look at incomplete markets is very similar to using VaR methodology. We can define the 1 percent VaR as the loss L such that $P[\Pi - \Sigma < L] = 1\%$ and set the price of the security as:

$$(p, \Pi)^* = \arg\max_{p,\Pi} \{L; P[\Pi - \Sigma < L] = 1\%\}$$

In this framework, the price of a security reflects the replication risk, considering scenarios that occur once every eight years. This allows risk limits to be defined in terms of quantiles.

For example, distribution of the size of a jump can be estimated historically and stressed in order to provide a simulation bench for replication strategies. The replicating portfolio can then be optimized to minimize the loss corresponding to the tracking error of the replication strategy. Finally, the trader can define the part of the VaR that will be financed with a bid-offer spread and the part that will be financed by capital.

2.3 Conclusion

Quantitative finance became extremely successful as soon as Black and Scholes introduced their simple options pricing formula. We have argued that such simple models should be used as communication tools for traders rather than as risk management tools. While the rapidity with which simple models have become popular can potentially lead to derivatives bubbles, the more complex models are more difficult to test and potentially lead to higher model risk. We therefore need to find a trade-off in order to successfully create innovative new products that rely neither on model risk nor on false assumptions in the long run.

References

Fisher, R., and L. Tippett. 1928. Limiting forms of the frequency distribution of the largest and smallest member of a sample. *Proceedings of the Cambridge Philosophical Society* 24.

Herzog, B., and J. Turc. 2011. Pricing and hedging with equity-credit models. Chapter 17 in this volume.

Overhaus, M., et al. 2001. *Equity derivatives: Theory and applications.* New York: John Wiley & Sons.

Soros, G. 2003. *The alchemy of finance.* Hoboken, NJ: John Wiley & Sons.

von Mises, R. 1936. La distribution de la plus grande de n valeurs. In *Selected Papers*, vol. 2. Providence, RI: American Mathematical Society.

PART II

Credit Derivatives: Methods

CHAPTER 3

An Introduction to Multiname Modeling in Credit Risk

Aurélien Alfonsi

Université Paris-Est, CERMICS

This chapter is intended to be an introductory survey on credit risk models for multiname products. We first present the intensity models for single defaults, which leads up to the copula model. We hint at its limits, especially concerning the dependence dynamics between defaults that it induces. As an alternative, we consider loss models and present several reduced-form models that are designed to have known distributions through their Fourier transform. We then present the Markovian projection of the loss process, and introduce the local intensity model and its extensions. Last, we focus on two forward loss models whose principle is to model directly the future loss distributions rather than the loss itself. This simultaneous presentation points out similarities and differences between them.

3.1 Introduction

Let us begin with a short introduction to the credit risk market. Credit derivatives are financial products that bring to their owner, under some prespecified conditions, a payment protection when default events occur. A default event can be a number of events, including the bankruptcy of a financial entity or its inability to reimburse its debt. In general, we divide these derivatives into two categories. The first category consists in the single-name credit derivatives that are products that deal with only one default. The most widespread product that belongs to that category is the credit default swap (CDS). Let us describe here briefly its mechanism. The owner of a CDS will receive a protection payment when a firm defaults, if this happens before the date of maturity. This maturity and the default entity are of course defined at the beginning of the CDS. In exchange, the owner will pay to the protection seller regular payments until the default or if it does not happen until the maturity. From a practical point of view, these products are well adapted if one has a strong exposure to an identified bankruptcy. However, in general, financial parties have diversified investments and are naturally exposed to many defaults. They would prefer to buy directly a product that takes into consideration their whole aggregated default exposure, instead of buying many single-name products. This motivates the other category of products, the multiname credit derivatives whose payment structure depends on many defaults. The most representative products of this category are the collateralized debt obligations (CDOs). For the owner, this mainly consists of being reimbursed of its loss generated by bankruptcies when its total loss due to defaults is between two prespecified values. In exchange, the owner has to give regular payments that are proportional to the outstanding notional of the CDO protection that one could expect in the future from the CDO contract. Multiname products such as CDOs are thus financial tools that allow one to be hedged according to a certain level of loss, without specifying a priori which entities will default. Therefore, they are really fitted to control one's exposure to defaults. All of these products were originally dealt over the counter. This is still the case for bespoke products. Nonetheless, some of them, such as CDSs on large companies and CDOs on standard pools, have been standardized in the recent past. We give here a precise description of these CDSs and CDOs.

Now, let us think about the two categories mentioned in terms of information. It is well known that market prices reflect some information on the economy, so what kind of information could we grasp from the prices of single-name and multiname credit derivatives products? Single-name prices will inform on the default probability of one firm in the future and, in this way, on the health of that firm. Of course, the more prices we have on a default, the more we know about its distribution and its fluctuation. Multiname prices clearly include too that information for each underlying default. But they also bring information on the dependence between underlying defaults. This is related to another risk, called credit risk contagion—that is, the risk of interdependent failures. Though very simple, it is interesting to keep in mind this interpretation of prices through information when modeling. For example, it helps to understand which product can be used to calibrate a parameter or what products can be priced within one model.

Now we would like to hint at the specificities of the credit risk market and especially their implication when modeling. First, it is intrinsically different from the other markets because the underlyings are unpredictable discrete events, while usually underlyings are nonnegative paths. Obviously, the prices observed in the credit risk market are nonnegative paths that could each be modeled as a diffusion with jumps as in the other markets. Doing this, however, it would be hard to catch the dependence between the prices of two products taking into account the same underlying default. Indeed, payoff structures are often directly constituted from the discrete default events. This is why modeling default events directly is an important issue to get consistency between prices. Another important feature of the credit risk market is that it is a rather young market. Therefore, there are still few products that are quoted in the market. This has to be taken into consideration because it means that we cannot fit a model with too many refinements. A last important feature is the similarity between the credit derivatives' payoff and that of the fixed-income products. This is not really due to blind chance, because they are often complementary such as bonds and CDSs (for a more detailed discussion on this, see Brigo and Mercurio 2006). As a consequence, many approaches coming from the fixed-income world have been adapted to credit risk, as we will see here.

The goal of this chapter is to give an overview of the modeling in credit risk when multiname products are considered and default dependence (or correlation) is a driver. In a first part, we introduce the copula model that arises naturally once we start from intensity models for the single-name defaults. Then, we point out the drawbacks of this approach and motivate the introduction of loss models. In the second part we focus on loss models whose dynamics have a reduced form. In the third part, we present the local intensity model for the loss. It is very similar to the local volatility model in equity. We also give extensions of this model. Last, we present two forward-loss models that, though being close in their conception, present nonetheless some differences. We hope that our parallel description will shed light on these models and thus help one to understand their mechanism. Last, we briefly point out the limits of the loss models presented here and state some main challenges that remain to be addressed.

It is important to mention that we do not address credit index options. These are multiname products that have as an underlying the future spread of the whole index, rather than a specific tranche. As such, in principle their valuation would not depend on the whole loss dynamics but only on the correlation-independent spread associated with the untranched loss. However, proper inclusion of front-end protection and problems related to the singularity of the pricing measure render this product correlation dependent as well. For a related discussion the reader is referred to Morini and Brigo (2009) and Rutkowski (2010).

3.1.1 Notations

Through all these models, we consider the same probabilistic background. We indeed assume that all the market events are described by the probabilistic filtered space $(\Omega, (\mathcal{G}_t)_{t \geq 0}, \mathcal{G}, \mathbb{P})$. Here, as usual, $\mathcal{G}_t$ is the σ-field that describes all the future events that can occur before time t and $\mathcal{G}$ describes all the future events. We also assume that $\mathbb{P}$ is a martingale measure. It means that prices of future cash flows are $(\mathcal{G}_t)$-martingales under $\mathbb{P}$, and practically that prices can be computed through expectations. We consider $m \geq 1$ defaultable entities and name $\tau^1, \ldots, \tau^m$ their time of default. We assume they are positive $(\mathcal{G}_t)$-stopping times. We suppose also that there exists a subfiltration $(\mathcal{F}_t)_{t \geq 0}$ that describes all default-risk-free assets such as riskless zero coupon bonds. These are products that give with certainty a unit payment at a fixed maturity. Let us introduce also some other standard notations. For $j \in \{1, \ldots, m\}$, let us denote $(\mathcal{H}_t^j)_{t \geq 0}$ the filtration generated by $(\tau^j \wedge t)_{t \geq 0}$ and $(\mathcal{F}_t^j)_{t \geq 0} = (\mathcal{F}_t \vee \mathcal{H}_t^j)_{t \geq 0}$. We also use the notation $\mathcal{F} = \bigvee_{t \geq 0} \mathcal{F}_t$, $\mathcal{F}^j = \bigvee_{t \geq 0} \mathcal{F}_t^j$, and so on. Last, we assume that:

$$\mathcal{G}_t = \bigvee_{j=1}^m \mathcal{F}_t^j$$

That is, the market events come from only the default-free assets and the default times $\tau^1, \ldots, \tau^m$.

3.2 The Copula Model

In this section, we present the copula approach for multiname modeling. We also introduce CDS and CDO payoffs and explain how in practice this model is fitted to market data. Let us first begin with the single-default products.

3.2.1 Default Intensity Models and Calibration to CDSs

Intensity models (or reduced-form default models) assume that the default is explained by an exogenous process that is called "intensity of default."

Definition 3.2.1   *Let us consider* $\tau : \Omega \to \mathbb{R}_+$ *a nonnegative random variable. We will say that* τ *follows a default intensity model with respect to the filtration* $(\mathcal{F}_t)_{t\geq 0}$ *if there exist a nonnegative* $(\mathcal{F}_t)$*-adapted càdlàg process* $(\lambda_t, t \geq 0)$ *and an exponential random variable* ξ *of parameter* 1 *that is independent from* $\mathcal{F}$ *such that:*

$$\tau = \inf\{t \geq 0, \int_0^t \lambda_s \, ds \geq \xi\}$$

The process $(\lambda_t, t \geq 0)$ *is called the extended intensity of the default* τ.

Usually, we assume moreover that the extended intensity satisfies the following two properties:

$$\forall t \geq 0, \mathbb{P}(\Lambda(t) < +\infty) = 1 \text{ and } \mathbb{P}(\lim_{t \to +\infty} \Lambda(t) = +\infty) = 1$$

where $\Lambda(t) = \int_0^t \lambda_s \, ds$. They are in general satisfied by most of the intensity models proposed in the literature. If the first one did not hold, this would mean, since $\{\Lambda(t) = +\infty\} \subset \{\tau \leq t\}$, that $\mathcal{F}_t$ can provide information on the default time for some $t > 0$. This is in contradiction with the modeling assumption that $(\mathcal{F}_t)_{t\geq 0}$ describes only the default-risk-free world, and we prefer in general to avoid it. The second property just means that every entity will collapse someday if we wait long enough.

In all of Section 3.2, we assume that $\tau^1, \ldots, \tau^m$ follow an intensity model with respect to $(\mathcal{F}_t)_{t\geq 0}$ and we denote $\lambda_t^1, \ldots, \lambda_t^m$ their respective intensities and $\xi^1, \ldots, \xi^m$ the associated exponential random variables.

A credit default swap is a product that offers protection against the default of a firm during a fixed period $[T_0, T_n]$. The protection buyer must in exchange at some predefined maturities $T_1, \ldots, T_n$ pay an amount that is usually proportional to the time elapsed since the last maturity. We denote by $\mathcal{T} = \{T_0, T_1, \ldots, T_n\}$ the maturities that define a CDS contract, $\alpha_i = T_i - T_{i-1}$ and $D(t, T)$ the discount factor between t and T ($t < T$) that is assumed $\mathcal{F}_T$-measurable. For $j \in \{1, \ldots, m\}$, we also name $\mathrm{LGD}^j \in [0, 1]$ the loss fraction generated by the default τ^j and assume it to be deterministic. Within this framework, the payoff of a CDS on τ^j at time T_0 reads (written for the protection seller):

$$\left(\sum_{i=1}^{n} D(T_0, T_i) \alpha_i R \mathbf{1}_{\tau^j > T_i} \right) + D(T_0, \tau^j) R (\tau^j - T_{\beta(\tau^j)-1}) \mathbf{1}_{\tau^j \leq T_n}$$

$$- \mathrm{LGD}^j D(T_0, \tau^j) \mathbf{1}_{\tau^j \leq T_n}$$

where $\beta(t)$ is the index such that $t \in (T_{\beta(t)-1}, T_{\beta(t)}]$. Here, R denotes the CDS rate or spread. In practice it is set initially such that the contract is zero-valued for the protection buyer and the protection seller.[1] The payments are usually made quarterly and the standard final maturities include one, three, five, seven, and ten years. Here, we have neglected the counterparty risk—that is, the risk that one of the two parties may default during the contract. For a CDS with counterparty risk, see, for example, Brigo and Capponi (2008); Brigo and Chourdakis (2008).

Let us assume now that $T_0 = 0$ (the current time) and that we have at our disposal market prices of the fair CDS rate on each default τ^j. Then, we can use these data to calibrate the intensities. More precisely, under the intensity model, the fair CDS rate is given by (see, for example, Brigo and Alfonsi 2005):

$$R^j(\mathcal{T}) = \frac{\mathrm{LGD}^j \mathbb{E}[D(0, \tau^j) \mathbf{1}_{\tau^j \leq T_n}]}{\mathbb{E}[\sum_{i=1}^{n} D(0, T_i) \alpha_i \mathbf{1}_{\tau^j > T_i} + D(0, \tau^j)(\tau^j - T_{\beta(\tau^j)-1}) \mathbf{1}_{\tau^j \leq T_n}]} \qquad (3.1)$$

$$= \frac{\mathrm{LGD}^j \mathbb{E}[\int_0^{T_n} D(0, t) \exp(-\Lambda^j(t)) \lambda_t^j \, dt]}{\sum_{i=1}^{n} \mathbb{E}[D(0, T_i) \exp(-\Lambda^j(T_i))] \alpha_i + \mathbb{E}[\int_0^{T_n} D(0, t)(t - T_{\beta(t)-1}) \exp(-\Lambda^j(t)) \lambda_t^j \, dt]}$$

where $\Lambda^j(t) = \int_0^t \lambda_s^j \, ds$. Therefore, specifying a parameterized model for the extended intensities λ^j and a model for the discount factors, we are able to fit the prices given by the market. This is the case for our example if one assumes that intensities are deterministic and piecewise linear or follow the shifted square-root diffusion (SSRD) model described in Brigo and Alfonsi (2005). Thus, in a general manner, intensity models are often chosen to be tractable when pricing the single-name products.

3.2.2 Dependence between Defaults and Calibration to CDO

The thresholds $\xi^1, \ldots, \xi^m$ that trigger the defaults each follow an exponential law of parameter 1. Therefore, the random variables $\exp(-\xi^1), \ldots, \exp(-\xi^m)$ follow an uniform distribution on $[0, 1]$.

Definition 3.2.2 *Let $m \geq 2$. The cumulative distribution function of a random variable vector $(U_1, \ldots, U_m)$*

$$(u_1, \ldots, u_m) \in [0, 1]^m \mapsto \mathbb{P}(U_1 \leq u_1, \ldots, U_m \leq u_m)$$

each coordinate U_i of which follows a uniform distribution on $[0, 1]$ is called a (m-dimensional) copula. We denote by $C^+(u_1, \ldots, u_m) = \min(u_1, \ldots, u_m)$ the comonotone copula, which is associated to $U_i = U_1$ and represents the perfect positive dependence.

Since we focus on credit risk issues, we will not go beyond this copula definition and we refer to the paper of Embrechts, Lindskog, and McNeil (2001) for a nice introduction to copula functions and dependence modeling. For a further reading on this topic, we mention the book by Nelsen (1999) and hint at a recent development made by Alfonsi and Brigo (2005) on a tractable copula family.

We denote C the copula that is the cumulative distribution function of the vector $(\exp(-\xi^1), \ldots, \exp(-\xi^m))$. Let us remark that for $t_1, \ldots, t_m \geq 0$, we have:

$$\begin{aligned}
\mathbb{P}(\tau^1 \geq t_1, \ldots, \tau^m \geq t_m | \mathcal{F}) &= \mathbb{P}(e^{-\xi^1} \leq \exp(-\Lambda^1(t_1)), \ldots, e^{-\xi^m} \\
&\leq \exp(-\Lambda^m(t_m)) | \mathcal{F}) \\
&= C(\exp(-\Lambda^1(t_1)), \ldots, \exp(-\Lambda^m(t_m)))
\end{aligned}$$

Now, let us turn to the collateralized debt obligation and describe a synthetic CDO payoff. To understand its practical interest in terms of hedging, we suppose that we have sold protections against defaults $\tau^1, \ldots, \tau^m$ through CDS contracts with the same schedule of payments $\mathcal{T} = \{T_0, \ldots, T_n\}$. We assume that the number of CDSs sold is the same for each underlying default, and our loss due to the bankruptcies at time t is thus proportional to the loss process

$$L(t) = \frac{1}{m} \sum_{j=1}^{m} \text{LGD}^j \mathbf{1}_{\tau^j \leq t} \tag{3.2}$$

Here, we have normalized the loss process $(L(t), t \geq 0)$ in order to have $L(t) = 1$ in the worst case (i.e., $\text{LGD}^j = 1$ for all j and every default before t). Let us assume, for example, that we do not want to undergo a loss that exceeds 3 percent of the largest loss that we may have. To do so, we conclude a contract with another firm that will reimburse the loss undergone above 3 percent (i.e., when $L(t) \geq 0.03$) in exchange of regular payments. Such contract is called the [3%, 100%] tranche CDO on the basket loss process $(L(t), t \geq 0)$. Most often in practice, tranches are thinner (for example, [3%, 6%], [6%, 9%], . . .) and bring protection when the relative loss $(L(t), t \geq 0)$ is within two values. Let us now describe precisely the payoff structure of a CDO tranche $[a, b]$ for $0 \leq a < b \leq 1$. We introduce for that scope the function

$$\forall x \in [0, 1], \ H_a^b(x) = \frac{(x-a)^+ - (x-b)^+}{b-a}$$

At time T_0, the cash flow scenario of a tranche CDO $[a, b]$ with payment schedule $\mathcal{T}$ is, for the protection seller:

$$\sum_{i=1}^n \alpha_i R[1 - H_a^b(L(T_i))]D(T_0, T_i) + \int_{T_0}^{T_n} R(t - T_{\beta(t)-1})D(T_0, t)d[H_a^b(L(t))]$$

$$- \int_{T_0}^{T_n} D(T_0, t)d[H_a^b(L(t))]$$

Here, R is called the rate (spread) of the CDO tranche $[a, b]$. Let us observe here that the regular payments are, as for the CDS, proportional to the elapsed time since the last maturity. For the CDO tranche, they are also proportional to the maximal loss that remains to cover within the tranche. For a few years, standard CDO tranches have been quoted on the market. As an example for the iTraxx index, there are $m = 125$ names and the quoted tranches are [0%, 3%], [3%, 6%], [6%, 9%], [9%, 12%], and [12%, 22%]. Recently, also the super-senior tranche [22%, 100%] has been traded. The full tranche [0, 100%] is also quoted and is called the index. The final maturities are three, five, seven, and ten years and the payments are quarterly. The riskiest tranche ([0%, 3%] for the iTraxx) is usually called the equity tranche, the intermediate ones are called the mezzanine tranche, and the least risky tranche ([12%, 22%] for the iTraxx) is called the senior tranche. Except for the equity tranche (for which an up-front payment value is quoted, even if recently junior mezzanine tranches are also being quoted up front), the market quotes the rate $R_a^b(T)$ that makes the contract zero-valued.

Now we turn to the valuation of that rate and assume that $T_0 = 0$, which means that the tranche starts at the current time. Under our assumption, the fair rate value is given by:

$$R_a^b(T) = \frac{\mathbb{E}\left[\sum_{i=1}^n \alpha_i[1 - H_a^b(L(T_i))]D(0, T_i) + \int_0^{T_n}(t - T_{\beta(t)-1})D(0, t)d[H_a^b(L(t))]\right]}{\mathbb{E}\left[\int_0^{T_n} D(0, t)d[H_a^b(L(t))]\right]}$$

(3.3)

Remark 3.2.1 *Let us assume that the interest rates are deterministic or more generally independent of the loss process $(L(t), t \geq 0)$, and we set $P(0, t) = \mathbb{E}[D(0, t)]$. Then, the*

CDO fair rate only depends on the marginal laws of the loss. Indeed, integrating by parts, we easily get that:

$$R_a^b(T) = \frac{\sum_{i=1}^n \alpha_i P(0, T_i) - \int_0^{T_n} P(0, t)\mathbb{E}[H_a^b(L(t))]dt - \int_0^{T_n}(t - T_{\beta(t)-1})\mathbb{E}[H_a^b(L(t))]dP(0, t)}{P(0, T_n)\mathbb{E}[H_a^b(L(T_n))] - \int_0^{T_n}\mathbb{E}[H_a^b(L(t))]dP(0, t)}$$

Let us explain how we can compute this price if we know the intensities dynamics $(\lambda_t^j, t \geq 0)$ and the copula C. Contrary to Remark 3.2.1, we do not assume that the interest rates are independent of the loss. There may be dependence between them and the default intensities. However, we can proceed similarly by conditioning with respect to the default-free filtration. Thus, we first calculate the conditional expectations given the σ-field $\mathcal{F}$. An integration by parts on the integrals gives, for example, on the denominator

$$\int_0^{T_n} D(0, t)d[H_a^b(L(t))] = D(0, T_n)H_a^b(L(T_n)) - \int_0^{T_n} H_a^b(L(t))d[D(0, t)]$$

and thus

$$\mathbb{E}\left[\int_0^{T_n} D(0, t)d[H_a^b(L(t))]\Big|\mathcal{F}\right] = D(0, T_n)\mathbb{E}[H_a^b(L(T_n))|\mathcal{F}]$$

$$- \int_0^{T_n} \mathbb{E}[H_a^b(L(t))|\mathcal{F}]d[D(0, t)]$$

since $D(0, t)$ is $\mathcal{F}$-measurable. Therefore, to calculate the expectations that define each tranche, it is sufficient to know for any t the law of $L(t)$ conditioned to $\mathcal{F}$. This is the case since we have:

$$\forall x \in [0, 1], \; \mathbb{P}(L(t) \leq x|\mathcal{F}) = \sum_{\substack{J \subset \{1,\ldots,m\} \\ s.t. \frac{1}{m}\sum_{k \in J} \text{LGD}^k \leq x}} \mathbb{P}(\forall j \in J, \tau^j \leq t, \forall j \notin J, \tau^j > t|\mathcal{F})$$

$$\text{(3.4)}$$

and (sieve formula):

$$\mathbb{P}(\forall j \in J, \tau^j \leq t, \forall j \notin J, \tau^j > t|\mathcal{F})$$
$$= \sum_{K \subset J}(-1)^{\#J - \#K}\mathbb{P}(\forall j \in K, \tau^j > 0, \forall j \notin K, \tau^j > t|\mathcal{F})$$
$$= \sum_{K \subset J}(-1)^{\#J - \#K} C(e^{-1_{1 \notin K}\Lambda^1(t)}, \ldots, e^{-1_{m \notin K}\Lambda^m(t)})$$

Then, we can calculate the expectation $\mathbb{E}[\int_0^{T_n} D(0, t)d[H_a^b(L(t))]]$ through a Monte Carlo method, and in the same manner the other expectations can be computed to deduce the fair price $R_a^b(T)$. However, for the sake of simplicity, one assumes often deterministic extended intensities and discount factors when computing CDO prices to avoid this last step that might be time-consuming. This does not render the model irrelevant, because the main risk that determines the price of the CDO is the interdependence of the defaults. Fluctuations of default intensities and risk-free interest rates usually play a minor role. This is, however, not true when the copula considered is close to the comonotone copula C^+, since the defaults are then basically ordered by their deterministic intensity (see Brigo and Capponi 2008).

The preceding formula implicitly requires that we are able to compute the value of a copula function although this is not always a trivial issue. For the copulas called factor copulas (such as some Gaussian copulas), Laurent and Gregory (2003) and Hull and White (2004) have proposed two rather efficient numerical integration methods; see also Rosen and Saunders (2009) for a multifactor setting. Both methods first compute the law of $L(t)$ conditioned to the factor(s) that define the copula C and then use a numerical integration with respect to the factor(s). This conditioned law is obtained through its Fourier transform in Laurent and Gregory (2003) and is approximated directly using a so-called bucket method in Hull and White (2004). Let us finally give standard special cases for which the preceding calculations are much simpler. First, if one assumes that the loss given defaults (LGDs) are identical ($\text{LGD}^j = \text{LGD}$), the loss is proportional to the number of defaults, and the sets J in equation (3.4) are simply $\#J \leq mx/\text{LGD}$. Moreover, if the copula is symmetrical in the sense that $C(u_1, \ldots, u_m) = C(u_{\sigma(1)}, \ldots, u_{\sigma(m)})$ for any permutation σ, and if the defaults have the same extended intensity (λ_t, $t \geq 0$), we have a simpler formula to characterize the loss distribution:

$$\forall j \in \{0, \ldots, m\}, \ \mathbb{P}(L(t) = \frac{j}{m}\text{LGD}|\mathcal{F})$$

$$= \binom{m}{j} \sum_{k=0}^{j} \binom{j}{k} (-1)^{j-k} C(\underbrace{1, \ldots, 1}_{k \text{ times}}, e^{-\Lambda(t)}, \ldots, e^{-\Lambda(t)})$$

A special case of this formulation is referred as large homogeneous portfolio (LHP).

3.2.3   Copula Model and Default Intensity Jumps

Here we would like to hint at the evolution of the rate of default when defaults occur. To that purpose, we need to introduce another definition of the intensity than the extended intensity introduced before.

Definition 3.2.3   *Let us consider $(\mathcal{G}'_t)_{t\geq 0}$ a subfiltration of $(\mathcal{G}_t)_{t\geq 0}$ and τ a $(\mathcal{G}'_t)$-stopping time. We will say that $(\lambda_t^{\tau|\mathcal{G}'}, t \geq 0)$ is the intensity of τ with respect to the filtration $(\mathcal{G}'_t)_{t\geq 0}$ if the two following properties hold:*

1. $(\lambda_t^{\tau|\mathcal{G}'}, t \geq 0)$ *is a $(\mathcal{G}'_t)$-adapted càdlàg process.*
2. $\mathbf{1}_{\tau \leq t} - \int_0^t \lambda_s^{\tau|\mathcal{G}'} ds$ *is a $(\mathcal{G}'_t)$-martingale.*

The intuitive meaning of the intensity is the following. Let us assume that we observe some evolution and have access to the information modeled by $(\mathcal{G}'_t)_{t \geq 0}$. From the martingale property, one has

$$\mathbb{P}(\tau \in (t, t+dt]|\mathcal{G}'_t) = \mathbb{E}\left[\int_t^{t+dt} \lambda_s^{\tau|\mathcal{G}'} ds \,\Big|\, \mathcal{G}'_t\right] \underset{dt \to 0^+}{\approx} \lambda_t^{\tau|\mathcal{G}'} dt$$

and thus $\lambda_t^{\tau|\mathcal{G}'}$ is the rate of probability that τ occurs in the immediate future knowing $\mathcal{G}'_t$. In particular, $\lambda_t^{\tau|\mathcal{G}'} = 0$ on $\{\tau \leq t\}$ and for $(\mathcal{G}'_t)_{t\geq 0} = (\mathcal{F}_t)_{t\geq 0} \vee \sigma(\tau \wedge t, t \geq 0)$, $\lambda_t^{\tau|\mathcal{G}'}$ coincides with the extended intensity λ_t for $t < \tau$.

Let us turn now to our model for the defaults $\tau^1, \ldots, \tau^m$. It is not hard to see that for any $j \in \{1, \ldots, m\}$, $\lambda_t^{\tau^j|\mathcal{F}^j} = \lambda_t^j \mathbf{1}_{\tau^j > t}$ is the intensity of τ^j with respect to $(\mathcal{F}_t^j)_{t\geq 0}$. It is equal to the extended intensity until the default occurs and then jumps to 0. This is the rate of default seen by someone that would have access only to the information modeled by $(\mathcal{F}_t^j)_{t\geq 0}$. However, one has in general access to the full information $\mathcal{G}_t = \bigvee_{j=1}^m \mathcal{F}_t^j$ and would like to know the intensity with respect to it. We have:

$$\lambda_t^{\tau^j|\mathcal{G}} = \lim_{dt\to 0^+} \frac{\mathbb{P}(\tau^j \in (t, t+dt]|\mathcal{G}_t)}{dt}$$

$$= \sum_{K \subset \{1, \ldots, m\} - \{j\}} \mathbf{1}_{Def_t(K)} \lim_{dt\to 0^+} \frac{1}{dt} \mathbb{P}(\tau^j \in (t, t+dt]|\mathcal{F}_t \vee Def_t(K) \vee \forall k \in K, \tau^k)$$

where $Def_t(K) := \{\forall k \in K, \tau^k \leq t, \forall k \notin K, \tau^k > t\}$. Let us consider for example $j = 1$ and suppose that no default has occurred at time t ($K = \emptyset$). Then we have

$$\mathbb{P}(\tau^1 \in (t, t+dt]|\mathcal{F}_t \vee Def_t(\emptyset))$$
$$= \frac{\mathbb{E}(C(e^{-\Lambda^1(t)}, \ldots, e^{-\Lambda^m(t)}) - C(e^{-\Lambda^1(t+dt)}, e^{-\Lambda^2(t)}, \ldots, e^{-\Lambda^m(t)})|\mathcal{F}_t)}{C(e^{-\Lambda^1(t)}, \ldots, e^{-\Lambda^m(t)})}$$

and therefore

$$\lambda_t^{\tau^1|\mathcal{G}} = \lambda_t^1 e^{-\Lambda^1(t)} \frac{\partial_1 C(e^{-\Lambda^1(t)}, \ldots, e^{-\Lambda^m(t)})}{C(e^{-\Lambda^1(t)}, \ldots, e^{-\Lambda^m(t)})} \text{ on } Def_t(\emptyset)$$

Let us suppose now that τ^m is the only one default that has occurred before time t at time t_m ($K = \{m\}$), so that $\tau^m = t_m < t$. We have:

$$\mathbb{P}(\tau^1 \in (t, t+dt]|\mathcal{F}_t \vee Def_t(\{m\}), \tau^m = t_m) = 1 - \mathbb{P}(\tau^1 > t+dt|\mathcal{F}_t \vee Def_t(\{m\}), \tau^m = t_m)$$
$$= \frac{\partial_m C(e^{-\Lambda^1(t)}, \ldots, e^{-\Lambda^{m-1}(t)}, e^{-\Lambda^m(t_m)}) - \partial_m C(e^{-\Lambda^1(t+dt)}, \ldots, e^{-\Lambda^{m-1}(t)}, e^{-\Lambda^m(t_m)})}{\partial_m C(e^{-\Lambda^1(t)}, \ldots, e^{-\Lambda^{m-1}(t)}, e^{-\Lambda^m(t_m)})}$$

and therefore

$$\lambda_t^{\tau^1|\mathcal{G}} = \lambda_t^1 e^{-\Lambda^1(t)} \frac{\partial_1 \partial_m C(e^{-\Lambda^1(t)}, \ldots, e^{-\Lambda^{m-1}(t)}, e^{-\Lambda^m(t_m)})}{\partial_m C(e^{-\Lambda^1(t)}, \ldots, e^{-\Lambda^{m-1}(t)}, e^{-\Lambda^m(t_m)})} \text{ on } Def_t(\{m\})$$

This way, we can calculate explicitly the intensity $\lambda_t^{\tau^1|\mathcal{G}}$ on the event $Def_t(K)$ for each K, if one assumes that the copula function is regular enough. We refer to the papers of Schönbucher and Schubert (2001) and Brigo and Chourdakis (2008) for further details.

Let us make now some comments on these calculations. First, we have seen that even without default, the current intensity of each default time depends on the copula function. This means in practice that even single-name products such as a CDS that starts at a future date contain some risk of interdependence of defaults. Second, the formulas that define the intensity $\lambda_t^{\tau^1|\mathcal{G}}$ are not the same on $Def_t(\emptyset)$ and $Def_t(\{m\})$; there is therefore in general a jump of this intensity when the first default τ^m occurs. In a general manner, $\lambda_t^{\tau^1|\mathcal{G}}$ jumps at each default time until it vanishes when τ^1 itself occurs. Intuitively, jumps are all the more significant as the dependence between the default that happens and τ^1 is strong. This fact has been widely studied in the literature, and we refer, for example, to Bielecki and Rutkowski (2003).

3.2.4 Strength and Weakness of the Copula Model

The main strength of the copula approach is undoubtedly its ability to catch the information from the CDS market. Let us suppose that for each default that defines the loss process $L(t)$, one or more CDSs are traded. We can then easily calibrate a deterministic intensity that fits exactly the prices observed (see Brigo and Alfonsi 2005 for details). If one assumes that the copula that describes the dependence between the defaults belongs to a parametrized family (e.g., the Gaussian copula family), one can then fit its parameters from the CDO market prices since we are able to compute these prices in a quite efficient manner. With this calibrated model, we can then price every credit risk product that depends on the defaults that define the loss $L(t)$. Thus, one has a model that is at first sight coherent with the single risk and multiname risk markets and allows one to price a rather broad set of credit risk products.

However, the situation is unfortunately not so idyllic. First, we have in practice at most five CDO prices for each tranche to calibrate the copula function. It is then likely to be a copula family with few parameters; otherwise, our calibration would not have a deep meaning. If the copula family depends on only one parameter, it is, however, not possible in general to fit all the prices well. When this parameter has an intuitive meaning, a common practice is to represent CDO prices with this parameter. This is exactly like the representation of European call prices by a Black-Scholes volatility. To do so, each tranche price corresponds ideally to a unique parameter. In general, this property does not hold; that is why in the one-factor Gaussian copula model, the base correlation mechanism has been introduced. However, in that case, the fitted parameter (the base correlation) depends in practice strongly on the tranche and the maturity. This skew observed shows that there is no one-factor Gaussian copula matching the prices on the market. The base correlation being a rather intuitive parametrization, the skew is used in practice to depict how the market anticipates the future losses. However, when the market is stressed like during the recent subprime crisis, base correlation values are fanciful and unreliable. Many works have been done to identify a copula family or an extension of the copula model that depends on few parameters and could approximate well the tranche prices observed on the market. We mention here the work of Burtschell, Gregory, and Laurent (2005). Extending the one-factor Gaussian copula model, several authors have considered models where defaults are assumed to be independent conditional on a more general factor. This factor encapsulates the dependence between defaults. Among them, we cite the works of Hull and White (2006) and Chapovsky, Rennie, and Tavares (2007), who implement the factor structure on the intensities rather than on the copula triggers.

Implied correlation also suffers from a number of problems related to possible violation of no-arbitrage constraints. Torresetti, Brigo, and Pallavicini (2006) illustrated precrisis the two main types of implied correlation one may obtain from market CDO tranche spreads. They noticed that compound correlation is more consistent at the single tranche level but for some market CDO tranche spreads cannot be implied. Base correlation is less consistent but more flexible and can be implied for a much wider set of CDO tranche market spreads. It is also noticed that base correlation is more easily interpolated and leads to the possibility to price nonstandard detachments. However, Torresetti et al. (2006) show examples of how base correlation may lead to negative expected tranche losses, thus violating basic no-arbitrage conditions.

Nonetheless, the copula model presents some weaknesses that go deeper than the base correlation skew and the calibration problem. The main one is that the copula model freezes the evolution of the dependence between the defaults. To illustrate this, let us assume that the defaults indeed follow the copula model with stochastic default intensities from time 0. Let us suppose, for example, that no default has been observed up to time t. Using the lack of memory property, the random variables $\xi^j - \Lambda^j(t)$ follow an exponential law of parameter 1 and we name C_t the copula defined as the cumulative distribution function of $(e^{-(\xi^1 - \Lambda^1(t))}, \ldots, e^{-(\xi^m - \Lambda^m(t))})$. Then, we have for $t_1, \ldots, t_m > t$:

$$\mathbb{P}(\tau^1 > t_1, \ldots, \tau^m > t_m | \mathcal{F} \vee \{\forall j, \tau^j > t\}) = \frac{C(\exp(-\Lambda^1(t_1)), \ldots, \exp(-\Lambda^m(t_m)))}{C(\exp(-\Lambda^1(t)), \ldots, \exp(-\Lambda^m(t)))}$$

$$=: C_t(\exp(-(\Lambda^1(t_1) - \Lambda^1(t))), \ldots, \exp(-(\Lambda^m(t_m) - \Lambda^m(t))))$$

The copula C_t is with this formula entirely determined by the initial copula C and the stochastic evolution up to time t of the intensities that describe the single defaults—more precisely $\Lambda^1(t), \ldots, \Lambda^m(t)$. We can have analogous formulas when defaults occur before t. There is therefore no way through this model to get an autonomous evolution of the copula C_t and thus of the dependence between defaults. This does not seem to be realistic. Moreover, one would like to use (as for other financial markets) further option prices such as CDO tranche options or options embedded in cancelable tranches as a tool to catch the future evolution of the dependencies between defaults as seen today by the market. In a general manner, the main advantage of market calibration in comparison with the historical estimation is its ability to grasp the market's idea of the future trend; this is precisely what we cannot get within the copula model since it fixes the future interdependence between defaults from the initial time. And there is no straightforward extension of this model that allows us to get rid of this deficiency. Essentially, a copula is a static multivariate distribution.

3.3 Reduced Form Loss Models

An alternative to the copula model is to try to model directly the loss process ($L(t)$, $t \geq 0$) without taking into consideration the individual default times. This is a rather natural idea since CDOs are products that depend on the defaults only through this process. In this section we give examples of reduced-form loss models coming from the works of Errais, Giesecke, and Goldberg (2006); Giesecke and Goldberg (2005); and Brigo, Pallavicini, and Torresetti (2007a). These examples, as we will see, belong to the general class of affine models (Errais, Giesecke, and Goldberg 2006) for which the law of $L(t)$ is known analytically or semianalytically for each time t through its Fourier transform. This ensures a rather time-efficient calibration to CDO prices. Last, we hint at the random thinning procedure introduced in Giesecke and Goldberg (2005) that provides a mean to get single-name intensities that are consistent with the loss model.

3.3.1 Generalized Poisson Loss Model (Brigo et al. 2007a)

We begin our little tour of reduced-form models with the generalized Poisson loss (GPL) model because it relies on Poisson processes that are simple and well-known processes. Let us first assume for the sake of simplicity that the losses given the default of each name are all equal to LGD $\in (0, 1]$ and deterministic. Thus, the loss is proportional to the number of defaults $N(t) = \sum_{j=1}^{m} \mathbf{1}_{\tau^j \leq t}$:

$$L(t) = \frac{\text{LGD}}{m} N(t)$$

Let us assume that there are $k \leq m$ independent standard Poisson processes $M_1(t), \ldots, M_k(t)$ with intensity 1 on the probability space $(\Omega, \mathcal{G}, \mathbb{P})$. We suppose that we have k intensity processes $\lambda_t^{N_1}, \ldots, \lambda_t^{N_k}$ that we suppose adapted to the default-free filtration $(\mathcal{F}_t)_{t \geq 0}$ and define the cumulative intensities $\Lambda^{N_l}(t) = \int_0^t \lambda_s^{N_l} ds$ for $l \in \{1, \ldots, k\}$. Last, we define the time-inhomogeneous Poisson processes:

$$\forall l \in \{1, \ldots, k\}, \ N_l(t) = M_l(\Lambda^{N_l}(t))$$

that we assume to be adapted with respect to the filtration $(\mathcal{G}_t)_{t\geq 0}$. Let us consider k integers such that $1 \leq j_1 < j_2 < \cdots < j_k \leq m$. The GPL model assumes that the number of defaults at time t is given by:

$$N(t) = \min(Z_t, m) \text{ where } Z_t = \sum_{l=1}^{k} j_l N_l(t)$$

Thus, it allows for the possibility of simultaneous defaults: A jump of $N_l(t)$ induces exactly j_l defaults (if $Z_t \leq m$). That models in a rather extreme way the dependence between the defaults. One knows then exactly the distribution of Z_t given $\mathcal{F}$ through its Fourier transform using the independence of the Poisson processes M_l:

$$\forall u \in \mathbb{R}, \ \mathbb{E}[e^{iuZ_t}|\mathcal{F}] = \prod_{l=1}^{k} \exp[\Lambda^{N_l}(t)(e^{ij_l u} - 1)] = \exp\left[\sum_{l=1}^{k} \Lambda^{N_l}(t)(e^{ij_l u} - 1)\right]$$

Let us now turn to the valuation of the CDO rate $R_a^b(T)$ defined in equation (3.3). We are exactly in the same situation as for the copula model since we know the distribution of the loss $L(t) = \frac{\text{LGD}}{m} \min(Z_t, m)$ given $\mathcal{F}$. Therefore, if one specifies a model for the discount factors and the intensities $\lambda^{N_l}(t)$ we can once again calculate the expectations in equation (3.3) using integrations by parts and conditioning first to $\mathcal{F}$. Typically, one assumes in a first implementation of this model that the discount factors and the intensities are deterministic; this allows one to compute in a rather efficient way the CDO rate value using an inverse Fourier method. This is obviously an important point for calibration purpose to get a reasonable computation time. A calibration procedure of this model to real CDO tranche data is discussed in detail in Brigo, Pallavicini, and Torresetti (2007a). It gives encouraging results: All tranche prices but the long-term maturity CDO prices are fitted correctly. A little modification of the definition of the loss process $[\frac{\text{LGD}}{m'} \min(Z_t, m')$ instead of $\frac{\text{LGD}}{m} \min(Z_t, m)$ for $m' > m]$ is proposed in Brigo, Pallavicini, and Torresetti (2007a) to correct this problem, though we lose through this method the interpretation of $\min(Z_t, m)$ as the number of defaults before t. Recently, Brigo, Pallavicini, and Torresetti (2010) have revisited their model, and have given an analysis and a new parametrization of their GPL model for data in crisis.

Last, we want to mention an easy extension to this model. As we have seen, the main features of the GPL model are to allow multiple defaults and to have an analytically tractable loss distribution. The properties of the Poisson processes that are crucial here are that they are unit-jump-increasing processes whose Fourier transform is known. Thus, one could extend the GPL model taking $\forall l \in \{1, \ldots, k\}$, $N_l(t) = \tilde{M}_l(\Lambda^{N_l}(t))$ where the processes $\tilde{M}_l(t)$ are chosen to be independent unit-jump-increasing processes with an analytical formula for their Fourier transform $u \mapsto \mathbb{E}[\exp(iu\tilde{M}_l(t))]$. A possible way is to take $\tilde{M}_l(t) = M_l(S_l(t))$, where $(S_l(t), t \geq 0)$ is an increasing process independent from M_l. In that case, the Fourier transform writes:

$$\forall u \in \mathbb{R}, \ \mathbb{E}[\exp(iu\tilde{M}_l(t))] = \mathbb{E}[\exp(S_l(t)(e^{iu} - 1))]$$

If we take for S_l a Lévy subordinator such as an inverse Gaussian or a gamma subordinator, we have an analytical formula for it (see Brigo, Pallavicini, and Torresetti (2007a) for the gamma case). This is also the case if one assumes $S_l(t)$ to be a primitive of a Cox-Ingersoll-Ross process, or more generally if $S_l(t)$ is a positive linear combination of these (independent) processes.

3.3.2 Hawkes Process and Affine Point Process Loss Model (Errais, Giesecke, and Goldberg 2006)

Contrary to the previous GPL model, the model proposed by Giesecke and Goldberg (2005) and detailed in Errais et al. (2006) excludes the possibility of simultaneous defaults. To take into consideration the contagion between defaults, they model directly the loss process as a pure jump process whose jump intensity increases when defaults occur. Namely, they model $L(t)$ as a $(\mathcal{G}_t)$-adapted Hawkes process. We consider here a particular case and assume that it has an intensity of jumps that solves

$$d\lambda_t^L = \kappa(\rho(t) - \lambda_t^L)dt + \delta dL(t) \text{ with } \delta, \kappa, \lambda_0^L \geq 0 \tag{3.5}$$

and a jump law distribution ν such that $\nu((0, 1/m]) = 1$. This means that the instantaneous rate of jumps is $\lim_{dt\to 0^+} \frac{\mathbb{P}(L(t+dt)-L(t)>0|\mathcal{G}_t)}{dt} = \lambda_t^L$ and thus $\lim_{dt\to 0^+} \frac{\mathbb{E}[f(L(t+dt))-f(L(t))|\mathcal{G}_t]}{dt} = \lambda_t^L(\int_0^{1/m} f(L(t) + x)\nu(dx) - f(L(t)))$ for any bounded measurable function f. More precisely, the jump events (i.e., triggering and jump size) are supposed to be independent from the default-free filtration $(\mathcal{F}_t)_{t\geq 0}$ and we assume the stronger condition:

$$\lim_{dt\to 0^+} \frac{\mathbb{E}[f(L(t+dt)) - f(L(t))|\mathcal{G}_t \vee \mathcal{F}]}{dt}$$
$$= \lambda_t^L \left(\int_0^{1/m} f(L(t) + x)\nu(dx) - f(L(t)) \right)$$

We also suppose that the process $\rho(t)$ is positive and adapted to $(\mathcal{F}_t)_{t\geq 0}$. In Errais et al. (2006), $\rho(t)$ is assumed to be deterministic, but we want to show here that it is easy to nest dependence with the default-free filtration. In a more general way, the other fixed parameters could have been considered time-dependent and adapted to $(\mathcal{F}_t)_{t\geq 0}$ for what follows.

Through the choice of ν, this model allows the possibility to have random recovery rate. Taking identical deterministic recovery rates across names would lead to $\nu(dx) = \delta_{\text{LGD}/m}(dx)$. Let us remark also that the loss process is not bounded from above with this model. If this has undesirable effects, one can cap it as for the GPL model. With the preceding parametrization, the meaning of the parameters is rather clear: the intensity process has a mean reversion toward $\rho(t)$ with a speed parametrized by κ. The parameter δ synthesizes the impact of a default on the subsequent bankruptcies.

Under that model, Errais et al. (2006) have shown that one can calculate the Fourier transform of the loss distribution $\mathbb{E}[\exp(iuL(t))|\mathcal{F}]$ solving numerically ordinary differential equations (ODEs). This allows one to calculate as for the previous GPL or copula models the CDO rate value [equation (3.3)]. More precisely, we have the following result.

Proposition 3.3.1 *Let us fix $s \geq t$. Under the preceding setting, the Fourier transform of the loss $L(s)$ conditioned to $\mathcal{G}_t \vee \mathcal{F}$ is given by*

$$\forall u \in \mathbb{R}, \ \mathbb{E}[\exp(iuL(s))|\mathcal{G}_t \vee \mathcal{F}] = \exp(iuL(t) + a(u,t,s) + b(u,t,s)\lambda_t^L) \quad (3.6)$$

where the coefficient functions $a(u,t,s)$ and $b(u,t,s)$ are $\mathcal{F}_s$-measurable and solve the following ordinary differential equations:

$$\partial_t b(u,t,s) = \kappa b(u,t,s) + 1 - \int e^{(iu+\delta b(u,t,s))x} \nu(dx) \quad (3.7)$$

$$\partial_t a(u,t,s) = -\kappa\rho(t)b(u,t,s) \quad (3.8)$$

with the final condition $a(u,s,s) = 0$ and $b(u,s,s) = 0$. When ρ is a deterministic function, $a(u,t,s)$ and $b(u,t,s)$ are also deterministic.

This kind of result is standard and we just sketch the proof. The following process $(\mathbb{E}[\exp(iuL(s))|\mathcal{G}_t \vee \mathcal{F}], t \leq s)$ is a $(\mathcal{G}_t \vee \mathcal{F})$-martingale. If equation (3.6) holds, one has

$$\frac{d \exp(iuL(t) + a + b\lambda_t^L)}{\exp(iuL(t-) + a + b\lambda_{t-}^L)} = \exp((iu + b\delta)\Delta L(t))$$

$$- 1 + [\partial_t a + \partial_t b\lambda_t^L + b\kappa(\rho(t) - \lambda_t^L)]dt$$

where $\Delta L(t) = L(t) - L(t-)$. It is a martingale increment if and only if:

$$\lambda_t^L \left(\int e^{(iu+\delta b)x} \nu(dx) - 1 + \partial_t b - b\kappa \right) + \partial_t a + b\kappa\rho(t) = 0 \ a.s.$$

and one deduces equations (3.7) and (3.8) since λ_t^L takes a.s. an infinite number of values.

This way, one can even get the Fourier transform of the joint law of $J(t) := (L(t), N(t))$, where $N(t)$ denotes the number of jumps of the loss process up to time t. This is done explicitly in the paper of Errais, Giesecke, and Goldberg (2006). They introduce in a more general manner d-dimensional affine point processes $(J(t), t \geq 0)$ for which the Fourier transform can be calculated in the same way as for the Hawkes process. Of course, the Fourier transform of a sum of d-dimensional independent affine point process also has a similar form. This broadens considerably the possible models for the loss process. Within this framework, a time-inhomogeneous Poisson process appears as a particular one-dimensional affine point process, and the GPL model as a sum of one-dimensional independent affine point processes. More generally, most of the extension of the GPL model we have considered in the previous section can also be seen as a sum of one-dimensional independent affine point processes. They are interesting particular cases for which the Fourier transform is known analytically and does not require one to solve ODEs.

3.3.3 Loss Models and Single Defaults

We conclude this section on the reduced-form loss models by giving some clue on the natural question: Once a loss model is given for $L(t)$, can we find a procedure to define the individual defaults $\tau^1, \ldots, \tau^m$ in a coherent manner with the loss process? This might be of interest if one aimed to price a credit risk product that relies on some of the defaults that define $L(t)$. This is the case in the example of a CDO tranche whose underlying loss brings on the default times $\tau^1, \ldots, \tau^j$ with $1 \leq j < m$. This approach that consists in first defining the aggregated loss and then the single defaults is called top-down in the literature. Instead, in the copula model, we have a bottom-up approach: We first define the single-default events and then define the loss with the formula (3.2). We do not have such a problem of coherency in bottom-up models.

We explain here the random thinning procedure that has been introduced by Giesecke and Goldberg (2005). Let us denote by $N(t) = \sum_{s \leq t} \mathbf{1}_{\Delta L(s) > 0}$ the number of loss jumps before time t. When $N(t) \leq m$, one would like to assign to each jump one of the default times $\tau^1, \ldots, \tau^m$ and we exclude then simultaneous defaults. Ideally, it would be nice to have a direct relationship between $N(t)$ and the single-default indicators $\mathbf{1}_{\tau^j \leq t}$ for $j \in \{1, \ldots, m\}$. Giesecke and Goldberg (2005) have investigated the following one, called strong random thinning:

$$\mathbf{1}_{\tau^j \leq t} = \int_0^t \zeta_s^j \, dN(s)$$

where the $(\zeta_t^j, t \geq 0)$ are $(\mathcal{G}_t)$-predictable processes satisfying some technical conditions. However, as they show, this default representation is too strong and implies that one knows before the next jump which name will default. This is rather unrealistic and one has to find a weaker binding between the loss and the single defaults. The random thinning procedure they propose binds the $(\mathcal{G}_t)$-intensities of the single default to the $(\mathcal{G}_t)$-intensity λ_t^N of the counting process $N(t)$. The last intensity is defined as the process such that:

$$N(t) - \int_0^t \lambda_s^N \, ds$$

is a $(\mathcal{G}_t)$-martingale.

In the Hawkes process loss model, this is also the intensity of jumps defined by equation (3.5). They assume that there are $(\mathcal{G}_t)$-adapted processes $(\zeta_t^j, t \geq 0)$ such that $\zeta_t^j \lambda_t^N$ is the $(\mathcal{G}_t)$-intensity of the stopping time τ^j according to Definition (3.2.4). Let us remind the reader that single intensities vanish after their related default so that we may write $\zeta_t^j = \zeta_t^j \mathbf{1}_{\tau^j > t}$. Since $\min(N(t), m) = \sum_{j=1}^m \mathbf{1}_{\tau^j \leq t}$, the process $\int_0^t \sum_{j=1}^m \zeta_s^j \mathbf{1}_{\tau^j > s} \lambda_s^N ds - \int_0^t \lambda_s^N \mathbf{1}_{N(s) \leq m} ds$ is a $(\mathcal{G}_t)$-martingale and therefore we have necessarily:

$$\sum_{j=1}^m \zeta_t^j \mathbf{1}_{\tau^j > t} = \mathbf{1}_{N(t) \leq m} \tag{3.9}$$

Reciprocally, if the processes $(N(t), t \geq 0)$ and $(\zeta_t^j, t \geq 0)$ are given and satisfy condition (3.9), it is easy to check that $\zeta_t^j \lambda_t^N$ is the $(\mathcal{G}_t)$-intensity of τ^j if one assumes at each jump that the default name is chosen independently according to the discrete probability law $(\zeta_t^1 \mathbf{1}_{\tau^1 > t}, \ldots, \zeta_t^m \mathbf{1}_{\tau^m > t})$ on $\{1, \ldots, m\}$.

Let us give an example of processes $(\zeta_t^j, t \geq 0)$ that satisfy equation (3.9) and consider m positive deterministic functions $z^j(t)$ for $j \in \{1, \ldots, m\}$. Then, one can simply choose $\zeta_t^j = \frac{z^j(t) \mathbf{1}_{\tau^j > t}}{\sum_{j=1}^m z^j(t) \mathbf{1}_{\tau^j > t}}$ on $\{N(t) < m\}$ and $\zeta_t^j = 0$ on $\{N(t) \geq m\}$. Through the random thinning procedure, the law of τ^j at time 0 is simply given by:

$$\mathbb{P}(\tau^j \leq t) = \mathbb{E}\left[\int_0^t \zeta_s^j \lambda_s^N ds\right]$$

If one has a fast enough way to compute it, one can then calibrate the processes $(\zeta_t^j, t \geq 0)$ using the single-CDS rate prices [equation (3.1)]. Let us suppose, for example, that the loss process $L(t)$ comes from a Hawkes process. If we assume deterministic recovery rates $[\nu(dx) = \delta_{\text{LGD}/m}(dx)]$ and cap the loss by LGD, it has then exactly m jumps. One can then fit this capped loss to the CDO prices and use the random thinning procedure to get a model that is consistent with single-CDS and CDO data. If $L(t)$ may have more than m jumps (as for the general Hawkes process model) and is already calibrated to CDO prices, then it will still be consistent with CDO and CDS prices if the expected loss beyond m jumps at the larger final maturity $T_{\max}$ is negligible. This will be mainly the case if the event $\{N(T_{\max}) > m\}$ is very rare. Otherwise, assigning a default name to each of the m first jumps is not appropriate.

Getting coherent single-default events starting from the loss process is a current topic of research. The thinning procedure has recently been revisited by Bielecki, Crépey, and Jeanblanc (2008). As an alternative to this method, we cite here the work of Brigo, Pallavicini, and Torresetti (2007b), who consider another approach based on the common Poisson model (Lindskog and McNeil 2001) and extend their GPL model to take into account the single defaults.

3.4 Markovian Projection, Local Intensity, and Stochastic Local Intensity Models

Up to now, we have considered different parametrized models for the loss distribution. Typically, they assume loss dynamics for which the CDO fair prices can be quickly computed. Thus, they can be calibrated in practice to get prices as close as possible to the market data.

In this section, we present an approach that is very similar to the well-known local volatility model proposed by Dupire (1994) for the equity options market. Let us recall briefly this result. Assuming deterministic interest rates, there is a local volatility function $\sigma(t, x)$ such that the model $d\bar{S}_t = r\bar{S}_t dt + \sigma(t, \bar{S}_t)\bar{S}_t dW_t$ perfectly matches all European call option prices. The local volatility and the European call prices are linked with a partial differential equation (PDE). In particular, since the knowledge of the European call prices is equivalent to the knowledge of the marginal laws of the stock, this shows that for any stock dynamics $dS_t = rS_t dt + \sigma_t S_t dW_t$, we can find a Markovian process $\bar{S}_t$ that has the same marginal laws. This result was already obtained by Gyöngy (1986), who showed that $\sigma(t, S_t) = \sqrt{\mathbb{E}[\sigma_t^2 | S_t]}$. Here, like European options, CDO prices only depend on the loss process through its marginal laws (see Remark 3.2.1). We present in the first part an analogous result and explain how to construct a Markov jump process that can match all the marginal laws of the loss. We also hint at different ways to calibrate this Markovian process that have been suggested in the literature.

This approach has the main advantage of allowing a theoretically exact calibration to the CDO rates. However, it freezes all the dynamics from the initial CDO data, which may not be flexible enough for valuing further more advanced contracts. To fill this deficiency, at least two ways have been suggested. Taking back the idea of the Heath-Jarrow-Morton and Brace-Gatarek-Musiela models for the interest rates, the forward loss models describe the dynamics of the Markovian process that matches the marginal laws of the loss. Section 3.5 is devoted to them. Here, we consider in Subsection 3.4.2 loss models with a stochastic jump intensity. The trick is to do so reusing the calibration made for the simple Markovian process in order to fit CDO rates. This is very similar to what is done in equity derivatives for stochastic volatility models. Once a local volatility function $\sigma(t, x)$ has been fitted to European call prices, any local stochastic volatility model $dS_t = rS_t dt + f(t, Y_t)\eta(t, S_t)S_t dW_t$ such that $\mathbb{E}[f(t, Y_t)^2 | S_t]\eta(t, S_t)^2 = \sigma(t, S_t)^2$ automatically fits the European call prices thanks to Gyöngy's result.

In all of this section, we assume that all the recovery rates are deterministic and equal to $1 - \text{LGD}$ for all the firms within the basket. Thus, we have:

$$L(t) = \frac{\text{LGD}}{m} \sum_{j=1}^{m} \mathbf{1}_{\tau^j \leq t} = \frac{\text{LGD}}{m} N(t) \tag{3.10}$$

where $N(t)$ is the number of defaults at time t. For $k \in \{0, \ldots, m\}$, we also set:

$$\ell_k = \frac{k\text{LGD}}{m}, \ \mathscr{L}_k = \{\ell_0, \ldots, \ell_k\} \text{ and } \mathscr{L}_k^* = \mathscr{L}_k \setminus \{0\} \tag{3.11}$$

3.4.1   Markovian Projection of the Loss Process

We consider the loss process described previously. It is a nondecreasing pure jump process that takes values in $[0, 1]$. We also set $\Delta L(t) = L(t) - L(t-) \in \mathscr{L}_{m-N(t)}$ the size of the loss jump at time t. Looking at the predictable compensator of the integer-valued random measure associated to $L(t)$, there exists a nondecreasing process Λ_t^L and probability measures $\nu(t, dx)$ on $\mathbb{R}_+$ (both $(\mathcal{G}_t)$-predictable) such that:

$$\sum_{s \leq t, \Delta L(s) > 0} F(s, \Delta L(s), L(s-)) - \int_0^t \int_{\mathbb{R}} F(s, x, L(s-))\nu(s, dx)d\Lambda_s^L$$

is a $(\mathcal{G}_t)$-martingale when $\mathbb{E}[\sum_{s>0, \Delta L(s)>0} |F(s, \Delta L(s), L(s-))|] < \infty$ (see Jacod and Shiryaev 2003, p. 66). This is automatically satisfied when F is bounded since there are at most m jumps. Taking $F(s, x, \ell) = \mathbf{1}_{x \notin \mathscr{L}_{m(1-\ell/\text{LGD})}^*}$, we get that $\nu(t, \mathscr{L}_{m-N(t-)}^*) = 1$ when $d\Lambda_t^L > 0$. Therefore, we have $\nu(t, dx) = \sum_{i=1}^{m-N(t-)} \nu_i(t)\delta_{\ell_i}(dx)$ with $\sum_{i=1}^{m-N(t-)} \nu_i(t) = 1$.

Moreover, we assume now that $d\Lambda_t^L = \lambda_t^L dt$, where $(\lambda_t^L, t \geq 0)$ is a nonnegative $(\mathcal{G}_t)$-predictable process. This in particular implies that $\mathbb{P}(L(t) = L(t-)) = 1$ for any $t \geq 0$ [take $F(s, x, \ell) = \mathbf{1}_{s=t}\mathbf{1}_{x>0}$], which means that no default can occur at a given time. Taking $F(s, x, \ell) = 1$, we also get that:

$$\sum_{s \leq t, \Delta L_s > 0} \mathbf{1}_{\Delta L_s > 0} - \int_0^t \lambda_s^L ds$$

is a $(\mathcal{G}_t)$-martingale. In other words, λ_t^L is the instantaneous rate of jumps.

Let f be a bounded function. We have, using the tower property of the conditional expectation:

$$\mathbb{E}[f(L(t))] = \mathbb{E}[f(L(0))] + \int_0^t \mathbb{E}\left[\sum_{i=1}^{m-N(s-)} (f(L(s-) + \ell_i) - f(L(s-)))\lambda_s^L \nu_i(s)\right] ds$$

$$= \mathbb{E}[f(L(0))] + \int_0^t \mathbb{E}\left[\sum_{i=1}^{m-N(s-)} (f(L(s-) + \ell_i) - f(L(s-)))\mathbb{E}[\lambda_s^L \nu_i(s)|L(s-)]\right] ds$$

We set $\lambda(t, L(t-)) = \mathbb{E}[\lambda_t^L|L(t-)]$ and $\nu_i(t, L(t-)) = \mathbb{E}[\lambda_t^L \nu_i(t)|L(t-)]/\lambda(t, L(t-))$, with $\nu_i(t, L(t-)) = 0$ when $\lambda(t, L(t-)) = 0$. Taking $f(\ell) = \mathbf{1}_{\ell=\ell_k}$ for $k = 0, \ldots, m$, we get:

$$\frac{d\mathbb{P}(L(t) = \ell_k)}{dt} = -\lambda(t, \ell_k)\mathbb{P}(L(t) = \ell_k) + \mathbf{1}_{k \geq 1} \sum_{j=0}^{k-1} \nu_{k-j}(t, \ell_j)\lambda(t, \ell_j)\mathbb{P}(L(t) = \ell_j)$$

Thus, $(\mathbb{P}(L(t) = \ell_k), k = 0, \ldots, m)$ appears as the unique solution of a linear ODE. This is precisely the Kolmogorov equation of a Markov chain on $\mathscr{L}_m$ with jump intensity $\lambda(t, \ell)$ and jump law $\sum_{i=1}^{m-\ell} \nu_i(t, \ell) \delta_{\ell_i}(dx)$. We get the following proposition.

Proposition 3.4.1 *Under the preceding assumptions, the Markov chain defined on $\mathscr{L}_m$ with the jump intensity*

$$\lambda(t, L(t-)) = \mathbb{E}[\lambda_t^L | L(t-)]$$

and the jump law

$$\nu(t, L(t-), dx) = \mathbb{E}[\lambda_t^L \nu(t, dx) | L(t-)] / \lambda(t, L(t-))$$

has the same marginal laws as the loss process. The function $\lambda(t, \ell)$ is then called the "local intensity" by analogy with the local volatility model.

In particular, excluding simultaneous defaults (i.e., $\nu_i(t) = \mathbf{1}_{i=1}$), this Markov chain has only jumps of size LGD/m that occur at rate $\lambda(t, L(t-))$. This Markovian projection of the loss process is usually called "local intensity model" since its law is characterized only by $\lambda(t, \ell)$.

This is analogous with the loss process [equation (3.10)] of Gyöngy's theorem for continuous SDEs. Recently, Bentata and Cont (2009) have unified these results by showing that a similar Markovian projection holds for general semimartingales.

In general, it is common to exclude simultaneous defaults and to consider the local intensity model as an approximation of the real loss process. In that case, the Kolmogorov equation has the simpler form:

$$0 \le k \le m, \quad \frac{d\mathbb{P}(L(t) = \ell_k)}{dt} = -\lambda(t, \ell_k)\mathbb{P}(L(t) = \ell_k)$$
$$+ \mathbf{1}_{k \neq 0} \lambda(t, \ell_{k-1})\mathbb{P}(L(t) = \ell_{k-1})$$

Assuming for a while that the marginal laws of the loss process are known for any $t \ge 0$, it is then straightforward to get the local intensity model, which gives the same marginal laws as the real loss process. In other words, there is in the local intensity model a bijection between the local intensity and the marginal laws of the loss. Of course, we do not have in practice the full knowledge of $(\mathbb{P}(L(t) = \ell_k), t \ge 0)$ for $t \ge 0$, $k \in \{0, \ldots, m\}$. However, according to Remark 3.2.1, CDO (and index) prices depend mainly on marginal distributions of the loss process and therefore bring a partial information on the marginal loss distributions. The idea is then to calibrate the local intensity to these prices. This calibration problem is ill-posed because different local intensities can lead to the same market prices. Different approaches have already been proposed. In Cont and Savescu (2008), an approach analogous to Dupire's formula is obtained for call options on the loss. Thus, $\lambda(t, \ell)$ can be recovered with this equation if it is assumed to be a piecewise constant between CDO maturities. Cont and Minca (2008) propose a nonparametric calibration procedure that minimizes a relative entropy criterion. Lopatin and Misirpashaev (2007) instead consider a specific parametrized form for the local intensity and then look at the parameters that best fit the market data.

In any case, once the local intensity is calibrated to market data, the loss dynamics are fully determined. This may be a drawback, because the local intensity itself can change in time. Said differently, the local intensity model may not be rich enough to take into account products that start in the future or pathwise options on the loss. To fill this deficiency, Schonbücher (2005) gives a way to model the dynamics of the local intensity. This is presented in Section 3.5. In another direction, Arnsdorf and Halperin (2007) and Lopatin and Misirpashaev (2007) suggest adding another source of randomness following the approach used for the stochastic local volatility model in equity. Their models are presented in the next paragraphs.

3.4.2   Stochastic Local Intensity (SLI) Loss Models

In these paragraphs, we present two similar models that have been proposed contemporarily. Arnsdorf and Halperin called their model a bivariate spread-loss portfolio (BSLP) model. Here, we rather called them stochastic local intensity (SLI) models by analogy with the stochastic local volatility models in equity.

The idea is to start with a local intensity function $\lambda(t, \ell)$ that is already calibrated and matches CDO and index prices. We then assimilate the marginal laws of the real loss process to the marginal laws of the local intensity model. Therefore, $\mathbb{P}(L(t) = \ell_k)$ is known for $t \geq 0, k \in \{0, \ldots, m\}$. We consider $(Y_t)_{t \geq 0}$ a general $(\mathcal{G}_t)$-adapted real process and two functions $f, \eta : \mathbb{R}_+ \times \mathbb{R} \to \mathbb{R}_+$. We assume that the loss process $L(t)$ has jumps of size LGD at the rate

$$\lambda_t^L = \eta(t, L(t-)) f(t, Y_t)$$

From Proposition 3.4.1, this model automatically fits CDO prices as soon as the following condition holds:

$$\eta(t, L(t-))\mathbb{E}[f(t, Y_t)|L(t-)] = \lambda(t, L(t-))$$

Of course, $\eta(t, L(t-)) = \lambda(t, L(t-))/\mathbb{E}[f(t, Y_t)|L(t-)]$ is unfortunately not a correct definition since $(L(t), t \geq 0)$ depends on η. In general, Y_t is assumed to solve:

$$dY_t = \mu(t, L(t), Y_t)dt + \sigma(t, L(t), Y_t)dW_t + \gamma(t, L(t-), Y_t)dL(t)$$

where $(W_t, t \geq 0)$ is a $(\mathcal{G}_t)$-Brownian motion, and one would like to have a loss process with a jump rate $\lambda(t, L(t-))/\mathbb{E}[f(t, Y_t)|L(t-)]$. Due to this conditional expectation, this dynamic is nonlinear and involves the joint law of $(Y_t, L(t))$. To the best of our knowledge, the existence and the uniqueness of such a process $(Y_t, L(t))_{t \geq 0}$ are still an open question.

However, it is possible to look at a numerical proxy of such a process. To do so, we assume that we have $\mathbb{P}(L(t) = \ell_k, Y_t \in dy) = p(t, \ell_k, y)dy$ for some smooth function p. We can write the Fokker-Planck equation for $k \in \{0, \ldots, m\}, y \in \mathbb{R}$:

$$\partial_t p(t, \ell_k, y) = \mathbf{1}_{k \geq 1} \eta(t, \ell_{k-1}) f(t, y) p(t, \ell_{k-1}, y) - \eta(t, \ell_k) f(t, y) p(t, \ell_k, y)$$
$$- \partial_y(\mu(t, \ell_k, y) p(t, \ell_k, y)) + \frac{1}{2} \partial_y^2 (\sigma^2(t, \ell_k, y) p(t, \ell_k, y))$$

Here, we have assumed $\gamma \equiv 0$ for the sake of simplicity. Let us consider a regular time grid $t_j = j\Delta t$ and assume that the initial distribution $p(t_0, \ell, y)$ is known. We write the Euler explicit scheme to express $p(t_1, \ell_k, y)$ in function of $p(t_0, \ell_{k-1}, y)$, $p(t_0, \ell_k, y)$, and their derivatives:

$$p(t_1, \ell_k, y) = p(t_0, \ell_k, y) + \Delta t \Big[\mathbf{1}_{k \geq 1} \eta(t_0, \ell_{k-1}) f(t_0, y) p(t_0, \ell_{k-1}, y)$$
$$- \eta(t_0, \ell_k) f(t_0, y) p(t_0, \ell_k, y) - \partial_y(\mu(t_0, \ell_k, y) p(t_0, \ell_k, y))$$
$$+ \frac{1}{2} \partial_y^2 (\sigma^2(t_0, \ell_k, y) p(t_0, \ell_k, y)) \Big]$$

Since $\mathbb{P}(L(t_1) = \ell_k) = \int p(t_1, \ell_k, y)dy$ is assumed to be known, we can deduce from the integrated Euler scheme with respect to y the values of $\eta(t_0, \ell_k)$ from $k = 0$ to $k = m$ that allow us to match the marginal laws. Then, it is possible to compute $p(t_1, \ell_k, y)$ using the Euler scheme. Thus, we can compute iteratively $\eta(t_j, \ell_k, y)$ and then $p(t_{j+1}, \ell_k, y)$ up to the desired maturity.

Even though this numerical scheme may seem rather intuitive, it is not proved (to the best of our knowledge) that it converges when the time step goes to zero under some general assumptions. We now give two recent models that belong to this framework.

3.4.2.1 Lopatin and Misirpashaev (2007) Model

In this model, we have $f(t, y) = y$, and

$$dY_t = \kappa(\rho(t, L(t)) - Y_t)dt + \sigma \sqrt{Y_t} dW_t$$

Using the same procedure as before, we could in principle find for any function ρ a corresponding η that allows it to match the marginal laws. Instead of this, Lopatin and

Misirpashaev suggest that we fit the function ρ in order to match directly the marginal laws (i.e., $\eta \equiv 1$). Therefore, $\lambda_t^L = Y_t$, and the loss intensity is in fact modeled directly. The procedure to calibrate ρ is very analogous to the one described earlier.

3.4.2.2 Arnsdorf and Halperin (2007) Model

In this model, $f(t, y) = y$ and Y_t solves:

$$dY_t = \mu(t, Y_t)dt + \sigma(t, Y_t)dW_t + \gamma(t, Y_t)dL(t)$$

with some specific choices of μ, σ, and γ that we do not give in detail here. Since $\gamma \not\equiv 0$, the Fokker-Planck equation becomes more complicated. To avoid this problem, Arnsdorf and Halperin suggest approximating $(Y_t, L(t))$ by a Markovian process $(\bar{Y}_t, L(t))$ that takes a finite number of values. Doing so, the Fokker-Planck (or Kolmogorov) equation becomes elementary and we can then apply the numerical procedure described earlier.

3.5 Forward Loss Models

We conclude our quick tour on the loss modeling with the presentation of two forward loss models proposed contemporaneously by Schönbucher (2005) and Sidenius, Piterbarg, and Andersen (2005). Forward loss models are to reduced-form models what Heath-Jarrow-Morton (HJM) and Brace-Gatarek-Musiela (BGM) models are to short interest rate models. In the fixed income case, forward (short or LIBOR) rates are thus directly specified; these rates are mainly the fair interest rates one should apply at a current time t for a future contract at time $T > t$. The forward loss models that we consider here target to model how the future loss distributions $L(T)$ are seen by the market at time t. Contrary to the previous models, the loss itself is not directly modeled. We have decided to present here both models at the same time with analogous notations to point out similarities and differences. We focus only on the main construction steps of these models and refer to the original papers for technical proofs and further developments. We keep the same filtered probability space as for the previous models. Last, we assume in this section that the loss process is independent from the interest rates so that the computation of the CDO rates [equation (3.3)] is straightforward once we know the future loss distributions (and the expected discount factors).

3.5.1 Schönbucher's Forward Model (2005)

3.5.1.1 Description of the Loss

Here, we assume that each default has the same deterministic recovery rate $1 - $ LGD. In that case, the loss is proportional to the number of defaults, and it is equivalent to model one or the other. We are then exactly in the same setting as equation (3.10), and we use as before the notation (3.11). The law of $L(T)$ seen at time $t \leq T$ is described by $\pi(t, T) \in \mathbb{R}^{m+1}$ where $\pi_k(t, T) = \mathbb{P}(L(T) = \ell_k|\mathcal{G}_t)$ for $k = 0, \ldots, m$. We have the following straightforward properties:

(i) $\pi_k(t, T) \geq 0$.
(ii) $\sum_{k=0}^{m} \pi_k(t, T) = 1$.
(iii) For each $n \in \{0, \ldots, m\}$, $T \mapsto \mathbb{P}(L(T) \leq \ell_n|\mathcal{G}_t) = \sum_{k=0}^{n} \pi_k(t, T)$ is nonincreasing.
(iv) $\pi_k(t, t) = \mathbf{1}_{\{L(t)=\ell_k\}}$.

These properties stem immediately from the fact that $(L(t), t \geq 0)$ is an increasing $(\mathcal{G}_t)$-adapted process taking values in $\mathcal{L}_m$. They are thus necessary arbitrage-free conditions on $\pi(t, T)$.

Assumptions on the loss process (A.1) *We assume that the loss process is defined by equation (3.10), and therefore $\pi(t, T)$ satisfies properties (i–iv). Moreover, we assume that*

$$T \mapsto \pi(t, T) \text{ is } C^1 \text{ and } \forall k, \ \pi_k(t, T) > 0 \implies \forall T' \geq T, \pi_k(t, T') > 0 \quad (3.12)$$

Under these assumptions **(A.1)**, it is shown in Schönbucher (2005) that there is a nondecreasing time-inhomogeneous Markov chain $(\tilde{L}_t(T), T \geq t)$ on $\mathcal{L}_m$ with transition matrices $(\lambda(t, T), T \geq t)$ such that $\lambda(t, T)$ is $\mathcal{G}_t$-measurable and

$$\forall T \geq t, \forall k \in \{0, \ldots, m\}, \ \pi_k(t, T) = \mathbb{P}(\tilde{L}_t(T) = \ell_k|\mathcal{G}_t) \quad (3.13)$$

This result is very similar to Proposition 3.4.1. The generator of $(\tilde{L}_t(T), T \geq t)$ can be written for a bounded function f:

$$\lim_{dT \to 0^+} \frac{\mathbb{E}\left[f(\tilde{L}_t(T + dT)) - f(\tilde{L}_t(T))|\mathcal{G}_T\right]}{dT}$$

$$= \sum_{k=0}^{m-1} \mathbf{1}_{\{\tilde{L}_t(T)=\ell_k\}} \sum_{l=k+1}^{m} \lambda_{k,l}(t, T) \left(f(\ell_l) - f(\ell_k)\right) \quad (3.14)$$

Reciprocally, if one starts from $\mathcal{G}_t$-measurable transition rates $\lambda(t, T)$, can we find a loss process satisfying **(A.1)** that is consistent with equation (3.13), that is, such that

$$\forall t \geq 0, \forall T \geq t, \forall k \in \{0, \ldots, m\}, \ \pi_k(t, T) = \mathbb{P}(\tilde{L}_t(T) = \ell_k|\mathcal{G}_t) \quad (3.15)$$

where $(\bar{L}_t(T), T \geq t)$ is defined by $\bar{L}_t(t) = L(t)$ and equation (3.14)? If this holds, $L(t + dt)$ and $\bar{L}_t(t + dt)$ have the same law conditioned to $\mathcal{G}_t$, and we get from equation (3.14) taken at $T = t$

$$\lim_{dt \to 0^+} \frac{\mathbb{E}\left[f(L(t + dt)) - f(L(t))|\mathcal{G}_t\right]}{dt} = \sum_{k=0}^{m-1} \mathbf{1}_{\{L(t) = \ell_k\}} \sum_{l=k+1}^{m} \lambda_{k,l}(t, t)\left(f(\ell_l) - f(\ell_k)\right)$$

(3.16)

Therefore, the loss dynamics is fully characterized by the transition rates if the consistency equality (3.15) holds. The idea of Schönbucher's model is to specify dynamics for the transition rates and identify conditions under which there exists a loss process that is consistent with those. The loss dynamics is then given by equation (3.16).

We will restrict the transition rate matrices that we consider. Indeed, it has been shown in Schönbucher (2005) that under additional assumptions on $\pi(t, T)$ that we do not specify here, the Markov chain $(\bar{L}_t(T), T \geq t)$ can be chosen to have only jumps of size LGD/m. This is a loss of generality, also with respect to the GPL model. This amounts to excluding simultaneous defaults after t. If these additional assumptions are not satisfied, a result stated in Schönbucher (2005) shows that one can, however, approximate closely the forward loss distributions by a nondecreasing Markov chain with LGD/m jumps. As a consequence, it does not seem so much restrictive to focus on the transition matrices that allow only LGD/m jumps ($\lambda_{k,l}(t, T) = 0$ for $l \geq k + 2$). We use then the shorter notation:

$$\lambda_k(t, T) = \lambda_{k,k+1}(t, T) \text{ for } k < m \text{ and set } \lambda_m(t, T) = 0 \qquad (3.17)$$

Model principle: We model the dynamics for the transition rates $\lambda_k(t, T)$, $k \in \{0, \ldots m - 1\}$ and look for conditions under which there exists a loss process satisfying **(A.1)** that is consistent in the sense of equation (3.15). The loss dynamics are then fully characterized by

$$\lim_{dt \to 0} \frac{\mathbb{E}\left[f(L(t + dt)) - f(L(t))|\mathcal{G}_t\right]}{dt} = \sum_{k=0}^{m-1} \mathbf{1}_{\{L(t) = \ell_k\}} \lambda_k(t, t)\left(f(\ell_{k+1}) - f(\ell_k)\right)$$

(3.18)

3.5.1.2   Consistency and Option Valuation

The model being specified, we would like to find forward rate dynamics for $\lambda_k(t, T)$ that are consistent with the loss distribution in the sense of equation (3.15). To do so, one has first to compute $\mathbb{P}(\bar{L}_t(T) = \ell_k|\mathcal{G}_t)$ as a function of the transition rates. We introduce as in Schönbucher (2005) $P_{k,l}(t, T) = \mathbb{P}(\bar{L}_t(T) = \ell_l|\mathcal{G}_t, \bar{L}_t(t) = \ell_k)$.

From equations (3.16) and (3.17), one gets the Kolmogorov equation $\partial_T P_{k,l}(t, T) = P_{k,l-1}(t, T)\lambda_{l-1}(t, T) - P_{k,l}(t, T)\lambda_l(t, T)$. Since $P_{k,l}(t, t) = \mathbf{1}_{l=k}$, we deduce

$$l < k, \qquad P_{k,l}(t, T) = 0$$

$$l = k, \qquad P_{k,k}(t, T) = \exp\left(-\int_t^T \lambda_k(t, s)ds\right) \qquad (3.19)$$

$$l > k, \qquad P_{k,l}(t, T) = \int_t^T P_{k,l-1}(t, s)\lambda_{l-1}(t, s)\exp\left(-\int_s^T \lambda_l(t, u)du\right)ds$$

Let us emphasize here that these are the transition probabilities of our representation of the loss $\tilde{L}_t$, not of the true loss process. The following key result stated in Schönbucher (2005) gives necessary and sufficient conditions to get a loss representation that is consistent with the real loss in the sense of equation (3.15).

Proposition 3.5.1 *Let us assume that the loss process $(L(t), t \geq 0)$ starts from $L(0) = 0$ and is such that $\pi(t, T)$ satisfy properties (i–iv) and condition (3.12). Let us assume that for each $k \in \{0, \ldots, m-1\}$, the transition rate $\lambda_k(t, T)$ is nonnegative and $(\mathcal{G}_t)$-adapted and satisfies $\mathbb{E}[\sup\limits_{t \leq T}\lambda_k(t, T)] < \infty$. Then the following conditions are equivalent:*

1. $\forall T \geq t \geq 0, \forall k \in \{0, \ldots, m\},\ \pi_k(t, T) = \mathbb{P}(\tilde{L}_t(T) = \ell_k|\mathcal{G}_t)$. *(consistency)*
2. $\forall T > 0, \forall l \in \{0, \ldots, m\},\ (P_{N(t),l}(t, T))_{t\in[0,T]}$ *is a $(\mathcal{G}_t)$-martingale.*
3. $\forall T > 0, \forall l \in \{0, \ldots, m\},\ (\lambda_l(t, T)P_{N(t),l}(t, T))_{t\in[0,T]}$ *is a $(\mathcal{G}_t)$-martingale and* $\lim\limits_{dt\to 0}\dfrac{\mathbb{P}(L(t+dt)-L(t)=\text{LGD}/m|\mathcal{G}_t)}{dt} = \lambda_{N(t)}(t, t)$.

3.5.1.3 Consistent Transition Rates Dynamics and Simulation

Our aim is now to specify transition rates that are consistent with the loss process. Following Schönbucher (2005), we assume that there is a d-dimensional $(\mathcal{G}_t)$-Brownian motion and $(\mathcal{G}_t)$-predictable coefficients $\mu_k(t, T) \in \mathbb{R}$ and $\sigma_k(t, T) \in \mathbb{R}^d$ such that

$$\forall k \in \{0, \ldots, m-1\},\ \lambda_k(t, T) = \lambda_k(0, T) + \int_0^t \mu_k(s, T)ds + \int_0^t \sigma_k(s, T)dW_s \qquad (3.20)$$

In preparation for applying Proposition 3.5.1 and finding a consistency condition, one has to know the transition probability dynamics. Schönbucher (2005) shows that

$$\forall k, l \in \{0, \ldots, m\}, t \leq T,\ dP_{k,l}(t, T) = u_{k,l}(t, T)dt + v_{k,l}(t, T)dW_t$$

and we refer to the original paper for the recursive explicit formulas of $u_{k,l}(t, T)$ and $v_{k,l}(t, T)$ in terms of the transition rate dynamics. Applying Proposition 3.5.1, it is then shown that the transition rates [equation (3.20)] are consistent with the loss if and only if:

$$\forall l \in \{0, \dots, m\}, \ P_{N(t),l}(t, T)\mu_l(t, T) = -\sigma_l(t, T)v_{N(t),l}(t, T) \text{ and}$$

$$\lim_{dt \to 0} \frac{\mathbb{P}(L(t + dt) - L(t) = \text{LGD}/m | \mathcal{G}_t)}{dt} = \lambda_{N(t)}(t, t)$$

Existence of coefficients $\mu_k(t, T)$ and $\sigma_k(t, T)$ that satisfy this condition is not directly addressed. It is, however, given a simulation scheme for the loss $(L(t), t \geq 0)$ that satisfies asymptotically this condition once $\lambda(0, T)$ and $\sigma(t, T)$ have been fixed for $0 \leq t \leq T$. At time 0, $\lambda(0, T)$ and $\sigma(t, T)$ have to be parametrized and calibrated to market data. Typically, since $\lambda(0, T)$ fully determines $\pi(0, T)$, it is chosen to fit exactly the prices of CDO tranches that start immediately (see Section 3.4.1 for some references on this calibration). The volatilities $\sigma(t, T)$ should then be fitted to other products (tranche options, cancelable tranches, etc.). We set $\hat{L}(0) = 0$, $\hat{N}(0) = 0$ and $\hat{\lambda}(0, T) = \lambda(0, T)$, and consider a time step Δt. Let us assume that we have simulated $\hat{L}$ and $\hat{\lambda}$ up to time $t = q\Delta t$ so that $\hat{L}(t)$ and $(\hat{\lambda}(t, T), T \geq t)$ are known. Now, one should remark from equation (3.19) (respectively from $v_{k,l}$'s formula in Schönbucher (2005)) that the transition probabilities $P_{k,l}(t, T)$ and the coefficients $v_{k,l}(t, T)$ are entirely determined by the transition rates $(\lambda(t, T), T \geq t)$ and $(\sigma(t, T), T \geq t)$. Therefore, we can estimate these with $(\hat{\lambda}(t, T), T \geq t)$ and $(\sigma(t, T), T \geq t)$, and we set:

$$\forall l \geq \hat{N}(t), \forall T \geq t, \ \hat{\mu}_l(t, T) = -\frac{\hat{v}_{\hat{N}(t),l}(t, T)}{\hat{P}_{\hat{N}(t),l}(t, T)}\sigma_l(t, T)$$

and $\hat{\mu}_l(t, T) = 0$ for $l < \hat{N}(t)$. Then, we set $\hat{N}(t + \Delta t) = \hat{N}(t) + B_q$ and $\hat{L}(t + \Delta t) = \hat{L}(t) + B_q\text{LGD}/m$ where B_q is an independent Bernoulli variable of parameter $\hat{\lambda}_{\hat{N}(t)}(t, t)\Delta t$ and:

$$\forall l, \forall T \geq t + \Delta t, \ \lambda_l(t + \Delta t, T) = \lambda_l(t, T) + \hat{\mu}_l(t, T)\Delta t + \sigma(t, T)(W_{t+\Delta t} - W_t)$$

In fact, only transition rates above $\hat{N}(t + \Delta t)$ will be useful next, and we can instead simply take $\lambda_l(t + \Delta t, T) = 0$ for $l < \hat{N}(t + \Delta t)$. We can then continue the iteration.

To conclude this section, one should mention that more sophisticated dynamics are also considered in Schönbucher (2005). In particular, extensions are proposed to take into account possible dependence of the loss to single defaults. In connection with that, let us mention also that the random thinning procedure introduced in Subsection 3.3.3 can be applied here to assign a default name to each loss jump.

3.5.2 The SPA Model (Sidenius, Piterbarg, and Andersen 2005)

3.5.2.1 Description of the Loss

Assumptions on the loss process (A.2) *Following Sidenius, Piterbarg, and Andersen (SPA), we consider a general loss process $(L(t), t \geq 0)$ valued in $[0, 1]$ that is a nondecreasing $(\mathcal{G}_t)$-adapted Markov process. More precisely, we assume it satisfies $L(0) = 0$ and*

$$\lim_{dt \to 0} \frac{\mathbb{E}\left[f(L(t+dt)) - f(L(t))|\mathcal{G}_t \vee \mathcal{F}\right]}{dt} = \mathcal{A}_t f(L(t))$$

The generator $\mathcal{A}_t$ is assumed to be defined on a domain $\mathcal{D}$ that is dense in the set of bounded measurable functions, and to satisfy: $\forall f \in \mathcal{D}$, $\forall l \in [0, 1]$, $\mathcal{A}_t f(l)$ is $\mathcal{F}_t$-measurable. Thus, the jump events (triggering and jump sizes) depend on only $\mathcal{G}_t \vee \mathcal{F}$ through $\mathcal{F}_t$ and $L(t)$.

We assume also that filtrations $(\mathcal{F}_t)_{t \geq 0}$ and $(\mathcal{G}_t)_{t \geq 0}$ are such that for each $\mathcal{G}_t$ integrable variable X, $\mathbb{E}[X|\mathcal{F}] = \mathbb{E}[X|\mathcal{F}_t]$. In comparison to the Schönbucher's model, the jumps may have different sizes that can take into account different recoveries. This is particularly relevant given the difficulties seen in 2008 and 2009 in calibrating super-senior tranches using fixed recoveries. Their number may also exceed m. With the loss dynamics depending only on the default-free filtration and the loss itself, there is no possible particular dependence to some single default.

Instead of dealing directly with the forward loss distributions $\pi(t, T) = (\pi_x(t, T), x \in [0, 1])$ where $\pi_x(t, T) = \mathbb{P}(L(T) \leq x|\mathcal{G}_t)$, the SPA model introduces for $t, T \geq 0$ (not only $T \geq t$), $p(t, T) = (p_x(t, T), x \in [0, 1])$ where $p_x(t, T) = \mathbb{P}(L(T) \leq x|\mathcal{F}_t)$. It satisfies the following properties:

(i) $x \mapsto p_x(t, T)$ is nondecreasing.
(ii) $p_1(t, T) = 1$.
(iii) For each $x \in [0, 1]$, $T \mapsto p_x(t, T)$ is nonincreasing.
(iv) $(p_x(t, T))_{t \geq 0}$ is a $(\mathcal{F}_t)$-martingale.

Except the last one, they reflect the fact that $(L(t), t \geq 0)$ is a nondecreasing process valued in $[0, 1]$ and are thus arbitrage-free conditions. For $t \geq T$, $\mathbf{1}_{L(T) \leq x}$ is both $\mathcal{G}_t$ and $\mathcal{G}_T$ measurable, and from $\forall X \in L^1(\mathcal{G}_t)$, $\mathbb{E}[X|\mathcal{F}] = \mathbb{E}[X|\mathcal{F}_t]$ we deduce

(v) $p_x(t, T) = p_x(T, T)$ for $t \geq T$.

The SPA model proposes to model the forward loss distributions $\pi(t, T)$ through $p(t, T) = \mathbb{E}[\pi(t, T)|\mathcal{F}_t]$. Clearly, $\pi(t, T)$ cannot in general be fully characterized by $p(t, T)$ since we may have $\pi(t, T) \neq \pi'(t, T)$ and $\mathbb{E}[\pi(t, T)|\mathcal{F}_t] = \mathbb{E}[\pi'(t, T)|\mathcal{F}_t]$. Thus, one needs to specify a model to determine in a unique and consistent manner a loss process that satisfies **(A.2)** from $p(t, T)$. Let us suppose that a family

$(p(t, T); t, T \geq 0)$ satisfying properties (i–v) is given. A loss process $(L(t), t \geq 0)$ satisfying **(A.2)** will be consistent with it if one has:

$$\forall t, T \geq 0, \forall x \in [0, 1], \; \mathbb{P}(L(T) \leq x | \mathcal{F}_t) = p_x(t, T) \qquad (3.21)$$

This condition is analogous to equation (3.15). In Schönbucher's model, it characterizes the loss dynamics and leads to overlapped conditions between the loss and the transition rates (Proposition 3.5.1). Here we have two levels: the probabilities $p(t, T)$ are first fixed and we look for a loss process that is consistent with them. In Sidenius, Piterbarg, and Andersen (2005), several constructions are proposed for the loss process, and we deal in the next section with the simplest one.

Model principle: The loss process is described through the $p(t, T)$ dynamics. To do so, one needs to have a univocal construction of a loss process satisfying **(A.2)** from $(p(t, T); t, T \geq 0)$ such that consistency condition (3.21) holds. The choice of this construction is free, but it induces, beyond conditions (i–v), necessary restrictions on $p(t, T)$ that should be satisfied. Last, this choice is not neutral for option valuation and is thus of importance.

3.5.2.2 Consistency and Option Valuation

Let us consider a family $(p(t, T); t, T \geq 0)$ that satisfies properties (i–v). Moreover, we assume that $p_x(t, T)$ is continuously differentiable w.r.t. T and also that there is a finite grid $x_0 = 0 < x_1 < \cdots < x_q = 1$ such that $\forall t \geq 0$, $p_{x_i}(t, t) < p_{x_{i+1}}(t, t)$. We construct a loss process $(L(t), t \geq 0)$ that is consistent in a slightly weaker sense with equation (3.21); that is,

$$\forall t, T \geq 0, \forall i \in \{0, \ldots, q\}, \; \mathbb{P}(L(T) \leq x_i | \mathcal{F}_t) = p_{x_i}(t, T) \qquad (3.22)$$

Let us suppose that the loss process $(L(t), t \geq 0)$ takes values on the grid and has the generator $\lim\limits_{dt \to 0} \frac{\mathbb{E}[f(L(t+dt)) - f(L(t)) | \mathcal{G}_t \vee \mathcal{F}]}{dt} = \sum_{i=0}^{q-1} \mathbf{1}_{\{L(t)=x_i\}} a_{x_i}(t) \, (f(x_{i+1}) - f(x_i))$ for any bounded function f. Defining $p_x^L(t, T) = \mathbb{P}(L(T) \leq x | \mathcal{F}_t)$, one deduces that $\partial_T p_{x_i}^L(t, t) = -a_{x_i}(t)(p_{x_i}^L(t, t) - p_{x_{i-1}}^L(t, t))$ [with the convention $p_{x_{-1}}^L(t, T) = 0$]. Therefore, if L is consistent, one has necessarily $a_{x_i}(t) = \frac{-\partial_T p_{x_i}(t,t)}{p_{x_i}(t,t) - p_{x_{i-1}}(t,t)}$ where $p_{x_{-1}}(t, T) = 0$.

We then define the loss process $(L(t), t \geq 0)$ with the generator:

$$\lim_{dt \to 0} \frac{\mathbb{E}\left[f(L(t + dt)) - f(L(t)) | \mathcal{G}_t \vee \mathcal{F} \right]}{dt}$$

$$= \sum_{i=0}^{q-1} \mathbf{1}_{\{L(t)=x_i\}} \frac{-\partial_T p_{x_i}(t, t) \, (f(x_{i+1}) - f(x_i))}{p_{x_i}(t, t) - p_{x_{i-1}}(t, t)}$$

and the initial condition $L(0) = 0$. One has to check that it is consistent (i.e., $\forall i,\ p_{x_i}^L(t, T) = p_{x_i}(t, T)$). Let us fix $t \geq 0$. One has $p_{x_i}^L(t, 0) = p_{x_i}(t, 0) = 1$, and for $T \leq t,\ \partial_T p_{x_i}^L(t, T) = \frac{\partial_T p_{x_i}(T, T)}{p_{x_i}(T, T) - p_{x_{i-1}}(T, T)}(p_{x_i}^L(t, T) - p_{x_{i-1}}^L(t, T))$. Since $p_{x_i}(t, T) = p_{x_i}(T, T)$ for $t \geq T$, one has also $\partial_T p_{x_i}(t, T) = \partial_T p_{x_i}(T, T)$ because $(p_{x_i}(t, T) - p_{x_i}(t, T - \varepsilon))/\varepsilon = (p_{x_i}(T, T) - p_{x_i}(T, T - \varepsilon))/\varepsilon$ and thus:

$$\partial_T p_{x_i}^L(t, T) = \frac{\partial_T p_{x_i}(t, T)}{p_{x_i}(t, T) - p_{x_{i-1}}(t, T)}(p_{x_i}^L(t, T) - p_{x_{i-1}}^L(t, T)) \qquad (3.23)$$

The vector $(p_{x_i}(t, T), i = 0, \ldots, q)$ solves the same linear ODE (3.23) as $(p_{x_i}^L(t, T), i = 0, \ldots, q)$ with the same initial value, and one deduces $p_{x_i}(t, T) = p_{x_i}^L(t, T)$ for $T \leq t$. In particular, we have $p_{x_i}(T, T) = p_{x_i}^L(T, T)$ for any $T \geq 0$ and then $p_{x_i}(t, T) = \mathbb{E}[p_{x_i}(T, T)|\mathcal{F}_t] = \mathbb{E}[p_{x_i}^L(T, T)|\mathcal{F}_t] = p_{x_i}^L(t, T)$ for $t \leq T$. We have therefore shown that there is only one Markov chain that jumps from x_i to x_{i+1} that is consistent in the sense of equation (3.22).

Other constructions of loss process are investigated in Sidenius, Piterbarg, and Andersen (2005). Let us stress that each construction may require additional assumptions on $p(t, T)$ beyond properties (i–v). In the preceding case, these are the continuous differentiation w.r.t. T and $\forall t \geq 0,\ p_{x_i}(t, t) < p_{x_{i+1}}(t, t)$. When specifying dynamics for the probabilities $p_x(t, T)$, one has then to be careful that these assumptions are also satisfied.

3.5.2.3 Probability Rates Dynamics and Simulation

In this section, we are concerned in specifying dynamics for the probabilities $(p_x(t, T), t \leq T)$ that satisfy the conditions (i–v). In Sidenius, Piterbarg, and Andersen (2005), two parametrizations of these probabilities are considered. The first one (HJM-like) models $p_x(t, T)$ through the forward instantaneous rate process $f_x(t, T) = -\frac{\partial_T p_x(t, T)}{p_x(t, T)}$, while the second one (BGM-like) describes them using the LIBOR rates $F_x(t, n) = \frac{p_x(t, T_n) - p_x(t, T_{n+1})}{p_x(t, T_{n+1})(T_{n+1} - T_n)}$ where $T_0 < T_1 < \ldots$ are fixed maturities.

We focus here on the HJM-like parametrization and consider a countable family $(W^\nu, \nu \geq 1)$ of independent $(\mathcal{F}_t)$-Brownian motions. To satisfy properties (iv) and (v), we assume:

$$\forall t \leq T,\ dp_x(t, T) = p_x(t, T) \sum_{\nu=1}^{\infty} \Sigma_x^\nu(t, T) dW_t^\nu$$

with $p_x(0, T) = 1$ and $p_x(t, T) = p_x(T, T)$ for $t \geq T$. Coefficients $\Sigma_x^\nu(t, T)$ are $\mathcal{F}_t$ measurable and supposedly regular enough for what follows. We also assume $\Sigma_x^\nu(T, T) = 0$. We then easily get the forward rate dynamics:

$$t \leq T,\ df_x(t, T) = \sum_{\nu=1}^{\infty} \left(\sigma_x^\nu(t, T) \left(\int_t^T \sigma_x^\nu(t, u) du \right) dt + \sigma_x^\nu(t, T) dW_t^\nu \right)$$

where $\sigma_x^\nu(t, T) = -\partial_T \Sigma_x^\nu(t, T)$. From $f_x(t, T) = -\frac{\partial_T p_x(t, T)}{p_x(t, T)}$, we get for $T \geq t$, $p_x(t, T) = p_x(t, t) \exp(-\int_t^T f_x(t, u) du)$. For $u \leq t$, one has $p_x(t, t) = p_x(u, u)$ and then $f_x(u, u) = -\partial_T \ln(p_x(t, u))$ so that $p_x(t, t) = \exp(-\int_0^t f_x(u, u) du)$. Therefore, we get:

$$\forall t, T \geq 0, \; p_x(t, T) = \exp\left(-\int_0^{t \wedge T} f_x(u, u) du - \int_{t \wedge T}^T f_x(t, u) du\right)$$

Therefore, we can rewrite properties (i–iii) with the forward rates $(f_x(t, T), 0 \leq t \leq T)$:

(i) $x \mapsto \int_0^t f_x(u, u) du + \int_t^T f_x(t, u) du$ is nonincreasing.
(ii) $f_1(t, T) = 0$.
(iii) for each $x \in [0, 1]$, $f_x(t, T) \geq 0$.

The property (i) is clearly satisfied if $x \mapsto f_x(t, T)$ is nonincreasing. In Sidenius, Piterbarg, and Andersen (2005), look for coefficients that write $\sigma_x^\nu(t, T) = \varphi^\nu(t, T, f_x(t, T))$ and give sufficient conditions on φ^ν such that these three conditions hold. Some practical examples are also presented.

Let us now address quickly the simulation issue. Once a forward rate dynamic has been selected to calibrate market data, one can simulate the forward rates up to a final maturity $T_{\max}$ using a Euler scheme. Typically, since $p(0, T) = \pi(0, T)$ $(\mathcal{F}_0 = \mathcal{G}_0)$, $f(0, T)$ is chosen to fit exactly the prices of CDO tranches that start at the current time and the dynamics of $f(t, T)$ should be fitted to other products. Then, $p(t, T)$ can be deduced easily for $t \geq 0$ and $T \leq T_{\max}$. Finally, one has to simulate the chosen loss process. If it is the one described in the previous section, this is a simple Markov chain that jumps from x_i to x_{i+1} with the intensity $\frac{-\partial_T p_{x_i}(t, t)}{p_{x_i}(t, t) - p_{x_{i-1}}(t, t)}$.

3.6   Further Issues in Credit Modeling

Though not being exhaustive, we have presented here several main research directions in credit risk. We have focused on the default modeling and have skipped some important topics related to credit risk such as recovery modeling. All the models presented here allow, at least theoretically, to price any option derivative on the loss process since they are designed for that. All of them are meant to be calibrated to prices of CDOs that start at the current time. Here, we have not discussed the robustness of the calibration procedure, which is an important issue to investigate. Last, we have not treated here the hedging problem in credit risk. This is of course another main topic of research. We mention here the connected work of Bielecki, Jeanblanc, and Rutkowski (2007).

Research on loss models is still very active. Though the weaknesses of the copula model were already known, the recent crisis has brought additional evidence of them, and has pointed out the need for a new robust standard model. The crisis has also stopped the growth of very sophisticated products. Therefore, the current need is not to propose new models for pricing new kinds of products. It is rather to strengthen the existing models, making them more robust and reliable.

The models that we have introduced here are related mainly to only one aggregated loss, but they do not cover all of the credit products that are dealt over the counter. Indeed, all these models need to be calibrated with some market data and are thus linked to a specific loss process $L(t)$. However, in practice, one has to price products such as the bespoke CDO whose associated loss is not traded on the markets. This loss may come from a subbasket of $L(t)$, may have only some common names with $L(t)$, or may have no name in common. In each case, how can we make use of the information on $L(t)$ to price our product? This is a tough question, and it is theoretically treated here only in the subbasket case because one can have a model for single defaults consistent with $L(t)$ (e.g., copula model or random thinning procedure). Other credit risk products such as CDO-squareds bring on many loss processes that may or may not have names in common. Each of them may have common names with the calibrated loss $L(t)$. Once again, how can we price such products using the market information in the best way? Currently, heuristic arguments (such as classification of the firms by size or sector); economic analysis; dubious mapping methods (see Reyfman, Ushakova, and Kong 2004; Baheti and Morgan 2007); and historical data are used to fill the lack of market prices and price these products. Nonetheless, beyond the problem of the information available on the market, designing an efficient and coherent model for many loss processes is certainly an important issue for the coming year.

Acknowledgments

I would like to thank Damiano Brigo for the many illuminating discussions with him during recent years. I am grateful to Abdelkoddousse Ahdida, Benjamin Jourdain, and Andrea Pallavicini for their comments. I acknowledge the support of the chair "Risques Financiers" of Fondation du Risque, and of the Credinext project from Finance Innovation.

Note

1. The International Swaps and Derivatives Association (ISDA) has recommended in early 2009 to switch and quote the CDS through an up-front value that is paid at the beginning of the contract. The CDS spread R is then standardized to some specific values (see www.cdsmodel.com/information/cds-model, and also Beumee et al. (2009) for a discussion on the quoting conversion).

References

Alfonsi, A., and D. Brigo. 2005. New families of copulas based on periodic functions. *Communications in Statistics: Theory and Methods* 34 (7): 1437–1447.

Arnsdorf, M., and I. Halperin. 2007. BSLP: Markovian bivariate spread-loss model for portfolio credit derivatives. JPMorgan Quantitative Research. http://arxiv.org/pdf/0901.3398v1.

Baheti, P., and S. Morgan. 2007. Base correlation mapping. *Lehman Brothers Quantitative Research, Quarterly* (Q1).

Bentata, A., and R. Cont. 2009. Matching marginal distributions of a semimartingale with a Markov process. *Comptes Rendus Mathématique, Académie des Sciences, Paris*, Series I, 347.

Beumee, J., D. Brigo, D. Schiemert, and G. Stoyle. 2009. Charting a course through the CDS Big Bang. Fitch Solutions research report. www.fitchratings.com/dtp/pdf2-09/qurc0804.pdf.

Bielecki, T. R., S. Crépey, and M. Jeanblanc. 2008. Up and down credit risk. Working paper. Available at www.defaultrisk.com.

Bielecki, T. R., M. Jeanblanc, and M. Rutkowski. 2007. Hedging of basket credit derivatives in CDS market. *Journal of Credit Risk* 3, no. 1 (Spring).

Bielecki, T. R., and M. Rutkowski. 2003. Dependent defaults and credit migrations. *Applicationes Mathematicae* 30:121–145.

Brigo, D., and A. Alfonsi. 2005. Credit default swap calibration and derivatives pricing with the SSRD stochastic intensity model. *Finance and Stochastics* 9 (1): 29–42.

Brigo, D., and A. Capponi. 2008. Bilateral counterparty risk valuation with stochastic dynamical models and application to credit default swaps. http://ssrn.com/abstract=1318024.

Brigo, D., and K. Chourdakis. 2008. Counterparty risk for credit default swaps: Impact of spread volatility and default correlation. *International Journal of Theoretical and Applied Finance* 12(7):1007–1026.

Brigo, D., and F. Mercurio. 2006. *Interest rate models—theory and practice with smile, inflation and credit.* 2nd ed. Springer Finance Series. New York: Springer.

Brigo, D., A. Pallavicini, and R. Torresetti. 2007a. Calibration of CDO tranches with the dynamical GPL model. *Risk* (May): 70–75.

Brigo, D., A. Pallavicini, and R. Torresetti. 2007b. Cluster-based extension of the generalized Poisson loss dynamics and consistency with single names. *International Journal of Theoretical and Applied. Finance* 10 (4): 315–339.

Brigo, D., A. Pallavicini, and R. Torresetti. 2010. *Credit models and the crisis: A journey into CDOs, copulas, correlations and dynamic models.* Chichester, UK: John Wiley & Sons.

Burtschell, X., J. Gregory, and J.-P. Laurent. 2005. A comparative analysis of CDO pricing models. Working paper.

Chapovsky, A., A. Rennie, and P. Tavares. 2007. Stochastic intensity modelling for structured credit exotics. In *Credit correlation: Life after copulas*, ed. A. Lipton and A. Rennie. Singapore: World Scientific.

Cont, R., and A. Minca. 2008. Recovering portfolio default intensities implied by CDO quotes. http://ssrn.com/abstract=1104855.

Cont, R., and I. Savescu. 2008. Forward equations for portfolio credit derivatives. http://ssrn.com/abstract=1124954.

Dupire, B. 1994. Pricing with a smile. *Risk* 7, no. 1 (January): 18–20.

Embrechts, P., F. Lindskog, and A. McNeil. 2001. Modelling dependence with copulas and applications to risk management. Working paper.

Errais, E., K. Giesecke, and L. R. Goldberg. 2006. Pricing credit from the top down with affine point processes. Working paper, updated version at http://ssrn.com/abstract=908045.

Giesecke, K., and L. R. Goldberg. 2005. A top-down approach to multi-name credit. Working paper, updated version at http://ssrn.com/abstract=1142152.

Gyöngy, I. 1986. Mimicking the one-dimensional marginal distributions of processes having an Itô differential. *Probability Theory and Related Fields* 71 (4): 501–516.

Hull, J., and A. White. 2004. Valuation of a CDO and an n-th to default CDS without Monte Carlo simulation. *Journal of Derivatives* 12, no. 2 (Winter): 8–23.

Hull, J., and A. White. 2006. Valuing credit derivatives using an implied copula approach. Working paper.

Jacod, J., and A. Shiryaev. 2003. *Limit theorems for stochastic processes.* 2nd ed. Springer, Grundlehren der Mathematischen Wissenschaften.

Laurent, J.-P., and J. Gregory. 2003. Basket default swaps, CDO's and factor copulas. Working paper.

Lindskog, F., and A. McNeil. 2001. Common Poisson shock models: Applications to insurance and credit risk modelling. *ASTIN Bulletin* 33 (2): 209–238.

Lopatin, A., and T. Misirpashaev. 2007. Two-dimensional Markovian model for dynamics of aggregate credit loss. Working paper. Available at www.defaultrisk.com.

Morini, M., and D. Brigo. 2009. No-Armageddon arbitrage-free equivalent measure for index options in a credit crisis. *Mathematical Finance.*

Nelsen, R. 1999. *An introduction to copulas.* New York: Springer.

Reyfman, A., K. Ushakova, and W. Kong. 2004. How to value bespoke tranches consistently with standard ones. Bear Stearns educational report.

Rosen, D., and D. Saunders. 2009. Analytical methods for hedging systematic credit risk with linear factor portfolios. *Journal of Economic Dynamics and Control* 33 (1): 37–52.

Rutkowski, M. 2010. Options on credit default swaps and credit default indexes. In ed. T. R. Bielecki, D. Brigo, and F. Patras. *Recent advancements in theory and practice of credit derivatives,* Princeton, NJ: Bloomberg Press.

Schönbucher, P. 2005. Portfolio losses and the term structure of loss transition rates: A new methodology for the pricing of portfolio credit derivatives. Working paper.

Schönbucher, P., and D. Schubert. 2001. Copula-dependent default risk in intensity models. Working paper.

Sidenius, J., V. Piterbarg, and L. Andersen. 2005. A new framework for dynamic credit portfolio loss modelling. Working paper.

Torresetti, R., D. Brigo, and A. Pallavicini. 2006. Implied correlation in CDO tranches: A paradigm to be handled with care. In *Credit models and the crisis: A journey into CDOs, copulas, correlations and dynamic models,* by D. Brigo, A. Pallavicini, and R. Torresetti. Chichester, UK: John Wiley & Sons, 2010. Available at http://ssrn.com/abstract=946755.

CHAPTER 4

A Simple Dynamic Model for Pricing and Hedging Heterogeneous CDOs

Andrei V. Lopatin

Numerix LLC

We present a simple bottom-up dynamic credit model that can be calibrated simultaneously to the market quotes on collateralized debt obligation (CDO) tranches and individual credit default swaps (CDSs) constituting the credit portfolio. The model is most suitable for the purpose of evaluating the hedge ratios of CDO tranches with respect to the underlying credit names. Default intensities of individual assets are modeled as deterministic functions of time and the total number of defaults accumulated in the portfolio. To overcome numerical difficulties, we suggest a semianalytic approximation that is justified by the large number of portfolio members. We calibrate the model to the recent market quotes on CDO tranches and individual CDSs and find the hedge ratios of tranches. Results are compared with those obtained within the static Gaussian copula model.

4.1 Introduction

One of the key challenges in the field of credit derivatives remains the construction of sophisticated mathematical models of collateralized debt obligations (CDOs). The interest is motivated by the practical demand of tractable models capable of reliable, arbitrage-free valuation of portfolio loss derivatives, as well as calculation of sensitivities with respect to the underlying assets required for hedging purposes. Most CDO models that are currently used in practice are static, the industry standard being the Gaussian copula (GC) model. In the static approach, the loss of the credit portfolio is modeled independently at each time step, disregarding the dynamics of the loss process.

71

Dynamic models suggested up to the present time can be loosely classified into two categories. Models that belong to the first category are constructed from the bottom up, such that the dynamics of the portfolio loss are built on top of default processes of underlying credit names. Default dynamics of each component, in turn, can be described either via the structural approach originated by Merton (1974) or via a reduced, intensity-based approach where default events are unpredictable. A CDO model based on a structural description of components was suggested by Inglis and Lipton (2007); see also Inglis, Lipton, Savescu, and Sepp (2008). The list of intensity-based bottom-up CDO models is extensive, and here we refer only to a few publications that are related most closely to the present work: Bielecki, Vidozzi, and Vidozzi (2006); Duffie and Garleanu (2001); Duffie, Saita, and Wang (2006); Eckner (2007); Feldhütter (2007); Frey and Backhaus (2007); and Mortensen (2006). The dynamic model recently suggested by Hull and White (2006) can also be attributed to the bottom-up framework, in spite of the fact that the authors assume the homogeneous portfolio case at the initial stage of model construction. The main problem of the models belonging to this class is complexity: In order to achieve numerical feasibility, one is often forced to either choose analytically tractable dynamics, thereby reducing calibration capability, or restrict considerations to the homogeneous portfolio case.

Models that belong to the second category postulate the dynamics for the portfolio loss directly, not referring to the underlying portfolio members. This framework was first suggested in works of Giesecke and Goldberg (2005), Schönbucher (2005), and Sidenius, Piterbarg, and Andersen (2005). Other models that were recently developed within this framework can be found in works by Arnsdorf and Halperin (2007); Brigo, Pallavicini, and Torresetti (2007); Errais, Giesecke, and Goldberg (2006); Ding, Giesecke, and Tomecek (2006); and Lopatin and Misirpashaev (2008). The top-down framework allows reducing the dimensionality of the problem, making it possible to formulate a numerically tractable model having sufficient flexibility for calibration to the market of CDO tranches. Models of this kind are natural candidates for pricing the dynamics-sensitive derivatives of the portfolio loss. This approach, however, obscures the relationship of the model to the underlying portfolio members, and requires special techniques to recover the dynamics of single-name intensities. Such a procedure, the so-called random thinning, was suggested in the work of Giesecke and Goldberg (2005). See also the recent paper by Halperin and Tomecek (2008). More detailed reviews of the two approaches can be found in the recent articles by Giesecke (2008) and Bielecki, Crépey, and Jeanblanc (2009).

In the present work, we suggest a simple dynamic bottom-up model having sufficient flexibility for simultaneous calibration to the market of credit default swaps (CDSs) and CDO tranches, and capable of evaluating tranche hedge ratios as well as simple instruments whose values can be expressed through a one-dimensional marginal distribution of the portfolio loss. The model is defined by specifying the form of the default intensity for each underlying asset as a function of time, t, and the number of defaults, $N(t)$, accumulated in the credit portfolio up to t. Our choice of the state variable can be better understood on examination of the simplest model within the top-down framework. This model, which in analogy with the local volatility model is sometimes called the local intensity model, represents the one-dimensional Markov chain, where default transitions $N \to N + 1$ are governed by intensity, $\lambda(N(t), t)$, which is a deterministic function of N and t. Remarkably, it can be shown that any top-down credit model with default intensity given by an adaptive stochastic process of a general kind can be brought to the form of the local intensity model as long as instruments under consideration can be expressed through the one-dimensional marginal distribution of the portfolio loss (Lopatin and Misirpashaev 2008). Thus, a minimal multiname dynamic model can be constructed as an extension of the local intensity model by choosing the default intensity of each name to be a deterministic function of $N(t)$.

Our model can also be viewed as a special case of the default contagion model (Davis and Lo 2001). In the default contagion framework, the default intensity of the kth asset is given by the deterministic function $\lambda_k(\mathbf{n}(t), t)$ of the portfolio state represented by the vector of asset default indicators $\mathbf{n} = (n_1, n_2, \ldots, n_{N_0})$, N_0 being the number of assets in the portfolio. Default of the kth asset thereby affects (typically increasing) the default intensities of other assets. In its general form, the default contagion model contains a huge number of free parameters and, in practice, one deals with default intensities of a particular functional form. Examples of specific models that belong to this framework can be found in papers by Davis and Lo (2001), Jarrow and Yu (2001), and Laurent, Cousin, and Fermanian (2007). Our model corresponds to the special case where each default intensity depends on the total number of defaults $N = n_1 + n_2 + \cdots + n_{N_0}$.

Default contagion models are Markovian and, thus, they support the application of many standard numerical techniques, including forward/backward induction and Monte Carlo simulations. However, the huge size of the configuration space, 2^{N_0}, makes application of the forward/backward induction unfeasible. Construction of an effective Monte Carlo scheme is also a difficult task because of the requirement of calibration to tranches and individual credits. We resolve this difficulty by developing a semianalytic approach that makes use of the fact that the number of portfolio members is large. This technique allows reducing the original multidimensional problem to the system of N_0 coupled one-dimensional Fokker-Planck equations. Further, we show that, within the developed forward induction scheme, the calibration to individual CDSs can be implemented automatically with essentially no extra computational cost. Calibration to tranches is implemented as a mixture of bootstrap and multidimensional solving procedures similar to the scheme used by Arnsdorf and Halperin (2007). As a result, the complete calibration procedure becomes computationally effective and, for typical market data, takes less than a minute on a laptop with an AMD Turion ML-40 (2.19 GHz) processor.

The rest of the chapter is organized as follows. In Section 4.2, we present the model. In Section 4.3, we describe the semianalytic approach to solving the model. In Section 4.4, we present the procedure of model calibration, along with numerical results for the fit to recent market data. Tranche hedge ratios are considered in Section 4.5, where results of the dynamic model are compared with those obtained within the GC model. In Section 4.6, we extend our approach to the case of a portfolio with heterogeneous recovery coefficients. In Section 4.7, we discuss the connection of the default contagion framework to the double stochastic one in general terms. In Section 4.8 we include the effect of negative correlations between the recovery coefficients and default intensity. We conclude in Section 4.9.

4.2 Model

Under the standard assumption of constant recovery coefficients, stripping each CDS allows us to reproduce the survival probabilities of individual portfolio members. This procedure relies on time interpolation of the implied default intensity, which, in the simplest case, is taken to be piece constant. Thus, we assume that the kth portfolio member is characterized by the survival probability, $p_k(t)$, and the recovery coefficient, R_k. We postulate the default intensity of the kth asset to be:

$$\lambda_t^k = a_k(t) + b_k(t)\,Y(N(t), t) \tag{4.1}$$

where $N(t)$ is the number of defaults accumulated in the portfolio up to time t. The function $Y(N, t)$ is the common (systemic) component that serves to model the correlations of default events. The functions $a_k(t)$ and $b_k(t)$ are specific to the kth asset. For a given $Y(N, t)$, functions $a_k(t)$ and $b_k(t)$ are used to fit the model to the survival curves of individual assets. The function $Y(N, t)$ provides a freedom for calibrating the model to CDO tranches. It is clear, however, that the model [equation 4.1] has too many free parameters, in addition to the freedom in interpolation of the function $Y(N, t)$, which will be discussed later since both functions $a_k(t)$ and $b_k(t)$ cannot be defined uniquely by fitting a single survival curve. For this reason, we choose a particular specification of model (4.1) containing no extra parametric freedom. We take $a_k(t) = 0$ such that the intensity of the kth asset becomes a product of the idiosyncratic component $b_k(t)$ and the systemic component, $Y(N, t)$. An alternative simple choice would be to take $b_k(t) = 1$ such that each single asset intensity would be a sum of the idiosyncratic component $a_k(t)$ and systemic component, $Y(N, t)$. We prefer the first choice because it guarantees the positivity of all default intensities by construction. Nonzero values of $a_k(t)$, however, will be used later for calculating the tranche hedge ratios. In Section 4.7, we comment on restrictions in applications of model (4.1) and compare it with models of the double stochastic framework.

For the sake of clarity we note that model (4.1) does not allow for simultaneous defaults of several assets. Indeed, the probability of defaults of two assets within the time interval δ_t scales as δ_t^2, while the probability of a single asset default scales as δ_t. This property is used throughout the chapter.

4.3 Semianalytic Approach

Model (4.1) could be treated directly by writing down the multidimensional Fokker-Planck equation on the full distribution function of defaults and then solving it numerically. This way, however, is practically unfeasible, since the size of the config-uration space of the full distribution function is given by 2^{N_0}, which, for a typical number of assets, $N_0 = 125$, exceeds the operating memory of modern computers by orders of magnitude. The simulation approach is certainly a possible alternative. However, one has to keep in mind that the model must be calibrated (at least) to the market of CDO tranches via iterative solving, and this, most likely, will make the simulation method unfeasible, too. Here we present a semianalytic approximate scheme to solving model (4.1) which is justified by a large number of assets in the credit basket.

Let us consider the probability that the kth asset has survived up to time t, and that, at the same time, N assets in total have defaulted,

$$P_k(N, t) = P[\, n_k(t) = 0, N(t) = N\,] \tag{4.2}$$

Here, n_k is the default indicator of the kth asset ($n_k = 1$ assumes default and $n_k = 0$ survival) and $N(t)$ is the number of defaults in the basket accumulated up to time t. We note that $P_k(N_0, t) = 0$. The probability $P_k(N, t)$ satisfies the following Fokker-Planck equation (see the derivation in Appendix 4A):

$$\frac{d}{dt}P_k(N, t) = \Lambda_k(N-1, t)P_k(N-1, t) - [\Lambda_k(N, t) + \lambda_k(N, t)]\, P_k(N, t) \tag{4.3}$$

where

$$\lambda_k(N, t) = \lim_{\delta_t \to 0} \frac{1}{\delta_t} E[\, n_k(t + \delta_t) - n_k(t) \mid N(t) = N\,] = a_k(t) + b_k(t)\, Y(N, t) \tag{4.4}$$

and $\Lambda_k(N, t)$ is the intensity of any asset other than the kth to default, conditioned that the total number of defaults in the basket is N, and that the kth asset has survived,

$$\Lambda_k(N, t) = \lim_{\delta_t \to 0} \frac{1}{\delta_t} \sum_{p \neq k} E[\, n_p(t + \delta_t) - n_p(t) \mid n_k(t) = 0\ N(t) = N\,] \tag{4.5}$$

Instead of writing the multiplier $\mathbf{1}_{N>0}$ in front of the first term in the right-hand side of equation (4.3), we define that $P_k(N, t) = 0$ at $N < 0$. We follow this conven-tion throughout the paper for the sake of brevity. To gain an intuitive understanding of this equation, it is instructive to imagine that the kth asset was extracted from the basket such that a system consisting of a single asset and the basket with re-maining $N - 1$ assets is formed. The meaning of the terms in equation (4.3) then becomes straightforward: Default transition in the reduced basket are described via the intensity $\Lambda_k(N, t)$, while the term containing $\lambda_k(N, t)$ is responsible for a possible default of the kth asset itself. The boundary condition for equation (4.3) at the origin $t = 0$ is:

$$P_k(N, 0) = \begin{cases} 1, & N = 0, \\ 0, & N \neq 0 \end{cases} \qquad (4.6)$$

The intensity of defaults in the basket having all but kth assets, $\Lambda_k(N, t)$, is unknown. Direct determination of this quantity is difficult and, in the case of a realistic CDO having 125 or even more members, would require an application of simulations. It is clear, however, that, in the case of a large portfolio, $\Lambda_k(N, t)$ is approximately given by the intensity of a default transition $N \to N + 1$ in the whole basket conditioned on the total number of defaults:

$$\Lambda_B(N, t) = \lim_{\delta_t \to 0} \frac{1}{\delta_t} P[N(t + \delta_t) = N + 1 \mid N(t) = N] \qquad (4.7)$$

Indeed, both $\Lambda_B(N, t)$, $\Lambda_k(N, t) \sim N_0$. At the same time these quantities must coincide in the case $b_k = 0$; thus in the leading in order in N_0 we must have $\Lambda_k(N, t) \approx \Lambda_B(N, t)$. The basket intensity, $\Lambda_B(N, t)$, can also be defined as:

$$\Lambda_B(N, t) = \lim_{\delta_t \to 0} \frac{1}{\delta_t} \sum_{k=1}^{N_0} E[n_k(t + \delta_t) - n_k(t) \mid N(t) = N] \qquad (4.8)$$

Equivalence of the two definitions can be shown starting from equation (4.8) as follows:

$$\Lambda_B(N, t) = \lim_{\delta_t \to 0} \frac{1}{\delta_t} E[N(t + \delta_t) - N(t) \mid N(t) = N] = \lim_{\delta_t \to 0} \frac{1}{\delta_t} P[N(t + \delta)$$
$$= N + 1 \mid N(t) = N]$$

The approximation $\Lambda_k(N, t) \approx \Lambda_B(N, t)$ can be improved by multiplying the basket intensity by $1 - 1/(N_0 - N)$; this ensures that the scheme becomes exact in the homogeneous portfolio case. Thus, we formulate the mean field approximation for $\Lambda_k(N, t)$ as follows:

$$\Lambda_k(N, t) \to \left(1 - \frac{1}{N_0 - N}\right) \Lambda_B(N, t) \qquad (4.9)$$

In the next section, we show that correction $1/(N_0 - N)$ plays an important role in making the scheme internally consistent, and we discuss possible alternatives to equation (4.9).

We note that the approximation (4.9) may not be applicable if an extremely risky asset is present in the basket, such that the basket intensity becomes dominated by a single-name contribution. So, for the present approach to be applicable the intensity of any asset in the basket must be much smaller than the total basket intensity. Note, however, that for a given dispersion of asset spreads, this requirement will always be satisfied if the basket is large enough. This clarifies the meaning of the large portfolio limit.

To complete the system of equations (4.1), (4.3), and (4.9), one needs to find the basket intensity $\Lambda_B(N, t)$. To fulfill this goal, we will first show that the probability distribution of defaults in the basket,

$$P_B(N, t) = \mathrm{P}[N(t) = N] \tag{4.10}$$

is related to the probabilities $P_k(N, t)$ via:

$$P_B(N, t) = \frac{1}{N_0 - N} \sum_{k=1}^{N_0} P_k(N, t) \tag{4.11}$$

This equation can be proven by presenting the basket default distribution function, $P_B(N, t)$, in the form

$$P_B(N, t) = \sum_{\mathbf{n}} p(\mathbf{n}, t) \, \mathbf{1}_{n_1 + n_2 + \ldots + n_{N_0} = N} \tag{4.12}$$

where $p(\mathbf{n}, t)$ is the probability density of the portfolio state represented by the vector of default indicators $\mathbf{n} = (n_1, n_2, \ldots, n_{N0})$, and where summation goes over all possible portfolio states. Similarly, one can write:

$$P_k(N, t) = \sum_{\mathbf{n}} p(\mathbf{n}, t) \, \mathbf{1}_{n_k = 0} \, \mathbf{1}_{n_1 + n_2 + \ldots + n_{N_0} = N} \tag{4.13}$$

Equation (4.11) can be proven by inserting equation (4.13) into its right-hand-side and further term-by-term comparison with equation (4.12).

The basket intensity $\Lambda_B(N, t)$ now can be found from the identity:

$$\Lambda_B(N, t) = \frac{\sum\limits_{k=1}^{N_0} \lambda_k(N, t) P_k(N, t)}{P_B(N, t)} \tag{4.14}$$

that follows from the definitions (4.2), (4.4), (4.8), and (4.10):

$$\Lambda_B(N, t) P_B(N, t) = \lim_{\delta_t \to 0} \frac{1}{\delta_t} \sum_{k=1}^{N_0} \mathrm{E}[(n_k(t + \delta_t) - n_k(t)) \mathbf{1}_{N(t) = N}]$$

$$= \sum_{k=1}^{N_0} \lambda_k(N, t) \, P_k(N, t) \tag{4.15}$$

The system of the equations (4.3), (4.4), (4.9), (4.11), and (4.14), along with the boundary condition (4.6), define uniquely the functions $p_k(N, t)$, $P_B(N, t)$, and $\Lambda_B(N, t)$. Indeed, assuming that the single-name intensities $\lambda_k(N, t)$ are given, one can integrate equation (4.3) simultaneously for all k using $\Lambda_k(N, t)$ defined through equations (4.9), (4.11), and (4.14) on each integration time step.

4.3.1 Self-Consistency Check

The functions $P_B(N, t)$ and $\Lambda_B(N, t)$ that represent, respectively, the probability density of defaults and the intensity of a default of any asset in the basket conditioned that $N(t) = N$ play an important role in formulation of the semianalytic scheme developed in the previous section. Because of their meanings, these two functions must be related by the following Fokker-Planck equation:

$$\frac{d}{dt} P_B(N, t) = \Lambda_B(N - 1, t) P_B(N - 1, t) - \Lambda_B(N, t) P_B(N, t) \qquad (4.16)$$

Validity of this equation can be confirmed with the help of the Markovian projection technique used in Lopatin and Misirpashaev (2008). The corresponding proof is presented in Appendix 4B.

Equation (4.16) was neither explicitly nor implicitly used in the formulation of the semianalytic scheme and, thus, it is important to be sure that functions $P_B(N, t)$ and $\Lambda_B(N, t)$ obtained within this scheme satisfy equation (4.16).

Here, we show that this equation is satisfied indeed. Under approximation (4.9), $\Lambda_k(N, t)$ is independent of k. Summing both parts of equation (4.3) over k and using equations (4.11) and (4.14), one can bring it to the form:

$$\frac{d}{dt} P_B(N, t) = \frac{N_s + 1}{N_s} \Lambda_k(N - 1, t) P_B(N - 1, t)$$
$$- \left(\Lambda_k(N, t) + \frac{\Lambda_B(N, t)}{N_s} \right) P_B(N, t) \qquad (4.17)$$

where $N_s = N_0 - N$ is the number of survived assets in the basket. Now, using equation (4.9) for $\Lambda_k(N, t)$, one can see that equation (4.17) is consistent with equation (4.16).

Note that equation (4.17) would not be satisfied if the term $1/(N_0 - N)$ in equation (4.9) were neglected. This correction, thus, plays an important role in ensuring internal consistency of the scheme. The form of this correction, however, is not unique. For example, one can show that the approximation

$$\Lambda_k(N, t) \rightarrow \Lambda_B(N, t) - \lambda_k(N, t) \qquad (4.18)$$

also leads to the internally consistent scheme. In Appendix 4C we consider the question of consistency in more general terms.

4.4 Model Calibration

The model equation (4.1) has to be calibrated to the market data on CDO tranches and individual CDSs. Recall that the single-name spreads can be fitted by choosing functions $b_k(t)$, while the spreads of CDO tranches are adjusted via the function $Y(N, t)$. Fast calibration to the single-name spreads is one of the key requirements for the model to be useful in practice. In the case of static models this problem is often solved via using the copula approach that respects the consistency with the single name survival probabilities by construction. A generalization of the copula approach to dynamic models can be found in Bielecki, Vidozzi, and Vidozzi (2008) (see also references therein). In the case of the present model we resolve the calibration problem by using a forward induction scheme that brings almost no extra computational cost to numerical integration of equation (4.3). Calibration to CDO tranches is implemented as a mixture of bootstrap and iterative fitting. The latter procedure is similar to calibration of the local intensity model to CDO tranches, with function $Y(N, t)$ playing a role similar to that of the local intensity (Arnsdorf and Halperin 2007; Lopatin and Misirpashaev 2008). In this section, we will first assume that the function $Y(N, t)$ is given and describe the calibration to the single-name survival probabilities. Then, we will turn to calibration of the function $Y(N, t)$ to CDO tranches.

4.4.1 Calibration to the Asset Survival Probabilities

We will consider the calibration procedure within the simplest, first order in time scheme. Fixing the set of times $t_0, t_1, \ldots, t_M$, where t_0 is the start time and t_M is the horizon, we write equation (4.3) in the form

$$
\frac{P_k(N, t_{i+1}) - P_k(N, t_i)}{\Delta_i} = \Lambda_k(N - 1, t_i) P_k(N - 1, t_i)
$$
$$
- [\Lambda_k(N, t_i) + \lambda_k(N, t_i)] P_k(N, t_i) \quad (4.19)
$$

where $\Delta_i = t_{i+1} - t_i$. The consistency with the market data on single-name CDS can be ensured by requiring that the single-name survival probabilities, $p_k(t)$, can be reproduced within the model:

$$
p_k(t_i) = \sum_{N=0}^{N_0-1} P_k(N, t_i) \quad (4.20)
$$

This equation must be satisfied on each integration time step by choosing the proper values of $b_k(t_i)$. This can be done with the help of equation (4.21):

$$
\lambda_k(t_i) = \frac{1}{p_k(t_i)} \sum_{N=0}^{N_0-1} \lambda_k(N, t_i) P_k(N, t_i) \quad (4.21)
$$

where $\lambda_k(t)$ is the marginal default intensity of the kth asset implied by the survival curve:

$$\lambda_k(t_i) = \frac{1}{p_k(t_i)} \frac{p_k(t_i) - p_k(t_{i+1})}{\Delta_i} \tag{4.22}$$

Equation (4.21) can be obtained via the summation of both parts of equation (4.19) over N, from $N = 0$ up to $N_0 - 1$, and has a straightforward meaning: It equals the marginal default intensity of the kth asset calculated from the survival curve with that obtained from the model. Now, inserting equation (4.4) into equation (4.21) and resolving the obtained equation with respect to $b_k(t)$, one obtains:

$$b_k(t_i) = \lambda_k(t_i)\, p_k(t_i) \left(\sum_{N=0}^{N_0-1} Y(N, t_i)\, P_k(N, t_i) \right)^{-1} \tag{4.23}$$

The procedure of model calibration to CDSs can be summarized in five steps:

1. Begin with initial date $i = 0$ and set the values of $P_k(N, 0)$ according to equation (4.6).
2. Find the values of $b_k(N, t_i)$ according to equation (4.23).
3. Find the values of $\lambda_k(N, t)$, $P_B(N, t)$, $\Lambda_B(N, t)$, and $\Lambda_k(N, t)$ according to equations (4.4), (4.11), (4.14), and (4.9), respectively.
4. Find the values of $P_k(N, t)$ at the next time node according to equation (4.19).
5. Set $i \to i + 1$ and repeat steps 2 to 5 until the horizon is reached.

4.4.2   Calibration to Tranches

We consider the calibration procedure to CDO tranches in a simplified case of a portfolio with homogeneous recovery coefficients, $R_k = R$, and notionals, $A_k = A$. This allows expressing the portfolio loss through the number of defaults as $L = hN$, where $h = A(1 - R)$ is the loss given default. The value of a CDO tranche in this case can be computed directly from the probability density of the number of defaults, $P_B(N, t)$. Generalization of our approach to a fully heterogeneous basket is presented in Section 4.6.

Market data on CDO tranches are not complete for uniquely determining the function $Y(N, t)$ and, thus, to proceed, one needs to assume that $Y(N, t)$ has a certain functional form. Choosing a particular form of $Y(N, t)$ we make use of experience with calibrating the local intensity model. Following Arnsdorf and Halperin (2007), we choose to use the piece-linear in loss interpolation. Dependence of $Y(N, t)$ on time, in the simplest case, is assumed to be piece-constant. Allowing nontrivial time dependence, however, often helps in calibrating low-maturity senior tranches (see later discussion).

Thus, we parametrize the $Y(N, t)$ surface via the linear interpolation in loss between the values $Y_k(t)$ defined at the loss levels $l_p(t)$:

$$Y(N, t) = Y_{p-1}(t) \frac{l_p(t) - Nh}{l_p(t) - l_{p-1}(t)} + Y_p(t) \frac{Nh - l_{p-1}(t)}{l_p(t) - l_{p-1}(t)}, \qquad l_{p-1} < Nh < l_p$$

(4.24)

In the simplest case, the functions $l_k(t)$ can be set to be losses corresponding to the detachment levels of tranches,

$$l_p(t) = L_p^{\text{tr}}$$

(4.25)

We also assume that functions $Y_k(t)$ are time independent within the intervals between the tranche maturities:

$$Y_p(t) = Y_{i,p}, \qquad T_{i-1} \leq t < T_i$$

(4.26)

where $T_1, T_2, \ldots, T_M$ is the set of tranche maturity dates and $T_0 = t_0$ is the start date. This form allows setting up a bootstrap calibration to CDO tranches with different maturities: First, one calibrates the model to tranches with maturity T_1 setting $Y_{1,p}$. Then, the model is calibrated to tranches that mature at T_2, adjusting $Y_{2,p}$, and keeping $Y_{1,p}$ unchanged. The procedure is repeated until the model is fully calibrated.

Our numerical experiments showed that the scheme just presented usually provided a good fit to the tranches for most of the market data before the credit crisis. However, the scheme often fails in fitting after-crisis tranche quotes with acceptable accuracy. Typically, the model significantly overprices the senior tranche and underprices the super-senior tranche at five-year maturity. We found that the assumption of time independence of the function $Y(N, t)$ within the intervals between adjacent tranche maturities was one of the key reasons for this failure. This assumption can be justified only by the smallness of the time intervals between the tranche maturity dates. In the case of the standard set of tranche maturities, five, seven, and ten years, it could be justified for the last two intervals, but it hardly holds for the first one. Indeed, when the time evolution just begins, the probability distribution function of losses is confined to a region of low losses lying within the equity tranche. At these times, only the $Y_{1,1}$ component, corresponding to the detachment level of the equity tranche, can affect the dynamics. The value $Y_{1,6}$, corresponding to the super-senior tranche, on the contrary begins to affect the dynamics only at later evolution stages, when the portfolio loss can reach the super-senior tranche with significant probability. This illustrates that values of Y corresponding to more senior tranches effectively have lower leverage for guiding the dynamics. To resolve this problem, we suggest scaling the loss levels l_k linearly in time for the first interval as:

$$l_p(t) = L_p^{\text{tr}} \frac{t - t_0}{T_1 - t_0}, \qquad t_0 < t < T_1$$

(4.27)

TABLE 4.1   Model and Market CDO Spreads in the Homogeneous Portfolio Case

	5-Year		7-Year		10-Year	
	Market	Model	Market	Model	Market	Model
0–3%	34.165	34.2	40.04	40.14	45	45.19
3–6%	370.4	370.9	462.9	460.8	591.8	588.2
6–9%	244.4	245.4	276	278.7	335.7	338.2
9–12%	167.5	166.3	189.7	189.4	218.6	217.6
12–22%	82.4	86	93.2	92.9	105.7	106.6
22–100%	32.2	30	36.6	35	38	36.8

Our numerical experiments showed that this modification results in a dramatic improvement of the calibration quality for all considered data. Calibration results presented next (as well as hedge ratios considered later) are obtained with the scaling that equation(4.27) used.

4.4.3   Numerical Results on Calibration

We present numerical data on calibration to the sets of iTraxx Series 9 tranches maturing at five, seven, and ten years and quoted on April 17, 2008. The index was quoted for maturities three, five, seven, and ten years with the corresponding spreads 65.8, 89.8, 95, 98.8 basis points (bps). Stripping of the single-name quotes was done assuming the piece-constant implied marginal default intensity. The market spreads for each CDS were taken at five, seven, and ten years, skipping the quotes at lower maturities even if they were available. To avoid a possible arbitrage between the index and single-name spreads, the survival curves were matched to index quotes via homogeneous rescaling of the obtained survival curves. This procedure is standard to all bottom-up credit models.

   Along with the heterogeneous portfolio with market-given CDS spreads, we also consider an artificial homogeneous situation where all CDSs are set to index quotes. Results of the fits to CDO tranches are presented in Tables 4.1 and 4.2 for homogeneous and heterogeneous situations, respectively. In both cases, the results of the fit are well within the market bid-offer spreads. Using other data, we generally have

TABLE 4.2   Model and Market CDO Spreads in the Heterogeneous Portfolio Case

	5-Year		7-Year		10-Year	
	Market	Model	Market	Model	Market	Model
0–3%	34.165	34.2	40.04	40.09	45	45.19
3–6%	370.4	370.9	462.9	460	591.8	588.3
6–9%	244.4	245.4	276	277.6	335.7	338.4
9–12%	167.5	168.1	189.7	188.6	218.6	217.6
12–22%	82.4	85.4	93.2	94.3	105.7	107.1
22–100%	32.2	29.4	36.6	34.7	38	36.6

FIGURE 4.1   Basket Default Intensity, $\Lambda_B(N, t)$, in the Heterogeneous Portfolio Case

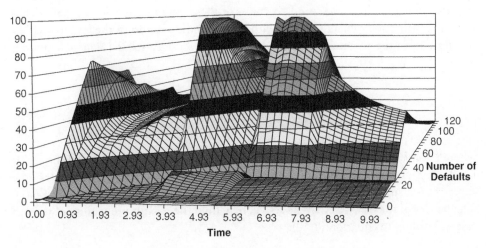

observed that calibration quality is essentially not sensitive to the heterogeneity of the portfolio. The basket default intensity, $\Lambda_B(N, t)$, in the heterogeneous portfolio case is presented in Figure 4.1.

4.5   Hedging a CDO Tranche

In this section, we consider the hedging of a CDO tranche against the market movements of spreads of the underlying CDSs. This question is usually addressed by defining the amount of protection, delta, that needs to be bought on each credit name in order to hedge a long position in a CDO tranche. Delta of the kth credit is defined as the ratio of the change in the tranche value, ΔV^{tr}, and the change in the value of kth CDS, $\Delta V_k^{\mathrm{cds}}$, occurring under a small shift of the kth CDS spread:

$$\delta_k = \frac{\Delta V^{\mathrm{tr}}}{\Delta V_k^{\mathrm{cds}}} \qquad (4.28)$$

This approach to hedging of the spread risk is similar to vega hedging in the Black-Scholes model. While it can hardly be rigorously justified, it is robust and now widely used in practice. Here we follow this standard, simplified scheme. Recent achievements in the rigorous approach to hedging of a credit derivative with respect to different kinds of risks can be found in the work by Bielecki, Jeanblanc, and Rutkowski (2008) (see also references therein).

4.5.1   Hedge Ratios in the Gaussian Copula Model

At present, the tranche deltas are most often calculated via the Gaussian copula (GC) model. This model is also frequently used to gain an intuitive understanding of the dependence of hedge ratios on tranche subordination, contract maturity, spreads of the underlying credits, and so on. Because of these reasons, we will compare deltas obtained within the dynamic model with corresponding results of the GC model.

Recall that the GC model is defined through the set of correlated Gaussian random variables:

$$X_k = \sqrt{1 - \beta_k^2} \, \xi_k + \beta_k \, Z \qquad (4.29)$$

where ξ_k and Z are uncorrelated univaried Gaussian random variables and the factor loadings, β_k, define the correlation matrix of variables X_k. At time t, the default of the kth asset is assumed to occur if the random variable X_k falls below the barrier $c_k(t)$. The barrier of the kth CDS can be set via matching the default probability of the kth asset according to equation (4.30):

$$N(c_k(t)) = p_k^{\mathrm{d}}(t) \qquad (4.30)$$

where $N(x)$ is the cumulative normal distribution and $p_k^{\mathrm{d}}(t)$ is the probability of the kth asset to default before time t. This way the GC model is calibrated to portfolio credits. To achieve a stable calibration to CDO tranches, it is common to use the so-called base correlation scheme. In this approach, the value of a tranche with attachment points (k_1, k_2) is presented as the difference of the values of two base tranches with attachment levels $(0, k_2)$ and $(0, k_1)$, respectively, which are taken at different correlations. Calibrating the tranches, consequently, in accordance with their seniority, one obtains the so-called base correlation curve. The base correlation approach is obviously not intrinsically consistent, which is the main drawback of the GC model (leaving aside fundamental drawbacks of the static approach).

To find the delta of a tranche with respect to the kth credit in the GC model, one shifts the kth spread by a small amount (typically 1 bp) by readjusting accordingly the default probabilities at the relevant dates t_i. The barriers $c_k(t_i)$ are then reset according to equation (4.30), the tranche value is recalculated, and delta is obtained from equation (4.28).

It is important to note that this procedure assumes the hedging of a tranche against the idiosyncratic change of the default probability of a given CDS. Indeed, shifting the barrier of the kth asset does not affect in any way the distribution of defaults of other assets in the portfolio. Formally, this can be written as:

$$\delta_k \sum_{n_k=0,1} p(\mathbf{n}, t) = 0 \qquad (4.31)$$

where δ_k denotes the variation corresponding to the shift of the barrier of the kth asset.

4.5.2 Hedge Ratios in the Dynamic Model

The recipe just presented for the calculation of the hedge ratios is to some extent uncertain because it does not prescribe which model parameters should be adjusted and which should stay constant when taking the derivative in equation (4.28). Calculation within the GC model, for example, is based on the intuitively natural assumption that base correlations are not perturbed. For the static factor models, this problem was discussed in Andersen and Sidenius (2005). The same uncertainty is present in the dynamic approach. To use equation (4.28), one has to identify the model parameters that, similar to correlation coefficients in the GC model, should stay unperturbed when taking the derivative in equation (4.28). We will identify the default correlations with the jumps in the intensities, λ_k, taking place at the default of an asset in the basket. Since, in our model, the individual intensities depend only on the number of defaults, N, and time, t, these jumps can be written as:

$$\kappa_k(N, t) = \lambda_k(N + 1, t) - \lambda_k(N, t) \tag{4.32}$$

Thus, we postulate that the tranche delta with respect to the kth credit is given by equation (4.28), where the derivative is taken under the constraint that the surface $\kappa_k(N, t)$ is kept unchanged. Given the expression for the default intensities (4.1), this assumes that functions $a_k(t)$ can be used for adjusting the model to the shifted single name spreads, while the systemic intensity $Y(N, t)$ and factors $b_k(t)$ should be kept unperturbed. The calibration procedure with adjusting coefficients $a_k(t)$ is very similar to the one described in Section 4.4, with the difference that equation (4.21) must be resolved with respect to the coefficients $a_k(t)$, which were kept zero. Inserting equation (4.4) into equation (4.21) and using equation (4.11), and (4.14) one obtains:

$$a_k(t_i) = \lambda_k(t_i) - \frac{b_k(t_i)}{p_k(t_i)} \sum_{N=0}^{N_0-1} Y(N, t_i) \, P_k(N, t_i) \tag{4.33}$$

The described procedure for calculation of the tranche delta with respect to the kth asset can be summarized in four steps:

1. Calibrate the dynamic model to CDO tranches and single-name spreads following the procedure of Section 4.4.
2. Find the perturbed values of the survival probability and default intensity of the kth asset corresponding to a 1 bp shift of the spread.
3. Recalibrate the model keeping the functions $b_k(t)$ and $Y(N, t)$ unchanged (as obtained on step 1) and adjusting functions $a_k(t)$ according to equation (4.33).
4. Obtain tranche delta via equation (4.28) with ΔV^{tr} being the differences of the tranche values obtained on steps 3 and 1.

We note that, while conceptually this procedure looks similar to the one used in the GC model, there is a significant qualitative difference between the two approaches: The GC model assumes that hedging ratios are calculated with condition (4.31) being satisfied, meaning that the change of the single-asset default probability does not affect other portfolio assets. This condition does not hold for the suggested dynamic definition of the hedge ratios. Changing the survival probability of a given asset, one immediately perturbs the default intensities of all other assets. When presenting our numerical results, we will refer to the procedure described earlier as "contagious." Next we consider an alternative idiosyncratic definition compatible with equation (4.31).

4.5.3   Recovering Idiosyncratic Risk in the Dynamic Model

Ignorance of the effect of default contagion is one of the drawbacks of the static GC approach. Indeed, the fact that the market fluctuations of single-name spreads are correlated can hardly be doubted and, therefore, the hedge ratios obtained in the idiosyncratic manner should be taken with caution. Yet, the idiosyncratic risk provides useful additional information and corresponding hedge ratios can also be of interest to practitioners. Here we present a recipe for deriving tranche deltas within the developed dynamical approach which is consistent with condition (4.31).

In the case of homogeneous recovery coefficients, the value of a CDO tranche is uniquely defined by the basket probability distribution $P_B(N, t)$. Therefore, to determine the tranche delta, it is enough to find the change in the basket probability density, $\delta_k P_B(N, t)$, under the idiosyncratic change of the survival probability of the kth asset. It turns out that $\delta_k P_B(N, t)$ can be expressed through the corresponding change of the probability density $P_k(N, t)$ defined by equation (4.2) as:

$$\delta_k P_B(N, t) = \delta_k(P_k(N, t) - P_k(N - 1, t)) \qquad (4.34)$$

This expression can be proven as follows. Let us present the basket probability density as:

$$P_B(N, t) = P_k(N, t) + P_k^d(N, t) \qquad (4.35)$$

where $P_k^d(N, t)$ is the probability that up to time t the kth asset defaulted and that the total number of defaults in the basket is N. Equation (4.35) has an obvious meaning: the probabilities for the kth asset to survive and to default conditioned on the total number of defaults must sum to one. Thus, the change in the basket probability density can be written as:

$$\delta_k P_B(N, t) = \delta_k P_k(N, t) + \delta_k P_k^d(N, t) \qquad (4.36)$$

But, according to equation (4.31), under the idiosyncratic change of the survival probability of the kth asset,

$$\delta_k(P_k(N, t) + P_k^d(N + 1, t)) = 0 \qquad (4.37)$$

Equation (4.34) now follows immediately from equations (4.36) and (4.37).

Thus, the problem of finding the change of the tranche value under the idiosyncratic perturbation of the survival probability of the kth asset is reduced to finding $\delta_k P_k(N, t)$ in equation (4.34). According to the Fokker-Planck equation (4.3), the probability density $P_k(N, t)$ is defined uniquely by the conditioned default intensity of the kth asset, $\lambda_k(N, t)$, and by the conditioned intensity of defaults in the basket having all but kth asset, $\Lambda_k(N, t)$. It is important to note that the latter, by definition, should be kept unperturbed when finding the delta as long as one deals with the idiosyncratic risk.

Finally, we have to specify the change of the single-asset default intensity. We choose to rescale the default intensity of the kth asset,

$$\lambda_k(N, t) \rightarrow \lambda'_k(N, t) = \kappa(t)\lambda_k(N, t) \qquad (4.38)$$

This definition is preferable to changing some model parameters in a specific way because it can be applied to any intensity-based bottom-up model. A similar procedure was used in Eckner (2007). Within the first order in time scheme, the probability of $P_k(N, t)$ is determined by equation (4.19). The perturbed probability $P'_k(N, t) = P_k(N, t) + \delta_k P_k(N, t)$ is, thus, defined by

$$\frac{P'_k(N, t_{i+1}) - P'_k(N, t_i)}{\Delta_i} = \Lambda_k(N - 1, t_i)P'_k(N - 1, t_i) - (\Lambda_k(N, t_i)$$
$$+ \kappa(t)\lambda_k(N, t_i))\, P'_k(N, t_i) \qquad (4.39)$$

The scaling function $\kappa(t)$ can be found by matching the perturbed survival probability of the kth asset using the procedure described in Section 4.4: Summing both parts of equation (4.39) over N from 0 to $N_0 - 1$, we obtain:

$$\lambda'_k(t_i) = \frac{\kappa(t_i)}{p'_k(t_i)} \sum_{N=0}^{N_0-1} \lambda_k(N, t_i)\, P'_k(N, t_i) \qquad (4.40)$$

Here, $p'_k(t)$ is the perturbed marginal survival probability of the kth asset and $\lambda'_k(t_i)$ is the corresponding marginal default intensity $\lambda'_k(t_i) = (p'_k(t_i) - p'_k(t_{i+1}))/p'_k(t_i)\Delta_i$. The scaling function $\kappa(t)$ now can be found from equation (4.40):

$$\kappa(t) = p'_k(t_i)\lambda'_k(t_i) \left(\sum_{N=0}^{N_0-1} \lambda_k(N, t_i)\, P'_k(N, t_i) \right)^{-1} \qquad (4.41)$$

Equation (4.39) can be solved numerically by going forward in time and taking the values of $\kappa(t_i)$ from equation (4.41) on each time step. For clarity, we summarize in four steps the calculation of the delta of the kth credit:

1. Calibrate the dynamic model to CDO tranches and single-name spreads following the procedure of Section 4.4.
2. Find the perturbed values of the survival probability and default intensity of the kth asset [$p'_k(t)$ and $\lambda'_k(t_i)$, respectively] in accordance with the shifted spread of the kth asset.
3. Find P'_k by solving equations (4.39) and (4.41) forward in time.
4. Find the change in the basket probability density according to equation (4.34), calculate the corresponding change in the tranche values, and obtain delta from equation (4.28).

This procedure will be further referred to as idiosyncratic.

4.5.4   Numerical Results on Tranche Deltas

Here, we present the numerical results on tranche deltas. We use the same market data as in Section 4.4.3 and calculate deltas for all available tranches with respect to CDSs that mature at the same dates with tranches. As in Subsection 4.4.3, along with the real market data on CDSs, we also consider an artificially homogeneous setup where all CDS spreads are set to corresponding index spreads.

Tranche deltas calculated within the two dynamic methods are presented in Tables 4.3 and 4.4 for homogeneous and heterogeneous cases, respectively, along with the values obtained via the GC model. In the heterogeneous case, we present our results for three representative portfolio members with low, moderate, and high values of the spreads.

TABLE 4.3 Tranche Delta in Homogeneous Portfolio Case

Maturity	5-Year			7-Year			10-Year		
Method	DC	DI	GC	DC	DI	GC	DC	DI	GC
CDS Spreads	85			91			94.9		
0–3%	0.2441	0.4408	0.2327	0.1859	0.3372	0.1800	0.1483	0.2270	0.1356
3–6%	0.1407	0.1420	0.1456	0.1562	0.2108	0.1516	0.1635	0.2445	0.1529
6–9%	0.0931	0.0848	0.0989	0.1024	0.1033	0.1035	0.1163	0.1528	0.1141
9–12%	0.0678	0.1310	0.0720	0.0703	0.1565	0.0768	0.0804	0.1689	0.0851
12–22%	0.1287	0.0854	0.1346	0.1298	0.0828	0.1465	0.1450	0.1117	0.1650
22–100%	0.3486	0.1516	0.3427	0.3864	0.1639	0.3749	0.3930	0.1798	0.3937

Deltas of tranches obtained in the dynamic model via contagious (DC) and idiosyncratic (DI) methods are presented, along with corresponding results calculated via the static Gaussian copula (GC) model in the homogeneous portfolio case.

TABLE 4.4 Tranche Deltas in Heterogeneous Portfolio Case

Maturity	5-Year			7-Year			10-Year		
Method	DC	DI	GC	DC	DI	GC	DC	DI	GC
CDS Spreads	29.3			33.4			32.4		
0–3%	0.2404	0.1740	0.1064	0.1613	0.1201	0.0753	0.1010	0.0835	0.0512
3–6%	0.1530	0.0570	0.0540	0.1548	0.0722	0.0595	0.1429	0.0846	0.0617
6–9%	0.1006	0.0292	0.0420	0.1072	0.0366	0.0419	0.1180	0.0529	0.0467
9–12%	0.0712	0.0653	0.0290	0.0749	0.0569	0.0296	0.0886	0.0657	0.0321
12–22%	0.1303	0.0275	−0.0035	0.1449	0.0345	−0.0031	0.1650	0.0425	0.0061
22–100%	0.3468	0.6740	0.7961	0.4144	0.7141	0.8248	0.4729	0.7240	0.8440
CDS Spreads	90.7			97			101.9		
0–3%	0.2571	0.4583	0.2064	0.1823	0.3449	0.1572	0.1347	0.2282	0.1165
3–6%	0.1553	0.1550	0.1333	0.1650	0.2199	0.1387	0.1626	0.2518	0.1417
6–9%	0.0994	0.0771	0.0968	0.1119	0.1094	0.0998	0.1217	0.1564	0.1104
9–12%	0.0679	0.1766	0.0734	0.0757	0.1594	0.0771	0.0864	0.1830	0.0853
12–22%	0.1224	0.0691	0.1483	0.1303	0.0944	0.1595	0.1524	0.1092	0.1786
22–100%	0.3211	0.1031	0.3657	0.3677	0.1306	0.3972	0.3893	0.1601	0.4075
CDS Spreads	200			207.5			213		
0–3%	0.2931	0.5560	0.3200	0.2392	0.4335	0.2577	0.1940	0.2975	0.2033
3–6%	0.1560	0.1767	0.2038	0.1828	0.2542	0.2131	0.1933	0.2947	0.2125
6–9%	0.0929	0.0759	0.1264	0.1117	0.1120	0.1372	0.1278	0.1660	0.1504
9–12%	0.0584	0.1440	0.0878	0.0693	0.1402	0.0973	0.0824	0.1695	0.1083
12–22%	0.1011	0.0520	0.1720	0.0956	0.0732	0.1960	0.1073	0.0889	0.2158
22–100%	0.2878	0.0185	0.0956	0.2893	0.0176	0.1046	0.2852	0.0294	0.1199

Deltas of tranches obtained in the dynamic model via contagious (DC) and idiosyncratic (DI) methods are presented, along with corresponding results obtained via the static Gaussian copula (GC) model in the heterogeneous portfolio case. Three representative members with low, moderate, and high spreads were chosen from a portfolio of 125 names.

We begin with the discussion of the homogeneous case. Comparing results obtained within the two dynamic methods, one can see that deltas of senior tranches obtained within the first (contagious) method are higher than those obtained within the second (idiosyncratic) one. This effect disappears with lowering the tranche seniority and turns to the opposite for the equity tranche. Such behavior is expected since the clustering of defaults, disregarded by the idiosyncratic approach, causes senior tranches to be more risky.

Tranche deltas obtained within the contagious dynamic approach turn out to be pretty close to the results obtained within the GC model. This observation is highly surprising since deltas of the GC model are obtained within the idiosyncratic framework, and one would naturally expect that those deltas will be closer to the corresponding dynamic idiosyncratic values. We have checked that, in the regime of flat correlations where the GC model represents a consistent static model, the results of the GC model are, indeed, closer to the idiosyncratic deltas of the dynamic model.

FIGURE 4.2   Tranche Deltas as Functions of Maturity in a Simple Artificial Setup

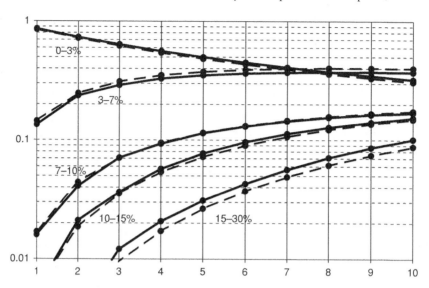

Tranche quotes are generated by the Gaussian copula model with constant correlations set to 0.2. Tranche attachment points were chosen to be 0, 3, 7, 10, 15, or 30 percent, and a fully homogeneous portfolio was considered with CDS spreads set to 50 bp and recovery coefficients 40 percent. Solid lines represent the values obtained via the dynamic idiosyncratic method (the dynamic model was calibrated to the tranche quotes generated by the GC model) while the dashed lines show results of the GC model.

This can be seen from Figure 4.2 showing idiosyncratic tranche deltas as functions of maturity obtained within the two models in the case of an artificial setup where tranche quotes are generated via the GC model with flat correlations. However, when significant base correlation skew is present, the situation changes to the opposite and results of the GC model get closer to the dynamic values obtained within the contagious approach. Thus, the inconsistency of the base correlation framework causes deltas of the GC model to deviate significantly from those obtained within the consistent idiosyncratic dynamic framework and, coincidentally, makes them closer to the values obtained with inclusion of the default contagion effect.

Deltas obtained in the heterogeneous case (see Table 4.4) turn out to be relatively close to the corresponding homogeneous values only for assets with moderate spreads, close to the spread of the index. While all three methods predict deltas to be rather sensitive to the values of the underlying spreads, results obtained within the dynamic contagious method are significantly more uniform over portfolio members. Such smoothing can be intuitively expected to be caused by the default contagion effect. It is important to note that the GC model predicts negative deltas for the senior tranche with respect to the asset with low default probability maturing in five and seven years. Neither dynamic method shows this problem. In the case of an asset with high default probability, the two idiosyncratic methods (GC and dynamic) predict very low deltas for senior and super-senior tranches. In the context of the GC model, this effect is well known and can be explained as follows: Under the condition that the portfolio loss has reached senior tranches, the probability of an unreliable asset to survive is close to zero and small changes of its spread become irrelevant. This consideration, however, is of an idiosyncratic nature because we assume that changing the spread of an asset will not affect the spreads of other assets. Thus, one expects that contagion effects will tend to smear this effect out, which is supported by our results: Deltas of senior tranches with respect to the high-spread asset are not small and are significantly larger than results obtained within the idiosyncratic framework.

4.6 Portfolio with Heterogeneous Recovery Coefficients

Throughout this chapter, we have considered a simplified case of a portfolio with homogeneous recovery coefficients. Here, we present a generalization of the developed method to fully heterogeneous portfolios. One of the ways to proceed would be to modify the model to make the asset default intensities be deterministic functions of the portfolio loss. Alternatively, one can try to recover the portfolio loss distribution, making no changes to the existing scheme. While the first way is feasible, it has two disadvantages. First, the loss variable requires a finer grid than that of the discrete number of defaults, and this will result in a significant decrease in the numerical efficiency. The second problem is that the tranche pricing formulas also include the amortization due to recovery, which, to find, requires the knowledge of the distributions of the portfolio recovery (for details see, for example, Antonov, Mechkov, and Misirpashaev 2007) that would be difficult to obtain if the state variable is chosen to be the portfolio loss. The contribution to the tranche value from this mechanism is not significant; nevertheless, the inclusion of this mechanism is a requirement for a model to be used in the industry applications. For these reasons, we prefer to choose the second way to proceed.

In the spirit of the developed semianalytic approach, we will make use of the fact that the number of assets in the portfolio is large. In this limit, the intensity of the transition with a given loss change, l, conditioned on the number of defaults, N, can be written as:

$$t(l, N, t) = \frac{1}{P_B(N, t)} \sum_{k=1}^{N_0} \lambda_k(N, t) \, P_k(N, t) \, \delta(l - h_k) \qquad (4.42)$$

where $\delta(x)$ is the Dirac delta function and $h_k = A_k(1 - R_k)$ is the loss given default of the kth asset. Equation (4.42) defines the instantaneous probability of the transition between the two portfolio states characterized by different losses and default numbers. Namely, given that, at time t, the portfolio loss is L, and the number of defaults is N, the generator $t(l, N, t)$ represents the transition $(L, N) \rightarrow (L + l, N + 1)$. Thereby, one can write the Fokker-Planck equation on the joint probability distribution of the loss and number of defaults, $P(L, N, t)$, as:

$$\frac{d}{dt} P(L, N, t) = \int dl \Big(t(l, N-1, t)\, P(L-l, N-1, t) - t(l, N, t)\, P(L, N, t) \Big)$$

$$(4.43)$$

Given the joint distribution, $P(L, N, t)$, the loss distribution function, $P(L, t)$, can be found as:

$$P(L, t) = \sum_{N=0}^{N_0} P(L, N, t) \qquad (4.44)$$

Equations (4.42), and (4.43) allow construction of the joint probability distribution $P(L, N, t)$ out of the probabilities $P_k(N, t)$. The probability distribution of the loss defining the spreads of CDO tranches can then be obtained from equation (4.44). Numerical solution of equation (4.43) requires discretization of the loss variable. This computationally expensive convolution operation can be bypassed by turning to the Fourier representation. Amortization due to recovery can be found in a similar way, changing the loss variable to recovery and setting $1 - R_i \to R_i$.

Finally, we comment on the parametrization of the surface $Y(N, t)$ in the case of heterogeneous recoveries. In Section 4.4.2, we presented the scheme that uses linear interpolation in the loss. This scheme used the simple relationship between the portfolio loss and number of defaults, $L = Nh$, which is not valid in the case of heterogeneous recoveries. To resolve this problem, one can introduce the expected loss conditioned on the number of defaults,

$$\bar{L}(N) = \mathrm{E}\,[\,L(t)\,|\,N(t) = N] \qquad (4.45)$$

which can be easily found from the joint default distribution function $P(L, N, t)$. Parametrization of $Y(N, t)$ can then be done exactly as in Subsection 4.4.2 with the substitution $hN \to \bar{L}(N)$.

4.7 Markovian Projection onto the Default Contagion Model

The model (4.1), as any model of the default contagion framework, can hardly provide an adequate description of the stochastic market fluctuations of CDS spreads (the market risk) that are very significant even in the absence of defaults. In this respect, the default contagion framework can be contrasted with the double stochastic approach. Consider, for example, the model used by Eckner (2007), which defines single asset intensities in the form:

$$\lambda_t^k = X_t^k + a_k Y_t \qquad (4.46)$$

where X_t^k and Y_t are, respectively, stochastic idiosyncratic and systemic components, each following Cox-Ingersoll-Ross (CIR) dynamics with jumps. Model (4.46) captures the market risk, but it does not include explicitly the default contagion effect. The market risk is important for pricing dynamics-sensitive instruments, such as, for example, options on tranches. Sensitivity of the option value to the stochastic dynamics of the default intensity was confirmed within the models of the top-down framework in works by Arnsdorf and Halperin (2007) and Lopatin and Misirpashaev (2008).

In this section, we show that double stochastic and contagion models are not fundamentally different as long as one deals with instruments whose values can be expressed completely through the full probability density of defaults $p(\mathbf{n}, t)$. In this case, the division of stochastic dynamics of default intensities into the "market" and "contagious" is to some extent illusory in the sense that only additional, more specific, market information would allow one to distinguish between the two. Here we show that the default contagion model can be viewed as a reduced form of a model with default intensities given by adaptive stochastic processes. This procedure can be viewed as a multidimensional generalization of the Markovian projection technique used by Lopatin and Misirpashaev (2008). The same multidimensional extension was recently used by Giesecke, Kakavand, Mousavi, and Takada (2009) in a context of developing an efficient simulation method. The most famous example of using the Markovian projection in finance is the projection of the stochastic volatility model onto the Dupire (1994) local volatility model. This projection was first suggested and proved by Gyöngy (1986) in no relation to finance. Detailed discussion of applications of Gyöngy's lemma is given by Piterbarg (2007); see also Antonov, Misirpashaev, and Piterbarg (2007) for an example of a multidimensional Markovian projection.

In the most general form, the default contagion model defines the default intensities of portfolio members as deterministic functions of the current portfolio state,

$$\lambda_t^k = \lambda_k(\mathbf{n}(t), t) \tag{4.47}$$

The model (4.1) is a special case of model (4.47) with intensities given by $\lambda_k(\mathbf{n}, t) = a_k(t) + b_k(t) Y(n_1 + n_2 + \cdots + n_{N_0}, t)$. Because the model is Markovian, the full basket probability density $p(\mathbf{n}, t)$ obeys the Fokker-Planck equation:

$$\frac{d}{dt} p(\mathbf{n}, t) = \sum_{k=1}^{N_0} \lambda_k(\mathbf{n} - \mathbf{e_k}, t) \, p(\mathbf{n} - \mathbf{e_k}, t) - \lambda_k(\mathbf{n}, t) \, p(\mathbf{n}, t) \tag{4.48}$$

where the vector $\mathbf{e}_k$ has kth element set to unity, all others being zeros. The default intensity, $\lambda_k(\mathbf{n}, t)$, is defined such that:

$$\lambda_k(n_1, \ldots, n_k = 1, \ldots, n_{N_0}, t) = 0 \tag{4.49}$$

ensuring that a defaulted asset may not default. Also, to avoid writing obvious constraints in summation in equation (4.48), we define that $p(n_1, \ldots,$

$n_m = -1, \ldots, n_{N_0}, t) = 0$ for any m. Equivalently, equation (4.48) can be written in the form:

$$\frac{d}{dt} p(\mathbf{m}, t) = \sum_{\mathbf{n}} p(\mathbf{n}, t) A(\mathbf{n}, \mathbf{m}, t) \qquad (4.50)$$

where the generator matrix $A(\mathbf{n}, \mathbf{m})$ is defined as:

$$A(\mathbf{n}, \mathbf{m}, t) = \begin{cases} -\sum_{k=1}^{N_0} \lambda(\mathbf{n}), & \mathbf{m} = \mathbf{n}, \\ \lambda_k(\mathbf{n}), & \mathbf{m} = \mathbf{n} + \mathbf{e}_k, \\ 0, & \text{all other cases} \end{cases} \qquad (4.51)$$

Now, let us consider the double stochastic model of a general kind with the default intensity of the kth asset being given by an arbitrary adaptive stochastic process μ_t^k. This model will reproduce the same default probability density $p(\mathbf{n}, t)$ as model (4.47) as long as:

$$\lambda_k(\mathbf{n}, t) = \mathrm{E}[\mu_t^k \,|\, \mathbf{n}(t) = \mathbf{n}] \qquad (4.52)$$

To prove this statement, let us write the probability density $p(\mathbf{n}, t)$ at time $t + \delta t$,

$$p(\mathbf{m}, t + \delta t) = \mathrm{P}[\mathbf{n}(t + \delta t) = \mathbf{m}] = \sum_{\mathbf{n}} \mathrm{P}[\mathbf{n}(t + \delta t) = \mathbf{m} \,|\, \mathbf{n}(t) = \mathbf{n}] \, \mathrm{P}[\mathbf{n}(t) = \mathbf{n}] \qquad (4.53)$$

and consider transition elements:

$$T(\mathbf{n}, \mathbf{m}, t, \delta t) = \mathrm{P}[\mathbf{n}(t + \delta_t) = \mathbf{m} \,|\, \mathbf{n}(t) = \mathbf{n}] \qquad (4.54)$$

in the limit $\delta_t \to 0$, keeping only terms of zero and linear order in δ_t. It is clear that, in this limit, one can leave only elements with $\mathbf{m} = \mathbf{n}$ and $\mathbf{m} = \mathbf{n} + \mathbf{e}_k$. In the latter case,

$$\lim_{\delta_t \to 0} \frac{1}{\delta_t} T(\mathbf{n}, \mathbf{n} + \mathbf{e}_k, t, \delta_t) = \lim_{\delta_t \to 0} \frac{1}{\delta_t} \mathrm{P}[\mathbf{n}(t + \delta_t) = \mathbf{n} + \mathbf{e}_k \,|\, \mathbf{n}(t) = \mathbf{n}]$$

$$= \mathrm{E}[\mu_t^k \,|\, \mathbf{n}(t) = \mathbf{n}] \qquad (4.55)$$

From condition $\sum_{\mathbf{m}} T(\mathbf{n}, \mathbf{m}, t, \delta_t) = 1$, we find the diagonal elements:

$$T(\mathbf{n}, \mathbf{n}, t, \delta_t) = 1 - \sum_{\mathbf{m} \neq \mathbf{n}} T(\mathbf{n}, \mathbf{m}, t, \delta_t)$$

$$= 1 - \delta_t \sum_k \mathbf{1}_{n_k = 0} \, \mathrm{E}[\mu_t^k \,|\, \mathbf{n}(t) = \mathbf{n}] + O(\delta t^2) \qquad (4.56)$$

Inserting expressions for matrix elements (4.55), and (4.56) into equation (4.53) and taking the limit $\delta t \to 0$, we reproduce equation (4.48) with $\lambda_k(\mathbf{n}, t)$ given by conditional expectation in accordance with equation (4.52).

The presented Markovian projection technique provides a link between the double stochastic and contagion models by showing that contagion effect can be generated via projecting the stochastic intensity on the portfolio state. This, of course, does not mean that any two models of the two frameworks are guaranteed to give the same or close results for the tranche hedge ratios. Indeed, starting, for example, from the model (4.46) and constructing the corresponding Markovian contagion model via equation (4.52), one would hardly obtain the deterministic intensities fitting the specific form [equation (4.1)]. Also, as we discussed in Section 4.5.2, the derivation of hedge ratios relies on the fixing of certain model parameters at the stage of recalibrating the model to the perturbed survival probabilities. This may also lead to discrepancies in the results obtained within the two models. Indeed, keeping certain parameters in model (4.46) constant, in general, would impose a rather complicated constraint on the effective intensities of the default contagion model.

4.8 Stochastic Recovery Coefficients

It is established empirically that asset recoveries are negatively correlated with the rate of defaults (see, for example, Hamilton, Varma, Ou, and Cantor 2005). Recent credit crisis has fully revealed the importance of this effect. During this turbulent time period spreads of senior tranches have widened so much that often they could not be fitted via the industry standard, Gaussian copula model under assumption of constant recovery coefficients (base correlations were hitting the unity bound). An extension of the Gaussian copula model allowing for inclusion of stochastic, factor correlated, recoveries was developed well before the credit crisis by Andersen and Sidenius (2004). Amraoui and Hitier (2008) have recently suggested a particular form of the dependence of recovery coefficients on a factor that automatically respects the consistency with static values of CDS recoveries. Inglis, Lipton, and Sepp (2009) use bivariate recovery distribution extending the static version of the Inglis and Lipton model. Hull and White (2006) include correlations between the recoveries and default intensity in order to improve the quality of calibration of their implied copula model.

The simplest way to include the effect of negative correlations between recoveries and intensity of defaults in our model is to assume that an asset recovery is a deterministic function of its default intensity. So, the loss given default (LGD) of the kth asset, $L_t^k = 1 - R_t^k$, (L_t^k is in units of asset notional) has a form:

$$L_t^k = f_k(\lambda_t^k) \qquad (4.57)$$

Prior to choosing a particular form for the dependence $f_k(\lambda)$, we note that special care should be taken to ensure consistency between equation (4.57) and static recovery coefficients, R_k, used on the stage of obtaining the survival probabilities, $p_k(t)$, from the market CDS spreads. As a reminder, CDS value is fully determined by the asset default probability, $d_k(t) = 1 - p_k(t)$, and expected loss $\bar{l}_k(t)$. Stripping the survival curve, one usually makes an assumption of constant recovery coefficients, or, equivalently, that an asset LGD defined as:

$$L_k = \frac{\bar{l}_k(t)}{d_k(t)} \tag{4.58}$$

is constant. We note that the realized values of asset losses may be (and in reality certainly are) stochastic, yet, in order to strip a CDS, one needs to know only the effective static LGD defined according to equation (4.58). Thus, one has to ensure that stochastic LGD given by equation (4.57) is consistent with the static LGD [equation (4.58)]. This can be guaranteed via imposing the requirement:

$$L_k = \frac{E[\, L_t^k \lambda_t^k \,]}{E[\, \lambda_t^k \,]} \tag{4.59}$$

In the case of the present model this general consistency requirement becomes:

$$L_k = \frac{\displaystyle\sum_{N=0}^{N_0-1} f_k(\lambda_k(N, t))\, \lambda_k(N, t)\, P_k(N, t)}{\displaystyle\sum_{N=0}^{N_0-1} \lambda_k(N, t)\, P_k(N, t)} \tag{4.60}$$

Now we turn to the specification of the function $f_k(\lambda)$. Following Hull and White (2006), we choose the linear dependence of the loss given default on intensity restricted by upper and lower bounds, $L_k^{\min}$ and $L_k^{\max}$, respectively. Whereas the natural values for these bounds are $L_k^{\min} = 0$ and $L_k^{\max} = 1$, we prefer to keep them arbitrary satisfying $0 \leq L_k^{\min} \leq L_k^{\max} \leq 1$. Thus, we assume:

$$f_k(\lambda) = B(a_k + \theta_k \lambda, L_k^{\min}, L_k^{\max}) \tag{4.61}$$

where $B(x, a, b)$ is:

$$B(x, a, b) = \begin{cases} b, & x > b \\ x, & a \leq x \leq b \\ a, & x < a \end{cases} \tag{4.62}$$

To make equation (4.61) consistent with constraint (4.59), we will assume that the slopes θ_k and bound values $L_k^{\min}$, $L_k^{\max}$ are fixed model parameters, while the values of a_k are chosen such that equation (4.60) is satisfied at all times. We note that, in general, it makes the coefficients a_k to be time dependent even when the input values $(\theta_k, L_k^{\min}, L_k^{\max})$ are constant. One can see that changing a_k one shifts the function

TABLE 4.5 Model Fit for CDO Tranches in the Case of CDX 12 Quoted on June 19, 2009

	5-Year		7-Year		10-Year	
	Market	Model	Market	Model	Market	Model
0–3%	63.82	63.82	68.90	68.91	73.30	73.30
3–7%	34.18	34.18	40.98	40.97	46.80	46.80
7–10%	14.74	14.74	19.59	19.61	25.34	25.35
10–15%	4.44	4.43	6.23	6.21	8.64	8.64
15–30%	−0.69	−0.71	−0.83	−0.79	−0.84	−0.81
30–100%	−2.79	−2.86	−3.50	−3.51	−4.01	−4.10

Tranche values are given in percents of notionals; spreads of all tranches are 100 bp. Parameters of stochastic recovery are $\theta = 2$, $L^{\min} = 0.2$, and $L^{\max} = 1$.

$f_k(\lambda)$ along the λ-axis such that $f_k(\lambda)$ takes the values $L_k^{\min}$, $L_k^{\max}$ in the limits $a_k \to -\infty$, $a_k \to \infty$, respectively. This guarantees the existence of the solution of equation (4.60) as long as the loss bounds include the static value of LGD, $L_k^{\min} < L_k < L_k^{\max}$.

Numerical implementation of the described procedure suits well the forward calibration scheme of Section 4.4. At each integration time step, t_i, equation (4.60) has to be solved numerically for the values of $a_k(t_i)$. Piece-linear form of the dependence in equation (4.61) allows one to find the root within just a few iterations such that numerical overhead due to this procedure turns out to be not significant. In many cases the overall calibration procedure may become even faster because negative correlations between the recoveries and default intensity often result in the reduction of the basket default intensity, which in turn allows one to choose smaller time steps in integration. Table 4.5 shows the results of model calibration to CDX 12 index tranches quoted on June 19, 2009. Parameters that set correlated recoveries in equation (4.61) were $\theta_k = 2$, $L_k^{\min} = 0.2$, $L_k^{\max} = 1$. For this market data the model could not be calibrated without inclusion of correlated recovery with acceptable accuracy.

4.9 Conclusion

We have presented a simple bottom-up credit model that can be calibrated simultaneously to CDO tranches and to the spreads of underlying CDSs. The model is solved within the semianalytic forward induction method that allows reduction of the original multidimensional problem to a system of coupled one-dimensional Fokker-Planck equations and is justified when the number of assets in the portfolio is large. While in the present chapter we have mostly concentrated on the case of homogeneous recovery coefficients, the method can be extended to handle heterogeneous recoveries as well.

We have used two different methods for calculating tranche hedge ratios with respect to market changes of spreads of underlying CDSs. The first method takes into account that perturbing the survival probability of an asset affects the dynamics of other portfolio members; the second deliberately disregards this effect. We found that the two methods in general produce rather different results, supporting the importance of inclusion of the default contagion effect. Surprisingly, we found that in the homogeneous portfolio case deltas calculated via the first method are close to the corresponding values obtained within the GC model. Even in the heterogeneous case, the results are still fairly close for those portfolio members that have spreads close to the spread of the index. In general, the tranche deltas obtained within the contagion method are more homogeneous over portfolio members than those obtained within the idiosyncratic scheme.

Appendix 4A: Derivation of the Fokker-Planck Equation (4.3)

We derive equation (4.3) for a default contagion model of a general kind defined in equation (4.47). In this case, the default intensity $\lambda_k(N, t)$ entering equation (4.3) should be understood as the default intensity of the kth asset, conditioned on the total number of defaults accumulated in the portfolio,

$$\lambda_k(N, t) = \frac{\sum_{\mathbf{n}} \lambda_k(\mathbf{n}, t)\, p(\mathbf{n}, t)\, \mathbf{1}_{n_1+n_2+\cdots+n_{N_0}=N}}{P_k(N, t)} \qquad (4.63)$$

This equation turns into identity when $\lambda_k(\mathbf{n}, t)$ depends on the current portfolio state through the total number of defaults, N, as in the case of model (4.1). Here and below we assume that equation (4.49) holds.

Similarly, based on the definition (4.5), we can express $\Lambda_k(N, t)$ through the full probability density $p(\mathbf{n}, t)$ and intensity of defaults (4.47) as:

$$\Lambda_k(N, t) = \frac{\sum_{\mathbf{n}} \sum_{m;\, m \neq k} \lambda_m(\mathbf{n}, t)\, p(\mathbf{n}, t)\, \mathbf{1}_{n_k=0}\, \mathbf{1}_{n_1+n_2+\ldots+n_{N_0}=N}}{P_k(N, t)} \qquad (4.64)$$

For the purpose of this appendix it is convenient to write equation (4.48) in a more compact form:

$$\frac{d}{dt}\, p(\mathbf{n}, t) = \sum_{k=1}^{N_0} \hat{\mathcal{L}}_k \lambda_k(\mathbf{n}, t)\, p(\mathbf{n}, t) - \lambda_k(\mathbf{n}, t)\, p(\mathbf{n}, t) \qquad (4.65)$$

where the action of the operator $\hat{\mathcal{L}}_k$ on an arbitrary function $f(\mathbf{n})$ is defined as:

$$\hat{\mathcal{L}}_k\, f(n_1, \ldots, n_k = 1, \ldots, n_{N_0}) = f(n_1, \ldots, n_k = 0, \ldots, n_{N_0})$$
$$\hat{\mathcal{L}}_k\, f(n_1, \ldots, n_k = 0, \ldots, n_{N_0}) = 0 \qquad (4.66)$$

The operator $\hat{\mathcal{L}}_k$ lowers the default indicator of the kth asset.

To derive equation (4.3), we multiply both sides of equation (4.65) by $\mathbf{1}_{n_k=0} \mathbf{1}_{n_1+n_2+\ldots+n_{N_0}=N}$ and sum over all realization of defaults:

$$\frac{d}{dt} P_k(N, t) = \sum_{\mathbf{n}} \sum_{m=1}^{N_0} \mathbf{1}_{n_k=0} \mathbf{1}_{n_1+\ldots+n_{N_0}=N} \left(\hat{\mathcal{L}}_m \lambda_m(\mathbf{n}, t) \, p(\mathbf{n}, t) - \lambda_m(\mathbf{n}, t) \, p(\mathbf{n}, t) \right)$$

(4.67)

The contribution from the first term in the brackets in equation (4.67) can be reduced to the first term in the right-hand side of equation (4.3) as:

$$\sum_{\mathbf{n}} \sum_{m} \mathbf{1}_{n_k=0} \mathbf{1}_{n_1+\ldots+n_{N_0}=N} \hat{\mathcal{L}}_m \, \lambda_m(\mathbf{n}, t) \, p(\mathbf{n}, t)$$

$$= \sum_{\mathbf{n}} \sum_{m;\, m \neq k} \hat{\mathcal{L}}_m \, \mathbf{1}_{n_k=0} \mathbf{1}_{n_1+\ldots+n_{N_0}+1=N} \lambda_m(\mathbf{n}, t) \, p(\mathbf{n}, t)$$

$$= \sum_{\mathbf{n}} \sum_{m;\, m \neq k} \mathbf{1}_{n_k=0} \mathbf{1}_{n_1+\ldots+n_{N_0}+1=N} \lambda_m(\mathbf{n}, t) \, p(\mathbf{n}, t)$$

$$= \Lambda_k(N-1, t) P_k(N-1, t)$$

(4.68)

The contribution of the second term in the brackets in equation (4.67) brings the term $(\Lambda_k(N, t) + \lambda_k(N, t)) P_k(N, t)$ of equation (4.3). This can be observed directly by summing equations (4.63) and (4.64).

Appendix 4B: Markovian Projection onto the One-Dimensional Markov Chain

Here we derive equation (4.16). Consider the basket probability density at the time $t + \delta_t$:

$$P_B(N, t + \delta_t) = \mathrm{P}[N(t + \delta_t) = N] = \sum_{M} \mathrm{P}[N(t + \delta_t)$$

$$= N | N(t) = M] \, \mathrm{P}[N(t) = M]$$

(4.69)

Keeping in mind that the limit $\delta_t \to 0$ will be taken, we consider only terms of $O(1)$ and $O(\delta_t)$. Thus, leaving only terms with $N = M$ and $M = N - 1$ in the sum in equation (4.69), we obtain:

$$P_B(N, t + \delta_t) = \mathrm{P}[N(t + \delta_t) = N \,|\, N(t) = N - 1] \, P_B(N-1, t) + \mathrm{P}[N(t + \delta_t)$$

$$= N \,|\, N(t) = N] \, P_B(N, t) + O(\delta_t^2)$$

(4.70)

Using equation (4.7) and the normalization condition $\sum_M P[N(t + \delta_t) = M \mid N(t) = N] = 1$ we can find the leading order in δ_t expressions for the transition elements

$$P[N(t + \delta_t) = N \mid N(t) = N - 1] = \Lambda_B(N - 1, t) \delta_t + O(\delta_t^2) \quad (4.71)$$

$$P[N(t + \delta_t) = N \mid N(t) = N] = 1 - \Lambda_B(N, t) \delta_t + O(\delta_t^2) \quad (4.72)$$

Inserting equations (4.71) and (4.72) into equation (4.70) and taking the limit $\delta_t \to 0$, we obtain equation (4.16).

Appendix 4C: Self-Consistency Criterion for the Semianalytic Approximation

In this appendix, we formulate the criterion that guarantees the self-consistency of the semianalytic approximation. Consider a general approximation for $\Lambda_k(N, t)$,

$$\Lambda_k(N, t) = \Lambda_B(N, t) + \Lambda'_k(N, t) \quad (4.73)$$

not specifying the form of the correction $\Lambda'_k(N, t)$. Functions $P_B(N, t)$ and $\Lambda_B(N, t)$ obtained via solution of equations (4.3), (4.4), (4.11), and (4.14) will satisfy equation (4.16) for any $\Lambda_{k'}(N, t)$ that obeys the following condition:

$$\sum_{k=1}^{N_0} \Lambda'_k P_k(N, 0) = -P_B(N, t)\Lambda_B(N, t) \quad (4.74)$$

First, we show that criterion (4.74) is the valid identity. Inserting $\Lambda'_k(N, t) = \Lambda_k(N, t) - \Lambda_B(N, t)$ into the left-hand side of equation (4.74) and then using equations (4.11) and (4.14), we write condition (4.74) in the equivalent form,

$$\sum_k \Lambda_k(N, t) P_k(N, t) = (N_0 - N - 1) \sum_{k=1}^{N_0} \lambda_k(N, t) P_k(N, t) \quad (4.75)$$

The validity of this equation can be proven analogously to the derivation of equation (4.11). The left-hand side of equation (4.75) can be written in terms of the full probability density $p(\mathbf{n}, t)$ as:

$$\sum_{p, k, k \neq p} \sum_{\mathbf{n}} \lambda_p(N, t) \, p(\mathbf{n}, t) \, \mathbf{1}_{n_k=0} \, \mathbf{1}_{n_p=0} \, \mathbf{1}_{n_1+n_2+\ldots+n_{N_0}=N} \quad (4.76)$$

where summation over indexes p and k goes from 1 to N_0 and the default indicators take values $n_k = 0, 1$. The right-hand side of equation (4.75) can be written as:

$$(N_0 - N - 1) \sum_{p=1}^{N_0} \sum_{\mathbf{n}} \lambda_p(N, t) \; p(\mathbf{n}, t) \, \mathbf{1}_{n_p=0} \, \mathbf{1}_{n_1+n_2+\ldots+n_{N_0}=N} \qquad (4.77)$$

Equality of equations (4.76), and (4.77) can be seen by observing that, for a fixed state vector $\mathbf{n}$ and index p, the sum over k in equation (4.76) reduces to multiplication by the factor $N_0 - N - 1$.

Now, we show that equation (4.74) guarantees the self consistency of the semi-analytic approach. We proceed analogously to the corresponding consideration in Subsection 4.3.1. Taking the sum of both sides of equation (4.3) over k and using equation (4.11), we obtain:

$$(N_0 - N) \frac{d}{dt} P_B(N, t) = -\Lambda_B(N, t) P_B(N, t) + \sum_{k=1}^{N_0} \Lambda_k(N - 1, t) P_k(N - 1, t)$$
$$- \Lambda_k(N, t) P_k(N, t) \qquad (4.78)$$

One can easily show that this equation can be brought to the form of equation (4.16) under the assumption that equation (4.74) is valid.

Acknowledgments

I would like to thank Alexandre Antonov, Igor Halperin, Serguei Issakov, Alex Lipton, Timur Misirpashaev, Frédéric Vrins, and Igor Zaoutine for useful discussions. I am grateful to my colleagues at Numerix and especially to Gregory Whitten for support of this work.

References

Amraoui, S., and S. Hitier. 2008. Optimal stochastic recovery for base correlation. Working paper, available at www.defaultrisk.com.

Andersen, L., and J. Sidenius. 2004. Extensions to the Gaussian copula: Random recovery and random factor loadings. *Journal of Credit Risk* 1 (1): 29–70.

Andersen, L., and J. Sidenius. 2005. CDO pricing with factor models: Survey and comments. *Journal of Credit Risk* 1 (3): 71–88.

Antonov, A., S. Mechkov, and T. Misirpashaev. 2007. Analytical techniques for synthetic CDOs and credit default risk measures. *Wilmott* (November–December): 84–105.

Antonov, A., T. Misirpashaev, and V. Piterbarg. 2007. Markovian projection onto a Heston model. Working paper, available at http://ssrn.com.

Arnsdorf, M., and I. Halperin. 2007. BSLP: Markovian bivariate spread-loss model for portfolio credit derivatives. Working paper, available at www.defaultrisk.com.

Bielecki, T. R., A. Vidozzi, and L. Vidozzi. 2006. An efficient approach to valuation of credit basket products and rating-triggered step-up bonds. Working paper, available at www.defaultrisk.com.

Bielecki, T. R., A. Vidozzi, and L. Vidozzi. 2008. A Markov copulae approach to pricing and hedging of credit index derivatives and ratings triggered step-up bonds. *Journal of Credit Risk* 4 (1).

Bielecki, T. R., M. Jeanblanc, and M. Rutkowski. 2008. Pricing and trading credit default swaps in a hazard process model. *Annals of Applied Probability* 18 (6): 2495–2529.

Bielecki, T. R., S. Crépey, and M. Jeanblanc. 2009. Up and down credit risk. Working paper, available at www.defaultrisk.com.

Brigo, D., A. Pallavicini, and R. Torresetti. 2007. Calibration of CDO tranches with the dynamical generalized-Poisson loss model. *Risk* (May): 70–75.

Davis, M., and V. Lo. 2001. Infectious defaults. *Quantitative Finance* 1:382–387.

Ding, X., K. Giesecke, and P. Tomecek. 2006. Time-changed birth processes and multi-name credit. Working paper, available at www.defaultrisk.com.

Duffie, D., and N. Garleanu. 2001. Risk and valuation of collateralized debt obligations. *Financial Analysts Journal* 57 (1): 41–59.

Duffie, D., L. Saita, and K. Wang. 2006. Multi-period corporate default prediction with stochastic covariates. *Journal of Financial Economics* 83 (3): 635–665.

Dupire, B. 1994. Pricing with a smile. *Risk* (January): 18–20.

Eckner, A. 2007. Computational techniques for basic affine models of portfolio credit risk. Working paper, available at www.defaultrisk.com.

Errais, E., K. Giesecke, and L. Goldberg. 2006. Pricing credit from the top down with affine point processes. Working paper, available at www.defaultrisk.com.

Feldhütter, P. 2007. An empirical investigation of an intensity-based model for pricing CDO tranches. Working paper, available at htttp://ssrn.com.

Frey, R., and J. Backhaus. 2007. Dynamic hedging of synthetic CDO tranches with spread and contagion risk. Working paper, available at www.defaultrisk.com.

Giesecke, K. 2008. Portfolio credit risk: Top-down vs. bottom-up approaches. In *Frontiers in quantitative finance: Credit risk and volatility modeling*, ed. R. Cont. Hoboken, NJ: John Wiley & Sons.

Giesecke, K., and L. Goldberg. 2005. A top-down approach to multi-name credit. Working paper, available at www.defaultrisk.com.

Giesecke, K., H. Kakavand, M. Mousavi, and H. Takada. 2009. Exact and efficient simulation of correlated defaults. Working paper, available at www.defaultrisk.com.

Gyöngy, I. 1986. Mimicking the one-dimensional marginal distributions of processes having an Itô differential. *Probability Theory and Related Fields* 71:501–516.

Halperin, I., and P. Tomecek. 2008. Climbing down from the top: Single name dynamics in credit top down models. Working paper, available at www.defaultrisk.com.

Hamilton, D. T., P. Varma, S. Ou, and R. Cantor. 2005. Default and recovery rates of corporate bond issuers. Moody's Investors Service, January.

Hull, J., and A. White. 2006. Valuing credit derivatives using an implied copula approach. *The Journal of Derivatives* 14 (2): 8–28.

Inglis, S., and A. Lipton. 2007. Factor models for credit correlation. *Risk* (December): 110–115.

Inglis, S., A. Lipton, I. Savescu, and A. Sepp. 2008. Dynamic credit models. *Statistics and Its Interface* 1 (2): 211–227.

Inglis, S., A. Lipton, and A. Sepp. 2009. Factor models for credit correlation. *Risk* (April): 106–107.

Jarrow, R. A., and F. Yu. 2001. Counterparty risk and the pricing of defaultable securities. *Journal of Finance* 53:2225–2243.

Laurent, J.-P., A. Cousin, and J.-D. Fermanian. 2007. Hedging default risks of CDOs in Markovian contagion models. Working paper, available at www.defaultrisk.com.

Lopatin, A., and T. Misirpashaev. 2008. Two-dimensional Markovian model for dynamics of aggregate credit loss. *Advances in Econometrics* 22:243–274.

Merton, R. 1974. On the pricing of corporate debt: The risk structure of interest rates. *Journal of Finance* 29:449–470.

Mortensen, A. 2006. Semi-analytical valuation of basket credit derivatives in intensity-based models. *Journal of Derivatives* 13:8–26.

Piterbarg, V. 2007. Markovian projection method for volatility calibration. *Risk* (April): 84–89.

Schönbucher, P. 2005. Portfolio losses and the term structure of loss transition rates: A new methodology for the pricing of portfolio credit derivatives. Working paper, available at www.defaultrisk.com.

Sidenius, J., V. Piterbarg, and L. Andersen. 2005. A new framework for dynamic credit portfolio loss modeling. *International Journal of Theoretical and Applied Finance* 11 (2): 163–197.

CHAPTER 5

Modeling Heterogeneity of Credit Portfolios: A Top-Down Approach

Igor Halperin

Quantitative Research, JPMorgan

Top-down models of credit portfolios have become popular in recent years due to their simplicity and computational efficiency. In terms of individual constituents of a credit portfolio, a top-down approach is usually associated with a limit of a homogeneous portfolio where all obligors have equal spreads, notionals, and recoveries. In this chapter, we present several extensions of such a classical top-down (TD) setting that account for heterogeneity in all these parameters. In particular, we introduce a simple and numerically efficient way of dissecting the portfolio risk into contributions of individual names, and show how this can be used in order to calculate single-name sensitivities in a top-down framework. Furthermore, we suggest a practical way of handling heterogeneity of individual notionals and recoveries, as well as a possible randomness of recoveries, using a biased urn model of portfolio defaults. In particular, for random recoveries, our model is shown to produce a negative codependence between defaults and recoveries, in agreement with empirical behavior of credit markets.

5.1 Introduction

Modeling of a dynamic credit portfolio can proceed according to two different paradigms. In a *bottom-up* approach, we start with single-name dynamics, which are constructed to fit individual credit spreads. At the second stage, one attempts to calibrate the dependence structure (introduced via common factors or a copula) to portfolio pricing data such as tranche prices. However, calibration to tranches across multiple strikes and maturities can be quite challenging in this framework.

Furthermore, the bottom-up approach makes it difficult—though not impossible (see Collin-Dufresne, Goldstein, and Helwege 2003; Schönbucher 2003)—to introduce default clustering (contagion) in a tractable way.

In many applications, the portfolio loss (or spread loss) process is all we need for pricing and risk management. In particular, this is the case when one wants to price a nonstandard index tranche off standard ones, and risk-manage it using the same standard tranches plus the credit index. Another example is an exotic portfolio derivative (such as a tranche option) that is hedged using tranches written on the same portfolio. In recognition of this fact, the alternative *top-down* approach, suggested by Giesecke and Goldberg (GG) (2005), directly models a portfolio-level (or economy-level) loss process, rather than loss processes for individual names. Such a process is generally much easier to calibrate to tranche prices than an aggregate portfolio loss process obtained with the bottom-up approach. Moreover, credit contagion is built in in this approach by construction (Errais, Giesecke, and Goldberg 2006; Giesecke and Goldberg 2005). Once a calibrated portfolio loss process is obtained, it can be used to price vanilla and exotic derivatives referencing the same portfolio. For a further comparison between the bottom-up and the top-down paradigms and a brief review of published models, see, for example, Bielecki, Crépey, and Jeanblanc (2008) and references therein.

The main modeling primitive of a top-down approach is an integer-value default process N_t giving the number of defaults in the portfolio by time t. As the payoff of a collateralized debt obligation (CDO) tranche is determined by the portfolio loss rather than the number of defaults, the default process N_t should be supplemented by a recovery model. The simplest link between the loss and default count processes is provided within a homogeneous pool approximation where all obligors have the same notionals $I_i = I$ and the same fixed recoveries $R_i = R$, or equivalently, the same losses given default (LGDs) $l_i = \bar{l}$.[1] Then the portfolio loss at time t is:

$$L_t = \sum_i I_i l_i 1_{\{\tau_i \leq t\}} = I\bar{l}N_t \tag{5.1}$$

where τ_i is a random default time of the ith obligor, and $1_{\{\tau_i \leq t\}}$ is its default indicator. Therefore, for a homogeneous portfolio the relationship between the number of defaults N_t and portfolio loss L_t is one-to-one. Such a single-name interpretation of top-down models within a homogeneous pool with equal recoveries is the most popular among practitioners. Other possible specifications include either stochastic i.i.d. recovery as in Ding, Giesecke, and Tomecek (2006), or recovery modeled as a deterministic function of either the number of defaults as in the BSLP model of Arnsdorf and Halperin (2008), or default intensity as suggested by Lopatin and Misirpashaev (2007). The common feature of all these approaches is that the jump size of the cumulative portfolio loss is independent of the defaulting firm. This is of course in line with the basic idea of the top-down approach.

5.1.1   Objectives

In practice, reference portfolios for collateralized debt obligation (CDO) tranches are typically heterogeneous in spreads and expected recoveries, as well as in notionals.[2] It is therefore important to quantify the impact of portfolio heterogeneity on valuation and risk management of portfolio credit derivatives within the top-down approach.

In this chapter, we present a number of modeling tools that could be used separately or in combination to account for impact of different aspects of heterogeneity of credit portfolios on valuation and risk management of CDO tranches and other portfolio derivatives.

Before presenting our solutions, we provide a general discussion of implications of heterogeneities in different parameters. We consider several cases in order.

5.1.2   Spread Heterogeneity and Top-Down Models

The first part of this chapter deals with heterogeneity in spreads. To formulate the problem, consider a portfolio that has constituent names with the same notionals and recoveries, but different spreads. The fact that spreads are different does not affect the top-down pricing framework, as the link between the loss and default processes remains the same as for a perfectly homogeneous portfolio. However, risk management of CDO tranches becomes more complicated. Indeed, for hedging spread and default risk on a single-name basis, we need a way to dissect the portfolio-level risk, as given by probabilities to have 0, 1, . . . defaults by a given time, into contributions of constituent names (i.e., to find a way to do a meaningful single-name calibration of a top-down model).

In the first part of this chapter, we present a simple and numerically efficient approach to calibration to constituent names and calculation of single-name sensitivities within a top-down model. Our method largely follows the framework of the random thinning procedure proposed by Giesecke and Goldberg (2005); see also Ding, Giesecke, and Tomecek (2006); Errais, Giesecke, and Goldberg (2006). The idea of this approach is to simplify the construction of a full-blown portfolio model by splitting it into two steps.

In the first step, we average over all single names, and calibrate the top part of a top-down model to the index and tranche spread data. In this way, one constructs a calibrated portfolio default intensity process. By supplying it with a recovery model (e.g., a constant recovery assumption), we obtain a portfolio loss model.

The second step of dissecting the portfolio loss intensity into contributions of constituent names in the portfolio is *optional*. This means that it is performed only if we want not only to price, but also to risk-manage our tranche positions on a single-name basis. To this end, we need to know the way to calculate single-name sensitivity parameters, in particular spread sensitivities of tranches in our book.

This information, additional to that contained in the knowledge of the calibrated portfolio default intensity, comes at an extra computational cost, which is time consuming. In a traditional bottom-up model, this information is by construction always an outcome of our model calibration, whether we want it or not. In constrast, the top-down approach achieves a useful reduction in the computational complexity, which now becomes user-driven.

Indeed, if we are interested only in the price discovery for different possible tranche trades, we need only the top part of the top-down model. If, however, we need both tranche prices and single-name sensitivities for the purpose of risk management of existing positions, we go to the second step of the algorithm, which calculates contributions of individual names in the total portfolio default intensity. Our use of a top-down formulation ensures consistency between two sets of prices, while saving computational time by *not* performing single-name calibration when it is not needed.

While our method largely follows the framework of the random thinning developed by Giesecke and Goldberg (2005), we differ from their approach in both the mathematical formalism and the numerical algorithm. We view the top part of a top-down model as producing incomplete information scenarios that yield a forecast of the timing of sequential defaults in the portfolio, but lose information on the defaulters' identities. In a sense, our problem thus becomes a problem of *inference*, where we probabilistically assign identities to all future defaulters. As will be clear in what follows, our approach bears resemblance to the well-known statistical problem of inference of a two-dimensional (2-D) probability distribution when only its 1-D marginals (corresponding, in our case, to portfolio-level and individual names default forecasts, respectively) are known. We show how this problem can be solved in a very efficient way using the so-called iterative scaling algorithm. Our presentation in this part follows Halperin and Tomecek (2008). An alternative approach is presented in Giesecke, Goldberg, and Ding (2009).

5.1.3   Notional and Recovery Heterogeneity

The second part of this chapter deals with heterogeneity in notionals and recoveries, which, to the best of the author's knowledge, has not been previously addressed in the literature on the top-down approach. Note that while heterogeneity in spreads impacts only risk management of portfolio credit derivatives, heterogeneity in notionals and recoveries breaks the one-to-one correspondence between the portfolio loss and default processes, and therefore impacts both valuation and risk management.

The simplest way to use a top-down model for a heterogeneous portfolio is to calculate portfolio-averaged notionals and recoveries, and then use them as in equation (5.1) to relate the portfolio loss and default counting processes. However, as a tranche payoff is a nonlinear function of portfolio loss, such a naive averaging misses certain "recovery convexity correction" (see Section 5.5 for details).

Another case when heterogeneity becomes important is the time resolution of portfolio loss. This can be illustrated as follows. Imagine we have a portfolio of $N - 1 = 99$ names $\{O_i\}_{i=1}^{N-1}$ with spreads equal to 100 basis points and notionals of \$1m, and another name O_N with a spread of 500 bp and notional of \$20m. If we assume that default probability of a name is proportional to its spread, then the probability that the first defaulter is name O_N conditional on the fact of first default can be estimated as $5/104 \simeq 0.048$. Assume all names have the same recovery of 50 percent. Then we can estimate the expected loss upon first default (expected loss given default [LGD]) as $0.048 \cdot 10 + 0.952 \cdot 0.5 \simeq \$0.96m$. For the second default, we can estimate the expected LGD as $\$0.92m$. In contrast, a naive averaging over all notionals would result in the expected LGD equal to $\$0.595m$ independently of the default order, which underestimates the true expected LGD upon the first default by nearly 40 percent. Clearly, if we want to use a top-down model in such a setting, we need something more sophisticated than a naive averaging over all notionals.[3]

5.1.4 Our Approach: A Biased Urn Model of Portfolio Defaults

Our approach to modeling heterogeneity of notionals and recoveries is similar to the previous problem of dissecting the portfolio risk into contributions of constituent names. Again, we develop a probabilistic approach to describe identities of defaulters, which is the only possible approach if we adopt a top-down paradigm. To this end, we view the portfolio default process as sampling of balls from an urn without replacement. We use a biased urn model to describe notional and recovery heterogeneity at default, and estimate corrections to naive formulas usually used in this context. We further show that the same biased urn model can be used for modeling of stochastic recovery. Moreover, it turns out that our simple framework allows one to mimic a negative codependence between default and recovery rates, which is observed in real markets.

It should be mentioned that approaches developed in this chapter assume a static (as seen today, $t = 0$), rather than dynamic view of credit portfolios. This refers, in particular, to the way we compute single-name sensitivities and impact of notional heterogeneity in Sections 5.4 and 5.5, respectively. Our objective is not to design a full-blown single-name dynamic model of a heterogeneous credit portfolio, but rather to develop probabilistic methods that allow one to account for impact or spread and notional heterogeneity onto valuation and risk management of portfolio credit derivatives, most notably CDO tranches, using simple and straightforward generalizations and extensions of a top-down framework initially formulated at the level of the total portfolio loss process. Note that as long as CDO tranches are static instruments themselves,[4] static methods developed should suffice.

5.1.5 Outline of the Chapter

The chapter is organized as follows. In Section 5.2 we introduce the so-called top-down (TD) matrices, which serve as the basic modeling primitives of our approach. Section 5.3 then introduces the iterative scaling algorithm for calibration of TD matrices to individual spreads. In Section 5.4 we calculate single-name sensitivities with our approach. Section 5.5 introduces the biased urn model and describes our approach to the modeling of portfolio heterogeneity within this model. In Section 5.6 we present another use of the biased urn model, this time to model recovery heterogeneity or random recovery within a top-down approach. The final Section 5.7 presents some discussion and conclusions.

5.2 Top-Down Default Time Matrices

The following notation will be used throughout this chapter:

- τ_i—default time of name i.
- τ^j—time of the jth default in the portfolio.
- $[T^{(1)}, \ldots, T^{(M)}]$—reference maturities.[5] We set $T^{(0)} = 0$.

Next, we introduce our modeling primitives. For each interval $m = 1, \ldots, M$, we consider the following matrix:

$$P_{ij}^{(m)}(t) = P\left[\{\tau^j = \tau_i\} \bigcap \{T^{(m-1)} \le \tau_i \le T^{(m)}\} \,|\mathcal{F}_t\right] \qquad (5.2)$$

In words, this is the joint probability that the ith name is the jth defaulter, and this event happens in the interval $[T^{(m-1)}, T^{(m)}]$, conditional on the currently available information $\mathcal{F}_t$. (Modeling of filtration $\mathcal{F}_t$ will be discussed later.) Note that we assume that instantaneous multiple default events are not possible. Clearly, we can equivalently write equation (5.2) as:

$$P_{ij}^{(m)}(t) = P\left[\{\tau_i = \tau^j\} \bigcap \{T^{(m-1)} \le \tau^j \le T^{(m)}\}\,\Big|\mathcal{F}_t\right] \qquad (5.3)$$

In what follows, we will occasionally refer to equation (5.2) or (5.3) as top-down default time matrices, or TD matrices for short. The definitions (5.2), (5.3) are inspired by the formalism used in the reliability theory and competing risk models,[6] where the object of inference is the joint probability $p(T, O)$ of the event T (e.g., a first failure in a system) and the type O of risk among a set of alternatives $O_1, O_2, \ldots$ that could cause the failure. In our setting, identities of defaulted names serve as risk types O_i, with an additional rule that they cannot repeat in the default history of a portfolio.[7]

Both the single-name and portfolio probabilities are obtained by marginalization:

$$\sum_i P_{ij}^{(m)}(t) = P\left[T^{(m-1)} \le \tau^j \le T^{(m)}\,\Big|\mathcal{F}_t\right]$$

$$\sum_j P_{ij}^{(m)}(t) = P\left[T^{(m-1)} \le \tau_i \le T^{(m)}\,\Big|\mathcal{F}_t\right] \qquad (5.4)$$

where we used equations (5.3) and (5.2), respectively. Both the top-down and bottom-up forward probabilities entering the right-hand side of equation (5.4) can be easily calculated as follows:

$$P\left[T^{(m-1)} \le \tau^j \le T^{(m)} \middle| \mathcal{F}_t \right] = w_t^{(m)}(j) - w_t^{(m-1)}(j)$$
$$P\left[T^{(m-1)} \le \tau_i \le T^{(m)} \middle| \mathcal{F}_t \right] = Q_{i,t}^{(m)} - Q_{i,t}^{(m-1)} \tag{5.5}$$

where $w_t^{(m)}(j)$ is the tail probability of having at least j defaults in the portfolio by time $T^{(m)}$.

$$w_t^{(m)}(j) = \sum_{j'=j}^{N} P\left[\tau^{j'} \le T^{(m)} \middle| \mathcal{F}_t \right] \tag{5.6}$$

(note that $w_0^{(0)}(j) = \delta_{j0}$), and $Q_{i,t}^{(m)}$ is the cumulative default probability of the ith name by time $T^{(m)}$. Note that we explicitly show dependence on t for both $w_t^{(m)}(j)$ and $Q_{i,t}^{(m)}$ to emphasize their dependence on the filtration $\mathcal{F}_t$.

5.2.1 Dynamics of TD Matrices

In the rest of this chapter, we work with TD matrices as seen at time zero (i.e., conditional on $\mathcal{F}_0$). Note that this is the only calculation needed to estimate hedge costs for our book today, at time $t = 0$. However, we might in principle be interested in analysis of *dynamic* evolution of the TD matrices at later times $t > 0$. This may be required to price hypothetic exotic credit derivatives whose payoffs depend on both portfolio loss and spread, as well as on losses or/and spreads of some (or all) individual names.

To get the single-name dynamics, we need to update the TD matrices dynamically based on observed information. In this section, we briefly outline a framework that can be used to this end. A more detailed exposition can be found in Halperin and Tomecek (2008). Material presented here is not used in what follows, and thus can be skipped at the first reading.

As will be discussed later, updating of TD matrices is done in two ways: by zeroing out rows and columns corresponding to observed (simulated) defaults, and by random perturbation (done in a particular way; see the following) of nonzero elements, to account for single-name spread volatilities. This is achieved by first modeling a properly constructed filtration $\mathcal{F}_t$, and then providing rules for adapting the TD matrices to filtration $\mathcal{F}_t$.

The primary filtration $(\mathcal{F}_t)_{t \ge 0}$ is constructed from the following definitions:

- $(\mathcal{G}_t)_{t \ge 0}$ is the natural filtration of the top-down default-counting process: $\mathcal{G}_t = \sigma(\{\tau^j < t\}; j = 1, \ldots, N)$.
- $(\mathcal{I}_t)_{t \ge 0}$ is the filtration generated by the defaulters' identities: $\mathcal{I}_t = \sigma(\{\tau^j = \tau_i, \tau^j < t\}; i, j = 1, \ldots, N)$. We assume that at time $t = 0$ the information set $\mathcal{I}_0$ is known, as it can be directly observed.[8]

- $(\mathcal{H}_t)_{t \geq 0}$ is a background filtration containing external market information, and possibly generated by several information processes; see later in the chapter.
- The filtrations $(\mathcal{G}_t)_{t \geq 0}$, $(\mathcal{I}_t)_{t \geq 0}$, and $(\mathcal{H}_t)_{t \geq 0}$ are assumed to be independent, and the filtration $(\mathcal{F}_t)_{t \geq 0}$ is defined by:

$$\mathcal{F}_t = \mathcal{G}_t \vee \mathcal{I}_t \vee \mathcal{H}_t \qquad (5.7)$$

According to these definitions, the ordered default times τ^j are $\mathcal{G}$-stopping times, but the single-name default times τ_i are typically not. However, both τ^j and τ_i are $\mathcal{F}$-stopping times.

Let us now consider how different components of our filtration $\mathcal{F}_t$ are used to update the TD matrices. First, subfiltration $(\mathcal{G}_t)_{t \geq 0}$ informs us of the next default arrival. Upon arrival of the nth default in the portfolio, we zero out the current nth next-to-default column in the TD matrices, so that the next $(n + 1)$th column becomes the next-to-default column.

Next, observing information revealed by subfiltration $(\mathcal{I}_t)_{t \geq 0}$, we identify the constituent name who has defaulted upon this portfolio-level event, and zero out the corresponding row in the TD matrices. Because information on the defaulter identities is not part of the natural filtration $(\mathcal{G}_t)_{t \geq 0}$ of a top-down model, the only way to describe defaulter identities is to use a probabilistic approach, and assign probabilities to events of observing particular names upon defaulters in the portfolio. In the setting of Halperin and Tomecek (2008), this is done by Monte Carlo simulation of the defaulter's identity upon a portfolio-level default event.

Finally, we want to account for effects of single-spread volatilities of names in the portfolio. In particular, due to nonzero spread volatilities, individual names in the portfolio are decorrelated to a certain extent. This means that it is unrealistic to expect that all names will keep their spreads in between events of portfolio defaults, or that they respond in a completely deterministic way to such events.

This effect can be modeled via random perturbations of our TD matrices driven by filtration $\mathcal{H}$. The market filtration $\mathcal{H}$ is similar to that introduced by Brody, Hughston, and Macrina (BHM) (2007), which they use to introduce bond price dynamics to their model. In their paper, the filtration is generated by a Brownian bridge. By including this information in our overall filtration $\mathcal{F}$, we use similar techniques to enrich the dynamics of $P_{ij}^{(m)}(t)$. In particular, by enlarging the filtration of interest, it proves possible to decorrelate (to a certain extent) the individual forward default probabilities from the index's; without it, they would be perfectly correlated. A detailed construction of this sort is presented in Halperin and Tomecek (2008).

5.2.2   Relationship to Conditional Forward Matrices

Note that for $m = 1$, our TD matrix $P_{ij}^{(1)}$ is simply related to a time-independent matrix p_{ij} introduced by Ding, Giesecke, and Tomecek (2006) as a matrix of *conditional* probabilities, provided we restrict it to the time horizon given by $T^{(1)}$, $p_{ij} \rightarrow p_{ij}^{(1)}(t) \equiv P\left[\tau^j = \tau_i | \tau^j < T^{(1)}, \mathcal{F}_t\right]$. Indeed, in this case we obtain:

$$P_{ij}^{(1)}(t) = P\left[\{\tau^j = \tau_i\} \bigcap \{0 \leq \tau^j \leq T^{(1)}\} | \mathcal{F}_t\right] \tag{5.8}$$
$$= P\left[\tau^j = \tau_i | \tau^j \leq T^{(1)}, \mathcal{F}_t\right] P\left[\tau^j \leq T^{(1)} | \mathcal{F}_t\right] \equiv p_{ij}^{(1)}(t) w_t^{(1)}(j)$$

In contrast, for a forward interval $[T^{(m-1)}, T^{(m)}]$, we can similarly introduce a *conditional* forward TD matrix:

$$p_{ij}^{(m)}(t) \equiv P\left[\tau^j = \tau_i | T^{(m-1)} \leq \tau^j \leq T^{(m)}, \mathcal{F}_t\right] \tag{5.9}$$

Using equation (5.5) leads to the relationship between the conditional and joint TD matrices:

$$P_{ij}^{(m)}(t) = p_{ij}^{(m)}(t)[w_t^{(m)}(j) - w_t^{(m-1)}(j)] \tag{5.10}$$

Applying equation (5.4) leads to the marginal constraints for the conditional p-matrices:

$$\sum_i p_{ij}^{(m)}(t) = 1$$

$$\sum_j p_{ij}^{(m)}(t)\left[w_t^{(m)}(j) - w_t^{(m-1)}(j)\right] = Q_{i,t}^{(m)} - Q_{i,t}^{(m-1)} \tag{5.11}$$

These are exactly the formulas presented earlier in Halperin (2007).

A comment is in order here. Equation (5.10) demonstrates equivalence of the descriptions based on the joint and conditional forward TD matrices in the sense that as long as tail probabilities $\{w_j\}$ are known from the top part of the model, conditional TD matrices are known once the joint matrices are known, and vice versa. However, as will be discussed later, the joint TD matrices are more convenient to work with when calculating sensitivities in the present formalism.

5.2.3 Relationship to Intensity-Based Formulation

For some applications, an equivalent formalism based on intensities, rather than probability matrices, may be preferred. To this end, we follow Giesecke and Goldberg (2005) and Ding, Giesecke, and Tomecek (2006) (see the end of this section for a discussion) and introduce the so-called Z-factors as the conditional probability that name i is the next defaulter given an imminent default in the interval $[t, t + dt]$:

$$Z_t^i = \sum_{n=1}^N P\left[\tau^n = \tau_i | \tau^n \leq t + dt, \mathcal{F}_t\right] 1_{\{\tau^{n-1} \leq t < \tau^n\}} \tag{5.12}$$

Note that equation (5.12) yields the following relationship between the single-name and portfolio intensities:

$$\lambda_t^i = Z_t^i \lambda_t^p, \quad \text{where} \quad \sum_{i=1}^{N} Z_t^i = 1 \tag{5.13}$$

As shown by Giesecke and Goldberg, the single-name default probability is given by the following relationship:

$$P\left[t < \tau_i \leq T | \mathcal{F}_t\right] = \int_t^T \mathbb{E}\left[\lambda_s^i | \mathcal{F}_t\right] ds = \int_t^T \mathbb{E}\left[Z_s^i \lambda_s^p | \mathcal{F}_t\right] ds \tag{5.14}$$

In general, one can take the Z-factors to be any $\mathcal{F}$-adapted stochastic processes satisfying equation (5.13). To establish the relationship with the probability-based formalism, we note that in our case of piecewise constant probabilities we can use the conditional forward TD matrices (5.9) in equation (5.12). This gives rise to the following ansatz for the Z-factors:

$$Z_t^i = \sum_{n=1}^{N} \left[p_{in}^{(1)} 1_{\{\tau^{n-1} \leq t < \tau^n\}} 1_{\{t \leq T_1\}} + p_{in}^{(2)} 1_{\{\tau^{n-1} \leq t < \tau^n\}} 1_{\{T_1 < t \leq T_2\}} + \cdots \right] \tag{5.15}$$

Substituting this into the Giesecke-Goldberg formula [equation (5.14)], we obtain for the default probability at the first maturity:

$$Q_{T_1}^i \equiv P\left[0 < \tau_i \leq T_1\right] = \int_t^{T_1} \mathbb{E}\left[Z_s^i \lambda_s^p\right] ds = \sum_{j=1}^{N} p_{ij}^{(1)} \int_0^{T_1} \mathbb{E}\left[\lambda_s^p 1_{\{N_s = j-1\}}\right] ds$$

$$= \sum_{j=1}^{n} p_{ij}^{(1)} w_{0,T_1}(j) \tag{5.16}$$

and for the second maturity:

$$Q_{T_2}^i \equiv P\left[0 < \tau_i \leq T_2\right] = \int_0^{T_2} \mathbb{E}\left[Z_s^i \lambda_s^p\right] ds = \int_0^{T_1} E\left[Z_s^i \lambda_s^p\right] ds + \int_{T_1}^{T_2} E\left[Z_s^i \lambda_s^p\right] ds$$

$$= Q_{T_1} + \sum_{j=1}^{n} P_{ij}^{(2)} \left(w_{0,T_2}(j) - w_{0,T_1}(j)\right) \equiv Q_{T_1} + \sum_{j=1}^{n} P_{ij}^{(2)} w_{T_1,T_2}(j) \tag{5.17}$$

In the general case, we reproduce equation (5.11).

5.3 Thinning by Bootstrap and Iterative Scaling

In this section we present an algorithm that enables calculation of conditional TD matrices $p_{ij}^{(m)}(t)$ (or, equivalently, joint TD matrices $P_{ij}^{(m)}$) as seen today, at $t = 0$.[9]

Note that our formalism assumes that initially (at $t = 0$) the portfolio contains no defaulted names; that is, filtration $\mathcal{I}_0$ (see equation [5.7]) is trivial. That means that as long as we condition on information $\mathcal{F}_0 = \mathcal{G}_0 \vee \mathcal{I}_0 \vee \mathcal{H}_0$, bottom-up filtration $\mathcal{I}_t$ is not needed, and thus the TD matrices can indeed be calculated using only a top-down filtration; see the remark in Subsection 5.2.1.

As the calibration scheme of TD matrices $p_{ij}^{(m)}(0)$ is identical for all periods $[T_{m-1}, T_m]$, $m = 1, \ldots, M$, in this section we assume some fixed value of m, and denote $p_{ij} \equiv p_{ij}^{(m)}(0)$, $w_j \equiv w_0^{(m)}(j) - w_0^{(m-1)}(j)$, and $Q_i \equiv Q_{i,0}^{(m)} - Q_{i,0}^{(m-1)}$.

Using this notation, our problem is to find a matrix p_{ij} that satisfies the following row and column constraints:

$$\sum_{j=1}^{N} p_{ij} w_j = Q_i, \quad i = 1, \ldots, N \tag{5.18}$$

$$\sum_{i=1}^{N} p_{ij} = 1, \quad j = 1, \ldots, N \tag{5.19}$$

Note that this problem is ill-posed (and underdetermined), as we have N^2 unknowns but only $2N$ constraints; therefore, it can have an infinite number of solutions, or no solution at all, which happens when the constraints are contradictory. Before presenting the solution, we therefore want to analyze necessary conditions for the existence of a solution.

5.3.1 Consistency Condition

If we sum equation (5.18) over i, we obtain:

$$\sum_{j=1}^{N} w_j = \sum_{i=1}^{N} Q_i \tag{5.20}$$

Note that the right-hand side of this equation $\sum_{i=1}^{N} Q_i = \langle N_T \rangle^{(CDS)}$ is the expected number of defaults according to single-name credit default swap (CDS) data, while the left-hand side gives the expected number of defaults according to the top-down model:

$$\sum_{j=1}^{N} w_j = \sum_{j=1}^{N} \sum_{n \geq j}^{N} p_n = \sum_{n=1}^{N} n p_n = \langle N_T \rangle^{(model)} \tag{5.21}$$

We thus have the following consistency condition:

$$\langle N_T \rangle^{(model)} = \langle N_T \rangle^{(CDS)} = \langle N_T \rangle \tag{5.22}$$

Unless equation (5.22) is satisfied, no set of top-down matrices can match both the "top" and "down" data. Note that the standard procedure of basis adjustment (see, e.g., O'Kane 2008) ensures that the theoretical formula for the index par spread S_{idx} in terms of CDS par spreads S_i and their risky durations $PV01_i$:

$$S_{idx} = \frac{\sum_i S_i PV01_i}{\sum_i PV01_i} \tag{5.23}$$

holds by adding a uniform additive or proportional tweak to all spreads S_i in the index portfolio. This procedure does *not* guarantee that the constraint (5.22) is met, and indeed one typically finds a small difference (of the order of 1 percent) between $\langle N \rangle^{(model)}$ and $\langle N \rangle^{(CDS)}$ even after the basis adjustment is made. While alternative schemes of basis adjustment where equation (5.22) would be enforced are certainly feasible, in this chapter we choose to further adjust (basis-adjusted) single-name default probabilities so that equation (5.22) holds.

5.3.2   Iterative Scaling (IS) Algorithm

We assume that an initial guess (a "prior") $q_{ij} \equiv p_{ij}^{(0)}$ for the solution is available (see the following for a particular choice). We then use the iterative scaling algorithm[10] to find the matrix p_{ij}. With this method, the matrix is updated iteratively $p^{(0)} \rightarrow p^{(1)} \cdots \rightarrow p^{(k)} \rightarrow p^{(k+1)} \cdots$ according to the following scheme:

$$p_{ij}^{(k+1)} = \begin{cases} p_{ij}^{(k)} \dfrac{Q_i}{\sum_j p_{ij}^{(k)} w_j} & \text{for } k \text{ odd} \\[2ex] \dfrac{p_{ij}^{(k)}}{\sum_i p_{ij}^{(k)}} & \text{for } k \text{ even} \end{cases} \tag{5.24}$$

In other words, we alternatively rescale the matrix to enforce the row and column constraints until convergence. The equivalent scheme for joint TD matrices P_{ij} reads:

$$P_{ij}^{(k+1)} = \begin{cases} P_{ij}^{(k)} \dfrac{Q_i}{\sum_j P_{ij}^{(k)}} & \text{for } k \text{ odd} \\[2ex] P_{ij}^{(k)} \dfrac{w_j}{\sum_i P_{ij}^{(k)}} & \text{for } k \text{ even} \end{cases} \tag{5.25}$$

5.3.3   Choice of the Initial Guess

Obviously, a solution of an ill-posed problem defined by equations (5.18) and (5.19), if it exists, should generally depend on an initial guess (a "prior") q_{ij} for the TD matrix p_{ij}. Here we present a few possible specifications of the prior matrix.

One possible choice is a factorized prior $q_{ij} = q_i k_j$. Consider the first three steps of the IS algorithm with this prior:

$$p_{ij}^{(1)} = q_i k_j \frac{Q_i}{q_i \sum_j k_j w_j} = \frac{k_j Q_i}{\sum_j k_j w_j}$$

$$p_{ij}^{(2)} = \frac{p_{ij}^{(1)}}{\sum_i p_{ij}^{(1)}} = \frac{k_j Q_i}{\sum_j k_j w_j} \frac{\sum_j k_j w_j}{k_j \sum_i Q_i} = \frac{Q_i}{\sum_i Q_i} = \frac{Q_i}{\langle N_T \rangle} \qquad (5.26)$$

$$p_{ij}^{(3)} = p_{ij}^{(2)} \frac{Q_i}{\sum_j p_{ij}^{(2)} w_j} = \frac{Q_i}{\langle N_T \rangle}$$

so that the algorithm converges to the solution $p_{ij} = Q_i / \langle N_T \rangle$, independently of the initial guess. This solution suggests that the relative riskiness of a name stays the same (i.e., independent of j) as defaults arrive. However, such a behavior looks unreasonable on physical grounds, as riskier names are expected to default earlier than less risky ones. We view this as an evidence against using factorized priors.

A simple and reasonable alternative to factorized priors that conforms to one's intuition about the order of defaulters in the portfolio is obtained if we assume a linear law for rows of a conditional p-matrix, such that for a risky name the probability that it defaults first, second, and so on will (linearly) decrease, while for tighter names it will increase. We can further assume that once some sufficiently high default level $\bar{n}$ is reached, the conditional TD matrix p_{ij} becomes uniform across names, so that $\bar{n}$ can be referred to as a "uniformization bound." This is summarized in the following ansatz for the prior matrix:

$$q_{ij} = \begin{cases} q_{i1} + \alpha_i j & i = 1, \ldots, N, j \leq \bar{n} \\ \frac{1}{N} & i = 1, \ldots, N, j > \bar{n} \end{cases} \qquad (5.27)$$

where

$$\alpha_i = \frac{1}{\bar{n}} \left(\frac{1}{N} - q_{i1} \right)$$

This ansatz parametrizes the p-matrix in terms of its first column. The latter can be chosen according to current values of CDS spreads. Note that $\sum_i q_{ij} = 1$ as long as $\sum_i q_{i1} = 1$. In Figure 5.1 we show three rows in such a prior matrix for the first maturity interval, corresponding to names with low, moderate, and high spreads (respectively, Baxter International, General Electric [GE], and Citigroup).

The ansatz (5.27) is certainly not the only possible model for the prior. Another method to construct the prior will be presented after we discuss the single-name sensitivities calculation.

FIGURE 5.1 Three Rows of the Prior Matrix $q_{ij}^{(1)}$ Corresponding to Low, Moderate, and High Spreads

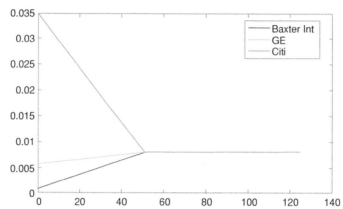

5.3.4 Numerical Examples

We have tested the IS algorithm on several data sets, and found in each case fast convergence (in less than 10 steps per maturity) to parameters matching single-name CDS spreads with relative errors below 1 percent. The whole calculation takes about two or three seconds on a standard PC. An example of calibrated conditional thinning matrices is given in Figure 5.2 for CDX IG8 data on 03/03/2008 (the same data set will be used for all numerical examples in what follows). Tail probabilities needed for this calculation are produced by our own version of a top-down model called the bivariate spread-loss portfolio (BSLP) model (Arnsdorf and Halperin 2008); however, any other top-down model can be used to this end. Tail probabilities produced by the BSLP by calibrating to the same data set are shown in Figure 5.3.

5.3.5 Information-Theoretic Interpretation of IS Algorithm

If we rescale our matrices $p_{ij} \to Np_{ij}$ and $q_{ij} \to Nq_{ij}$ so that now $\sum_{i,j} p_{ij} = \sum_{i,j} q_{ij} = 1$, then $\{p_{ij}\}, \{q_{ij}\}$ can be thought of as two-dimensional probability

FIGURE 5.2 Calibrated Thinning Matrices $p_{ij}^{(1)}, p_{ij}^{(2)}, p_{ij}^{(3)}$ for Intervals $[0, 3Y]$, $[3Y, 5Y]$, $[5Y, 7Y]$ for CDX IG8 Data on 03/03/2008, Obtained with Linear Prior (5.27). The fourth matrix is similar and is not shown here to save space.

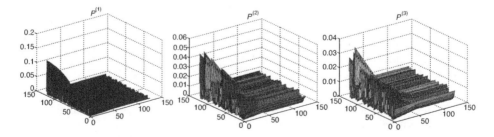

FIGURE 5.3 Tail Probabilities for Horizons of Three, Five, Seven and Ten Years for CDX IG8 Data on 03/03/2008 Calculated with the BSLP Model

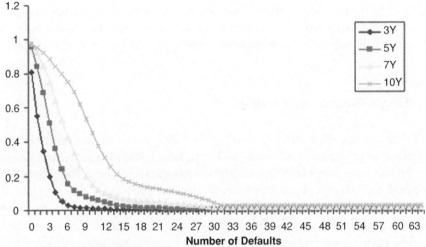

distributions. As was shown by Ireland and Kullback (1968) and Csiszár (1975) (see also Csiszár (n.d.), the IS algorithm can be interpreted as an alternative minimization of the Kullback-Leibler (KL) divergence (relative entropy; see, e.g., Cover and Thomas 1991) between these two measures:

$$D[p||q] = \sum_{ij} p_{ij} \log \frac{p_{ij}}{q_{ij}} \qquad (5.28)$$

subject to constraints $\sum_{j=1}^{N} p_{ij} w_j = \frac{1}{N} Q_i$ and $\sum_{i=1}^{N} p_{ij} = 1/N$. The standard approach to this problem uses the method of Lagrange multipliers to enforce the constraints, leading to the following Lagrangian function:

$$\mathcal{L} = D[p||q] - \sum_j \lambda_j \left(\sum_i p_{ij} - \frac{1}{N} \right) - \sum_i \xi_i \left(\sum_j p_{ij} w_j - \frac{Q_i}{N} \right) \qquad (5.29)$$

which can be solved using convex duality (Cover and Thomas 1991), with dimensionality of the problem being the number of Lagrange multipliers ξ_i (i.e., equal to the number of constraints). The approach of Ireland and Kullback and Csiszár uses instead an *alternative* recursive minimization of the KL distance [equation (5.28)], where we alternate between enforcing the row constraints only at odd steps and column constraints only at even steps. This can be shown to precisely correspond to the alternating rescaling of the IS algorithm. This method may be computationally less expensive than the direct minimization of equation (5.29), especially for large-scale problems, and it allows one to prove convergence of the IS algorithm under certain technical conditions.

We note that the information-theoretic reformulation of the problem can be easily generalized to the case when one matches single-name spreads approximately (e.g., in the least-square sense) rather than exactly, and thus can be used to ensure stability of single-name calibration. We will not pursue this approach further in this chapter.

5.4   Single-Name Sensitivities

The TD matrices calibrated as of today can be used for calculation of single-name sensitivities, as proposed by Giesecke and coauthors (Ding, Giesecke, and Tomecek 2006; Errais, Giesecke, and Goldberg 2006; Giesecke and Goldberg 2005). Specifically, once a calibrated set of TD matrices is found, sensitivity to a given name i is calculated as follows. First we rescale the ith row in the unconditional TD matrix to accommodate the new (bumped) spread of the ith name. Once this is done, summation of the new perturbed matrix over i produces a new set of bumped tail probabilities, which is equivalent to bumping tranche prices. The ratio of changes of the marked-to-market (MTM) of a given tranche to that of the underlying names is the name delta of the tranche.

Let us consider the calculation in more details, focusing for simplicity on the first maturity interval $[0, T_1]$. Assume that we want to calculate sensitivity of tranche prices to a given name i. To this end, we tweak only the ith row of the joint TD matrix $P_{ij} = P_{ij}^{(1)}$. We consider the simplest proportional tweak of all elements in the ith row:[11]

$$\delta P_{ij} = \varepsilon P_{ij} \qquad (5.30)$$

Using equation (5.4), we obtain the following tweaks of the default probability $Q_i(T)$ and tail probabilities w_j:

$$\delta Q_i = \sum_{j=1}^{N} \delta P_{ij} = \varepsilon \sum_{j=1}^{N} P_{ij} = \varepsilon Q_i$$
$$\delta w_j = \delta P_{ij} = \varepsilon P_{ij} \qquad (5.31)$$

Note that as long as the rule (5.30) of the tweak of P_{ij} is specified, the tweak of the conditional TD matrix p_{ij} is not arbitrary but is rather fixed by the relationship:

$$\delta P_{ij} = w_j \delta p_{ij} + p_{ij} \delta w_j \qquad (5.32)$$

Substituting equation (5.30) and the second of equation (5.31) and rearranging, this yields:

$$\delta p_{ij} = \varepsilon p_{ij} \left(1 - p_{ij}\right) \tag{5.33}$$

Equation (5.31) expresses the sought-after duality between tweaks of single-name default probability and the tail probability, which both stem from a tweak of the joint TD matrix P_{ij}. It is exactly this duality that enables the whole calculation of single-name sensitivities in our framework.[12] What remains now for calculation of those single-name sensitivities is to establish a relationship between changes of the marked-to-market of name i and a tranche with changes δQ_i and δw_j, respectively.

In what follows, we establish approximate, rather than exact, relationships for single-name sensitivities. Generalizations of formulas to follow to make them exact (i.e., include contributions of all cash flows) are straightforward, but lead to bulky expressions and hence will be omitted here. Furthermore, as will be shown later on, our approximate formulas can be inverted, leading to some interesting insights (see Section 5.4.1).

We start with establishing relevant formulas for name i. Let us approximate a change of MTM, δMTM_i, of CDS referencing the ith name by a change δDL_i of its default leg. (Note that this approximation becomes exact if the CDS premium is paid up front rather than as a running spread. Corrections to this approximation will be considered later.) In turn, δDL_i can be approximated by the (discounted) change in the expected loss on this name—that is, the default probability times $(1 - R)/N$, assuming a unit portfolio notional. This yields:

$$\delta MTM_i \simeq \frac{1 - R}{N} B(0, T) \delta Q_i(T) \tag{5.34}$$

where $B(0, T)$ is a discount factor to time T.[13]

We can now use the same approximation for the MTM change of the tranche, so that the latter is approximated by the (discounted) change of the tranche expected loss (EL). We assume an ordered set of strikes $K_1, \ldots, K_{N_{tr}}$ expressed as a fraction of the total portfolio notional, with $K_0 = 0$ and $K_{N_{tr}} = 1$. Let $EL_k \equiv EL_{[K_{k-1}, K_k]}$ (where $k = 1, \ldots, N_{tr}$) be the expected loss of the kth tranche, expressed as a percentage of the tranche notional, is defined as follows (here $I = \frac{1}{N}$ is the CDS notional):

$$EL_k = \frac{S_{k-1} - S_k}{K_k - K_{k-1}} \tag{5.35}$$

where

$$S_k = \sum_{n=1}^{N} ((1 - R)nI - K_k NI)^+ \rho_n \tag{5.36}$$

and ρ_n is the probability of having n defaults by a given time horizon, which can be expressed in terms of the tail probabilities $\{w_n\}$ defined in Section 5.2:

$$\rho_n = \begin{cases} w_n - w_{n+1} & n = 1, \ldots, N-1 \\ w_N & n = N \end{cases} \tag{5.37}$$

After some algebra, we obtain for S_k:

$$S_k = \frac{1-R}{N} 1_{(\hat{K}_k < 1)} \left(\sum_{n=\lfloor \hat{K}_k N \rfloor}^{N} w_n + \left(\lfloor \hat{K}_k N \rfloor - \hat{K}_k N \right) w_{\lfloor \hat{K}_k N \rfloor} \right)$$

$$\simeq \frac{1-R}{N} 1_{(\hat{K}_k < 1)} \sum_{n=\lfloor \hat{K}_k N \rfloor}^{N} w_n$$

where $\hat{K}_k \equiv K_k/(1-R)$ and $\lfloor x \rfloor$ stands for the smallest integer equal or larger than x. For the tranche expected loss with $\hat{K}_{k-1}, \hat{K}_k < 1$ we therefore have:

$$EL_k \simeq \frac{1-R}{K_k - K_{k-1}} \frac{1}{N} \sum_{n=\lfloor \hat{K}_{k-1} N \rfloor}^{\lfloor \hat{K}_k N \rfloor} w_n \tag{5.38}$$

Using equations (5.38), (5.34), and (5.31), we arrive at the following approximate formula for the single-name delta of the kth tranche in the random thinning framework:

$$\Delta_i^k \equiv \frac{(\delta MTM)_{tranche}^k}{(\delta MTM)_i} \simeq \frac{1}{K_k - K_{k-1}} \frac{1}{N} \frac{\sum_{n=\lfloor \hat{K}_{k-1} N \rfloor}^{\lfloor \hat{K}_k N \rfloor - 1} \delta P_{in}}{\sum_{n=1}^{N} \delta P_{in}}$$

$$= \frac{1}{K_k - K_{k-1}} \frac{1}{N} \frac{\sum_{n=\lfloor \hat{K}_{k-1} N \rfloor}^{\lfloor \hat{K}_k N \rfloor - 1} w_n p_{in}}{\sum_{n=1}^{N} w_n p_{in}} \tag{5.39}$$

Note that this formula readily demonstrates that tweaks $\delta P_{in} = \varepsilon w_n p_{in}$ should be different for different names, as otherwise our approximation would produce the same deltas for all names.

We can also calculate the index delta from all single-name deltas as follows. If we tweak all single names at once using a proportional tweak with the same ε for all names, then the change of tranche MTM is:

$$(\delta MTM)_{tranche}^k = \sum_i \Delta_i^k (\delta MTM)_i \tag{5.40}$$

while, in contrast, by definition it is equal to:

$$(\delta MTM)^k_{tranche} = \Delta^k_{idx}(\delta MTM)_{idx} \qquad (5.41)$$

Comparing these two formulas and taking into account the relationship:

$$(\delta \text{MTM})_{idx} = \sum_i \frac{1}{N}(\delta MTM)_i = \varepsilon(1-R)B(0,T)\sum_{i=1}^{N}\sum_{n=1}^{N} w_n p_{in} \qquad (5.42)$$

we obtain two relationships for the index delta. The first one is a bottom-up formula expressing the index delta as a weighted average of single-name deltas:

$$\Delta^k_{idx} = N\frac{\sum_{i=1}^{N}\Delta^k_i(\delta MTM)_i}{\sum_{i=1}^{N}(\delta MTM)_i} \qquad (5.43)$$

and the second one is a top-down relationship:

$$\Delta^k_{idx} = \frac{(\delta MTM)^k_{tranche}}{(\delta MTM)_{idx}} \simeq \frac{1}{K_k - K_{k-1}}\frac{\sum_{i=1}^{N}\sum_{n=\lfloor \hat{K}_{k-1}N\rfloor}^{\lfloor \hat{K}_k N\rfloor - 1} w_n p_{in}}{\sum_{i=1}^{N}\sum_{n=1}^{N} w_n p_{in}} \qquad (5.44)$$

Note that approximate deltas calculated according to equation (5.44), and rescaled by the tranche widths $K_k - K_{k-1}$, sum up to 1 across all tranches in the capital structure, whereas single-name deltas sum up to $1/N$. Also note the following simple relationship between the index delta and single-name deltas:

$$\Delta^k_{idx} \simeq \sum_i \Delta^k_i \qquad (5.45)$$

which follows from equation (5.43) as long as all spreads in the index portfolio are approximately equal and tweaked in the same way (i.e., using the same value of ε).

We would like to note that the accuracy of approximate formulas (5.39) and (5.45) can be improved without adding complexity. This is done by assuming a continuous coupon, and approximating the premium legs of a CDS and a tranche using the a constant riskless rate r and a constant hazard rate h_i so that the survival probability of name i reads:

$$Q_i(T) = e^{-h_i T} \qquad (5.46)$$

TABLE 5.1 Single Name Sensitivities for a Low Spread Name (Baxter)

Tranche	0–3%	3–7%	7–10%	10–15%	15–30%	30–100%
BC delta	0.0546	0.0086	−0.0022	−0.0034	−0.0093	0.0109
RT delta (prior 1)	0.0521	0.0218	0.0152	0.0102	0.0085	0.0057
RT delta (prior 2)	0.0283	0.0035	0.0011	0.0005	0.0009	0.0101

and a similar formula for the survival probability of a tranche. This yields the following value for the premium leg of a tranche:

$$
PL_{[K_d,K_u]} = s \int_0^T dt e^{-rt} e^{-ht} = \frac{1}{r+h}\left(1 - e^{-(r+h)T}\right) \simeq sT\left(1 - \frac{1}{2}T(r+h)\right)
$$

$$
\simeq sT\left(1 - \frac{1}{2}rT - \frac{1}{2}EL_{[K_d,K_u]}\right) \tag{5.47}
$$

where h is the continuous coupon rate. This produces the following refinement to the approximate relationship (5.39):

$$
\Delta_i^k \simeq \frac{1}{K_k - K_{k-1}} \frac{1}{N} \frac{B(0,T) + \frac{1}{2}s_{tr}^k T}{B(0,T) + \frac{1}{2}s_i T} \frac{\sum_{n=\lfloor \hat{K}_{k-1}N \rfloor}^{\lfloor \hat{K}_k N \rfloor} w_n p_{in}}{\sum_{n=1}^N w_n p_{in}} \tag{5.48}
$$

Numerical experiments indicate that accuracy of the approximate formula (5.48) in comparison with an exact expression that includes contributions of all cash flows is not worse than 10 percent.

The results of single-name sensitivities calculated using (5.48) are given in Tables 5.1, 5.2, and 5.3 for three names representing low, moderate, and high spread names, respectively.

A few comments are in order here in regard to these numbers. The first row in these tables, labeled "BC delta," shows sensitivities calculated with the base correlation method. Negative entries in Table 5.1 (and Table 5.3) clearly show that the base correlation methodology is wrong in the sense that for positive asset correlations all single-name sensitivities in a right model should be positive, not negative.[14] Nevertheless, in view of the absence of a market-standard alternative to the base correlation methodology, we will keep base correlation sensitivities as a reference point for our RT scheme. The second row ("RT delta (prior 1)") in the tables refers to single-name sensitivities calculated with the linear prior (5.27), while the third row gives the RT delta calculated with the base correlation prior, which is explained in Section 5.4.1. One

TABLE 5.2 Single-Name Sensitivities for a Medium Spread Name (GE)

Tranche	0–3%	3–7%	7–10%	10–15%	15–30%	30–100%
BC delta	0.0900	0.0314	0.0153	0.0136	0.0172	0.0006
RT delta (prior 1)	0.1180	0.0334	0.0175	0.0097	0.0056	0.0034
RT delta (prior 2)	0.1025	0.0345	0.0212	0.0159	0.0156	0.0014

TABLE 5.3 Single-Name Sensitivities for a High Spread Name (Sprint)

Tranche	0–3%	3–7%	7–10%	10–15%	15–30%	30–100%
BC delta	0.1914	0.0487	0.0116	0.0028	0.0001	−4.75e-10
RT delta (prior 1)	0.1744	0.0433	0.0195	0.0093	0.0032	0.0013
RT delta (prior 2)	0.1725	0.0595	0.0316	0.0144	0.0021	0.0002

sees that the RT method produces numbers of the same order of magnitude as the base correlation model, with largest differences being for mezzanine and senior tranches.

At this point, a question that could be asked is which set of deltas is the right one. Generally, the ultimate answer to this question requires exploring the behavior of the profit and loss (P&L) distribution of the hedged position, where hedges are calculated according to the model. While we do not pursue such an analysis in this chapter, we note that RT deltas are likely to be less wrong than base correlation deltas, as they arise from a consistent, arbitrage-free model. For example, unlike the latter, positivity of RT deltas is guaranteed by construction. More on the comparison between RT sensitivities calculated with prior 1 and prior 2 will be said in Section 5.4, after the base correlation prior ("prior 2") is introduced.

5.4.1 Base Correlation Prior

Assume we are given some set of target single-name sensitivities that we would like to match as closely as possible. These sensitivities can come from any bottom-up model such as CreditMetrics, approximately calibrated to tranche quotes of interest. Using the results of the preceding section, we can then invert the relationship (5.48) or (5.39) and construct the p-matrices such that these deltas are approximately matched. We then use these p-matrices as priors that need to be corrected by the IS algorithm to match the single-name and portfolio data. The new true sensitivities are then calculated using the calibrated TD matrices.

Note that each row in the p-matrix has N elements (e.g., $N = 125$ for CDX.NA.IG and iTraxx portfolios), while for the same portfolios we have only six deltas per name. This means that the problem is severely underdetermined. To reduce the number of free parameters, we assume that for each i and m, elements of $p_{ij}^{(m)}$ are piecewise-constant between default counts j that correspond to strikes of tranches in the calibration set.[15] Thus, we set $p_{in} = \bar{p}_i^1$ for $j \in [1, j_1]$, $p_{in} = \bar{p}_i^2$ for $j \in [j_1 + 1, j_2]$, and so on. Equation (5.39) with a proportional tweak $(\delta p)_{in} = \varepsilon p_{in}$ produces the following formula for the delta of the kth tranche with respect to name i:

$$
\Delta_i^k \simeq \frac{1}{K_k - K_{k-1}} \frac{1}{N} \frac{\sum_{n=\lfloor \hat{K}_{k-1}N \rfloor}^{\lfloor \hat{K}_k N \rfloor} w_n p_{in}}{\sum_{n=1}^{N} w_n p_{in}} = \frac{1}{K_k - K_{k-1}} \frac{1}{N} \frac{\sum_{n=\lfloor \hat{K}_{k-1}N \rfloor}^{\lfloor \hat{K}_k N \rfloor} w_n p_{in}}{Q_i(T_1)}
$$

$$
= \frac{1}{K_k - K_{k-1}} \frac{1}{N} \frac{\bar{p}_i^k \sum_{n=\lfloor \hat{K}_{k-1}N \rfloor}^{\lfloor \hat{K}_k N \rfloor} w_n}{Q_i(T_1)} = \frac{1}{K_k - K_{k-1}} \frac{1}{N} \frac{\bar{p}_i^k \bar{w}^k}{Q_i(T_1)} \tag{5.49}
$$

FIGURE 5.4 Three Rows of the Prior Matrix $q_{ij}^{(1)}$ Corresponding to Low, Moderate, and High Spreads, with the Base Correlation Prior

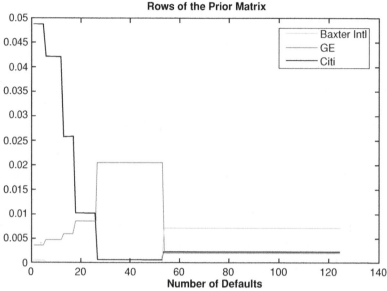

where $\bar{w}^k \equiv \sum_{n=\lfloor \hat{K}_{k-1} N \rfloor}^{\lfloor \hat{K}_k N \rfloor} w_n$. Inverting this relationship, we obtain:

$$\bar{p}_i^k = \Delta_i^k Q_i(T_1)\frac{N(K_k - K_{k-1})}{\bar{w}^k} \tag{5.50}$$

Similar to equation (5.48), this relationship can be improved by taking into account nonvanishing spreads paid by a CDS and a tranche:

$$\bar{p}_i^k = \Delta_i^k Q_i(T_1)\frac{N(K_k - K_{k-1})}{\bar{w}^k} \frac{B(0, T) + \frac{1}{2}s_i T}{B(0, T) + \frac{1}{2}s_{tr}^k T} \tag{5.51}$$

The result is shown in Figure 5.4 for the same three names that were used for illustration of our linear prior matrices. Resulting calibrated thinning matrices are shown in Figure 5.5. They can be compared with the profiles displayed in Figure 5.4. One sees that the direction behavior is similar in both cases.

Going back to comparison of sensitivity parameters obtained with different RT schemes (see Tables 5.1–5.3), the numbers shown there for three selected names do not really demonstrate that sensitivities obtained with the base correlation prior are considerably closer to base correlation sensitivities than those obtained with the linear prior. That this is indeed the case is illustrated in Figure 5.6 where we show the relative difference between the RT and BC equity delta across different names in the portfolio for both the linear and the base correlation choice for the prior.[16] What can be clearly

FIGURE 5.5 Calibrated Thinning Matrices $p_{ij}^{(1)}$, $p_{ij}^{(2)}$, $p_{ij}^{(3)}$ Obtained with the Base Correlation Prior

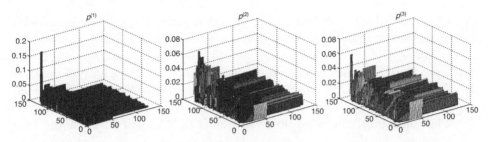

seen, though, is that with the first prior our equity delta is generally higher than the BC delta, while with base correlation prior the situation is reversed.

Thus, our numerical experiment shows that the idea of having a sort of calibration of TD matrices to base correlation deltas does not really work, as the subsequent rescaling of TD matrices (needed to match single-name and portfolio data) substantially alternates the prior matrices. While we are not aware of any compelling financial explanation of this behavior, perhaps a more interesting practical conclusion that can be drawn from our experiments with different priors is that single-name deltas are not unique, and depend on fine details of the model (in our case, the choice of the prior). As discussed in more detail in Halperin and Tomecek (2008), this situation is in fact quite common, and occurs not only in top-down but in bottom-up models as well.

FIGURE 5.6 Relative Difference of Equity Delta Obtained with the Random Thinning (RT) and Base Correlation (BC) Methods, for the Linear and Base Correlation Choices of the Prior

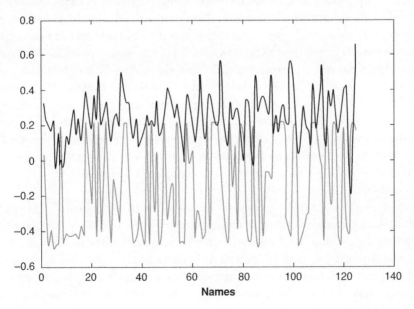

5.5 Modeling Notional Heterogeneity

In terms of a portfolio's constituents, the top-down setting is usually associated with the assumption of a homogeneous portfolio with all notionals I_i and recoveries R_i being equal: $I_i = I$ and $R_i = R$ for $i = 1, \ldots, N$ where N is the number of names in the portfolio. Equivalently, this means that the total loss in the portfolio upon n defaults in $L_n = n(1 - R)I \equiv n\bar{L}$, where $\bar{L}$ is the loss given default (LGD) common for all names.

While the standard index portfolios such as CDX.NA.IG or iTraxx Europe have equal notionals for all names, most bespoke portfolios are usually heterogeneous in their notionals. Furthermore, recoveries for either index or bespoke portfolios are not known beforehand, and should be treated as random, with generally different expected recoveries for different names. It is therefore important to understand the impact of the notional and recovery heterogeneity, as well as possible randomness of recoveries, on the valuation of portfolio derivatives, most notably CDO tranches.

In this section, we concentrate on the notional heterogeneity, leaving a discussion of recovery heterogeneity and randomness for the next section. We develop a systematic way of accounting for notional heterogeneity in a top-down modeling framework, by constructing a representation of a *heterogeneous* credit portfolio in terms of an equivalent *homogeneous* pool whose default probabilities are adjusted in such a way that tranche expected losses for both portfolios match. In what follows, we refer to this procedure as *homogenization*.

5.5.1 The General Idea

In a bottom-up model, account for the notional heterogeneity is straightforward and explicit. Indeed, as individual names are distinguishable, the total loss for any given time horizon is uniquely (for fixed recoveries) specified by their default times. On the contrary, a natural filtration of a top-down model contains only portfolio-level default times but does not reveal identities of individual defaulters. Therefore, the top-down approach does not allow for a straightforward account of the notional heterogeneity.

To explain our approach, it is convenient to visualize two observers: a bottom-up observer O_{BU} who registers identities of all defaulters that have defaulted by time t, and a top-down observer O_{TD} who only registers events of defaults in the portfolio, but does not know identities of the defaulters. In the nomenclature of Section 5.2.1, observers O_{BU} and O_{TD} have access to information revealed by filtration $\mathcal{G}_t \vee \mathcal{I}_t$ and $\mathcal{G}_t$, respectively.

Even though observer O_{TD} does not see identities of the defaulters, the observer can assess them *probabilistically* by assigning probabilities to observe individual obligors among defaulted names based on the initial characteristics of the portfolio.

In our approach, we take the viewpoint of observer O_{TD}. By viewing the identity (and hence the notional) of the next defaulter as a random quantity, we effectively substitute *explicit* account of notional heterogeneity by modeling it in a *statistical* sense.

To explain how it works, consider the problem of valuation of a tranche with strikes K_1, K_2. It involves calculation of the following expectation:

$$EL_K(t) \equiv \mathbb{E}\left[\left(L(t) - K\right)^+ \big| \mathcal{F}_0\right] \equiv \langle(L_t - K)^+\rangle \tag{5.52}$$

where $K = K_1$ or K_2, $L(t) = \sum_{i=1}^{N}(1 - R_i)I_i 1_{\{\tau_i \leq t\}}$ is the portfolio loss at time t, and the notation $\langle\ldots\rangle$ stands for the expected value. The expectation in equation (5.52) should be taken with respect to all sources of randomness, which we discuss next.

First, the expectation (5.52) should involve averaging over different default scenarios across names in the portfolio. However, information available to observer O_{TD} is *incomplete* as the observer is able to register only default events but not defaulter identities.

Let p_n be probabilities of incomplete information scenarios with n defaults in the portfolio. Note that probabilities p_n depend on assumptions on default dependencies in the portfolio, and hence should be calibrated to available prices of CDO tranches. Furthermore, let $L_{n,t}$ be the portfolio loss in a scenario with n defaults at time t. Note that as we take the viewpoint of the top-down observer O_{TD}, we do not know the identity of defaulters. As our information is incomplete, the total loss $L_{n,t}$ in the scenario with n defaults should be viewed as *random*, unless all names have the same notionals and recoveries. Thus we can formally evaluate equation (5.52) as follows:

$$EL_K(t) = \sum_{n=1}^{N} p_n \left\langle \left(L_{n,t} - K\right)^+ \right\rangle \tag{5.53}$$

where $\langle\ldots\rangle$ now stands for averaging over identities of defaulters.

To proceed, assume that all names in the portfolio at hand can be bucketed into N_c reasonably homogeneous groups, such that all names in group k (where $k = 1, \ldots, N_c$) have approximately the same notionals and expected recoveries, and thus the same absolute LGDs $l = l_k$. Then the total portfolio loss in a scenario with n defaults is:

$$L_{n,t} = \sum_{k=1}^{N_c} l_k n_{k,t} \tag{5.54}$$

where $n_{k,t}$ is the total number of names from group k among the defaulters at time t. Using the convention in the mathematical literature, we will label different homogeneous groups by different colors.

The following important remark is in order here. Consider application of decomposition equation (5.53) to a standardized index tranche. Assume that all recoveries are fixed and equal across constituent names. In this case, averaging $\langle\ldots\rangle$ over defaulters' identities in equation (5.53) becomes redundant. This means that, under the assumption of a constant recovery rate, the set of probabilities p_n is the only piece of information about the market that can be learned from observing prices of index tranches.

Now consider a more general case of a heterogeneous bespoke portfolio where the identity averaging operator $\langle \ldots \rangle$ is not redundant anymore.[17] Let us think of the portfolio default process as sampling (without replacement) from an urn that initially contains N balls, each ball belonging to one of the homogeneous groups introduced earlier. By defining probabilities of sampling balls of different colors upon sequential defaults in the portfolio, we provide rules for calculation of the averaging over defaulters' identities $\langle \ldots \rangle$ in equation (5.53).

We thus arrive at a method for calculation of tranche expected loss that factorizes the result into dynamic and static components. A dynamic component controls the pace with which we draw balls from the urn. This information is carried by probabilities p_n, which are inferred from market prices of traded tranches and indexes. The second, static or geometric component specifies tranche losses in scenarios with a given total number n of defaults counted by a given time horizon. We assume that this contribution does not depend on the market prices of index tranches (as the latter information is already incorporated in probabilities p_n), but is rather driven by purely geometric, correlation-independent factors such as notionals and expected recoveries. The latter either are directly observed or can be inferred from the CDS market. This leads to a practically important conclusion that the latter averaging over defaulter identities (or equivalently over possible values of random L_n) can be performed *prior* to calibration of the model to prices of CDO tranches.

Such a method, referred to as a *homegenization*, will be presented later. Note that our homegenization procedure is time-homogeneous (i.e., independent of a particular time horizon t), and thus needs to be done only once, rather than for all nodes on a time grid used for the pricing. Because of time-homogeneity of our method, the time argument of the portfolio loss $L_{n,t}$ will be omitted in this section.

We further note that equation (5.53) is useful because it suggests an intuitive decomposition of the total risk into contributions of scenarios with different numbers of defaults n. Parameter n offers a convenient one-dimensional risk space for a credit portfolio book, which is intuitive for risk managers who typically ask questions like: "What are my possible losses in a scenario with $n = 5$ defaults in my portfolio?"[18] It is exactly the decomposition (5.53) that suggests such an intuitive decomposition of the total risk into contributions of scenarios with different numbers of defaults n.

To summarize, in order for expression (5.53) to be meaningful in the context of heterogeneous portfolios, we should treat identities of defaulters in each given portfolio-level scenario as random, and perform explicit averaging over them. Clearly, such an approach is not able to produce a model of single-name dynamics like those obtained in a bottom-up model or with a dynamic random thinning of a top-down model. The objective here is rather to find a way to account for a possible heterogeneity of a credit portfolio in a top-down setting.

5.5.2 Heterogeneity Bias

Before moving on to a proposed solution, we want to discuss what can be said on the impact of portfolio heterogeneity on general grounds.

Irrespective of the exact meaning of the averaging procedure in equation (5.53), as long as $(x - K)^+$ is a convex function of x, by Jensen's inequality we have:

$$\langle (L_n - K)^+ \rangle \geq (\langle L_n \rangle - K)^+ \tag{5.55}$$

Here $\langle L_n \rangle$ stands for the portfolio loss averaged with regard to the same distribution of notionals that is used in the LHS. Hence, Jensen tells us that for any fixed set of probabilities p_n, taking the expectation inside a nonlinear payoff would lead to underestimation of the expression (5.52). However, such interchange of computing the payoff and taking the expectation is *not* what we typically do in a top-down model. Indeed, within an approach to be presented later, a model-based calculation of $\langle L_n \rangle$ would involve averaging with a certain multivariate distribution whose parameters depend, in particular, on spreads of names in the portfolio. On the contrary, in the naive top-down approach, we instead simply divide the total notional of the portfolio by the number of names to get the average loss per default. Assuming we have N_c groups of names such that group i has n_i names in it (so that $\sum_{i=1}^{N_c} n_i = N$) and all names in group i have the same notionals $\mathcal{N}_i$, the average LGD is:

$$\bar{L} = \frac{\sum_{i=1}^{N_c}(1 - R_i)n_i\mathcal{N}_i}{\sum_{i=1}^{N_c} n_i} = (1 - R)\frac{\sum_{i=1}^{N_c} n_i\mathcal{N}_i}{N}$$

(where we take $R_i = R$), and thus the average fractional loss in the scenario with n defaults is:

$$\langle L_n \rangle_{naive} = \frac{n\bar{L}}{\sum_{i=1}^{N_c} n_i\mathcal{N}_i} = (1 - R)\frac{n}{N} \tag{5.56}$$

We put the subscript "naive" in order to distinguish this expression from $\langle L_n \rangle$ that appears in equation (5.55) and stands for a proper average with a distribution of notionals; see the next pages). Thus, in the naive top-down setting, we effectively substitute the left-hand side of equation (5.55) by the expression $(\langle L_n \rangle_{naive} - K)^+$. In what follows, we will refer to this prescription as the *naive homogenization* rule.

We want to emphasize that while Jensen's inequality [equation (5.55)] implies that for any fixed set of probabilities p_n, substitution of the left-hand side of equation (5.55) by its right-hand side underestimates the expectation (5.52), no such general statement can be made once we use the naive homogenization rule instead. Indeed, as will be illustrated with numerical examples that follow, the direction of the bias depends on the portfolio, and can be of any sign.

5.5.3 The Biased Urn Model

Our objective is to calculate the expectations in equation (5.53) in a way that remains faithful to the modeling paradigm of the top-down approach, with the number of defaults n being the prime object of modeling.

To this end, we propose to use a biased urn model (see, e.g., Fog 2008 or Johnson, Kotz, and Balakrishnan 1997 for a review). Imagine we have an urn that contains $N = \sum_{i=1}^{N_c} m_i$ balls of N_c different colors, where m_i is the number of balls of color $i \in C = [1, \ldots, N_c]$. We sample n balls one by one without replacement, assuming that the probability that a particular ball is sampled at a given draw is proportional to a *weight* $\omega_i > 0$. The weight ω_i of a ball depends only on its color i. Let $\mathbf{N}(n) = (n_1, n_2, \ldots, n_{N_c})$ be the numbers of balls of colors $C_1, C_2, \ldots, C_{N_c}$ sampled in the first n draws, so that $\sum_{i=1}^{N_c} n_i = n$. The probability that the next draw gives a ball of color i is:

$$q_i = \frac{\omega_i(m_i - n_i)}{\sum_{j=1}^{N_c} \omega_j(m_j - n_j)} \equiv \frac{\omega_i g_i}{\sum_{j=1}^{N_c} \omega_j g_j} \tag{5.57}$$

Note that a simultaneous rescaling of all coefficients ω_i by the same factor does not change the probabilities [equation (5.57)] and hence keeps the model intact. This can be used to rescale all parameters ω_i such that they are normalized to one:

$$\sum_{i=1}^{N_c} \omega_i = 1 \tag{5.58}$$

Note that if all m_i are the same, then the probability to observe a ball of color i upon the first draw is $P_i = \omega_i$. Therefore, ω_i can be interpreted as probability that the first ball drawn is of color i, when the urn initially has equal numbers of balls of all colors; see Manly (1974).

The total probability of having $\mathbf{N}(n) = (n_1, n_2, \ldots, n_{N_c})$ in the first n draws is given by the Wallenius's noncentral multivariate hypergeometric distribution (Johnson, Kotz, and Balakrishnan 1997):

$$W[\mathbf{n}] \equiv Pr[\mathbf{N}(n) = \mathbf{n}] = \prod_{i=1}^{N_c} \binom{m_i}{n_i} \int_0^1 \prod_{i=1}^{N_c} \left(1 - t^{\frac{\omega_i}{d}}\right)^{n_i} dt, \quad \sum_{i=1}^{N_c} n_i = n \tag{5.59}$$

where

$$d = \sum_{i=1}^{N_c} \omega_i(m_i - n_i), \quad n_i \leq m_i \tag{5.60}$$

5.5.4 Application to Credit Portfolios

To apply these mathematical ideas to modeling losses in credit portfolios, let us start with bucketing all names in the portfolio into buckets chosen to be approximately homogeneous in notionals and spreads. We assign the same color C_i to all names in the ith bucket, where $i = 1, \ldots, N_c$. Furthermore, as names with higher spreads are expected to default sooner than names with lower spreads, we can choose weights ω_i as follows:

$$\omega_i = \frac{\sum_k S_{ik}}{\sum_{i,k} S_{ik}} \tag{5.61}$$

where S_{ik} is the spread of the ith name in the kth color group. Thus, the numerator in equation (5.61) stands for the total spread for all names in bucket i, while the denominator stands for the total spread across all names in the portfolio.

Note that assigning weights according only to spreads of names in the portfolio is not the only possible choice. Another (and probably more realistic) way of constructing weights ω_i could incorporate betas of different names. Indeed, if name i defaults by a time horizon T, then, all other things being equal, probabilities that other names default as well could be sorted according to default correlations $\beta_i \beta_j$. We leave this idea for a future exploration.

5.5.5 Homogenization Method

Let us rewrite equation (5.53) by multiplying and dividing by $(\langle L_n \rangle_{naive} - K)^+$:

$$EL_K(t) = \sum_{n=1}^{N} p_n \frac{\langle (L_n - K)^+ \rangle}{(\langle L_n \rangle_{naive} - K)^+} (\langle L_n \rangle_{naive} - K)^+ \equiv \sum_{n=1}^{N} p_n \alpha_{nK} (\langle L_n \rangle_{naive} - K)^+ \tag{5.62}$$

where $\langle L_n \rangle_{naive}$ is defined in equation (5.56), and

$$\alpha_{nK} = \frac{\langle (L_n - K)^+ \rangle}{(\langle L_n \rangle_{naive} - K)^+} \tag{5.63}$$

are the *heterogeneity correction factors* (HCFs).

Equation (5.62) decomposes the tranche expected loss into a weighted sum of loss contributions obtained with the naive top-down averaging over notionals of constituent names. The weights are given by the values of the product $p_n \alpha_{nK}$. All the impact of heterogeneity of the portfolio is now hidden in HCF parameters (5.63).

We calculate HCF coefficients using Monte Carlo integration. Let N_c be the total number of buckets (colors), with L_i being the LGD for all names in the ith bucket. Then we obtain:

$$\alpha_{nK} = \frac{1}{(\langle L_n \rangle_{naive} - K)^+} \sum_{n_1 + \cdots + n_{N_c} = n} \left(\sum_{i=1}^{N_c} n_i L_i - K \right)^+ W[\mathbf{n}] \qquad (5.64)$$

where Wallenius's noncentral hypergeometric distribution $W(\mathbf{n})$ is defined in equation (5.59).

The simplest method to sample from Wallenius's noncentral hypergeometric distribution is to simulate the bias urn as just described. Other methods of sampling are described in Fog (2008). Note that we have to do one Monte Carlo integration per portfolio default state $n = 1, 2, \ldots, N$. There is no need to redo this calculation during the calibration stage of the model, as equation (5.64) involves only the CDS data (to construct weights) and tranche specification (strikes) but not the tranche market data (tranche spreads). This means that the HCF coefficients α_{nK} should be calculated only *once*, and then cached for the calibration of the top-down model.

Once the HCF coefficients α_{nK} are calculated, the model calibration proceeds as follows. We assume that the implementation of a top-down model is flexible enough to allow for default-order-dependent strikes K_n and portfolio notional. In this case, we can incorporate the effect of HCF coefficients α_{nk} by doing a proper simultaneous n-dependent rescaling of both the portfolio notional and tranche strike. After that, one should proceed with the usual calibration of the top-down model that amounts to finding a set of market-implied probabilities p_n.

We would like to note that the homogenization trick comes with a price tag: It works for only one tranche at a time, as the HCF coefficients α_{nK} depend on the strike K. To price a tranche with a different strike, one should recompute the HCF coefficients, and then recalibrate probabilities p_n. The latter thus effectively become strike-dependent. This may pose a problem for pricing of exotic contracts that require a simultaneous pricing of several tranches. However, for a more standard case of valuing a single tranche, our proposed solution of extending the classical top-down setting using a biased urn model appears to be a viable solution for a more accurate pricing. We consider examples next.

5.5.6   Numerical Examples

We consider a few examples with both synthetic and real portfolios. In all cases we consider a portfolio of $N = 100$ names. Our test amounts to comparison of the tranche expected loss (equation [5.53]) calculated using the homogenization method of the previous section versus the result obtained using the naive homogenization rule. We look at the specific tranche strike $K = 7\%$.

The first example deals with a portfolio with four groups of notionals of $\$[1.0, 5.0, 10.0, 15.0]$ mm. The number of names in each group, respectively, are $10, 30, 40$, and 20. The weights are chosen to be $\omega = (1/15, 5/15, 3/15, 6/15)$. The result is shown in Figure 5.7. The second example is more heterogeneous. We have

FIGURE 5.7 Example of Moderately Heterogeneous Portfolio

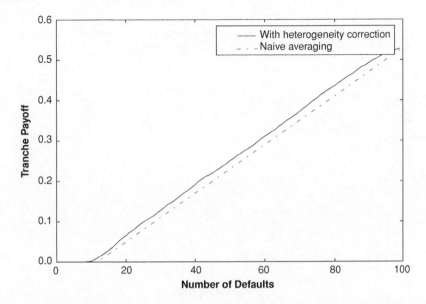

two groups only, with notionals of $1 and 10 mm, respectively. The number of names in these groups are 10 and 90, respectively. Weights are 5/6 and 1/6. The result is shown in Figure 5.8. The third example is as the second one, except now the weights are 1/6 and 5/6. The result is shown in Figure 5.9. The difference in behavior between Figures 5.8 and 5.9 is easy to understand. Indeed in the second example, names with

FIGURE 5.8 Example of Strongly Heterogeneous Portfolio

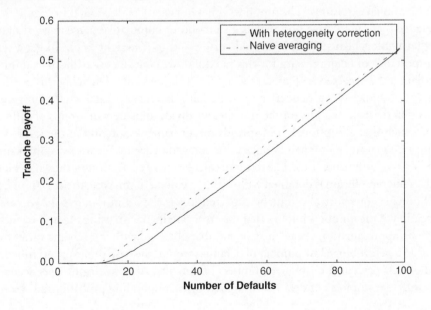

FIGURE 5.9   Example of Strongly Heterogeneous Portfolio

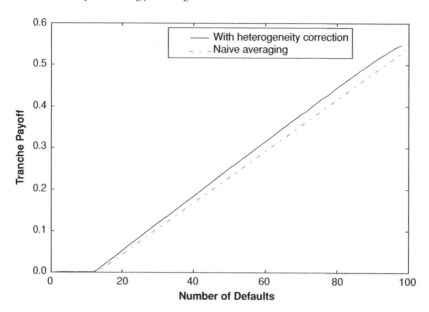

a below-average notional are expected to default sooner than names with an above-average notional, while in the third example, the situation is reversed. Therefore, the tranche expected loss line goes below the naive profile in the former case, and above in the latter case.

Our next example deals with a real traded portfolio, which will be referred to as the XYZ portfolio in what follows. The XYZ portfolio is quite heterogeneous in terms of the notional exposures. The amount of heterogeneity is illustrated in Figure 5.10, where we plot cumulative notional as a function of cumulative percentage of names (so that homogeneous portfolio would correspond to a straight line). To get a sense of importance of heterogeneity for this portfolio, we consider an artificial example of calculation the expected loss for a tranche $(7 - 100)$ percent referencing this portfolio (the actual tranches are defined by a waterfall scheme). To calculate heterogeneity correction for expected loss on the tranche, we divide all issuers in groups of different colors, such that all notionals and spreads for all names belonging to the same color group are equal and set to their average value across that group. We use a decomposition into $N = 10$ different colors. The result of calculation of corrections is shown in Figure 5.11. A finer resolution is obtained with $N = 15$ colors. In this case, the deviation from the homogeneous portfolio tranche expected loss is shown in Figure 5.12. A careful inspection of the numbers implies that the error obtained with using the homogeneous portfolio approximation versus the true number obtained with our scheme varies from about 150 percent for a low number of defaults (around the cusp in the payoff function) to about 20 percent for a higher numbers of defaults. After averaging over scenarios with different numbers of defaults (weighted by corresponding probabilities), we may

FIGURE 5.10   Notional Heterogeneity of the XYZ Portfolio

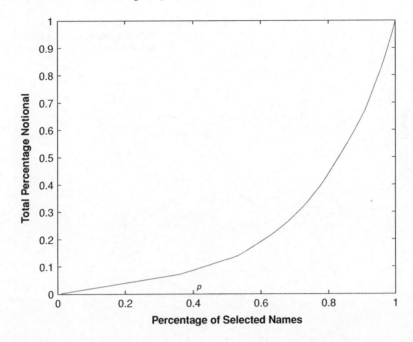

FIGURE 5.11   Heterogeneity Correction for the XYZ Portfolio with 10 Colors

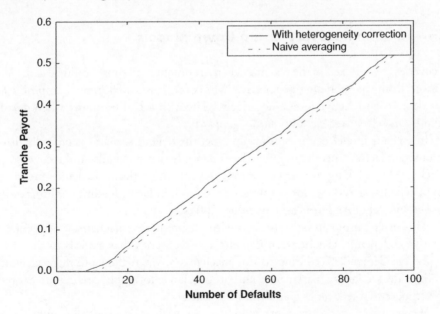

FIGURE 5.12   Heterogeneity Correction for the XYZ Portfolio with 15 Colors

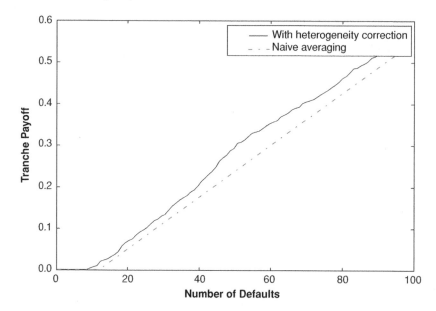

therefore expect that the true tranche expected loss may be larger than that predicted by the homogeneous model by about 25 to 30 percent.

5.6   Random Recovery in Top-Down Models

Recoveries are not fixed in the real market environment, and thus should be considered random from the modeling perspective. Moreover, it is a well-known empirical fact that defaults and recoveries are negatively related: In a bad economy when defaults build up massively, recoveries typically go down.

In a factor model of the bottom-up type, the default scenario is typically driven by a market factor; thus the negative dependence between defaults and recoveries can be achieved by making recoveries inversely dependent on the same market factor that drives defaults, as is done, for example, in the random factor loadings (RFL)/random recovery model of Andersen and Sidenius (2004).

This mechanism can be contrasted with an alternative mechanism of generating negative codependencies between defaults and recoveries that appeals to the law of supply and demand. According to this mechanism, when there are many defaulted bonds in the secondary market, demand drops relative to supply, driving prices down. This implies that recoveries go down in this scenario.

We want to model impact of random recoveries in credit portfolio within a top-down approach. Before moving on to presenting technicalities, it is important to clarify what it means. Random recoveries can be interpreted in two ways. At the level of individual constituent names, random recoveries mean that for any given name, the recovered value is not known beforehand, and is rather known to take values from a set $\mathcal{R}$ with probabilities $p_i = P(R = R_i)$. At the portfolio level, in contrast, random recovery means that the portfolio loss is a jump process with random jump sizes. A negative codependence between defaults and recoveries means that, on average, the size of a jump increases with the number of defaults.

In a top-down framework, we cannot keep the first interpretation of random recovery because we lose the single-name information. However, we can, and will, model the second, portfolio-level specification of random recoveries. The key observation that allows us to apply the top-down setting to model stochastic recovery in the portfolio-level meaning is the fact that we condition only on information $\mathcal{F}_0$ available today, $t = 0$. As discussed in Section 5.2.1, a top-down framework suffices in this case for modeling future default patterns, without a need for a full-blown bottom-up model.

As top-down approaches do not typically employ a factor framework, we prefer to incorporate the second mechanism based on the supply-and-demand balance. We assume that a default pattern of a given credit portfolio in terms of low-default versus high-default scenarios can be viewed as a proxy for the whole market. In this case, one simple way to incorporate a negative codependence between defaults and recoveries in a descriptive way is to postulate a deterministic dependence between them, such that recovery becomes a decreasing function of the number of defaults n. This is done, for example, in the BSLP model of Arnsdorf and Halperin (2008). While it was empirically observed that some simple two-point parametrizations (e.g., 40 percent recovery up to 10 defaults, and zero recovery thereafter) often improves quality of calibration, such a procedure is ad hoc, and does not attempt to link to randomness of actual recoveries upon defaults.

Our purpose here is to suggest a simple model for stochastic recovery in a top-down model where negative codependence between defaults and recoveries would be built in. It is shown that the deterministic dependence of recoveries on the default order n arises as an approximation to stochastic dynamics of recoveries in this framework. This can be used to mark the profile of the recovery as a function of n based on a recovery model rather than on an ad hoc method.

5.6.1 The General Idea

Consider a portfolio of N constituent names, all having different, and generally random, recoveries R_i or, equivalently, random LGDs $L_i = 1 - R_i$. The simplest possibility is to characterize the random LGD for name i by a two-point (Bernoulli) distribution with two possible values $l = l_1$ and $l = l_2$ and corresponding probabilities $p_{1i} = p_i$ and $p_{2i} = 1 - p_i$, so that the expected LGD μ_i for name i is $\mu_i = p_i l_1 + (1 - p_i) l_2$. We assume that different names have generally different expected LGDs μ_i, or equivalently different low LGD probabilities p_i. Also note that the deterministic case corresponds to the limit $l_1 = l_2$.

If we take a viewpoint of observer O_{BU} (see Section 5.5), we know the identity i of the defaulter, and hence we know the expected LGD μ_i at the next default, as well as uncertainty around this value, which is controlled by variance σ_i^2 of the Bernoulli distribution.

If, however, we take the viewpoint of the top-down observer O_{TD}, the situation changes as now we do *not* know the identity of the defaulter. Instead, we *simulate* the identity of the defaulter by setting up a Monte Carlo scheme with the biased urn model. Therefore, even if we start with a top-down model with heterogeneous but fixed LGDs, the LGD of the next defaulter effectively becomes random as long as identity of the defaulter is treated as random. As long as parameters μ_i are different for different names, this means that the next LGD is uncertain not only due to variance around the given mean, but also due to uncertainty of the mean itself!

Let us compare this case to the problem of modeling the fixed recovery case within the top-down approach. Assume all notionals in the portfolio are the same, while LGDs are different (but fixed). Within the framework of the biased urn model, the only difference between this case and the previous one is that now all $\sigma_i = 0$. This means that within the top-down approach, uncertainties due to notional or/and LGD heterogeneity and random recovery are undistinguishable, and can be described within the same model with possibly adjusted parameters.

This suggests a simple way to account for random recoveries in the top-down approach using the same biased urn model as we used for modeling notional heterogeneity. We keep LGDs of individual names fixed, but increase uncertainty of picking names with different values of LGD in comparison with the fixed recovery case. To isolate the impact of randomness of recoveries from notional heterogeneity, in this section we assume that all constituent names in the portfolio have the same notional. Each name is deterministically assigned one of the possible values l_1 and l_2. Such a binary partition of all names in the portfolio provides the simplest framework for modeling nonequal (and random) recoveries upon actual defaults. That is, we combine all names in two groups of low and high LGDs, and fit parameters l_1 and l_2 to approximately match the expected LGDs of all names in both groups. To further specify the model, we need to choose weights ω_1 and $\omega_2 = 1 - \omega_1$. Note that it is the latter parameters that determine the nontrivial dependence of the incremental portfolio loss on default order (the number of defaults in the portfolio at time t). As will be shown later, these parameters can be chosen such that they become broadly consistent with empirical behavior of recovery rates.

5.6.2   The Biased Urn Model: Approximate Mean and Variance

We now want to demonstrate that the empirically observed behavior of recoveries, namely their negative correlation with default levels, can be mimicked in this model, and emerges as a joint effect of the selection bias and the no-replacement rule of the sampling procedure.

We want to calculate the expected recovery upon the next default in the portfolio, conditional on previously observing $n = 0, 1, \ldots, N$ defaults. In terms of the biased urn model, this means that we want to know the probability to observe a given LGD $L_{n+1} = l_k$ with $k = 1$ or $k = 2$ at the event of the $(n + 1)$th portfolio default.

However, as seen from today, this probability is *random* as it depends on the number of remaining balls g_i ($i = 1, 2$) of both colors after n defaults, which is information not available at time $t = 0$. That is, parameters g_i in equation (5.57) should be viewed at $t = 0$ as random.

To investigate the behavior of losses in this model, one possible way thus would be to simulate many possible scenarios of portfolio defaults, and then average over them in order to calculate the expected pattern of losses given default. Such Monte Carlo simulation could be performed using, for example, sampling methods described by Fog (2008).

There exists, however, a simpler way to predict the expected profile of the portfolio loss processes, by using approximate formulas for the *expected* value and variance of the next loss given default (5.57), which were derived by Manly (1974).

Let μ_{ij} be the expected value of the number g_i of balls of color i remaining in the urn after j draws. It (approximately) satisfies the following recursive relationship:

$$\mu_{ij} = \mu_{i,j-1} - \frac{\omega_i \mu_{ij}}{\sum_i \omega_i \mu_{ij}} \equiv \mu_{i,j-1} - \theta_{i,j-1} \qquad (5.65)$$

The formula for approximate *expected* probabilities of drawing balls of different colors is then obtained if we substitute random parameters g_i in equation (5.57) by their expected values [equation (5.65)].

The approximate formula for the variance of g_i after j draws reads:

$$c_{iij} = \left(1 - 2\frac{\omega_i}{\sum_k \omega_k \mu_{i,j-1}}\right) c_{ii,j-1} + \theta_{i,j-1} \left(2\frac{\sum_k \omega_k c_{ii,j-1}}{\sum_k \omega_k \mu_{i,j-1}} + 1 - \theta_{i,j-1}\right) \qquad (5.66)$$

5.6.3   Application for Modeling Random Recovery

Here we see the applications of the urn model framework for the modeling of random recovery/LGD. To have the simplest two-point model of LGD distribution, we consider the case of $c = 2$ colors. We note that while the following analysis is based on the approximate analytical formula (5.65), it can be confirmed by explicit Monte Carlo simulation.

The way we choose the rest of the parameters depends on what we want to match.

5.6.3.1   *Matching the Expected Recovery Only*

In this case, we can assume that the portfolio is composed of two groups of equal size $m_1 = m_2$ with LGD equal to l_1 and l_2 for all names from the first and the second groups, respectively (so that $l_1 < l_2$). Furthermore, we choose weights ω_1 and $\omega_2 = 1 - \omega_1$ in such a way that the expected recovery (prior to observing defaults) would match a target value.

FIGURE 5.13 Expected LGD as a Function of Number of Defaults for $l_1 = 0.565$, $l_2 = 0.9$, $\omega_1 = 0.9$ and $\omega_2 = 0.1$

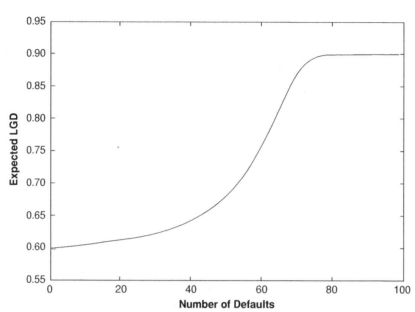

The resulting profile of the expected LGD as a function of number of defaults is shown in Figure 5.13. Thus, at least in the average sense, scenarios with a large number of defaults will be accompanied by increase of LGD for a next defaulter. Therefore, our model is able to produce a negative codependence between default and recovery rates without introducing any explicit *causal* dependence between them in the spirit of, say, the RFL model, where they are both made functions of the common market factor. In our framework, the effect holds *statistically* (as it does in the real market), and arises as a result of the bias in defaulter selected (controlled by parameter ω_1) and the fact that that the portfolio default process is identified with a sampling without replacement.

5.6.3.2 *Matching Both Mean and Variance of Recovery Distribution*

Parameters of the model can be tuned further if we want to tie them to a given level of variance of recovery rate, in addition to the expected recovery. The simplest way to do it is to choose parameters l_1, l_2, and ω_1 in such a way that both target mean and variance numbers are matched. For example, if the LGD has mean $\bar{L} = 0.6 = 1 - \bar{R}$ with $\bar{R} = 0.4$ and standard deviation of 15 percent (i.e., variance $\sigma^2 = 0.022$), we can assume that these should be the mean and variance of recovery for the first default event. This produces two equations:

$$p_1 l_1 + (1 - p_1) l_2 = \bar{L}$$
$$p_1 (l_1 - \bar{L})^2 + (1 - p_1)(l_2 - \bar{L})^2 = \sigma^2 \qquad (5.67)$$

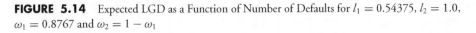

FIGURE 5.14 Expected LGD as a Function of Number of Defaults for $l_1 = 0.54375$, $l_2 = 1.0$, $\omega_1 = 0.8767$ and $\omega_2 = 1 - \omega_1$

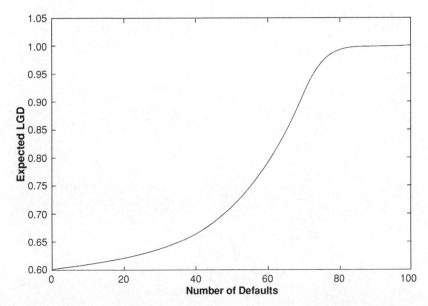

which can be resolved if we fix one of these parameters. For example, if we set $l_2 = 1$, then the solution for p_1 and $l_1 \equiv 1 - R_1$ is:

$$R_1 = \bar{R} + \frac{\sigma^2}{\bar{R}}$$

$$p_1 = \frac{\bar{R}}{R_1} = \frac{\bar{R}^2}{\bar{R}^2 + \sigma^2} \tag{5.68}$$

For the values $\bar{R} = 0.4$ and $\sigma = 0.15$, this results in the following set of parameters: $l_1 = 0.54375$, $l_2 = 1$, $\omega_1 = p_1 = 0.8767$, and $\omega_2 = p_2 = 1 - p_1$. The resulting profile of expected LGD is shown in Figure 5.14.

5.6.3.3 Controlling the Slope

To control the slope of the LGD curve, we can play with the initial numbers m_1 and $m_2 = N - m_1$ of balls of two colors, in addition to parameters l_1, l_2, ω_1. An example is shown in Figure 5.15, where we compare profiles of expected LGDs for two sets $(m_1, m_2) = (50, 50)$ and $(m_1, m_2) = (30, 70)$. Note that in order to have the same initial point, parameter ω_1 is set here to be 0.9432 (and $\omega_2 = 1 - \omega_1 = 0.0568$).

5.6.3.4 Implementation Issues

Handling the stochastic recovery in the tree setting can be done in a similar way to the method of treating notional heterogeneity proposed in the preceding section. Namely,

FIGURE 5.15 Expected LGD as a Function of Number of Defaults for $(m_1, m_2) = (50, 50)$, $\omega_1 = 0.8767$, and $(m_1, m_2) = (30, 70)$, $\omega_1 = 0.9432$

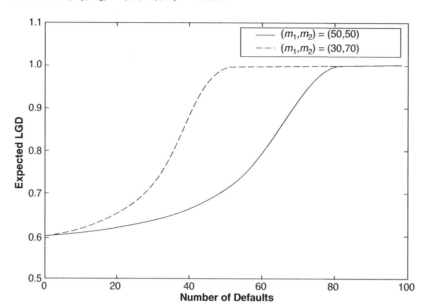

we can calculate tranche expected losses $(L_n - K)^+$ for all nodes n on the tree once *before* calibration of the default tree determining state probabilities p_n, and cache these values for all runs of calibration and pricing. Alternatively, in a Monte Carlo setting the recovery can be directly sampled using probabilities [equation (5.57)].

Finally, for a specific setting of the BSLP model of Arnsdorf and Halperin (2008), our resulting LGD profiles like those shown in Figures 5.13 and 5.14 can be used to produce a deterministic recovery schedule that can be used instead of ad hoc piecewise-flat deterministic profiles.

5.7 Conclusion

In this chapter we presented several probabilistic methods that can be used on top of a classical top-down model in order to assess the impact of portfolio heterogeneity on the valuation and risk management of CDO tranches and possibly other portfolio credit derivatives. We have first addressed spread heterogeneity. We established a link of this problem to the problem of calculation of single-name sensitivities. To this end, we developed an approach based on a view of the single-name calibration of a top-down model as a problem of statistical inference. We have then shown how this idea can be implemented within a simple and numerically efficient algorithm.

In the second part of the paper, we addressed the problem of modeling the notional and recovery heterogeneity of credit portfolios. To this end, we proposed to model portfolio defaults dynamics as a biased sampling without replacement from an urn containing balls of different colors. We have shown how modeling portfolio defaults within this model splits the problem into dynamic and static components. That is, the dynamic component controls the speed with which we draw balls from the urn, and thus should be calibrated to available tranche prices. On the contrary, the static component is controlled by observable, geometric parameters such as notionals and expected recovery, independent of tranche prices. Therefore, this part of the model can be calibrated indepedently of tranche pricing data.

Acknowledgments

Opinions expressed in this chapter are those of the author, and do not necessarily reflect the view of JPMorgan. I would like to thank Andrew Abrahams, Anil Bangia, Kay Giesecke, Peter Rappoport, Philipp Schönbucher, Jakob Sidenius, and Pascal Tomecek for very helpful discussions. If any errors remain, they are my own.

Notes

1. Usually, all constituent names in a homogeneous pool are further assumed to have the same spread, but this assumption is not necessary here.
2. The latter is for bespoke portfolios only, as standardized index portfolios such as CDX or iTraxx are constructed to have the same notional for all of their constituent names.
3. This example is not as contrived as it might seem at the first sight. For example, strong heterogeneity in notionals is rather typical for CDOs referencing pools of commercial mortgage-backed securities (CMBS CDOs).
4. In the sense that their prices are determined by marginal loss distributions at different maturities, rather than a joint distribution of defaults across maturities.
5. The choice of the grid $[T^{(1)}, \ldots, T^{(M)}]$ is determined by the desired resolution in calibration to single-name default probabilities.
6. I want to thank Philipp Schönbucher for showing me formulas nearly identical to equations (5.2), (5.3). While the formalism based on joint probabilities (5.2) turns out to be equivalent to one previously employed in Halperin (2007), which instead uses conditional probabilities (see later in the chapter), I find it convenient to start the exposition by introducing them first.
7. This rule is easy to impose in a Monte Carlo setting; see Halperin and Tomecek (2008) for details.
8. A bottom-up model differs from a top-down one in that the former models filtration $\mathcal{I}_t$ for $t > 0$, while the latter does not. But, as long as information $\mathcal{I}_0$ is observed directly without any need for a model, this means that any expectations conditional on information $\mathcal{I}_0$ can be calculated using a top-down model that completely sidesteps modeling filtration $\mathcal{I}_{t>0}$, without any need for a bottom-up model. This observation will be used later in

our calculation of top-down matrices, single-name sensitivities, and notional and recovery heterogeneities.

9. Some of the results of this section have been previously reported in Halperin (2007).

10. The method was originally developed in 1937 by Kruithof to estimate telephone traffic matrices. For more information on the IS method and its relationship to information theory, see Csiszár (n.d.) and also the following pages.

11. We choose a proportional tweak as another simple one-parametric scheme with an additive tweak $\delta P_{ij} = \varepsilon$, which would lead to nearly equal sensitivities for different names; see a comment after equation (5.39).

12. We note that such a tying of spread shifts to particular shifts of tail probabilities (and hence correlation parameters) is akin to the local volatility approach in equity derivative modeling.

13. Corrections to the right-hand side of this equation are $O(r)$ where r is a short risk-free rate, and thus can be neglected as long as r is small enough.

14. This deficiency of the base correlation model is well known to practitioners.

15. Note that these values of j are easily found as long as we assume a fixed recovery: $j_k = \lfloor \hat{K}_k N \rfloor$.

16. On average, RT sensitivities obtained with prior 2 are in fact somewhat closer to base correlation deltas than those obtained with prior 1, but this difference does not appear significant.

17. Note that probabilities p_n for this portfolio are generally different from the corresponding probabilities obtained for an index portfolio. Finding the correspondence between these two sets amounts to solving the so-called bespoke mapping problem in this particular modeling approach. We do not expand on this topic here, and instead refer the reader to Halperin (2009) and references therein.

18. A related picture is presented in Rappoport and Ghigliazza (2008). I thank Peter Rappoport for a discussion.

References

Andersen, L., and J. Sidenius. 2004. Extensions to the Gaussian copula: Random recovery and random factor loadings. *Journal of Credit Risk* 1:29.

Arnsdorf, M., and I. Halperin. 2008. BSLP: Bivariate spread loss portfolio model, *Journal of Computational Finance* 12:77.

Bielecki, T. R., S. Crépey, and M. Jeanblanc. 2008. Up and down credit risk. Working paper.

Brody, D. C., L. P. Hughston, and A. Macrina. 2007. Beyond hazard rates: A new framework credit-risk modeling. Working paper.

Collin-Dufresne, P., R. Goldstein, and J. Helwege. 2003. Is credit event risk priced? Modeling contagion via the updating of beliefs. Available at www.defaultrisk.com.

Cover, T. M., and J. L. Thomas. 1991. *Elements of Information Theory.* New York: John Wiley & Sons.

Csiszár, I. 1975. I-divergence geometry of probability distributions and minimization problems. *Annals of Probability* 3:146.

Csiszár, I. n.d. Information theoretic methods in probability and statistics. Available at www.itsoc.org/review/01csi.pdf.

Ding, X., K. Giesecke, and P. Tomecek. 2006. Time-changed birth processes and multi-name credit. Working paper.

Errais, E., K. Giesecke, and L. Goldberg. 2006. Pricing credit from top down with affine point processes. Working paper, available at www.defaultrisk.com.

Fog, A. 2008. Sampling methods for Wallenius' and Fisher's noncentral hypergeometric distributions.

Giesecke, K., and L. Goldberg. 2005. A top-down approach to multi-name credit. Available at www .defaultrisk.com.

Giesecke, K., L. Goldberg, and X. Ding. 2009. A top-down approach to multi-name credit. Working paper. This paper is a revision of Giesecke and Goldberg (2005).

Halperin, I. 2007. The "top" and the "down" in credit top-down models. Presented at Credit Risk Summit, New York, November.

Halperin, I. 2009. Implied multi-factor model for bespoke CDO tranches and other portfolio credit derivatives. http://xxx.lanl.gov/abs/0910.2696.

Halperin, I., and P. Tomecek 2008. Climbing down from the top: Single name dynamics in credit top-down models. Working paper, available at http://lanl.arxiv.org/abs/0901.3404.

Ireland, C.T., and S. Kullback. 1968. Contingency tables with given marginals. *Biometrica* 55:179.

Johnson, N.L., S. Kotz, and N. Balakrishnan. 1997. Discrete multivariate distributions. New York: John Wiley & Sons.

Lopatin, A.V., and T. Misirpashaev. 2007. Two-dimensional Markovian model for dynamics of aggregate credit loss. Working paper, available at www.defaultrisk.com.

Manly, B. F. G. 1974. A model for certain types of selection experiments. *Biometrics* 30:281.

McGinty, L., M. Harris, and J. Due. 2005. Delta blues. J.P. Morgan.

O'Kane, D. 2008. *Modelling single name and multi-name credit derivatives*. Hoboken, NJ: John Wiley & Sons.

Rappoport, P., and R. M. Ghigliazza. 2008. Hedging default risk in portfolios of credit tranches. J.P. Morgan, August.

Schönbucher, P. 2003. Information-driven default contagion. Available at www.defaultrisk.com.

Dynamic Hedging of Synthetic CDO Tranches: Bridging the Gap between Theory and Practice

Areski Cousin

Université de Lyon, Université Lyon 1, ISFA

Jean-Paul Laurent*

Université Paris 1 Panthéon-Sorbonne and BNP Paribas

This chapter intends to provide insights about the topical issue of risk managing synthetic collateralized debt obligations (CDOs). We stand in the gray zone between mathematical finance and financial econometrics, between academic and market practitioners' approaches. We chose to first present two scholar models, each of them leading to perfect replication of CDO tranches with credit default swaps (CDSs). Though they rely on rather simplistic assumptions and are built upon different premises, they lead to similar hedge ratios. We also stress that the study of the hedging issue in these two approaches involves the same basic theoretical ingredients. We then discuss various problems related to the use of such models in designing hedging strategies for CDO tranches and back-testing or assessing hedging performance. At this stage, it appears that model-based hedging strategies do help in the risk management process. Even though correlation markets had to face serious tests, more data related to short-term-maturity equity tranche spreads and plain CDSs are required to discriminate against competing modeling approaches.

6.1 Introduction

The theory is when you know everything and nothing works. The practice is when everything works and nobody knows why. We have put together the theory and practice: there is nothing that works . . . and nobody knows why!

—Albert Einstein

---

*The opinions expressed here are those of the author and do not reflect the views of BNP Paribas.

The risk management and the hedging of collateralized debt obligations (CDOs) and related products are topics of tremendous importance, yet much has to be done on both theoretical and empirical grounds. The risks at hand are usually split into different categories that may sometimes overlap, such as credit spread and default risks, correlation and contagion risks. These will be the center of our discussion. This does not mean that these risks are orthogonal; for instance, an increase in credit spreads is likely to increase the occurrence of defaults; due to contagion effects, the arrival of defaults may trigger jumps in credit spreads and changes in the dependence structure between default times; and so on. For simplicity, we focus on the hedging of synthetic CDO tranches on reference indexes such as iTraxx Europe or CDX NA IG. The 2007–2008 crisis also drove attention to liquidity, counterparty risks, and related issues such as recovery risk, collateral management, downgrading of guarantors, and basis risks, which we briefly address. Focus was concentrated on the risks within senior tranches and tail risks. Conversely, the 2005 crisis was driven by some rather specific event, namely the widening of spreads in the automobile sector, and led to some disruptions between equity and junior mezzanine tranches, associated with idiosyncratic gamma risks and unwinding of positive carry trades.

Before going any further with hedging of CDO tranches, we need to account for the way models are used and the reliance on market data. We take as an example the modeling of dependence of default dates of names within a credit portfolio. A quick glance at the literature should convince us that it is a key point in disentangling the hedging puzzle.

Ingenuously, we could think of a probabilistic construction of default times that matches the actual behavior of defaults, spreads, and tranche quotes; we could assume that this probabilistic construction could be perfectly determined and that given some set of well-identified hedging instruments, we would end up with, maybe, a self-financing replicating strategy for CDO tranches. Then, the hedging and risk management puzzle would be solved thanks to good computational skills, and eventually some kind of algorithmic hedging would consecrate the reign of robots and expel from the trading rooms all sorts of quantitative analysts, traders, and risk managers, who are nowadays considered by a number of bright minds as a hybridization of dummies and crooks abusing and misusing mathematics. This would likely be the final stage in the evolutionary process and the end of history as far as credit derivatives are concerned.

Actually, we subsequently describe two scholar models, one belonging to the category of contagion models, the other one to that of structural models, so that *within the model*, perfect hedging strategies of CDO tranches can be computed. This is somehow good news since credit might eventually no longer be the ugly duckling of mathematical finance.

However, when it comes to putting models to work, the issue appears trickier than it looked at first sight and the picture becomes blurred. Let us assume for a while that the ingenuous modeler with superlative skills reaches the holy grail[1] of designing the true probabilistic description of default times. Such a probabilistic model is likely to involve a small set of correlation parameters (say it is a parametric model). There should be some parameters such that CDO tranches of any maturity and attachment and detachment point should be matched at one fell swoop at any time. But, even if we were to restrict to CDO quotes for a given maturity, all parametric models we have in mind fail the perfect calibration test and are thus misspecified.[2] As a consequence, one cannot predict from scratch what would be the hedging performance of such a model, assuming that perfect replication of CDO tranches is meaningful within the model; that is, some form of market completeness is achieved. For instance, the structural model associated with an underlying multivariate Brownian motion would most likely fail to price junior, mezzanine, and senior tranches with some flat correlation matrix.[3] In terms of model specification, this means that the model is rejected with certainty, since it predicts deterministic relationships across prices, which are inconsistent with observed data.

In order to circumvent this issue, the usual way is to relax some assumptions, such as constant correlation, Brownian increments in asset prices, introducing some clustering effects through stochastic volatility.[4] This is not priceless. First, it leads to increased complexity both on numerical grounds and in understanding the relevant dynamics. Then, one might lose some suitable properties of the simpler model, such as the existence of self-financing replicating strategies, which leads to difficulties in designing optimal hedging strategies (in incomplete markets). Parsimony is for sure an important property of a relevant model. When it comes to models where the number of parameters is large, sometimes even larger than the number of liquid calibrating prices, one can rightfully question the usefulness of such an approach. Also, one may feel growing unease looking at this data-driven inference, where the purpose is to find some probability distribution over default times that matches observed data.[5] Looking at the world of defaults through such glasses and entering a risk management process from that premise is a perilous adventure.

The culmination of the inverse problem of model design from market prices leads to some nonparametric approaches, such as the local volatility model in the equity field and its local intensity counterpart in the credit domain (see Cont and Minca 2008; Cont, Deguest, and Kan 2010). This relies on some hidden though not innocuous assumptions such as the absence of simultaneous defaults. Moreover, given some sparse market data, one usually needs to parametrize the local intensity, for instance assuming piecewise linear dependence on the number of defaults. The devil is in this kind of detail since credit deltas may actually greatly depend on such a kind of arbitrary numerical scheme. For instance, when computing a default hedge in a local intensity loss model, one would need to assess the change of the loss intensity after a first default, something that cannot be directly inferred from CDO tranche quotes. It is worth remarking that these implied dynamics are usually associated with a one-dimensional Markov process, which is quite convenient for simplicity but is likely to shrink the risks to be handled.

If one model as just described would be deemed worthy, it should be time consistent. For instance, in the case of a parametric model, calibrated parameters should remain constant over time. As this is never the case, one actually deals with some unknown dynamics, possibly some kind of incompleteness due to jumps in calibrated parameters. It is also likely that implied parameters are actually correlated with the underlying assets, say credit default swap spreads; thus one has to choose to compute either the total or the partial derivative to derive hedge ratios. We just want to stress that given that recalibration process, the possibly desirable properties of the initial theoretical model are likely to be lost.

Moreover, given any model, market practice consists in bumping initial conditions rather than computing derivatives with respect to the underlying assets (assuming a Markovian framework). For instance, when using an intensity model, instead of computing sensitivities with respect to short-term intensities,[6] one will shift the credit curves, recalibrate the model, and look for the changes in the prices of CDO tranches. The computed deltas have little connection, if any, with the theoretical deltas.

Self-financing replicating strategies are usually set up within a theoretical context and, when applied in a market context, have no reason to lead to a replication of the promised payoff. It is not surprising, then, that the corresponding theoretical models are not dealt with by market practitioners according to the theory when it comes to computing hedging ratios. Hedging strategies derived from a hypothetical complete markets framework can be seen as a convenient benchmark for further analysis, but there is no guarantee that these would perform better than a model with poorer theoretical or dynamical properties. This is not to say that financial models are useless; actually, empirical evidence tends to show that model-based hedging outperforms statistically based hedging and leads to a significant reduction in risk. Let us also point out that hedging performance can be dramatically improved whenever a CDO book is statically hedged; that is, CDO tranches are hedged with other similar CDO tranches, and the dynamic hedging with credit default swaps addresses only residual risks.

Trying to encompass such a large topic, we chose to discuss, in a first part, the theory that underpins the two most documented and understood pricing and hedging models as far as CDO tranches are concerned. In a second part, we focus on a number of methodological and implementation issues related to the use of such models.[7]

6.2 Hedging of CDO Tranches: Theoretical Issues and Perspectives

> As far as the laws of mathematics refer to reality, they are not certain. As far as they are certain, they do not refer to reality.
>
> —Albert Einstein

6.2.1 Default Times and Aggregate Loss Process

Throughout this chapter, we consider a credit portfolio with n risky obligors. The corresponding default times $\tau_1, \ldots, \tau_n$ are assumed to be nonnegative and finite random variables defined on a common probability space (Ω, A, P), where P is the historical probability measure. The evolution of default states in the portfolio is driven by default indicator processes $N_t^1 = 1_{\{\tau_1 \leq t\}}, \ldots, N_t^n = 1_{\{\tau_n \leq t\}}$. That is, for any name $i = 1, \ldots, n$, $N_t^i = 1$ if firm i has defaulted before t or $N_t^i = 0$ otherwise.

Let us remark that default times can be reinterpreted in terms of a marked point process—that is, a sequence of ordered credit events $(T_i)_{i \in I}$ satisfying $T_i < T_{i+1}$

associated with some other random elements $(Z_i)_{i \in I}$, called marks, containing further information about defaults, such as the identity of names that have defaulted. In the general case where simultaneous defaults are possible, each mark may contain a set of names and the size of the mark space is possibly equal to 2^n. This has a direct consequence on the completeness of the market, since in that case, the hedging of defaultable claim would require nonstandard instruments whose default payments are contingent to the arrival of joint defaults. Conversely, when simultaneous defaults are precluded, the size of the mark space is reduced to n. In what follows, we consider that the latter assumption is satisfied.

Regarding the pricing of CDO tranches, the key quantity is the fractional cumulative loss process $L_t = \frac{1}{n} \sum_{i=1}^{n} (1 - R_i) N_t^i$, where $R_1, \ldots, R_n$ denote the recovery rates in case of default of names $i = 1, \ldots, n$. The loss process L_t is thus an increasing right-continuous pure jump process.

6.2.2 CDO Tranche Cash Flows

A synthetic CDO tranche is a structured product based on an underlying portfolio of equally weighted reference entities subject to credit risk.[8] The cash flows associated with a synthetic CDO tranche only depend on the realized path of the cumulative losses on the reference portfolio. Default losses on the credit portfolio are split along some thresholds (attachment and detachment points) and allocated to the various tranches. A CDO tranche with attachment point a, detachment point b, and maturity T is essentially a bilateral contract between a protection seller and a protection buyer. We describe later on the cash flows associated with the default payments leg (payments received by the protection buyer) and the premium payments leg (payments received by the protection seller).

6.2.2.1 Default Payments Leg

The protection seller agrees to pay the protection buyer default losses each time they impact the tranche $[a, b]$ of the reference portfolio. More precisely, the cumulative default payment $L_t^{[a,b]}$ on the tranche $[a, b]$ is equal to zero if $L_t \leq a$, to $L_t - a$ if $a \leq L_t \leq b$ and to $b - a$ if $L_t \geq b$. Let us remark that $L_t^{[a,b]}$ has a call spread payoff with respect to L_t and can be expressed as $L_t^{[a,b]} = (L_t - a)^+ - (L_t - b)^+$. Default payments are simply the increment of $L_t^{[a,b]}$; that is, there is a payment of $L_t^{[a,b]} - L_{t-}^{[a,b]}$ from the protection seller at every jump time of $L_t^{[a,b]}$ occurring before contract maturity T. If r_t denotes the continuously compounded default-free interest rate and $B_t = \exp\left(-\int_0^t r_s \, ds\right)$ the associated discount factor, the discounted payoff corresponding to default payments can written as:

$$\int_0^T B_t \, dL_t^{[a,b]} = \sum_{i=1}^{n} B_{\tau_i} \left(L_{\tau_i}^{[a,b]} - L_{\tau_i-}^{[a,b]}\right) 1_{\{\tau_i \leq T\}}$$

6.2.2.2 *Premium Payments Leg*

The protection buyer has to pay the protection seller a periodic premium (quarterly for standardized indexes) based on a fixed spread or premium S and proportional to the current outstanding nominal of the tranche $b - a - L_t^{[a,b]}$. Let us denote by t_i, $i = 1, \ldots, I$ the premium payment dates with $t_I = T$ and by Δ_i the length of the ith period $[t_{i-1}, t_i]$ (in fractions of a year and with $t_0 = 0$). The CDO premium payments are equal to $S\Delta_i\left(b - a - L_{t_i}^{[a,b]}\right)$ at regular payment dates t_i, $i = 1, \ldots, I$. Moreover, when a default occurs between two premium payment dates and when it affects the tranche, an additional payment (the accrued coupon) must be made at default time to compensate the change in value of the tranche outstanding nominal. For example, if name j defaults between t_{i-1} and t_i, the associated accrued coupon is equal to $S\left(\tau_j - t_{i-1}\right)\left(L_{\tau_j}^{[a,b]} - L_{\tau_j-}^{[a,b]}\right)$. Eventually, the discounted payoff corresponding to premium payments can be expressed as:

$$\sum_{i=1}^{I}\left(B_{t_i} S\Delta_i\left(b - a - L_{t_i}^{[a,b]}\right) + \int_{t_{i-1}}^{t_i} B_t S\left(t - t_{i-1}\right) dL_t^{[a,b]}\right)$$

6.2.3 Filtration

A CDO tranche position is typically hedged by entering opposite positions on a portfolio of liquid hedging instruments such as credit default swaps referencing names in the reference portfolio. Other examples of hedging instruments are credit default swaps standardized indexes or standard tranches referencing these indexes. The composition of the hedging portfolio needs to be regularly adjusted as the market environment quickly evolves. In order to tackle the hedging issue in a dynamical way, one needs to specify how information is progressively disclosed to the market.

We first investigate the framework of contagion intensity models for which the hedging of CDO tranches can be fully described in a dynamical way. In a second step, we try to establish some connections with other hedging approaches.

As we consider the hedging of CDO tranches whose cash flows are driven by the realization of defaults in the portfolio, the smallest filtration one shall consider may include information associated with the arrival of defaults. Let us denote by $H_t^i = \sigma\left(N_s^i, s \leq t\right)$, $i = 1, \ldots, n$, $H_t = \bigvee_{i=1}^{n} H_{i,t}$. The filtration $(H_t)_{t \in \mathbb{R}^+}$ is referred to as the natural filtration associated with the default times.

We moreover assume that there exist some (P, H_t)-intensities associated with the counting processes N_t^i, $i = 1, \ldots, n$; that is, there exist some (nonnegative) H_t-predictable processes $\alpha^{1,P}, \ldots, \alpha^{n,P}$, such that the processes defined by:

$$M_t^{i,P} := N_t^i - \int_0^t \alpha_s^{i,P} ds, \quad i = 1, \ldots, n$$

are (P, H_t)-martingales. This implies in particular that, for any name $i = 1, \ldots, n$, the default intensity process $\alpha^{i,P}$ must vanish after the default of name i; that is, $\alpha_t^{i,P} = 0$ on the set $\{t > \tau_i\}$. Let us recall that simultaneous defaults are precluded in this framework; that is, $P\left(\tau_i = \tau_j\right) = 0$ for $i \neq j$.

6.2.4   Predictable Representation Theorem and Equivalent Changes of Probability Measure

The main theoretical tool for the analysis of the hedging issue is a predictable representation theorem (see Brémaud 1981, Chapter 3). It states that, for any H_T-measurable P-integrable random variable A, there exists some H_t-predictable processes $\theta^1, \ldots, \theta^n$ such that:

$$A = E^P[A] + \sum_{i=1}^n \int_0^T \theta_s^i \left(dN_s^i - \alpha_s^{i,P} ds\right).$$

This result provides a way to express any default-contingent payoff as a sum of stochastic integrals with respect to the fundamental martingales $M_t^{i,P}$, $i = 1, \ldots, n$.

Interestingly, it can also be used to characterize equivalent changes of probability measure. From the predictable representation theorem, one can show that any Radon-Nikodym derivative ζ (i.e., a strictly positive martingale with expectation equal to 1) can be written as:

$$d\zeta_t = \zeta_{t-} \sum_{i=1}^n \pi_t^i dM_t^{i,P}, \quad \zeta_0 = 1$$

where $\pi^1, \ldots, \pi^n$ are some H_t-predictable processes. Conversely, the unique solution of the latter stochastic differential equation is the local martingale (Doléans-Dade exponential):

$$\zeta_t = \exp\left(-\sum_{i=1}^n \int_0^t \pi_s^i \alpha_s^{i,P} ds\right) \prod_{i=1}^n \left(1 + \pi_{\tau_i}^i\right)^{N_t^i}$$

Note that, in order that ζ is indeed a nonnegative local martingale, one needs that $\pi_t^i > -1$. Moreover, the process ζ is a true martingale under some integrability conditions on the π^i's (e.g., $\pi^1, \ldots, \pi^n$ bounded) or if $E^P[\zeta_t] = 1$ for any t. We can now define a new probability measure Q from P thanks to the Radon-Nikodym derivative ζ:

$$dQ\big|_{H_t} = \zeta_t dP\big|_{H_t}$$

Eventually, it can be proved that under this new probability measure Q the default intensity $\alpha^{i,Q}$ of τ_i is proportional to the default intensity $\alpha^{i,P}$ of τ_i under P. More precisely, for any name $i = 1, \ldots, n$ the process $M^{i,Q}$ defined by:

$$M_t^{i,Q} := N_t^i - \int_0^t \left(1 + \pi_s^i\right) \alpha_s^{i,P} ds$$

is a (Q, H_t)-martingale. We refer the reader to Cousin, Jeanblanc, and Laurent (2010) for more details on the construction of equivalent changes of probability measure in this framework.

6.2.5 Hedging Instruments

For the sake of simplicity, let us assume for a while that instantaneous digital credit default swaps are traded on the names. An instantaneous digital credit default swap on name i traded at t, provides a payoff equal to $dN_t^i - \alpha_t^i dt$ at $t + dt$. The quantity dN_t^i corresponds to the payment on the default leg, and $\alpha_t^i dt$ is the (short-term) premium on the default swap. Note that considering such instantaneous digital default swaps rather than actually traded credit default swaps is not a limitation of our purpose. This can rather be seen as a convenient choice of basis from a theoretical point of view.[9]

We assume that contractual spreads $\alpha^1, \ldots, \alpha^n$ are nonnegative processes adapted to the filtration H_t of default times. The natural filtration of default times can thus be seen as the relevant information on economic grounds. Since we deal with the filtration generated by default times, the credit default swap premiums are deterministic between two default events. Therefore, we restrain ourselves to a market where only default risk occurs and credit spreads themselves are driven by the occurrence of defaults. In our simple setting, there is no specific credit spread risk. This corresponds to the framework of Bielecki, Jeanblanc, and Rutkowski (2007) and Bielecki, Crépey, Jeanblanc, and Rutkowski (2007).

For simplicity, we further assume that (continuously compounded) default-free interest rates are constant and equal to r. Given some initial investment V_0 and some H_t-predictable processes $\delta^1, \ldots, \delta^n$ associated with some self-financed trading strategy in instantaneous digital credit default swaps, we attain at time T the payoff $V_0 e^{rT} + \sum_{i=1}^n \int_0^T \delta_s^i e^{r(T-s)} \left(dN_s^i - \alpha_s^i ds\right)$. By definition, δ_s^i is the nominal amount of instantaneous digital credit default swap on name i held at time s. This induces a net cash flow of $\delta_s^i \times \left(dN_s^i - \alpha_s^i ds\right)$ at time $s + ds$, which has to be invested in the default-free savings account up to time T.

6.2.6 Pricing Measure and Perfect Hedging

We define a pricing measure as a probability measure Q equivalent to P and such that, under Q, the default intensities associated with default times are exactly equal to the short-term credit spreads $\alpha^1, \ldots, \alpha^n$. From the previous analysis on equivalent changes of probability measure, one can readily describe the (unique) pricing measure.

First, it is natural to assume that $\left\{\alpha_t^i > 0\right\} \overset{P-a.s.}{=} \left\{\alpha_t^{i,P} > 0\right\}$ for all time t and all name $i = 1, \ldots, n$. Indeed, from the absence of arbitrage opportunity, the short-term premium on a given name i at any date t is positive ($\alpha_t^i > 0$) if and only if the default of that name is likely to occur at time t ($\alpha_t^{i,P} > 0$). As a consequence, for any $i = 1, \ldots, n$, the process π^i defined by:

$$\pi_t^i = \left(\frac{\alpha_t^i}{\alpha_t^{i,P}} - 1\right)\left(1 - N_{t-}^i\right)$$

is a H-predictable process such that $\pi^i > -1$.

Second, following the previous analysis, the process ζ defined by:

$$\zeta_t = \exp\left(-\sum_{i=1}^{n}\int_0^t \pi_s^i \alpha_s^{i,P} ds\right)\prod_{i=1}^{n}\left(1 + \pi_{\tau_i}^i\right)^{N_t^i}$$

is a true Radon-Nikodym derivative. Moreover, under the probability Q built from P thanks to the equivalent change of probability measure $dQ\big|_{H_t} = \zeta_t dP\big|_{H_t}$, the processes:

$$M_t^i := N_t^i - \int_0^t \alpha_s^i ds, \quad i = 1, \ldots, n$$

are (Q, H_t)-martingales. In particular, the short-term credit spreads $\alpha^1, \ldots, \alpha^n$ are the intensities of default times under the new probability Q. Given a specification of default intensities under the historical probability measure P, it is important to remark that the pricing measure is uniquely determined by the dynamics of short-term credit spreads. In the rest of the study, we will work under the pricing measure Q.

Unsurprisingly, the possibility of perfect hedging is related to a martingale representation theorem under the pricing measure. Let us consider some H_T-measurable Q-integrable payoff A. Since A depends on the default indicators of the names up to time T, this encompasses the cases of CDO tranches and basket default swaps, provided that recovery rates are deterministic.[10] It is possible to show that the predictable representation theorem described earlier also holds under the probability Q. There exists some H_t-predictable processes $\theta^1, \ldots, \theta^n$ such that:

$$A = E^Q[A] + \sum_{i=1}^{n}\int_0^T \theta_s^i\left(dN_s^i - \alpha_s^i ds\right)$$

Let us remark that, due to the predictable property of the θ's, the processes defined by $t \to \int_0^t \theta_s^i \left(dN_s^i - \alpha_s^i ds \right)$ are also (Q, H_t)-martingales. As a consequence,

$$A = E^Q\left[A|\, H_t\right] + \sum_{i=1}^{n} \int_t^T \theta_s^i \left(dN_s^i - \alpha_s^i ds \right)$$

The latter expression can be interpreted in the following way. Starting from t, one can replicate the payoff A with the initial investment $V_t = E^Q\left[e^{-r(T-t)}A|\, H_t\right]$ (in the savings account) and the trading strategy based on instantaneous digital credit default swaps defined by $\delta_s^i = \theta_s^i e^{-r(T-s)}$ for $0 \le s \le T$ and $i = 1, \ldots, n$. As there is no charge to enter an instantaneous digital credit default swap, $V_t = E^Q\left[e^{-r(T-t)}A|\, H_t\right]$ corresponds to the time t replication price of the claim A.

Let us remark that it is theoretically possible to build up a replication strategy based on actually traded credit default swaps. Thanks to the predictable representation theorem, one can express the dynamics of credit default swaps in terms of the dynamics of instantaneous digital CDSs. The next step consists of inverting a linear system to obtain the representation of any H_T-measurable payoff with respect to the dynamics of actually traded CDSs. The reader is referred to the first chapter of Cousin, Jeanblanc, and Laurent (2009) for a thorough presentation of this method in the case of two names. Interestingly, as explained in Cousin and Jeanblanc (2010), the dynamics of portfolio loss derivatives can be fully described using the dynamics of the underlying CDSs when default times are assumed to be ordered. In this particular case, the hedging strategies can be computed explicitly in a general n-dimensional framework.

While the use of the predictable representation theorem guarantees that, in our framework, any basket default swap can be perfectly hedged with respect to default risks, it does not provide a practical way of constructing hedging strategies. As is the case with interest rate or equity derivatives, exhibiting hedging strategies involves some Markovian assumptions.

6.2.7 Computation of Hedging Strategies in a Homogeneous Markovian Setting

When going to implementing actual hedging strategies, one needs extra assumptions, both for the implementation to be feasible and to cope with quoted CDO tranches. We therefore consider the simplest way to specialize the aforementioned model: we assume that all risk-neutral predefault intensities are equal and only depend on the current number of defaults; that is,

$$\alpha_t^i = \bar{\alpha}\,(t, N_t)\, 1_{\{t < \tau_i\}}, \quad i = 1, \ldots, n$$

where $N_t = \sum_{i=1}^{n} N_t^i$ denotes the total number of defaults that have occurred in the portfolio up to time t. We also assume that all recovery rates are constant across names and time. As a consequence, the loss process is merely proportional to the number of defaults process N_t whose intensity is simply equal to the predefault intensity times the number of nondefaulted names:

$$\lambda\,(t,\,N_t) = (n - N_t)\,\bar{\alpha}\,(t,\,N_t)$$

In that framework, it can be shown that the aggregate loss process is a continuous-time Markov chain, more precisely a pure death process (thanks to the no simultaneous defaults assumption) with generator matrix:

$$\Lambda(t) = \begin{pmatrix} -\lambda(t,0) & \lambda(t,0) & 0 & 0 & 0 \\ 0 & -\lambda(t,1) & \lambda(t,1) & 0 & 0 \\ & & \ddots & \ddots & \\ 0 & 0 & 0 & -\lambda(t,n-1) & \lambda(t,n-1) \\ 0 & 0 & 0 & 0 & 0 \end{pmatrix}$$

Moreover, the replication price of a European-type CDO tranche payoff $\Phi\,(N_T)$ can be written as $V\,(t,\,k) = E\left[e^{-r(T-t)}\Phi\,(N_T)\,|\,N_t = k\right]$ and solves the backward Kolmogorov differential equations:

$$\frac{\partial V(t,\,k)}{\partial t} = r\,V(t,\,k) - \lambda(t,\,k)\,(V(t,\,k+1) - V(t,\,k)),\quad k = 0,\dots,n-1$$

Regarding the hedging issue, homogeneous Markovian models are appealing because replication strategies are the same for all (nondefaulted) names, which results in a dramatic dimensionality reduction. In that case, it is enough to consider the index portfolio as a single hedging instrument, which is consistent with some market practices. If we denote by $V^I\,(t,\,N_t) = E\left[e^{-r(T-t)}\Phi^I\,(N_T)\,|\,N_t\right]$ the time t replication price of the CDS index (European-type payoff), then by standard Itô's calculus, one can show that:

$$dV(t,\,N_t) = \delta^I(t,\,N_t)dV^I(t,\,N_t) + \left(V(t,\,N_t) - \delta^I(t,\,N_t)V^I(t,\,N_t)\right)r\,dt$$

where

$$\delta^I(t,\,N_t) = \frac{V(t,\,N_t + 1) - V(t,\,N_t)}{V^I(t,\,N_t + 1) - V^I(t,\,N_t)}$$

is the credit delta (i.e., the proportion of the self-financing hedging portfolio invested in the CDS index). In other words, the change in value of a CDO tranche in a short period $[t,\,t+dt]$ can be fully replicated by holding at time t a position $\delta^I(t,\,N_t)$ in the CDS index, for a total value of $\delta^I(t,\,N_t)V^I(t,\,N_t)$, and by investing the remaining part of the portfolio value, $V(t,\,N_t) - \delta^I(t,\,N_t)V^I(t,\,N_t)$, in the risk-free asset. The numerical implementation of hedging strategies can be achieved in a more realistic case through a binomial tree as detailed in Laurent, Cousin, and Fermanian (2007) or by means of Markov chain techniques.

Eventually, we have built up a complete market model in which CDO tranche prices can be fully replicated by dynamically trading the CDS index and the risk-free asset, and the associated hedging strategies can be derived explicitly. On practical grounds, another nice feature of the model concerns the estimation of model parameters from CDO tranche market quotes. As described in Laurent et al. (2007), the knowledge of up-front premiums of equity CDO tranches with different maturities and detachment points (and given some recovery rate) is equivalent to the knowledge of marginal distributions of the number of defaults at different time horizons. Thanks to the forward Kolmogorov equations, one can then perfectly compute the intensities of the aggregate loss process or the predefault intensities. Such a fully calibrated and Markov model is also known as the local intensity model. This parallels the local volatility approach of Dupire (1994) in the equity derivatives context where the dynamics of underlying assets are driven by a diffusion process as opposed to a finite-state Markov chain in the case of credit portfolio derivatives. As in local volatility models, local intensity models allow for a perfect match of unknown parameters from a complete set of CDO tranches quotes. In this context, Cont, Deguest, and Kan (2010) have computed an analogue, for credit portfolio derivatives, of Dupire's well-known formula. This is based, however, on the (rather hidden) assumption of no simultaneous defaults.

Another promising approach regarding hedging in a Markovian environment is the Markov copula approach developed by Bielecki, Vidozzi, and Vidozzi (2008). In this fully dynamic bottom-up framework, default indicators form a multivariate Markov process. The important point is that each individual default indicator is assumed to be a Markov process (in its own filtration). Under the latter assumption, there is no contagion effect in the sense that the default of a given name does not yield a change in the default intensities of the nondefaulted names. However, as this is also the case in common-shocks models, defaults may occur simultaneously.[11] The latter assumption is crucial on practical grounds, since it allows the calibration of model parameters to be dealt with exactly the same way as in a standard static copula setup. Indeed, the calibration process can be performed in two separate steps. First, individual default intensities can be precalibrated on single-name CDS curves, and second, dependence parameters (intensities of joint defaults) can be fitted on CDO tranche quotes. Bielecki, Cousin, Crépey, and Herbertsson (2010) provide a common-shocks model interpretation of this framework so that efficient convolution recursion procedures are also available for pricing and hedging static basket instruments like CDO tranches. Additionally, the Markovian structure of the model allows one to address the hedging issue in a dynamic and theoretically consistent way.

Until now, we have considered that credit spreads are driven by defaults and we have stressed that this feature leads to a complete CDO tranche market where the hedging can be fully described in a dynamic way. We will now use the same methodology to analyze the hedging issue in a completely different framework where spreads and defaults are both driven by a multivariate diffusion process. This corresponds to a multivariate extension of the Black-Cox (1976) structural model.

6.2.8 Hedging Credit Portfolio Derivatives in Multivariate Structural Models

One may compare the previous framework with the standard structural approach, where default time of a given name is defined as the first hitting time of a barrier by a geometric Brownian motion associated with the asset process of the corresponding name. Hull, Predescu, and White (2005) investigate the pricing of CDO tranches within a Gaussian multivariate structural model, similar to the one presented in this section. Let $(W_t)_{t \geq 0}$, $W_t = \left(W_t^1, \ldots, W_t^n \right)$ be an n-dimensional Brownian motion whose components are correlated by the same dependence parameter ρ; that is, for any $i \neq j$, $\left\langle W^i, W^j \right\rangle_t = \rho t$. We denote by $\left(F_t^i \right)_{t \geq 0}$ the natural filtration associated with W^i, $i = 1, \ldots, n$ and $(F_t)_{t \geq 0}$, $F_t = \vee_{i=1}^n F_t^i$ the natural filtration associated with W. For any firm $i = 1, \ldots, n$, we consider that the asset value A^i follows a nonnegative diffusion process under the historical probability measure P; that is,

$$\frac{dA_t^i}{A_t^i} = \mu_i dt + \sigma_i dW_t^i, \quad i = 1, \ldots, n$$

where the expected rate of return $\mu = (\mu_i)_{1 \leq i \leq n}$ and the diffusion rate $\sigma = (\sigma_i)_{0 \leq i \leq n}$ are real-valued column vectors. In this framework, the default times are defined by $\tau_i = \inf \left\{ t \geq 0 \, \middle| \, A_t^i \leq b_i \right\}$, where b_i denotes the threshold associated with firm i. In that structural model, dependence between default times stems from the correlation between the asset values. For calibration of default probabilities over different time horizons, however, the barrier needs to be time dependent, which does not change the main features of the model.

Roughly speaking, the value of assets for a given firm i can be replicated by holding the debt and the equity part of its liabilities, which can both be seen as tradable securities. This legitimates, at least on theoretical grounds, the role of the firm's assets as primary hedging instruments in this framework. Using a multivariate extension of the Girsanov's theorem for correlated Brownian motion, it is possible to define a pricing measure Q, equivalent to the historical probability measure P, and such that discounted asset values are Q-martingales. Moreover, the latter change of probability measure does not perturb the dependence structure among dynamics of asset values. More specifically, the new Brownian motions $\tilde{W}^1, \ldots, \tilde{W}^n$ driving the dynamics of $A^1, \ldots, A^n$ under the probability Q are still correlated with the same dependence parameter ρ; that is, for any $i \neq j$, $\left\langle \tilde{W}^i, \tilde{W}^j \right\rangle_t = \rho t$. Furthermore, it is well known that the completeness of the market is guaranteed in this framework as far as the correlation matrix of W involving parameters $\sigma_1, \ldots, \sigma_n$ and ρ is invertible. One can then perfectly replicate any F_T-measurable payoff by holding a self-financing portfolio composed of the firm's assets $A^1, \ldots, A^n$ and the risk-free asset.

In this first-passage structural model, the cash flows of credit default swaps written on name $i = 1, \ldots, n$ can be synthesized as a combination of barrier options. Indeed, the cash flows on the default leg are the same as the ones of a down-and-in barrier option with a fixed loss payment at the time when the value of assets falls below the prespecified threshold. As for the premium leg, it can be replicated using a set of down-and-out barrier options with maturity dates equal to premium payment dates. It is then possible to relate the replicating price of a credit default swap to replicating prices of barrier options. Clearly, the price of a CDS written on a given name i is a Markov process with respect to the natural filtration associated with $\tilde{W}^i$ since the cash flows are only driven by the dynamics of $\tilde{W}^i$. As a result, the dynamics of CDS i only involves the dynamics of $\tilde{W}^i$.

Credit default swaps are described here as derivative instruments, but they can be used to dynamically hedge more complex products such as CDO tranches. This process relies on the building of a self-financing portfolio including the risk-free asset and the dividend-bearing credit default swaps. Once the dynamics of each individual CDS has been found, it is straightforward to describe the dynamics of the replicating portfolio, given some prespecified hedging strategies (predictable processes).

The hedging of the CDO tranche price is then theoretically feasible thanks to the predictable representation theorem for multivariate Brownian martingales that holds under the pricing measure Q.[12] Let us consider some F_T-measurable Q-integrable payoff A. This typically includes the payoff of CDO tranches or basket default swaps[13] maturing at date T. Then there exists some F_t-predictable processes $\theta^1, \ldots, \theta^n$ such that:

$$A = E^Q[A\,|F_t] + \sum_{j=1}^{n} \int_t^T \theta_s^j \, d\tilde{W}_s^j$$

Hence, the dynamics of CDO tranche prices can be described in terms of the dynamics of the correlated Brownian motions $\tilde{W}^1, \ldots, \tilde{W}^n$. Theoretically, the hedging strategies can be found by identifying the Brownian terms in the dynamics of the replicating portfolio and in the dynamics of CDO tranche prices.[14]

Let us note that when a default event occurs, the hedging position in the corresponding CDS is used to cover the loss. Then, from that time, the hedging portfolio contains one fewer CDS than before. But, since future cash flows of CDO tranches are driven by the possible defaults of the nondefaulted names, CDSs are no longer required for hedging after extinction. This feature should be captured by the hedging strategies computed in this framework.

On practical grounds, one can remark that prices of credit default swaps and CDO tranches are Markovian processes in this framework and, by Feynman-Kac's theorem, they are also solutions of particular partial differential equations (PDEs).[15]

While the former Markov chain approach focused on default risk, neglecting credit spread risk, the structural approach deals with credit spread risk only. Default times are predictable stopping times with respect to the Brownian filtration and do not constitute an extra source of risk. Finally, the structural approach defines a complete CDO tranche market governed by spread risk, and in that sense it can be seen as the dual counterpart of the Markovian contagion approach.

Fermanian and Vigneron (2009) tackle the problem from a slightly different perspective. Starting from a one-factor Gaussian copula model, they are able to specify the dynamics of zero coupon CDSs (or equivalently conditional survival probabilities) that leads to perfect replication of European-type payoffs. Unsurprisingly, the completeness of the market is guaranteed when the correlation parameter used in the one-factor Gaussian copula model corresponds to the correlation between Brownian motion driving the dynamics of zero coupon CDSs. Subsequently, they attempt to relate their framework with the multivariate extension of the structural model presented earlier, but numerical investigation in that case seems to be cumbersome and is postponed for further research. Using market quotes of CDO tranches on recent series of iTraxx and CDX main indexes, they instead perform a back-test investigation of correlation parameters (called break-even correlation) that would have been plugged in the one-factor Gaussian copula model in order to perfectly replicate a CDO tranche with the underlying single-name CDS, given a spread scenario. This method is a first step toward the practical implementation of hedging strategies in a complete market model driven by credit spread risks.

Multivariate structural models are consistent with popular dynamic credit risk models such as CreditMetrics and Moody's KMV. They permit one to deal with joint credit migration (changes of credit ratings) among a wide range of names and with stochastic recovery, following the lines of Krekel (2008). Clearly, the multivariate Gaussian assumption is simplistic and questionable, but as in the previous Markov chain it allows one to derive unambiguous self-financing replicating strategies for CDO tranches.

6.2.9   Comparison with Other Approaches

We have presented a dual view of complete market models, the former focusing on default risks and the latter concentrating on credit spread risks. The nature of default times differs from one case to the other. In the former, default times are totally inaccessible stopping times, whereas in the latter case, default times are predictable. Given these two scholar models, we will set out the main theoretical features of hedging CDO tranches, bringing to light whatever the underlying model might be. We will also try to highlight the commonalities (if any) between the approaches.

6.2.9.1   Filtration

A first issue is related to the choice of filtration. In order to deal with the hedging issue in a consistent dynamical way, one must start with the specification of a filtration. However, there are several ways of defining the information flow that is available to the modeler.

Enlargement of Filtration

A first approach (generally associated with reduced-form models) involves a reference or background filtration, generally driven by a jump-diffusion process, which captures the evolution of some macroeconomic factors or prices of default-free assets. An important point is that the background filtration does not provide enough information to predict with certainty at a given date whether the default of a name occurs. In other words, default times are not stopping times with respect to the background filtration. One needs some extra information to predict defaults. A natural idea is to expand this initial filtration with the flow of information provided by the dynamics of defaults. This is referred to as the progressive enlargement of filtration technique, which has been extensively studied in the literature. An important issue associated with this technique is the so-called immersion property or H-hypothesis under which martingales in the reference filtration remain martingales in the global enlarged filtration. Indeed, to preclude arbitrage opportunities in the default-free market, discounted default-free asset prices are assumed to be martingales with respect to the reference filtration (under a risk-neutral measure). Under the H-hypothesis, the no-arbitrage property is preserved in the global filtration, which is the case only in very particular situations. This has been pointed out by Jeanblanc and Le Cam (2009) in a single-name setting or by Bielecki, Crépey, and Jeanblanc (2010) for top-down credit risk models. For instance, it is well known that the H-hypothesis is satisfied in a single-name Cox model where the default time corresponds to the first jump instant of a doubly stochastic Poisson process. This is also the case in some very particular multivariate extensions of the latter framework where default times are assumed to be independent or ordered as shown in Ehlers and Schönbucher (2009).

Direct Specification of the Entire Set of Information

Another interesting and promising approach is the one proposed by Hitier and Huber (2009). This construction follows the opposite direction from the previous approach. Hitier and Huber (2009) consider a filtration for which default times are totally inaccessible stopping times and admit default intensities adapted to this filtration. Using the terminology of Jeanblanc and Le Cam (2007), this corresponds to an "intensity-based approach" as opposed to the previous enlargement of filtration approach, also called the "hazard process approach." The idea is then to divide the initial filtration into two subfiltrations, the first being associated with a background intensity process independent of default events, and the second being driven by defaults. They, however, assume that the background intensities are equal to the initial intensities before the arrival of the corresponding default and show that this hypothesis is implied by the classical H-hypothesis. An alternative route (generally associated with structural models) is to start with a filtration under which default times are predictable stopping times (or at least accessible, i.e., not totally inaccessible). This is typically the case for jump-diffusion structural models for which the initial filtration contains information associated with the asset value process and possibly related to a random barrier.

Alteration or Reduction of the Initial Set of Information

However, it is reasonable to assume that CDS or bond investors do not have the same information set as firm managers. Starting from a structural approach, there are several ways of specifying how the information set can be altered or obscured. Duffie and Lando (2001) build up the investor's filtration by first adding noise to the asset value process and sampling this noisy information set at some particular discrete dates. Goldberg and Giesecke (2004) start with a random-barrier structural model and assume that the threshold level is not known by the investor. Çetin, Jarrow, Protter, and Yildirim (2004) assume that the investor observes only whether the firm's cash flows are positive or negative. In the approach by Guo, Jarrow, and Zeng (2005), the asset value is available only at some discrete dates and with an additional delay or lag. In all the latter approaches, it is assumed that the investor can also observe the default event. As a consequence, the set of information available to the investor is defined by the smallest filtration containing the set of altered information and such that default times are stopping times. Interestingly, under this coarser filtration, default times are totally inaccessible stopping times and admit default intensities yielding to a reduced-form modeling approach. As we fall into the class of the reduced-form approach, a natural investigation is to check whether the immersion property holds. When the asset value process is obscured by a diffusion process, this is effectively the case, as shown in Coculescu, Geman, and Jeanblanc (2008). The reader is referred to Jarrow and Protter (2004) for a detailed analysis of the link between structural and reduced-form models in the case of incomplete information.

Whatever techniques are used to specify how information is dynamically disclosed to the modeler, default times are finally always defined as stopping times with respect to a given filtration. However, depending on the modeler's access to the overall information, default times can be either predictable, totally inaccessible stopping times but also stopping times that are neither predictable nor totally inaccessible (as is the case, for instance, for jump-diffusion structural models where negative jumps can impact firms assets' dynamics).

6.2.9.2 Martingale Representation Theorem and Completeness of the Market

The existence of a martingale representation theorem is a key ingredient regarding the hedging issue. Given a model specification (i.e., introduction of an underlying probability measure, description of sources of randomness, and construction of an information set), it provides a nice representation of martingale processes in terms of fundamental elementary martingales such as Brownian motions or compensated (marked) point processes. More precisely, it states that the dynamics of any martingale process can be expressed as a linear combination of some fundamental martingales, the weights being associated with some predictable processes. In particular, it allows one to represent the dynamics of any contingent claim in terms of the dynamics of the fundamental martingales. The martingale representation theorem is thus the right mathematical tool to study the completeness of the market model.

6.2.9.3 Hedging Instruments

Another common ingredient associated with the hedging issue concerns the specification of tradable hedging instruments. Let us note, obviously, that the question of the market completeness has to be addressed in connection with both the specification of a market model and the description of some liquid hedging instruments. Typically, one could think of credit index default swaps or CDSs on names with possibly different maturities, standardized synthetic single-tranche CDOs. However, to simplify the theoretical analysis, it is often convenient to assume in a first stage that stylized default-contingent products are traded in the market, provided that actually traded hedging instruments can be fully replicated using these simplified products.

6.2.9.4 Change of Probability Measure

The natural way of defining a credit risk model is to start with the construction of default times under the physical probability measure. However, when arbitrage opportunities are precluded, one can find an equivalent probability measure, also called pricing or risk-neutral measure, under which discounted prices of (non-dividend-bearing) primary assets are martingales. This is very convenient on both practical and theoretical grounds. The pricing measure is built up thanks to an equivalent change of probability measure involving a Radon-Nikodym density similar to the one involved in the classical Girsanov's theorem. However, Coculescu, Jeanblanc, and Nikeghbali (2007) show that in an intensity model the immersion property is not preserved by an equivalent change of probability measure, which may explain why in so many approaches the model is directly specified under a given risk-neutral measure.

6.3 From Theory to Hedging Effectiveness

> In theory, theory and practice are the same. In practice, they are not.
>
> —Albert Einstein

Starting from the simplest case of a complete market and either Markov chain or structural models, we have tried to show that most multivariate models of defaults involve more or less the same basis ingredients, though we still lack a simple-to-state and comprehensive mathematical framework.

Rather than concentrating on the internal features of a pricing (and possibly hedging) model, such as the relevant filtrations, conditional default probabilities, aggregate loss, or credit spread dynamics, we should think of the outcomes of a hedging model for CDO tranches. These are rather simple: a set of hedging instruments, CDSs in most cases (sometimes other CDO tranches are also considered), and hedge ratios with respect to the hedging instruments. A key point is that the outputs are the same—for instance, in the structural or in the Markov chain models described earlier. Thus, it will be possible to derive some comparisons between models built upon different premises, for instance their ability to reduce the risk of a CDO tranche through a dynamic trading strategy. This will lead to back-testing approaches, and it turns out to be an econometric rather than a theoretical issue.

More precisely, a pricing and hedging model is usually associated with a parametrized set of trading strategies and, to proceed with any comparison, we must specify how the parameters (for instance, some correlation or contagion parameters) are set and updated. As will be discussed, such a choice is likely of first importance with respect to hedging performance, though such calibration or estimation of hedging parameters is usually neglected in theoretical approaches.

We do not claim that pricing is irrelevant with respect to the hedging problem. Usually, pricing models are calibrated on liquid market quotes.[16] Then, such a calibrated model can be used in a predictive way. If we assume that the implied parameters—say, correlation parameters for base tranches—are constant over some (short) time interval or evolve according to some predefined rule, then, given some new quotes of underlying CDSs (say), one should be able to predict the change in market value of a tranche and thus the required amount of hedging CDSs. Thus, pricing models that are associated with implied parameters with smooth patterns over time are likely to be useful for risk management purposes, too. The same line of reasoning will be detailed later when considering the connection between hedging and the pricing of bespoke CDO tranches.

Going further along these general statements, we also recall that any pricing and hedging model associated with perfect replication will be rejected by data with probability one: First, such models are associated with nonnoisy relationships between CDO tranches. Then, completeness precludes any hedging residual. We thus deal with misspecified models and should not consider such misspecification as a rejection a priori of a pricing and risk management framework. We should rather focus on the degree of misspecification, as, for instance, assessed by hedging performance.[17]

Another important practical topic is related to stability of hedging performance over different periods and under different economic regimes or market contexts. Certainly, one would most likely choose an all-roader that could cope with both the idiosyncratic auto crisis of 2005 and the systemic crisis of 2007–2009. This view is also related to a stationary world and objective probabilities, which is rather comfortable but is also questionable when dealing with financial markets. The notion of regimes of volatility, which has been popularized by Derman (1999) in equity markets, might also be applicable in correlation markets. Clearly, identifying the relevant regime is an issue, but it seems a rather unrealistic objective that a simple-to-implement hedging strategy would supersede its competitors in any context.[18]

The preceding remarks may look thought-provocative from the standard mathematical finance and modeling point of view. We do not claim that a model does not need to rely on understandable, sound, and clear economic intuition and internal consistency. But looking for the perfect fit leads to extra implementation costs, blurs the key and ancillary features, obscures internal and external communication about risk management, and increases operational risks.

This is why we deliberately favored the multivariate structural model and the Markovian loss models.[19] Both allow the derivation of replicating strategies of CDO tranches. Calibration is, at least at first sight, rather easy. Moreover, the one-factor Gaussian copula has become the standard model, as measured by market acceptance, for pricing and hedging purposes (see Finger 2009). From Hull, Predescu, and White (2005) or Cousin and Laurent (2008a), we know that the Gaussian copula dependence is quite similar to the one that comes out of the multivariate structural model: At least for investment-grade names, default is not likely to occur shortly after inception. The Gaussian copula might be viewed as a one-step version of the multivariate structural model. Thus, deltas with respect to underlying CDSs are likely to be quite similar in the two approaches. We will follow thereafter this route.[20] Since deltas associated with the multivariate structural model are well understood and lead to perfect replication of CDO tranches when concentrating on spread risk (defaults are predictable), we can think of deltas coming out of the Gaussian copula model to have some economic significance.[21] As discussed earlier, Fermanian and Vigneron (2009) propose a different approach. They look for some dynamic models consistent with the credit spread deltas obtained from the Gaussian copula model.

6.3.1   Hedging with CDO Tranches

> If you want to know the value of a security, use the price of another security that is as similar to it as possible. All the rest is modeling.
>
> —Emanuel Derman

Hedging of CDO tranches with other tranches on similar underlying portfolios with close attachment-detachment points and maturities is likely to be the more efficient and least costly way of pricing and risk-managing a book. To go a bit further, we could speak of spatial versus dynamic hedging. To properly implement such a static hedging, some kind of metrics or proximity between payoffs is required, and this usually involves a model. For instance, given a joint distribution of default times in a bottom-up model, one might use a set of liquid CDO tranches to minimize the ℓ_2-norm hedging error within a book of bespoke tranches.[22]

One could proceed with a linear regression based on historical data. Obviously, to go along this approach, historical data is required.[23] Let us, for instance, consider the hedging of an equity tranche with a junior mezzanine tranche on a standard index such as iTraxx Europe Main or CDX NA IG. Here, one has to keep in mind that the historical and the model-based approaches to static hedging are rather different. There is no reason why the static hedge ratio (i.e., the coefficient in the regression of the payoff to be hedged on the hedging payoff) has to be constant over time. For instance, going further in the preceding example, as the expected loss on the underlying portfolios changes over time, the moneyness of the equity and junior mezzanine tranches does not change accordingly and the ratio of theoretical deltas (in almost any theoretical hedging model) is likely to vary. This first point is fairly obvious. Also, at different points in times, the market views may change. This does not concern only the mean of the underlying portfolio, but other statistical features, such as, say, the degree of dependence between default times. Eventually, there is no reason for a stable and linear relationship between tranches over time, which weakens the purely statistical approach and calls for the use of a model for conditional (upon the current information) and epistemic[24] distributions of default times.

Designing hedging strategies using CDO tranches does not require the minimization of some hedging error and can be conducted through a pricing model, usually some variant of the Gaussian copula model.

Based on a simple implementation of the Gaussian copula model,[25] Ammann and Brommundt (2009) report that the standard deviation of the changes in value of a delta-hedged tranche, with an adjacent tranche, is about two times smaller than that of an unhedged portfolio. One could expand upon that, and use the Gaussian copula model to hedge, say, a junior mezzanine tranche against an equity tranche and the credit default swap index. In theory, one should be able to hedge against both small and large movements of the index—that is, both delta and (parallel) gamma risks. Actually, since equity tranches are associated with large idiosyncratic gamma risks, such an approach is perilous. Some still remember that similar trades with positive carry were popular up to the 2005 auto crisis, when some investors had to cut positions with heavy losses; see Petrelli, Siu, Zhang, and Kapoor (2006) and Petrelli, Zhang, Jobst, and Kapoor (2007). We can also mention that this kind of Taylor expansion–based approach to hedging lacks some theoretical rigor since higher-order terms may not be associated with vanishing risks. Given this, it is not surprising that hedging a given CDO tranche with two different tranches may lead to a decrease in hedging performance (Ammann and Brommundt 2009).

An important and practical topic is the pricing and risk management of bespoke tranches. These are tranches based on credit portfolios that differ from standard indexes, usually with higher credit spread names. Turc, Benhamou, Herzog, and Teyssier (2006) and Baheti and Morgan (2007) describe different ways to compute correlation parameters depending on the average credit spread of the bespoke portfolio. Ding and Sherris (2009) use these ideas to build and check different hedging strategies of standard CDO tranches. Given some stated dependence between correlation and credit spreads, one can compute the total derivative of a CDO tranche with respect to a shift in credit spreads. For instance, using the moneyness matching approach in Turc et al. (2006), an increase in credit spreads is associated with an increase in the expected loss and thus a decrease in the detachment point of the equivalent equity tranche. Since base correlations curves are usually upward sloping, an increase in credit spreads is thus associated with a decrease in base correlations. Of course, keeping the correlation parameters constant is a special case corresponding to usual delta computations.

Another common issue is the hedging of nonstandard tranches on standard indexes, such as iTraxx or CDX. It may also concern super-senior tranches or, on the contrary, first-losses tranches; thin tranchelets, for instance a 5 percent to 6 percent tranche on the iTraxx; and eventually short-term contracts, especially as older series mature. Some commonly described approaches lead to difficulties.[26] One has to deal with standard no-arbitrage constraints on expected tranche losses, which are also related to super-replication prices, as discussed in Walker (2008). This actually provides some help, but still leads to a wide range of admissible prices and hedge ratios in a number of cases. This also raises the issue of the availability and reliability of prices of such nonstandard tranches. During the liquidity and credit crisis, the spreads of super-senior tranches widened dramatically. This was partly due to the fear of systemic and contagion effects in the credit world. But it may also be that huge short positions by major participants, such as American International Group (AIG), could not be held due to the lack of collateral, and possibly some predatory trading has emphasized the price of super-senior protection. In such a period of stress and market dislocation, one can rightfully wonder about the significance of transaction prices.

6.3.2   Back to Back-Testing

> A theory is something nobody believes, except the person who made it. An experiment is something everybody believes, except the person who made it.
>
> —Albert Einstein

Let us now go back to comparing dynamic hedging strategies of CDO tranches based on credit default swaps. We focus on a number of methodological issues and discuss some results that come out of the small number of empirical studies.

Our message is twofold:

First, there are numerous statistical and practical issues, when assessing hedging performance, that cannot clearly be seen from the bird's-eye view of academic mathematical finance. These will be detailed hereafter, and as a consequence drawing comparisons between different models is difficult.

Then, credit spread deltas of CDO tranches, with respect to credit default swap indexes, as obtained from the Gaussian copula approximation of the structural model and default deltas, are not that different from one another. Moreover, static deltas obtained from dynamic Cox models are not different, either. The discrepancies between the models can be given some economic intuition, based on the correlation dynamics or equivalently the mechanism of default contagion. These deltas lead to risk-reducing hedging strategies. Actually, this suggests that market practice is far from being vacuous, since risk management among trading desks relies mainly upon variations of the Gaussian copula approach. This is rather good news at the level of an investment bank, though it does not necessarily solve for systemic issues, where major trading firms appear to have similar long or short exposures to be hedged.

Our main focus regarding comparing models will be the use of the Gaussian copula and of the Markov loss model described before. As discussed earlier, the Gaussian copula is viewed here as some approximation of a costly-to-implement structural model. Both models are widely used among practitioners and have sound and easy-to-understand theoretical foundations. We will not pay a lot of attention to so-called intensity models or models based on Cox processes, due to their difficulties in dealing with the high degree of dependence between default events, as seen during the credit and liquidity crisis.[27] Similarly, we will only briefly deal with incomplete market approaches even though some seem to be associated with appealing hedging efficiency. These approaches are a bit trickier on theoretical grounds, since the connection between the pricing and the hedging is not as obvious as in the case of complete market models.

Before going further in comparing hedging strategies, a few points need to be stated.

At this stage, partly due to practical constraints, back-test studies have involved the use of indexes rather than individual credit default swaps. In other words, the amount of credit default swap used in the hedging portfolio is name independent. This is questionable, especially when the dispersion of credit spreads in the underlying portfolio is significant. For instance, such name heterogeneity is likely to involve higher credit deltas in equity tranches for risky names. This issue is discussed later where we consider the scattering of individual name deltas.

When trying to simultaneously deal with default and credit spread risk, a view shared by some academics is to deal with credit default swap indexes of different maturities. However, we still lack some empirical studies to support such a view and there might be some operational difficulties in implementing these ideas. For instance, hedge ratios could be of opposite signs and large magnitudes. In the studies we are aware of, the preferred hedging instrument is thus the credit default swap index of the same maturity as the considered CDO tranche. It would definitely be an interesting investigation to assess whether the use of credit default swaps of different maturities actually increases hedging performance. Preliminary and indirect evidence discussed later tends to show that credit spread deltas and default deltas are not too far away and suggests that a given position in the underlying credit portfolio could lead to a good hedge against both default and credit spread risks.

Regarding the computation and the calibration of parameters, there are different issues.[28] We have already mentioned that the Markovian loss model, in its simplest form, involves a set of contagion parameters that has the same dimension as the number of names (say 125), while there are many fewer pricing constraints (typically six for one horizon). Depending on the calibration method, the dependence of the loss intensities on the number of defaults may vary. This is not innocuous from the point of view of delta computations.

In the Gaussian copula model, there are also a number of issues related to the way correlation parameters are determined, whether base or implied correlations are being used, and whether these correlations are kept constant or updated as credit spreads change (correlation regimes). The principles of the hedging and risk management are fairly simple: The pricing tools are used to compute sensitivities to market inputs and to market parameters, such as credit spreads of the constituents of the reference credit portfolio. The main focus is put on credit spread risk, while default risk is usually dealt with a reserve policy. Such risks are managed thanks to credit index default swaps or CDSs on the underlying names of the basket. Other risks, such as idiosyncratic and parallel gamma[29] credit spread risks or correlation exposure, can be in principle managed by trading liquid index tranches across the capital structure.

Let us emphasize a key issue when computing credit deltas in the one-factor Gaussian copula model with base correlations. There are actually two approaches that can be denoted as "sticky strike" and "sticky delta," to parallel the terminology used in equity derivatives markets (see Derman 1999). In the sticky strike approach, the base correlations are kept unchanged when bumping the credit curves. When

FIGURE 6.1 Negative Deltas Due to the Steepness of the Base Correlation Curve

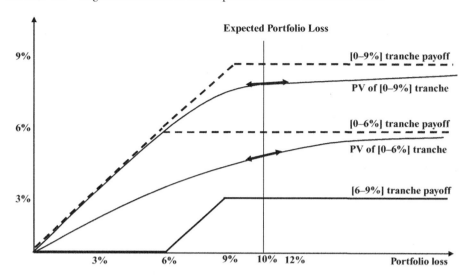

computing sticky deltas, one takes into account the change in base correlations due to the change in the moneyness of the tranche when credit spreads move up; the equity tranche becomes more junior, which actually leads to using a smaller base correlation. In other words, in the sticky delta approach an increase in credit spreads is associated with a smaller dependence between default events. As a consequence, the sticky delta of an equity tranche is lower than the delta computed under the sticky strike approach.

Morgan and Mortensen (2007) have investigated some anomalies when using the base correlation for the computation of sensitivities. They show that credit spread deltas on the iTraxx S7 5Y 12 to 22 percent tranche can be negative due to the steepness of the base correlation curve. Such a counterintuitive effect[30] is illustrated in Figure 6.1.

Example: Consider a mezzanine 6 to 9 percent tranche on a bespoke portfolio. The expected loss on the portfolio at inception is equal to 10 percent. Figures in solid lines show the present value of the default leg of the 0 to 6 percent and 0 to 9 percent base correlation tranches as a function of the expected loss on the portfolio. The base correlation for the 0 to 9 percent tranche is assumed to be very high; thus the volatility of the reference portfolio is quite small compared to the time value of the base tranche. Conversely, the base correlation of the 0 to 6 percent tranche is much smaller, which is consistent with steep upward base correlation curves. Thus, the volatility of the (same) reference portfolio is much higher than the time value of the option. The present value of the default leg of the mezzanine 6 to 9 percent tranche is the difference between the present values of the 0 to 6 percent and 0 to 9 percent base correlation tranches and should remain between 0 and 3 percent to avoid plain arbitrage opportunities. Given this constraint, it may be (see Figure 6.1) that the delta of the more junior tranche is smaller than the delta of the more senior tranche for some levels of expected portfolio loss. In such regions, the present value of the mezzanine tranche will decrease as the expected loss on the underlying portfolio increases (which is rather unlikely).

Also, when considering a bump in credit spreads in order to compute a hedging exposure in the credit default swap index, one may, for instance, operate a translation or rather choose a multiplicative effect, which clearly will not lead to the same magnitude of credit deltas for the different tranches. Recently, recovery rate assumptions of key importance have appeared. Prior to the liquidity and credit crisis, most market participants relied upon a standard though arbitrary recovery rate assumption of 40 percent. Since then, it has appeared that such an assumption would not be consistent with the large spreads quoted on senior tranches. Various amendments, including a recovery markdown or different specifications of state-dependent stochastic recovery rate, have been proposed by the industry (see Amraoui, Cousot, Hitier, and Laurent 2009). This has actually a significant impact on hedge ratios, especially at the individual name level. Typically, the use of a stochastic recovery rate or a recovery rate markdown will tend to lower the exposure of senior tranches to tight names. The basis risk between the spread of the credit default swap index and the average spread of its constituents is another seemingly minor issue when computing hedge ratios. Such basis risk is mostly related to transaction costs and can fluctuate widely, especially during times of turmoil. This raises some doubts regarding the effective level of spreads and thus of expected loss and can have some effect on the computation of hedge ratios. Various choices and adjustments can be envisaged, and none of them could actually be neglected when considering hedging efficiency. Other seemingly minor issues have to be dealt with in order to compute correlation parameters that are consistent with market quotes, such as the amortization of premium legs and the term structure of CDO tranche spreads.[31]

Let us stress that, when constructing hedge ratios, the use of parameters that calibrate prices may not be the first-best. Gouriéroux and Laurent (1996) have developed a concept of objective-based inference and implied hedging parameter, which might be well suited when conducting back-tests with misspecified models.

Regarding hedging efficiency, we would first like to emphasize some similarities between the deltas associated with dissimilar models, Gaussian copula models, Markov loss models, and affine intensity models.

Eckner (2009) or Feldhütter (2008) rely on an affine specification of default intensities. Conditionally on the path of default intensities, default times are independent; that is, there are no contagion effects at default times. The model is parametric with respect to the term structure of credit spreads and to CDO tranches. Eckner (2009) calibrates model parameters to credit spreads and liquid tranche quotes associated with the CDX NA IG5 index. Hedge ratios with respect to the credit default swap index are then computed.[32] The sensitivities of CDO tranche and index prices are calculated with respect to uniform and relative shifts of individual intensities. The model deltas can be compared with those computed from the Gaussian copula model. As can be seen from Table 6.1, though the figures differ, the orders of magnitude are roughly the same. The equity tranche deltas computed in Eckner (2009) are slightly larger than those computed under the Gaussian copula, as in a sticky delta approach. Such

TABLE 6.1   Market Deltas and Model Deltas as in Eckner (2009)

Tranches	0–3%	3–7%	7–10%	10–15%	15–30%
Market deltas	18.5	5.5	1.5	0.8	0.4
Model deltas	21.7	6.0	1.1	0.4	0.1

a result is consistent with a market where an increase in the average credit spread is the outcome of some idiosyncratic shifts and an increase in the dispersion of credit spreads. This is typical of the May 2005 correlation crisis, which was actually associated with smaller correlations on the equity tranches. At this stage, some methodological points are worth mentioning. First, while the model is dynamic, the way hedge ratios are computed is typically static. One shifts some parameters related to credit spreads without relating such bumps to a theoretical approach of dynamic hedging. More importantly, on practical grounds, there are different ways to inflate credit spreads, associated with different hedge ratios. For instance, one can privilege a shift associated with the systemic component of the intensity; such a shift will be therefore associated with an increase in the dependence between defaults.

Arnsdorf and Halperin (2007) consider a Markov chain that accounts for the dynamics of defaults and credit spreads. This can be seen as a two-dimensional Markov chain. Contrary to the previous model, defaults are informative and credit spreads jump at the arrival of defaults. The theoretical properties of the model with respect to completeness are not studied, but Arnsdorf and Halperin (2007) compute deltas of standard iTraxx tranches with respect to the corresponding credit default swap index. As in Eckner (2007), the deltas with respect to individual credit default swaps are not provided. However, one could think of using the random thinning procedure discussed in Giesecke and Goldberg (2005) or Giesecke (2008) to provide such individual deltas.

Table 6.2 shows some market (computed under the Gaussian copula model) and model (corresponding to "model B" in Arnsdorf and Halperin 2007) deltas in March 2007 for five-year CDO tranches. As in Table 6.1, it can be seen that the figures are roughly the same. However, it is noticeable that equity tranche deltas are smaller when using the Markov chain.

From a risk management perspective, an interesting feature is that the deltas with respect to underlying credit default swaps have the same order of magnitude in the different approaches. Let us first recall that, in the case of zero default-free interest rates, the default leg of a senior CDO tranche can be seen as a call option on a portfolio

TABLE 6.2   Market and Model Deltas as in Arnsdorf and Halperin (2007)

Tranches	0–3%	3–6%	6–9%	9–12%	12–22%
Market deltas	26.5	4.5	1.3	0.7	0.3
Model deltas	21.9	4.8	1.6	0.8	0.4

of discount bonds maturing with the CDO tranche. The delta feature suggests that at a portfolio level, say an iTraxx or CDX index, a shift of credit spreads or a default event would have roughly the same effect on the expected portfolio loss dynamics. In other words, the same amount of CDS would lead to protection against both credit spread and default risks. This is quite preliminary and needs to be further confirmed by using an embedding framework.

Though the pricing methodologies differ, Eckner (2009); Arnsdorf and Halperin (2007); Laurent, Cousin, and Fermanian (2007); Cont and Kan (2008); Feldhütter (2008); Cont, Deguest, and Kan (2010); and Cousin, Crépey, and Kan (2010) provide some examples of the use of dynamic arbitrage-free pricing models to compute sensitivities with respect to credit spreads and thus hedge ratios with respect to credit default swaps. As mentioned earlier, driving comparisons is never an easy task since one has to decide about the way model parameters are determined. This can actually explain some discordance between empirical studies regarding hedging efficiency of different models, especially since there is not so much difference between the computed deltas. While, unsurprisingly, the authors stress the divergences between hedging strategies associated with different modeling approaches, the relative errors, as measured by root mean squared error or the mean average hedge error, do not differ that much.

Regarding statistical issues, when assessing hedging performance, one should be cautious about the issues related to data snooping, multiple hypothesis testing, or false discovery rate. It is tempting to embed a simple model in a larger one, which is likely to be more flexible and involve more parameters. Then, the simple model appears to be a restricted version of a more sophisticated one and we can check this restriction on parameters.[33] If the base model is not rejected, then most likely researchers will look for another extension until a new model is found that is claimed to supersede the older one. This is not a fair contest since the best alternative is chosen and one has to correct test statistics accordingly. In- and out-of-sample data do not correct for this data-driven model selection, because comparing out-of-sample hedging performance is part of the standard model selection methodology. This strengthens our focus on simple models.[34]

6.3.3 Delta Scattering

Up to now, we mainly concentrated on the hedging of CDO tranches with respect to the underlying credit default swap index. However, in many cases it makes sense to hedge at the name level, especially when the spreads associated with the index constituents are dispersed. A name with a large spread is more likely to contribute to the value of an equity tranche, and thus should be associated with a larger hedge ratio than a tight name. Likewise, an increase in dispersion of spreads should be associated with an increase in the value of the default leg of an equity tranche (and conversely for senior tranches).

By construction, bottom-up models and especially copula-type models allow a name-per-name derivation of hedge ratios.[35] Regarding top-down models, the building of individual deltas is currently being investigated; random thinning, as some researchers advocate, might do the job. We leave this point for further discussion.

Another issue with models that involve some kind of contagion is the scope of contagion effects. For instance, failure of a name within the CDX index may lead to jumps in the credit spreads of names in the iTraxx. In theory, such exposure should be hedged, which may be forgotten if one would consider the North American world separately. Likewise, such hidden name dependence appears in bespoke CDOs due to the mapping onto liquid indexes.

As mentioned in the first part of this section, one is likely to expect a smooth and increasing pattern of credit deltas with respect to the spreads of the underlying names for an equity tranche, a decreasing pattern for senior tranches, and possibly a humped shape for some mezzanine tranches.

However, other issues came to light, such as huge discrepancies between individual name deltas and subsequently very large positive or negative idiosyncratic gammas in high-correlation regimes, as observed in 2008 on the iTraxx and CDX markets. Actually, when the dependence level between default dates becomes quite high, as could be seen during the liquidity and credit crisis, strange phenomena occur. Names cluster together according to the level of credit spreads, and credit deltas are equal to either zero or one; see Burtschell, Gregory, and Laurent (2009) for a detailed analysis. For instance, when looking at an equity tranche, the names with the highest credit spreads have a delta equal to one,[36] whereas the remaining names have a delta equal to zero. Such a phenomenon also occurs in the stochastic correlation model described by Burtschell, Gregory, and Laurent (2007). The bumps in Figure 6.2 are related to the comonotonic (perfect dependence) state and the heterogeneity among credit spreads.

FIGURE 6.2 Irregular Patterns of Individual Names Deltas in Regimes of High Correlation

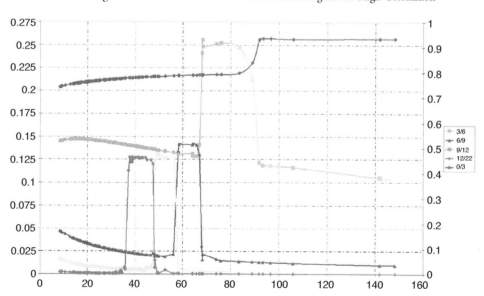

Such a rather counterintuitive pattern precludes the use of the credit default swap index as a hedging tool for CDO tranches. Other heterogeneity effects in individual credit deltas are reported by Houdain (2006).

Figure 6.2 exhibits CDO tranche deltas with respect to the level of credit spreads computed on August 31, 2005. Nominal is equal to 125. Five-year credit spreads on the x-axis are expressed in basis points per annum. Credit deltas of the equity tranche are on the right axis. Figure 6.2 shows that individual credit deltas may actually differ significantly from one name to another.

Such irregular patterns of credit spread deltas will occur whenever pricing models involve some kind of threshold. This is the case, for instance, with the popular random factor loading approach of Andersen and Sidenius (2005). We want to stress that these patterns of credit spread deltas with respect to the level of credit spreads convey a lot of information. They almost directly show the amount of idiosyncratic gamma risk by looking at the slope of such a curve. The higher the increase of credit spread deltas with respect to the level of spreads, the higher the corresponding idiosyncratic gamma.[37]

The increased efficiency of hedging at a name level is an important issue for trading desks, but, as mentioned earlier, it cannot be fully assessed unless the details of the hedging strategy, including the ways hedging parameters are calibrated, are disclosed.

6.4 Conclusion

> The wise man bridges the gap by laying out the path by means of which he can get from where he is to where he wants to go.
>
> —John Pierpont Morgan

This chapter has dealt with the usefulness of pricing and hedging models for the risk management of synthetic CDOs. We have shown that CDO tranches can be replicated with self-financing strategies within the basic implementations of the multivariate structural model and of the Markovian loss (or local intensity) model. The former approach is primarily designed to hedge credit spread risks. In the latter approach, focus is put on hedging default risks and may involve a high degree of default contagion. In both cases, credit default swaps are traded to hedge CDO tranches, and the involved mathematical tools, such as conditional default probabilities or the use of some martingale representation theorem, are the same. On other grounds these models are strikingly different, and each of them could be criticized as too simple and missing some desirable empirical features. The mathematics of the multivariate structural model are well known.[38] The Gaussian copula model, widely used in the banking industry, may be seen as a one-step approximation of the multivariate structural model, especially for investment-grade names associated with small default probabilities. This might explain some kind of robustness of the model and lays the path for a better understanding of its limitations. Such an issue has already been studied as far as pricing is concerned, but a formal investigation is still required for hedging.

The overall picture regarding risk management of CDOs looks quite gloomy in the aftermath of the liquidity and credit crisis. Misconceptions about CDOs of subprime mortgages, such as the understatement of dependence across minitranches, are now well known and discussed (see Crouhy, Jarrow, and Turnbull 2008).[39] If one dares to look at facts with eyes wide open, it seems clear that trading desks managing synthetic CDOs had dissimilar performances, which is not surprising, regarding the number of technical issues briefly addressed within this chapter. This does not invalidate various quantitative developments in the credit correlation field. According to Karl Popper's evolutionary view of science (Popper 1992), researchers look for falsification of a theory or a model that represents the state of the art. For this reason, the burgeoning of credit risk models and more recently of back-testing approaches testifies to a vivid research field rather than rigor mortis. Let us consider the supplementary (and somehow challenging) view of T. Kuhn (1996): "No theory ever solves all the puzzles with which it is confronted at a given time; nor are the solutions already achieved often perfect. On the contrary, it is just the incompleteness and imperfection of the existing data-theory fit that, at any given time, define many of the puzzles that characterize normal science." Whether it is time to shift to another paradigm or even abandon the current quantitative finance "research programme"[40] is thus still not obvious.

Notes

1. For instance, some academics tend to think that the use of a Gumbel, Clayton, or *t*-copula would have avoided the pitfalls of the Gaussian copula approach. We refer to Burtschell, Gregory, and Laurent (2009); Cousin and Laurent (2008a, 2008c); or Gregory and Laurent (2008) for reviews of a number of popular pricing approaches.

2. For this reason, some authors have considered models where the expected tranche loss surface is an input parameter. While consistency with traded tranche quotes at a given point in time is fulfilled by construction, this approach has its own difficulties. It is not clear whether the loss dynamics will be consistent with the recalibration process. Moreover, as is known in equity markets, a dynamic model (say a local volatility model) that is consistent with market data can be associated with poor hedging properties.

3. By "flat" correlation matrix, we mean that pairwise correlation parameters are constant across names.

4. Here, we have implicitly assumed that the new model embeds the older one. One could also switch to a distinct approach. In the credit field, there are actually different seeds, say for simplicity, such as structural and reduced-form models. Some footbridges have already been thrown over the gap, and we will mention the useful effort to integrate the probabilistic framework. Much as the claim that stock prices are semimartingales, we will be left with a very small set of testable restrictions as the counterpart of our broad mathematical view, which is clearly an issue for the purpose of building useful models. As the French say, "*Qui trop embrasse, mal étreint.*"

5. The best use of such an approach is to provide a consistent interpolation procedure to compute consistent prices of less liquid prices for accounting purposes.

6. Assuming that name predefault intensities follow a multivariate diffusion process.

7. We refer to Laurent, Cousin, and Fermanian (2007); Cousin and Laurent (2008b), and Cousin, Jeanblanc, and Laurent (2009) for contributions related to this chapter.

8. We refer the reader to the Meissner (2008) and De Servigny and Jobst (2007) textbooks or to Kakodkar, Galiani, Jónsson, and Gallo (2006) for a detailed analysis of the CDO market and credit derivatives cash flows.

9. Of course, it is possible to compute credit deltas with respect to traded credit default swaps in this framework. We refer the reader to Laurent, Cousin, and Fermanian (2007) for more details on this point.

10. Or albeit H_T-measurable.

11. The possibility of simultaneous defaults may also be seen as an extreme contagion effect.

12. Let us note that this theorem is usually written for martingales adapted to a filtration generated by a standard Brownian motion with independent components. However, as an intermediary step, the correlated Brownian motion $\tilde{W}$ can be expressed as the product of the square root of its correlation matrix with a standard n-dimensional Brownian motion with independent components. As a result, any payoff contingent to the dynamics of $\tilde{W}$ up to time T can be described as a sum of stochastic integrals with respect to $\tilde{W}^1, \ldots, \tilde{W}^m$.

13. At least when recovery rates are assumed to be deterministic.

14. Let us note, however, that the dynamics of CDO tranche prices is very difficult to make explicit in this framework since it involves the joint law of some correlated first-passage times.

15. In the case of CDSs, these PDEs can be solved numerically using either finite difference methods or algorithms based on recombining trees. Regarding CDO tranche prices, the dimension of the PDE is too large to consider a direct numerical resolution method. CDO tranche prices should be computed using Monte Carlo simulations instead.

16. Provided that these are available, an assumption that is problematic during periods of market disruption.

17. One could argue that the new generation of top-down models takes the loss surface or equivalently the set of CDO tranches quotes as inputs, as is the case with Heath-Jarrow-Morton models in the interest rates framework. However, such models are not aimed at risk-managing plain CDOs, which seems to be the key issue today, but rather focus on more complex payoffs, such as constant proportion debt obligations (CPDOs), or leverage super-senior tranches.

18. In a recent work, Cousin, Crépey, and Kan (2010) investigate the hedging abilities of the Gaussian copula model and of the Markovian contagion model (local intensity model in their terminology). They look for regimes where one model would outperform the other. They show some robustness of the Gaussian copula approach.

19. Frey and Backhaus (2008, 2010) and Arnsdorf and Halperin (2007) provide some Markovian loss models that are more versatile, but also more difficult to handle.

20. We might have alternatively considered the Gaussian copula as a (non-Markovian) contagion model. If one restricts to the natural filtration of default times, defaults are informative; they bring some information about the latent Gaussian variables of the nondefaulted names. The jumps of credit spreads at default times depend on derivatives of the survival function, and there is a singularity at time zero. This is not, however, the common way to appraise the Gaussian copula. If one were to observe the path of assets associated with

different names instead of the terminal values, contagion would disappear. About 10 years ago, while one of the authors was working on basket credit derivatives, the preferred model was a structural model based on multidimensional normal-inverse Gaussian (NIG) processes and a factor structure. Prices and Greeks were computed by Monte Carlo, which was quite slow, especially for the Greeks. At one point in time, the model was downgraded to a static one, but in most cases, prices and Greeks were quite similar. We would definitely need a more systematic investigation of this point.

21. In theory, one should start with the computation of the derivatives of the value of the CDO tranche and of hedging CDSs with respect to underlying state variables, here the asset values at the current time. Then, the amount of hedging CDSs is the ratio of the derivatives. Market practitioners rather make the derivation with respect to the default barrier, or in a static approach with respect to the default threshold. This can also be seen as a shift in credit spreads, often of one basis point.

22. Given a conditional (upon current information) joint distribution of default times, it is possible to compute the covariances of the bespoke payoff and of the liquid tranche payoffs and thus to derive the optimal static hedge.

23. Typically, daily or weekly data are used. This requires prices for the payoffs to be hedged and the hedging instruments. As a consequence, this approach is not well suited to hedge nonstandard tranches.

24. Reflecting risk managers' views about the future.

25. Large homogeneous portfolio approximation.

26. For instance, careless approaches based on the interpolation of base correlations may lead to negative tranchelets prices, the use of base correlations is associated with nonlocal effects in correlation analysis, and extrapolation is often hazardous. Moreover, hedge ratios also depend on somehow arbitrary recovery rate assumptions. See later in the chapter about delta scattering and model implementation.

27. Regarding hedging issues, Laurent (2006) deals with such models. It is shown that due to default diversification in large portfolios, the hedging error can be controlled by hedging credit spread risk only.

28. We already briefly discussed some issues regarding the computation of hedge ratios when considering affine intensity models.

29. Idiosyncratic gamma is also denoted as iGamma and referred to as "microconvexity." Parallel gamma is also known as index gamma and referred to as "macroconvexity."

30. Schloegl, Mortensen, and Morgan (2008) show that such effects can also occur in arbitrage-free models.

31. We refer to Jobst (2007) or Meissner, Hector, and Rasmussen (2008) (Meissner 2008, chap. 18) for further discussions about hedging CDOs within the Gaussian copula framework. On the numerical side, Andersen, Sidenius, and Basu (2003) and Iscoe and Kreinin (2007), among many other authors, provide semianalytical techniques to compute sensitivities within the Gaussian copula framework. Joshi and Kainth (2004), Rott and Fries (2005), and Chen and Glasserman (2008) detail some improvements of the Monte Carlo approach that are applicable to the pricing and hedging of CDO tranches, especially when one falls outside the factor framework.

32. Let us remark that this model would hardly be calibrated during the 2008 crisis on CDX and iTraxx tranches.

33. This first step may not be straightforward since the distribution of hedging errors needs to be derived.

34. Even though, looking in greater detail, there are still a lot of rather arbitrary and often unnoticed modeling choices.

35. See Cousin and Laurent (2008a, 2008c) or Burtschell, Gregory, and Laurent (2009) for reviews of such bottom-up models within a factor copula framework. The sensitivity approach applies to copula models that, contrary to the base correlation approach, provide arbitrage-free CDO tranche quotes. Schloegl, Mortensen, and Morgan (2008) prove that tranchelet sensitivities are always positive in such a framework. Dealing with large amounts of data and the cost of numerical implementation drove early back-test studies toward using credit default swap indexes.

36. There is always a matter of norm. Here the reference is the credit default swap index. One also has to care about the notional of the tranche in certain cases.

37. Such a reasoning is not rigorous and holds at the first order. However, the approximation is usually quite good.

38. However, some details are, surprisingly enough, not yet described in the academic literature. We can think of using hedging instruments that vanish before the maturity of the CDO tranche, but are no longer required after extinction.

39. We can, however, notice that it does not invalidate the Gaussian copula model per se, provided that this is applied at the lowest level rather than at the minitranche level. When considering well-diversified mortgage-backed security (MBS) mezzanine tranches, the idiosyncratic risks are wiped out and only systemic risks such as the price level in the residential mortgage market remains. It is not surprising therefore that the correlation between these minitranches would be much higher than assessed by rating agencies and that senior tranches of asset-backed securities (ABSs) were overpriced.

40. See Lakatos (1978) regarding the concept of a "research programme" and an attempt to reconcile the views of Popper and Kuhn. Feyerabend (1975) provides a sharper criticism of Popper's falsification concept.

References

Ammann, M., and B. Brommundt. 2009. Hedging collateralized debt obligations. Working paper, University of St. Gallen.

Amraoui, S., L. Cousot, S. Hitier, and J.-P. Laurent. 2009. Pricing CDOs with state dependent stochastic recovery rates. Working paper, ISFA Actuarial School, University of Lyon and BNP Paribas.

Andersen, L., and J. Sidenius. 2005. Extensions to the Gaussian copula: Random recovery and random factor loadings. *Journal of Credit Risk* 1 (1): 29–70.

Andersen, L., J. Sidenius, and S. Basu. 2003. All your hedges in one basket. *Risk* (November): 67–72.

Arnsdorf, M., and I. Halperin. 2007. BSLP: Markovian bivariate spread-loss model for portfolio credit derivatives. Working paper, JPMorgan.

Baheti, P., and S. Morgan. 2007. Base correlation mapping. *Lehman Brothers, Quantitative Research Quarterly* (Q1).

Bielecki, T. R., A. Cousin, S. Crépey, and A. Herbertsson. 2010. Pricing and hedging portfolio credit derivatives in a bottom-up model with simultaneous defaults. Working paper, Evry University.

Bielecki, T. R., S. Crépey, and M. Jeanblanc. 2010. Up and down credit risk. *Quantitative Finance*, forthcoming.

Bielecki, T. R., S. Crépey, M. Jeanblanc, and M. Rutkowski. 2007. Valuation of basket credit derivatives in the credit migrations environment. In *Handbook of financial engineering*, ed. J. Birge and V. Linetsky. Elsevier.

Bielecki, T. R., M. Jeanblanc, and M. Rutkowski. 2007. Hedging of basket credit derivatives in default swap market. *Journal of Credit Risk* 3 (1): 91–132.

Bielecki, T. R., A. Vidozzi, and L. Vidozzi. 2008. A Markovian copulae approach to pricing and hedging of credit index derivatives and ratings triggered step-up bonds. *Journal of Credit Risk* 4 (1).

Black, F., and J. C. Cox. 1976. Valuing corporate securities: Some effects of bond indenture provisions. *Journal of Finance* 31 (2): 351–367.

Brémaud, P. 1981. Point processes and queues: Martingale dynamics. New York: Springer-Verlag.

Burtschell, X., J. Gregory, and J.-P. Laurent. 2007. Beyond the Gaussian copula: Stochastic and local correlation. *Journal of Credit Risk* 3 (1): 31–62.

Burtschell, X., J. Gregory, and J.-P. Laurent. 2009. A comparative analysis of CDO pricing models under the factor copula framework. *Journal of Derivatives* 16 (4): 9–37.

Çetin, U., R. Jarrow, P. Protter, and Y. Yildirim. 2004. Modeling credit risk with partial information. *Annals of Applied Probability* 14:1167–1178.

Chen, Z., and P. Glasserman. 2008. Sensitivity estimates for portfolio credit derivatives using Monte Carlo. *Finance and Stochastics* 12 (4): 507–540.

Coculescu, D., H. Geman, and M. Jeanblanc. 2008. Valuation of default-sensitive claims under imperfect information. *Finance and Stochastics* 12 (2): 195–218.

Coculescu, D., M. Jeanblanc, and A. Nikeghbali. 2007. Default times, nonarbitrage conditions and change of probability measures. Working paper, Evry University.

Cont, R., R. Deguest, and Y. Kan. 2010. Recovering default intensities from CDO spreads: Inversion formula and model calibration. *SIAM Journal on Financial Mathematics* 1:555–585.

Cont, R., and Y. Kan. 2008. Dynamic hedging of portfolio credit derivatives. Financial Engineering Report 2008-08, Columbia University.

Cont, R., and A. Minca. 2008. Recovering portfolio default intensities implied by CDO quotes. Financial Engineering Report 2008-01, Columbia University.

Cousin, A., S. Crépey, and Y. Kan. 2010. Delta hedging correlation risk? Working paper, ISFA Actuarial School, University of Lyon.

Cousin, A., and M. Jeanblanc. 2010. Hedging portfolio loss derivatives with CDSs. Working paper, Evry University.

Cousin, A., M. Jeanblanc, and J.-P. Laurent. 2010. Hedging CDO tranches in a Markovian environment. Paris-Princeton Lectures on Mathematical Finance 2010. Springer.

Cousin, A., and J.-P. Laurent. 2008a. Comparison results for exchangeable credit risk portfolios. *Insurance: Mathematics and Economics* 42 (3): 1118–1127.

Cousin, A., and J.-P. Laurent. 2008b. Hedging issues for CDOs. In *The definitive guide to CDOs*, ed. G. Meissner, chap. 17, 461–480. London: Risk Books.

Cousin, A., and J.-P. Laurent. 2008c. An overview of factor modeling for CDO pricing. In *Frontiers in quantitative finance: Credit risk and volatility modeling*, ed. R. Cont, chap. 7, 185–216. Hoboken, NJ: John Wiley & Sons.

Crouhy, M. G., R. J. Jarrow, and S. M. Turnbull. 2008. The subprime credit crisis of 2007. *Journal of Derivatives* 16 (4): 81–110.

Derman, E. 1999. Regimes of volatility. *Quantitative Strategies Research Notes*, Goldman Sachs.

De Servigny, A., and N. Jobst. 2007. *The Handbook of Structured Finance*. New York: McGraw-Hill.

Ding, J. J., and M. Sherris. 2009. Pricing and hedging synthetic CDO tranche spread risks. Working paper, Australian School of Business, University of New South Wales.

Duffie, D., and D. Lando. 2001. Term structures of credit spreads with incomplete accounting information. *Econometrica* 69:633–664.

Dupire, B. 1994. Pricing with a smile. *Risk* (January): 18–20.

Eckner, A. 2009. Computational techniques for basic affine models of portfolio credit risk. *Journal of Computational Finance* 13:63–97.

Ehlers, P., and P. J. Schönbucher. 2009. Background filtrations and canonical loss processes for top-down models of portfolio credit risk. *Finance and Stochastics* 13:79–103.

Feldhütter, P. 2008. An empirical investigation of an intensity-based model for pricing CDO tranches. Working paper, Copenhagen Business School.

Fermanian, J.-D., and O. Vigneron. 2009. On break-even correlation: The way to price structured credit derivatives by replication. Working paper.

Feyerabend, P. 1975. *Against method: Outline of an anarchistic theory of knowledge.* New York: Humanities Press.

Finger, C. 2009. Testing hedges under the standard tranched credit pricing model. *RiskMetrics Journal* 9, no. 1 (Winter).

Frey, R., and J. Backhaus. 2010. Dynamic hedging of synthetic CDO tranches with spread and contagion risk. *Journal of Economic Dynamics and Control* 34:710–724.

Frey, R., and J. Backhaus. 2008. Pricing and hedging of portfolio credit derivatives with interacting default intensities. *International Journal of Theoretical and Applied Finance* 11 (6): 611–634.

Giesecke, K. 2008. Portfolio credit risk: Top-down vs. bottom-up approaches. Working paper, Stanford University.

Giesecke, K., and L. R. Goldberg. 2005. A top down approach to multi-name credit. Working paper, Stanford University.

Goldberg, L. R., and K. Giesecke. 2004. Forecasting default in the face of uncertainty. *Journal of Derivatives* 12 (1): 14–25.

Gouriéroux, C., and J.-P. Laurent. 1996. Estimation of dynamic hedge. Working paper, CREST.

Gregory, J., and J.-P. Laurent. 2008. Practical pricing of synthetic CDOs. In *The definitive guide to CDOs—Market, application, valuation, and hedging,* ed. G. Meissner. London: Risk Books.

Guo, X., R. A. Jarrow, and Y. Zeng. 2005. Credit risk models with incomplete information. To appear in *Mathematics of Operations Research.*

Hitier, S., and E. Huber. 2009. CDO pricing: Copula implied by risk neutral dynamics. Working paper, BNP Paribas.

Houdain, J. 2006. Valorisation et gestion de dérivés de crédit: Les CDOs synthétiques ou la croissance exponentielle des produits de corrélation. PhD thesis, ENS Cachan.

Hull, J., M. Predescu, and A. White. 2005. The valuation of correlation-dependent derivatives using a structural model. Working paper, University of Toronto.

Iscoe, I., and A. Kreinin. 2007. Valuation of synthetic CDOs. *Journal of Banking and Finance* 31 (11): 3357–3376.

Jarrow, R., and P. Protter. 2004. Structural versus reduced form models: A new information based perspective. *Journal of Investment Management* 2 (2): 1–10.

Jeanblanc, M., and Y. Le Cam. 2007. Reduced form modelling of credit risk. Working paper, Evry University.

Jeanblanc, M., and Y. Le Cam. 2009. Immersion property and credit risk modelling. In *Optimality and risk—Modern trends in mathematical finance,* 99–132. New York: Springer.

Jobst, N. 2007. An introduction to the risk management of collateral debt obligations. In *The handbook of structured finance,* ed. A. de Servigny and N. Jobst, 295–338. New York: McGraw-Hill.

Joshi, M., and D. Kainth. 2004. Rapid and accurate development of prices and Greeks for *n*th to default swaps in the Li model. *Quantitative Finance* 4 (3): 266–275.

Kakodkar, A., S. Galiani, J. Jónsson, and A. Gallo. 2006. *Credit derivatives handbook.* Vol. 2. New York: Merrill Lynch.

Krekel, M. 2008. Pricing distressed CDOs with base correlation and stochastic recovery. Working paper, UniCredit Markets & Investment Banking.

Kuhn, T. S. 1996. *The structure of scientific revolutions.* 3rd ed. Chicago: University of Chicago Press.

Lakatos, I. 1978. *The methodology of scientific research programmes: Philosophical papers.* Vol. 1. New York: Cambridge University Press.

Laurent, J.-P. 2006. A note on the risk management of CDOs. Working paper, ISFA Actuarial School, University of Lyon and BNP Paribas.

Laurent, J.-P., A. Cousin, and J.-D. Fermanian. 2007. Hedging default risk of CDOs in Markovian contagion models. Working paper, ISFA Actuarial School, University of Lyon; to appear in *Quantitative Finance*.

Meissner, G., ed. 2008. *The definitive guide to CDOs*. London: Risk Books.

Meissner, G., R. Hector, and T. Rasmussen. 2008. Hedging CDOs within the Gaussian copula framework. In *The definitive guide to CDOs—Market, application, valuation, and hedging*, ed. G. Meissner. London: Risk Books.

Morgan, S., and A. Mortensen. 2007. CDO hedging anomalies in the base correlation approach. *Lehman Brothers, Quantitative Credit Research Quarterly* (October): 49–61.

Petrelli, A., O. Siu, J. Zhang, and V. Kapoor. 2006. Optimal static hedging of defaults in CDOs. Working paper, available at www.defaultrisk.com.

Petrelli, A., J. Zhang, N. Jobst, and V. Kapoor. 2007. A practical guide to CDO trading risk management. In *The handbook of structured finance*, ed. A. de Servigny and N. Jobst, 339–371. New York: McGraw-Hill.

Popper, K. R. 1992. *The logic of scientific discovery*. Rev. ed. London: Routledge.

Rott, M. G., and C. P. Fries. 2005. Fast and robust Monte Carlo CDO sensitivities. Working paper.

Schloegl, L., A. Mortensen, and S. Morgan. 2008. Strange risk in a correlation model. *Lehman Brothers, Quantitative Credit Research Quarterly* (Q1): 1–7.

Turc, J., D. Benhamou, B. Herzog, and M. Teyssier. 2006. Pricing bespoke CDOs: Latest developments. *Quantitative Strategy*, Société Générale.

Walker, M. B. 2008. The static hedging of CDO tranche correlation risk. Working paper, University of Toronto.

CHAPTER 7

Filtering and Incomplete Information in Credit Risk

Rüdiger Frey

Department of Mathematics, Universität Leipzig

Thorsten Schmidt

TU Chemnitz

This chapter studies structural and reduced-form credit risk models under incomplete information using techniques from stochastic filtering. We start with a brief introduction to stochastic filtering. Next we cover the pricing of corporate securities (debt and equity) in structural models under partial information. Furthermore, we study the construction of a dynamic reduced-form credit risk model via the innovations approach to nonlinear filtering, and we discuss pricing, calibration, and hedging in that context. The chapter closes with a number of numerical case studies related to model calibration and the pricing of credit index options.

7.1 Introduction

The recent turmoil in credit markets highlights the need for a sound methodology for managing books of credit derivatives. In particular, it is commonly agreed that the pricing and the risk management of relatively liquid products such as corporate bonds, credit default swaps (CDSs), or index-based derivatives (e.g., synthetic collateralized debt obligation [CDO] tranches) should be based on *dynamic* credit risk models. The development of such models is, however, a challenging problem: A successful model needs to capture the dynamic evolution of credit spreads and the dependence structure of defaults in a realistic way, while being at the same time tractable and parsimonious.

In this chapter we show that incomplete information and filtering techniques are a very useful tool in this regard. We begin with a short introduction to stochastic filtering in Section 7.2. In Section 7.3 we give an overview of the application of filtering to credit risk models. Next we discuss in detail structural models with incomplete information on the asset value. In particular, we explain that the pricing of many corporate securities naturally leads to a nonlinear filtering problem; this problem is then solved by a Markov chain approximation. This part of the exposition (Sections 7.4 and 7.5) is based on the seminal paper by Duffie and Lando (2001) and on our own work Frey and Schmidt (2009).

Sections 7.6 and 7.7 are devoted to filtering in reduced-form models. We present in detail the construction of a dynamic credit portfolio model via the innovations approach to nonlinear filtering. Moreover, pricing of credit derivatives, model calibration, hedging, and various aspects of the numerical implementation of the model are considered. A number of numerical case studies in Section 7.7 illustrate practical aspects of the model. In particular, we discuss the performance of calibration strategies and present new results on the pricing of credit index options. This part of the chapter largely follows our own paper Frey and Schmidt (2010).

A survey on nonlinear filtering in interest rate and credit risk models with a focus default-free term structure models can be found in Frey and Runggaldier (2008). Further related literature is discussed in the body of the chapter.

7.2 A Short Introduction to Stochastic Filtering

Factor models are frequently employed in financial mathematics, since they lead to fairly parsimonious models. Stochastic filtering comes into play when these factors are observed only indirectly, possibly because they are hidden in additional noise. We present a small introduction to filtering, which is inspired by Davis and Marcus (1981); for a detailed exposition we refer to Bain and Crisan (2009). We start with a small example.

Example 7.2.1 Consider a normally distributed random variable $X \sim \mathcal{N}(0, \sigma^2)$ (the so-called signal). Assume that X cannot be observed directly but with additional noise; that is, an analyst of the system observes the sequence $Y = (Y_1, Y_2, \ldots, Y_n)$, where:

$$Y_i = X + W_i \tag{7.1}$$

and $W_1, W_2, \ldots, W_n$ are independent and indentically distributed (i.i.d) with $W_i \sim \mathcal{N}(0, s^2)$, independent of X. The natural estimate of X given the observation Y is the conditional expectation $\mathbb{E}(X|Y_1, \ldots, Y_n)$. As X and Y are jointly normal, X can be decomposed in the following way:

$$X = a_1 Y_1 + \cdots + a_n Y_n + \xi \tag{7.2}$$

where ξ is normally distributed and independent of Y. The coefficients a_i can be computed as follows. Consider for simplicity the case $n = 2$. Then:

$$\mathrm{Cov}(X, Y_1) = \mathrm{Cov}(X, X + W_1) = \mathrm{Var}(X) = \sigma^2 = \mathrm{Cov}(X, Y_2)$$

By contrast,

$$\mathrm{Cov}(X, Y_1) = \mathrm{Cov}(a_1 Y_1 + a_2 Y_2 + \xi, Y_1) = a_1 \mathrm{Var}(Y_1) + a_2 \mathrm{Var}(X)$$
$$= a_1(\sigma^2 + s^2) + a_2\sigma^2$$

and similarly, $\mathrm{Cov}(X, Y_2) = a_1\sigma^2 + a_2(\sigma^2 + s^2)$. This gives two linear equations for a_1 and a_2 and we obtain $a_1 = a_2 = \sigma^2/(2\sigma^2 + s^2)$. Hence, the estimate of X turns out to be:

$$\mathbb{E}(X \mid Y_1, Y_2) = a_1 Y_1 + a_2 Y_2 = \frac{\sigma^2}{2\sigma^2 + s^2}\left(Y_1 + Y_2\right)$$

More generally, the estimate of X for arbitrary n is given by:

$$\mathbb{E}(X \mid Y_1, \ldots, Y_n) = \frac{\sigma^2}{n\sigma^2 + s^2} \sum_{i=1}^{n} Y_i \qquad (7.3)$$

The conditional variance $\mathrm{Var}(X \mid Y_1, \ldots, Y_n)$ is given by the variance of ξ in equation (7.2) and computes to $(\sigma^2 s^2)/(n\sigma^2 + s^2)$.

7.2.1 Stochastic Filtering

Generalizing this example, stochastic filtering is concerned with the following problem: Consider a set of time points $\mathcal{T}$; in the discrete setting typically $\mathcal{T} = \{1, 2, \ldots\}$ or in continuous-time $\mathcal{T} = [0, \infty)$. The unobservable variable of interest X is called *signal* or *state process*. It is a stochastic process $X = (X_t)_{t \in \mathcal{T}}$. The observation is given by the *observation process* $Y = (Y_t)_{t \in \mathcal{T}}$, and we denote by $\mathcal{F}_t^Y = \sigma(Y_s : s \leq t)$ the information generated by the observation until time t.

In filtering, one wants to estimate X based on the observation of Y. A major goal is to describe the conditional distribution of X_t given the $\mathcal{F}_t^Y$. The conditional distribution can be computed if one knows:

$$\mathbb{E}(\phi(X_t)|\mathcal{F}_t^Y) \qquad (7.4)$$

for a reasonably large class of functions ϕ. For computational reasons it is important to obtain this expression in a recursive way. In the sequel we describe several standard filtering problems and the corresponding recursive algorithms for evaluating the conditional expectation (7.4) in each of the models.

7.2.2   The Kalman-Bucy Filter in Discrete Time

The Kalman-Bucy filter is the simplest practically relevant case where the filtering problem has an explicit solution. The setup is an extension of Example 7.2.1. As before, X stands for the unobserved factor process, while Y represents the observation process. Consider the following model on $\mathcal{T} = \{1, 2, \dots\}$:

$$X_t = a(t)X_{t-1} + b(t)W_t \tag{7.5}$$
$$Y_t = c(t)X_t + d(t)V_t$$

where $W = (W_1, W_2, \dots)$ and $V = (V_1, V_2, \dots)$ are sequences of independent, standard normally distributed random variables and where the distribution of X_0 is given. This setup has the following interpretation: The factor process X evolves through a stochastic difference equation; note that (7.1) is the special case with $a(t) = 1$ and $b(t) = 0$. The observation Y contains $c(t)X_t$ plus additive noise. For simplicity, we assume that a, b, c, and d are deterministic, real-valued functions.[1] It is well-known that in this case the conditional distribution of X_t given $\mathcal{F}_t^Y$ is normal, so that it suffices to determine the mean and the variance of this distribution.

The Kalman-Bucy filter is a recursive procedure for computing the conditional mean and variance of X. It works in two steps: Assume that until time t,

$$X_{t|t} := \mathbb{E}\big(X_t | \mathcal{F}_t^Y\big)$$

has been computed. A first observation is that from t to $t+1$ the process X evolves according to equation (7.5). Taking this into account, one computes the *prediction*:

$$X_{t+1|t} := \mathbb{E}\big(X_{t+1} | \mathcal{F}_t^Y\big) = a(t)X_{t|t}$$

The next step incorporates the new observation at $t+1$ given by Y_{t+1}. A part of Y_{t+1}, namely $X_{t+1|t}$, can be predicted on the basis of the information available at time t, so that the *innovation* (the part of Y_{t+1} that actually carries new information) is given by $Y_{t+1} - X_{t+1|t}$. Only the innovation therefore matters for the updating to $X_{t+1|t+1}$. It can be shown that $X_{t+1|t+1}$ is given by a recursive updating rule of the form:

$$X_{t+1|t+1} = X_{t+1|t} + L_t(Y_{t+1} - X_{t+1|t}) \tag{7.6}$$

where

$$L_t = \frac{c(t)P_{t+1|t}}{c(t)^2 P_{t+1|t} + d(t)^2}$$
$$P_{t+1|t} = a(t)^2 P_{t|t} + b(t)^2, \text{ and } P_{t+1|t+1} = P_{t+1|t}(1 - L_t c(t))$$

Here P is the conditional variance; that is, $P_{s|t} = \mathbb{E}\big((X_s - X_{s|t})^2|\mathcal{F}_t^Y\big)$. Note that P is a deterministic function of time and independent of the particular realization of the observation process Y.

The Kalman-Bucy has also been applied to Gaussian models that are nonlinear by linearizing the nonlinear coefficient functions around the current estimate of X_t. This procedure is called *extended Kalman filter*. Kalman filtering is frequently employed in the empirical analysis of swap and credit spreads; see, for instance, Feldhütter and Lando (2008).

7.2.3 Filtering in Continuous Time

The standard continuous-time filtering problem is of the form:

$$
\begin{aligned}
dX_t &= a(t, X_t)dt + b(t, X_t)dW_t \\
dY_t &= c(t, X_t)dt + dV_t
\end{aligned}
\tag{7.7}
$$

for independent Brownian motions W and V. The model (7.7) can be viewed as a continuous-time version of a discrete-time filtering setup such as equation (7.5), as is illustrated in the following example.

Example 7.2.2 Translating equation (7.5) to more general time points $t_k := k\Delta$, we consider the observation $\bar{c}(t_k)X_{t_k} + \varepsilon_k$ for $\varepsilon_k \sim N(0, \Delta)$ and $\bar{c}(\cdot) = \Delta c(\cdot)$. In continuous time one considers instead the *cumulative observation process*:

$$
Y_t := \sum_{t_k \leq t} \Big(\bar{c}(t_k)X_{t_k} + \varepsilon_k\Big)
$$

Then one has for Δ small:

$$
Y_t \approx \int_0^t c(s)X_s\,ds + V_t
\tag{7.8}
$$

The generalization of this equation leads to equation (7.7).

In the innovations approach to nonlinear filtering, the conditional distribution of X_t given $\mathcal{F}_t^Y$ in the model (7.7) is characterized by a stochastic differential equation (SDE) as follows. First, denote by $\mathscr{L}$ the generator of the Markovian diffusion X:

$$
\mathscr{L}\phi(t, x) = \phi_t a(t, x) + \phi_x(t, x) + \frac{1}{2}\sum_{i,j=1}^n v_{ij}(t, x)\phi_{x_i x_j}(t, x)
$$

for any function $\phi(t, x) \in C^{1,2}$, where we set $v(t, x) := b(t, x)b(t, x)^\top$. Note that by the Itô formula $\phi(t, X_t) - \int_0^t \mathscr{L}\phi(t, X_s)ds$ is a (local) martingale so that locally

$\mathscr{L}\phi(t, X_t)dt$ gives the expected change of the process $\phi(t, X_t)$. Denote for a generic function $f(t, x)$:

$$\widehat{f}_t := \mathbb{E}\big(f(t, X_t)|\mathcal{F}_t^Y\big)$$

The innovations approach leads to the following SDE, called the *Kushner-Stratonovich equation*:

$$d\widehat{\phi}_t = \widehat{(\mathscr{L}\phi)}_t dt + \big(\widehat{c\phi}_t - \widehat{c}_t\widehat{\phi}_t\big) \cdot \big(dY_t - \widehat{c}_t\,dt\big) \tag{7.9}$$

This equation is driven by the *innovation*:

$$dY_t - \widehat{c}_t\,dt = dY_t - \mathbb{E}\big(dY_t|\mathcal{F}_t^Y\big)$$

As in the case of the Kalman-Bucy filter, the filter equation (7.9) contains two parts: $\widehat{\mathscr{L}\phi}_t$ represents the expected change of $\phi(X_t)$, and the second term gives the update with respect to the new information, which we called innovation.

Equation (7.9) is in general an infinite-dimensional equation: In order to determine $\widehat{\phi}$ one needs $\widehat{c\phi}$; this in turn requires $\widehat{c^2\phi}$ and so on. A substantial part of the modern filtering literature is concerned with finding finite-dimensional approximations to this equation that can be implemented on a computer; see, for instance, Budhiraja, Chen, and Lee (2007) or Part II of Bain and Crisan (2009).

Equation (7.9) remains true if the diffusion X is replaced by a general Markov process; just the generator $\mathscr{L}$ and the class of functions ϕ need to be adjusted in a proper way. For instance, in the case of a finite-state Markov chain the generator is given by the matrix of transition intensities. The corresponding filter formulas can be found in Section 7.2.5.

7.2.4 Observations as a Jump Process

Alternatively, the observations could be given by a doubly stochastic Poisson process with intensity depending on the factor process X. For a concrete example, suppose that N is a standard Poisson process with intensity one, that X is a diffusion, and that the observation Y is a time-changed Poisson process. Formally,

$$dX_t = a(t, X_t)dt + b(t, X_t)dW_t$$
$$Y_t = N_{\Lambda_t} \text{ for } \Lambda_t = \int_0^t \lambda(X_s)ds \tag{7.10}$$

In applications to credit risk the jump-process Y typically represents default events in a given reference portfolio. The Kushner-Stratonovich equation for the model (7.10) takes the form:

$$d\widehat{\phi}_t = \widehat{\mathscr{L}\phi}_t dt + \frac{1}{\widehat{\lambda}_t}\left(\widehat{\lambda\phi}_t - \widehat{\lambda}_t\widehat{\phi}_t\right) \cdot \left(dY_t - \widehat{\lambda}_t\, dt\right) \tag{7.11}$$

See, for instance, Brémaud (1981) for a detailed derivation.

7.2.5   The Case of Markov Chains

If X is a finite-state Markov chain, the Kushner-Stratonovich equation (7.9) reduces to a finite-dimensional SDE system. Assume, without loss of generality, that X has values $\{1, \ldots, K\}$ and denote the transition intensities of X by $(q(i, j))_{1 \le i, j \le K}$. The conditional distribution of X_t given $\mathcal{F}_t^Y$ is given by the probabilities:

$$\pi_t^k := \mathbb{P}(X_t = k|\mathcal{F}_t^Y)$$

From equation (7.9) one obtains, letting $\phi(x) = 1_{\{x=k\}}$, the dynamics of the conditional distribution π:

$$d\pi_t^k = \sum_{i=1}^N \pi_t^i q(i, k)dt + \pi_t^k\left(c(t, k) - \sum_{i=1}^N \pi_t^i c(t, i)\right) \cdot \left(dY_t - \sum_{i=1}^N \pi_t^i c(t, i)dt\right) \tag{7.12}$$

An illustration of the filter is given in Figure 7.1. Similar formulas can be given if Y follows a jump process. For further details on filtering in the case of finite-state

FIGURE 7.1   A Simulated Trajectory of the Unobservable Markov Chain X (Circles) and the Filter Estimate $\widehat{X} = \mathbb{E}(X_t \mid \mathcal{F}_t^Y)$

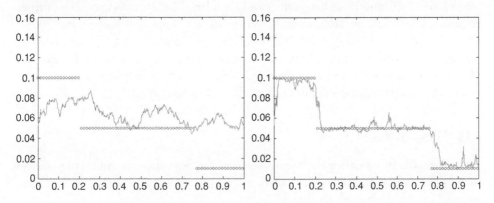

The left figure has high observation noise σ_V, while the right one has low observation noise. High noise translates to a low precision in the filter estimate and vice versa.

Markov chains, consider Elliott (1993). We use the Kushner-Stratonovich equation for finite-state Markov chains in the construction of a reduced-form credit risk model in Section 7.6.

Markov-chain approximations can be used as a computational tool for computing the filter for more general state variables; see, for instance, Budhiraja, Chen, and Lee (2007) for details. There are other situations where the Kushner-Stratonovich equation admits a finite-dimensional solution. The most prominent example is the continuous-time Kalman-Bucy filter; see, for instance, Bain and Crisan (2009).

7.3 Credit Risk Models under Incomplete Information

In this section we explain how incomplete information (the fact that some state variables are not fully observed by investors) frequently arises in credit risk models, so that filtering techniques naturally come into play.

We start with some notation. Consider a portfolio of m firms. The default time of firm i is denoted by the random variable $\tau_i > 0$. Let $D_{t,i} = 1_{\{\tau_i \leq t\}}$ denote the current default state of firm i. $D_{t,i}$ is zero if the company did not default until t and jumps to one at the default time. The current default state of the portfolio is $D_t = (D_{t,1}, \ldots, D_{t,m})$, and the default history up to time t is given by $\mathcal{F}_t^D := \sigma(D_s : s \leq t)$. The corresponding filtration is denoted by $\mathbb{F}^D$. Throughout we work on a filtered probability space $(\Omega, \mathcal{G}, \mathbb{G}, Q)$ and all stochastic processes considered will be $\mathbb{G}$-adapted. Typically Q will be the risk-neutral measure used for pricing. Moreover, we assume for simplicity that default-free interest rates are deterministic and equal to $r > 0$.

Existing dynamic credit risk models can be grouped into two classes: *structural* and *reduced-form models*. Structural models originated from Black and Scholes (1973), Merton (1974), and Black and Cox (1976). Important contributions to the literature on reduced-form models are Jarrow and Turnbull (1995), Landor (1998), Duffie and Singleton (1999), and Blanchet-Scalliet and Jeanblanc (2004), among others. Further details on credit risk models can be found in McNeil, Frey, and Embrechts (2005), Schmidt and Stute (2004), Schönbucher (2003), or Lando (2004). In structural as well as in reduced-form models it makes sense to assume that investors have imperfect information on some of the state variables of the models. A rich literature on credit risk models under incomplete information deals with this aspect.

7.3.1 Structural Models

Here one starts by modeling the asset value A of the firm under consideration. Given some, possibly random, default barrier $K = (K_t)_{t \geq 0}$, default happens at the first time when A crosses the barrier K; that is,

$$\tau = \inf\{t \geq 0 : A_t \leq K_t\} \tag{7.13}$$

The default barrier is often interpreted as the value of the liabilities of the firm; then default happens at the first time that the asset value of a firm is too low to cover its liabilities. If A is a diffusion, then the default time τ is a predictable stopping time with respect to the global filtration $\mathbb{G}$ to which A and K are adapted. It is well documented that this fact leads to very low values for short-term credit spreads, contradicting most of the available empirical evidence.

The natural state variables in a structural model are thus the asset value A of the firm and, if liabilities are stochastic, the liability-level K. It is difficult for investors to assess the value of these variables. There are many reasons for this: accounting reports offer only noisy information on the asset value; market and book values can differ as intangible assets are difficult to value; part of the liabilities are usually bank loans whose precise terms are unknown to the public, and many more. Starting with the seminal work of Duffie and Lando (2001), a growing literature therefore studies models where investors have only noisy information about A and/or K; the conditional distribution of the state variables given investor information is then computed by Bayesian updating or filtering arguments. Examples of this line of research include Duffie and Lando (2001); Nakagawa (2001); Coculescu, Geman, and Jeanblanc (2008); Schmidt and Novikov (2008); and Frey and Schmidt (2009); we discuss the works of Duffie and Lando (2001) and Frey and Schmidt (2009) in detail later. Interestingly, it turns out that the distinction between structural and reduced-form models is in fact a distinction between full and partial observability of asset values and liabilities (see Jarrow and Protter 2004): In the models mentioned the default time is predictable with respect to the global filtration $\mathbb{G}$ but becomes totally inaccessible with respect to the investor filtration $\mathbb{F}$. As a consequence, the default time admits an intensity in the investor filtration and the short-term credit spreads achieve realistic levels, as is explained in Section 7.4.

7.3.2 Reduced-Form Models

In this model class one models directly the law of the default time τ. Typically, τ is modeled as a totally inaccessible stopping time with respect to the global filtration $\mathbb{G}$, and it is assumed that τ admits a $\mathbb{G}$-intensity λ. This intensity is termed *risk-neutral default intensity* (recall that we work under the risk-neutral measure Q). Formally, $\lambda = (\lambda_t)_{t \geq 0}$ is a $\mathbb{G}$-predictable process such that

$$1_{\{\tau \leq t\}} - \int_0^{t \wedge \tau} \lambda_s \, ds \tag{7.14}$$

is a $\mathbb{G}$-martingale. Dependence between defaults is typically generated by assuming that the default intensities depend on a common factor process X. Denote by $\mathbb{F}^X :=$ $(\mathcal{F}_t^X)_{t \geq 0} = (\sigma(X_s : s \leq t))_{t \geq 0}$ the filtration generated by the factor X. The simplest construction is that of *conditionally independent, doubly stochastic default times*: Here it is assumed that given the realization of the factor process, the default times τ_i are conditionally independent with intensities $\lambda_i(X_t)$; that is,

$$Q(\tau_1 > t_1, \ldots, \tau_m > t_m \mid \mathcal{F}_\infty^X) = \prod_{i=1}^{m} \exp\left(-\int_0^{t_i} \lambda_i(X_s)\, ds \right) \qquad (7.15)$$

In applications, X is usually treated as a latent process whose current value must be inferred from observable quantities such as prices or the default history. A theoretically consistent way for doing this is to determine via filtering the conditional distribution of X_t given investor information $\mathbb{F}$. Models of this type include the contributions by Schönbucher (2004); Collin-Dufresne, Goldstein, and Helwege (2003); Duffie et al. (2009); Frey and Schmidt (2010); and Frey and Runggaldier (2010). The last two papers are discussed in Section 7.6.

Remark 7.3.1   We will see that the introduction of incomplete information generates *information-driven default contagion* (both in structural and in reduced-form models): *The news that some obligor has defaulted causes an update in the conditional distribution of the unobserved factor and hence to a jump in the $\mathbb{F}$-default intensity of the surviving firms. This in turn leads to interesting dynamics of credit spreads; compare the discussion following Proposition 7.6.1.*

7.4   Structural Models I: Duffie and Lando (2001)

In this section we discuss the influential paper by Duffie and Lando (2001). As previously, let Q be the risk-neutral measure and $\mathbb{G} = (\mathcal{G}_t)_{t \geq 0}$ be the filtration that represents full information. The asset value A is assumed to follow a geometric Brownian motion with drift μ, volatility σ, and initial value A_0, such that:

$$A_t = A_0 \exp\left(\left(\mu - \frac{1}{2}\sigma^2 \right)t + \sigma W_t \right) \qquad (7.16)$$

where W is a Brownian motion. The default barrier K and the inital value A_0 are taken to be constant and therefore the default time is $\tau := \inf\{t \geq 0: A_t \leq K\}$. It is assumed that A is not directly observable. Rather, investors observe default, and they receive *noisy accounting reports* at deterministic times $t_1, t_2, \ldots$. This is modeled by assuming they observe the random variables:

$$Y_i := \ln A_{t_i} + U_i$$

at t_i, where $U_1, U_2, \ldots$ is a sequence of independent, normally distributed random variables, independent of A. Formally, with $D_t := 1_{\{\tau \le t\}}$, the information available to investors is given by:

$$\mathcal{F}_t := \sigma(D_s : s \le t) \vee \sigma(\{Y_i : t_i \le t\})$$

We now study the computation of survival probabilities, default intensities, and credit spreads. We start with the situation under full information. By the Markov property of A one has, for $T \ge t$,

$$Q(\tau > T \mid \mathcal{G}_t) = 1_{\{\tau > t\}} Q\left(\inf_{s \in (t, T)} A_s > K \mid \mathcal{G}_t\right)$$

$$= 1_{\{\tau > t\}} Q\left(\inf_{s \in (t, T)} A_s > K \mid A_t\right)$$

$$=: 1_{\{\tau > t\}} F_\tau(t, T, A_t)$$

Note that the mapping $T \mapsto F_\tau(t, T, v)$ gives the risk-neutral survival probabilities of the firm under full information at time t, given that $A_t = v$. This probability is easily computed using standard results on the first passage time of Brownian motions with drift. Using iterated conditional expectations, one obtains the survival probability in the investor filtration:

$$Q(\tau > T \mid \mathcal{F}_t) = \mathbb{E}\Big(Q(\tau > T \mid \mathcal{G}_t) \mid \mathcal{F}_t\Big)$$

$$= 1_{\{\tau > t\}} \int_{\log K}^\infty F_\tau(t, T, v)\, \pi_{A_t \mid \mathcal{F}_t}(dv)$$

Here $\pi_{A_t \mid \mathcal{F}_t}$ denotes the conditional distribution of A_t given $\mathcal{F}_t$. In Duffie and Lando (2001), this distribution is computed in an elementary way, involving Bayes's formula and properties of first passage time of Brownian motion. Section 7.5.1 shows how filtering techniques can be used in this context.

Next we turn to the *default intensity* in the model with incomplete information. It can be shown that under some regularity conditions the default intensity is given by:

$$\lambda_t = \lim_{h \downarrow 0} \frac{1}{h} Q\big(t < \tau \le t + h \mid \mathcal{F}_t\big) \tag{7.17}$$

provided this limit exists for all $t \ge 0$ almost surely (see Aven 1985 for details). Duffie and Lando show that such a λ_t exists and is given on $\{\tau > t\}$ by:

$$\lambda_t = \frac{\sigma^2 K}{2} \frac{\partial}{\partial v} f_{A_t \mid \mathcal{F}_t}(K) \tag{7.18}$$

where $f_{A_t|\mathcal{F}_t}$ denotes the Lebesgue density of the conditional distribution of A_t given $\mathcal{F}_t$.

7.4.1   Bonds and Credit Spreads

A defaultable zero coupon bond with zero recovery pays one unit of account at maturity T if no default happened and zero otherwise. Hence, in this setup its price $p(t, T)$ at time t equals:

$$1_{\{\tau > t\}} e^{-r(T-t)} Q\big(\tau > T \mid \mathcal{F}_t\big) = 1_{\{\tau > t\}} e^{-r(T-t)} \int_{\log K}^{\infty} F_\tau(t, T, v)\, \pi_{A_t|\mathcal{F}_t}(dv)$$

Therefore zero coupon bond prices can be expressed as an average with respect to the filter distribution. The credit spread $c(t, T)$ of the bond gives the yield over the risk-free short-term rate. Formally it is given by:

$$c(t, T) = -\frac{1}{T-t}\Big(\log p(t, T) - \log p_0(t, T)\Big) \tag{7.19}$$

where $p_0(t, T)$ denotes the price at time t of the risk-free zero coupon bond with maturity T. Hence we get on $\{\tau > t\}$ that $c(t, T) = \frac{-1}{T-t}\log Q(\tau > T \mid \mathcal{F}_t)$. In particular, we obtain:

$$\lim_{T \to t} c(t, T) = -\lim_{T \to t}\Big(\frac{\partial}{\partial T} Q(\tau > T \mid \mathcal{F}_t)\Big) = \lambda_t$$

where the second equation follows from equation (7.17). This shows that the introduction of incomplete information typically leads to nonvanishing short-term credit spreads.

Other debt-related securities such as credit default swaps (CDSs) can be priced in a straightforward fashion once the conditional survival function given investor information is at hand.

7.5   Structural Models II: Frey and Schmidt (2009)

In Frey and Schmidt (2009), the Duffie-Lando model is extended in two directions: First, nonlinear filtering techniques based on Markov chain approximations are employed in order to determine the conditional distribution of the asset value given the investor information; second, the paper introduces dividend payments and discusses the pricing of the firm's equity under incomplete information. We begin with a discussion of the filtering part.

7.5.1 The Filtering Part

7.5.1.1 The Model

Here we present a slightly simplified version of the model discussed in Frey and Schmidt (2009). Similarly to in the Duffie-Lando model, the asset value A is given by the geometric Brownian motion [equation (7.16)], so that the log-asset value $X_t := \log A_t$ satisfies $X_t = X_0 + \left(\mu - \frac{1}{2}\sigma^2\right) t + \sigma W_t$. The default time τ is:

$$\tau := \inf\{t \geq 0 : A_t \leq K\} = \inf\{t \geq 0 : X_t \leq \log K\}$$

Investors observe the default state of the firm; moreover, they receive information related to the state of the company, such as information (news) given by analysts, articles in newspapers, and so on. It is assumed that this information is discrete, corresponding, for instance, to buy/hold/sell recommendations or rating information. Formally, news events on the company are issued at time points t_n^I, $n \geq 1$; the news obtained at t_n^I is denoted by I_n, which takes values in the discrete state space $\{\ell_1, \ldots, \ell_{M^I}\}$. The conditional distribution of I_n given the asset value of the company at t_n^I is denoted by $\nu_I(I_n|x)$ where:

$$\nu_I(\ell_j|x) := Q(I_n = \ell_j | X_{t_n^I} = x)$$

Summarizing, the information of investors at time t is given by:

$$\mathcal{F}_t := \mathcal{F}_t^D \vee \sigma\left(I_n : t_n^I \leq t\right) \tag{7.20}$$

7.5.1.2 Filtering

In order to determine the conditional distribution $\pi_{X_t|\mathcal{F}_t}$ with minimal technical difficulties, the log-asset value process X is approximated by a finite-state discrete-time Markov chain as follows: Define for a $\Delta > 0$ the grid:

$$\{t_k^\Delta = k\Delta : k \in \mathbb{N}\}$$

Let $(X_k^\Delta)_{k \in \mathbb{N}}$ be a discrete-time finite-state Markov chain with state space $\{m_1^\Delta, \ldots, m_{M^\Delta}^\Delta\}$ and transition probabilities p_{ij}^Δ. Define the induced process X^Δ by $X_t^\Delta = X_k^\Delta$ for $t \in [t_k^\Delta, t_{k+1}^\Delta)$. In Frey and Schmidt (2009) it is assumed that the chain $(X_k^\Delta)_{k \in \mathbb{N}}$ is close to the continuous log-asset-value process X in the sense that X^Δ converges in distribution to X as $\Delta \to 0$; it is shown that this implies that the conditional distribution $\pi_{X_t^\Delta|\mathcal{F}_t}$ converges weakly to $\pi_{X_t|\mathcal{F}_t}$ as $\Delta \to 0$. The approximating Markov chain can be chosen to be trinomial with transition probabilities determined by matching the first and second moment of the transition probabilities of X^Δ with those of X; see Frey and Schmidt (2009) for details.

In the sequel we keep Δ fixed and therefore mostly omit it from the notation. The conditional distribution $\pi_{X_{t_k}^{\Delta} | \mathcal{F}_{t_k}}$ is summarized by the probability vector $\pi(k) = (\pi^1(k), \ldots, \pi^M(k))$ with:

$$\pi^j(k) := Q(X_k = m_j \mid \mathcal{F}_{t_k})$$

The initial filter distribution $\pi(0)$ can be inferred from the initial distribution of X_0, which is a model primitive. There is a simple explicit recursive updating rule for the probability vector $\pi(k)$, as we show next. It is convenient to formulate the updating rule in terms of *unnormalized probabilities* $\sigma(k) \propto \pi(k)$ ($\propto$ standing for proportional to); the vector $\pi(k)$ can then be obtained by normalization:

$$\pi^j(k) = \frac{\sigma^j(k)}{\sum_{i=1}^{M} \sigma^i(k)}$$

Proposition 7.5.1 *For $k \geq 1$ and $t_k < \tau$ denote by $N_k := \{n \in \mathbb{N} : t_{k-1} < t_n^I \leq t_k\}$ the set of indexes of news arrivals in the period $(t_{k-1}, t_k]$, and recall that p_{ij} are the transition probabilities of the approximating Markov chain X. Then for $j = 1, \ldots, M$ we have that:*

$$\sigma^j(k) = 1_{\{m_j > \log K\}} \sum_{i=1}^{M} \left(p_{ij} \sigma^i(k-1) \prod_{n \in N_k} v_I(I_n | m_i) \right) \tag{7.21}$$

Here we use the convention that the product over an empty set is equal to one.

Formula (7.21) explains how to obtain $\sigma(k)$ from $\sigma(k-1)$ and the new observation received over $(t_{k-1}, t_k]$. The derivation of this formula is quite instructive. First note that given the new information arriving in $(t_{k-1}, t_k]$, equation (7.21) forms a linear and in particular a positively homogeneous mapping Γ such that $\sigma(k) = \Gamma\sigma(k-1)$. Hence it is enough to show that $\pi(k) \propto \Gamma\pi(k-1)$. In order to compute $\pi(k)$ from $\pi(k-1)$ and the new observation, we proceed in two steps. In step 1 we compute (up to proportionality) an auxiliary vector of probabilities $\bar{\pi}(k-1)$ with:

$$\bar{\pi}^i(k-1) = Q(X_{k-1} = m_i \mid \mathcal{F}_k^-), \ 1 \leq i \leq M \tag{7.22}$$

where $\mathcal{F}_k^- := \mathcal{F}_{t_{k-1}} \vee \sigma(\{I_n : n \in N_k\})$. In filtering terminology this is a smoothing step, as the conditional distribution of X_{k-1} is updated using the new information arriving in $(t_{k-1}, t_k]$. In step 2 we determine (again up to proportionality) $\pi(k)$ from the auxiliary probability vector $\bar{\pi}(k-1)$ using the dynamics of (X_k) and the additional information that $\tau > t_k$. We begin with step 2. Since $\{\tau > t_k\} = \{\tau > t_{k-1}\} \cap \{X_k > \log K\}$, we get:

$$Q\left(X_k = m_j \mid \mathcal{F}_{t_k}\right) \propto Q\left(X_k = m_j, X_k > \log K \mid \mathcal{F}_k^-\right)$$

$$= \sum_{i=1}^{M} Q\left(X_k = m_j, X_k > \log K, X_{k-1} = m_i \mid \mathcal{F}_k^-\right)$$

$$= 1_{\{m_j > \log K\}} \sum_{i=1}^{M} p_{ij} \, \bar{\pi}^i(k-1) \tag{7.23}$$

Next we turn to the smoothing step. Note that given $X_{k-1} = m_i$, the likelihood of the news observed over $(t_{k-1}, t_k]$ equals $\prod_{n \in N_k} \nu_I(I_n \mid m_i)$, and we obtain:

$$\bar{\pi}^i(k-1) \propto \pi^i(k-1) \cdot \prod_{n \in N_k} \nu_I(I_n \mid m_i)$$

Combining this with equation (7.23) gives equation (7.21).

7.5.2 Pricing the Firm's Equity

Next we discuss the pricing of the firm's equity or shares. This is of interest for at least two reasons: On the theoretical side, this analysis sheds some light on the relationship between share price and asset value in the presence of incomplete information; on the practical side this is a prerequisite for the pricing of certain hybrid corporate securities such as equity default swaps.

In Frey and Schmidt (2009) the predefault value of the firm's equity S is defined as the expected value of the future discounted dividends up to the default of the firm. Simplifying slightly the original setup of Frey and Schmidt (2009), we assume that dividends are paid at dividend dates t_n^d; the dividend paid at t_n^d is given by the random variable:

$$d_n = \delta_n A_{t_n^d}, \quad \text{for } \delta_n \in [0, 1) \text{ i.i.d., independent of } A \text{ with mean } \bar{\delta}$$

Formally we thus have:

$$S_t = \mathbb{E}\left(\sum_{t < t_n^d < \tau} e^{-r(t_n^d - t)} \delta_n A_{t_n^d} \mid \mathcal{F}_t \right) \tag{7.24}$$

Denote by $\mathbb{E}\left(\sum_{t < t_n^d < \tau} e^{-r(t_n^d - t)} \delta_n A_{t_n^d} \mid \mathcal{G}_t \right)$ the equity value under full information. Since A is a Markov process, on $\{\tau > t\}$ the latter is given by some function $S(t, A_t)$ of time and the current equity value. Using the tower property of conditional expectations we thus get:

$$S_t = \mathbb{E}\left(\mathbb{E}\left(\sum_{t<t_n^d<\tau} e^{-r(t_n^d-t)}\delta_n A_{t_n^d} \mid \mathcal{G}_t \right) \mid \mathcal{F}_t \right) = 1_{\{\tau>t\}}\mathbb{E}\left(S(t, A_t) \mid \mathcal{F}_t \right)$$

and the conditional distribution of the right can be computed using the approximation of the filter distribution given in Proposition 7.5.1.[2]

Example 7.5.1 This is a closed-form solution for the equity value under full information. A slight modification of the setup leads to a closed-form expression for the function $S(\cdot)$. For this we assume that the dividend dates are the jump times of a Poisson process with intensity λ^d, corresponding to the average number of dividend dates per year. With frequent dividend payments, such as quarterly or semiannually, the equity value obtained under the assumption of Poissonian dividend dates is a good approximation of its counterpart for fixed dividend dates. The advantage of this assumption is that the predefault equity value becomes independent of calendar time t. Proposition 2.4 of Frey and Schmidt (2009) states that for $\mu < r$ the full-information value of the firm's equity equals $1_{\{\tau>t\}}S(A_t)$ with:

$$S(v) = \frac{\lambda^d\bar{\delta}}{r-\mu}\left[v - \left(\frac{v}{K} \right)^{\alpha^*} K \right] \tag{7.25}$$

Here $\alpha^* < 0$ is the unique negative root of the quadratic equation,

$$\alpha\mu + \frac{1}{2}\sigma^2\alpha(\alpha-1) = r$$

Note that S is concave in v and approaches the line $v \mapsto v \cdot \frac{\lambda^d\bar{\delta}}{(r-\mu)}$ as v tends to infinity. This line corresponds to the value of the firm's equity for $K = 0$ and therefore $\tau = \infty$. The qualitative behavior of S is illustrated in Figure 7.2.

7.5.3 Further Applications

We briefly discuss further results obtained in Frey and Schmidt (2009).

7.5.3.1 Estimating the Asset Values from Equity Values

The filter estimate of the previous section corresponds to a fundamental valuation approach: One tries to assess the value of the firm's assets from economic information such as news. When the stock of the firm is liquidly traded, one could alternatively compute a market implied estimator of the asset value by inverting some pricing formula that relates asset and equity value. The KMV methodology is a typical example

FIGURE 7.2 Value of the Firm's Equity as a Function of the Asset Value According to Equation (7.25) for Different σ and with $K = 60$

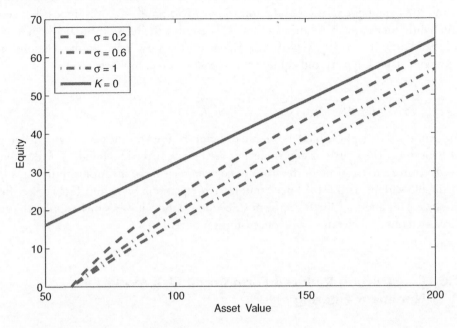

The straight line is the equity value for $K = 0$.

where this approach is used; see Crosbie and Bohn (1997–2001). Formally, given the current equity value S^* observed in the market and a valuation formula under full information of the form $S_t = S(t, A_t)$, S strictly increasing in v, the corresponding *equity-implied estimator* EE_t is given by the solution of the equation $S(t, \mathrm{EE}_t) = S^*$.

In Frey and Schmidt (2009) it is shown that this estimator performs well if the conditional variance of A_t given the investor information $\mathcal{F}_t$ is small—that is, if the observations received by investors carry a lot of information about the true value of A_t. However, the estimator performs poorly if the conditional variance of A_t is comparatively large. Moreover, it is possible to study the bias of the equity estimator via Jensen's inequality. If the function $v \mapsto S(t, v)$ is concave as in Example 7.5.1, one obtains that:

$$\mathrm{EE}_t \leq \mathbb{E}(A_t | \mathcal{F}_t)$$

If $v \mapsto S(t, v)$ is convex, the inequality is reversed.

7.5.3.2 Equity Value and Default Intensity

It can be shown that relation (7.18) for the default intensity under incomplete information in the Duffie-Lando model carries over to the setup of Frey and Schmidt

(2009). Given this result, in Frey and Schmidt (2009) the relationship between equity value and default intensity λ_t is studied. It turns out that for fixed firm characteristics μ and σ a hyperbolic relation of the form $\lambda_t = h(S_t) := \frac{\alpha}{S^\rho}$—as it is imposed in certain hybrid models such as Linetsky (2006)—describes the relationship between stock price and default intensity well. If these characteristics vary, however, the relationship between default intensity and equity value breaks down completely.

7.5.3.3   Pricing of Hybrid Securities

As mentioned before, the model could in principle be used for the pricing and hedging of hybrid securities such as equity default swaps or convertible bonds. For this one needs to give a description of the stock price dynamics in the investor filtration, using a suitable variant of the Kushner-Stratonovich equations (7.9) and (7.11); see, for instance, Frey and Lu (2010). In the next section we show how a similar approach can be carried out in the context of reduced-form models.

7.6   Constructing Reduced-Form Credit Risk Models via Nonlinear Filtering

Now we turn our attention to reduced-form models under incomplete information. We discuss in detail our own model proposed in Frey and Schmidt (2010). A key idea in that paper is to use the innovations approach to nonlinear filtering in order to derive the price dynamics of credit derivatives. We will show that this leads to a fairly tractable model with rich dynamics of credit spreads and a lot of flexibility for calibration.

7.6.1   The Setup

We consider a portfolio that contains credit derivatives on m firms. As before, the default state of the portfolio is described by the process $D = (D_{t,1}, \ldots, D_{t,m})_{t \geq 0}$ with $D_{t,i} = 1_{\{\tau_i \leq t\}}$, $\mathbb{G}$ represents the global filtration to which all processes are adapted, and we work directly under the risk-neutral pricing measure Q. The model is driven by some factor process X, modeled as a finite-state Markov chain with state space $S^X := \{1, \ldots, K\}$. The default time τ_i has $\mathbb{G}$-default intensity $\lambda_i(X_t)$ where $\lambda_1, \ldots, \lambda_m$ are given functions from S^X to $(0, \infty)$. Then, as in equation (7.14), $D_{t,i} - \int_0^{\tau_i \wedge t} \lambda_i(X_s) \, ds$ is a martingale with respect to the full-information filtration $\mathbb{G}$. Moreover, we assume that the τ_i are conditionally independent given X; compare equation (7.15). In this setup the process (X, D) is jointly Markov.

However, we assume that X is unobservable and that prices of traded securities are given as conditional expectation with respect to a filtration $\mathbb{F} = (\mathcal{F}_t)_{t \geq 0}$, which is called *market information*. The filtration $\mathbb{F}$ is generated by a process Y giving observations of

X in additive noise and by the default history of the firms under consideration; that is, $\mathbb{F} = \mathbb{F}^Y \vee \mathbb{F}^D$. Y is of the form:

$$Y_t = \int_0^t a(X_s)ds + V_t \qquad (7.26)$$

with a Brownian motion V, independent of X and D. As intended, X is not $\mathbb{F}$-adapted. The process Y models the information contained in security prices; it is not directly linked to observable economic quantities. We come back to this point when we discuss calibration strategies for the model in Section 7.6.4. Throughout the rest of the chapter we denote by $\widehat{U}_t := \mathbb{E}(U_t | \mathcal{F}_t)$ the *projection* of a generic process U on the market filtration $\mathbb{F}$.

Example 7.6.1   This is a *one-factor model*. In the numerical part we will consider a one-factor model where X represents the global state of the economy. For this we model the default intensities under full information as *increasing* functions λ_i : $\{1, \ldots, K\} \to (0, \infty)$. Note that this implies that 1 represents the best state (lowest default intensities) and that K corresponds to the worst state; moreover, the default intensities are comonotonic. In the special case of a homogeneous model, the default intensities of all firms are identical: $\lambda_i(\cdot) \equiv \lambda(\cdot)$. In that situation one could assume that $a(\cdot) = c \ln \lambda(\cdot)$. Here the constant $c \geq 0$ models the information content of Y: for $c = 0$, Y carries no information, whereas for c large the state X_t can be observed with high precision.

Denote by $(q(i, k))_{1 \leq i, k \leq K}$ the generator matrix of X so that $q(i, k)$, $i \neq k$, giving the intensity of a transition from state i to state k. In this chapter we consider two possible choices for this matrix. First, let the factor process be constant, $X_t \equiv X$ for all t. In that case $q(i, k) \equiv 0$, and filtering reduces to Bayesian analysis. A model of this type is known as *frailty model*; see also Schönbucher (2004). Later we will see that the frailty model can be viewed as a dynamic version of the implied copula model of Hull and White (2006). Second, we consider the case where X has *next-neighbor dynamics*; that is, the chain jumps from X_t only to the neighboring points $X_t \pm 1$ (with the obvious modifications for $X_t = 0$ and $X_t = K$).

7.6.1.1   Nonlinear Filtering Problems

In this setup the computation of important economic quantities leads to nonlinear filtering problems in a natural way. Consider first the pricing of credit derivatives. The payoff H of a typical credit derivative depends on the default state of the portfolio at the maturity date T; in mathematical terms H is an $\mathcal{F}_T^D$-measurable random variable. Examples include defaultable zero coupon bonds, CDSs, or CDOs; see Subsection 7.6.3 for details. In line with risk-neutral pricing we define the price of the claim by the conditional expectation of the discounted payoff under the risk-neutral measure:

$$\widehat{H}_t := \mathbb{E}\big(e^{-r(T-t)} H \mid \mathcal{F}_t\big)$$

Note that this definition involves the market filtration $\mathcal{F}_t$. As (X, Y) is Markovian, it follows that for typical payoffs $\mathbb{E}\big(e^{-r(T-t)} H \mid \mathcal{G}_t\big)$ is a function of t, X_t and D_t, which we denote by $h(t, X_t, D_t)$. By the tower property of the conditional expectation we obtain:

$$\widehat{H}_t = \mathbb{E}\Big(\mathbb{E}\big(e^{-r(T-t)} H \mid \mathcal{G}_t\big) \mid \mathcal{F}_t\Big) = \mathbb{E}\big(h(t, X_t, D_t) \mid \mathcal{F}_t\big) \qquad (7.27)$$

Since D_t is observable, in order to compute $\widehat{H}_t$ we need to determine the conditional distribution of X_t given $\mathcal{F}_t$; that is, we have to solve a nonlinear filtering problem. This problem is studied in the next section.

The intensity of τ_i with respect to a smaller information set $\mathbb{F}$ with $\mathbb{F}^D \subset \mathbb{F} \subset \mathbb{G}$ is given by projecting the $\mathbb{G}$-default intensity on the smaller filtration $\mathbb{F}$ (see Chapter 2 of Brémaud (1981)). Hence in our setup the $\mathbb{F}$-default intensity of firm i is given by:

$$\hat{\lambda}_{t,i} := \mathbb{E}\left(\lambda_i(X_t) \mid \mathcal{F}_t\right), \quad t \leq \tau_i \qquad (7.28)$$

That is, the computation of default intensities in the market filtration leads to a nonlinear filtering problem as well.

7.6.1.2   Model Performance

We are convinced that this model has a number of attractive features. First, actual computations are done mostly in the context of the hypothetical model where X is fully observable. Since the latter has a simple Markovian structure, computations become relatively straightforward. Second, the fact that prices of traded securities are constructed by projection on the market filtration $\mathbb{F}$ leads to rich credit-spread dynamics: The proposed approach accommodates *spread risk* (random fluctuations of credit spreads between defaults) and *default contagion*; see, for instance, Figure 7.3. Finally, the approach gives great flexibility in terms of calibration methodologies, as is discussed in detail in Section 7.6.4.

7.6.2   Filtering and Factor Representation of Market Prices

Since X is a finite-state Markov chain, the conditional distribution of X_t given $\mathcal{F}_t$ is described by the vector $\pi_t = (\pi_t^1, \ldots, \pi_t^K)^\top$ with $\pi_t^k := Q(X_t = k \mid \mathcal{F}_t)$.

In particular, we have for a generic function $a \colon \{1, \ldots, K\} \to \mathbb{R}$ the relationship

$$\widehat{a_t} := \widehat{a(X_t)} = \sum_{k=1}^{K} \pi_t^k a(k)$$

Proposition 7.6.1 shows that π is the solution of a K-dimensional SDE system. This system is driven by the $\mathbb{F}$-Brownian motion m^Y given by:

$$m_t^Y := Y_t - \int_0^t \widehat{a}_s \, ds \tag{7.29}$$

and by the compensated default indicator process $M = (M_{t,1}, \ldots, M_{t,m})'_{t \geq 0}$ with:

$$M_{t,j} := D_{t,j} - \int_0^t (1 - D_{s-,j}) \, (\widehat{\lambda_j})_s \, ds \tag{7.30}$$

Recall that $(q(i, k))_{1 \leq i, k \leq K}$ is the generator matrix of X. In Frey and Schmidt (2010) the following result is established.

Proposition 7.6.1 *The vector* $\pi_t = (\pi_t^1, \ldots, \pi_t^K)'$ *solves the SDE system:*

$$d\pi_t^k = \sum_{i=1}^{K} q(i, k)\pi_t^i dt + (\gamma^k(\pi_{t-}))^\top dM_t + (\alpha^k(\pi_t))^\top dm_t^Y \tag{7.31}$$

with coefficients given by:

$$\gamma_j^k(\pi_t) = \pi_t^k \Big(\frac{\lambda_j(k)}{\sum_{i \in S^X} \lambda_j(i)\pi_t^i} - 1 \Big), \quad 1 \leq j \leq m \tag{7.32}$$

$$\alpha^k(\pi_t) = \pi_t^k \Big(a(k) - \sum_{i \in S^X} \pi_t^i a(i) \Big) \tag{7.33}$$

Note that the diffusion part of equation (7.31) and in particular the function α^k from equation (7.33) has the same form as in equation (7.12); the form of γ^k from equation (7.32) is closely related to the Kushner-Stratonovich equation for point process observation (7.11).

Proposition 7.6.1 permits us to give an explicit expression for *contagion effects* induced by incomplete information. More precisely, consider two firms $i \neq j$. Then it follows from equation (7.32) that the jump in the default intensity of firm i at the default time τ_j of firm j is given by:

$$\widehat{\lambda}_{\tau_j,i} - \widehat{\lambda}_{\tau_j-,i} = \sum_{k=1}^{K} \lambda_i(k) \cdot \pi_{\tau_j-}^k \left(\frac{\lambda_j(k)}{\sum_{l=1}^{K} \lambda_j(l)\pi_{\tau_j-}^l} - 1 \right) = \frac{\mathrm{cov}^{\pi_{\tau_j-}}(\lambda_i, \lambda_j)}{\mathbb{E}^{\pi_{\tau_j-}}(\lambda_j)} \quad (7.34)$$

Here cov^π as well as $\mathbb{E}^\pi$ denote the covariance (expectation) with respect to the probability measure π on S^X, and π_{τ_j-} gives the conditional distribution of X immediately prior to the default event. According to equation (7.34), default contagion increases with increasing correlation of the random variables $\lambda_i(\cdot)$ and $\lambda_j(\cdot)$ under π_{τ_j-}, which is perfectly in line with economic intuition.

In Frey and Schmidt (2010) it is shown that the process $(D_t, \pi_t)_{t\geq}$ is a Markov process in the market filtration $\mathbb{F}$; the generator $\mathscr{L}$ of this process is an integro-differential operator. Hence the prices of credit derivatives can be expressed in terms of D_t and π_t, as is discussed in detail in the next section. The process (D, π) will therefore be called the *market state* process. The following algorithm can be used to generate a trajectory of the market state process:

Algorithm 7.6.1

(i) Generate a trajectory of X using a standard algorithm for the simulation of Markov chains.

(ii) Generate for the trajectory of X constructed in step (i) a trajectory of the default indicator D and the noisy information Y. For the simulation of D one can use known methods for simulating conditionally independent, doubly stochastic random times as given in Section 9.6 of McNeil, Frey, and Embrechts (2005).

(iii) Solve (numerically) for the given trajectory of D and Y the SDE system (7.31) (e.g., via Euler approximation).

Once a trajectory of the market state process (D, π) is at hand, the price path of a credit derivative can be simulated using the relationship $\widehat{H}_t = \sum_{k=1}^{K} h(t, k, D_t)\pi_t^k$, $h(\cdot)$ the full-information value of the claim as in (7.27).

7.6.3 Pricing

In this section we discuss the pricing of credit derivatives in more detail. Basically all credit derivatives common in practice fall into one of the following two classes:

1. *Options on the default state* This class comprises derivatives with a cash flow stream that depends on the default history of the underlying portfolio so that it is $\mathbb{F}^D$-adapted; examples are corporate bonds, CDSs, and CDOs.

2. *Options on traded assets* This class contains derivatives whose payoffs depend on the future market value of traded credit products. Examples include options on corporate bonds or options on CDS indexes and CDO tranches.

The pricing methodologies for these product classes differ, so they are discussed separately.

7.6.3.1 Options on the Default State

Let the $\mathbb{F}^D$-adapted process $(H_t)_{0 \le t \le T}$ be the cumulative cash flow stream associated with the claim. Then by risk-neutral pricing its ex-dividend price at time t is defined to be:

$$\widehat{H}_t = \mathbb{E}\Big(\int_t^T e^{-r(s-t)} \, dH_s \mid \mathcal{F}_t \Big) \tag{7.35}$$

Denote by $h(t, k, d) := \mathbb{E}\big(\int_t^T e^{-r(s-t)} \, dH_s \mid (X_t, D_t) = (k, d) \big)$ the full-information price of the claim. Similarly as in equation (7.27), double conditioning on the full-information filtration $\mathbb{G}$ leads to the relationship:

$$\widehat{H}_t = \sum_{k=1}^K \pi_t^k h(t, k, D_t) \tag{7.36}$$

Note that $\widehat{H}_t$ depends only on the current market state (D_t, π_t) and on the function $h(\cdot)$ that gives the hypothetical value under full information; the precise form of the function $a(\cdot)$ from equation (7.26) and thus of the dynamics of π is irrelevant. The dynamics of π do, however, matter in the computation of hedging strategies; see Frey and Schmidt (2010) for details.

Example 7.6.2 We discuss zero coupon bonds and CDSs.

- Consider a zero coupon bond on firm i with maturity T and zero recovery. Here $H_t \equiv 0$ for $t < T$ and $H_T \equiv 1_{\{\tau_i > T\}}$. By standard results on bond pricing with doubly stochastic default times (see, for instance, Lando 1998) the full-information value is given by:

$$h_i(t, k, d) = 1_{\{d_i = 0\}} \mathbb{E}\Big(e^{-\int_t^T r + \lambda_i(X_s) ds} \mid X_t = k \Big) \tag{7.37}$$

The price of the bond at time t is then given by $\widehat{H}_{t,i} = \sum_{k=1}^K \pi_t^k h_i(t, k, D_t)$.
- Next consider a CDS on name i. Denote by $t_1 < \cdots < t_N = T$ the premium payment dates and by x the spread of the contract. The cumulative cash flow stream of the premium leg is then given by $H_t^{\text{prem}} = x \sum_{t_n \le t} 1_{\{\tau_i > t_n\}}$, whereas the

cumulative cash flow stream of the default leg equals $H_t^{\text{def}} = \delta \int_0^t dD_{s,i}, \delta \in (0, 1)$, the loss given default of the firm. It is well known that the full-information value of the premium leg at time t is equal to $x 1_{\{\tau_i > t\}} V_i^{\text{prem}}(t, k)$ with:

$$V_i^{\text{prem}}(t, k) = \sum_{t_n > t} \mathbb{E}\left(e^{-\int_t^{t_n} r + \lambda_i(X_s)ds} | X_t = k\right) \tag{7.38}$$

The full-information value of the default leg equals $\delta 1_{\{\tau_i > t\}} V_i^{\text{def}}(t, k)$ with:

$$V_i^{\text{def}}(t, k) = \mathbb{E}\left(\int_t^T \lambda_i(X_s)e^{-\int_t^s r + \lambda_i(X_u)du} ds | X_t = k\right) \tag{7.39}$$

Given the spread x, the value at time t, is thus given by $\sum_{k=1}^K \pi_t^k \left(x V_i^{\text{prem}}(t, k) - V_i^{\text{def}}(t, k)\right)$, and the fair spread at time t is:

$$x_t^* := \frac{\delta \sum_{k=1}^K \pi_t^k V_i^{\text{def}}(t, k)}{\sum_{k=1}^K \pi_t^k V_i^{\text{prem}}(t, k)}$$

Analogous arguments are used in the pricing of CDS indexes and CDOs.

Remark 7.6.1 (Computation of full-information value $h(\cdot)$). *For bonds and CDSs the computation of h amounts to computing equations (7.37) and (7.38), respectively. There is an easy solution to this task involving the exponential of the generator matrix of X; see Elliott and Mamon (2003). In the case of CDOs, a solution of this problem via Laplace transforms can be found in di Graziano and Rogers (2009). Alternatively, a two-stage method that employs the conditional independence of defaults given $\mathcal{F}_\infty^X$ can be used. For this one, first generate a trajectory of X via Monte Carlo. Given this trajectory, the loss distribution can then be evaluated using one of the known methods for computing the distribution of the sum of independent (but not identically distributed) Bernoulli variates. Finally, the loss distribution is computed by averaging over the sampled trajectories of X. An extensive numerical case study comparing the different approaches is given in Wendler (2009).*

7.6.3.2   Options on Traded Assets

Assume now that N basic options on the default state are traded on the market, and denote their ex-dividend price at time t by $\widehat{p}_{t,1}, \ldots, \widehat{p}_{t,N}$. Then the payoff of an option on traded assets is of the form $\tilde{g}(D_{\tilde{T}}, \widehat{p}_{\tilde{T},1}, \ldots, \widehat{p}_{\tilde{T},N})$, to be paid at maturity $\tilde{T} \leq T$ (T is the maturity of the underlying products). From equation (7.36), the payoff of the option can be written in the form $g\left(D_{\tilde{T}}, \pi_{\tilde{T}}\right)$, where g is implicitly defined. Since the market state (D, π) is an $\mathbb{F}$-Markov process, the price of the option at time $t < \bar{T}$ is given by a function of time and the current market state,

$$\mathbb{E}\left(e^{-r(\bar{T}-t)}g(D_{\bar{T}}, \pi_{\bar{T}})|\mathcal{F}_t\right) = g(t, D_t, \pi_t) \tag{7.40}$$

By standard results from Markov process theory, the function g is a solution of the backward equation:

$$\partial_t g(\cdot) + \mathscr{L}g(\cdot) = 0$$

where $\mathscr{L}$ is the generator of (D, π). However, the market state is usually a high-dimensional process so that the practical computation of $g(\cdot)$ has to be based on Monte Carlo methods, using Algorithm 7.6.1. Note that for an option on the default state the function $g(\cdot)$ does typically depend on the entire generator $\mathscr{L}$ of (D, π) and hence on the form of $a(\cdot)$.

Example 7.6.3 This is an example of options on a CDS index. Index options are a typical example for an option on a traded asset. Denote by $\bar{T} < T$ the maturity of the contract and of the underlying CDS index. Upon exercise the owner of the option holds a protection-buyer position on the underlying index with a prespecified spread $\bar{x}$ (the exercise spread of the option); moreover, the owner obtains the cumulative portfolio loss up to time $\bar{T}$ given by:

$$L_{\bar{T}} = \sum_{i=1}^{m} \delta 1_{\{\tau_i \leq \bar{T}\}}$$

Denote by $V^{\mathrm{def}}(t, X_t, D_t)$ and $V^{\mathrm{prem}}(t, X_t, D_t)$ the full-information value of the default and the premium payment leg of the CDS index. In our setup the value of the option at maturity $\bar{T}$ is then given by the following function of the market state at $\bar{T}$:

$$g(D_{\bar{T}}, \pi_{\bar{T}}) = \left(L_{\bar{T}} + \sum_{k \leq K} \pi_{\bar{T}}^k \left(V^{\mathrm{def}}(\bar{T}, k, D_{\bar{T}}) - \bar{x} V^{\mathrm{prem}}(\bar{T}, k, D_{\bar{T}})\right)\right)^+ \tag{7.41}$$

Numerical examples are given in Subsection 7.7.3.

7.6.4 Calibration

As we have just seen, the price of the credit derivatives common in practice is given by a function of the current market state (D, π). Here a major issue arises: We view the process Y generating the market filtration $\mathbb{F}$ as some kind of abstract information. Then the process π is not directly observable for investors. However, pricing formulas need to be evaluated using only publicly available information. A key point for the application of the model is therefore to determine π_t from prices of traded securities observed at time t—that is, model calibration. We discuss two approaches, standard calibration based on linear or convex optimization and a calibration approach via filtering proposed by Frey and Runggaldier (2010).

7.6.4.1　Standard Calibration

Standard calibration means that we determine π_t by minimizing some distance between market prices and model prices at time t. This is facilitated substantially by the observation that the set of all probability vectors consistent with the price information at a given point in time t can be described in terms of a set of linear inequalities.

Example 7.6.4　We discuss zero coupon bonds and CDSs as representative examples:

- Consider a zero coupon bond on firm i and suppose that at t we observe bid and ask quotes $\underline{p} \leq \overline{p}$ for the bond. In order to be consistent with this information, a solution π of the calibration problem at t needs to satisfy the linear inequalities:

$$\underline{p} \leq \sum_{k=1}^{K} p_i(t, k)\pi^k \leq \overline{p}$$

- Consider a CDS contract on firm i and suppose that at time t we observe bid and ask spreads $\underline{x} \leq \overline{x}$ for the contract. Then π must satisfy the following two inequalities:

$$\sum_{k=1}^{K} \pi^k \left(\underline{x} V_i^{\text{prem}}(t, k) - \delta V_i^{\text{def}}(t, k) \right) \leq 0$$

$$\sum_{k=1}^{K} \pi^k \left(\overline{x} V_i^{\text{prem}}(t, k) - \delta V_i^{\text{def}}(t, k) \right) \geq 0$$

Moreover, π needs to satisfy the obvious linear constraints $\pi^k \geq 0$ for all k and $\sum_{k=1}^{K} \pi^k = 1$.

Standard linear programming techniques can be used to detect if the system of linear inequalities corresponding to the available market quotes is nonempty and to determine a solution π. In case there is more than one probability vector π consistent with the given price information at time t, a unique solution π^* of the calibration problem can be determined by a suitable *regularization procedure*. For instance, one could choose π^* by minimizing the relative entropy to the uniform distribution. This leads to the convex optimization problem:

$$\pi^* = \text{argmin} \left\{ \sum_{k=1}^{K} \pi^k \ln \pi^k : \pi \text{ is consistent with the price information in } t \right\}$$

7.6.4.2 Calibration via Filtering

Alternatively, π_t can be estimated from historical price data by nonlinear filtering. By equation (7.36), the price of a traded credit product in the market filtration is given by a function $g(t, D_t, \pi_t)$ of time and of the current market state. Assume that investors observe this price with a small amount of noise. The noise represents observation errors such as bid-ask spreads and transmission errors as well as errors in the model specification. As explained in Subsection 7.2.3, the noisy price observation can be modeled by the process U with dynamics:

$$dU_t = g(t, D_t, \pi_t)dt + w d\bar{V}_t \tag{7.42}$$

where $\bar{V}$ is a Brownian motion independent of all other processes, and where the constant $w > 0$ models the error variance in the price observation. In this context, estimating π_t amounts to finding the mean of conditional distribution of π_t given the information available to investors at time t, where the latter is described by the σ-field $\mathcal{F}_t^I := \mathcal{F}_t^D \vee \mathcal{F}_t^U$. Recall that π_t solves the SDE (7.31). In order to determine the conditional distribution of π_t given $\mathcal{F}_t^I$, one therefore has to solve a second nonlinear filtering problem with signal process $(\pi_t)_{t \geq 0}$ and observations given by the default state D and the noisy price information U. From a filtering viewpoint this is a challenging problem with usually high-dimensional signal π, observations of mixed type (diffusion and marked point processes), and common jumps of observation D and signal π. This problem is studied in detail in Frey and Runggaldier (2010); in particular, that paper proposes a numerical solution via particle filtering. Numerical results are presented in the next section.

Calibration via filtering is appealing conceptually: New price information at t is used to update the a priori distribution of π_t given past price information up to time $t - 1$, say, but this a priori distribution (and hence the history of prices) is not disregarded altogether. In that sense the method provides an interpolation between historical estimation of model parameters and standard calibration procedures.

Remark 7.6.2 *Of course, in order to use the model one needs to determine also the parameters of $a(\cdot)$ and—in case of next-neighbor dynamics—parameters of the generator matrix of X.*

7.6.5 Hedging

Hedging is a key issue in the management of portfolios of credit derivatives. The standard practice adopted on credit markets is to use sensitivity-based hedging strategies computed by ad hoc rules within the static base-correlation framework; see, for instance, Neugebauer (2006). Clearly, it is desirable to work with hedging strategies that are based on a methodologically sound approach instead. Using the previous results on the dynamics of credit derivatives it is possible to derive model-based dynamic hedging strategies. A detailed derivation of these strategies can be found in the original paper (Frey and Schmidt 2010). A key issue in the computation of hedging strategies is the fact the market is typically incomplete (that is, most claims cannot be replicated perfectly), as the price of the traded credit derivatives follows a jump-diffusion process. In order to deal with this problem, the concept of risk minimization as introduced by Föllmer and Sondermann (1986) is therefore used. Risk minimization is well suited for the hedging of credit derivatives, as the ensuing hedging strategies are relatively easy to compute and as it suffices to know the risk-neutral dynamics of credit derivatives prices.

The dynamic hedging of credit derivatives is also studied in Frey and Backhaus (2010); Laurent, Cousin, and Fermanian (2007); and Cont and Kan (2008), albeit in a different setup.

7.7 Numerical Case Studies

In order to illustrate the application of the model to practical problems, we present a number of small numerical case studies on model dynamics, calibration, and the pricing of credit index options. We concentrate on homogeneous models throughout, while the inhomogeneous situation is covered in Frey and Schmidt (2010).

7.7.1 Dynamics of Credit Spreads and of π

As remarked earlier, the fact that in our model the prices of traded securities are given by the conditional expectation with respect to the market filtration leads to rich credit-spread dynamics with random fluctuations of credit spreads between defaults and default contagion. This is illustrated in Figure 7.3 by a simulated credit-spread trajectory. The fluctuation of credit spreads between defaults as well as contagion

FIGURE 7.3 Simulated Credit-Spread Trajectory

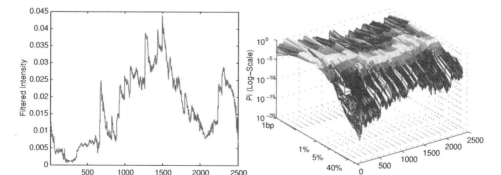

A simulated path of credit spreads under zero recovery (*left*) and the corresponding trajectory of the solution π of the Kushner-Stratonovich equation (*right*); time is measured in days. Note that on the right graph logarithmic scaling is being used.

effects at default times (e.g., around $t = 600$) can be spotted clearly. The right graph gives the corresponding trajectory of the solution π of the Kushner-Stratonovich equation (7.31). State probabilities fluctuate in response to the fluctuations of D; moreover, there are shifts in the distribution π at default events. Both graphs have been created for the case where X is a Markov chain with next-neighbor dynamics.

7.7.2 Calibration

We discuss calibration for the frailty model where $X_t \equiv X$ and hence the generator matrix of X is identically zero; see also Example 7.6.1. In the frailty model default times are independent, exponentially distributed random variables given $X = k$, and dependence is created by mixing over the states of X. A static model of this form (no dynamics of π) has been proposed by Hull and White (2006) under the label *implied copula model*; see also Rosen and Saunders (2009). Since prices of CDS indexes and CDO tranches are independent of the dynamics of π (recall the discussion surrounding equation (7.36)), for these products pricing and standard calibration in the dynamic frailty model and in the static implied copula models coincide. However, our framework permits the pricing of tranche and index options and the derivation of model-based hedging strategies. Both issues cannot be addressed in the static implied copula models.

Since in the frailty model default times are independent given the current value of X, computing the full-information value of traded securities is particularly easy. The long-run dynamics of credit spreads implied by the frailty model are quite unrealistic, though, as the filter learns the true value of X over time. However, since prices of CDS indexes and CDO tranches are independent of the dynamics of π, this is not a problem for the calibration of the model to index data and tranche data or for the pricing of bespoke tranches. The frailty model is, however, not well suited for the pricing of options on traded assets if the maturity $\bar{T}$ of the option is large.

7.7.2.1 Standard Calibration to iTraxx Spreads

We begin with an example for a calibration of the model to observed tranche and index spreads of the iTraxx. We consider a homogeneous model with $|S^X| = 9$; the values of the one-year default intensity are given in Table 7.1. The model was calibrated to tranche and index spread data from 2004, 2006, 2008, and 2009. The data from 2004 and 2006 are typical for tranche and index spreads before the credit crisis; the data from 2008 and 2009, in contract, represent the state of the market during the crisis. In order to determine a solution π^* of the calibration problem, we use the methodology described in Section 7.6.4, with very satisfactory results. The resulting values for π are given in Table 7.1. We clearly see that with the emergence of the credit crisis the calibration procedure puts more mass on states where the default intensity is high; in particular, the extreme state where $\lambda = 70$ percent gets a probability of around 3 percent. This reflects the increased awareness of future defaults and the increasing risk aversion in the market after the advent of the crisis. The fact that the

TABLE 7.1 Results of the Calibration to iTraxx Spread Data (Index and Tranches) for Different Data Sets from Several Years

λ (in %)	0.01	0.3	0.6	1.2	2.5	4.0	8.0	20	70
π^*, data from 2004	12.6	22.9	42.0	17.6	2.5	1.45	0.54	0.13	0.03
π^*, data from 2006	22.2	29.9	39.0	7.6	1.2	0.16	0.03	0.03	0.05
π^*, data from 2008	1.1	7.9	57.6	10.8	11.7	4.9	1.26	1.79	2.60
π^*, data from 2009	0.0	13.6	6.35	42.2	22.3	12.5	0.0	0.00	3.06

The components of π^* are given in percentage points.

model-implied probability of "Armageddon scenarios" increases as the credit crisis unfolds can also be observed in other model types; see, for instance, Brigo, Pallavicini, and Torresetti (2009).

7.7.2.2   Calibration via Filtering

Next we illustrate the filter approach to model calibration with numerical results from Frey and Runggaldier (2010). The quantity to be estimated via filtering is the default intensity in the market filtration $\widehat{\lambda}_t$ which can be viewed as approximation for the short-term credit spread. Numerical results are given in Figure 7.4, where the filter estimate $\mathbb{E}(\widehat{\lambda}_t \mid \mathcal{F}_t^I)$ is given for a high and a low value of the observation noise w.

FIGURE 7.4   A Trajectory of the Market Default Intensity $\widehat{\lambda}_t$ and of the Investor Estimate $E(\widehat{\lambda}_t \mid \mathcal{F}_t^I)$ for Different Observation Noise

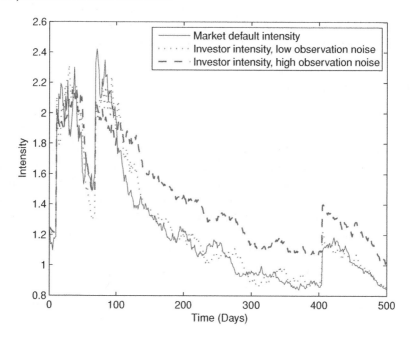

TABLE 7.2 Implied Volatilities for an Option to Buy Protection on the CDS Index with Implied Volatilities Are Computed via the Pedersen (2003) Approach

c	0.5	1.	2	5
Moneyness $\bar{x}/x_0 = 0.8$	1.53	1.56	1.62	1.83
Moneyness $\bar{x}/x_0 = 1$	1.75	1.75	1.76	1.93
Moneyness $\bar{x}/x_0 = 1.2$	1.95	1.95	1.95	2.04

Note that for low observation noise the estimator $\mathbb{E}(\widehat{\lambda}_t \mid \mathcal{F}_t^I)$ tracks $\widehat{\lambda}_t$ quite well. Further details are given in Frey and Runggaldier (2010).

7.7.3 Pricing of Credit Index Options

Options on a CDS index introduced in Example 7.6.3 are a typical example for an option on a traded asset. In practice this contract is usually priced by a fairly ad hoc procedure: It is assumed that the so-called loss-adjusted spread (the sum of the value of the default payments over the time period $(\bar{T}, T]$ and of the front-end protection $L_{\bar{T}}$, divided by the value of the premium payments over $(\bar{T}, T]$) is lognormally distributed under a suitable martingale measure so that the value of the option can be computed via the Black formula. Prices are then quoted in terms of implied volatilities; see Pedersen (2003) and Brigo and Morini (2007) for further details. Beyond convenience there is no justification for the lognormality assumption in the literature. In particular, it is unclear if a dynamic model for the evolution of spreads and credit losses can be constructed that supports the lognormality assumption, and the use of the Black formula, and there is no empirical justification for this assumption, either.

The filter model discussed here, however, offers the possibility to price this product in the context of a consistent model for the joint evolution of defaults and credit spreads. In our numerical experiments we worked in the following setup: We used the same frailty model as in the calibration to iTraxx data; the function $a(\cdot)$ from equation (7.26) was given by $a(k) = c \ln \lambda(k)$ for varying values of c; the value π_0 at the starting day of the contract was the 2009 value from Table 7.1; that is, the model was calibrated to tranche spreads and index spreads on that date; the time to maturity $\bar{T}$ of the option was taken equal to three months.[3] Prices were computed using Monte Carlo simulation.

Table 7.2 presents our pricing results for varying values of c (varying local spread volatility) and varying moneyness $\bar{x}/x_0$ ($\bar{x}$ the exercise spread of the option as given in equation (7.41) and x_0 the index spread at inception of the option). We can see the following:

- The model generates *volatility skews*: options with high moneyness (out-of-the-money options) tend to have higher implied volatilities than in-the-money options. This appears reasonable: Out-of-the-money options provide protection against the adverse scenario of rising spreads and/or many losses during the run time of the option. Such a protection tends to be more expensive than the protection against benign scenarios. The obvious analogy is the skew for equity options, where implied volatilities for out-of-the-money put options (which offer protection against the adverse scenario of falling markets) are higher than implied volatilities for out-of-the-money calls.

- Increasing the value of c tends to lead to higher implied volatilities. Nonetheless it shows that for options on traded assets the choice of the function $a(\cdot)$ does indeed have an impact on the price of the option. Given market quotes for credit index options, this observation could of course be used to calibrate parameters of $a(\cdot)$.

We also used next-neighbor dynamics for X to price the option. This led to a slightly smoother distribution of the credit spread at $\bar{T}$, but the impact on option prices and implied volatilities was found to be very small. Finally, we looked at the distribution of the loss-adjusted spread in our model. Recall that in the literature it is frequently assumed that this spread is lognormally distributed. In Figure 7.5 we therefore give a quantile-quantile plot of logarithmic loss-adjusted spreads in our model against the normal distribution. The S-shaped form of the plot clearly points to heavy tails.

Unfortunately, market quotes for index options are relatively scarce, so we could not test our pricing results empirically. However, our findings clearly caution against the thoughtless use of the Black formula and of market models in credit index markets, despite the obvious success of this methodology in the default-free interest world.

FIGURE 7.5 Quantile-Quantile Plot of Logarithmic Loss-Adjusted Spread against the Normal Distribution.

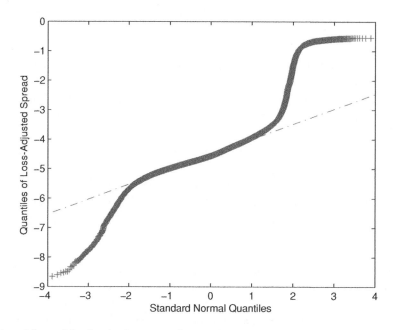

The S-shaped form of the plot clearly points to heavy tails.

Notes

1. The Kalman-Bucy filter can be generalized to the multidimensional case and $a, \ldots, d$ may be adapted with respect to the filtration $\mathcal{F}_t^Y = \sigma(Y_s : s \leq t)$.
2. Strictly speaking, observed dividends contain information about A as well and should therefore be included in the filtering result. This can be done analogously as in Proposition 7.5.1; for details we refer to Frey and Schmidt (2009).
3. Short maturities of three to six months are the market standard for index options; longer-term contracts are hardly overtraded, as the composition of the underlying index changes every six months.

References

Aven, T. 1985. A theorem for determining the compensator of a counting process. *Scandinavian Journal of Statistics* 12 (1): 69–72.

Bain, A., and D. Crisan. 2009. *Fundamentals of stochastic filtering.* New York: Springer.

Black, F., and J. C. Cox. 1976. Valuing corporate securities: Some effects of bond indenture provisions. *Journal of Finance* 31:351–367.

Black, F., and M. Scholes. 1973. The pricing of options and corporate liabilities. *Journal of Political Economy* 81:637–654.

Blanchet-Scalliet, C., and M. Jeanblanc. 2004. Hazard rate for credit risk and hedging defaultable contingent claims. *Finance and Stochastics* 8:145–159.

Brémaud, P. 1981. *Point processes and queues.* New York: Springer-Verlag.

Brigo, D., and M. Morini. 2007. Arbitrage-free pricing of credit index options. the no-armageddon-pricing measure and the role of correlation after the subprime crisis. Preprint, available on www.defaultrisk.com.

Brigo, D., A. Pallavicini, and R. Torresetti. 2009. Credit models and the crisis, or: How I learned to stop worrying and love the CDO. Working paper, Imperial College, London.

Budhiraja, A., L. Chen, and C. Lee. 2007. A survey of nonlinear methods for nonlinear filtering problems. *Physica D* 230:27–36.

Coculescu, D., H. Geman, and M. Jeanblanc. 2008. Valuation of default sensitive claims under imperfect information. *Finance and Stochastics* 12:195–218.

Collin-Dufresne, P., R. Goldstein, and J. Helwege. 2003. Is credit event risk priced? Modeling contagion via the updating of beliefs. Preprint, Carnegie Mellon University.

Cont, R., and Y. H. Kan. 2008. Dynamic hedging of portfolio credit derivatives. Working paper.

Crosbie, P., and J. R. Bohn. 1997–2001. *Modeling default risk.* KMV Corporation. www.kmv.kom/insight/index.html.

Davis, M. H. A., and S. I. Marcus. 1981. An introduction to nonlinear filtering. In *Stochastic systems: The mathematics of filtering and identifications and applications,* ed. M. Hazewinkel and J. C. Willems, 53–75. Dortrecht, Netherlands: Reidel Publishing Company.

Duffie, D., A. Eckner, G. Horel, and L. Saita. 2009. Frailty correlated default. *Journal of Finance* 64:2089–2123.

Duffie, D., and D. Lando. 2001. Term structures of credit spreads with incomplete accounting information. *Econometrica* 69:633–664.

Duffie, D., and K. Singleton. 1999. Modeling term structures of defaultable bonds. *Review of Financial Studies* 12:687–720.

Elliott, R. 1993. New finite-dimensional filters and smoothers for noisily observed Markov chains. *IEEE Transactions on Information Theory*, IT-39:265–271.

Elliott, R.J., and R. S. Mamon. 2003. A complete yield curve description of a Markov interest rate model. *International Journal of Theoretical and Applied Finance* 6:317–326.

Feldhütter, P., and D. Lando. 2008. Decomposing swap spreads. *Journal of Financial Economics* 88:375–405.

Föllmer, H., and D. Sondermann. 1986. Hedging of non-redundant contingent-claims. In *Contributions to mathematical economics* ed. W. Hildenbrand and A. Mas-Colell, 147–160. Amsterdam: North Holland.

Frey, R., and J. Backhaus. 2010. Dynamic hedging of synthetic CDO-tranches with spread - and contagion risk. *Journal of Economic Dynamics and Control* 34:710–724.

Frey, R., and D. Lu. 2010. Pricing of hybrid credit products: A nonlinear filtering approach. Preprint, Universität Leipzig.

Frey, R., and W. Runggaldier. 2008. Nonlinear filtering in models for interest-rate and credit risk. In *Handbook of nonlinear filtering.* Oxford University Press.

Frey, R., and W. J. Runggaldier. 2010. Pricing credit derivatives under incomplete information: A nonlinear-filtering approach. *Finance and Stochastics* 14 (4): 495–526.

Frey, R., and T. Schmidt. 2009. Pricing corporate securities under noisy asset information. *Mathematical Finance* 19 (3): 403–421.

Frey, R., and T. Schmidt. 2010. Pricing and hedging of credit derivatives via the innovations approach to nonlinear filtering. Preprint, Universität Leipzig. To appear in *Finance and Stochastics.*

Hull, J., and A. White. 2006. The implied copula model. *Journal of Derivatives.*

Jarrow, R., and P. Protter. 2004. Structural versus reduced-form models: A new information based perspective. *Journal of Investment Management* 2:1–10.

Jarrow, R., and S. Turnbull. 1995. Pricing options on financial securities subject to default risk. *Journal of Finance* 5:53–86.

Lando, D. 1998. On Cox processes and credit risky securities. *Review of Derivatives Research* 2:99–120.

Lando, D. 2004. *Credit risk modeling: Theory and applications.* Princeton, NJ: Princeton University Press.

Laurent, J., A. Cousin, and J. Fermanian. 2007. Hedging default risk of CDOs in Markovian contagion models. Working paper, ISFA Actuarial School, Université de Lyon.

Linetsky, V. 2006. Pricing equity derivatives subject to bankruptcy. *Mathematical Finance* 16 (2): 255–282.

McNeil, A., R. Frey, and P. Embrechts. 2005. *Quantitative risk management: Concepts, techniques and tools.* Princeton, NJ: Princeton University Press.

Merton, R. 1974. On the pricing of corporate debt: The risk structure of interest rates. *Journal of Finance* 29:449–470.

Nakagawa, H. 2001. A filtering model on default risk. *Journal of Mathematical Science, University of Tokyo* 8:107–142.

Neugebauer, M. 2006. Understanding and hedging risks in synthetic CDO tranches. Fitch special report, August.

Pedersen, C. 2003. Valuation of portfolio credit default swaptions. Working paper, Lehman Brothers Quantitative Credit Research.

Rosen, D., and D. Saunders. 2009. Valuing CDOs of bespoke portfolios with implied multi-factor models. *Journal of Credit Risk.*

Schmidt, T., and A. Novikov. 2008. A structural model with unobserved default boundary. *Applied Mathematical Finance* 15 (2): 183–203.

Schmidt, T., and W. Stute. 2004. Credit risk—A survey. *Contemporary Mathematics* 336:75–115.

Schönbucher, P. 2003. *Credit derivates pricing models.* New York: John Wiley & Sons.

Schönbucher, P. 2004. Information-driven default contagion. Preprint, Department of Mathematics, ETH Zürich.

Wendler, R. A. 2009. Über die Bewertung von Kreditderivaten unter unvollständiger Information. *Blätter der DGVFM* 30:379–394.

CHAPTER 8

Options on Credit Default Swaps and Credit Default Indexes

Marek Rutkowski

School of Mathematics and Statistics, University of Sydney

We focus on derivations of valuation formulas and hedging strategies for credit default swaptions and credit default index swaptions. Most results presented in this chapter are independent of a particular convention regarding the specification of fee and protection legs, so that they can also be applied to valuation of other credit derivatives that exhibit similar features as credit default swaptions, for instance, options on CDO tranches. The main tool is a judicious choice of the reference filtration combined with a suitable specification of the risk-neutral dynamics for the predefault (loss-adjusted) fair market spreads. We first deal with options on single-name credit default swaps: we rederive here the conventional market formula and we provide pricing and hedging results within the intensity-based setup. General results are exemplified by explicit computations for the price and hedging strategy for the CIR default intensity model. Subsequently, we extend the valuation results to options on CDS indexes. In the last section, we present constructions of several variants of market models for forward CDS spreads, as first proposed by Brigo (2006, 2008). We provide explicit representations for the joint dynamics for some families of forward CDS spreads under a common probability measure. Specifically, we derive the joint dynamics for the family of one- and two-period forward CDS spreads, as well as for the family of one-period and coterminal forward CDS spreads.

8.1 Introduction

A *credit default swap* (CDS) is a contract between two counterparties—the protection buyer and the protection seller—in which protection against the risk of default by the underlying reference entity is provided to the buyer. The protection buyer pays a premium at regular intervals to the protection seller in order to obtain the right to receive a contingent payment from the seller following a credit event by the reference entity. Examples of a *credit event* include default, restructuring, a ratings downgrade, or a failure to pay; for simplicity, we refer to a credit event as being a *default*. If no default event takes place, then the only cash flows are those from the protection buyer, who pays at periodic intervals (usually quarterly) a predetermined premium κ—termed hereafter the CDS spread—until the contract expires.

If, however, there is a default event prior to the maturity of a CDS, the protection buyer stops making premium payments at the time of the event after making one final accrual payment at default time. At the moment of default the protection seller pays the protection payment, which is computed according to a predetermined rule. We make here the standing assumption that the protection payment amount is deterministic, which is tantamount to the postulate that the recovery rate for the underlying entity is known in advance at the moment when a credit default swap is entered into.

A plain-vanilla credit default swaption is a European option on the value of the underlying forward credit default swap. An essential feature of this contract is that it is canceled if default occurs prior to the swaption's maturity. It thus can formally be seen as an example of a *survival claim*, that is, a claim that yields a nonzero payoff at the maturity date only provided that default does not occur prior to or at maturity date. It is worth mentioning here that, due to the *front-end protection* clause, this feature is no longer valid for credit default index swaptions.

This chapter is organized as follows.

We start by presenting in Section 8.2 the most important features of credit default swaps. We introduce the valuation formulas for the protection and fee leg of a credit default swap within the so-called *intensity-based* framework. This method is also known as the *reduced-form* approach, as opposed to the *structural* approach, which is based on the specification of the total value of the firm's assets. The most important ingredient of the reduced-form approach is the concept of a *survival process* of the random time modeling the date of occurrence of a default event. The main result of Section 8.2 is the formula for the predefault fair spread of a forward credit default swap.

Section 8.3 analyzes the valuation and hedging of single-name credit default swaptions within the intensity-based framework. We present some general pricing results and we show how to justify the Black formula for credit default swaptions, which was adopted as a conventional market pricing formula.

Section 8.4 deals with a particular intensity-based model in which the stochastic default intensity is postulated to follow the Cox-Ingersoll-Ross dynamics. It appears that in that case the value of the credit default swaption and the form of the hedging strategy can be computed explicitly.

Section 8.5 extends results of Section 8.3 to the case of credit default indexes. The generalization is nontrivial, due to the quite peculiar way in which the cash flows of credit default indexes and related swaptions are specified.

Section 8.6 addresses the issue of constructing market models for certain families of single-name credit default swap spreads that correspond to some choice of start and expiration dates. To be more specific, it is shown how to derive the joint dynamics under a single probability measure of the family of one- and two-period forward CDS spreads, as well as of the family of one-period and coterminal forward CDS spreads.

The content of this chapter is based on several papers, which are explicitly referred to in the following pages. Of course, it is not possible to review all results and models related to the valuation and hedging of credit default (index) swaptions.

Let us mention that throughout this chapter, we refer to the more traditional market convention, which stipulates that the value of a credit default swap equals zero at the time of its issuance, so that no up-front fee is required from the protection buyer. This convention was recently replaced by another one, in which the fee leg is composed of the up-front payment by the protection buyer upon entering the contract and the fixed annuity paid until maturity or default, whichever comes first. The fixed spread is set to equal either 100 or 500 bps, depending on the credit quality of the underlying credit entity. Similarly, the recovery rate is also standardized to two possible values, 20 percent or 40 percent, depending on the credit quality of the underlying name.

It is worth stressing that most methods and results presented in this chapter can be rather easily adjusted to the new convention. In particular, the dynamics of the price process of a credit default swap are given by the same expression under both market conventions, of course, except for the initial value. For the sake of consistency with the quoted papers, we thus decided to follow the traditional market convention, which was used in all of them, except for the paper by Beumee et al. (2009), where a detailed comparison of the two alternative conventions is provided. In particular, Beumee et al. deal with the issue of conversion of the up-front CDS spread quotes into running quotes (or vice versa) using a consistent term structure of default rates.

8.2 Credit Default Swaps

A strictly positive random variable τ defined on a probability space $(\Omega, \mathcal{G}, \mathbb{Q})$ is called a *random time*; it will also be later referred to as the *default time*. We introduce the jump process $H_t = \mathbb{1}_{\{\tau \leq t\}}$ associated with τ and we denote by $\mathbb{H}$ the filtration generated by this process. The filtration $\mathbb{H}$ models the jump risk associated with the default event.

We assume that we are given, in addition, some *reference filtration* $\mathbb{F}$ and we set $\mathbb{G} = \mathbb{H} \vee \mathbb{F}$, meaning that $\mathcal{G}_t = \sigma(\mathcal{H}_t, \mathcal{F}_t)$ for every $t \in \mathbb{R}_+$. The filtration $\mathbb{G}$ is called the *full filtration*, since at any date t the σ-field $\mathcal{G}_t$ represents the full information available to investors. An additional filtration $\mathbb{F}$ is introduced in order to address the issue of the spread volatility risk.

Let the process F be defined by the equality $F_t = \mathbb{Q}(\tau \leq t \mid \mathcal{F}_t)$, for every $t \in \mathbb{R}_+$, and let

$$G_t = 1 - F_t = \mathbb{Q}(\tau > t \mid \mathcal{F}_t) \tag{8.1}$$

be the *survival process* with respect to the filtration $\mathbb{F}$. Note that if $G_t > 0$ for every $t \in \mathbb{R}_+$ then τ is not an $\mathbb{F}$-stopping time.

The following result underpins the computations in the intensity-based framework (see, for instance, Chapter 5 in Bielecki and Rutkowski (2002) or Chapter 3 in Bielecki, Jeanblanc, and Rutkowski (2009)).

Lemma 8.2.1   *For any $s > t$ and any $\mathbb{Q}$-integrable and $\mathcal{F}_s$-measurable random variable X we have that:*

$$\mathbb{E}_{\mathbb{Q}}(\mathbb{1}_{\{s<\tau\}}X \mid \mathcal{G}_t) = \mathbb{1}_{\{t<\tau\}}\, G_t^{-1}\, \mathbb{E}_{\mathbb{Q}}(G_s X \mid \mathcal{F}_t) \qquad (8.2)$$

Let Y be a $\mathbb{G}$-adapted stochastic process. Then there exists a unique $\mathbb{F}$-adapted process $\widetilde{Y}$ such that, for every $t \in \mathbb{R}_+$,

$$\mathbb{1}_{\{t<\tau\}}Y_t = \mathbb{1}_{\{t<\tau\}}\widetilde{Y}_t \qquad (8.3)$$

The process $\widetilde{Y}$ is termed the predefault value *of the process Y.*

Let us recall that we may attach to the strictly positive survival process G the *hazard process* Γ, defined as $\Gamma_t = -\ln G_t$. If the hazard process Γ is absolutely continuous, so that $\Gamma_t = \int_0^t \gamma_u\, du$ for some $\mathbb{F}$-predictable process γ, then we say that τ admits the $\mathbb{F}$-*intensity process* γ or, simply, that γ is the *default intensity*. In the special case when the default intensity γ is well defined, some formulas given later can be represented in terms of this process. Neither the existence of the default intensity nor even the continuity of the survival process G are required for the further developments presented in Sections 8.2 and 8.3. By contrast, in Section 8.4 we deal with a specific model of default, which is based on the specification of the intensity process γ.

8.2.1   Forward Credit Default Swap

We write $T_0 < T_1 < \cdots < T_m$ to denote the *tenor structure* of a forward-start credit default swap with the following interpretation:

- T_0 is the CDS inception date.
- T_m is the maturity date of the CDS.
- T_j is the jth fee payment date for $j = 1, 2, \ldots, m$.

Let τ be a strictly positive random variable representing the moment of default of the reference credit name. We set $v(\tau) = j - 1$ on the event $\{T_{j-1} \le \tau < T_j\}$ and we write $\alpha_j = T_j - T_{j-1}$ for every $j = 1, 2, \ldots, m$. Let B be an $\mathbb{F}$-adapted, strictly positive process modeling the savings account (or any other strictly positive numéraire). From now on, the underlying probability measure $\mathbb{Q}$ is interpreted as a martingale measure associated with the choice of B as the numéraire asset. We consider the case of a constant protection payment given as $1 - \delta$, where δ is the recovery rate, assumed to be constant.

It is essential to assume that the inequality $G_t > 0$ holds for every $t \in [0, T_1]$. In view of the definition of the process G, to ensure the positivity of G_t for every $t \in [0, T_1]$, it suffices to make the standing assumption that $G_{T_1} > 0$.

In the following, we frequently use the notation $\beta_t = B_t^{-1}$ and $\beta(t, T) = B_t B_T^{-1}$. Also, let $\mathbb{1}_A$ stand for the indicator function of an event A, so that $\mathbb{1}_A(\omega) = 1$ if ω belongs to A and $\mathbb{1}_A(\omega) = 0$ otherwise. The following definition formalizes the concept of the forward credit default swap and introduces the notation for the discounted payoffs of the two legs of this contract.

Definition 8.2.1 *The forward credit default swap issued at time $s \in [0, T_0]$, with the unit notional, the protection payment $1 - \delta$ and the $\mathcal{F}_s$-measurable spread κ, is determined by its discounted payoff, which equals $D_t = P_t - \kappa A_t$ for every $t \in [s, T_0]$, where in turn the discounted payoff of the* protection leg *equals:*

$$P_t = (1 - \delta)\beta(t, \tau)\mathbb{1}_{\{T_0 \leq \tau \leq T_m\}} \tag{8.4}$$

and the discounted payoff of the fee leg *(also known as the* premium leg*) per one unit of the spread equals:*

$$A_t = \sum_{j=1}^{m} \alpha_j \beta(t, T_j)\mathbb{1}_{\{T_j < \tau\}} + \beta(t, \tau)(\tau - T_{v(\tau)})\mathbb{1}_{\{T_0 < \tau \leq T_m\}} \tag{8.5}$$

The valuation of the forward CDS at time t is based on the risk-neutral formula under $\mathbb{Q}$ applied to the discounted future payoffs. We consider here only the case $t \in [s, T_0]$, though an extension to the general case $t \in [s, T_m]$ is readily available as well.

Definition 8.2.2 *The price at the time $t \in [s, T_0]$ of the forward credit default swap for the protection buyer equals:*

$$S_t(\kappa) = \mathbb{E}_{\mathbb{Q}}(D_t \mid \mathcal{G}_t) = \mathbb{E}_{\mathbb{Q}}(P_t \mid \mathcal{G}_t) - \kappa \, \mathbb{E}_{\mathbb{Q}}(A_t \mid \mathcal{G}_t) \tag{8.6}$$

Note that in equation (8.6) we used, in particular, the property that κ is $\mathcal{F}_s$-measurable, and thus it is also $\mathcal{G}_t$-measurable for every $t \in [s, T_0]$.

Remark 8.2.1 *Brigo (2005, 2006, 2008) proposed and studied the following simplified versions D_t^i, $i = 1, 2$ of the actual discounted payoff D_t:*

$$D_t^1 = (1 - \delta) \sum_{j=1}^{m} \alpha_j \beta(t, T_j)\mathbb{1}_{\{T_{j-1} < \tau \leq T_j\}} - \kappa \sum_{j=1}^{m} \alpha_j \beta(t, T_j)\mathbb{1}_{\{T_j < \tau\}} \tag{8.7}$$

and

$$D_t^2 = (1 - \delta) \sum_{j=1}^{m} \alpha_j \beta(t, T_j) \mathbb{1}_{\{T_{j-1} < \tau \leq T_j\}} - \kappa \sum_{j=1}^{m} \alpha_j \beta(t, T_j) \mathbb{1}_{\{T_{j-1} < \tau\}} \qquad (8.8)$$

These conventions prove useful when dealing with market models for CDS spreads, which are examined in some detail in Section 8.6.

Let us stress that most results for credit default swaptions can be established for a fairly general choice of a convention regarding the protection and fee leg payment schedules. The only crucial properties are that all cash flows should occur after the inception date T, as well as the *knockout* feature, that is, the fact that the contract becomes void if default occurs prior to or at T. Put more formally, it is enough to assume that the discounted payoff at time $t \in [s, T_0]$ of a studied contract has the form:

$$D_t = P_t - \kappa A_t \qquad (8.9)$$

where P_t and A_t represent discounted payoffs of some T_0-*survival claims*, meaning that the following equalities are satisfied for every $t \in [s, T_0]$:

$$P_t = \mathbb{1}_{\{T_0 < \tau\}} P_t, \qquad A_t = \mathbb{1}_{\{T_0 < \tau\}} A_t \qquad (8.10)$$

To sum up, the concepts and results examined cover in fact various conventions regarding the timing and size of cash flows of forward credit default swaps.

Lemma 8.2.2 *The price at time $t \in [s, T_0]$ of the forward CDS issued at time $s \in [0, T_0]$ satisfies*

$$S_t(\kappa) = \mathbb{1}_{\{t < \tau\}} G_t^{-1} \mathbb{E}_{\mathbb{Q}}(D_t \,|\, \mathcal{F}_t) = \mathbb{1}_{\{t < \tau\}} \widetilde{S}_t(\kappa) \qquad (8.11)$$

where the predefault price satisfies $\widetilde{S}_t(\kappa) = \widetilde{P}_t - \kappa \widetilde{A}_t$, where we denote

$$\widetilde{P}_t = G_t^{-1} \mathbb{E}_{\mathbb{Q}}(P_t \,|\, \mathcal{F}_t), \qquad \widetilde{A}_t = G_t^{-1} \mathbb{E}_{\mathbb{Q}}(A_t \,|\, \mathcal{F}_t) \qquad (8.12)$$

If the discounted payoffs P_t and A_t are given by equations (8.4) and (8.5), respectively, then:

$$\widetilde{P}_t = (1 - \delta) G_t^{-1} \mathbb{E}_{\mathbb{Q}} \left(\sum_{j=1}^{m} \beta(t, \tau) \mathbb{1}_{\{T_{j-1} < \tau \leq T_j\}} \,\bigg|\, \mathcal{F}_t \right) \qquad (8.13)$$

and

$$\widetilde{A}_t = G_t^{-1}\,\mathbb{E}_{\mathbb{Q}}\Big(\sum_{j=1}^{m}\alpha_j\beta(t,\,T_j)\mathbb{1}_{\{T_j<\tau\}} + \beta(t,\tau)(\tau - T_{v(\tau)})\mathbb{1}_{\{T_0<\tau\leq T_m\}}\,\Big|\,\mathcal{F}_t\Big)\quad(8.14)$$

Proof. Recall that by definition:

$$S_t(\kappa) = \mathbb{E}_{\mathbb{Q}}(D_t\,|\,\mathcal{G}_t) = \mathbb{E}_{\mathbb{Q}}(P_t\,|\,\mathcal{G}_t) - \kappa\,\mathbb{E}_{\mathbb{Q}}(A_t\,|\,\mathcal{G}_t)$$

By combining equation (8.2) with equation (8.10), we obtain:

$$\mathbb{E}_{\mathbb{Q}}(P_t\,|\,\mathcal{G}_t) = \mathbb{1}_{\{t<\tau\}}G_t^{-1}\,\mathbb{E}_{\mathbb{Q}}(P_t\,|\,\mathcal{F}_t) = \mathbb{1}_{\{t<\tau\}}\widetilde{P}_t$$

and:

$$\mathbb{E}_{\mathbb{Q}}(A_t\,|\,\mathcal{G}_t) = \mathbb{1}_{\{t<\tau\}}G_t^{-1}\,\mathbb{E}_{\mathbb{Q}}(A_t\,|\,\mathcal{F}_t) = \mathbb{1}_{\{t<\tau\}}\widetilde{A}_t$$

which proves equation (8.12). To derive equations (8.13) and (8.14), it suffices to make use of equation (8.14) and explicit representations (8.4) and (8.5) for P_t and A_t.

The quantity $\widetilde{P}_t$ is the predefault value at time $t \in [s,\,T_0]$ of the protection leg per unit of the nominal, whereas $\widetilde{A}_t$ represents the predefault value at time $t \in [s,\,T_0]$ of the fee leg per one basis point of the spread. The latter is commonly known as the (predefault) *present value of a basis point* (*PVBP*) of the CDS, but it is also sometimes termed the *risky PVBP* or the *CDS annuity*. In the sequel, it will be sometimes referred to as the *swap annuity*. It is worth noting that neither $\widetilde{P}_t$ nor $\widetilde{A}_t$ depend on the initiation date s of the forward CDS, and thus they can be defined for every $t \in [0,\,T_0]$.

Under the standing assumption that $G_{T_1} > 0$, it can be deduced easily from equation (8.14) that $\widetilde{A}_t > 0$ for every $t \in [s,\,T_0]$. Indeed, using equation (8.14), we obtain:

$$\widetilde{A}_t \geq G_t^{-1}\,\mathbb{E}_{\mathbb{Q}}\big(\alpha_1\beta(t,\,T_1)\mathbb{1}_{\{T_1<\tau\}}\,\big|\,\mathcal{F}_t\big) = G_t^{-1}\,\mathbb{E}_{\mathbb{Q}}\big(\alpha_1\beta(t,\,T_1)\mathbb{Q}(\tau > T_1\,|\,\mathcal{F}_{T_1})\,\big|\,\mathcal{F}_t\big)$$
$$= G_t^{-1}\,\mathbb{E}_{\mathbb{Q}}\big(\alpha_1\beta(t,\,T_1)G_{T_1}\,\big|\,\mathcal{F}_t\big) > 0$$

8.2.2 Predefault Fair Forward CDS Spread

Since the forward CDS contract is terminated at default with no further payments, the concept of the fair (or par) forward CDS spread is only meaningful prior to default. However, it is also possible, and in fact more convenient, to introduce the notion of the *predefault* fair forward CDS spread, which can be formally defined for any date

$t \in [0, T_0]$. To this end, we propose the following definition in which the issuance date s of a particular forward CDS is irrelevant.

Definition 8.2.3 *The* predefault fair forward CDS spread *at time $t \in [0, T_0]$ is the $\mathcal{F}_t$-measurable random variable κ_t such that $\widetilde{S}_t(\kappa_t) = 0$, where $\widetilde{S}_t(\kappa_t) = \widetilde{P}_t - \kappa_t \widetilde{A}_t$ and the processes $\widetilde{P}$ and $\widetilde{A}$ are given by equations (8.13) and (8.14), respectively.*

Note that the predefault fair spread is simply denoted by κ_t, although the symbol $\widetilde{\kappa}_t$ would perhaps be more consistent with the notation used for other predefault quantities. It is possible to formally set the fair forward CDS spread to be equal to zero after default of the underlying name, but this additional convention is not essential, and thus it will not be used in what follows.

The next result is a simple consequence of Lemma 8.2.2. It shows that the fair forward CDS spread play the same role as the forward rate in a default-free interest rate swap.

Lemma 8.2.3 *The predefault fair forward CDS spread satisfies, for any $t \in [0, T_0]$,*

$$\kappa_t = \frac{\widetilde{P}_t}{\widetilde{A}_t} = \frac{\mathbb{E}_{\mathbb{Q}}\left((1 - \delta) \sum_{j=1}^{m} B_\tau^{-1} \mathbb{1}_{\{T_{j-1} < \tau \le T_j\}} \,\Big|\, \mathcal{F}_t\right)}{\mathbb{E}_{\mathbb{Q}}\left(\sum_{j=1}^{m} \alpha_j B_{T_j}^{-1} \mathbb{1}_{\{T_j < \tau\}} + B_\tau^{-1}(\tau - T_{v(\tau)}) \mathbb{1}_{\{T_0 < \tau \le T_m\}} \,\Big|\, \mathcal{F}_t\right)} = \frac{\widehat{P}_t}{\widehat{A}_t} \tag{8.15}$$

where the $(\mathbb{Q}, \mathbb{F})$-martingales $\widehat{P}$ and $\widehat{A}$ are defined by the following expressions:

$$\widehat{P}_t = G_t B_t^{-1} \widetilde{P}_t = \mathbb{E}_{\mathbb{Q}}\left((1 - \delta) \sum_{j=1}^{m} B_\tau^{-1} \mathbb{1}_{\{T_{j-1} < \tau \le T_j\}} \,\Big|\, \mathcal{F}_t\right) \tag{8.16}$$

and

$$\widehat{A}_t = G_t B_t^{-1} \widetilde{A}_t = \mathbb{E}_{\mathbb{Q}}\left(\sum_{j=1}^{m} \alpha_j B_{T_j}^{-1} \mathbb{1}_{\{T_j < \tau\}} + B_\tau^{-1}(\tau - T_{v(\tau)}) \mathbb{1}_{\{T_0 < \tau \le T_m\}} \,\Big|\, \mathcal{F}_t\right) \tag{8.17}$$

The price of the forward CDS issued at $s \in [0, T_0]$ with an arbitrary $\mathcal{F}_s$-measurable spread κ admits the following representation, for every $t \in [s, T_0]$,

$$S_t(\kappa) = \mathbb{1}_{\{t < \tau\}} \widetilde{A}_t (\kappa_t - \kappa) \tag{8.18}$$

Proof. Since κ_t is $\mathcal{F}_t$-measurable, from Lemma 8.2.2, we obtain that $\widetilde{S}_t(\kappa) = \widetilde{P}_t - \kappa_t \widetilde{A}_t$. It is thus clear that the first equality in equation (8.15) holds, provided that

$\widetilde{A}_t > 0$. The second equality in equation (8.15) follows from equations (8.13) and (8.14). To derive (8.18), we observe that:

$$\widetilde{S}_t(\kappa) = \widetilde{S}_t(\kappa) - \widetilde{S}_t(\kappa_t) = \widetilde{P}_t - \kappa\widetilde{A}_t - (\widetilde{P}_t - \kappa_t\widetilde{A}_t) = \widetilde{A}_t(\kappa_t - \kappa)$$

where we used the equality $\widetilde{S}_t(\kappa_t) = 0$ (cf. Definition 8.2.3).

The practical use of equation (8.18) hinges on the evaluation of the quantity $\widetilde{A}_t$, which is defined by equation (8.14). Indeed, the market quote for this term is not readily available. The computation of $\widetilde{A}_t$ relies on the well-known concept of the *implied risk-neutral default probabilities*. For a single-name case, they can be obtained from the market quotes for CDS spreads for different maturities, that is, from the market CDS spread curve observed at time t.

8.3 Options on Credit Default Swaps

A *credit default swaption* gives its holder, who pays an upfront fee, the right—but not the obligation—to buy (or sell) the protection on a prearranged single-name CDS. It thus can be seen as a call (or put) option with strike zero written on the market value of the underlying CDS at the option's expiry date. In the sequel, we will focus on the case of the call option.

An important feature of a credit default swaption is the *knock out* feature at default. For a single-name swaption, if the reference entity of the underlying CDS defaults before the exercise date of the swaption then the contract is knocked out, meaning that the swaption is nullified and thus terminates with zero value. We will later see that this is different from the case of a *credit default index swaption* where, if several (but not all) of reference entities default then the swaption continues until its expiration date.

It is postulated throughout that the underlying contract is the forward CDS issued at time $s \in [0, T_0]$ with an $\mathcal{F}_s$-measurable spread κ, as specified by Definition 8.2.1. The exercise date U of the swaption satisfies $s < U \leq T_0$, that is, the swaption expires either before or at the start date T_0 of the underlying forward CDS.

Definition 8.3.1 *The* credit default swaption *to enter a forward CDS with an $\mathcal{F}_s$-measurable spread κ at a future date $s < U \leq T_0$ has the payoff at maturity equal to* $C_U = (S_U(\kappa))^+$.

The feature that the credit default swaption is knocked out if default occurs prior to exercise date U is already encoded in the payoff C_U, since we have that

$$C_U = (S_U(\kappa))^+ = \left(\mathbb{1}_{\{U<\tau\}}S_U(\kappa)\right)^+ = \mathbb{1}_{\{U<\tau\}}(S_U(\kappa))^+ \qquad (8.19)$$

The price at time $t \in [s, U]$ of the European claim C_U is given by the risk-neutral valuation formula

$$C_t = \mathbb{E}_{\mathbb{Q}}\Big(\beta(t, U)\big(S_U(\kappa)\big)^+ \,\Big|\, \mathcal{G}_t\Big) = \mathbb{E}_{\mathbb{Q}}\Big(\mathbb{1}_{\{U < \tau\}}\beta(t, U)\widetilde{A}_U(\kappa_U - \kappa)^+ \,\Big|\, \mathcal{G}_t\Big) \quad (8.20)$$

where we employed equation (8.18) to obtain the second equality.

The next lemma furnishes a representation for the price of the credit default swaption in terms of the reference filtration $\mathbb{F}$.

Lemma 8.3.1   *The price of the credit default swaption equals, for every $t \in [s, U]$,*

$$C_t = \mathbb{1}_{\{t < \tau\}} G_t^{-1} \, \mathbb{E}_{\mathbb{Q}}\Big(G_U \beta(t, U)\widetilde{A}_U(\kappa_U - \kappa)^+ \,\Big|\, \mathcal{F}_t\Big) \quad (8.21)$$

Proof. It is clear that the random variable $Y := \beta(t, U)\widetilde{A}_U(\kappa_U - \kappa)^+$ is $\mathcal{F}_U$-measurable. Therefore, equality (8.21) is an immediate consequence of formulas (8.2) and (8.20).

The crucial observation is that the pricing formula (8.21) can be further simplified by a suitable change of a probability measure, as pointed out by Brigo (2005), Brigo and Morini (2005), and Jamshidian (2004). To this end, we define an equivalent probability measure $\widehat{\mathbb{Q}}$ on $(\Omega, \mathcal{F}_U)$ by postulating that the Radon-Nikodým density of $\widehat{\mathbb{Q}}$ with respect to $\mathbb{Q}$ equals:

$$\frac{d\widehat{\mathbb{Q}}}{d\mathbb{Q}} = c\,\widehat{A}_U =: \eta_U, \quad \mathbb{Q}\text{-a.s.} \quad (8.22)$$

where $c = \big(\mathbb{E}_{\mathbb{Q}}(\widehat{A}_U)\big)^{-1}$ is the normalizing constant, which ensures that $\mathbb{E}_{\mathbb{Q}}(\eta_U) = 1$, so that $\widehat{\mathbb{Q}}$ is indeed a probability measure on $(\Omega, \mathcal{F}_U)$. The process $\eta_t = c\,\widehat{A}_t$, $t \in [s, U]$, is a strictly positive $(\mathbb{Q}, \mathbb{F})$-martingale, which in turn implies that, for every $t \in [s, U]$,

$$\frac{d\widehat{\mathbb{Q}}}{d\mathbb{Q}}\Big|\, \mathcal{F}_t = \mathbb{E}_{\mathbb{Q}}(\eta_U \,|\, \mathcal{F}_t) = \eta_t, \quad \mathbb{Q}\text{-a.s.}$$

The next result yields a simplified representation for the price of the credit default swaption.

Lemma 8.3.2   *The price of the credit default swaption satisfies $C_t = \mathbb{1}_{\{t < \tau\}}\widetilde{C}_t$, where the predefault price of the swaption equals, for every $t \in [s, U]$,*

$$\widetilde{C}_t = \widetilde{A}_t \, \mathbb{E}_{\widehat{\mathbb{Q}}}\big((\kappa_U - \kappa)^+ \,\big|\, \mathcal{F}_t\big) \quad (8.23)$$

Proof. Recall that we denote $\widehat{A}_t = G_t B_t^{-1} \widetilde{A}_t$ and $\eta_t = c \widehat{A}_t$. Formula (8.21) yields

$$
\begin{aligned}
C_t &= \mathbb{1}_{\{t<\tau\}} B_t G_t^{-1} \, \mathbb{E}_{\mathbb{Q}} \left(\widehat{A}_U (\kappa_U - \kappa)^+ \,\big|\, \mathcal{F}_t \right) \\
&= \mathbb{1}_{\{t<\tau\}} \widetilde{A}_t \eta_t^{-1} \, \mathbb{E}_{\mathbb{Q}} \big(\eta_U (\kappa_U - \kappa)^+ \,\big|\, \mathcal{F}_t \big) \\
&= \mathbb{1}_{\{t<\tau\}} \widetilde{A}_t \, \mathbb{E}_{\widehat{\mathbb{Q}}} \big((\kappa_U - \kappa)^+ \,\big|\, \mathcal{F}_t \big)
\end{aligned}
$$

where the last equality is an immediate consequence of the abstract Bayes formula (see Lemma A.1.4 in Musiela and Rutkowski 2007).

The next important lemma shows that the change of the probability measure from $\mathbb{Q}$ to $\widehat{\mathbb{Q}}$ makes the fair forward CDS spread κ a driftless process, more precisely, a martingale with respect to $\widehat{\mathbb{Q}}$.

Lemma 8.3.3 *The predefault fair forward CDS spread $(\kappa_t,\ t \in [s,\, U])$ is a strictly positive $(\widehat{\mathbb{Q}},\ \mathbb{F})$-martingale.*

Proof. We observe that the product $\kappa \eta$ is manifestly a $(\mathbb{Q},\ \mathbb{F})$-martingale, since it satisfies, for every $t \in [s,\, U]$,

$$
\kappa_t \eta_t = c \kappa_t \widehat{A}_t = c \, \widehat{P}_t = c \, \mathbb{E}_{\mathbb{Q}} \bigg((1 - \delta) \sum_{j=1}^m B_\tau^{-1} \mathbb{1}_{\{T_{j-1} < \tau \le T_j\}} \,\bigg|\, \mathcal{F}_t \bigg)
$$

Let us recall the well-known result from the martingale theory stating, using the present notation, that a process κ is a $(\widehat{\mathbb{Q}},\ \mathbb{F})$-martingale whenever the product $\kappa \eta$ is a $(\mathbb{Q},\ \mathbb{F})$-martingale. Using this property, which is an almost immediate consequence of the abstract Bayes formula (see the proof of Lemma A.14.1 in Musiela and Rutkowski 2007), we immediately arrive at a conclusion that the process κ follows a $(\widehat{\mathbb{Q}},\ \mathbb{F})$-martingale.

8.3.1 Hedging of Credit Default Swaptions

Hedging of the credit default swaption is by no means a trivial issue. Of course, any approach to this problem will heavily rely on the choice of traded instruments that are assumed to be available for the purpose of hedging. In the present setup, it is natural to postulate that the forward CDS with an $\mathcal{F}_s$-measurable rate κ is traded. As the second traded instrument, we take a portfolio of corporate bonds that formally corresponds to the CDS annuity. This choice is motivated by a simple observation that $\widetilde{A}_t$ corresponds to the predefault value at time $t \in [s,\, T_0]$ of a specific portfolio of corporate bonds with zero recovery, referred to hereafter as the *swap portfolio*. If the default event occurs at some date $t \in [s,\, T_0]$, the wealth of this portfolio necessarily falls to zero. Clearly, the same feature is enjoyed by the forward CDS, as well as by the credit default swaption we wish to hedge. This explains why it will suffice in our computations to focus on the dynamics of the predefault value of the swaption and the predefault wealth of the hedging portfolio.

Let $A_t = \mathbb{1}_{\{t < \tau\}} \widetilde{A}_t$ be the value of the swap portfolio at time $t \in [s, T_0]$. Recall also that the swaption's price satisfies $S_t(\kappa) = \mathbb{1}_{\{t < \tau\}} \widetilde{S}_t(\kappa)$ for any date $t \in [s, T_0]$.

We write $\varphi = (\varphi^1, \varphi^2)$ to denote a *trading strategy*, where φ^1 and φ^2 are $\mathbb{G}$-predictable processes. It is considered the wealth of a trading strategy between the date s and the expiry date U of the swaption, where by assumption $U \le T_0$. For any $t \in [s, U]$, the *wealth* $V_t(\varphi)$ of a portfolio φ is defined by the equality

$$V_t(\varphi) = \varphi_t^1 S_t(\kappa) + \varphi_t^2 A_t$$

and this immediately entails that the *predefault wealth* of φ satisfies, for every $t \in [s, U]$,

$$\widetilde{V}_t(\varphi) = \varphi_t^1 \widetilde{S}_t(\kappa) + \varphi_t^2 \widetilde{A}_t$$

Of course, the equality $V_t(\varphi) = \mathbb{1}_{\{t < \tau\}} \widetilde{V}_t(\varphi)$ holds for any $t \in [s, U]$ and thus it suffices to examine a replicating strategy on the interval $[s, s \vee \tau \wedge U]$.

Put another way, it is enough to search for $\mathbb{F}$-predictable processes $\widetilde{\varphi}^i$, $i = 1, 2$ such that for every $t \in [s, U]$ we have that $\mathbb{1}_{\{t < \tau\}} \varphi_t^i = \widetilde{\varphi}_t^i$ for $i = 1, 2$. We then say that a trading strategy φ *replicates* a credit default swaption with the price process C and the predefault price $\widetilde{C}$ if the equality $\widetilde{V}_t(\widetilde{\varphi}) = \widetilde{C}_t$ is valid for every $t \in [s, U]$ or, equivalently, if the equality $V_t(\varphi) = C_t$ holds for every $t \in [s, U]$.

A replicating strategy φ is required to be *self-financing*, in the sense that:

$$d\widetilde{V}_t(\varphi) = d\widetilde{V}_t(\widetilde{\varphi}) = \widetilde{\varphi}_t^1 \, d\widetilde{S}_t(\kappa) + \widetilde{\varphi}_t^2 \, d\widetilde{A}_t$$

It can be easily shown by Itô's formula that the relative predefault wealth $\widetilde{V}(\widetilde{\varphi})/\widetilde{A}$ satisfies

$$d(\widetilde{V}_t(\widetilde{\varphi})/\widetilde{A}_t) = \widetilde{\varphi}_t^1 \, d(\widetilde{S}_t(\kappa)/\widetilde{A}_t) \tag{8.24}$$

To proceed further, we make an additional assumption that the filtration $\mathbb{F}$ is generated by a one-dimensional Brownian motion W under $\mathbb{Q}$. Let us mention that this assumption is satisfied, for instance, in the case of the market model considered in Section 8.4, provided that the interest rate is assumed to be either deterministic or governed by the same Brownian motion as the default intensity.

Since $\widehat{P}$ and $\widehat{A}$ are strictly positive $(\mathbb{Q}, \mathbb{F})$-martingales, we deduce from the predictable representation theorem for the Brownian filtration that there exist $\mathbb{F}$-predictable processes σ^P and σ^A such that, for every $t \in [s, T_0]$,

$$\widehat{P}_t = \widehat{P}_s + \int_s^t \widehat{P}_u \sigma_u^P \, dW_u, \qquad \widehat{A}_t = \widehat{A}_s + \int_s^t \widehat{A}_u \sigma_u^A \, dW_u$$

The next result is an immediate consequence of the Girsanov theorem.

Lemma 8.3.4 *Let the filtration $\mathbb{F}$ be generated by a one-dimensional Brownian motion W under $\mathbb{Q}$. Then the forward CDS rate $(\kappa_t, \ t \in [s, U])$ is a $(\widehat{\mathbb{Q}}, \mathbb{F})$-martingale and*

$$d\kappa_t = \kappa_t \sigma_t^\kappa \, d\widehat{W}_t \tag{8.25}$$

where the $\mathbb{F}$-predictable process σ^κ satisfies $\sigma^\kappa = \sigma^P - \sigma^A$ and the $(\widehat{\mathbb{Q}}, \mathbb{F})$-Brownian motion $\widehat{W}$ is defined by the formula

$$\widehat{W}_t = W_t - \int_s^t \sigma_u^A \, du, \quad \forall t \in [s, U]$$

We are in a position to state the result, which provides an explicit, though admittedly rather abstract, representation for the hedging strategy. In the next section, we show that one can derive closed-form expressions for processes arising in equation (8.26) in a particular intensity-based model.

Proposition 8.3.1 *The replicating strategy $\widetilde{\varphi} = (\widetilde{\varphi}^1, \widetilde{\varphi}^2)$ for the credit default swaption is given by, for every $t \in [s, U]$,*

$$\widetilde{\varphi}_t^1 = \frac{\widetilde{\xi}_t}{\kappa_t \sigma_t^\kappa}, \quad \widetilde{\varphi}_t^2 = \frac{\widetilde{C}_t - \widetilde{\varphi}_t^1 \widetilde{S}_t(\kappa)}{\widetilde{A}_t} \tag{8.26}$$

where $\widetilde{\xi}$ is the process satisfying

$$\frac{\widetilde{C}_U}{\widetilde{A}_U} = \frac{\widetilde{C}_s}{\widetilde{A}_s} + \int_s^U \widetilde{\xi}_t \, d\widehat{W}_t \tag{8.27}$$

Proof. The existence of $\widetilde{\xi}$ is a consequence of the predictable representation theorem for the Brownian filtration. Formula (8.18) established in Lemma 8.2.3 gives $\widetilde{S}_t(\kappa) = \widetilde{A}(\kappa_t - \kappa)$. Using also equations (8.25) and (8.24), we obtain

$$d(\widetilde{V}_t(\widetilde{\varphi})/\widetilde{A}_t) = \widetilde{\varphi}_t^1 \, d(\widetilde{S}_t(\kappa)/\widetilde{A}_t) = \widetilde{\varphi}_t^1 \, d\kappa_t = \widetilde{\varphi}_t^1 \kappa_t \sigma_t^\kappa \, d\widehat{W}_t \tag{8.28}$$

A comparison of equations (8.27) and (8.28) provides the expression for the hedge ratio $\widetilde{\varphi}^1$. Standard arguments show that the strategy $\widetilde{\varphi}$ given by equation (8.26) is self-financing and its predefault wealth satisfies $\widetilde{V}_t(\widetilde{\varphi}) = \widetilde{C}_t$ for every $t \in [s, U]$. As already mentioned, if default occurs prior to or at expiration date U of the credit default swaption, then the wealth of the portfolio φ falls to zero and the same property is satisfied by the price process of the credit default swaption.

In view of the last result, the problem of replication of the credit default swaption is reduced to the computation of the quantities $\widetilde{\xi}_t$, κ_t and σ_t^κ appearing in equation (8.26). To a large extent, this result is model independent; for instance, if the process

σ^κ is deterministic it yields the Black formula for the predefault price of a credit default swaption. The assumption of a deterministic character of σ^κ is quite constraining, however, as explained in Brigo and El Bachir (2010). In Section 8.4, we present the pricing and hedging results within the set-up in which σ^κ is not deterministic, but closed-form expressions for the price and hedging strategy for a credit default swaption are available.

8.3.2   Black Formula for Credit Default Swaptions

The goal of this section is to examine the case of a deterministic volatility of the forward CDS rate. For a more detailed discussion of applicability of some variant of the Black formula to valuation of credit default swaptions, the interested reader is referred to Brigo (2005), Brigo and Morini (2005), Jamshidian (2004), Li and Rutkowski (2010), Morini and Brigo (2007), and Rutkowski and Armstrong (2009). Let us only mention here that although an arbitrage-free model of a family of forward CDS rates underpinning Proposition 8.3.2 is not easy to construct, the pricing formula (8.29) was nevertheless adopted as the market convention for quoting credit default swaptions. Let N denote the cumulative distribution function of the standard normal (Gaussian) distribution.

Proposition 8.3.2 *Assume that the volatility σ^κ of the forward CDS rate $(\kappa_t, t \in [0, T_0])$ is deterministic for every $t \in [s, U]$. Then the predefault value of the credit default swaption with an $\mathcal{F}_s$-measurable strike κ and the expiry date $U \le T_0$ equals, for every $t \in [s, U]$,*

$$\widetilde{C}_t = \widetilde{A}_t \Big(\kappa_t N \big(d_+(\kappa_t, t, U) \big) - \kappa N \big(d_-(\kappa_t, t, U) \big) \Big) \tag{8.29}$$

where

$$d_{\pm}(\kappa_t, t, U) = \frac{\ln(\kappa_t/\kappa) \pm \frac{1}{2} \int_t^U (\sigma_u^\kappa)^2 \, du}{\sqrt{\int_t^U (\sigma_u^\kappa)^2 \, du}}$$

Equivalently,

$$\widetilde{C}_t = \widetilde{P}_t \, N \big(d_+(\kappa_t, t, U) \big) - \kappa \widetilde{A}_t \, N \big(d_-(\kappa_t, t, U) \big) \tag{8.30}$$

The replicating strategy $\widetilde{\varphi} = (\widetilde{\varphi}^1, \widetilde{\varphi}^2)$ is given by $\widetilde{\varphi}_t^1 = N \big(d_+(\kappa_t, t, U) \big)$ and

$$\widetilde{\varphi}_t^2 = \kappa \Big(N \big(d_+(\kappa_t, t, U) \big) - N \big(d_-(\kappa_t, t, U) \big) \Big)$$

Proof. The proof of the proposition is analogous to the derivation of the classic Black and Scholes formula for an equity option and the corresponding hedging strategy. For this reason, we will merely sketch its main steps.

First, the derivation of the pricing formula (8.29) relies on explicit computations using equality (8.23). It suffices to observe that, under the assumptions of the proposition, the process κ has the lognormal probability distribution under $\mathbb{Q}$ and $\widehat{\mathbb{Q}}$. Since these arguments are fairly standard, they are omitted.

Second, to find the hedging strategy, it suffices to observe that by applying the Itô formula to the right-hand side of the equality

$$\frac{C_t}{\widetilde{A}_t} = \kappa_t N\big(d_+(\kappa_t, t, U)\big) - \kappa N\big(d_-(\kappa_t, t, U)\big)$$

we obtain, for every $t \in [s, U]$,

$$d(\widetilde{C}_t/\widetilde{A}_t) = \kappa_t \sigma_t^\kappa \, N\big(d_+(\kappa_t, t, U)\big) \, d\widehat{W}_t = N\big(d_+(\kappa_t, t, U)\big) \, d\kappa_t$$

so that we may identify the process $\widetilde{\xi}$ arising in equality (8.27) as being given by

$$\widetilde{\xi}_t = \kappa_t \sigma_t^\kappa \, N\big(d_+(\kappa_t, t, U)\big)$$

This in turn is equivalent to the equality $\widetilde{\varphi}_t^1 = N\big(d_+(\kappa_t, t, U)\big)$. The second component of the replicating strategy can now be found directly by combining equation (8.26) with equation (8.29).

For examples of market models for certain families of forward CDS spreads, in which the assumptions of Proposition 8.3.2 are satisfied, we refer to Section 8.6.

8.4 CIR Default Intensity Model

The goal of this section, in which we follow Brigo and Alfonsi (2003, 2005) and Bielecki, Jeanblanc, and Rutkowski (2008), is to illustrate some abstract results from the preceding section by providing a detailed analysis of a particular intensity-based model. Since the stochastic intensity is described by the Cox, Ingersoll, and Ross (1985) dynamics, the model is referred to as the *CIR default intensity* model. The main results of this section show that not only the value of a credit default swaption (see Proposition 8.4.3), but also the hedging strategy for the swaption (see Corollary 8.4.2), are given by closed-form expressions. For the second result, an important step is an explicit computation of the volatility process σ^κ of forward CDS spread (see Proposition 8.4.1).

Let us first describe some general features, which hold in the intensity-based setup when the reference filtration is generated by a Brownian motion W. We start by postulating that we are given a nonnegative and $\mathbb{F}$-predictable process γ defined on some probability space $(\Omega, \mathbb{G}, \mathbb{Q})$ endowed with the filtration $\mathbb{F}$ and we set $\Gamma_t = \int_0^t \gamma_u \, du$. The default time is then defined through the so-called *canonical construction*, that is, by the formula

$$\tau = \inf \left\{ t \in \mathbb{R}_+ : \Gamma_t \geq \theta \right\} \qquad (8.31)$$

where θ is a random variable with the unit exponential distribution, independent of the filtration $\mathbb{F}$. Note that the random time τ defined by equation (8.31) can be seen as the moment of the first jump of a Cox process with the stochastic intensity γ.

For any $u > 0$, we define the $(\mathbb{Q}, \mathbb{F})$-martingale $(G_t^u, \ t \in [0, T_m])$ by setting

$$G_t^u = \mathbb{E}_{\mathbb{Q}}\left(e^{-\Gamma_u} \, \big| \, \mathcal{F}_t\right) \text{ for } t \in [0, u[, \quad G_t^u = e^{-\Gamma_u} \text{ for } t \in [u, T_m]$$

so that $G_t = e^{-\Gamma_t}$ for every $t \in [0, T_m]$. Moreover, for any fixed $x > 0$, we define the $(\mathbb{Q}, \mathbb{F})$-martingale $(f_t^x, \ t \in [0, T_m])$ by the formula

$$f_t^x = \mathbb{E}_{\mathbb{Q}}\left(\gamma_x e^{-\Gamma_x} \, \big| \, \mathcal{F}_t\right) \text{ for } t \in [0, x[, \quad f_t^x = \gamma_x e^{-\Gamma_x} \text{ for } t \in [x, T_m]$$

Let us now describe the underlying forward credit default swap. In this section, we consider the following specification of the two legs of the forward CDS

$$D_t = (1 - \delta)\beta(t, \tau)\mathbb{1}_{\{T_0 \leq \tau \leq T_m\}} - \kappa \sum_{j=1}^m \alpha_j \beta(t, T_j)\mathbb{1}_{\{T_j < \tau\}} \qquad (8.32)$$

In order to simplify some formulas, we define the stepwise function $\Theta : \mathbb{R} \to \mathbb{R}$ by setting

$$\Theta(t) = \sum_{j=1}^m \alpha_j \mathbb{1}_{\{t \geq T_j\}}, \quad \forall \, t \in [0, T_m] \qquad (8.33)$$

Using this notation, we may rewrite equation (8.32) as follows:

$$D_t = \int_{]0, t \wedge T_m]} (1 - \delta)\beta(t, u) \, dH_u - \kappa \int_{]0, t \wedge T_m]} (1 - H_u)\beta(t, u) \, d\Theta(u) \qquad (8.34)$$

where, as usual, the process H is defined by the formula $H_t = \mathbb{1}_{\{\tau \leq t\}}$. Under the present convention, the price of the forward CDS equals, for every $t \in [s, U]$,

$$S_t(\kappa) = \mathbb{E}_{\mathbb{Q}}\left((1 - \delta)\beta(t, \tau)\mathbb{1}_{\{T_0 \leq \tau \leq T_m\}} - \kappa \int_{]\tau \wedge T_0, \tau \wedge T_m]} \beta(t, u) \, d\Theta(u) \, \bigg| \, \mathcal{G}_t\right)$$

Remark 8.4.1 *It is worth stressing that some other conventions for the fee leg (for instance, the convention represented by equation (8.8)) are also covered by the foregoing results. It suffices to modify the choice of the auxiliary function Θ, which in fact is any stepwise function or indeed an arbitrary function of finite variation on the interval $[T_0, T_m]$. Hence the method presented below is flexible enough to cover several alternative specifications of the fee payments. One could also include the accrual term in the fee leg (as in equation (8.5)), but the resulting expression would become too cumbersome. Similarly, the protection leg can also be modified (e.g., as in equation (8.7)), but this would require modifying some explicit computations presented in this section. To conclude, the approach developed in this section is fairly general, but for definiteness we have chosen to deal with convention (8.34) for some function Θ.*

Let us return to the issue of valuation of a forward CDS under convention (8.32) within the present setup. The following auxiliary result is borrowed from Bielecki, Jeanblanc, and Rutkowski (2008).

Lemma 8.4.1 *The price $S_t(\kappa) = \mathbb{1}_{\{t<\tau\}}\widetilde{S}_t(\kappa)$ satisfies, for every $t \in [s, T_0]$,*

$$S_t(\kappa) = \mathbb{1}_{\{t<\tau\}} \frac{1}{G_t}\left((1-\delta)\int_{T_0}^{T_m}\beta(t,u)f_t^u\,du - \kappa\int_{]T_0,T_m]}\beta(t,u)G_t^u\,d\Theta(u)\right)$$

$$(8.35)$$

8.4.1 Dynamics of the Default Intensity

For the remaining part of this section, we work under the standing assumption that the default intensity γ is governed by the CIR dynamics (see Cox, Ingersoll, and Ross 1985):

$$d\gamma_t = (a - b\gamma_t)\,dt + c\sqrt{\gamma_t}\,dW_t, \quad \gamma_0 > 0 \qquad (8.36)$$

where a, b, and c are strictly positive constants and W is a one-dimensional Brownian motion, which generates the filtration $\mathbb{F}$. It is assumed throughout that the short-term interest rate r, and thus also the savings account B, are deterministic.

It is well known that under the assumption that $2a > c^2$ the unique solution to the stochastic differential equation (8.36) is strictly positive. We postulate that the default time τ is defined by formula (8.31), so that $G_t = e^{-\Gamma_t}$. Let us denote, for arbitrary $0 \le t \le u \le T_m$,

$$H_t^u = \mathbb{E}_{\mathbb{Q}}\left(e^{-(\Gamma_u - \Gamma_t)} \,\big|\, \mathcal{F}_t\right) = \frac{G_t^u}{G_t} \qquad (8.37)$$

It is known (see, e.g., Section 3.2.3 in Brigo and Mercurio 2006, Section 6.3.4 in Jeanblanc, Yor, and Chesney 2009, or page 357 in Musiela and Rutkowski 2007) that H_t^u equals:

$$H_t^u = e^{m(t,u)-n(t,u)\gamma_t} = \widehat{H}(\gamma_t, t, u) \tag{8.38}$$

where we denote

$$\widehat{H}(y, t, u) = e^{m(t,u)-n(t,u)y} \tag{8.39}$$

and the functions m and n are given by the following expressions:

$$m(t, u) = \frac{2a}{c^2} \ln \left\{ \frac{de^{b(u-t)/2}}{d \cosh d(u-t) + \frac{1}{2}b \sinh d(u-t)} \right\}$$

and

$$n(t, u) = \frac{\sinh d(u-t)}{d \cosh d(u-t) + \frac{1}{2}b \sinh d(u-t)}$$

where in turn $2d = (b^2 + 2c^2)^{1/2}$. It is important to observe that, for any fixed $t \in \mathbb{R}_+$, the function $n(t, u)$, $u \geq t$, is strictly increasing. Moreover, the function n is strictly positive and thus, for any fixed u and t, the auxiliary function $\widehat{H}(y, t, u)$ is decreasing and continuous in $y \in \mathbb{R}_+$.

Let $D^0(t, u)$ stand for the price at time t of the unit defaultable zero coupon bond, which matures at time $u \geq t$ and is subject to the zero recovery scheme. Also, let $B(t, u)$ denote the price at time t of the default-free unit zero coupon bond maturing at $u \geq t$. Since the interest rate r is deterministic, the price $D^0(t, u)$ can be easily computed as follows [we make use here of formula (8.2)]:

$$D^0(t, u) = B_t \, \mathbb{E}_{\mathbb{Q}}(B_u^{-1}\mathbb{1}_{\{u<\tau\}} \mid \mathcal{G}_t) = \mathbb{1}_{\{t<\tau\}}B(t, u)H_t^u = \mathbb{1}_{\{t<\tau\}}\widetilde{D}^0(t, u) \tag{8.40}$$

where $B(t, u) = B_t B_u^{-1} = \beta(t, u)$ and where we write $\widetilde{D}^0(t, u)$ to denote the *predefault value* of the bond at time t.

8.4.2 Volatility of the CDS Spread

As in Section 8.3, we consider a credit default swaption, with expiry date U (where $0 < U \leq T_0$) and zero strike, which is written on the value of the underlying forward start CDS. We will now assume that the underlying CDS was issued at time $s = 0$, has the start date T_0 and maturity T_m. Finally, κ is a constant spread.

The swaption's payoff C_U at its expiry date is given by the equality $C_U = (S_U(\kappa))^+$ or, equivalently (cf. Lemma 8.2.1):

$$C_U = \mathbb{1}_{\{U<\tau\}}\widetilde{A}_U(\kappa_U - \kappa)^+$$

The first step in the valuation of this contract is the computation of the volatility of the fair CDS spread. For the proof of Proposition 8.4.1, which is based on Lemma 8.4.1, the interested reader is referred to Bielecki, Jeanblanc, and Rutkowski (2008).

Proposition 8.4.1 *The volatility of the forward CDS satisfies* $\sigma^\kappa = \sigma^P - \sigma^A$, *where*

$$\sigma_t^P = c\sqrt{\gamma_t}\,\frac{\beta_{T_m}H_t^{T_m}n(t, T_m) - \beta_{T_0}H_t^{T_0}n(t, T_0) + \int_{T_0}^{T_m} r_u\beta_u H_t^u n(t, u)\,du}{\beta_{T_0}H_t^{T_0} - \beta_{T_m}H_t^{T_m} - \int_{T_0}^{T_m} r_u\beta_u H_t^u\,du} \quad (8.41)$$

and

$$\sigma_t^A = -c\sqrt{\gamma_t}\,\frac{\int_{]T_0,\,T_m]}\beta_u H_t^u n(t, u)\,d\Theta(u)}{\int_{]T_0,\,T_m]}\beta_u H_t^u\,d\Theta(u)} \quad (8.42)$$

Under the assumptions made in this section, the price $B(t, u)$ at time t of the unit (default-free) discount bond maturing at time u satisfies $B(t, u) = \beta(t, u)$. Let us write $\gamma_t^u = f_t^u G_t^{-1}$. It can be easily checked that

$$\gamma_t^u = \widehat{h}(\gamma_t, t, u)$$

where we denote $\widehat{h}(y, t, u) = -\partial_u \widehat{H}(y, t, u)$ and the function $\widehat{H}$ is given by equation (8.39). It is then not difficult to establish the following equality:

$$C_U = \mathbb{1}_{\{U<\tau\}}\left((1-\delta)\int_{T_0}^{T_m} B(U, u)\gamma_U^u\,du - \kappa\int_{]T_0,\,T_m]} B(U, u)H_U^u\,d\Theta(u)\right)^+$$

This in turn leads to the following representation:

$$C_U = \mathbb{1}_{\{U<\tau\}}\left((1-\delta)B(U, T_0)H_U^{T_0} - \int_{]T_0,\,T_m]} B(U, u)H_U^u\,d\chi(u)\right)^+ \quad (8.43)$$

where the function $\chi : \mathbb{R}_+ \to \mathbb{R}$ with $\chi(0) = 0$ is defined by the formula

$$d\chi(u) = -(1-\delta)\frac{\partial\ln B(U, u)}{\partial u}\,du + \kappa\,d\Theta(u) + (1-\delta)\,d\mathbb{1}_{[T_m,\infty[}(u) \quad (8.44)$$

Let us define auxiliary functions $\zeta : \mathbb{R}_+ \to \mathbb{R}_+$ and $\psi : \mathbb{R} \to \mathbb{R}_+$ by setting

$$\zeta(x) = (1-\delta)B(U, T_0)\widehat{H}(x, U, T_0), \quad \psi(y) = \int_{]T_0,\,T_m]} B(U, u)\widehat{H}(y, U, u)\,d\chi(u) \quad (8.45)$$

We note that χ generates a finite, nonnegative measure μ_χ on $(]T_0, T_m], \mathcal{B}(]T_0, T_m]))$ such that $\mu_\chi(]T_0, T_m]) > 0$. Therefore, the strictly positive function ψ is strictly decreasing. Moreover, since for any $u > U$ we have that $\lim_{y \to -\infty} \widehat{H}(y, U, u) = \infty$ and $\lim_{y \to \infty} \widehat{H}(y, U, u) = 0$, we see that $\lim_{y \to -\infty} \psi(y) = \infty$ and $\lim_{y \to \infty} \psi(y) = 0$. Let us observe that since ψ is strictly decreasing and continuous, the inverse function $\psi^{-1} :]0, \infty[\to \mathbb{R}$ enjoys the same properties.

Formula (8.43) can be rewritten as follows:

$$C_U = \mathbb{1}_{\{U < \tau\}} \left(\zeta(\gamma_U) - \psi(\gamma_U) \right)^+ \tag{8.46}$$

Our next goal is to examine representation (8.46) in more detail. Toward this end, we shall analyze the existence of a solution to the equation $\zeta(\gamma_U(\omega)) = \psi(\gamma_U^*(\omega))$ for any fixed $\omega \in \Omega$. Put another way, we deal with the following random equation:

$$(1 - \delta) B(U, T_0) \widehat{H}(\gamma_U, U, T_0) = \int_{]T_0, T_m]} B(U, u) \widehat{H}(\gamma_U^*, U, u) \, d\chi(u) \tag{8.47}$$

where we search for a solution γ_U^*. In view of the properties of ζ and ψ, the following result is obvious (note that the second statement in the lemma follows from the strict positivity of γ_U).

Lemma 8.4.2 *There exists a unique $\mathcal{F}_U$-measurable random variable $\gamma_U^* = \psi^{-1}(\zeta(\gamma_U))$ such that*

$$\zeta(\gamma_U) = (1 - \delta) B(U, T_0) \widehat{H}(\gamma_U, U, T_0) = \int_{]T_0, T_m]} B(U, u) \widehat{H}(\gamma_U^*, U, u) \, d\chi(u)$$
$$= \psi(\gamma_U^*) \tag{8.48}$$

On the set $\{\zeta(\gamma_U) \geq \psi(0)\}$, we have $\gamma_U^* \leq 0$ and thus the inequality $\zeta(\gamma_U) = \psi(\gamma_U^*) > \psi(\gamma_U)$ holds.

We are in a position to prove the crucial result, which is borrowed from Brigo and Alfonsi (2003) and Bielecki et al. (2008). It furnishes a convenient representation for the payoff of the credit default swaption for any expiry date U that satisfies $0 < U \leq T_0$.

Proposition 8.4.2 *The payoff of the credit default swaption admits the following representation:*

$$C_U = \mathbb{1}_{\{U < \tau\}} \int_{]T_0, T_m]} B(U, u) \left(\widehat{H}(\gamma_U^*, U, u) - \widehat{H}(\gamma_U, U, u) \right)^+ d\chi(u) \tag{8.49}$$

Proof. In view of equations (8.43) and (8.48), we obtain:

$$C_U = \mathbb{1}_{\{U < \tau\}} \left(\int_{]T_0, T_m]} B(U, u) \big(\widehat{H}(\gamma_U^*, U, u) - \widehat{H}(\gamma_U, U, u) \big) \, d\chi(u) \right)^+$$

$$= \mathbb{1}_{\{U < \tau\}} \left(\int_{]T_0, T_m]} B(U, u) \big(\widehat{H}(\gamma_U^*, U, u) - \widehat{H}(\gamma_U, U, u) \big) \, \mu_\chi(du) \right)^+$$

Since μ_χ is a nonnegative measure and the sign of the expression $\widehat{H}(\gamma_U^*, U, u) - \widehat{H}(\gamma_U, U, u)$ is constant with respect to u, the validity of equality (8.49) is clear.

We are in a position to state the following corollary to Proposition 8.4.2. Let us note that equality (8.50) is an immediate consequence of equation (8.49) combined with equation (8.40).

Corollary 8.4.1 *The payoff of the credit default swaption equals*

$$C_U = \int_{]T_0, T_m]} \big(K(u) D^0(U, U) - D^0(U, u) \big)^+ d\chi(u) \tag{8.50}$$

where the random variable $K(u)$ satisfies $K(u) = B(U, u) \widehat{H}(\gamma_U^*, U, u)$ and χ is given by equation (8.44).

8.4.3 Hedging of the Credit Default Swaption

Throughout Section 8.4.3, we work under the standing assumption that $U = T_0$. In that case, the function ζ is constant, specifically, the equality $\zeta(x) = 1 - \delta$ holds for every $x \in \mathbb{R}_+$. Therefore, equation (8.47) simplifies to

$$\zeta(\gamma_{T_0}) = 1 - \delta = \int_{]T_0, T_m]} B(T_0, u) \widehat{H}(\gamma_{T_0}^*, T_0, u) \, d\chi(u)$$

The unique solution $\gamma_{T_0}^*$ is deterministic and it is strictly positive whenever $1 - \delta < \psi(0)$. If, on the contrary, the inequality $1 - \delta \geq \psi(0)$ holds then the credit default swaption is formally equivalent to a portfolio of defaultable bonds with zero recovery and thus its valuation and hedging problem becomes trivial.

From now on, we will thus focus on the case when the inequality $1 - \delta < \psi(0)$ is valid. By applying Corollary 8.4.1, we obtain

$$C_{T_0} = \int_{]T_0, T_m]} \big(K(u) D^0(T_0, T_0) - D^0(T_0, u) \big)^+ d\chi(u) = \int_{]T_0, T_m]} C_{T_0}^u \, d\chi(u) \tag{8.51}$$

Formula (8.51) shows that the credit default swaption is formally equivalent to a weighted portfolio of survival claims maturing at T_0 and indexed by $u \in \,]T_0, T_m]$, where $C_{T_0}^u$ equals

$$C_{T_0}^u = \left(K(u)D^0(T_0, T_0) - D^0(T_0, u)\right)^+ = \mathbb{1}_{\{T_0 < \tau\}}\left(K(u) - \widetilde{D}^0(T_0, u)\right)^+ \quad (8.52)$$

where $K : \,]T_0, T_m] \to \mathbb{R}_+$ is a deterministic function and $\widetilde{D}^0(T_0, u)$ stands for the predefault value at time T_0 of the defaultable bond with zero recovery maturing at time u.

We will now adapt to the present setup the general hedging results of Section 8.3.1. Recall that we have shown there that the hedge ratio $\widetilde{\varphi}^1$ is given by the generic expression [cf. formula (8.26)]:

$$\widetilde{\varphi}_t^1 = \frac{\widetilde{\widetilde{\xi}}_t}{\kappa_t \sigma_t^\kappa} \quad (8.53)$$

where the process $\widetilde{\widetilde{\xi}}$ is implicitly defined by equation (8.27) with $U = T_0$, and the process $\sigma^\kappa = \sigma^P - \sigma^A$ represents the volatility of the forward CDS spread (see Proposition 8.4.1). To make formula (8.53) useful for practical purposes, we need, of course, to compute explicitly the process $\widetilde{\widetilde{\xi}}$.

To achieve this goal, we will adopt the following strategy. We will first use equality (8.50) in order to derive an explicit pricing formula for the swaption in terms of the intensity process γ. Subsequently, we will employ the pricing formula for an explicit evaluation of the process $\widetilde{\widetilde{\xi}}$.

Proposition 8.4.3 *The predefault price of the credit default swaption equals, for every $t \in [0, T_0]$:*

$$\widetilde{C}_t = \int_{]T_0, T_m]} B(t, u) P(\gamma_t, t, T_0, u, \widehat{K}(u)) \, d\chi(u) \quad (8.54)$$

where $\widehat{K}(u) := K(u)/B(T_0, u) = \widehat{H}(\gamma_{T_0}^*, T_0, u)$ *and where* $P(\gamma_t, t, T_0, u, \widehat{K}(u))$ *stands for the price at time t of a put bond option with strike $\widehat{K}(u)$ and expiry T_0 written on a zero coupon bond maturing at u computed in the CIR model with the short-term interest rate modeled by the process γ.*

The advantage of the pricing formula (8.54) is the well-known fact that the arbitrage price $P_t^u := P(\gamma_t, t, T_0, u, \widehat{K}(u))$ of the put bond option in the CIR interest rate model can be computed explicitly (see, for instance, Proposition 10.3.4 in Musiela and Rutkowski 2007). Using the present notation, it can be represented as follows:

$$P_t^u = \widehat{K}(u)\widehat{H}(\gamma_t, t, T_0) \, \mathbb{P}_{T_0}(\widehat{H}(\gamma_{T_0}, T_0, u) \le \widehat{K}(u) \mid \gamma_t)$$
$$- \widehat{H}(\gamma_t, t, u) \, \mathbb{P}_u(\widehat{H}(\gamma_{T_0}, T_0, u) \le \widehat{K}(u) \mid \gamma_t)$$

where the probability measures $\mathbb{P}_{T_0}$ and $\mathbb{P}_u$ are the forward martingale measures for the dates T_0 and u, respectively, in the CIR interest rate model. Equivalently,

$$P_t^u = \widehat{K}(u)\widehat{H}(\gamma_t, t, T_0)\,\mathbb{P}_{T_0}(\gamma_{T_0} \geq \bar{K}(T_0, u) \mid \gamma_t) - \widehat{H}(\gamma_t, t, u)\,\mathbb{P}_u(\gamma_{T_0}$$
$$\geq \bar{K}(T_0, u) \mid \gamma_t) \tag{8.55}$$

where $\widehat{H}(\gamma_t, t, u)$ can be interpreted as the price at time t of the zero coupon bond maturing at u in the CIR interest rate model with the short-term rate modeled by the process γ. For any $u \in]T_0, T_m]$, the constant $\bar{K}(T_0, u)$ appearing in equation (8.55) can be easily computed using equation (8.39), specifically,

$$\bar{K}(T_0, u) = \frac{m(T_0, u) - \ln \widehat{K}(u)}{n(T_0, u)}$$

It is well known that the conditional probability density functions of γ_{T_0} given γ_t, under the forward martingale measures $\mathbb{P}_{T_0}$ and $\mathbb{P}_u$ in the CIR interest rate model, can be expressed in terms of the transition probability density function of the ν-dimensional squared Bessel process with $\nu = 4a/c^2$, that is, in term of the noncentral χ^2-distribution.

Let us denote

$$p_{T_0}(\gamma_t, t, T_0, u) = \mathbb{P}_{T_0}(\gamma_{T_0} \geq \bar{K}(T_0, u) \mid \gamma_t)$$

and

$$p_u(\gamma_t, t, T_0, u) = \mathbb{P}_u(\gamma_{T_0} \geq \bar{K}(T_0, u) \mid \gamma_t)$$

Then we can rewrite formula (8.55) as follows:

$$P_t^u = \widehat{K}(u)H_t^{T_0}p_{T_0}(\gamma_t, t, T_0, u) - H_t^u p_u(\gamma_t, t, T_0, u) \tag{8.56}$$

This also means that

$$P_t^u = \widehat{K}(u)H_t^{T_0}\Psi_{T_0}(Z_t^{T_0,u}, t, T_0, u) - H_t^u \Psi_u(Z_t^{T_0,u}, t, T_0, u) \tag{8.57}$$

where we set $Z_t^{T_0,u} = H_t^u / H_t^{T_0}$ and where the functions Ψ_{T_0} and Ψ_u are obtained by expressing γ_t in terms of $Z_t^{T_0,u}$.

To obtain equation (8.57) from equation (8.56), it suffices to note that the ratio $H_t^u / H_t^{T_0}$ is a strictly decreasing function of γ_t for any fixed $u > T_0$, since it is clear that the inequality $n(t, u) > n(t, T_0)$ holds in that case. More explicitly,

$$Z_t^{T_0,u} = H_t^u / H_t^{T_0} = \exp\left(m(t, u) - m(t, T_0) - (n(t, u) - n(t, T_0))\gamma_t\right)$$

and thus

$$\gamma_t = \frac{m(t, u) - m(t, T_0) - \ln Z_t^{T_0, u}}{n(t, u) - n(t, T_0)}$$

To find the hedging strategy, it remains to identify the process $\widetilde{\xi}$ arising in equation (8.53), that is, the process $\widetilde{\xi}$ implicitly defined by the equality [cf. (8.27)]:

$$d(\widetilde{C}_t / \widetilde{A}_t) = \widetilde{\xi}_t \, d\widehat{W}_t$$

where $\widehat{W}$ is the Brownian motion under the swap measure $\widehat{\mathbb{Q}}$ introduced in Section 8.3.1. This task appears to be feasible in the present framework, as shown by the following result, which was established in Bielecki et al. (2008a).

Proposition 8.4.4 *We have that, for every $t \in [0, T_0]$,*

$$\widetilde{\xi}_t = \frac{1}{\widetilde{A}_t} \left(\int_{]T_0, T_m]} B(t, u) \left(\vartheta_t^{T_0, u} H_t^u \left(b_t^u - b_t^{T_0} \right) - P_t^u b_t^{T_0} \right) d\chi(u) - \widetilde{C}_t \sigma_t^A \right) \quad (8.58)$$

where $\widetilde{A}_t = \widetilde{A}_t$, $H_t^u = \widehat{H}(\gamma_t, t, u)$, $b_t^u = c\, n(t, u)\sqrt{\gamma_t}$, $P_t^u = P(\gamma_t, t, T_0, u, \widehat{K}(u))$, the volatility process σ^A is given by equation (8.42), and the processes $\vartheta^{T_0, u}$, $u \in]T_0, T_m]$, are given by, for every $t \in [0, T_0]$,

$$\vartheta_t^{T_0, u} = \widehat{K}(u) \frac{\partial \Psi_{T_0}}{\partial Z}(Z_t^{T_0, u}, t, T_0, u) - \Psi_u(Z_t^{T_0, u}, t, T_0, u)$$

$$- Z_t^{T_0, u} \frac{\partial \Psi_u}{\partial Z}(Z_t^{T_0, u}, t, T_0, u) \quad (8.59)$$

We are in a position to state an important corollary to Propositions 8.4.1, 8.4.3, and 8.4.4.

Corollary 8.4.2 *Let us consider the CIR default intensity model with a deterministic short-term interest rate. The replicating strategy $\widetilde{\varphi} = (\widetilde{\varphi}^1, \widetilde{\varphi}^2)$ for the credit default swaption with expiration date $U = T_0$ equals, for any $t \in [0, T_0]$,*

$$\widetilde{\varphi}_t^1 = \frac{\widetilde{\xi}_t}{\kappa_t \sigma_t^\kappa}, \quad \widetilde{\varphi}_t^2 = \frac{\widetilde{C}_t - \widetilde{\varphi}_t^1 \widetilde{S}_t(\kappa)}{\widetilde{A}_t}$$

where the processes σ^κ, $\widetilde{C}$, and $\widetilde{\xi}$ are given in Propositions 8.4.1, 8.4.3, and 8.4.4, respectively. Moreover,

$$\widetilde{A}_t = B(t) \int_{]T_0, T_m]} \beta_u H_t^u \, d\Theta(u) \quad (8.60)$$

$$\widetilde{S}_t(\kappa) = -(1 - \delta) B_t \int_{T_0}^{T_m} \beta_u \partial_u H_t^u \, du - \kappa B_t \int_{]T_0, T_m]} \beta_u H_t^u \, d\Theta(u) \quad (8.61)$$

and

$$\kappa_t = -\frac{(1-\delta)\int_{T_0}^{T_m}\beta_u\,\partial_u H_t^u\,du}{\int_{]T_0,\,T_m]}\beta_u H_t^u\,d\Theta(u)} \tag{8.62}$$

It is fair to say, despite the fact that the replicating strategy for the credit default swaption is given here in the semianalytical form, that the practical implementation of this strategy is by no means straightforward, due to numerical difficulties that arise in the context of formulas (8.41)–(8.42) and (8.58)–(8.59).

8.5 Options on Credit Default Indexes

A *credit default index swap* (CDIS) is a standardized contract that is based upon a fixed portfolio of reference entities. The two main indexes to which CDSs are referenced are CDX, referring to companies within North America and iTraxx, which refers to companies within Europe and Asia. We look at the case of the CDX, although iTraxx and other indexes have very similar characteristics. At its conception, the CDX is referenced to $n = 125$ fixed companies that are chosen by market makers. These 125 reference entities are specified to have equal weights within the CDX. If we assume each has a nominal value of one then, because of the equal weighting, the total notional would be 125. In effect, one CDX provides on average the same protection to that of 125 single-name CDSs upon the same reference entities.

By contrast to a standard single-name CDS, the buyer of the CDX provides protection to the market makers. In other words, by purchasing a CDX from market makers the investor is not receiving protection; rather, they are providing it to the market makers. In exchange for the protection the investor is providing, the market makers pay the investor a periodic fixed premium, otherwise known as the *credit default index spread*. Such standardized contracts promote liquidity within the derivatives market.

Typically, the recovery rate $\delta \in [0, 1]$ is predetermined and constant for all reference entities in the index. By purchasing the index the investor is agreeing to pay the market makers $1 - \delta$ for any default that occurs before maturity. That is, following a default the investor has to cover the loss incurred, which is achieved by paying to the market maker the amount of $1 - \delta$. Following this, the nominal value of the CDX is reduced by one. Once a removal has taken place there is no replacement of the defaulted firm on the CDX series. This process repeats after every default and the CDX continues on until maturity.

The standard maturities of a CDX are five and 10 years with payments occurring quarterly. However, in more recent times, three- and seven-year products have been introduced. New CDXs are defined semiannually and the fixed rate, reference entities, and maturities are reconfigured by the market makers according to current market conditions. Such changes do not alter preexisting contracts. iTraxx and other credit default index swaps operate analogously with the CDX, with the only distinctions being in the contract details—the premium, the number, and choice of reference entities and reconfiguration procedures.

The presentation in this section is largely based on the paper by Rutkowski and Armstrong (2009). Similar results were obtained in the independent work by Morini and Brigo (2007).

8.5.1   Default Times and Reference Filtration

As we are now working within the multiname case, the appropriate notation needs to be introduced. We denote by $(\Omega, \mathcal{G}, \mathbb{Q})$ the underlying probability space. Let $\mathbb{G}$ be the filtration generated by the reference filtration $\mathbb{F}$ and filtrations $\mathbb{H}^1, \ldots, \mathbb{H}^n$, where $\mathbb{H}^i$ is the filtration generated by the default indicator $H_t^i = \mathbb{1}_{\{\tau_i \leq t\}}$ of the default time of the ith credit name. We postulate that simultaneous defaults are excluded in our model, and we introduce the sequence $\tau_{(1)} < \cdots < \tau_{(n)}$ of ordered default times associated with the original sequence of default times $\tau_1, \ldots, \tau_n$. Let $\mathbb{H}^{(i)}$ is the filtration generated by the indicator process $H_t^{(i)} = \mathbb{1}_{\{\tau_{(i)} \leq t\}}$ of the ith default.

We thus have $\mathbb{G} = \mathbb{H}^{(n)} \vee \bar{\mathbb{F}}$, where the filtration $\mathbb{H}^{(n)}$ is generated by the indicator process $H_t^{(n)} = \mathbb{1}_{\{\tau_{(n)} \leq t\}}$ of the last default and where we set $\bar{\mathbb{F}} = \mathbb{F} \vee \mathbb{H}^{(1)} \vee \cdots \vee \mathbb{H}^{(n-1)}$. For brevity, in what follows we will write $\bar{\tau} = \tau_{(n)}$ to denote the random time when all firms in a given portfolio are in default. In the context of valuation of credit default index swaptions, the usefulness of this particular decomposition of the full filtration $\mathbb{G}$ was noted independently by Morini and Brigo (2007) and Rutkowski and Armstrong (2009).

We will frequently focus on the events $\{\bar{\tau} \leq t\}$ and $\{\bar{\tau} > t\}$ for a fixed t. In their 2007 paper, Morini and Brigo refer to these events as the *Armageddon event* and the *no-Armageddon event*, respectively. Following Rutkowski and Armstrong (2009), we use here the terms *collapse event* and *precollapse event*, respectively. The event $\{\bar{\tau} \leq t\}$ corresponds to the total collapse of the reference portfolio, in the sense that all underlying credit names default either prior to or at time t.

As in Section 8.2 [cf. formula (8.1)], we start by defining the auxiliary process $\bar{F}$, which is now given by the following expression, for every $t \in \mathbb{R}_+$,

$$\bar{F}_t = \mathbb{Q}(\bar{\tau} \leq t \mid \bar{\mathcal{F}}_t)$$

Let us denote by $\bar{G}_t = 1 - \bar{F}_t = \mathbb{Q}(\bar{\tau} > t \mid \bar{\mathcal{F}}_t)$ the corresponding survival process with respect to the filtration $\bar{\mathbb{F}}$ and let us temporarily assume that the inequality $\bar{G}_t > 0$ holds for every $t \in \mathbb{R}_+$. In what follows, we require only that the inequality $\bar{G}_t > 0$ holds for every $t \in [s, T_1]$, so that, in particular, $\bar{G}_{T_1} = \mathbb{Q}(\bar{\tau} > T_1 \mid \bar{\mathcal{F}}_{T_1}) > 0$.

Then for any $\mathbb{Q}$-integrable and $\bar{\mathcal{F}}_T$-measurable random variable X we have that [cf. equation (8.2)]:

$$\mathbb{E}_{\mathbb{Q}}(\mathbb{1}_{\{T < \bar{\tau}\}} X \mid \mathcal{G}_t) = \mathbb{1}_{\{t < \bar{\tau}\}} \, \bar{G}_t^{-1} \, \mathbb{E}_{\mathbb{Q}}(\bar{G}_T X \mid \bar{\mathcal{F}}_t) \tag{8.63}$$

For the reader's convenience, let us state the following immediate consequence of Lemma 8.2.1.

Lemma 8.5.1 *Let Y be a $\mathbb{G}$-adapted stochastic process. Then there exists a unique $\mathbb{F}$-adapted process $\tilde{Y}$ such that, for every $t \in \mathbb{R}_+$,*

$$\mathbb{1}_{\{t<\tilde{\tau}\}} Y_t = \mathbb{1}_{\{t<\tilde{\tau}\}} \tilde{Y}_t \tag{8.64}$$

The process $\tilde{Y}$ is termed the precollapse value *of the process Y.*

8.5.2 Forward-Start Credit Default Index Swap

We write $T_0 < T_1 < \cdots < T_m$ to denote the *tenor structure* of the forward-start CDIS, where

- $T_0 = T$ is the inception date.
- T_m is the maturity date.
- T_j is the jth fee payment date for $j = 1, 2, \ldots, m$.

Let $\alpha_j = T_j - T_{j-1}$ for every $j = 1, 2, \ldots, m$. We assume that the savings account process B is strictly positive and $\mathbb{F}$-adapted or, at least, $\tilde{\mathbb{F}}$-adapted. The probability measure $\mathbb{Q}$ is interpreted as a martingale measure associated with the choice of B as the numéraire asset.

Definition 8.5.1 *The discounted cash flows for the seller (that is, for the protection buyer) of the* forward CDIS *issued at time $s \in [0, T_0]$ with an $\mathcal{F}_s$-measurable spread κ are, for every $t \in [s, T_0]$,*

$$D_t^n = P_t^n - \kappa A_t^n \tag{8.65}$$

where

$$P_t^n = (1 - \delta) B_t \sum_{i=1}^{n} B_{\tau_i}^{-1} \mathbb{1}_{\{T_0 < \tau_i \le T_m\}} \tag{8.66}$$

and

$$A_t^n = B_t \sum_{j=1}^{m} \alpha_j B_{T_j}^{-1} \sum_{i=1}^{n} \left(1 - \mathbb{1}_{\{T_j \ge \tau_i\}}\right) \tag{8.67}$$

are discounted payoffs of the protection leg and the fee leg per one basis point, respectively. The fair price *at time* $t \in [s, T_0]$ *of a forward credit default index swap for the protection buyer equals*

$$S_t^n(\kappa) = \mathbb{E}_{\mathbb{Q}}(D_t^n \mid \mathcal{G}_t) = \mathbb{E}_{\mathbb{Q}}(P_t^n \mid \mathcal{G}_t) - \kappa \mathbb{E}_{\mathbb{Q}}(A_t^n \mid \mathcal{G}_t)$$

From equations (8.66) and (8.67), we obtain the following properties of P_t^n and A_t^n:

$$P_t^n = \mathbb{1}_{\{T_0 < \bar{\tau}\}} P_t^n, \qquad A_t^n = \mathbb{1}_{\{T_0 < \bar{\tau}\}} A_t^n \tag{8.68}$$

Let us note that the quantities P_t^n and A_t^n are well defined for any $t \in [0, T_0]$ and they do not depend on the issuance date s of the forward CDIS under consideration.

The cash flows of the protection leg of the forward credit default index swap are similar to summing the cash flows of n individual single-name forward CDS cash flows. Indeed, the right-hand side of equation (8.66) is simply the discounted sum of constant protection payouts $(1 - \delta)$ for all the reference entities that have defaulted during the lifetime of the forward CDIS, that is, between the inception date T_0 and the maturity date T_m.

The fee leg is somewhat different, however. The premium payment of the forward CDIS decreases following every default, since the constant premium is only paid on the nominal value of the surviving entities. Hence the nominal value reduces after every default and the investor's fee payment decreases in proportion to the change in nominal value. The total nominal of a portfolio of single-name CDSs also decreases after each default, but the total premium paid after defaults depends also on the identities of defaulted names, since spreads of individual CDSs are typically different.

We write J_t to denote the *reduced nominal* at time $t \in [s, T_0]$, as given by the formula

$$J_t = n - \sum_{i=1}^{n} \mathbb{1}_{\{t \geq \tau_i\}} = \sum_{i=1}^{n} \left(1 - \mathbb{1}_{\{t \geq \tau_i\}}\right) = \sum_{i=1}^{n} \mathbb{1}_{\{\tau_i > t\}} \tag{8.69}$$

It is useful to observe that

$$J_t \geq \frac{1}{n} \mathbb{1}_{\{\bar{\tau} > t\}}$$

and thus

$$\mathbb{E}_{\mathbb{Q}}(J_t \mid \bar{\mathcal{F}}_t) \geq \frac{1}{n} \mathbb{Q}(\bar{\tau} > t \mid \bar{\mathcal{F}}_t) = \frac{1}{n} \bar{G}_t \tag{8.70}$$

The proof of the following pricing result is exactly the same as the proof of Lemma 8.2.2. It is based on formulas (8.63) and (8.68).

Lemma 8.5.2 *The price at time $t \in [s, T_0]$ of the forward CDIS satisfies*

$$S_t^n(\kappa) = \mathbb{1}_{\{t < \bar{\tau}\}} \bar{G}_t^{-1} \, \mathbb{E}_{\mathbb{Q}}(D_t^n \mid \tilde{\mathcal{F}}_t) = \mathbb{1}_{\{t < \bar{\tau}\}} \tilde{S}_t^n(\kappa) \tag{8.71}$$

where the precollapse price *of the forward CDIS satisfies $\tilde{S}_t^n(\kappa) = \tilde{P}_t^n - \kappa \, \bar{A}_t^n$, where in turn*

$$\tilde{P}_t^n = \bar{G}_t^{-1} \, \mathbb{E}_{\mathbb{Q}}(P_t^n \mid \tilde{\mathcal{F}}_t), \quad \bar{A}_t^n = \bar{G}_t^{-1} \, \mathbb{E}_{\mathbb{Q}}(A_t^n \mid \tilde{\mathcal{F}}_t) \tag{8.72}$$

or, more explicitly,

$$\tilde{P}_t^n = (1 - \delta) \bar{G}_t^{-1} B_t \, \mathbb{E}_{\mathbb{Q}}\Big(\sum_{i=1}^{n} B_{\tau_i}^{-1} \mathbb{1}_{\{T_0 < \tau_i \le T_m\}} \Big| \tilde{\mathcal{F}}_t \Big) \tag{8.73}$$

and

$$\bar{A}_t^n = \bar{G}_t^{-1} B_t \, \mathbb{E}_{\mathbb{Q}}\Big(\sum_{j=1}^{m} \alpha_j B_{T_j}^{-1} J_{T_j} \Big| \tilde{\mathcal{F}}_t \Big) \tag{8.74}$$

The process $\bar{A}_t^n$ may be thought of as the precollapse present value of receiving risky one basis point on the forward CDIS payment dates T_j on the residual nominal value J_{T_j}. Similarly, the process $\tilde{P}_t^n$ represents the precollapse present value of the protection leg of the contract.

8.5.2.1 Precollapse Fair CDIS Spread

Since the forward CDIS is terminated at the moment of the nth default with no further payments, it makes sense to define the forward CDS spread only prior to $\bar{\tau}$. It is thus natural to introduce the concept of the *precollapse* fair forward CDIS spread, rather than the fair forward CDS spread.

Definition 8.5.2 *The* precollapse fair forward CDIS spread *at time $t \in [0, T_0]$ is the $\tilde{\mathcal{F}}_t$-measurable random variable κ_t^n such that $\tilde{S}_t^n(\kappa_t^n) = 0$.*

The following result, which is a counterpart of Lemma 8.2.3, is a straightforward consequence of Lemma 8.5.2. It is worth noting that the quantity κ_t^n is well defined for every $t \in [0, T_0]$ and, manifestly, it does not depend on the issuance date s. Observe also that the $(\mathbb{Q}, \tilde{\mathbb{F}})$-martingales $\widehat{P}^n$ and $\widehat{A}^n$ correspond to $(\mathbb{Q}, \mathbb{F})$-martingales $\widehat{A}$ and $\widehat{P}$ introduced in Section 8.2 (see formulas (8.16) and (8.17)).

Lemma 8.5.3 *Assume that* $\bar{G}_{T_1} = \mathbb{Q}(\bar{\tau} > T_1 \mid \bar{\mathcal{F}}_{T_1}) > 0$. *Then the precollapse fair forward CDIS spread satisfies, for every* $t \in [0, T_0]$,

$$\kappa_t^n = \frac{\bar{P}_t^n}{\bar{A}_t^n} = \frac{(1-\delta)\,\mathbb{E}_{\mathbb{Q}}\Big(\sum_{i=1}^n B_{\tau_i}^{-1}\mathbb{1}_{\{T_0 < \tau_i \le T_m\}}\Big| \bar{\mathcal{F}}_t\Big)}{\mathbb{E}_{\mathbb{Q}}\Big(\sum_{j=1}^m \alpha_j B_{T_j}^{-1} J_{T_j}\Big| \bar{\mathcal{F}}_t\Big)} = \frac{\widehat{P}_t^n}{\widehat{A}_t^n} \tag{8.75}$$

where the $(\mathbb{Q}, \bar{\mathbb{F}})$-*martingales* $\widehat{P}^n$ *and* $\widehat{A}^n$ *are given by*

$$\widehat{P}_t^n = \bar{G}_t B_t^{-1} \bar{P}_t^n = (1-\delta)\mathbb{E}_{\mathbb{Q}}\Big(\sum_{i=1}^n B_{\tau_i}^{-1}\mathbb{1}_{\{T_0 < \tau_i \le T_m\}}\Big| \bar{\mathcal{F}}_t\Big) \tag{8.76}$$

and

$$\widehat{A}_t^n = \bar{G}_t B_t^{-1} \bar{A}_t^n = \mathbb{E}_{\mathbb{Q}}\Big(\sum_{j=1}^m \alpha_j B_{T_j}^{-1} J_{T_j}\Big| \bar{\mathcal{F}}_t\Big) \tag{8.77}$$

The price of the forward CDIS admits the following representation, for every $t \in [0, T_0]$,

$$S_t^n(\kappa) = \mathbb{1}_{\{t < \bar{\tau}\}} \bar{A}_t^n(\kappa_t^n - \kappa) \tag{8.78}$$

8.5.2.2 Market Convention for Valuing a CDIS

The crucial difficulty in the analysis of a credit default index swaption is that the market quote for the quantity $\bar{A}_t^n$ is not directly available. For this reason, some ad hoc approximations for the value of A_t^n were proposed in order to enable marking to market of a CDIS. Usually, they hinge on the following postulates:

- All firms are identical (homogeneous portfolio); in fact, we formally just deal with an artificial single-name case, meaning that either all firms default or none do.
- The implied risk-neutral default probabilities for different maturities are computed using a flat single-name CDS curve with a constant spread equal to κ_t^n.

In view of these postulates, the right-hand side in equation (8.74) can approximate as follows:

$$\bar{A}_t^n \approx J_t PV_t(\kappa_t^n)$$

where $PV_t(\kappa_t)$ is the risky present value of receiving one basis point at all CDIS payment dates calibrated to a flat CDS curve with spread equal to κ_t^n, where κ_t^n is the quoted CDIS spread at time t. Consequently, the conventional market formula for the market value of the CDIS with fixed spread κ reads, on the precollapse event $\{t < \bar{\tau}\}$,

$$\bar{S}_t(\kappa) = J_t PV_t(\kappa_t^n)(\kappa_t^n - \kappa) \tag{8.79}$$

In particular, if the credit default index swap was issued at time 0 with the spread κ_0^n, then its marked-to-market value at time t equals

$$\bar{S}_t(\kappa_0^n) = \mathbb{1}_{\{t < \bar{\tau}\}} PV_t(\kappa_t^n) J_t(\kappa_t^n - \kappa_0^n) \tag{8.80}$$

As was explained earlier, the quantity $PV_t(\kappa_t^n)$ is computed as if it was a single-name case, not a multiname case. For this very reason, we underline the importance of this step in the market convention. As we will argue, from the theoretical viewpoint, it would be much easier to work with the mathematically correct formula (8.78), rather than with the conventional expression (8.79).

8.5.2.3 Market Payoff of a Credit Default Index Swaption

In Section 8.3, we dealt with the valuation of options on a single-name credit default swap. This is now extended to options on a credit default index swap, referred to as *credit default index swaptions*. Credit default index swaptions are European options and thus can only be exercised at expiry at the preset exercise spread κ. Standard contracts have maturities of either three or six months. For example, in a standard CDX swaption contract the specifics would be: the underlying CDX, the expiry date, the strike level κ, and the type (payer or receiver).

Let us first present briefly the market convention regarding the payoff of the payer credit default index swaption; for more details and comments, the interested reader is referred to Pedersen (2003). It is assumed here that the credit default index swap was issued at time 0, with the constant spread κ_0^n and κ_U^n representing the corresponding market quote at time U.

Definition 8.5.3 *The conventional market formula for the payoff at maturity $U \leq T_0$ of the* payer credit default index swaption *with strike level κ reads*

$$C_U = \left(\mathbb{1}_{\{U < \bar{\tau}\}} PV_U(\kappa_U^n) J_U(\kappa_U^n - \kappa_0^n) - \mathbb{1}_{\{U < \bar{\tau}\}} PV_U(\kappa) n (\kappa - \kappa_0^n) + L_U \right)^+ \tag{8.81}$$

where the reduced nominal J is given by equation (8.69) and L stands for the loss process for our portfolio so that, for every $t \in \mathbb{R}_+$,

$$L_t = (1 - \delta) \sum_{i=1}^{n} \mathbb{1}_{\{\tau_i \leq t\}}$$

Note first that in Definition 8.5.3 we set our underlying forward CDIS to have inception date T_0 and maturity T_m. However, the losses from the portfolio are computed from time 0 onward. Hence the holder of the swaption has the right to enter the underlying forward CDIS at time U and, if this option is exercised, he also gains protection against losses from the portfolio between time 0 and time U. The key difference between this cash flow and the cash flow of single-name credit default swaption is that here we no longer deal with the knockout feature, even after the nth default. This lack of knockout proves to be difficult in the valuation and hedging of index swaptions. No longer may the standard Black formula be used to price the credit default index swaptions as this formula only works for options that do knockout at default.

The market convention (8.81) is due to the fact that the swaption has physical settlement and the CDIS with spread κ is not traded. If the swaption is exercised, its holder takes a long position in the on-the-run index and is compensated for the difference between the value of the on-the-run index and the value of the (nontraded) index with spread κ, as well as for defaults that occurred in the interval $[0, U]$.

Recall that $PV_U(\kappa)$ is the risky present value at time U of receiving one basis point at all CDIS payment dates calibrated to a flat single-name CDS curve with spread equal to κ. It is worth observing that $PV_U(\kappa)$ is random only in the interest rates (typically, forward LIBORs), whereas $PV_U(\kappa_U^n)$ is random in both interest rates and the index spread κ_U^n. In order to make $PV_U(\kappa)$ completely deterministic, one may use the standard assumption that the interest rate for some future date lies on the current forward curve for that same date. Under this additional assumption, the quantity $PV_U(\kappa_U^n)$ will only be random via its dependence on the index spread.

8.5.2.4 Put–Call Parity for Credit Default Index Swaptions

For the sake of brevity, let us denote, for any fixed $\kappa > 0$,

$$f(\kappa, L_U) = L_U - \mathbb{1}_{\{U < \bar{\tau}\}} PV_U(\kappa) n(\kappa - \kappa_0^n)$$

Then the payoff of the payer credit default index swaption entered at time 0 and maturing at U equals

$$C_U = \left(\mathbb{1}_{\{U < \bar{\tau}\}} PV_U(\kappa_U^n) J_U(\kappa_U^n - \kappa_0^n) + f(\kappa, L_U) \right)^+$$

whereas the payoff of the corresponding *receiver credit default index swaption* satisfies

$$P_U = \left(\mathbb{1}_{\{U < \bar{\tau}\}} PV_U(\kappa_U^n) J_U(\kappa_0^n - \kappa_U^n) - f(\kappa, L_U) \right)^+$$

This leads to the following equality, which holds at maturity date U

$$C_U - P_U = \mathbb{1}_{\{U<\tilde{\tau}\}}PV_U(\kappa_U^n)J_U(\kappa_U^n - \kappa_0^n) + f(\kappa, L_U)$$

8.5.3 Model Payoff of a Credit Default Index Swaption

The actual payoff [equation (8.81)] of a credit default index swaption is rather difficult to handle analytically, in general. The advantage of this formula is that it is based on market data and it is easy to implement. The major drawback is that it is internally inconsistent since the quantities $PV_U(\kappa_U^n)$ and $PV_U(\kappa)$ are computed on the basis of a single-name case and thus are not consistent with any model for default times $\tau_1, \dots, \tau_n$. For this reason, we will consider in what follows the simplified version of the swaption's payoff.

Definition 8.5.4 *The* model payoff *of the payer credit default index swaption entered at time* 0 *with maturity date* U *and strike level* κ *equals*

$$C_U = (S_U^n(\kappa) + L_U)^+ \tag{8.82}$$

or, more explicitly equation [cf. (8.78)]:

$$C_U = \left(\mathbb{1}_{\{U<\tilde{\tau}\}}\bar{A}_U^n(\kappa_U - \kappa) + L_U\right)^+ \tag{8.83}$$

To formally derive equation (8.83) from equation (8.81), it suffices to postulate that

$$PV_U(\kappa)n \approx PV_U(\kappa_U)J_U \approx \bar{A}_U^n$$

We will first use representation (8.82) to establish, in Subsection 8.5.3.3, the pricing formula for a credit default index swaption, which was proposed in Morini and Brigo (2007). Next, in Subsection 8.5.5, equality (8.83) will be used to justify the market pricing formula for a credit default index swaption. The crucial difference between the two approaches is that the market pricing formula (8.98) refers to the fair CDIS spread κ^n, whereas the model formula (8.95) of Morini and Brigo (2007), as well as the related Pedersen's (2003) formula, are based on the loss-adjusted fair CDIS spread κ^a, which will be introduced in Subsection 8.5.3.2.

8.5.3.1 Loss-Adjusted CDIS

Since $L_U \geq 0$ and, obviously, $L_U = \mathbb{1}_{\{U<\tilde{\tau}\}}L_U + \mathbb{1}_{\{U\geq\tilde{\tau}\}}L_U$, the payoff [equation (8.83)] can also be represented as follows:

$$C_U = (S_U^n(\kappa) + \mathbb{1}_{\{U<\tilde{\tau}\}}L_U)^+ + \mathbb{1}_{\{U\geq\tilde{\tau}\}}L_U = (S_U^a(\kappa))^+ + C_U^L \tag{8.84}$$

where we denote

$$S_U^a(\kappa) = S_U^n(\kappa) + \mathbb{1}_{\{U<\tilde{\tau}\}} L_U, \quad C_U^L = \mathbb{1}_{\{U\geq\tilde{\tau}\}} L_U$$

The quantity $S_U^a(\kappa)$ represents the payoff at time U of the loss-adjusted forward CDIS, which is formally defined as follows.

Definition 8.5.5 *The discounted cash flows for the seller of the* loss-adjusted forward CDIS *(that is, for the buyer of the protection) are, for every $t \in [0, U]$,*

$$D_t^a = P_t^a - \kappa A_t^n$$

where we denote:

$$P_t^a = P_t^n + B_t B_U^{-1} \mathbb{1}_{\{U<\tilde{\tau}\}} L_U$$

It is essential to observe that the payoff D_U^a is the U-survival claim, in the sense that

$$D_U^a = \mathbb{1}_{\{U<\tilde{\tau}\}} D_U^a$$

Let us note that any other adjustments to the payoff P_t^n (or A_t^n) of the CDIS is also admissible, provided that the property $P_U^a = \mathbb{1}_{\{U<\tilde{\tau}\}} P_U^a$ (or $A_U^a = \mathbb{1}_{\{U<\tilde{\tau}\}} A_U^a$) holds. Therefore, if we wish to define a particular adjustment of the fair CDIS spread for any date $t \in [0, U]$, we only need to ensure that the modified protection and fee payoffs are U-survival claims.

Lemma 8.5.4 *The price of the loss-adjusted forward CDIS equals, for every $t \in [0, U]$,*

$$S_t^a(\kappa) = \mathbb{1}_{\{t<\tilde{\tau}\}} \tilde{G}_t^{-1} \mathbb{E}_{\mathbb{Q}}(D_t^a \mid \tilde{\mathcal{F}}_t) = \mathbb{1}_{\{t<\tilde{\tau}\}} \tilde{S}_t^a(\kappa)$$

where the precollapse price satisfies $\tilde{S}_t^a(\kappa) = \tilde{P}_t^a - \kappa \tilde{A}_t^n$, where in turn

$$\tilde{P}_t^a = \tilde{G}_t^{-1} \mathbb{E}_{\mathbb{Q}}(P_t^a \mid \tilde{\mathcal{F}}_t), \quad \tilde{A}_t^n = \tilde{G}_t^{-1} \mathbb{E}_{\mathbb{Q}}(A_t^n \mid \tilde{\mathcal{F}}_t)$$

or, more explicitly,

$$\tilde{P}_t^a = \tilde{G}_t^{-1} B_t \mathbb{E}_{\mathbb{Q}}\left((1-\delta) \sum_{i=1}^n B_{\tau_i}^{-1} \mathbb{1}_{\{T_0<\tau_i\leq T_m\}} + \mathbb{1}_{\{U<\tilde{\tau}\}} B_U^{-1} L_U \Big| \tilde{\mathcal{F}}_t\right)$$

and

$$\bar{A}_t^n = \bar{G}_t^{-1} B_t \, \mathbb{E}_{\mathbb{Q}} \Big(\sum_{j=1}^m \alpha_j B_{T_j}^{-1} J_{T_j} \, \Big| \, \bar{\mathcal{F}}_t \Big)$$

8.5.3.2 Precollapse Loss-Adjusted Fair CDIS Spread

We are in a position to define the loss-adjusted fair forward CDIS spread.

Definition 8.5.6 *The precollapse loss-adjusted fair forward CDIS spread at time $t \in [0, U]$ is the $\bar{\mathcal{F}}_t$-measurable random variable κ_t^a such that $\bar{S}_t^a(\kappa_t^a) = 0$.*

Then we have the following result, which corresponds to Lemma 8.5.3. Recall that $\widehat{A}^n$ is given by formula (8.77). In addition, we define the $(\mathbb{Q}, \bar{\mathbb{F}})$-martingale $\widehat{P}^a$ by setting

$$\widehat{P}_t^a = \bar{G}_t B_t^{-1} \bar{P}_t^a = \mathbb{E}_{\mathbb{Q}} \Big((1 - \delta) \sum_{i=1}^n B_{\tau_i}^{-1} \mathbb{1}_{\{T_0 < \tau_i \le T_m\}} + \mathbb{1}_{\{U < \bar{\tau}\}} B_U^{-1} L_U \, \Big| \, \bar{\mathcal{F}}_t \Big) \quad (8.85)$$

Note that according to this convention, the losses between U and T_0 are not accounted for in the definition of $\widehat{P}^a$. This mismatch is natural, however, since U is the expiry date of the swaption and T_0 is the start date of the underlying forward credit default index swap. Of course, the gap disappears when $U = T_0$, that is, when the credit default index swap starts at the swaption's expiration date.

Lemma 8.5.5 *Assume that $\bar{G}_{T_1} = \mathbb{Q}(\bar{\tau} > T_1 \mid \bar{\mathcal{F}}_{T_1}) > 0$. Then the precollapse loss-adjusted fair forward CDIS spread satisfies, for every $t \in [0, U]$,*

$$\kappa_t^a = \frac{\bar{P}_t^a}{\bar{A}_t^n} = \frac{\mathbb{E}_{\mathbb{Q}} \Big((1 - \delta) \sum_{i=1}^n B_{\tau_i}^{-1} \mathbb{1}_{\{T_0 < \tau_i \le T_m\}} + \mathbb{1}_{\{U < \bar{\tau}\}} B_U^{-1} L_U \, \Big| \, \bar{\mathcal{F}}_t \Big)}{\mathbb{E}_{\mathbb{Q}} \Big(\sum_{j=1}^m \alpha_j B_{T_j}^{-1} J_{T_j} \, \Big| \, \bar{\mathcal{F}}_t \Big)} = \frac{\widehat{P}_t^a}{\widehat{A}_t^n}$$

$$(8.86)$$

The price of the forward CDIS admits the following representation, for every $t \in [0, T_0]$,

$$S_t^a(\kappa) = \mathbb{1}_{\{t < \bar{\tau}\}} \bar{A}_t^n (\kappa_t^a - \kappa) \quad (8.87)$$

Proof. The proof of this result is essentially the same as the proof of Lemma 8.5.3 and thus it is omitted.

8.5.3.3   Model Pricing Formula for Credit Default Index Swaptions

It is easy to check that the model payoff [equation (8.83)] of the credit default index swaption can be represented as follows:

$$C_U = \mathbb{1}_{\{U < \bar\tau\}} \bar{A}_U^n (\kappa_U^a - \kappa)^+ + \mathbb{1}_{\{U \geq \bar\tau\}} L_U \qquad (8.88)$$

This equality should be seen as the loss-adjusted simplification of formula (8.84). The price at time $t \in [0, U]$ of the claim C_U is thus given by the risk-neutral valuation formula

$$C_t = B_t \, \mathbb{E}_{\mathbb{Q}} \big(B_U^{-1} C_U \,\big|\, \mathcal{G}_t \big) = B_t \, \mathbb{E}_{\mathbb{Q}} \big(\mathbb{1}_{\{U < \bar\tau\}} B_U^{-1} \bar{A}_U^n (\kappa_U^a - \kappa)^+ \,\big|\, \mathcal{G}_t \big)$$
$$+ B_t \, \mathbb{E}_{\mathbb{Q}} \big(\mathbb{1}_{\{U \geq \bar\tau\}} B_U^{-1} L_U \,\big|\, \mathcal{G}_t \big)$$

Using the filtration $\bar{\mathbb{F}}$, we can obtain a more explicit representation for the first term in the formula above, as the following result shows.

Lemma 8.5.6   *The price at time $t \in [0, U]$ of the payer credit default index swaption equals*

$$C_t = \mathbb{1}_{\{t < \bar\tau\}} B_t \bar{G}_t^{-1} \, \mathbb{E}_{\mathbb{Q}} \big(\widehat{A}_U^n (\kappa_U^a - \kappa)^+ \,\big|\, \bar{\mathcal{F}}_t \big) + B_t \, \mathbb{E}_{\mathbb{Q}} \big(\mathbb{1}_{\{U \geq \bar\tau\}} B_U^{-1} L_U \,\big|\, \mathcal{G}_t \big) \quad (8.89)$$

Proof. The random variable $Y = B_U^{-1} \bar{A}_U^n (\kappa_U^a - \kappa)^+$ is manifestly $\bar{\mathcal{F}}_U$-measurable and it satisfies $Y = \mathbb{1}_{\{U < \bar\tau\}} Y$. Hence the equality is an immediate consequence of formula (8.63).

Let us first note that, on the collapse event $\{t \geq \bar\tau\}$ we have that $\mathbb{1}_{\{U \geq \bar\tau\}} B_U^{-1} L_U = B_U^{-1} n(1 - \delta)$ and thus the pricing formula (8.89) reduces to

$$C_t = B_t \, \mathbb{E}_{\mathbb{Q}} \big(\mathbb{1}_{\{U \geq \bar\tau\}} B_U^{-1} L_U \,\big|\, \mathcal{G}_t \big) = n(1 - \delta) B_t \, \mathbb{E}_{\mathbb{Q}} \big(B_U^{-1} \,\big|\, \mathcal{G}_t \big) = n(1 - \delta) B(t, U)$$
$$(8.90)$$

where $B(t, U)$ is the price at time t of the U-maturity default-free zero coupon bond. This case is thus easy to handle, and thus it is not examined in what follows.

Let us thus concentrate on the precollapse event $\{t < \bar\tau\}$. We now have $C_t = C_t^a + C_t^L$, where

$$C_t^a = B_t \bar{G}_t^{-1} \, \mathbb{E}_{\mathbb{Q}} \big(\widehat{A}_U^n (\kappa_U^a - \kappa)^+ \,\big|\, \bar{\mathcal{F}}_t \big) \qquad (8.91)$$

and

$$C_t^L = B_t \, \mathbb{E}_{\mathbb{Q}} \big(\mathbb{1}_{\{U \geq \bar\tau > t\}} B_U^{-1} L_U \,\big|\, \bar{\mathcal{F}}_t \big)$$

where the last equality follows from the well known fact that on $\{t < \bar{\tau}\}$ any $\mathcal{G}_t$-measurable event can be represented by an $\bar{\mathcal{F}}_t$-measurable event, in the sense that for any event $A \in \mathcal{G}_t$ there exists an event $\bar{A} \in \bar{\mathcal{F}}_t$ such that $\mathbb{1}_{\{t<\bar{\tau}\}}A = \mathbb{1}_{\{t<\bar{\tau}\}}\bar{A}$ (cf. Lemma 8.5.1).

The computation of C_t^L requires only the knowledge of the risk-neutral conditional distribution of $\bar{\tau}$ given $\bar{\mathcal{F}}_t$ and the term structure of interest rates, since on the event $\{U \geq \bar{\tau} > t\}$ we have that $B_U^{-1}L_U = B_U^{-1}n(1-\delta)$.

By contrast, the computation of C_t^a hinges on exactly the same arguments as in the single-name case. First, we define the equivalent probability measure $\widehat{\mathbb{Q}}$ on $(\Omega, \bar{\mathcal{F}}_U)$ by postulating that the Radon-Nikodým density of $\widehat{\mathbb{Q}}$ with respect to $\mathbb{Q}$ equals

$$\frac{d\widehat{\mathbb{Q}}}{d\mathbb{Q}} = c\,\widehat{A}_U^n, \quad \mathbb{Q}\text{-a.s.}$$

The quantity $c = \left(\mathbb{E}_{\mathbb{Q}}(\widehat{A}_U^n)\right)^{-1} > 0$ is the normalizing constant, which ensures that $\widehat{\mathbb{Q}}$ given by equation (8.92) is indeed a probability measure on $(\Omega, \bar{\mathcal{F}}_U)$.

We note that the process $\widehat{\eta}_t = c\,\widehat{A}_t^n$, $t \in [0, U]$, is a $(\mathbb{Q}, \bar{\mathbb{F}})$-martingale, since

$$\widehat{\eta}_t = c\,\widehat{A}_t^n = c\,\mathbb{E}_{\mathbb{Q}}\Big(\sum_{j=1}^m \alpha_j B_{T_j}^{-1} J_{T_j}\,\Big|\,\bar{\mathcal{F}}_t\Big)$$

Moreover, the process $\widehat{\eta}$ is strictly positive, since we have assumed that $\mathbb{Q}(\bar{\tau} > T_1 \mid \bar{\mathcal{F}}_{T_1}) = \bar{G}_{T_1} > 0$, so that inequality (8.70) is valid. Consequently,

$$\widehat{\eta}_t \geq c\,\mathbb{E}_{\mathbb{Q}}\Big(\alpha_1 B_{T_1}^{-1} J_{T_1}\,\Big|\,\bar{\mathcal{F}}_t\Big) = c\,\mathbb{E}_{\mathbb{Q}}\Big(\alpha_1 B_{T_1}^{-1} \mathbb{E}_{\mathbb{Q}}(J_{T_1} \mid \bar{\mathcal{F}}_{T_1})\,\Big|\,\bar{\mathcal{F}}_t\Big)$$
$$\geq \frac{c}{n}\,\mathbb{E}_{\mathbb{Q}}\Big(\alpha_1 B_{T_1}^{-1} \bar{G}_{T_1}\,\Big|\,\bar{\mathcal{F}}_t\Big) > 0$$

We conclude that the Radon-Nikodým density of $\widehat{\mathbb{Q}}$ with respect to $\mathbb{Q}$ equals, for every $t \in [0, U]$,

$$\frac{d\widehat{\mathbb{Q}}}{d\mathbb{Q}}\Big|\bar{\mathcal{F}}_t = \mathbb{E}_{\mathbb{Q}}(\widehat{\eta}_U \mid \bar{\mathcal{F}}_t) = \widehat{\eta}_t, \quad \mathbb{Q}\text{-a.s.} \tag{8.92}$$

Lemma 8.5.7 *On the collapse event $\{t \geq \bar{\tau}\}$, the price at time $t \in [0, U]$ of the payer credit default index swaption is given by equation (8.90). On the precollapse event $\{t < \bar{\tau}\}$, the price equals*

$$C_t = \bar{A}_t^n\,\mathbb{E}_{\widehat{\mathbb{Q}}}\big((\kappa_U^a - \kappa)^+ \mid \bar{\mathcal{F}}_t\big) + B_t\,\mathbb{E}_{\mathbb{Q}}\big(\mathbb{1}_{\{U \geq \bar{\tau} > t\}} B_U^{-1} L_U \mid \bar{\mathcal{F}}_t\big) \tag{8.93}$$

Proof. It suffices to examine C_t^a. Using equation (8.91) and (8.92), we obtain

$$
\begin{aligned}
C_t^a &= B_t \bar{G}_t^{-1} \, \mathbb{E}_{\mathbb{Q}} \left(\widehat{A}_U^n (\kappa_U^a - \kappa)^+ \,\Big|\, \bar{\mathcal{F}}_t \right) \\
&= \bar{A}_t^n \widehat{\eta}_t^{-1} \, \mathbb{E}_{\mathbb{Q}} \left(\widehat{\eta}_U (\kappa_U^a - \kappa)^+ \,\Big|\, \bar{\mathcal{F}}_t \right) \\
&= \bar{A}_t^n \, \mathbb{E}_{\widehat{\mathbb{Q}}} \left((\kappa_U^a - \kappa)^+ \,\big|\, \bar{\mathcal{F}}_t \right)
\end{aligned}
$$

where the last equality follows from the abstract Bayes formula.

The next lemma establishes the martingale property of the process κ^a under $\widehat{\mathbb{Q}}$.

Lemma 8.5.8 *The precollapse loss-adjusted fair forward CDIS spread κ_t^a, $t \in [0, U]$, is a strictly positive $(\widehat{\mathbb{Q}}, \bar{\mathbb{F}})$-martingale.*

Proof. Similarly as in the proof of Lemma 8.3.3, it suffices to observe that the product $\kappa^a \widehat{\eta}$ satisfies

$$
\kappa_t^a \widehat{\eta}_t = c \kappa_t^a \widehat{A}_t^n = c \widehat{P}_t^a
$$

and thus the process $\kappa^a \widehat{\eta}$ is a $(\mathbb{Q}, \bar{\mathbb{F}})$-martingale, since clearly $\widehat{P}^a$ is a $(\mathbb{Q}, \bar{\mathbb{F}})$-martingale. By the well-known argument, we conclude that κ^a is a $(\widehat{\mathbb{Q}}, \bar{\mathbb{F}})$-martingale.

8.5.4 Black Formula for Credit Default Index Swaptions

Our next goal is to establish a suitable version of the Black formula for the credit default index swaption. To this end, we postulate that the precollapse loss-adjusted fair forward CDIS spread satisfies, for every $t \in [0, U]$,

$$
\kappa_t^a = \kappa_0^a + \int_0^t \sigma_u^a \kappa_u^a \, d\widehat{W}_u \tag{8.94}
$$

where $\widehat{W}$ is the one-dimensional standard Brownian motion under $\widehat{\mathbb{Q}}$ with respect to $\bar{\mathbb{F}}$ and σ is an $\bar{\mathbb{F}}$-predictable process. Let us emphasize that the assumption that the filtration $\bar{\mathbb{F}}$ is the Brownian filtration would be too restrictive, since $\bar{\mathbb{F}} = \mathbb{F} \vee \mathbb{H}^{(1)} \vee \cdots \vee \mathbb{H}^{(n-1)}$ and thus the filtration $\bar{\mathbb{F}}$ obviously supports also discontinuous martingales (which is, of course, not the case when the filtration is generated by a Brownian motion).

Proposition 8.5.1 *Assume that the volatility σ^a of the precollapse loss-adjusted fair forward CDIS spread is a positive function. Then the predefault price of the payer* *credit default index swaption equals, for every* $t \in [0, U]$ *on the precollapse event* $\{t < \bar{\tau}\}$,

$$C_t = \bar{A}_t^n \Big(\kappa_t^a N\big(d_+(\kappa_t^a, t, U)\big) - \kappa N\big(d_-(\kappa_t^a, t, U)\big) \Big) + C_t^L \qquad (8.95)$$

or, equivalently,

$$C_t = \bar{P}_t^a \, N\big(d_+(\kappa_t^a, t, U)\big) - \kappa \bar{A}_t^n \, N\big(d_-(\kappa_t^a, t, U)\big) + C_t^L \qquad (8.96)$$

where

$$d_\pm(\kappa_t^a, t, U) = \frac{\ln(\kappa_t^a/\kappa) \pm \frac{1}{2} \int_t^U (\sigma_u^a)^2 \, du}{\big(\int_t^U (\sigma_u^a)^2 \, du \big)^{1/2}}$$

Proof. It suffices to focus on C_t^a. In view of (8.93) and (8.94), we obtain

$$C_t^a = \bar{A}_t^n \, \mathbb{E}_{\widehat{\mathbb{Q}}}\big((\kappa_U^a - \kappa)^+ \,|\, \bar{\mathcal{F}}_t\big) = \bar{A}_t^n \Big(\kappa_t^a N\big(d_+(\kappa_t^a, t, U)\big) - \kappa N\big(d_-(\kappa_t^a, t, U)\big) \Big)$$

where the second equality follows by standard computations.

A slightly different approach to valuation of a credit default index swaption was proposed by Pedersen (2003). The derivation of Pedersen's formula hinges on the simplification of the actual payoff of the swaption, combined with the assumption that not all reference entities will default prior to the swaption's maturity date $U \leq T$. Formally, it is enough to postulate that

$$L_U = \mathbb{1}_{\{U < \bar{\tau}\}} L_U \qquad (8.97)$$

so that $C_U^L = 0$. Under this assumption, the second term in pricing formulas (8.89), (8.93), and (8.95) vanishes and thus, for instance, expression (8.95) reduces to the standard Black swaptions formula.

Under usual circumstances, the probability of all defaults occurring prior to U is expected to be very low, and thus assumption (8.97) seems to be reasonable. As argued by Morini and Brigo (2007), however, this assumption is not always justified; in particular, it is not suitable for periods when the market conditions deteriorate. Moreover, since in options pricing we deal with the risk-neutral probability measure, it is worth stressing that the risk-neutral default probabilities are known to drastically exceed statistically observed default frequencies, which correspond to default probabilities under the physical probability measure.

Let us finally mention that Jackson (2005) proposed an alternative approach to valuation of a credit default index swaption by conditioning on the number of defaults prior to the swaption's maturity. He was able to derive, albeit under fairly stringent model assumptions, the pricing formula in the form of a weighted average of suitable variants of the Black formula.

8.5.5   Market Pricing Formula for Credit Default Index Swaptions

Before concluding this section, let us briefly examine one of the conventional market formulas for valuing credit default index swaption. Let us emphasize that the pricing formula (8.98) refers to the quoted fair forward CDIS spread κ^n and its (deterministic) volatility σ^n, rather than to its loss-adjusted (and thus not directly observed) version κ^a. To account for a potential loss prior to the swaption's maturity, a suitable (although somewhat ad hoc) adjustment to the strike level κ is introduced.

Proposition 8.5.2   *Assume that the volatility σ^n of the fair forward CDIS spread κ^n is deterministic. The price of a payer credit default index swaption can be approximated as follows, for every $t \in [0, U]$,*

$$
C_U \approx \mathbb{1}_{\{t < \bar{\tau}\}} \bar{A}_t^n \Big(\kappa_t^n N\big(d_+(\kappa_t^n, t, U)\big) - (\kappa - \bar{L}_t) N\big(d_-(\kappa_t^n, t, U)\big) \Big) \tag{8.98}
$$

where

$$
d_\pm(\kappa_t^n, t, U) = \frac{\ln(\kappa_t^n / (\kappa - \bar{L}_t)) \pm \frac{1}{2} \int_t^U (\sigma_u^n)^2 \, du}{\left(\int_t^U (\sigma_u^n)^2 \, du \right)^{1/2}}
$$

where in turn $\bar{L}_t = \mathbb{E}_{\widehat{\mathbb{Q}}}\big((A_U^n)^{-1} L_U \mid \bar{\mathcal{F}}_t \big)$.

Proof. Let us sketch the proof. We start by approximating the model payoff, which is given by the expression [cf. equation (8.83)]:

$$
C_U = \Big(\mathbb{1}_{\{U < \bar{\tau}\}} \bar{A}_U^n (\kappa_U^n - \kappa) + L_U \Big)^+
$$

in the following way:

$$
C_U \approx \mathbb{1}_{\{U < \bar{\tau}\}} \bar{A}_U^n \Big(\kappa_U^n - \kappa + \bar{L}_t \Big)^+
$$

where we denote

$$
\bar{L}_t = \mathbb{E}_{\widehat{\mathbb{Q}}}\big((\bar{A}_U^n)^{-1} L_U \mid \bar{\mathcal{F}}_t \big)
$$

The last equality may be written as

$$
C_U \approx \mathbb{1}_{\{U < \bar{\tau}\}} \bar{A}_U^n \Big(\kappa_U^n - (\kappa - \bar{L}_t) \Big)^+
$$

where the random variable $\bar{L}_t$ is manifestly $\bar{\mathcal{F}}_t$-measurable. By applying the risk-neutral valuation and proceeding as in the proof of Proposition 8.5.1, we obtain the stated formula.

8.6 Market Models for CDS Spreads

The traditional approach to modeling interest rates based on the short-term interest rate has been radically changed to modeling with observable market variables such as the forward LIBORs, as studied in Brace, Gątarek, and Musiela (1997); Miltersen, Sandmann, and Sondermann (1997); and Musiela and Rutkowski (1997), and forward swap rates examined in Jamshidian (1997). The success of market models for interest rates motivates the development of an analogous approach in the context of valuation and hedging of plain-vanilla CDS options and exotic credit derivatives. The main advantage is that these models are based on observable market variables, whereas more traditional approaches hinge on the nonobservable quantities such as the value of the firm or default intensity. This chapter focuses on obtaining market models by using some particular families of forward CDS spreads as the underlying variables. For the purpose of modeling, the simplified protection and fee payment legs will be used throughout.

In Section 8.6.3, we present the model proposed in Brigo (2006, 2008), where one- and two-period forward CDS spreads are modeled by providing their joint dynamics under a single probability measure. Subsequently, in Section 8.6.4, we study an alternative model briefly outlined in Brigo (2008). In this version of the market model, we focus on the specification of the joint dynamics of one-period and coterminal forward CDS spreads under a common probability measure. The aforementioned models are also presented in Section 23.3 of Brigo and Mercurio (2006). For more general results in this vein, we refer to Li and Rutkowski (2010), who examined several variants of market models driven by general semimartingales.

8.6.1 Forward Credit Default Swaps

As usual, we write $T_0 < T_1 < \cdots < T_m$ to denote the *tenor structure*. For any $l = 0, \ldots, m-1$ and $p = l+1, \ldots, m$ we consider a forward-start credit default swap of type (l, p) where:

- T_l is the CDS inception date.
- T_p is the maturity date of the CDS.
- T_j is the jth fee payment date for $j = l+1, 2, \ldots, p$.

Throughout this section, we adopt the postponed running CDS convention [equation (8.7)], proposed in papers by Brigo (2006, 2008). However, for the simplicity of presentation, we will now use the usual notation for the discounted payoffs of the two legs of the forward CDS of type (l, p). Specifically, we denote

$$P_t^{l,p} = (1 - \delta) \sum_{j=l+1}^{p} \beta(t, T_j) \mathbb{1}_{\{T_{j-1} < \tau \le T_j\}} \tag{8.99}$$

and

$$A_t^{l,p} = \sum_{j=l+1}^{p} \beta(t, T_j) \alpha_j \mathbb{1}_{\{T_j < \tau\}} \tag{8.100}$$

In addition, we write

$$\widetilde{P}_t^{l,p} = G_t^{-1} \mathbb{E}_{\mathbb{Q}}(P_t^{l,p} \mid \mathcal{F}_t) \tag{8.101}$$

and

$$\widetilde{A}_t^{l,p} = G_t^{-1} \mathbb{E}_{\mathbb{Q}}(A_t^{l,p} \mid \mathcal{F}_t) \tag{8.102}$$

so that, for every $t \in [0, T_l]$,

$$\mathbb{E}_{\mathbb{Q}}(P_t^{l,p} \mid \mathcal{G}_t) = \mathbb{1}_{\{t < \tau\}} G_t^{-1} \mathbb{E}_{\mathbb{Q}}(P_t^{l,p} \mid \mathcal{F}_t) = \mathbb{1}_{\{t < \tau\}} \widetilde{P}_t^{l,p}$$

and

$$\mathbb{E}_{\mathbb{Q}}(A_t^{l,p} \mid \mathcal{G}_t) = \mathbb{1}_{\{t < \tau\}} G_t^{-1} \mathbb{E}_{\mathbb{Q}}(A_t^{l,p} \mid \mathcal{F}_t) = \mathbb{1}_{\{t < \tau\}} \widetilde{A}_t^{l,p}$$

We observe that under the assumption that $G_t > 0$ the inequality $\widetilde{A}_t^{l,p} > 0$ holds for every $t \in [0, T_l]$. It follows immediately from Lemma 8.2.3, that the corresponding predefault fair forward CDS spread satisfies, for any $t \in [0, T_l]$,

$$\kappa_t^{l,p} = \frac{\widetilde{P}_t^{l,p}}{\widetilde{A}_t^{l,p}} = \frac{\mathbb{E}_{\mathbb{Q}}\left((1 - \delta) \sum_{j=l+1}^{p} B_{T_j}^{-1} \mathbb{1}_{\{T_{j-1} < \tau \le T_j\}} \mid \mathcal{F}_t\right)}{\mathbb{E}_{\mathbb{Q}}\left(\sum_{j=l+1}^{p} \alpha_j B_{T_j}^{-1} \mathbb{1}_{\{T_j < \tau\}} \mid \mathcal{F}_t\right)} = \frac{\widehat{P}_t^{l,p}}{\widehat{A}_t^{l,p}} \tag{8.103}$$

where the $(\mathbb{Q}, \mathbb{F})$-martingales $\widehat{P}$ and $\widehat{A}$ are given by the following expressions, for every $t \in [0, T_l]$,

$$\widehat{P}_t^{l,p} = G_t B_t^{-1} \widetilde{P}_t^{l,p} = (1 - \delta) \mathbb{E}_{\mathbb{Q}}\left(\sum_{j=l+1}^{p} B_{T_j}^{-1} \mathbb{1}_{\{T_{j-1} < \tau \le T_j\}} \mid \mathcal{F}_t\right) \tag{8.104}$$

and

$$\widehat{A}_t^{l,p} = G_t B_t^{-1} \widetilde{A}_t^{l,p} = \mathbb{E}_{\mathbb{Q}}\left(\sum_{j=l+1}^{p} \alpha_j B_{T_j}^{-1} \mathbb{1}_{\{T_j < \tau\}} \,\Big|\, \mathcal{F}_t \right) \qquad (8.105)$$

Assuming that the forward CDS was issued at $s \in [0, T_l]$ and thus κ is $\mathcal{F}_s$-measurable, we obtain the following expression for its price at time t, for every $t \in [s, T_0]$,

$$S_t^{l,p}(\kappa) = \mathbb{1}_{\{t < \tau\}} \widetilde{A}_t^{l,p}(\kappa_t^{l,p} - \kappa) \qquad (8.106)$$

8.6.2 Change of a Numéraire

The goal of this subsection is to summarize the most essential features of the change of numéraire technique. Let us start by stating the following well-known result, whose proof is based on a rather straightforward application of the abstract Bayes formula.

Proposition 8.6.1 *Suppose that* $(N_t, \ t \in [0, T])$ *and* $(\widetilde{N}_t, \ t \in [0, T])$ *are positive,* $\mathbb{F}$-*adapted processes such that the process* $\frac{\widetilde{N}}{N}$ *is a strictly positive* $\mathbb{Q}$-*martingale. Let the Radon-Nikodým density process* ζ *of an equivalent probability measure* $\widetilde{\mathbb{Q}}$ *with respect to* $\mathbb{Q}$ *satisfy*

$$\zeta_t := \frac{d\widetilde{\mathbb{Q}}}{d\mathbb{Q}} \,|\, \mathcal{F}_t = \frac{N_0}{\widetilde{N}_0} \frac{\widetilde{N}_t}{N_t} \qquad (8.107)$$

If $(X_t, \ t \in [0, T])$ *is any process such that the following equality holds under* $\mathbb{Q}$, *for every* $t \in [0, T]$,

$$\frac{X_t}{N_t} = \mathbb{E}_{\mathbb{Q}}\left(\frac{X_T}{N_T} \,\Big|\, \mathcal{F}_t \right)$$

then the following equality holds under $\widetilde{\mathbb{Q}}$, *for every* $t \in [0, T]$,

$$\frac{X_t}{\widetilde{N}_t} = \mathbb{E}_{\widetilde{\mathbb{Q}}}\left(\frac{X_T}{\widetilde{N}_T} \,\Big|\, \mathcal{F}_t \right)$$

Essentially, this result shows that X/N is a $(\mathbb{Q}, \mathbb{F})$-martingale whenever the process $X/\widetilde{N}$ is a $(\widetilde{\mathbb{Q}}, \mathbb{F})$-martingale. However, the dynamics of X under the two equivalent martingale measures are different and we are typically interested in explicit representations for both dynamics. Let us briefly examine this issue in the context of a process X driven by a $(\mathbb{Q}, \mathbb{F})$-Brownian motion W. In that case, it suffices to make use of the classic Girsanov theorem.

Let $(W_t, \ t \in [0, \ T])$ be an $\mathbb{R}^d$-valued process such that $W_1, \ldots, W_d$ are standard Brownian motions under $\mathbb{Q}$ with the following correlations:

$$d \langle W_k, \ W_l \rangle_t = \rho_{k,l} \, dt$$

for some constants $\rho_{k,l} \in [-1, 1]$ with $\rho_{l,k} = \rho_{k,l}$ and $\rho_{k,k} = 1$. Suppose that a real-valued process $(X_t, \ t \in [0, \ T])$ satisfies under $\mathbb{Q}$

$$dX_t = \mu_t \, dt + \sigma_t \, dW_t \qquad (8.108)$$

where μ_t is a real-valued process, σ_t is an $\mathbb{R}^d$-valued process represented as $1 \times d$ row vector, and W_t is represented as $d \times 1$ column vector. Equivalently,

$$dX_t = \mu_t \, dt + \sum_{k=1}^{d} \sigma_t^k \, dW_k(t)$$

We wish to find the dynamics of X under the martingale measure $\widetilde{\mathbb{Q}}$ associated with the numéraire $\widetilde{N}$, that is, the representation

$$dX_t = \widetilde{\mu}_t \, dt + \sigma_t \, d\widetilde{W}_t \qquad (8.109)$$

where the process $\widetilde{W}$ is an $\mathbb{R}^d$-valued process such that $\widetilde{W}_1, \ldots, \widetilde{W}_d$ are standard Brownian motions under $\mathbb{Q}$ with the following correlations:

$$d \langle \widetilde{W}_k, \ \widetilde{W}_l \rangle_t = \rho_{k,l} \, dt$$

In order to compute the drift term $\widetilde{\mu}$ in formula (8.109), it suffices to provide a link between the processes W and $\widetilde{W}$ and to make use of equation (8.108).

Let $(V_t(Y), \ t \in [0, \ T])$ be defined as the $1 \times d$ row vector process $(v_t, \ t \in [0, \ T])$ in the dynamics of the real-valued process $Y = (Y_t, \ t \in [0, \ T])$ that satisfies

$$dY_t = v_t \, dW_t \qquad (8.110)$$

Note that the map V is linear, meaning that

$$V(c_1 Y^1 + c_2 Y^2) = c_1 V(Y^1) + c_2 V(Y^2)$$

where and c_1 and c_2 are arbitrary real numbers and the processes Y^1 and Y^2 are assumed to be driven by a common Brownian motion W. Manifestly, $V(c) = 0$ for any real number c.

Assume that Y is a strictly positive process satisfying equation (8.110). Then, using the Itô formula, one can show that

$$V(\ln(Y)) = \frac{V(Y)}{Y} = \frac{v}{Y} \tag{8.111}$$

In that case, by combining equation (8.110) with equation (8.111), we obtain

$$dY_t = Y_t V_t(\ln(Y))\, dW_t$$

This shows that the process $V_t(\ln(Y))$ represents the *volatility* vector of a strictly positive (local) $(\mathbb{Q}, \mathbb{F})$-martingale Y with respect to W.

The following proposition is an immediate consequence of the classic Girsanov theorem. We denote by R the d-dimensional square matrix $R = [\rho_{k,l}]$. Also, v' stands for the transpose of v.

Proposition 8.6.2 *The $(\mathbb{Q}, \mathbb{F})$-Brownian motion $(W_t,\ t \in [0,\ T])$ and the $(\widetilde{\mathbb{Q}}, \mathbb{F})$- Brownian motion $(\widetilde{W}_t,\ t \in [0,\ T])$ satisfy the following relationship:*

$$d\widetilde{W}_t = dW_t - RV_t\left(\ln\left(\frac{\widetilde{N}}{N}\right)\right)' dt$$

or, equivalently,

$$d\widetilde{W}_t = dW_t - RV_t\big(\ln\zeta\big)' dt \tag{8.112}$$

where the Radon-Nikodým density process ζ is given by formula (8.107). Consequently, the drift term $\widetilde{\mu}$ in the dynamics of the process X under $\widetilde{\mathbb{Q}}$ equals

$$\widetilde{\mu}_t = \mu_t + \sigma_t RV_t(\ln\zeta)'$$

Formula (8.112) yields, for every $k = 1, \ldots, d$,

$$d\widetilde{W}_k(t) = dW_k(t) - \sum_{l=1}^{d} \rho_{k,l} V_t^l\big(\ln\zeta\big) dt \tag{8.113}$$

If, in addition, the process $\ln\zeta$ satisfies

$$d\ln\zeta_t = v_t\, dW_t = \sum_{l=1}^{d} v_t^l\, dW_l(t)$$

for some process v, then equation (8.113) becomes

$$d\widetilde{W}_k(t) = dW_k(t) - \sum_{l=1}^{d} \rho_{k,l} v_t^l \, dt$$

and thus the drift term of X under $\widetilde{\mathbb{Q}}$ equals

$$\widetilde{\mu}_t = \mu_t + \sum_{k,l=1}^{d} \sigma_t^k \rho_{k,l} v_t^l$$

8.6.3   One- and Two-Period Forward CDS Spreads

In this section, we construct the *market model* for the family of one- and two-period forward CDS spreads. To be more specific, our aim is to derive the joint dynamics under a single probability measure of the family of CDS spreads $\kappa^j = \kappa^{j-1,j}$, $j = 1, \ldots, m$, and $\widehat{\kappa}^j = \kappa^{j-2,j}$, $j = 2, \ldots, m$.

Let us recall that

$$\widehat{A}_t^{j-1,j} = \alpha_j \, \mathbb{E}_{\mathbb{Q}} \left(B_{T_j}^{-1} \mathbb{1}_{\{\tau > T_j\}} \,\Big|\, \mathcal{F}_t \right)$$

and

$$\widehat{P}_t^{j-1,j} = (1 - \delta) \left\{ \mathbb{E}_{\mathbb{Q}} \left(B_{T_j}^{-1} \mathbb{1}_{\{\tau > T_{j-1}\}} \,\Big|\, \mathcal{F}_t \right) - \mathbb{E}_{\mathbb{Q}} \left(B_{T_j}^{-1} \mathbb{1}_{\{\tau > T_j\}} \,\Big|\, \mathcal{F}_t \right) \right\}$$

with the one-period spread κ^j given by the following expression, for every $j = 1, \ldots, m$ and every $t \in [0, T_{j-1}]$,

$$\kappa_t^j = \frac{\widetilde{P}_t^{j-1,j}}{\widetilde{A}_t^{j-1,j}} = \frac{\widehat{P}_t^{j-1,j}}{\widehat{A}_t^{j-1,j}}$$

Similarly,

$$\widehat{A}_t^{j-2,j} = \alpha_{j-1} \, \mathbb{E}_{\mathbb{Q}} \left(B_{T_{j-1}}^{-1} \mathbb{1}_{\{\tau > T_{j-1}\}} \,\Big|\, \mathcal{F}_t \right) + \alpha_j \, \mathbb{E}_{\mathbb{Q}} \left(B_{T_j}^{-1} \mathbb{1}_{\{\tau > T_j\}} \,\Big|\, \mathcal{F}_t \right)$$

and

$$\widehat{P}_t^{j-2,j} = (1 - \delta) \left\{ \mathbb{E}_{\mathbb{Q}} \left(B_{T_j}^{-1} \mathbb{1}_{\{\tau > T_{j-1}\}} \,\Big|\, \mathcal{F}_t \right) - \mathbb{E}_{\mathbb{Q}} \left(B_{T_j}^{-1} \mathbb{1}_{\{\tau > T_j\}} \,\Big|\, \mathcal{F}_t \right) \right.$$
$$\left. + \mathbb{E}_{\mathbb{Q}} \left(B_{T_{j-1}}^{-1} \mathbb{1}_{\{\tau > T_{j-2}\}} \,\Big|\, \mathcal{F}_t \right) - \mathbb{E}_{\mathbb{Q}} \left(B_{T_{j-1}}^{-1} \mathbb{1}_{\{\tau > T_{j-1}\}} \,\Big|\, \mathcal{F}_t \right) \right\}$$

and the two-period spread $\widehat{\kappa}^j$ satisfies, for every $j = 2, \ldots, m$ and every $t \in [0, T_{j-2}]$,

$$\widehat{\kappa}_t^j = \frac{\widetilde{P}_t^{j-2,j}}{\widetilde{A}_t^{j-2,j}} = \frac{\widehat{P}_t^{j-2,j}}{\widehat{A}_t^{j-2,j}}$$

We start by recalling that the process $\widehat{A}^{m-1,m}$ is a positive $(\mathbb{Q}, \mathbb{F})$-martingale and thus it defines, after suitable normalization, the probability measure $\mathbb{P}^m$ on $(\Omega, \mathcal{F}_T)$ by setting, for every $t \in [0, T_m]$,

$$\frac{d\mathbb{P}^m}{d\mathbb{Q}} \mid \mathcal{F}_t = d_m \widehat{A}_t^{m-1,m} \tag{8.114}$$

where d_m is the normalizing constant. Using the abstract Bayes formula, one can easily check that the process κ^m is a $(\mathbb{P}^m, \mathbb{F})$-martingale and thus, in this sense, the probability measure $\mathbb{P}^m$ is the martingale measure for the forward spread κ^m. In the sequel, we will deal with a full spectrum of martingale measures associated with the family of one- and two-period forward CDS spreads.

Remark 8.6.1 *It is tempting to interpret the probability measure $\mathbb{P}^m$ as a martingale measure associated with the choice of the predefault price process $\widetilde{A}^{m-1,m}$ of the fee leg as the numéraire asset. More precisely, we should rather point at the process $B\widehat{A}^{m-1,m}$ as the numéraire asset associated with $\mathbb{P}^m$, since this process is a $(\mathbb{Q}, \mathbb{F})$-martingale when divided by the savings account. By a slight abuse of the terminology, in what follows we will simply refer to the process $\widehat{A}^{m-1,m}$ as the numéraire asset corresponding to the martingale measure $\mathbb{P}^m$.*

The following simple algebraic result is in fact crucial for our further purposes.

Lemma 8.6.1 *The following equality holds, for every $j = 1, \ldots, m$ and every $t \in [0, T_j]$,*

$$\frac{\widehat{A}_t^{j-1,j}}{\widehat{A}_t^{m-1,m}} = \prod_{l=j+1}^{m} \frac{\widehat{\kappa}_t^l - \kappa_t^l}{\kappa_t^{l-1} - \widehat{\kappa}_t^l} \tag{8.115}$$

Proof. It suffices to check that the following equality holds:

$$\frac{\widehat{A}_t^{j-1,j}}{\widehat{A}_t^{j,j+1}} = \frac{\widehat{\kappa}_t^{j+1} - \kappa_t^{j+1}}{\kappa_t^j - \widehat{\kappa}_t^{j+1}}$$

This can be done by straightforward computations and thus the details are left to the reader.

We argue that the processes defined in equation (8.115) are $(\mathbb{P}^m, \mathbb{F})$-martingales. Indeed, if we multiply the right-hand side of equation (8.115) by $\widehat{A}_t^{m-1,m}$, we obtain a $(\mathbb{Q}, \mathbb{F})$-martingale and thus, in view of equation (8.114), the ratios given in equation (8.115) are manifestly $(\mathbb{P}^m, \mathbb{F})$-martingales.

Given the family of positive $(\mathbb{P}^m, \mathbb{F})$-martingales given by equation (8.115), we can define a family of probability measures $\mathbb{P}^j$ for $j = 1, \ldots, m - 1$, by setting, for every $t \in [0, T_j]$,

$$\frac{d\mathbb{P}^j}{d\mathbb{P}^m} \Big|_{\mathcal{F}_t} = c_j \frac{\widehat{A}_t^{j-1,j}}{\widehat{A}_t^{m-1,m}} \tag{8.116}$$

where c_j is the normalizing constants. One can observe that the probability measures $\mathbb{P}^j$ can equivalently be defined by setting [cf. equation (8.114)]:

$$\frac{d\mathbb{P}^j}{d\mathbb{Q}} \Big|_{\mathcal{F}_t} = d_j \widehat{A}_t^{j-1,j} \tag{8.117}$$

where d_j is another normalizing constant. In view of equation (8.117), it is easily seen that the one-period forward spread κ^j is a $(\mathbb{P}^j, \mathbb{F})$-martingale for every $j = 1, \ldots, m - 1$. In other words, the probability measure $\mathbb{P}^j$ is the martingale measure for the forward spread κ^j.

We note that the following process is a positive $(\mathbb{P}^j, \mathbb{F})$-martingale, for every $j = 2, \ldots, m$,

$$\begin{aligned}
\frac{\widehat{A}_t^{j-2,j}}{\widehat{A}_t^{j-1,j}} &= \frac{\alpha_{j-1} \mathbb{E}_{\mathbb{Q}} \left(B_{T_{j-1}}^{-1} \mathbb{1}_{\{\tau > T_{j-1}\}} \Big| \mathcal{F}_t \right) + \alpha_j \mathbb{E}_{\mathbb{Q}} \left(B_{T_j}^{-1} \mathbb{1}_{\{\tau > T_j\}} \Big| \mathcal{F}_t \right)}{\alpha_j \mathbb{E}_{\mathbb{Q}} \left(B_{T_j}^{-1} \mathbb{1}_{\{\tau > T_j\}} \Big| \mathcal{F}_t \right)} \\
&= \frac{\widehat{A}_t^{j-2,j-1}}{\widehat{A}_t^{j-1,j}} + 1 = \frac{\widehat{\kappa}_t^j - \kappa_t^j}{\kappa_t^{j-1} - \widehat{\kappa}_t^j} + 1 = \frac{\kappa_t^{j-1} - \kappa_t^j}{\kappa_t^{j-1} - \widehat{\kappa}_t^j}
\end{aligned} \tag{8.118}$$

where we have also used equation (8.115). Therefore, we can also define a family of the associated probability measures $\widehat{\mathbb{P}}^j$ on $(\Omega, \mathcal{F}_{T_{j-1}})$ for $j = 2, \ldots, m$. It suffices to set

$$\frac{d\widehat{\mathbb{P}}^j}{d\mathbb{P}^j} \Big|_{\mathcal{F}_t} = \widehat{c}_j \frac{\widehat{A}_t^{j-2,j}}{\widehat{A}_t^{j-1,j}} \tag{8.119}$$

where $\widehat{c}_j$ is the normalizing constant. It is easily seen that the two-period forward spread $\widehat{\kappa}^j$ follows a $(\widehat{\mathbb{P}}^j, \mathbb{F})$-martingale, for every $j = 2, \ldots, m$.

We summarize the above considerations in the following commutative diagram, which represents the family of equivalent martingale measures associated with different numéraire assets or, equivalently, with different forward CDS spreads:

$$
\mathbb{Q} \xrightarrow{\frac{d\mathbb{P}^m}{d\mathbb{Q}}} \mathbb{P}^m \xrightarrow{\frac{d\mathbb{P}^{m-1}}{d\mathbb{P}^m}} \mathbb{P}^{m-1} \xrightarrow{\frac{d\mathbb{P}^{m-2}}{d\mathbb{P}^{m-1}}} \dots \xrightarrow{\frac{d\mathbb{P}^2}{d\mathbb{P}^3}} \mathbb{P}^2 \xrightarrow{\frac{d\mathbb{P}^1}{d\mathbb{P}^2}} \mathbb{P}^1
$$

$$
\downarrow^{\frac{d\widehat{\mathbb{P}}^m}{d\mathbb{P}^m}} \quad \downarrow^{\frac{d\widehat{\mathbb{P}}^{m-1}}{d\mathbb{P}^{m-1}}} \qquad\qquad \downarrow \qquad \downarrow^{\frac{d\widehat{\mathbb{P}}^2}{d\mathbb{P}^2}}
$$

$$
\widehat{\mathbb{P}}^m \xrightarrow{\frac{d\widehat{\mathbb{P}}^{m-1}}{d\widehat{\mathbb{P}}^m}} \widehat{\mathbb{P}}^{m-1} \xrightarrow{\frac{d\widehat{\mathbb{P}}^{m-2}}{d\widehat{\mathbb{P}}^{m-1}}} \dots \xrightarrow{\frac{d\widehat{\mathbb{P}}^2}{d\widehat{\mathbb{P}}^3}} \widehat{\mathbb{P}}^2
$$

where the Radon-Nikodým densities satisfy

$$
\frac{d\mathbb{P}^m}{d\mathbb{Q}} \,\big|\, \mathcal{F}_t \simeq \widehat{A}_t^{m-1,m}
$$

$$
\frac{d\mathbb{P}^j}{d\mathbb{P}^{j+1}} \,\big|\, \mathcal{F}_t \simeq \frac{\widehat{A}_t^{j-1,j}}{\widehat{A}_t^{j,j+1}} = \frac{\widehat{\kappa}_t^{j+1} - \kappa_t^{j+1}}{\kappa_t^j - \widehat{\kappa}_t^{j+1}}
$$

$$
\frac{d\widehat{\mathbb{P}}^j}{d\mathbb{P}^j} \,\big|\, \mathcal{F}_t \simeq \frac{\widehat{A}_t^{j-2,j}}{\widehat{A}_t^{j-1,j}} = \frac{\kappa_t^{j-1} - \kappa_t^j}{\kappa_t^{j-1} - \widehat{\kappa}_t^j}
$$

where the symbol $\simeq$ is used instead of the equality sign to emphasize the fact that, for simplicity of notation, the normalizing constants were omitted. It is worth stressing that the normalizing constants play no role in the following pages, anyway. Our aim is to find the joint dynamics of the $(2m - 1)$-dimensional process $(\kappa^1, \dots, \kappa^m, \widehat{\kappa}^2, \dots, \widehat{\kappa}^m)$ under some martingale measure, for instance, under the martingale measure $\mathbb{P}^m$.

In view of Lemma 8.6.1 and equality (8.118), the proof of the following auxiliary result is rather obvious.

Lemma 8.6.2 *The following relationships are satisfied by the Radon-Nikodým density processes:*

$$
\zeta_t^j := \frac{d\mathbb{P}^j}{d\mathbb{P}^m} \,\big|\, \mathcal{F}_t \simeq \frac{\widehat{A}_t^{j-1,j}}{\widehat{A}_t^{m-1,m}} = \prod_{l=j+1}^m \frac{\widehat{\kappa}_t^l - \kappa_t^l}{\kappa_t^{l-1} - \widehat{\kappa}_t^l}
$$

$$
\widehat{\zeta}_t^j := \frac{d\widehat{\mathbb{P}}^j}{d\mathbb{P}^m} \,\big|\, \mathcal{F}_t \simeq \frac{\widehat{A}_t^{j-2,j}}{\widehat{A}_t^{m-1,m}} = \frac{\kappa_t^{j-1} - \kappa_t^j}{\kappa_t^{j-1} - \widehat{\kappa}_t^j} \prod_{l=j+1}^m \frac{\widehat{\kappa}_t^l - \kappa_t^l}{\kappa_t^{l-1} - \widehat{\kappa}_t^l}
$$

These relationships appear to be crucial in the subsequent derivation of the joint dynamics for one- and two-period CDS spreads. This goal can be achieved in a general semimartingale setup studied in Li and Rutkowski (2009b). However, for the clarity of presentation, we will focus here on the special case of the market model driven by a multidimensional Brownian motion, as was postulated in Brigo (2006, 2008).

We need first to introduce suitable notation. Following Brigo (2006, 2008), we assume that the market model is driven by the $2m - 1$ correlated Brownian motions $W_1, \ldots, W_m, \widehat{W}_2, \ldots, \widehat{W}_m$ under $\mathbb{Q}$. To be more specific, it is postulated that

$$\begin{cases} d\kappa_t^j = \kappa_t^j \Big(\mu_j(t) \, dt + \sigma_t^j \, dW_j(t) \Big) \\ d\widehat{\kappa}_t^j = \widehat{\kappa}_t^j \Big(\varphi_j(t) \, dt + v_t^j \, d\widehat{W}_j(t) \Big) \end{cases}$$

for some $\mathbb{F}$-adapted drifts μ_j and φ_j. The correlations between the $(\mathbb{Q}, \mathbb{F})$-Brownian motions $W_1, \ldots, W_m, \widehat{W}_2, \ldots, \widehat{W}_m$ are specified by setting

$$d \langle W_i, W_j \rangle_t = \rho_{i,j} \, dt$$
$$d \langle \widehat{W}_i, \widehat{W}_j \rangle_t = \eta_{i,j} \, dt$$
$$d \langle W_i, \widehat{W}_j \rangle_t = \theta_{i,j} \, dt$$

Our aim is to obtain the dynamics of processes κ^j and $\widehat{\kappa}^j$ under a single probability measure. To this end, it is more convenient to work directly with the set of martingale measures associated with the numéraires $\widehat{A}^{j-1,j}$ and $\widehat{A}^{j-2,j}$, rather than with the martingale measure $\mathbb{Q}$ associated with the savings account as the numéraire asset.

Let $W_i^{j-1,j}$ denote the $(\mathbb{P}^j, \mathbb{F})$-Brownian motion obtained from the $(\mathbb{Q}, \mathbb{F})$-Brownian motion W_i, when we change the probability measure from $\mathbb{Q}$ to the martingale measure $\mathbb{P}^j$ associated with the numéraire $\widehat{A}^{j-1,j}$. Similarly, $W_i^{j-2,j}$ stands for the $(\widehat{\mathbb{P}}^j, \mathbb{F})$-Brownian motion obtained from the $(\mathbb{Q}, \mathbb{F})$-Brownian motion W_i by changing the probability measure from $\mathbb{Q}$ to the martingale measure $\widehat{\mathbb{P}}^j$, which corresponds to the numéraire $\widehat{A}^{j-2,j}$.

By the same token, $\widehat{W}_i^{j-1,j}$ is the $(\mathbb{P}^j, \mathbb{F})$-Brownian motion obtained from the $(\mathbb{Q}, \mathbb{F})$-Brownian motion $\widehat{W}_i$, when we change the probability measure from $\mathbb{Q}$ to the martingale measure $\mathbb{P}^j$ associated with the numéraire $\widehat{A}^{j-1,j}$. $\widehat{W}_i^{j-2,j}$ stands for the $(\widehat{\mathbb{P}}^j, \mathbb{F})$-Brownian motion obtained from the $(\mathbb{Q}, \mathbb{F})$-Brownian motion $\widehat{W}_i$ by changing the probability measure from $\mathbb{Q}$ to the martingale measure $\widehat{\mathbb{P}}^j$, which corresponds to the numéraire $\widehat{A}^{j-2,j}$.

Of course, in both cases an equivalent change of the probability measure is performed using the classic Girsanov theorem. For the reader's convenience, the change of the numéraire technique is summarized in Subsection 8.6.2.

Since the forward CDS spreads follow martingales under the respective martingale measures, the dynamics of one-period and two-period forward CDS rates can also be represented as follows:

$$\begin{cases} d\kappa_t^j = \kappa_t^j \sigma_t^j \, dW_j^{j-1,j}(t) \\ d\widehat{\kappa}_t^j = \widehat{\kappa}_t^j v_t^j \, d\widehat{W}_j^{j-2,j}(t) \end{cases} \tag{8.120}$$

In the next result, according to the notation introduced previously, the processes $W_j^{m-1,m}$ and $\widehat{W}_j^{m-1,m}$ are $(\mathbb{P}^m, \mathbb{F})$-Brownian motions associated with the $(\mathbb{Q}, \mathbb{F})$-Brownian motions W_j and $\widehat{W}_j$, respectively. The probability measure $\mathbb{P}^m$ can be interpreted as the *terminal* martingale measure for the market model at hand, since it corresponds to the last one-period forward CDS, starting at T_{m-1} and expiring at T_m.

Proposition 8.6.3 *The joint dynamics of the family of one- and two-period forward CDS spreads* $(\kappa^1, \ldots, \kappa^m, \widehat{\kappa}^2, \ldots, \widehat{\kappa}^m)$ *under the martingale measure* $\mathbb{P}^m$ *are*

$$
\begin{cases}
d\kappa_t^j = \kappa_t^j \left(\mu_j^m(t)\,dt + \sigma_t^j\,dW_j^{m-1,m}(t) \right) \\
d\widehat{\kappa}_t^j = \widehat{\kappa}_t^j \left(\varphi_j^m(t)\,dt + v_t^j\,d\widehat{W}_j^{m-1,m}(t) \right)
\end{cases}
$$

where the $(\mathbb{P}^m, \mathbb{F})$*-Brownian motions* $W_1^{m-1,m}, \ldots, W_m^{m-1,m}, \widehat{W}_2^{m-1,m}, \ldots, \widehat{W}_m^{m-1,m}$ *satisfy*

$$
d\langle W_i^{m-1,m}, W_j^{m-1,m} \rangle_t = \rho_{i,j}\,dt
$$

$$
d\langle \widehat{W}_i^{m-1,m}, \widehat{W}_j^{m-1,m} \rangle_t = \eta_{i,j}\,dt
$$

$$
d\langle W_i^{m-1,m}, \widehat{W}_j^{m-1,m} \rangle_t = \theta_{i,j}\,dt
$$

and the processes μ_j^m *and* φ_j^m *are given by* $\mu_j^m = \sigma^j \bar{\mu}_j^m$ *and* $\varphi_j^m = v^j \bar{\varphi}_j^m$, *where in turn*

$$
\bar{\mu}_j^m(t) = -\sum_{l=j+1}^{m} \frac{\theta_{j,l} v_t^l \widehat{\kappa}_t^l - \rho_{j,l} \sigma_t^l \kappa_t^l}{\widehat{\kappa}_t^l - \kappa_t^l} + \sum_{l=j+1}^{m} \frac{\rho_{l-1,j} \sigma_t^{l-1} \kappa_t^{l-1} - \theta_{j,l} v_t^l \widehat{\kappa}_t^l}{\kappa_t^{l-1} - \widehat{\kappa}_t^l}
$$

and

$$
\bar{\varphi}_j^m(t) = -\sum_{l=j+1}^{m} \frac{\eta_{j,l} v_t^l \widehat{\kappa}_t^l - \theta_{j,l} \sigma_t^l \kappa_t^l}{\widehat{\kappa}_t^l - \kappa_t^l} + \sum_{l=j+1}^{m} \frac{\theta_{j,l-1} \sigma_t^{l-1} \kappa_t^{l-1} - \eta_{j,l} v_t^l \widehat{\kappa}_t^l}{\kappa_t^{l-1} - \widehat{\kappa}_t^l}
$$
$$
- \frac{\theta_{j-1,j} \sigma_t^{j-1} \kappa_t^{j-1} - \theta_{j,j} \sigma_t^j \kappa_t^j}{\kappa_t^{j-1} - \kappa_t^j} + \frac{\theta_{j,j-1} \sigma_t^{j-1} \kappa_t^{j-1} - \eta_{j,j} v_t^j \widehat{\kappa}_t^j}{\kappa_t^{j-1} - \widehat{\kappa}_t^j}
$$

Proof. We will first find the relationship between the processes $W_j^{j-1,j}$ and $W_j^{m-1,m}$. To this end, we will make use of the Girsanov theorem (cf. Proposition 8.6.2).

For the Radon-Nikodým density process ζ^j defined in Lemma 8.6.2 we obtain, for every $j = 1, \ldots, m$,

$$
\begin{aligned}
V\left(\ln \left(\zeta^j \right) \right) &= V\left(\ln \left(\frac{\widehat{A}_t^{j-1,j}}{\widehat{A}_t^{m-1,m}} \right) \right) \\
&= V\left(\ln \left(\prod_{l=j+1}^{m} \frac{\widehat{\kappa}^l - \kappa^l}{\kappa^{l-1} - \widehat{\kappa}^l} \right) \right) \\
&= \sum_{l=j+1}^{m} V\left(\ln \left(\frac{\widehat{\kappa}^l - \kappa^l}{\kappa^{l-1} - \widehat{\kappa}^l} \right) \right) \\
&= \sum_{l=j+1}^{m} V\left(\ln \left(\widehat{\kappa}^l - \kappa^l \right) \right) - \sum_{l=j+1}^{m} V\left(\ln \left(\kappa^{l-1} - \widehat{\kappa}^l \right) \right) \\
&= \sum_{l=j+1}^{m} \frac{V(\widehat{\kappa}^l) - V(\kappa^l)}{\widehat{\kappa}^l - \kappa^l} - \sum_{l=j+1}^{m} \frac{V(\kappa^{l-1}) - V(\widehat{\kappa}^l)}{\kappa^{l-1} - \widehat{\kappa}^l}
\end{aligned}
$$

Using Proposition 8.6.2, we thus obtain the following relationship between the $(\widehat{\mathbb{P}}^j, \mathbb{F})$-Brownian motion $W_j^{j-2,j}$ and the corresponding $(\mathbb{P}^m, \mathbb{F})$-Brownian motion $W_j^{m-1,m}$

$$
\begin{aligned}
dW_j^{j-1,j}(t) = {} & dW_j^{m-1,m}(t) - \sum_{l=j+1}^{m} \frac{\theta_{j,l} v_t^l \widehat{\kappa}_t^l - \rho_{j,l} \sigma_t^l \kappa_t^l}{\widehat{\kappa}_t^l - \kappa_t^l} \, dt \\
& + \sum_{l=j+1}^{m} \frac{\rho_{l-1,j} \sigma_t^{l-1} \kappa_t^{l-1} - \theta_{j,l} v_t^l \widehat{\kappa}_t^l}{\kappa_t^{l-1} - \widehat{\kappa}_t^l} \, dt
\end{aligned}
$$

By combining the preceding formula with equation (8.120), we obtain the stated formula for the drift μ_j^m of the one-period forward spread κ^j under $\mathbb{P}^m$ for every $j = 1, \ldots, m$ (note that, as expected, $\mu_m^m = 0$).

To compute the drift $\varphi_j^m(t)$ of the two-period forward spread $\widehat{\kappa}^j$ under $\mathbb{P}^m$, we need to find the transformation from the $(\widehat{\mathbb{P}}^j, \mathbb{F})$-Brownian motion $\widehat{W}_j^{j-2,j}$ to the $(\mathbb{P}^m, \mathbb{F})$-Brownian motion $\widehat{W}_j^{m-1,m}$. For the corresponding Radon-Nikodým density process $\widehat{\zeta}^j$ defined in Lemma 8.6.2 we obtain, for every $j = 2, \ldots, m$,

$$
\begin{aligned}
V\left(\ln \left(\widehat{\zeta}^j \right) \right) &= V\left(\ln \left(\frac{\widehat{A}_t^{j-2,j}}{\widehat{A}_t^{m-1,m}} \right) \right) \\
&= V\left(\ln \left(\frac{\kappa^{j-1} - \kappa^j}{\kappa^{j-1} - \widehat{\kappa}^j} \prod_{l=j+1}^{m} \frac{\widehat{\kappa}^l - \kappa^l}{\kappa^{l-1} - \widehat{\kappa}^l} \right) \right)
\end{aligned}
$$

$$
= \sum_{l=j+1}^{m} V\left(\ln \left(\frac{\widehat{\kappa}^l - \kappa^l}{\kappa^{l-1} - \widehat{\kappa}^l} \right) \right) + V\left(\ln \left(\frac{\kappa^{j-1} - \kappa^j}{\kappa^{j-1} - \widehat{\kappa}^j} \right) \right)
$$

$$
= \sum_{l=j+1}^{m} V\left(\ln \left(\widehat{\kappa}^l - \kappa^l \right) \right) - \sum_{l=j+1}^{m} V\left(\ln \left(\kappa^{l-1} - \widehat{\kappa}^l \right) \right)
$$

$$
+ V\left(\ln \left(\kappa^{j-1} - \kappa^j \right) \right) - V\left(\ln \left(\kappa^{j-1} - \widehat{\kappa}^j \right) \right)
$$

$$
= \sum_{l=j+1}^{m} \frac{V(\widehat{\kappa}^l) - V(\kappa^l)}{\widehat{\kappa}^l - \kappa^l} - \sum_{l=j+1}^{m} \frac{V(\kappa^{l-1}) - V(\widehat{\kappa}^l)}{\kappa^{l-1} - \widehat{\kappa}^l}
$$

$$
+ \frac{V(\kappa^{j-1}) - V(\kappa^j)}{\kappa^{j-1} - \kappa^j} - \frac{V(\kappa^{j-1}) - V(\widehat{\kappa}^j)}{\kappa^{j-1} - \widehat{\kappa}^j}
$$

Consequently, the transformation from the $(\widehat{\mathbb{P}}^j, \mathbb{F})$-Brownian motion $\widehat{W}_j^{j-2,j}$ to the $(\mathbb{P}^m, \mathbb{F})$-Brownian motion $\widehat{W}_j^{m-1,m}$ is given by the formula

$$
d\widehat{W}_j^{j-2,j}(t) = d\widehat{W}_j^{m-1,m}(t) - \sum_{l=j+1}^{m} \frac{\eta_{j,l} v_t^l \widehat{\kappa}_t^l - \theta_{j,l} \sigma_t^l \kappa_t^l}{\widehat{\kappa}_t^l - \kappa_t^l} \, dt
$$

$$
+ \sum_{l=j+1}^{m} \frac{\theta_{j,l-1} \sigma_t^{l-1} \kappa_t^{l-1} - \eta_{j,l} v_t^l \widehat{\kappa}_t^l}{\kappa_t^{l-1} - \widehat{\kappa}_t^l} \, dt
$$

$$
- \frac{\theta_{j-1,j} \sigma_t^{j-1} \kappa_t^{j-1} - \theta_{j,j} \sigma_t^j \kappa_t^j}{\kappa_t^{j-1} - \kappa_t^j} \, dt
$$

$$
+ \frac{\theta_{j,j-1} \sigma_t^{j-1} \kappa_t^{j-1} - \eta_{j,j} v_t^j \widehat{\kappa}_t^j}{\kappa_t^{j-1} - \widehat{\kappa}_t^j} \, dt
$$

Using equation (8.120) and the preceding formula, we obtain the desired expression for the drift φ_j^m. Since the drifts μ_j^m and φ_j^m are completely determined by the family of one- and two-period forward CDS spreads, their volatilities and correlations between Brownian motions, we have obtained here a closed system of stochastic differential equations driven by the $2m - 1$ correlated $(\mathbb{P}^m, \mathbb{F})$-Brownian motions $W_1^{m-1,m}, \ldots, W_m^{m-1,m}, \widehat{W}_2^{m-1,m}, \ldots, \widehat{W}_m^{m-1,m}$.

Let us observe that the relationships between different Brownian motions established in the proof of Proposition 8.6.3 can be used to derive the joint dynamics of forward CDS spreads under any martingale measure $\mathbb{P}^j$ for $j = 1, \ldots m$, and $\widehat{\mathbb{P}}^j$ for $j = 2, \ldots, m$.

It is also important to notice that the joint dynamics of CDS spreads provide a necessary condition for the market model to be arbitrage-free, but they do not provide a sufficient condition. The predefault price of a defaultable zero coupon bond with zero recovery, denoted as $\widetilde{D}(t, T_j)$, should be a strictly positive process decreasing in maturity. Therefore, the model for the joint dynamics of forward CDS spreads should ensure that this property holds. For instance, to ensure that the following inequality holds, for every $j = 1, \ldots, m$,

$$0 < \frac{\widetilde{D}(t, T_j)}{\widetilde{D}(t, T_{j-1})} < 1$$

it suffices to postulate that $\widehat{\kappa}_t^j$ belongs to the following random interval:

$$\left(\min \left(\kappa_t^{j-1}, \frac{\alpha_j \kappa_t^j + \alpha_{j-1} \kappa_t^{j-1}}{(\alpha_{j-1} + \alpha_j)} \right), \ \max \left(\kappa_t^{j-1}, \frac{\alpha_j \kappa_t^j + \alpha_{j-1} \kappa_t^{j-1}}{(\alpha_{j-1} + \alpha_j)} \right) \right)$$

However, to guarantee that the condition is satisfied by the modeled family of spreads, one needs to make a judicious choice of volatility processes for CDS spreads. This appears to be a very challenging problem and, to the best of our knowledge, no solution is readily available.

8.6.4   One-Period and Coterminal Forward CDS Spreads

In this section, we study in detail the market model for a family of one-period and coterminal forward CDS spreads (cf. Li and Rutkowski 2010 and Phung 2009). This particular model of CDS spreads can be seen as a counterpart of the model of coterminal forward swap rates proposed by Jamshidian (1997). It is thus worth mentioning that Jamshidian's model can be seen as an alternative for the market model of forward LIBORs, as developed in papers by Brace et al. (1997) and Musiela and Rutkowski (1997). The main goals of Jamshidian's approach were to formally derive the market swaptions formula within an arbitrage-free framework and to facilitate the valuation of exotic swap derivatives, such as Bermudan swaptions.

   In the context of CDS spreads, the corresponding model was first put forward by Brigo (2008). The idea behind this approach is to define the dynamics of a family of one-period forward CDS spreads $\kappa^{0,1}, \kappa^{1,2}, \ldots, \kappa^{m-1,m}$ and the *coterminal* forward CDS spreads $\kappa^{0,m}, \kappa^{1,m}, \ldots, \kappa^{m-1,m}$ under a single probability measure. As in the case of a default-free model, the advantage of dealing with this particular family of forward CDS spreads becomes clear when addressing the issues of valuation and hedging of Bermudan CDS options.

   The method is very much similar to that used in Section 8.6.3 and thus we will leave details to the reader. It should be emphasized, however, that throughout Section 8.6.4 each forward CDS spread is indexed by its starting date rather than expiration date (unlike in Section 8.6.3). The one-period forward CDS spread is thus denoted as

$$\kappa_t^k := \kappa_t^{k,k+1} = \frac{\widetilde{P}_t^{k,k+1}}{\widetilde{A}_t^{k,k+1}}, \quad \forall\, t \in [0, T_k]$$

for every $k = 0, \ldots, m - 1$. The coterminal CDS spread with start date T_i and maturity T_n will be denoted by

$$\widehat{\kappa}_t^k := \kappa_t^{k,m} = \frac{\widetilde{P}_t^{k,m}}{\widetilde{A}_t^{k,m}}, \quad \forall \, t \in [0, \, T_k]$$

for $k = 0, \ldots, m - 1$. This notation is chosen here for the sake of consistency with the paper by Li and Rutkowski (2010). It is clear that $\kappa^{m-1} = \widehat{\kappa}^{m-1}$ and thus it suffices to consider the forward spreads $\widehat{\kappa}^k$ for $k = 0, \ldots, m - 2$.

Since we now deal with the family of spreads $(\kappa^0, \ldots, \kappa^{m-1}, \widehat{\kappa}^0, \ldots, \widehat{\kappa}^{m-2})$, it is natural to postulate that the model is driven by the $2m - 1$ correlated Brownian motions $W_0, \ldots, W_{m-1}, \widehat{W}_0, \ldots, \widehat{W}_{m-2}$ under $\mathbb{Q}$. Therefore, we work hereafter under the assumption that

$$\begin{cases} d\kappa_t^j = \kappa_t^j \left(\mu_j(t) \, dt + \sigma_t^j \, dW_j(t) \right) \\ d\widehat{\kappa}_t^j = \widehat{\kappa}_t^j \left(\varphi_j(t) \, dt + \nu_t^j \, d\widehat{W}_j(t) \right) \end{cases} \tag{8.121}$$

where the $\mathbb{F}$-adapted drift processes μ_j and φ_j are not yet known. The correlations between the $(\mathbb{Q}, \mathbb{F})$-Brownian motions $W_0, \ldots, W_{m-1}, \widehat{W}_0, \ldots, \widehat{W}_{m-2}$ are specified as follows:

$$d \langle W_i, W_j \rangle_t = \rho_{i,j} \, dt$$
$$d \langle \widehat{W}_i, \widehat{W}_j \rangle_t = \eta_{i,j} \, dt$$
$$d \langle W_i, \widehat{W}_j \rangle_t = \theta_{i,j} \, dt$$

For any $j = 0, \ldots, m - 1$, let $W_i^{j,j+1}$ denote the $(\mathbb{P}^j, \mathbb{F})$-Brownian motion obtained from the $(\mathbb{Q}, \mathbb{F})$-Brownian motion W_i, when we change the probability measure from $\mathbb{Q}$ to the martingale measure $\mathbb{P}^j$ associated with the numéraire $\widehat{A}^{j,j+1}$. Similarly, for any $j = 0, \ldots, m - 1$ we denote by $W_i^{j,m}$ the $(\widehat{\mathbb{P}}^j, \mathbb{F})$-Brownian motion obtained from the $(\mathbb{Q}, \mathbb{F})$-Brownian motion W_i by changing the probability measure from $\mathbb{Q}$ to the martingale measure $\widehat{\mathbb{P}}^j$ corresponding to the numéraire $\widehat{A}^{j,m}$.

The same convention applies to $(\mathbb{Q}, \mathbb{F})$-Brownian motions $\widehat{W}_0, \ldots, \widehat{W}_{m-2}$. Hence $\widehat{W}_i^{j,j+1}$ for any $j = 0, \ldots, m - 1$ is the $(\mathbb{P}^j, \mathbb{F})$-Brownian motion obtained from the $(\mathbb{Q}, \mathbb{F})$-Brownian motion $\widehat{W}_i$, when we change the probability measure from $\mathbb{Q}$ to the martingale measure $\mathbb{P}^j$ associated with the numéraire $\widehat{A}^{j,j+1}$. Finally, $\widehat{W}_i^{j,m}$ denotes the $(\widehat{\mathbb{P}}^j, \mathbb{F})$-Brownian motion obtained from the $(\mathbb{Q}, \mathbb{F})$-Brownian motion $\widehat{W}_i$ when the probability measure is changed from $\mathbb{Q}$ to the martingale measure $\widehat{\mathbb{P}}^j$ corresponding to the numéraire $\widehat{A}^{j,m}$ for any $j = 0, \ldots, m - 2$.

Let us observe that we now deal with the following family of equivalent martingale measures:

$$
\mathbb{Q} \xrightarrow{\frac{d\widehat{\mathbb{P}}^0}{d\mathbb{Q}}} \widehat{\mathbb{P}}^0 \xrightarrow{\frac{d\widehat{\mathbb{P}}^1}{d\widehat{\mathbb{P}}^0}} \widehat{\mathbb{P}}^1 \xrightarrow{\frac{d\widehat{\mathbb{P}}^2}{d\widehat{\mathbb{P}}^1}} \quad \cdots \quad \xrightarrow{\frac{d\widehat{\mathbb{P}}^{m-2}}{d\widehat{\mathbb{P}}^{m-3}}} \widehat{\mathbb{P}}^{m-2} \xrightarrow{\frac{d\widehat{\mathbb{P}}^{m-1}}{d\widehat{\mathbb{P}}^{m-2}}} \widehat{\mathbb{P}}^{m-1} = \mathbb{P}^{m-1}
$$

$$
\frac{d\mathbb{P}^0}{d\widehat{\mathbb{P}}^0} \Bigg\downarrow \qquad \frac{d\mathbb{P}^1}{d\widehat{\mathbb{P}}^1} \Bigg\downarrow \qquad \qquad \Bigg\downarrow \qquad \frac{d\mathbb{P}^{m-2}}{d\widehat{\mathbb{P}}^{m-2}} \Bigg\downarrow
$$

$$
\mathbb{P}^0 \xrightarrow{\frac{d\mathbb{P}^1}{d\mathbb{P}^0}} \mathbb{P}^1 \xrightarrow{\frac{d\mathbb{P}^2}{d\mathbb{P}^1}} \quad \cdots \quad \xrightarrow{\frac{d\mathbb{P}^{m-2}}{d\mathbb{P}^{m-3}}} \mathbb{P}^{m-2} \xrightarrow{\frac{d\mathbb{P}^{m-1}}{d\mathbb{P}^{m-2}}} \qquad \mathbb{P}^{m-1}
$$

Recall that [cf. equation (8.105)]:

$$
\widehat{A}_t^{k,m} = G_t B_t^{-1} \widetilde{A}_t^{k,m} = \sum_{i=k+1}^{m} \alpha_i \, \mathbb{E}_{\mathbb{Q}} \left(B_{T_i}^{-1} \mathbb{1}_{\{\tau > T_i\}} | \mathcal{F}_t \right) \tag{8.122}
$$

The following simple result will play a role analogous to Lemma 8.6.2. Recall that we may identify here $\mathbb{P}^{m-1}$ with $\widehat{\mathbb{P}}^{m-1}$, since $\kappa^{m-1} = \widehat{\kappa}^{m-1}$.

Lemma 8.6.3 *The following relationships are satisfied by the Radon-Nikodým density processes, for every $j = 0, \ldots, m-2$,*

$$
\widehat{\zeta}_t^j = \frac{d\widehat{\mathbb{P}}^j}{d\mathbb{P}^{m-1}} \Big| \, \mathcal{F}_t \simeq \frac{\widehat{A}_t^{j,m}}{\widehat{A}_t^{m-1,m}} = \prod_{k=j}^{m-2} \frac{\widehat{\kappa}_t^{k+1} - \kappa_t^k}{\widehat{\kappa}_t^k - \kappa_t^k}
$$

$$
\zeta_t^j = \frac{d\mathbb{P}^j}{d\mathbb{P}^{m-1}} \Big| \, \mathcal{F}_t \simeq \frac{\widehat{A}_t^{j,j+1}}{\widehat{A}_t^{m-1,m}} = \frac{\widehat{\kappa}_t^{j+1} - \widehat{\kappa}_t^j}{\widehat{\kappa}_t^j - \kappa_t^j} \prod_{k=j+1}^{m-2} \frac{\widehat{\kappa}_t^{k+1} - \kappa_t^k}{\widehat{\kappa}_t^k - \kappa_t^k}
$$

Proof. To establish the first equality, it suffices to show that for arbitrary $k = 0, \ldots, m-2$

$$
\frac{\widehat{A}_t^{k,m}}{\widehat{A}_t^{k+1,m}} = \frac{\widehat{\kappa}_t^{k+1} - \kappa_t^k}{\widehat{\kappa}_t^k - \kappa_t^k} \tag{8.123}
$$

The right-hand side in equation (8.123) equals

$$
\frac{\widehat{A}_t^{k,m}}{\widehat{A}_t^{k+1,m}} = \frac{\sum_{i=k+1}^{m} \alpha_i \, \mathbb{E}_{\mathbb{Q}} \left(B_{T_i}^{-1} \mathbb{1}_{\{\tau > T_i\}} \mid \mathcal{F}_t \right)}{\sum_{i=k+2}^{m} \alpha_i \, \mathbb{E}_{\mathbb{Q}} \left(B_{T_i}^{-1} \mathbb{1}_{\{\tau > T_i\}} \mid \mathcal{F}_t \right)} \tag{8.124}
$$

We recall that

$$
\widehat{\kappa}_t^k = \frac{\widehat{P}_t^{k,m}}{\widehat{A}_t^{k,m}} = \frac{(1-\delta) \sum_{i=k+1}^{m} \mathbb{E}_{\mathbb{Q}} \left(B_{T_i}^{-1} \mathbb{1}_{\{T_{i-1} < \tau \le T_i\}} | \mathcal{F}_t \right)}{\sum_{i=k+1}^{m} \alpha_i \, \mathbb{E}_{\mathbb{Q}} \left(B_{T_i}^{-1} \mathbb{1}_{\{\tau > T_i\}} | \mathcal{F}_t \right)}
$$

where, for every $i = 1, \ldots, m$,

$$(1 - \delta)\, \mathbb{E}_{\mathbb{Q}}\left(B_{T_i}^{-1}\mathbb{1}_{\{T_{i-1} < \tau \leq T_i\}}\,|\mathcal{F}_t\right) = \kappa_t^{i-1}\alpha_i\, \mathbb{E}_{\mathbb{Q}}\left(B_{T_i}^{-1}\mathbb{1}_{\{\tau > T_i\}}\,|\mathcal{F}_t\right)$$

Hence the following equality is valid:

$$\widehat{\kappa}_t^k = \frac{\sum_{i=k+1}^{m}\kappa_t^{i-1}\alpha_i\, \mathbb{E}_{\mathbb{Q}}\left(B_{T_i}^{-1}\mathbb{1}_{\{\tau > T_i\}}\,|\mathcal{F}_t\right)}{\sum_{i=k+1}^{m}\alpha_i\, \mathbb{E}_{\mathbb{Q}}\left(B_{T_i}^{-1}\mathbb{1}_{\{\tau > T_i\}}\,|\mathcal{F}_t\right)}$$

Consequently, we obtain

$$\widehat{\kappa}_t^k - \kappa_t^k = \frac{\sum_{i=k+1}^{m}\kappa_t^{i-1}\alpha_i\, \mathbb{E}_{\mathbb{Q}}\left(B_{T_i}^{-1}\mathbb{1}_{\{\tau > T_i\}}\,|\mathcal{F}_t\right)}{\sum_{i=k+1}^{m}\alpha_i\, \mathbb{E}_{\mathbb{Q}}\left(B_{T_i}^{-1}\mathbb{1}_{\{\tau > T_i\}}\,|\mathcal{F}_t\right)} - \kappa_t^k$$

$$= \frac{\sum_{i=k+2}^{m}(\kappa_t^{i-1} - \kappa_t^k)\alpha_i\, \mathbb{E}_{\mathbb{Q}}\left(B_{T_i}^{-1}\mathbb{1}_{\{\tau > T_i\}}\,|\mathcal{F}_t\right)}{\sum_{i=k+1}^{m}\alpha_i\, \mathbb{E}_{\mathbb{Q}}\left(B_{T_i}^{-1}\mathbb{1}_{\{\tau > T_i\}}\,|\mathcal{F}_t\right)}$$

By similar computations, we find that

$$\widehat{\kappa}_t^k - \kappa_t^k = \frac{\sum_{i=k+2}^{m}(\kappa_t^{i-1} - \kappa_t^k)\alpha_i\, \mathbb{E}_{\mathbb{Q}}\left(B_{T_i}^{-1}\mathbb{1}_{\{\tau > T_i\}}\,|\mathcal{F}_t\right)}{\sum_{i=k+2}^{m}\alpha_i\, \mathbb{E}_{\mathbb{Q}}\left(B_{T_i}^{-1}\mathbb{1}_{\{\tau > T_i\}}\,|\mathcal{F}_t\right)}$$

By combining the formulas, we obtain:

$$\frac{\widehat{\kappa}_t^{k+1} - \kappa_t^k}{\widehat{\kappa}_t^k - \kappa_t^k} = \frac{\sum_{i=k+1}^{m}\alpha_i\, \mathbb{E}_{\mathbb{Q}}\left(B_{T_i}^{-1}\mathbb{1}_{\{\tau > T_i\}}\,|\mathcal{F}_t\right)}{\sum_{i=k+2}^{m}\alpha_i\, \mathbb{E}_{\mathbb{Q}}\left(B_{T_i}^{-1}\mathbb{1}_{\{\tau > T_i\}}\,|\mathcal{F}_t\right)}$$

In view of equation (8.124), this completes the proof of the first equality.

For the second equality, we observe that for arbitrary $j = 0, \ldots, m-2$ we have that $\widehat{A}_t^{j,j+1} = \widehat{A}_t^{j,m} - \widehat{A}_t^{j+1,m}$ and thus:

$$\frac{\widehat{A}_t^{j,j+1}}{\widehat{A}_t^{m-1,m}} = \frac{\widehat{A}_t^{j,m}}{\widehat{A}_t^{m-1,m}} - \frac{\widehat{A}_t^{j+1,m}}{\widehat{A}_t^{m-1,m}} = \frac{\widehat{\kappa}_t^{j+1} - \widehat{\kappa}_t^j}{\widehat{\kappa}_t^j - \kappa_t^j}\prod_{k=j+1}^{m-2}\frac{\widehat{\kappa}_t^{k+1} - \kappa_t^k}{\widehat{\kappa}_t^k - \kappa_t^k}$$

as required.

It is rather clear that rather than starting from equation (8.121), we may start by postulating that the dynamics of forward CDS spreads under the respective martingale measures are given by the following expressions:

$$\begin{cases} d\kappa_t^j = \kappa_t^j \sigma_t^j \, dW_j^{j,j+1}(t) \\ d\widehat{\kappa}_t^j = \widehat{\kappa}_t^j v_t^j \, d\widehat{W}_j^{j,m}(t) \end{cases} \tag{8.125}$$

We wish to derive the joint dynamics of the $(2m-1)$-dimensional process $(\kappa^0, \ldots, \kappa^{m-1}, \widehat{\kappa}^0, \ldots, \widehat{\kappa}^{m-2})$ under some probability measure. For this purpose, we may choose, for instance, the martingale measure $\mathbb{P}^{m-1}$ associated with the positive $(\mathbb{Q}, \mathbb{F})$-martingale $\widehat{A}^{m-1,m}$. In the next result, the joint dynamics of the family of one-period and coterminal CDS spreads are explicitly stated under the martingale measure $\mathbb{P}^{m-1} = \widehat{\mathbb{P}}^{m-1}$. Once again, this probability measure can be seen as the terminal martingale measure for the model at hand.

Proposition 8.6.4 *The joint dynamics of the family forward one-period and coterminal CDS spreads $(\kappa^0, \ldots, \kappa^{m-1}, \widehat{\kappa}^0, \ldots, \widehat{\kappa}^{m-2})$ under the martingale measure $\mathbb{P}^{m-1}$ are*

$$\begin{cases} d\kappa_t^j = \kappa_t^j \left(\mu_j^{m-1}(t) \, dt + \sigma_t^j \, dW_j^{m-1,m}(t) \right) \\ d\widehat{\kappa}_t^j = \widehat{\kappa}_t^j \left(\varphi_j^{m-1}(t) \, dt + v_t^j \, d\widehat{W}_j^{m-1,m}(t) \right) \end{cases}$$

where the $(\mathbb{P}^{m-1}, \mathbb{F})$-Brownian motions $W_0^{m-1,m}, \ldots, W_{m-1}^{m-1,m}, \widehat{W}_0^{m-1,m}, \ldots, \widehat{W}_{m-2}^{m-1,m}$ satisfy

$$d \langle W_i^{m-1,m}, W_j^{m-1,m} \rangle_t = \rho_{i,j} \, dt$$

$$d \langle \widehat{W}_i^{m-1,m}, \widehat{W}_j^{m-1,m} \rangle_t = \eta_{i,j} \, dt$$

$$d \langle W_i^{m-1,m}, \widehat{W}_j^{m-1,m} \rangle_t = \theta_{i,j} \, dt$$

The drift $\mu_{m-1}^{m-1}(t) = 0$ and for every $j = 0, \ldots, m-2$ we have that $\mu_j^{m-1}(t) = \sigma^j \bar{\mu}_j^{m-1}(t)$ and $\varphi_j^{m-1}(t) = v^j \bar{\varphi}_j^{m-1}(t)$, where in turn

$$\bar{\mu}_j^{m-1}(t) = -\sum_{k=j+1}^{m-2} \frac{\theta_{j,k+1} v_t^{k+1} \widehat{\kappa}_t^{k+1} - \rho_{j,k} \sigma_t^k \kappa_t^k}{\widehat{\kappa}_t^{k+1} - \kappa_t^k} + \sum_{k=j+1}^{m-2} \frac{\theta_{j,k} v_t^k \widehat{\kappa}_t^k - \rho_{j,k} \sigma_t^k \kappa_t^k}{\widehat{\kappa}_t^k - \kappa_t^k}$$

$$- \frac{\theta_{j,j+1} v_t^{j+1} \widehat{\kappa}_t^{j+1} - \theta_{j,j} v_t^j \widehat{\kappa}_t^j}{\widehat{\kappa}_t^{j+1} - \widehat{\kappa}_t^j} + \frac{\theta_{j,j} v_t^j \widehat{\kappa}_t^j - \rho_{j,j} \sigma_t^j \kappa_t^j}{\widehat{\kappa}_t^j - \kappa_t^j}$$

and

$$\bar{\varphi}_j^{m-1}(t) = -\sum_{k=j}^{m-2} \frac{\eta_{j,k+1} v_t^{k+1} \widehat{\kappa}_t^{k+1} - \theta_{j,k} \sigma_t^k \kappa_t^k}{\widehat{\kappa}_t^{k+1} - \kappa_t^k} + \sum_{k=j}^{m-2} \frac{\eta_{j,k} v_t^k \widehat{\kappa}_t^k - \theta_{j,k} \sigma_t^k \kappa_t^k}{\widehat{\kappa}_t^k - \kappa_t^k}$$

Proof. We start by noting that for the Radon-Nikodým density process $\widehat{\zeta}^j$, which was defined in Lemma 8.6.3, we obtain

$$
\begin{aligned}
V\big(\ln(\widehat{\zeta}^j)\big) &= V\left(\ln\left(\frac{\widehat{A}_t^{j,m}}{\widehat{A}_t^{m-1,m}}\right)\right) \\
&= V\left(\ln\left(\prod_{k=j}^{m-2} \frac{\widehat{\kappa}^{k+1} - \kappa^k}{\widehat{\kappa}^k - \kappa^k}\right)\right) \\
&= \sum_{k=j}^{m-2} V\left(\ln\left(\frac{\widehat{\kappa}^{k+1} - \kappa^k}{\widehat{\kappa}^k - \kappa^k}\right)\right) \\
&= \sum_{k=j}^{m-2} V\left(\ln\big(\widehat{\kappa}^{k+1} - \kappa^k\big) - \ln\big(\widehat{\kappa}^k - \kappa^k\big)\right) \\
&= \sum_{k=j}^{m-2} \left(\frac{V(\widehat{\kappa}^{k+1} - \kappa^k)}{\widehat{\kappa}^{k+1} - \kappa^k} - \frac{V(\widehat{\kappa}^k - \kappa^k)}{\widehat{\kappa}^k - \kappa^k}\right) \\
&= \sum_{k=j}^{m-2} \left(\frac{V(\widehat{\kappa}^{k+1}) - V(\kappa^k)}{\widehat{\kappa}^{k+1} - \kappa^k}\right) - \sum_{k=j}^{m-2} \left(\frac{V(\widehat{\kappa}^k) - V(\kappa^k)}{\widehat{\kappa}^k - \kappa^k}\right)
\end{aligned}
$$

Using Proposition 8.6.2, we obtain, for every $j = 0, \dots, m-2$,

$$
\begin{aligned}
d\widehat{W}_j^{j,m}(t) = {}& d\widehat{W}_j^{m-1,m}(t) - \sum_{k=j}^{m-2} \frac{\eta_{j,k+1} v_t^{k+1} \widehat{\kappa}_t^{k+1} - \theta_{j,k} \sigma_t^k \kappa_t^k}{\widehat{\kappa}_t^{k+1} - \kappa_t^k} \, dt \\
&+ \sum_{k=j}^{m-2} \frac{\eta_{j,k} v_t^k \widehat{\kappa}_t^k - \theta_{j,k} \sigma_t^k \kappa_t^k}{\widehat{\kappa}_t^k - \kappa_t^k} \, dt
\end{aligned}
$$

This in turn yields the stated formula for the process $\bar{\varphi}_j^{m-1}$ and thus for the drift of $\widehat{\kappa}^j$ under $\mathbb{P}^{m-1}$. Similarly, for the Radon-Nikodým density process ζ^j introduced in Lemma 8.6.3, we get

$$
\begin{aligned}
V\big(\ln(\zeta^j)\big) &= V\left(\ln\left(\frac{\widehat{A}_t^{j,j+1}}{\widehat{A}_t^{m-1,m}}\right)\right) \\
&= V\left(\ln\left(\frac{\widehat{\kappa}^{j+1} - \widehat{\kappa}^j}{\widehat{\kappa}^j - \kappa^j} \prod_{k=j+1}^{m-2} \frac{\widehat{\kappa}^{k+1} - \kappa^k}{\widehat{\kappa}^k - \kappa^k}\right)\right) \\
&= \sum_{k=j+1}^{m-2} V\left(\ln\left(\frac{\widehat{\kappa}^{k+1} - \kappa^k}{\widehat{\kappa}^k - \kappa^k}\right)\right) + V\left(\ln\left(\frac{\widehat{\kappa}^{j+1} - \widehat{\kappa}^j}{\widehat{\kappa}^j - \kappa^j}\right)\right)
\end{aligned}
$$

$$
= \sum_{k=j+1}^{m-2} V\Big(\ln \big(\widehat{\kappa}^{k+1} - \kappa^k \big) \Big) - \sum_{k=j+1}^{m-2} V\Big(\ln \big(\widehat{\kappa}^k - \kappa^k \big) \Big)
$$

$$
+ V\Big(\ln \big(\widehat{\kappa}^{j+1} - \widehat{\kappa}^j \big) \Big) - V\Big(\ln \big(\widehat{\kappa}^j - \kappa^j \big) \Big)
$$

$$
= \sum_{k=j+1}^{m-2} \frac{V(\widehat{\kappa}^{k+1}) - V(\kappa^k)}{\widehat{\kappa}^{k+1} - \kappa^k} - \sum_{k=j+1}^{m-2} \frac{V(\widehat{\kappa}^k) - V(\kappa^k)}{\widehat{\kappa}^k - \widehat{\kappa}^k}
$$

$$
+ \frac{V(\widehat{\kappa}^{j+1}) - V(\widehat{\kappa}^j)}{\widehat{\kappa}^{j+1} - \widehat{\kappa}^j} - \frac{V(\widehat{\kappa}^j) - V(\kappa^j)}{\widehat{\kappa}^j - \kappa^j}
$$

Using once again Proposition 8.6.2, we find that, for every $j = 0, \ldots, m - 2$,

$$
dW_j^{j,j+1}(t) = dW_j^{m-1,m}(t) - \sum_{k=j+1}^{m-2} \frac{\theta_{j,k+1} v_t^{k+1} \widehat{\kappa}_t^{k+1} - \rho_{j,k} \sigma_t^k \kappa_t^k}{\widehat{\kappa}_t^{k+1} - \kappa_t^k} \, dt
$$

$$
+ \sum_{k=j+1}^{m-2} \frac{\theta_{j,k} v_t^k \widehat{\kappa}_t^k - \rho_{j,k} \sigma_t^k \kappa_t^k}{\widehat{\kappa}_t^k - \kappa_t^k} \, dt - \frac{\theta_{j,j+1} v_t^{j+1} \widehat{\kappa}_t^{j+1} - \theta_{j,j} v_t^j \widehat{\kappa}_t^j}{\widehat{\kappa}_t^{j+1} - \widehat{\kappa}_t^j} \, dt
$$

$$
+ \frac{\theta_{j,j} v_t^j \widehat{\kappa}_t^j - \rho_{j,j} \sigma_t^j \kappa_t^j}{\widehat{\kappa}_t^j - \kappa_t^j} \, dt
$$

This yields the stated formula for the process $\bar{\mu}_j^{m-1}$ and thus also the dynamics of κ^j under the martingale measure $\mathbb{P}^{m-1}$.

It is essential to find additional conditions that the one-period and coterminal forward CDS spreads need to satisfy in order for the model to be arbitrage-free. They appear even more difficult to handle than in case of the model of one- and two-period forward CDS spreads, and thus they are not examined here.

8.7 Acknowledgments

This research was supported under the Australian Research Council's Discovery Projects funding scheme (DP0881460).

References

Beumee, J., D. Brigo, D. Schiemert, and G. Stoyle. 2009. Charting a course through the CDS Big Bang. Fitch Solutions, Quantitative Research, Global Special Report, April 7.

Bielecki, T. R., M. Jeanblanc, and M. Rutkowski. 2008. Hedging of a credit default swaption in the CIR default intensity model. *Finance and Stochastics*.

Bielecki, T. R., M. Jeanblanc, and M. Rutkowski. 2009. *Credit risk modeling*. Osaka University, CSFI Lecture Notes Series 02. Osaka, Japan: Osaka University Press.

Bielecki, T. R., and M. Rutkowski. 2002. *Credit risk: Modeling, valuation and hedging*. New York: Springer-Verlag.

Brace, A., D. Gątarek, and M. Musiela. 1997. The market model of interest rate dynamics. *Mathematical Finance* 7:127–154.

Brigo, D. 2005. Market models for CDS options and callable floaters. *Risk* (January). Reprinted in *Derivatives trading and option pricing*, ed. N. Dunbar. London: Risk Books.

Brigo, D. 2006. Constant maturity CDS valuation with market models. *Risk* (June).

Brigo, D. 2008. CDS options through candidate market models and the CDS-calibrated CIR++ stochastic intensity model. In *Credit risk: Models, derivatives and management*, ed. N. Wagner, 393–426. Chapman & Hall/CRC Financial Mathematics Series.

Brigo, D., and A. Alfonsi. 2003. Credit default swaps calibration and option pricing with the SSRD stochastic intensity and interest-rate model. Working paper.

Brigo, D., and A. Alfonsi. 2005. Credit default swaps calibration and derivatives pricing with the SSRD stochastic intensity and interest-rate model. *Finance and Stochastics* 9:29–42.

Brigo, D., and N. El-Bachir. 2010. An exact formula for default swaptions pricing in SSRJD stochastic intensity model. *Mathematical Finance* 20:365–382.

Brigo, D., and F. Mercurio. 2006. *Interest rate models: Theory and practice—with smile, inflation and credit*. 2nd ed. New York: Springer-Verlag.

Brigo, D., and M. Morini. 2005. CDS market formulas and models. Working paper, Banca IMI.

Cox, J. C., J.E. Ingersoll, and S.A. Ross. 1985. A theory of the term structure of interest rates. *Econometrica* 53:385–407.

Jackson, A. 2005. A new method for pricing index default swaptions. Working paper, Global Credit Derivatives Research, Citigroup, London.

Jamshidian, F. 1997. LIBOR and swap market models and measures. *Finance and Stochastics* 1:293–330.

Jamshidian, F. 2004. Valuation of credit default swaps and swaptions. *Finance and Stochastics* 8:343–371.

Jeanblanc, M., M. Yor, and M. Chesney. 2009. *Mathematical models for financial markets*. New York: Springer-Verlag.

Li, L., and M. Rutkowski. 2010. Market models of forward CDS spreads. Working paper, University of Sydney.

Miltersen, K., K. Sandmann, and D. Sondermann. 1997. Closed form solutions for term structure derivatives with log-normal interest rates. *Journal of Finance* 52:409–430.

Morini, M., and D. Brigo. 2007. No-Armageddon arbitrage-free equivalent measure for index options in a credit crisis. *Mathematical Finance*.

Musiela, M., and M. Rutkowski. 1997. Continuous-time term structure models: Forward measure approach. *Finance and Stochastics* 1:261–291.

Musiela, M., and M. Rutkowski. 2007. *Martingale methods in financial modelling*. 2nd ed., corrected 2nd printing. New York: Springer-Verlag.

Pedersen, C.M. 2003. Valuation of portfolio credit default swaptions. *Quantitative Credit Research Quarterly*, Lehman Brothers (November): 1–11.

Phung, Q. P. V. 2009. Market models for credit default swaptions. Master's project, University of New South Wales, October.

Rutkowski, M., and A. Armstrong. 2009. Valuation of credit default swaptions and credit default index swaptions. *International Journal of Theoretical and Applied Finance* 12:1027–1053.

PART III

Credit Derivatives: Products

CHAPTER 9

Valuation of Structured Finance Products with Implied Factor Models

Jovan Nedeljkovic

R² Financial Technologies

Dan Rosen

R² Financial Technologies and The Fields Institute

David Saunders

University of Waterloo, Canada

The recent credit crisis has highlighted limitations of the industry's general understanding and risk management practices regarding structured credit portfolios. Market participants clearly misunderstood and underestimated the risks in many securities, especially with respect to the default correlation, systematic risk, and contagion effects. In particular, pricing models for asset-backed security (ABS) types and collateralized debt obligation (CDO) securities have been often overly simplistic, with many institutions placing too much reliance on dealer quotes and simple models based on credit ratings.

In contrast to synthetic CDOs, the application of stochastic models for ABSs and cash CDOs is fairly new. Given the complexity of the collateral and their waterfall structures, these models are computationally intensive. Also, standardized calibration is more difficult to achieve, due to the illiquidity in the market.

In this chapter, we apply the implied factor methodology to value structured finance instruments such as ABSs and CDOs. The model can be used in a parsimonious way, through a small number of factors that drive the joint defaults and prepayments in the pool. It also results in a framework where cash flow simulations are used effectively, leading to an efficient calibration as well as subsequent consistent pricing of new instruments. We demonstrate the performance of the model by calibrating it to the ABX indexes, and show the implications when pricing other illiquid securities.

[F]irms that performed better . . . had established, before the turmoil began, rigorous internal processes . . . and consequently had developed in-house expertise to conduct independent assessments. . . . In contrast, firms that faced more significant challenges . . . generally lacked relevant internal valuation models and sometimes relied too passively on external views of credit risk from rating agencies and pricing services to determine values for their exposures.

—Senior Supervisors Group, "Observations on Risk Management Practices during the Recent Market Turbulence," 2008

9.1 Introduction

The recent credit crisis, which nearly brought down the entire financial system, has highlighted limitations of the industry's general understanding and risk management practices of structured credit portfolios. Several reports have been written that explore the underlying causes of the crisis and discuss lessons for structurers, investors, and regulators.[1] In particular, regulators and industry associations have highlighted both the need for greater transparency as well as the inadequacy, in general, of some standard valuation and risk modeling approaches used by industry participants, relying too heavily on external credit ratings and dealer quotes.

In its broadest definition, *structured finance* is a generic term referring to financings more complicated than traditional loans, bonds, and common equity. More specifically, it is also used as a broad term to describe financing transactions that help transfer risk as applied to securitizations of various assets (mortgages, credit card receivables, auto loans, etc.). Structured finance brings some tangible economic benefits such as opening up new sources of financing to consumers, reducing funding costs, and freeing balance sheet capacity or restructuring its composition. However, it has arguably also played an important contributing role in the degradation of underwriting standards for some financial assets, such as mortgages, and has helped give rise to both the credit bubble and the subsequent crash and financial crisis of 2007 to 2009.

Structured finance instruments are complex financial structures with specific features, which makes their valuation challenging when compared to simple bonds. *Asset-backed securities* (ABSs) are bonds whose cash flows are based on underlying pools of assets. Generally, a special purpose trust or instrument is set up that takes title to the assets, and the cash flows are "passed through" to the investors in the form of various tranched securities. The types of assets that can be securitized range from residential mortgages to student loans, car loans, and credit card receivables. Since these assets are usually illiquid and private in nature, the securitization essentially makes them available for investment to a much broader range of investors. In contrast, a *collateralized debt obligation* (CDO) is a generic term for a subset of securitizations. It generally encompasses collateralized bond obligations (CBOs), collateralized loan obligations (CLOs), collateralized mortgage obligations (CMOs), collateralized fund

FIGURE 9.1 Asset-Backed Security (ABS) Structure

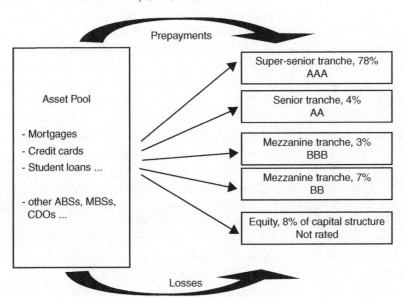

obligations (CFOs), and more. CDOs are generally backed by any type or combination of types of debt: tranches of other collateralized debt obligations, asset-backed bonds, notes issued by a special purpose entity that purchases other underlying assets, which are used as collateral to back the notes, hedge fund obligations, bonds, loans, future receivables, or any other type of debt.

Figure 9.1 gives an example of an ABS structure. A key feature of ABSs and CDOs is that investors bear the *credit risk* of the collateral. In addition, these securities may also bear *prepayment risk* stemming from the underlying collateral. Multiple tranches of securities are issued by the ABS or CDO, offering investors various maturity and credit risk characteristics. Tranches are categorized as senior, mezzanine, and subordinated/equity, according to their degree of credit risk. If there are defaults or the CDO's collateral otherwise underperforms, scheduled payments to senior tranches take precedence over those of mezzanine tranches, which in turn take precedence over subordinated/equity tranches. Senior and mezzanine tranches are typically rated (in the figure, the former receive ratings of AA to AAA at inception and the latter receive BB to BBB). The ratings are meant to reflect both the credit quality of the underlying collateral as well as how much protection a given tranche is afforded by tranches that are subordinate to it.

Accurate modeling, valuation, and risk measurement of structured finance products is challenging, given the complexity of the structures and underlying risks. Investors have in practice generally relied on periodic valuations and reports provided by dealers (or "opinions"). This black-box approach has resulted in a lack of transparency in prices and limited risk capabilities (risk measures, stress-testing, concentration reports, etc.). During the housing and credit boom of the past decade, structured finance instruments generally performed very well. There was a widespread perception that their risks were small and contained. This view proved to be wrong.

Valuation and risk solutions for structured finance portfolios are computationally intensive, rely on multiple data sources, and thus require important investments in methodology, systems, and people. Several difficulties in valuing them and measuring their risk include:

- *Complex risk profile.* Portfolios contain market risk (interest rates and spreads), credit risk, and prepayment risk (as well as liquidity risk). These risks are entangled, and it is difficult to capture their interaction effectively. Correlations are very important and difficult to assess—they are not widely used or standardized. Systematic concentrations have proven to be key drivers of losses as well as possible contagion (between obligors in a market, as well as across markets).
- *Complex structures.* The cash flow structures are complex and generally opaque for a standard investor. They are difficult to model and are computationally involved.
- *Lack of reliable pricing data.* Pricing, as well as fundamental credit data, comes from multiple data sources and is often incomplete or unreliable. The lack of liquidity[2] in the market increases this problem.

Pricing methods for ABS/CDOs can be essentially divided into two classes: *Bond pricing* (single-scenario) methods and *stochastic* (option-based, or simulation) methods. The predominant pricing framework for ABSs and cash CDOs, widely used by dealers and investors, is based on simple bond models and matrix pricing, where the yields of these securities are expressed in a similar way to those of typical corporate bonds. These models have two key characteristics. First, they employ a *single-scenario valuation*; that is, they generally assume a deterministic stream of cash flows from the collateral and the structure. Second, they generally *rely on credit ratings* as determinants of yields (spreads) and risk measurement.

The practical application of more robust stochastic, option-pricing models to value structured credit products is less than a decade old. Most of this advanced modeling work has focused on the valuation of synthetic CDOs with underlying corporate CDSs. These instruments are analytically more tractable since they have simple, standardized waterfalls that can be readily modeled. Also, the models can be more objectively calibrated to observable indexes and tranches, which are commonly traded. The prevailing synthetic CDO valuation framework is based on the Gaussian copula model, originally developed by Li (2000), with the additional use of base correlations to match quoted prices of index tranches (see, e.g., McGinty and Ahluwalia 2004). Extensions of the Gaussian copula model include allowing for random parameters (e.g., Andersen and Sidenius 2005) and copulas other than the Gaussian one (Burtschell, Gregory, and Laurent 2009). In spite of its many well-documented deficiencies, this framework is widely used throughout the industry. In particular, the pricing of bespoke portfolios is still difficult and not standardized, with the industry applying generally ad hoc *mapping* models to relate the prices of traded indexes to those of tranches of different bespoke portfolios (St. Pierre et al. 2004).

Second-generation models include *dynamic CDO models* and *implied factor models* for bespoke portfolios with detailed collateral modeling. In general, copula models are referred to as *static* because credit risk is determined by a single set of random factors, rather than by random processes that evolve through time. Dynamic models remedy this situation by linking credit dynamics to stochastic processes. Models in this vein include Brigo, Pallavicini, and Torresetti (2007), Schönbucher (2005), and Hull and White (2008a). These models generally require a *top-down* approach in practice, where the modeling object is directly the portfolio loss distribution, and not the individual names in the credit portfolio.

Bottom-up approaches, where the underlying pool is modeled in detail, are required to value structures with names that are different from the indexes and benchmark instruments used for calibration (i.e., bespoke portfolios). In particular, *implied factor models* are powerful tools that can achieve consistent valuations across different portfolios and specifically model bespoke portfolios. In this approach, a (small) set of factors is used to drive the joint credit (and prepayment) events within the underlying portfolio. The calibration of the model searches for an optimal joint distribution of the factors, such that the market prices of a set of reference securities (such as the tranches of various indexes) are matched, possibly within allowable error limits. The first such model was the "implied copula model" of Hull and White (2006), which is actually a top-down approach. Several others have followed, including the "implied factor model" of Rosen and Saunders (2009) and Nedeljkovic, Rosen, and Saunders (2010); the "implied Archimedean copula" of Vacca (2008); papers based on minimum entropy (Dempster, Medova, and Yang 2007; Meyer-Dautrich and Wagner 2007; Halperin 2009); and others (Hull and White 2008b; Walker 2006).

In contrast to synthetic CDOs, the application of stochastic models for ABS and cash CDOs is fairly new. Given the complexity of the collateral and their waterfall structures, these models are computationally intensive—each computation of the cash flows accruing to a tranche as a result of a particular set of assumed default and prepayment rates consumes a large amount of computation time. Also, standardized calibration is more difficult to achieve, due to the illiquidity in the market.

In this chapter, we apply the implied factor methodology of Rosen and Saunders (2009), and Nedeljkovic, Rosen, and Saunders (2010) to value structured finance instruments such as ABSs and CDOs. The model can be used in a parsimonious way, through a small number of factors that drive the joint defaults and prepayments in the pool. It also results in a framework where cash flow simulations are used effectively, leading to an efficient calibration as well as subsequent consistent pricing of new instruments. We demonstrate the performance of the model by calibrating it to the ABX indexes, and show the implications when pricing other illiquid securities.

The remainder of the chapter is structured as follows: The second section reviews the methods commonly employed for pricing structured finance instruments. The third section introduces the implied factor methodology. The fourth section briefly discusses the ABX indexes. The fifth section presents an application of the implied factor methodology to ABS securities, showing a calibration of the model to the ABX indexes before and during the credit crisis. The sixth section presents some conclusions and discusses directions for future research.

9.2 Valuation of Structured Finance Instruments

As discussed in the introductory section, pricing methods for ABSs and CDOs (with underlying ABSs) can be essentially divided into two classes: *bond pricing* (single-scenario) methods and *stochastic* (option-based, or simulation) methods.[3] In this section, we briefly review these methods, and summarize their advantages and disadvantages. This section is intended to provide some basic methodological background. The implied factor model is then described in more detail in Section 9.3 and throughout the example.

9.2.1   Bond Models (Single-Scenario)

A simple bond model assumes a single cash flow scenario—that is, a deterministic amortization that produces a single stream of cash flows from the collateral and then the structure. The price of the security is given by summing the discounted cash flows, computed using an appropriate spread that reflects the riskiness of the structure. Dealers generally construct comparable spread matrices, based on several instrument characteristics such as ratings, asset class, geography, and vintage. Thus, this model can be seen as a simple *price-yield* calculator.

Bond pricing models (using a matrix approach) allow comparative pricing of "similar" instruments by:

- Providing standards for generating "representative" cash flows based on consistent scenario assumptions.
- Applying consistent discount spreads (premiums) to instruments, based on similar "risk characteristics".

In the case of a corporate bond, the spread essentially captures the default (and recovery) risk of the issuer, as well as perhaps liquidity. For an ABS, the discount spread embeds all the risks not modeled beyond the deterministic scenario, including:

- Credit risk of the underlying pool (default and recovery).
- Volatility and correlations of the cash flows in the underlying loans (resulting from the prepayment uncertainty).
- Nonlinearities and embedded optionality of the instrument's waterfall.

FIGURE 9.2 Cash Flow Waterfall and Pricing

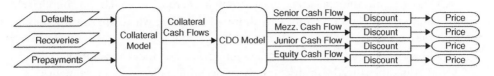

Figure 9.2 depicts the bond-pricing approach. It can be summarized as a four-step procedure:

1. *Scenario definition.* A scenario contains detailed assumption vectors to generate cash flows (i.e., the projections of default, prepayment, and recovery rates over the life of the deal). It also contains a realization of the interest-rate term structure and other financial factors if necessary (e.g., foreign exchange [FX] rates). In principle, great detail is required when modeling the instrument's cash flows in a scenario based on either pool-level assumptions or loan-level assumptions and using perhaps some clustering methods, for example by collateral type, geography, or loan-to-value (LTV) ratios.
2. *Collateral cash flows.* Under the given scenario, the cash flows of the collateral pool are modeled in detail when the information is available, or are proxied in some reasonable way when information is missing.
3. *Waterfall cash flows.* Based on the collateral cash flows and a detailed definition of the ABS waterfall, the instrument's cash flows are obtained.[4] If the detailed waterfall is not available, then it is approximated based on the instrument's indicative data.
4. *Net present value (NPV).* The ABS cash flows are discounted applying the appropriate discount rates composed of the (risk-free) interest rates and the applicable spread (based on the instrument characteristics and market-comparable matrices).

The cash flow generation for CDOs backed by ABSs involves an additional level of complexity. First one computes the detailed pool cash flows for each underlying ABS, then the cash flow waterfall of each ABS bond, and finally the overall CDO cash flow waterfall.

The NPV calculation formula (expressed in continuous compounding) is given by:

$$PV = \sum_{j=1}^{T} CF_j(Y) \cdot \exp\left(-\left(r(t_j) + s(X)\right) \cdot t_j\right) \quad (9.1)$$

where

$CF_j(Y)$ is the cash flow at time t_j, which depends on the pool assumptions defined by the vector Y.

$Y = (PP, Def, LGD, \ldots)$ gives the levels of the parameters defining the scenario (prepayment, default, and loss given default [LGD] rates over time, interest rates, etc.).

$r(t)$ is the risk-free interest rate for borrowing until time t.

$s(X)$ is the applicable spread for the instrument (here assumed flat, for simplicity), and may depend on various attributes of the pool, which are summarized in the vector X.

$X =$ (asset type, rating, sector, region, vintage, . . .) defines the parameters determining the spreads (or discount margins) applicable to the instrument.

The single-scenario approach provides a useful stress-testing framework, since it allows exploration of the price impact of different assumptions on spreads and collateral behavior. In some cases, practitioners have resorted to pricing using several scenarios. The final price is obtained by weighting the prices in each scenario, generally in an ad hoc way.

9.2.2   Stochastic Models and Monte Carlo Techniques

Option-theoretic approaches based on stochastic models are standard valuation techniques for derivatives. The practical application of stochastic option-pricing models to value structured credit products is less than a decade old, and is now best industry practice for corporate synthetic CDOs. These instruments are analytically tractable since they have simple, standardized waterfalls that can be readily modeled. Also, the models can be more objectively calibrated to observable indexes and tranches, which are commonly traded (e.g., CDX or iTraxx). The prevailing synthetic CDO valuation framework is based on the Gaussian copula model (using base correlations). In spite of its many well-documented deficiencies, this framework is widely used throughout the industry. In particular, the pricing of bespoke portfolios is still difficult and not standardized, with the industry applying generally ad hoc mapping models to relate the prices of traded indexes to those of tranches of different bespoke portfolios.

In contrast to synthetic CDOs, the application of stochastic models for ABS and cash CDOs is rather new. Given the complexity of the collateral and their waterfall structures, the valuation of structured finance instruments is more involved and computationally intensive, generally requiring Monte Carlo simulation methods. The underlying risk profiles are also more complex. In addition to default and recovery risks, there is prepayment and potentially other market risks. Finally, standardized calibration is also more difficult to achieve, due to the illiquidity in the market and lack of reference instruments.

The stochastic valuation methodology is conceptually simple, and can be seen as a sophisticated extension of the single-scenario methodology. It can be described in the following five steps:

1. *Scenario generation.* A sample of scenarios is generated (typically very large), where each scenario contains detailed assumptions to generate cash flows (default, prepayment, and recovery rates), as well realizations of interest rates and other financial factors. Scenarios are generated from a well-defined joint stochastic process for all the factors, which accounts for their volatilities, correlations, and so on.

Similar to the single scenario case, under each scenario, we compute:

2. Conditional collateral cash flows.
3. Conditional waterfall cash flows.
4. Conditional net present value (NPV). In contrast to the single-scenario case, where an applicable spread is used, cash flows are discounted applying the risk-free rate.

The final value is given by averaging the conditional NPVs over all the scenarios:

5. *Instrument's final value* (unconditional present value).

The parameters of the processes used to generate the scenarios are calibrated from market prices, where available (e.g., based on indexes such as the iTraxx, CDX, LCDX, ABX, and CMBX) or to a standard set of market quotes for representative, more liquid instruments.

Some important features of this approach include:

- It is a structured, multiscenario approach that effectively uses advances in credit models, Monte Carlo methods, and CDO analytics developed over the past decade.
- It explicitly models the key risks: credit (default, LGD, spread), prepayment, and market risk, as well as their interactions.
- It is a portfolio risk-based approach where correlations and concentration risks are captured.
- It can be implemented as an arbitrage-free approach, and can also be complemented with liquidity premiums, subjective views, and so on.
- It provides consistent valuation of all the deals based on the same collateral pool (by using consistent parameters), as well as valuation of various asset classes (synthetics, cash, ABSs, CLOs, CDOs, CDO2s) through the consistent use of scenarios.
- It naturally provides sensitivities to various risks, as well as hedge ratios (this may be computationally intensive).

The practical application of these methods presents several challenges for ABS instruments. First, their implementation may be involved, and the solutions are computationally intensive. Second, their calibration can be difficult. It involves the following steps:

- The parameters of the general model are first derived to match quoted tranche prices (for example, for an index or a set of observable quotes). These parameters would be directly applicable for nonstandard tranches on the same collateral pool (or a very similar basket).
- Since the ABS has a different underlying pool than the index (it is a bespoke portfolio), common practice requires a mapping procedure from the standard model parameters to the bespoke portfolio model. Mapping procedures have generally relied on some judgment and ad hoc treatment.

In the next section we describe the implied factor model approach, originally developed in Rosen and Saunders (2009) and Nedeljkovic, Rosen, and Saunders (2010) for bespoke synthetic CDOs and CLOs, and apply it later in Section 9.5 to the ABX indexes and cash residential mortgage-backed securities (RMBSs).

9.3 Implied Factor Models and Weighted Monte Carlo

In this section, we review the implied factor model approach for pricing portfolio credit derivative securities. A special case is developed and calibrated to the ABX.HE indexes in Section 9.5. The methodology combines the application of factor models, commonly used to measure portfolio credit risk and value (synthetic) structured credit products and weighted Monte Carlo methods (e.g., Avellaneda et al. 2001). In Rosen and Saunders (2009) the method is applied to calculate implied distributions for multifactor credit risk models over several CDO examples including multiple indexes, and Nedeljkovic, Rosen, and Saunders (2010) apply it to value CLOs. For a general review of factor models applied to portfolio credit risk the reader is referred to McNeil, Embrechts, and Frey (2005).

We focus on the static version of the model. We begin by assuming that credit risk is driven by two sets of random variables:

- *Systematic credit factors.* These factors (Z_k, $k = 1, \ldots, K$), can represent the influence of different sectors, geographic regions, and economic variables on credit portfolio cash flows. We assume an a priori distribution for the factors, coming for example from a standard credit portfolio model (in the dynamic version we assume their underlying joint process). The objective of the implied factor methodology is to find the distribution of the systematic factors that allows us to match observed market prices of a set of reference instruments (e.g., tranches of some indexes or other liquid credit instruments).
- *Idiosyncratic factors.* These factors (ε_n, $n = 1, \ldots, N$), are independent of the systematic factors, and of each other. It is often the case, although not strictly necessary, that there is a single idiosyncratic factor for each name in the underlying portfolios under consideration. The distribution of idiosyncratic risk is assumed known.

Let f_Z and f_ε denote the marginal distributions of the systematic and idiosyncratic credit factors, respectively. Since systematic and idiosyncratic risk are assumed to be independent, the joint distribution of all risk factors is the product of the marginal distributions:

$$f_{Z,\varepsilon}(z, \varepsilon) = f_Z(z) \cdot f_\varepsilon(\varepsilon) \tag{9.2}$$

An outcome of the systematic and idiosyncratic factors (a scenario), determines the timing of credit events of every obligor in the underlying portfolio. These credit events include defaults (and in this case what the recoveries are), and prepayments. Thus, an important part of the methodology is a (precalibrated) credit portfolio model. For example, for the case of default events, we can express such a credit portfolio model in general terms through a link function h, which provides the marginal default probability before time t of every obligor i given the systematic factor Z as:

$$F_{i,t}(Z) = h\left(a_{it} + \sum_{k=1}^{K} b_{ik}Z_k\right) \qquad (9.3)$$

The credit model can resemble the commonly used standard copula model or a logit model. We assume that similar equations apply for prepayment and loss given default (LGD) (or recoveries). The model, together with the distribution of the factors, determines the codependence of credit events in the portfolio. The factor loadings b for each obligor are assumed given (from the credit portfolio model), but, in general, the constant terms a are used to calibrate the model to individual name prices where available (e.g., when CDSs are available).

The basic strategy is then to assume that the distribution of idiosyncratic risk is given (i.e., is equal to its prior distribution), and then infer the distribution of the systematic factors from the observed market prices. Once this distribution has been determined, it can be used to price any instrument whose underlying portfolio depends on the same factors. To put it succinctly: *The implied systematic factor distribution is the vehicle used to transfer the information contained in observable market prices to obtain comparable prices and hedge parameters for other less liquid instruments.*

The method proceeds as follows. Assume that there are M instruments (e.g., credit default swaps, credit indexes, index tranches, etc.) whose prices are observable in the market, denoted by π_m, $m = 1, \ldots, M$. Denote by $PV_m(Z, \varepsilon)$ the present value of the mth instrument's cash flows under a given realization of the systematic and idiosyncratic risk factors, and by $PV_m(z)$ its (conditional) expected present value of the cash flows, given that $Z = z$:

$$PV_m(z) = E[PV_m|Z = z] = \int PV_m(z, \varepsilon) \cdot f_\varepsilon(\varepsilon)d\varepsilon \qquad (9.4)$$

Since the distribution of idiosyncratic risk is given, the preceding function can be computed explicitly for many common factor models and credit-derivative securities. In order to match the observed distribution of market prices exactly, the systematic factor distribution $f_Z(z)$ should satisfy:

$$E[PV_m(Z)] = \int PV_m(z) \cdot f_Z(z)dz = \pi_m, \quad m = 1, \ldots, M \qquad (9.5)$$

in the event that Z has a continuous distribution, or:

$$E[PV_m(Z)] = \sum_{s=1}^{S} PV_m(z_s) \cdot q_s, \quad s = 1, \ldots, S, \quad m = 1, \ldots, M \qquad (9.6)$$

in the event that Z has a discrete distribution assigning probability q_s to the outcome $Z = z_s, s = 1, \ldots, S$.

The preceding constraints form a set of conditions to be satisfied by the distribution of the systematic credit risk factors Z. In general, there may be many probability distributions that satisfy these M constraints exactly, or perhaps none. The approach is to select the distribution that satisfies all the pricing constraints and maximizes a measure of the fitness G of the distribution. In the case of a continuous Z, this optimization problem can be stated as:

$$
\begin{aligned}
\max\ & G(f_Z) \\
& \int PV_m(z) \cdot f_Z(z)dz = \pi_m, \quad m = 1, \ldots, M \\
& \int f_Z(z)dz = 1 \\
& f_Z(z) \geq 0
\end{aligned}
\tag{9.7}
$$

In the case of a discrete Z, the problem is:

$$
\begin{aligned}
\max\ & G(q) \\
& \sum_{s=1}^{S} q_s \cdot PV_m(z_s) = \pi_m, \quad m = 1, \ldots, M \\
& \sum_{s=1}^{S} q_s = 1 \\
& q_s \geq 0, \quad s = 1, \ldots, S
\end{aligned}
\tag{9.8}
$$

Once the implied factor distribution has been determined by solving one of the preceding optimization problems, it can be used to compute prices and hedge parameters[5] for other instruments.

A number of observations regarding the general problem formulation are in order:

- Additional constraints are also possible. For example, it may be stipulated that the distribution of Z lies in some parametric family of distributions.
- There are a number of possible choices of the measure of distribution fitness, G, which are popular in such calibration problems (see, e.g., Rubinstein 1994). Common choices include minimizing the distance from a prior distribution p, for example in the discrete case; minimizing the vector norm $\|q - p\|_r$ for some convenient r (e.g., $r = 1, 2, \infty$); maximizing the smoothness of the probability distribution (e.g., Hull and White [2006] minimize a discretized integral of the squared second derivative of the probability density); and minimizing the relative entropy with respect to a prior distribution p:

$$
G(q) = \sum_{s=1}^{S} p_s \cdot \ln(q_s / p_s)
\tag{9.9}
$$

- A simple modification to the optimization problem is to replace the hard constraints with penalized terms in the objective function.

$$\max G(q) - \sum_{m=1}^{M} C_m \left(\sum_{s=1}^{S} P V_m(z_s) - \pi_m \right)^2$$

$$\sum_{s=1}^{S} q_s = 1 \tag{9.10}$$

$$q_s \geq 0, \quad s = 1, \ldots, S$$

This may reflect the belief that market prices cannot be considered perfectly accurate (noting, for example, the relative illiquidity of the reference pricing securities in the calibration). The coefficients $C_m \geq 0$ can be used to set the relative importance of matching the observed prices of each instrument. Alternatively, one could consider matching prices within the bid-ask spread (either using hard constraints to bound prices or using penalties for prices that fall outside the bid-ask spread).

- For reasons of computational efficiency, we would like to generate a minimum number of well-chosen scenarios that span the factor space to generate solutions with a given numerical accuracy. This is particularly important when the simulation of instrument cash flows conditional on the systematic factor Z is expensive, as in the case of cash instruments for which the waterfall must be evaluated. For single-factor models, one can use equally spaced scenarios, quadrature points, or other simple methods. Similarly, some simple grids can be used for two-factor models. More general Monte Carlo methods are necessary for high dimensions.[6]

- Scenario coverage is a factor. Scenario sets must reflect outcomes of the factors that are reasonably produced by the (a priori unknown) implied factor distribution. In particular, this requires enough outcomes in the tails to reproduce market prices. For example, if scenarios are sampled from a prior factor distribution with thin tails (e.g., a normal distribution), the optimizer is left with insufficient scenarios in the tails of the factor distributions to match observed market prices (particularly for senior tranches). In practice, implied factor distributions often have fat tails, with significant excess kurtosis. Therefore it is important to include sufficient scenarios far out in the tails.

9.4 The ABX Indexes

The Markit ABX.HE indexes provide representative price information on the performance of residential mortgage-backed securities (RMBSs) and serve as a market benchmark for the pricing of RMBSs and CDOs of RMBSs. Each index consists of a collection of 20 tranches of RMBSs that were at approximately the same level of the capital structure when they were issued. The first ABX.HE indexes, series

ABX.HE.06-1, were introduced in January 2006, and were based on deals issued during the second half of 2005. New versions, or rolls, of the index were planned to be defined every six months afterward. Once a roll of the index is determined, it continues trading until the maturity of all the underlying collateral. Rolls of the index were introduced in July 2006 (ABX.HE.06-2), January 2007 (ABX.HE.07-1), and July 2007 (ABX.HE.07-2). Each version of the index is constructed based on RMBS deals issued in the previous six months. Owing to the paucity of RMBS issuance since the onset of the financial crisis, no new versions of the index have been defined since July 2007.

Originally, there were five ABX indexes in a series. The indexes were defined in terms of the ratings of their underlying tranches by the major rating agencies to be ABX.HE.AAA, ABX.HE.AA, ABX.HE.A, ABX.HE.BBB, and ABX.HE.BBB–. In RMBS deals (even those backed by subprime mortgages), the largest portion of the underlying collateral (typically about 80 percent) serves to back a number of AAA tranches. The ABX.HE.AAA index was constructed from the AAA tranche from each of the underlying deals with the largest duration (hence interpreted to be the riskiest AAA tranche). Later, in order to provide a fuller representation of the risk of the RMBS market across the capital structure, the ABX.HE.PENAAA (penultimate AAA) indexes were introduced, constructed from the second-to-last AAA tranches of the capital structure of the underlying RMBS.

The RMBSs underlying each roll of the ABX are chosen by a poll of the sponsoring dealers, and are subject to a set of criteria to ensure proper diversification (e.g., no more than four deals can be connected to a single issuer, and no more than six deals to a single master servicer). For a detailed description of the mechanics of the index rolls, see Markit (2006).

The synthetic credit default swaps (CDSs) underlying the ABX.HE indexes are defined using the International Swaps and Derivatives Association (ISDA) pay as you go (PAUG) template.[7] There are two legs of the CDS, which exchange payments as follows:

- The protection buyer makes regular payments of a fixed percentage of the index notional.
- In return, the protection seller makes payments to the protection buyer in the event of interest or principal shortfall or principal write-down.

An important characteristic of these CDSs, which is different from standard CDSs, is that the principal that has been written down, owing, for example, to delinquencies in payment of the underlying collateral, can be written up again if the collateral pool performance improves. In the event of a *write-up*, the protection buyer must make a payment to the protection seller (essentially returning all or a portion of an earlier write-down payment made by the protection seller). This requirement to make a payment in the event of a write-up applies even if the CDS on the ABX.HE was entered into after the original write-down payment was made (see the ISDA novation protocol and PAUG template).

The ABX.HE indexes are quoted on a price basis. These are interpreted on a percentage basis of the current notional, with prices greater than 100 indicating that the index is currently priced at a premium and prices less than 100 indicating that the index is currently priced at a discount. If the index is priced at a premium, the protection seller must make an up-front payment of (Price – 100) per dollar of current notional to the protection buyer at the initiation of the CDS. For example, a quoted price of 101.5 would result in an initial up-front payment of $1.50 per dollar of current notional. Similarly, if the index is priced at a discount, the protection buyer must make an up-front payment of (100 – Price) per dollar of current notional to the protection seller at contract initiation. The general equation for the price of the index is thus:

$$\text{Notional} \times (\text{Price} - 100) = \text{PV(Fixed Leg)} - \text{PV(Floating Leg)} \quad (9.11)$$

The fixed leg includes all payments made by the protection buyer, including scheduled coupon payments, as well as payments that return earlier write-downs. The floating leg encompasses all payments made by the protection seller, including payments of interest and principal shortfall, as well as write-downs.

Owing to their relative liquidity and coverage of a large part of the RMBS market, market participants have employed the ABX.HE indexes as price benchmarks and indicators of the values of other securities backed by subprime mortgages. For example, UBS, Morgan Stanley, and Citigroup all acknowledged using the ABX.HE indexes as guidelines when writing down losses on investments in subprime mortgages (*Wall Street Journal* 2007). However, the volatility and illiquidity of the index led some market participants to question its use as a benchmark, further noting that the two most popular trades for which it was used (financial institutions using it to hedge mortgage risk and hedge funds using it to short mortgages) would tend to depress the index value (See *Wall Street Journal* (2007), *Economist* (2008)).

Furthermore, as observed earlier when discussing the introduction of the ABX.PENAAA indexes, the indexes only cover part of the capital structure of the 20 underlying deals. These deals may also not cover a sufficient portion of the mortgage market to serve as a full benchmark (see Fender and Scheicher [2008] for further discussion of these points). Fender and Scheicher (2008) perform a regression analysis on ABX.HE returns, and find that heightened risk aversion and market illiquidity played a sizable role in the collapse of the indexes. Stanton and Wallace (2008) also undertake a regression analysis, and find that credit events are insufficient to explain the indexes' declines. They rather find evidence that "returns on ABX.HE indexes of all credit qualities are consistently and statistically significantly related to short-sale demand imbalances in the option and equity markets of publicly traded builders, the commercial banks, and investment banks and the government sponsored enterprises (GSEs)." This suggests that the indexes may have been used as a vehicle to short these companies indirectly, another popular trade that would tend to depress index levels. All these concerns must be borne in mind when the index is used as a benchmark with which to price subprime mortgage-related securities, and particularly in our case, when a mathematical model is calibrated to index prices.

9.5 Examples

In this section we present a series of examples where we calibrate a simple implied factor model to the quoted prices of the ABX.HE indexes, and then price a tranche of another RMBS structure. We first present the simple factor model used in the examples. We then calibrate each series of the index at a point in time close to its first release (i.e., when the series of the index was on-the-run, and hence was the most recently released). We present the implied factor distributions and discuss various issues in their calibration and their characteristics. We then show the calibration of all the ABX.HE series at a recent date at the beginning of 2010. Finally, we demonstrate the impact of pricing on another RMBS structure on this date.

Throughout this section, we use a very simple single-factor model to calibrate each index series separately, for illustration purposes only. We also assume simple homogeneous credit parameters for each pool. However, the detailed pool and cash flow waterfall is modeled and simulated in each scenario. We stress the fact that even a simple model performs actually quite well before and even after the crisis. As we can see from the sensitivity of the RMBS prices to the ABX.HE index series used for calibration, in practice it is advisable to use a more robust model, with detailed bottom-up analysis of the underlying pool.

9.5.1 Underlying Credit Model

We use as a prior, a single-factor Gaussian copula model, which drives jointly defaults and prepayments for each obligor; severities are also stochastic and correlated (e.g., Nedeljkovic, Rosen, and Saunders 2010). The credit risk model is based on the Vasicek portfolio credit model (Vasicek 2002). For simplicity, we assume a homogeneous portfolio. Corresponding to each obligor n, there is a creditworthiness indicator CWI_n satisfying:

$$CWI_n = \sqrt{\rho} \cdot Z + \sqrt{1 - \rho} \cdot \varepsilon_n \qquad (9.12)$$

where Z and ε_n are independent standard normal random variables. The random variable Z is common to all names and represents systematic risk, which in the applications in this chapter may be regarded as the general credit performance of the subprime mortgage market. In a more general multifactor model, Z would be a vector and could include elements representing different geographic regions, industries, and market segments, thus allowing for a fuller modeling of systematic risk. The idiosyncratic risk variable ε_n represents the risk that is unique to the given name.

Defaults occur when the value of CWI_n is low, and prepayments occur when the value of CWI_n is high. Specifically, we consider that:

$$\text{Name } n \begin{cases} \text{Defaults if} & CWI_n \leq \Phi^{-1}(PD) \\ \text{Prepays if} & CWI_n \geq \Phi^{-1}(1 - PP) \end{cases} \qquad (9.13)$$

where Φ is the standard normal cumulative distribution function, and PD and PP denote the (unconditional) default and prepayment probabilities. Then, on a given scenario ($Z = z$), the annual conditional default and prepayment probabilities for obligors in the collateral pool, $PD(z)$ and $PP(z)$, are given respectively by:

$$PD(z) = \Phi\left(\frac{\Phi^{-1}(PD) - \sqrt{\rho} \cdot z}{\sqrt{1-\rho}}\right), \quad PP(z) = \Phi\left(\frac{\Phi^{-1}(PP) + \sqrt{\rho} \cdot z}{\sqrt{1-\rho}}\right)$$

(9.14)

Finally, default probabilities and loss severities (LGDs) are correlated, by making the severities a (nondecreasing) piecewise linear function of the default rates.

We use the following specific parametrization for the *prior model* in these examples. The asset correlation ρ is set to be 0.15, the value for this asset class in the Basel Capital Accord (Basel Committee on Banking Supervision 2006). The annual default and prepayment probabilities are $PD = 0.15$ and $PP = 0.135$. The average LGD is 45 percent, with this chosen to have a value of 60 percent at a PD level of 20 percent (empirically observed levels) and a minimum and maximum levels of 10 percent and 90 percent (reasonable bounds). We find it more natural to consider scenarios directly on the annual default rate $PD(z)$. Thus, we employ a linear discretization in this variable. Equation (9.14) can then be used to determine the corresponding prepayment rates. Figure 9.3 shows the conditional PD, PP, and LGD in each scenario, as well as the prior probability density (there are a total of 141 systematic scenarios). The horizontal axis indexes the scenario number; as is apparent from the shape of its graph, the discretization of the scenarios is linear in the PD (PD values correspond to the left vertical axis). Note that the prior density of the systematic factor Z is standard normal, and this gives the resulting scenario probabilities in Figure 9.3 (scenario probabilities appear on the right vertical axis). Prepayments (PP) in each scenario are determined by applying

FIGURE 9.3 Prior Model and Scenarios

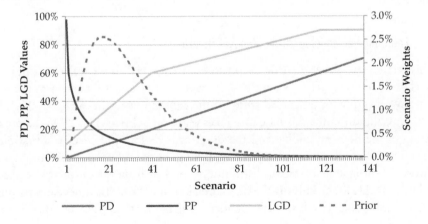

equation (9.14) to solve for $PP(z)$ as a function of $PD(z)$ (PP values are on the left vertical axis), while LGD values are determined as a piecewise linear function of PDs (LGD
values are on the left vertical axis). Finally, owing to the size of the underlying collateral
pools, we can safely assume that idiosyncratic risk is diversified away, and hence we can
apply the law of large numbers. Thus, when the value of the systematic factor is $Z = z$,
the collateral pools default and prepay with the constant rates $PD(z)$ and $PP(z)$.

Several comments on the choice of credit model are in order. First, we have chosen
the simplest factor model for illustrative purposes, and more complex factor models
could be employed in practice (see Rosen and Saunders 2009). Second, homogeneous
pools are used for convenience; practitioners generally have the data to perform a
more detailed analysis of the underlying collateral in order to obtain more accurate
default, prepayment, and severity profiles for loans in the pools (as well as, perhaps, a
factor model that accounts for risk concentrations). Third, note that the prior model
fixes the joint scenarios of PDs, PPs, and LGDs, but not the actual probabilities
(or any moments or correlations), since the weights of the factor distribution are
going to adjust to match the observed market prices of the reference securities (in
the next section these are various ABX indexes). Thus, getting the overall, qualitative
relationships between these variables is very important, with the absolute levels taking
a secondary role. Here, too, a model with more than one factor may provide further
flexibility (although one has to consider the scarce amount of price data to calibrate
the model). Fourth, note that in this case we do not have individual obligor prices,
or the prices of the overall pools to set the average PDs, as is the case with synthetic
CDOs on indexes with corporate names; this allows us essentially to set the constant
terms a in equation (9.3). Thus, we obtain these mean values from the matching of
all the observed prices.[8]

In all examples presented in this chapter, the implied distribution is calibrated by
solving the optimization problem (9.10) with $G(q)$ taken to be the negative of the
relative entropy (equation (9.9)) with respect to the prior distribution p that corresponds to a normal distribution for Z (i.e., the probabilities depicted in Figure 9.3).
Per scenario prices of the index tranches (i.e., the $PV_m(z_s)$ in equation (9.10)) are
calculated based on the default, prepayment, and LGD assumptions in each scenario
using equation (9.11).

9.5.2   Calibration of Model to On-the-Run ABX Indexes

In this section, we show the calibration to each ABX.HE index series at a point in
time close to its release (i.e., when the series was on-the-run, and hence was the most
recent). We begin with a detailed study of the calibration to the ABX.HE.06-1 as a
base case. Calibration for this base case takes place on February 24, 2006, before the
bursting of the housing bubble and the onset of the subprime crisis. Calibration to
later vintages then allows us to view the beginnings of the subprime crisis through the
evolution of the systematic factor distributions implied from the on-the-run indexes.

The ABX.HE.06-1 index is the first vintage of the ABX.HE index, and its prices
for each credit grade have historically tended to be higher than those of other indexes,

TABLE 9.1 ABX.HE.06-1 Calibration on February 24, 2006

Component	Market Price	Prior Price	Prior Error	Model Price	Model Error	Closest Copula Price	Closest Copula Error	Tranche Correlation
AAA	100.31	84.91	15.35%	100.37	0.06%	100.19	0.12%	5.82%
AA	100.34	66.29	33.94%	100.30	0.04%	97.66	2.67%	3.51%
A	100.32	57.89	42.29%	100.19	0.13%	94.73	5.57%	2.78%
BBB	100.32	52.37	47.79%	99.32	1.00%	93.70	6.60%	3.17%
BBB–	100.64	52.98	47.35%	101.23	0.59%	96.80	3.82%	4.36%

owing to the fact that their underlying subprime mortgages, issued in the second half of 2005, are regarded as being of better quality than those issued later (see Goodman et al. 2008).

The valuation date is February 24, 2006, about six weeks after the initial introduction of the ABX.HE indexes in January 2006. Market prices for all of the ABX.HE.06-1 indexes are given in the second column of Table 9.1.[9] The valuation date precedes the dramatic decline in U.S. housing prices, as well as (presumably) the significant use of short positions on the ABX.HE by hedge funds to short mortgage-related companies. Indeed, on this date, all the indexes are actually trading at a premium. Figure 9.4 plots the prices of the ABX.HE.06-1 series over the past two years, where we can observe the dramatic hit that the prices of these securities have endured during the credit crisis.

Figure 9.5 gives the present value[10] of the cash flows of each of the components of the ABX.HE.06-1 series under the factor scenarios (Figure 9.3).[11]

A striking feature of Figure 9.5 is the fact that most tranches experience a threshold effect where at some point their values drop precipitously within a few default scenarios. This effect is most pronounced for the more junior tranches in the capital structure,

FIGURE 9.4 Historical Prices of ABX.HE.06-1 Indexes

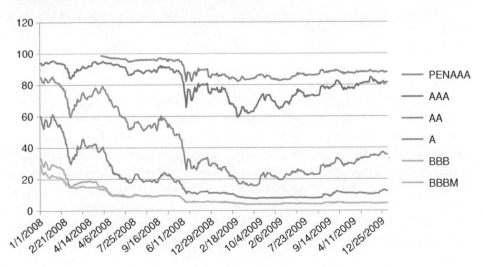

FIGURE 9.5 Present Value of ABX.HE.06-1 Indexes across Factor Scenarios (February 24, 2006)

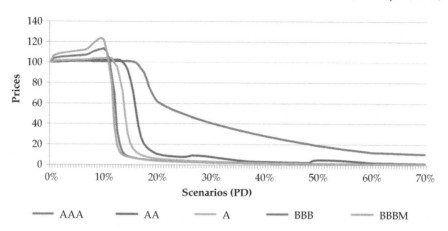

and least significant for the AAA tranche. This feature is reflective of the binary nature of the subordinate tranches, which are prone to be wiped out once defaults exceed a certain level. The AAA tranche value declines more modestly, as it benefits from the credit enhancement provided by the subordinate tranches. Note also that the tranches are priced at par under the zero-default scenario, largely since prepayments are very high and the principal is paid right away. Senior tranches remain at or near par for low default (high prepayment) scenarios, and then decline in value as defaults become more likely. Note, however, the sharp increase in value of the junior tranches before they experience their precipitous drop in value. Take, for example, the BBB– tranche. At a level of about 10 percent PD it goes above 120, and drops as the defaults hit the underlying ABSs. However, as PDs decrease, prepayments simultaneously increase, resulting in faster payback of principal and a corresponding loss of income from a high coupon.

Table 9.1 shows the results of the factor model calibration to the ABX.HE.06-1 prices.

In Table 9.1, the column labeled "Prior Price" gives the value of the index under the prior distribution (corresponding to the systematic credit factor Z having a standard normal distribution). In contrast to the market, with the prior distribution, all index components are priced at a discount, with the level of the discount steepening as we move downward through the capital structure. Pricing errors for this prior model are quite significant, and become very large for the mezzanine tranches. The implied factor distribution optimization problem is solved using as objective function minimum relative entropy (with respect to the prior distribution), and with the pricing constraints in penalized form. The model achieves a very close match to the market prices, with all errors remaining below 1 percent. Also shown in Table 9.1 are the prices of the indexes using the "closest Gaussian copula", which matches the first two moments (mean and standard deviation) of the implied PD distribution. Finally, the table presents

FIGURE 9.6 Factor Distributions (in PDs) for the ABX.HE.06-1 on February 24, 2006

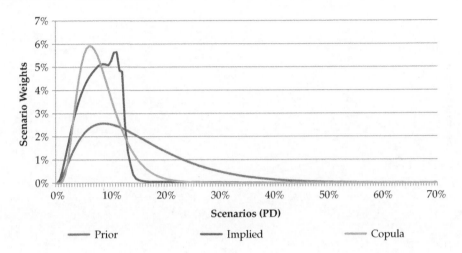

the implied tranche correlations, which are obtained by fixing the mean to that of the implied PD distribution, and then finding the correlations that match each of the tranche prices. Note that these correlations are generally very low (and much lower than for corporate obligors), consistent with empirical default correlations of retail obligors.

Figure 9.6 gives the implied distribution (expressed in PD space), and compares it with the prior and the closest copula. Summary statistics of the implied factor distribution are given in Table 9.2.

From Figure 9.6, we can see that the implied distribution is less conservative than the prior since it puts more mass on lower PD scenarios, and has a thinner right tail (corresponding to high defaults). The closest Gaussian copula distribution is much closer to the implied distribution, with less skew but a thicker tail. With the benefit of hindsight, we can interpret these results as an indication that the market was underpricing the default risk of subprime RMBSs before the subprime crisis. Observe also that the probability density of the implied distribution peaks and then drops precipitously near the threshold where the scenario prices of the mezzanine tranches begin their dramatic decline. We will see this feature recur in other calibrations.

We now move to calibrating the model to the other ABX.HE series at their inceptions. This allows us to follow the progress of the onset of the crisis, through the initial bursting of the housing bubble to the week of the quant fund meltdown.

TABLE 9.2 Moments for the Implied PD Distribution of the ABX.HE.06-1 on February 24, 2006

Mean	Standard Deviation	Skewness	Kurtosis
8.11%	3.86%	2.19	19.59

FIGURE 9.7 Factor Distributions (in PDs) for the ABX.HE.06-2 on July 19, 2006

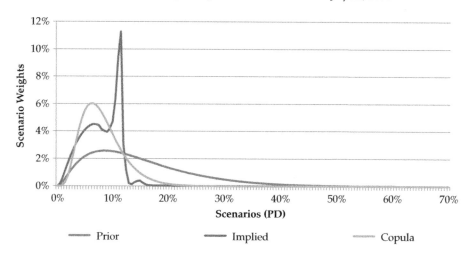

At each date, we are viewing prices and implied distributions of the ABX.HE index based on prices of RMBSs that were issued in the previous two quarters. Thus the underlying collateral RMBSs are of comparable ages at each valuation date, which is important given the typical manner in which defaults and prepayments affect these securities, through time, after issuance.

Figure 9.7 and Table 9.3 show the results of the calibration of the model to ABX.HE.06-2 index prices on July 19, 2006.[12] The valuation date is immediately after the index roll, and consequently all of the indexes are priced at par. This point in time is near the peak of U.S. home prices. Again, the model calibrates well to the market prices. In this case, the implied distribution features a big spike near the point where the mezzanine tranches begin the precipitous drop in their prices over the scenarios. Note, again with hindsight, that we still find an implied distribution that understates the risk lurking in the RMBS market, as evidenced by the thin right tail giving low implied probabilities of high default rates.

Figure 9.8 and Table 9.4 present the model calibration to the ABX.HE.07-1 series on February 23, 2007. By this point in time, the onset of the crisis was beginning to

TABLE 9.3 ABX.HE.06-2 Calibration on July 19, 2006

Component	Market Price	Prior Price	Prior Error	Model Price	Model Error	Closest Copula Price	Closest Copula Error	Tranche Correlation
AAA	100.00	84.82	15.18%	100.13	0.13%	99.85	0.15%	5.32%
AA	100.00	66.13	33.87%	99.73	0.27%	97.33	2.67%	3.00%
A	100.00	58.12	41.88%	100.35	0.35%	94.74	5.26%	2.62%
BBB	100.00	52.36	47.64%	99.80	0.20%	93.22	6.78%	2.83%
BBB−	100.00	52.56	47.44%	100.60	0.60%	95.90	4.10%	3.94%

FIGURE 9.8 Factor Distributions (in PDs) for the ABX.HE.07-1 on February 23, 2007

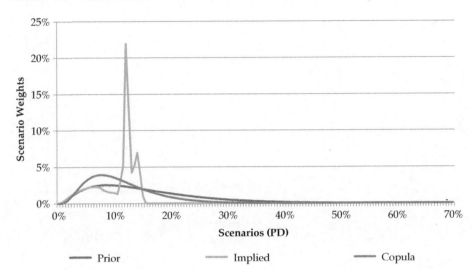

be felt in force. Housing prices had decreased significantly, and subprime lenders were in serious trouble, announcing huge losses, and, in many cases, filing for bankruptcy protection. The pronounced deterioration in market conditions is evidenced by the price of the BBB– index from the 07-1 roll, which was trading on the valuation date at 68.50, after being issued at par only a few weeks earlier. The simple model however still fits observed market prices well. At this point we begin to see the implied factor distribution reflect the heightened risk aversion in the market. In particular, part of the probability spike that appears before the steep drop in price for the more junior tranches over the scenarios has now been transferred to higher default rate scenarios, under which these tranches are worth significantly less. The beginning of the panic is also evident in the closest Gaussian copula distribution, which now has a much thicker right tail and does not resemble at all the implied distribution, and produces larger errors. This is also evidenced by the implied tranche correlations (where also note that for two mezzanine tranches we are not able to obtain them).

TABLE 9.4 ABX.HE.07-1 Calibration on February 23, 2007

Component	Market Price	Prior Price	Prior Error	Model Price	Model Error	Closest Copula Price	Closest Copula Error	Tranche Correlation
AAA	99.15	86.08	13.19%	99.33	0.18%	95.57	3.61%	3.28%
AA	99.15	65.28	34.16%	98.99	0.16%	84.05	15.23%	1.16%
A	92.50	58.49	36.77%	92.52	0.02%	78.37	15.28%	1.62%
BBB	75.21	55.78	25.84%	75.14	0.10%	76.92	2.27%	—
BBB–	68.50	58.19	15.05%	68.57	0.10%	80.83	18.01%	—

FIGURE 9.9 Factor Distributions (in PDs) for the ABX.HE.07-1 on August 6, 2007

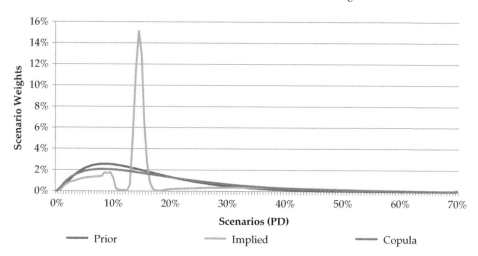

Finally, Figure 9.9 and Table 9.5 show the calibration of the model to the ABX.HE.07-2 series on August 6, 2007. By this time the subprime crisis was in full effect. Subprime lenders had been virtually wiped out, with New Century and Countrywide (among many others) having filed for bankruptcy months earlier. The Bear Stearns highly leveraged quantitative funds, which focused on structured credit, had suffered massive public losses. We see the panic in the RMBS market reflected in the ABX prices and the corresponding implied distribution. The BBB– index had already plummeted to 38.94 not long after its issuance at par, and all tranches except the AAA lost more than 25 percent of their value within a matter of weeks. The model fits the prices well, at the expense of creating a less smooth distribution. In addition to the usual spike near (but now clearly after) the point at which the junior tranches experience their dramatic price drop, the implied distribution now also exhibits a thick right tail, placing over 2 percent probability on scenarios with over 20 percent annual default rates.

Table 9.6 traces the evolution of the first part of the crisis through the summary statistics of the implied PD distributions based on the calibration to the

TABLE 9.5 ABX.HE.07-2 Calibration on August 6, 2007

Component	Market Price	Prior Price	Prior Error	Model Price	Model Error	Closest Copula Price	Closest Copula Error	Tranche Correlation
AAA	90.63	90.28	0.39%	91.10	0.52%	84.28	7.01%	2.00%
AA	83.14	74.42	10.49%	83.09	0.07%	65.61	21.08%	99.90%
A	60.43	71.75	18.73%	60.45	0.03%	62.91	4.11%	15.23%
BBB	42.18	66.06	56.62%	42.26	0.18%	57.89	37.24%	7.13%
BBB–	38.94	62.27	59.90%	38.87	0.18%	54.63	40.28%	7.76%

TABLE 9.6 Moments of the Implied Distributions

Index Vintage	Calibration Date	Mean	Standard Deviation	Skewness	Kurtosis
ABX.HE.06-1	February 24, 2006	8.11%	3.86%	2.19	19.59
ABX.HE.06-2	July 19, 2006	8.18%	3.74%	1.81	18.25
ABX.HE.07-1	February 23, 2007	11.00%	5.91%	4.32	35.09
ABX.HE.07-2	August 6, 2007	17.47%	11.92%	1.71	5.75

on-the-run ABX indexes. A striking feature of the data is the dramatic growth of the first two moments. Over an 18-month period, the mean implied default rates more than double and their standard deviation more than triples. The pattern in the skewness is more difficult to discern. The kurtosis doubles in the first year, but then drops dramatically (to a still significant level, and only once the mean default rate has become very high).

These examples show how the implied factor model is able to calibrate well to ABX prices throughout the initial onset of the subprime crisis. It is important to note that while the examples provide intriguing snapshots of the evolution of the early days of the crisis, the resulting distributions need to be interpreted with care. Since the collateral underlying different vintages of the ABX is not the same, the resulting distributions are for *different* pools of loans.[13] It is a well known and much discussed fact that underwriting standards for subprime mortgages deteriorated significantly in the run-up to the subprime crisis. Consequently, the examples reveal simultaneously the market's heightened awareness of systematic risk as well as the declining quality of the collateral of the index constituent RMBSs. The need to disentangle these two effects, and the corresponding requirement to select an appropriate comparable index when using the implied factor model to price a given structured instrument is discussed further in Section 9.5.4.

9.5.3 Calibration to the ABX Indexes after the Crisis

We now calibrate all four vintages of the ABX.HE indexes on January 12, 2010, a date we (perhaps optimistically) refer to as "after the crisis."[14] It is important to keep in mind that, since we are calibrating the indexes on the same date, we are looking at implied default distributions of collateral pools based on subprime mortgages of different ages. Given the typical default and prepayment patterns for these mortgages through time (see, e.g., Goodman et al. 2008), the examples must be interpreted with some care. This is particularly important when choosing which index to employ as a comparable when pricing another MBS structure, as we will see in the next section.

The prices of all the indexes on the valuation date are given in Table 9.7. Given the dearth of RMBS issuance and liquidity since the crisis, the 07-2 roll is the most recent ABX series. The mortgages underlying the subprime securitizations that serve as index constituents have suffered heavy defaults (particularly for the later rolls), and the indexes have endured massive write-downs.

TABLE 9.7   ABX Index Prices, January 12, 2010

	ABX.HE.06-1	ABX.HE.06-2	ABX.HE.07-1	ABX.HE.07-2
PENAAA	88.21	72.66	42.20	37.75
AAA	81.94	46.54	34.17	34.16
AA	34.74	11.00	4.00	4.88
A	10.44	5.13	3.63	4.44
BBB	4.50	5.00	3.57	3.50
BBB–	4.50	5.00	3.42	3.50

Details of the calibration to the ABX.HE.06-1 series are provided in Figures 9.10 and 9.11 and Table 9.8.

The model is able to match all the index prices closely, even while minimizing relative entropy with respect to a prior distribution that has enormous pricing errors. In this case, the implied distribution has become far more risky than in the early days in the crisis. Indeed, the mean of the implied PD distribution is now 35 percent (the standard deviation is 12.6 percent, skewness is 0.15, and kurtosis is 2.5). The closest Gaussian copula distribution now places nontrivial probability for default rates above 70 percent (indicated by the probability spike in Figure 9.11, which represents the mass of the distribution lying beyond the range of the horizontal axis). Figure 9.10, which gives the present values of the indexes over the scenarios, also reveals some important features of pricing after the crisis. In particular, note the high values under low default scenarios for the mezzanine (BBB and BBB–) indexes. Three important considerations should be kept in mind when looking at these prices. First, the price is quoted on the basis of the *current* underlying notional. For the ABX.HE.06-1 BBB index this

FIGURE 9.10   Present Value of ABX.HE.06-1 Indexes across Factor Scenarios (January 12, 2010)

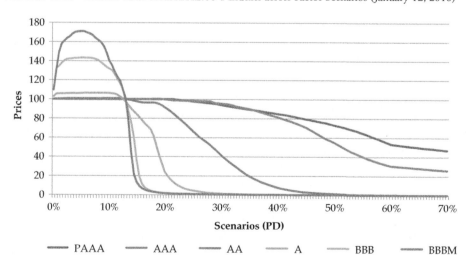

FIGURE 9.11 Factor Distributions (in PDs) for the ABX.HE.06-1 on January 12, 2010

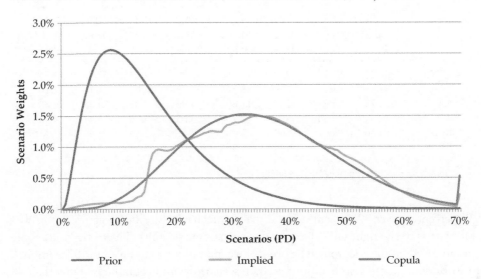

is 47 percent of the original notional, and for the BBB– index it is 32.6 percent, as both these tranches have already experienced substantial write-downs. Second, in low default scenarios, excess spread will accumulate quickly for these tranches and they may pay off in full. Additionally, the PAUG novation protocol (see Section 9.4) may require protection buyers to make payments reversing earlier write-downs.

Table 9.9 summarizes the results of the calibration to each of the ABX series separately on January 12, 2010. Figure 9.12 and Table 9.10 show the corresponding implied distributions, with their summary statistics.

The model cannot calibrate simultaneously the indexes in the 06-2 and 07-2 series (and some tranches are left out of the final optimization). For example, for the 07-2 series, the implied distribution is computed without including the BBB and BBB– indexes. The prices of these indexes under the implied distribution are 7.51 (114.53 percent error) and 6.22 (77.80 percent error), respectively.

The implied distributions calibrated to the different indexes have a number of similarities. All distributions have very high implied mean default rates (ranging from

TABLE 9.8 ABX.HE.06-1 Calibration on January 12, 2010

Component	Market Price	Prior Price	Prior Error	Model Price	Model Error	Closest Copula Price	Closest Copula Error	Tranche Correlation
PENAAA	88.21	98.83	12.04%	87.16	1.19%	87.22	1.12%	7.08%
AAA	81.94	98.78	20.55%	82.14	0.25%	82.47	0.65%	12.80%
AA	34.74	88.58	154.97%	34.75	0.04%	34.94	0.57%	11.20%
A	10.44	72.37	593.20%	10.44	0.01%	10.01	4.14%	11.86%
BBB	4.50	74.97	1,556.06%	4.51	0.30%	4.93	9.65%	10.98%
BBB–	4.50	80.99	1,699.74%	4.50	0.08%	4.06	3.61%	11.28%

TABLE 9.9   Calibration Results for Different ABX.HE Series on January 12, 2010

	ABX.HE.06-1		ABX.HE.06-2		ABX.HE.07-1		ABX.HE.07-2	
	Market Price	Model Price	Market Price	Model Price	Market Price	Model Price	Market Price	Model Price
PENAAA	88.21	87.16	72.66	72.66	42.20	42.33	37.75	37.75
AAA	81.94	82.14	46.54	46.54	34.17	34.08	34.16	34.16
AA	34.74	34.75	11.00	11.00	4.00	4.01	4.88	4.88
A	10.44	10.44	5.13	5.13	3.63	3.62	4.44	4.44
BBB	4.50	4.51	5.00	5.00	3.57	3.56	3.50	7.51*
BBB–	4.50	4.50	5.00	6.58*	3.42	3.43	3.50	6.22*

*Indicates a tranche not included in the optimization.

35 percent to over 42 percent). The distributions have also shifted significant probability mass to the right tail corresponding to extreme defaults. These effects are more pronounced for the later rolls. The probability spike at the right tail of the 07-2 implied distribution indicates probability placed on scenarios with default rates higher than 70 percent. We reiterate that the underlying RMBS pools are different for each series, and the collateral underlying the later ones is generally regarded to be of poorer quality.

Finally, note that calibration of the model becomes significantly more difficult in the later stages of the crisis and the postcrisis period. While Table 9.9 indicates that pricing errors with the implied factor model are small for the 06-1 index, this is not true for all indexes. Consider, for example, the 07-2 series. The prices over all model scenarios are given in Figure 9.13. Note the extremely high values of the mezzanine tranches under low PD scenarios, due to the payments by the protection buyers reversing earlier write-downs due to the novation protocol. Also note that the

FIGURE 9.12   Factor Distributions (in PDs) for the ABX.HE Series on January 12, 2010

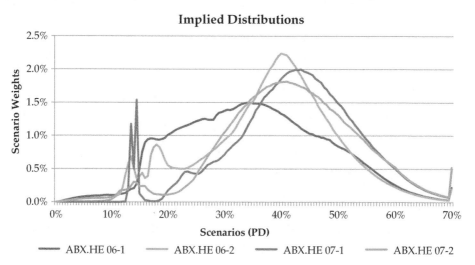

TABLE 9.10 Summary Statistics of Implied Distributions on January 12, 2010

Calibration Index	Mean	Standard Deviation	Skewness	Kurtosis
ABX.HE.06-1	35.22%	12.58%	0.15	2.53
ABX.HE.06-2	37.97%	11.46%	−0.25	2.86
ABX.HE.07-1	42.29%	11.29%	−0.33	3.16
ABX.HE.07-2	41.53%	11.59%	−0.27	3.34

price of the BBB is greater than that of the BBB– under almost all scenarios. However, both indexes have the same market price. This makes it very difficult to calibrate the model in the absence of arbitrage. It further seems difficult to find an implied distribution that simultaneously matches the prices of the indexes composed of senior and mezzanine tranches.

The preceding calibration exercise indicates that it is still possible to calibrate the implied factor model, even in times of crisis with extreme market dislocation and illiquidity. However, there are a number of limitations to the calibration methodology as presented. Data limitations required the imposition of homogeneity assumptions on pool parameters that would not hold in practice. In particular, we are unable to model any segmentation of the credit (or prepayment) risk of the underlying collateral. Furthermore, we have restricted ourselves to the use of a single systematic factor. Given the existence of local bubbles (and crises) in real estate markets, a production implementation of the model would likely feature geographic factors to account for any concentration in the underlying collateral (together with a global factor modeling contagion and the possibility of a national or global real estate market crash). The ideal implementation of the model would indeed proceed from a bottom-up approach, utilizing detailed information on the underlying RMBS tranches, as well on the performance and structure of their collateral.

FIGURE 9.13 Present Value of ABX.HE.07-2 Indexes across Factor Scenarios (January 12, 2010)

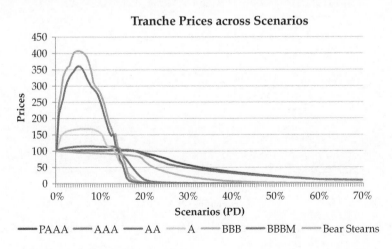

9.5.4   Pricing a Cash Structured Finance Instrument

We now demonstrate the pricing of another RMBS structure, which does not have a
liquid price, based on the implied factor model calibration. We will see that an underlying detailed credit model and choice of comparable index can make a substantial
difference in the RMBS price. The exercise is carried out for illustration purposes
only, with limited analysis on the underlying collateral of the RMBS, rather than as an
example of how a reliable valuation is carried out in practice. In particular, we stress
the critical point that bottom-up modeling, based on detailed collateral information,
is vital for pricing of structured finance products.

The deal is a senior tranche of an RMBS security issued in the first half of 2007.
The price of the deal (PV of cash flows) over the systematic scenarios is plotted
in Figure 9.14, together with the implied distributions of the ABX.HE indexes on
January 12, 2010, for reference. In practice, the scenarios used for the RMBS must
account for the instruments' characteristics, and thus one must apply a proper shift
or adjustment to the implied distribution (or scenario parameters) to account for the
differences between the index collateral pool and the collateral pool of the instrument
to be priced.

While the RMBS is likely not trading at this date, it has a dealer quote of 23.25
(source: Lehman Live). From Figure 9.14, we see that the single scenario that comes
closest to matching this quote represents a default probability of 29 percent (with a
prepayment rate of almost 4 percent and a severity of 67 percent).

As we have not applied a full bottom-up approach, we wish at a minimum to
select a comparable index through some examination of the collateral pools underlying
the RMBS and the indexes. Table 9.11 summarizes some pool-indicative characteristics, which represent the creditworthiness of the collateral of the RMBS, as well as

FIGURE 9.14   Present Value of RMBS across Factor Scenarios (January 12, 2010)

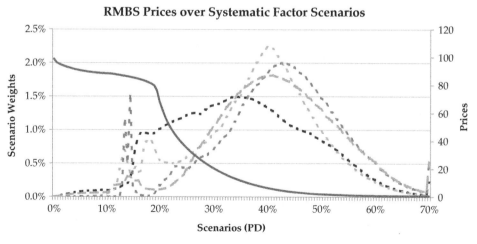

TABLE 9.11 Pool Characteristics for RMBSs and Indexes

Instrument	FICO		LTV		Delinq. 30		Delinq. 60		Delinq. 90		Age		Implied PD	
	Mean	StDev	Mean	StDev	Mean	StDev	Mean	StDev	Mean	StDev	Mean	StDev	Mean	StDev
ABX.HE.06-1	633.01	59.45	79.25	13.63	4.70%	21.16%	3.07%	17.25%	13.72%	34.41%	52.49	2.63	35.22%	12.58%
ABX.HE.06-2	583.57	164.71	78.66	14.11	4.30%	20.29%	3.07%	17.24%	15.62%	36.31%	40.16	16.00	37.97%	11.46%
ABX.HE.07-1	624.55	57.20	79.23	13.51	5.09%	21.98%	3.64%	18.73%	21.45%	41.04%	44.37	14.39	42.29%	11.29%
ABX.HE.07-2	619.71	56.57	80.54	13.64	4.94%	21.68%	3.55%	18.52%	17.95%	38.38%	38.76	8.18	41.53%	11.59%
BSH07HE2	609.90	53.52	80.20	NA	3.66%	18.79%	4.38%	20.47%	42.76%	49.47%	35.37	0.81		

TABLE 9.12 RMBS Prices Calculated with
Various Factor Distributions

Distribution		Price
Market		23.25
ABX.HE.06-1	Implied	24.28
	Copula	23.97
ABX.HE.06-2	Implied	18.31
	Copula	17.07
ABX.HE.07-1	Implied	11.60
	Copula	10.91
ABX.HE.07-2	Implied	12.20
	Copula	12.16

underlying each of the ABX series. Based on most of the characteristics, the closest comparable is the ABX 07-2 series. This vintage comes nearest to matching the RMBS based on FICO scores (both mean and standard deviation); loan-to-value (LTV) statistics are virtually identical across all the ABX indexes, and the mean LTV ratios match closely that of the RMBS. The 30-day delinquency rate of the RMBS is significantly below those of any of the ABX indexes (closest to the 06-2), while the 60-day RMBS delinquency rate is significantly higher than those of the ABX indexes (closest to those of the 07-1 and 07-2 rolls). The 90-day delinquency rate of the RMBS is different from the ABX indexes. At 42.76 percent, it is nearly twice that of the closest ABX index roll (the 07-1 at 21.45 percent). The mean age is also closest to the most recent index roll (07-2).

Table 9.12 shows the prices of the RMBSs calculated using the scenarios and implied factor distribution of each ABX series. Prices computed with the closest Gaussian copula are also given for each of the series.

According to the analysis, the actual price of the RMBSs should be around $12 to $13, based on the 07-2 series's factor distribution. The RMBS dealer quote is almost twice this value, somewhat surprisingly close to that obtained from the 06-1 factor distribution, which has much better quality collateral. Generally, prices computed using the closest Gaussian copulas are near those computed using the implied distributions directly. There are, of course, several possible explanations for this price discrepancy. First, we point to the fact that in recent history market participants (and RMBS holders in particular) have been somewhat reluctant to mark down the prices of MBSs because of the consequent write-down losses suffered. Second, there is a general lack of liquidity in the market, giving rise to large errors in the quotes for both the indexes, and especially the RMBSs. Third, the homogeneous pool assumptions that we are using for the RMBSs and the indexes are not ideal, and are a potential source of model error in this somewhat simplistic analysis. Also, a more detailed analysis of the credit quality of the collateral underlying the RMBSs and the indexes may be required in practice. A more robust prior model could be used, which uses more detailed bottom-up assumptions for the indexes and the RMBSs, leveraging pool-level performance information.

9.6 Conclusion

The role played by the mispricing of structured finance securities in the lead-up to the recent financial meltdown leaves little doubt that the development of better methods for pricing, hedging, and risk management of these instruments is an important priority. Historically, market participants have tended to rely on overly simplistic pricing methods, such as single-scenario models based on credit ratings. Full-scale Monte Carlo approaches have been considered only recently, and remain computationally demanding owing to the requirements of simulating the performance of underlying collateral and the cash flow waterfall.

In this chapter, we have studied a simple and robust method for calibrating the distributions of systematic factors in factor models of portfolio credit risk to the prices of liquid structured instruments, such as indexes of RMBSs. The resulting distributions may then be employed to determine prices (and hedge parameters) of less liquid instruments. The distribution of the systematic factors serves as the vehicle through which information is transferred from observable market prices to bespoke instruments. Since a single implied systematic distribution is employed, it is possible to price all other instruments in a consistent manner.

An illustrative example is presented, which calibrates the distribution of the systematic factor to prices of the ABX indexes. We show how a simple model parametrization performs quite well before and through the credit crisis. Indeed, we can observe the onset of the subprime crisis through the evolution of the implied systematic factor distribution in time. We also present an example illustrating how the implied factor distribution might be used to price an illiquid RMBS.

One of the major advantages of the implied factor distribution approach to pricing structured credit products is its flexibility, which facilitates a complete and consistent bottom-up approach to determining prices of illiquid instruments that are consistent with observed market information. We present a simple parametrization of the model based on homogeneous pool assumptions; a more complete implementation of the model in practice goes beyond the examples presented herein, and employs detailed information regarding the underlying deal collateral. In this manner, structured credit valuations can simultaneously become more sensitive to risk concentrations and more consistent with information provided by the market.

Acknowledgments

Thanks to Benoit Fleury for many helpful comments and suggestions. The authors also gratefully acknowledge financial support from R^2 Financial Technologies (JN, DR, DS), The Fields Institute (DR), the Natural Sciences and Engineering Research Council of Canada (NSERC) (DS), and Fitch Solutions (DR, DS).

Notes

1. See, for example, IOSCO (2008), Senior Supervisors Group (2008), IIF (2008), and Smithson (2008).
2. The word *liquidity* is used in different contexts in the financial literature. In this paper, when we refer to the liquidity of an instrument or market, we mean trading liquidity (i.e., the ability to transact in a timely fashion with low transaction costs, and without undue effect on market prices).
3. In addition, practitioners commonly use a third approach, the collateral market value (net asset value [NAV]) method to monitor these investments (see, for example, Prince 2006). In this case, the underlying collateral is first marked to market (MTM), and one can compute various coverage ratios reflecting how this collateral's MTM covers the different bonds in the structure (if it were to be liquidated).
4. As part of the application of the cash flow waterfall, any requisite overcollateralization (O/C) and interest coverage (I/C) tests are carried out.
5. Hedge parameters, such as sensitivities to default and prepayment rates, can be calculated using the implied distribution and the dual variables of the optimization problem. See Nedeljkovic et al. (2010) for a detailed discussion.
6. It is well known that standard Monte Carlo simulation leads to scenario sets where some scenarios cluster, and does not provide an optimal span of the probability space (see Glasserman 2004). Quasi Monte Carlo (QMC) methods, based on low-discrepancy sequences, for example using Sobol points, provide effective sampling techniques for problems with moderate dimensionality.
7. See Nomura Fixed Income Research (2005) for a description of the PAUG protocol, as well as the mechanics of CDSs on ABSs.
8. Note that the homogeneity assumption, together with the linear discretization in PDs and constant default rates over time, resembles the implied copula model of Hull and White. Here, the factor model plays a more significant role to add correlated stochastic recoveries and prepayments.
9. Note that this is before the introduction of the PEN.AAA index, and consequently market prices for this index are not available on this date.
10. As is common practice, and consistent to available funding, discounting is done with the London Interbank Offered Rate (LIBOR) on the date.
11. The detailed cash flow generation under each scenario is done using Intex.
12. The picture of present values of the indexes' cash flows over the model scenarios is very similar for all the series, and hence we do not reproduce them.
13. The distributions are comparable in the sense that the underlying pools are of roughly the same age at the calibration dates.
14. ABX prices and IR curves for this date are from DataStream.

References

Andersen, L., and J. Sidenius. 2005. Extensions to the Gaussian copula: Random recovery and random factor loadings. *Journal of Credit Risk* 1 (1): 29–70.

Avellaneda, M., R. Buff, C. Friedman, N. Grandchamp, L. Kruk, and J. Newman. 2001. Weighted Monte Carlo: A new technique for calibrating asset-pricing models. *International Journal of Theoretical and Applied Finance* 1:447–472.

Basel Committee on Banking Supervision. 2006. International convergence of capital measurement and capital standards: A revised framework (comprehensive version). (June). Available at www.bis.org.

Brigo, D., A. Pallavacini, and R. Torresetti. 2007. Cluster-based extension of the generalized Poisson loss dynamics and consistency with single names. *International Journal of Theoretical and Applied Finance* 10 (4).

Burtschell, X., J. Gregory, and J.-P. Laurent. 2009. A comparative analysis of CDO pricing models. Available at www.defaultrisk.com.

Dempster, M. A. H., E. A. Medova, and S. W.Yang. 2007. Empirical copulas for CDO tranche pricing using relative entropy. *International Journal of Theoretical and Applied Finance* 10 (4): 679–701.

Economist. 2008. Don't mark to Markit. (March 8).

Fender, I., and M. Scheicher. 2008. The ABX: How do the markets price subprime mortgage risk? *BIS Quarterly Review* (September): 67–81.

Glasserman, P. 2004. *Monte Carlo methods in financial engineering*. New York: Springer.

Goodman, L. S., S. Li, D. J. Lucas, T. A. Zimmerman, and F. J. Fabozzi. 2008. *Subprime mortgage credit derivatives*. Hoboken, NJ: John Wiley & Sons.

Halperin, I. 2009. Implied multi-factor model for bespoke CDO tranches and other portfolio credit derivatives. Working paper, available at www.defaultrisk.com.

Hull, J., and A. White. 2006. Valuing credit derivatives using an implied copula approach. *Journal of Derivatives* (Winter): 1–41.

Hull, J., and A. White. 2008a. Dynamic models of portfolio credit risk: A simplified approach. *Journal of Derivatives* 15 (4): 9–28.

Hull, J., and A. White. 2008b. An improved implied copula model and its application to the valuation of bespoke CDO tranches. Available at www.defaultrisk.com.

IIF (International Institute of Finance). 2008. Final report of the IIF Committee on Market Best Practices: Principles of conduct and best practice recommendations. Available at www.iif.com/regulatory/cmbp.

IOSCO (Technical Committee of the International Organization of Securities Commissions). 2008. Report on the subprime crisis. Available at www.iosco.org/library/pubdocs/pdf/IOSCOPD273.pdf.

Li, D. 2000. On default correlation: A copula function approach. *Journal of Fixed Income* 9:43–54.

Markit. 2006. ABX transactions standard terms supplement. Available at www.markit.com.

McGinty, L., and R. Ahluwalia. 2004. A model for base correlation calculation. JPMorgan Credit Derivatives Strategies.

McNeil, A., P. Embrechts, and G. Frey. 2005. *Quantitative risk management*. Princeton, NJ: Princeton University Press.

Meyer-Dautrich, S., and C. Wagner. 2007. Minimum entropy calibration of CDO tranches. Working paper, UniCredit MIB.

Nedeljkovic, J., D. Rosen, and D. Saunders. 2010. Pricing and hedging CLOs with implied factor models. To appear in the *Journal of Credit Risk*.

Nomura Fixed Income Research. 2005. Synthetic ABS 101: PAUG and ABX.HE. Nomura.

Prince, J. 2006. A general review of CDO valuation methods. *Journal of Structured Finance* 12 (2): 14–21.

Rosen, D., and D. Saunders. 2009. Valuing CDOs of bespoke portfolios with implied multi-factor models. *Journal of Credit Risk* 5 (3): 3–36.

Rubinstein, M. 1994. Implied binomial trees. *Journal of Finance* 49 (3): 771–818.

Schönbucher, P. 2005. Portfolio losses and the term structure of loss transition rates: A new methodology for the pricing of portfolio credit derivatives. Working paper, available at www.defaultrisk.com.

Senior Supervisors Group. 2008. Observations on risk management practices during the recent market turbulence. Available at www.newyorkfed.org/newsevents/news/banking/2008/SSG_Risk_Mgt_doc_final.pdf.

Smithson, C. 2008. Valuing hard-to-value assets. *Risk* (September).

St. Pierre, M., E. Rousseau, J. Zavattero, O. van Esyseren, A. Arora, D. Pugachevsky, M. Fourny, and A. Reyfman. 2004. Valuing and hedging synthetic CDO tranches using base correlations. Bear Stearns Credit Derivatives.

Stanton, R., and N. Wallace. 2008. ABX.HE indexed credit default swaps and the valuation of subprime MBS. University of California–Berkeley, Fisher Center for Real Estate and Urban Economics. Retrieved from http://escholarship.org/uc/item/5s75x0ns.

Vacca, L. 2008. Market implied Archimedian copulas. *Risk* (January).

Vasicek, O. 2002. The distribution of loan portfolio value. *Risk* (December): 160–162.

Walker, M. 2006. CDO models—Towards the next generation: Incomplete markets and term structure. Working paper, available at www.defaultrisk.com.

Wall Street Journal. 2007. A "subprime" gauge in many ways? (December 12).

CHAPTER 10

Toward Market-Implied Valuations of Cash-Flow CLO Structures

Philippos Papadopoulos

ABN Amro Bank

The market for the debt tranches of cash-flow collateralized loan obligations (CLOs) has been historically a ratings-based buy-and-hold market with little secondary trading activity. With the onset of the credit crisis of 2007–2008, this market structure created significant valuation difficulties. In this work we adopt the hypothesis that an observable, derivatives-based tranche market exists, and we build a framework for deriving implied valuations for the various elements of a simplified cash-flow CLO structure. This is achieved by on the one hand transcribing the complex cash flow structure into a term sheet that can be valued using a market-based pricing framework, and on the other hand identifying an adequate loss model to calibrate to market data. The method is implemented via the simulation of a suitably defined Markov chain. We illustrate its use by performing comparisons between synthetic and cash flow structures and illustrating the potentially complex dependence of CLO liability valuation on structural elements. We enumerate further aspects of the CLO that have impact on valuation (such as embedded options) and the model extensions required to capture those.

10.1 Introduction

A typical cash-flow collateralized loan obligation (CLO) is a complex true sale securitization, whereby a diversified pool of credit assets (collateral) is sold into a special purpose vehicle, which in turn issues multiple classes of notes (Lucas 2001). These CLO liabilities are serviced exclusively by the cash flows generated by the collateral assets. One of the key structural features is *subordination*, namely the prioritization of losses to various notes according to their assigned *seniority*. In this respect the cash flow

319

structure is similar to the synthetic CDO contract that is implemented using portfolio credit derivatives technology (Batchvarov and Davletova 2005). The closeness of the naming acronyms belies the substantial differences between the two financial products. Cash-flow CLOs are typically characterized by a large number of structural elements and covenants, which govern very precisely the distribution of income and principal to the issued notes, whereas synthetic structures tend to be considerably simpler.

The market for debt tranches of cash CLOs has been historically a ratings-based, buy-and-hold market with limited market activity after the initial investment. The ratings attached to various rated notes served as indicators of credit quality but also as key drivers for valuation decisions. With the onset of the credit crisis, this market structure created significant valuation difficulties, as ratings became less reliable and the lack of trading prohibited market-based valuation (Basel Committee on Banking Supervision 2008). However, markets for portfolio credit derivatives, in particular those linked to credit indexes, profess to deliver an accessible assessment of market value assigned to different levels of credit loss.[1] Conditional on liquidity of such markets, it is natural to pose the question whether they can serve as an alternative basis for the valuation of various CLO structures. Exploring the answer to this question will be the main preoccupation of this piece. Before we embark on this task, it is worthwhile to review some of the existing techniques for cash-flow CLO valuation.

A common valuation approach is to infer a *credit rating* for a CLO note and then use the rating to compare with observed valuations of other similarly rated notes. The credit rating assignment step is typically done using simulations that capture the individual credit risk profile of entities in the portfolio, along with default correlations. The tools and assumptions used in the calculation are controlled by credit rating agencies, albeit with some parametric flexibility. The simulation and credit rating are thus obtained under some built-in historical measure. The essence of this approach is to identify a market risk premium for tranches that, under the simulation, are shown to exhibit similar loss characteristics (e.g., similar expected loss, or similar probability of loss).

A first observation is that estimating portfolio losses under the historical measure is far from trivial, due to scarcity of data. For example, confidence intervals around estimated historical correlations, to the extent that they are reported at all, are very wide (Servigny and Renault 2003). Those estimates are generally held fixed in time, which implies that valuation differences over time will only be linked to individual asset credit quality changes, not correlation estimate changes. A further weakness of this method is that it cannot provide valuations for the nonrated elements of the structure (management fees, equity), so it does not offer a complete and consistent framework for valuation. The method is also of questionable use when there are significant structural differences between tranches, which cannot be adequately discriminated by a one-dimensional rating measure. In such cases, even if the calculated ratings are similar, the applicable risk premiums may be vastly different.[2] Last, but not least, a collapse of market confidence in the rating methodology eliminates its ability to serve as a benchmark.

An alternative technique is based on an asset-and-liability modeling of the CLO *balance sheet*. Asset cash flows are obtained by simulating a large number of portfolio realization scenarios. Liability cash flows are estimated by processing the portfolio cash flows through the indenture (the CLO contract) and finally computing their present value using an appropriate risky discount factor. This method has a clear advantage over a ratings-based method in that it can, at least in a first step, include nonrated elements of the structure. Also, in this setup contractual features affect directly the cash flow profile, rather than indirectly through the impact on ratings. As with the ratings-based method, the simulation is done under an objective measure, with the same heavy data requirements. The usefulness of this method is limited by the availability of identifiable risk premiums for the various elements of the structure, for example CLO equity. Essentially there is a circularity problem, for if similar CLO structures were traded so as to infer a risk premium per liability class, there would be no need for this mark-to-model exercise. Finally, the method is obviously geared toward valuing the CLO balance sheet on a discounted cash flow (DCF) basis; the various embedded options are difficult to disentangle in this approach.

The starting observation for our work is that if we were to perform the described asset and liability cash flow CLO simulation under a market (pricing) measure and then averaged the cash flows discounted with a risk-free curve, we would indeed have the elements for building a complete valuation framework. Any cash flow structure that prioritizes interest and/or principal payments to CLO notes is thus essentially treated as a correlation product. The immediately required step, then, is to identify a market standard for a calibration of a portfolio loss model to observed synthetic tranche prices. For a robust valuation, the most desirable option would be to obtain as much as possible *model-free* information in the spirit of Walker (2006) and Torresetti, Brigo, and Pallavicini (2007). Unfortunately the path dependency of the CLO requires us to infer a set of consistent loss *paths*, covering all tenors and all loss levels. Hence some model element must be introduced. Alas, the current market standard model, the so-called *base correlation* approach (McGinty, Beinstein, Ahluwalia, and Watts 2004), is structurally unsuitable for the task, as it does not produce a set of loss paths that can simultaneously price all maturities and subordinations. In this chapter we explore, instead, how a general *top-down* modeling framework can be used for the valuation of the different elements of the CLO structure. For our purposes, a top-down approach (see Giesecke 2008 and Bielecki, Crépey, and Jeanblanc 2008 for recent reviews) is attractive, since it can calibrate to the entire set of market information (prices for tranches of various tenors and subordination levels) but retains a certain modeling simplicity that is lost in a multidimensional, name-level, specification (Duffie and Garleanu 2001). We caution, though, that the problem of calibrating a top-down loss process to tranche spreads is still a research topic (Cont and Minca 2008), and a market standard is not apparent. For this reason we adopt here a simplified framework and we will not advocate any particular specification.

The structure of the chapter is as follows: In Section 10.2 we discuss a complete, if somewhat simplified, mathematical translation of a cash-flow CLO structure. Such a step is essential for the transparent application of a valuation framework (CLO prospectuses provide generally lengthy *verbal* descriptions of the structure and pay-offs). Section 10.3 outlines a valuation framework based on a discrete time–discrete state version of the so-called top-down approach for credit risk modeling. The emphasis here is on an adequate set of principles rather than a production-oriented specification and calibration. Ideally, a market standard set of assumptions should develop, on which to base valuations of more complex structures. We illustrate how this framework can be, in principle, calibrated to synthetic tranche markets and then used to value the more complex CLO liabilities. In Section 10.4 we illustrate the application of the method to a typical structure and make a preliminary exploration of the key sensitivities. We conclude with Section 10.5, where we review the many simplifications and approximations that were required along the road and some possibilities for future work that may enhance the applicability of the method in a practical context.

10.2 Description of the Cash-Flow CLO Structure

We begin with a description of the cash-flow CLO structure. The definitive description of the the structure and the contractual arrangements under diverse sets of circumstances is always given in the so-called offering circular or prospectus, which is a legal document (indenture) describing in great detail all aspects of the CLO.[3]

While some commonalities and patterns are apparent in different CLOs, the very large number of elements in the prospectus means that variability can be introduced very easily. For example, the omission or inclusion of a few lines can substantially change the benefits of subordination to the various liabilities. In the following we abstract some of those common patterns, with no claim for completeness. An incomplete list of elements that are omitted is given in Section 10.5. There is, though, one aspect of CLOs that is of such importance that we discuss it here: Most CLOs are *managed*; that is, an asset manager is mandated to actively acquire, monitor, and steer the portfolio, including buy and sell decisions for individual assets and, if required, entering into workout procedures for defaulted assets. Even with the portfolio constraints usually outlined in the prospectus, the valuation of a structure allowing so much freedom is beyond the scope of the current work. Instead, we imagine the CLO already set up and in operation and the portfolio in a frozen run-off mode. This is a valid simplifying assumption that will, in principle, produce an unambiguous and useful valuation. Unfortunately, the maturity mismatch of typical assets (three- to five-year loans) versus the CLO notes (10 or more years) means that a frozen portfolio view cannot be taken too literally. In reality the asset manager is required to use repayments to purchase new assets at future times (there are, for example, minimum portfolio spread covenants). To a first approximation those future purchases do not, individually, add or subtract present value to the *asset portfolio*, as they are assumed to occur at future market prices. But those reinvestment choices can have an uneven impact on the value of the *liabilities* (a classic example is the systematic purchase of deeply discounted loans that still conform with rating criteria). In any case we will sidestep

FIGURE 10.1 Schematic Representation of a Discrete Time–Discrete State Approximation of the Portfolio Default Process

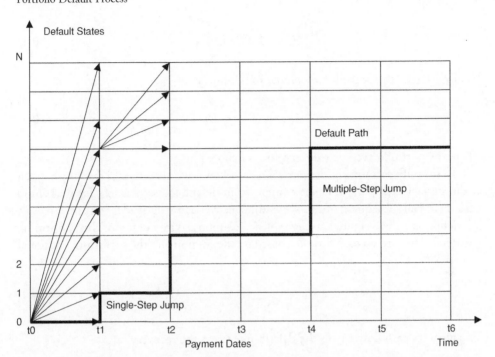

In the most general specification, all transition rates are freely specifiable. This creates significantly more degrees of freedom than market data. Ideally one would want to see more limited and natural degrees of freedom (i.e., those that best capture market sentiment about loss paths).

this difficult issue and throughout this study we assume maturity-matched assets and liabilities.

The first step will be a simplified description of the portfolio state and the associated cash flows. We introduce a time grid (discrete time approximation), with the current time denoted as $t_0 = 0$ and n subsequent periods separated by time points t_k. It is simple and convenient to identify this time grid with the schedule of payment dates (e.g., quarterly), but in the concrete numerical examples we will use an annual grid. The normalized default process D_k captures the fraction of the defaulted portfolio. It starts at zero, is nondecreasing in time, and is bounded by unity (see Figure 10.1). D_k takes discrete values, $D_k = \delta_i$, with $i \in [0, N]$. Those discrete values represent approximations to the actual defaulted fraction of the portfolio. While we will never actually specify the number of underlying credits, implicitly the assumption is that this number is substantially larger than N.

Linked to the default process is the surviving portfolio process, N_k, which denotes the fraction of the portfolio surviving at time t_k and is defined as one minus the default process at any time t, $N_k = 1 - D_k$, with ($N_0 = 1$). The hazard rate, λ_k, denotes the fraction of the surviving portfolio that is lost between time t_{k-1} and time t_k.

The reduction of the performing portfolio due to defaults is then governed by the iterative equation:

$$N_k = (1 - \lambda_k)N_{k-1} \tag{10.1}$$

Finally, we take the portfolio *loss process* to be simply:

$$L_k = (1 - g)D_k \tag{10.2}$$

where the portfolio average recovery rate is denoted by g.[4]

To simplify accounting the portfolio cash flows, we assume that defaults happen at the start of each period; hence coupon from defaulted assets is lost for that entire period (and all subsequent ones). We assume recoveries are delayed by one period only. We define as c the weighted average spread (coupon payment rate) of the performing collateral. The interest cash flow w_k, based on the coupon and the performing notional is then

$$w_k = c \ N_k \tag{10.3}$$

The recovery cash flow equals the default rate times the recovery rate:

$$r_k = g \ \lambda_k \ N_{k-1} \tag{10.4}$$

Throughout the document we will ignore the level of the risk-free interest rates. This is to avoid further loading up the notation and is motivated by the fact that the interest rate risk of the CLO is (in theory) hedged. We keep track of portfolio cash flow collections with the *interest proceeds* account I_k and the *principal proceeds* account P_k. The interest and recovery cash flows will accumulate during each period into the interest proceeds, respectively principal proceeds accounts. At least one additional account present in most structures is a cash or reserve account a_k. This account absorbs any cash that either is left incidentally or must be maintained contractually within the structure.

The CLO liability structure involves M *bonds*, indexed by $m = 1, \ldots, M$ in order of decreasing seniority, plus an equity position. We denote B_0^m the initial bond sizes and E_0 the initial equity size. The bond size may be reduced by contractual repayments or be increased by the addition of deferred interest (payment-in-kind feature). In contrast to typical synthetic structures, the notional of a CLO bond is *not* contractually reduced due to defaults during the life of the transaction (except for the adjustments mentioned earlier). Such reduction may be implicit in accumulating notional losses in the portfolio, but is normally only revealed as an explicit notional write-down (loss) when, as per the terms of the indenture, the bond must be redeemed and there are no available funds.

It is useful to define the *supported debt level* for a bond; that is, the sum of total bond sizes down to and including the mth bond:

$$\sigma_k^m = \sum_{j=1}^{m} B_k^j \tag{10.5}$$

The *overcollateralization* (OC) for the various bonds is then defined as:

$$L_k^m = \frac{\bar{N}_k}{\sigma_k^m} \tag{10.6}$$

We used in the numerator an *adjusted outstanding notional*:

$$\bar{N}_k = N_k + r_k \tag{10.7}$$

which includes in the ratio principal recoveries, in order to properly reflect the current leverage.[5]

Each CLO bond has an associated bond spread, c^m, which at any given period leads to *scheduled* interest payments, $S_k^m = c^m B_k^m$. Subject to the availability of funds and payment waterfall, each note will receive an *actual* bond payment b_k^m. Residual cash flows, after all debt servicing and costs, are paid out as dividend d_k to the equity interest. Scheduled interest that is *not* paid during a payment period (i.e., when $b_k^m < S_k^m$) is added to the outstanding notional of the bond as deferred interest[6]

$$B_k^m := B_k^m + S_k^m - b_k^m \tag{10.8}$$

This treatment is generally not applicable to senior notes, where missed interest payments will trigger an event of default and lead to an unwinding of the structure. For simplicity we assume that this deferred interest property applies to all notes.

The liabilities of a CLO also include asset manager fees. Those typically accrue on the par amount of the collateral. In order to align the interests of the manager with the various stakeholders, the fees are split into senior and mezzanine (or junior). There may be also contingent incentive fees that are linked to the performance of the CLO's equity tranche. We assume a simple fee schedule, with two fee components: senior fees denoted ϕ^{sen} and mezzanine fees denoted ϕ^{mez}. The absolute amount of scheduled fee payments in period k are then given by $F_k^{sen} = \phi^{sen} N_k$ and $F_k^{mez} = \phi^{mez} N_k$.

In addition to these leverage considerations, we define interest coverage ratios as running measures of the debt service payment ability. This measure is defined as the ratio of the *interest coverage amount* (IC), $\bar{w}_k = w_k - F_k^{sen}$ (defined as the current interest proceeds minus scheduled senior fees), over the cumulative scheduled interest payments down to the bond under consideration:

$$l_k^m = \frac{\bar{w}_k}{\kappa_k^m} \tag{10.9}$$

where we have defined the *supported debt service level*, κ_k^m:

$$\kappa_k^m = \sum_{j=1}^m c^j B_k^j = \sum_{j=1}^m S_k^j \tag{10.10}$$

10.2.1   Early Amortization Triggers

The cash flow structure is distinguished by the fact that the running leverage and debt service ratios (L_k^m, l_k^m) are checked at payments dates against some prespecified (and constant) triggers or barriers (L_B^m, l_B^m). Depending on the outcome of those comparisons, the indenture may modify the manner in which interest and principal payments are distributed to the various notes and equity. For the sake of simplicity, we assume here that each bond has an associated overcollateralization and interest coverage (OC/IC) pair of tests, whereas in practice several bonds may share a pair of tests. Those triggers are designed to protect the senior notes by diverting cash from subordinated notes and equity. The trigger coverage ratios are generally set lowest for the subordinated notes, next lowest for the mezzanine notes and highest for the senior notes. Hence subordinated note tests are breached earlier than mezzanine note tests and so on. We assume, as is usual in practice, that the two types of tests are examined in pairs and only the joint outcome affects the waterfall; that is, we are primarily interested in the joint indicator

$$J_k^m = 1_{\{L_k^m > L_B^m, l_k^m > l_B^m\}} \tag{10.11}$$

If the mth OC test fails during a period, the payment waterfall may require that at that point principal is (re)paid sequentially to all notes senior to or equal to the seniority of the test level, until the failing mth test is met. For example, if the second (Class B) OC/IC test fails, we need to repay notional to the Class A and Class B notes. For each OC test we define the supportable notional size Q_k^m:

$$Q_k^m = \frac{\bar{N}_k}{L_B^m} \tag{10.12}$$

This is the (reduced) size of the various bonds that will restore the OC indicator for this period to performing. The *scheduled notional reduction* of the lth bond for curing the mth OC test will be given (recursively, starting from the senior-most bond) by the expression

$$\delta T_k^{lm} = \max(\min(\sigma_k^m - \sum_{j=1}^{l-1} \delta T_k^{jm} - Q_k^m, B_k^l), 0) \tag{10.13}$$

The meaning of this expression is simply that the currently supported debt level σ_k^m must be reduced, iteratively, by repaying one bond at a time, to the supportable level Q_k^m by pursuing all possible bond reductions, starting from the senior-most ($m = 1$) bond and at each iteration taking into account previous reductions while taking care that bonds can only be paid down to zero.

Similarly, if the mth IC test is failing, the indenture requires that principal is repaid sequentially to all senior notes until the test is met. We define the supportable bond notional for each IC test:

$$R_k^m = \frac{\bar{w}_k}{l_B^m} \tag{10.14}$$

The *scheduled debt service reduction* of the lth bond, for curing the mth IC test, will be given (recursively) by the expression

$$\Delta P_k^{lm} = \max(\min(\kappa_k^m - \sum_{j=1}^{l-1} \Delta P_k^{jm} - R_k^m, S_k^l), 0) \tag{10.15}$$

Obviously, reducing the debt service can be achieved only via a corresponding *notional* reduction of the notes. Once we have computed the required spread reduction, using the bond coupon we calculate the required notional reduction of the lth bond, for curing the mth IC test:

$$\Delta T_k^{lm} = \frac{\Delta P_k^{lm}}{c^l} \tag{10.16}$$

Due to the customary joint application of the OC/IC tests, we combine the reduction requirements δT_k^{lm} and ΔT_k^{lm} into:

$$\partial T_k^{lm} = \max(\delta T_k^{lm}, \Delta T_k^{lm}) \tag{10.17}$$

Obviously, the required joint reduction ∂T_k^{lm} can be achieved only up to available funds. To keep track of the success of the leverage reduction operations, we introduce the indicator

$$C_k^m = 1_{\{\sum_{j=1}^{m} \partial T_k^{jm} = 0\}} \tag{10.18}$$

which at any point in the payment flow identifies whether the required payments for the mth test have been reduced to zero (hence satisfying the test). With the definitions given so far we are ready to provide a precise definition of the cash flow waterfall.

10.2.2   Priority of Payments (Waterfall)

The priority of payments (also known as the *payment waterfall*) refers to the sequence in which payments must be made to the various liabilities. Most CDOs make sequential repayment of principal. This means that the principal of the senior-most outstanding class is repaid fully before any repayment of principal is made to the next class. Occasionally notes with different interest rate characteristics may still be paired from a credit perspective and hence be repaid pro rata, namely according to the size of each bond. In most payment waterfalls, payments are made first from interest proceeds and then, if required and possible, from principal proceeds. In more detail, during a regular payment date, the waterfall goes through the following flowchart:

1. *Payment of senior fees.* Use the available interest proceeds account I_k to pay the senior fees F_k^{sen}. We denote *actual* fee payments made to senior and mezzanine bonds as f_k^{sen} and f_k^{mez} respectively. Here and later on, we denote this type of payment mathematically via the vector payment function $\mathcal{P}$,

$$\{F_k^{sen}, I_k, f_k^{sen}\} := \mathcal{P}(F_k^{sen}, I_k, f_k^{sen}) \tag{10.19}$$

   which acts on a triplet of inputs and produces a triplet of outputs as follows:

$$f_k^{sen} = \min(F_k^{sen}, I_k) \tag{10.20}$$

$$I_k := \max(0, I_k - F_k^{sen}) \tag{10.21}$$

$$F_k^{sen} := F_k^{sen} - f_k^{sen} \tag{10.22}$$

   where, as noted before, the sequence of equations is important and the $:=$ symbol denotes an update. Hence the payment function calculates the actual payment made f_k^{sen}, debits the paying account I_k, and adjusts the scheduled payment F_k^{sen} to reflect the transaction.

   If there is a shortfall in senior fees payment, the waterfall uses the principal proceeds account P_k to compensate:

$$\{F_k^{sen}, P_k, f_k^{sen}\} := \mathcal{P}(F_k^{sen}, P_k, f_k^{sen}) \tag{10.23}$$

2. *Payment of interest to senior bonds.* Use any remaining interest proceeds I_k to pay scheduled interest to senior notes. At this point the interest waterfall receives funds from the principal waterfall and any fund in the reserve account to make up (if possible) for any shortfall in paying the senior notes coupon. After all is said

and done, we increment the senior bond notional B_k^1 with any interest payment shortfall:

$$\{S_k^1, I_k, b_k^1\} := \mathcal{P}(S_k^1, I_k, b_k^1) \tag{10.24}$$

$$\{S_k^1, P_k, b_k^1\} := \mathcal{P}(S_k^1, P_k, b_k^1) \tag{10.25}$$

$$\{S_k^1, a_k, b_k^1\} := \mathcal{P}(S_k^1, a_k, b_k^1) \tag{10.26}$$

$$B_k^1 := B_k^1 + S_k^1 \tag{10.27}$$

3. *Mezzanine bond interest payments loop.* In this portion of the waterfall, a loop of identical operations is performed for every OC/IC test $m = 1, \ldots, M - 1$. For each test, we check the mth joint indicator J_k^m. (The junior-most OC/IC test J_k^M will allow equity payments rather than bond payments and is hence treated separately.)

(a) If $J_k^m = 1$, pay scheduled interest to the $m + 1$ notes from the interest proceeds I_k. (So, e.g., the Class B notes will receive payment if the Class A passes the OC/IC test).

$$\{S_k^{m+1}, I_k, b_k^{m+1}\} := \mathcal{P}(S_k^{m+1}, I_k, b_k^{m+1}) \tag{10.28}$$

$$B_k^{m+1} := B_k^{m+1} + S_k^{m+1} \tag{10.29}$$

Once the payments have been made, the loop proceeds to the next lower OC/IC test.

(b) If $J_k^m = 0$, we enter into OC/IC cure mode. In the first instance we use interest proceeds I_k, to sequentially amortize principal on notes down to the mth note, and then attempt to meet any shortfall using notional reduction from principal proceeds P_k or the reserve account a_k. In sequence for each of the notes $j = 1, \ldots, m$ this leads to the following updates.

$$\{\partial T_k^{jm}, I_k, \widetilde{b}_k^j\} := \mathcal{P}(\partial T_k^{jm}, I_k, \widetilde{b}_k^j) \tag{10.30}$$

$$\{\partial T_k^{jm}, P_k, \widetilde{b}_k^j\} := \mathcal{P}(\partial T_k^{jm}, P_k, \widetilde{b}_k^j) \tag{10.31}$$

$$\{\partial T_k^{jm}, a_k, \widetilde{b}_k^j\} := \mathcal{P}(\partial T_k^{jm}, a_k, \widetilde{b}_k^j) \tag{10.32}$$

where we introduced the auxiliary variable $\widetilde{b}_k^j$. This variable is initialized at zero before each update and stores temporarily the principal repayment that is possible from the various cash sources, as indicated in equations (10.30), (10.31), and (10.32). After each of the updates, the computed principal repayment is assigned to the actual bond (re)payment [equation (10.33)] and the corresponding bond size reduction [equation (10.34)].

$$b_k^j := b_k^j + \widetilde{b}_k^j \tag{10.33}$$

$$B_k^j := B_k^j - \widetilde{b}_k^j \tag{10.34}$$

We next check the indicator C_k^m, which expresses whether there were enough funds to achieve the necessary reductions.

(i) If $C_k^m = 1$, the required notional reduction has been achieved. Now the waterfall reverts back to Point 3a of the mezzanine portion.

(ii) If $C_k^m = 0$, the required reduction was not successful. We now have exhausted all funds and simply defer interest on notes from $(m + 1)$ onward, while equity receives no dividend this period. Hence for $j = m + 1, \ldots, M$:

$$b_k^j = 0 \qquad (10.35)$$

$$B_k^j := B_k^j + S_k^j \qquad (10.36)$$

$$d_k = 0 \qquad (10.37)$$

After the adjustments, we proceed directly to the next period.

4. *Payment of mezzanine fees.* Use the available interest proceeds account I_k to pay the mezzanine fees F_k^{mez}. In contrast to the senior fees, principal cash flows are not used to pay mezzanine fees.

$$\{F_k^{mez}, I_k, f_k^{mez}\} := \mathcal{P}(F_k^{mez}, I_k, f_k^{mez}) \qquad (10.38)$$

5. *Payment of equity dividends.* In this portion of the waterfall, passing the junior-most OC/IC test J_k^M leads to equity payments. The leftover interest proceeds reaching this stage are commonly referred to as *excess spread*. Leftover principal proceeds are held in a reserve account.

(a) If $J_k^M = 1$, pay any remaining interest proceeds I_k to equity:

$$d_k = I_k$$

$$a_k := a_{k-1} + P_k$$

$$I_k := 0$$

$$P_k := 0$$

The payment waterfall is now complete and we move to the next period.

(b) If $J_k^M = 0$, similarly to the mezzanine loop, we use any remaining interest and principal proceeds to sequentially amortize *all* the notes, until the test is cured. Hence for each of the notes $j = 1, \ldots, M$:

$$\{\partial T_k^{jM}, I_k, \tilde{b}_k^j\} := \mathcal{P}(\partial T_k^{jM}, I_k, \tilde{b}_k^j) \qquad (10.39)$$

$$\{\partial T_k^{jM}, P_k, \tilde{b}_k^j\} := \mathcal{P}(\partial T_k^{jM}, P_k, \tilde{b}_k^j) \qquad (10.40)$$

$$\{\partial T_k^{jM}, a_k, \tilde{b}_k^j\} := \mathcal{P}(\partial T_k^{jM}, a_k, \tilde{b}_k^j) \qquad (10.41)$$

where again $\widetilde{b}_k^j$ is used to store intermediate results and assign them (per repayment source) to bond payments and bond size reductions:

$$b_k^j := b_k^j + \widetilde{b}_k^j \qquad (10.42)$$

$$B_k^j := B_k^j - \widetilde{b}_k^j \qquad (10.43)$$

We now check whether the Mth (junior) OC/IC cure has been successful. We check the indicator C_k^M.

(i) If $C_k^M = 1$, the required notional reduction has been achieved. The waterfall reverts back to Point 5a.

(ii) If $C_k^M = 0$, the required reduction was not successful. Equity receives no payment for this period.

$$d_k = 0 \qquad (10.44)$$

We now have exhausted all funds and simply move on to the next period.

At maturity (t_n), all notes receive final scheduled coupon and principal (if possible). Schematically:

- Accumulate the interest and principal proceeds into the reserve account a_n.

$$a_n := a_{n-1} + N_n + I_n + P_n \qquad (10.45)$$

- For all bonds $j = 1, \ldots, M$, attempt sequential repayment of principal and accrued coupons.

$$\{S_n^j, a_n, b_n^j\} := \mathcal{P}(S_n^j, a_n, b_n^j) \qquad (10.46)$$

- Any remaining funds accumulate to the equity interest.

$$d_T = a_T \qquad (10.47)$$

A similar sequential scheme would apply also in the event of liquidation, if such event is triggered during the life of the transaction, with the proviso that it is market value rather than par value that will be collected.

10.3 Description of the Valuation Framework

After a substantial amount of notational gymnastics, we managed to describe the CLO cash flow payments within a few pages. This rococo facade should not obscure the fact that it is ultimately only the cash flow variables, (I_k, P_k), that drive all payments. Hence in order to value general payoffs defined in terms of these, we only need the market-implied distribution of the default process D_k (i.e., a set of loss paths with attached market-implied probabilities).

The discrete-time, discrete default rate framework (Figure 10.1) we adopted is still very general. At this stage it is generally assumed that the default process has the Markov property. The validity of this assumption can be answered empirically with the successful calibration to market data. For simple contracts that are primarily sensitive to marginal distributions of the loss process this may be always the case,[7] but a priori there seems to be no reason to suppose that a market of path-dependent contracts can be fit by a Markov process, as it can well be the case that the market is implying non-Markov dependence. It is, for example, rather implausible that the probability of reaching a certain loss level at a given time t_2 is priced identically (once given the loss level at an earlier time t_1), irrespectively of the loss history up to time t_1.

In a continuous-time framework one then has the further separation into single-jump approaches versus multiple-jump approaches. See Brigo, Pallavicini, and Torresetti (2006) for the related discussion. In our discrete time framework the natural specification is a multiple-jump approach. Hence the default process will be developing according to the equation

$$P(D_k = \delta_i) = \sum_{j=0}^{i} P(D_{k-1} = \delta_j) P(D_k = \delta_i | D_{k-1} = \delta_j) \qquad (10.48)$$

or in more concise notation

$$p_k^i = \sum_{j=0}^{i} p_{k-1}^j T_{k,k-1}^{ji} \qquad (10.49)$$

Any of the Markov top-down models for the loss process proposed in the literature, once calibrated to current market data, can be integrated between given time points to derive market-consistent transition matrices $T_{k,k-1}^{ji}$. Hence, we do not dwell on this further and we will take the calibration for granted. For exploratory purposes we will use transition matrices that conform to the following specification:

$$T_{k,k-1}^{ji} = \alpha_k^{i-j} \lambda_k^j \qquad (10.50)$$

where

$$\lambda_k^j = \frac{1}{\sum_{h=0}^{N-j} \alpha_k^h} \qquad (10.51)$$

This family ensures that the number of transition rates per period is the same as the number of states per period and hence may lead to a potentially unique calibration if the number of traded tranches is sufficiently dense, but it is at present unclear under what conditions this uniqueness would be guaranteed.

10.3.1 Synthetic Tranche Valuation

In order to facilitate the comparison with the cash CLO structure, we will assume that a family $m = 1, \ldots M$ of synthetic tranches, available for each tenor t_k, with $k = 1, \ldots n$, are structured in a funded, credit-linked note form.[8] The mth tranche with tenor t_k has attachment point L^m and detachment point U^m (attachment and detachment points are assumed independent of tenor) and offers a spread of s_k^m. For simplicity we take the available tenors to coincide with the interest payment periods. The protection seller purchases (at time t_0) a note at par value $U^m - L^m$ and receives a fixed premium s_k^m per period, applied to the outstanding tranche size at the beginning of the period, in return for accepting principal losses on the tranche during the period. Portfolio losses are attributed to the mth tranche if they exceed point L^m but not point U^m. Hence the cumulative tranche loss TL_k^m of a tranche with tenor t_k is given by the expression:

$$\text{TL}_k^m = \min(U^m - L^m, \max(L_k - L^m, 0)) \tag{10.52}$$

Note that by definition we have $\text{TL}_0^m = 0$. Also, in our simplified time grid, the variable TL_l^m indicates the tranches' losses at time t_l for all tranches with tenor larger than or equal to t_l.

Since we assumed deterministic and fixed recovery, the expected tranche losses are linked to the default process via

$$E[\text{TL}_k^m] = E[\min(U^m - L^m, \max((1 - g)D_k - L^m, 0))] \tag{10.53}$$

The value of interest cash flows is the sum of spread income over all periods $l = 1, \ldots k$, taking into account the outstanding tranche notional applicable for each period:

$$\text{PV}(I_k^m) = s_k^m \sum_{l=1}^k E[U^m - L^m - \text{TL}_{l-1}^m] \tag{10.54}$$

$$= k \, s_k^m (U^m - L^m) - s_k^m \sum_{l=1}^k E[\text{TL}_{l-1}^m] \tag{10.55}$$

The principal cash flows of the mth tranche will be the original principal ($U^m - L^m$), repaid at maturity (t_k), minus the loss compensation payments, with a PV of

$$\text{PV}(P_k^m) = U^m - L^m - E[\text{TL}_k^m] \tag{10.56}$$

The value of the mth tranche is thus

$$\text{PV}(I_k^m + P_k^m) = (1 + k \, s_k^m)(U^m - L^m) - s_k^m \sum_{l=1}^k E[\text{TL}_{l-1}^m] - E[\text{TL}_k^m] \tag{10.57}$$

In the context of a finite-state Markov chain we will approximate the expected tranche loss calculation as

$$E[\text{TL}_k^m] = \sum_{i=0}^{N} p_k^i \min(U^m - L^m, \max((1-g)\delta_i - L^m, 0)) \qquad (10.58)$$

Hence, as one might have expected, given a calibrated set of transition matrices $T_{k,k-1}^{ji}$, or the state probabilities p_k^i, the valuation of a synthetic tranche is an analytic exercise.

10.3.2   Cash-Flow CLO Valuation

The value of each of the bonds, senior and mezzanine management fees, and equity will be the sum of the respective expected payments:

$$\text{PV}(B^m) = \sum_{k=1}^{n} E[b_k^m] \qquad (10.59)$$

$$\text{PV}(f^{sen}) = \sum_{k=1}^{n} E[f_k^{sen}] \qquad (10.60)$$

$$\text{PV}(f^{mez}) = \sum_{k=1}^{n} E[f_k^{mez}] \qquad (10.61)$$

$$\text{PV}(E) = \sum_{k=1}^{n} E[d_k] \qquad (10.62)$$

These expressions are at first glance too complex for analytic computation. Payments are path dependent and we must average over all paths with their respective probabilities. A bond payment b_k^m at a given period is primarily a function of the current cash flows (I_k, P_k), but via the state of the OC/IC test indicators, the possibly deferred interest state of any bond, the state of the reserve account, and so on, it also depends on the cash flows of previous periods.

While for each given path it is easy to compute the associated probability, the number of paths is exploding as the number of discrete states increases. This state of affairs can be contrasted with the use of a single-factor model to derive credit risk measures for CLOs (Papadopoulos and Tan 2007). There, conditional on a factor realization, the path is completely described; hence, path-dependent entities can easily be computed and the expectation is reduced to an integral. Here we will instead resort to simulation of the Markov chain as a means for estimating the expectations. The procedure is fairly straightforward: For each simulated path we compute the set (I_k, P_k) and calculate payments to liabilities by applying for each period the waterfall of payments.

10.4 Numerical Examples

Here we explore the valuation framework for plausible sets of input values and for schematic structures. Our valuation target is a simplified, senior-mezzanine cash flow structure that we juxtapose to a three-tranche synthetic configuration. As mentioned previously, in this first investigation we do not use market data but instead a more controllable parametric specification for the transition matrix. More precisely, we take the first-period jumps to be given by a Gaussian copula derived model, which produces known distribution moments. Subsequent periods see transitions according to a simple replicating pattern: The relative probability of a jump of a given size versus no jump is always the same as the ratio observed in the first period, as per the specification of equation (10.50). This prescription fixes the transition probabilities for all periods and states. A concrete set of marginal probability distributions is illustrated in Figure 10.2.

FIGURE 10.2   The Evolution of the Probability Distribution of the Default Rate

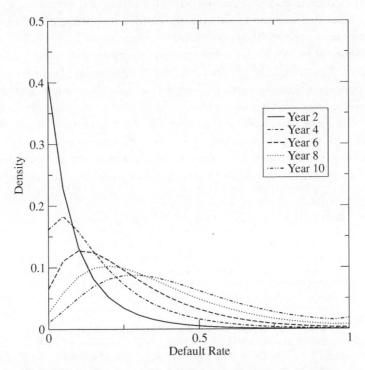

The time interval spans 10 periods, of which only the even periods are shown. The first-year transition matrix is injected directly as a precomputed model. Subsequent period matrices are simple repetitions (i.e., there is no time inhomogeneity). The state space consists of 21 states, with the 0th state corresponding to zero defaults in the portfolio and the 21st state corresponding to a fully defaulted portfolio. As the density evolves, the boundary condition on the right becomes visible.

TABLE 10.1 Parameters of Synthetic Structure

	Tranche Parameters			Zero-Loss Cash Flows		
Name	Lower Bound	Upper Bound	Spread	Per Annum	Total Coupon	Total
Equity	0.00	0.15	0.1	0.015	0.15	0.3
Mezzanine	0.15	0.30	0.01	0.0015	0.015	0.165
Senior	0.30	1.00	0.005	0.0035	0.035	0.735
Sum				0.02	0.2	1.2

10.4.1 Comparison of a Synthetic versus Cash Flow Structure

The parameters of the synthetic structure are shown in Table 10.1. In order to align as much as possible with the cash flow configuration, we calculate the zero-loss cash flows explicitly (right-hand side of the table).

The cash flow structure must be simplified substantially before we can attempt a comparison. In this direction we ignore (in this subsection only) the triggers of cash flow diversion. We also assume there are no management fees. The tranche and bond sizes are arranged so that they match initially. The spreads of the synthetic tranches are arranged so that the total spread matches the coupon rate of the cash flow portfolio. The parameters of the simplified configuration are shown in Table 10.2.

It is important to note here that the cash flow equity position is contractually quite distinct from the synthetic equity tranche, as it receives *residual* cash flows only and those can be obtained only from the performing portfolio. In contrast, synthetic equity has a guaranteed spread. The impact of this difference can most vividly be illustrated by performing a valuation under the assumption of *full recoveries*. That is, we assume that defaults do not lead to material loss (but they do remove performing loans from the portfolio!). In this case, the synthetic tranche notional would never decrease. In contrast, the spread income available to the cash flow structure is decreasing with each

TABLE 10.2 Parameters of Simplified Cash-Flow Structure

	Asset Parameters		Zero-Loss Cash Flows		
Portfolio	Size	Spread	Per Annum	Total Coupon	Total
Loans	1.0	0.02	0.02	0.2	1.2

	Liability Parameters		Zero-Loss Cash Flows		
Name	Size	Spread	Per Annum	Total Coupon	Total
Equity	0.15	N/A	0.015	0.15	0.3
Mezzanine	0.15	0.01	0.0015	0.015	0.165
Senior	0.70	0.005	0.0035	0.035	0.735
Sum			0.02	0.2	1.2

TABLE 10.3   Synthetic versus Cash Flow Valuation in Case of Full Recovery

Synthetic Structure		Cash Structure					
Equity	0.3000	Equity	0.2886	0.2771	0.2536	0.2092	0.1534
Mezzanine	0.1650	Mezzanine	0.1650	0.1650	0.1650	0.1650	0.1652
Senior	0.7350	Senior	0.7350	0.7350	0.7350	0.7350	0.7351
		Default rate	10.0%	20.0%	40.0%	76.6%	95.0%

additional default. The impact on valuation can be seen in Table 10.3, for a range of different expected terminal default rates. The cash flow equity valuation asymptotes to the principal-only value, as it is expected to receive progressively less and less income. The bonds, in contrast, retain their value (and may even gain slightly, since payment shortfalls will get capitalized). In practice the differences in equity performance will not be that extreme, because under a typical indenture the recoveries must be reinvested in performing assets.

Next we examine the sensitivity of the two structures to the expected loss rate and the volatility of the loss rate. We make an assumption of 60 percent recovery rate. The fixed recovery assumption does have the unfortunate implication that the senior tranche losses can never exceed a certain level (here maximum portfolio losses are 40 percent and hence principal losses for the senior tranches that have 30 percent subordination are limited to about 14 percent of notional).

As mentioned already, we control the multiperiod loss distributions only by modifying the first period input. Out of the many sensitivities that can be computed, we focus on the terminal (last period) expected loss rate and the volatility of the last period loss rate.

The valuation sensitivity to expected loss rate is shown in Figure 10.3. Probably the most interesting aspect is the fact that the cash equity retains marginally higher value as losses increase. This is the balance of two effects: As losses increase, performing assets are removed from the portfolio, which we assumed are not replaced. Hence spread income available to cash equity decreases. But whereas the synthetic equity notional decreases with each default (and hence future income decreases), this is not the case for cash equity.

Moving on to the sensitivities to higher moments of the distribution, we examine the volatility of the loss rate. This is obviously linked to the concept of *default correlation*. The valuation sensitivity to the volatility of the loss rate is shown in Figure 10.4. The familiar patterns are seen (e.g., equity tranches increasing in value with increased volatility). The most conclusive result is that the cash equity retains more value for low volatility.

10.4.2   Impact of OC Triggers and Management Fees

We introduce the next layer of structure into the cash-flow CLO, namely the OC/IC triggers. For simplicity we explore OC triggers only. Given the presence of two bonds,

FIGURE 10.3   Illustration of the Dependence of Tranche Values on the Expected Loss Rate

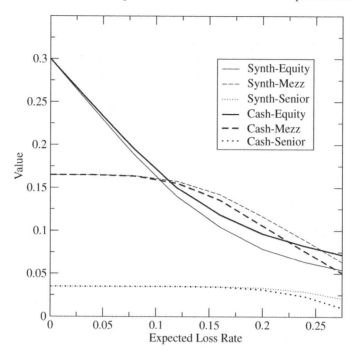

Our standard pair of synthetic and cash flow structures is valued using a loss model with an increasing terminal expected loss rate. For very low expected loss rates, the valuation converges to the zero-loss valuations of Tables 10.1 and 10.2. For the senior tranche we subtract the par value of 0.7 for clarity. Of course with increasing loss expectations all tranches lose value and the convexity is, as expected, positive for equity and negative for mezzanine/senior. It is quite noticeable that cash equity retains better valuation, at the expense of mezzanine and senior cash bonds.

there will be two OC ratios and two OC triggers to monitor L_B^1, L_B^2. Hence there is a two-dimensional parameter space. In the limit of very low OC trigger levels (i.e., cash flow diversion occurs only for very low OC ratios, or equivalently very high leverage), the diversion mechanism will have minimal impact and the valuation asymptotes to a trigger-less structure. In the limit of very high trigger levels, the diversion will be highly likely, which will amortize the notes. For values in between, the valuation depends rather sensitively on the trigger levels. Figure 10.5 illustrates this point for the mezzanine bond. The presence of triggers is generally beneficial to the bonds, as it leads to early repayment in precisely those loss paths that might later lead to principal losses.

The most obvious impact of management fees is the draining of interest income, which affects the valuation of all other liabilities. Most straightforward are the senior management fees, as those are paid ahead of bond interest payments. In Table 10.4 we see that the impact is predominantly on the equity piece, as expected, given the fact that the equity accrues all residual interest income.

FIGURE 10.4 Illustration of the Dependence of Tranche Values on the Volatility of the Loss Rate

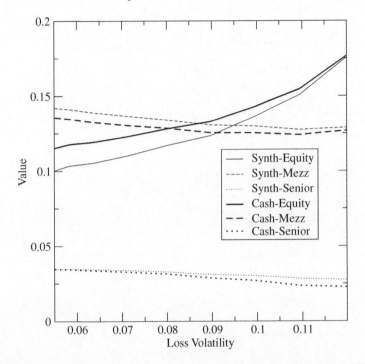

Our standard pair of synthetic and cash flow structures is valued using a loss model with increasing terminal loss rate volatility. The equity tranches gain in value with increased volatility, whereas mezzanine and senior tranches lose. This is in line with the intuition about the impact of correlation.

The value of the senior fees themselves is a constant fraction of the par value, namely the scheduled fees for the full maturity of the transaction. That discount reflects the sensitivity of the senior fees to collateral prepayments (here due to defaults only).

The impact of mezzanine fees (shown in Table 10.5) shows a similar picture, but with some interesting differences. For example, the relative impact of increasing mezzanine fees on equity value is higher compared to the corresponding impact of senior fees. Most interestingly, the relative value of the fees themselves *reduces* for higher fees (albeit slightly). Hence higher mezzanine fees reduce the fraction of scheduled fees that will be paid, as they decrease the ability of the structure to survive longer.

10.5 Summary and Discussion of Open Issues

Motivated by the shortcomings of existing valuation methodologies for collateralized loan obligations, we have explored the possibility of developing a valuation framework

FIGURE 10.5 Illustration of the Complex Dependence of Value of the Mezzanine Note on the Level of the Senior and Mezzanine OC Trigger Levels (L_B^1, L_B^2)

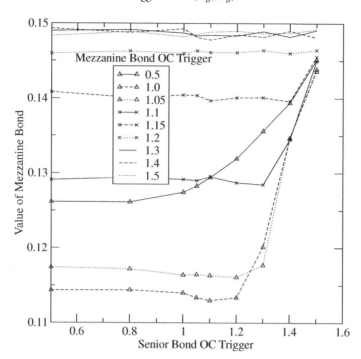

We vary both trigger levels between 0.5 and 1.5. The value of the mezzanine bond is generally an increasing function of its own trigger level, and it reaches its maximum when this reaches around $L_B^2 = 1.3$. When keeping L_B^2 fixed and increasing L_B^1, the value of the mezzanine bond is generally insensitive until L_B^1 reaches a threshold. At that point the value starts increasing with increasing L_B^1 and asymptotic toward its maximum value. It is worth noting that the inflection point does depend on the L_B^2 level!

that is based, to the degree possible, on market-observable inputs. The ideal source of market data would be tranche prices referencing credit indexes closely correlated to the CLO assets.

This framework has two essential components, on the one hand transcribing the complex cash flow structure into a term sheet that can be valued using a risk-neutral pricing framework and on the other hand identifying an adequate loss model to

TABLE 10.4   Value of Liabilities as Function of Senior Fees

Senior fees per annum	0.0000	0.0005	0.001	0.0015	0.002	0.0025	0.0030
Equity value	0.1122	0.1086	0.1043	0.1014	0.0983	0.0951	0.0916
Mezzanine value	0.1285	0.1279	0.1273	0.1272	0.1267	0.1258	0.1255
Senior value	0.7254	0.7254	0.7253	0.7252	0.7250	0.7249	0.7248
Senior fees value	0.0000	0.0041	0.0081	0.0122	0.0163	0.0203	0.0244
Fraction of par		81.2%	81.2%	81.3%	81.3%	81.3%	81.3%

TABLE 10.5　Value of Liabilities as a Function of Mezzanine Fees

Mezzanine fees per annum	0.0000	0.0010	0.0020	0.0030	0.0040	0.0050	0.0060
Equity value	0.1122	0.1046	0.0976	0.0918	0.0844	0.0782	0.0718
Mezzanine value	0.1285	0.1282	0.1274	0.1264	0.1256	0.1253	0.1238
Senior value	0.7254	0.7254	0.7253	0.7252	0.7251	0.7253	0.7250
Mezzanine fees value	0.0000	0.0076	0.0151	0.0226	0.0300	0.0374	0.0446
Fraction of par		75.9%	75.6%	75.4%	75.0%	74.8%	74.3%

calibrate to market data. Once those two components are in place, deriving a market-consistent valuation is accomplished (e.g., via implementing a simulation application).

Tackling the first component, we focused on the aspects of the cash flow structure that are most amenable to quantification (e.g., the precise accounting of the path-dependent payoffs of a CLO). The following discussion of open issues covers some other aspects that are relevant for valuation but were difficult to address at this stage. The second component (loss modeling framework) was kept deliberately general, as this task should ideally be performed using a market standard model that is hopefully used for multiple purposes besides CLO valuation. It appears that currently such a standard is lacking. The main design choice we did make in this direction was the adoption of a Markovian top-down approach, which in any case is promising as a developing market standard because of its parsimonious nature. While the Markov property may not be a valid model property for path-dependent contracts, it is certainly a topic of future research to identify the possible limitations of this assumption. Further, we considered here only the static aspects of the model (i.e., calibration to market prices at the current time), as this is sufficient for a first study. Interestingly, a dynamic extension of the model is required for capturing some of the notorious embedded options of the CLO.

We demonstrated the practical feasibility of the framework with some concrete numerical calculations. In this first instance we used simple and controlled numerical experiments to perform comparisons and sensitivity analyses. The overall conclusion points to the broad similarities of the CLO valuation to the (much more understood) synthetic structure, but also to the complicated interactions of the many elements of the structure that can have material impact on valuation.

10.5.1　Open Issues

• *Portfolio mapping.* In general the CLO portfolio will contain assets that are not part of a tradable index. In fact, the CLO structure offers considerable freedom in the type of assets that can be included, for example loans of different seniority characteristics (and hence very different recovery expectations). Even to the extent that reference portfolios or indexes are available for all types of assets included, there is still the challenge of combining this information into a consistent model. CLOs can include more exotic assets (e.g., other CLO bonds), which, while restricted to smaller fractions of notional, may carry larger fractions of the portfolio's risk.

- *Portfolio trading.* We assumed that the CLO portfolio is fully ramped up and static, and its maturity is matched to the liabilities. Generally CLO portfolios are rather more dynamic with a degree of trading (substitutions, reinvestments, etc.) permissible or even required, subject to not breaching related covenants. Valuation in the presence of active trading (i.e., considering the options of the asset manager) introduces significant complexity. A more specialized type of trading option concerns the treatment of assets that default. Such assets can be either held in the portfolio (taken through a workout process) or sold. In perfect markets this option would have zero value, but clearly it is a valuable option in less liquid markets.

- *Haircuts and collateral quality tests.* Collateral quality tests put restrictions on credit rating, maturity, and facility type of assets to ensure that the portfolio is managed within some guidelines. For example, there may be a limit to the CCC bucket of a portfolio. Breach of such guidelines may restrict active trading, trigger alternative cash flow waterfalls, and so on. Collateral quality tests pose a modeling challenge at two levels. First, they bring into the picture external agents (credit rating agencies) and the expected future assigned ratings. Second, they require the introduction of a more finely grained model of the portfolio (e.g., to at least have at hand the forward population distribution of the underlying asset spreads). Similarly, calculation of the leverage ratios may be requiring market-value-based haircuts for deteriorating credits. This requires the same augmentation of the model into one including spread dynamics for the portfolio constituents.

- *Prepayment option.* Bank loans can typically be prepaid after a lockout period. Given the floating-rate nature of the loans, the prepayment incentive is primarily linked to the credit spreads available to the borrowing entity. Hence, prepayments will affect a fixed portfolio by systematically removing the good risks, but also by reducing available spread income. As with other valuation problems involving prepayment, modeling can focus on the prepayment option (i.e., derive the theoretically optimal prepayment behavior or also incorporate empirical elements). In any case, prepayment performance will also be linked to the future development of credit spreads for portfolio assets.

- *Event-of-default option.* Senior bonds typically benefit from event-of-default clauses. In certain circumstances (e.g., where there is insufficient interest income to pay interest on the senior bonds) an event of default is declared and, unless cured in a short period, the structure may go into liquidation. The deciding option is held by senior note holders, but possibly subject to various restrictions (e.g., that the proceeds can also redeem the mezzanine notes). The event-of-default occurrence can be determined by the loss process, but evaluating the liquidation option at that time implies that a market value of the portfolio is available. Exercise is optimal if liquidation proceeds to senior bond holders exceed future expected payments under the indenture.

- *Equity call option.* The equity investors have the option of calling the CLO after the so-called noncall period (optional redemption). The option can be exercised only if liquidation proceeds (determined by future market value) exceed liabilities. In such cases, there is an incentive to exercise when the residual after liquidation exceeds the present value of expected future equity cash flows. This can be the case if assets have appreciated significantly since acquired for the CLO portfolio.

- *Interest rates.* The CLO aims to largely hedge away any interest rate or exchange rate sensitivity. To the extent that the hedges employed to this effect are imperfect, the valuation will be influenced directly.

Acknowledgement

The author would like to thank Damiano Brigo, Tom Bielecki, Frederic Patras, and the participants of the conference Recent Advancements in the Theory and Practice of Credit Derivatives, Nice 2009, for encouragement and constructive comments on this work. Any remaining errors are certainly the author's. The views and opinions presented in this article are exclusively the author's own and not of his employer.

Notes

1. For CLOs, relevant indexes are, for example, Markit's LevX Senior and Subordinated indexes.
2. An illustration of this problem is the rating of tranches with equal probability of loss but different expected losses.
3. Many CLO securities are actually exchange-listed, so obtaining examples of offering circulars, documents typically running into hundreds of pages, is fairly straightforward.
4. A more realistic recovery model might be to have the recovery be a deterministic declining function of the default rate or to introduce a second stochastic component.
5. Generally a market value haircut is also applied to the outstanding notional. The purpose of this haircut is to provide protection against a market value decline of deteriorating credits. In practice this haircut is applied only to the most deteriorated credits in the collateral pool (i.e., the part that would be expected to sell at a discount to par value due to downward credit migration).
6. In equation (10.8) we introduced the := symbol to denote the update of a variable during the distributions occurring on a payment date. This notation implies that the actual final values of any assigned variable depend on the ordering of those distributions and adjustments, as per the specific waterfall, which we define later in this section. An important note here is that due to deferred interest and possible unscheduled amortization (in order to comply with debt covenants), the scheduled payments are path dependent.
7. In this respect the analysis of Cont and Minca (2008) is relevant.
8. Tranches trading in unfunded—swap—format might be more affected by the different liquidity and counterparty exposure characteristics of such contracts versus a cash CLO.

References

Basel Committee on Banking Supervision. 2008. Fair value measurement and modelling: An assessment of challenges and lessons learned from the market stress.

Batchvarov, A., and A. Davletova. 2005. Synthetic CDO guidebook. Merrill Lynch Report.

Bielecki, T., S. Crépey, and M. Jeanblanc. 2008. Up and down credit risk. Working paper.

Brigo, D., A. Pallavicini, and R. Torresetti. 2006. Calibration of CDO tranches with the dynamical generalized-Poisson loss model. Working paper.

Cont, R., and A. Minca. 2008. Recovering portfolio default intensities implied by CDO quotes. Working paper.

Duffie, D., and N. Garleanu. 2001. Risk and valuation of collateralized debt obligations. *Financial Analysts Journal* 57, no. 1 (January): 41–59.

Giesecke, K. 2008. Portfolio credit risk: Top-down vs. bottom-up. In *Frontiers in quantitative finance: Credit risk and volatility modeling*, ed. R. Cont. Hoboken, NJ: John Wiley & Sons.

Lucas, D. 2001. CDO handbook. JPMorgan Report.

McGinty, L., E. Beinstein, R. Ahluwalia, and M. Watts. 2004. Credit correlation: A guide. JP Morgan Report.

Papadopoulos, P., and C. Tan. 2007. Credit risk analysis of cashflow CDO structures. Working paper.

Servigny, A., and O. Renault. 2003. Correlation evidence. *Risk* (July): 90–94.

Torresetti, R., D. Brigo, and A. Pallavicini. 2007. Implied expected tranched loss surface from CDO data. Working paper.

Walker, M. 2006. CDO models: Towards the next generation; incomplete markets and term structure. Working paper.

CHAPTER 11

Analysis of Mortgage-Backed Securities: Before and After the Credit Crisis

Harvey J. Stein

Bloomberg LP

Alexander L. Belikoff

Bloomberg LP

Kirill Levin

Bloomberg LP

Xusheng Tian

Bloomberg LP

There has been substantial turmoil and change in the financial markets over the past few years. We saw a housing bubble collapse trigger a subprime crisis that caused banks to fail, leading to a credit crisis and a recession requiring substantial government intervention. Among other things, this has led to renewed interest in analysis of mortgage-backed securities.

Valuation of mortgage-backed securities (MBSs) and collateralized mortgage obligations (CMOs) is the big science of the financial world. There are many moving parts, each one drawing on expertise in a different field. Prepayment modeling draws on statistical modeling of economic behavior. Data selection draws on risk analysis. Interest rate modeling draws on classic arbitrage pricing theory applied to the fixed income market. Index projection draws on statistical analysis. Making the Monte Carlo analysis tractable requires working with numerical methods and investigation of a variety of variance reduction techniques. Tractability also requires parallelization, which draws on computer science in building computation clusters, applying new technology such as graphical processing units (GPUs), and analysis and optimization of parallel algorithms.

Here we detail the different components, describing the approach we have taken at Bloomberg in each area, where we can accurately price individual securities in real time, and the entire universe of CMOs and MBSs can be analyzed overnight. Of particular interest is how the credit crisis that started in 2007 has impacted the modeling.

11.1 Market Structure

11.1.1 Market Size and the Credit Crisis

It is customary to begin papers on security valuation with a critique of the size of the market for said security. Market size can be categorized in a number of ways—outstanding notional, transaction volume, new issuance, and so on. While it is common to choose the measure and comparison making the market in question the largest market out of the set, we will break from tradition and look at a number of measures.

The mortgage debt market is the largest debt market in the United States. In terms of outstanding debt, as of June 2009, it weighed in at $10.3 trillion, comprising 48 percent of the total outstanding U.S. debt, and far exceeding the U.S. federal debt of $7.6 trillion (see Figure 11.1), but this is a somewhat deceptive comparison. Before the credit crisis, the housing market was expanding at a high rate. From mid-2003, when interest rates fell to 5.1 percent, through the beginning of the credit crisis (mid-2008), the debt outstanding grew 63 percent (see Figure 11.2). Since then, it has fallen

FIGURE 11.1 Outstanding U.S. Debt as of September 2009

N100 Equity**ALLX**

US Debt Outstanding - Sector — Page 1/1

Source	Federal Reserve	Current Value	Current Date	Previous Value	Previous Date (08/30/09)	Pct Chng
1) Debt Outstanding DomNonFin	DOUTTOTL	34551.9	09/09	34310.5	06/09	.70
2) Debt Outstanding Fed Govt	DOUTFED	7566.5	09/09	7195.2	06/09	5.16
3) Debt Outstanding Nonfed Tot	DOUTNONT	21408.5	09/05	20861.1	06/05	2.62
4) Debt Outstanding Houshld	DOUTHHLD	13614.4	09/09	13702.2	06/09	-.64
5) Debt Outstanding Home Mrtge	DOUTMORT	10291.9	09/09	10384.4	06/09	-.89
6) Debt Outstanding Cnsmr Crdt	DOUTCONC	2519.4	09/09	2539.8	06/09	-.80
7) Debt Outstanding Business	DOUTBUS	11062.0	09/09	11132.9	06/09	-.64
8) Debt Outstanding Corporate	DOUTCORP	7207.4	09/09	7183.8	06/09	.33
9) Debt Outstanding State&Locl	DOUTSTAL	2309.1	09/09	2280.2	06/09	1.27
10) Debt Outstanding Domstc Fin	DOUTDOMF	16065.3	09/09	16482.7	06/09	-2.53
11) Debt Outstanding Foreign	DOUTFRGN	2030.2	09/09	1957.3	06/09	3.72

Australia 61 2 9777 8600 Brazil 5511 3048 4500 Europe 44 20 7330 7500 Germany 49 69 9204 1210 Hong Kong 852 2977 6000
Japan 81 3 3201 8900 Singapore 65 6212 1000 U.S. 1 212 318 2000
SN 221453 26-Jan-2010 13:45:16

FIGURE 11.2 Debt Growth over Time from 1998 to 2010

The solid line is the total outstanding mortgage debt. The dashed line is total outstanding corporate debt. The dotted line is the federal debt. The dashed/dotted line is the overnight national average for the 30-year mortgage rate.

2.4 percent. While low rates caused an explosion of mortgage debt, they had little overall impact on corporate and federal debt. Corporate debt has grown slowly and independently from interest rates. Federal debt grew steadily since mid-2001, only to take off due to the government's attempts to remedy the crisis, growing 43 percent since then. Prior to the government's response to the credit crisis, the mortgage market stood at $10.5 trillion, compared to the federal debt of $5.3 trillion.

The growth in different sectors' debts gives some insight into the mechanism whereby low rates fueled the economy. While we cannot say that corporations did not benefit from low interest rates, one would have expected their debt to have grown faster with low rates if their borrowing played a major part in fueling the economy through its previous woes (the Internet bubble, the effects of the 9/11 terrorist attack, the 2002 stock market crash, etc.). And, while we do not know exactly what was done with the money borrowed by home buyers and homeowners, the huge growth in mortgage debt does lead one to suspect that homeowners made substantial use of low rates and high home prices to remove large amounts of equity from their homes.

The large growth in mortgage debt compared to the relatively flat level of corporate and federal debt leads one to believe that the previous economic troubles were largely mitigated through homeowner spending fueled by their use of low rates to leverage

FIGURE 11.3   Agency Pool New Issuance

N100 Mtge   **IMBS**

Bloomberg   **AGENCY MBS POOL ISSUANCE**   Page 2 of 4
$ Billion Most Recent

	Jan 10	Dec	Nov	Oct	Sep	Aug	Jul	Jun	May	Apr	Mar	'10	YTD '09	'08
TOTAL	84	130	101	105	130	154	169	236	212	138	180	84	1724	1153
Issuer														
FHLMC	19.9	35.5	25.8	26.0	30.8	47.4	42.9	60.1	43.7	46.3	57.6	20	462	341
FNMA	29.6	52.0	39.9	40.8	59.4	62.1	79.8	132	130	56.0	87.9	30	806	541
GNMA1	12.8	19.3	16.7	19.0	22.6	25.8	28.3	29.8	28.5	28.3	28.6	13	286	146
GNMA2	21.2	23.2	18.8	19.6	17.1	19.0	17.9	13.9	10.5	7.2	5.9	21	169	125
Loan Type														
30yr	67.1	103	81.4	84.6	110	128	143	188	185	116	158	67	1448	951
15yr	9.6	14.5	10.3	11.0	12.2	16.6	18.5	37.6	17.2	16.4	15.9	10	181	93
ARM	5.9	6.4	5.2	5.7	3.8	3.5	2.2	2.6	.8	.6	.5	6	33	78
Other	1.0	5.7	4.2	4.2	4.0	6.1	5.4	8.4	9.1	4.3	5.4	1	61	31
Coupon (30yr Fixed)														
<4.0-	.1	.3	.2	.1	.1	.2	.3	.5	.3	.2	.2	0	3	0
4.0-	3.8	6.4	4.4	3.6	7.9	11.9	31.1	39.0	31.1	23.4	31.0	4	209	0
4.5-	36.4	55.6	36.0	32.5	39.6	64.0	82.6	112	77.4	67.6	95.8	36	715	18
5.0-	24.8	37.8	36.1	42.2	49.8	42.9	24.4	19.0	36.0	21.1	25.5	25	376	201
5.5-	1.8	2.8	4.1	5.5	8.9	8.0	3.4	3.9	24.0	2.6	3.8	2	89	385
6.0-	.1	.4	.4	.6	2.3	.9	.6	3.2	16.2	.9	1.4	0	39	257
6.5-	.0	.0	.1	.1	1.2	.1	.2	7.0	.2	.2	.4	0	13	70
>7.0	.0	.0	.0	.0	.1	.0	.0	3.0	.0	.4	.1	0	4	19

the housing bubble. This also leads one to question the mechanism by which low rates will be able to help in the current crisis, given that borrowing is now difficult and no home equity remains to be drawn on.

We can also look at the market in terms of issuance. Over $1.7 trillion in agency pools was issued in 2009, and $1.2 trillion was issued in 2008. With $342 billion of CMO issuance in 2009 and $191 billion issued in 2008, we can see that only a small proportion of this debt (15 percent to 20 percent) was used for securitization of CMOs (see Figures 11.3 and 11.4). This was quite different before the crisis. In 2004 and 2005, $1 trillion and $987 billion in agency pools were issued, whereas $822 billion and $1 trillion of CMOs were issued, putting issuance on par with securitization.

More information on issuance is shown in Figure 11.5. Pool issuance exploded from 2001 to 2003, due to the tremendous drop in mortgage rates we saw in this period (from 8 percent to 5 percent) and the subsequent growth in the housing market. It experienced a drop back to 2001 levels in 2004, as rates stabilized and people found exotic loans to be financially advantageous over conforming debt. Issuance rebounded during and after the credit crisis, to close to peak levels in 2009. This is believed to be due to the banks' unwillingness to issue loans they could not in turn sell off, pushing borrowers back into the conforming markets. For example, one can potentially make a larger down payment so that a jumbo loan is not needed, or put together the necessary documentation so that an Alt-A loan is not needed.

However, CMO issuance tracked MBS issuance through 2004, but fell off dramatically during the crisis and remains at low levels. This is due to flat yield curves

FIGURE 11.4 CMO New Issuance

	Jan 10 Dec	Nov	Oct	Sep	Aug	Jul	Jun	May	Apr	Mar	Feb	YTD '10	'09	'08
Bloomberg CMO ISSUANCE $ Billion 2008-2010												Page 2 of 7		
TOTAL	- 39.8	29.0	37.5	28.7	44.0	32.7	41.3	33.0	25.3	13.9	8.8	-	342	191
Collateral Source														
FHLMC	- 5.8	7.5	7.2	6.6	10.8	7.4	11.8	7.0	4.6	2.7	2.4	-	76	51
FNMA	- 7.1	6.0	9.8	5.7	12.7	4.1	7.9	3.8	3.2	2.4	2.1	-	69	56
GNMA	- 24.4	11.1	16.5	10.7	18.0	9.9	10.5	9.8	5.5	4.1	3.0	-	124	34
WHOLE	- 2.5	4.4	3.9	5.6	2.6	11.2	11.1	12.4	12.0	4.8	1.2	-	73	50
Collateral Type														
30yr	- 35.9	22.2	30.3	20.4	40.7	19.3	30.0	18.9	15.2	8.7	6.4	-	252	128
15yr	- .5	.1	.4	2.2	.3	1.7	-	.2	.6	.2	.6	-	7	2
ARM	- 1.1	2.0		.1	-	-	.3	2.2	1.1	-	-	-	7	13
Other	- 2.2	4.7	6.7	6.0	3.0	11.7	11.0	11.6	8.4	5.0	1.8	-	76	48
Collateral WAC (Fixed Rate)														
<5.5	- 24.2	8.9	9.4	12.2	15.5	14.6	24.3	17.8	19.6	6.1	1.7	-	155	37
5.5-	- 10.4	10.1	14.9	10.4	22.2	10.5	9.6	7.2	2.2	3.0	1.1	-	101	23
6.0-	- 3.3	6.6	9.8	4.5	5.8	6.1	6.5	5.4	1.0	3.2	4.0	-	59	58
6.5-	- .7	1.5	3.4	.4	.5	1.5	.5	.3	1.1	1.3	2.1	-	17	45
7.0-	- -	-	-	-	-	-	-	-	.2	.3	-	-	1	14
7.5-	- -	-	-	- 1.0	-	-	.1	-	-	-	-	-	1	1
8.0-	- -	-	-	-	-	-	-	-	-	-	-	-	0	-
>8.5	- -	-	-	-	-	-	-	.2	-	-	-	-	0	-

FIGURE 11.5 Historical Issuance of Agency CMOs and MBSs

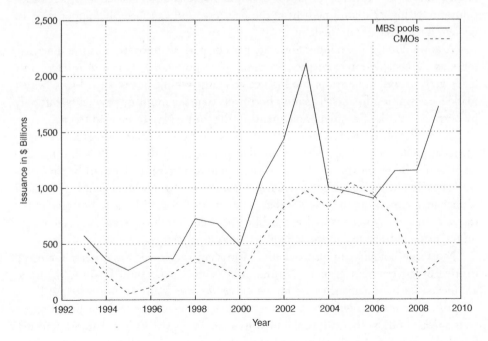

making securitization less profitable, and a lack of capital, leaving the banks unwilling or unable to keep the collateral on hand. In 2009 we saw a steepening of the yield curve and an easing of credit at the banks, and subsequently an increase in issuance.

11.1.2   Underlying Collateral

Mortgages are loans issued against real estate. They are the subatomic particles of the MBS and CMO market—MBSs and CMOs are built out of them, but they are not traded directly. Payments are typically monthly and take the form of a payment of some amount of principal plus the interest accrued over the course of the month.

Fixed-rate mortgages have a fixed coupon that is accrued on a monthly basis against the outstanding principal. Principal payments are scheduled so that the monthly payments are equal—it is a self-amortizing loan. Typically, the principal is fully repaid at the end of the loan, with a term of 15 to 30 years, although there is also issuance of balloons, which amortize on a 30-year basis but expire in five to seven years, requiring payment of the outstanding balance at expiration.

Adjustable-rate mortgages (ARMs) have a coupon that is tied to some index— London Interbank Offered Rate (LIBOR), Treasury rates, and so on. They often have clauses protecting the holder from extreme rate moves (lifetime caps, annual resets, maximum annual resets, etc.). For example, a 3/1 ARM with a 1/2/6 cap structure has a fixed coupon for the first three years (potentially a low teaser rate) and resets at that time and once each year after that. The first reset cannot adjust up more than 1 percent, each additional reset cannot adjust up more than 2 percent, and the maximum the rate can increase is 6 percent. So, for example, if the coupon started at 4 percent, it cannot reset higher than 5 percent at the first reset and can never be higher than 10 percent during the life of the loan.

Around 2005, the extended low-rate period sparked innovation in the mortgage markets. Adjustable-rate mortgages became more popular. Issuance of interest-only loans grew as well. The subprime market was largely built out of such loans, which made it easy for less financially sound borrowers to make monthly payments, but only by bearing the risk of far higher payments in the future (when the loan resets).

When people refinance, move, or otherwise pay down their mortgages, the payments are reflected as larger than scheduled payments in the cash flow stream. The loans could be reamortized, changing the remaining stream of monthly payments while leaving the maturity date fixed. More typically, the monthly scheduled payment is unchanged, meaning that the number of payments is reduced due to both the initial excess principal payment as well as the difference between the interest due each month on the reduced balance and the scheduled interest payments.

Mortgage holders can also default. Mortgages that meet the criteria for being insured by government agencies (Fannie Mae, Ginnie Mae, and Freddie Mac) and are picked up by the agencies are known as *conforming* loans, or *prime* loans. These are primary loans for owner-occupied residences, with sufficiently high FICO scores (was at least 660), sufficiently small loan-to-value ratios (LTVs less than 80 percent), full documentation for three years of income, sufficiently small payment-to-income ratios (starting with less than 28 percent and ending with less than 38 percent), and of sufficiently small loan size. These comprise about 40 percent of the market (Veale 2008).

The remaining 60 percent of the market consists of *nonconforming* loans. They range from *jumbos*, which are conforming in all respects except for the size of the loan, through Alt-A loans, which fail to conform in a second respect, such as incomplete income documentation or higher LTVs, to loans that deviate further from the conforming criteria. Some refer to this entire class as *subprime*, but we will reserve the term for the last-named class.

The subprime crisis was precipitated by the "innovative" subprime loans being issued during the low rate regime. Subprime holders who could not maintain their payments had been using rising prices to regularly refinance and cash out. Rising rates caused home prices to flatten, making it impossible for these borrowers to cash out again. They started to default. The second wave of defaults occurred when the remaining loans reset to higher rates. This occurred when rates themselves were high, so refinancing into a more affordable monthly payment was difficult. Furthermore, due to high rates, the housing market fell to the point where the selling price of the home was lower than the principal outstanding on the mortgage, inducing people to default on the loans, and causing losses for the holders of the loans. This devalued banks' leveraged positions in CDOs backed by the loans, causing losses sufficiently large to sink some investment banks and requiring influxes of capital to maintain solvency (i.e., the credit crisis).

11.1.3 MBS Pools

MBS pools are resecuritized sets of mortgages. If mortgages are the subatomic particles, then MBS pools are the atoms.

In 1938, the collapse of the national housing market led to the federal government's formation of the *government-sponsored enterprise* (GSE) known as the *Federal National Mortgage Association* (aka Fannie Mae) to help rebuild the market. This was done through the agency's bearing of mortgage default risk through government guarantees. Subsequently, two additional agencies were established—the *Federal Home Loan Mortgage Corporation* (Freddie Mac), and the *Government National Mortgage Association* (Ginnie Mae).

Mortgages are sold by issuing banks to agencies or other organizations. These organizations issue pools backed by specific mortgages. Investors purchase shares of the pools. The shares receive monthly principal and interest payments consisting of the principal and interest payments made to the underlying mortgages minus a servicing fee. The loans themselves are the collateral backing the MBS pool.

By buying the loans, the agencies remove the loans from the banks' books. This removes prepayment and default risk from the banks, and gives the banks the money to make more loans, thus fueling home ownership. The agencies then recoup the money by selling the pools, thus ultimately transferring the debt and the prepayment risk from the banks to the market itself. Default risk is borne by the agency. In the event of default, after partial payment of the principal is had via foreclosure, the remaining principal is paid by the agency.

FIGURE 11.6 Detail of an MBS Pool

```
DES                                                                    P155 Mtge  DES
                                                                             SCHEMA MODE
                                                                         Security Description
┌──────────────────────────────────────────────────────────────────────────────────────┐
│Agency    FG          Issue Date      01/01/06   Originator                              │
│Pool      A41492      Mty Date        01/01/36   Gmac Mortgage, Llc                      │
│CUSIP     3128K1UR0                               1100 Virginia Drive, Mc: 190-ftw-a65 , Fo│
│Type      (A4)  Conventional 30 years                                                    │
│Traits    30/360                                                                         │
│Generic   FGLMC 6 2006                           Coupon              6.000               │
├──────────────────────────────────────────────────────────────────────────────────────┤
│Information As Of    Jan10                                                               │
│                                                      Prepayments                        │
│WAC       6.862  Orig WAC      6.862  Factor       0.42155101            CPR    PSA      │
│WARM        304  Orig WAM        359  Orig Amt     11,447,452  1 Mon     0.1      2      │
│WALA         49                       Curr Amt      4,825,685  3 Mon     5.3     89      │
│Curtailed     7                                               6 Mon     24.9    414      │
│                 WAOLT           360  AOLS            143,278  1 Year    27.3    455      │
│                 WAOLTV           78  WAOLS           163,404  Life      18.4    419      │
│# Loans      36  WAOCS           634  MAX LS         315,000  Geographics (Top 3)        │
│                                                                  State      %UPB        │
│                 WAOCLTV          79                          PA              12         │
│Delay     44 ( 14 )  WAODTI       40  Curr TPO         37.53  FL             12         │
│1 Month CPR       21) More Historical Data                    IL             11         │
│  Jan10  Dec09  Nov09  Oct09  Sep09  Aug09  Jul09  Jun09  May09  Apr09  Mar09  Feb09    │
│   0.1    0.2   14.9   36.2   17.8   59.5   62.8   0.0    0.0    0.0   67.4   0.0        │
│1) Summary  2) Generic  3) Prepay  4) Geo/LOY  5) Loans                                 │
└──────────────────────────────────────────────────────────────────────────────────────┘
Australia 61 2 9777 8600 Brazil 5511 3048 4500 Europe 44 20 7330 7500 Germany 49 69 9204 1210 Hong Kong 852 2977 6000
Japan 81 3 3201 8900        Singapore 65 6212 1000    U.S. 1 212 318 2000    Copyright 2010 Bloomberg Finance L.P.
                                                              SN 221453 H283-220-3 20-Jan-2010 17:50:37
```

The security description screen for an MBS pool (in this case FGA41492) shows the general characteristics of the pool, such as the CUSIP, the type of collateral in the pool, the issue date, and the current and original weighted average coupon (WAC) of the underlying collateral, as well as some loan-level characteristics, such as the maximum loan size and the weighted average LTV. Data for a generic pool similar to this one are on the second tab, prepayment history is on the third tab, and loan-level data are on the fourth and fifth tabs.

Mortgage pools are known as pass-through securities, since the interest and principal payments (minus fees) pass through to the owners of shares of the pools. See, for example, FGA41492 <Mtge><Go> (as in Figure 11.6) and FNCL 5<Mtge><Go> on the Bloomberg terminal.

When originally formed, Fannie Mae was a government agency. The guarantee that it gave was backed by the U.S. government. In 1968, Fannie Mae was converted to a private corporation, largely to remove its liabilities from the federal government's balance sheet (Green and Schnare 2009). Nonetheless, its guarantees were considered to be in no danger of failing. The only default considerations applied to MBS pools were of homeowner default as reflected by early repayment of principal to the pool holder.

The credit crisis has reversed the status of the agencies. Both Fannie and Freddie held huge volumes of Alt-A and subprime debt. When homeowner defaults skyrocketed and these positions deteriorated in value, the agencies lost enough to become insolvent. In fact, their 2008 losses were higher than their total profits from 1990 through 2007. On September 7, 2008, the government stepped in and took ownership of both agencies (Green and Schnare 2009).

The last chapter in the story of the agencies remains to be written. On one hand, Representative Barney Frank (D-MA), the chairman of the House Financial Services Committee, recently recommended abolishing Fannie Mae and Freddie Mac. On the other hand, Treasury Secretary Timothy Geithner said that an overhaul of the agencies was unlikely to begin this year. One can only guess at what might happen and how it will impact the holders of agency debt and MBS pools.

While the credit crisis has had a major impact on the agencies, their guarantees are still being priced as if they are sound. In fact, while the spread between agency debt and U.S. Treasuries spiked as high as 140 basis points during the crisis, it has since come down to as little as 15 to 25 basis points. MBS pool spreads have behaved similarly. The spread from the 30-year Fannie current coupon to the 10-year Treasury tended to be around 100 to 150 basis points during the low rate regime at the end of 2002 through the tightening of rates until mid-2006, when spreads started to fluctuate more, peaking at almost 240 basis points in 2008. Subsequently, spreads have dropped substantially, down to as little as 70 basis points. This is attributable at least in part to the government's buying of mortgage pools in an effort to keep mortgage rates low.

FNCL 5 is what is known on the Bloomberg system as a generic pool. It is a fictitious Fannie pool whose attributes are an average of actual Fannie pools. One can also specify variants as arguments to the command, such as `FNCL 5 NEW<Mtge><Go>` to select a 5 percent coupon Fannie generic based on newly issued mortgages (with age less than 30 months). Other tails are "`SEAS`" for seasoned (older) mortgages (with age greater than 60 months), and "`MOD`," for moderately seasoned (with age between 30 and 60 months). Also available is "TBA," for mortgage pools traded now for delivery in a future month, with the pool details unspecified (i.e., To Be Announced [TBA]).

11.1.4   CMOs

In 1983, Lewis S. Ranieri led Salomon Brothers and First Boston to create the first *collateralized mortgage obligation* (CMO). They realized that more pools could be sold if the pool cash flows were carved up to stratify risk. By creating desirable risk profiles, tranches could be sold to a wider audience and at a larger profit than the underlying collateral.

CMOs are resecuritized mortgage collateral, typically mortgage pools. Agency deals are resecuritized sets of MBS pools. There are also CMOs backed by individual loans (typically jumbos), or even other CMOs. Being built out of MBS pools or other CMOs makes them the molecules of the mortgage market.

In the case of agency deals, MBS pools are purchased by or retained by the agency issuing the CMO. Tranches (bonds) are issued against these shares. The principal and interest paid by the pools is distributed among the tranches according to rules determined when the deal is designed (structured). This is the collateral backing the CMO. It could consist of as many as 20,000 pools. Nonagency deals are the same except that they are backed by individual loans instead of shares of pools. CMOs can also be backed by tranches from other CMOs. These are called *reremics*.

Consider as an example a CMO backed by one MBS pool and having two tranches. One tranche (the interest-only or IO tranche) receives the interest payments from the collateral, and the other tranche (the principal-only or PO tranche) receives the principal payments. If the pool prepays, the PO bond gets a larger than usual cash flow, and the IO suddenly starts receiving less interest (the interest is now on a lower principal). In general, the PO gets a fixed amount of money at indeterminate times, while the IO, in that it only gets interest on the remaining balance, can receive anything from $0 (if prepayment occurs immediately) to whatever the original scheduled interest payments were (if no prepayment occurs). Increases in prepayment increase the value of POs while decreasing the value of IOs.

In general, the rules defining CMO tranches segregate into two classes, those driving interest handling and those driving principal handling. By controlling interest payments, one can control interest rate risk. By controlling principal payments, one can control prepayment risk.

Interest rate rules can make a tranche pay a fixed coupon at a selected level, or a stepped coupon, or a floating coupon, and so on. By creating PO tranches, the interest that would otherwise go to them can be delivered to a fixed coupon tranche, increasing the interest payments. A floater can be synthesized from fixed coupon loans by balancing it with a second tranche that is an inverse floater.

Principal handling rules include sequential-pay bonds, *planned amortization classes* (PACs) and *targeted amortization classes* (TACs). Sequential-pay bonds are a classic waterfall structure, where the first tranche gets principal payments until paid off, then the second tranche gets the principal payments, and so on. The last tranche is the most protected from prepayment risk and behaves the most like an ordinary bond. PACs amortize based on a schedule, as long as prepayment remains in a specified band. When prepayment crosses outside the band, the PAC stops following the schedule and is said to be *broken*. TACs follow an amortization schedule as long as prepayment is at a specific level.

The rules constituting the structure of a deal can be arbitrarily complex. We have even seen tranches that were structured to have large cash flows only when prepayment closely matched specific prepayment speeds (for example, constant prepayment rates [CPRs] of 2, 4, 6, etc.).

Agency deals are backed by agency pools, so homeowner defaults are experienced as an early return of principal in the underlying collateral. For them, homeowner defaults will not cause losses of principal. This does not hold for nonagency deals. As a result, the rules for specifying the cash flows of the individual tranches include rules for how losses are distributed. Loss modeling for nonagency deals has become far more important as the subprime crisis has evolved. CMOs backed by subprime deals are currently analyzed largely by looking at the issuers (to get an idea of the quality of the underwriting) and the delinquencies, defaults, and loss severities of the underlying collateral.

The credit crisis has also increased regulatory risks. Governments and central banks are proposing and enacting a variety of regulations in an effort to prevent future financial crises. The courts are also getting involved. A U.S. bankruptcy court has recently overruled contractual stipulations of seniority for a particular CDO deal of Lehman Brothers. This could have a wide-ranging impact on securitization.

Given the reduced issuance of CMOs and the ongoing changes to regulations, only time will tell how the structures evolve in the face of the credit crisis. The market will have to balance its postcrisis shyness for exotic structures and risk with its thirst for yield.

The Bloomberg functions DES and DES2 describe CMO tranches and their collateral, respectively. The CLC function shows the composition of the collateral, and the VAC function shows all the tranches of the deal. Of interest for nonagency deals is the DQRP function, which lists deals by delinquency and default information, and CLP and SEV, which display more detailed delinquency and default data for the collateral of a specific deal.

11.2 Prepayment

Prepayments historically were modeled as fixed rates. People would look at security value as a function of these fixed rates. As the markets matured, prepayment models were developed to estimate prepayments as a function of the overall rate environment and the particulars of the individual loans or pools in question.

11.2.1 Prepayment Speeds

Before prepayments were modeled, a small sample of prepayment speeds were used for valuing mortgages. The simplest is SMM, which stands for *single monthly mortality.* This is the percentage of the remaining balance above scheduled that was paid, and thus ranges from 0 percent to 100 percent, where following the scheduled payments is an SMM of 0 percent and prematurely paying off the loan is an SMM of 100 percent. If P_i is the scheduled principal payment for the ith payment, P_i' is the actual principal payment made (which is the payment made minus the interest due on the outstanding balance), and B_i is the actual remaining balance after the ith payment, then

$$\text{SMM}_i = 100 \left(\frac{P_i' - P_i}{B_{i-1} - P_i} \right)$$

The *constant prepayment rate* (CPR) is the annualized equivalent of a given SMM. So,

$$\text{CPR} = 100 \left(1 - \left(1 - \frac{\text{SMM}}{100} \right)^{12} \right)$$

Note that this is *not* exactly the percentage of balance paid down if the SMM is fixed over the next 12 months. To compute the latter, one would need to reamortize each month.

MBS pools and CMO tranches can be valued at fixed SMMs or CPRs, but it is not especially realistic, given that prepayment seldom occurs at a constant rate.

The *prepayment speed assumption* (PSA) was the first attempt to take into account that prepayments tend to vary with the age of the loan. A PSA of 100 percent assumes a CPR of 0.2 percent for the origination month, increasing by 0.2 percent per month for the first 30 months and 6.0 percent per month until the loan pays off; 200 percent

PSA assumes twice this; and so on. However, this is not especially realistic, either, in that eventually prepayment tends to drop down as well.

On the Bloomberg, the CCPR function converts SMM to CPR, the CSSM function converts CPR to SMM, and the SMMT function gives a table of equivalent CPRs and SMMs.

11.2.2   Prepayment Modeling

Prepayment modeling was born to overcome the stark contrast between fixed prepayment speeds and observed prepayment behavior. Prepayment modeling is a critical component of MBS and CMO valuation. It is a research area in its own right, requiring substantial statistical analysis combined with insight into and experience with the behavior of the mortgage markets. Salient features of prepayment are proposed, evidence for them is collected from statistical analysis of historical prepayment patterns, and if the evidence supports the theory, models are developed for these relationships.

For MBS pools, the major components are housing turnover, refinancing, curtailment, and default. We model these as three independent components (lumping the last two together), with each component having its own parameters for capturing the behavior of that component. When relevant, these parameters are tuned to the specific collateral type (Xia and Liu 2008).

11.2.3   Housing Turnover

The Bloomberg housing turnover component consists of a seasonality-adjusted base turnover rate tempered by a seasoning curve, the lock-in effect, and home price appreciation.

The base turnover rate is the seasonally adjusted ratio of total home sales to total U.S. housing stock. It is seasonal because people move less often in the winter than in the summer. This is adjusted by seasoning because of the observance that housing turnover in a given pool tends to increase and then level off over time. Our seasoning function takes into account the pool's age, loan type, and coupon spread, slowing prepayment when refinancing rates are higher than the pool's coupon. We also take into account the lock-in effect, where housing turnover is reduced when it is less affordable to close out one's existing mortgage and take out a mortgage on a new property. This happens if the outstanding balance is large and rates are high relative to the loan coupon.

During the housing market growth and through the housing bubble we saw an overall increase in housing turnover. People took advantage of low rates by trading up to more expensive homes and by speculating in the housing market. This led us to adjust this component. Once the bubble popped and credit became tight, housing turnover slowed down. The model handled this change well through its home price appreciation dependency.

The importance of the housing turnover component is illustrated in Figure 11.7, which compares overall prepayment speed and model prepayment speed with the housing turnover component. While housing turnover rarely contributes more than 10 percent to the CPR, it dominates prepayment behavior when rates are high.

FIGURE 11.7　Actual and Predicted Prepayment Speeds

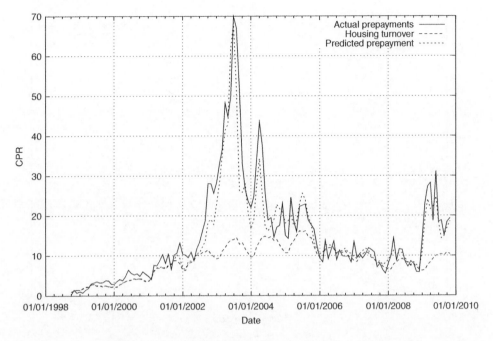

Actual prepayment speed and model prepayment speed compared to the housing turnover component for a 30-year 5.5 percent FNMA pool originated in 1998.

Figure 11.7 also illustrates the predictive power of the Bloomberg prepayment model, showing excellent agreement between model-predicted prepayment and observed prepayment.

11.2.4　Refinancing

Refinancing is the major interest rate dependent component, and is the major component when rates are low relative to the loan's coupon. Refinancing will typically be zero when rates are above the pool's rate, pick up as rates drop, and top out at some maximum level (because not everyone can refinance). Hence the commonly used S-curve for refinancing prepayment rates (see Figure 11.8). Factored into this are a number of qualitative features:

- Refinancing is dampened in new loans due to up-front costs. This tapers off as the loan ages or if refinancing incentive is sufficiently high.
- Credit quality affects prepayment. Borrowers with poor credit are less able to refinance. Credit quality can be gotten directly from FICO scores (where available), or detected by a high loan coupon relative to the current coupon at issuance, indicating credit concerns by the lender.
- Pools that have experienced substantial prepayment are less likely to prepay in the future. This is the *burnout effect*. It is due to refinancing removing borrowers from the pool who are willing to refinance, leaving only the borrowers who are unaware

FIGURE 11.8 Sample Refinancing S-Curves

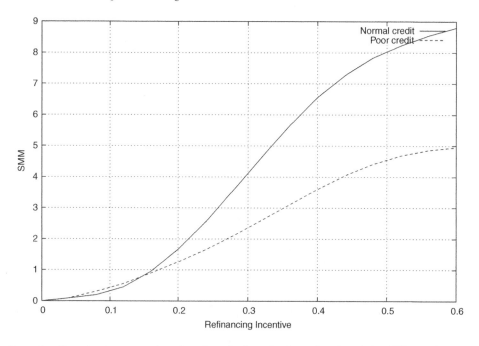

Example refinancing rate curves (as a function of refinancing incentive, the relative difference between the coupon and the refinancing rate) for normal and poor credit. Different refinancing rate curves are used for different levels of credit quality and for different types of collateral.

of or unable to take advantage of refinancing opportunities. This could be due to declining property values, deteriorating creditworthiness, high loan-to-value ratios, and so on. We model it based on accumulated refinancing exposure.

- Prepayment often jumps when rates hit historic lows, presumably due to press coverage encouraging people to refinance. We call this the *media effect*. We model it based on the ratio between the current mortgage rate and weighted mortgage rates of the prior five years.

- Prepayment is asymmetrical in the neighborhood of a mortgage rate low (the *pipeline effect*). Prepayment does not drop when rates rise as quickly as it grew when rates dropped. This is due to mortgage broker capacity limits causing a backup in refinancing applications, favoring the ones the broker finds more valuable. This tends to occur only at spikes in prepayment, and thus only around historic lows.

The housing bubble presented a refinancing environment that had not been seen before in the data history. Prepayment models tended to underestimate the prepayment in this period and needed adjustment. Similarly, during the credit crisis it became difficult for homeowners to refinance, leading us to flatten the refinancing S-curves. In anticipation of credit becoming more available, we have recently moved to time-dependent S-curves. We start with a flatter S-curve and progress to a steeper one as the recession fades and credit eases. This can be seen in Figure 11.7. The spike in prepayment in 2009 was far smaller than the one in 2003 despite rates reaching similar lows due to the postcrisis tight credit situation (Liu 2009).

11.2.5 Default and Curtailment

Default occurs when the borrower fails to make loan payments. The lending institution forecloses and sells the property. The sale triggers closing the loan with the repayment of its outstanding principal.

Curtailment occurs when the borrower pays more than the scheduled monthly payment. Since loans typically are not reamortized, this reduces the loan maturity. The outstanding balance is reduced, which reduces the interest due each month, so that each monthly payment further pays down the principal by the difference between the scheduled interest and the actual interest due. Curtailment also occurs toward the end of the life of a mortgage, when some borrowers choose to pay off the remaining principal rather than continuing to pay interest.

While default was a fundamental instigator of the credit crisis, it was largely in the subprime market, and especially in the more exotic ARMs where payments shot up when the loans reset. As such, it had a much smaller impact on the conforming loans, where borrowers had high credit, low LTVs, and fixed-coupon loans that did not demand immediate action. The biggest impact was in the loans originated at the peak in the market. While their original LTVs were low, housing prices dropped, increasing LTVs. Coupled with harder economic times, these loans show both higher default rates as well as losses.

The Bloomberg prepayment model incorporates default and curtailment through aggregate default and curtailment curves that are a function of the loan age, such as in Figure 11.9.

More recently, we have observed a change in the behavior of the GSEs (agency buyouts) that has required a corresponding modeling change. In February 2010, Freddie Mac announced that it would essentially buy out all mortgages delinquent by 120 days or more. Shortly thereafter, Fannie Mae announced similar plans. The first payments resulting from this action occurred in March.

From the perspective of an agency-backed mortgage pool, an agency buyout appears the same as a default—a principal payment comes into the pool that pays off one of the underlying loans. The difference is that before having taken this action, principal would have been repaid some time after the homeowner in question actually defaulted. Now, the principal is paid much sooner. It could even be paid out on loans taken by homeowners that do not ultimately default.

This was modeled at Bloomberg by expanding and enriching the default modeling component (Liu and Xia 2010). The changes made were as follows:

- Different default prepayment curves are used for different coupons to account for the relationship between coupon and delinquency.
- Unemployment rate projections are incorporated into default estimation to model the fact that delinquency increases when unemployment is up.

FIGURE 11.9   Aggregate Default and Curtailment Prepayment Speed Curve

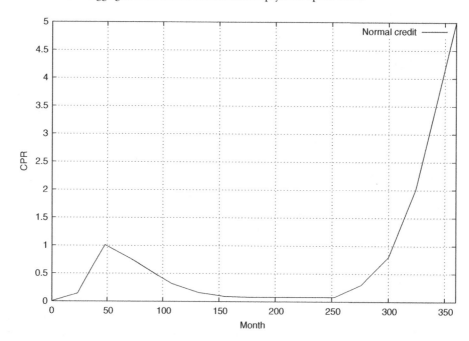

Sample default and curtailment curve for 30-year agency collateral.

- We use home price index projections to better model the LTV and hence the impact of home prices on default rates.
- The spread at origination and credit scores are used to better model homeowner credit impairment.

Since agency buyouts change the composition of the pools, the housing turnover and refinancing components were recalibrated as well. The end result is that higher-risk pools are seeing higher projected prepayment speeds.

11.2.6   Loan-Level Characteristics

As additional loan-level data becomes available, we continue to analyze it and incorporate it into the Bloomberg prepayment model if it is found to be a good predictor of prepayment behavior. For example, the loan-to-value ratio (LTV), credit score, loan size, and occupancy type were found to have much more predictive power than property type and loan purpose. As such, we classify LTV, credit score, loan size, and occupancy type as primary loan attributes, and the remaining attributes as secondary attributes. When available, we use the primary loan attributes to adjust prepayment rates.

Borrowers will reap larger monthly benefits from refinancing a large loan than from refinancing a small loan. One would expect that this would lead to higher prepayment rates for larger loans. Analysis of the data has traditionally borne this out and led us to steepen the refinancing S-curve as loan size increases. More recently, frequent changes of loan size limits by the agencies has polluted the signal of this indicator.

Similarly, borrowers with higher credit scores are able to more easily refinance, and can do so at better rates. We find that while low credit scores significantly dampen prepayment rates, there is a tapering off of the effect as credit scores improve. The Bloomberg prepayment model incorporates this observation into a second S-curve adjustment. As underwriting standards are tightened, we are seeing the credit score become a better indicator of prepayment rates.

High-LTV loans are harder to refinance than low-LTV loans. Using LTVs to adjust prepayment rates can be complicated because they depend not only on how the mortgage has paid down but on how home prices have grown. Making use of our home price appreciation model enabled us to estimate the current LTV. The Bloomberg prepayment model incorporates the current LTV by steepening the refinancing S-curve for lower-LTV loans.

Analysis of historical prepayment rates has shown that loans for owner-occupied properties repay at substantially higher rates than those for non-owner-occupied properties, leading to as much as a 20-point spread in CPRs at high prepayment incentive levels. This is incorporated by steepening the refinancing S-curve as a function of the percentage of owner-occupied properties in the pool.

11.2.7   ARM Modeling

The yield curve steepened toward the end of the housing bubble, leading to growth in the ARM market. ARMs accounted for about 11 percent of the market in 2007.

ARM prepayment analysis is similar to fixed coupon prepayment analysis. It uses the same components (housing turnover, refinancing, and curtailment and default) as are used in fixed-coupon prepayment analysis, with the added complication that the loan coupon changes over time. The refinancing incentive can jump when the coupon resets. Borrowers will often refinance in anticipation of a rate jump. Growth in the refinancing incentive coming from drops in rates does not cause as much prepayment as the same refinancing incentive coming from an increase in the coupon.

Different products also behave differently: 3/1 ARMs exhibit higher prepayment rates than 5/1 ARMs, which in turn prepay faster than 7/1 ARMs. Borrowers who take 7/1 ARMs are presumably planning to stay in the property longer than those taking 5/1 ARMs. Otherwise they would have taken advantage of the lower teaser rate of the 5/1 ARMs. Similarly, holders of 3/1 ARMs have to be more wary of market rates because their loans reset sooner.

11.3   Yields and OAS

Yield calculations and option adjusted spread (OAS) calculations are two ways to value mortgage-backed securities. Yield calculations compute the internal rate of return for the pool or CMO tranche at a given price assuming a particular prepayment scenario.

OAS calculations compute the overall shift to interest rates implied by a given price and with respect to a variety of prepayment and interest rate scenarios.

11.3.1 Yield Calculations

Yields are computed relative to a prepayment scenario. One picks a prepayment speed (such as 200 percent PSA), generates the cash flows, and solves for the yield. While this is simple conceptually, it can be quite intensive when the CMO is backed by 20,000 pools, each of which must be amortized according to the chosen prepayment speed, with cash flows distributed across 100 tranches.

As alluded to earlier, yields can also be computed using prepayment models. In general, one would need to generate an interest rate scenario, project the prepayment model inputs, and run the prepayment model. One can assume flat projections, project based on the current yield curve, or generate a scenario based on an interest rate model. On the Bloomberg, in the YT function, one can do this for the stock 32 scenarios of Bloomberg's one-factor interest rate model. These are the individual path prices that go into the OAS1 calculation. The paths themselves can be viewed on OASV (Figure 11.20). See Figure 11.10 for example yield calculations with respect to varying interest rate levels and prices.

FIGURE 11.10 Yield Calculations

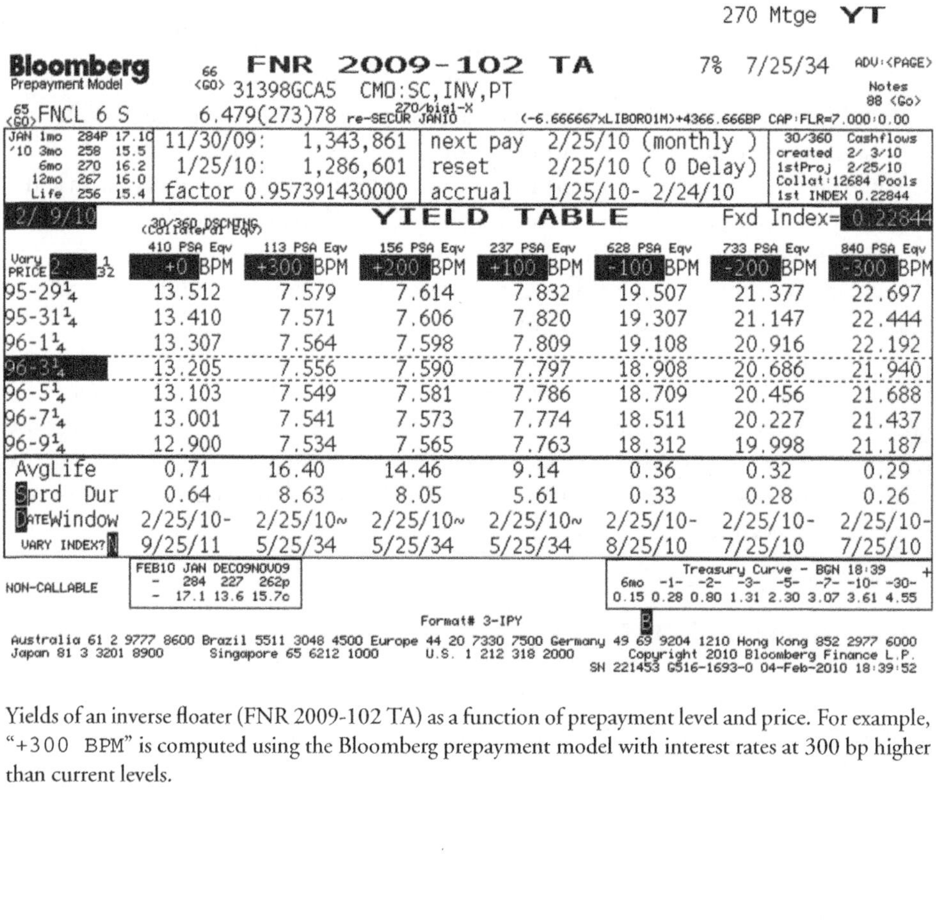

270 Mtge **YT**

Bloomberg 66 **FNR 2009-102 TA**	7% 7/25/34 ADV:⟨PAGE⟩

Prepayment Model ⟨GO⟩ 31398GCA5 CMO:SC,INV,PT — Notes 88 ⟨Go⟩
65⟨GO⟩ FNCL 6 S 6.479(273)78 re-SECUR JAN10 270/biol-X (-6.666667×LIBOR01M)+4366.666BP CAP:FLR=7.000:0.00

JAN 1mo 284P 17.10	11/30/09: 1,343,861	next pay 2/25/10 (monthly)	30/360 Cashflows created 2/ 3/10
'10 3mo 258 15.5	1/25/10: 1,286,601	reset 2/25/10 (0 Delay)	1stProj 2/25/10
6mo 270 16.2	factor 0.957391430000	accrual 1/25/10- 2/24/10	Collat:12684 Pools
12mo 267 16.0			1st INDEX 0.22844
Life 256 15.4			

2/ 9/10 **YIELD TABLE** Fxd Index= 0.22844
30/360 PSCHING (30 Reference Eqv)

Vary PRICE 1 32	410 PSA Eqv +0 BPM	113 PSA Eqv +300 BPM	156 PSA Eqv +200 BPM	237 PSA Eqv +100 BPM	628 PSA Eqv -100 BPM	733 PSA Eqv -200 BPM	840 PSA Eqv -300 BPM
95-29¼	13.512	7.579	7.614	7.832	19.507	21.377	22.697
95-31¼	13.410	7.571	7.606	7.820	19.307	21.147	22.444
96-1¼	13.307	7.564	7.598	7.809	19.108	20.916	22.192
96-3¼	13.205	7.556	7.590	7.797	18.908	20.686	21.940
96-5¼	13.103	7.549	7.581	7.786	18.709	20.456	21.688
96-7¼	13.001	7.541	7.573	7.774	18.511	20.227	21.437
96-9¼	12.900	7.534	7.565	7.763	18.312	19.998	21.187
AvgLife	0.71	16.40	14.46	9.14	0.36	0.32	0.29
Sprd Dur	0.64	8.63	8.05	5.61	0.33	0.28	0.26
DateWindow	2/25/10-	2/25/10~	2/25/10~	2/25/10~	2/25/10-	2/25/10-	2/25/10-
VARY INDEX?	9/25/11	5/25/34	5/25/34	5/25/34	8/25/10	7/25/10	7/25/10

NON-CALLABLE
FEB10 JAN DEC09NOV09
- 284 227 262p
- 17.1 13.6 15.7c

Treasury Curve - BGN 18:39 +
6mo -1- -2- -3- -5- -7- -10- -30-
0.15 0.28 0.80 1.31 2.30 3.07 3.61 4.55

Format# 3-IPY B
Australia 61 2 9777 8600 Brazil 5511 3048 4500 Europe 44 20 7330 7500 Germany 49 69 9204 1210 Hong Kong 852 2977 6000
Japan 81 3 3201 8900 Singapore 65 6212 1000 U.S. 1 212 318 2000 Copyright 2010 Bloomberg Finance L.P.
SN 221453 G516-1693-0 04-Feb-2010 18:39:52

Yields of an inverse floater (FNR 2009-102 TA) as a function of prepayment level and price. For example, "+300 BPM" is computed using the Bloomberg prepayment model with interest rates at 300 bp higher than current levels.

In the case of floaters, the index needs to be projected as well. Again, one can do this on a fixed basis, or can relate it to the current Treasury or swap curve forward rates, or can generate an interest rate model scenario.

Relevant functions include:

- YT—yield tables as a function of price and prepayment. Enter a price shift to get a full table. 0BPM as a prepayment speed means to run the Bloomberg prepayment model with flat projections. 100BPM means to run it with projections 1 percentage point higher (i.e., use an 8 percent coupon instead of a 7 percent coupon). 4BOB uses the fourth scenario of a 32-path OAS calculation as input for the prepayment model. 0BOB is the 0 percent volatility scenario.
- VALL—Prepayment speed quotes.

11.3.2 OAS Methodology

More powerful than computing yields under specific scenarios would be to compute the average value under a large set of realistic scenarios. The OAS is the shift to discount rates needed in this process to arrive at a specified price.

Because of the complexity of the prepayment model and the CMO tranche payment rules, this calculation must be done using Monte Carlo. The calculation takes a number of steps:

- The interest rate model is calibrated to observed rates and option prices.
- Interest rate scenarios are generated. Each scenario consists of discount rates, longer tenor rates, and par rates for each month for as many as 30 years.
- Indexes such as current coupons and the District 11 Cost of Funds are projected based on interest rate scenario projections.
- The prepayment vector for each scenario and each piece of collateral is computed.
- Based on the collateral cash flows and rate and index projections, the tranche cash flows are computed.
- The cash flows are discounted according to the rates from the corresponding scenario, shifted by the OAS.

The average of the discounted cash flows is the security price at the given OAS.

11.3.3 OAS and Prepayment

Some consider it problematic to use prepayment modeling in the context of OAS analysis. The thinking is that prepayment modeling, being a historical analysis, needs some sort of risk-neutral adjustment when being used in a risk-neutral option valuation context, and liken it to using historical volatility instead of implied volatility when valuing options.

This analysis is misguided. The historical analysis used in prepayment modeling is not trying to gauge pricing model parameters. The analysis is attempting to deduce the characteristics of the contingent claim held by the homeowner.

To clarify, consider a population holding European call options on a particular stock with varying maturity dates. Assume they all have the same strike, but we do not know what it is. All we have is historical data on the stock price and the payoff of the options when they are exercised. This data would essentially be a discrete random sampling of $\max(S - K, 0)$, where S is the stock price and K is the common strike. Historical analysis of this data would yield a good characterization of the actual payoff function. It would be perfectly correct to use this historically estimated payoff function for option pricing. No risk-neutral adjustment need be applied.

To the extent that prepayment is truly a contingent claim on interest rates, then there is no logical inconsistency in deducing it via historical analysis and using it directly in OAS analysis.

The problems that arise from using a prepayment model in OAS analysis come from other sources. Prepayment is far more complicated than a simple option. Errors in deducing homeowner behavior can cause pricing errors. Changes in the markets can effect homeowner behavior as well. Aggregation of behavior also introduces errors—it hinges on the assumption that the remaining drivers of prepayment behavior are independent of interest rates. Furthermore, applying a risk-neutral valuation on the aggregate behavior treats the market as if it is complete, when in fact prepayment cannot be perfectly hedged by pure interest rate instruments.

Some research (Levin and Davidson 2008; Brunson, Kau, and Keenan 2001) has tried to bridge these gaps through more direct modeling of the prepayment option held by the homeowner. More research is needed in this area.

11.4 Selection of Calibration Instruments

Realistic interest rate modeling requires good data on interest rates and volatility. A simple model calibrated to the right data will perform better than a sophisticated model calibrated to the wrong data. The right data is characterized by having good pricing and capturing the risks of the security being analyzed.

11.4.1 Treasury Market Calibration

Traditionally, mortgage OAS valuation was done relative to the Treasury curve. This was motivated by the thinking that agency-backed mortgages should be close to Treasuries in creditworthiness. However, it also has its drawbacks. The Treasury market is heterogeneous in that older bonds trade differently from new issuance, and volatility data (in terms of option prices) is sparse.

11.4.2 Swap Market Calibration

An alternative choice is to value mortgage market securities relative to the swap market. This has a number of advantages. The swap market is quoted more uniformly and densely, with the short end being given by Eurodollar futures and the longer end quoted on an annual basis as a par rate. Furthermore, caps, floors, and swaptions are also quoted. The caps and floors are quoted across strikes, giving information about the volatility smile. Swaptions are quoted across maturities and tenors, yielding rich information about the term structure of volatility. Quotes for swaption skews can be gotten as well. Another advantage of calibrating to swap market data is that mortgage-backed securities are typically hedged via the swap market. Calibrating to the swap market makes it easy to directly compute the appropriate hedges.

Due to these issues, the mortgage market has evolved to value securities relative to the swap market.

The credit crisis has complicated the situation. We first observed widening spreads between LIBOR rates and Treasury rates. Next, we observed dislocations between LIBOR rates of different tenors. For example, basis spreads in the U.S. market between three-month and six-month LIBOR swaps were plus or minus a basis point through the middle of 2007. As the crisis evolved, these spreads ramped up to as high as 45 basis points in March 2009. This has led to a flurry of research into the varying disconnects between LIBOR rates and risk-free forward rates, leading to various approaches that try to adapt the handling of basis spreads between currencies (Boenkost and Schmidt 2005; Fruchard, Zammouri, and Willems 1995) to spreads between rates of different tenors (Bianchetti 2010; Mercurio 2009; Morini 2009). Subsequently, basis spreads have dropped off to 5 to 10 basis points, and the needs for these approaches has diminished, but ideally basis spreads should still be taken into account at least in a basic way.

We believe the richness of volatility data in the swap market outweighs the complications that the credit crisis has introduced.

11.4.3 Capturing the Smile and Term Structure of Volatility

While calibration to the swap curve is straightforward, calibrating to the volatility data is more difficult. How closely the volatility data can be matched depends on the interest rate model being used. Single-factor models with time-dependent instantaneous volatility can calibrate to the term structure of one tenor of volatility, but not to the full volatility cube. Multifactor models have the advantage of calibrating to multiple strips of tenors, but at an increase in complexity and opacity.

In the mortgage markets, the two-year and 10-year tenor swaptions are often used for hedging. If model prices of the two-year and 10-year swaptions are off, then hedges probably will not be accurate, either. Conversely, calibrating to a large set of securities complicates pricing and hedge construction. If a subset of the securities captures most of the risk, then the hedges would be clearer and cheaper if one calibrated to the subset. This suggests that calibration should be to the two-year and 10-year swaptions.

For simpler models, the skew that can be captured is driven by the choice of model, with lognormal short-rate models exhibiting flat implied Black volatilities (as a function of strike), and normal short-rate models exhibiting a downward-sloping skew in Black volatility (a flat normal volatility). More complicated models such as rate-dependent volatility models (like the constant elasticity of variance model [CEV])

FIGURE 11.11   Swaption Skews at One Year

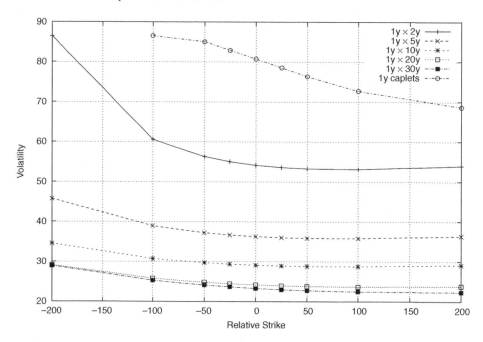

Black swaption volatility as a function of strike relative to the at-the-money (ATM) swap rate for swaptions maturing in one year and a variety of tenors.

or stochastic volatility models (like the stochastic alpha, beta, rho model [SABR]) can be calibrated to the volatility skew, but are harder to work with. To keep the modeling simple, we look for a model that can calibrate to the two cited strips of options and that also captures the skew.

It always pays to look at the data. Figures 11.11 and 11.12 are typical. Skews for different tenors at a given maturity tend to be parallel, although sometimes the market deviates from this, as we see here, where the short-maturity caplets show a markedly different skew from the longer-tenor swaptions. There is substantial change in volatilities both as a function of strike (skew) and as a function of maturity (term structure). Changes in volatility as a function of tenor are less pronounced, although they are substantial for very short maturities and tenors.

One way to analyze the skew is by fitting a skew model (such as the CEV model, $dr = \sigma r^{\beta} dW$) to each smile. In this model, a β of zero implies normally distributed rates, a β of one corresponds to lognormally distributed rates, and a β of $\frac{1}{2}$ corresponds to rates distributed as in the Cox-Ingersoll-Ross (CIR) process.

In Figures 11.13 and 11.14, we see the fit and the fitting error for the USD market from 2002 to 2010. The figures show that aside from some of the six-month maturity points, and except for 2007, the fitted volatilities are off by roughly 1 percent to 4 percent, so the CEV betas for these are reasonable indicators of the skew. Where they are off, there is a certain amount of smile that the CEV model cannot capture.

FIGURE 11.12 Swaption Skews at Five Years

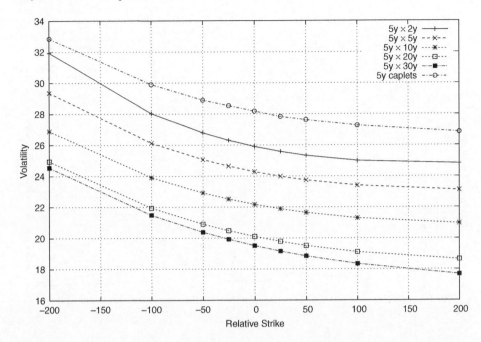

Black swaption volatility as a function of strike (relative to the ATM swap rate) for swaptions maturing in five years and a variety of tenors (taken from 2/9/2010).

FIGURE 11.13 CEV βs

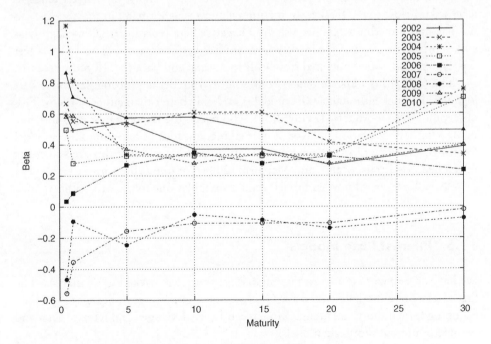

Fitted CEV β as a function of maturity for caplet skews on different dates.

FIGURE 11.14 CEV β Fitting Errors

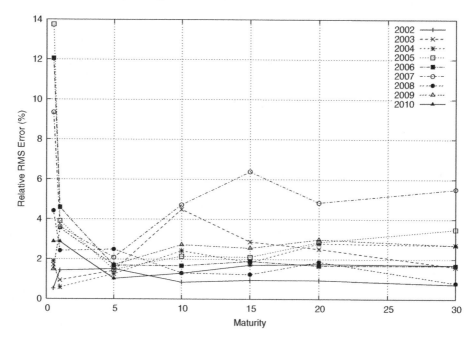

CEV model fitting errors as a function of maturity for the data sets of Figure 11.13.

From the betas we can see that aside from the short tenors, the market tends to have a skew close to a CIR skew, sometimes closer to lognormal, but mostly closer to normal, and sometimes exhibits a slightly negative beta (volatilities falling slightly as strikes increase). The change in skew over time is better seen in Figure 11.15. Over this time period, skews migrated from CIR to normal and back to CIR more recently.

The CIR β fits indicate that overall a normal model is probably favorable to a lognormal model, although a CIR model is probably better than either of them. This observation is supported by Levin (2004), who rejects the use of lognormal short-rate models for MBS valuation in favor of normal models. Ideally, one would use a model for which the skew can evolve over time, but methods for doing this are still being researched. See Errais, Mauri, and Mercurio (2004) for one approach.

Overall, the use of normal models remains popular due to their tractability.

11.5   Interest Rate Models

We have developed two interest rate models for mortgage-backed OAS analysis. The first interest rate model we used for OAS was developed over 10 years ago—a one-factor lognormal short rate model. More recently, we developed and released one- and two-factor normal short rate models.

FIGURE 11.15   CEV β Migration

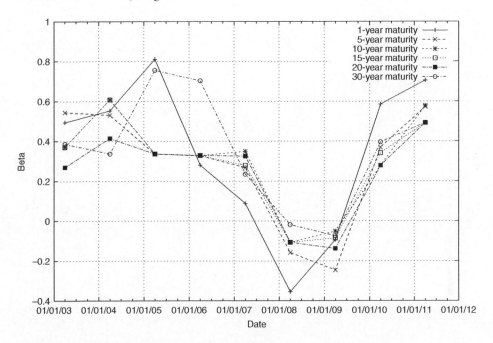

Fitted CEV β as a function of time for different maturities.

11.5.1   Lognormal Short Rate Models

Lognormal short rate models have been popular for many years in the fixed income markets. They are simple and intuitive, and lognormal processes have the property of always staying positive, which, a priori, is an attractive feature for a rate process. One example is Bloomberg's lognormal mean-reverting model, where the short rate process r_t is defined by the following risk-neutral dynamics with respect to the money market numéraire[1] ($N_t = e^{\int_0^t r_t dt}$):

$$dR_t = -aR_t dt + \sigma\, dW_t$$
$$r_t = e^{R_t + \theta t}$$

where a and σ are constants and θ_t is a function of time. θ_t is chosen so that discounting matches the yield curve. Under this model, R_t is Gaussian and mean-reverting to zero, so r_t is lognormal and mean-reverting as well.

While this is an attractive and straightforward model, in one-factor short rate models, rates of different tenors are fully correlated. When the short rate goes up, all the rates go up; and when the short rate goes down, all the rates go down. This model will never test the behavior of securities under any other type of yield curve movement (such as the short rates decreasing while the long rates increase). While there is some evidence that adding such movements has little impact on MBS pool pricing, it can

FIGURE 11.16   LIBOR versus 10-Year Swap Rate

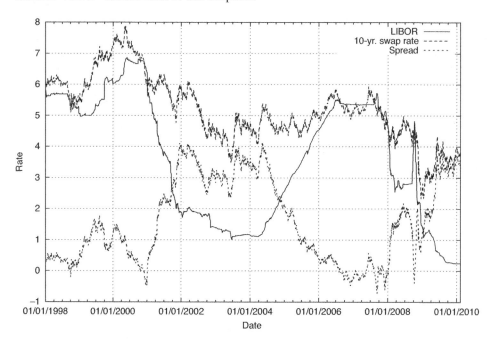

The spread between three-month LIBOR and the 10-year swap rate over time gives an indication of how the slope of the yield curve varies.

have a greater impact on CMO tranches. It is also not realistic. Since 1998, the spread between 3-month LIBOR and the 10-year swap rate has ranged from a low of −72 basis points (an inverted curve on 9/10/2007) to a high of 413 basis points, with a standard deviation of 132 basis points (Figure 11.16).

One could try to remedy this by using a two-factor lognormal model, but since there are no closed-form formulas for the yield curve as a function of the model state, it is difficult to make this practical.

The one-factor lognormal short rate model also suffers from a rigidity in calibration. The model has a time-dependent shift (θ_t) and two constant parameters (a and σ). This at best allows calibration to only the yield curve and two options. Calibrating to more options would have to be on a best fit basis. This would make the model prices of calibrating instruments different from their observed prices, essentially using the model to smooth observed option prices.

This could be remedied by making a and σ time or rate dependent. Making σ time dependent would allow calibration to one term structure of volatility. Making a time dependent as well would allow calibration to two term structures of volatility, but calibration of mean reversion is known to be difficult. Alternatively, making σ both rate and time dependent (a local volatility version of this model) would allow calibration to a full set of caps and floors, but still would not necessarily capture swaption pricing as well (which are European options on longer rates).

11.5.2 The Two-Factor LGM Model

Because of their tractability and flexibility, it has become common to use normal interest rate models. One family of models that are especially tractable is the linear Gaussian Markovian (LGM) family of models.

One way to specify a fixed income model is to specify the price processes of the zero coupon bonds. Let P_t^T of the value at time t of \$1 received at time T (the price at time t of a zero coupon bond maturing at time T). Then, $P_T^T = 1$, so given a numéraire N_t, an equivalent martingale measure is a measure Q such that

$$P_t^T = E^Q \left[\frac{1}{N_T} \bigg| \mathcal{F}_t \right] N_t$$

The LGM models are a family of models that specify P_t^T indirectly. Rather than specifying the P_t^T processes themselves, we select a numéraire N_t and a measure Q and use the preceding to specify P_t^T. This then guarantees the market is arbitrage free.[2]

For example, the one-factor LGM model is given by the numéraire:

$$dX_t = \alpha(t) dW_t$$
$$\eta(t) = \int_0^t \alpha^2(s) ds$$
$$N_t = \frac{1}{P_0^t} e^{H(t)X_t + \frac{1}{2} H^2(t)\eta(t)}$$

where W_t is Brownian motion. This formulation of the numeraire immediately guarantees calibration to the observed yield curve.

This is very similar to the Markov functional approach to interest rate modeling (Hunt, Kennedy, and Pelsser 2000). That method also picks a process and makes the numéraire a function of the process state. But rather than specifying the numéraire in closed form, it computes the numéraire numerically so as to fit an appropriate slice of the volatility cube. This is a powerful approach, but is not as tractable as the LGM approach.

The LGM model is equivalent to the one-factor Hull-White model, where the risk-neutral process for the short rate (r_t) with respect to the money market numéraire $(e^{\int_0^t r_t dt})$ is:

$$dr_t = (\theta(t) - \kappa(t)r_t)dt + \sigma(t)dW_t$$

where

$$\kappa(t) = -H''(t)/H'(t)$$
$$\sigma(t) = H'(t)\alpha(t)$$
$$\theta(t) = -(\log D(t))' H''(t)/H'(t) + (\log D(t))'' - (H'(t))^2 \eta(t)$$

or equivalently,

$$r_t = \theta^*(t) + X_t$$
$$dX_t = -a^*(t)X_t dt + \sigma^*(t)dW_t$$

where

$$\theta^*(t) = r_0 e^{-\int_0^t k(u)du} + \int_0^t e^{-\int_u^t k(s)ds} \theta(u)du$$
$$X_0 = 0$$
$$a^* = k$$
$$\sigma^* = \sigma$$

The particular member of this family that we have used is a two-factor version, which we will express in terms of the money market numéraire and in the latter form, namely:

$$r_t = \theta_t + X_t + Y_t$$
$$dX_t = -a_X X_t dt + \sigma_X(t)dW_1$$
$$dY_t = -a_Y Y_t dt + \sigma_Y(t)dW_2$$
$$dW_1 dW_2 = \rho dt$$

This is, in fact, equivalent to the two-factor Hull-White model and is also known as the G2++ model in Brigo and Mercurio (2001).

The two-factor LGM model is flexible enough to fit overall historically observed option prices, while calibrating as well to two strips of swaptions. Under this model, historical data indicates that one of the mean reversions is high, the other is low, and the correlation is close to -1. Our current defaults are $a_X = 0.03$, $a_Y = 0.5$, and $\rho = -0.7$.

Since high mean reversion dampens volatility, one can think of the low mean reversion factor as contributing to the volatility of long rates, and the two of them as contributing to the volatility of the short rates. Changes in the short rates are then the same as changes in the long rates, plus an additional noise component. The negative correlation between the two factors reduces the volatility of the short tenors, thus better fitting volatilities as a function of tenor. While the time-dependent volatilities could also be used to fit this market feature, using negative correlation allows it to persist in time. The current volatility term structure is shown in Figure 11.17. Figure 11.18 shows the model's volatility term structure after fitting to the swaption data. Figure 11.19 shows the fitting error.

While one would think that a two-factor model would allow for twists of the yield curve, it turns out that although this model allows some twisting, at the aforementioned parameter settings this behavior is minimal. The long rates and the short rates, while not having correlation one, still have extremely high correlation. More research needs

FIGURE 11.17 Swaption Term Structures

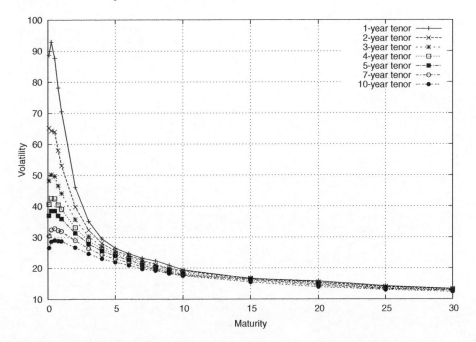

Market quotes for Black swaption volatilities as a function of maturity for various tenors.

FIGURE 11.18 LGM Model's Swaption Term Structures

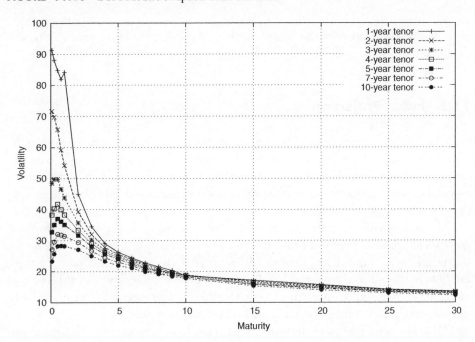

Black swaption implied volatility term structure from the LGM model fitted to 2-year and 10-year swaptions.

FIGURE 11.19   Term Structure Comparison

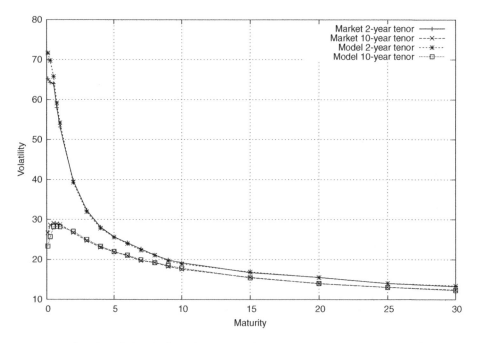

Comparison of market Black volatilities for 2-year and 10-year swaptions to Black implied volatilities from the LGM model fitted to the same data. The chart illustrates that relative fitting error is on the order of 2.5 percent, which translates to about $\frac{1}{2}$ a volatility point.

to be done on the impact of this and on further decoupling the movement of different tenors.

11.6   Index Projection

Scenario information impacts CMO tranche cash flow generation at two points in the calculation—during amortization of the collateral, and during paying of the bonds. During amortization, the scenario information is needed to feed the prepayment model. During cash flow generation, scenario information is used only when generating cash flows for floating rate tranches.

When the scenario information needed is discount rate information, be it a forward rate or a par rate, it is derived from the interest rate model. If the interest rate model is driven by the swap market, then the discount rates are swap market rates, so these imply LIBOR rates and swap rates. If the interest rate model is driven by the Treasury market, then these are Treasury discount rates and constant maturity Treasury (CMT) rates. Rates that are implied by the model we call *discount rates*.

Discount rates are straightforward to generate. In some models (such as the two-factor LGM model), there are formulas for these rates as a function of the model parameters and state variables of the model. In this case, the formulas are used to compute the discount rates directly. When formulas do not exist, the rates must be generated numerically. In the case of the one-factor lognormal model, this involves building a lattice for the short rate and discounting back from level to level to compute the discount factor implied for each rate at each level and for each tenor needed. From these discount factors, both implied forward rates and par rates can be computed. Scenario discount rates are then determined by interpolation on the lattice to give the discount rate as a function of the monthly short rate in the scenario.

However, rates other than discount rates are needed as well. The Bloomberg prepayment model uses the current coupon to derive prepayment rates. CMO tranches can float on LIBOR, Treasury rates, CMT rates, the District 11 Cost of Funds index, and other rates. The inputs needed that are economically related but are not discount rates we call *indexes*.

Index projection requires modeling the index as a function of the discount rates from the underlying interest rate model. The index projection method can be simple or complex. If the volatility of the index relative to the discount rates is ignored, then one can simply regress historically to determine the relationship and use this relationship to project the rates going forward. More complicated models can take lags between markets as well as volatility into account.

At Bloomberg, we chose to follow the simpler approach. For example, the current coupon rates are proxied by a linear combination of the two-year and 10-year par rates. The linear combination is derived through regression. To correct for 0th order errors, the projection is shifted to match the actual value of the current coupons. The regressions are periodically checked and adjusted to correct for changes in the relationships between the indexes and the discount rates.

Some rates (such as the District 11 Cost of Funds index) require more sophisticated treatment. For this index, we follow the approach from Stanton and Wallace (1995). If D_i is the index in month i, and T_i is the six-month Treasury rate, then the model sets $D_i = 0.889 * D_{i-1} + 0.112 * T_i + 5.6$ bp. No research has been done since then on the extent to which this model still fits the District 11 Cost of Funds index.

11.7 Monte Carlo Analysis

The accuracy of a Monte Carlo analysis is the standard deviation of the prices (or the calculated OAS at a given price) observed when repeating the Monte Carlo over and over again. Given appropriate statistical assumptions (i.i.d. samples, law of large numbers) this is approximately the standard deviation of the prices from the individual scenarios divided by the square root of the number of scenarios. For a general introduction to Monte Carlo analysis and variance reduction techniques, see Glasserman (2003). Akesson and Lehoczky (2000) compare quasi Monte Carlo techniques for MBS pricing under the one-factor Hull-White model and a simpler prepayment model.

Pricing options with naive Monte Carlo techniques can require as many as 100,000 scenarios for high accuracy. Using this many paths even for MBS pool valuation is prohibitively time consuming, primarily due to the time involved in the prepayment modeling. With CMOs backed by thousands of pieces of collateral, or even by other CMOs, needing so many paths would make the calculation intractable.

11.7.1 Variance Reduction in the One-Factor Lognormal Model

In the one-factor lognormal model, we speed up convergence by using a pseudo Monte Carlo. Paths are not random. They are chosen to best fit the stochastic differential equation (SDE) defining the short-rate process. The short rate path is generated by picking a set of bifurcation times (which always include $t = 0$). At each bifurcation time, each path is split into two paths and a semiannual step is taken with spacing chosen so that the first and second moments of R_t are matched (with up and down probabilities of 0.5). We can then solve for θ_t so that r_t yields the correct discounting.

To match the distribution for R_t, if the last bifurcation for this pair of paths occurred at time b and had value R, then the two values of R used at time t are given by

$$R^u = \mathbf{E}[R_t | R_b = R] + \sqrt{\mathrm{Var}[R_t | R_b = R]}$$
$$R^d = \mathbf{E}[R_t | R_b = R] - \sqrt{\mathrm{Var}[R_t | R_b = R]}$$

The expectation and variance can be solved for by solving the SDE for R. Trying to solve for a function $f(t, x)$ such that $R_t = f(t, W_t)$ does not work, but using integrating factors does. Multiplying the SDE for R_t by e^{at} and moving the dt term to the left side yields:

$$e^{at} dR_t + ae^{at} R_t dt = \sigma e^{at} dW_t$$

Since $d(e^{at} R_t) = e^{at} dR_t + ae^{at} R_t dt$, we immediately have that

$$\int_b^t d(e^{as} R_s) = e^{at} R_t - e^{ab} R_b = \int_b^t \sigma e^{as} dW_s$$

Solving for R_t yields

$$R_t = e^{a(b-t)} R_b + \int_b^t \sigma e^{a(s-t)} dW_s$$

The latter integral is a martingale, so

$$\mathbf{E}[R_t | R_b] = R_b e^{-a(t-b)}$$

FIGURE 11.20 Short Rate Paths

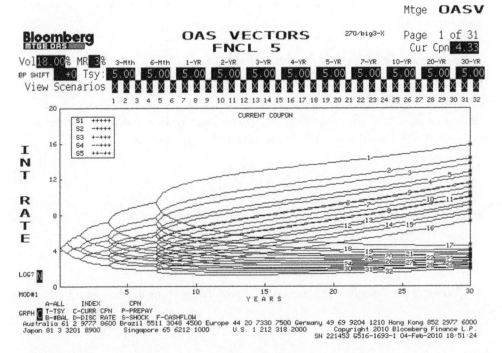

Short rate paths for the one-factor lognormal model with a flat 5 percent yield curve, 18 percent volatility, and 3 percent mean reversion, using 5 bifurcation points.

and the variance is $\mathbf{E}[(\int_b^t \sigma e^{a(s-t)} dW_s)^2] = \int (\sigma e^{a(s-t)})^2 ds$, so

$$\text{Var}[R_t | R_b] = \frac{\sigma^2}{2a}(1 - e^{-2a(t-b)})$$

Once all of the R^u and R^d are computed for time t, we then choose θ_t so that discounting \$1 from time t along all the paths and averaging gives the time t discount factor.

The short rate scenarios are then the set of paths through the bifurcation tree. For N bifurcation times there are 2^N paths. See Figure 11.20 for an example of the outcome of this process.

With a mean reversion of zero ($a = 0$) and the number of bifurcation points equal to the number of levels, the bifurcation method becomes a binary lattice for r.

The bifurcation method has the advantage of generating correct conditional distributions at the bifurcation points, and of being calibrated to the yield curve. Using this technique gives reasonable results with fairly small numbers of paths. However, variability is coarse with semiannual steps, and it is unclear that the overall variance is captured. It also does not extend well to the multifactor case. Similar to finite difference approaches, the bifurcation method suffers from the curse of dimensionality. For example, a two-factor model would require at least 3^n paths for n splittings. This would yield 59,049 paths for 10 splittings, whereas in a one-factor model, 10 splittings is only 1,024 paths.

11.7.2   Variance Reduction in the Two-Factor LGM Model

For the LGM model, we employ a variety of variance-reduction techniques. First, consider the choice of numéraire. To value an option, one must first select a numéraire N and change to a corresponding equivalent martingale measure Q. Under this measure, if V is the value of a self-financing portfolio or asset, then

$$\frac{V_s}{N_s} = E^Q\left[\frac{V_t}{N_t}\middle|\mathcal{F}_s\right], \; s < t$$

so

$$V_0 = N_0 E^Q\left[\frac{V_t}{N_t}\right]$$

If N' is another numéraire with associated equivalent martingale measure Q', then

$$\frac{N_t/N_0}{N_t'/N_0'} = \frac{dQ}{dQ'}$$

where dQ/dQ' is the Radon-Nikodým derivative of Q with respect to Q', and we have that

$$V_0 = N_0 E^Q\left[\frac{V_t}{N_t}\right] = N_0' E^{Q'}\left[\frac{V_t}{N_t'}\right]$$

While the two expectations give the same results, different measures weight the paths differently, and thus the choice of numéraire has an importance sampling effect on the Monte Carlo computation. A numéraire that is higher on high rates will have an equivalent martingale measure that is correspondingly higher as well, and thus the Monte Carlo associated with the higher numéraire will sample more heavily from this region.

Because prepayment is more stable in high-rate environments than in low-rate environments, MBS pools tend to behave more stably in high-rate environments. Thus, it is important to sample more from low-rate paths than from high-rate paths. This can be achieved by using a numéraire that is low for high-rate paths and high for low-rate paths.

Working with the native LGM numéraire is convenient for option pricing formulas. However, the native numéraire causes poor Monte Carlo behavior. The money market numéraire behaves much better. Although it is more difficult to work with the money market numéraire, it does better importance sampling of the rate space for MBS valuation.

Our second basic variance reduction technique is to shift θ_t for the specific set of paths generated so that discounting matches the yield curve. Combining these two methods gives a standard deviation of about 1 basis point for 2,000 paths. With 2,000 paths, the OAS is expected to be within 1 basis point of the calculated OAS about 30 percent of the time, and within 2 basis points about 66 percent of the time. We can compute this in about 15 seconds using our Linux clusters.

To further speed up the analysis, we use the principal component analysis (PCA) of the correlation matrix. Naive Monte Carlo analysis is done by simulating dW. We randomly generate the independent increments and sum them to generate a path. Another way to do Monte Carlo is to generate paths directly.

In the Monte Carlo for the two-factor LGM model, we ultimately need to randomly generate paths for X_t and Y_t. In other words, we need to randomly generate vectors of the form

$$P = (X_{t_1}, \ldots, X_{t_n}, Y_{t_1}, \ldots, Y_{t_n})$$

In the LGM model, X_{t_i} and Y_{t_i} are jointly distributed as a $2n$-dimensional Gaussian with zero mean. Let C be the covariance matrix of these $2n$ random variables. If

$$Z = (z_1, \ldots, z_{2n})^t$$

where the z_i are i.i.d. $N(0, 1)$, and $C = AA^t$, then AZ has the same distribution as P. Thus, we can generate paths P by generating the i.i.d. z_i and computing AZ.

One such matrix A satisfying $C = AA^t$ is given by the Cholesky decomposition of C. Another is the matrix whose columns are the eigenvectors of C, scaled by the square roots of their eigenvalues. The latter has the property that the best k-factor approximation to P is given by the sum of the first k columns of A (times z_1 through z_k), in the sense that it captures more of the variance than any other k-factor approximation. See Figures 11.21, 11.22, 11.23, and 11.24 for example eigenvectors.

While standard PCA analysis is helpful, it can still be improved on for mortgages and in general for fixed income. Because a mortgage generates monthly cash flows over potentially a 30-year period, each path is a 360-element vector. Roughly speaking, PCA generates this vector as a sum of sine functions of period 360, 180, 90, and so on. Since in fixed income, cash flows that are more distant in the future contribute less to the price than cash flows that are closer in time, variation this far in the future is wasted. This is doubly true for MBS pools, where principal pay-downs further shorten the duration.

To improve on PCA-based variance reduction for MBSs, we weight the near-term variance higher than the distant variance. This then generates sets of paths that less optimally capture the variance of P, but better capture the variance of MBS sensitivity to rates. Since discounting is exponential, it is natural to use exponential weighting of the PCA as well.

One additional step is necessary in the weighted PCA variance reduction technique. This is to take into account the differing impact of the two factors. The long

FIGURE 11.21 First Five Eigenvectors, First Factor, Unweighted PCA

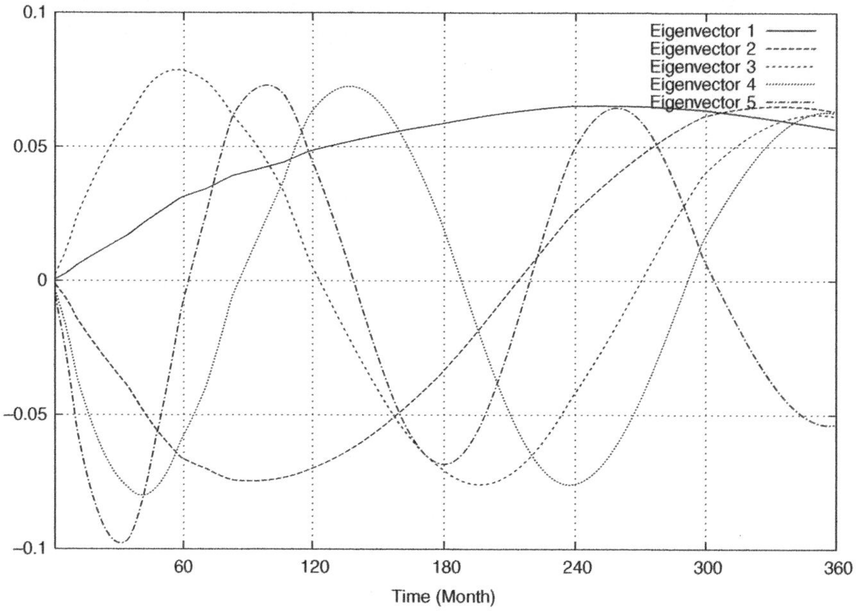

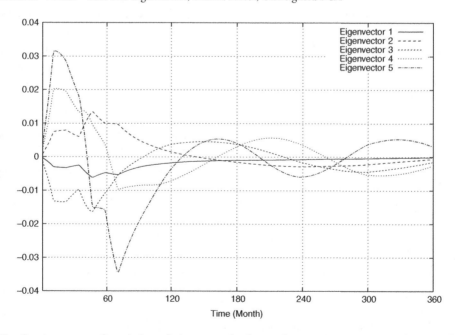

First five eigenvectors of a typical correlation matrix for the two-factor LGM. Eigenvectors shown are for the first factor using an unweighted PCA.

FIGURE 11.22 First Five Eigenvectors, Second Factor, Unweighted PCA

First five eigenvectors of a typical correlation matrix for the two-factor LGM. Eigenvectors shown are for the second factor using an unweighted PCA.

FIGURE 11.23 First Five Eigenvectors, First Factor, Weighted PCA

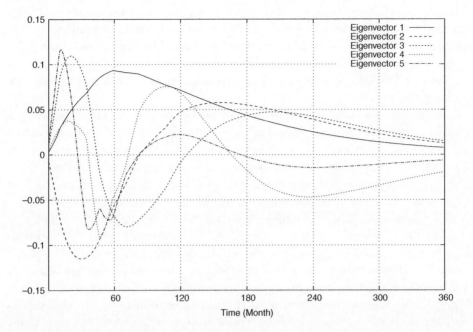

First five eigenvectors of a typical correlation matrix for the two-factor LGM. Eigenvectors shown are for the first factor using a weighted PCA.

FIGURE 11.24 First Five Eigenvectors, Second Factor, Weighted PCA

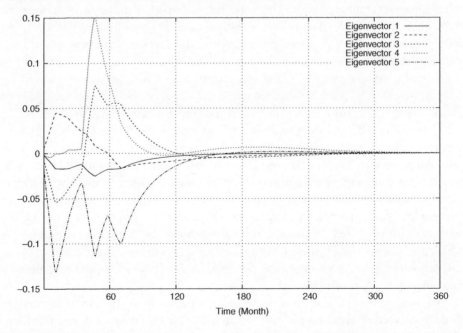

First five eigenvectors of a typical correlation matrix for the two-factor LGM. Eigenvectors shown are for the second factor using a weighted PCA.

rates are predominantly driven by the low mean-reversion factor, while short rates are driven by both factors. Thus, it makes sense to weight the high mean-reversion factor less in the Monte Carlo. The weighted PCA variance reduction technique reduces variance by roughly a factor of 2 compared to the baseline approach of using the money market numéraire with discounting adjustments. A factor of 2 reduction in the variance translates to a factor of 4 reduction in the number of paths needed for the same variance.

We tested two additional techniques to further reduce variance. One is local antithetic sampling. Antithetic sampling generates two paths for each vector of random numbers—the vector itself and its reflection relative to the distribution in question. Antithetic sampling often reduces variance, but is not very effective in interest rate Monte Carlo. However, we have found that local antithetic sampling coupled with PCA works well. Local antithetic sampling was first introduced in Dupire and Savine (1998), where it was called the uniform with antithetic noise (UWAN) method.

The local antithetic technique combines integration on a grid with antithetic sampling. The idea is to lay down a grid, randomly select one point from each grid element, and then choose the antithetic reflection from within each grid element. This combines the advantages of integrating on a grid with the noise cancellation of Monte Carlo. We have found that using this technique on the first two eigenvectors further reduces the variance, yielding pricing variances for weighted PCA with locally antithetic sampling of a factor of 4 lower than in the base case of using the money market numéraire with discounting adjustments, and thus reducing the number of paths for the same accuracy by a factor of 16.

Another method we have found to work well is using Sobol sequences. In fact, Sobol sequences combined with PCA works better than local antithetic sampling with PCA, in both the weighted and the unweighted cases. Even without weighting, using Sobol sequences with PCA gives slightly better variance reduction than weighted PCA with local antithetic sampling on the first two eigenvectors. Because of this, and to avoid any bias that weighted PCA might introduce in CMO pricing, we settled on using unweighted PCA with Sobol sequences as our variance-reduction technique of choice. Figure 11.25 summarizes the behavior of the different approaches.

One curious effect of PCA analysis is that despite reducing the number of paths, it can slow down the overall computation. Computing the eigenvectors of a 720×720 matrix can take 5 seconds on our Linux boxes. Doing it for computing the OAS, as well as for three shifted calculations (for computing duration, convexity, and vega) yields an additional 20 seconds of computation. For MBSs, where each path can be computed fairly quickly, this largely outweighs the savings given by reducing the number of paths needed. We tried to solve this problem by computing the four PCA calculations themselves in parallel, but this then requires distributing the results of the calculation to all the nodes, increasing the network time beyond the savings gotten by parallelizing the PCA calculations.

We worked around this problem by using a partial PCA. Instead of computing all the eigenvectors, we compute only the first 50. This is far faster than a full PCA, taking less than a second. Nonetheless, the first 50 eigenvectors capture almost all of

FIGURE 11.25 Monte Carlo Accuracy

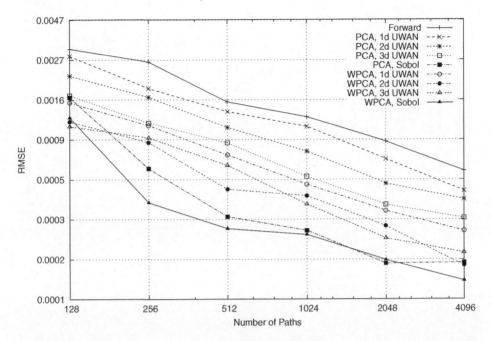

The "Forward" case is using the money market numéraire with discounting adjustments. PCA stands for principal component analysis. WPCA stands for weighted principal component analysis. The UWAN methods are done with one, two, and three eigenvectors.

the variance and thus have little impact on the variance reduction of the PCA method. Using partial PCA instead of full PCA enables us to compute a 500-path MBS OAS in about 6 seconds.

11.8 Parallelization

Even with variance-reduction techniques, interactive calculation of OASs for large CMOs is slow on a single CPU. Parallel processing is needed. At Bloomberg, we built Linux clusters to speed up response time, making it possible to run hundreds of paths for a large CMO in just a few seconds. Our Linux clusters originally consisted of 50 dual-CPU Linux boxes, on which we parallelize at the path level. We started building Linux clusters in 1997, with the first cluster based on the DEC Alpha, which was the fastest microprocessor at the time. Over time, we have built new clusters and retired old clusters. Our newest cluster is based on 32 quad-core dual-CPU blades for a total of 256 compute cores.

For MBSs, efficiency drops off rapidly as the number of slaves increases. This is because only one piece of collateral needs to be processed for each path, so the computation is dominated by communication time (Figure 11.26). For CMOs, efficiency

FIGURE 11.26 Parallelization Gain on an MBS

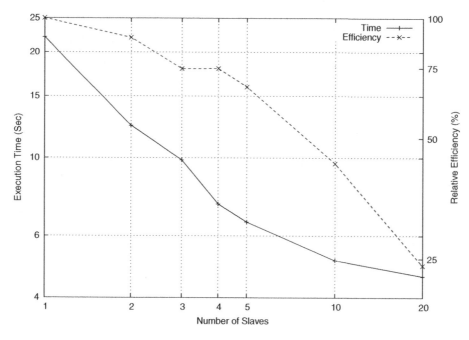

Effectiveness of path level parallelization for MBSs on non-GPU clusters.

also drops off as the number of slaves increases, but because far more computational effort is involved for each path, the parallelization maintains high efficiency (Figure 11.27).

Advances in the computational power of the graphical processing units (GPUs) of video cards has made running computations on GPUs increasingly popular. To capitalize on this computational power, we ported our CMO computations to the Compute Unified Device Architecture (CUDA) to run on GPUs. GPUs do not easily support variance-reduction techniques efficiently, and it would be time-consuming to port the entire computation to GPUs. To circumvent this, we used a hybrid approach of running the most time-consuming component of the computation on the GPUs and the rest on the CPUs. The end result is that the CPUs generate the interest rate paths and pay the tranches, and the GPUs run the prepayment model, collateral amortization, and cash flow computations.

Like CPUs, GPUs have layers of memory available that are accessible at different latencies, from small amounts of memory local to each core that can be accessed with low latency to larger amounts of memory globally accessible to all cores within the GPU and is very slow to access. Additional latency is introduced by the Single Instruction, Multiple Data (SIMD) architecture of the GPU, where threads operating in parallel can work on different data, but must be executing the same instructions. Due to the memory and SIMD latencies inherent in GPU calculations, parallelization

FIGURE 11.27   Parallelization Gain on a CMO

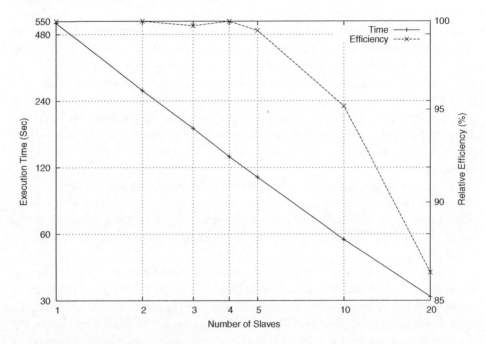

Effectiveness of parallelization for CMOs.

for the GPUs required simultaneous parallelization both by path and by piece of collateral. The parallelization is quite effective for CMOs backed by large numbers of individual pools or loans.

Comparing the performance of different hardware platforms is difficult. On the one hand, a PC with a GPU card can perform some CMO calculations 50 times faster than singly threaded code run on a PC without a GPU. However, the PC without a GPU is cheaper, and given that most CPUs now have multiple cores, the CPU is underutilized. A fairer comparison would be to compare a GPU-equipped PC to an equivalent dollar cost non-GPU system. The latter would be about 2.5 dual-CPU, quad-core PCs versus one dual-CPU quad-core PC equipped with four GPUs. But, while this is comparable in dollar terms, it is different in energy costs and footprint (which also has a cost).

To do the comparison, work must be done to efficiently parallelize the CPU version of the test as well. And, since the code that runs on a GPU is usually hand tuned for optimal performance, the same should be done for the CPU-based version. One should also note that optimization does not just include tuning a particular algorithm. It can also require changing algorithms. For example, for a finite difference computation, while on a CPU an implicit method could be optimal, on a GPU, latency and memory issues might make an explicit method optimal. Similarly, Monte Carlo variance-reduction techniques that are required for efficient computation on

CPUs could be so inefficient on GPUs that the optimal approach on the latter is to merely increase the number of scenarios.

Finally, there are different ways to parallelize, and different parallelizations are appropriate for different applications. Computing risks for the universe of CMOs on a nightly basis is different from an interactive application that computes OAS and key rate risks for individual CMOs. For the former, optimal performance might be gotten from running each deal as a separate process, with the number of simultaneous processes approximately the number of available cores (possibly a little higher, to take advantage of some pipelining and interleaving of computation and communications), whereas the latter may require spreading individual pricing calculations across multiple cores.

Due to these considerations, while performance comparisons are needed for making design decisions, they are rarely unbiased. Quoted comparisons must always be judged skeptically with an eye toward exactly what is being compared, how fairly it is being compared, and how representative the comparison is to the actual application at hand.

In our case, a GPU-based cluster of 12 nodes running Linux, each node with four NVIDIA Tesla GPUs and quad-core dual Intel CPUs (48 GPUs, 240 cores each) is comparable in price to a non-GPU cluster of 32 nodes, each with two quad-core CPUs (256 cores). Comparing the GPU-based cluster to the non-GPU Linux cluster, the slowest deals get over a factor of 10 improvement in speed. Because of differences in parallelization efficiency, there are some deals that run faster on the non-GPU cluster. We've observed some deals that for interactive computation are two times faster on the non-GPU cluster. But the bulk of them run faster on the GPU cluster. More importantly, because the slowest deals are orders of magnitude slower than the fastest deals, the GPU-based solution is an overall win for the overnight calculations. This is also with a reduced footprint and reduced power requirements (Hook and Tian 2009).

Another comparison we can do is with our nightly production cash flow runs. We have a nightly process that computes OAS, duration, and convexity for the universe of CMOs. This consists of doing three price computations (an OAS calculation is about the same amount of computation as a price calculation). With 32 paths per calculation, and computing some additional scenarios, we run a total of about 100 path calculations. We run this on a 48-core Sun Fire 6800 (cores running at 1.6 GHz), using 36 threads (leaving 12 cores available for other functionality). The current universe of CMOs that we do this for contains about 30,000 deals, for a total of about 3,000,000 path calculations. The entire calculation takes about six hours, yielding approximately 14,000 path calculations per hour per CPU core, ignoring the fact that some of the slowest deals are not processed because they take too long to complete.

We also compute OASs nightly for the same universe of CMOs on our GPU-based clusters. We have four GPU-based clusters, each with 12 nodes running Linux. All of the CPUs are Intel Xeons running at 3 GHz. The clusters use NVIDIA Tesla GPUs running at 1.44 GHz on two of the clusters and at 1.3 GHz on the other two clusters. Each machine has two quad-core CPUs and four GPUs. Each GPU has 240 cores. This gives each machine a total of eight conventional cores and 960 GPU cores.

Over the four clusters, this amounts to a grand total of 96 conventional CPUs and 192 GPUs, or, in terms of cores, 384 conventional cores and 46,080 GPU cores.

On the GPU clusters, instead of computing OASs using 32 paths and the one-factor model, we use 256 paths and the two-factor model. In addition to duration and convexity, we also compute key rate risks and vega volatility. This yields about 22 price calculations, or about 5,600 path calculations, 56 times the work we do for the one-factor OAS computation. Over the universe of CMOs, this amounts to 169,000,000 path calculations each night, and takes about three hours to complete, yielding about 147,000 paths per hour per GPU augmented conventional CPU core, or a factor of 10 over an unaided Sun core.

In addition to enabling us to run the two-factor OAS calculations nightly on the universe of CMOs, we are also able to run the universe of MBS pools. We do the same calculation as for CMOs, but for about 1,000,000 pools. We have not yet developed the code for efficiently running the MBS calculations on the GPUs, so we use four conventional clusters. Two of the clusters consist of 32 machines running Linux with two quad-core 2.3 GHz AMD CPUs each. The other two clusters have 48 machines also running Linux, but with two dual-core 2.4 GHz AMD CPUs each, for a grand total of 896 cores. The MBS calculation process starts running on these four clusters at the same time that the CMO calculations start on the GPU clusters. When the CMO calculations complete, the GPU clusters are used conventionally for MBS OAS. The entire run (MBS and CMO) takes 12 hours.

11.9 Calculating Greeks

Greeks are generally hard to calculate for Monte Carlo–based pricing. This is due to the noise in the price calculations.

11.9.1 Noisy Greeks

If $P(S)$ is the price of a security given a parameter value S (such as a shift of the volatilities or a shift of the interest rate environment), then the change in price with respect to a change in this parameter can be approximated by

$$\frac{dP}{dS} \approx \frac{P(S+h) - P(S-h)}{2h}$$

When P is the price of 100 par of an MBS pool or CMO tranche, and S is a shift of the interest rate environment (in percent, not in basis points), this yields the sensitivity of the price to interest rate shifts. From this, the duration is then D, where

$$D = \frac{-100\,dP/dS}{P(S)}$$

We can analyze the error in approximating the derivative by a difference using the Taylor expansion of P around S.

$$P(S + h) = P(S) + P'(S)h + \frac{1}{2}P''(S)h^2 + \frac{1}{3!}P'''(S)h^3 + \ldots$$

so

$$\frac{P(S + h) - P(S - h)}{2h} = P'(S) + \frac{1}{3!}P'''(S)h^2 + \ldots$$

The lowest order error term is thus quadratic in h and proportional to the third derivative of P. However, numerical calculations are rarely exact. Let $\bar{P}$ be what we actually compute. Then $\bar{P}(S) - P(S) = \epsilon(S)$ is the error seen in the price when computed at parameter value S. Then

$$\frac{\bar{P}(S + h) - \bar{P}(S - h)}{2h} = \frac{P(S + h) + \epsilon(S + h) - (P(S - h) + \epsilon(S - h))}{2h}$$

$$= P'(S) + \frac{1}{3!}P'''(S)h^2 + \cdots + \frac{\Delta\epsilon}{2h}$$

To avoid the derivative being tainted by higher-order nonlinearity, one must choose a small h. However, it is always tainted by the pricing error ϵ. Further compounding problems is the difference $\bar{P}(S + h) - \bar{P}(S - h)$ itself. As h tends to zero, $P(S + h) - P(S - h)$ tends to zero as well. However, $\epsilon(S + h) - \epsilon(S - h)$ does not tend to zero. So in fact, as h tends to zero, all that is left of $\bar{P}(S + h) - \bar{P}(S - h)$ is noise, rendering the derivative calculation nothing but noise as well. In fact, as h tends to zero, the actual calculated derivative will tend to infinity.

To get a good approximation for the derivative, one must balance the nonlinearity error introduced by a large h with the relatively large cancellation error in computing ΔP that is introduced by a small h, and one must try to keep ϵ relatively constant as well (to make $\frac{\Delta\epsilon}{2h}$ as small as possible).

Even for a common computation that can be done at machine precision (such as computing the difference derivative of a cumulative normal function), care must be taken in the choice of step size, and the step size needed is surprisingly large. The errors for a step size of 10^{-6} are noisy, and those for 10^{-4} are dominated by the convexity error. A step size of 10^{-5} nicely balances the two (Figure 11.28).

In numerical methods such as finite difference, ϵ tends to be fairly flat. The same holds for the bifurcation tree approach used in the lognormal one-factor model. But when the price is computed by a true Monte Carlo, $\epsilon(S + h)$ will typically be substantial and random. This can be overcome by using a large h, but at a cost of increasing the error due to nonlinearity.

A better way of controlling the error term in Monte Carlo calculations is to not compute $P(S + h)$ and $P(S - h)$ independently. By using the same paths (or even just the same random number seed), one can force $\epsilon(S + h)$ to be close to $\epsilon(S - h)$,

FIGURE 11.28 Difference Derivative Errors

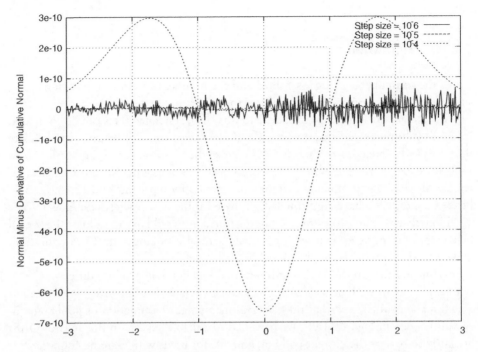

Error for difference derivative of the cumulative normal distribution for different step sizes.

thus controlling the error in the duration. We have had good success with durations calculated with 200 paths and 25 basis point shifts even though the pricing error is about 6 basis points.

11.9.2 Which Duration?

Durations are also affected by how other calibration instruments are handled. Given that $P(S)$ is computed by calibrating the model to the yield curve and to swaptions, should the same be done when computing $P(S + h)$? To be consistent within the pricing framework, it should. But this can actually be inconsistent with the interest rate model. The swaption volatilities are quoted in Black volatility, which is from a lognormal process. Using the same lognormal volatility when the rates are shifted increases the normal volatility when rates are moved up and decreases it when rates are moved down. This enforces lognormal behavior on top of the underlying interest rate model. This is irrelevant for a lognormal model, but the assumption in a normal model is that interest rate changes in absolute terms are independent of the level of rates. To maintain this assumption, one must hold the *normal* volatility of the options constant when shifting.

In the LGM model, to be consistent with the underlying interest rate process, we default to the latter. For those who are interested in seeing the impact of holding the quoted swaption volatilities constant, we allow the user to select this option on the screen.

11.10 Validation

Given the components being assembled and the number of assumptions being made, substantial work must be done to validate the results.

To validate the interest rate model Monte Carlo, generated rates can be compared to the distribution calculated analytically. Bullet bonds can also be priced to validate that the yield curve is correctly fitted. Of course, the convergence of the Monte Carlo itself must be checked as well. One would also like one's interest rate model to be reasonably close to reproducing currently observed option pricing, and also have some historic validity. We have confirmed all of these for the new interest rate model.

Nonetheless, when everything is put together, one would like to validate the overall behavior in the mortgage market. We have done this by looking at the OASs, duration, and convexities produced by the model.

While it is known that different interest rate models will produce different OASs, one would like to see that the OASs produced are relatively stable over time (modulo actual market shifts), and that they are reasonably flat as a function of pool coupon. As can be seen in Figure 11.29, we have had reasonable success in this regard. OASs are fairly close near the current coupon, and rise for pools with extreme coupons.

FIGURE 11.29 OAS

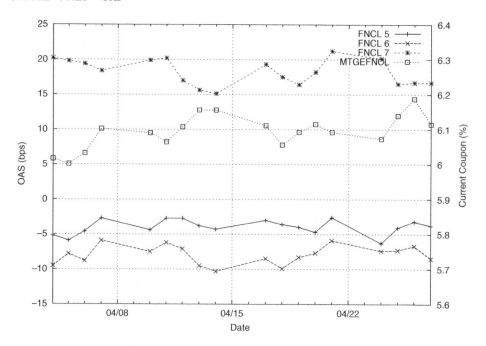

OASs computed from prices for pools of different coupons. Computations are for April 2006.

FIGURE 11.30   OAS Duration

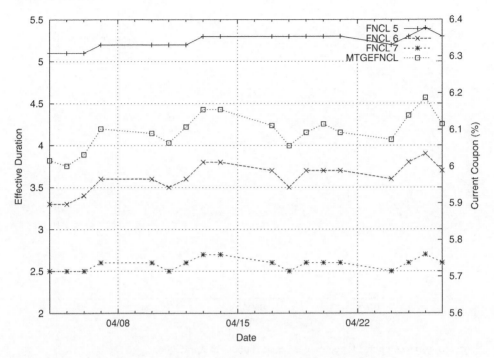

OAS durations computed for MBS pools of different coupons in April 2006.

Durations are a little harder to validate. Prepayment increases as rates drop, causing duration to drop as well. This is one behavior to look for. Another is agreement with history. In that duration is the relative change in price with respect to change in yield, one can compute it historically by regressing yield against price. This is known as *empirical duration*. Different choices of yield (short or long rates, Treasury or swap rates) and different historical window sizes will yield different results. Also, empirical duration is a trailing indicator, while OAS duration is a leading indicator. This means that while rates are trending down, empirical duration should be higher than OAS duration, and while rates are trending up, the opposite should hold. Thus while OAS duration and empirical duration cannot necessarily be directly compared, one can at least look for these sorts of relationships.

Figure 11.30 shows that we have been reasonably successful in generating stable OAS durations that behave rationally. Durations drop when the current coupon drops, with the drop having the greatest impact on the coupons near but below the current coupon.

Finally, prepayment activity should cause negative convexity. As rates rise and prepayment drops (and the security thus starts to behave more like a fixed payment bond), convexity should increase. Figure 11.31 shows that we have achieved this behavior as well.

FIGURE 11.31 OAS Convexities

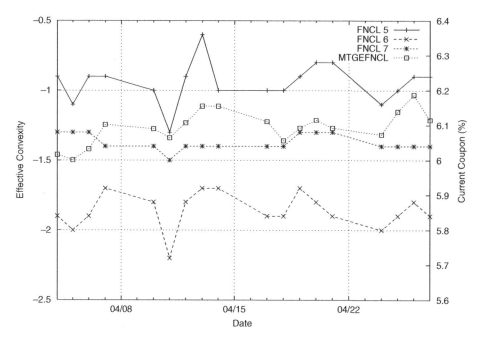

OAS convexities computed for pools of different coupons in April 2006.

11.11 Conclusion

There has been substantial turmoil and change in the markets over the past few years. We have seen a substantial housing bubble collapse, triggering a subprime crisis that caused banks to fail, leading to a credit crisis and a recession that required substantial governmental intervention. These events have demanded reevaluation of the methodologies used in CMO valuation.

We have reviewed the methodologies used in CMO valuation and how the credit crisis has impacted it. As we've seen, the big science of CMO valuation has lots of moving parts, with each one drawing on a different area. Prepayment modeling draws on statistical modeling of economic behavior. Data selection draws on risk analysis. Interest rate modeling draws on classic arbitrage pricing theory applied to the fixed income market. Index projection draws on statistical analysis. Making the Monte Carlo analysis tractable requires working with numerical methods and investigation of a variety of variance-reduction techniques. Tractability also requires parallelization, which draws on computer science in building computation clusters, applying new technology such as GPUs, and analysis and optimization of parallel algorithms. As Emanuel Derman (2004) says, quantitative finance is an interdisciplinary endeavor. CMO valuation proves the point.

We have detailed the different components, describing the approach we have taken at Bloomberg, with particular emphasis on how the credit crisis has impacted valuation.

We have detailed the validation of these components, showing that everything works well together and yields good MBS and CMO valuation. And we have discussed the technology used for doing nightly analyses of the entire universe of MBSs and CMOs.

While the events of the recent crisis have required tuning and revisiting the valuation methodologies used in MBS and CMO valuation, the overall techniques and approaches have remained valid.

Acknowledgments

Special thanks to Warren Xia and Sherman Liu, Prepayment Modeling Group, Bloomberg LP, for their work on prepayment modeling; Liuren Wu, Quantitative Finance R&D Group, Bloomberg LP, for his work on the two-factor normal model; Michael Geller for discussions about the CMO market; and James Hook for his work on porting the calculations to GPUs and for discussions about GPUs.

Notes

1. A numéraire is an asset or portfolio that always has positive value. The risk-neutral dynamics are the dynamics under the equivalent martingale measure. This is an equivalent measure Q under which V/N is a martingale whenever V is the value of a self-financing portfolio or asset. Under this measure, the time t value of a contingent claim with value V_T at time $T > t$ is $E^Q[V_T/N_T|F_t]N_t$. The first fundamental theorem of option pricing says that the market is arbitrage free if and only if Q exists.
2. The first fundamental theorem of arbitrage pricing theory requires the numéraire to be the price process of an admissible strategy. While this may not hold when the zero coupon bond price processes are constructed as described earlier from an arbitrary numéraire (the model may not be complete), the numéraire can always be added to the market without introducing arbitrage, thus satisfying the requirements of the first fundamental theorem.

References

Akesson, F. and J. P. Lehoczky. 2000. Path generation for quasi-Monte Carlo simulation of mortgage-backed securities. *Management Science* 46, no. 9 (September): 1171–1187.

Bianchetti, M. 2010. Two curves, one price: Pricing & hedging interest rate derivatives decoupling forwarding and discounting yield curves. (January 11). Available at http://ssrn.com/abstract=133435.

Boenkost, W. and W. M. Schmidt. 2005. Cross currency swap valuation. (May 6). Available at http://ssrn.com/abstract=1375540.

Brigo, D., and F. Mercurio. 2001. *Interest rate models—theory and practice*. New York: Springer-Verlag.

Brunson, A. L., J. B. Kau, and D. C. Keenan. 2001. A fixed-rate mortgage valuation model in three state variables. *Journal of Fixed Income* (June).

Derman, E. 2004. *My life as a quant: Reflections on physics and finance*. Hoboken, NJ: John Wiley & Sons.

Dupire, B., and A. Savine. 1998. Dimension reduction and other ways of speeding Monte Carlo simulation. In *Monte Carlo: Methodologies and applications for pricing and risk management*. London: Risk Books.

Errais, E., G. Mauri, and F. Mercurio. 2004. Capturing the skew in interest rate derivatives: A shifted lognormal LIBOR model with uncertain parameters. (November 22). www.fabiomercurio.it/sllmup.pdf.

Fruchard, E., C. Zammouri, and E. Willems. 1995. Basis for change. Risk 8, no. 10 (October): 70–75.

Glasserman, P. 2003. *Monte Carlo methods in financial engineering*. New York: Springer.

Green, R., and A. Schnare. 2009. The rise and fall of Fannie Mae and Freddie Mac: Lessons learned and options for reform. (November 19). Available at http://ssrn.com/abstract=1509722.

Hook, J., and X. Tian. 2009. GPU acceleration of CMO OAS. GPU Technology Conference. www.nvidia.com/content/GTC/videos/GTC09-1431.flv.

Hunt, P., J. Kennedy, and A. Pelsser. 2000. Markov-functional interest rate models. *Finance and Stochastics* 4 issue 4 (August): 391–408, doi:10.1007/PL00013525, www.springerlink.com/content/en3. Working paper available at http://ssrn.com/abstract=49240 or doi:10.2139/ssrn.49240.

Levin, A. 2004. Interest rate model selection. *Journal of Portfolio Management* 30, no. 2 (Winter): 74–86, doi:10.3905/jpm.2004.319932.

Levin, A., and A. Davidson. 2008. The concept of credit OAS in valuation of MBS. *Journal of Portfolio Management* (Spring).

Liu, S. 2009. The "new normal" for prepayment behavior. Bloomberg mortgage research.

Liu, S., and W. Xia. 2010. Bloomberg prepayment models updated for agency buyout. BMMI<Go> on the Bloomberg terminal.

Mercurio, F. 2009. Interest rates and the credit crunch: New formulas and market models. (February 5). Bloomberg Portfolio Research Paper No. 2010-01-FRONTIERS. Available at http://ssrn.com/abstract=1332205.

Morini, M. 2009. Solving the puzzle in the interest rate market (Parts 1 & 2). (October 12). Available at http://ssrn.com/abstract=1506046.

Stanton, R., and N. Wallace. 1995. ARM wrestling: Valuing adjustable rate mortgages indexed to the eleventh district cost of funds. *Real Estate Economics* 23.

Veale, S. 2008. The credit crisis of 2008–2009??–2010??? Bloomberg seminar, April 14.

Xia, W., and S. Liu. 2008. The Bloomberg fixed-rate MBS prepayment model. PBPM<Go> on the Bloomberg terminal.

PART IV

Counterparty Risk Pricing and Credit Valuation Adjustment

CHAPTER 12

CVA Computation for Counterparty Risk Assessment in Credit Portfolios

Samson Assefa

Équipe Analyse et Probabilité, Université d'Évry Val d'Essonne, and CRIS Consortium

Tomasz R. Bielecki

Professor of Applied Mathematics, Illinois Institute of Technology

Stéphane Crépey

Université d'Évry Val d'Essonne and CRIS Consortium

Monique Jeanblanc

Université d'Évry Val d'Essonne, Europlace Institute of Finance, and CRIS Consortium

We first derive a general counterparty risk representation formula for the credit valuation adjustment (CVA) of a netted and collateralized portfolio. This result is then specified to the case, most challenging from the modeling and numerical point of view, of counterparty credit risk. Our general results are essentially model free. Thus, although they are theoretically pleasing, they do not immediately lend themselves to any practical computations. We therefore subsequently introduce an underlying stochastic model, in order to put the general results to work. We thus propose a Markovian model of portfolio credit risk in which dependence between defaults and the wrong-way risk are represented by the possibility of simultaneous defaults among the underlying credit names. Specifically, single-name marginals in our model are themselves Markov, so that they can be precalibrated in the first stage, much like in the standard (static) copula approach. One can then calibrate the few model dependence parameters in the second stage. The numerical results show a good agreement of the behavior of expected positive exposure (EPE) and CVA in the model with stylized features.

12.1 Introduction

Counterparty risk is one of the most primitive forms of risk associated with contracts (financial and otherwise) between two or more counterparties. The understanding and ability to measure and manage counterparty risk associated with the over-the-counter (OTC) financial contracts have been growing along with the growing volume of the literature on the subject. The brief discussion that follows of some of the works studying counterparty risk is by no means complete and comprehensive; it is rather meant to give a flavor of what has been done in this area so far.

In Canabarro and Duffie (2003) an introduction to methods used to measure, mitigate, and price counterparty risk is given. In addition, the authors provide a discussion of use of the Monte Carlo simulation to measure counterparty risk. Also, they discuss practical calculation of credit valuation adjustment (CVA) in the case of OTC derivatives by considering currency and interest rate swap agreements between two defaultable counterparties.

A discussion of counterparty risk and credit mitigation techniques at the portfolio level is given in De Prisco and Rosen (2005). In particular the authors provide a discussion of how Monte Carlo simulation and approximation methods, such as add-on approaches (as in Basel I, for example), as well as some analytical approximations, can be used to calculate various statistics related to the measurement of counterparty credit risk. Their paper provides a discussion of practical implementation of collateral modeling, and the calculation of expected exposure in credit derivatves portfolios with wrong-way risk.

Zhu and Pykhtin (2007) provide a discussion of the simulation of credit exposure and collateral modeling in the presence of a call period. They also discuss calculation of expected exposure (EE) and credit valuation adjustment (CVA) assuming the wrong-way risk.

Redon (2006) gives two different analytical methods to calculate expected exposure in order to account for the wrong-way risk. The first analytical method accounts for wrong-way risk due to currency depreciation in the case of country risk. This method gives expected exposure as a weighted average of the expected exposure when assuming there is a country crisis and of the expected exposure when assuming there is no country crisis. The second analytical method is based on the Merton-like model of default risk (cf. Bielecki and Rutkowski 2002) and the calculation of expected exposure assuming a Brownian motion model for the mark-to-market value of the portfolio subject to counterparty risk. These assumptions allow the author to account for wrong-way risk by correlating the Brownian motions used to model default and mark-to-market. Moreover, using this modeling framework it was possible to derive analytical expressions for expected exposure.

Gibson (2005) provides both an analytical and a Monte Carlo simulation method to calculate expected exposure and expected positive exposure to a margined and collateralized counterparty. The analytical method is based on a Gaussian model for the mark-to-market value of the portfolio exposed to counterparty risk, while the Monte Carlo simulation is based on a Gaussian random walk. Using the Gaussian model the author investigates the dependence of a collateralized exposure on: the initial mark-to-market, the threshold, the remargining period, the grace period, and the minimum transfer amount.

Brigo and Tarenghi (2004) price equity swaps with counterparty risk in a first passage structural model of credit risk using tractable formulas and indicate that it is much less tractable to use a reduced form of credit risk to do the pricing.

Using a reduced form of credit risk where the default intensity of the counterparty is assumed to be deterministic, Brigo and Masetti (2005) consider how to calculate the CVA of interest rate swaps assuming unilateral counterparty credit risk. In the case of a single interest rate swap they show CVA can be calculated tractably while if there are netting agreements they provide approximation formulas that enable the calculation of CVA at the portfolio level.

Brigo and Pallavicini (2008) consider unilateral counterparty risk in interest rate payoffs in the presence of correlation between the interest rates and the default event. Using a reduced form model of credit risk, the authors show that counterparty risk has a significant impact on CVA and the magnitude of CVA depends on the correlation. They also consider the calculation of CVA for a portfolio of interest swaps with netting agreements, European swaptions, Bermudan swaptions, and constant-maturity swap spread options.

In Brigo, Pallavicini, and Papatheodorou (2010) the valuation of interest rate swaps assuming bilateral counterparty credit risk is considered, generalizing the work in Brigo and Pallavicini (2008). The effect of correlation between the default spread of the counterparty, the default spread of the investor, and interest rates on CVA is analyzed. The authors also provide results on the calculation of CVA for a portfolio of interest rate swaps.

Brigo and Chourdakis (2008) analyze unilateral counterparty risk in CDSs using a reduced form model of credit risk where default events are connected using a bivariate copula on the exponential triggers. They show that in the absence of volatility in the default intensities CVA decreases as the correlation parameter for the copula approaches 1. Hence the authors point to the importance of having volatility in the default intensities to account for wrong-way risk.

Brigo and Capponi (2008) consider bilateral counterparty risk. They provide a general formula for the representation of CVA in the absence of joint defaults. Using a trivariate Gaussian copula for modeling the default dependence of the investor, the counterparty, and the underlying CDS name, they show that in the absence of spread volatility the CVA decreases as the correlation between the investor and the counterparty is close to 1. Hence they conclude that pure contagion models could be inappropriate to model CVA as they underestimate the risk in a high-correlation environment. Moreover, it is shown that simple add-on approaches cannot be used effectively to capture the behavior of CVA.

Calculation of CVA in the case of bilateral credit risk on a portfolio consisting of over-the-counter derivatives is considered in Gregory (2009). Using a Gaussian copula model and allowing for simultaneous defaults, the author finds that the contribution of simultaneous default (which represents systematic risk) to the calculation of CVA is not significant. The paper concludes with a cautionary note regarding the use of bilateral CVA.

Lipton and Sepp (2009) study counterparty credit risk in CDS contracts via a structural model based on the jump-diffusion process. They develop original methods for computation of CVA in this context.

12.1.1   What Is Done in This Chapter

We consider in this chapter several issues related to the valuation and mitigation of counterparty credit risk (CCR) on an OTC credit-derivative contract, or, more generally, on a portfolio of OTC credit derivatives, written between two counterparties, relative to a pool of credit names. In particular, we study bilateral counterparty risk on a credit default swap (CDS), and unilateral counterparty risk on a portfolio of CDSs, in a suitable model of dependence for the underlying default times. In addition, we consider the issues of mitigation of counterparty credit risk by means of netting and/or collateralization (or margining).[1]

Remark 12.1.1 *We need to stress, though, that in order to simplify our presentation we give a highly stylized model for the collateral process. In particular we do not explicitly account for such aspects of the collateral formation as:*

- *Haircut provisions*
- *Margin period of risk*
- *Minimum transfer amounts*
- *Discrete tenor remargining*
- *Various classes of assets used as collateral*
- *Collateral thresholds*

We shall incorporate these important considerations into our model in a future paper.

In this context we discuss the problem of representation and computation of the credit valuation adjustment (CVA). It is generally accepted that (cf. Canabarro and Duffie 2003, 128) the *CVA of an OTC derivatives portfolio with a given counterparty is the market value of the credit risk due to any failure to perform on agreements with that counterparty.* Thus, essentially, we have that (cf. Section 12.2.1)

$$CVA = P - \Pi$$

where P represents the market value of the portfolio not accounting for the counterparty risk, and Π is the market value of the portfolio with accounting for the counterparty risk.

However, CVA can be represented as (cf. equation (12.6))

$$CVA = \mathbb{E}(discounted\ PFED)$$

where $\mathbb{E}$ represents a suitable mathematical expectation, and PFED is the potential future exposure at default. We characterize the PFED random variable in Lemma 12.2.1.

Remark 12.1.2 *It needs to be stressed that typically, when assessing the counterparty risk, practitioners begin with modeling the flow of so-called potential future exposure (PFE) and then they derive from the PFE various measures of the counterparty risk, such as the CVA (cf. De Prisco and Rosen 2005). In this regard we proceed in an opposite direction: We start with CVA defined as $P - \Pi$ and then deduce the relevant potential future exposure at default (PFED). It also needs to be noted that there are various ways in which financial institutions define PFE. Our definition of PFED is in line of the way the potential future exposure is understood in De Prisco and Rosen (2005) or in Zhu and Pykhtin (2007).*

In case of a deterministic discount factor we provide yet another representation of the CVA in terms of an appropriate integral of the so-called expected positive exposures (EPEs); see equations (12.14) and (12.15).

12.1.1.1 Outline of the Chapter

Section 12.2 presents preparatory results about general counterparty risk. In Section 12.3 these results are specified to the case of counterparty credit risk. All the developments done in these first two sections are essentially model free. Thus, although they are theoretically pleasing, they do not immediately lend themselves to any practical computations. In Section 12.4 we propose an underlying stochastic model that is able to put the previous results to work, also guaranteeing a satisfactory performance of the proposed methodology. In Section 12.5 numerical results are presented and discussed.

12.2 General Counterparty Risk

We consider two parties of a financial contract. We call them *the investor* and *the counterparty*. Furthermore, we denote by τ_{-1} and τ_0 the default times of the investor and of the counterparty, respectively. We will study unilateral counterparty risk from the perspective of the investor (i.e., $\tau_{-1} = \infty$ and $\tau_0 < \infty$), as well as the bilateral counterparty risk (i.e., $\tau_{-1} < \infty$ and $\tau_0 < \infty$).

We start by deriving a general (not specific to credit markets) representation formula for bilateral counterparty risk valuation adjustment for a fully netted and collateralized portfolio of contracts between the investor and his/her counterparty. This result can be considered as general since, for any partition of a portfolio into netted subportfolios, the results of this section may be applied separately to every subportfolio. The exposure at the portfolio level is then simply derived as the sum of the exposures of the subportfolios. This result is thus a generalization of that of Brigo and Capponi (2008) to a possibly *collateralized* portfolio.

It needs to be emphasized that we do not exclude simultaneous defaults of the investor and his/her counterparty,[2] since our model in Section 12.4 precisely builds upon the possibility of simultaneous default as a way to account for default dependence. We do assume, however, that the default times cannot occur at fixed times, as is for instance satisfied in all the intensity models of credit risk, such as the one introduced in Section 12.4.

For $i = -1$ or 0, representing the two counterparties, let H^i and J^i stand for the default and nondefault indicator processes of τ_i, so $H^i_t = \mathbb{1}_{\tau_i \leq t}$, $J^i_t = 1 - H^i_t$. We also denote $\tau = \tau_{-1} \wedge \tau_0$, with related default and nondefault indicator processes denoted by H and J, respectively. In case where unilateral counterparty credit risk is considered, one simply sets $\tau_{-1} = +\infty$, so in this case $\tau = \tau_0$.

We fix the portfolio time horizon $T \in \mathbb{R}_+$, and we fix the underlying risk-neutral pricing model $(\Omega, \mathbb{F}, \mathbb{P})$ with a filtration $\mathbb{F} = (\mathcal{F}_t)_{t \in [0, T]}$ such that τ_{-1} and τ_0 are $\mathbb{F}$-stopping times. One assumes that all the *processes* considered are $\mathbb{F}$-adapted, all the *random variables* are $\mathcal{F}_T$-measurable, all the random times are $[0, T] \cup \{+\infty\}$-valued, and all the semimartingales are càdlàg. We denote by $\mathbb{E}_\tau$ the conditional expectation under $\mathbb{P}$ given $\mathcal{F}_\tau$, for any stopping time τ. All the cash flows and prices (mark-to-market values of cash flows) are considered from the perspective of the investor. In accordance with the usual convention regarding *ex-dividend* valuation, $\int_a^b$ is to be understood as $\int_{]a,b]}$ (so in particular $\int_a^b = 0$ whenever $a \geq b$).

Let D and $\mathcal{D}$ represent the counterparty clean and counterparty risky cumulative dividend processes of the portfolio over the time horizon $[0, T]$, assumed to be finite variation processes. By *counterparty clean cumulative dividend process* we mean the cumulative dividend process that does not account for the counterparty risk, whereas by *counterparty risky cumulative dividend process* we mean the cumulative dividend process that does account for the counterparty risk.

Let β denote a finite variation and continuous *discount factor* process. The following definitions are consistent with the standard theory of arbitrage (cf. Delbaen and Schachermayer 2006).

Definition 12.2.1 (i) *The* counterparty clean price process (or counterparty clean mark-to-market (MTM) process) *of the portfolio is given by* $P_t = \mathbb{E}_t[p^t]$, *where the random variable* $\beta_t p^t$ *represents the* cumulative discounted cash flows of the portfolio on the time interval $]t, T]$, not accounting for counterparty risk, *so, for* $t \in [0, T]$,

$$\beta_t p^t = \int_t^T \beta_s \, dD_s \tag{12.1}$$

(ii) *The* counterparty risky MTM *process of the portfolio is given by* $\Pi_t = \mathbb{E}_t[\pi^t]$, *where the random variable* π^t *represents the* cumulative discounted cash flows of the portfolio adjusted for the counterparty risk *on the time interval* $]t, T]$, so, for $t \in [0, T]$,

$$\beta_t \pi^t = \int_t^T \beta_s \, d\mathcal{D}_s \tag{12.2}$$

Remark 12.2.2 *Recall* $\tau = \tau_{-1} \wedge \tau_0$, $J = 1 - H$. *In the counterparty risky case there are no cash flows after* $\tau \wedge T$, *so the* ($\mathcal{F}_T$-*measurable*) *random variable* π^t *is in fact* $\mathcal{F}_{\tau \wedge T}$-*measurable, and* $\pi^t = \Pi_t = 0$ *for* $t \geq \tau \wedge T$.

We consider collateralized portfolios. In this regard we consider a *cumulative margin process* and we assume that no lump margin cash flow can be asked for at time τ. Accordingly, given a finite variation cumulative margin process of the form $\gamma = J\mu + H\mu_{\tau-}$, so $\gamma_t = \mu_t \mathbb{1}_{t < \tau} + \mu_{\tau-} \mathbb{1}_{t \geq \tau}$ (note that γ does not jump at time τ), we define the *cumulative discounted margin process* by

$$\beta\Gamma = \int_{[0,\cdot]} \beta_t J_t \, d\gamma_t \tag{12.3}$$

So, in particular, $\Gamma_0 = \gamma_0 - \gamma_{0-}$, and since J is killed at τ and γ does not jump at τ, one has for $\tau < \infty$,

$$\beta_\tau \Gamma_\tau = \int_{[0,\tau)} \beta_t \, d\gamma_t$$

Comments 12.2.1 **(i)** *Collateralization is a key modeling issue, particularly with regard to the development of centralized clearinghouses for CDSs. Indeed, in the case of a centralized market, the counterparty risk is transferred from the market participants to the clearinghouse, and from the level of contracts or portfolios of contracts to the level of the margin calls. More precisely, the question becomes whether the clearinghouse will be able to face nonrecovered margin amounts called at times of default of market participants. If the counterparty risk model of the clearinghouse is good enough so that the degree of confidence of the market participants in the clearinghouse is sufficiently high, then the centralization of the market will have a beneficial effect. Otherwise the centralization may have little impact.*
(ii) *As postulated before, we consider just one collateral account, which may take either positive or negative value. Of course, a negative value from the perspective of one of the two counterparties means a positive value from the perspective of the other counterparty, and vice versa.*
(iii) *The restriction that no margin can be asked for at time* τ *is of course motivated by the financial interpretation. In fact, to be more realistic in this regard, it would be important to introduce a notion of delay as in Zhu and Pykhtin (2007).*
(iv) *Note that we are implicitly assuming in equation (12.3) that the margin account consists of cash, which is put into a margin account and reinvested at the risk-free rate.*

According to the Basel Committee on Banking Supervision (cf. Basel Committee on Banking Supervision 2004, 31), other forms of collateral may be used, such as:

- *Gold.*
- *Debt securities rated by a recognized external credit assessment institution where these are either:*
  - *At least BB– when issued by sovereigns or public sector entities (PSEs) that are treated as sovereigns by the national supervisor.*
  - *At least BBB– when issued by other entities (including banks and securities firms).*
  - *Or at least A-3/P-3 for short-term debt instruments.*
- *Debt securities not rated by a recognized external credit assessment institution where:*
  - *They are issued by a bank, listed on a recognized exchange, and classified as senior debt.*
  - *All rated issues of the same seniority by the issuing bank that are rated at least BBB– or A-3/P-3 by a recognized external credit assessment institution; and the bank holding the securities as collateral has no information to suggest that the issue justifies a rating below BBB– or A-3/P-3 (as applicable).*
  - *The supervisor is sufficiently confident about the market liquidity of the security.*
- *Equities (including convertible bonds) that are included in a main index.*
- *Undertakings for collective investments in transferable securities (UCITS) and mutual funds.*

However, according to the ISDA (2003) survey it is mostly cash that is used for collateral, with some instances of sovereign bonds that are used for this purpose. It is not clear whether credit derivatives have ever been or are used as collateral, although the European Central Bank (2009) indicates that CDS contracts can be used for this purpose. In a future work we will investigate how well default-sensitive instruments (such as CDS contracts) can mitigate, if used as a collateral, the value of default of the counterparty.
(v) Here we take the margining process as given. In particular the issue of optimal collateralization (in some sense, cf., e.g., Aparicio and Cossin 2001) is not considered here, and is left for future research.

We assume for notational simplicity that γ and Γ are killed at T (so $\Gamma_t = \gamma_t = 0$ for $t \geq T$) and we define a random variable $\chi_{(\tau)}$ as

$$\chi_{(\tau)} = P_{(\tau)} + \Delta D_\tau - \Gamma_\tau \text{ if } \tau < T, \text{ and zero otherwise} \qquad (12.4)$$

in which, for $\tau < \infty$, $\Delta D_\tau = D_\tau - D_{\tau-}$ denotes the jump of D at τ,[3] and where the so-called *legal value* $P_{(\tau)}$ is an $\mathcal{F}_\tau$-measurable random variable representing an (ex-dividend) fair value of the portfolio at time τ (in a sense to be specified later, cf. in particular Remark 12.2.4).

Let D^* denote the dividend process corresponding to the cash flows of D stopped at $\tau-$, that is,

$$D^* = JD + HD_{\tau-}$$

Assumption 12.2.1 The counterparty risky portfolio cumulative dividend process is given by

$$\mathcal{D} = D^* + \Gamma_\tau H + \left(R_0 \chi^+_{(\tau)} - \chi^-_{(\tau)}\right)[H, H^0]$$
$$- \left(R_{-1} \chi^-_{(\tau)} - \chi^+_{(\tau)}\right)[H, H^{-1}] - \chi_{(\tau)}[[H, H^0], H^{-1}] \qquad (12.5)$$

where the $\mathcal{F}_{\tau_0}$—and $\mathcal{F}_{\tau_{-1}}$—measurable random variables R_0 and R_{-1}, respectively, denote the recovery rates of the investor and of its counterparty upon default, and $[\cdot, \cdot]$ is the covariation process; that is, in the case of pure jumps processes, it is the sum of products of common jumps.

Remark 12.2.3 *Though the previous structural assumption on the cash flows makes perfect sense with respect to the financial interpretation of netting and margining, one may object that in case of the default of a counterparty the cash flow [equation (12.5)] always has the same functional form regardless of what happens with the reference dividend process. For example, in case of modeling the counterparty risk relative to an underlying CDS contract, we postulate that the recovery structure in case of a default of a counterparty is the same regardless of whether the counterparty defaults at the same time as the default time of the obligor referencing the CDS contract. It might seem at first sight that this tacit assumption excludes* wrong-way risk *(Redon 2006) from the model, namely the risk that the value of the contract be particularly high from the perspective of the other party at the moment of default of the counterparty, which is a major issue regarding counterparty risk. In fact, the recovery* structure *in case of a default of a counterparty is the same, but the* ingredients *of the structure ($\chi_{(\tau)}$, specifically) may support wrong-way risk, with for instance a significant chance that ΔD_τ in $\chi_{(\tau)}$ be more important than a typical ΔD_t, as will be the case in our credit risk applications and models.*

12.2.1 CVA Representation Formula

As we will now see, (cf. also, e.g., Brigo and Capponi 2008), one can represent the *credit valuation adjustment* process CVA $:= J(P - \Pi)$ in the form

$$\beta_t \text{CVA}_t = J_t \mathbb{E}_t\left[\beta_\tau \xi_{(\tau)}\right] \qquad (12.6)$$

where $\xi_{(\tau)}$ is a suitable $\mathcal{F}_\tau$-measurable random variable called *potential future exposure at default* (PFED).

Comments 12.2.2 **(i)** *Since we consider the general case of the bilateral counterparty risk, the CVA process may take any real value. In case of the unilateral counterparty risk,* *this process always takes either nonnegative values or nonpositive values, depending on which of the two parties entails the counterparty risk.*

(ii) *In general, the representation given in equation (12.6) does not uniquely define $\xi_{(\tau)}$. It is an open question under what assumptions on the model filtration $\mathbb{F}$ the representation (12.6) uniquely defines $\xi_{(\tau)}$.*

The following result is of interest:

Lemma 12.2.1   *A version of PFED is given by:*

$$\xi_{(\tau)} = P_\tau - P_{(\tau)} + (1 - R_0)\mathbb{1}_{\tau=\tau_0}\chi^+_{(\tau)} - (1 - R_{-1})\mathbb{1}_{\tau=\tau_{-1}}\chi^-_{(\tau)} \qquad (12.7)$$

Proof.   One has,

$$J_t\mathbb{E}_\tau \int_t^T \beta_s\left(dD_s - dD_s^*\right) = J_t\mathbb{E}_\tau \int_{[\tau,\,T]} \beta_s\,dD_s$$
$$= J_t\beta_\tau\left(P_\tau + \Delta D_\tau\right) = J_t\beta_\tau\left(P_\tau - P_{(\tau)} + \chi_{(\tau)} + \Gamma_\tau\right)$$

So, taking conditional expectation given $\mathscr{F}_t$,

$$J_t\mathbb{E}_t\left\{\int_t^T \beta_s\left(dD_s - dD_s^*\right) - \beta_\tau\Gamma_\tau\right\} = J_t\mathbb{E}_t\left\{\beta_\tau\left(P_\tau - P_{(\tau)} + \chi_{(\tau)}\right)\right\}$$

Thus, by Definition 12.2.1 and in view of equation (12.5),

$$J_t\beta_t(P_t - \Pi_t) = J_t\mathbb{E}_t\left\{\beta_\tau\left(P_\tau - P_{(\tau)} + \chi_{(\tau)}\right)\right\}$$
$$- J_t\mathbb{E}_t\left\{\beta_\tau\left(\mathbb{1}_{\tau=\tau_0}\left(R_0\chi^+_{(\tau)} - \chi^-_{(\tau)}\right) - \mathbb{1}_{\tau=\tau_{-1}}\left(R_{-1}\chi^-_{(\tau)} - \chi^+_{(\tau)}\right) - \mathbb{1}_{\tau_0=\tau_{-1}}\chi_{(\tau)}\right)\right\}$$

which can be checked by inspection to coincide with $J_t\mathbb{E}_t\left[\beta_\tau\xi_{(\tau)}\right]$, with $\xi_{(\tau)}$ here defined by the right-hand side of equation (12.7). The result follows by definition (12.6) of a PFED.

In the rest of the chapter we impose the following standing hypothesis:

Assumption 12.2.2 $P_{(\tau)} = P_\tau$.

Remark 12.2.4   *This assumption appears to be considered as the current market standard. Arguably (see Crépey, Jeanblanc, and Zargari 2010a), a more consistent choice, but also a more intensive one from the computational point of view, might be $P_{(\tau)} = \Pi_{\tau-}$. We observed in Crépey, Jeanblanc, and Zargari (2010a) that, in the simple reduced-form setup of that paper, adopting either convention made little difference in practice. One should be aware that this might not be the case in different (like structural) setups, however.*

So, henceforth,

$$\xi_{(\tau)} = (1 - R_0)\mathbb{1}_{\tau=\tau_0}\chi_{(\tau)}^+ - (1 - R_{-1})\mathbb{1}_{\tau=\tau_{-1}}\chi_{(\tau)}^- \tag{12.8}$$

with

$$\chi_{(\tau)} = P_\tau + \Delta D_\tau - \Gamma_\tau \tag{12.9}$$

In case β is deterministic, the following alternative representation of the CVA at time 0 immediately follows from equations (12.6) and (12.8):

$$\beta_0 \text{CVA}_0$$
$$= \mathbb{E}[\beta_\tau \xi_{(\tau)}] = \mathbb{E}\left(\beta_\tau(1 - R_0)\mathbb{1}_{\tau=\tau_0}\chi_{(\tau)}^+\right) - \mathbb{E}\left(\beta_\tau(1 - R_{-1})\mathbb{1}_{\tau=\tau_{-1}}\chi_{(\tau)}^-\right)$$
$$= \int_0^T \beta_s \mathbb{E}\left((1 - R_0)\mathbb{1}_{\tau=\tau_0,\,\tau_0\in ds}\chi_{(\tau)}^+\right) - \int_0^T \beta_s \mathbb{E}\left((1 - R_{-1})\mathbb{1}_{\tau=\tau_{-1},\,\tau_{-1}\in ds}\chi_{(\tau)}^-\right)$$
$$= \int_0^T \beta_s \mathbb{E}\left((1 - R_0)\chi_{(\tau)}^+ \mid \tau_0 = s,\, \tau_0 \leq \tau_{-1}\right)\mathbb{P}(\tau_0 \in ds,\, s \leq \tau_{-1})$$
$$\quad - \int_0^T \beta_s \mathbb{E}\left((1 - R_{-1})\chi_{(\tau)}^- \mid \tau_{-1} = s,\, \tau_{-1} \leq \tau_0\right)\mathbb{P}(\tau_{-1} \in ds,\, s \leq \tau_0)$$
$$= \int_0^T \beta_s \text{EPE}_+(s)\mathbb{P}(\tau_0 \in ds,\, \tau_{-1} \geq s) - \int_0^T \beta_s \text{EPE}_-(s)\mathbb{P}(\tau_{-1} \in ds,\, \tau_0 \geq s)$$
$$\tag{12.10}$$

where the *expected positive exposures* $\text{EPE}_\pm$, also known as the *asset charge* and the *liability benefit*, respectively, are the functions of time defined by, for $t \in [0, T]$,

$$\text{EPE}_+(t) = \mathbb{E}\left[(1 - R_0)\chi_{(\tau)}^+|\tau_0 = t \leq \tau_{-1}\right],$$
$$\text{EPE}_-(t) = \mathbb{E}\left[(1 - R_{-1})\chi_{(\tau)}^-|\tau_{-1} = t \leq \tau_0\right] \tag{12.11}$$

Remark 12.2.5 *Note that the following representation for CVA$_0$ may be better for computational purposes:*

$$\beta_0 CVA_0 = \int_0^T \int_s^T \beta_s \mathbb{E}\left((1 - R_0)\chi_{(\tau)}^+ \mid \tau_0 = s \; \tau_{-1} = u\right)\mathbb{P}(\tau_0 \in ds,\, \tau_{-1} \in du)$$
$$\quad - \int_0^T \int_s^T \beta_s \mathbb{E}\left((1 - R_{-1})\chi_{(\tau)}^+ \mid \tau_{-1} = s,\, \tau_0 = u\right)\mathbb{P}(\tau_{-1} \in ds,\, \tau_0 \in du)$$
$$= \int_0^T \int_s^T \beta_s \widetilde{EPE}_+(s, u)\mathbb{P}(\tau_0 \in ds,\, \tau_{-1} \in du)$$
$$\quad - \int_0^T \int_s^T \beta_s \widetilde{EPE}_-(u, s)\mathbb{P}(\tau_{-1} \in ds,\, \tau_0 \in du) \tag{12.12}$$

$$\widetilde{EPE}_+(t, r) = \mathbb{E}\left[(1 - R_0)\chi_{(\tau)}^+ | \tau_0 = t, \tau_{-1} = r\right],$$

$$\widetilde{EPE}_-(r, t) = \mathbb{E}\left[(1 - R_{-1})\chi_{(\tau)}^- | \tau_0 = r, \tau_{-1} = t\right] \qquad (12.13)$$

In the context of unilateral counterparty risk, that is, $\tau_{-1} = \infty$, equation (12.10) of course reduces to:

$$\beta_0 CVA_0 = \int_0^T \beta_s \, EPE(s)\mathbb{P}(\tau \in ds) \qquad (12.14)$$

where the *expected positive exposure* (*EPE*) is the function of time defined by, for $t \in [0, T]$,

$$EPE(t) = \mathbb{E}\left[\xi_{(\tau)} | \tau = t\right] = \mathbb{E}\left[(1 - R_0)\chi_{(\tau)}^+ | \tau_0 = t\right] \qquad (12.15)$$

Remark 12.2.6 *Frequently, in the case of unilateral counterparty risk, the EPE is computed under the assumption that $R_0 = 0$.*

Remark 12.2.7 *In a future paper we plan to study dynamics of the CVA process to see how it reacts to varying credit quality of both counterparties, and, in case of counterparty credit risk, to the credit quality of the reference portfolio.*

Comments 12.2.3 **(i)** *As we already observed, the terminology used in the literature dealing with counterparty risk is quite fluid. For example, what we call expected positive exposure, and what we denote as EPE(t), is frequently called* expected (conditional) exposure *and is denoted as EE(t). Then the expected positive exposure over, say, the nominal lifetime of the portfolio—that is, over the interval [0, T]—is defined as the average,*

$$\frac{1}{T}\int_0^T EE(t)dt$$

(ii) *CVA is one of the possible measures of the PFED.*[4] *In the context of unilateral counterparty risk, alternative commonly used measurements of PFED are:*

The effective EPE *(efEPE), computed at the time horizon one year (1y) as [to be compared with equation (12.14)],*

$$\beta_0 efEPE = \mathbb{E}(\beta_\tau \xi_\tau | \tau < 1y) = \frac{\int_0^{1y} \beta_s \, EPE(s)\mathbb{P}(\tau \in ds)}{\mathbb{P}(\tau < 1y)} \qquad (12.16)$$

The exposure at default *profile EAD(t) defined by, for t typically taken as the portfolio time horizon T, or, in case of credit limits with term structure (such as 1y, 2y, 5y . . .), t varying in the term structure,*

$$\beta_0 EAD(t) = \alpha \max_{s \in [0,t]} \mathbb{E}(\beta_\tau \xi_\tau | \tau < s) \tag{12.17}$$

for some conservative factor $\alpha > 1$; *or, alternatively to equation (12.17), no conservative factor* α, *but consideration of a high-level quantile* q_α *(with, e.g.,* $\alpha = 95\%$*) instead of the conditional expectation in equation (12.17), so,*

$$\beta_0 EAD(t) = \max_{s \in [0,t]} q_\alpha (\beta_\tau \xi_\tau | \tau < s)$$

12.2.2 Collateralization Modeling

Modeling the margin process is very important, too. In particular, for

$$\gamma_t = P_0 + \int_{(0,t]} J_s \beta_s^{-1} d(\beta_s P_s), \quad \Gamma_\tau = P_{\tau-} \tag{12.18}$$

one gets,

$$\xi_{(\tau)} = \xi_{(\tau)}^1 = (1 - R_0)\mathbb{1}_{\tau=\tau_0} (\Delta(D + P)_\tau)^+ - (1 - R_{-1})\mathbb{1}_{\tau=\tau_{-1}} (\Delta(D + P)_\tau)^- \tag{12.19}$$

The choice $\Gamma_\tau = P_{\tau-}$ (cf. equation (12.18)) is, arguably, the extreme case of the collateral.

More generally, the good understanding of the principles of accumulation of the collateral is a crucial issue. Apart from the previous extreme case, here is a possible suggestion in case of bilateral risk when both counterparties are contractually obliged to post the collateral whenever called for.

We assume that adjustments of the account are done according to a discrete tenor, say $0 < t_1 < t_2 < \cdots < t_n < T$. Here is the description of the mechanics of the collateral account, where $\Delta_{i,i+1}$ stands for $\Gamma_{t_{i+1}} - \frac{\beta_{t_i}}{\beta_{t_{i+1}}}\Gamma_{t_i}$:

- If $\Gamma_{t_i} > 0$ and if $\Delta_{i,i+1} > 0$, then counterparty 0 needs to post, at time t_{i+1}, the collateral amount equal to $\Delta_{i,i+1}$.
- If $\Gamma_{t_i} > 0$ and if $\Delta_{i,i+1} \leq 0$, then counterparty 0 receives back, at time t_{i+1}, the amount equal to $-\Delta_{i,i+1}$ from the collateral account in case $\Gamma_{t_{i+1}} > 0$; however, if $\Gamma_{t_{i+1}} \leq 0$ then counterparty 0 receives back, at time t_{i+1}, the amount equal to $\frac{\beta_{t_i}}{\beta_{t_{i+1}}}\Gamma_{t_i}$ from the collateral account, and counterparty -1 posts, at time t_{i+1}, the collateral in the amount of $-\Gamma_{t_{i+1}} \leq 0$.

- If $\Gamma_{t_i} \leq 0$ and if $\Delta_{i,i+1} < 0$, then counterparty -1 needs to post, at time t_{i+1}, the collateral amount equal to $-\Delta_{i,i+1}$.
- If $\Gamma_{t_i} \leq 0$ and if $\Delta_{i,i+1} \geq 0$, then counterparty -1 receives back, at time t_{i+1}, the amount equal to $\Delta_{i,i+1}$ from the collateral account in case $\Gamma_{t_{i+1}} < 0$; however, if $\Gamma_{t_{i+1}} \geq 0$ then counterparty -1 receives back, at time t_{i+1}, the amount equal to $-\frac{\beta_{t_i}}{\beta_{t_{i+1}}}\Gamma_{t_i}$ from the collateral account, and counterparty 0 posts, at time t_{i+1}, the collateral in the amount of $\Gamma_{t_{i+1}} \leq 0$.

Now, we come to the issue of how to compute the quantities Γ_{t_i}. Let V_t be the generic symbol for the value of the contract's exposure at time t due to bilateral counterparty risk. For example:

- $V_t = CVA_t^0$, where CVA_t^0 is the uncollateralized CVA, that is, CVA computed setting $\Gamma \equiv 0$.
- $V_t = \Pi_t^0$, where Π^0 is the uncollateralized risky MTM process.
- $V_t = P_t$, the intrinsic MTM process.
- $V_t =$ the intrinsic MTM process adjusted for margin period of risk, for minimum transfer amount, for thresholds, for haircuts, and so on.

Remark 12.2.8 *At first sight it might seem reasonable to consider that the collateral cash flow should be somehow decided based on the fluctuations of the discounted CVA process, rather than based on the fluctuations of the MTM process. However, in view of equations (12.8) and (12.9) (under our standing Assumption 12.2.2), the choice $V_t = P_t$ is probably the most appropriate.*

The general idea for accumulating the collateral should be that the collateral amount changes in the same direction as the process V. For example, we might postulate that

$$\Gamma_{t_{i+1}} = \frac{\beta_{t_i}}{\beta_{t_{i+1}}}\Gamma_{t_i} + f(\beta_{t_i}, \beta_{t_{i+1}}, \Gamma_{t_i}, V_{t_i}, V_{t_{i+1}}) \tag{12.20}$$

where f is a function satisfying two general conditions:

$$f(\beta', \beta'', c, a, b) \geq 0 \text{ if } \frac{\beta'}{\beta''}a < b, \quad f(\beta', \beta'', c, a, b) \leq 0 \text{ if } \frac{\beta'}{\beta''}a > b$$

$$f(\beta', \beta'', c, a, b) = 0 \text{ iff } |\frac{\beta'}{\beta''}a - b| \leq \epsilon$$

for some $\epsilon > 0$.

Comments 12.2.4 **(i)** *The preceding formulas need to be appropriately adjusted in case of the unilateral counterparty risk exposure. In particular, one will then need to take either positive or negative parts of* V_t, *depending on the point of view.*
(ii) *Zhu and Pykhtin (2007), who consider the case of unilateral counterparty risk only, compute the collateral using the following specifications:*

- $V_t = \Pi_t$
- $f(\beta', \beta'', c, a, b) = \max(a - H, 0) - \frac{\beta'}{\beta''} c$

where H represents a threshold, so that $\Gamma_{t_{i+1}} = \max(\Pi_{t_i} - H, 0)$.

12.3 Counterparty Credit Risk

We now specify the general setup presented earlier to the situation of the counterparty credit risk.

Toward this end we postulate that the contracts comprising the portfolio between the investor and his/her counterparty reference defaultable credit names. Next, we denote by τ_i, for $i = 1, \ldots, n$, the default times of n credit names underlying the portfolio's contracts. We set $\mathbb{N}_n = \{-1, 0, 1, \ldots, n\}$, $\mathbb{N}_n^* = \{1, \ldots, n\}$. For $i \in \mathbb{N}_n$, we let H^i and J^i stand for the default and nondefault indicator processes of τ_i (assumed to be an $\mathbb{F}$-stopping time), so $H_t^i = \mathbb{1}_{\tau_i \le t}, J_t^i = 1 - H_t^i$. We assume that the default times τ_i's cannot occur at fixed times. We do not, however, exclude simultaneous jumps of the credit names.

12.3.1 General Credit-Risky Portfolio

We shall consider in this section counterparty credit risk associated with portfolios of contracts between two counterparties and referencing *single underlyings*. Let thus the portfolio constituents cumulative dividend processes be given by, for $i = 1, \ldots, n$,

$$D^i = \int_{[0, \cdot]} J_u^i \, dC_u^i + \int_{[0, \cdot]} \delta_u^i \, dH_u^i = J^i C^i + H^i \left(C_{\tau_i-}^i + \delta_{\tau_i}^i \right)$$

for a bounded variation *coupon process* $C^i = (C_t^i)_{t \in [0, T]}$, and a *recovery process* $\delta^i = (\delta_t^i)_{t \in [0, T]}$. We assume for simplicity that the C^i's do not jump at the τ_j's (otherwise this would induce further terms in some of the identities that follow).

The counterparty clean portfolio cumulative dividend process is thus $D = \sum_{i \in \mathbb{N}_n^*} D^i$. So, by linearity, the portfolio MTM process is given as $P = \sum_{i \in \mathbb{N}_n^*} P^i$, where for $i = 1, \ldots, n$,

$$P_t^i = \mathbb{E}_t p_i^t \text{ with } \beta_t p_i^t = \int_t^T \beta_s \, dD_s^i \tag{12.21}$$

Note that

$$\Delta D_\tau = \sum_{i \in \mathbb{N}_n^*} \mathbb{1}_{\tau_i = \tau} \delta_\tau^i \qquad (12.22)$$

So in particular, for the collateralization policy $\Gamma_\tau = P_{\tau-}$ (cf. equation (12.18)), we have that equation (12.19) yields

$$\xi_{(\tau)} = \xi_{(\tau)}^1 = (1 - R_0)\mathbb{1}_{\tau = \tau_0} \left(\sum_{i \in \mathbb{N}_n^*} \mathbb{1}_{\tau_i = \tau} \delta_\tau^i + \Delta P_\tau \right)^+$$

$$- (1 - R_{-1})\mathbb{1}_{\tau = \tau_{-1}} \left(\sum_{i \in \mathbb{N}_n^*} \mathbb{1}_{\tau_i = \tau} \delta_\tau^i + \Delta P_\tau \right)^- \qquad (12.23)$$

which typically reduces to (assuming the P^i's do not jump at τ unless $\tau = \tau_i$):

$$\xi_{(\tau)}^1 = (1 - R_0)\mathbb{1}_{\tau = \tau_0} \left(\sum_{i \in \mathbb{N}_n^*} \mathbb{1}_{\tau_i = \tau < T_i} (\delta_\tau^i - P_{\tau-}^i) \right)^+$$

$$- (1 - R_{-1})\mathbb{1}_{\tau = \tau_{-1}} \left(\sum_{i \in \mathbb{N}_n^*} \mathbb{1}_{\tau_i = \tau < T_i} (\delta_\tau^i - P_{\tau-}^i) \right)^- \qquad (12.24)$$

We thus see that the choice $\Gamma_\tau = P_{\tau-}$ corresponds to an extreme case of the collateral: that is, the collected collateral balances the predefault MTM at default of the counterparty; that is, it balances $P_{\tau-}$, although it does not balance the ith value of default if the counterparty defaults at the default time of the ith reference obligor.

Remark 12.3.1 *In case of the unilateral counterparty risk exposure, the extreme collateralization policy corresponds to the choice $\Gamma_\tau = P_{\tau-}^+$ (see Comment 12.2.4 (i)). The unilateral counterparty risk analog of formula (12.23) is thus, with $R = R_0$,*

$$\xi_{(\tau)} = \xi_{(\tau)}^1 = (1 - R) \left(\sum_{i \in \mathbb{N}_n^*} \mathbb{1}_{\tau_i = \tau} \delta_\tau^i + P_\tau - P_{\tau-}^+ \right)^+ \qquad (12.25)$$

We assume henceforth for simplicity that the face value of all the credit derivatives under consideration is equal to monetary unit and that all spreads are paid continuously in time.

12.3.2 Bilateral CDS Counterparty Credit Risk (Market Maker's Perspective)

The first practical issue we want to consider is that of bilateral CCR on a CDS, which is important from the marking-to-market perspective (determination of a spread accounting for bilateral CCR).

Remark 12.3.2 *We consider the pre–Big Bang (cf. Markit 2009) covenants regarding the cash flows of the CDS contract. That is, we do not include the up-front payment in the cash flows. The following developments can, however, be easily adapted to the post–Big Bang universe of CDS contracts.*

We consider a counterparty risky *payer CDS* on name 1 (CDS protection on name 1 bought by the investor, or credit name -1, from its counterparty, represented by the credit name 0). Denoting by T the maturity, κ the contractual spread and $R_1 \in [0, 1]$ the recovery, this corresponds to the special case of Section 12.3.1 in which $n = 1$ (so we delete unnecessary indexes in the notation), and

$$C_t = -\kappa(t \wedge T), \quad \delta_t = (1 - R_1)\mathbb{1}_{t < T} \tag{12.26}$$

The following result follows by application of equations (12.8), (12.9), (12.22), and (12.24).

Proposition 12.3.1 *For a counterparty risky payer CDS, one has,*

$$\xi_{(\tau)} = \xi_{(\tau)}(pay; -1, 0, 1) = (1 - R_0)\mathbb{1}_{\tau=\tau_0}\left(P_\tau + \mathbb{1}_{\tau_1=\tau<T}(1 - R_1) - \Gamma_\tau\right)^+$$
$$-(1 - R_{-1})\mathbb{1}_{\tau=\tau_{-1}}\left(P_\tau + \mathbb{1}_{\tau_1=\tau<T}(1 - R_1) - \Gamma_\tau\right)^- \tag{12.27}$$

So, in case of no collateralization ($\Gamma = 0$)

$$\xi_{(\tau)} = \xi^0_{(\tau)} = (1 - R_0)\mathbb{1}_{\tau=\tau_0}\left(P_\tau^+ + \mathbb{1}_{\tau_1=\tau<T}(1 - R_1)\right) - (1 - R_{-1})\mathbb{1}_{\tau=\tau_{-1}}P_\tau^- \tag{12.28}$$

and in the case of extreme collateralization ($\Gamma_\tau = P_{\tau-}$, cf. equation (12.24)),

$$\xi^1_{(\tau)} = (1 - R_0)\mathbb{1}_{\tau=\tau_0=\tau_1<T}(1 - R_1 - P_{\tau-})^+$$
$$-(1 - R_{-1})\mathbb{1}_{\tau=\tau_{-1}=\tau_1\leq T}(1 - R_1 - P_{\tau-})^- \tag{12.29}$$

Remark 12.3.3 *To derive equation (12.28) we used that $P_\tau = \mathbb{1}_{\tau<\tau_1}P_\tau$, and therefore*

$$\left(P_\tau + \mathbb{1}_{\tau_1=\tau<T}(1 - R_1)\right)^+ = P_\tau^+ + \mathbb{1}_{\tau_1=\tau<T}(1 - R_1)$$

The symmetric concept of the receiver counterparty risky CDS complements the concept of the payer counterparty risky CDS. In case of a receiver counterparty risky CDS (CDS protection on name 1 sold by the investor, or credit name -1, to its counterparty, represented by the credit name 0), one of course has, symmetrically to equation (12.26),

$$C_t = \kappa(t \wedge T), \quad \delta_t = -(1 - R_1)\mathbb{1}_{t<T} \tag{12.30}$$

and one gets likewise,

$$\xi_{(\tau)} = \xi_{(\tau)}(rec; -1, 0, 1) = -\xi_{(\tau)}(pay; 0, -1, 1)$$
$$\xi^1_{(\tau)} = \xi^1_{(\tau)}(rec; -1, 0, 1) = -\xi^1_{(\tau)}(pay; 0, -1, 1) \tag{12.31}$$

12.3.2.1   Decomposition of the Fair Spread

Note that the decomposition of the (fair) MTM at time $t = 0$ for a CDS subject to the credit counterparty risk can be written as

$$0 = \Pi_0(\hat{\kappa}) = P_0(\hat{\kappa}) - CVA_0(\hat{\kappa}) = P_0(\hat{\kappa}) - \mathbb{E}_0(\beta_\tau \xi_\tau(\hat{\kappa})) \tag{12.32}$$

where we denoted by $\hat{\kappa}$ the CCR adjusted fair spread at initiation of the CDS, and we explicitly recorded dependence on $\hat{\kappa}$ of the relevant quantities. Of course, by the CCR adjusted fair spread we mean the constant $\hat{\kappa}$ that solves equation (12.32).

Likewise, the clean fair spread, say $\bar{\kappa}$, solves

$$0 = P_0(\bar{\kappa}) \tag{12.33}$$

In general, it is not possible to provide a closed-form formula for the difference

$$\epsilon = \hat{\kappa} - \bar{\kappa} \tag{12.34}$$

and thus, we do not have, in general, an explicit formula for the spread decomposition

$$\hat{\kappa} = \bar{\kappa} + \epsilon \tag{12.35}$$

12.3.3   Unilateral Portfolio CCR (Bank's Perspective)

Here, we consider a bank that holds a portfolio of credit contracts referencing various credit names. This portfolio is subject to a counterparty credit risk with regard to a single counterparty. A bank typically disregards its own counterparty risk when assessing the counterparty risk of a portfolio with another party. Thus, we are led to consider unilateral counterparty risk from the perspective of the bank.

Remark 12.3.4 *A further issue not dealt with in this chapter is the case where a bank faces CCR with regard to several counterparties.*

So in this section we have that $\tau_{-1} = +\infty$ and $\tau = \tau_0$ is the default time of the investor's (bank's) counterparty, with recovery R_0 simply denoted as R.

More specifically, we now consider on each firm i, with $i = 1, \ldots, n$, a payer (default protection bought by the investor from the counterparty) or receiver (default protection sold by the investor to the counterparty) CDS with maturity T_i, contractual spread κ_i, and recovery R_i. Let P_i conventionally denote here the counterparty clean price of a *payer CDS* on the ith firm, for every $i = 1, \ldots, n$, so that the counterparty clean portfolio value is $P = \left(\sum_i \text{pay} - \sum_i \text{rec} \right) P_i$.

One thus gets by application of equations (12.8), (12.9), (12.22), and (12.25),

Proposition 12.3.2 *For a portfolio of CDSs with unilateral CCR, one has,*

$$\xi_{(\tau)} = (1 - R) \left(P_\tau + \Big(\sum_{i \ pay} - \sum_{i \ rec} \Big) \mathbb{1}_{\tau_i = \tau < T_i} (1 - R_i) - \Gamma_\tau \right)^+ \qquad (12.36)$$

with $\Gamma = 0$ in the no-collateralization case and $\Gamma_\tau = P_{\tau-}^+$ in the unilateral extreme collateralization case.

12.4 Multivariate Markovian Default Model

In this section we propose an underlying stochastic model, that will be able to put the previous results to work. Toward this end we define a Markovian bottom-up model of multivariate default times with factor process $X = (X^{-1}, \ldots, X^n) = (X^i)_{i \in \mathbb{N}_n}$ (recall $\mathbb{N}_n = \{-1, 0, \ldots, n\}$), which will have the following key features (see Bielecki, Vidozzi, and Vidozzi 2008; Bielecki et al. 2010):

(i) The pair (X, H) is Markov in its natural filtration $\mathbb{F}$.
(ii) Each pair (X^i, H^i) is a Markov process.
(iii) At every instant, either each alive obligor can default individually or all the surviving names whose indexes are in the set I_l, where the I_l's are a few prespecified subsets of the pool, can default simultaneously.

Remark 12.4.1 *Property (ii) grants quick valuation of single-name credit derivatives and independent calibration of each model marginal (X^i, H^i), whereas (iii) will allow us to account for dependence between defaults. Given property (i), various computational methods are, in principle, also available for basket derivatives. Since the Markovian dimension of the model will be of the order of, in general, 2^n, pricing of basket instruments by deterministic numerical schemes for the related Kolmogorov equations is precluded by the curse of dimensionality as soon as n exceeds a few units. However, in the special* *case of static basket instruments with payoff of the form $\phi(N_T)$ where $N_t = \sum_{i=1}^{n} H_t^i$, efficient convolution recursion pricing schemes are also available (see Bielecki et al. 2010). In general, a practical alternative is to use Monte Carlo simulation methods (see Section 12.4.2).*

We thus define a certain number of groups $I_l \subseteq \mathbb{N}_n$, of obligors who are likely to default simultaneously. Let $\mathcal{I} = (I_l)$. We define the generator of process $(X, H) = (X^i, H^i)_{i \in \mathbb{N}_n}$ as, for $u = u(t, \chi, \epsilon)$ with $\chi = (x_{-1}, \ldots, x_n) \in \mathbb{R}^{n+2}$, $\epsilon = (e_{-1}, \ldots, e_n) \in \{0, 1\}^{n+2}$:

$$
\begin{aligned}
\mathcal{A}_t u(t, \epsilon, \chi) = \sum_{i \in \mathbb{N}_n} & \left(b_i(t, x_i) \partial_{x_i} u(t, \chi, \epsilon) + \frac{1}{2} \sigma_i^2(t, x_i) \partial_{x_i^2}^2 u(t, \chi, \epsilon) \right) \\
& + \sum_{i, j \in \mathbb{N}_n; i < j} \varrho_{i,j}(t) \sigma_i(t, x_i) \sigma_j(t, x_j) \partial_{x_i, x_j}^2 u(t, \chi, \epsilon) \\
& + \sum_{i \in \mathbb{N}_n} \left(\eta_i(t, x_i) - \sum_{I \in \mathcal{I}; I \ni i} \lambda_I(t, \chi) \right) \left(u(t, \chi, \epsilon^i) - u(t, \chi, \epsilon) \right) \\
& + \sum_{I \in \mathcal{I}} \lambda_I(t, \chi) \left(u(t, \chi, \epsilon^I) - u(t, \chi, \epsilon) \right)
\end{aligned}
\tag{12.37}
$$

where, for $i, j \in \mathbb{N}_n$, and $I \in \mathcal{I}$:

- b_i, σ_i^2, $\varrho_{i,j}(t)$, and η_i denote suitable *drift, variance, correlation,* and *predefault intensity* function-coefficients.
- ϵ^i, resp. ϵ^I, denotes the vectors obtained from ϵ by replacing the component e_i, resp. the components e_j for $j \in I$, by number one.
- The nonnegative bounded functions $\lambda_I(t, \chi)$ are chosen so that the following holds, for every $i, t, \chi = (x_{-1}, \ldots, x_n)$:

$$
\sum_{I \in \mathcal{I}; I \ni i} \lambda_I(t, \chi) \leq \eta_i(t, x_i)
\tag{12.38}
$$

For instance, one can set, for every $I \in \mathcal{I}$ and $t, \chi = (x_{-1}, \ldots, x_n)$,

$$
\lambda_I(t, \chi) = \alpha_I \inf_{i \in I} \eta_i(t, x_i)
\tag{12.39}
$$

for some nonnegative parameters α_I, such that $\sum_{I \in \mathcal{I}} \alpha_I \leq 1$, which provide the model with a dependence structure.

Remark 12.4.2 *It is possible to consider the situation of a* common factor process $X^i = X$ *by letting* $b_i = b$, $\sigma_i = \sigma$, $\varrho = 1$, *and* $X_0^i = x$. *On the opposite the choice* $\varrho = 0$ *will correspond to independent factor processes X^is. In the latter case dependency* *between defaults is then only represented in the model by the possibility of simultaneous defaults.*

One can then verify (see Bielecki, Vidozzi, and Vidozzi 2008) that for $i \in \mathbb{N}_n$, the pair (X^i, H^i) is a jointly Markov process admitting the following generator, for $u = u(t, x_i, e_i)$ with $(x_i, e_i) \in \mathbb{R} \times \{0, 1\}$:

$$\mathcal{A}^i_t u(t, x_i, e_i) = b_i(t, x_i) \partial_{x_i} u(t, x_i, e_i) + \frac{1}{2} \sigma_i^2(t, x_i) \partial^2_{x_i^2} u(t, x_i, e_i)$$
$$+ \eta_i(t, x_i)\big(u(t, x_i, 1) - u(t, x_i, e_i)\big) \qquad (12.40)$$

12.4.1 Model Calibration

In the remainder of the chapter we apply the Markovian model introduced earlier to valuation of the counterparty risk in the portfolio of CDS contracts, where the recovery rate associated with the ith contract is R_i. It is implicit in the specification (12.37) (see also equation (12.40)) for the model generator that one will work with constant recoveries R_i's, for simplicity. In the case of affine coefficients, and assuming a constant interest rate r and a constant recovery rate R_i, the time $t = 0$ fair spread for the ith CDS contract, say κ_0^i, is then given by an explicit formula $\kappa_0^i = \kappa^i(0, X_0^i)$ in terms of r, R_i, T_i, and the parameters of the coefficients b_i, σ_i^2, and η_i (see, e.g., Crépey, Jeanblanc, and Zargari 2010b; Duffie and Garleanu 2001). Given predetermined values of r and R_i, the parameters of the coefficients can then be calibrated so to match the spread curve of the related CDS.

Remark 12.4.3 *More generally, assuming random recovery R_i with a suitably parametrized distribution, one could calibrate this distribution jointly with calibration of b_i, σ_i^2, and η_i using the corresponding CDS spread curve (cf. Bielecki et al. (2010)).*

The few residual model dependence parameters α_I with $I \in \mathcal{I}$ can then be calibrated to target prices of basket instruments, which can, for instance, be done by simulation.

Remark 12.4.4 *We do not engage in any calibration exercise of the preceding Markovian model in this chapter, as we intend only to illustrate qualitative features of our model. Calibration of the kind of Markov copula models that we use here is investigated in Bielecki et al (2010).*

12.4.2 Model Simulation

Given that $\mathcal{I}$ consists of only a few (no more than three or four, say) prespecified subsets of the pool, the simulation of a set of random times $(\tau_i)_{i \in \mathbb{N}_n}$ is quite fast. Given a previously simulated trajectory of X, one essentially needs to simulate i.i.d. exponential random variables $\mathcal{E}_\iota$, for $\iota \in \mathcal{I} \cup \mathbb{N}_n$. Then one computes, for every $I \in \mathcal{I}$,

$$\hat{\tau}_I = \inf\{t > 0; \int_0^t \lambda_I(s, X_s)ds \geq \mathcal{E}_I\}$$

and for every $i \in \mathbb{N}_n$,

$$\hat{\tau}_i = \inf\{t > 0; \int_0^t \lambda_i(s, X_s)ds \geq \mathcal{E}_i\}$$

with for t, $\chi = (x_{-1}, \ldots, x_n)$,

$$\lambda_i(t, \chi) = \eta_i(t, x_i) - \sum_{I \in \mathcal{I};\, I \ni i} \lambda_I(t, \chi)$$

One sets finally, for every $i \in \mathbb{N}_n$,

$$\tau_i = \hat{\tau}_i \wedge \left(\bigwedge_{I \in \mathcal{I};\, I \ni i} \hat{\tau}_I \right)$$

12.5 Numerical Results

We present here some numerical results illustrating applications of the theory. The computations are carried out by running 2×10^6 crude Monte Carlo simulations using MATLAB R2009a on a laptop with an Intel Core 2 Duo, 2.66 GHz CPU. *In the tables the number between parentheses in each cell denotes the empirical standard deviation of the related Monte Carlo estimate (empirical average on its left).*[5]

All recovery rates are fixed at 0.4. The intensities of default $\eta_i(t, X_t^i)$, $i \in \mathbb{N}_n$, are assumed to be of the affine form:

$$\eta_i(t, X_t^i) = a_i + X_t^i \tag{12.41}$$

where a_i is a constant, and where X^i is a homogeneous Cox-Ingersoll-Ross (CIR) process generated by

$$dX_t^i = \zeta_i(\mu_i - X_t^i)\, dt + \sigma_i\sqrt{X_t^i}\, dW_i \tag{12.42}$$

12.5.1 Application to Bilateral CDS CCR

We first consider application of the preceding model to bilateral counterparty credit risk valuation on a one-payer CDS. We thus consider a credit pool made of an investor,

TABLE 12.1 Parameters for CIR Process

Credit Risk Level	a	ζ	μ	σ	X_0	κ
Low	a^l	0.90	0.001	σ^l	0.001	10
Middle	a^m	0.80	0.02	σ^m	0.02	120
High	a^h	0.50	0.05	σ^h	0.05	300

a counterparty, and a reference name on which the CDS contract is written between the investor and the counterparty. So $n = 1$, and the PFEDs in the case of no collateralization and extreme collateralization are given by formulas (12.28) and (12.29), respectively. In this section each collection of the parameters $(a_i, \zeta_i, \mu_i, \sigma_i)$, $i = -1, 0, 1$, in (12.41)–(12.42) may take values corresponding to a low, a medium, or a high regime. These values are shown in Table 12.1.[6]

The values of parameters a and σ will vary, but in such a way that the spreads showing in the last column of the table are kept constant.

We consider two scenarios regarding the credit quality of the three names involved: the investor, the counterparty, and the reference name. In each case we assume that the two riskiest names, with set referred to by I, can default jointly (but all three names cannot default together). The joint default intensity $\lambda_I(t, \chi)$ is defined by formula (12.39) where $\alpha_I \geq 0$ is chosen in such a way that equation (12.38) holds.

Example 12.5.1 The first scenario that we consider is similar to the one in Brigo and Capponi (2008) and consists of:

- An investor with a very low risk profile.
- A counterparty that has a middle credit risk profile.
- A reference name with a high risk profile.

We set $I = \{0, 1\}$ so that the counterparty and the reference name can default together.

The numerical results are summarized in Table 12.2. In column one of this table, we set $\sigma_1^h = 0.01$ and we increase the joint default intensity $\lambda_I(t, \chi)$, by increasing α_I from 0 to 1, to see whether CVA increases in the case of increasing default dependence. Note that in Brigo and Capponi (2008) this is not the case for too-low levels of volatilities in the model. In the second column of Table 12.2, we set $\sigma_1^h = 0.2$ to additionally see the impact of increased volatility of the reference on CVA.

Both columns are further divided into the part representing the case of no margining (no collateralization), and the part representing extreme margining (extreme collateralization). We observe that the extreme collateralization convention adopted for these calculations does not reduce the CVA by any significant amount. This is probably due to the fact that the collateralization does not mitigate the risk associated with the value of default.

TABLE 12.2 CVA in Basis Points for the Case $\sigma_{-1}^l = \sigma_0^m = 0.01$

α_I	$\sigma_1^b = 0.01$		$\sigma_1^b = 0.20$	
	No Margining	Margining	No Margining	Margining
0	0.22 (0.00)	0.0 (0.00)	3.8 (0.02)	0.0 (0.00)
0.1	27.4 (0.21)	27.2 (0.21)	27.8 (0.20)	24.4 (0.20)
0.2	54.7 (0.29)	54.5 (0.29)	52.0 (0.28)	48.9 (0.28)
0.3	82.1 (0.36)	82.0 (0.36)	77.0 (0.34)	74.2 (0.34)
0.4	109.6 (0.41)	109.5 (0.41)	101.7 (0.39)	99.2 (0.39)
0.5	137.6 (0.46)	137.5 (0.46)	126.6 (0.44)	124.6 (0.44)
0.6	165.5 (0.50)	165.4 (0.50)	152.0 (0.48)	150.3 (0.48)
0.7	194.1 (0.54)	194.0 (0.54)	177.7 (0.52)	176.3 (0.52)
0.8	223.2 (0.58)	223.2 (0.58)	203.3 (0.55)	202.2 (0.55)
0.9	252.3 (0.61)	252.3 (0.61)	229.0 (0.59)	228.3 (0.58)
1.0	281.7 (0.64)	281.7 (0.64)	255.0 (0.62)	254.6 (0.61)

Furthermore, we see from the results of column one in Table 12.2 that in our model, unlike in the Gaussian copula contagion model used in Brigo and Capponi (2008), CVA increases as default dependence gets higher, even in the case of low volatilities of the factor processes.

In case of no collateralization, the CVA values in rows 1 and 2 of the second column of Table 12.2 are higher than the values in column one. With regard to row 1, this behavior can be explained as follows: When σ_1^b increases from $\sigma_1^b = 0.01$ to 0.2, the mark-to-market value of the reference CDS when positive, that is, $(P_t^1)^+$, becomes higher. As there is no possibility of joint default, the main contribution to CVA is due to $(P_t^1)^+$, and consequently CVA gets higher.

The following more specific observations can be made with regard to the effect of margining that shows in Table 12.2:

- First, with regard to the first row, as there is no joint default, the use of extreme collateral removes counterparty risk.
- As the joint default intensity of the counterparty and reference, λ_I, increases, CVA will depend more and more on the loss due to the joint default of the counterparty and reference. The magnitude of the loss due to joint default is much larger than the extreme collateral value P_t^1; hence, the impact of collateral on CVA decreases as α_I increases. Moreover, when there is joint default and $P_{\tau-}^1 < 0$, extreme collateralization will actually increase the loss since the investor incurs not only the loss $(1 - R_0)(1 - R_1)$ but also the value of the extreme collateral that was posted to the counterparty just before default.
- Moving from column one to column two in Table 12.2, the increase of $(P_t^1)^+$ due to a higher volatility makes it possible for extreme collateralization to have more impact in reducing counterparty risk. However, as α_I increases, extreme collateralization will have less impact as the loss due to joint default is much larger compared to the

value $(P_t^1)^+$ and, as noted earlier, there is a chance of increasing the loss due to lost collateral if $P_{\tau-}^3 < 0$.

Example 12.5.2   The second scenario is that of:

- A reference name with a very low risk profile.
- An investor that has a middle credit risk profile.
- A counterparty with a high risk profile.

In this scenario we choose the joint default intensities in such a way that the investor and counterparty can default together but all three names cannot default together. We thus set $I = \{-1, 0\}$.

Note that in Example 12.5.1 the CVA is calculated based on the loss due to possible joint default of the counterparty and reference name, as well as based on the the mark-to-market value of the reference CDS. In the current scenario the CVA values are based on the mark-to-market value of the reference CDS only, as the joint default of the counterparty and reference is not possible. Hence the CVA values in the current scenario are much lower (see Table 12.3). This shows that the contribution of joint default toward CVA is much larger than the contribution of the mark-to-market value of the reference CDS. The very low CVA values can be further explained by calculating numerically the average of $(P_t^1)^+$ and $(P_t^1)^-$, which is found to be in the order of less than a basis point due to the very low risk profile of the reference.

Similarly to how we did this in Example 12.5.1, in column one of Table 12.3 we increase the joint default intensity $\lambda_I(t, \chi)$ by increasing α_I from 0 to 1 to see the impact on CVA of the increase of the intensity of joint default λ_I. And, as in Example 12.5.1, we see that increasing dependence between the counterparty and the investor leads to an increase in CVA.

TABLE 12.3   CVA in Basis Points for the Case $\sigma_{-1}^m = \sigma_1^l = 0.01$

α_I	$\sigma_1^h = 0.01$		$\sigma_1^h = 0.20$	
	No Margining	Margining	No Margining	Margining
0	0.030 (0.00)	0.0 (0.00)	0.030 (0.00)	0.0 (0.00)
0.1	0.034 (0.00)	0.0 (0.00)	0.034 (0.00)	0.0 (0.00)
0.2	0.038 (0.00)	0.0 (0.00)	0.037 (0.00)	0.0 (0.00)
0.3	0.042 (0.00)	0.0 (0.00)	0.041 (0.00)	0.0 (0.00)
0.4	0.046 (0.00)	0.0 (0.00)	0.045 (0.00)	0.0 (0.00)
0.5	0.050 (0.00)	0.0 (0.00)	0.049 (0.00)	0.0 (0.00)
0.6	0.055 (0.00)	0.0 (0.00)	0.053 (0.00)	0.0 (0.00)
0.7	0.059 (0.00)	0.0 (0.00)	0.056 (0.00)	0.0 (0.00)
0.8	0.063 (0.00)	0.0 (0.00)	0.060 (0.00)	0.0 (0.00)
0.9	0.068 (0.00)	0.0 (0.00)	0.064 (0.00)	0.0 (0.00)
1.0	0.072 (0.00)	0.0 (0.00)	0.068 (0.00)	0.0 (0.00)

With regard to the effect of margining in Table 12.3, the CVA values are all zero because counterparty risk due to the loss of the mark-to-market value is removed by extreme collateralization.

12.5.2   Application to Unilateral Portfolio CCR

We now consider the issue of valuation of the unilateral counterparty credit risk on a portfolio of CDSs. We thus assume that we have a risk-free investor that is trading a portfolio of payer and receiver CDSs with a defaultable counterparty. In the fully netted case, the PFEDs corresponding to a portfolio with no collateralization and to a portfolio with extreme collateralization are given by formula (12.36) for $\Gamma = 0$ or $\Gamma_\tau = P_{\tau-}^+$, respectively (see Proposition 12.3.2).

We conducted numerical experiments for the preceding two cases, and for comparison we also considered the nonnetted (and noncollateralized) case. By summation over the CDSs composing the portfolio, one has in the latter case that the corresponding PFED is given by:

$$\xi_{(\tau)} = (1 - R) \left(\sum_{i \text{ pay}} \left(P_\tau^i + \mathbb{1}_{\tau=\tau_i < T_i}(1 - R_i) \right)^+ + \sum_{i \text{ rec}} P_\tau^{i,-} \right) \quad (12.43)$$

where P^i denotes the counterparty clean price of a payer CDS on name i in the portfolio (see Section 12.3.3).

Here we consider an underlying portfolio of 100 CDS contracts. The corresponding market spreads (in basis points) are presented in the listing in equation (12.44):

$(\kappa_1, \ldots, \kappa_{100})$
$= (405.936, 225.937, 620.786, 195.083, 37.97, 32.17, 1,743.673, 348.411,$
$\qquad 399.788, 297.902, 3,013.286, 359.909, 327.962, 2,085.618, 145.519,$
$\qquad 234.948, 212.135, 120.000, 124.000, 304.845, 225.904, 39.78, 28.320,$
$\qquad 229.577, 291.100, 349.071, 132.982, 889.620, 28.110, 25.110,$
$\qquad 311.131, 210.919, 368.858, 480.993, 359.483, 200.581, 164.500,$
$\qquad 127.000, 456.170, 130.027, 229.912, 343.500, 361.515, 300.346,$
$\qquad 583.736, 342.688, 133.451, 141.984, 2,440.458, 579.000, 306.745,$
$\qquad 324.709, 647.019, 433.597, 201.960, 192.860, 243.031, 296.210, 333.747,$
$\qquad 295.873, 374.750, 270.432, 436.182, 430.537, 127.000, 145.043,$
$\qquad 52.270, 29.070, 123.000, 45.880, 29.930, 31.560, 190.000, 361.990,$
$\qquad 36.980, 31.440, 33.880, 16.570, 39.000, 73.560, 70.470, 24.840, 21.270,$
$\qquad 47.880, 53.450, 31.190, 499.517, 1,092.000, 26.770, 49.810, 60.400,$
$\qquad 180.000, 27.960, 130.876, 123.000, 47.110, 190.000, 38.170,$
$\qquad 42.730, 200.000) \qquad\qquad\qquad\qquad\qquad\qquad\qquad\qquad\qquad (12.44)$

Now, we divide the portfolio into two categories: the first category composed of $p = 70$ payer CDSs, and the second category composed of $r = 30$ receiver CDSs. The choice of the names for the payer CDSs and receiver CDSs is made by taking the first 70 names from equation (12.44) and declaring them to represent payer contracts, and declaring the remaining 30 names to represent the receiver contracts.[7]

Next, setting $n = 100$, for $l \in L := \{20, 70, 101\}$, we define I_l as the set, possibly including the counterparty indexed by 0, containing the indexes of the l riskiest obligors, as measured by the spread of the corresponding five-year market CDS quote, and we set $\mathcal{I} = (I_l)_{l \in L}$, where each I_l stands for a specific subset of $\mathbb{N}_n^*$. More specifically, we consider a *nested* grouping of reference names of the CDS contracts in the portfolio, as well as the counterparty, which can default together. Thus, we have:

$$I_{20} \subseteq I_{70} \subseteq I_{101} = \mathbb{N}_n^* = \{0, 1, 2, \ldots, 100\}$$

These groups were created using the market CDS spreads given in equation (12.44). The riskiness of the obligors was assessed based on the list obtained by sorting equation (12.44) in descending order.

The obligors in I_{20} are assumed to have high credit risk, while the obligors in $I_{70} \setminus I_{20}$ are assumed to have middle credit risk and the obligors in $I_{101} \setminus I_{70}$ are assumed to have low credit risk.

The default intensities of the obligors are given as shifted CIR processes [cf. equations (12.41)–(12.42)]. We assume that all obligors having high credit risk have the same credit risk parameters; hence I_{20} is a homogeneous group with the CIR parameters given in the bottom row of Table 12.4. Similarly, all the obligors with middle credit risk (that is, obligors belonging to $I_{70} \setminus I_{20}$) have the same CIR parameters that are in the middle row of Table 12.4. We also assume that the obligors with low credit risk; that is, obligors belonging to $I_{101} \setminus I_{70}$, have the same CIR parameters that are in the upper row of Table 12.4. Note we use the word *homogeneous* to indicate that the obligors have the same credit risk profile and that their default intensities differ only by a constant.

The default intensities of the reference names and of the counterparty are assumed to be of the form $a_i + X^i$ where X^i is the CIR process common for the lth group in case $i \in I_l$. This setup corresponds to taking a common factor process for each

TABLE 12.4 Parameters for CIR Process for CDS Portfolio

Credit Risk Level	ζ	μ	σ	X_0
Low	0.9	0.001	0.01	0.001
Middle	0.80	0.02	0.1	0.02
High	0.50	0.05	0.2	0.05

homogeneous group (see Remark 12.4.2). The constants a_i of the reference names are calibrated to match spreads listed in equation (12.44), and they are given in the listing in equation (12.45):

$$(a_1, \ldots, a_{100})$$
$$= (0.0194, 0.0178, 0.0552, 0.0126, 0.0053, 0.0044, 0.2424, 0.0382, 0.0184,$$
$$0.0297, 0.4540, 0.0401, 0.0348, 0.2993, 0.0044, 0.0193, 0.0155, 0.0001,$$
$$0.0008, 0.0309, 0.0177, 0.0056, 0.0037, 0.0184, 0.0286, 0.0383, 0.0023,$$
$$0.1000, 0.0037, 0.0032, 0.0320, 0.0153, 0.0132, 0.0319, 0.0400, 0.0135,$$
$$0.0075, 0.0013, 0.0278, 0.0018, 0.0184, 0.0373, 0.0404, 0.0302, 0.0490,$$
$$0.0372, 0.0023, 0.0038, 0.3585, 0.0482, 0.0312, 0.0342, 0.0596, 0.0240,$$
$$0.0138, 0.0122, 0.0206, 0.0295, 0.0357, 0.0294, 0.0142, 0.0252, 0.0244,$$
$$0.0235, 0.0013, 0.0043, 0.0077, 0.0038, 0.0006, 0.0066, 0.0040, 0.0043,$$
$$0.0118, 0.0404, 0.0052, 0.0042, 0.0046, 0.0018, 0.0055, 0.0113, 0.0107,$$
$$0.0031, 0.0025, 0.0070, 0.0079, 0.0042, 0.0350, 0.1337, 0.0035, 0.0073,$$
$$0.0091, 0.0101, 0.0037, 0.0019, 0.0006, 0.0069, 0.0118, 0.0054, 0.0061,$$
$$0.0134) \hspace{4cm} (12.45)$$

Since we assume a risk-free investor, the margining process is assumed to be unilateral, where by unilateral we mean that only the counterparty posts collateral provided the value of the portfolio is positive for the investor at the margin date. Hence if the portfolio has negative (positive) value for the investor (counterparty), there is no collateral posted by the investor. The margin process is thus assumed to be $\Gamma_\tau = P_{\tau-}^+$; see Remark 12.3.1 and equation (12.25).

Example 12.5.3   The scenario is that of:

- A nondefaultable investor.
- A defaultable counterparty with a *constant default intensity* such that the market CDS spread of the counterparty κ_0 is either $1, 20, 40, 60, 80, 100, 120$, or 300 basis points.
- The portfolio of $p = 70$ payer CDSs and $r = 30$ receiver CDSs based on the description given in this section.

In Table 12.5 we examine the behavior of the CVA with respect to the default intensity of the counterparty, in three different cases: no netting and no margining, netting and no margining, and both netting and margining. The heading "Counterparty Risk Type" for the first column is to indicate the classification of the counterparty into one of the homogeneous groups I_{20}, $I_{70} \setminus I_{20}$, or $I_{101} \setminus I_{70}$, whose respective

TABLE 12.5 CVA for Portfolio of CDSs When $\eta_0(t, X_t^0) = \eta_0$ Is Constant and $(\alpha_{I_{20}}, \alpha_{I_{70}}, \alpha_{I_{101}}) = (0.3, 0.3, 0.3)$

Counterparty Risk Type	κ_0	η_0	CVA No Netting No Margining	CVA Netting No Margining	CVA Netting with Margining
Low	1	0.00017	50.7 (2.2)	27.1 (1.2)	26.6 (1.2)
Low	20	0.00333	808.2 (8.9)	433.8 (4.9)	422.8 (4.8)
Low	40	0.00667	822.2 (8.9)	441.9 (4.8)	419.7 (4.8)
Low	60	0.0100	834.2 (8.9)	448.6 (4.8)	415.8 (4.8)
Low	80	0.01333	847.4 (8.9)	456.1 (4.8)	412.9 (4.8)
Low	100	0.01667	860.5 (8.8)	463.2 (4.8)	409.8 (4.8)
Middle	120	0.0200	4,729.1 (20.1)	3,737.2 (16.0)	3,675.8 (15.9)
Middle	300	0.0500	5,348.0 (21.0)	4,230.8 (16.9)	4,083.4 (16.8)

default intensities are modeled using CIR parameters corresponding to high, middle, and low credit risk regimes, respectively. From the results obtained we see that CVA increases as the counterparty has a higher market CDS spread κ_0 (which corresponds to a higher intensity of default).

Netting appears to have a higher impact as the counterparty becomes riskier. However, this does not seem to be the case of margining. Essentially, margining mitigates all the counterparty risk that it can mitigate, regardless of the riskiness of the counterparty, and the remaining risk, due to composition of the credit names and possible joint defaults, simply can't be mitigated by the kind of margining that we use here. In the margining case with extreme collateralization, the CVA is essentially due to joint defaults. As increasing the riskiness of the counterparty does not increase $\lambda_{I_{101}}(t, \chi)$, so the joint default intensity of the counterparty is constant for all rows in this scenario (except for the last two rows—see end of the paragraph), and the CVA does not really change, either. This is of course true only to the extent that the joint default intensity of the counterparty stays unchanged, that is, as long as the counterparty stays in the low risk group. So, in the last two rows of the table, with spreads κ_0 of 120 or 300 bps, the counterparty belongs to the middle risk group, its joint default intensity is thus higher, and the net effect is an increase of the CVA, even in the case of extreme collateralization.

In Figures 12.1, 12.2, 12.3, 12.4, 12.5, 12.6, and 12.7, we give the EPE(t) curves in the cases of no netting and no margining, netting and no margining, and netting and margining with extreme collateralization, respectively. In each case the EPE(t) curves are given for a selection of κ_0 (i.e., $\kappa_0 = 20$ basis points, $\kappa_0 = 60$ basis points, and $\kappa_0 = 100$ basis points). The curves were obtained by fitting a quadratic polynomial (*nonlinear regression*) through the $\xi_{(\tau)}$ values for $\tau = \tau_0 < T$.

Remark 12.5.1 *Another way to calculate EPE(t) is to divide the time interval* $[0, T]$ *into time buckets and calculate the average loss incurred in each time bucket. But the EPE curves obtained in this way are very oscillatory, which indicates that there is a high variance*

FIGURE 12.1   EPE(t) for Portfolio

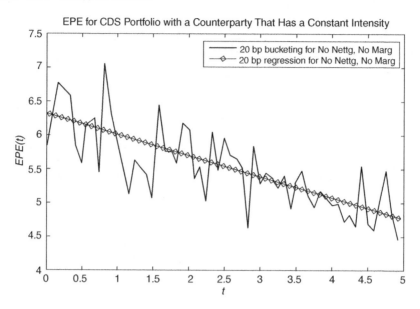

in this method, even with two million Monte Carlo simulations. When superimposing the EPE(t) curve obtained through the bucketing and the nonlinear regression, one obtains that the two results are in good qualitative agreement, though (see Figure 12.1).

Let η_0 denote the constant intensity of default of the counterparty; that is, $\eta_0(t, X_t^0) = \eta_0$. To explain the pattern of the EPE(t) curves observed in the CDS

FIGURE 12.2   EPE(t) for Portfolio

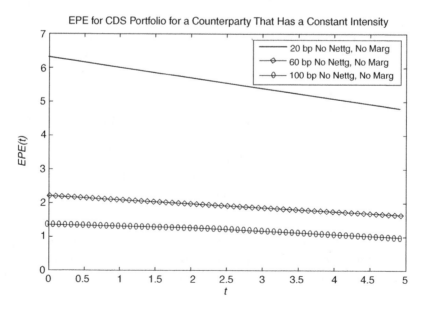

FIGURE 12.3 EPE(t) for Portfolio

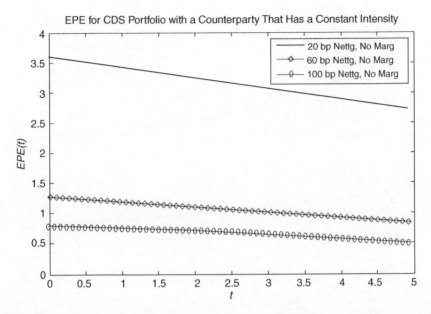

portfolio case, one needs to consider the ratio $\mathbb{1}_{0\in I_l}\frac{\mathbb{E}[\lambda_{I_l}(t,X_t)]}{\eta_0}$, which gives the probability of a *joint* default of the counterparty, *conditionally to its default* (alone or jointly). Provided that the counterparty risk profile does not change as the CDS spread of the counterparty κ_0 increases, the numerator in this ratio remains the same, whereas the denominator increases. Therefore the ratio decreases, meaning that the conditional

FIGURE 12.4 EPE(t) for Portfolio

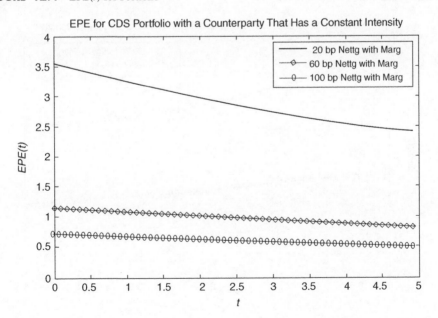

FIGURE 12.5   EPE(t) for Portfolio

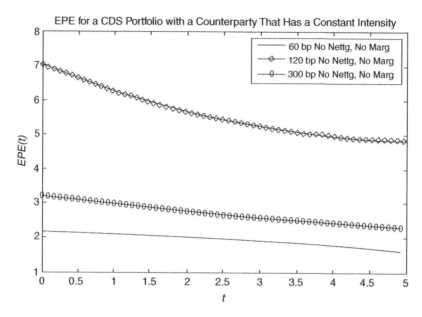

probability of a joint default decreases (see Table 12.6). Since joint defaults are responsible for the most part of the PFED, therefore, as κ_0 increases, the EPE(t) curves
become lower, as we can see in the figures. However, if the riskiness of the counterparty increases such that it can default jointly with the group I_{70} and/or I_{101}, then
the joint default probability will generally increase as there are 61 reference names

FIGURE 12.6   EPE(t) for Portfolio

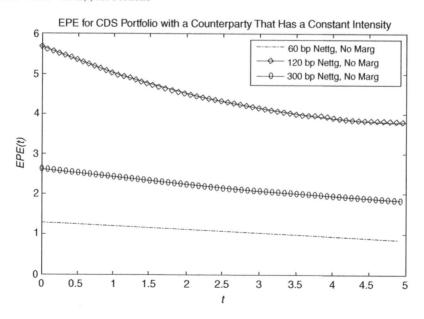

FIGURE 12.7   EPE(*t*) for Portfolio

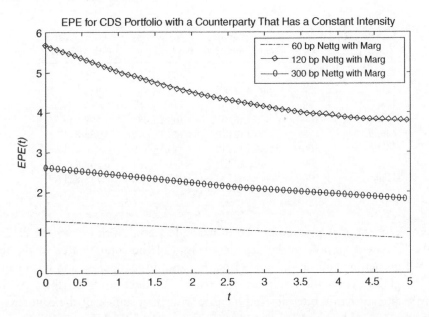

(corresponding to 61 payer CDSs) in I_{70}, which can jointly default with the counterparty. Hence as κ_0 increases such that the counterparty risk profile changes to a more risky type, the EPE(*t*) curve becomes higher, as we can see in the figures.

Example 12.5.4   The scenario is that of:

- A nondefaultable investor.
- A defaultable counterparty with a *stochastic intensity* such that it has a market CDS spread κ_0 equal to 10, 20, 60, 100, 120, 300, 400, or 500 basis points.
- A portfolio of $p = 70$ payer CDSs and $r = 30$ receiver CDSs based on the description given in this section.

TABLE 12.6   Dependence of EPE on $\frac{\mathbb{E}[\lambda_{I_l}(t,\chi)]}{\eta_0}$, with $t = \frac{1}{12}$ (*One Month*), for Portfolio of CDSs When $\eta_0(t, X_t^0) = \eta_0$ Is Constant

Counterparty Risk Type	κ_0	η_0	$\dfrac{\mathbb{1}_{0 \in I_{20}} \times \mathbb{E}[\lambda_{I_{20}}(t, X_t)]}{\eta_0}$	$\dfrac{\mathbb{1}_{0 \in I_{70}} \times \mathbb{E}[\lambda_{I_{70}}(t, X_t)]}{\eta_0}$	$\dfrac{\mathbb{1}_{0 \in I_{101}} \times \mathbb{E}[\lambda_{I_{101}}(t, X_t)]}{\eta_0}$
Low	20	0.0033	0	0	0.2511
Low	60	0.0100	0	0	0.0829
Low	100	0.01667	0	0	0.0166
Middle	120	0.0200	0	0.2808	0.0414
Middle	300	0.0500	0	0.1240	0.0166

TABLE 12.7   CVA for Portfolio of CDSs When $\eta_0(t, X_t^0)$ Is Stochastic
$((\alpha_{I_{20}}, \alpha_{I_{70}}, \alpha_{I_{101}}) = (0.3, 0.3, 0.3))$

Counterparty Risk Type	κ_0	CVA No Netting No Margining	CVA Netting No Margining	CVA Netting with Margining
Low	10	488.4 (7.0)	262.1 (3.8)	256.7 (3.8)
Low	20	808.4 (8.9)	433.9 (4.9)	423.0 (4.8)
Low	60	834.2 (8.9)	448.5 (4.8)	415.9 (4.8)
Low	100	860.4 (8.8)	463.2 (4.8)	409.8 (4.8)
Middle	120	5,440.2 (21.4)	4,338.1 (17.2)	4,256.6 (17.1)
Middle	300	5,364.1 (21.0)	4,243.1 (16.9)	4,076.8 (16.8)
High	400	8,749.9 (22.1)	7,211.3 (18.1)	6,943.0 (18.0)
High	500	8,543.5 (21.8)	7,017.9 (17.8)	6,713.8 (17.7)

Table 12.7 is the analog of Table 12.5 in Example 12.5.3; it thus gives the behavior of the CVA with respect to the default intensity of the counterparty, in the three cases of no netting and no margining, netting and no margining, and both netting and margining. From the results we see that CVA values are larger for a counterparty with a stochastic intensity and increase with the riskiness of the counterparty. In Figures 12.8, 12.9, 12.10, 12.11, 12.12, 12.13, 12.14, 12.15, and 12.16, we give the EPE(t) curves for the no netting with no margining, netting with no margining, and netting with margining cases. This time the behavior of the EPE(t) curves is explained by the ratio $\mathbb{E}[\frac{\lambda_{I_f}(t,X_t)}{\eta_0(t,X_t^0)}]$ (see Table 12.8).

FIGURE 12.8   EPE(t) for Portfolio

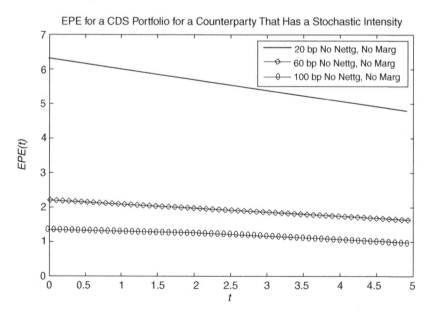

FIGURE 12.9   EPE(t) for Portfolio

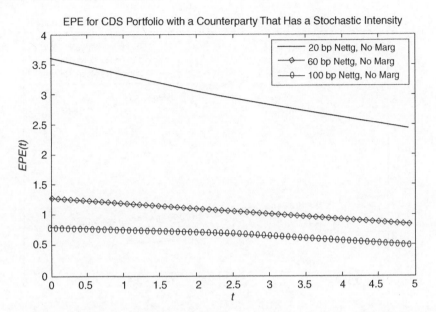

FIGURE 12.10   EPE(t) for Portfolio

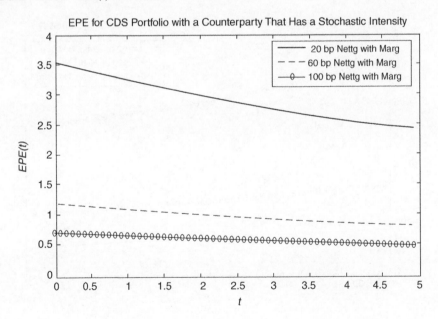

FIGURE 12.11   EPE(t) for Portfolio

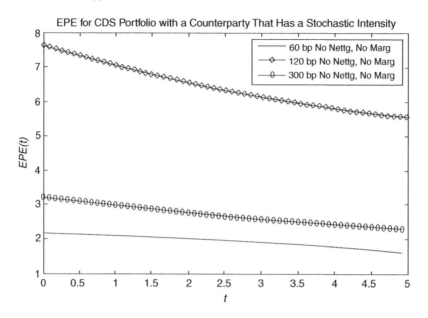

FIGURE 12.12   EPE(t) for Portfolio

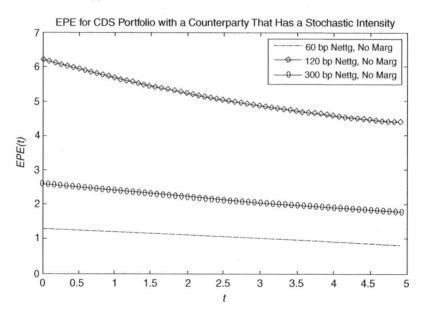

FIGURE 12.13 EPE(t) for Portfolio

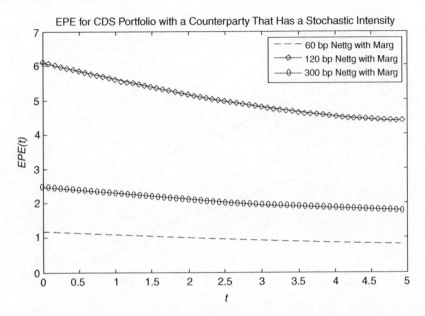

FIGURE 12.14 EPE(t) for Portfolio

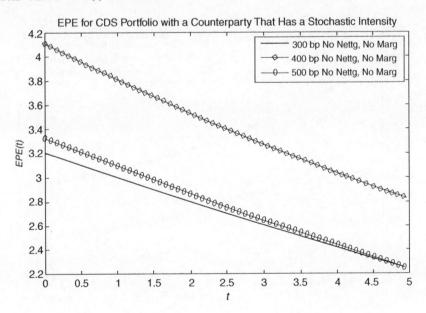

FIGURE 12.15 EPE(t) for Portfolio

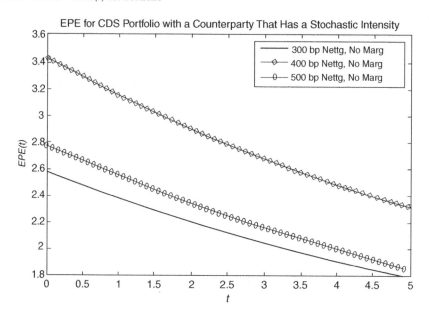

FIGURE 12.16 EPE(t) for Portfolio

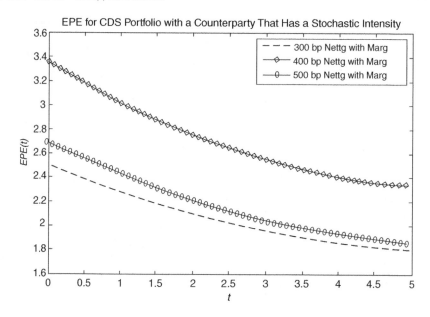

TABLE 12.8 Dependence of EPE on $\mathbb{E}\left[\frac{\lambda_{I_l}(t,X_t)}{\eta_0(t,X_t^0)}\right]$, with $t = \frac{1}{12}$, for Portfolio of CDSs When $\eta_0(t, X_t^0)$ Is Stochastic

Counterparty Risk Type	κ_0	$\mathbb{1}_{0 \in I_{20}} \times \mathbb{E}\left[\frac{\lambda_{I_{20}}(t,X_t)}{\eta_0(t,X_t^0)}\right]$	$\mathbb{1}_{0 \in I_{70}} \times \mathbb{E}\left[\frac{\lambda_{I_{70}}(t,X_t)}{\eta_0(t,X_t^0)}\right]$	$\mathbb{1}_{0 \in I_{101}} \times \mathbb{E}\left[\frac{\lambda_{I_{101}}(t,X_t)}{\eta_0(t,X_t^0)}\right]$
Low	20	0	0	0.2485
Low	60	0	0	0.0828
Low	100	0	0	0.0497
Middle	120	0	0.3000	0.0429
Middle	300	0	0.1222	0.0166
High	400	0.2809	0.0937	0.0126
High	500	0.2247	0.0744	0.0100

12.6 Acknowledgments

The research of the other authors benefited from the support of the DGE. The research of T. R. Bielecki was supported by NSF Grant DMS–0604789 and NSF Grant DMS–0908099.

Notes

1. We refer to *ISDA Collateral Guidelines* (2005) for a detailed discussion setting industry standards for collateral formation.
2. We also allow for simultaneous defaults among the names in the underlying portfolio.
3. Recall that all processes are assumed to be càdlàg.
4. As already remarked, in the literature the term *potential future exposure* (PFE) is used, rather than PFED, as well as the related term *PFE profile* (PFE as a function of future time). Accordingly, the terms: *measures of PFE* (cf. Delta Hedge GmbH n.d., 6), and *risk measures of PFE profile* (cf. De Prisco and Rosen 2005, 11) are used.
5. The random number generation was sufficiently rich to justify the large number of generated paths: The uniform random numbers were generated using MATLAB's rand function that is based on the modified *subtract with borrow* generator, which has a period of 2^{1492}. The normally distributed random numbers were generated using MATLAB rand function, which is an implementation of Marsaglia's shift-register generator summed with linear congruential generator, which has a period of 2^{64}.
6. The values of ζ and μ given in Table 12.1 are the same as in Brigo and Capponi (2008). It needs to be stressed, though, that our dependence model is completely different from the one used in that paper.
7. We stress that the partition of the portfolio into payer and receiver CDSs was not based on the sorted list but on the original list of market CDS spreads given in equation (12.44).

References

Aparicio, F., and D. Cossin. 2001. Control of credit risk collateralization using quasi-variational inequalities. *Journal of Computational Finance* 4 (3): 5–38.

Basel Committee on Banking Supervision. 2004. International convergence of capital measurement and capital standards. Bank for International Settlements, June.

Bielecki, T. R., A. Cousin, S. Crépey, and A. Herbertsson. 2010. Pricing and hedging portfolio credit derivatives in a bottom-up model with simultaneous defaults. Working paper.

Bielecki, T. R., and M. Rutkowski. 2002. *Credit risk: Modeling, valuation and hedging.* Berlin: Springer-Verlag.

Bielecki, T. R., A. Vidozzi, and L. Vidozzi. 2008. A Markov copulae approach to pricing and hedging of credit index derivatives and ratings triggered step-up bonds. *Journal of Credit Risk* 4 (1).

Brigo, D., and A. Capponi. 2008. Bilateral counterparty risk valuation, with stochastic dynamical models and application to credit default swaps. Working paper.

Brigo, D., and K. Chourdakis. 2008. Counterparty risk for credit default swaps: Impact of spread volatility and default correlation. *International Journal of Theoretical and Applied Finance* 12 (7): 1007–1026.

Brigo, D., and M. Masetti. 2005. A formula for interest rate swaps valuation under counterparty risk in the presence of netting agreements. Working paper.

Brigo, D., and A. Pallavicini. 2008. Counterparty risk and contingent CDS valuation under correlation between interest-rates and default. *Risk* (February).

Brigo, D., A. Pallavicini, and V. Papatheodorou. 2010. Bilateral counterparty risk valuation for interest-rate products: Impact of volatilities and correlations. Working paper.

Brigo, D., and M. Tarenghi. 2004. Credit default swap calibration and equity swap valuation under counterparty risk with a tractable structural model. Working paper.

Canabarro, E., and D. Duffie. 2003. Measuring and marking counterparty risk. Chapter 9 of *Asset/liability management of financial institutions.* Euromoney Books.

Crépey, S., M. Jeanblanc, and B. Zargari. 2010a. Counterparty risk on a CDS in a Markov chain copula model with joint defaults. In *Recent Advances in Financial Engineering 2009.* M. Kijima, C. Hara, Y. Muromachi, and K. Tanaka, eds. Singapore: World Scientific Publishing Co.

Crépey, S., M. Jeanblanc, and B. Zargari. 2010b. Counterparty risk on a CDS with joint defaults and stochastic spreads. Working paper.

Delbaen, F., and W. Schachermayer. 2006. *The mathematics of arbitrage.* New York: Springer Finance.

Delta Hedge GmbH. n.d. *Counterparty credit risk.* Available at www.delta-hedge.com/pdf/Delta Hedge Counterparty Credit Risk.pdf.

De Prisco, B., and D. Rosen. 2005. Modelling stochastic counterparty credit exposures for derivatives portfolios. Chapter 1 of *Counterparty credit risk modelling: Risk management, pricing and regulation,* ed. Michael Pykhtin. London: Risk Books.

Duffie, D., and N. Gârleanu. 2001. Risk and the valuation of collateralized debt obligations. *Financial Analysts Journal* 57:41–62.

European Central Bank. 2009. *Credit default swaps and counterparty credit risk.* (August).

Gibson, M. 2005. Measuring counterparty credit exposure to a margined counterparty. Chapter 2 of *Counterparty credit risk modelling: Risk management, pricing and regulation,* ed. Michael Pykhtin. London: Risk Books.

Gregory, J. 2009. Being two-faced over counterparty risk. *Risk* (February).

International Swaps and Derivatives Association. 2003. *Annex 1—ISDA-LIBA-TBMA counterparty risk market survey.* ISDA Inc.

Lipton, A., and A. Sepp. 2009. Credit value adjustment for credit default swaps via the structural default model. *Journal of Credit Risk* 5 no. 2 (Summer).

Markit. 2009. *The CDS Big Bang: Understanding the changes to the global CDS contract and North American conventions.* (March).

Redon, C. 2006. Wrong way risk modelling. *Risk* (April).

Zhu, S., and M. Pykhtin. 2007. A guide to modeling counterparty credit risk. *GARP Risk Review* (July/August).

CHAPTER 13

Structural Counterparty Risk Valuation for Credit Default Swaps

Christophette Blanchet-Scalliet

Université de Lyon

Frédéric Patras

Université de Nice and Zeliade Systems

The valuation of counterparty risk for single-name credit derivatives is often based on reduced models where defaults intensities drive the jump-to-default of the counterparty. Whereas efficient and relatively easy to calibrate to credit default swaps (CDS) spreads and market data, we argue that this approach should be supplemented by the structural approach familiar in multiname credit risk (e.g., in the Gaussian copula models or in many widespread credit portfolios risk assessment tools). We discuss Merton-type structural models for counterparty risk, their advantages, soundness, and potential shortcomings, and address the question of their numerical tractability. We focus then on the derivation of closed formulas for counterparty risk on a (possibly collateralized) CDS—extending the ones familiar in the pricing of multiname barrier options. Most of our results are meaningful more generally for derivatives on two default-prone assets: multiple barrier conditions or equity-to-credit modeling.

13.1 Introduction

Default risk computations are directly involved in four closely connected, but still separated, areas: first, the pricing of single- and multiname credit derivatives (ABS, CDS, CDOs, etc.); second, risk valuation for regulatory, risk management, and economic capital valuation purposes; third, rating assignments; and fourth, equity-to-credit modeling. The present chapter is focused mainly on the first two aspects of credit risk valuation, but its methods and ideas could be applied to the two other fields. More generally, its theoretical content can be viewed as a general contribution to the field of probabilistic methods in multiname risk and valuation.

Although deriving new formulas for credit derivative transactions on two assets, our main interest will be on counterparty risk. Once again, this is a central argument, both for regulatory purposes (counterparty risk was already a key issue in the Basel I agreements, but its relevance and complexity was emphasized by the later improvements of the set of rules; see, e.g., Bank for International Settlements 1998; Basel Committee on Banking Supervision 2005; Hull 2007) and also for practical risk management.

The field of counterparty risk has evolved dramatically recently, due in particular to the seminal work by D. Brigo and his coauthors. Our present contribution rests largely on similar ideas. We should refer in particular to the pioneering work by Hull-White (2001) and to Brigo-Tarenghi (2004, 2007). Further references will be given later. This field undergoes currently rapid changes due to new rules, regulations, and market practices (Markit 2009), however, the underlying theoretical needs will remain important in the future.

On the mathematical side, we derive formulas for the joint distribution of the default events—and of other relevant joint probabilities—of two default-prone entities in a Merton or Black-Cox type of setting. We discuss in particular some natural extensions of the Black-Cox model that handle problems such as the one of short-term maturities, following largely Patras (2006a). Closed formulas for counterparty risk on a CDS transaction or for a first-to-default swap on two underlyings follow.

We refrain from seeking the outmost generality or for a complete list of pricing formulas that could be obtained using the methods developed in the present chapter. Most credit derivatives on two underlyings with time-dependent payoffs can actually be priced in the structural approach using our results. The exercise of deriving the corresponding formulas is left to the interested reader. For more sophisticated models than the ones we consider here (e.g., with arbitrary jump-diffusion dynamics or time-dependent thresholds), the derivation of closed formulas is not possible in general. We refer, in this broader setting, to Chapter 21, by P. Del Moral and the second author, investigating recent general Monte Carlo techniques suited to the computation of default times and rare events analysis in a higher-dimensional setting.

We include in Appendix 13A and Appendix 13B, besides technical lemmas, a study of the distribution of first hitting times in a polyhedral domain.

13.2 Modeling Two-Dimensional Default Risk

13.2.1 Reduced versus Structural Models

We follow here Merton's structural approach to risk, where the default of a company is triggered by its firm value V falling below a threshold (see Merton 1974 or, e.g.,

Bielecki and Rutkowski 2002 chap. 3). The risk-neutral dynamics of the processes V is given by:

$$\frac{dV(t)}{V(t)} = (r - k)dt + \sigma\,dB(t)$$

As in Black-Cox (1976), the threshold is described by a time-dependent deterministic process $v(t) := Ke^{\gamma t}$. Here, r is the constant short-term interest rate and B a standard Brownian motion. The coefficient k is a payout ratio representing net payouts/inflows by the firm (see, e.g., Bielecki and Rutkowski 2002, chap. 2). Notice that we will use mainly a risk-neutral dynamics, but the same construction would hold with a real-life dynamics (just replace $r - k$ by the drift under the historical probability). One of the interesting features of this approach to credit risk is that the underlying processes can be interpreted as closely related to fundamental information on the firm (for example, K is naturally related to the outstanding debt). This observation allows use of the model even in situations where market prices are not available (for example, when one can not approximate the value of the firm as the sum of its debt and stock market capitalization) or in a credit-to-equity approach. The other advantage of this class of model with respect to intensity models (where the default is measured by the intensity of a jump process) is that, contrary to intensity models, their extension to several assets is straightforward—modeling the correlation between the assets amounts to correlate the Brownian motions driving the two asset values.

It is well-known, however, that the original Merton methodology, where the threshold is determined by the firm's liabilities, as well as its natural refinements such as the Black-Cox (1976) first passage time formulas, give qualitatively good but numerically poor results. For example, the structural method will rank correctly the risks of two companies but it will not be able to predict the spreads of the corresponding CDS. For pricing purposes, the correct way to use the Merton and Black-Cox models is to calibrate their parameters on the market prices of the securities issued by the companies. Doing so ensures that the models price the risk correctly. This is the ground for their various uses, either in credit risk measurement (think of the Basel II Vasicek-type large pool formulas, see Hull 2007; Vasicek 1987), or for pricing purposes (think of the one-factor Gaussian copula model for CDO tranches, see Schönbucher 2003).

Another classical problem raised by Merton-type models is that defaults are predictable and the calibration of short maturities CDS spreads is quite difficult. This is not a serious problem for old-fashioned CDSs, where the spread was computed so that the mark-to-market (MTM) value of the contract was 0 at inception. This convention implies indeed that the MTM value of the contract remains low for short-term maturities, so that a default of the counterparty at such maturities has a limited effect. In other terms, counterparty defaults at short maturities have a relatively small impact on the counterparty default leg of the contract. This issue of short-term maturities becomes, however, more important when the CDS Big Bang conventions are adopted (Markit 2009) (since up-front payments are made), at least if the CDSs are not negotiated through a clearing house.

One classical solution to remedy these difficulties is to allow general curvilinear default thresholds (at the price of computational tractability, although some forms of the threshold curve still allow the derivation of closed formulas [see Bielecki and Rutkowski 2002]), or to allow jumps in the firm value as in Zhou (2001b) or Lipton (2002). More recently, Brigo and Tarenghi introduced several improvements of these models; in particular, they showed that the introduction of a time-dependent or random volatility allows for higher short-term spreads (Brigo and Tarenghi 2004, 2007). Another alternative model was proposed by Lipton and Sepp (2009). They introduce a multiname structural default model based on correlated jump-diffusion processes. In their model, a typical default of a single name is triggered by a sudden drop in the asset value followed by its gradual deterioration. In a multiname setting, they allow for both collective and idiosyncratic jumps—a classical way to correlate jump processes in view of applications to credit risk. Following the general techniques developed in Lipton (2001), they are able to derive integro-differential equations and compute Green functions adapted to the problem and, ultimately, pricing equations.

We will discuss a simple way to accommodate the Merton and Black-Cox types of models so as to capture short-term CDS spreads, with the same degree of higher-dimensional tractability as the classical models.

13.2.2   Higher-Dimensional Default Risk

The approach to higher-dimensional default risk in the structural setting was pioneered in the industry by risk valuation softwares and, in the academic literature, by Hull-White (2001) who used correlated Brownian motions with thresholds calibrated on default probabilities for the study of multiname credit risk. The analytical study of higher-dimensional default risk was initiated by Zhou (2001a) (with previously an important contribution to the general topic by He-Keirstead-Rebholz 1998). More recent works include Brigo-Tarenghi (2004, 2005), who studied in particular counterparty risk on equity swaps and hybrid equity/credit derivatives; see also Brigo-Morini-Tarenghi, Chapter 14 of the present volume.

Recall that we are interested in modeling the counterparty risk on a credit risk transaction. This involves (in general and depending on the particular features of the transaction) the computation of various joint laws. For example, for a vanilla credit default swap, the computation relies on the distribution of the default time of the counterparty and the conditional distribution (with respect to the default of the counterparty) of the values of the CDS contract. The same methodology can be applied to the valuation of first-to-default contracts on two underlyings when the payoff is time-dependent; see Section 13.4 of the present chapter; the time-independent case has been addressed in He, Keirstead, and Rebholz (1998); Patras (2006b); and Zhou (2001a).

The construction of first passage times of thresholds for a two-asset portfolio was investigated systematically by Lipton (2001), who pointed out the relevance of the method of images in the setting of universal (Riemann-type) coverings of a wedge. Lipton's seminal contribution largely relies on analytical tools. The same idea was developed independently in Patras (2006b) from a probabilistic point of view (here, the accent was drawn on the strong Markov properties of Brownian motions to introduce the method of images on the universal covering). A nice numerical feature of this approach is that it points out, through the method of images, that the formal series showing up in the formulas that we will introduce below should decay rapidly for geometrical reasons. Intuitively, the density of a Brownian motion decays exponentially with the distance, and this decay should be reflected in a fast convergence of the corresponding series—these (fairly technical) numerical properties are discussed in Lipton's book; we won't discuss them further in this chapter.

Notice that the computations we are interested in require going beyond the existing formulas for two-dimensional credit risk in the structural approach. Indeed, these formulas rely mainly on the computation of the probability that one (and only one) out of two firms defaults or that the two firms default before a given maturity, whereas pricing counterparty risk for a CDS transaction requires (among others) the exact knowledge of default times distributions.

We have tried to keep some balance between generality and the choice of too restrictive assumptions. The model for which we will derive explicit formulas is a generic two-dimensional version of the Black-Cox model (see, however, the next section for some simple generalizations that do not affect its numerical tractability).

We label 1 and 2 the two default-prone entities. In view of applications to counterparty risk, the counterparty will be labeled 2. We write τ_1 (resp. τ_2) for the random time when the first (resp. second) entity defaults. Defaults are triggered when two lognormal processes V_1 and V_2 with the risk-neutral dynamics

$$\frac{dV_i(t)}{V_i(t)} = (r - k_i)dt + \sigma_i dB_i(t)$$

associated respectively to the first and second entity fall below barriers $v_i(t) := K_i e^{\gamma_i t}$. Last, we assume that the Brownian motions B_1 and B_2 are correlated: $Cov(B_1(t), B_2(t)) = \varrho t$. This is an important assumption that reflects the fact that the counterparty (the protection seller) of a CDS transaction is often a well-rated company that will not default except in a very bad macroeconomic environment. In particular, if the counterparty defaults, one may expect CDS spreads on other entities to widen considerably simultaneously. This phenomenon is accounted for by a positive correlation coefficient. It is the main reason, together with the dynamical aspects of the problem, why simplistic counterparty risk models fail, both theoretically and empirically, to account for counterparty-driven loss expectations on derivative contracts.

13.2.3 Extending the Lardy-Finkelstein Model

In this section, we address briefly the problem of short-term maturities in the structural approach. The model we refer to in the title of this section, the idea of which is attributed to Lardy and Finkelstein (Inglis, Lipton, Savescu, and Sepp 2008; Schönbucher 2003), essentially underlies risk valuation methods such as the ones of CreditGrades or E2C. This is a simple but robust and intuitive model, close to the classical Black-Cox model, except for the introduction of a random recovery rate on the liabilities of the firm. Namely, the asset value $V(t)$ behaves lognormally, as in the usual Black-Cox model, but a default occurs now when $V(t)$ cross the random barrier LD, where D stands for the debt (or an equivalent quantity, implied either from fundamental analysis or from market data) and $L = \overline{L}e^{\lambda Z - \frac{\lambda^2}{2}}$ for a random recovery rate with a lognormal behavior (here, $\overline{L}$ and λ are constant parameters and Z stands for a standard Gaussian variable).

Notice the meaningfulness of this feature of the model in view of the recent developments that occurred during the turmoil of the subprime crisis: It has been indeed realized that introducing random recoveries was necessary in multiname credit risk in order to make sense of the spreads on the CDOs' super-senior tranches. The extra assumption in the Lardy-Finkelstein model (with respect to Black-Cox) amounts to consider a random barrier or to introduce randomness in the present value of the firm's assets (CreditGrades 2002). These equivalent assumptions also make sense on their own (for example, a firm's asset value is not an observable quantity).

Allowing for this randomness implies the possibility of nonzero short-term CDS spreads. Still, the model is not fully satisfactory for dynamic risk management purposes and may imply, in practice, small default probabilities at the start of the contract, failing to explain fully the observations of short-term debt (Inglis, Lipton, Savescu, and Sepp 2008). A further extension is then possible, namely, adding jumps to the asset value process. Lipton (2002) considers, for example, log-exponentially distributed jumps—an approach that preserves some analytical tractability of the model.

As far as higher-dimensional credit events are concerned, the problem of the numerical tractability is certainly even more an issue. In Patras (2006a), we suggested the simple solution of introducing an independent Poisson process to model, together with the random recovery rate, short-term defaults and short-term spreads. The independence hypothesis ensures the tractability of the model. The calibration of the intensity of the jump-to-default process component on the short-term spreads allows for an idiosyncratic component of the firm's credit risk. In other terms, the model results in a kind of "composite spread" approach to the credit risk of the firm that decomposes into (1) uncertainty on the asset value and/or recovery rate on the liabilities (this follows from the randomness of the recovery rate), (2) idiosyncratic risk (corresponding to the jump-to-default component of the dynamics), and (3) a classical structural Black-Cox type component corresponding to the mid- and long-term performance of the firm. These questions are discussed in Patras, (2006a), to which we refer for details. They are closely related to current issues in the equity-to-credit modeling (see, e.g., Turc et al. 2008).

The key point for the present chapter is that there is a convenient way to extend the Lardy-Finkelstein model to the multiname setting. Namely, for a family of N assets, assume that the asset value processes $V_1(t), \ldots, V_N(t)$ are correlated as usual in a Black-Cox model, that is, by correlating the corresponding Brownian motions

$B_1, \ldots, B_N$ driving their respective dynamics. If one assumes further that the standard deviation parameters $\lambda_1, \ldots, \lambda_N$ in the definition of the random barriers $L_1 D_1, \ldots, L_N D_N$ are proportional to the volatility of the assets, and that the Gaussian variables $Z_1, \ldots, Z_N$ showing up in the definition of the L_i are correlated as the B_is, then it can be shown easily (Patras 2006a) that the numerical tractability of the model is the same as the numerical tractability of the usual Black-Cox model. In particular, it was shown in Patras (2006b) that the formulas obtained from the two-dimensional method of images (Lipton 2001; Patras 2006b) do apply to the Lardy-Finkelstein model. The same conclusion holds *mutatis mutandis* for our forthcoming developments.

Here we stop this discussion, the purpose of which was to point out that some easy (and less easy) adaptations of the Black-Cox model allow us to handle the problem of the calibration of short-term spreads in the structural setting. As we mentioned before, such adaptations are necessary in practice to handle counterparty risk on over-the-counter (OTC) CDS contracts, in particular under Big Bang type conventions (fixed spreads, floating up fronts).

We turn now to the problem of deriving closed formulas for counterparty risk on CDSs (and similar quantities) in this setting.

13.3 Counterparty Risk

Recall that a CDS is a contract between a protection buyer against default of the underlying name in exchange for periodic coupon payments until the termination of the contract. The default of the underlying being hedged by the CDS contract, the protection buyer is still exposed to two risks: market risk (induced by the variations of the mark-to-market (MTM) value of the contract) and, for OTC contracts, credit risk—losses that happen if the counterparty defaults when the mark-to-market value of the contract is positive to the protection buyer. Notice that even netted or collateralized contracts keep some residual amount of credit risk. The counterparty default leg of the contract is particularly sensitive to the correlation between the counterparty and the underlying—as the markets experienced after Lehman Brothers' collapse.

Of course, in full generality, counterparty risk is two-sided (the protection seller is exposed to mark-to-market losses if the protection buyer goes bankrupt). This other side of the risk is partially mitigated by the observation that, on average, the protection seller will incur losses if the protection buyer defaults in a context of decreasing spreads (i.e., lower credit risk)—that is, in a bullish macroeconomic environment, which makes the default of the protection buyer less likely. For the same reason, valuing the credit valuation adjustment (CVA) associated to the possible default of the protection buyer is less problematic and is more satisfactorily treated with simple adjustments techniques than the one of the CVA associated to the protection seller, which is much more sensitive to correlation effects. For that reason we won't consider here two-sided counterparty risk, and refer to Gregory (2009), for example, for further details on the subject.

In this section, we derive a closed formula for the counterparty default leg of a CDS contract, that is the present value (PV) of the expected losses on a vanilla single-name credit derivative transaction due to the default of the protection seller. We emphasize that the notion of counterparty default leg should not be confused with the usual notion of default leg for a CDS contract, that is, the present value of future payments by the protection seller.

The classical reference for general insights on counterparty risk is Brigo-Masetti (2006), to which we refer for details on the overall subject that are omitted here.

13.3.1 Margin Agreements

In the presence of margin agreements, there is still some residual counterparty risk. The extent of this risk depends on the particular features of the margin agreements and on some technically difficult issues such as margin period of risk effects. For example, the counterparty may at some point stop posting collateral due to financial difficulties without the default event or bankruptcy being necessarily and immediately triggered. Specific models have to be devised for that particular risk that are out of the scope of the present chapter; see Pykhtin (2009) and Chapter 16 of the present volume.

We consider here a simple case of margin agreements. For consistency, and since we are interested in the risks incurred by the protection buyer, we assume that only the counterparty (protection seller) has to post collateral (the other side of the margin agreements, if existing, being largely irrelevant for our purposes). In other terms, we consider a unilateral agreement and follow Pykhtin's (2009 and Chapter 16) approach and conventions. The agreement is characterized by a counterparty threshold H_c and a minimum transfer amount (MTA). If the contract value less the already posted collateral exceeds the threshold, the counterparty must post extra collateral to bring this collateralized value back to the threshold. If the contract value less the already posted collateral is below the threshold, part of the posted collateral (if there is any) must be returned to the counterparty to bring the collateralized value back to the threshold. To reduce the frequency of collateral exchange, no collateral is transferred if the amount that needs to be transferred is less than the MTA.

The exact modeling of collateralization subject to MTA is difficult because it involves theoretically the computation of passage times related to the MTA condition. Therefore, in practice, the threshold H_c can be replaced with the effective threshold H_e defined as $H_e = H_c + MTA$. The margin agreement is then treated as if it had zero MTA and H_e as a threshold. In the remainder of the chapter, we adopt this approximation. Notice that the (however simplified) model includes as a meaningful subcase the one of a full collateralization ($H_c = 0$) with, however, a nonzero MTA.

13.3.2 Counterparty Default Leg

We follow standard market practices. Namely, we assume that the CDS contract has a notional value C and that, if the underlying entity defaults, the buyer of protection receives $(1 - R_u) \cdot C$ from the seller of protection, where R_u stands for the recovery rate of the underlying entity. Similarly, if the counterparty (the protection seller) defaults at t on the CDS contract, we assume that the buyer of protection receives $l(p_t) = R_c \cdot p_t^+$, where $p_t^+ = \sup(0, p_t)$ stands for the positive part of the market value p_t of the CDS contract at t, and where R_c stands for the counterparty recovery rate. In the presence of margin agreements, the buyer receives instead $l(p_t) = 0$ if $p_t < 0, l(p_t) = R_c p_t$ if $0 \leq p_t < H_e$ and $l(p_t) = p_t - (1 - R_c) H_e$ else. Notice that other margin agreements than the ones we considered would simply result into a different formula for the function l (however possibly involving other parameters than p_t).

Using the joint law of the default time of the counterparty and of the underlying entity for the CDS, we compute now the default probability of the underlying entity conditional to the default of the counterparty, and obtain a closed formula for the counterparty default leg. The present moment is normalized to $t = 0$ in what follows, it may or may not coincide with the inception of the CDS contract.

The coupon payments rate (CDS spread) by the protection buyer is denoted by s. We assume continuous payments of the fees: in practice, fees are payed quarterly (and sometimes semiannually), but due to the payments-in-arrears conventions, the continuous payments assumption is a reasonable one.

The theoretical counterparty default leg D_c is given by

$$D_c = E[e^{-r\tau_2} \cdot l(p(V_1(\tau_2), \tau_2)) 1_{\tau_2 < (T \wedge \tau_1)}]$$

where $p(V_1(\tau_2), \tau_2)$ is the market price of the CDS contract at $t = \tau_2$ (when $\tau_1 \geq \tau_2$). The value $p(V_1(\tau_2), \tau_2)$ is obtained as the difference between the (counterparty risk free) default and fee legs, that is:

$$p(V_1(\tau_2), \tau_2) = D_l(V_1(\tau_2), \tau_2) - \frac{sC}{r} \cdot E[(1 - e^{-r((T \wedge \tau_1) - \tau_2)}) 1_{\tau_1 \geq \tau_2} | \mathcal{F}_{\tau_2}]$$

where

$$D_l(V_1(\tau_2), \tau_2) = E[C(1 - R_u) e^{-r(\tau_1 - \tau_2)} 1_{\tau_2 \leq \tau_1 \leq T} | \mathcal{F}_{\tau_2}]$$

and where we write $\mathcal{F}_t$, as usual, for the natural filtration of the probability space underlying the two Brownian motions $B_1(t)$, $B_2(t)$.

Notice that the term $T \wedge \tau_1$ can be, in most situations, safely replaced by T in the formula. This is because, for standard values for the spreads and implied default probabilities in single-name default risk computations, the computation of the fee leg conditional to the hypothesis that no default occurs is a good first-order approximation to the unconditional fee leg. The following computations could be simplified accordingly.

Without margin agreements, we get:

Theorem 13.3.1   *The counterparty default leg D_c is given by:*

$$D_c = CR_c$$

$$*E\left[1_{\tau_2<(T\wedge\tau_1)}e^{-r\tau_2}\left(\left(1-R_u+\frac{s}{r}\right)\left(e^{-\mu_{\tau_2}(\beta-\eta)}N\left(\frac{-\mu_{\tau_2}-\eta(T-\tau_2)}{\sqrt{T-\tau_2}}\right)\right.\right.\right.$$

$$\left.+e^{-\mu_{\tau_2}(\beta+\eta)}N\left(\frac{-\mu_{\tau_2}+\eta(T-\tau_2)}{\sqrt{T-\tau_2}}\right)\right)$$

$$-\frac{s}{r}\left(1-e^{-r(T-\tau_2)}\left(1-N\left(\frac{-\mu_{\tau_2}-\beta(T-\tau_2)}{\sqrt{T-\tau_2}}\right)\right.\right.$$

$$\left.\left.\left.\left.\left.-e^{-2\mu_{\tau_2}\beta}N\left(\frac{-\mu_{\tau_2}+\beta(T-\tau_2)}{\sqrt{T-\tau_2}}\right)\right)\right)\right)\right)^+\right]$$

where $v_1 := r - k_1 - \gamma_1 - \frac{1}{2}\sigma_1^2$, $\eta := \sqrt{\frac{v_1^2}{\sigma_1^2}+2r}$, $\beta := \frac{v_1}{\sigma_1}$, $\mu_{\tau_2} := \frac{\ln\left(\frac{V_1(\tau_2)}{v_1(\tau_2)}\right)}{\sigma_1}$.

Indeed,

$$p(V_1(\tau_2),\tau_2)1_{\tau_2<(T\wedge\tau_1)}$$

$$= C1_{\tau_2<(T\wedge\tau_1)}E\left[(1-R_u)e^{-r(\tau_1-\tau_2)}1_{\tau_2\le\tau_1<T}-\frac{s}{r}1_{\tau_2<\tau_1}\right.$$

$$\left.+\frac{s}{r}e^{-r(\tau_1-\tau_2)}1_{\tau_2\le\tau_1<T}+\frac{s}{r}e^{-r(T-\tau_2)}1_{\tau_2\le T<\tau_1}\Big|\mathcal{F}_{\tau_2}\right]$$

$$= C1_{\tau_2<(T\wedge\tau_1)}\left(E\left[\left(1-R_u+\frac{s}{r}\right)e^{-r(\tau_1-\tau_2)}1_{\tau_2\le\tau_1<T}\Big|\mathcal{F}_{\tau_2}\right]-E\left[\frac{s}{r}1_{\tau_2<\tau_1}\Big|\mathcal{F}_{\tau_2}\right]\right.$$

$$\left.+E\left[\frac{s}{r}e^{-r(T-\tau_2)}1_{\tau_2\le T<\tau_1}\Big|\mathcal{F}_{\tau_2}\right]\right)$$

The theorem follows by standard computations of integrals over Gaussian densities that are sketched in Appendix 13A. In the presence of margin agreements, the function $R_c(\ )^+$ should be replaced by $l(\ )$ in the theorem. The same observation holds for our forthcoming developments and we won't repeat it.

13.3.3   Explicit Formulas

Recall that $\tau_i = \inf\{t,\ V_i(t) \le K_i e^{\gamma_i t}\}$. The condition $V_i(t) \le K_i e^{\gamma_i t}$ can be rewritten: $W_i(t) \ge y_0^i$, where $W_i(t) = \ln(\frac{K_i e^{\gamma_i t}}{V_i(t)}) - \ln(\frac{K_i}{V_i(0)})$ and $y_0^i = \ln V_i(0) - \ln K_i$. Equivalently, $W_i(t)$ is the diffusion process:

$$dW_i(t) = -v_i t - \sigma_i dB_i(t)$$

with $\mathbf{W}_i(0) = 0$ and $v_i := r - k_i - \gamma_i - \frac{1}{2}\sigma_i^2$.

Let us define $\mathbf{Z}(t)$ by:

$$\mathbf{Z}(t) = (Z_1(t), Z_2(t))^* = \frac{1}{\sqrt{1-\varrho^2}} \begin{pmatrix} \sigma_1^{-1} & -\varrho\sigma_2^{-1} \\ 0 & \sqrt{1-\varrho^2}\sigma_2^{-1} \end{pmatrix} \begin{pmatrix} y_0^1 - W_1(t) \\ y_0^2 - W_2(t) \end{pmatrix}$$

We get:

$$dZ_1(t) = \phi_1 dt + dX_1(t), \ dZ_2(t) = \phi_2 dt + dX_2(t)$$

where $\mathbf{X}(t) = (X_1(t), X_2(t))$ is a standard planar Brownian motion and

$$\phi_1 = \frac{v_1\sigma_2 - v_2\sigma_1\varrho}{\sigma_1\sigma_2\sqrt{1-\varrho^2}}, \phi_2 = \frac{v_2}{\sigma_2}$$

In particular, $\mathbf{Z}(t)$ is a 2-dim. Brownian motion with drift and the barrier conditions $V_i(t) = v_i(t)$ now read: $Z_2(t) = 0$ and $\sqrt{1-\varrho^2}Z_1(t) + \varrho Z_2(t) = 0$.

We want to compute the default leg D_c, that is, equivalently:

$$E[h(B_1(\tau_2), \tau_2)1_{\tau_2 \leq (T \wedge \tau_1)}]$$
$$= E[\bar{h}(Z_1(\tau_2), \tau_2)1_{\tau_2 \leq (T \wedge \tau_1)}] = \int_0^T \int_0^{+\infty} \bar{h}(a, s)P(\tau_2 \in ds,$$
$$\tau_2 = \tau_2 \wedge \tau_1, Z_1(\tau_2) \in da) da ds$$

where $h(x, t) :=$

$$\left(e^{-rt}\left(1 - R_u + \frac{s}{r}\right)\left(e^{-\mu_{x,t}(\beta-\eta)}N\left(\frac{-\mu_{x,t} - \eta(T-t)}{\sqrt{T-t}}\right)\right.\right.$$
$$\left. + e^{-\mu_{x,t}(\beta+\eta)}N\left(\frac{-\mu_{x,t} + \eta(T-t)}{\sqrt{T-t}}\right)\right)$$
$$- \frac{s}{r}\left(1 - e^{-r(T-t)}\left(1 - N\left(\frac{-\mu_{x,t} - \beta(T-t)}{\sqrt{T-t}}\right)\right.\right.$$
$$\left.\left.\left.\left. - e^{-2\mu_{x,t}\beta}N\left(\frac{-\mu_{x,t} + \beta(T-t)}{\sqrt{T-t}}\right)\right)\right)\right)\right)^+$$

$\mu_{x,t} := \sigma_1^{-1}(v_1 t + \sigma_1 x + \ln V_1(0) - \ln K_1)$ and $\bar{h}(z, t) = h(\frac{-y_0^1 - v_1 t}{\sigma_1} + \sqrt{1-\rho^2} \cdot z, t)$. Applying the Girsanov theorem, $(Z_1(t), Z_2(t))^*$ is a classical Brownian motion for the probability law $\mathbf{Q}$:

$$\frac{d\mathbf{Q}}{d\mathbf{P}} = e^{-\phi_1 X_1(T) - \phi_2 X_2(T) - \left[\frac{\phi_1^2}{2} + \frac{\phi_2^2}{2}\right]T} \ \mathbf{P}_{a.s.}.$$

Let $r_0 e^{i\theta_0} := Z_1(0) + i Z_2(0) = \frac{y_0^1 \sigma_2 - \varrho y_0^2 \sigma_1}{\sigma_1 \sigma_2 \sqrt{1-\varrho^2}} + i \frac{y_0^2}{\sigma_2}$.

Lemma 13.3.1   *We have, for $(a, 0) \in \mathbf{R}^2$ s.t. $a > 0$:*

$$\mathbf{P}(\tau_2 \in dt, \tau_2 = \tau_2 \wedge \tau_1, Z_1(\tau_2) \in da) = e^{\phi_1(a - r_0 \cos(\theta_0)) - \phi_2 r_0 \sin(\theta_0) - \frac{||\vec{\phi}||^2 t}{2}} \frac{\pi}{\alpha^2 t a} e^{-(a^2 + r_0^2)/2t}$$

$$\times \sum_{n=0}^{\infty} n \sin \frac{n \pi \theta_0}{\alpha} I_{n\pi/\alpha} \left(\frac{a r_0}{t} \right) da dt$$

where $||\vec{\phi}||^2 := \phi_1^2 + \phi_2^2$, $\alpha := \arcsin(\varrho) + \frac{\pi}{2}$ and $I_{n\pi/\alpha}$ is the modified Bessel function of index $n\pi/\alpha$.

Proof. The lemma follows from Theorem 13.B.1 in Appendix 13B (up to a straightforward adaptation since we consider here a polyhedral domain $D := \{(x, y) \in \mathbf{R}^2 | y \geq 0, \sqrt{1 - \varrho^2} x + \varrho y \geq 0\}$ with a horizontal lower—instead of an upper—boundary, so that the signs have to be changed accordingly in the formulas). Indeed, according to Carslaw and Jaeger (1988) or Patras (2006b, 697), we have, for (a, b) in a neighborhood of $(a, 0)$ with $b > 0$:

$$f(a, b, t) da db = \mathbf{Q}(\mathbf{Z}(t) \in (da, db), \tau_1 \wedge \tau_2 > t)$$

$$= \frac{2\mu}{\alpha t} e^{-(\mu^2 + r_0^2)/2t} \sum_{n=0}^{\infty} \sin \frac{n \pi \theta}{\alpha} \sin \frac{n \pi \theta_0}{\alpha} I_{n\pi/\alpha} \left(\frac{\mu r_0}{t} \right) d\mu d\theta$$

where $\theta := arctg(\frac{b}{a})$, $\mu := \sqrt{a^2 + b^2}$. Therefore, we get

$$\mathbf{Q}(\tau_2 = \tau_2 \wedge \tau_1, \tau_2 \in dt, Z_1(\tau_2) \in da)$$

$$= \frac{\pi}{\alpha^2 t a} e^{-(a^2 + r_0^2)/2t} \sum_{n=0}^{\infty} n \sin \frac{n \pi \theta_0}{\alpha} I_{n\pi/\alpha} \left(\frac{a r_0}{t} \right) da dt$$

and the proof follows.

Theorem 13.3.2   *The counterparty default leg D_c of the CDS is given by:*

$$D_c = CR_c \int_0^T \int_0^{+\infty} \bar{h}(\mu, t) e^{\phi_1(\mu - r_0 \cos(\theta_0)) - \phi_2 r_0 \sin(\theta_0) - \frac{||\vec{\phi}||^2 t}{2}}$$

$$\times \frac{\pi}{\alpha^2 t \mu} e^{-(\mu^2 + r_0^2)/2t} \sum_{n=0}^{\infty} n \sin \frac{n \pi \theta_0}{\alpha} I_{n\pi/\alpha} \left(\frac{\mu r_0}{t} \right) dt d\mu$$

Notice that although involving a double integral on Gaussian densities and Bessel function (which asymptotic behavior is well understood, making numerical approximations easy and efficient), this kind of higher-order integral is familiar in physics (heat conduction in solids, cross-sections computations, acoustics, etc.).

13.3.4   Fair Price of a CDS

In this section, we take advantage of our computation of the counterparty default leg to compute the fair price of a CDS contract at an arbitrary time (normalized again to $t = 0$ in this section) between the inception of the contract and its maturity T. As usual, it is obtained as the difference between the default and fee legs, but, contrary to the usual pricing formulas, we take into account exactly the effect of the counterparty default leg.

Notice that, as a contribution to the general theory of multiname credit risk, we insist in deriving exact formulas and general methods but, for practical purposes, it may be convenient to use approximation schemes to simplify the use of the formulas and fasten the computations. For example, in order to compute the fee leg, it may be convenient to assume that defaults can occur only at times t_i, $i = 1 \ldots n$, so that the following integral expressions can be safely replaced by finite sums involving only the computation of the default probabilities $\mathbf{P}(\tau_1 \wedge \tau_2 \leq t_i)$.

Let us write D_s for the standard default leg of the CDS, that is, the present value of the cash flows corresponding to payments by the seller of protection if there is a default occurring on the assets underlying the CDS contract. The total default leg D_{tot} of the CDS contract is given by the sum $D_s + D_c$, where D_c is given by Theorem 13.3.2.

Lemma 13.3.2   *The standard default leg is given by:*

$$
D_s = C(1 - R_u) \int_0^T \int_0^{+\infty} e^{\phi_1(\mu \cos(\alpha) - r_0 \cos(\theta_0)) + \phi_2(\mu \sin(\alpha) - r_0 \sin(\theta_0)) - \frac{\|\vec{\phi}\|^2 T}{2}} \frac{\pi}{\alpha^2 t \mu}
$$

$$
e^{-(\mu^2 + r_0^2)/2t} \sum_{n=0}^{\infty} (-1)^{n+1} n \sin \frac{n\pi \theta_0}{\alpha} I_{n\pi/\alpha}\left(\frac{\mu r_0}{t}\right) d\mu dt
$$

The proof follows from the same reasoning as the one of Lemma 13.3.1 and can be omitted.

Notice that:

$$
\mathbf{Q}(\tau_1 \in dt, \tau_1 = \tau_1 \wedge \tau_2, Z_1(t) + iZ_2(t) = d\mu \cdot e^{i\alpha})
$$

$$
= \frac{\pi}{\alpha^2 t \mu} e^{-(\mu^2 + r_0^2)/2t} \sum_{n=0}^{\infty} (-1)^{n+1} n \sin \frac{n\pi \theta_0}{\alpha} I_{n\pi/\alpha}\left(\frac{\mu r_0}{t}\right) d\mu dt
$$

Recall that the fee leg of a credit derivative contract is the present value of cumulated payments by the protection buyer. We write from now on τ for $\tau_1 \wedge \tau_2$.

Lemma 13.3.3   *The fee leg F of the CDS contract is given by:*

$$Fs^{-1} = \frac{1 - e^{-rT}}{r}\mathbf{P}(\tau \geq T) + E\left[\frac{1 - e^{-r\tau}}{r}1_{\tau \leq T}\right]$$

$$= \frac{1 - e^{-rT}}{r}\int_0^\infty \int_0^\alpha e^{\phi_1(\mu\cos(\kappa) - r_0\cos(\theta_0)) + \phi_2(\mu\sin(\kappa) - r_0\sin(\theta_0)) - \frac{\|\vec{\phi}\|^2 T}{2}}\frac{2\mu}{\alpha T}$$

$$e^{-(\mu^2 + r_0^2)/2T}\sum_{n=1}^\infty \sin\frac{n\pi\kappa}{\alpha}\sin\frac{n\pi\theta_0}{\alpha}I_{n\pi/\alpha}\left(\frac{\mu r_0}{T}\right)d\mu d\kappa$$

$$+ \int_0^T \int_0^{+\infty} \frac{1 - e^{-rt}}{r}e^{\phi_1(\mu\cos(\alpha) - r_0\cos(\theta_0)) + \phi_2(\mu\sin(\alpha) - r_0\sin(\theta_0)) - \frac{\|\vec{\phi}\|^2 t}{2}}\frac{\pi}{\alpha^2 t\mu}$$

$$e^{-(\mu^2 + r_0^2)/2t}\sum_{n=0}^\infty (-1)^{n+1}n\sin\frac{n\pi\theta_0}{\alpha}I_{n\pi/\alpha}\left(\frac{\mu r_0}{t}\right)d\mu dt$$

$$+ \int_0^T \int_0^{+\infty} \frac{1 - e^{-rt}}{r}e^{\phi_1(\mu - r_0\cos(\theta_0)) - \phi_2 r_0\sin(\theta_0) - \frac{\|\vec{\phi}\|^2 t}{2}}\frac{\pi}{\alpha^2 t\mu}$$

$$e^{-(\mu^2 + r_0^2)/2t}\sum_{n=0}^\infty n\sin\frac{n\pi\theta_0}{\alpha}I_{n\pi/\alpha}\left(\frac{\mu r_0}{t}\right)dt d\mu$$

The first term was computed in Patras (2006b, 698); the last two follow from our previous computations.

Theorem 13.3.3   *The fair price of a CDS, taking into account the counterparty risk, is given by:*

$$D_{tot} - F$$

where F and D_{tot} are given by the previous lemmas.

13.4 First-to-Default on Two Underlyings

As was mentioned in the introduction, most credit derivative transactions on two default-prone instruments with time-dependent payoffs can be priced (at least theoretically) using the techniques developed in the present chapter. As an example, we derive the fair spread of a first-to-default contract on two underlyings.

Most notations are as stated earlier, when we were dealing with the counterparty risk on a CDS, and we do not recall them except when necessary. The only difference is that, now, the two default-prone entities are treated on the same footing. We still write C for the notional value of the contract and assume a given recovery rate R (e.g., 40 percent) so that, at the first default occuring before the maturity of the contract, the buyer of protection will receive $C(1 - R)$ (recall this is the very definition of a first-to-default contract; on the other hand, the buyer of protection pays a continuous fee—still called the spread—until the first default occurs or until the maturity of the contract if no default occurs before the maturity).

Lemma 13.4.1 *The default leg of the contract is given by:*

$$
D = C(1 - R)\left[\int_0^T \int_0^{+\infty} e^{-rt} e^{\phi_1(\mu\cos(\alpha) - r_0\cos(\theta_0)) + \phi_2(\mu\sin(\alpha) - r_0\sin(\theta_0)) - \frac{\|\vec{\phi}\|^2 T}{2}} \frac{\pi}{\alpha^2 t \mu}\right.
$$

$$
e^{-(\mu^2 + r_0^2)/2t} \sum_{n=0}^{\infty} (-1)^{n+1} n \sin\frac{n\pi\theta_0}{\alpha} I_{n\pi/\alpha}\left(\frac{\mu r_0}{t}\right) d\mu dt
$$

$$
+ \int_0^T \int_0^{+\infty} e^{-rt} e^{\phi_1(\mu - r_0\cos(\theta_0)) - \phi_2 r_0\sin(\theta_0) - \frac{\|\vec{\phi}\|^2 t}{2}}
$$

$$
\left.\frac{\pi}{\alpha^2 t \mu} e^{-(\mu^2 + r_0^2)/2t} \sum_{n=0}^{\infty} n \sin\frac{n\pi\theta_0}{\alpha} I_{n\pi/\alpha}\left(\frac{\mu r_0}{t}\right) dt d\mu\right]
$$

On the other hand, the fee leg is given by the same formula as in Lemma 13.3.3; this is because the coupon is served by the protection buyer until a first default occurs in both cases (a CDS with counterparty risk or a first-to-default swap on two underlyings).

Theorem 13.4.1 *The fair spread s of a first-to-default swap on two underlyings at inception of the contract is given by*

$$
s = \frac{D}{F'}
$$

where D is given by Lemma 13.4.1 and $F' = Fs^{-1}$ by Lemma 13.3.3.

Appendix 13A: Theoretical Default Legs for CDS

We include in this section a proof of the formulas for the market price of a CDS conditional on the default of the counterparty. These are classical computations and/or variations thereof. We give therefore only short indications and refer to Bielecki and Rutkowski (2002, chap. 3) for further details.

The notations are as in Section 13.3; N stands as usual for the cumulated standard normal distribution.

Lemma 13A.1 *On the set $\tau_2 < \tau_1$, we have:*

$$
P(\tau_1 \leq T | \mathcal{F}_{\tau_2}) = N\left(\frac{-Y_{\tau_2} - \nu_1(T - \tau_2)}{\sigma_1\sqrt{T - \tau_2}}\right) + e^{-2\nu_1\sigma_1^{-2}Y_{\tau_2}} N\left(\frac{-Y_{\tau_2} + \nu_1(T - \tau_2)}{\sigma_1\sqrt{T - \tau_2}}\right)
$$

where $Y_t := \ln\left(\frac{V_1(t)}{v_1(t)}\right) = \ln\left(\frac{V_1(0)}{K_1}\right) + v_1 t + \sigma_1 B_1(t)$, $v_1 := r - k_1 - \gamma_1 - \frac{1}{2}\sigma_1^2$.

The lemma is a direct application of Cor. 3.1.1 in Bielecki and Rutkowski (2002).

Lemma 13A.2 *For $a, b, c \in \mathbf{R}$ with $b < 0$ and $c^2 > a$:*

$$\int_0^y e^{ax} dN\left(\frac{b-cx}{\sqrt{x}}\right) = \frac{d+c}{2d}g(y) + \frac{d-c}{2d}h(y)$$

with $d = \sqrt{c^2 - 2a}$, $g(y) := e^{b(c-d)} N\left(\frac{b-dy}{\sqrt{y}}\right)$, $h(y) := e^{b(c+d)} N\left(\frac{b+dy}{\sqrt{y}}\right)$

See Lemma 3.2.1, equation (3.16) in Bielecki and Rutkowski (2002).

Corollary 13A.1 *We have, on $\tau_1 > \tau_2$:*

$$E[e^{-r(\tau_1-\tau_2)}1_{\tau_1 < T}|\mathcal{F}_{\tau_2}]$$
$$= e^{-\mu_{\tau_2}(\beta-\eta)} N\left(\frac{-\mu_{\tau_2} - \eta(T-\tau_2)}{\sqrt{T-\tau_2}}\right) + e^{-\mu_{\tau_2}(\beta+\eta)} N\left(\frac{-\mu_{\tau_2} + \eta(T-\tau_2)}{\sqrt{T-\tau_2}}\right)$$

where $\eta := \sqrt{\frac{v_1^2}{\sigma_1^2} + 2r}$, $\beta := \frac{v_1}{\sigma_1}$, $\mu_{\tau_2} := \frac{Y_{\tau_2}}{\sigma_1}$

Indeed, by the previous lemmas,

$$E[e^{-r(\tau_1-\tau_2)}1_{\tau_1 < T}|\mathcal{F}_{\tau_2}]$$
$$= \int_{\tau_2}^T e^{-r(s-\tau_2)} dP(\tau_1 \leq s|\mathcal{F}_{\tau_2}) = \int_{\tau_2}^T e^{-r(s-\tau_2)}\left[dN\left(\frac{-Y_{\tau_2} - v_1(s-\tau_2)}{\sigma_1\sqrt{s-\tau_2}}\right)\right.$$
$$\left. + e^{-2v_1\sigma_1^{-2}Y_{\tau_2}} dN\left(\frac{-Y_{\tau_2} + v_1(s-\tau_2)}{\sigma_1\sqrt{s-\tau_2}}\right)\right]$$
$$= \frac{\eta+\beta}{2\eta} e^{-\mu_{\tau_2}(\beta-\eta)} N\left(\frac{-\mu_{\tau_2} - \eta(T-\tau_2)}{\sqrt{T-\tau_2}}\right)$$
$$+ \frac{\eta-\beta}{2\eta} e^{-\mu_{\tau_2}(\beta+\eta)} N\left(\frac{-\mu_{\tau_2} + \eta(T-\tau_2)}{\sqrt{T-\tau_2}}\right)$$
$$+ e^{-2v_1\sigma_1^{-2}Y_{\tau_2}}\left[\frac{\eta-\beta}{2\eta} e^{-\mu_{\tau_2}(-\beta-\eta)} N\left(\frac{-\mu_{\tau_2} - \eta(T-\tau_2)}{\sqrt{T-\tau_2}}\right)\right.$$
$$\left. + \frac{\eta+\beta}{2\eta} e^{-\mu_{\tau_2}(-\beta+\eta)} N\left(\frac{-\mu_{\tau_2} + \eta(T-\tau_2)}{\sqrt{T-\tau_2}}\right)\right]$$

and the formula follows.

Appendix 13B: First Hitting Time in a Polyhedral Domain

Our results rely largely on the following two-dimensional extension of a theorem of Daniels; see Daniels (1982, equation 3.1). This natural extension is important in view of applications to multidimensional Brownian processes, particularly in the setting of credit risk. It was first announced without a proof in Iyengar (1985) and could be easily extended to higher-dimensional cases. We could not find a proof in the literature, and include therefore a short demonstration in this appendix.

Let $Z_t^{(x_0, y_0)}$ (abbreviated to Z_t when no confusion can arise), a planar Brownian starting at (x_0, y_0) evolving in a polyhedral domain D with absorbing boundary ∂D. We write τ for the first hitting time of the boundary and $f(x_0, y_0, x, y, t)$ (abbreviated to $f(x, y, t)$ when no confusion can arise) for the density of the surviving process:

$$f(x, y, t)dxdy := P(Z_t \in (dx, dy), \tau > t)$$

We look for the distribution of hitting times: $P(\tau \in dt, Z_\tau \in dp)$, $dp \in \partial D$ and can assume (up to a planar rotation) that ∂D is horizontal and an upper boundary for D in the neighborhood of p, so that dp is a horizontal line element: $dp = (da, b)$, with $p = (a, b) \in \partial D$.

Theorem 13B.1 *We have:*

$$P(\tau \in dt, Z_\tau = (da, b)) = -\frac{1}{2}\frac{\partial}{\partial b}f(a, b, t)dadt \qquad (13.1)$$

Sketch of the proof: Let us write $\phi(x, y, \Delta t)dadt$ for $P(\tau \in dt, Z_\tau \in (da, b)|Z_{t-\Delta t} = (x, y))$, where in practice we will choose $\Delta t << 1$ and study the asymptotics when Δt goes to 0. From Daniels's theorem (1982, Fla 3.1), which computes the first exit density for a one-dimensional BM, together with the independence of the horizontal and vertical components of a two-dimensional BM, we get, in the neighborhood of (a, b):

$$\phi(x, y, \Delta t) \cong \frac{1}{2\pi\Delta t^2}\exp-\frac{(a-x)^2}{2\Delta t}\cdot\exp-\frac{(b-y)^2}{2\Delta t}\cdot(b-y)$$

Then,

$$P(\tau \in dt, Z_\tau \in (da, b))da^{-1}dt^{-1} = \int_D f(x, y, t-\Delta t)\phi(x, y, \Delta t)dxdy$$

$$\cong \int_D \left[f(a, y, t-\Delta t) + (x-a)f_x'(a, y, t-\Delta t) \right.$$

$$\left. +\frac{(x-a)^2}{2}f_x''(a, y, t-\Delta t) \right]\phi(x, y, \Delta t)dxdy$$

By symmetry, in the neighborhood of (a, b) in D, $\phi(x, y, \Delta t) \cong \phi(2a - x, y, \Delta t)$, so that the second term of the expansion vanishes. Since ∂D is an absorbing boundary, $f(a, b, t - \Delta t) = f'_x(a, b, t - \Delta t) = f''_x(a, b, t - \Delta t) = 0$ and the third term reads:

$$\int_D \frac{(x-a)^2}{2} f''_x(a, y, t - \Delta t)\phi(x, y, \Delta t)dxdy$$

$$\cong -\frac{1}{\Delta t} \int_{-\infty}^{+\infty} \frac{(x-a)^2}{2} \frac{1}{\sqrt{2\pi \Delta t}} e^{-\frac{(x-a)^2}{2\Delta t}} dx$$

$$* \int_{-\infty}^{b} (b-y)^2 \frac{1}{\sqrt{2\pi \Delta t}} e^{-\frac{(b-y)^2}{2\Delta t}} \frac{\partial f''_x}{\partial y}(a, b, t - \Delta t)dy$$

$$= O(\Delta t)$$

Similarly, the first term reads:

$$\int_D f(a, y, t - \Delta t)\phi(x, y, \Delta t)dxdy$$

$$\cong \int_{-\infty}^{b} \frac{(b-y)}{\sqrt{2\pi}\Delta t^{3/2}} e^{-\frac{(b-y)^2}{2dt}} f(a, y, t - \Delta t)dy \int_{-\infty}^{\infty} \frac{1}{\sqrt{2\pi}\Delta t^{1/2}} e^{-\frac{(x-a)^2}{2\Delta t}} dx$$

$$= \int_{-\infty}^{b} \frac{(b-y)}{\sqrt{2\pi}\Delta t^{3/2}} e^{-\frac{(b-y)^2}{2\Delta t}} f(a, y, t - \Delta t)dy$$

$$= -\int_{-\infty}^{b} \frac{(b-y)^2}{\sqrt{2\pi}\Delta t^{3/2}} e^{-\frac{(b-y)^2}{2\Delta t}} f'_y(a, b, t - \Delta t)dy$$

$$= -\frac{1}{2} f'_y(a, b, t - \Delta t)$$

The theorem follows.

References

Bank for International Settlements. 1998. OTC derivatives: Settlement procedures and counterparty risk management. Basel (September).

Basel Committee on Banking Supervision. 2005. The application of Basel II to trading activities and the treatment of double default effects. (July).

Black, F., and J. C. Cox. 1976. Valuing corporate securities: Some effects of bond indenture provisions. *Journal of Finance* 31:351–367.

Bielecki, T., and M. Rutkowski. 2002. *Credit risk: Modeling, valuation and hedging.* Springer Finance. Berlin: Springer-Verlag.

Brigo, D., and M. Masetti. 2006. Risk neutral pricing of counterparty risk. In *Counterparty credit risk modeling: Risk management, pricing and regulation,* ed. M. Pykhtin. London: Risk Books.

Brigo, D., and M. Tarenghi. 2004. Credit default swap calibration and equity swap valuation under counterparty risk with a tractable structural model. Proceedings of the FEA 2007. Available at www.ssrn.com and www.arxiv.org.

Brigo, D., and M. Tarenghi. 2005. Credit default swap calibration and counterparty risk valuation with a scenario based first passage mode. Available at www.ssrn.com and www.arxiv.org.

Carslaw, H. S., and J. C. Jaeger. 1988. *Conduction of heat in solids*. New York: Clarendon Press.

CreditGrades. 2002. Technical document. May.

Daniels, H. (1982). Sequential tests constructed from images. *Annals of Statistics* 10:394–400.

Gregory, J. 2009. Being two-faced over counterparty risk. *Risk* 22 (2): 86–90.

He, H., W. Keirstead, and J. Rebholz. 1998. Double lookbacks. *Mathematical Finance* 8 (3): 201–228.

Hull, J. 2007. *Risk management and financial institutions*. Englewood Cliffs, NJ: Pearson.

Hull, J., and A. White. 2001. Valuing credit default swaps II: Modeling default correlations. *Journal of Derivatives* 10 (3): 12–22.

Inglis, S., A. Lipton, I. Savescu, and A. Sepp. 2008. Dynamic credit models. *Statistics and Its Interface* 1: 211–227.

Iyengar, S. 1985. Hitting lines with two-dimensional Brownian motion. *SIAM Journal of Applied Mathematics* 45 (6): 983–989.

Lipton, A. 2001. *Mathematical methods for foreign exchange*. Singapore: World Scientific.

Lipton, A. 2002. Assets with jumps. *Risk* 15 (9): 149–153.

Lipton, A., and A. Sepp. 2009. Credit value adjustment for credit default swaps via the structural model. *Journal of Credit Risk* 5 (2): 123–146.

Markit. 2009. The CDS Big Bang: Understanding the changes to the global CDS contract and North American conventions. (March).

Merton, R. C. 1974. On the pricing of corporate debt: The risk structure of interest rates. *Journal of Finance* 29:449–470.

Patras, F. 2006a. Corrélation et défauts: Évaluation de first-to-default swaps dans un modèle multi-name à la Lardy-Finkelstein. *Banque et Marchés* 80:1–5.

Patras, F. 2006b. A reflection principle for correlated defaults. *Stochastic Processes and Their Applications* 116:690–698.

Pykhtin, M. 2009. Modeling credit exposure for collateralized counterparties. *Journal of Credit Risk* 5, no. 4 (Winter): 3–27.

Schönbucher, P. 2003. *Credit derivatives pricing models*. New York: John Wiley & Sons.

Turc, J., et al. 2008. The S2C model: An integrated framework for equity-credit relative value. Société Générale, Credit Research.

Vasicek, O. 1987. Probability of loss on a loan portfolio. Working paper, KMV. Published as "Loan portfolio value." *Risk* (December 2002).

Zhou, C. 2001a. An analysis of default correlations and multiple defaults. *Review of Financial Studies* 14 (2): 555–576.

Zhou, C. 2001b. The term structure of credit spreads with jump risk. *Journal of Banking and Finance* 25 (2): 2015–2040.

CHAPTER 14

Credit Calibration with Structural Models and Equity Return Swap Valuation under Counterparty Risk

Damiano Brigo

Gilbart Professor of Financial Mathematics, King's College, London

Massimo Morini

Bocconi University and Banca IMI

Marco Tarenghi

Mediobanca

In this chapter we develop structural first passage models—analytically tractable first passage (AT1P) and scenario barrier time-varying volatility (SBTV)—with time-varying volatility and characterized by high tractability, moving from the original work of Brigo and Tarenghi (2004, 2005) and Brigo and Morini (2006). The models can be calibrated exactly to credit spreads using efficient closed-form formulas for default probabilities. In these models default events are caused by the value of the firm assets hitting a safety threshold, which depends on the financial situation of the company and on market conditions. In AT1P this default barrier is deterministic. Instead SBTV assumes two possible scenarios for the initial level of the default barrier, for taking into account uncertainty on balance sheet information. While in Brigo and Tarenghi (2004, 2005) the models are analyzed across Parmalat's history, here we apply the models to exact calibration of Lehman credit default swap (CDS) data during the months preceding default, as the crisis unfolds. The results we obtain with AT1P and SBTV have reasonable economic interpretation, and are particularly realistic when SBTV is considered.

The pricing of counterparty risk in an equity return swap is a convenient application we consider, also to illustrate the interaction of our credit models with equity models in a hybrid products context.

14.1 Introduction

Modeling firms default is an important issue, especially in recent times where the crisis begun in 2007 has led to bankruptcy of several companies all over the world. Credit pricing models can be traditionally divided into two main categories: (1) reduced-form models and (2) structural models.

Reduced-form models (also called *intensity models* when a suitable context is possible) describe default by means of an exogenous jump process; more precisely, the default time is the first jump time of a Poisson process with deterministic or stochastic (Cox process) intensity. Here default is not triggered by basic market observables but has an exogenous component that is independent of all the default-free market information. Monitoring the default-free market does not give complete information on the default process, and there is no economic rationale behind default. This family of models is particularly suited to model credit spreads and in its basic formulation is easy to calibrate to credit default swap (CDS) data. See references at the beginning of Chapter 8 in Bielecki and Rutkowski (2001) for a summary of the literature on intensity models. We cite here Duffie and Singleton (1999), Lando (1998), and Brigo and Alfonsi (2005) as a reference for explicit calibration of a tractable stochastic intensity model to CDS data, and Brigo and El-Bachir (2008) for CDS options pricing formulas within such model class.

Structural models are based on the work by Merton (1974), in which a firm life is linked to its ability to pay back its debt. Let us suppose that a firm issues a bond to finance its activities and also that this bond has maturity T. At final time T, if the firm is not able to reimburse all the bondholders we can say that there has been a default event. In this simplified context default may occur only at final time T and is triggered by the value of the firm being below the debt level. In a more realistic and sophisticated structural model—Black and Cox (BC) (1976), part of the family of *first passage time models*—default can happen also before maturity T. In first passage time models the default time is the first instant where the firm value hits from above either a deterministic (possibly time varying) or a stochastic barrier, ideally associated with safety covenants forcing the firm to early bankruptcy in case of important credit deterioration. In this sense the firm value is seen as a generic asset and these models use the same mathematics of barrier options pricing models. For a summary of the literature on structural models, possibly with stochastic interest rates and default barriers, we refer for example to Chapter 3 of Bielecki and Rutkowski (2001). Here we just mention works generalizing the form of the default barrier to account for the debt level, such as Briys and de Varenne (1997); Hsu, Saa-Requejo, and Santa-Clara (2002); Hui, Lo, and Tsang (2003); and Dorfleitner, Schneider, and Veza (2007).

It is important to notice that structural models make some implicit but important assumptions: They assume that the firm value follows a random process similar to the one used to describe generic stocks in equity markets, and that it is possible to observe this value or to obtain it from equity information. Therefore, unlike intensity models, here the default process can be completely monitored based on default-free market information and comes less as a surprise. However, structural models in their basic formulations and with standard barriers (Merton, BC) have few parameters in their dynamics and cannot be calibrated exactly to structured data such as CDS quotes along different maturities.

In this chapter we follow Brigo and Tarenghi (2004, 2005) and Brigo and Morini (2006) to effectively use two families of structural models (AT1P and SBTV) in the ideal "territory" of intensity models (i.e., to describe default probabilities in a way that is rich enough to calibrate CDS quotes). First of all, in Section 14.2 we present the analytically tractable first passage model (AT1P), which has a deterministic default barrier and is a generalization of the classic Black and Cox model; we show how this model, differently from the Black and Cox model, mantains analytical formulas for default probabilities even when allowing asset volatility to be realistically time-varying. In Section 14.3 we show how this feature can be exploited in order to calibrate the parameters of the model to market prices of single name CDS's (in a way similar to the procedure used to calibrate intensities in reduced form models). While in Brigo and Tarenghi (2004) and Brigo and Morini (2006) we had tested AT1P and SBTV calibration on Parmalat data as Parmalat approached default, here in Section 14.4 we consider the concrete case of another firm, Lehman Brothers, approaching default, and we show how our proposed structural model calibration changes as the company credit quality (as summarized by its CDS quotes) deteriorates in time. The analysis of the model behavior in representing Lehman approaching default leads us to introduce in Section 14.5 an extension of the model, aimed at adding further realism to the model. This extension, called scenario barrier time-varying volatility (SBTV) model, assumes two possible scenarios for the initial level of the default barrier, to take into account uncertainty on balance sheet information, and in particular the difficulty in evaluating the liability portfolio of the company. Also in this case we mantain analytical tractability and in Section 14.6 we present the results of calibration to CDS quotes.

Due to their intrinsic nature, structural models result to be a natural method to price equity-credit hybrid products and also to evaluate counterparty risk in equity products. The counterparty risk adjustment (credit valuation adjustment [CVA]) has received a lot of attention in an exploding literature, and in several asset classes. We recall here the work of Sorensen and Bollier (1994); Huge and Lando (1999); Brigo and Pallavicini (2007); Brigo and Masetti (2005); and Brigo, Pallavicini, and Papatheodorou (2009) for CVA on interest rate products, both unilateral and bilateral (last paper). For credit products, especially CDSs, CVA has been analyzed in Leung and Kwok (2005); Blanchet-Scalliet and Patras (2008); Brigo and Chourdakis (2008); Crépey, Jeanblanc, and Zargari (2009); Lipton and Sepp (2009), who resort to a structural model; and Walker (2005), while Brigo and Capponi (2008) study the bilateral case. CVA on commodities is analyzed in Brigo and Bakkar (2009), whereas CVA on equity is analyzed in Brigo and Tarenghi (2004, 2005). CVA with netting is examined in Brigo and Masetti (2005); Brigo and Pallavicini (2007); and Brigo, Pallavicini, and Papatheodorou (2009). CVA with collateral margining is analyzed in Assefa, Bielecki, Crépey, and Jeanblanc (2009) and in Alavian et al. (2009), whereas collateral triggers are considered in Yi (2009). In Section 14.7 we consider the particular case of an equity return swap with counterparty risk. In this context we have to take care of the correlation between the counterparty and the underlying, and this is done much more conveniently in structural models than in intensity models. Here for CVA results in equity payoffs we follow Brigo and Tarenghi (2004, 2005), also reported in the final part of Brigo and Masetti (2005).

14.2 The Analytically Tractable First Passage (AT1P) Model

The fundamental hypothesis of the model we resume here is that the underlying process is a geometric Brownian motion (GBM), which is also the kind of process commonly used for equity stocks in the Black-Scholes model. This choice is the typical choice of classical structural models (Merton, Black-Cox), which postulate a GBM (Black and Scholes) lognormal dynamics for the value of the firm V. This lognormality assumption is considered to be acceptable. Crouhy, Galai, and Mark (2000) report that "this assumption [lognormal V] is quite robust and, according to KMVs own empirical studies, actual data conform quite well to this hypothesis." Therefore, let us assume that the value of the firm V risk-neutral dynamics is governed by the following SDE:

$$dV_t = V_t (r_t - k_t) \, dt + V_t \sigma_t \, dW_t, \quad V(0) = V_0 \tag{14.1}$$

where r_t is the risk-free rate, k_t is the firm payout ratio, and σ_t is the volatility of the firm value, and all these parameters are time-dependent.

Before presenting our AT1P model, let us recall the main features of basic structural models.

14.2.1 Basic Structural Models

The first structural model is due to Merton (1974) and assumes that the value of the firm V is governed by a GBM like equation (14.1) where all the dynamics parameters are constant in time (that is, $r_t \equiv r$, $k_t \equiv k$, and $\sigma_t \equiv \sigma$).

In this model the value of the firm V is the sum of the firm equity value S and of the firm debt value D. The firm equity value S, in particular, can be seen as a kind of option on the value of the firm V. Merton typically assumes a zero coupon debt at a terminal maturity $\bar{T}$, a debt face value L and the company defaults at final maturity (and only then) if the value of the firm $V_{\bar{T}}$ is below the debt L to be paid.

The debt value at time $t < \bar{T}$ is thus:

$$D_t = \mathbb{E}_t[D(t, \bar{T})\min(V_{\bar{T}}, L)] = \mathbb{E}_t[D(t, \bar{T})[V_{\bar{T}} - (V_{\bar{T}} - L)^+]]$$
$$= \mathbb{E}_t[D(t, \bar{T})[L - (L - V_{\bar{T}})^+]] = P(t, \bar{T})L - \text{Put}(t, \bar{T}; V_t, L)$$

where Put(time, maturity, underlying, strike) is a put option price, and the stochastic discount factor at time t for maturity T is denoted by $D(t, T) = B(t)/B(T)$, where $B(t) = \exp(\int_0^t r_u du)$ denotes the bank-account numéraire, r being the instantaneous short interest rate. Since we will assume deterministic interest rates, in our case $D(t, T) = P(t, T)$, the zero coupon bond price at time t for maturity T.

The equity value can be derived as a difference between the value of the firm and the debt:

$$S_t = V_t - D_t = V_t - P(t, \bar{T})L + \text{Put}(t, \bar{T}; V_t, L) = \text{Call}(t, \bar{T}; V_t, L)$$

so that, as is well known, in Merton's model the equity can be interpreted as a call option on the value of the firm. The main drawback of Merton's model is that the default event can happen only at maturity: obviously, this assumption is too strong to be realistic.

Let us now move to the Black-Cox (BC) model. Black and Cox assume, besides a possible zero coupon debt, safety covenants forcing the firm to declare bankruptcy and pay back its debt with what is left as soon as the value of the firm V_t goes below a "safety level" barrier $H(t)$. The choice of this safety level is not easy. Assuming a debt face value of L at final maturity $\bar{T}$ as before, an obvious candidate for this safety level is the final debt present value discounted back at time t; that is, $LP(t, \bar{T})$. However, one may want to cut some slack to the counterparty, giving it some time to recover even if the level goes below $LP(t, \bar{T})$, and the safety level can be chosen to be lower than $LP(t, \bar{T})$. Black and Cox assume the following definition for the default barrier:

$$H(t) = \begin{cases} L & \text{if} \quad t = \bar{T} \\ Ke^{-\gamma(\bar{T}-t)} & \text{if} \quad t < \bar{T} \end{cases} \qquad (14.2)$$

where γ and K are positive parameters. Black and Cox assume also $Ke^{-\gamma(\bar{T}-t)} \leq Le^{-r(\bar{T}-t)}$. For simplicity, we will assume $L = K$. So, the debt value L is paid at maturity $\bar{T}$ if and only if the value $V(t)$ touches the barrier $H(t)$ either after $\bar{T}$ or never. The value of the debt at time 0 is therefore

$$D(0) = \mathbb{E}_0\left[L\, D(0, \bar{T})\, \mathbf{1}_{\{\tau > \bar{T}\}}\right] \qquad (14.3)$$

where τ is the default time—that is, the firm time instant where the process V crosses the barrier. This is a knockout digital barrier option that can be rewritten as

$$D(0) = L\, P(0, \bar{T})\, \mathbb{E}_0\left[\mathbf{1}_{\{\tau > \bar{T}\}}\right] = L\, P(0, \bar{T})\, \mathbb{Q}\left(\tau > \bar{T}\right) \qquad (14.4)$$

where $\mathbb{Q}(\tau > \bar{T})$ is the survival probability of the firm. By making use of standard barrier option pricing techniques, we can compute the survival probability in the Black-Cox case for all $T \le \bar{T}$ as

$$\mathbb{Q}(\tau > T) = \Phi\left(\frac{\ln\left(\frac{V_0}{H(0)}\right) + \bar{\nu}\,T}{\sigma\sqrt{T}}\right) - \left(\frac{H(0)}{V_0}\right)^{2\bar{a}} \Phi\left(\frac{\ln\left(\frac{H(0)}{V_0}\right) + \bar{\nu}\,T}{\sigma\sqrt{T}}\right) \quad (14.5)$$

with $\bar{\nu} = r - k - \gamma - \frac{1}{2}\sigma^2$ and $\bar{a} = \frac{\bar{\nu}}{\sigma^2}$.

Even if we have an analytical formula for the survival probability, unfortunately the model is not flexible enough to be exactly calibrated to a large number of CDS market quotes. In the following section we face this issue by presenting a model that is an extension of the Black-Cox model, and has all the required flexibility.

14.2.2   AT1P Model (Brigo and Tarenghi 2004)

Formula (14.5) is based on two fundamental assumptions: (1) time constant parameters in the dynamics, and (2) an exponential default barrier. Here we want to relax these assumptions; we state the following:[1]

Proposition 14.2.1   (Analytically tractable first passage (AT1P) model) *Assume the risk-neutral dynamics for the value of the firm V is characterized by a risk-free rate r_t, a payout ratio k_t, and an instantaneous volatility σ_t, according to equation (14.1); that is,*

$$dV_t = V_t\,(r_t - k_t)\,dt + V_t\,\sigma_t\,dW_t$$

and assume a default barrier $H(t)$ (depending on the parameters H and B) of the form

$$H(t) = H \exp\left(\int_0^t \left(r_u - k_u - B\sigma_u^2\right) du\right)$$

and let τ be defined as the first time where $V(t)$ hits $H(t)$ from above, starting from $V_0 > H$,

$$\tau = \inf\{t \ge 0 : V_t \le H(t)\}$$

Then the survival probability is given analytically by

$$\mathbb{Q}(\tau > T) = \left[\Phi\left(\frac{\log\frac{V_0}{H} + \frac{2B-1}{2}\int_0^T \sigma_u^2 du}{\sqrt{\int_0^T \sigma_u^2 du}}\right) - \left(\frac{H}{V_0}\right)^{2B-1} \Phi\left(\frac{\log\frac{H}{V_0} + \frac{2B-1}{2}\int_0^T \sigma_u^2 du}{\sqrt{\int_0^T \sigma_u^2 du}}\right)\right] \quad (14.6)$$

A couple of remarks are in order. First, we notice that in the formula for the survival probability in Proposition 14.2.1, H and V never appear alone, but always in ratios like V/H; this homogeneity property allows us to rescale the initial value of the firm $V_0 = 1$, and express the barrier parameter H as a fraction of it. In this case we do not need to know the real value of the firm, neither its real debt situation. Also, we can rewrite the barrier as

$$H(t) = H \exp \left(\int_0^t \left(r_u - k_u - B\sigma_u^2 \right) du \right)$$

$$= \frac{H}{V_0} \mathbb{E}_0 \left[V_t \right] \exp \left(-B \int_0^t \sigma_u^2 du \right) \tag{14.7}$$

Therefore the behavior of $H(t)$ has a simple economic interpretation. The backbone of the default barrier at t is a proportion, controlled by the parameter H, of the expected value of the company assets at t. H may depend on the level of liabilities, on safety covenants, and in general on the characteristics of the capital structure of the company. This is in line with observations in Giesecke (2004), pointing out that some discrepancies between the Black-Cox model and empirical regularities may be addressed with the realistic assumption that, like the firm value, the total debt grows at a positive rate, or that firms maintain some target leverage ratio as in Collin-Dufresne and Goldstein (2001).

Also, depending on the value of the parameter B, it is possible that this backbone is modified by accounting for the volatility of the company's assets. For example, $B > 0$ corresponds to the interpretation that when volatility increases—which can be independent of credit quality—the barrier is slightly lowered to cut some more slack to the company before going bankrupt. In the following tests we simply assume $B = 0$, corresponding to a case where the barrier does not depend on volatility and the "distance to default" is simply modeled through the barrier parameter H.

14.3　Calibration of the Structural Model to CDS Data

Since we are dealing with default probabilities of firms, it is straightforward to think of financial instruments depending on these probabilities and whose final aim is to protect against the default event. One of the most representative protection instruments is the credit default swap (CDS). CDSs are contracts that have been designed to offer protection against default. Here we introduce CDSs in their traditional "running" form. For a methodology for converting running CDSs to up-front CDSs, as from the so-called Big Bang by the International Swaps and Derivatives Association (ISDA); see Beumee et al. (2009).

Consider two companies, "A" (the *protection buyer*) and "B" (the *protection seller*), which agree on the following. If a third reference company "C" (the *reference credit*) defaults at a time $\tau_C \in (T_a, T_b]$, "B" pays to "A" at time $\tau = \tau_C$ itself a certain protection cash amount L$_{GD}$ (loss given the default of "C"), supposed to be deterministic in the present chapter. This cash amount is a *protection* for "A" in case "C" defaults. A typical stylized case occurs when "A" has bought a corporate bond issued from "C" and is waiting for the coupons and final notional payment from this bond: If "C" defaults before the corporate bond maturity, "A" does not receive such payments. "A" then goes to "B" and buys some protection against this risk, asking "B" a payment that roughly amounts to the bond notional in case "C" defaults.

Typically L$_{GD}$ is equal to a notional amount, or to a notional amount minus a recovery rate. We denote the recovery rate by R$_{EC}$.

In exchange for this protection, company "A" agrees to pay periodically to "B" a fixed running amount R, called CDS spread, at a set of times $\{T_{a+1}, \ldots, T_b\}$, $\alpha_i = T_i - T_{i-1}$, $T_0 = 0$. These payments constitute the premium leg of the CDS (as opposed to the L$_{GD}$ payment, which is termed the protection leg), and R is fixed in advance at time 0; the premium payments go on up to default time τ if this occurs before maturity T_b, or until maturity T_b if no default occurs.

$$B \to \text{ protection L}_{GD} \text{ at default } \tau_C \text{ if } T_a < \tau_C \leq T_b \to \text{"A"}$$

$$B \leftarrow \text{ rate } R \text{ at } T_{a+1}, \ldots, T_b \text{ or until default } \tau_C \leftarrow \text{"A"}$$

Formally, we may write the RCDS (R stands for running) discounted value at time t seen from "A" as

$$\Pi_{RCDS_{a,b}}(t) := - D(t, \tau)(\tau - T_{\beta(\tau)-1}) R \mathbf{1}_{\{T_a < \tau < T_b\}}$$

$$- \sum_{i=a+1}^{b} D(t, T_i)\alpha_i R \mathbf{1}_{\{\tau \geq T_i\}} + \mathbf{1}_{\{T_a < \tau \leq T_b\}} D(t, \tau) \text{L}_{GD} \quad (14.8)$$

where $t \in [T_{\beta(t)-1}, T_{\beta(t)})$; that is, $T_{\beta(t)}$ is the first date among the T_i's that follows t, and where α_i is the year fraction between T_{i-1} and T_i.

Sometimes a slightly different payoff is considered for RCDS contracts. Instead of considering the exact default time τ, the protection payment L$_{GD}$ is postponed to the first time T_i following default (i.e., to $T_{\beta(\tau)}$). If the grid is three or six months spaced, this postponement consists of a few months at worst. With this formulation, the CDS discounted payoff can be written as

$$\Pi_{PRCDS_{a,b}}(t) := - \sum_{i=a+1}^{b} D(t, T_i)\alpha_i R \mathbf{1}_{\{\tau \geq T_i\}} + \sum_{i=a+1}^{b} \mathbf{1}_{\{T_{i-1} < \tau \leq T_i\}} D(t, T_i) \text{L}_{GD}$$

$$(14.9)$$

which we term *postponed running CDS* (PRCDS) discounted payoff. Compare with the earlier discounted payout [equation (14.8)], where the protection payment occurs exactly at τ: The advantage of the postponed protection payment is that no accrued-interest term in $(\tau - T_{\beta(\tau)-1})$ is necessary, and also that all payments occur at the canonical grid of the T_i's. The postponed payout is better for deriving market models of CDS rates dynamics and for relating CDSs to floaters; see, for example, Brigo (2004a, 2004b).

Let us consider again the basic RCDS: The pricing formula for this payoff depends on the assumptions on the interest rates dynamics and on the default time τ. Let $\mathcal{F}_t$ denote the basic filtration without default, typically representing the information flow of interest rates and possibly other default-free market quantities (and also intensities in the case of reduced-form models), and $\mathcal{G}_t = \mathcal{F}_t \vee \sigma(\{\tau < u\}, u \leq t)$ the extended filtration including explicit default information. In our current structural model framework with deterministic default barrier, the two sigma-algebras coincide by construction (i.e., $\mathcal{G}_t = \mathcal{F}_t$), because here the default is completely driven by default-free market information. This is not the case with intensity models, where the default is governed by an external random variable and $\mathcal{F}_t$ is strictly included in $\mathcal{G}_t$ (i.e., $\mathcal{F}_t \subset \mathcal{G}_t$).

We denote by CDS$(t, [T_{a+1}, \dots, T_b], T_a, T_b, R, \text{L}_{\text{GD}})$ the price at time t of the aforementioned standard running CDS. At times some terms are omitted, such as for example the list of payment dates $[T_{a+1}, \dots, T_b]$. In general we can compute the CDS price according to risk-neutral valuation (see, for example, Bielecki and Rutkowski 2001):

$$\text{CDS}(t, T_a, T_b, R, \text{L}_{\text{GD}}) = \mathbb{E}\{\Pi_{\text{RCDS}_{a,b}}(t)|\mathcal{G}_t\}$$
$$= \mathbb{E}\{\Pi_{\text{RCDS}_{a,b}}(t)|\mathcal{F}_t\} =: \mathbb{E}_t\{\Pi_{\text{RCDS}_{a,b}}(t)\} \quad (14.10)$$

in our structural model setup. A CDS is quoted through its fair R, in that the rate R that is quoted by the market at time t satisfies CDS$(t, T_a, T_b, R, \text{L}_{\text{GD}}) = 0$. Let us assume, for simplicity, deterministic interest rates; then we have

$$\text{CDS}(t, T_a, T_b, R, \text{L}_{\text{GD}})$$
$$:= -R\,\mathbb{E}_t\{P(t, \tau)(\tau - T_{\beta(\tau)-1})\mathbf{1}_{\{T_a < \tau < T_b\}}\}$$
$$- \sum_{i=a+1}^{b} P(t, T_i)\alpha_i R\,\mathbb{E}_t\{\mathbf{1}_{\{\tau \geq T_i\}}\} + \text{L}_{\text{GD}}\mathbb{E}_t\{\mathbf{1}_{\{T_a < \tau \leq T_b\}}P(t, \tau)\}$$
$$= -R\left[\sum_{i=a+1}^{b}\left(P(t, T_i)\alpha_i\,\mathbb{Q}\{\tau \geq T_i\} + \int_{T_{i-1}}^{T_i}(u - T_{i-1})P(t, u)d\mathbb{Q}(\tau \leq u)\right)\right]$$
$$+ \text{L}_{\text{GD}}\int_{T_a}^{T_b}P(t, u)d\mathbb{Q}(\tau \leq u) \quad (14.11)$$

From our earlier definitions, straightforward computations lead to the price at initial time 0 of a CDS, under deterministic interest rates, as

$$\mathrm{CDS}_{a,b}(0, R, \mathrm{L_{GD}}) = R \int_{T_a}^{T_b} P(0, t)(t - T_{\beta(t)-1})d\mathbb{Q}(\tau > t)$$

$$- R \sum_{i=a+1}^{b} P(0, T_i)\alpha_i \mathbb{Q}(\tau \geq T_i) - \mathrm{L_{GD}} \int_{T_a}^{T_b} P(0, t)d\mathbb{Q}(\tau > t) \quad (14.12)$$

so that if one has a formula for the curve of survival probabilities $t \mapsto \mathbb{Q}(\tau > t)$, as in our AT1P structural model, one also has a formula for CDSs. It is clear that the fair rate R strongly depends on the default probabilities. The idea is to use quoted values of these fair Rs with different maturities to derive the default probabilities assessed by the market.

Formula (14.6) can be used to fit the model parameters to market data. However, the only parameter left that can account for time dependence is the volatility. If we use exogenous volatility (deduced perhaps from historical or implied equity volatility) we are left with no freedom. However, we may infer the first year volatility $\sigma(0 - 1y) := \{\sigma(t) : t \in [0, 1]\}$ from equity data and use H as a first fitting parameter, and then use the remaining later volatilities $\sigma(1y - 2y)$, $\sigma(2y - 3y)$, and so on as further fitting parameters. Therefore, $\sigma(2y-)$ will be determined by credit quality as implied by CDS data rather than by equity data. To sum up, we can choose piecewise constant volatility, and look for those volatility values after the first year that make the quoted CDSs fair when inserting in their premium legs the market-quoted Rs. In this way we find as many volatilities as many CDSs we consider minus one. In this first case H is determined by CDSs.

Alternatively, if we aim at creating a one to one correspondence to volatility parameters and CDS quotes, we can exogenously choose the value H and B, leaving all the unknown information in the calibration of the volatility. If we do so, we find exactly one volatility parameter for each CDS maturity, including the first one. In our tests we have followed this second approach, where H has been chosen externally before calibration.

In general the preceding CDS calibration procedures are justified by the fact that in the end we are not interested in estimating the real process of the firm value underlying the contract, but only in reproducing risk-neutral default probabilities with a model that makes sense also economically. While it is important that the underlying processes have an economic interpretation, we are not interested in sharply estimating them or the capital structure of the firm, but rather we appreciate the structural model interpretation as a tool for assessing the realism of the outputs of calibrations, and as an instrument to check economic consequences and possible diagnostics.

In the following section we analyze how the AT1P model works in practice; in particular, we consider the case of Lehman Brothers, one of the world's major banks that fell into a deep crisis, ending up with the bank's default. For simplicity our tests have been performed using the approximated postponed payoff (14.9). An analysis of the same model on the Parmalat crisis, terminating in the 2003 default, is available in Brigo and Tarenghi (2004) and Brigo and Morini (2006).

14.4　A Case Study with AT1P: Lehman Brothers Default History

- *August 23, 2007:* Lehman announces that it is going to shut one of its home lending units (BNC Mortgage) and lay off 1,200 employees. The bank says it would take a $52 million charge to third-quarter earnings.
- *March 18, 2008:* Lehman announces better than expected first-quarter results (but profits have more than halved).
- *June 9, 2008:* Lehman confirms the booking of a $2.8 billion loss and announces plans to raise $6 billion in fresh capital by selling stock. Lehman shares lose more than 9 percent in afternoon trade.
- *June 12, 2008:* Lehman shakes up its management; its chief operating officer and president, and its chief financial officer are removed from their posts.
- *August 28, 2008:* Lehman prepares to lay off 1,500 people. The Lehman executives have been knocking on doors all over the world seeking a capital infusion.
- *September 9, 2008:* Lehman shares fall 45 percent.
- *September 14, 2008:* Lehman files for bankruptcy protection and hurtles toward liquidation after it failed to find a buyer. (See Figure 14.1.)

FIGURE 14.1　Lehman Brothers Stock Price (*solid line, left axis*); CDS Spread One-Year in Basis Points (*dashed line, right axis*)

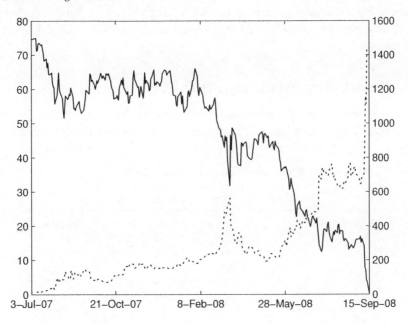

Here we show how the AT1P model calibration behaves when the credit quality of the considered company deteriorates in time (perceived as a widening of CDS spreads).[2] We are going to analyze three different situations: (1) a case of relatively stable situation, before the beginning of the crisis, (2) a case in the middle of the crisis, and (3) a last case just before the default.

During our calibration we fix $R_{EC} = 40$ percent, $B = 0$, and $H = 0.4$; this last choice is a completely arbitrary choice and has been suggested by the analogy with the CDS recovery rate. Also, as a comparison, we report the results of the calibration obtained using an intensity model. In simple intensity models, the survival probability can be computed as $\mathbb{Q}(\tau > t) = \exp(-\int_0^t \lambda(u)du)$, where λ is the *intensity function* or *hazard rate* (assumed here to be deterministic). We choose a piecewise constant shape for $\lambda(t)$ and calibrate it to CDS quotes.

14.4.1   Lehman Brothers CDS Calibration: July 10, 2007

On the left part of Table 14.1 we report the values of the quoted CDS spreads on July 10, 2007, before the beginning of the crisis. We see that the spreads are very low, indicating a stable situation for Lehman. In the middle of Table 14.1 we have the results of the calibration obtained using an intensity model, while on the right part of the table we have the results of the calibration obtained using the AT1P model.

It is important to stress the fact that the AT1P model is flexible enough to achieve exact calibration.

We can see that, in terms of survival probabilities, the two models return very similar results, confirming that survival probabilities are model independent when rates and default are independent. Also, looking at the calibrated volatilities, we see that they are nearly the same on all buckets, with the exception of the first one where it is higher: this is a common feature to all the cases we have considered and is related to difficulty of traditional structural models in producing high short-term credit spreads.

14.4.2   Lehman Brothers CDS Calibration: June 12, 2008

In Table 14.2 we report the results of the calibration on June 12, 2008, in the middle of the crisis. We see that the CDS spreads R_i have increased with respect to the

TABLE 14.1   Results of Calibration for July 10, 2007

T_i	R_i (bps)	λ_i (bps)	Surv (Int)	σ_i	Surv (AT1P)
July 10, 2007			100.0%		100.0%
1y	16	0.267%	99.7%	29.2%	99.7%
3y	29	0.601%	98.5%	14.0%	98.5%
5y	45	1.217%	96.2%	14.5%	96.1%
7y	50	1.096%	94.1%	12.0%	94.1%
10y	58	1.407%	90.2%	12.7%	90.2%

TABLE 14.2 Results of Calibration for June 12, 2008

T_i	R_i (bps)	λ_i (bps)	Surv (Int)	σ_i	Surv (AT1P)
June 12, 2008			100.0%		100.0%
1y	397	6.563%	93.6%	45.0%	93.5%
3y	315	4.440%	85.7%	21.9%	85.6%
5y	277	3.411%	80.0%	18.6%	79.9%
7y	258	3.207%	75.1%	18.1%	75.0%
10y	240	2.907%	68.8%	17.5%	68.7%

previous case, but are not very high, indicating the fact that the market is aware of the difficulties suffered by Lehman but thinks that it can come out of the crisis. The survival probability resulting from calibration is lower than in the previous case; since the barrier parameter H has not changed, this translates into higher volatilities.

14.4.3 Lehman Brothers CDS Calibration: September 12, 2008

In Table 14.3 we report the results of the calibration on September 12, 2008, just before Lehman's default. We see that the spreads are now very high, corresponding to lower survival probability and higher volatilities than before.

14.4.4 Comments

We have seen that the AT1P model can calibrate exactly CDS market quotes, and the survival probabilities obtained are in accordance with those obtained using an intensity model. This confirms the well-known fact that, when interest rates are assumed independent of default, survival probabilities can be implied from CDSs in a model-independent way (formula (14.12)). Anyway, after a deeper analysis of the results, we find:

- *Scarce relevance of the barrier in calibration.* The barrier parameter H has been fixed before calibration and everything is left to the volatility calibration.
- *High discrepancy between first volatility bucket and the following values.*

TABLE 14.3 Results of Calibration for September 12, 2008

T_i	R_i (bps)	λ_i (bps)	Surv (Int)	σ_i	Surv (AT1P)
September 12, 2008			100.0%		100.0%
1y	1,437	23.260%	79.2%	62.2%	78.4%
3y	902	9.248%	65.9%	30.8%	65.5%
5y	710	5.245%	59.3%	24.3%	59.1%
7y	636	5.947%	52.7%	26.9%	52.5%
10y	588	6.422%	43.4%	29.5%	43.4%

The problem is that when the default boundary is deterministic, diffusion models tend to calibrate a relevant probability of default by one year (shortest horizon credit spread) only by supposing particularly high one-year volatility. This is due to the fact that, initially, with low volatilities the trajectories of a model like equation (14.1) do not widen fast enough to hit a deterministic barrier frequently enough to generate relevant default probabilities. One has therefore to choose a high initial volatility to achieve this. The problem is also related to the fundamental assumption that the default threshold is a deterministic, known function of time, based on reliable accounting data. This is a very strong assumption and usually it is not true: Balance sheet information is not certain, possibly because the company is hiding information, or because a real valuation of the firm assets is not easy (for example, in case of derivative instruments). Public investors, then, may have only a partial and coarse information about the true value of the firm assets or the related liability-dependent firm condition that would trigger default.

In AT1P model, H is the ratio between the initial level of the default barrier and the initial value of the company assets. To take market uncertainty into account in a realistic albeit simple manner, H can be replaced by a random variable assuming different values in different scenarios. This is the main idea that leads us to introduce the SBTV model.

14.5   SBTV Model (Brigo and Morini 2006)

Where may one consider explicitly market uncertainty on the situation of the company, due to the fact that balance sheet information is not always reliable or easy to value? This is a possibility in case the company is hiding information, or in case illiquidity causes the valuation of the firm assets and liabilities to be uncertain. In the first case, following for example Giesecke (2004) who refers to scandals such as Enron, Tyco, and WorldCom, a crucial aspect in market uncertainty is that public investors have only a partial and coarse information about the true value of the firm assets or the related liability-dependent firm condition that would trigger default. This was our motivation to introduce randomness in H when we dealt with Parmalat in Brigo and Tarenghi (2005) and Brigo and Morini (2006). In particular, randomness in the initial level H of the barrier was used in Brigo and Morini (2006) to represent the uncertainty of market operators on the real financial situation of Parmalat, due to lack of transparency and actual fraud in Parmalat's accounting. Here it can represent equally well the uncertainty of market operators on the real financial situation of Lehman. But in this case the uncertainty is related to an objective difficulty in assigning a fair value to a large part of the assets and liabilities of Lehman (illiquid mortgage-related portfolio credit derivatives) and to the intrinsic complexity of the links between the bank and the related structured investment vehicles (SIVs) and conduits.

Therefore, in order to take market uncertainty into account in a realistic, albeit simple, manner, in the following H is replaced by a random variable assuming different values in different scenarios, each scenario with a different probability.

As in Brigo and Morini (2006), in this work we deem scenarios on the barrier to be an efficient representation of the uncertainty on the balance sheet of a company, while deterministic time-varying volatility can be required for precise and efficient calibration of CDS quotes. The resulting model is called the scenario barrier time-varying volatility (SBTV) AT1P model. In this way we can achieve exact calibration to all market quotes. Let the assets value V risk neutral dynamics be given by equation (14.1). The default time τ is again the first time where V hits the barrier from above, but now we have a scenario barrier

$$H^I(t) = H^I \exp\left(\int_0^t (r_u - k_u - B\sigma_u^2)du\right) = \frac{H^I}{V_0}\mathbb{E}\left[V_t\right]\exp\left(-B\int_0^t \sigma_u^2 du\right)$$

where H^I assumes scenarios $H^1, H^2, \ldots, H^N$ with $\mathbb{Q}$ probabilities $p^1, p^2, \ldots, p^N$. All probabilities are in $[0, 1]$ and add up to one, and H^I is independent of W. Thus now the ratio H^I / V_0 depends on the scenario I. If we are to price a default-sensitive discounted payoff Π, by iterated expectation we have

$$\mathbb{E}\left[\Pi\right] = \mathbb{E}\left[\mathbb{E}\left[\Pi|H^I\right]\right] = \sum_{i=1}^N p^i\,\mathbb{E}\left[\Pi|H^I = H^i\right]$$

so that the price of a security is a weighted average of the prices of the security in the different scenarios, with weights equal to the probabilities of the different scenarios. For CDS, the price with the SBTV model is

$$\mathrm{SBTV}\mathbf{CDS}_{a,b} = \sum_{i=1}^N p^i \cdot \mathrm{AT1P}\mathbf{CDS}_{a,b}(H^i) \tag{14.13}$$

where $AT1P\mathbf{CDS}_{a,b}(H^i)$ is the CDS price computed according to the AT1P survival probability formula (14.6) when $H = H^i$. Hence, the SBTV model acts like a mixture of AT1P scenarios.

14.6 A Case Study with SBTV: Lehman Brothers Default History

Here we want to show how the SBTV model calibration behaves with respect to the AT1P model. We consider the Lehman Brothers example as before. We limit our analysis to only two barrier scenarios (H^1 with probability p^1 and H^2 with probability $p^2 = 1 - p^1$), since, according to our experience, further scenarios do not increase the calibration power.

TABLE 14.4 Scenario Barriers and Probabilities

Scenario	H	p
1	0.4000	96.2%
2	0.7313	3.8%

In the calibration, we set the lower barrier parameter $H^1 = 0.4$. If we consider M CDS quotes, we have $M + 2$ unknown parameters: H^2, p^1 ($p^2 = 1 - p^1$) and all the volatilities σ_j corresponding to the M buckets. It is clear that a direct fit like in the AT1P case (where we have one unknown volatility σ_j for each CDS quote R_j) is not possible. Exact calibration could be achieved using a two-step approach:

1. We limit our attention to the first three CDS quotes, and set $\sigma_1 = \sigma_2 = \sigma_3 = \bar{\sigma}$. Now we have three quotes for three unknowns (H^2, p^1, and $\bar{\sigma}$) and can run a best fit on these parameters (not exact calibration, since the model could not be flexible enough to attain it).
2. At this point we go back to consider all the M CDS quotes and, using H^2 and the p's just obtained, we can run a second step calibration on the M volatilities σ_j to get an exact fit. Notice that if the first-step calibration is good enough, then the refinement to $\sigma_{1,2,3}$ due to second-step calibration is negligible.

14.6.1   Lehman Brothers CDS Calibration: July 10, 2007

In Table 14.4 we report the values of the calibrated barrier parameters with their corresponding probabilities, while in Table 14.5 we show the results of the calibration.

Looking at the results in Tables 14.4 and 14.5 we see that, in the case of the quite stable situation for Lehman, we have a lower barrier scenario (better credit quality) with very high probability, and a higher barrier scenario (lower credit quality) with low probability. Also, when comparing the results with the AT1P calibration, we see that now the calibrated volatility is nearly constant on all maturity buckets, which is a desirable feature for the firm value dynamics.

TABLE 14.5 Results of Calibration for July 10, 2007

T_j	R_j (bps)	σ_j (bps)	Surv (SBTV)	σ_j	Surv (AT1P)
July 10, 2007			100.0%		100.0%
1y	16	16.6%	99.7%	29.2%	99.7%
3y	29	16.6%	98.5%	14.0%	98.5%
5y	45	16.6%	96.1%	14.5%	96.1%
7y	50	12.6%	94.1%	12.0%	94.1%
10y	58	12.9%	90.2%	12.7%	90.2%

TABLE 14.6 Scenario Barriers and Probabilities

Scenario	H	p
1	0.4000	74.6%
2	0.7971	25.4%

14.6.2 Lehman Brothers CDS Calibration: June 12, 2008

Looking at the results in Tables 14.6 and 14.7 we see that the (worse credit quality) barrier parameter H^2 has both a higher value (higher proximity to default) and a much higher probability with respect to the calibration case of July 10, 2007. This is due to the higher CDS spread values. Moreover, by noticing that the fitted volatility has not increased too much, we can argue that the worsened credit quality can be reflected into a higher probability of being in the scenario with higher default barrier (worsened credit quality).

14.6.3 Lehman Brothers CDS Calibration: September 12, 2008

Here we have a large increase in CDS spreads, which can be explained by a very large probability of 50 percent for the higher barrier scenario and a higher value for the scenario itself, that moves to 0.84 from the preceding cases of 0.79 and 0.73. Tables 14.8 and 14.9 show the results of calibration. We see that there are not greater differences in volatilities than before, and the larger default probability can be explained by a higher level of proximity to default and high probability of being in that proximity (high H scenario). In this particular case we have equal probability of being in either the risky or the stable scenario.

14.6.4 Comments

We have seen that the calibration performed with the SBTV model is comparable, in terms of survival probabilities, with the calibration obtained using the AT1P model. Also, the calibration is exact in both cases. However, we have seen that the SBTV

TABLE 14.7 Results of Calibration for June 12, 2008

T_j	R_j (bps)	σ_j (bps)	Surv (SBTV)	σ_j	Surv (AT1P)
June 12, 2008			100.0%		100.0%
1y	397	18.7%	93.6%	45.0%	93.5%
3y	315	18.7%	85.7%	21.9%	85.6%
5y	277	18.7%	80.1%	18.6%	79.9%
7y	258	17.4%	75.1%	18.1%	75.0%
10y	240	16.4%	68.8%	17.5%	68.7%

TABLE 14.8 Scenario Barriers and Probabilities

Scenario	H	p
1	0.4000	50.0%
2	0.8427	50.0%

model returns a more stable volatility term structure, and also has a more robust economic interpretation.

One of the main drawbacks of structural models is that they usually are not able to explain short-term credit spreads; in fact, usually the diffusion part of the GBM is not enough to explain a nonnull default probability in very small time intervals. The introduction of default barrier scenarios could be a way to overcome this problem; in fact, a very high scenario barrier could be enough to account for short-term default probabilities.

At this point, a natural extension of the family of structural models we have presented here is the valuation of hybrid equity/credit products. In the following part of this chapter, we are going to deal with this application.

14.7 A Fundamental Example: Pricing Counterparty Risk in Equity Return Swaps

In this section we present an example of pricing with the calibrated structural model. This follows Brigo and Tarenghi (2004), and is reported also in the last part of Brigo and Masetti (2005). This example concerns the valuation of an equity return swap where we take into account counterparty risk, and is chosen to highlight one case where the calibrated structural model may be preferable to a reduced-form intensity model calibrated to the same market information. This is an illustration of a more general situation that typically occurs when one tries to price the counterparty risk in an equity payoff. We will see that it is possible to split the expectation of the payoff, and that the decomposition roughly involves the valuation of the same payoff without counterparty risk and the valuation of an option on the residual NPV of the considered payoff at the default time of the counterparty. Therefore including the counterparty risk adds an optionality level to the payoff.

TABLE 14.9 Results of Calibration for September 12, 2008

T_j	R_j (bps)	σ_j (bps)	Surv (SBTV)	σ_j	Surv (AT1P)
September 12, 2008			100.0%		100.0%
1y	1,437	19.6%	79.3%	62.2%	78.4%
3y	902	19.6%	66.2%	30.8%	65.5%
5y	710	19.6%	59.6%	24.3%	59.1%
7y	636	21.8%	52.9%	26.9%	52.5%
10y	588	23.7%	43.6%	29.5%	43.4%

Let us consider an equity return swap payoff. Assume we are a company "A" entering a contract with company "B," our counterparty. The reference underlying equity is company "C." We assume "A" to be default-free (i.e., we consider unilateral counterparty risk). For a discussion on unilateral versus bilateral risk, see Brigo and Capponi (2008) and Brigo, Pallavicini, and Papatheodorou (2009). The contract, in its prototypical form, is built as follows. Companies "A" and "B" agree on a certain amount K of stocks of a reference entity "C" (with price S) to be taken as nominal ($N = K S_0$). The contract starts in $T_a = 0$ and has final maturity $T_b = T$. At $t = 0$ there is no exchange of cash (alternatively, we can think that "B" delivers to "A" an amount K of "C" stock and receives a cash amount equal to $K S_0$). At intermediate times "A" pays to "B" the dividend flows of the stocks (if any) in exchange for a periodic rate (for example a semiannual LIBOR or EURIBOR rate L) plus a spread X. At final maturity $T = T_b$, "A" pays $K S_T$ to "B" (or gives back the amount K of stocks) and receives a payment $K S_0$. This can be summarized as in equation (14.14).

$$
\begin{array}{cccc}
\text{Initial time 0:} & \text{No flows, or} & & \\
\boxed{A} \longrightarrow & K S_0 \text{ cash} & \longrightarrow & \boxed{B} \\
\longleftarrow & K \text{ equity} & \longleftarrow & \\
& \cdots & & \\
\text{Time } T_i: \longrightarrow & \text{Equity dividends} & \longrightarrow & \qquad (14.14)\\
\boxed{A} \longleftarrow & \text{LIBOR + Spread} & \longleftarrow & \boxed{B} \\
& \cdots & & \\
\text{Final time } T_b: \longrightarrow & K \text{ equity or } K S_{T_b} \text{ cash} & \longrightarrow & \\
\boxed{A} \longleftarrow & K S_0 \text{ cash} & \longleftarrow & \boxed{B}
\end{array}
$$

The price of this product can be derived using risk-neutral valuation, and the (fair) spread is chosen in order to obtain a contract whose value at inception is zero. We ignore default of the underlying "C," thus assuming it has a much stronger credit quality than the counterparty "B." This can be the case for example when "C" is an equity index (Pignatelli 2004). It can be proved that if we do not consider default risk for "B," the fair spread is identically equal to zero. But when taking into account counterparty default risk in the valuation, the fair spread is no longer zero. In case an early default of the counterparty "B" occurs, the following happens. Let us call $\tau = \tau_B$ the default instant. Before τ everything is as before, but if $\tau \leq T$, the net present value (NPV) of the position at time τ is computed. If this NPV is negative for us (i.e., for "A"), then its opposite is completely paid to "B" by us at time τ itself. On the contrary, if it is positive for "A," it is not received completely but only a recovery fraction R$_{\text{EC}}$ of that NPV is received by us. It is clear that to us ("A") the counterparty risk is a problem when the NPV is large and positive, since in case "B" defaults we receive only a fraction of it.

Analytically, the risk-neutral expectation of the discounted payoff is ($L(S, T)$ is the simply compounded rate at time S for maturity T):

$$\Pi_{ES}(0) = \mathbb{E}_0\left\{ \mathbf{1}_{\{\tau > T_b\}}\left[- K\,\mathrm{NPV}^{0-T_b}_{dividends}(0) + KS_0 \sum_{i=1}^{b} D(0, T_i)\alpha_i \big(L(T_{i-1}, T_i)\right.\right.$$

$$\left. + X\big) + D(0, T_b)\big(KS_0 - KS_{T_b}\big)\right]$$

$$+ \mathbf{1}_{\{\tau \le T_b\}}\left[- K\,\mathrm{NPV}^{0-\tau}_{dividends}(0) + KS_0 \sum_{i=1}^{\beta(\tau)-1} D(0, T_i)\alpha_i \big(L(T_{i-1}, T_i)\right.$$

$$\left.\left. + X\big) + D(0, \tau)\big(\mathrm{R}_{\mathrm{EC}}(\mathrm{NPV}(\tau))^+ - (-\mathrm{NPV}(\tau))^+\big)\right]\right\} \qquad (14.15)$$

where

$$\mathrm{NPV}(\tau) = \mathbb{E}_\tau\left\{ - K\,\mathrm{NPV}^{\tau-T_b}_{dividends}(\tau) + KS_0 \sum_{i=\beta(\tau)}^{b} D(\tau, T_i)\alpha_i\,(L(T_{i-1}, T_i) + X)\right.$$

$$\left. + \big(KS_0 - KS_{T_b}\big) D(\tau, T_b)\right\} \qquad (14.16)$$

We denote by $\mathrm{NPV}^{s-t}_{dividends}(u)$ the net present value of the dividend flows between s and t computed in u.

We state the following:[3]

Proposition 14.7.1 (Equity return swap price under counterparty risk) *The fair price of the equity swap defined earlier [i.e., equation (14.15)], can be simplified as follows:*

$$\Pi_{ES}(0) = KS_0 X \sum_{i=1}^{b} \alpha_i P(0, T_i) - L_{GD} \mathbb{E}_0\left\{ \mathbf{1}_{\{\tau \le T_b\}} P(0, \tau)(\mathrm{NPV}(\tau))^+\right\} \qquad (14.17)$$

The first term is the equity swap price in a default-free world, whereas the second one is the optional price component due to counterparty risk.

Remark 14.7.1 (Different choice for the NPV) *Let us focus for a second on the NPV term in equation (14.16). In particular let us concentrate on the interval $[T_{\beta(\tau)-1}, T_{\beta(\tau)})$ containing the default time τ. If τ is strictly inside the interval, the LIBOR + spread resetting at the earlier $T_{\beta(\tau)-1}$ is paid for the whole interval.*

A different formulation is the following. In case the default time is inside a certain interval, the LIBOR + spread term for the part of this interval preceding default is *immediately paid and we add the remaining part, to be paid at the end of the interval, discounted back from the end of the interval to the current (default) time. This amounts to letting the summation in equation (14.16) start from $\beta(\tau) + 1$ rather than from $\beta(\tau)$ and adding the following term in the NPV payoff:*

$$
\begin{aligned}
&\left(L\left(T_{\beta(\tau)-1}, T_{\beta(\tau)}\right) + X\right)\left(\tau - T_{\beta(\tau)-1}\right) \\
&+ \left(L\left(T_{\beta(\tau)-1}, T_{\beta(\tau)}\right) + X\right)\left(T_{\beta(\tau)} - \tau\right) D\left(\tau, T_{\beta(\tau)}\right)
\end{aligned}
$$

Formulation (14.16) reads like postponing the default τ to the first T_i following τ and then discounting it back to the current (default) time.

Both formulations make sense, so contract specifications are important in order to price this kind of product. Analytical pricing formulas with our choice result in being more tractable than with the alternative choice presented in this remark, where small accruing terms appear. Such accruing terms are very small in general and can be ignored.

If we try to find the preceding price by computing the expectation through a Monte Carlo simulation, we have to simulate both the behavior of the equity "C" underlying the swap, which we call $S_t = S_t^C$, and the default of the counterparty "B." In particular we need to know exactly $\tau = \tau_B$. Obviously the correlation between "B" and "C" could have a relevant impact on the contract value. Here the structural model can be helpful: Suppose to calibrate the underlying process V to CDSs for name "B," we find the appropriate default barrier and volatilities according to the procedure outlined earlier in this chapter with the AT1P or SBTV model. We could set a correlation between the processes V_t^B for "B" and S_t for "C," derived, for example, through historical estimation directly based on equity returns, and simulate the joint evolution of $[V_t^B, S_t]$. As a proxy of the correlation between these two quantities we may consider the correlation between S_t^B and S_t^C (i.e., between equities).

Remark 14.7.2   (Using reduced-form models?) *At this point it may be interesting to consider the alternatives offered by an intensity reduced-form model. If one takes a deterministic intensity, since Poisson processes and Brownian motions defined on the same space are independent, there is no way to introduce a correlation between the default event for "B" and the value of the equity "C." To take into account this correlation we may have to move to stochastic intensity. However, correlating the stochastic intensity of "B" to the equity of "C" may lead to a poorly tractable model, even under tractable intensities as in Brigo and Alfonsi (2005), and the amount of correlation induced in this way may be too small for practical purposes.*

Going back to our equity swap, now it is possible to run the Monte Carlo simulation, looking for the spread X that makes the contract fair. The simulation itself is simpler when taking into account the following computation included in the discounted NPV:

$$P(\tau, T_b)\mathbb{E}_\tau\{S_{T_b}\} = S_\tau - \text{NPV}_{dividends}^{\tau-T_b}(\tau) \tag{14.18}$$

so that we have

$$
\begin{aligned}
P(0,\tau)\text{NPV}(\tau) &= K S_0 \sum_{i=\beta(\tau)}^{b} P(0, T_i)\alpha_i(L(T_{i-1}, T_i) + X) + K S_0 P(0, T_b) \\
&\quad - K P(0, \tau)S_\tau \\
&= K S_0 \sum_{i=\beta(\tau)}^{b} P(0, T_i)\alpha_i X + K S_0 P(0, T_{\beta(\tau)-1}) \\
&\quad - K P(0, \tau)S_\tau
\end{aligned}
\tag{14.19}
$$

The reformulation of the original expected payoff [equation (14.15)] as in equation (14.17) presents an important advantage in terms of numerical simulation. In fact in equation (14.15) we have a global expectation, hence we have to simulate the exact payoff for each path. In equation (14.17), with many simplifications, we have isolated a part of the expected payoff out of the main expectation. This isolated part has an expected value that we have been able to calculate, so that it does not have to be simulated. Simulating only the residual part is helpful because now the variance of the part of the payoff that has been computed analytically is no longer affecting the standard error of our Monte Carlo simulation. The standard error is indeed much lower when simulating equation (14.17) instead of equation (14.15). The expected value we computed analytically involves terms in S_{T_b} that would add a lot of variance to the final payoff. In equation (14.17) the only S_{T_b} term left is in the optional NPV part.

We performed some simulations under different assumptions on the correlation between "B" and "C." We considered five cases: $\rho = -1$, $\rho = -0.2$, $\rho = 0$, $\rho = 0.5$, and $\rho = 1$. In Table 14.11 we present the results of the simulation. For counterparty "B" we used the CDS rates reported in Table 14.10. For the reference stock "C" we used a hypothetical stock with initial price $S_0 = 20$, volatility $\sigma = 20$ percent, and constant dividend yield $q = 0.80$ percent. The simulation date is September 16,

TABLE 14.10 CDS Spreads Used for the Counterparty "B" Credit Quality in the Valuation of the Equity Return Swap

T_i	R_i^{BID} (bps)	R_i^{ASK} (bps)
1y	25	31
3y	34	39
5y	42	47
7y	46	51
10y	50	55

TABLE 14.11   Fair Spread X (in Basis Points) of the
Equity Return Swap in Five Different Correlation Cases for
AT1P and SBTV Models

ρ	X (AT1P)	X (SBTV)
-1	0.0	0.0
-0.2	3.0	3.6
0	5.5	5.5
0.5	14.7	11.4
1	24.9	17.9

2009. The contract has maturity $T = 5y$ and the settlement of the LIBOR rate has a semiannual frequency. Finally, we included a recovery rate $R_{EC} = 40$ percent. Since the reference number of stocks K is just a constant multiplying the whole payoff, without losing generality we set it equal to one.

In order to reduce the errors of the simulations, we adopted a variance reduction technique using the default indicator (whose expected value is the known default probability) as a control variate. In particular we have used the default indicator $1_{\{\tau < T\}}$ at the maturity T of the contract, which has a large correlation with the final payoff. Even so, a large number of scenarios are needed to obtain errors with a lower order of magnitude than X.

We notice that X increases together with ρ. This fact can be explained in the following way. Let us consider the case of positive correlation between "B" and "C": This means that, in general, if the firm value for "B" increases, moving away from the default barrier, also the stock price for "C" tends to increase due to the positive correlation. Both processes will then have high values. Instead, again under positive correlation, if V_t^B lowers toward the default barrier, also S_t^C will tend to do so, going possibly below the initial value S_0. In this case $NPV(\tau)$ has a large probability to be positive (see equation (14.19)), so that one needs a large X to balance it, as is clear when looking at the final payoff [equation (14.17)]. On the contrary, for negative correlation, the same reasoning can be applied, but now if V_t^B lowers and tends to the default barrier, in general S_t^C will tend to move in the opposite direction and the corresponding $NPV(\tau)$ will probably be negative, or, if positive, not very large. Hence the balancing spread X we need will be quite small.

Also we notice that, for $\rho \neq 0$, the fair spread X is different when computed either with the AT1P or the SBTV model. This can be explained by the fact that the payoff depends strongly on the dependence structure between τ and S_T, while ρ is an instantaneous correlation that ignores randomness in the barrier that defines τ; because of the different volatility term structure obtained with the two models, but especially because of the random barrier in the SBTV model, we have that the same value of ρ corresponds to different dependence structures between τ and S_T, and hence to different values for the fair spread X. This shows that counterparty risk pricing is quite subject to model risk, since two models calibrated to the same data give different answers.

Finally, as a comparison, we computed X also with a calibrated intensity model, and obtained $X = 5.5$ bps, a value consistent with the case $\rho = 0$, representing the independence case.

14.8 Conclusion

In general the link between default probabilities and credit spreads is best described by intensity models. The credit spread to be added to the risk-free rate represents a good measure of a bond credit risk, for example. Yet, intensity models present some drawbacks: They do not link the default event to the economy but rather to an exogenous jump process whose jump component remains unexplained from an economic point of view.

In this paper we have introduced two analytically tractable structural models (AT1P and SBTV) that allow for a solution to these points. In these models the default has an economic cause, in that it is caused by the value of the firm hitting the safety barrier value, and all quantities are basic market observables. The extension to hybrid equity/credit products turns out to be natural, given the possibility to model dependency between equity assets and firms asset just by modeling the correlation between the two dynamics.

We showed how to calibrate the AT1P and SBTV model parameters to actual market data: Starting from CDS quotes, we calibrated the value of the firm volatilities that are consistent with CDS quotes and also leading to analytical tractability. We also explained the analogies with barrier option pricing, in particular the case with time-dependent parameters.

As a practical example, we also applied the model to a concrete case, showing how it can describe the proximity of default when time changes and the market quotes for the CDSs reflect increasing credit deterioration. When the market detects a company crisis, it responds with high CDS quotes and this translates into high default probabilities (i.e., high probabilities for the underlying process to hit the safety barrier) that in turn translate in high calibrated volatilities for the firm value dynamics.

Also, we showed how these two models can be used in practice: We analyzed the case of an equity return swap, evaluating the cost embedded in the instrument due to counterparty risk.

Appendix 14A: AT1P Model: Proof

Let us consider an asset X^* with the following risk-neutral dynamics:

$$dX_t^* = X_t^* \left(r_t - q_t^*\right) dt + X_t^* \sigma_t dW_t \tag{14.20}$$

where r_t, q_t^* and σ_t are time-dependent deterministic functions. As it is known, it is not possible to find analytical formulas for barrier options when the underlying dynamics have nonconstant parameters. But, following the work of Lo, Lee, and Hui (2003) and Rapisarda (2003), it is possible to find analytical formulas for barrier options with maturity T when the barrier has the following shape:

$$H^*(t) = H \exp\left(-\int_t^T \left(r_s - q_s^* - B\sigma_s^2\right) ds\right) \qquad (14.21)$$

depending on a parameter B and on the constant reference value H.

In this framework, we can price a *down-and-out binary barrier option* as

$$\mathrm{BinBarr}^{\mathrm{D\&O}} = P(0, T)\left[\Phi\left(\frac{\ln\left(\frac{X_0^*}{H}\right) + \int_0^T v_s\, ds}{\sqrt{\int_0^T \sigma_s^2 ds}}\right) - \left(\frac{H^*(0)}{X_0^*}\right)^{2B-1} \Phi\left(\frac{\ln\left(\frac{H^*(0)^2}{X_0^* H}\right) + \int_0^T v_s\, ds}{\sqrt{\int_0^T \sigma_s^2 ds}}\right)\right]$$

where $v_t = r_t - q_t^* - \frac{\sigma_t^2}{2}$. This means that the probability of not touching the barrier before T is

$$\mathbb{Q}(\tau > T) = \left[\Phi\left(\frac{\ln\left(\frac{X_0^*}{H}\right) + \int_0^T v_s\, ds}{\sqrt{\int_0^T \sigma_s^2 ds}}\right) - \left(\frac{H^*(0)}{X_0^*}\right)^{2B-1} \Phi\left(\frac{\ln\left(\frac{H^*(0)^2}{X_0^* H}\right) + \int_0^T v_s\, ds}{\sqrt{\int_0^T \sigma_s^2 ds}}\right)\right] \qquad (14.22)$$

However, the barrier $H^*(t)$ in equation (14.21) depends on the maturity T of the chosen option (that is $H^*(t) = H_T^*(t)$); we want to avoid such dependency, so we impose

$$H_{T_1}^*(t) = H_{T_2}^*(t)$$

for $t \leq T_1 \leq T_2$ and for every pair of maturities T_1 and T_2. This condition implies, for each t:

$$r_t - q_t^* - B\sigma_t^2 = 0, \quad \text{or} \quad q_t^* = r_t - B\sigma_t^2 \qquad (14.23)$$

Substituting equation (14.23) in equations (14.20) and (14.21), we get

$$dX_t^* = X_t^* B\sigma_t^2 dt + X_t^* \sigma_t dW_t$$
$$H^*(t) \equiv H \qquad (14.24)$$

where the barrier is now flat and the dynamic depends only on σ (and B). Obviously, however, in general equation (14.23) does not hold.

We can still manage to preserve analytical tractability as follows. Let us assume from now on that the real risk-neutral dynamic of the asset is

$$dX_t = X_t (r_t - q_t) \, dt + X_t \sigma_t dW_t \tag{14.25}$$

with $X_0 = X_0^*$, and define a barrier

$$H(t) = H \exp\left(-\int_0^t (q_s - q_s^*) \, ds \right) \tag{14.26}$$

Then, by integrating X^* and X's equations it is easy to show that the first time $X^*(t)$ hits $H^*(t) = H$ is the same as the first time the real process $X(t)$ hits $H(t)$. Therefore, probabilities of touching the barrier computed with $(X^*(t), H^*(t))$ are the same as those computed with $(X(t), H(t))$.

Now, moving from equity barrier options to the firm default framework, we can identify X with the firm value process V, and use the auxiliary process $V^*(= X^*)$ (with $q_t^* = r_t - B\sigma_t^2$) to compute the survival probabilities. Substituting equation (14.23) in equation (14.22), we get

$$\mathbb{Q}(\tau > T) = \left[\Phi\left(\frac{\ln\left(\frac{V_0}{H}\right) + \frac{2B-1}{2} \int_0^T \sigma_s^2 ds}{\sqrt{\int_0^T \sigma_s^2 ds}} \right) \right.$$
$$\left. - \left(\frac{H}{V_0} \right)^{2B-1} \Phi\left(\frac{\ln\left(\frac{H}{V_0}\right) + \frac{2B-1}{2} \int_0^T \sigma_s^2 ds}{\sqrt{\int_0^T \sigma_s^2 ds}} \right) \right] \tag{14.27}$$

that is the survival probability for the AT1P model.

Remark 14A.1   *We do not need to know the actual dynamics of the firm value V, since we can use the auxiliary process V^* defined in equation (14.24). Neither do we need the true barrier $H(t)$, since we can use the flat barrier $H^*(t) = H$.*

This fact is useful in simulation: In fact, to price a barrier option with a constant barrier, we can use the Brownian bridge technique as explained, for example, in Metwally and Atiya (2002), thus avoiding the need to simulate the dynamics of V on a very large number of time steps.

Notes

1. A proof of the proposition can be found in Appendix 14A.
2. It is market practice for CDSs of names with deteriorating credit quality to quote an up-front premium rather than a running spread. After the so-called ISDA Big Bang, it is likely

that several names will quote an up-front on top of a fixed prespecified running spread even when the credit quality has not deteriorated. In our tests we directly deal with the equivalent running spread alone, which can be obtained by up-front premiums by means of standard techniques; see, for example, Beumee et al. (2009).

3. A proof of the proposition is given in the most general setup in Brigo and Masetti (2005).

References

Alavian, S., J. Ding, P. Whitehead, and L. Laudicina. 2009. Counterparty valuation adjustment (CVA). Working paper, available at www.defaultrisk.com.

Assefa, S., T. Bielecki, S. Crépey, and M. Jeanblanc. 2009. *CVA computation for counterparty risk assessment in credit portfolio.* Preprint.

Beumee, J., D. Brigo, D. Schiemert, and G. Stoyle. 2009. Charting a course through the CDS Big Bang. Fitch Solutions research report.

Bielecki, T., and M. Rutkowski. 2001. *Credit risk: Modeling, valuation and hedging.* New York: Springer-Verlag.

Black, F., and J. C. Cox. 1976. Valuing corporate securities: Some effects of bond indenture provisions. *Journal of Finance* 31:351–367.

Blanchet-Scalliet, C., and F. Patras. 2008. Counterparty risk valuation for CDS. Available at www.defaultrisk.com.

Brigo, D. 2004a. Candidate market models and the calibrated CIR++ stochastic intensity model for credit default swap options and callable floaters. In *Proceedings of the 4th ICS Conference*, Tokyo, March 18–19. Available at www.damianobrigo.it. Short version in "Market models for CDS options and callable floaters," *Risk* (January 2005).

Brigo, D. 2004b. Constant maturity credit default swap pricing with market models. Available at http://ssrn.com. Short version in *Risk* (June 2006).

Brigo, D., and A. Alfonsi. 2005. Credit default swap calibration and derivatives pricing with the SSRD stochastic intensity model. *Finance and Stochastics* 9 (1): 2005. Extended verison available at www.damianobrigo.it. See also *Proceedings of the 6th Columbia–JAFEE International Conference*, Tokyo, March 15–16, 2003, 563–585.

Brigo, D., and I. Bakkar. 2009. Accurate counterparty risk valuation for energy-commodities swaps. *Energy Risk* (March).

Brigo, D., and A. Capponi. 2008. Bilateral counterparty risk valuation with stochastic dynamical models and application to credit default swaps. Working paper. Available at http://ssrn.com and www.arXiv.org. Short version in *Risk* (March 2010).

Brigo, D., and K. Chourdakis. 2009. Counterparty risk for credit default swaps: Impact of spread volatility and default correlation. *International Journal of Theoretical and Applied Finance* 12 (7): 1007–1026.

Brigo, D., and N. El-Bachir. 2008. An exact formula for default swaptions pricing in the SSRJD stochastic intensity model. To appear in *Mathematical Finance.* Available at www.defaultrisk.com, http://ssrn.com, and www.arXiv.org.

Brigo, D., and M. Masetti. 2005. Risk neutral pricing of counterparty risk. In *Counterparty credit risk modeling: Risk management, pricing and regulation*, ed. M. Pykhtin. London: Risk Books.

Brigo, D., and M. Morini. 2006. Structural credit calibration. *Risk* (April).

Brigo, D., and A. Pallavicini. 2007. Counterparty risk under correlation between default and interest rates. In *Numerical methods for finance*, ed. J. Miller, D. Edelman, and J. Appleby. Chapman Hall.

Brigo, D., A. Pallavicini, and V. Papatheodorou. 2009. Bilateral counterparty risk valuation for interest-rate products: Impact of volatilities and correlations. Working paper. Available at http://ssrn.com and www.arXiv.org.

Brigo, D., and M. Tarenghi. 2004. Credit default swap calibration and equity swap valuation under counterparty risk with a tractable structural model. Proceedings of the FEA 2004 Conference at MIT, Cambridge, Massachusetts, November 8–10. Available at http://ssrn.com, www.arXiv.org and defaultrisk.com.

Brigo, D., and M. Tarenghi. 2005. Credit default swap calibration and counterparty risk valuation with a scenario based first passage model. Available at http://ssrn.com, www.arXiv.org, and www.defaultrisk.com.

Briys, E., and F. de Varenne. 1997. Valuing risky fixed rate debt: An extension. *Journal of Financial and Quantitative Analysis* 32 (2): 239–248.

Collin-Dufresne, P., and R. Goldstein. 2001. Do credit spreads reflect stationary leverage ratios? *Journal of Finance* 56:1929–1958.

Crépey, S., M. Jeanblanc, and B. Zargari. 2009. CDS with counterparty risk in a Markov chain copula model with joint defaults. Working paper.

Crouhy, M., D. Galai, and R. Mark. 2000. A comparative analysis of current credit risk models. *Journal of Banking and Finance* 24:59–117.

Dorfleitner, G., P. Schneider, and T. Veza. 2007. Flexing the default barrier. Working paper. Available at http://ssrn.com.

Duffie, D., and K. Singleton. 1999. Modeling term structures of defaultable bonds. *Review of Financial Studies* 12:687–720.

Giesecke, K. 2004. Credit modelling and valuation: An introduction. To appear in *Credit risk: Models and management*, vol. 2. London: Risk Books.

Hsu, J. C., J. Saa-Requejo, and P. Santa-Clara. 2002. Bond pricing with default risk. Working paper, Anderson School, UCLA.

Huge, B., and D. Lando. 1999. Swap pricing with two-sided default risk in a rating-based model. *European Finance Review* 3:239–268.

Hui, C. H., C. F. Lo, and S. W. Tsang. 2003. Pricing corporate bonds with dynamic default barriers. *Journal of Risk* 5 (3).

Lando, D. 1998. On Cox processes and credit-risky securities. *Review of Derivatives Research* 2:99–120.

Leung, S. Y., and Y. K. Kwok. 2005. Credit default swap valuation with counterparty risk. *Kyoto Economic Review* 74 (1): 25–45.

Lipton, A., and A. Sepp. 2009. Credit value adjustment for credit default swaps via the structural default model. *Journal of Credit Risk* 5 (2): 123–146.

Lo, C. F., H. C. Lee, and C. H. Hui. 2003. A simple approach for pricing barrier options with time-dependent parameters. *Quantitative Finance* 3.

Merton, R. 1974. On the pricing of corporate debt: The risk structure of interest rates. *Journal of Finance* 29:449–470.

Metwally, S. A. K., and A. F. Atiya. 2002. Using Brownian bridge for fast simulation of jump-diffusion processes and barrier options. *Journal of Derivatives*.

Pignatelli, M. 2004. Private communication, Banca IMI.

Rapisarda, F. 2003. Pricing barriers on underlyings with time-dependent parameters. Working paper.

Sorensen, E. H., and T. F. Bollier. 1994. Pricing swap default risk. *Financial Analysts Journal* 50 (3): 23–33.

Walker, M. 2005. Credit default swaps with counterparty risk: A calibrated Markov model. Working paper.

Yi, C. 2009. Dangerous knowledge: Credit value adjustment with credit triggers. Bank of Montreal research paper.

CHAPTER 15

Counterparty Valuation Adjustments

Harvey J. Stein

Bloomberg LP

Kin Pong Lee

Bloomberg LP

The financial crisis that began in 2007 has highlighted the importance of assessing counterparty credit risk. Regulations, accounting practices, and investment practices are all being reshaped to better manage counterparty risk.

Here we review the need for counterparty credit risk analysis, focusing on accurate computation of the counterparty valuation adjustment (CVA). We

- *Provide a general framework for computing CVA*
- *Relate the CVA to the value of a portfolio of options*
- *Compare the CVA of bonds to swaps*
- *Analyze other approaches to CVA management (such as discount shifts, current exposure, and bilateral CVA)*
- *Discuss hedging methodologies*

15.1 Introduction

Despite the recent market upheavals, the OTC derivatives markets continue to comprise one of the largest components of the financial markets, with an overall outstanding notional of $547 trillion in December 2008, 70 percent of which are in interest rate derivatives. As of June 2009, this has grown to $605 trillion. And in spite of market contractions, gross values in the over-the-counter (OTC) markets are up. From June 2008 to December 2008, OTC gross market value increased 60 percent, from $20 trillion to $32 trillion (Bank for International Settlements 2009). Interest rate derivatives' gross market value doubled from $9 trillion to $18 trillion.

Prompted by the desire to weather or even reduce market turmoil, regulations, accounting practices, and investment practices have been under reevaluation. In particular, approaches for analyzing and mitigating counterparty risk have garnered renewed interest. Regulators have been advocating greater usage of clearinghouses. Accounting boards have been refining and codifying fair market valuation, placing additional emphasis on careful consideration of counterparty risk. The International Accounting Standards Board (IASB) has even issued a request for comment on counterparty risk calculation methodologies. And investors and traders have been trying to better factor some notion of counterparty risk into their trading and risk management practices.

Here we investigate the notion of counterparty risk and the associated counterparty valuation adjustment (CVA) in the fixed income markets. We outline the CVA calculation, detail the underlying model assumptions, give examples of the calculation, and discuss the impact the CVA has in the value of these instruments.

15.2 Counterparty Risk

Counterparty risk is the exposure the investor has to loss due to a specific counterparty failing to meet contractual obligations. This is the default risk of a position or portfolio.

When holding an uncovered contract with a counterparty, one's immediate counterparty exposure is to the loss (if any) that would incur if the counterparty were to default. If the investor is long a bond, then the exposure is to the bond issuer, and the loss that would incur is the value of the bond minus the amount that would be recovered by the investor. If the investor is short the bond, then the investor bears no counterparty risk.

The immediate exposure on an uncovered swap is different. With a swap, one is simultaneously long the receiving leg and short the paying leg. At some times, this one contract can be an asset and thus exposed to counterparty default, while at other times it can be a liability and engender no counterparty exposure at all.

Another difference between bond exposure and swap exposure is in recovery. With bonds, investors receive a percentage of the principal (recovery on principal) (Altman and Kishore 1996). The remaining interest payments of the contract are lost. With a swap, as per the ISDA master agreement, recovery is on the market value of the swap, which values both principal and interest payments (Cooper and Mello 1991).

The final difference between bond and swap counterparty exposure is that swap counterparty exposure is often modified or mitigated by other contracts. If the parties involved have activated the netting agreement in the ISDA master agreement, then the overall exposure at a given time is not to the loss on each individual contract, but to the net value of all contracts covered by the netting agreement. In particular, without a netting agreement, one would receive recovery on each swap with positive value, while still owing the full market value of swaps with negative values. With a netting agreement in place, swaps with negative value will decrease the overall exposure (Brigo and Masetti 2005).

The other agreement that modifies credit risk is the ISDA credit support annex (CSA). When undertaken, this agreement stipulates that positions must be collateralized and details exactly how this must be done. The parties maintain an account with collateral against the value of the swap (or net value of all the instruments under the netting agreement). When the difference between the net value of the securities and the amount of collateral posted exceeds the margin requirements, additional collateral must be posted to make up the difference. This limits exposure to the size of market moves before additional posting is demanded, plus the size of the margin requirement (Alvian et al. 2009).

15.3 Counterparty Valuation Adjustment (CVA)

Exposure to default is quantified by the counterparty valuation adjustment (CVA) (Alvian et al. 2009). This is the price deficit of the instrument that arises from default risk. It is the difference between the price of the instrument and the price it would have were the counterparty free of default risk (the risk-free price minus the risky price). This is the cost of hedging the default risk, or equivalently, the price of the embedded default risk.

Counterparty risk calculations are fairly straightforward for instruments and portfolios that are long-only. In a long only position (like a bond position), counterparty risk can be judged by using models that are able to incorporate a discount curve shift. CVAs depend on interest rates and default risks, and are sensitive to volatility only if the underlying structure itself is volatility sensitive.

For positions that can be long or short depending on market conditions, counterparty risk calculations are more complicated. This applies to interest rate swaps. For these instruments, CVAs do not just depend on interest rates and default risk. They also depend on volatility.

For example, consider a five-year at-the-money receive fixed interest rate swap in a flat interest rate environment. At zero volatility, the swap will for the most part have a nearly zero market value, and thus little default risk. However, at high volatility, the swap has the potential to be fairly valuable in the future. Under those conditions, default would cause a substantial loss.

Swaps, in that exposure is to the market value and not to the principal, also have more exposure than bonds to the shape of the yield curve. Even at zero volatility, if the swap curve is steep, then the swap can be heavily in-the-money for much of its life, and thus will exhibit far more counterparty risk than in a flat curve environment.

15.4 Modeling the CVA

Consider a contract with a given counterparty[1] that matures at time T and has price process $V(t)$ when neglecting the embedded default risk. Let $P(t)$ be the principal at time t. For example, if this is a position in a bond issued by a risky company, then $V(t)$ is the price at time t of the equivalent risk-free bond and $P(t)$ is constant if the bond is not amortizing. Let R_v (R_p) be the recovery rate on the price (principal), which we assume to be a known constant.

If the counterparty were to default right now and the position currently has positive value ($V(0) > 0$), then the investor receives $R_v \times V(0) + R_p \times P(0)$ for the contract, effectively losing $(1 - R_v)V(0) - R_p P(0)$. If the value is negative, there is no loss—the investor still owes the liability. Thus, the immediate exposure to default is:

$$(1 - R_v)\max(V(0), 0) - R_p P(0)1_{v(0)>0}$$

where $1_{v(0)>0}$ is the indicator function (it is 1 when $V(0) > 0$ and otherwise 0). Similarly, if τ is the time of default, then our loss at that time is:

$$(1 - R_v)\max(V(\tau), 0) - R_p P(\tau)1_{v(\tau)>0}$$

The cost of this payoff is the counterparty valuation adjustment (CVA) for the contract. It is the cost of the default risk, or equivalently, the cost of hedging the counterparty risk. The first term is the loss after recovery on the market value (CVA$_V$). The second term is the loss after recovery on the principal (CVA$_P$). For individual securities, either R_v or R_p will typically be zero. For a portfolio with mixed recoveries, one would need to sum over the value and principal processes of the constituents.

In the case of being long bonds, the market value recovery is zero $R_v = 0$, and the market value is nonnegative, so the loss at default time reduces to:

$$V(\tau) - R_p P(\tau)$$

In the case of a swap, where recovery is on the market value alone ($R_p = 0$), the loss at default time reduces to:

$$(1 - R_v)\max(V(\tau), 0)$$

The quantity $\max(V(t), 0)$ is the payoff of a call option to purchase the contract at time t. Taking expectations with respect to the risk-neutral measure for a numéraire N, we see that this component of the CVA, namely the loss from recovery on the market value, is given by:

$$N(0)E\left[(1 - R_v)\frac{\max(V(\tau), 0)}{N(\tau)}1_{\tau < T}\right]$$

$$= (1 - R_v)N(0)E\left[\int_0^T \frac{\max(V(t), 0)}{N(\tau)}\delta(t - \tau)dt\right]$$

$$= (1 - R_v)N(0)\left[\int_0^T E\left[\frac{\max(V(t), 0)}{N(\tau)}\delta(t - \tau)\right]dt\right]$$

where δ is the Dirac delta function. If under the equivalent martingale measure, default is independent of both the contract value and the numéraire, then the expectation of the product is the product of the expectations, and we see that the CVA$_V$ is:

$$(1 - R_v)N(0)\left[\int_0^T E\left[\frac{\max(V(t), 0)}{N(t)}\right]E[\delta(t - \tau)]dt\right]$$

$$= (1 - R_v)\left[\int_0^T N(0)E\left[\frac{\max(V(t), 0)}{N(t)}\right]E[\delta(t - \tau)]dt\right]$$

The second expectation in the integrand is the default probability density function $p(t)$. The remainder of the integrand is the time zero value of the call option to enter into the tail of the swap at time t. If we denote this value by $C(0, t)$, then the CVA$_V$ is:

$$(1 - R_v) \int_0^T C(0, t) p(t) dt$$

Similarly, if $P(0, t)$ denotes the time zero value of the time t principal $P(t)$, and it is deterministic, or otherwise independent of $V(t)$ then the CVA$_P$ is:

$$-R_p \int_0^T N(0) E \left[\frac{P(t)}{N(t)} 1_{V(t)>0} \right] p(t) dt$$

$$= -R_p \int_0^T P(0, t) \Pr(V(t) > 0) p(t) dt$$

where $\Pr(V(t) > 0)$ is the probability that $V(t)$ is positive. So the full CVA formula is:

$$(1 - R_v) \int_0^T C(0, t) p(t) dt - R_p \int_0^T P(0, t) \Pr(V(t) > 0) p(t) dt$$

If the contract value is always positive, then the CVA becomes:

$$(1 - R_v) \int_0^T V(0, t) p(t) dt - R_p \int_0^T P(0, t) p(t) dt$$

$$= \int_0^T [(1 - R_v) V(0, t) - R_p P(0, t)] p(t) dt$$

where $V(0, t)$ is the time zero value of the remainder of the contract at time t (the time t tail of the contract).

15.5 CVA Calculations for Bonds

If a risk-free bond with a coupon of C pays f times per year at times t_i, with maturity t_n, the value of the bond is the discounted value of its cash flows:

$$\sum_{i}^{n} \frac{C}{f} D(t_i) + 100 D(t_n)$$

where $D(t)$ is the risk-free discount factor for time t (Stein 2007).

For bonds, recovery is on the principal ($R_v = 0$), the current value of the principal payment is the discounted value of the time at which it is paid, and the bond value is never negative. So,

$$P(0, t) = D(t)100$$

and

$$V(0, t) = \sum_{t=t} \frac{C}{f} D(t_i) + 100 D(t_n)$$

Assuming independence of rates and default, the counterparty valuation adjustment is:

$$\int_0^{t_n} [V(0, t) - R_p D(t)100] p(t) dt$$

Consider the contribution of one term from $V(0, t)$ to this integral. It is

$$\int_0^{t_i} \frac{C}{f} D(t_i) p(t) dt$$
$$= \frac{C}{f} D(t_i)(1 - S(t_i))$$

where $S(t_i)$ is the survival probability for time t (the probability of no default before time t, namely $1 - \int^t p(s) ds$). So, the CVA for the bond is:

$$\sum^n \frac{C}{f} D(t_i)(1 - S(t_i)) + 100 D(t_n)(1 - S(t_n)) - R_p \int^{t_n} 100 D(t) p(t) dt$$

This is just the sum of the values of the discounted cash flows times the odds of losing them, minus the value of the recovery. Subtracting from the value of the risk-free bond, we get the value of the risky bond:

$$\sum^n \frac{C}{f} D(t_i) S(t_i) + 100 D(t_n) S(t_n) + \int^{t_n} 100 R_p D(t) p(t) dt$$

The value of the risky bond is the sum of the discounted cash flows times the odds of getting them plus the value of the recovery of the principal in the event of default. This is the standard CDS model applied to a bond.

FIGURE 15.1 Spread Conversion on YASN

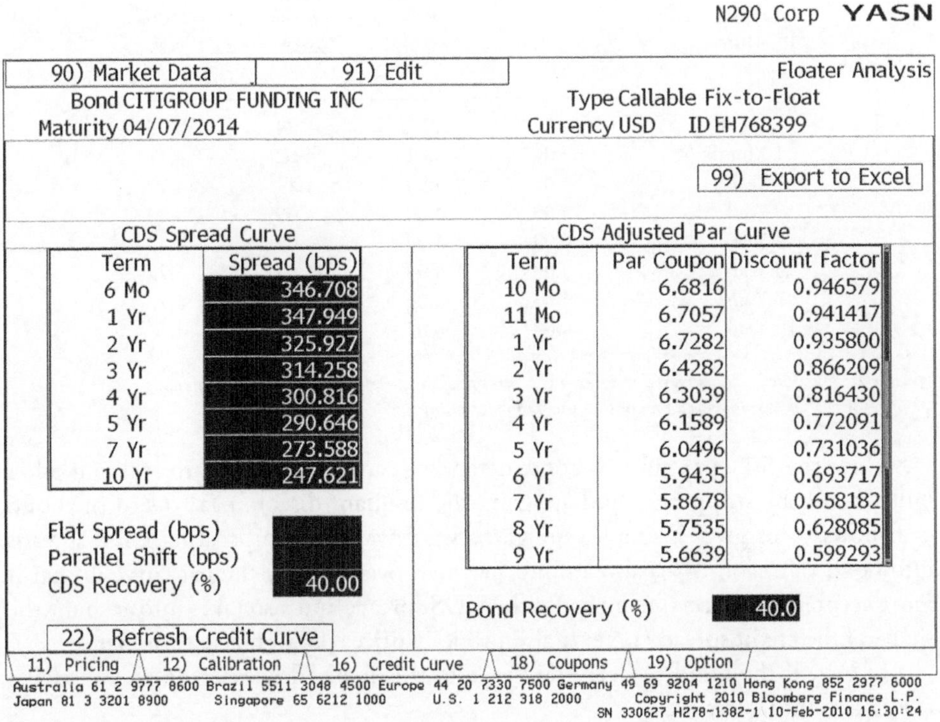

N290 Corp **YASN**

90) Market Data	91) Edit	Floater Analysis

Bond CITIGROUP FUNDING INC   Type Callable Fix-to-Float
Maturity 04/07/2014   Currency USD   ID EH768399

99) Export to Excel

CDS Spread Curve		CDS Adjusted Par Curve		
Term	Spread (bps)	Term	Par Coupon	Discount Factor
6 Mo	346.708	10 Mo	6.6816	0.946579
1 Yr	347.949	11 Mo	6.7057	0.941417
2 Yr	325.927	1 Yr	6.7282	0.935800
3 Yr	314.258	2 Yr	6.4282	0.866209
4 Yr	300.816	3 Yr	6.3039	0.816430
5 Yr	290.646	4 Yr	6.1589	0.772091
7 Yr	273.588	5 Yr	6.0496	0.731036
10 Yr	247.621	6 Yr	5.9435	0.693717
		7 Yr	5.8678	0.658182
Flat Spread (bps)		8 Yr	5.7535	0.628085
Parallel Shift (bps)		9 Yr	5.6639	0.599293
CDS Recovery (%)	40.00			

Bond Recovery (%)   40.0

22) Refresh Credit Curve

11) Pricing	12) Calibration	16) Credit Curve	18) Coupons	19) Option

Australia 61 2 9777 8600 Brazil 5511 3048 4500 Europe 44 20 7330 7500 Germany 49 69 9204 1210 Hong Kong 852 2977 6000
Japan 81 3 3201 8900   Singapore 65 6212 1000   U.S. 1 212 318 2000   Copyright 2010 Bloomberg Finance L.P.
SN 330627 H278-1382-1 10-Feb-2010 16:30:24

YASN, the structured notes analysis function, converts CDS curves to credit adjusted par curves for the purpose of doing OAS analysis on structured notes.

To get a feel for the impact of the credit spreads on bond values, we can compute the credit-adjusted par curve. For $t_i = \frac{i}{f}$, and for each n, solve for $C = C(t_n)$ such that

$$100 = \sum^{n} \frac{C}{f} D(t_i) S(t_i) + 100 D(t_n) S(t_n) + \int^{t_n} 100 R D(t) p(t) dt$$

Then $C(t)$ gives the credit adjusted implied par curve—the coupons that an issuer with this CDS spread curve would theoretically use to issue debt at par.

We do this calculation in the YASN function—Bloomberg's structured notes analysis function (see Figure 15.1).

With a flat 100 bp CDS spread curve and a flat 3 percent swap curve, the entire process roughly corresponds to adding the CDS spread to the swap par rates (aside from the impact of default between trade date and settlement date, which increases the par coupon at short maturities). When the CDS recovery rate differs from the bond recovery rate (or when CDS spreads are very large), the equivalent par curve can be significantly different from a shift of the risk-free curve by the credit spread, although it is still a shift. When the CDS and swap curves are not flat, this relationship no longer holds. (See Table 15.1.)

TABLE 15.1   Credit-Adjusted Par Rates

CDS Recovery:	0 %	40 %	80 %	40 %
Bond Recovery:	0 %	40 %	80 %	0 %
Term				
1 Week	4.22	4.22	4.24	5.08
1 Month	4.00	4.01	4.02	4.71
1 Year	4.02	4.04	4.11	4.72
2 Years	4.03	4.04	4.09	4.73
3 Years	4.03	4.04	4.09	4.73
5 Years	4.03	4.04	4.08	4.72
7 Years	4.03	4.04	4.08	4.72
10 Years	4.03	4.04	4.08	4.72

Credit-adjusted par rates for a flat 100 bp CDS spread curve and a flat 3 percent swap curve as a function of the CDS and bond recovery rates.

Once the risky par curve is constructed, we can use it directly for valuing other bullet bonds by stripping it and applying the resultant discount factors to the bond cash flows. This gives a simple, straightforward way of incorporating CDS spreads into bond valuations. It is also an improvement over shifting the par curve in that it more accurately reflects the impact of the CDS spreads and also takes into account the shape of the credit spread curve. It also properly prices par bonds back to par.

In fact, if the bond recovery rate is zero, this method is exact. In this case, the risky discount factors are

$$D(t)S(t)$$

which makes the risky spot rate curve

$$\bar{R}(t) = -\frac{1}{t}\log(D(t)S(t)) = R(t) - \frac{1}{t}\log S(t)$$

where $R(t)$ is the risk-free spot curve (in continuous compounding). In this case, the survival probabilities add a spread of $-\frac{1}{t}\log S(t)$ (the average hazard rate) to the risk-free rate. This is roughly the CDS spread adjusted by the CDS recovery rate.

However, as bonds deviate from par and the recovery rate grows, this method will deviate from the CDS model-based method. It can lead to 5 to 15 basis points of error with a 100 bp CDS spread when a bond is several hundred basis points away from par. However, given other general uncertainties (such as the value of the recovery rate itself, or the spread between the bond market and the CDS market), it is a reasonable approximation, and errors can be folded into the option adjusted spread (OAS) as an additional shift of the forward curve.

Once a bond has a more complicated structure (such as embedded calls or puts, or complicated floating coupons, such as range accruals), one must do more than just discount cash flows. For complicated bonds, one can use the risk-adjusted par curve with an interest rate model, as is done in the YASN function, where we calibrate the

FIGURE 15.2 The YASN Function

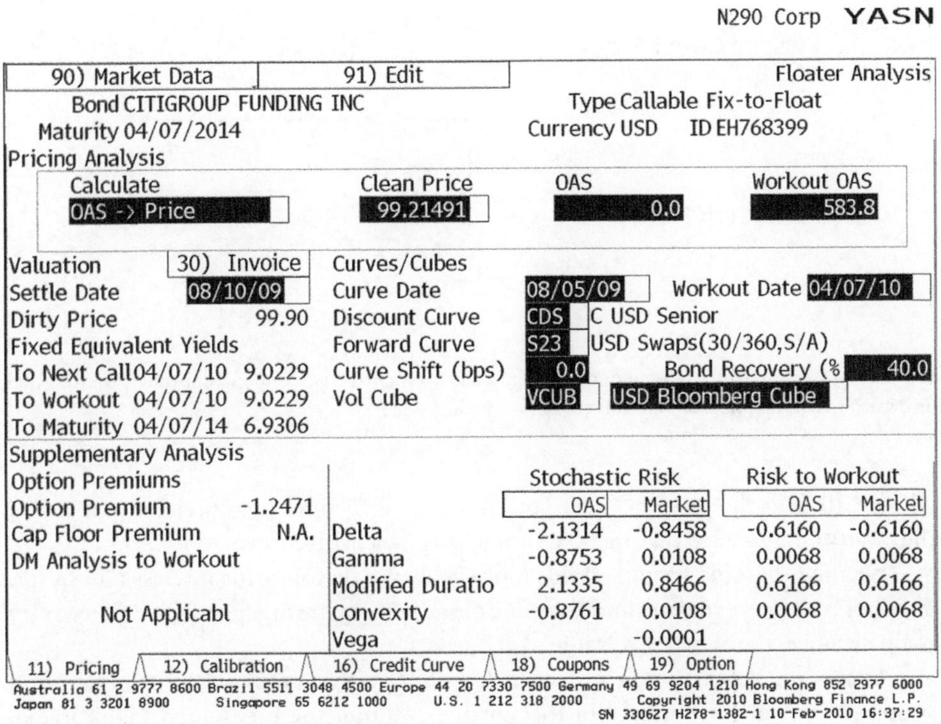
N290 Corp YASN
90) Market Data
91) Edit
Floater Analysis
Bond CITIGROUP FUNDING INC
Type Callable Fix-to-Float
Maturity 04/07/2014
Currency USD ID EH768399
Pricing Analysis
Calculate
OAS -> Price
Clean Price
99.21491
OAS
0.0
Workout OAS
583.8
Valuation
30) Invoice
Settle Date 08/10/09
Dirty Price 99.90
Fixed Equivalent Yields
To Next Call04/07/10 9.0229
To Workout 04/07/10 9.0229
To Maturity 04/07/14 6.9306
Curves/Cubes
Curve Date 08/05/09
Workout Date 04/07/10
Discount Curve CDS C USD Senior
Forward Curve S23 USD Swaps(30/360,S/A)
Curve Shift (bps) 0.0
Bond Recovery (% 40.0
Vol Cube VCUB USD Bloomberg Cube
Supplementary Analysis
Option Premiums
Option Premium -1.2471
Cap Floor Premium N.A.
DM Analysis to Workout
Not Applicabl
Stochastic Risk
Risk to Workout
OAS Market
OAS Market
Delta -2.1314 -0.8458 -0.6160 -0.6160
Gamma -0.8753 0.0108 0.0068 0.0068
Modified Duratio 2.1335 0.8466 0.6166 0.6166
Convexity -0.8761 0.0108 0.0068 0.0068
Vega -0.0001
11) Pricing
12) Calibration
16) Credit Curve
18) Coupons
19) Option
Australia 61 2 9777 8600 Brazil 5511 3048 4500 Europe 44 20 7330 7500 Germany 49 69 9204 1210 Hong Kong 852 2977 6000
Japan 81 3 3201 8900 Singapore 65 6212 1000 U.S. 1 212 318 2000 Copyright 2010 Bloomberg Finance L.P.
SN 330627 H278-1382-1 10-Feb-2010 16:37:29

The YASN function applies volatility to the swap curve and is calibrated to quoted swaptions. The risk-adjusted par curve is applied on top of this process to value risky cash flows.

Hull-White short rate model with time-dependent volatility to the swaptions that most closely hedge the bond. (See Figure 15.2.) The model is then calibrated to the risky par curve by imposing a time-dependent shift of the model's forward rates. We have found this approach to be a reasonable compromise among accuracy, complexity, and tractability.

15.6 CVA Calculations for Swaps

CVA calculations for swaps demand more finesse. The fundamental difference between the calculations for swaps and for bonds is that swaps can be assets or liabilities. When they are liabilities there is no counterparty default exposure. Taking this into account requires the introduction of swaptions.

For a swap, the principal recovery rate is zero, and the swap can be positive or negative in value. So, assuming independence of default and the contract price, the CVA is:

$$(1 - R_v) \int_0^T C(0, t) p(t) dt$$

FIGURE 15.3 Swaption Cash Flows versus Default Cash Flow Losses

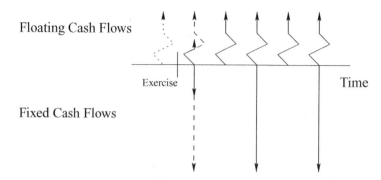

A swaption exercised between coupon payments has a prorated first coupon (illustrated by the solid arrows), whereas upon default the full cash flows are lost.

where $C(0, t)$ is the value of a call option maturing at time t to enter into the tail of the swap. Thus, we see that the CVA for a swap is sensitive to volatility.

We note that this formula holds more generally than just for interest rate swaps. This holds whenever default and the value of the security are independent, and recovery is a percentage of the risk free value of the security.

The value of the option on the tail, $C(0, t)$ differs from the usual value of a swaption with exercise time t in that in the swaption the first coupon is prorated, whereas in the option to enter into the tail, the loss is of the entire first coupon. The difference between the two payoffs is illustrated in Figure 15.3. The difference is further exacerbated by the fact that in a typical swap, the fixed and floating cash flows have different periodicities. As can be seen in Figure 15.4, since the first payment in a

FIGURE 15.4 Forward Swap Values and Forward Tail Values

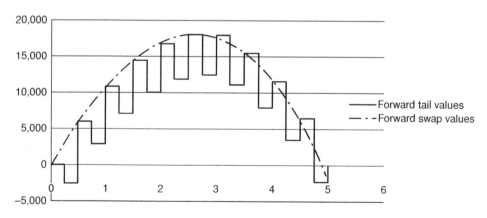

Comparison of forward swap values to forward tail values for a five-year at the money payer swap.

FIGURE 15.5   Swaption and Tail Option Prices: 20 Percent Volatility

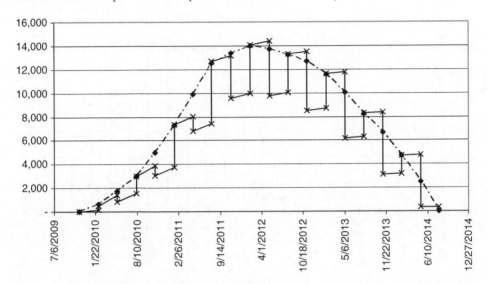

Swaption prices as a function of maturity are given by the broken line. The prices of options to enter into the tail of an existing payer swap are given by the solid line. The underlying swap is a five-year swap on a $1 million notional paying 4 percent fixed against three-month U.S. LIBOR. The options and swaptions are valued under a flat 20 percent volatility.

swaption is prorated, the forward swap values are much smoother than for the values of the tail of the swap in question.

The difference in forward values has an analogous impact on the value of the corresponding options, as illustrated in Figure 15.5. Again, while the swaption values are relatively smooth as a function of maturity, the option to enter into the tail of the swap jumps as cash flow dates are passed. One can also see that volatility has a huge impact on the overall exposure, with peak expected exposure changing from \$5,957 to \$14,418, and with the peak occurring earlier as well (see Figure 15.6).

To calculate the CVA for a swap, we approximate the integral by a sum. For optimal accuracy, the calculation could be done on a daily basis, but this is extremely time-consuming. Since default probabilities and option prices are relatively linear between cash flows, we can get good approximations if we (1) use the midpoint of the interval for the option exercise, and (2) take care to adjust for the difference between swaptions and options to enter into the tail of the swap.

The difference between the swaptions and the tail options can be accounted for by adjusting volatilities, strikes, and forward rates. Consider the pay fixed swap with fixed rate F that the holder of a swaption would receive on exercise (at time t). Let the underlying floating (fixed) leg pay at times t_i (t_i'). Let $L(w, x, y)$ be the time w forward LIBOR rate setting at time x and paying at time y, $Z(x, y)$ be the time x price of a zero coupon bond paying at time y, and a_i (a_i') be the accrual fractions for

FIGURE 15.6   Swaption and Tail Option Prices: 0 Percent Volatility

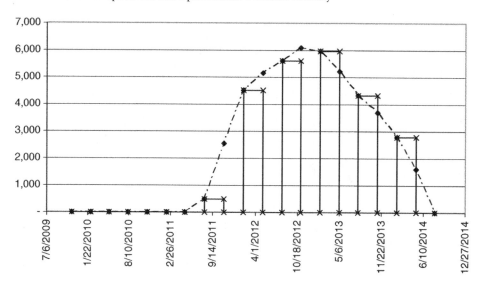

The same comparison as in Figure 15.5, but with 0 percent volatility.

the floating (fixed) payment periods from t_i to t_{i+1} (from t_i' to t_{i+1}'). Then the time t value of the swap is:

$$S(t) = \sum L(t, t_i, t_{i+1}) Z(t, t_{i+1}) a_i - \sum F a_i' Z(t, t_i')$$

Since $t \leq t_i$,

$$L(t, t_i, t_{i+1}) = \left(\frac{1}{a_i''} \right) \left(\frac{Z(t, t_i)}{Z(t, t_{i+1})} - 1 \right)$$

(with LIBOR accrual factor a_i''). If we assume $a_i = a_i''$, then $S(t)$ can be written in terms of Z as:

$$S(t) = Z(t, t_2) - Z(t, t_n) - \sum F a_i' Z(t, t_i')$$

This gives us the standard expression for the time t value of a forward start swap (Stein 2007).

If we use $\bar{t}_i$, $\bar{a}_i$, and so on to denote the same information for the option to enter into the tail of the existing swap, then all the values are the same, except that the first reset date ($\bar{t}_1$) is earlier than the valuation time (t), and the first accrual factors correspond to the full period rather than the partial period. The time t value of the first floating cash flow is:

$$\frac{Z(t, t_2)}{Z(\bar{t}_1, t_2)} - Z(t, t_2)$$

So the value of the tail is:

$$
\begin{aligned}
\bar{S}(t) &= \frac{Z(t, t_z)}{Z(\bar{t}_1, t_2)} - Z(t, t_2) + \sum_{i \geq 2} L(t, t_i, t_{i+1}) Z(t, t_{i+1}) a_i \\
&\quad - F \bar{a}'_1 Z(t, t'_1) - \sum_{i \geq 2} F a'_i Z(t, t'_i) \\
&= \frac{Z(t, t_z)}{Z(\bar{t}_1, t_2)} - Z(t, t_n) - F \bar{a}'_1 Z(t, t'_1) - \sum_{i \geq 2} F a'_i Z(t, t'_i)
\end{aligned}
$$

The difference between the two is

$$
\bar{S}(t) - S(t) = \frac{Z(t, t_z)}{Z(\bar{t}_1, t_z)} - Z(t, t_1) - F(\bar{a}'_1 - a'_1) Z(t, t'_1)
$$

This is the adjustment that needs to be made to convert the swaption payoff to the payoff of the option on the tail of the swap. If $D = \bar{S}(t) - S(t)$, then the payoff of the option to exercise into the tail of the swap is

$$
\max(\bar{S}(t), 0) = \max(S(t) + D, 0) = \max(S(t), -D) + D
$$

This can be approximated by replacing D by its time zero value, and using it to approximate the value of the option on the tail by the swaption with an adjusted strike, forward rate, and volatility.

The impact of these adjustments is illustrated in Table 15.2. Cash flows are annual, yet annual sampling at the beginning or end of the period gives rise to substantial errors. Midpoint sampling is quite accurate even when just sampling once per year. The table also illustrates the impact of ignoring the difference between the options to enter into the tail of the swap and the swaptions.

TABLE 15.2 CVAs from Different Methodologies

Sampling Frequency (in Months)	CVA (Anticipated)	CVA (Postponed, Using Swaptions)	CVA (Postponed, Using Tail Options)	CVA (Midpoint, Using Tail Options)
2	$4,468.03	$4,529.87	$4,763.81	$4,615.92
4	$4,324.49	$4,445.17	$4,924.06	$4,613.98
6	$4,132.73	$4,315.81	$5,070.28	$4,651.73
12	$3,635.04	$3,953.62	$5,482.16	$4,656.87

We compare computing the CVA using swaptions at the beginning of the default period (anticipated), at the midpoint, and at the end of the period (postponed). The underlying interest rate swap is a five-year swap on $1 million notional, paying a 3.5 percent fixed coupon annually against 12-month U.S. LIBOR, with a 40 percent recovery rate and a flat 500 bp CDS spread. Calculations use market quotes of swap rates and swaption prices.

15.7 Example Calculation

Consider a 10-year at-the-money (ATM) interest rate swap receiving fixed and paying U.S. LIBOR 3-month on a $1 million notional. At a recovery rate of 40 percent and a flat CDS spread of 100 bp, the CVA is $2,174.68, as is illustrated by the Bloomberg CVA function (Figure 15.7).

As can be expected, not only is the risky swap less valuable than the riskless swap, but it also has credit and volatility exposure.

The details of the calculation are available on the second page (Figure 15.8). Here we see the interval default probabilities used with each swaption, the resultant present value of each potential loss, and the time *t* losses (assuming no default before that time).

It is interesting to note the difference in CVA values between payer and receiver swaps. In Figure 15.4, we show the forward values of a payer swap as a function of time. With an upward-sloping yield curve, the swap is mostly of positive value. Contrast this with a receiver swap. In the same environment, a receiver swap's value will be the negative of this—the forward value will be negative over the life of the swap. Because of this, the payer swap spends much more time as an asset, and its CVA will be much

FIGURE 15.7   The CVA Function

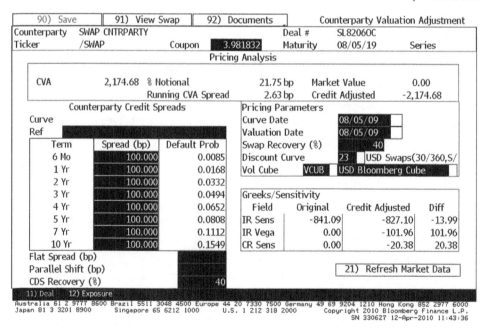

The CVA function computes counterparty valuation adjustments for OTC derivatives. Here we compute the CVA for a 10-year ATM receive fixed interest rate swap on $1 million notional with a 40 percent recovery rate and a flat 100 bp CDS spread. Calculations are using the swap curve and swaption volatilities from 8/5/09.

FIGURE 15.8 Breakdown of the CVA Calculation

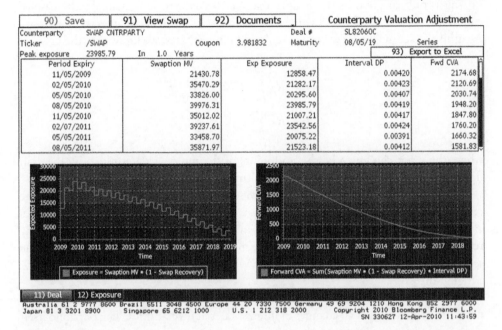

The Exposure tab of the CVA function displays the swaption prices and default probabilities used in the CVA calculation.

higher than the equivalent receiver swap. For the swap in Table 15.3, the CVA goes up by a factor of 2 if the swap is flipped from payer to receiver. Table 15.3 shows the CVA for at the money payer and receiver swaps, along with the par coupon adjustments these CVAs would imply. More discussion of this subtlety can be found in (Bielecki and Rutkowski 2002).

TABLE 15.3 CVA and Effective Par Coupons

CDS Spread (bps)	Reciever Swap CVA	Payer Swap CVA	Receiver Swap Par Coupon	Payer Swap Par Coupon
10	$ 230.15	$ 484.59	3.985 %	3.976 %
20	$ 457.38	$ 962.68	3.987 %	3.970 %
50	$1,121.93	$ 2,358.79	3.995 %	3.953 %
100	$2,174.68	$ 4,563.37	4.008 %	3.926 %
200	$4,090.56	$ 8,548.83	4.032 %	3.875 %
300	$5,780.38	$12,028.01	4.054 %	3.828 %
400	$7,272.53	$15,063.43	4.074 %	3.785 %
500	$8,591.68	$17,709.67	4.092 %	3.746 %

CVAs and effective par coupons for payer and receiver swaps as a function of CDS spread. The underlying swap is a 10-year ATM swap on $1 million notional with swap rate 3.982 percent.

15.8 Hedging

Pricing is only as good as the hedges that can be used to lock it in. In the case of counterparty risk, the hedges can be problematic. Consider an interest rate swap. Assuming no correlation between default and interest rates, we know that the CVA is:

$$= (1 - R) \int_0^T C(0, t) p(t) dt$$

$$\simeq (1 - R) \sum C(0, t_i) \bar{p}(t_i)$$

where the t_i are chosen to be the midpoints of the intervals determined by the cash flows, and $\bar{p}(t_i)$ is the probability of defaulting in the ith interval.

This suggests two ways of replicating the CVA. We can take positions $\bar{p}(t_i)$ in the corresponding swaptions, or we can take positions $C(0, t_i)$ in securities whose values are the interval default probabilities (if we can find them). Neither of these will actually replicate the CVA statically, because the positions themselves do not exhibit the same sensitivities to market conditions as the CVA does. But they can serve as a basis for hedging the CVA.

Consider hedging via the portfolio of swaptions. By holding the swaptions, this portfolio hedges against all changes of interest rates and volatilities. The portfolio itself is unaffected by credit spread changes. It would have to be rebalanced when credit spreads change.

Hedging the credit side is more complicated. When credit spreads increase, the CVA increases, so if we try to hedge with one credit default swap, we need to be long protection. Augmenting the above portfolio with the appropriate CDS position to neutralize the credit spread sensitivity will require being long CDS protection.

The main difficulty in using CDS in this fashion to hedge the CVA is that while we are hedged against shifts of the CDS spread curve, we are not necessarily hedged against the default event.[2] To see this, consider having sold protection against default loss on an ATM swap. We would have been paid the CVA for this protection. To apply the hedge, we would use the money to buy the above swaption portfolio and entered into this credit default swap. If default occurs immediately, because the swap is at the money, there would be no loss and we wouldn't have to pay anything. We could liquidate our swaption portfolio, recover the CVA value, and on top of that, because we are long protection from the CDS, receive additional income from the CDS position. Thus, an immediate default results in making money, so this position is not a perfect hedge—we end up overhedged. Similarly, if the swap was heavily in-the-money and credit spreads were small, we could potentially be underhedged by following this strategy.

Alternatively, we can take positions in CDS equal to the forward market values of the swap, minus the value of the corresponding swaption portfolio. This would properly hedge against the default event, but not necessarily hedge against changes in credit spreads. In either case, there is also the issue that the hedge bleeds—it incurs a loss over time due to the cost of the CDS protection. This loss would have to be factored into the hedge, which further complicates matters because it is also dependent on the default time.

In practice, since credit spreads change more frequently than default events occur, one typically hedges against credit spread changes with a portfolio of CDS positions. This hedge has to be managed in an attempt to make sure that one is sufficiently long protection before default becomes imminent, lest one be caught with insufficient coverage when the default event actually occurs. This can be managed to the extent that the default arrival is not Poisson (i.e., there is some knowledge in the market about the default time beyond just the hazard rate).

Another hedging complication arises from the cross gamma (the sensitivity of the CVA to the second derivative with respect to credit spreads and interest rates). If interest rates or volatilities change, the swaption portfolio hedges the change. If credit spreads change, the CDS position hedges the change. The hedging problem that arises from the cross gamma is when both change at the same time. Because the CVA depends on the product of the default probabilities and the swaption values, the cross gamma is a function of the product of the first-order derivatives, whereas the hedge is not exposed to this product—it has roughly zero cross gamma. So when both change, the CVA move includes a cross gamma–related move, while the hedge does not.

In all, more work can be done on practical, effective methods of hedging counterparty risk.

15.9 Wrong-Way Risk and Recovery Risk

Assuming independence of the underlying position and the default event works only as long as the market complies with this assumption. Making this assumption can be a mistake when the counterparty has a close relationship with the underlying contract. When default risk increases as the position value increases, this is known as *wrong-way risk* (Pykhtin and Zhu 2007). One classic example is buying a put from a company on its own stock. The value of the put peaks when the company goes bankrupt and is unable to pay. Another example is entering into a receiver oil swap with an oil company. As oil prices drop, the company's profits drop, but the value of the swap increases. A more subtle example is in credit default swaps. Consider buying credit default swaps from one bank to insure against default of another bank. If the latter bank defaults, it could very well be in an environment where the former bank is unable to pay (Redon 2006).

Accounting for wrong-way risk requires a model linking the value of the underlying contract with the default of the counterparty. For credit default swaps, this could be done by considering three separate events, each with its own hazard rate and Poisson arrival—the default of the first party, the default of the second party, and their joint default. Defaults are linked both through the joint default process and/or by driving the hazard rates by correlated processes (such as Brownian motions).

For contracts that do not involve defaults (like interest rate swaps), linking the counterparty default to the contract value is more subtle. One can, for example, make the hazard rate stochastic and driven by a Brownian motion that is correlated to the

Brownian motions driving interest rates (Jarrow and Yu 2001), but if the default event itself is a Poisson arrival (and hence uncorrelated to rates) this often doesn't yield as high a correlation as one would like. Some argue on this basis for structural models where default occurs when the firm value crosses a barrier (Lipton and Sepp 2009). Nonetheless, even with a Poisson default arrival, correlation in this model still can have a sizable impact on the pricing (Brigo and Pallavicini 2008).

The biggest difficulty in handling wrong-way risk is in judging and hedging the correlation. While it is possible to model the correlation, how should one calibrate the model correlation to the market? Lacking derivatives that directly expose pricing of the correlation, one can only access the correlation indirectly, either through historical analysis or as a by-product of the behavior of the model in question. In the former case, one is looking backward instead of forward, and is not necessarily operating under the pricing measure. In the latter case, one is assuming that certain characteristics of the market (like the shape of the volatility smile) are arising from the correlation. The lack of derivatives that directly expose the correlation makes hedging the correlation impact difficult as well.

Another weakness is related to recovery risk. Given that we will not know the recovery rate until some time after the default occurs, one should model the uncertainty of the recovery rate itself. Much work has been done on estimation of recovery rates and their incorporation into risk modeling (Altman, Resti, and Sironi 2003). Little work has been done in incorporating their uncertainty into CVA calculations, let alone calibrating and hedging it. One would expect difficulties similar to those in handling correlation, although some of the risk can be mitigated by credit default swaps, which are also exposed to recovery rate risk.

15.10 Accounting Considerations

Accounting for the counterparty risk in one's positions is required by accounting standards FASB 157 in the United States and IAS 39 in Europe. For example, paragraph 5 of Appendix B of FASB 157 states:

> B5. Risk-averse market participants generally seek compensation for bearing the un-
> certainty inherent in the cash flows of an asset or liability (risk premium). A fair value
> measurement should include a risk premium reflecting the amount market partici-
> pants would demand because of the risk (uncertainty) in the cash flows. (Financial
> Accounting Standards Board 2007)

While accounting rules are being updated (FASB and IAS are working jointly on refinements), the replacement for the preceding paragraph from FASB 157, namely Topic 820, Subtopic 10, Section 55, Paragraph 55, strengthens the position that credit risks need to be accounted for:

> 55-8. A fair value measurement should include a risk premium reflecting the amount
> market participants would demand because of the risk (uncertainty) in the cash flows.
> Otherwise, the measurement would not faithfully represent fair value. In some cases,

TABLE 15.4   Discount Shift Errors—In the Money Swaps

CDS Rate	CVA	Discount Shift
0	0	0
100	1,761	1,528
200	3,575	2,997
300	5,295	4,425
400[a]	6,918	5,809

CVAs computed with option volatilities compared to those computed by discount shifts for a heavily in-the-money swap—a 5 percent five-year receiver swap on a $1 million notional using market swap rates and market volatilities. (The five-year swap rate is 3.16 percent.)

determining the appropriate risk premium might be difficult. However, the degree of difficulty alone is not a sufficient basis on which to exclude a risk adjustment. (Financial Accounting Standards Board 2009)

While accurate valuation of the embedded default risk is preferred, a number of alternative approaches have traditionally been accepted. The simplest approach is to follow the same method as is used for bonds, namely to shift the discount curve to account for the credit spread. When all the corresponding swaptions are in-the-money, this corresponds to the zero volatility version of the CVA. For swaps that are heavily in-the-money, this approach can give a rough idea of the CVA (as illustrated in Table 15.4). Here the volatility accounts for about 15 percent to 20 percent to the CVA.

If any of the relevant swaptions are out of the money, or the swaptions are close enough to at-the-money that the volatility plays a larger role, then this approximation can go seriously wrong. This can even happen for in the money swaps if the curve is sufficiently steep. The errors are illustrated in Table 15.5, where we see that for an at-the-money swap, the discount curve shift underestimates the CVA by as much as 38 percent.

The worst-case scenario for this methodology is an at-the-money swap in a flat interest rate environment. In this case, if the payment frequency of the two legs is

TABLE 15.5   Discount Shift Errors—ATM Swaps

CDS Rate	CVA	Discount Shift
0	0	0
100	1,185	735
200	2,287	1,432
300	3,311	2,092
400	4,262	2,719

CVAs computed with option volatilities compared to those computed by discount shifts for an ATM five-year receiver swap on a $1 million notional using market swap rates and market volatilities. (The five-year swap rate is 3.16 percent.)

equal, shifting the curve will have no impact on the swap value at all. The curve shift method will produce a zero CVA regardless of the default risk.

For an out-of-the-money swap, this approximation cannot be used at all. It will cause an increase in the value of the swap, not an increase in the counterparty valuation adjustment. The same holds for pay fixed swaps in the typical positively sloped interest rate environment. For example, switching the swap to a pay fixed swap would make all the discount shift values negative.

To compensate for the latter shortcoming, the discount method is modified. Positions that are of positive value are treated as assets and their value is reduced as above according to the counterparty's credit risk. Positions with negative values are treated as liabilities. Instead of depressing their value according to the counterparty's credit, their value is *increased* according to the *investor's* credit. This is by symmetry and based on the theory that the money is owed to the counterparty and only a fraction of it will be paid if the investor defaults. While treating positive and negative positions separately helps to salvage the discount shift approach, it also adds the problems that bilateral CVA causes. These will be discussed shortly.

Another approach that can be used is the current net exposure approach. This is a portfolio level method that can take netting agreements and collateralization into account. The sum of the values of the positions under a given netting agreement is the current net exposure. It is the amount that is subject to immediate default risk. If it is positive, then an immediate default of the counterparty would yield a loss for the investor. The loss could be insured by a position in a credit default swap against default of the counterparty with notional equal to the current net exposure. The maturity of the CDS contract would be chosen based on some notion of the average maturity or duration of the portfolio. The CVA would be the cost of the CDS contract's fixed leg (the leg paying the spread) which is often approximated by the credit spread for the CDS contract applied over the life of the contract. Collateralization can be taken into account by reducing the current net exposure to the threshold level (the level beyond which the position must be collateralized).

The current net exposure approach can be analyzed in terms of the CDS hedge for the default risk of a portfolio. Considering that the forward values of the portfolio are varying, one could consider improving this method by using a portfolio of CDS contracts of varying maturities and notionals so that the net CDS notional at any given time matches the forward value of the portfolio. The set of CDS contracts with this property would then be the CDS hedge for the portfolio assuming zero interest rate volatility. The current net exposure approach is a rough approximation of this with just one CDS contract.

The advantages of the current net exposure approach are that it is very easy to implement and it easily takes netting agreements into account. On the negative side, being a zero volatility approach, it suffers from similar problems to the discount shift approach in that the valuations neglect the value coming from interest rate volatility, which can be substantial.

A practical problem with the method is that it tends to be unstable. The CDS notional fluctuates with the market value of the portfolio, and so does the computed

CVA. It is not dampened by the price diffusion as the accurate calculation of the CVA itself would be. Consider, for example, the CVA calculations in Figure 15.7. The sensitivities show that a 1 basis point move of interest rates moves the market value by $827, but moves the CVA by only $14.

Another modification often found in accounting practices is to use what is known as the bilateral CVA instead of the preceding calculation of the embedded counterparty default risk (known as unilateral CVA). Instead of computing the value of the contract subject to default of the counterparty, the investor would compute the value subject to default of either the counterparty or the investor. This complicates the calculation, but is often approximated as the difference between the investor's CVA to the counterparty and the counterparty's CVA to the investor. This approximation can have significant error depending on the relationship between the value of the contract and the order in which the defaults occur.

Bilateral CVA is often employed in accounting. It is also looked upon favorably by investors because it reduces the CVA charge. However, it has a number of undesirable properties. If the investor's credit is worse than the counterparty's, it can actually increase the value of the derivative. Similarly, a drop in credit of the investor could potentially cause an improvement in the balance sheet. Some, however, argue that this is a feature of mark-to-market accounting and not a drawback, noting that bonds issued by a firm will impact the balance sheet in a similar fashion. See Gregory (2009) or Brigo and Capponi (2009) for further discussions. The latter also includes a detailed example of how CVAs are impacted by changes in credit spreads and correlations.

Another problem with bilateral CVA is that the price of a derivative should be associated with a hedge. But there is no realistic hedge an investor can establish for the investor's own default risk. This renders the bilateral CVA less than a realistic market price.

Because of these issues, accounting boards have been lobbied to reject bilateral CVA as an acceptable approach. We can hope that these issues will be addressed as the IASB, U.S. Financial Accounting Standards Board (FASB), and other accounting standards boards work together on global convergence of accounting standards.

15.11 Conclusion

The financial crisis that began in 2007 has highlighted the importance of assessing counterparty credit risk. Counterparty credit risk can be quantified by the counterparty or credit valuation adjustment (CVA). The CVAs for a bond and other securities that are long only can be calculated by using curve shifts. However, for securities that combine long and short positions (such as interest rate swaps), discount curve shifts are of limited utility. In this case, calculations must be done taking volatility into account, and essentially consist of combining appropriately adjusted swaption prices with default rates (as can be derived from CDS spreads). We have:

- Outlined the general CVA calculation.
- Detailed the application to bonds and interest rate swaps.

- Presented hedging methodologies.
- Discussed the impact of the underlying model assumptions.
- Analyzed the relationship between the CVA and some of the commonly accepted approaches to accounting for credit risk on balance sheets.

Notes

1. This could also be a portfolio of securities, all under a netting agreement with a given counterparty.
2. This holds even if we expand the CDS spread to hedge against moves of all the points of the CDS spread curve by using a portfolio of CDS positions based on the sensitivity of the CVA value to moves of the individual curve points.

References

Altman, E. I., and V. M. Vellore. 1996. Almost everything you wanted to know about recoveries on defaulted bonds. *Financial Analysts Journal* 52 (6) (November/December).

Altman, E., A. Resti, and A. Sironi. 2003. Default recovery rates in credit risk modeling: A review of the literature and empirical evidence http://citeseerx.ist.psu.edu/viewdoc/summary?doi=10.1.1.62.4799, December.

Alvian, S., J. Ding, P. Whitehead, and L. Laudicina. 2009. Counterparty valuation adjustment (CVA). Working paper. Available at www.ibdx.com/shahram/Files/CVAShahram.pdf.

Bank for International Settlements. 2009. Detailed tables on semiannual OTC derivatives statistics at end—June 2009.

Bielecki, T., and M. Rutkowski. 2002. *Credit risk: Modelling, valuation and hedging.* New York: Springer-Verlag.

Brigo, D., and A. Capponi. 2009. Bilateral counterparty risk valuation with stochastic dynamical models and application to credit default swaps. Working paper. Available at SSRN: http://ssrn.com/abstract=1318024.

Brigo, D., and M. Masetti. 2005. A formula for interest rate swap valuation under counterparty risk in presence of netting agreements. In *Counterparty credit risk modelling: Risk management, pricing and regulation*, M. Pykhtin London: Risk Books.

Brigo, D., and A. Pallavicini. 2008. Counterparty risk and contingent CDS under correlation *Risk* (February).

Cooper, I. A., and A. S. Mello. 1991. The default risk of swaps. *Journal of Finance* 46 (2) (June).

Financial Accounting Standards Board. 2007. Statement of Financial Accounting Standards No. 157, fair value measurements.

Financial Accounting Standards Board. 2009. Topic 820, fair value measurements and disclosures.

Gregory, J. 2009. Being two-faced over counterparty credit risk. *Risk* (February).

Jarrow, R. A., and F. Yu. 2001. Counterparty risk and the pricing of defaultable securities. *Journal of Finance* 56 (6) (October).

Lipton, A., and A. Sepp. 2009. Credit value adjustment for credit default swaps via the structural default model. *Journal of Credit Risk* 5 (2) (Summer).

Pykhtin, M., and S. Zhu. 2007. A guide to modelling counterparty credit risk. *Global Association of Risk Professionals* 37 (July/August).

Redon, C. 2006. Wrong way risk modelling. *Risk* (April).

Stein, H. J. 2007. Valuation of exotic interest rate derivatives—Bermudans and range accruals. (December) Available at http://ssrn.com/abstract=1068985.

CHAPTER 16

Counterparty Risk Management and Valuation

Michael Pykhtin*

Federal Reserve Board

In this chapter, we give an overview of approaches to managing counterparty credit risk (CCR) and review different aspects of modeling CCR. We define counterparty credit exposure for a stand-alone derivative contract and then extend this definition to a portfolio of contracts. We show how netting agreements reduce counterparty-level exposure and briefly describe the basic principles of simulating exposure. We introduce the concept of exposure profile and illustrate it with examples. Then we turn to collateralization and show how margin agreements can further reduce credit exposure. We formally define collateralized exposure and discuss popular approaches to modeling available collateral. We use several simple examples to illustrate the basic properties of collateralized exposure profiles. We also discuss how CCR is priced and introduce the concepts of unilateral and bilateral credit valuation adjustment (CVA). We pay specific attention to modeling CVA in the presence of wrong-way risk. We conclude the chapter by discussing modeling portfolio loss and economic capital in the context of CCR.

16.1 Introduction

High-profile defaults (and near defaults) accompanying the financial crisis of 2007 to 2009 (collapse of Bear Stearns, Lehman Brothers, Wachovia, etc.) have emphasized the importance for financial institutions to measure and manage counterparty credit risk

---

*The opinions expressed here are those of the author, and do not necessarily reflect the views or policies of the Federal Reserve Board or its staff.

(CCR). Counterparty credit risk is the risk that a counterparty in a financial contract will default prior to the expiration of the contract and will fail to make all the payments required by the contract. Only the contracts privately negotiated between the counterparties—over-the-counter (OTC) derivatives and securities financing transactions (SFTs)—bear CCR. Exchange-traded derivatives are not subject to CCR because all contractual payments promised by these derivatives are guaranteed by the exchange.

Counterparty credit risk is similar to other forms of credit risk (such as lending risk) in that the source of economic loss is an obligor's default. However, CCR has two unique features that set it apart from lending risk:

1. *Uncertainty of credit exposure.* Credit exposure of one counterparty to another is determined by the market value of all the contracts between these counterparties. While one can obtain the current exposure from the current contract values, the future exposure is uncertain because the future contract values are not known at present.

2. *Bilateral nature of credit exposure.* Since both counterparties can default and the value of many financial contracts (such as swaps) can change sign, the direction of future credit exposure is uncertain. Counterparty A may be exposed to default of counterparty B under one set of future market scenarios, while counterparty B may be exposed to default of counterparty A under another set of scenarios.

The uncertainty of future credit exposure makes managing and modeling CCR of the trading book challenging. For a comprehensive introduction to CCR see Arvanitis and Gregory (2001), Canabarro and Duffie (2003), or Pykhtin and Zhu (2007). For a more extensive coverage, see Pykhtin (2005), Canabarro (2010), or Gregory (2010).

16.2 Managing and Mitigating Counterparty Credit Risk

One of the most conventional techniques of managing credit risk is setting counterparty-level *credit limits*. If a new transaction with the counterparty would result in the counterparty-level exposure exceeding the limit, the transaction is not allowed. The limits usually depend on the counterparty's credit quality: Higher-rated counterparties have higher limits. To compare uncertain future exposure with deterministic limit, *potential future exposure* (PFE) profiles are calculated from exposure probability distributions at future time points. PFE profiles are obtained by calculating a quantile of exposure at a high confidence level (typically, above 90 percent). Some institutions use different exposure measures, such as *expected exposure* (EE) profiles, for comparing with credit limit. It is important to understand that a given credit limit amount is meaningful only in the context of a given exposure measure (e.g., 95-percent-level quantile).

Future credit exposure can be greatly reduced by means of risk-mitigating agreements between two counterparties, which include *netting agreements*, *margin agreements*, and *early termination agreements*.

- *Netting agreements.* A netting agreement is a legally binding contract between two counterparties that, in the event of default of one of them, allows aggregation of transactions between these counterparties. Instead of each trade between the counterparties being settled separately, the entire portfolio covered by the netting agreement is settled as a single trade whose value equals the net value of the portfolio. Nowadays most netting agreements in the developed countries have the form of an International Swaps and Derivatives Association (ISDA)[1] Master Agreement. All the trades covered by an ISDA Master Agreement are subject to closeout netting.
- *Margin agreements.* Margin agreements limit the potential exposure of one counterparty to another by means of requiring collateral should the unsecured exposure exceed a predefined threshold. The threshold value may depend on the credit quality of the counterparty dynamically: If the counterparty is downgraded, the threshold will drop. Most margin agreements in the developed countries have the form of a Credit Support Annex (CSA) to an ISDA Master Agreement. A CSA may cover all the trades under a Master Agreement or a subset of trades.
- *Early termination agreements.* Two types of early termination agreements are often used: *termination clauses* and *downgrade provisions*. A termination clause is specified at the trade level. A unilateral (bilateral) termination clause gives one (both) of the counterparties the right to terminate the trade at the fair market value at a predefined set of dates. A downgrade provision is specified for the entire portfolio between two counterparties. Under a unilateral (bilateral) downgrade provision, the portfolio is settled at its fair market value the first time the credit rating of one (either) of the counterparties falls below a predefined level.

16.3 Credit Exposure

Let us consider a financial institution (we will call it a *bank* for brevity) that has a portfolio of derivative contracts with a counterparty. The bank's *exposure* to the counterparty at given future time is given by the bank's economic loss in the event of the counterparty's default at that time. If the counterparty defaults, the bank must close out all its positions with the counterparty. To determine the loss arising from the counterparty's default, it is convenient to assume that the bank enters into an equivalent portfolio of trades with another counterparty in order to maintain its market position. Since the bank's market position is unchanged after replacing the trades, the loss is determined by the portfolio's replacement cost at the time of default.

16.3.1 Stand-Alone Contract-Level Exposure

Suppose that the bank has a single trade i with the counterparty. We denote the mark-to-market (MTM) value of this trade at time t from the bank's perspective via $V_i(t)$. Suppose that the counterparty defaults at time t and that there are no recoveries. Let us consider two types of future market scenarios:

1. $V_i(t) \leq 0$: The bank receives the amount of $|V_i(t)|$ when it replaces the trade with another counterparty, but has to forward this amount to the defaulting counterparty when it settles the trade, so that the net loss for the bank is zero.
2. $V_i(t) > 0$: The bank pays the amount of $V_i(t)$ to another counterparty when it replaces the trade, but receives nothing from the defaulting counterparty, so that the net loss is equal to the trade value $V_i(t)$.

Combining these scenarios, we can write the bank's credit exposure $E_i(t)$ to the counterparty, created by contract i at future time t as:

$$E_i(t) = \max\{V_i(t), 0\} \tag{16.1}$$

Since the contract MTM value changes unpredictably over time as the market moves, only the current exposure is known with certainty, while the future exposure is uncertain.

Figure 16.1 illustrates the concept of stand-alone contract-level credit exposure of the bank to the counterparty's default. Contract value from the bank's perspective is shown along the time line: by a single line for the past (the value is known), and by multiple lines for the future (the value is unknown). The multiple lines for the future region illustrate possible future scenarios, each of which can materialize. At any future time point the contract MTM value can be described by a probability distribution. The density of such a distribution is shown schematically on the plot. Only scenarios with positive contract value result in nonzero credit exposure of the bank to the counterparty – this part of the distribution is shaded on the plot. The "negative" scenarios result in zero exposure for the bank.

FIGURE 16.1 Contract Mark-to-Market (MTM) Value and Stand-Alone Contract-Level Counterparty Credit Exposure

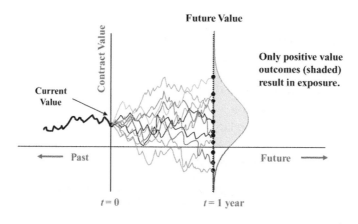

We can also look at Figure 16.1 from the counterparty's perspective. For the counterparty, the trade MTM value is the negative of that for the bank. Therefore, we should flip the plot over so that the positive value scenarios become negative value scenarios and vice versa. Only the nonshaded part of the distribution results in nonzero credit exposure of the counterparty to default of the bank.

16.3.2 Counterparty-Level Exposure

Very often a bank has multiple trades with a counterparty. Some of these trades may be fully or partially offsetting others. However, from a legal point of view, each trade with the counterparty must be settled separately in the event of the counterparty's default *unless* there are legally enforceable agreements between the bank and the counterparty that say otherwise. Settling each trade separately means that the bank's exposure to the counterparty is equal to the sum of the stand-alone contract-level exposures:

$$E_c(t) = \sum_i E_i(t) = \sum_i \max\{V_i(t), 0\} \tag{16.2}$$

Let us consider a situation when a bank and a counterparty have a single trade that both of them want to get out of. Instead of canceling the trade, they may prefer to unwind it (i.e., to enter into the reverse transaction). While the market value of such a portfolio is identically zero, the credit exposure calculated according to equation (16.2) is not. Table 16.1 illustrates this point assuming that there are only two states of the world, in which the trades can assume values +$10 and −$10.

When the counterparty defaults, the bank has to forward $10 to the counterparty to settle the trade with the negative value for the bank. However, in the worst case of zero recovery, the bank is not going to receive anything from the counterparty when it settles the trade with the positive value. Thus, the bank's credit exposure to the counterparty is $10 under either scenario.

The situation where the market value of the portfolio is zero, but the exposure is not, is not a natural one. Netting agreements are designed to rectify this. A netting agreement is a legally binding contract between two counterparties that, in the event of default of one of them, allows aggregation of transaction before settling claims. The values of all trades covered by a netting agreement are added together, and the resulting portfolio value is settled as a single trade.

TABLE 16.1 Two Equal and Opposite Trades With and Without Netting

	Market Value			Exposure (No Netting)		
	Trade 1	Trade 2	Total	Trade 1	Trade 2	Total
Scenario 1	10	−10	0	10	0	10
Scenario 2	−10	10	0	0	10	10

Suppose that there is a netting agreement between the bank and the counterparty that covers the entire portfolio. Then, the bank's exposure to the counterparty created by this portfolio is given by:

$$E_c(t) = \max \left\{ \sum_i V_i(t), 0 \right\} \qquad (16.3)$$

where the summation is over all trades that the bank has with the counterparty. If there is a netting agreement between the bank and the counterparty in the example of two opposite trades considered earlier, application of equation (16.3) results in exposure that is identically zero.

From a risk management point of view, a single netting agreement covering all the trades between two counterparties would be an ideal solution. However, because of operational constraints (e.g., an international bank that works under different jurisdictions) or some other factors (e.g., some firms prefer to avoid cross-asset-class netting), it is not uncommon for counterparties to have multiple netting agreements that cover nonoverlapping subsets of the entire portfolio. There may also be trades that are not covered by any of the existing netting agreements. Counterparty-level exposure in this most general case is given by:

$$E_c(t) = \sum_k \max \left\{ \sum_{i \in \mathrm{NA}_k} V_i(t), 0 \right\} + \sum_{i \notin \{\mathrm{NA}\}} \max[V_i(t), 0] \qquad (16.4)$$

The inner summation in the first term of equation (16.4) aggregates the values of all trades covered by the kth netting agreement (hence, $i \in \mathrm{NA}_k$ notation), while the outer summation aggregates exposures across all netting agreements. The second term in equation (16.4) is simply the sum of the stand-alone contract-level exposures of all trades that do not belong to any netting agreement (hence, $i \notin \{\mathrm{NA}\}$ notation).

16.3.3   Simulating Credit Exposure

Because of the complex nature of banks' portfolios, exposure distribution at future time points is usually obtained via Monte Carlo simulation process. This process typically consists of three major steps:

1. *Scenario generation.* Dynamics of market risk factors (e.g., interest rates, foreign exchange [FX] rates, etc.) is specified via relatively simple stochastic processes (e.g., geometric Brownian motion). These processes are calibrated either to historical data or to market implied data. Future values of the market risk factors are simulated for a fixed set of future time points.

2. *Instrument valuation.* For each simulation time point and for each realization of the underlying market risk factors, valuation is performed for each trade in the counterparty portfolio.
3. *Aggregation.* For each simulation time point and for each realization of the underlying market risk factors, counterparty-level exposure is obtained by applying the necessary netting rules, conceptually described by equation (16.4).

The outcome of this process is a set of realizations of the counterparty-level exposure (each realization corresponds to one market scenario) at each simulation time point.

Because of the computational intensity required to calculate counterparty exposures—especially for a bank with a large portfolio—certain compromises between the accuracy and the speed of the calculation are usually made: relatively small number of market scenarios (typically, a few thousand) and simulation time points (typically, in the 50 to 200 range), simplified valuation methods, and so on.

For more details on simulating credit exposure, see De Prisco and Rosen (2005) or Pykhtin and Zhu (2007).

16.3.4 Credit Exposure Profiles

The most complete characterization of future credit exposure is given by its probability distribution at each future time point. However, for many risk management applications, a single deterministic quantity characterizing exposure at a given time point is needed. For example, to determine whether credit exposure for a given counterparty is above its credit limit, a single number characterizing the exposure would be useful. A collection of such numbers obtained by applying the same procedure to exposure distributions at all simulation time points is known as an *exposure profile*. Two types of exposure profiles are widely used in practice: potential future exposure (PFE) and expected exposure (EE). A potential future exposure profile is obtained by calculating a high-confidence-level (e.g., 95 percent) quantile of exposure at each simulation time point. An expected exposure profile is obtained by calculating the sample mean of the simulated exposure realizations at each simulation time point. In this subsection we show several illustrative examples of exposure profiles.

16.3.4.1 The Case with No Cash Flows

Let us first consider a forward-starting interest rate payer swap (i.e., the bank pays fixed rate and receives floating rate). The swap is initiated today, starts in five years, and ends 10 years from today. Figure 16.2 shows the EE and the 95 percent PFE of this swap in the units of the swap notional over the first five years. These profiles start at zero (the swap is at-the-money at inception) and are monotonically increasing with time, indicating that exposure distribution is getting wider as one moves further into the future. This behavior is explained by the simple fact that more uncertainty is

FIGURE 16.2 Expected Exposure (EE) and Potential Future Exposure (PFE) Profiles for Forward-Starting Swap

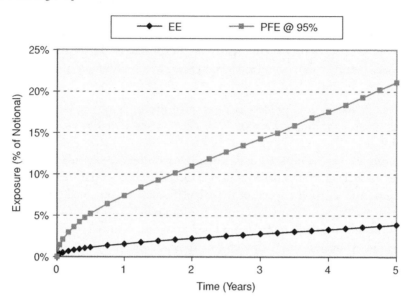

associated with the more distant future. Such profiles are characteristic of any trade or portfolio that does not have cash flows in the given time interval.

16.3.4.2   The Case with Cash Flows

Let us now consider an immediately starting five-year interest rate payer swap. Since there are cash flows in the time period of interest, the timing of these cash flows is extremely important. Let us assume that the payments of the fixed leg and of the floating leg occur simultaneously with the annual frequency. Figure 16.3 shows the profiles of EE and PFE at 95 percent for this swap obtained from a simulation with monthly time points. These profiles rise between the payment dates, but jump downward at each payment date. The *diffusion* effect is responsible for the rising behavior between the payment dates. As our simulation time crosses one of the payment dates, one fewer cash flows remain between the simulation time and the swap maturity. Fewer remaining cash flows mean less uncertainty, so the width of the trade value distribution (measured today) is reduced, and the exposure profiles jump down. This behavior is known as the *amortization* effect.

16.4   Credit Exposure under Collateralization

One of the most popular and effective techniques of mitigating and controlling counterparty credit risk is collateralization. The idea of collateralization of counterparty

FIGURE 16.3 EE and PFE Profiles for Immediately Starting Swap with Annual Payments

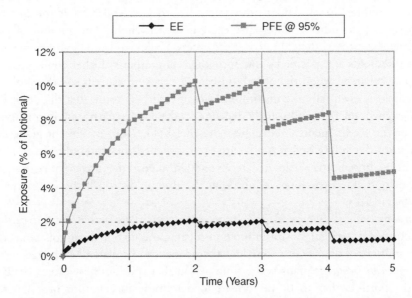

risk is very similar to the way collateral is used to mitigate lending risk: Collateral is used to reduce credit exposure. However, because of the uncertainty of counterparty credit exposure and the bilateral nature of counterparty credit risk, collateral management is much more complex in the case of counterparty risk. Exposure of one counterparty to another one changes every day as the markets move. Therefore, to keep the current exposure under control, it is not sufficient to post collateral once. Instead, collateral must be posted and returned frequently, preferably on a daily basis. Moreover, because MTM value of many types of OTC derivatives can change sign, credit exposure can change direction. If both counterparties want to limit their exposure, then either counterparty is required to post collateral when the other's exposure rises.

16.4.1 Margin Agreements

The rules of posting collateral are specified in a legally enforceable margin agreement signed by both counterparties. Some of the most important contractual features of margin agreements are:

- *Unilateral/bilateral.* Margin agreement can be either unilateral (in one of the counterparties' favor) or bilateral. Under a unilateral agreement, one of the counterparties is required to post collateral when the unsecured exposure (i.e., exposure calculated without taking into account any collateral) of the other counterparty rises above a threshold. Under a bilateral agreement, either party posts collateral. If the credit quality of the counterparties is comparable, the agreement is usually bilateral. If the credit quality of one of the counterparties is significantly worse than that of the other, the stronger counterparty may insist on a unilateral agreement in its favor.

- *Threshold(s).* Under a unilateral margin agreement, a threshold is specified for one of the counterparties. This counterparty has to post collateral if the unsecured exposure of the other counterparty exceeds the threshold. The amount of posted collateral must be sufficient to cover the excess. Under a bilateral margin agreement, two thresholds are specified—one for either counterparty. Either counterparty has to post collateral when the other's unsecured exposure exceeds the threshold. The threshold is essentially the maximum level of credit exposure that the other counterparty will tolerate, and usually depends on the counterparty's credit quality: The better the credit quality, the higher the threshold. Non-investment-grade counterparties (including hedge funds) are often assigned the threshold of zero. High-credit-quality counterparties may receive a high value of the threshold. Furthermore, the margin agreement may require that the threshold drop if the counterparty is downgraded.
- *Minimum transfer amount (MTA).* If the amount of collateral that needs to be posted or returned is less than the minimum transfer amount, no transfer of collateral occurs. The purpose of the MTA is to reduce the frequency of collateral exchange.
- *Margin call frequency.* This is the time period that specifies how often revaluation of the portfolio has to be performed to determine the amount of collateral (if any) that needs to be posted or returned. Daily margin call frequency has become standard.

Let us consider the mechanics of margin agreements. Suppose that two counterparties, A and B, have a portfolio of nettable trades supported by a unilateral margin agreement in A's favor with a daily margin call frequency. Counterparty A follows this procedure on a daily basis: It evaluates the entire portfolio and compares the portfolio MTM value to counterparty B's threshold and the amount of cash-equivalent collateral counterparty B has already posted to counterparty A. If the portfolio value is below the threshold, counterparty A should return any collateral that it holds to counterparty B, subject to the MTA. If the portfolio value is above the threshold, the collateral amount required by counterparty A is equal to the difference between the portfolio value and the threshold. If the required collateral exceeds the value of the posted collateral and the excess is greater than the MTA, a margin call is made. If the required collateral is less than the value of the posted collateral by more than the MTA, counterparty A returns this difference to counterparty B. In a bilateral agreement, counterparty B follows the same procedure as counterparty A.

16.4.2   Collateralized Credit Exposure

Suppose now that there is a single netting agreement between the bank and the counterparty that covers the entire portfolio. Suppose also that this netting agreement is covered by a margin agreement. In the presence of the margin agreement, exposure at time t is reduced by the amount of collateral $C(t)$ available to the bank at time t. Still, exposure is floored at zero because, in the event of the counterparty's default, any collateral in excess of the bank's replacement cost must be returned to the counterparty.

We can easily formalize this and define the collateralized credit exposure of the bank to the counterparty via:

$$E_c(t) = \max \left\{ \sum_i V_i(t) - C(t), 0 \right\} \tag{16.5}$$

where the summation is over all trades that the bank has with the counterparty. Equation (16.5) is the collateralized version of equation (16.3).

If there are multiple netting agreements, we can similarly generalize equation (16.4) by specifying collateral amount $C_k(t)$ available to the bank under netting agreements NA_k at time t:

$$E_c(t) = \sum_k \max \left[\sum_{i \in NA_k} V_i(t) - C_k(t), 0 \right] + \sum_{i \notin \{NA\}} \max[V_i(t), 0] \tag{16.6}$$

For netting agreements that are not covered by a margin agreement, collateral in equation (16.6) is identically zero.

We have written equations (16.5) and (16.6) implicitly assuming that the bank can only receive collateral. It is less obvious that collateral posted by the bank can also result in the bank's exposure to the counterparty's default and that this credit exposure can still be described by equations (16.5) and (16.6). For these equations to be valid regardless of whether the bank posts or receives collateral, we have to assume the following convention: $C(t)$ is positive if the bank holds collateral at time t, and negative if the bank has posted collateral at time t.

To simplify notations, from now on we consider a single netting set covered by a margin agreement. Let us verify that if we use this convention, equation (16.5) will describe the bank's credit exposure for the scenarios when the bank posts collateral. Suppose that at time t the bank has posted collateral in the amount $|C(t)|$, so that the received collateral under our convention is $C(t) = -|C(t)| < 0$. Suppose also that the counterparty defaults at time t. To determine the bank's loss, let us consider three possible types of scenarios for the portfolio MTM value $V(t) = \sum_i V_i(t)$:

1. $V(t) \leq C(t)$: Since the portfolio value is negative, the bank receives the amount $|V(t)|$ from another counterparty when it replaces the portfolio. This amount is greater than the collateral amount $|C(t)|$ that the bank has posted. To settle the portfolio with the defaulting counterparty, the bank needs to pay the amount $|V(t)|$, but it withholds the amount $|C(t)|$ to recover collateral that it has posted. There is no loss to the bank under this scenario.
2. $C(t) < V(t) \leq 0$: The portfolio value is still negative; so the bank receives the amount $|V(t)|$ from another counterparty when it replaces the portfolio. However, this amount is not sufficient to recover the collateral amount $|C(t)|$ that the bank has posted. Even if the bank does not pay anything to the defaulting counterparty, it still loses the amount $|C(t)| - |V(t)| = V(t) - C(t)$.

3. $V(t) > 0$: Under this scenario the bank pays the amount $V(t)$ to replace the portfolio. The posted collateral $|C(t)|$ is completely lost. The net loss is $V(t) + |C(t)| = V(t) - C(t)$.

Combining these three scenario types into a single expression produces the bank's loss equal to $\max\{V(t) - C(t), 0\}$, which is precisely the right-hand side of equation (16.5).

Thus, if we know both the portfolio MTM value and collateral received or posted by the bank at a given point in time for a given scenario, we can easily calculate the collateralized credit exposure at that time point for that scenario. The missing piece in this simple calculation is a model of collateral, which would relate the portfolio value to the collateral amount.

16.4.3   Modeling Collateral

The simplest approach to modeling collateral is to limit the future exposure from above by the threshold (i.e., for all scenarios with portfolio value above the threshold, set the exposure equal to the threshold). However, this approach is too simplistic because it ignores the time lag between the last delivery of collateral and the time when the loss is realized. Even when the counterparty is willing to post collateral, it may take several days between a margin call and the time when the bank actually receives collateral. However, we have to assume a longer delay: since we are interested in exposure *at default*, we have to assume that the counterparty has financial difficulties and is not willing to post collateral. The counterparty may pretend to dispute the margin call, and it may take the bank several days to realize that the counterparty is actually defaulting rather than disputing the call. When the bank is certain of the counterparty's default, it issues a notice of default. Usually a notice of default has a grace period of several days. During this grace period the counterparty can still post collateral and avoid default. Only if the counterparty does not post collateral by the expiration of the grace period, the counterparty is officially in default and the bank can start settling the trades with the counterparty. Settling the trades requires their valuation, which is often done by requesting third-party quotes on equivalent trades. The quotes can be obtained quickly for simple trades (e.g., vanilla interest rate swaps), but it may take longer to obtain quotes for more exotic trades. Only when the portfolio is closed out does the magnitude of the bank's loss due to the counterparty's default become certain.

The delay between the margin call that the counterparty does not respond to and the time by which the bank is able to close out and/or replace the counterparty portfolio is known as the *margin period of risk* (*MPR*). Generally, it is impossible to predict how long this delay is going to be, as it involves many uncertain factors mentioned earlier. In spite of this, it is usually assumed that the MPR is a deterministic quantity. It is prudent to allow different values of MPR for different margin agreements to account for different contractual margin call frequencies and for different levels of trade liquidity in the portfolios. For daily contractual margin call frequency and portfolios of liquid trades, a two-week MPR is usually assumed. For less frequent margin calls or more exotic trades, longer periods should be used.

Suppose that the bank closes out the defaulting counterparty's portfolio by time t. For modeling purposes, time t is the counterparty's default time because this is when the bank's loss on the counterparty materializes. Then, any margin call that happened at time t is irrelevant because the defaulting counterparty is not going to respond to it. Moreover, if the counterparty defaults at time t, we should assume that the latest margin call that the counterparty would respond to is at time $t - \delta t$, where δt denotes the MPR appropriate for a given margin agreement. Thus, any change in portfolio MTM value between $t - \delta t$ and t will not be covered by collateral.

16.4.3.1 Unilateral Margin Agreements

Let us consider a single unilateral (in the bank's favor) margin agreement with the counterparty's threshold $H_c \geq 0$ and the minimum transfer amount MTA. When the portfolio value exceeds the threshold, the counterparty must post collateral to keep the bank's exposure from rising above the threshold. As the exposure drops below the threshold, the bank returns collateral to the counterparty. MTA limits the frequency of collateral exchange. It is difficult to model collateral subject to MTA exactly because this would require daily simulation time points, which is not feasible given the long-term nature of exposure modeling. In practice, the actual threshold H_c is often replaced with the effective threshold defined as $H_c^{(e)} = H_c + \text{MTA}$. After this replacement, the margin agreement is treated as if it had zero MTA.

Applying the rules of posting collateral under the assumption of the effective threshold with zero MTA and taking into account the MPR, the collateral $C(t)$ available to the bank at time t is given by

$$C(t) = \max\left\{ V(t - \delta t) - H_c^{(e)}, 0 \right\} \tag{16.7}$$

where $V(t)$ is the portfolio value from the bank's perspective at time t.

Collateralized exposure is obtained by substituting equation (16.7) into equation (16.5), which yields

$$E_c(t) = \begin{cases} [H_c^{(e)} + V(t) - V(t - \delta t)]^+ & \text{if } V(t - \delta t) > H_c^{(e)} \\ [V(t)]^+ & \text{if } V(t - \delta t) \leq H_c^{(e)} \end{cases} \tag{16.8}$$

where we have used the notation $x^+ = \max\{x, 0\}$. The top line of the right-hand side of equation (16.8) describes the scenarios when the bank receives collateral from the counterparty, while the bottom line describes the scenarios when collateral is zero. When collateral held by the bank is zero, exposure coincides with the noncollateralized exposure. When the bank receives collateral, exposure can be above or below the effective threshold, depending on the sign of the portfolio value increment. If the

MPR is set to zero, the portfolio value increment would also be zero—so that the exposure would be equal to the threshold for all collateral-receiving scenarios.

16.4.3.2 Bilateral Margin Agreements

Under a bilateral margin agreement, both the counterparty and the bank have to post collateral: The counterparty posts collateral when the bank's exposure to the counterparty exceeds the counterparty's threshold, while the bank posts collateral when the counterparty's exposure to the bank exceeds the bank's threshold. Since we are doing our analysis from the bank's point of view, we will keep the counterparty's threshold H_c *nonnegative*, but will specify the bank's threshold H_b as *nonpositive*. Then, the bank posts collateral when the portfolio MTM value (defined from the bank's perspective) is *below* the bank's threshold. The minimum transfer amount is the same for the bank and the counterparty, and MTA > 0.

Similarly to the unilateral case, we will create effective thresholds for the bank and for the counterparty. Effective threshold for the counterparty, $H_c^{(e)}$, remains unchanged. From the counterparty's point of view, the effective threshold for the bank must be defined in exactly the same way. After taking into account that we do not switch our point of view and $H_b \leq 0$, the definition of the effective threshold for the bank will be $H_b^{(e)} = H_b - \text{MTA}$. Now the bilateral agreement can be treated as if it had zero MTA.

Collateral available to the bank at time t under the bilateral agreement is modeled as:

$$C(t) = \max\left\{ V(t - \delta t) - H_c^{(e)}, 0 \right\} + \min\left\{ V(t - \delta t) - H_b^{(e)}, 0 \right\} \qquad (16.9)$$

The first term in the right-hand side of equation (16.9) describes the scenarios when the bank receives collateral (i.e., $C(t) > 0$), while the second term describes the scenarios when the bank posts collateral (i.e., $C(t) < 0$).

Substituting equation (16.9) into equation (16.5), we obtain collateralized credit exposure

$$E_c(t) = \begin{cases} [H_c^{(e)} + V(t) - V(t - \delta t)]^+ & \text{if } V(t - \delta t) > H_c^{(e)} \\ [V(t)]^+ & \text{if } H_b^{(e)} \leq V(t - \delta t) \leq H_c^{(e)} \\ [H_b^{(e)} + V(t) - V(t - \delta t)]^+ & \text{if } V(t - \delta t) < H_b^{(e)} \end{cases} \qquad (16.10)$$

The top line of the right-hand side of equation (16.10) describes scenarios when the bank receives collateral from the counterparty, the middle line describes scenarios when the bank neither receives nor posts collateral, and the bottom line describes scenarios when the bank posts collateral.

Earlier in the chapter, when we introduced the concept of collateralized exposure, we discussed the possibility that collateral posted by the bank to the counterparty can generate credit exposure for the bank. However, we did not have any collateral model

FIGURE 16.4   Credit Exposure Arising from Posted Collateral

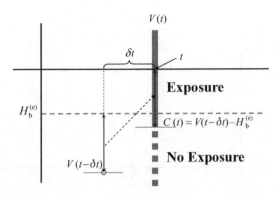

at that point. Now, when we have a collateral model, it is straightforward to verify that posting collateral can result in credit exposure. This fact immediately follows from the bottom row of the right-hand side of equation (16.10): If the bank posts collateral (i.e., $V(t - \delta t) < H_{\mathrm{b}}^{(e)}$), credit exposure is positive when $H_{\mathrm{b}}^{(e)} + V(t) - V(t - \delta t) > 0$ (i.e., when the portfolio value increment from time point $t - \delta t$ to time point t is greater than the magnitude of the bank's effective threshold).

It is easy to see that it is the nonzero MPR that allows for nonzero credit exposure from posting collateral. If we shrink the MPR δt to zero, the bottom row of the right-hand side of equation (16.10) degenerates to $[H_{\mathrm{b}}^{(e)}]^+$, which is equal to zero because $H_{\mathrm{b}}^{(e)} < 0$.

Figure 16.4 illustrates this behavior by showing two ranges of portfolio MTM value $V(t)$ at time point t, given a single realization of the portfolio value $V(t - \delta t)$ at the time point $t - \delta t$: The upper range results in exposure, while the lower range does not.

16.4.4   Simulating Collateralized Exposure

As we discussed earlier in this chapter, exposure distribution is usually obtained via the Monte Carlo simulation process. Simulating collateralized exposure has its own specifics, which we will now briefly outline.

Suppose that we want to simulate collateralized exposure on a fixed set of time points $\{t_k\}$ ($k = 1, 2, \ldots$), which we will call the *primary* time points. To be able to simulate collateralized exposure at time point t_k, we need to know the portfolio MTM value at two time points: the primary point t_k and the *look-back* point $t_k - \delta t$. The short-term time points can be densely spaced, and we might have already simulated trade values at $t_k - \delta t$ as at one of the previous primary time points. However, the interval between two adjacent time points typically increases with the simulation time. Very soon this interval becomes larger than the MPR δt, so that the inequality $t_{k-1} < t_k - \delta t$ holds for all k's above a certain value. Thus, to simulate collateralized exposure at a primary time point t_k, we need to include the look-back time point $t_k - \delta t$

FIGURE 16.5   Simulating the Collateralized Exposure

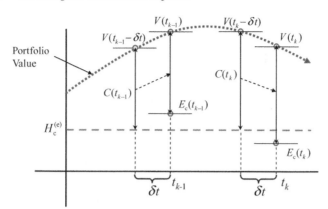

in the simulation set for trade MTM values, unless the look-back point coincides with one of the previous primary points. Trade values are simulated in the path-by-path manner at the extended time point set, which includes all the primary and look-back time points. Collateralized exposure is calculated only at the primary time points.

Figure 16.5 illustrates the process of simulating collateralized exposure. The horizontal dashed line shows the counterparty's effective threshold. The dotted curve shows one of the continuous portfolio value scenarios that happens to be above the effective counterparty threshold $H_c^{(e)}$. Two primary simulation time points are shown: t_{k-1} and t_k. To obtain collateralized exposure at these *two* time points, portfolio value needs to be simulated at *four* time points in this order: the look-back point $t_{k-1} - \delta t$, the primary point t_{k-1}, the look-back point $t_k - \delta t$, and the primary point t_k. These simulated portfolio values are shown as small circles on the scenario curve. Collateral available to the bank at the primary point is calculated as the difference between the portfolio value at the look-back point and the effective threshold, subject to a floor of zero. Then collateralized exposure is obtained by subtracting this collateral amount from the portfolio value at the primary time point, subject to a floor of zero. After following this procedure in Figure 16.5, we can observe that the collateralized exposure is above the threshold for t_{k-1} and is below the threshold for t_k. This is consistent with our analysis of equation (16.8): The portfolio value is rising from $t_{k-1} - \delta t$ to t_{k-1} and is falling from $t_k - \delta t$ to t_k.

While the full Monte Carlo approach for collateralized exposure is very flexible, its clear disadvantage is that for collateralized counterparties the simulation time is doubled due to inclusion of the look-back time points. The only way to avoid this doubling is to use an approximation. Pykhtin (2009) has developed an approximate semianalytical method for calculating collateralized expected exposure (EE) that does not require simulation of the trade MTM values at the look-back time points. Gibson (2005) has calculated collateralized EE analytically, without any exposure simulation at all, but the price he had to pay was the assumption that the portfolio MTM value at any time point is normally distributed with a known mean and standard deviation.

16.4.5   Collateralized Exposure Profiles

Collateralized exposure profiles look very different from the noncollateralized ones—even for exactly the same trades. In this subsection we show several examples of collateralized exposure profiles for the same two trades we have considered in Subsection 16.3.4. We consider margin agreements with two values of the threshold(s): 0.5 percent of the swap notional (the small threshold) and 2.0 percent of the swap notional (the large threshold).

16.4.5.1   Potential Future Exposure

Figure 16.6 shows collateralized PFE at the confidence level of 95 percent for the *forward* starting swap under two unilateral margin agreements that differ by the value of the effective threshold. To make the visual analysis easier, we used the same scale for both panels that represent different threshold values. Three curves on either panel correspond to three different values for the MPR: zero, two weeks (2W), and one month (1M).

The PFE profiles in Figure 16.6 start rising quickly, but come to a plateau soon after they cross the threshold. The profile for zero MPR stays exactly at the threshold. The amount by which the other two curves exceed the threshold is nearly the same for both values of the threshold. The one-month curve is always above the two-week curve.

We can understand this behavior by realizing that, unless the threshold is extremely high, the PFE is determined by the states of the world where the bank receives collateral. Exposure for these scenarios is given by the top line of the right-hand side of equation (16.8), which can be written as:

$$E_c^{(rec)}(t) = [H_c^{(e)} + \delta V(t - \delta t, t)]^+ \tag{16.11}$$

where we have introduced the notation $\delta V(t - \delta t, t) \equiv V(t) - V(t - \delta t)$ for the increment of the portfolio value over the MPR. The time interval δt for the portfolio value increment is the same for all t. Therefore, in the absence of cash flows, the tail of $\delta V(t - \delta t, t)$ does not change much with time, and the collateralized PFE profile is relatively flat. Since the distribution of $\delta V(t - \delta t, t)$ does not depend on the level of threshold, the amount by which the collateralized PFE profile exceeds the threshold does not depend on the threshold, either. The distribution of $\delta V(t - \delta t, t)$ is always wider for larger values of δt because of more uncertainty associated with larger times. Therefore, the larger is the assumed MPR, the higher above the threshold the collateralized PFE profile will be. Finally, in the limit of zero MPR (i.e., $\delta t = 0$), the increment of the portfolio value is zero, so that $E_c^{(rec)}(t) = H_c^{(e)}$ and the PFE is equal to the threshold.

Figure 16.7 shows collateralized PFE at the confidence level of 95 percent for the *immediately* starting swap under margin agreements with the same two values of the effective threshold. As before, the curves on either panel correspond to the MPR of zero, two weeks (2W), and one month (1M), and the same scale is used for both plots.

FIGURE 16.6 Collateralized PFE at 95 Percent for the Forward-Starting Swap for the Cases of: (a) Small Threshold and (b) Large Threshold

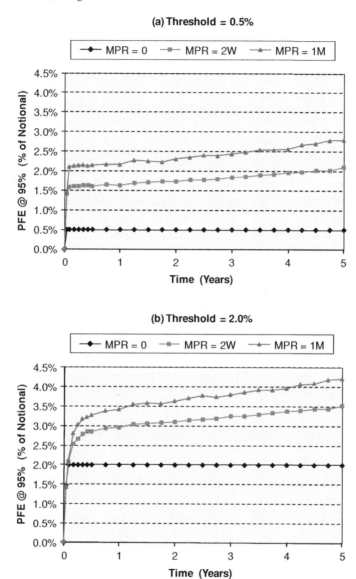

All the effects that we have discussed for the case of the forward-starting swap are still present in Figure 16.7. The key difference between Figures 16.6 and 16.7 is that, as the simulation time progresses, the PFE curves approach the threshold in a jumpy manner instead of staying on a plateau. It is not difficult to understand why this happens. The jumps occur at the swap payment dates. As we have discussed, when we considered the noncollateralized exposure profiles, the distribution of the swap MTM value (measured today) becomes narrower after each payment date. As a consequence,

FIGURE 16.7 Collateralized PFE at 95 Percent for the Immediately Starting Swap for the Cases of: (a) Small Threshold and (b) Large Threshold

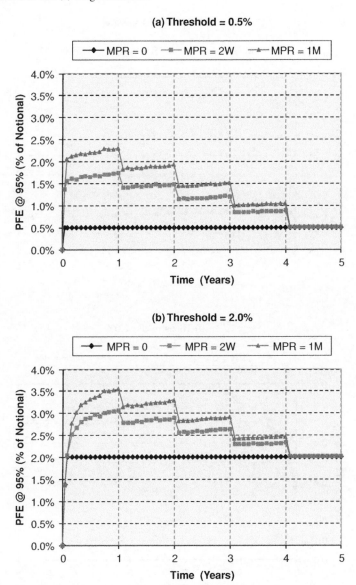

the width of the distribution of the increment of the swap value, $\delta V(t - \delta t, t)$, which determines the collateralized PFE, also jumps down after each cash flow.

16.4.5.2 Expected Exposure

Figure 16.8 shows collateralized EE for the *forward*-starting swap under margin agreements with the same two values of the counterparty's effective threshold as earlier.

FIGURE 16.8 Collateralized EE for the Forward-Starting Swap for the Cases of: (a) Small Threshold and (b) Large Threshold

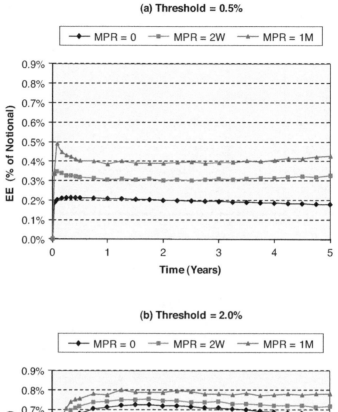

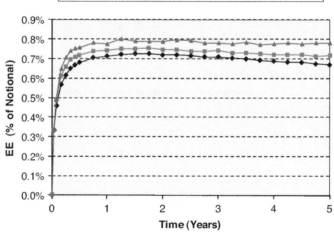

As before, the curves on each panel correspond to the MPR of zero, two weeks (2W), and one month (1M) and the same scale is used for both plots.

Similarly to the collateralized PFE profiles, the collateralized EE profiles in Figure 16.8 start rising quickly, but come to a plateau. Another common feature is that the one-month curve is always above the two-week curve. However, there are two important features of collateralized EE profiles that are different from the collateralized PFE profiles of Figure 16.6:

- *In most cases, the plateau is below the counterparty's effective threshold.* In fact, for zero MPR, this is always the case. Indeed, collateralized EE is the simple average of all simulated collateralized exposure scenarios. When the MPR is zero, any collateralized exposure scenario is bounded by zero from below and by the threshold from above, so the average is also between zero and the threshold. For nonzero MPR, collateralized exposure can go above the threshold, but the excess over the threshold is determined by the portfolio value increment over the MPR, which cannot be very large due to the small magnitude of the MPR. Unless the threshold is very small or time zero portfolio MTM value is very large, the contribution from the scenarios above the threshold is not sufficient to bring the average above the threshold.
- *Including nonzero MPR in the model becomes less and less important as the magnitude of the counterparty's threshold increases.* Indeed, the difference between the collateralized EE profiles for margin agreements with nonzero MPR and zero MPR in Figure 16.9 becomes smaller as the counterparty's threshold becomes larger. This behavior is in striking contrast with the collateralized PFE profiles, where this difference did not change much as the threshold increased. This can be explained as follows: Collateralized expected exposure can be viewed as the sum of two expectations: one over the scenarios with zero collateral and one over the scenarios with positive collateral (i.e., the bank receives collateral). Exposure under collateral-receiving scenarios is given by equation (16.11), which we repeat here for the reader's convenience:

$$E_c^{(rec)}(t) = [H_c^{(e)} + \delta V(t - \delta t, t)]^+$$

When the counterparty's threshold $H_c^{(e)}$ is small in comparison to the range of potential changes of the portfolio MTM value over the MPR, the zero floor skews the average over all collateral-receiving scenarios upward, resulting in the EE contribution well above the threshold. As the threshold becomes larger, the effect of the zero floor on the average decreases. As the threshold becomes significantly larger than the standard deviation of $\delta V(t - \delta t, t)$, the effect of the zero floor can be practically neglected, and the average of the collateralized exposure over the collateral-receiving scenarios becomes approximately equal to the threshold plus the average increment of portfolio value. The latter term is often quite small, so that the contribution of the collateral-receiving scenarios to the collateralized EE is approximately equal to $H_c^{(e)}$ for large values of the threshold, which is precisely the contribution of the collateral-receiving scenarios in the zero-MPR case.

Figure 16.9 shows the collateralized EE for the immediately starting swap under the same margin agreements as stated earlier. All the effects that we have discussed for the case of the forward-starting swap are still present in Figure 16.9. The key difference between Figures 16.8 and 16.9 is the presence of jumps at the swap payment dates. We have already explained the nature of these jumps when we discussed the collateralized PFE profiles.

FIGURE 16.9 Collateralized EE for the Immediately Starting Swap for the Cases of: (a) Small Threshold and (b) Large Threshold

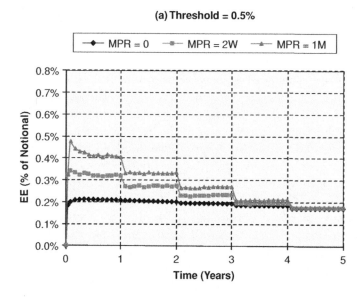

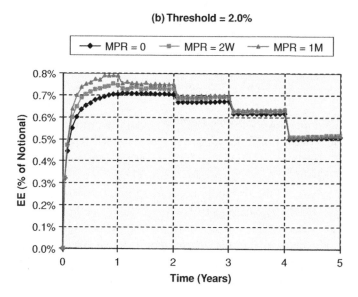

16.5 Pricing Counterparty Risk

16.5.1 Unilateral Pricing

Let us assume that the bank is default-risk-free. Then, when pricing transactions with a counterparty, the bank should require a risk premium to be compensated for the risk of the counterparty defaulting. The market value of this risk premium, defined for the entire portfolio of trades with the counterparty, is known as unilateral *credit valuation adjustment* (CVA).

A risk-neutral valuation framework is used for pricing CCR. Suppose that the counterparty defaults at a random time τ_c and T is the maturity of the longest trade in the counterparty portfolio. Then, the bank's economic loss $L_{u\text{-}l}$ arising from the counterparty's default and discounted to today is given by:

$$L_{u\text{-}l} = 1_{\{\tau_c \leq T\}}(1 - R_c)E_c(\tau_c)\frac{B(0)}{B(\tau_c)} \tag{16.12}$$

where $1_{\{A\}}$ is the indicator function that assumes value 1 if Boolean variable A is true and value 0 otherwise, $E_c(t)$ is the bank's exposure to the counterparty's default at time t, R_c is the counterparty recovery rate (i.e., the percentage of the bank's exposure to the counterparty that the bank will be able to recover in the event of the counterparty's default), and $B(t)$ is the value of the money market account at time t. One should keep in mind that the counterparty-level exposure $E_c(t)$ incorporates all netting and margin agreements between the bank and the counterparty, as discussed earlier.

Unilateral CVA is obtained by taking the risk-neutral expectation of the loss in equation (16.12). Under the assumption that the recovery rate is independent of the market factors and the time of default, this expectation can be written as:

$$\mathrm{CVA}_{u\text{-}l} = (1 - \bar{R}_c)\int_0^T \mathrm{EE}_c^*(t)d\mathrm{PD}_c(t) \tag{16.13}$$

where $\bar{R}_c$ is the expected counterparty recovery rate, $\mathrm{PD}_c(t)$ is the cumulative risk-neutral probability of the counterparty's default from today (time 0) to time t, estimated today, and $\mathrm{EE}_c^*(t)$ is the risk-neutral discounted expected exposure at time t, conditional on the counterparty defaulting at time t, given by:

$$\mathrm{EE}_c^*(t) = \mathbb{E}\left[\frac{B(0)}{B(t)}E_c(t)\bigg| \tau_c = t\right] \tag{16.14}$$

The term structure of the risk-neutral PDs is obtained from the credit default swap (CDS) spreads quoted in the market (see, for example, Schönbucher 2003).

In practice, the dependence between exposure and the counterparty's credit quality is often ignored, and conditioning on default in equation (16.14) is removed. Discounted EE is calculated for a set of simulation time points $\{t_k\}$ under the exposure simulation framework outlined earlier. Then, CVA is calculated by approximating the integral in equation (16.13) by a sum:

$$\mathrm{CVA}_{u\text{-}l} \approx (1 - \bar{R}_c)\sum_k \mathrm{EE}_c^*(t_k)\left[\mathrm{PD}_c(t_k) - \mathrm{PD}_c(t_{k-1})\right] \tag{16.15}$$

Since the exposure expectation in equation (16.15) is risk neutral, scenario models for all market risk factors should be arbitrage free. This is achieved by appropriate calibration of drifts. Moreover, risk factor volatilities should be calibrated to the available market prices of options on the risk factors.

For more details on unilateral CVA, see Brigo and Masetti (2005).

16.5.2   Bilateral Pricing

In reality, banks are not default risk free. Because of the bilateral nature of credit exposure, the bank and the counterparty will never agree on the fair price of CCR if they apply unilateral pricing, outlined earlier: Either of them will demand a risk premium from the other. The bilateral approach specifies a single quantity—known as bilateral CVA—that accounts both for the bank's loss caused by the counterparty's default and the counterparty's loss caused by the bank's default.

Bilateral loss from the bank's perspective is given by:

$$
\begin{aligned}
L_{b\text{-}l} = \; & 1_{\{\tau_c \leq T\}} 1_{\{\tau_c < \tau_b\}} (1 - R_c) E_c(\tau_c) \frac{B(0)}{B(\tau_c)} \\
& - 1_{\{\tau_b \leq T\}} 1_{\{\tau_b < \tau_c\}} (1 - R_b) E_b(\tau_b) \frac{B(0)}{B(\tau_b)}
\end{aligned}
\tag{16.16}
$$

where τ_b is the random time of default of the bank, $E_b(t)$ is the counterparty's exposure to the bank's default at time t, and R_b is the bank recovery rate (i.e., the percentage of the counterparty's exposure to the bank that the counterparty will be able to recover in the event of the bank's default).

The first term in equation (16.16) describes the bank's loss when the counterparty defaults, but the bank does not default. The second term describes the loss of the counterparty in the event of the bank's default and the counterparty's survival. From the bank's point of view, the counterparty's loss is a gain arising from the bank's option not to pay the counterparty when the bank defaults, so this term is subtracted from the bank's loss. Equation (16.16) is completely symmetrical: If we change the sign of the right-hand side, we will obtain the bilateral loss of the counterparty.

Bilateral CVA is obtained by taking the risk-neutral expectation of equation (16.16):

$$
\begin{aligned}
\text{CVA}_{b\text{-}l} = \; & (1 - \bar{R}_c) \int_0^T \text{EE}_c^*(t) \Pr[\tau_b > t | \tau_c = t] d\text{PD}_c(t) \\
& - (1 - \bar{R}_b) \int_0^T \text{EE}_b^*(t) \Pr[\tau_c > t | \tau_b = t] d\text{PD}_b(t)
\end{aligned}
\tag{16.17}
$$

where $\text{EE}_c^*(t)$ is the discounted expected exposure of the bank to the counterparty at time t, conditional on the counterparty defaulting at time t, defined in equation

(16.14), and $\mathrm{EE}_b^*(t)$ is the discounted expected exposure of the counterparty to the bank at time t, conditional on the bank defaulting at time t, defined as:

$$\mathrm{EE}_b^*(t) = \mathbb{E}\left[E_b(t)\frac{B_0}{B_t} \middle| \tau_b = t \right] \tag{16.18}$$

If the dependence between the credit exposure and the credit quality of the counterparty and of the bank can be ignored, the conditional expectations in equations (16.14) and (16.18) should be replaced with the unconditional ones. As expected, equation (16.17) is symmetrical between the bank and the counterparty, so that the bank and the counterparty will always agree on the price of CCR for their portfolio.

One can use a copula model to express the conditional probabilities in equation (16.17) as functions of the counterparty's and the bank's risk-neutral unconditional PDs. For example, if the normal copula model (see Li 2000) is used to describe the dependence between τ_c and τ_b, the conditional probabilities in equation (16.17) take this form:

$$\mathrm{Pr}[\tau_b > t | \tau_c = t] = 1 - \Phi\left(\frac{\Phi^{-1}[\mathrm{PD}_b(t)] - \rho\Phi^{-1}[\mathrm{PD}_c(t)]}{\sqrt{1 - \rho^2}} \right) \tag{16.19}$$

and

$$\mathrm{Pr}[\tau_c > t | \tau_b = t] = 1 - \Phi\left(\frac{\Phi^{-1}[\mathrm{PD}_c(t)] - \rho\Phi^{-1}[\mathrm{PD}_b(t)]}{\sqrt{1 - \rho^2}} \right) \tag{16.20}$$

where ρ is the normal copula correlation, $\Phi(\cdot)$ is the standard normal cumulative distribution function, and $\Phi^{-1}(\cdot)$ is its inverse.

For more details on bilateral CVA, see Gregory (2009).

16.5.3 Exposure Dependent on Counterparty's Credit Quality

So far we have ignored the fact that the expectation of the discounted exposure at time t in equation (16.14) is conditional on the counterparty's default occurring at time t. However, this conditioning is material when there is a significant dependence between the exposure and the counterparty's credit quality. This dependence may come from two sources:

1. *Wrong-way/right-way risk.* The risk is called wrong-way if exposure tends to increase when the counterparty credit quality worsens, and it is called right-way when exposure tends to decrease. Strictly speaking, wrong-way/right-way risk is always present, but it is often ignored to simplify exposure modeling. However, there are cases when wrong-way/right-way risk is too significant to be ignored (e.g., credit derivatives, equity derivatives, commodity trades with a producer of that

commodity, etc.). Wrong-way/right-way risk was first considered in Levin and Levy (1999) and Finger (2000).

2. *Exposure-limiting agreements that depend on the counterparty's credit quality.* One example of such agreements is a margin agreement with the threshold dependent on the counterparty's credit rating. Another example is an early termination agreement, under which the bank can terminate the trades with the counterparty when the counterparty's rating falls below a predefined level.

To account for any dependence between exposure and the counterparty's credit quality, one has to model them jointly. Let us characterize the counterparty's credit quality by a stochastic default intensity process $\lambda_c(t)$, without specifying its underlying dynamics.[2] Higher values of the intensity correspond to lower credit quality of the counterparty. The counterparty's PD can be defined via the default intensity process according to:

$$
PD_c(t) = 1 - \mathbb{E}\left[\exp\left(-\int_0^t \lambda_c(s)ds\right)\right]
\tag{16.21}
$$

We can use the intensity process to express the expectation conditional on default at time t in equation (16.14) via unconditional expectations:

$$
EE_c^*(t) = \frac{1}{PD_c'(t)}\mathbb{E}\left[\lambda_c(t)\exp\left(-\int_0^t \lambda_c(s)ds\right)\frac{B(0)}{B(t)}E_c(t)\right]
\tag{16.22}
$$

where $PD_c'(t)$ is the first derivative of $PD_c(t)$, which is related to the intensity process via:

$$
PD_c'(t) = \mathbb{E}\left[\lambda_c(t)\exp\left(-\int_0^t \lambda_c(s)ds\right)\right]
\tag{16.23}
$$

as one can verify by differentiating the right-hand side of equation (16.21) with respect to t.

The conditional discounted EE in equation (16.22) can be easily calculated during the joint simulation process. Suppose that the counterparty credit exposure, the money market account, and the counterparty default intensity processes are simulated jointly for M scenarios (paths) for a set of time points $t_1, t_2, \ldots, t_k$ and that t_0 is today's time. All possible dependence between the exposure and the counterparty's credit quality is accounted for in this simulation. Then, the conditional discounted EE for time point t_k can be calculated according to:

$$
\mathrm{EE}_c^*(t_k) = \frac{\dfrac{1}{M} \sum_{m=1}^{M} \lambda_c^{(m)}(t_k) \exp\left(-\sum_{j=1}^{k} \lambda_c^{(m)}(t_{j-1})(t_j - t_{j-1})\right) \dfrac{B(0)}{B^{(m)}(t_k)} E_c^{(m)}(t_k)}{\dfrac{1}{M} \sum_{m=1}^{M} \lambda_c^{(m)}(t_k) \exp\left(-\sum_{j=1}^{k} \lambda_c^{(m)}(t_{j-1})(t_j - t_{j-1})\right)}
$$

(16.24)

where $E_c^{(m)}(t_k)$, $B^{(m)}(t_k)$, and $\lambda_c^{(m)}(t_k)$ are the values of the exposure, money market account, and intensity, respectively, simulated for scenario m and time point t_k.

For more details on modeling right-way/wrong-way risk, see Hille, Ring, and Shimamoto (2005), Redon (2006), and Brigo and Pallavicini (2008).

16.6 Portfolio Loss and Economic Capital

Until now we have discussed modeling credit exposure and losses at the counterparty level. However, the distribution of the credit loss of the bank's entire trading book provides more complete information about the risk the bank is taking. Portfolio loss distribution is needed for such risk management tasks as calculation and allocation of economic capital (EC). For a comprehensive introduction to EC for CCR, see Picoult (2005).

Portfolio credit loss $L(T)$ for time horizon T can be expressed as the sum of the counterparty-level losses over all the counterparties of the bank:

$$
L(T) = \sum_{j} 1_{\{\tau_j \leq T\}} (1 - R_j) E_j(\tau_j) \frac{B_0}{B_{\tau_j}}
$$

(16.25)

where τ_j is the time of default of counterparty j, R_j is the recovery rate for counterparty j, and $E_j(t)$ is the bank's exposure at time t created by all the trades that the bank has with counterparty j. As before, the counterparty-level exposure incorporates all netting and margin agreements between the bank and the counterparty.

Economic capital $\mathrm{EC}_q(T)$ for time horizon T and confidence level q is given by:

$$
\mathrm{EC}_q(T) = Q_q[L(T)] - \mathbb{E}[L(T)]
$$

(16.26)

where $Q_q[X]$ is the quantile of random variable X at confidence level q; in risk management, this quantity is often referred to as value at risk (VaR). The distribution of portfolio loss $L(T)$ can be obtained from equation (16.25) via joint Monte Carlo simulation of trade values for the entire bank portfolio and of default times of individual counterparties.

However, the joint simulation process is very expensive computationally and is often replaced by a simplified approach, where simulation of counterparty defaults is completely separate from exposure simulation. The simplified approach is a two-stage process. During the first stage, exposure simulation is performed and a deterministic loan equivalent exposure (LEQ) is calculated from the exposure distribution for each counterparty. The second stage is a simulation of counterparty default events according to one of the credit risk portfolio models that are used for loan portfolios. Portfolio credit loss is calculated as:

$$L(T) = \sum_j 1_{\{\tau_j \leq T\}} (1 - R_j) \mathrm{LEQ}_j(T) \tag{16.27}$$

where $\mathrm{LEQ}_j(T)$ is the loan equivalent exposure of counterparty j for time horizon T.

Note that many loan portfolio models do not produce the time of default explicitly. Instead, they only distinguish between two events: "Default has happened prior to the horizon (i.e., $\tau_j \leq T$)" and "Default has not happened prior to the horizon (i.e., $\tau_j > T$)." Note also that, because the time of default is not known, discounting to the present is not applied in equation (16.27).

For an infinitely fine-grained portfolio with independent exposures, it has been shown (see Canabarro, Picoult, and Wilde 2003; Wilde 2005) that LEQ is given by the EE averaged from zero to T—this quantity is often referred to as expected positive exposure (EPE):

$$\mathrm{EPE}_j(T) \equiv \frac{1}{T} \int_0^T \mathrm{EE}_j(t)dt \tag{16.28}$$

If one uses LEQ given by equation (16.28) for a real portfolio, the EC will be understated because both exposure volatility and correlation between exposures are ignored. However, this understated EC can be used in defining a scaling parameter commonly known as *alpha*:

$$\alpha_q(T) = \frac{\mathrm{EC}_q^{(\mathrm{Real})}(T)}{\mathrm{EC}_q^{(\mathrm{EPE})}(T)} \tag{16.29}$$

where $\mathrm{EC}_q^{(\mathrm{Real})}(T)$ is the economic capital of the real portfolio with stochastic exposures, and $\mathrm{EC}_q^{(\mathrm{EPE})}(T)$ is the economic capital of the same portfolio with stochastic exposures replaced with EPE.

If alpha of a real portfolio can be estimated, its LEQ can be defined according to:

$$\mathrm{LEQ}_j(T) = \alpha_q(T)\mathrm{EPE}_j(T) \tag{16.30}$$

Because EC of a portfolio with deterministic exposures is a homogeneous function of the exposures, using LEQ defined in equation (16.30) will produce the correct $EC_q^{(Real)}(T)$. The caveat of this approach is that one has to run a joint simulation of trade values and counterparties' defaults to calculate alpha.

Several estimates of typical values of alpha for a large dealer portfolio and the time horizon $T = 1$ year are available. An ISDA survey (see ISDA-TBMA-LIBA 2003) has reported alpha calculated by four large banks for their actual portfolios to be in the 1.07 to 1.10 range. Theoretical estimates of alpha under a set of simplifying assumptions (see Canabarro et al. 2003 and Wilde 2005) are 1.1 when market-credit correlations are ignored, and 1.2 when they are not.

The LEQ framework just described has found its place in the regulatory capital calculations under Basel II: A slightly modified version of equation (16.30) is used to calculate exposure at default (EAD) under the Internal Models Method for CCR (see Basel Committee on Banking Supervision 2006). Basel II fixes alpha at 1.4, but it allows banks to calculate their own alphas, subject to the supervisory approval and a floor of 1.2.

Notes

1. ISDA is a global trade association that represents leading participants in the over-the-counter (OTC) derivatives industry.
2. For an overview of stochastic default intensity and the associated Cox process, see Chapter 5 in Schönbucher (2003).

References

Arvanitis, A., and J. Gregory. 2001. *Credit: The complete guide to pricing, hedging and risk management.* London: Risk Books.

Basel Committee on Banking Supervision. 2006. International convergence of capital measurement and capital standards: A revised framework. (June).

Brigo, D., and M. Masetti. 2005. Risk neutral pricing of counterparty credit risk. In *Counterparty credit risk modelling*, ed. M. Pykhtin. London: Risk Books.

Brigo, D., and A. Pallavicini. 2008. Counterparty risk and contingent CDS under correlation. *Risk* (February): 84–88.

Canabarro, E. 2010. *Counterparty credit risk.* London: Risk Books.

Canabarro, E., and D. Duffie. 2003. Measuring and marking counterparty risk. In *Asset/liability management for financial institutions*, ed. L. Tilman. Institutional Investor Books.

Canabarro, E., E. Picoult, and T. Wilde. 2003. Analysing counterparty risk. *Risk* (September): 117–122.

De Prisco, B., and D. Rosen. 2005. Modelling stochastic counterparty credit exposures for derivatives portfolios. In *Counterparty credit risk modelling*, ed. M. Pykhtin. London: Risk Books.

Finger, C. 2000. Toward a better estimation of wrong-way credit exposure. *Journal of Risk Finance* 1, no. 3 (Spring): 43–51.

Gibson, M. 2005. Measuring counterparty credit exposure to a margined counterparty. In *Counterparty credit risk modelling*, ed. M. Pykhtin. London: Risk Books.

Gregory, J. 2009. Being two-faced over counterparty credit risk. *Risk* (February): 86–90.

Gregory, J. 2010. *Counterparty credit risk.* Hoboken, NJ: John Wiley & Sons.

Hille, C., J. Ring, and H. Shimamoto. 2005. Modelling counterparty credit exposure for credit default swaps. *Risk* (May): 65–69.

ISDA-TBMA-LIBA. 2003. Counterparty risk treatment of OTC derivatives and securities. *Financing Transactions* (June).

Levin, R., and A. Levy. 1999. Wrong way exposure—Are firms underestimating their credit risk? *Risk* (July): 52–55.

Li, D. 2000. On default correlation: A copula approach. *Journal of Fixed Income* 9 (4): 43–54.

Picoult, E. 2005. Calculating and hedging exposure, credit value adjustment and economic capital for counterparty credit risk. In *Counterparty credit risk modelling*, ed. M. Pykhtin. London: Risk Books.

Pykhtin, M. 2005. *Counterparty credit risk modelling*. London: Risk Books.

Pykhtin, M. 2009. Modeling credit exposure for collateralized counterparties. *Journal of Credit Risk* 5, no. 4 (Winter): 3–27.

Pykhtin, M., and S. Zhu. 2007. A guide to modeling counterparty credit risk. *GARP Risk Review* (July/August): 16–22.

Redon, C. 2006. Wrong way risk modelling. *Risk* (April): 90–95.

Schönbucher, P. 2003. *Credit derivatives pricing models*. Hoboken, NJ: John Wiley & Sons.

Wilde, T. 2005. Analytic methods for portfolio counterparty risk. In *Counterparty credit risk modelling*, ed. M. Pykhtin. London: Risk Books.

PART V

Equity to Credit

CHAPTER 17

Pricing and Hedging with Equity-Credit Models

Benjamin Herzog

Société Générale

Julien Turc

Société Générale

Equity-credit models are pricing tools designed to value both equity and credit derivatives within a unified framework. These models are based on the assumption that any equity or credit derivative product can be hedged using common tradable assets. A typical equity-credit model identifies two major risks—mark-to-market and jump-to-default—and then hedges the former using stocks and the latter using short-term credit default swap (CDS) contracts. We start with a description of a new equity-credit model that provides enough flexibility to extract information from both the equity smile and the CDS curve. We then show how linking the model's parameters to financial ratios allows us to highlight discrepancies.

17.1 Introduction

Equity-credit models provide an interesting link between the credit and equity markets, using modern pricing theory and stochastic calculus. In more concrete terms, equity-credit models offer an interesting parametric form linking both markets. If ample historical and cross-sectional data were available, one could analyze relative value between credit and equity using purely statistical means, which would be the best solution of all. However, as the credit market is still young, estimating the

FIGURE 17.1   Equity-Credit Pricing Models

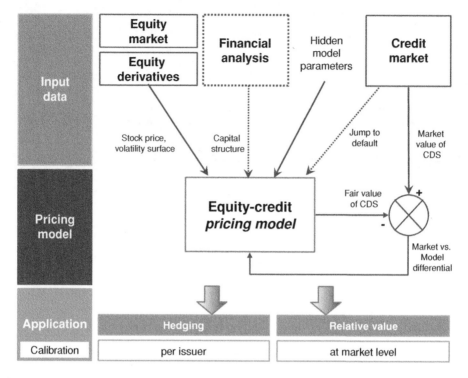

Source: SG Cross Asset Research.

credit-equity relationship across the capital structure and the credit cycle is a daunting if not impossible task. Parametric forms help greatly to compensate for the lack of data—provided they can tell the right story about market patterns and their changes over time.

Equity-credit models are usually based on equity prices and equity volatility data. Some models also consider companies' capital structures. Historical volatility is a natural input for these models, but implied volatility is a better indicator when available. Some models use all of this information to produce a theoretical CDS spread, while others, on the contrary, imply equity volatility from CDS spreads. We call a model that is calibrated to all markets at the same time a market model.

At the center of each equity-credit model considered here is a pricing model designed to value credit derivatives using equity data, equity implied volatility, possibly some additional financial data, and hidden model parameters that usually are very hard to estimate (see Figure 17.1). Such a pricing model can also be used to calculate equity volatility using credit spreads. Pricing models estimated through the equity market usually fail to correctly price credit spreads on average, let alone for each individual company. So, unless issuers are really confident about the theory that underlies the pricing model and about the real value of all its hidden parameters, such naive models are of little use in practice. In this chapter, we discuss two possible uses of equity-credit models, each of which demands a specific calibration to the credit market:

1. A *relative value model* that identifies CDSs (or other credit products) that trade richly or cheaply. Proper relative value models must be able to calibrate to the credit market on average, or possibly per sector. This is done by adjusting hidden parameters in the underlying pricing model.
2. A *market model* that finds the right hedge ratio for the capital structure. The value of various derivative products can be simulated against a change in the main dynamic factor(s) of the model. This provides a base-case scenario against which any relative value trade can be hedged. For hedging purposes, an equity-credit model must be fitted to all products involved in the transaction, at issuer level.

17.1.1 Relative Value Models

Firm value models, also known as structural models, are all derived from Robert Merton's seminal article in the *Journal of Finance* from 1973 (Merton 1973a). The main factor in Merton's model is the market value of a company's assets. Merton assumed that these assets could be traded on financial markets, and defined a default as an event whereby a company is worth less than the face value of its debt. Considering a company with a simple one-loan debt structure, Merton applied a Black-Scholes formula to value the loan as a risk-free loan minus a put option indexed on the assets.

Merton's approach gave birth to popular models and sometimes whole-scale risk solutions designed to estimate credit risk and price credit products. Evolutions from Merton's initial framework included adding jumps and stochastic volatility to enable the extreme extrapolation of the volatility smile required by the pricing of credit risk.

Firm value models tend to be most useful for issuers with wide spreads, traded equity, and options, but usually give poor results for investment-grade issuers with low gearing and relatively low equity implied volatility. In this part of the market, jump-to-default matters, and CDSs, which are viewed as far out-of-the-money options, are poorly extrapolated from the volatility smile.

17.1.2 Market Models

When it comes to hedging CDSs with shares, firm value models are of little use, at least on the investment-grade market. There are many other ways to approach the relationship between credit and equity, one of which relates short-term default probability (hazard rate) to the stock price in a parametric manner.

We can, for example, assume the hazard rate to be inversely proportional to the squared stock price, or proportional to squared debt per share. Such a model can be calibrated to five-year CDSs and to one-year at-the-money (ATM) equity implied volatility. We can show that a short CDS/short stock portfolio hedged using such a model would have been reasonably stable during the 2002 crisis through 2004.

17.2 Introducing the "Smile to Credit" Pricing Model

Smile to credit (S2C) is a capital structure arbitrage (CSA) model that can simultaneously price credit and equity derivatives. The originality of this model lies in the fact that it provides both a credit relative value framework and a comprehensive hedging tool at the same time.

The S2C model consists of three building blocks:

1. The *pricing model* provides a unified framework to price CDS curves and vanilla equity derivative products.
2. The *market model* is a version of the S2C model that is fitted to entire CDS curves and volatility smiles for each issuer. This model can be used to find the right hedge ratio for relative value trades involving various products indexed on the same issuer. Parameters estimated within the market model are also an essential component of the relative value process.
3. The *relative value model* identifies CDSs that trade richly or cheaply against the rest of the market, given additional model inputs like equity volatility and financial data.

The pricing kernel is itself composed of two building blocks:

1. A model for the issuer's stock price.
2. A model for default risk. In the S2C model, an issuer defaults whenever its stock price drops below a specific threshold. The model also considers a *hard default* scenario where the issuer suddenly and unexpectedly defaults on its debt.

17.2.1 Modeling a Company's Stock Price

Firm value models are usually based on a variable that is supposed to describe the market value of a company's assets. So we need to choose the random variable that best represents the asset value in the S2C model, and then define a stochastic process to simulate future possible scenarios for this variable.

The original Merton model reduces the whole debt structure to a single loan, and the issuer is supposed to default at loan maturity if its assets are worth less than the loan face value. In order to price credit curves, more recent firm value models assume that a default occurs whenever firm value falls below net debt or below a proportion of net debt.

This approach makes sense for companies with no traded equity and for issuers that are close to default, because in these cases the model can be used to price recovery rates on various tranches of the capital structure. However, this comes at a cost: Firm value models rely on a hidden parameter that is neither tradable nor observable, the asset value, and this raises serious technical problems. For companies with traded equity, it is much more convenient to use the share price as the underlying factor.

The S2C model is compatible with both approaches. It uses the stock price as the underlying variable and does not directly apply to companies with no traded equity. However, the relative value section of this article shows that the main parameters of the model can be regressed against financial data, which provides an indirect way to use the model for companies with no traded equity.

17.2.2 Using the Heston Model to Simulate Stock Dynamics

17.2.2.1 Modeling the Smile

The Heston model (Heston 1993) is an industry standard for pricing volatility surfaces in the equity option market. It makes stock price and volatility two correlated stochastic processes. The variance (volatility squared) is designed as a Cox-Ingersoll-Ross (CIR) process (Cox, Ingersoll, and Ross 1985). A CIR ensures that the variance of the stock price remains positive and reverts toward a long-term value.

$$\frac{dS_t}{S_t} = \mu dt + \sigma_t dW_t$$

$$d\sigma_t^2 = -a(\sigma_t^2 - \sigma_\infty^2)dt + \eta\sigma_t dZ_t, d\langle W, Z\rangle_t = \rho dt$$

where μ is the stock price's drift and σ_t its volatility. The initial value of the volatility is σ_0 while its long-term value is σ_∞. Finally, η stands for the volatility of volatility and ρ is the correlation between the Brownian motion of the stock's diffusion and that of volatility's diffusion.

The Heston model has several advantages:

- This model is the standard pricing tool for equity options and allows the capture of implied volatility information and simulation of the stock price in the most consensual way. Pricing default risk using such dynamics turns the equity volatility surface into credit fair value—hence our model's name: smile to credit.
- Use of a CIR process for the stock variance allows a consistent interpolation and extrapolation of the volatility term structure thanks to mean reversion. It is therefore possible to calibrate the Heston model using relatively short-term options and use it to value a full credit curve up to the 10-year maturity.

17.2.2.2 A Technical Remark

The Heston model is a stochastic volatility model, and as such involves complex and time-consuming numerical techniques when it comes to pricing barrier options. To avoid these problems, we use a projection of the Heston model into a *local volatility* model:

$$\frac{dS_t}{S_t} = \mu dt + \sigma\,(S_t,\,t)\,dW_t$$

where *local volatility* designates the equity's short-term volatility and is a function of share price and time. The formula for local volatility $\sigma(S,\,t)$ is provided later in this chapter in the appendix; see Gatheral (2004) for more details.

The S2C model therefore remains a traditional one-factor model for the stock price, but considers a change in volatility when the stock price moves. Typically, local volatility increases when the equity goes down, and Black-Scholes volatility increases sharply for out-of-the-money put options.

The projection of the stochastic volatility Heston model into a one-factor local volatility model remains valid as long as the correlation between stock and volatility is highly negative. The projection is a first-order approximation that does not address the issue of convexity in the smile. The parameter that determines convexity in the Heston model is the volatility of volatility, σ. Please refer to the appendix for more details.

So the projected model depends on three parameters only:

1. Short-term volatility σ_0.
2. Long-term volatility σ_∞.
3. $\rho\eta$, the product of stock-volatility correlation and volatility of volatility.

Note that mean-reversion speed is considered an exogenous variable, set to a corresponding half-life of one year.

17.2.3   Modeling Default Risk

Default risk is considered in two different manners in the S2C model. A company can default abruptly (hard default or jump to default), for example when specific negative news come up. Or it can default more progressively (soft default) as its situation deteriorates over time (see Figure 17.2).

While soft default risk can be estimated by evaluating the probability that the stock price will drop below a predefined default threshold, hard default risk requires the addition of jumps to our stochastic process.

17.2.3.1   Hard Default

In order to include jump-to-default risk, we allow our stock price to jump to zero. This means adding a jump component J to our stochastic process:

$$\frac{dS_t}{S_t} = \mu dt + \sigma_t dW_t - dJ_t,\; E[dJ_t] = \lambda dt$$

FIGURE 17.2 Different Default and Survival Scenarios for the Stock Price

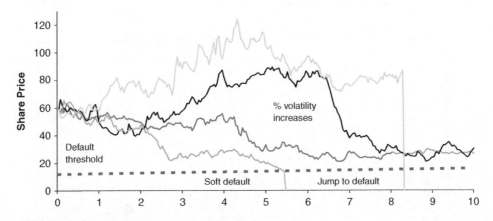

Source: SG Cross Asset Research.

At any point in time, the model assumes that there is a constant hazard rate λ. This hazard rate is supposed to be constant over time. When a jump to default occurs, shares lose all of their value and CDS protection is exercised.

If we view hard default as an extreme version of soft default, then a CDS may be seen as a far out-of-the-money option, which could then be extrapolated out of the volatility smile. However, the model then explains the whole Black-Scholes volatility smile through default risk. This is questionable, and in practice the model tends to be highly sensitive to fluctuations in the volatility smile.

The S2C model estimates jump to default directly from one-year CDS quotes. This approach is more realistic in our view, as it does not try to gain jump-to-default information from equity derivatives. Then, based on the hard-default risk estimated from the one-year CDS, the S2C model prices the five-year CDS using equity volatility.

In practice, however, market spreads for one-year CDSs are closely correlated to five-year CDSs and clearly price more soft-default risk than actual jump to default. We show how to overcome this difficulty in Section 17.3.2 on relative value.

17.2.3.2 Soft Default

In the S2C model, an issuer can also default if its share price falls below a specific level. We define this default threshold ξ such that the issuer goes bankrupt as soon as its stock price S_t falls below $\xi \times S_0$. Soft default therefore depends on this parameter and on stock volatility.

The default threshold ξ is a key parameter that is quite difficult to estimate:

- It could be estimated statistically by looking at historical default events. If enough sector data were available, that would the best way to do so.
- It could also be estimated using balance sheet data. Similarly to traditional firm value models, this would relate default to the ratio between net debt and asset value.

FIGURE 17.3 Hard Default Is Estimated Using the One-Year CDS While Soft Default Is Estimated Using Equity Implied Volatility and the Five-Year CDS

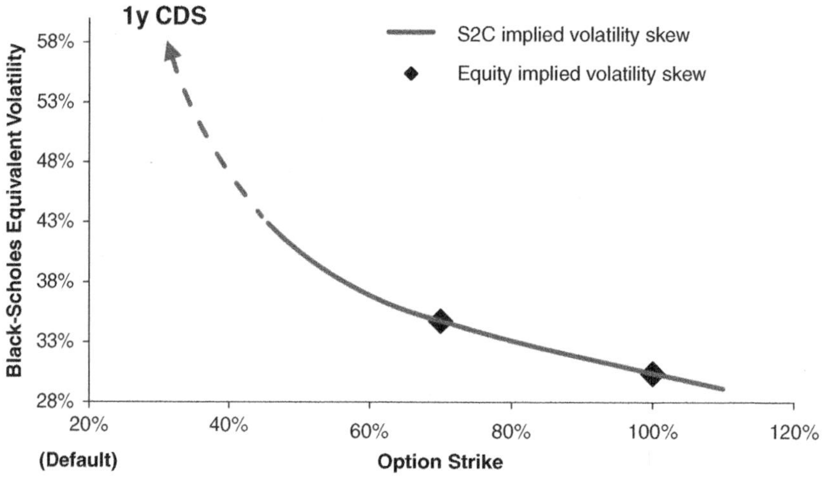

Source: SG Cross Asset Research.

However, as not enough data are available to perform a statistical analysis, and balance sheet data do not provide satisfactory results, we decided to calibrate this parameter to market prices along with other model parameters. The section on relative value shows how this parameter is linked to financial data in a second step.

To summarize, the one-year CDS is used to estimate jump-to-default risk (e.g., massive fraud risk), and the one- to five-year CDS curve is used to value soft-default risk (progressive credit deterioration) based on equity implied volatility information (see Figure 17.3).

17.3 A Market Model: Fitting the S2C Model

So far, we have described stock price dynamics in the S2C model and the way default risk is defined through jump to default and soft default. This section covers the estimation of the various parameters involved in the model. The market model version of the S2C model is designed to fit to the CDS curves and equity volatility smiles at the issuer level.

17.3.1 Putting the S2C Model Together

17.3.1.1 Initial Calibration

In the modeling of the Heston process, the drift μ is traditionally considered equal to the dividend-adjusted risk-free rate. The mean-reversion speed of the variance process a is set arbitrarily to a corresponding half-life of one year.

FIGURE 17.4 Overview of the Smile to Credit Model

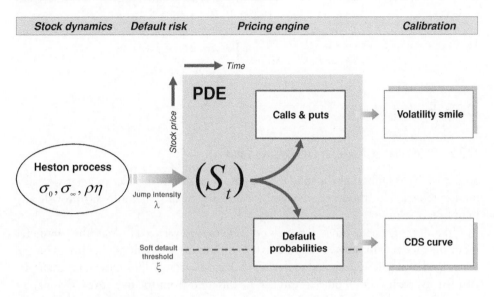

Source: SG Cross Asset Research.

We are left with three variance-specific parameters to determine for equity volatility:

1. The short-term volatility σ_0.
2. The long-term mean σ_∞.
3. The stock/volatility correlation $\rho\eta$.

And for the modeling of default risk, we need to determine (see Figure 17.4):

- The jump intensity λ that represents hard default.
- The default threshold ξ defined in the previous section, as a percentage of initial share price.

Our model therefore contains five degrees of freedom and must be calibrated to the price of at least five financial products. We calibrate it to:

- Two option prices (an ATM put and a 70 percent out-of-the-money one).
- Three CDS spreads (one-year, three-year, and five-year).

17.3.1.2 Fitting the S2C Model to CDS Curves

The S2C model has been initially calibrated to the shorter end of the CDS curve (one, three, and five years). We subsequently introduce a long-term debt growth rate (*dgr*) term structure that allows the model to be fitted to the longer end of the CDS curve:

$$\xi_t = \xi e^{\delta(t)}, \ \delta(t) = \begin{cases} r \times t, t < 5y \\ dgr(t), t > 5y \end{cases}$$

with r the risk-free rate.

17.3.2   Using the S2C Model for CDS Relative Value

So far, we have calibrated the model for each issuer in our data set in what we call a market model. This model can be used for hedging purposes but doesn't provide any kind of fair value.

In order to generate buy/sell signals on CDS curves, we need to stress the parameter set of the model. This new set of parameters will not perfectly fit market prices on the issuer level, but will be designed to fit the market on average. This means, for example, that the five-year CDS model spread can be different from the five-year CDS market spread for each issuer in the basket, but that average model and market spreads are close to each other.

17.3.2.1   Finding the Right Proxy for a Relative Value Model

In order to build our relative value model, we need to choose which parameters to stress and how to estimate them. The choice of the model parameter(s) that will be used is crucial as they will be the pivot point of our relative value analysis. Since we want to analyze the relative value of the CDS curve, it makes sense to use default-related parameters as proxies—the default threshold ξ and the jump intensity λ.

In order to perform our relative value analysis, we try to find rules of thumb to express these two default parameters in terms of company financial ratios:

- Intuitively, the default threshold ξ should be related to a relatively long-term indicator of creditworthiness. We have used the net debt/EBITDAR financial ratio, as the reflection of a company's profitability on a long-term horizon.
- In order to estimate the jump intensity, we use a different financial ratio that should be a better early indicator of short-term trouble: free cash flow/net debt.

Following our initial model calibration, the graphs in Figure 17.5 suggest several ways to estimate the default threshold ξ using the net debt/EBITDAR financial ratio and the jump intensity λ from the logarithm of the free cash flow/net debt ratio. We can, for example, use a second-order polynome for the default threshold and a loglinear regression for the jump intensity.

As shown in the jump intensity graph of Figure 17.5, it is usually convenient to split the regressions by sector, rating, or even spread level. In the following example, we

FIGURE 17.5 Estimating (a) Default Threshold and (b) Jump Intensity

(a) Default Threshold vs. Net Debt/EBITDAR

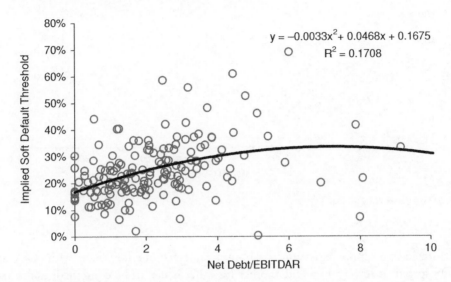

(b) Jump Intensity vs. FCF/Net Debt

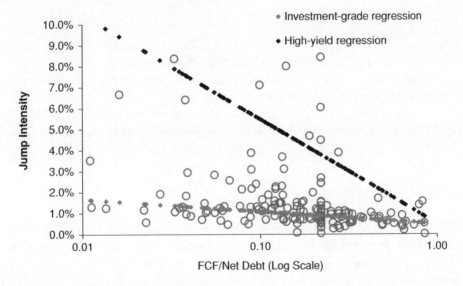

Source: SG Cross Asset Research.

FIGURE 17.6   Five-Year CDS Relative Value

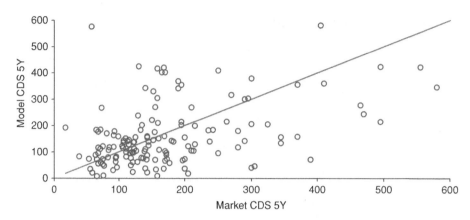

Source: SG Cross Asset Research.

performed two simple regressions for both parameters: one for issuers with one-year CDS spreads below 150 bp and another for other issuers. The combined results are shown in Figure 17.6.

17.3.2.2   A Flexible Framework

It is important to highlight the fact that based on the initial market model it is possible to generate many different versions of the relative value model.

For example, a sector or a rating split would allow a refinement of the relationships between default parameters and financial ratios.

It is also possible to drop the financial ratios and use historical data instead. That would integrate a different type of information, potentially generating different signals.

17.4   Conclusion

The S2C model is one that focuses mainly on market data (i.e., CDS spreads and the implied volatility surface). As such, it is mostly intended for trading credit derivatives against equity options. The market model is also designed to provide realistic sensitivities and can therefore provide theoretical deltas that can be used for short-term arbitrage between credit derivatives and stocks.

Although not its main purpose, we have shown that the S2C model could also be used as a fair value model that takes balance sheet data as inputs. The model can then be used to design credit long/short baskets. Finally, the model can be used to simulate dramatic changes in the balance sheet or value illiquid credit instruments on high-yield names.

Appendix: From Stochastic Volatility to Local Volatility

The Heston model is a popular tool in the equity markets, as option prices can be obtained in closed form. In the S2C model, however, we need to price a barrier option, which requires using a numerical solving technique. Although a Monte Carlo type of solving would do the job, we need a more efficient pricer as we will calibrate our model in five dimensions over large data sets. We use finite differences and solve the problem through its partial differential equation.

In order to make the Heston model compatible with such a framework, we need to turn the stochastic volatility into a local volatility. This means finding a function $\sigma(S_t, t)$ given a Heston process S_t, such that $dS_t = \mu S_t dt + \sigma(S_t, t)S_t dW_t$.

Gatheral (2004) proposes a simple way to do that. This comes at a cost, though, as we need to make an approximation that will reduce the flexibility of the model. Following Gatheral (2004), we note x_t the log-moneyness $\ln(S_t/K)$ and v_t the instantaneous variance σ_t^2.

Using these notations, the Heston SDE can be written as follows:

$$d\sigma_t^2 = -a(\sigma_t^2 - \sigma_\infty^2)dt + \rho\eta\left(dx_t + \frac{1}{2}\sigma_t^2 dt\right) + \sqrt{1 - \rho^2}\eta\sigma_t dW_t \qquad (17.1)$$

Taking the conditional expectation of the previous equation leads to an equation that can be solved (see Gatheral 2004), if not for the last term: $\sqrt{1 - \rho^2}\eta\sigma_t E[dW_t|x_T]$. Neglecting that last term comes down to assuming that either ρ is close to 100 percent or -100 percent, or the volatility of volatility η is small. Yet more importantly, if we remove the last term, we are left with a simpler equation where only $\rho\eta$ appears and the two parameters cannot be distinguished. This gives less flexibility to our model, but usually fits well with equity implied volatility smiles, which typically look more like skews.

Gatheral shows how to solve equation (17.1) following the approximation and derives a formula for the instantaneous variance v_t. We can then obtain the local variance $\sigma^2(S_t, t)$ as the conditional expectation of v_t.

Finally, we note $a' = a - \rho\eta/2$ and obtain:

$$\sigma^2(S_t, t) = \left(\sigma_0^2 - \frac{a}{a'}\sigma_\infty'^2\right)e^{-a't} + \frac{a}{a'}\sigma_\infty^2 + \frac{\rho\eta x_T}{(\sigma_0^2 - \sigma_\infty^2)\dfrac{1 - e^{-at}}{a} + \sigma_\infty^2 t}$$

$$\times\left[\frac{\sigma_0^2 - \sigma_\infty^2}{\rho\eta/2}\left(e^{-a't} - e^{-at}\right) + \sigma_\infty^2\frac{1 - e^{-a't}}{a'}\right] \qquad (17.2)$$

References

Cox, J. C., J. E. Ingersoll, and S. A. Ross. 1985. A theory of the term structure of interest rates. *Econometrica* 53.

Gatheral, J. 2004. *Case studies in financial modelling course notes*. Courant Institute of Mathematical Sciences.

Heston, S. 1993. A closed-form solution for options with stochastic volatility with applications to bond and currency options. *Review of Financial Studies*.

Merton, R. 1973a. On the pricing of corporate debt: The risk structure of interest rates. *Journal of Finance*.

CHAPTER 18

Unified Credit-Equity Modeling

Vadim Linetsky

McCormick School of Engineering and Applied Sciences, Northwestern University

Rafael Mendoza-Arriaga

McCombs School of Business, University of Texas at Austin

This chapter surveys a modeling framework for the unified valuation of corporate debt, credit, and equity derivatives. In this framework, the defaultable stock price is seen as the fundamental observable state variable. Corporate debt, credit, and equity derivatives on a given firm are seen as contingent claims on the defaultable stock. We model the defaultable stock price as a jump-to-default extended diffusion. In particular, we survey the jump-to-default extended constant elasticity of variance (JDCEV) model of Carr and Linetsky (2006) and the time-changed JDCEV model of Mendoza-Arriaga, Carr, and Linetsky (2009) with state-dependent jumps exhibiting leverage effect and stochastic volatility.

18.1 Introduction

In the celebrated Black-Scholes-Merton options pricing model, the firm's stock price is assumed to follow geometric Brownian motion, a strictly positive diffusion process with infinite lifetime. This assumption precludes the possibility of corporate bankruptcy rendering equity worthless. In contrast, the literature on credit risk is concerned with modeling bankruptcy and credit spreads. Until relatively recently, there was a disconnect between equity options pricing models that focus on modeling implied volatility smiles and ignore the possibility of default and models used to value corporate debt and credit derivatives that focus on default exclusively and ignore the information available in the equity options market.

553

As equity derivatives markets and credit derivatives markets have developed over the past decade, it has become increasingly clear to market participants that there are close linkages between credit derivatives, such as credit default swaps (CDSs), and equity options. It has been repeatedly observed in the markets that sharp stock price drops and accompanying increases in implied volatilities of stock options tend to happen contemporaneously with sharp increases in market credit spreads on corporate debt and credit default swaps. In particular, deep out-of-the-money puts derive most of their value from the positive probability of bankruptcy that will render equity worthless. Time and again, we have seen that when credit market participants become particularly concerned about default of a firm on its debt, transaction volumes in both the firm's CDSs and deep out-of-the-money puts on the firm's stock sharply increase. Moreover, implied volatility values extracted from deep out-of-the-money puts sharply increase to very high values. This market behavior is not surprising, as deep out-of-the-money puts can be used to hedge against corporate default, thus effectively blurring the line between credit derivatives and equity derivatives; see Carr and Wu (2009) for an empirical investigation of the connection between CDSs and deep out-of-the-money puts. In fact, this line is already blurred when one thinks of hybrid corporate securities such as convertible bonds that have both equity and credit features. This line is further blurred with the recent introduction of new hybrid derivatives, such as equity default swaps (EDSs).

Among recent empirical studies documenting linkages between equity volatility and credit spreads, Campbell and Taksler (2003) show that firm-level volatility can explain as much cross-sectional variation in bond yields as can credit ratings. Cremers et al. (2008) show that CDS spreads are positively correlated with both stock option implied volatility levels and the (negative) slope of the implied volatility as a function of moneyness. Hilscher (2008), using Merton's (1974) model, calculates a measure of implied volatility from corporate bond yield spreads and finds that this measure is highly significant when forecasting volatility. Carr and Wu (2009) show that stock return volatility and credit spreads have close links, specially at short maturities, due to positive comovements between the diffusion variance rate and the default arrival rate. Zhang, Zhou, and Zhu (2009) also examine the relationship between stock volatility and credit spreads, finding that equity volatility and a jump risk measure together explain 75 percent of the variation in credit spreads.

In light of this, a new generation of hybrid credit-equity models is needed allowing one to value and risk manage all securities related to a given firm, including equity and credit derivatives, in a unified fashion. On one hand, one might contemplate development of a comprehensive structural model that explicitly models the capital structure of a firm with its debt and equity as contingent claims on the value of the assets of the firm. However, such models would be exceedingly difficult to implement and calibrate in practice, as equity derivatives would be treated as compound options on the unobserved value of the assets of the firm. Practical considerations necessitate one to turn to reduced-form models instead.

The precursor of such models is Merton's (1976) model with a jump to default, where the stock of a firm evolves according to geometric Brownian motion punctuated with a single jump that takes the stock price from a positive value to zero (default or bankruptcy state). In Merton's original model the jump to default arrives according to a Poisson process with constant arrival rate (default intensity) independent of the firm's stock price. This is clearly not empirically realistic, as one would expect the probability of a jump to default to increase at lower stock prices and decrease at higher stock prices. It is thus natural to take the default intensity to be a decreasing function of the stock price. Indeed, it is in the convertible bonds pricing literature where such a specification for the default intensity first emerged. Davis and Lischka (2002), Andersen and Buffum (2003/2004) and Ayache, Forsyth, and Vetzal (2003) have all specified the default intensity as the negative power of the stock price. These references have treated the model numerically (e.g., by solving the pricing partial differential equation [PDE] by numerical methods). This specification of the default intensity as the negative power of the stock price has become quite popular for the pricing of convertible bonds and other hybrid products (e.g., Das and Sundaram 2007).

In contrast to the numerical approaches in the literature, recently Linetsky (2006) has solved the negative power intensity model in closed form, obtaining explicit analytical solutions for both corporate bonds and stock options in this model. Analysis of these solutions makes it clear that introducing a default intensity specified as the negative power of the stock price induces implied volatility skews in the stock options prices, with the *steepness of the skew controlled by the parameters of the default intensity*. We call this model *jump-to-default extended Black-Scholes*. While this model establishes a link between the implied volatility of equity options and the probability of default, since the local diffusion volatility of the stock price process remains constant in this model, the probability of default explains *all* of the volatility skew in this model.

Carr and Linetsky (2006) relaxed the assumption of constant diffusion volatility and replaced it with the constant elasticity of variance (CEV) assumption, thus introducing a *jump-to-default extended CEV (JDCEV) model*. The stock price follows a diffusion process with the CEV local diffusion volatility punctuated by a jump to default (jump to zero that renders the stock worthless). The arrival rate of default is specified to be an affine function of the local CEV variance. Since the CEV volatility is a negative power of the stock price, the JDCEV default intensity is also a negative power of the stock price (plus a constant or a deterministic function of time independent of the stock price). Carr and Linetsky solved the JDCEV model in closed form by exploiting a close connection of the CEV process to Bessel processes. Part of the implied volatility skew in the JDCEV options prices is explained by the leverage effect in the CEV volatility controlled by the CEV elasticity parameter, while part of the skew is explained by the probability of default controlled by the parameters in the default intensity specification. Vidal-Nunes (2009) has derived analytical approximations for American-style options in the JDCEV model. Le (2007) has conducted an empirical investigation of the JDCEV model. The JDCEV model has recently been applied to the pricing of equity default swaps (EDS) by Mendoza-Arriaga and Linetsky (2009), who solve the first passage time problem for the JDCEV process through a lower positive barrier, investigate the term structure of EDS spreads as a function of the EDS triggering barrier, and recover the JDCEV CDS spreads in the limiting case of the default barrier at the zero stock value. Related literature on EDS and other hybrid credit-equity derivatives includes Albanese and Chen (2005), Atlan and Leblanc (2005, 2006), Campi and Sbuelz (2005), and Campi, Polbennikov, and Sbuelz (2009).

Carr and Linetsky (2006) also present a general framework for *jump-to-default extended diffusion* models with general local volatility $\sigma(S, t)$ and default intensity $\lambda(S, t)$ functions. This framework introduces the possibility of bankruptcy in the one-dimensional diffusion model with local volatility taken to be a function of the stock price and time. Carr and Madan (2010) conduct further mathematical and empirical analysis of this modeling framework. In particular, they estimate the model jointly on CDS and equity options data. Bielecki et al. (2009) study convertible bonds and more general convertible securities in the jump-to-default extended diffusion framework.

Limitations of the jump-to-default extended diffusion framework are the absence of jumps in the stock price other than the single jump to default and the absence of an independent stochastic volatility component. A class of jump-to-default extended stochastic volatility models introduces stochastic volatility both into the instantaneous diffusion volatility, as well as into the default intensity. Carr and Wu (2008a, 2008b) propose and empirically test an affine model that is a jump-to-default extension of Heston's stochastic volatility model. The stock price follows an affine process with Cox-Ingersoll-Ross (CIR) stochastic volatility correlated with the stock price process punctuated by a jump to default. The default intensity is taken to be an affine function of the instantaneous stock price variance, as well as an additional default intensity factor also modeled by a CIR process. The model thus has three stochastic factors: the stock price, stochastic volatility, and the default intensity factor. Since the model is in the affine class, its characteristic function is known in closed form, and the pricing is accomplished by Fourier inversion. Carr and Wu estimate the model jointly on CDS and equity options data. Kovalov and Linetsky (2008) study convertible bond pricing in a four-factor extension of Carr and Wu's model that also includes stochastic interest rates. They obtain analytical solutions for European-style derivatives and develop finite element methods for numerical solution of a nonlinear PDE arising in the penalty formulation of a differential game with conversion and call.

The limitations of the jump-to-default extended Heston model are the absence of jumps and the inability to introduce direct dependence of the local volatility on the stock price (such as in stochastic alpha, beta, rho [SABR]-type models) without destroying the affine structure of the model. Mendoza-Arriaga, Carr, and Linetksy (2009) introduce a far-reaching generalization of the JDCEV model that removes both of these limitations. They introduce both jumps and stochastic volatility into the JDCEV model via the mechanism of stochastic time changes and, at the same time, preserve analytical tractability. They introduce a rich class of hybrid credit-equity models with state-dependent jumps, local-stochastic volatility, and default intensity. When the time change is a Lévy subordinator, the stock price process exhibits jumps with state-dependent Lévy measure. When the time change is a time integral of an activity rate process, the stock price process has local-stochastic volatility and default intensity. When the time change process is a Lévy subordinator in turn time changed with a time integral of an activity rate process, the stock price process has state-dependent jumps, local-stochastic volatility, and default intensity. Mendoza-Arriaga et al. (2009) develop analytical approaches to the pricing of credit and equity derivatives in this class of models based on the Laplace transform inversion and the spectral expansion approach.

The rest of this survey is organized as follows. In Section 18.2 we present a survey of the jump-to-default extended diffusion modeling framework, following Carr and Linetsky (2006) and Mendoza-Arriaga and Linetsky (2009). In Section 18.3 we present a survey of the JDCEV model of Carr and Linetsky (2006). In Section 18.4 we present a survey of the time-changed JDCEV model of Mendoza-Arriaga et al. (2009) with state-dependent jumps, stochastic volatility, and default.

18.2 Jump-to-Default Extended Diffusions (JDEDs)

18.2.1 The Modeling Framework

We start with a probability space given by $(\Omega, \mathcal{G}, \mathbb{Q})$ carrying a standard Brownian motion $\{B_t, t \geq 0\}$ and an exponential random variable $e \sim Exp(1)$ with unit parameter independent of B_t. We assume frictionless markets, no arbitrage, and take an equivalent martingale measure (EMM) $\mathbb{Q}$ as given. We model the *predefault* stock dynamics under the EMM as a time-inhomogeneous diffusion process $\{S_t, t \geq 0\}$ solving a stochastic differential equation (SDE):

$$dS_t = [r(t) - q(t) + h(S_t, t)]S_t dt + \sigma(S_t, t)S_t dB_t, \quad S_0 = S > 0 \qquad (18.1)$$

where $r(t) \geq 0$, $q(t) \geq 0$ are the time-dependent risk-free interest rate and time-dependent dividend yield (assumed to be deterministic functions of time), respectively. The time- and state-dependent functions $\sigma(S_t, t) > 0$ and $h(S_t, t) \geq 0$ are the volatility and default intensity, respectively. For simplicity, we assume that $r(t)$ and $q(t)$ are continuously differentiable in time on $[0, \infty)$ and that $\sigma(S_t, t)$ and $h(S_t, t)$ are continuously differentiable in the stock price and time on $(0, \infty) \times [0, \infty)$. In addition, we also assume that $\sigma(S_t, t)$ and $h(S_t, t)$ remain uniformly bounded as $S \to \infty$. Consequently, the process S does not explode to infinity. However, we do not impose any restriction as $S \to 0$. Therefore, the process may hit zero depending on the behavior of $\sigma(S_t, t)$ and $h(S_t, t)$ as $S \to 0$. If the process can hit zero in finite time, we kill the process at the first hitting time of zero, $T_0 = \inf\{t \geq 0 : S_t = 0\}$, and it is sent to a *cemetery state* Δ, where it remains forever. If zero is unattainable, S has infinite lifetime, and $T_0 = \infty$ by convention. We extend the state space for the process S to include the absorbing state Δ, by $E^\Delta = (0, \infty) \cup \{\Delta\}$. We denote by $\mathbb{F} = \{\mathcal{F}_t, t \geq 0\}$ the filtration generated by the process S. The term with $h(S_t, t)$ in the drift in equation (18.1) is needed to compensate for the jump to default to ensure the correct martingale dynamics of the gains process.

The jump-to-default event is modeled as the first jump time $\tilde{\zeta}$ of a doubly stochastic Poisson process (Cox process) with a jump-to-default *hazard process* $\{\Lambda_t, t \geq 0\}$. That is, $\tilde{\zeta}$ is the first time when the process Λ is greater than or equal to a random level $e \sim Exp(1)$:

$$\tilde{\zeta} = \inf\{t : \Lambda_t \geq e\} \tag{18.2}$$

If $h(S, t)$ remains bounded as $S \to 0$, we define $\Lambda_t = \int_0^t h(S_u, u)du$. If the default intensity $h(S, t)$ explodes at T_0 (i.e., $h(S, t) \to \infty$ as $S \to 0$), we define Λ_t by:

$$\Lambda_t = \begin{cases} \int_0^t h(S_u, u)du, & t < T_0 \\ \infty, & t \geq T_0 \end{cases} \tag{18.3}$$

At time $\tilde{\zeta}$, the stock jumps to the cemetery (bankruptcy) state Δ, where it remains forever. The cemetery (default) state Δ can be identified with zero by setting $\Delta = 0$. We assume that absolute priority applies and equity holders do not receive any recovery in the event of default. Thus, the stock price subject to bankruptcy is a diffusion process $S^\Delta = \{S_t^\Delta, t \geq 0\}$ with the extended state space E^Δ. We call S_t^Δ the *defaultable stock process*. We notice that, in general, in this model default can happen either at time T_0 via diffusion to zero or at time $\tilde{\zeta}$ via a jump to default, whichever comes first. The time of default ζ (lifetime of the process S^Δ in the terminology of Markov processes) is then decomposed into a predictable and totally inaccessible part:

$$\zeta = T_0 \wedge \tilde{\zeta} \tag{18.4}$$

In our notation, $\{S_t, t \geq 0\}$ is the predefault stock price process [equation (18.1)], while $\{S_t^\Delta, t \geq 0\}$ is the defaultable stock price process, so that $S_t^\Delta = S_t$ for $t < \zeta$ and $S_t^\Delta = \Delta$ for all $t \geq \zeta$. We also notice that if $h(S, t) \to \infty$ as $S \to 0$, it is possible that the diffusion process S^Δ with killing at rate $h(S, t)$ never hits zero, while the process S [equation (18.1)] without killing can hit zero. Intuitively, as the jump-to-default intensity increases toward infinity as the process diffuses toward zero, the process will be almost surely killed through a jump to default from a positive value (will be sent to the cemetery state Δ from a positive value) before it has the opportunity to diffuse down to zero. In such a case, $\tilde{\zeta} < T_0, \zeta = \tilde{\zeta}$, and $S_{\zeta-}^\Delta > 0$ almost surely.

To keep track of how information is revealed over time, we introduce a default indicator process $\{D_t, t \geq 0\}$, $D_t = \mathbf{1}_{\{t \geq \zeta\}}$, a filtration $\mathbb{D} = \{\mathcal{D}_t, t \geq 0\}$ generated by D, and an enlarged filtration $\mathbb{G} = \{\mathcal{G}_t, t \geq 0\}$, $\mathcal{G}_t = \mathcal{F}_t \vee \mathcal{D}_t$ (recall that $\mathbb{F}$ is the filtration generated by the predefault process S).

If we identify the cemetery state $\Delta = 0$, then we can write the process for the stock price subject to bankruptcy in the form

$$dS_t^\Delta = S_t^\Delta((r(t) - q(t))dt + \sigma(S_{t-}^\Delta, t)dB_t - dM_t)$$

where the compensated default indicator process M_t is a martingale,

$$M_t = D_t - \int_0^{t \wedge \zeta} h(S_u, u) du$$

where $\int_0^{\tau \wedge t} h(S_u, u) du$ is the $\mathbb{G}$-compensator of D_t. The default hazard rate needs to be added in the drift rate in the predefault dynamics [equation (18.1)] to compensate for the default jump and to ensure that the total expected rate of return to the stockholder is equal to the risk-free rate in the risk-neutral economy, and the discounted gains process is a martingale under the EMM $\mathbb{Q}$. The addition of the jump-to-default intensity to the drift rate was already discussed in Merton (1976) and more recently by Davis and Lischka (2002).

18.2.2 Unified Valuation of Corporate Debt, Credit, and Equity Derivatives

We view the stock price as the fundamental observable state variable and, within the framework of our reduced-form model, view all securities related to a given firm, such as corporate debt, credit derivatives, and equity derivatives, as contingent claims written on the stock price process (18.1). A fundamental building block for the valuation of contingent claims on defaultable stock is the (risk-neutral) *survival probability*, or the probability of no default prior to time T, conditional on the information available at time $0 \le t < T$:

$$\mathbb{Q}(\zeta > T|\mathcal{G}_t) = \mathbf{1}_{\{\zeta > t\}} \mathbb{E}\left[\mathbf{1}_{\{\bar{\zeta} \wedge T_0 > T\}} |\mathcal{G}_t \right]$$

$$= \mathbf{1}_{\{\zeta > t\}} \mathbb{E}\left[\mathbf{1}_{\{\bar{\zeta} > T\}} \mathbf{1}_{\{T_0 > T\}} |\mathcal{G}_t \right] = \mathbf{1}_{\{\zeta > t\}} \mathbb{E}\left[e^{-\int_t^T h(S_u, u) du} \mathbf{1}_{\{T_0 > T\}} |\mathcal{F}_t \right]$$

$$(18.5)$$

where $\mathcal{G}_t = \mathcal{F}_t \vee \mathcal{D}_t$ is the enlarged filtration of the previous section. The last equality of equation (18.5) holds since $\mathbf{1}_{\{T_0 > T\}}$ is $\mathcal{F}_T$-measurable; see Bielecki and Rutkowski (2004, Corollary 5.1.1) and Jeanblanc, Yor, and Chesney (2009, Corollary 7.3.4.2).

The price of a recovery claim that pays a fixed recovery amount R at maturity T if default occurs by T is expressed in terms of the survival probability $\mathbb{Q}(\zeta > T|\mathcal{G}_t)$:

$$Re^{-\int_t^T r(u) du}[1 - \mathbb{Q}(\zeta > T|\mathcal{G}_t)] \tag{18.6}$$

Then the price of a defaultable zero coupon bond with unit face value and with recovery amount R $(0 \le R \le 1)$ paid at maturity T if default occurs by time T is given by:

$$Re^{-\int_t^T r(u) du}[1 - \mathbb{Q}(\zeta > T|\mathcal{G}_t)] + e^{-\int_t^T r(u) du} \mathbb{Q}(\zeta > T|\mathcal{G}_t) \tag{18.7}$$

A European contingent claim with maturity at time $T > 0$ and payoff $\Psi(S_T)$ at T, given no default by T, and no recovery if default occurs by T, is valued according to:

$$\mathbf{1}_{\{\zeta > t\}} e^{-\int_t^T r(u)du} \mathbb{E}\left[\Psi(S_T)\mathbf{1}_{\{\zeta > T\}}|\mathcal{G}_t\right]$$

$$= \mathbf{1}_{\{\zeta > t\}} e^{-\int_t^T r(u)du} \mathbb{E}\left[e^{-\int_0^T h(S_u,u)du}\Psi(S_T)\mathbf{1}_{\{T_0 > T\}}|\mathcal{F}_t\right] \qquad (18.8)$$

A recovery claim that pays a fixed recovery at the default time ζ, as opposed to at maturity, is valued according to:

$$\mathbf{1}_{\{\zeta > t\}}\mathbb{E}\left[e^{-\int_t^\zeta r(u)du}\mathbf{1}_{\{\zeta \leq T\}}|\mathcal{G}_t\right]$$

$$= \mathbf{1}_{\{\zeta > t\}} \int_t^T e^{-\int_t^u r(v)dv}\mathbb{E}\left[e^{-\int_t^u h(S_v,v)dv}h(S_u, u)\mathbf{1}_{\{T_0 > u\}}|\mathcal{F}_t\right]$$

$$+ \mathbf{1}_{\{\zeta > t\}}\mathbb{E}\left[e^{-\int_t^{T_0}\left(r(u)+h(S_u,u)\right)du}\mathbf{1}_{\{t < T_0 \leq T\}}|\mathcal{F}_t\right] \qquad (18.9)$$

This contingent claim models the CDS protection payoff.

18.2.3   Equity Options

A *European call option* with strike $K > 0$ with the payoff $\Psi(S_T) = (S_T - K)^+$ at expiration T has no recovery if the firm defaults. A *European put option* with strike $K > 0$ with the payoff $\Psi(S_T) = (K - S_T)^+$ can be decomposed into two parts: the put payoff $(K - S_T)^+\mathbf{1}_{\{\zeta > T\}}$, given no default by time T, and a recovery payment equal to the strike K at expiration in the event of default $\zeta \leq T$. Assuming no default by time $t \in [0, T)$, the pricing formulas for European-style call and put options take the form:

$$C(S_t, t; K, T) = e^{-\int_t^T r(u)du}\mathbb{E}\left[e^{-\int_t^T h(S_u,u)du}(S_T - K)^+\mathbf{1}_{\{T_0 > T\}}|\mathcal{F}_t\right] \qquad (18.10)$$

and

$$P(S_t, t; K, T) = P_0(S_t, t; K, T) + P_D(S_t, t; K, T) \qquad (18.11)$$

where

$$P_0(S_t, t; K, T) = e^{-\int_t^T r(u)du}\mathbb{E}\left[e^{-\int_t^T h(S_u,u)du}(K - S_T)^+\mathbf{1}_{\{T_0 > T\}}|\mathcal{F}_t\right] \qquad (18.12)$$

and

$$P_D(S_t, t; K, T) = Ke^{-\int_t^T r(u)du}[1 - \mathbb{Q}(\zeta > T|\mathcal{G}_t)] \qquad (18.13)$$

respectively. One notes that the put pricing formula (18.11) consists of two parts: the present value $P_0(S_T, t; K, T)$ of the put payoff conditional on no default given by equation (18.12) (this can be interpreted as the down-and-out put with the down-and-out barrier at zero), as well as the present value $P_D(S_T, t; K, T)$ of the cash payment equal to the strike K in the event of default given by equation (18.13). The recovery part of the put is a European-style default claim, a credit derivative that pays a fixed cash amount equal to the strike K at maturity T if and only if the underlying firm has defaulted by time $t < \zeta \leq T$. *Thus, the put option contains an embedded credit derivative.*

18.2.4 Equity Default Swaps

Equity default swaps (EDSs) are a class of hybrid credit-equity products that link credit default swaps (CDSs) to equity derivatives with barriers. An EDS is structured similarly to the CDS, with the transparency of the former based on the observable stock price. That is, an EDS delivers a protection payment to the EDS buyer at the time of the triggering event ζ_L, defined as the stock price decline below a prespecified lower triggering barrier level L. In exchange, the EDS buyer makes periodic premium payments at time intervals δ at the equity default swap rate ϱ up to the triggering event time ζ_L or the final maturity T, whichever comes first. If the triggering event occurs midperiod between the two premium payments, the buyer pays the accrued interest from the time of the last premium payment up to the time of the triggering event. The protection payment is the specified percentage $(1 - R)$ of the EDS notional amount $\mathcal{N}$ (by analogy with the CDS, here R is the recovery rate and $1 - R$ is the loss given default, or rather the loss given the triggering barrier crossing event, that the EDS seller pays to the EDS buyer). The valuation problem is to determine the swap rate ϱ so that the present value of the EDS contract is zero at the contract inception. This swap rate equates the present value of the protection payoff to the present value of the premium payments, including accrued interest up to the triggering event:

$$PV(Protection) = PV(Premium + Accrued\ Interest)$$

Mathematically, the problem of finding the arbitrage-free swap rate ϱ is reduced to investigating the first passage time ζ_L of a JDED process through a barrier level L. Since the stock price process evolves continuously except for possibly a single jump to zero (jump to default), the first passage time ζ_L of the stock price through a lower barrier $L > 0$ is the first time in which the predefault diffusion hits the barrier level L or the time of the jump to default $\bar{\zeta}$, whichever occurs first. That is, the triggering event time is given by $\zeta_L = T_L \wedge \bar{\zeta}$. Evidently, $\zeta_{L_1} \leq \zeta_{L_2}$ for $L_1 > L_2$ and, in particular,

$\zeta_L \le \zeta_0$ for $L > 0$. Thus, the CDS rate is the lower bound for EDS rates with positive triggering barriers.

Let N be the total number of premium payments, $\delta = T/N$ be the time between premium payments, and $t_i = i\delta$ with $i = 1, \ldots, N$ be ith periodic premium payment date. Then, the time zero value of the protection payoff is given by:

$$PV(Protection) = (1 - R) \cdot \mathbb{E}\left[e^{-\int_0^{\zeta_L} r(u)du} \mathbf{1}_{\{\zeta_L \le T\}} \right]$$

$$= (1 - R) \cdot \left(\int_0^T e^{-\int_0^u r(v)dv} \mathbb{E}_{0, S_0}\left[e^{-\int_0^{T_L} \left(r(u) + h(S_u, u) \right) du} \mathbf{1}_{\{T_L \le T\}} \right] \right.$$

$$\left. + \mathbb{E}_{0, S_0}\left[e^{-\int_0^u h(S_v, v)dv} h(S_u, u) \mathbf{1}_{\{T_L > u\}} \right] du \right)$$

The first term in parentheses is the present value of the payoff triggered by a jump to default from a positive stock price, if it occurs prior to maturity and prior to hitting zero via diffusion. The second term is the present value of the payoff if the stock price hits the barrier level L via diffusion, if it occurs prior to maturity and prior to the jump to default.

The present value of periodic premium payments up to ζ_L is given by:

$$PV(Premium) = \varrho \cdot \delta \sum_{i=1}^N e^{-\int_0^{t_i} r(u)du} \mathbb{E}_{0, S_0}\left[e^{-\int_0^{t_i} h(S_u, u)du} \mathbf{1}_{\{T_L \ge t_i\}} \right]$$

If the triggering event occurs between the two periodic payments dates t_i and t_{i+1} (i.e., $\zeta_L \in (t_i, t_{i+1})$), the EDS buyer pays the interest accrued since the previous payment date t_i up to the triggering event time ζ_L. The expression for the present value of the accrued interest is given in Mendoza-Arriaga and Linetsky (2009) and we do not reproduce it here.

To explicitly evaluate the protection and premium legs of the EDS contract requires one to solve the first passage time problem for the predefault diffusion process, as the first hitting time T_L enters these expressions. Mendoza-Arriaga and Linetsky (2009) obtain analytical solutions under the jump-to-default extended CEV process with time-homogeneous parameters by applying the eigenfunction expansion approach.

18.3 The Jump-to-Default Extended CEV Model (JDCEV)

To be consistent with the leverage effect and the implied volatility skew, in the CEV model the instantaneous volatility is specified as that of a constant elasticity of variance (CEV) process (see Cox (1975), Schroder (1989), Delbaen and Shirakawa (2002), Davydov and Linetsky (2001, 2003), Linetsky (2004c), Jeanblanc et al. (2009,

Chapter 6), and Mendoza and Linetsky (2010) for background on the CEV process):

$$\sigma(S, t) = a(t)S^\beta \qquad (18.14)$$

where $\beta < 0$ is the volatility elasticity parameter and $a(t) > 0$ is the time-dependent volatility scale parameter. To be consistent with the empirical evidence linking corporate bond yields and CDS spreads to equity volatility, the default intensity in the JDCEV model is specified as an affine function of the instantaneous variance of the underlying stock price:

$$h(S, t) = b(t) + c\,\sigma^2(S, t) = b(t) + c\,a^2(t)S^{2\beta} \qquad (18.15)$$

where $b(t) \geq 0$ is a deterministic nonnegative function of time and $c > 0$ is a positive constant parameter governing the sensitivity of h to σ^2. The functions $b(t)$ and $a(t)$ can be determined by reference to given term structures of credit spreads and at-the-money implied volatilities.

For $c \geq 1/2$, the SDE (18.1) with σ and h specified by (18.14)–(18.15) has a unique nonexploding solution. This solution is a diffusion process on $(0, \infty)$ where zero and infinity are both unattainable boundaries. For $c \in (0, 1/2)$, infinity is an unattainable (natural) boundary for all $\beta < 0$, while zero is an exit boundary for $\beta \in [c - 1/2, 0)$. For $c \in (0, 1/2)$ and $\beta < c - 1/2$, zero is a regular boundary, and we specify it as a killing boundary by adjoining a killing boundary condition. Thus, for $c \in (0, 1/2)$ the process S can hit zero and is sent to the cemetery state Δ at the first hitting time of zero, T_0. Note that for $c \geq 1/2$, $T_0 = \infty$ since zero is an unattainable boundary. Even though for $c \in (0, 1/2)$ the predefault process S can hit zero, since the intensity $h(S, t)$ goes to infinity as S goes to zero, zero is an unattainable boundary for the process S^Δ killed at the rate $h(S, t)$ ($\tilde\zeta < T_0$ a.s., and $\zeta = \tilde\zeta$ a.s.). Intuitively, on all sample paths in which the predefault stock price S diffuses down toward zero, the inverse relationship between h and S causes the process to be killed from a positive value before it can reach zero via diffusion. Consequently, the second term in the expression for the price of the recovery at default [equation (18.9)] vanishes identically in the JDCEV model.

To summarize, in the JDCEV model the defaultable stock is a (time-inhomogeneous) diffusion process $\{S_t^\Delta, t \geq 0\}$ with state space $E^\Delta = (0, \infty) \cup \{\Delta\}$, initial value $S_0 = x > 0$, diffusion coefficient $a(t)x^{\beta+1}$, drift $[r(t) - q(t) + b(t) + c\,a^2(t)x^{2\beta}]x$, and killing rate $h(x, t) = b(t) + c\,a^2(t)x^{2\beta}$. Predefault, the diffusion solves the JDCEV SDE:

$$dS_t = [r(t) - q(t) + b(t) + c\,a^2(t)X_t^{2\beta}]S_t dt + a(t)S_t^{\beta+1} dB_t, \quad S_0 = x \quad (18.16)$$

The defaultable stock price process is then $S_t^\Delta = X_t$ for all $t < \zeta$ and $S_t = \Delta$ for all $t \geq \zeta$.

Carr and Linetsky (2006) show that the JDCEV model is fully analytically tractable due to its close connection with the Bessel process; see Revuz and Yor

(1999, chap. 11); Borodin and Salminen (2002); Göing-Jaeschke and Yor (2003); and Jeanblanc et al. (2009, chap. 6) for background on Bessel processes.

Theorem 18.3.1 *Let* $\{S_t, t \geq 0\}$ *be the solution of the JDCEV SDE* (18.16). *Let* $\{R_t^{(v)}, t \geq 0\}$ *be a Bessel process of index* v *and started at* x, $BES^{(v)}(x)$. *Then, for* $c \geq 1/2$, *the process* (18.16) *can be represented as a rescaled and time-changed power of a Bessel process:*

$$\{S_t = e^{\int_0^t \alpha(u)du}(|\beta| R_{\tau(t)}^{(v)})^{\frac{1}{|\beta|}}, t \geq 0\} \tag{18.17}$$

where the deterministic time change is:

$$\tau(t) = \int_0^t a^2(u)e^{-2|\beta|\int_0^u \alpha(s)ds} du \tag{18.18}$$

and

$$v = \frac{c - 1/2}{|\beta|} \in \mathbb{R}, \quad R_0^{(v)} = x = \frac{1}{|\beta|} S^{|\beta|} > 0, \quad \alpha(t) = r(t) - q(t) + b(t) \tag{18.19}$$

For $c \in (0, 1/2)$ ($v < 0$), *the same representation holds before the first hitting time of zero:*

$$\{S_t = e^{\int_0^t \alpha(u)du}(|\beta| R_{\tau(t)}^{(v)})^{\frac{1}{|\beta|}}, 0 \leq t < T_0^S = \tau^{-1}(T_0^R)\} \tag{18.20}$$

where $T_0^S = \tau^{-1}(T_0^R)$ ($T_0^R = \tau(T_0^S)$) *is the first hitting time of zero for the process* S_t ($R_t^{(v)}$) *and* τ^{-1} *is the inverse function of the deterministic time change function* τ *(both processes are killed and sent to the cemetery state* Δ *at the first hitting time of zero).*

Using this reduction to Bessel processes, Carr and Linetsky (2006) show that the survival probability and European call and put options prices in the JDCEV model are expressed in closed form in terms of the noncentral chi-square distribution.

Lemma 18.3.1 *Let* X *be a* $\chi^2(\delta, \alpha)$ *random variable,* $v = \delta/2 - 1$, $p > -(v + 1)$, *and* $k > 0$. *The* pth *moment and truncated* pth *moments are given by:*

$$\mathcal{M}(p; \delta, \alpha) = E^{\chi^2(\delta,\alpha)}[X^p] = 2^p e^{-\frac{\alpha}{2}} \frac{\Gamma(p + v + 1)}{\Gamma(v + 1)} {}_1F_1(p + v + 1, v + 1, \alpha/2) \tag{18.21}$$

$$\Phi^+(p, k; \delta, \alpha) = E^{\chi^2(\delta,\alpha)}[X^p \mathbf{1}_{\{X>k\}}] = 2^p \sum_{n=0}^{\infty} e^{-\frac{\alpha}{2}} \left(\frac{\alpha}{2}\right)^n \frac{\Gamma(v + p + n + 1, k/2)}{n!\Gamma(v + n + 1)} \tag{18.22}$$

$$\Phi^-(p, k; \delta, \alpha) = E^{\chi^2(\delta,\alpha)}[X^p \mathbf{1}_{\{X \le k\}}] = 2^p \sum_{n=0}^{\infty} e^{-\frac{\alpha}{2}} \left(\frac{\alpha}{2}\right)^n \frac{\gamma(v + p + n + 1, k/2)}{n!\Gamma(v + n + 1)}$$

(18.23)

where $\Gamma(a)$ is the standard gamma function, $\gamma(a, x) = \int_0^x y^{a-1}e^{-y}dy$ is the incomplete gamma function, $\Gamma(a, x) = \Gamma(x) - \gamma(a, x)$ is the complementary incomplete gamma function, and:

$$_1F_1(a, b, x) = \sum_{n=0}^{\infty} \frac{(a)_n}{(b)_n} \frac{x^n}{n!}, \quad where \ (a)_0 = 1,$$

$$(a)_n = a(a + 1)\ldots(a + n - 1), n > 0$$

is the Kummer confluent hypergeometric function.

The JDCEV survival probability and call and put option pricing formulas are then expressed in terms of these moments and truncated moments of the noncentral chi-square distribution.

Theorem 18.3.2 *Let x and v be as defined in equation (18.19), and define $v_+ = v + 1/|\beta|$, $\delta_+ = 2(v_+ + 1)$ and $\tau = \tau(t, T) = \int_t^T a^2(u)e^{-2|\beta|\int_t^u \alpha(s)ds} du$. Assume that default has not happened by time $t \ge 0$; that is, $\zeta > t$, and $S_t = S > 0$.*
(i) The risk-neutral survival probability (18.5) is given by:

$$\mathbb{Q}(\zeta > T|\mathcal{G}_t) = Q(S, t; T) = e^{-\int_t^T b(u)du} \left(\frac{x^2}{\tau}\right)^{\frac{1}{2|\beta|}} \mathcal{M}\left(-\frac{1}{2|\beta|}; \delta_+, \frac{x^2}{\tau}\right)$$
(18.24)

(ii) The claim that pays one dollar at the time of jump to default ζ (first part of equation (18.9)) is given by:

$$\int_t^T e^{-\int_t^u [r(s)+b(s)]ds} \left\{ b(u) \left(\frac{x^2}{\tau(t, u)}\right)^{\frac{1}{2|\beta|}} \mathcal{M}\left(-\frac{1}{2|\beta|}; \delta_+, \frac{x^2}{\tau(t, u)}\right) \right.$$

$$\left. + ca^2(u)S^{2\beta}e^{-2|\beta|\int_t^u \alpha(s)ds} \left(\frac{x^2}{\tau(t, u)}\right)^{\frac{1}{2|\beta|}+1} \mathcal{M}\left(-\frac{1}{2|\beta|} - 1; \delta_+, \frac{x^2}{\tau(t, u)}\right) \right\} du$$

(18.25)

(The second part of equation (18.9) vanishes identically since the JDCEV process is killed by a jump to default before it has the opportunity to diffuse to zero.)
(iii) The call option price (18.10) is given by:

$$
C(S, t; K, T) = e^{-\int_t^T q(u)du} S\Phi^+\left(0, \frac{k^2}{\tau}; \delta_+, \frac{x^2}{\tau}\right)
$$

$$
- e^{-\int_t^T [r(u)+b(u)]du} K\left(\frac{x^2}{\tau}\right)^{\frac{1}{2|\beta|}} \Phi^+\left(-\frac{1}{2|\beta|}, \frac{k^2}{\tau}; \delta_+, \frac{x^2}{\tau}\right)
$$

$$(18.26)$$

where

$$
k = k(t, T) = \frac{1}{|\beta|} K^{|\beta|} e^{-|\beta|\int_t^T \alpha(u)du}
\tag{18.27}
$$

(iv) The price of the put payoff conditional on no default by time T [equation (18.12)] is given by:

$$
P_0(S, t; K, T) = e^{-\int_t^T [r(u)+b(u)]du} K\left(\frac{x^2}{\tau}\right)^{\frac{1}{2|\beta|}} \Phi^-\left(-\frac{1}{2|\beta|}, \frac{k^2}{\tau}; \delta_+, \frac{x^2}{\tau}\right)
$$

$$
- e^{-\int_t^T q(u)du} S\Phi^-\left(0, \frac{k^2}{\tau}; \delta_+, \frac{x^2}{\tau}\right)
$$

$$(18.28)$$

and the recovery part of the put option $P_D(S, t; K, T)$ is given by equation (18.13) with the survival probability (18.24).

Mendoza-Arriaga and Linetsky (2009) obtain analytical solutions for the first passage time problem and the EDS valuation problem for the JDCEV problem in the time-homogeneous case (i.e., assuming the parameters r, q, a, and b are time-independent). Vidal-Nunes (2009) obtains analytical approximations for American options in the JDCEV model.

Remark 18.3.1 *In the JDCEV model $\beta < 0$; if one sets $\beta = 0$ and specifies the default intensity by $h(S) = \alpha S^{-p}$, one obtains the jump-to-default extended Black-Scholes. This model has been solved analytically by Linetsky (2006) by different mathematical means from the solution to the JDCEV model of Carr and Linetsky (2006) surveyed here.*

18.4 Introducing Jumps and Stochastic Volatility via Time Changes

18.4.1 Time-Changing Jump-to-Default Extended Diffusions

In this section we survey credit-equity models with state-dependent jumps, local-stochastic volatility, and default intensity based on the time-changed jump-to-default extended diffusion framework developed by Mendoza-Arriaga, Carr, and Linetsky (2009). We start by defining the defaultable stock price dynamics under the EMM by:

$$S_t = \mathbf{1}_{\{t < \tau_d\}} e^{\rho t} X_{T_t} \equiv \begin{cases} e^{\rho t} X_{T_t}, & t < \tau_d \\ 0, & t \geq \tau_d \end{cases} \tag{18.29}$$

where $\{X_t, t \geq 0\}$ is a time-homogeneous diffusion starting from a positive value $X_0 = x > 0$ and solving the SDE:

$$dX_t = [\mu + h(X_t)]X_t \, dt + \sigma(X_t)X_t \, dB_t \tag{18.30}$$

where $\sigma(x)$ is the state-dependent instantaneous volatility, $\mu \in \mathbb{R}$ is a constant, and $h(x)$ is a function to be used as the killing rate in equation (18.32). In this section we restrict our attention to the time-homogeneous case. The functions $\sigma(x)$ and $h(x)$ are assumed Lipschitz continuous on $[\epsilon, \infty)$ for each $\epsilon > 0$, $\sigma(x) > 0$ on $(0, \infty)$, $h(x) \geq 0$ on $(0, \infty)$, and $\sigma(x)$ and $h(x)$ remain bounded as $x \to \infty$. We do not assume that $\sigma(x)$ and $h(x)$ remain bounded as $x \to 0$. Under these assumptions the process X does not explode to infinity, but, in general, may reach zero, depending on the behavior of $\sigma(x)$ and $h(x)$ as $x \to 0$. The SDE (18.30) has a unique solution up to the first hitting time of zero, $T_0 = \inf\{t \geq 0 : X_t = 0\}$. If the process can reach zero, we kill it at T_0 and send it to the cemetery state Δ, where it remains for all $t \geq T_0$ (zero is a *killing boundary*). If zero is an inaccessible boundary, we set $T_0 = \infty$ by convention. We call X the *background diffusion process*.

The process $\{T_t, t \geq 0\}$ is a random *time change* assumed independent of X. It is a right-continuous with left limits increasing process starting at zero, $T_0 = 0$, and with finite expectation, $\mathbb{E}[T_t] < \infty$ for every $t > 0$. We consider two important classes of time changes: *Lévy subordinators* (Lévy processes with positive jumps and nonnegative drift) that are employed to introduce jumps, and *absolutely continuous time changes*: $T_t = \int_0^t V_u \, du$ with a positive process $\{V_t, t \geq 0\}$ called the *activity rate* that are employed to introduce stochastic volatility. We also consider *composite time changes*:

$$T_t = T^1_{T^2_t} \tag{18.31}$$

by time changing a Lévy subordinator T^1_t with an absolutely continuous time change T^2_t.

The stopping time τ_d models the time of default. Let T_0 be the first time the diffusion X reaches zero. Let e be an exponential random variable with unit mean, $e \sim Exp(1)$, and independent of X and T. Define:

$$\zeta := \inf\{t \in [0, T_0] : \int_0^t h(X_u)du \geq e\} \qquad (18.32)$$

It can be interpreted as the first jump time of a doubly stochastic Poisson process with the state-dependent intensity $h(X_t)$ if it jumps before time T_0, or T_0 if there is no jump in $[0, T_0]$. At time ζ we kill the process X and send it to the cemetery state Δ, where it remains for all $t \geq \zeta$. The process X is thus a Markov process with killing with *lifetime* ζ.

After applying the time change T to the process X with lifetime ζ, the lifetime of the time changed process X_{T_t} is:

$$\tau_d := \inf\{t \geq 0 : T_t \geq \zeta\} \qquad (18.33)$$

While the process X_t is in the cemetery state for all $t \geq \zeta$, the time-changed process X_{T_t} is in the cemetery state for all times t such that $T_t \geq \zeta$ or, equivalently, $t \geq \tau_d$ with τ_d defined by equation (18.33). That is, τ_d defined by equation (18.33) is the first time the time-changed process X_{T_t} is in the cemetery state. We take τ_d to be the time of default. Since we assume that the stock becomes worthless in default, we set $S_t = 0$ for all $t \geq \tau_d$, so that $S_t = 1_{\{t < \tau_d\}} e^{\rho t} X_{T_t}$.

The *scaling factor* $e^{\rho t}$ with some constant $\rho \in \mathbb{R}$ is introduced in order to ensure that the discounted stock price process is a martingale under Q:

$$\mathbb{E}[S_t] < \infty \text{ for every } t \qquad (18.34)$$

and

$$\mathbb{E}[S_{t_2}|\mathcal{F}_{t_1}] = e^{(r-q)(t_2-t_1)} S_{t_1} \text{ for every } t_1 < t_2 \qquad (18.35)$$

where $r \geq 0$ is the risk-free interest rate and $q \geq 0$ is the dividend yield. The martingale condition (18.34)–(18.35) imposes some restrictions on the model parameters μ and ρ. Namely, if the time change T is a Lévy subordinator with Laplace exponent ϕ, then μ can be any value such that $\mathbb{E}[e^{\mu T_t}] < \infty$ and $\rho = r - q + \phi(-\mu)$. If T is an absolutely continuous time change or a composite time change, than $\mu = 0$ and $\rho = r - q$.

18.4.2 Time Changes

A *Lévy subordinator* $\{T_t, t \geq 0\}$ is a nondecreasing Lévy process with positive jumps and nonnegative drift with the Laplace transform:

$$\mathbb{E}[e^{-\lambda T_t}] = e^{-t\phi(\lambda)} \tag{18.36}$$

with the Laplace exponent given by the Lévy-Khintchine formula:

$$\phi(\lambda) = \gamma\lambda + \int_{(0,\infty)} (1 - e^{-\lambda s})v(ds) \tag{18.37}$$

with the Lévy measure $v(ds)$ satisfying $\int_{(0,\infty)}(s \wedge 1)v(ds) < \infty$, with nonnegative drift $\gamma \geq 0$, and the transition probability $\mathbb{Q}(T_t \in ds) = \pi_t(ds)$, $\int_{[0,\infty)} e^{-\lambda s}\pi_t(ds) = e^{-t\phi(\lambda)}$. The standard references on subordinators include Bertoin (1996, 1999) and Sato (1999); see also Geman, Madan, and Yor (2001) for finance applications. A subordinator starts at zero ($T_t = 0$ for $t = 0$), drifts at the constant nonnegative drift rate γ, and experiences positive jumps controlled by the Lévy measure $v(ds)$ (we exclude the trivial case of constant time changes with $v = 0$ and $\gamma > 0$). The Lévy measure v describes the arrival rates of jumps so that jumps of sizes in some Borel set A bounded away from zero occur according to a Poisson process with intensity $v(A) = \int_A v(ds)$. If $\int_{\mathbb{R}^+} v(ds) < \infty$, the subordinator is of compound Poisson type with the Poisson arrival rate $\alpha = \int_{\mathbb{R}^+} v(ds)$ and the jump size probability distribution $\alpha^{-1}v$. If the integral $\int_{\mathbb{R}^+} v(ds)$ is infinite, the subordinator is of infinite activity. Subordinators are processes of finite variation and, hence, the truncation of small jumps is not necessary in the Lévy-Khintchine formula (18.37).

An absolutely continuous time change $\{T_t, t \geq 0\}$ is defined as the time integral of an activity rate process. A key example is given by the CIR activity rate:

$$dV_t = \kappa(\theta - V_t)dt + \sigma_V\sqrt{V_t}dW_t$$

where the standard Brownian motion W is independent of the Brownian motion B driving the SDE (18.30), the activity rate process starts at some positive value $V_0 = v > 0$, $\kappa > 0$ is the rate of mean reversion, $\theta > 0$ is the long-run activity rate level, $\sigma_V > 0$ is the activity rate volatility, and it is assumed that the Feller condition is satisfied $2\kappa\theta \geq \sigma_V^2$ to ensure that the process never hits zero. Due to the Cox, Ingersoll, and Ross (1985) result giving the closed-form solution for the zero coupon bond in the CIR interest rate model, we have a closed-form expression for the Laplace transform of the time change:

$$\mathcal{L}_v(t, \lambda) = E_v[e^{-\lambda\int_0^t V_u du}] = A(t, \lambda)e^{-B(t,\lambda)v} \tag{18.38}$$

where $V_0 = v$ is the initial value of the activity rate process, $\varpi = \sqrt{2\sigma_V^2 \lambda + \kappa^2}$, and

$$A(t, \lambda) = \left(\frac{2\varpi e^{(\varpi + \kappa)t/2}}{(\varpi + \kappa)(e^{\varpi t} - 1) + 2\varpi} \right)^{\frac{2\kappa\theta}{\sigma_V^2}}, \quad B(t, \lambda) = \frac{2\lambda(e^{\varpi t} - 1)}{(\varpi + \kappa)(e^{\varpi t} - 1) + 2\varpi}$$

Carr et al. (2003) use the CIR activity rate process to time-change Lévy processes to introduce stochastic volatility in the popular Lévy models, such as the variance gamma process (VG), the normal inverse Gaussian process (NIG), and the Carr, Geman, Madan, Yor model (CGMY).

For the composite time change, $T_t = T_{T_t^2}^1$, where T_t^1 is a subordinator with Laplace exponent ϕ and T_t^2 is an absolutely continuous time change, by conditioning on T^2, the Laplace transform of the composite time change is:

$$\mathbb{E}[e^{-\lambda T_t}] = \mathbb{E}\left[\mathbb{E}\left[\exp\left(-\lambda T_{T_t^2}^1 \right) \Big| T_t^2 \right] \right] = \mathbb{E}[e^{-T_t^2 \phi(\lambda)}] = \mathcal{L}_z(t, \phi(\lambda)) \quad (18.39)$$

18.4.3   Pricing Corporate Debt, Credit, and Equity Derivatives

We begin with the (risk-neutral) survival probability. Conditioning on the time change, we have:

$$\mathbb{Q}(\tau_d > t) = \mathbb{Q}(\zeta > T_t) = \int_0^\infty \mathbb{Q}(\zeta > s)\pi_t(ds) = \int_0^\infty P_s(x, (0, \infty))\pi_t(ds)$$
$$(18.40)$$

where $P_t(x, (0, \infty)) = \mathbb{Q}(\zeta > t)$ is the survival probability for the diffusion X with lifetime ζ (transition probability for the Markov process X with lifetime ζ from the state $x > 0$ into $(0, \infty)$, $P_t(x, (0, \infty)) = 1 - P_t(x, \{\Delta\})$) and $\pi_t(ds)$ is the probability distribution of the time change T_t. If the survival probability for X and the distribution of the time change $\pi_t(ds)$ are known in closed form, we can obtain the survival probability by integration. The survival probability [equation (18.12)] of the defaultable stock price [equation (18.29)] can be interpreted as the survival probability up to a random time T_t of the background process X.

A European-style contingent claim with the payoff $\Psi(S_t)$ at maturity $t > 0$, given no default by time t and no recovery if default occurs, is valued by conditioning on the time change similar to the calculation for the survival probability:

$$e^{-rt}\mathbb{E}[\mathbf{1}_{\{\tau_d > t\}}\Psi(S_t)] = e^{-rt}\mathbb{E}[\mathbf{1}_{\{\zeta > T_t\}}\Psi(e^{\rho t} X_{T_t})]$$

$$= e^{-rt} \int_0^\infty \mathbb{E}\left[\mathbf{1}_{\{\zeta > s\}}\Psi(e^{\rho t} X_s) \right] \pi_t(ds) \quad (18.41)$$

In particular, for call and put options we have:

$$C(x; K, t) = e^{-rt}\mathbb{E}[(e^{\rho t}X_{T_t} - K)^+ \mathbf{1}_{\{\tau_d > t\}}]$$

$$= e^{-rt}\int_0^\infty \mathbb{E}[(e^{\rho t}X_s - K)^+ \mathbf{1}_{\{\zeta > s\}}]\pi_t(ds) \qquad (18.42)$$

and

$$P(x; K, t) = P_0(x; K, t) + P_D(x; K, t) \qquad (18.43)$$

where

$$P_0(x; K, t) = e^{-rt}\int_0^\infty \mathbb{E}[(K - e^{\rho t}X_s)^+ \mathbf{1}_{\{\zeta > s\}}]\pi_t(ds) \qquad (18.44)$$

and

$$P_D(x; K, t) = Ke^{-rt}[1 - \mathbb{Q}(\tau_d > t)] \qquad (18.45)$$

respectively.

Calculating expectations in the preceding expressions involves first computing the expectation $\mathbb{E}\left[\mathbf{1}_{\{\zeta > s\}} f(X_s)\right]$ for the background diffusion X and then integrating the result in time with the distribution of the time change T_t. For general Lévy subordinators and for the integral of the CIR process, the distributions are not available in closed form. Instead, their Laplace transforms are available [equations (18.36), (18.38), and (18.39)]. In principle, the distribution can be recovered by numerically inverting the Laplace transform. The second step is then to compute the integral in equations (18.40) and (18.41). Thus, even if we can determine the expectation $\mathbb{E}\left[\mathbf{1}_{\{\zeta > s\}} f(X_s)\right]$ for the background diffusion X in closed form, we still need to perform double numerical integration in order to compute equation (18.41) for the time-changed process.

Mendoza-Arriaga, Carr, and Linetsky (2009) propose two alternative approaches that avoid any need for Laplace inversion and numerical integration and are based on the resolvent operator and the spectral expansion, respectively. We now briefly summarize these two approaches that yield explicit analytical representations of the expectation operator:

$$\mathcal{P}_t f(x) = \mathbb{E}_x \left[\mathbf{1}_{\{\zeta > t\}} f(X_t)\right] \qquad (18.46)$$

associated with a one-dimensional diffusion X with lifetime ζ that are in the form suitable to perform time changes (the time t enters only through the exponentials).

Remark 18.4.1 *The two approaches presented in Sections 18.4.4 and 18.4.5 rely on properties of* one-dimensional time-homogeneous *diffusion processes. In particular, Section 18.4.5 requires that the semigroup $\{\mathcal{P}_t, t \geq 0\}$ of expectation operators associated with the diffusion is symmetric in the Hilbert space of functions on $(\ell, r) \subseteq \mathbb{R}$ square-integrable with the speed density of the diffusion process X.*

18.4.4 Valuation of Contingent Claims on Time-Changed Markov Processes: A Resolvent Operator Approach

We start by defining the *resolvent operator* $\mathcal{R}_s$ (e.g., Ethier and Kurtz 1986) as the Laplace transform of the expectation operator (18.46),

$$\mathcal{R}_s f(x) := \int_0^\infty e^{-st} \mathcal{P}_t f(x) dt \tag{18.47}$$

For one-dimensional diffusions, the resolvent operator can be represented as an integral operator (e.g., Borodin and Salminen 2002):

$$\mathcal{R}_s f(x) = \int_\ell^r f(y) G_s(x, y) dy = \frac{\phi_s(x)}{w_s} \int_\ell^x f(y) \psi_s(y) \mathrm{m}(y) dy$$

$$+ \frac{\psi_s(x)}{w_s} \int_x^r f(y) \phi_s(y) \mathrm{m}(y) dy \tag{18.48}$$

where the *resolvent kernel* or *Green's function* $G_s(x, y)$ is the Laplace transform of the transition probability density, $G_s(x, y) = \int_0^\infty e^{-st} p(t; x, y) dt$. It admits the following explicit representation:

$$G_s(x, y) = \frac{\mathrm{m}(y)}{w_s} \begin{cases} \psi_s(x)\phi_s(y), & x \leq y \\ \psi_s(y)\phi_s(x), & y \leq x \end{cases} \tag{18.49}$$

where the function $\mathrm{m}(x)$ is the *speed density* of the diffusion process X and is constructed from the diffusion and drift coefficients, $a(x)$ and $b(x)$ as follows; see Borodin and Salminen (2002, p.17):

$$\mathrm{m}(x) = \frac{2}{a^2(x)\mathfrak{s}(x)}, \quad \text{where } \mathfrak{s}(x) = \exp\left(-\int_{x_0}^x \frac{2b(y)}{a^2(y)} dy\right) \tag{18.50}$$

where $x_0 \in (\ell, r)$ is an arbitrary point in the state space (ℓ, r) of the 1D diffusion. When X is a predefault stock price process, the state space is $(0, \infty)$. The function $\mathfrak{s}(x)$ is called the *scale density* of the diffusion process X.

For $s > 0$, the functions $\psi_s(x)$ and $\phi_s(x)$ can be characterized as the unique (up to a multiplicative factor independent of x) solutions of the *Sturm-Liouville equation* associated with the infinitesimal generator $\mathcal{G}$ of the one-dimensional diffusion process,

$$\mathcal{G}u(x) = \frac{1}{2}a^2(x)\frac{d^2u}{dx^2}(x) + b(x)\frac{du}{dx}(x) - c(x)u(x) = s\,u(x) \qquad (18.51)$$

by first demanding that $\psi_s(x)$ is increasing in x and $\phi_s(x)$ is decreasing, and second, imposing boundary conditions at regular boundary points. The functions $\psi_s(x)$ and $\phi_s(x)$ are called *fundamental solutions* of the Sturm-Liouville equation (18.51). Their *Wronskian* defined with respect to the scale density is independent of x:

$$w_s = \frac{1}{\mathfrak{s}(x)}(\psi_s'(x)\phi_s(x) - \psi_s(x)\phi_s'(x)) \qquad (18.52)$$

In equation (18.48) we interchanged the Laplace transform integral in t and the expectation integral in y. This interchange is allowed by Fubini's theorem if and only if the function f is such that

$$\int_\ell^x |f(y)\psi_s(y)|\mathfrak{m}(y)dy < \infty \text{ and } \int_x^r |f(y)\phi_s(y)|\mathfrak{m}(y)dy < \infty \ \forall \ x \in (\ell, r),$$

$$s > 0 \qquad (18.53)$$

For f satisfying these integrability conditions, we can then recover the expectation (18.46) by first computing the resolvent operator (18.48) and then inverting the Laplace transform via the Bromwich Laplace transform inversion formula; see Pazy (1983) for the Laplace inversion formula for operator semigroups:

$$\mathcal{P}_t f(x) = \mathbb{E}_x\left[\mathbf{1}_{\{\zeta>t\}}f(X_t)\right] = \frac{1}{2\pi i}\int_{\varepsilon-i\infty}^{\varepsilon+i\infty} e^{st}\mathcal{R}_s f(x)ds \qquad (18.54)$$

A crucial observation is that in the representation (18.54) *time only enters through the exponential e^{st}*. We can thus write:

$$\mathbb{E}[\mathbf{1}_{\{\zeta>T_t\}}f(X_{T_t})] = \frac{1}{2\pi i}\int_{\varepsilon-i\infty}^{\varepsilon+i\infty}\mathbb{E}[e^{sT_t}]\mathcal{R}_s f(x)ds = \frac{1}{2\pi i}\int_{\varepsilon-i\infty}^{\varepsilon+i\infty}\mathcal{L}(t, -s)\mathcal{R}_s f(x)ds$$

$$(18.55)$$

where $\mathcal{L}(t, \lambda) = \mathbb{E}[e^{-\lambda T_t}]$ is the Laplace transform of the time change (here we require that $\mathbb{E}[e^{\varepsilon T_t}] = \mathcal{L}(t, -\varepsilon) < \infty$). We notice that this result does not require the knowledge of the transition probability measure of the time change, and only requires the knowledge of the Laplace transform of the time change (e.g., equations (18.36), (18.38), and (18.39)). Furthermore, it does not require the knowledge of the expectation $\mathbb{E}[\mathbf{1}_{\{\zeta>t\}}f(X_t)]$ for the background process X, and only requires the knowledge of the resolvent $\mathcal{R}_s f(x)$ given by equation (18.48). The Laplace transform inversion in (18.55) can be performed by appealing to the Cauchy residue theorem to calculate the Bromwich integral in the complex plane.

18.4.5   Valuation of Contingent Claims on Time-Changed Markov Processes: A Spectral Expansion Approach

We observe that the transition probability density $p(t; x, y)$ of a one-dimensional diffusion X can be obtained from the Green's function by inverting the Laplace transform. The Laplace inversion yields the *spectral representation of the transition density* $p(t; x, y)$ originally obtained by McKean (1956); see also Ito and McKean (1974, sect. 4.11); Wong (1964); Karlin and Taylor (1981); and Linetsky (2004c, 2007) for applications in finance.

Define the inner product $(f, g) := \int_{\ell}^{r} f(x)g(x)\mathfrak{m}(x)dx$ and let $L^2((\ell, r), \mathfrak{m})$ be the Hilbert space of functions on (ℓ, r) square-integrable with the speed density $\mathfrak{m}(x)$, that is, with $\|f\| < \infty$, where $\|f\|^2 = (f, f)$. Then the semigroup $\{\mathcal{P}_t, t \geq 0\}$ of expectation operators associated with a one-dimensional diffusion is symmetric in $L^2((\ell, r), \mathfrak{m})$; that is, $(\mathcal{P}_t f, g) = (f, \mathcal{P}_t g)$ for every $f, g \in L^2((\ell, r), \mathfrak{m})$ and $t \geq 0$. It follows that the infinitesimal generator $\mathcal{G}$ of a symmetric semigroup, as well as the resolvent operators $\mathcal{R}_s$, are self-adjoint, and we can appeal to the spectral theorem for self-adjoint operators in Hilbert space to obtain their spectral representations.

In the important special case when the spectrum of $\mathcal{G}$ in $L^2((\ell, r), \mathfrak{m})$ is purely discrete, the spectral representation has the following form. Let $\{\lambda_n\}_{n=1}^{\infty}$, $0 \leq \lambda_1 < \lambda_2 < \ldots$, $\lim_{n\uparrow\infty} \lambda_n = \infty$, be the eigenvalues of $-\mathcal{G}$ and let $\{\varphi_n\}_{n=1}^{\infty}$ be the corresponding eigenfunctions normalized so that $\|\varphi_n\|^2 = 1$. The pair (λ_n, φ_n) solves the *Sturm-Liouville eigenvalue-eigenfunction problem* for the (negative of the) differential operator in equation (18.51): $-\mathcal{G}\varphi_n = \lambda_n \varphi_n$. Dirichlet boundary condition is imposed at an endpoint if it is a killing boundary. Then the spectral representations for the transition density $p(t; x, y)$ and the expectation operator $\mathcal{P}_t f(x)$ for $f \in L^2((\ell, r), \mathfrak{m})$ take the form of *eigenfunction expansions*; for $t > 0$ the eigenfunction expansion (18.56) converges uniformly on compact squares in $(\ell, r) \times (\ell, r)$:

$$p(t; x, y) = \mathfrak{m}(y) \sum_{n=1}^{\infty} e^{-\lambda_n t} \varphi_n(x)\varphi_n(y) \qquad (18.56)$$

$$\mathcal{P}_t f(x) = \mathbb{E}_x \left[\mathbf{1}_{\{\zeta > t\}} f(X_t) \right] = \sum_{n=1}^{\infty} c_n e^{-\lambda_n t} \varphi_n(x) \qquad (18.57)$$

with the expansion coefficients $c_n = (f, \varphi_n)$ satisfying the Parseval equality $\|f\|^2 = \sum_{n=1}^{\infty} c_n^2 < \infty$. The eigenfunctions $\{\varphi_n(x)\}_{n=1}^{\infty}$ form a complete orthonormal basis in the Hilbert space $L^2((\ell, r), \mathfrak{m})$; that is, $(\varphi_n, \varphi_n) = 1$ and $(\varphi_n, \varphi_m) = 0$ for $n \neq m$. They are also eigenfunctions of the expectation operator, $\mathcal{P}_t \varphi_n(x) = e^{-\lambda_n t} \varphi_n(x)$, with eigenvalues $e^{-\lambda_n t}$, and of the resolvent operator, $\mathcal{R}_s \varphi_n(x) = \varphi_n(x)/(s + \lambda_n)$, with eigenvalues $1/(s + \lambda_n)$.

More generally, the spectrum of the infinitesimal generator $\mathcal{G}$ in $L^2((\ell, r), m)$ may be continuous, in which case the sums in equations (18.56)–(18.57) are replaced with the integrals. We do not reproduce general results on spectral expansions with continuous spectrum here and instead refer the reader to Davydov and Linetsky (2003), Lewis (1998, 2000), Linetsky (2004a, 2004b, 2004c, 2007), Lipton (2001), and Lipton and McGhee (2002) for further details on the spectral representation for one-dimensional diffusions and their applications in finance.

We notice that in the expression (18.57) *time enters only through the exponentials* $e^{-\lambda_n t}$. Then computing expectations for $f \in L^2((\ell, r), m)$ can be done as follows:

$$\mathbb{E}[\mathbf{1}_{\{\zeta > T_t\}} f(X_{T_t})] = \sum_{n=1}^{\infty} c_n \mathbb{E}[e^{-\lambda_n T_t}] \varphi_n(x) = \sum_{n=1}^{\infty} c_n \mathcal{L}(t, \lambda_n) \varphi_n(x) \qquad (18.58)$$

where $\mathcal{L}(t, \lambda)$ is the Laplace transform of the time change. Due to the fact that time enters the spectral expansion only through the exponentials $e^{-\lambda_n s}$, integrating this exponential against the distribution of the time change $\pi_t(ds)$, the integral in s in (18.57) reduces to the Laplace transform of the time change, $\int_{[0,\infty)} e^{-\lambda_n s} \pi_t(ds) = \mathcal{L}(t, \lambda_n)$.

Remark 18.4.2 *A key feature of the resolvent approach and spectral representation approach is that in both methodologies the temporal and spatial variables are separated. Furthermore, since the time variable t enters the expressions (18.54) and (18.57) only through the exponential function ($e^{-\mu t}$, for some μ), then the analytical tractability of* $\mathbb{E}[\mathbf{1}_{\{\zeta > T_t\}} f(X_{T_t})]$ *is feasible upon knowing the Laplace transform of the time change,* $\mathcal{L}(t, \mu)$.

18.4.6 Time-Changing the JDCEV Model

We now assume that the process X in equation (18.29) follows a time-homogeneous JDCEV process. That is, the parameters r, q, and b are nonnegative constants while a is a strictly positive constant. The infinitesimal generator of this diffusion on $(0, \infty)$ has the form:

$$\mathcal{G}f(x) = \frac{1}{2} a^2 x^{2\beta+2} \frac{d^2 f}{dx^2}(x) + (\mu + b + c\, a^2 x^{2\beta}) x \frac{df}{dx}(x) - (b + c\, a^2 x^{2\beta}) f(x) \qquad (18.59)$$

When applying a time change T_t to the JDCEV process, the parameter μ is assumed to be such that $\mathbb{E}[e^{\mu T_t}] < \infty$. The parameter ρ in equation (18.29) is assumed to be such that the stock price process S_t of equation (18.29) is a discounted martingale. For the JDCEV time-changed with a Lévy subordinator with the Laplace exponent $\phi(\lambda)$, this fixes ρ in terms of μ by $\rho = r - q + \phi(-\mu)$. For the JDCEV models with absolutely continuous and composite time changes, this restricts the parameters as follows: $\mu = 0$, $\rho = r - q$.

The scale and speed densities of the JDCEV diffusion are:

$$\mathfrak{m}(x) = \frac{2}{a^2} x^{2c-2-2\beta} e^{Ax^{-2\beta}}, \quad \mathfrak{s}(x) = x^{-2c} e^{-Ax^{-2\beta}}, \quad \text{where} \quad A := \frac{\mu+b}{a^2|\beta|} \quad (18.60)$$

The following theorem presents the fundamental solutions $\psi_s(x)$ and $\phi_s(x)$ entering the expression for the Green's function [Equation (18.49)] and their Wronskian w_s [Equation (18.52)]. Here we present the results for $\mu + b > 0$.

Theorem 18.4.1 *For a JDCEV diffusion process with the infinitesimal generator [equation (18.59)] with parameters $\beta < 0$, $a > 0$, $b \geq 0$, $c \geq 0$ and such that $\mu + b > 0$, the increasing and decreasing fundamental solutions $\psi_s(x)$ and $\phi_s(x)$ are:*

$$\psi_s(x) = x^{\frac{1}{2}+\beta-c} e^{-\frac{1}{2}Ax^{-2\beta}} M_{\varkappa(s),\frac{v}{2}}(Ax^{-2\beta}) \quad (18.61)$$

$$\phi_s(x) = x^{\frac{1}{2}+\beta-c} e^{-\frac{1}{2}Ax^{-2\beta}} W_{\varkappa(s),\frac{v}{2}}(Ax^{-2\beta}) \quad (18.62)$$

where $M_{k,m}(z)$ and $W_{k,m}(z)$ are the first and second Whittaker functions with indexes

$$v = \frac{1+2c}{2|\beta|}, \quad \varkappa(s) = \frac{v-1}{2} - \frac{s+\xi}{\omega}, \quad \text{where} \quad \omega = 2|\beta|(\mu+b), \quad \xi = 2c(\mu+b) + b$$
$$(18.63)$$

and the constant A is defined in equation (18.60). The Wronskian w_s defined by equation (18.52) reads:

$$w_s = \frac{2(\mu+b)\Gamma(1+v)}{a^2\Gamma(v/2 + 1/2 - \varkappa(s))} \quad (18.64)$$

The Green's function is given by equation (18.49). Inverting the Laplace transform leads to the spectral representation of the transition density [equation (18.56)].

Theorem 18.4.2 *When $\mu + b > 0$, the spectrum of the negative of the infinitesimal generator [equation (18.59)] is purely discrete with the eigenvalues and eigenfunctions:*

$$\lambda_n = \omega n + \xi, \quad \varphi_n(x) = A^{\frac{v}{2}} \sqrt{\frac{(n-1)!(\mu+b)}{\Gamma(v+n)}} x e^{-Ax^{-2\beta}} L_{n-1}^{(v)}(Ax^{-2\beta}), \quad n = 1, 2, \ldots$$
$$(18.65)$$

where $L_n^{(v)}(x)$ are the generalized Laguerre polynomials and ξ and ω are defined in equation (18.63). The spectral representation (eigenfunction expansion) of the JDCEV transition density is given by equation (18.56) with these eigenvalues and eigenfunctions and the speed density [equation (18.60)].

The closed-form solutions for the survival probability and call and put options given in Proposition 18.3.2 are not suitable for time changes since they depend on time in a nontrivial manner. Mendoza-Arriaga, Carr, and Linetsky (2009) obtain alternative representations based on the theory in Sections 18.4.4 and 18.4.5 and Theorems 18.4.1 and 18.4.2 with time entering only through exponentials.

Theorem 18.4.3 *For a JDCEV diffusion process with the infinitesimal generator [equation (18.59)] with parameters $\beta < 0$, $a > 0$, $b \geq 0$, $c \geq 0$, $\mu + b > 0$, and started at $x > 0$, the survival probability $\mathbb{Q}(\zeta > t)$ is given by:*

$$\mathbb{Q}(\zeta > t) = \sum_{n=0}^{\infty} e^{-(b+\omega n)t} \frac{\Gamma(1 + \frac{c}{|\beta|}) \left(\frac{1}{2|\beta|}\right)_n}{\Gamma(\nu + 1)n!} A^{\frac{1}{2|\beta|}} x e^{-Ax^{-2\beta}}$$

$$\times \, {}_1F_1\left(1 - n + \frac{c}{|\beta|}; \nu + 1; Ax^{-2\beta}\right) \tag{18.66}$$

where $_1F_1(a; b; x)$ is the confluent hypergeometric function, $(a)_n := \Gamma(a + n)/\Gamma(a) = a(a + 1)\dots(a + n - 1)$ is the Pochhammer symbol, and the constants A, ν, and ω are as defined in Theorem 18.4.1.

The proof is based on first computing the resolvent [equation (18.47)] with $f(x) = 1$ and then inverting the Laplace transform (18.54) analytically. Since constants are not square-integrable on $(0, \infty)$ with the speed density (18.60), we cannot use the spectral expansion approach of Section 18.4.5 and instead follow the Laplace transform approach of Section 18.4.4.

We now present the result for the put option. The put option price in the model [equation (18.29)] is given by equations (18.43)–(18.45). In particular, in order to compute the price of the put payoff conditional on no default before expiration, $P_0(x; K, t)$, we need to compute the expectation $\mathbb{E}[(K - e^{\rho t} X_s)^+ \mathbf{1}_{\{\zeta > s\}}] = e^{\rho t} \mathbb{E}[(e^{-\rho t} K - X_s)^+ \mathbf{1}_{\{\zeta > s\}}]$ for the JDCEV process [equation (18.59)]. The put payoff $f(x) = (k - x)^+$ is in the Hilbert space $L^2((0, \infty), \mathfrak{m})$ of functions square-integrable with the speed density (18.60) and, hence, the expectation has a spectral expansion. The eigenfunction expansion coefficients are computed in closed form.

Theorem 18.4.4 *For a JDCEV diffusion process with the infinitesimal generator [equation (18.59)] with parameters $\beta < 0$, $a > 0$, $b \geq 0$, $c \geq 0$, and such that $\mu + b > 0$, the expectation $\mathbb{E}[(k - X_t)^+ \mathbf{1}_{\{\zeta > t\}}]$ is given by the eigenfunction expansion (18.57) with* *the eigenvalues λ_n and eigenfunctions $\varphi_n(x)$ given in Theorem 18.4.2 and expansion coefficients:*

$$
c_n = \frac{A^{\nu/2+1} k^{2c+1-2\beta} \sqrt{\Gamma(\nu + n)}}{\Gamma(\nu + 1) \sqrt{(\mu + b)(n - 1)!}}
$$

$$
\times \left\{ \frac{|\beta|}{c + |\beta|} {}_2F_2 \left(\begin{matrix} 1 - n, \frac{c}{|\beta|} + 1 \\ \nu + 1, \frac{c}{|\beta|} + 2 \end{matrix} ; Ak^{-2\beta} \right) - \frac{\Gamma(\nu + 1)(n - 1)!}{\Gamma(\nu + n + 1)} L_{n-1}^{(\nu+1)} \left(Ak^{-2\beta} \right) \right\}
$$

$$(18.67)$$

where ${}_2F_2$ is the generalized hypergeometric function.

The survival probability entering the put pricing formula is already computed in Theorem 18.4.3. The survival probability for the time-changed JDCEV process is immediately obtained from equation (18.66) by replacing $e^{-(b+\omega n)t}$ with $\mathcal{L}(t, b + \omega n)$, the Laplace transform of the time change). For the put pricing formula, the factors $e^{-\lambda_n t}$ in the eigenfunction expansion are replaced with $\mathcal{L}(t, \lambda_n)$, the Laplace transform of the time change evaluated at the eigenvalue; see equation (18.58). The pricing formula for the call option is obtained via the put-call parity.

18.5 Numerical Illustration

We start with the JDCEV process with $\mu = 0$ and time-change it with a composite time change process $T_t = T_{T_t^2}^1$, where T^1 is the inverse Gaussian (IG) subordinator with the Lévy measure $\nu(ds) = Cs^{-3/2}e^{-\eta s}$ and the Laplace exponent $\phi(s) = \gamma s + 2C\sqrt{\pi}(\sqrt{s + \eta} - \sqrt{\eta})$, and T^2 is the time integral of the activity rate following the CIR process. In order to satisfy the martingale condition, we set $\rho = r - q$. The parameter values in our numerical example are listed in Table 18.1.

The JDCEV process parameter a entering into the local volatility function $\sigma(x) = a x^\beta$ is selected so that the local volatility is equal to 20 percent when the stock price is $50 (i.e., $a = 0.2 * 50^{-\beta} = 10$ with $\beta = -1$). We consider a pure jump process

TABLE 18.1 Parameter Values

JDCEV						
S	a	β	c	b	r	q
50	10	−1	0.5	0.01	0.05	0

CIR				IG		
V	θ	σ_V	κ	γ	η	C
1	1	1	4	0	8	$2\sqrt{2/\pi}$

FIGURE 18.1 Implied Volatility Smile/Skew Curves as Functions of the Strike Price for Times to Maturity from One-Fourth to Three Years

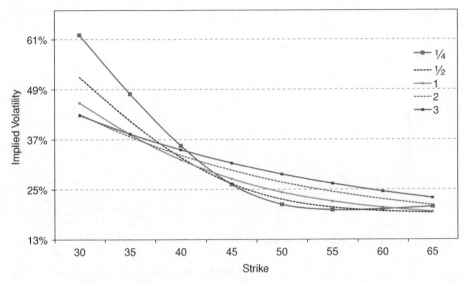

The current stock price level is 50.

with no diffusion component ($\gamma = 0$). For this choice of parameters of the IG time change and the CIR activity rate process the time change has the mean and variance $E[T_1] = 1$ and $Var[T_1] = 1/16$ at $t = 1$.

Figure 18.1 plots the implied volatility smile/skew curves of options priced under this model for several different maturities. We compute options prices in this model using Theorem 18.4.4 and then compute implied volatilities of these options by inverting the Black-Scholes formula. We observe that in this model shorter-maturity skews are steeper and flatten out as maturity increases, consistent with empirical observations in options markets. In the time-changed JDCEV model, short-maturity options exhibit a true volatility smile with the increase in implied volatilities both to the right and to the left of the at-the-money strike. This behavior cannot be captured in the pure diffusion model since in the JDCEV the implied volatility skew results from the leverage effect (the local volatility is a decreasing function of stock price) and the possibility of default (the default intensity is a decreasing function of stock price). The resulting implied volatility skew is a decreasing function of strike. After the time change with jumps, the resulting jump process has both positive and negative jumps. This results in the implied volatility smile pattern with volatility "smiling" on both sides of the at-the-money level.

Figure 18.2 plots the default probability and the credit spread (assuming zero recovery in default) as functions of time to maturity for several initial levels of the stock price. As the stock price decreases, the credit spreads of all maturities increase, but the shorter and intermediate maturities increase the fastest. This results in a pronounced hump in the term structure of credit spreads around these intermediate

FIGURE 18.2 Credit Spreads and Default Probabilities as Functions of Time to Maturity for the Initial Stock Price Levels $S = 30, 40, 50, 60, 70$

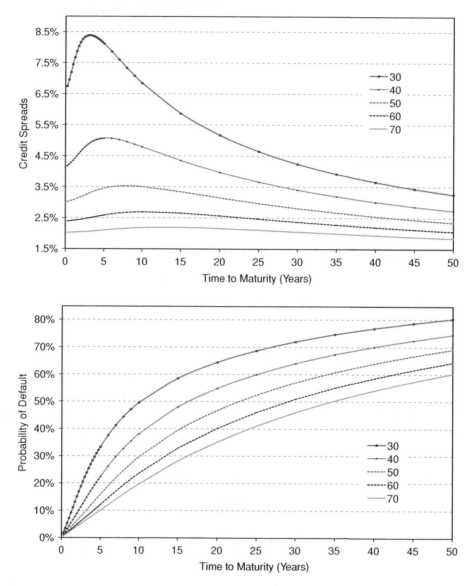

maturities. As the stock price falls, the hump becomes more pronounced and shifts toward shorter maturities. This increase in credit spreads with the decrease in the stock price is explained by both the leverage effect through the increase in the local volatility of the original diffusion and, hence, more jump volatility for the jump process after the time change, as well as the increase in the default intensity of the original diffusion process and the jump process after the time change.

Acknowledgment

This research was supported in part by the grants from the National Science Foundation under grant DMS-0802720.

References

Albanese, C., and O. X. Chen. 2005. Pricing equity default swaps. *Risk* 18 (6): 83–87.

Andersen, L., and D. Buffum. 2003/2004. Calibration and implementation of convertible bond models. *Journal of Computational Finance* 7 (2): 1–34.

Atlan, M., and B. Leblanc. 2005. Hybrid equity-credit modelling. *Risk* (August): 8.

Atlan, M., and B. Leblanc. 2006. Time-changed Bessel processes and credit risk. Working paper.

Ayache, E., P. Forsyth, and K. Vetzal. 2003. Valuation of convertible bonds with credit risk. *Journal of Derivatives* 11 (Fall): 9–29.

Bertoin, J. 1996. *Lévy processes.* New York: Cambridge University Press.

Bertoin, J. 1999. *Lectures on probability theory and statistics: Ecole d'Ete de Probabilities de Saint-Flour XXVII—1997.* Chapter "Subordinators: Examples and applications." New York: Springer.

Bielecki, T. R., S. Crépey, M. Jeanblanc, and M. Rutkowski. 2009. Convertible bonds in a defaultable diffusion model. Working paper.

Bielecki, T. R., and M. Rutkowski. 2004. *Credit risk: Modeling, valuation and hedging.* New York: Springer.

Borodin, A., and P. Salminen. 2002. *Handbook of Brownian motion: Facts and formulae.* 2nd rev. ed. Probability and Its Applications. Basel: Birkhauser Verlag AG.

Campbell, J., and G. Taksler. 2003. Equity volatility and corporate bond yields. *Journal of Finance* 58 (6): 2321–2349.

Campi, L., S. Polbennikov, and A. Sbuelz. 2009. Systematic equity-based credit risk: A CEV model with jump to default. *Journal of Economic Dynamics and Control* 33 (1): 93–108.

Campi, L., and A. Sbuelz. 2005. Closed-form pricing of benchmark equity default swaps under the CEV assumption. *Risk Letters* 1 (3): 107.

Carr, P., H. Geman, D. B., Madan, and M. Yor. 2003. Stochastic volatility for Lévy processes. *Mathematical Finance* 13 (3): 345–382.

Carr, P., and V. Linetsky. 2006. A jump to default extended CEV model: An application of Bessel processes. *Finance and Stochastics* 10 (3): 303–330.

Carr, P., and D. B. Madan. 2010. Local volatility enhanced by a jump to default. Forthcoming in *SIAM Journal on Financial Mathematics.*

Carr, P., and L. Wu. (2008a). Leverage effect, volatility feedback, and self-exciting market disruptions: Disentangling the multi-dimensional variations in S&P 500 index options. Working paper.

Carr, P., and L. Wu. (2008b). A simple robust link between American puts and credit protection. Working paper.

Carr, P., and L. Wu. 2009. Stock options and credit default swaps: A joint framework for valuation and estimation. *Journal of Financial Econometrics* (July 21): 1–41.

Cox, J. C. 1975. Notes on option pricing I: Constant elasticity of variance diffusions. Reprinted in *Journal of Portfolio Management* 23 (December 1996): 15–17.

Cox, J. C., J. E. Ingersoll, and S. A. Ross. 1985. A theory of the term structure of interest rates. *Econometrica* 53 (2): 385–407.

Cremers, M., J. Driessen, P. Maenhout, and D. Weinbaum. 2008. Individual stock-option prices and credit spreads. *Journal of Banking & Finance* 32 (12): 2706–2715.

Das, S. R., and R. K. Sundaram. 2007. An integrated model for hybrid securities. *Management Science* 53 (9): 1439–1451.

Davis, M., and F. R. Lischka. 2002. Convertible bonds with market risk and credit risk. In ed. R. H. Chan, Y.-K. Kwok, D. Yaho, and Q. Zhang, Studies in advanced mathematics, Vol. 26, 45–58. Cambridge, MA: International Press.

Davydov, D., and V. Linetsky. 2001. Pricing and hedging path-dependent options under the CEV process. *Management Science* 47:949–965.

Davydov, D., and V. Linetsky. 2003. Pricing options on scalar diffusions: An eigenfunction expansion approach. *Operations Research* 51:185–209.

Delbaen, F., and H. Shirakawa. 2002. A note of option pricing for constant elasticity of variance model. *Asia-Pacific Financial Markets* 9 (2): 85–99.

Ethier, S. N., and T. G. Kurtz. 1986. *Markov processes: Characterization and convergence.* Wiley Series in Probability and Statistics. New York: John Wiley & Sons.

Geman, H., D. B. Madan, and M. Yor. 2001. Time changes for Lévy processes. *Mathematical Finance* 11 (1): 79–96.

Göing-Jaeschke, A., and M. Yor. 2003. A survey and some generalizations of Bessel processes. *Bernoulli* 9 (2): 313–349.

Hilscher, J. 2008. Is the corporate bond market forward looking? Working paper.

Ito, K., and H. P. McKean. 1974. *Diffusion processes and their sample paths.* Corrected 2nd ed. Classics in Mathematics. London: Springer.

Jeanblanc, M., M. Yor, and M. Chesney. 2009. *Mathematical methods for financial markets.* Springer Finance. London: Springer.

Karlin, S., and H. M. Taylor. 1981. *A second course in stochastic processes.* New York: Academic Press.

Kovalov, P., and V. Linetsky. 2008. Valuing convertible bonds with stock price, volatility, interest rate, and default risk. Working paper.

Le, A. 2007. Separating the components of default risk: A derivatives-based approach. Working paper.

Lewis, A. L. 1998. Applications of eigenfunction expansions in continuous-time finance. *Mathematical Finance* 8 (4): 349–383.

Lewis, A. L. 2000. *Option valuation under stochastic volatility.* Newport Beach, CA: Finance Press.

Linetsky, V. 2004a. Computing hitting time densities for CIR and OU diffusions: Applications to mean-reverting models. *Journal of Computational Finance* 7 (4): 1–22.

Linetsky, V. 2004b. Lookback options and diffusion hitting times: A spectral expansion approach. *Finance and Stochastics* 8 (3): 343–371.

Linetsky, V. 2004c. The spectral decomposition of the optionl value. *International Journal of Theoretical and Applied Finance* 7 (3): 337–384.

Linetsky, V. 2006. Pricing equity derivatives subject to bankruptcy. *Mathematical Finance* 16 (2): 255–282.

Linetsky, V. 2007. *Handbook of financial engineering.* Vol. 15 of *Handbooks in operations research and management sciences.* Chapter "Spectral methods in derivatives pricing," 223–300. Amsterdam: Elsevier.

Lipton, A. 2001. *Mathematical methods for foreign exchange: A financial engineer's approach.* Singapore: World Scientific.

Lipton, A., and V. McGhee. 2002. Universal barriers. *Risk* 15 (5): 81–85.

McKean, H. P. 1956. Elementary solutions for certain parabolic partial differential equations. *Transactions of the American Mathematical Society* 82 (2): 519–548.

Mendoza, R., and V. Linetsky. 2010. The constant elasticity of variance model. In *Encyclopedia of Quantitative Finance,* ed. R. Cont. Hoboken, NJ: John Wiley & Sons.

Mendoza-Arriaga, R., P. Carr, and V. Linetsky. 2009. Time changed Markov processes in credit-equity modeling. Forthcoming in *Mathematical Finance.*

Mendoza-Arriaga, R., and V. Linetksy. 2009. Pricing equity default swaps under the jump to default extended CEV model. Forthcoming in *Finance and Stochastics.*

Merton, R. C. 1974. On the pricing of corporate debt: The risk structure of interest rates. *Journal of Finance* 29 (2): 449–470.

Merton, R. C. 1976. Option pricing when underlying stock returns are discontinuous. *Journal of Financial Economics* 3 (1): 125–144.

Pazy, A. 1983. *Semigroups of linear operators and applications to partial differential equations.* Berlin: Springer.

Revuz, D., and M. Yor. 1999. *Continuous martingales and Brownian motion.* Grundlehren der Mathematischen Wissenschaften. Berlin: Springer.

Sato, K. 1999. *Lévy processes and infinitely divisible distributions.* New York: Cambridge University Press.

Schroder, M. 1989. Computing the constant elasticity of variance option pricing formula. *Journal of Finance* 44 (1): 211–219.

Vidal-Nunes, J. P. 2009. Pricing American options under the constant elasticity of variance model and subject to bankruptcy. *Journal of Financial and Quantitative Analysis* 44 (5): 1231–1263.

Wong, E. 1964. *Stochastic processes in mathematical physics and engineering.* Chapter "The construction of a class of stationary Markoff processes," 264–276. Providence, RI: American Mathematical Society.

Zhang, B. Y., H. Zhou, and H. Zhu. 2009. Explaining credit default swap spreads with the equity volatility and jump risks. *Review of Financial Studies* 22 (12): 5099–5131.

PART VI

Miscellanea: Liquidity, Ratings, Risk Contributions, and Simulation

CHAPTER 19

Liquidity Modeling for Credit Default Swaps: An Overview

Damiano Brigo

Gilbart Professor of Financial Mathematics, King's College, London

Mirela Predescu

BNP Paribas, London

Agostino Capponi

School of Industrial Engineering, Purdue University

We review different theoretical and empirical approaches for measuring the impact of liquidity on CDS prices. We start with reduced-form models incorporating liquidity as an additional discount rate. We review Chen, Fabozzi, and Sverdlove (2008); Chen, Cheng, and Wu (2005); and Buhler and Trapp (2006, 2008), adopting different assumptions on how liquidity rates enter the CDS premium rate formula, about the dynamics of liquidity rate processes and about the credit-liquidity correlation. Buhler and Trapp (2008) provides the most general and realistic framework, incorporating correlation between liquidity and credit, liquidity spillover effects between bonds and CDS contracts, and asymmetric liquidity effects on the bid and ask CDS premium rates. We then discuss the Bongaerts, De Jong, and Driessen (2009) study, which derives an equilibrium asset pricing model incorporating liquidity effects. Findings include that both expected illiquidity and liquidity risk have a statistically significant impact on expected CDS returns, but only compensation for expected illiquidity is economically significant, with higher expected liquidity being associated with higher expected returns for the protection sellers. This finding is contrary to Chen, Cheng, and Wu (2005) and Chen, Fabozzi, and Sverdlove (2008), who found protection buyers to earn the liquidity premium instead. We finalize our review with a discussion of Predescu et al. (2009), who analyze also data in-crisis, and Tang and Yan (2007). The first one is a statistical model that associates an ordinal liquidity score with each CDS reference entity and allows one to compare liquidity of over 2,400 reference entities. This study points out that credit and illiquidity are correlated, with a smile pattern. Tang and Yan (2007) go back to a cardinal model that decomposes quantitatively CDS spreads into credit and liquidity components, and uses liquidity measures that again include bid-ask CDS information. All of these studies highlight that CDS premium rates are not pure measures of credit risk. CDS liquidity varies cross-sectionally and over time. CDS expected liquidity and liquidity risk premiums are priced in CDS expected returns and spreads. Further research is needed to measure liquidity premium at CDS contract level and to disentangle liquidity from credit effectively.

19.1 Introduction

Liquidity is a notion that has gained increasing attention following the credit crisis that started in 2007. As a matter of fact, this has been a liquidity crisis besides a credit crisis. For many market players, problems have been aggravated by the lack of reserves when they need to maintain positions in order to avoid closing deals with large negative mark-to-markets. This lack of reserves forced fire sales at the worst possible moments and started a domino effect leading to the collapses of several financial institutions.

19.1.1 Funding, Trading, and Systemic Liquidity

Szegö (2009) illustrates, among other factors, a negative loop involving illiquidity as fueling the crisis development. We can consider, for example, the following seven-step schematization:

1. (Further) liquidity reduction on asset trade.
2. (Further) price contraction due to liquidity decline.
3. (Further) decline of value of bank assets portfolio.
4. Difficulty in refinancing, difficulty in borrowing, being forced to (further) sale of assets.
5. Assets left? If so, go back to 1. If not:
6. Impossibility of refinancing.
7. Bankruptcy.

This sketchy and admittedly simplified representation highlights the three types of liquidity that market participants generally care about. One is the market/trading liquidity, generally defined as the ability to trade quickly at a low cost (O'Hara 1995). This generally means low transaction costs coming from bid-ask spreads, low price impact of trading large volumes, and considerable market depth. This notion of market liquidity can be applied to different asset classes (equities, bonds, interest rate products, foreign exchange (FX) products, credit derivatives, etc.) and to the overall financial markets. In addition to trading liquidity, banks and financial institutions also closely monitor funding liquidity, which is the ease with which liabilities can be funded through different financing sources.

Market and funding liquidity are related, since timely funding of liabilities relies on the market liquidity risk of assets, given that a bank may need to sell some of its assets to match liability-side obligations at certain points in time. The recent crisis prompted regulators and central banks to look very closely at both types of liquidity and to propose new guidelines for liquidity risk management (see Bank for International Settlements 2008; Financial Services Authority 2009).

A third kind of liquidity that is, however, implicit in the aforementioned schematization is the systemic liquidity risk associated with a global financial crisis, characterized by a generalized difficulty in borrowing.

As with other types of risks, liquidity needs to be analyzed from both a pricing perspective and a risk management one.

19.1.2   Liquidity as a Pricing Component

In the pricing space, Amihud, Mendelson, and Pedersen (2005) provide a thorough survey of theoretical and empirical papers that analyze the impact of liquidity on asset prices for traditional securities such as stocks and bonds. Other papers (Cetin, Jarrow, Protter, and Warachka (2005); Garleanu, Pedersen, and Poteshman (2009)) investigated the impact of liquidity on option prices. More generally, Cetin, Jarrow, and Protter (2004) extend the classical arbitrage pricing theory to include liquidity risk by considering an economy with a stochastic supply curve where the price of a security is a function of the trade size. This leads to a new definition of self-financing trading strategies and to additional restrictions on hedging strategies, all of which have important consequences in valuation. Their paper also reports a good summary of earlier literature on transaction costs and trade restrictions, to which we refer the interested reader.

Morini (2009) analyzes the liquidity and credit impact on interest rate modeling, building a framework that consistently accounts for the divergence between market forward rate agreements (FRA) rates and the London Interbank Offered Rate (LIBOR)-replicated FRA rates. He also accounts for the divergence between overnight indexed swap rates (Euro Overnight Index Average [EONIA]) and LIBOR rates. The difference between the two rates can only be attributed to liquidity or counterparty risk, the latter being almost zero in EONIA due to the very short (practically daily) times between payments. For illustration purposes, we report in Figure 19.1 the differences between EONIA and LIBOR rates for Europe and the analogous difference for the United States. It is clear from the graphs in Figure 19.1 that starting from the end of 2007 and till mid-2008, there is a noticeable increase in the difference between one-month LIBOR and the overnight index swap rate, which is instead very small in the beginning of the observation period. This is not surprising as the end of 2007 corresponds to the start of the subprime mortgage crisis, which then exacerbated and became the credit crunch crisis of 2008.

The analysis done by Morini (2009) makes use of basis swaps between LIBOR with different tenors, and takes into account collateralization. Morini is able to reconcile the divergence in rates even under simplifying assumptions. His analysis, however,

FIGURE 19.1 Difference between One-Month EU (U.S.) LIBOR and EU (U.S.) Overnight
Index Swap

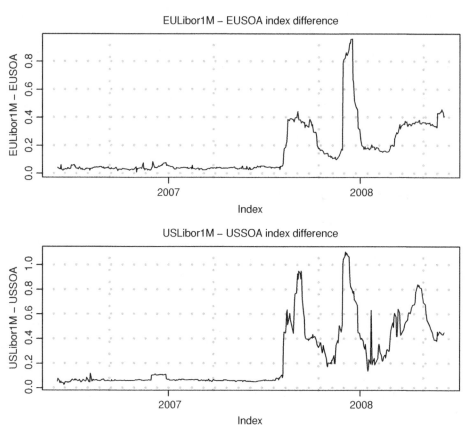

implicitly views liquidity as a consequence of credit rather than as an independent
variable, although he does not exclude the possibility that liquidity may have a more
independent component.

19.1.3 Liquidity in Risk Measurement

Several studies (Angelidis and Benos 2005; Bangia et al. 1999; Earnst, Stange, and
Kaserer 2009; Jarrow and Protter 2005; Jarrow and Subramanian 1997; Stange and
Kaserer 2008, among others) propose different methods of accounting for liquidity risk
in computing risk measures. Bangia et al. (1999) classify market liquidity risk in two
categories: (1) the exogenous illiquidity that depends on general market conditions, is
common to all market players, and is unaffected by the actions of any one participant,
and (2) the endogenous illiquidity that is specific to one's position in the market, varies
across different market players, and is mainly related to the impact of the trade size
on the bid-ask spread. Bangia et al. (1999) and Earnst et al. (2009) only consider the
exogenous illiquidity risk and propose a liquidity-adjusted value at risk (VaR) measure

built using the distribution of the bid-ask spreads. The other studies mentioned model and account for endogenous risk in the calculation of liquidity-adjusted risk measures.

In the context of the coherent risk measures literature, the general axioms a liquidity measure should satisfy are discussed in Acerbi and Scandolo (2008). They propose a formalism for liquidity risk that is compatible with the axioms of coherency of the earlier risk measures literature. They emphasize the important but easily overlooked difference between coherent risk measures defined on portfolio values and coherent risk measures defined on the vector space of portfolios. The key observation is that in the presence of liquidity risk the value function on the space of portfolios is not necessarily linear. From this starting point a theory is developed, introducing a nonlinear value function depending on a notion of liquidity policy based on a general description of the microstructure of illiquid markets and the impact that this microstructure has when marking a portfolio to market.

19.1.4   This Survey: Liquidity in CDS Pricing

In this chapter we focus on liquidity modeling in the valuation space, to which we return now, and more specifically, in the context of credit derivatives instruments, on the impact of liquidity on credit default swap (CDS) premium rates. CDSs represent the most liquid credit instruments and are highly standardized. The basic idea to include liquidity as a spread, leading to a liquidity stochastic discount factor, follows the approach adopted, for example, by Chen, Cheng, and Wu (2005) (CCW); Buhler and Trapp (2006, 2008) (BT06 and BT08); and Chen, Fabozzi, and Sverdlove (2008) (CFS), among others. All approaches but BT08 are unrealistic in that they assume the liquidity rate to be independent of the hazard rate associated with defaults of the relevant CDS entities. BT08 and Predescu et al. (2009) show, although in different contexts, that liquidity and credit are correlated. We discuss their results.

We will then analyze a different approach, by Bongaerts, De Jong, and Driessen (2009) (BDD), who use capital asset pricing model (CAPM)–like arguments to deduce liquidity from CDS data. None of these works use data in-crisis (i.e., after June 2007) except Predescu et al. (2009) (PTGLKR), where liquidity scores for CDS data are produced starting from contributors' bid-ask or mid CDS quotes across time. This is an ordinal liquidity measure, as opposed to a more attractive cardinal one, but it represents—to the best of our knowledge—the only work dealing with CDS liquidity also using crisis data. After the ordinal model by Predescu et al. (2009), we go back to works that decompose CDS premiums into liquidity and credit components quantitatively. One such study is Tang and Yan (2007) (TY), which also includes bid-ask information, among other variables chosen as liquidity measures: volatility to volume, number of contracts outstanding, trade-to-quote ratio, and volume.

We then conclude the chapter by comparing the often contradictory findings of these works, pointing out remaining problems in liquidity estimation and pricing in the credit market.

19.2   Liquidity as a Spread in Reduced-Form Models

The basic idea in this approach is to include liquidity as a (possibly stochastic) spread, leading to a liquidity (possibly stochastic) discount factor.

In order to be able to work on liquidity for CDS, we need to introduce the CDS contract and its mechanics. To this end we follow Brigo and Mercurio (2006, chap. 21).

19.2.1   Credit Default Swaps

The running CDS contract is defined as follows. A CDS contract ensures protection against default. Two parties, "A" (protection buyer) and "B" (protection seller), agree on the following.

If a third party, "C" (reference credit), defaults at time $\tau = \tau_C$, with $T_a < \tau < T_b$, "B" pays to "A" a certain amount L_{GD} (loss given default of the reference credit "C"). In turn, "A" pays to "B" a premium rate S at times $T_{a+1}, \ldots, T_b$ or until default. Set $\alpha_i = T_i - T_{i-1}$ and $T_0 = 0$. We can summarize the structure as:

| Protection Seller "B" | $\rightarrow$ | Protection L_{GD} at default τ_C if $T_a < \tau_C \leq T_b$ | $\rightarrow$ | Protection |
| | $\leftarrow$ | Rate S at $T_{a+1}, \ldots, T_b$ or until default τ_C | $\leftarrow$ | Buyer "A" |

(protection leg and premium leg, respectively). The amount L_{GD} is a *protection* for "A" in case "C" defaults. Typically, L_{GD} = notional, or "notional − recovery" = $1 - R_{EC}$.

Formally, we may write the CDS discounted value at time t as seen from "B" as:

$$\Pi_{RCDS_{a,b}}(t) := D(t, \tau)(\tau - T_{\beta(\tau)-1})S\mathbf{1}_{\{T_a < \tau < T_b\}}$$

$$+ \sum_{i=a+1}^{b} D(t, T_i)\alpha_i S\mathbf{1}_{\{\tau \geq T_i\}} - \mathbf{1}_{\{T_a < \tau \leq T_b\}}D(t, \tau)\,L_{GD} \tag{19.1}$$

where $t \in [T_{\beta(t)-1}, T_{\beta(t)})$; that is, $T_{\beta(t)}$ is the first date among the T_is that follows t and $D(t, T)$ is the risk-free discount factor at time t for maturity T.

A note on terminology: In the market S is usually called "CDS spread." However, we will use "spread" both to denote the difference between the ask and bid quotes of a security and to indicate the additional risk premium on top of the default-free instantaneous rate r. To avoid confusion we will refer to S as the CDS premium rate rather than CDS spread.

Usually, at inception time (say 0) the amount S is set at a value $S_{a,b}(0)$ that makes the contract fair (i.e., such that the present value of the two exchanged cash flows is zero). This is how the market quotes running CDSs: CDSs are quoted via their fair Ss (bid and ask).

Recently, there has been some interest in up-front CDS contracts with a fixed premium rate in the premium leg.[1] In these contracts the premium rate S is fixed to some preassigned canonical value $\bar{S}$, typically 100 or 500 basis points (bps, 1 bp $= 10^{-4}$), and the remaining part of the protection is paid up front by the party that is buying protection. In other words, instead of exchanging a possible protection payment for some coupons that put the contract in equilibrium at inception, one exchanges it with a fixed coupon and compensates for the difference with an up-front payment.

We denote by $\mathrm{CDS}(t, [T_{a+1}, \ldots, T_b], T_a, T_b, S, \mathrm{L_{GD}})$ the price at time t of the standard running CDS [equation (19.1)]. At times some terms are omitted, such as, for example, the list of payment dates $[T_{a+1}, \ldots, T_b]$, and to shorten notation further we may write $\mathrm{CDS}_{a,b}(t, S, \mathrm{L_{GD}})$.

The pricing formulas for these payoffs depend on the assumptions on interest rate dynamics and on the default time τ. If τ is assumed to be independent of interest rates, then model-independent valuation formulas for CDSs involving directly default (or survival) probabilities and default-free zero coupon bonds are available.

Proper valuation of CDSs should also take into account counterparty risk; see, for example, Brigo and Chourdakis (2009, unilateral case) and Brigo and Capponi (2008, bilateral case). Here, however, we focus on works that do not consider counterparty risk in the CDS valuation.

In general, whichever the model, we can compute the CDS price according to risk-neutral valuation:

$$\mathrm{CDS}_{a,b}(t, S, \mathrm{L_{GD}}) = \mathbb{E}_t\{\Pi_{\mathrm{RCDS}_{a,b}}(t)\} \tag{19.2}$$

where $\mathbb{E}_t$ is the risk-neutral expectation conditional on the market information at time t.

If we define the fair premium of the CDS at a given time t as the value of the premium rate $S = S_{a,b}(t)$ such that $\mathrm{CDS}_{a,b}(t, S_{a,b}(t), \mathrm{L_{GD}}) = 0$ (i.e., such that the two legs of the CDS have the same value), we can write, conditional on $\{\tau > t\}$,

$$S_{a,b}(t) = \frac{\mathbb{E}_t[\mathrm{L_{GD}}\, \mathbf{1}_{\{T_a < \tau \leq T_b\}} D(t, \tau)]}{\mathbb{E}_t[D(t, \tau)(\tau - T_{\beta(\tau)-1})\mathbf{1}_{\{T_a < \tau < T_b\}} + \sum_{i=a+1}^{b} D(t, T_i)\alpha_i \mathbf{1}_{\{\tau \geq T_i\}}]} \tag{19.3}$$

If we assume independence between rates and the default time, or more in particular deterministic interest rates, then the default time τ and interest rate quantities r, $D(s, t), \ldots$ are independent. It follows that the (receiver) CDS valuation, for a CDS selling protection at time 0 for defaults between times T_a and T_b in exchange of a periodic premium rate S becomes (PL = Premium leg, DL = Default leg or Protection leg).

$$\text{CDS}_{a,b}(0, S, \text{L}_\text{GD}; \mathbb{Q}(\tau > \cdot)) = \text{PL}_{a,b}(0, S; \mathbb{Q}(\tau > \cdot)) - \text{DL}_{a,b}(0, \text{L}_\text{GD}; \mathbb{Q}(\tau > \cdot)) \quad (19.4)$$

$$\text{PL}_{a,b}(0, S) = S\left[-\int_{T_a}^{T_b} P(0, t)(t - T_{\beta(t)-1})d_t\mathbb{Q}(\tau \geq t) + \sum_{i=a+1}^{b} P(0, T_i)\alpha_i\mathbb{Q}(\tau \geq T_i)\right]$$
$$(19.5)$$

$$\text{DL}_{a,b}(0, \text{L}_\text{GD}) = -\text{L}_\text{GD}\left[\int_{T_a}^{T_b} P(0, t)\, d_t\mathbb{Q}(\tau \geq t)\right] \quad (19.6)$$

where $P(t, u) = \mathbb{E}_t[D(t, u)]$ is the price of a default-risk-free zero coupon bond. In case rates are deterministic we have $D(t, u) = P(t, u)$ for all t, u. The CDS formula is model independent. In particular, for a spot CDS with $T_a = 0$ at $t = 0$ we have that the fair premium rate formula (19.3) becomes:

$$S_{0,b}(0) = \frac{-\text{L}_\text{GD}\int_0^{T_b} P(0, t)\, d_t\mathbb{Q}(\tau \geq t)}{-\int_0^{T_b} P(0, t)(t - T_{\beta(t)-1})d_t\mathbb{Q}(\tau \geq t) + \sum_{i=1}^{b} P(0, T_i)\alpha_i\mathbb{Q}(\tau \geq T_i)}$$
$$(19.7)$$

This means that if we strip survival probabilities from CDSs in a model independent way at time 0, to calibrate a chosen model for τ to the market CDS quotes, we just need to make sure that the survival probabilities we strip from CDSs are correctly reproduced by the chosen τ model, whichever it is.

Equations (19.5) and (19.6) are no longer valid in general if we remove the independence between τ and interest rates. This complicates matters considerably and it represents the reason why most of the works on liquidity risk with CDSs tend to assume independence between default-free interest rates and default.

Most of the approaches to liquidity we discuss in this chapter are based on the intensity approach (or reduced-form approach) to modeling τ. In this approach, default is not induced by basic market observables and/or economic fundamentals, but has an exogenous component that is independent of all the default-free market information. Monitoring the default-free market (interest rates, exchange rates, etc.) does not give complete information on the default process, and there is no economic rationale behind default. This family of models is particularly suited to model credit spreads and in its basic formulation is easy to calibrate to credit default swap (CDS) or corporate bond data.

19.2.2   Intensity Models for CDSs

We now introduce intensity models. First we need a few definitions from probability theory. We place ourselves in a probability space $(\Omega, \mathcal{G}, \mathcal{G}_t, \mathbb{Q})$. The filtration $(\mathcal{G}_t)_t$ models the flow of information of the whole market, including credit and defaults.

$\mathbb{Q}$ is the risk-neutral measure. This space is endowed also with a right-continuous and complete subfiltration $\mathcal{F}_t$ representing all the observable market quantities but the default events; hence $\mathcal{F}_t \subseteq \mathcal{G}_t := \mathcal{F}_t \vee \mathcal{H}_t$ where $\mathcal{H}_t = \sigma(\{\tau \leq u\} : u \leq t)$ is the right-continuous filtration generated by the default event.

We set $\mathbb{E}_t(\cdot) := \mathbb{E}(\cdot|\mathcal{G}_t)$, the risk-neutral expectation leading to prices.

Intensity models are based on the assumption that the default time τ is the first jump of a Cox process with intensity h_t; see, for example, Bielecki and Rutkowski (2001) for more details, or Brigo and Mercurio (2006). This in particular implies

$$\mathbb{Q}\{\tau \in [t, t+dt)|\tau \geq t, \mathcal{F}_t\} = h_t\, dt$$

where the stochastic process h is the intensity. This reads, if $t = $ now: "probability that reference entity defaults in (small) dt years given that it has not defaulted so far and given the default-free-market information so far is $h_t\, dt$."

Intensity is usually assumed to be at least an $\mathcal{F}_t$-adapted and right-continuous (and thus progressive) process and is denoted by h_t, and the *cumulated intensity* or *hazard process* is the stochastic process $T \mapsto H(T) = \int_0^T h_t dt$. We assume $h_t > 0$. We recall that the requirement to be $\mathcal{F}_t$-adapted means that given $\mathcal{F}_t$ (i.e., the default-free market information up to time t), we know h from 0 to t. This intuitively says that the randomness we allow into the intensity is induced by the default-free market. In a Cox process with stochastic intensity h, conditional on $\mathcal{F}_t$ [or just on $\mathcal{F}_t^h = \sigma(\{h_s : s \leq t\})$, i.e., just on the paths of h], we have a Poisson process structure with intensity h_t. In particular, we have that the first jump time of the process, transformed through its cumulated intensity, is an exponential random variable independent of $\mathcal{F}_t$:

$$H(\tau) = \xi$$

with ξ standard (unit-mean) exponential random variable independent of $\mathcal{F}_t$. Then we have that default can be defined as:

$$\tau := H^{-1}(\xi)$$

that provides us with suggestions on how to simulate the default time in this setting.

Notice that in this setting not only is ξ random, but h itself is stochastic. This is why Cox processes are at times called doubly stochastic Poisson processes.

For the survival probability in intensity models we have:

$$\mathbb{Q}\{\tau \geq t\} = \mathbb{Q}\{H(\tau) \geq H(t)\} = \mathbb{Q}\left\{\xi \geq \int_0^t h(u)du\right\}$$

$$= \mathbb{E}\left[\mathbb{Q}\left\{\xi \geq \int_0^t h(u)du \Big| \mathcal{F}_t^h\right\}\right] = \mathbb{E}\left[e^{-\int_0^t h(u)du}\right]$$

which is completely analogous to the bond price formula in a short interest rate model with interest rate h. This is the reason why the intensity can be seen also as an instantaneous credit spread. This is further illustrated by computing the price of a zero coupon defaultable bond in the intensity setting. The price at time t of a zero coupon defaultable bond with maturity T and zero recovery turns out to be

$$\mathbb{E}\{D(t, T)1_{\{\tau > T\}}|\mathcal{G}_t\} = 1_{\{\tau > t\}}\mathbb{E}\left[e^{-\int_t^T (r_u + h_u)\, du}|\mathcal{F}_t\right] \tag{19.8}$$

where r_t is the instantaneous (possibly stochastic) default-free interest rate at time t, so that $D(t, u) = \exp(-\int_t^u r_s ds)$.

Cox processes allow us to borrow the stochastic interest rates technology and paradigms into default modeling, although ξ remains independent of all default-free market quantities (of $\mathcal{F}$, of h, of r ...) and represents an external source of randomness that makes reduced-form models incomplete.

In this setting, the time-varying nature of h may account for the term structure of credit spreads, while the stochasticity of h can be used to introduce credit spread volatility. For example, in a diffusion setting, one has:

$$dh_t = b(t, h_t)dt + \sigma(t, h_t)\, dW_t$$

for suitable choices of the drift b and diffusion coefficient σ functions. These functions b and σ can be chosen so as to reproduce desired levels of credit spreads and credit spreads volatilities.

Intensity models have been introduced, for example, in the seminal work of Duffie and Singleton (1999). For tractable models and their calibration to the CDS term structure also in relation with CDS option pricing, see, for example, Brigo and Alfonsi (2005) and Brigo and El-Bachir (2008).

19.2.3   Intensity Models for Liquidity

In most of the models we review in this chapter, liquidity enters the picture as a further spread, or intensity. The idea is starting from a formula like equation (19.8) and adding a new rate term ℓ_t to discounting.

In other terms, the price of a zero coupon bond changes from (19.8), where no liquidity component is included, to:

$$\mathbb{E}\{D(t, T)L(t, T)1_{\{\tau > T\}}|\mathcal{G}_t\} = 1_{\{\tau > t\}}\mathbb{E}\left[e^{-\int_t^T (r_u + h_u + \ell_u)\, du}|\mathcal{F}_t\right] \tag{19.9}$$

where $L(t, u) = \exp(-\int_t^u \ell_s ds)$ is a stochastic discount factor component due to illiquidity, and ℓ is the instantaneous rate associated to this discount.

We can get a feeling for this use of the spread with the following example. As we have seen before, for running CDSs, the market quotes at a point in time the value of $S = S_{0,b}$ such that:

$$CDS_{0,b}(0, S_{0,b}, L_{GD}) = 0$$

This quote may come with a bid and an ask quote. Let us call them S^{bid} and S^{ask}. The (positive) difference $S^{ask} - S^{bid}$ is called the CDS bid-ask spread (BAS), or sometimes more colloquially just the CDS bid-ask.

It is known that if we assume h_t to be deterministic and constant in time and we take the premium leg of the CDS paying continuously instead of quarterly, the equilibrium premium rate S balancing the two legs at a given time is linked to h by the formula:

$$h = \frac{S_{0,b}}{L_{GD}} \Rightarrow S_{0,b} = h L_{GD} \tag{19.10}$$

(See, for example, Brigo and Mercurio 2006). Now, since S has a bid and an ask quote, we can apply this formula to both. We obtain:

$$h^{ask} = S_{0,b}^{ask}/L_{GD}, \quad h^{bid} = S_{0,b}^{bid}/L_{GD}$$

One possible, very rough first approach is to define the liquidity spread ℓ (in this framework deterministic and constant) as:

$$\ell := \frac{h^{ask} - h^{bid}}{2}$$

If we do that, and we define:

$$h^{mid} := \frac{h^{bid} + h^{ask}}{2} = \frac{S_{0,b}^{bid} + S_{0,b}^{ask}}{2 L_{GD}}$$

we notice that by definition then:

$$h^{bid} = h_{mid} - \ell, \quad h^{ask} = h_{mid} + \ell$$

and using again formula (19.10):

$$S_{0,b}^{mid} = h^{mid} L_{GD} = \frac{S_{0,b}^{bid} + S_{0,b}^{ask}}{2}$$

so that we have consistency with a meaningful definition of quoted mid S.

According to this simple calculation, the true credit spread of a name is the mid, whereas the range between bid and ask is due to illiquidity. For a perfectly liquid name $\ell = 0$ because the bid-ask spread is zero. For a very illiquid name with a large bid-ask spread, ℓ will be large. So strictly speaking, ℓ would be an *illiquidity spread*, although it is called by abuse of language a *liquidity spread*. In this chapter whenever we mention "liquidity spread" we mean an illiquidity spread. This means that if the spread increases, liquidity decreases (illiquidity increases).

The framework sees the mid CDS premium rate to be centered in the middle of the bid-ask range. However, it does not follow that the NPV of the CDS position also has the mid centered between bid and ask. This is illustrated in the simplified framework with continuous payments in the premium leg, flat hazard rates $h_t = h$, and constant deterministic interest rates r. In that case, the CDS default leg NPV corresponding to bid and ask becomes:

$$\mathrm{DL}_{0,b}^{bid}(\phi, \mathrm{L_{GD}}) = \mathrm{L_{GD}}\, h^{bid}\, \frac{(1 - \exp(-(r + h^{bid})\, T_b))}{r + h^{bid}},$$

$$\mathrm{DL}_{0,b}^{ask}(\phi, \mathrm{L_{GD}}) = \mathrm{L_{GD}}\, h^{ask}\, \frac{(1 - \exp(-(r + h^{ask})\, T_b))}{r + h^{ask}}$$

and we can see that:

$$\mathrm{L_{GD}}\, h^{mid}\, \frac{(1 - \exp(-(r + h^{mid})\, T_b))}{r + h^{mid}} \neq \frac{\mathrm{DL}_{0,b}^{bid} + \mathrm{DL}_{0,b}^{ask}}{2}$$

If we approximate the exponential at the first order we get back symmetry, but otherwise we do not observe that the NPV corresponding to the CDS mid quote is the midpoint between the NPV based on the CDS bid and ask quotes. More generally, when fitting also more sophisticated hazard rate processes to CDS bid and ask premium quotes, we will suffer from the same problem. The mid feature of the premium rates will not translate in mid NPVs. Despite this inconvenience, the idea is to use a process for ℓ in the instantaneous spread space to explain liquidity in the CDS prices. As a consequence, a formula similar to equation (19.9) is used to price the CDS under liquidity risk.

For example, Chen, Fabozzi, and Sverdlove (2008) in the first stage of their investigation fit a constant hazard rate h to S^{ask} and then calibrate the liquidity term ℓ (to be subtracted from h when discounting) to reprice the CDS mid quotes. In their view illiquidity always reduces the CDS premium and the CDS premium in the real market is less than a hypothetically perfectly liquid CDS premium. Because the latter is unobservable, they choose as benchmark the ask CDS premium. The liquidity premium will be reflected in the difference between the transaction CDS premium (mid) and the ask. In our example with flat hazard rates and continuous payments in the premium leg, this amounts to setting:

$$h^{ask} := \frac{S^{ask}}{\text{L}_{\text{GD}}}, \quad h^{mid} + \ell =: h^{ask} := \frac{S^{ask}}{\text{L}_{\text{GD}}}$$

This also implicitly suggests that:

$$h^{bid} := \frac{S^{mid}}{\text{L}_{\text{GD}}} - \ell$$

so that again $\ell = (h^{ask} - h^{bid})/2$.

Chen, Fabozzi, and Sverdlove (CFS) also argue that the liquidity correction should affect only the default leg of the CDS, since the premium leg is basically an annuity numéraire. This is not clear to us, since in a way also the premium leg is part of a traded asset subject to marking to market. And indeed, BT06 and BT08 make a different choice, and assume that the CDS liquidity discount appears in the payment/fix leg of the CDS and that there is a bond liquidity discount for the recovery part of the default leg. We discuss this more in detail later.

Having clarified the structure of the liquidity term with respect to the usual terms in CDS valuation with hazard rate/intensity models, we notice that the preceding picture considers the CDS bid and ask quotes to be perturbed by liquidity, so that CDS quotes do not express pure credit risk.

One may also think that the CDS expresses pure credit risk (see, for example, Longstaff, Mithal, and Neis 2005), but this is now considered to be unrealistic as illustrated in the papers discussed in this survey.

More generally, we will see that the model for both hazard rates and liquidity are stochastic. Typically, in the literature, under the risk-neutral probability measure, one assumes stochastic differential equations of diffusion type,

$$dh_t = b^h(t, h_t)dt + \sigma^h(t, h_t)dW_t^h, \quad d\ell_t = b^\ell(t, \ell_t)dt + \sigma^\ell(t, \ell_t)dW_t^\ell \quad (19.11)$$

where the two processes are possibly correlated. In most works in the literature, though, the two processes are unrealistically assumed to be independent. The advantage of assuming independence is that whenever we need to compute a formula similar to equation (19.9), its relevant component in credit and liquidity can be factored as:

$$\mathbb{E}_t\left[e^{-\int_t^T (h_u + \ell_u)\,du}\right] = \mathbb{E}_t\left[e^{-\int_t^T h_u\,du}\right]\mathbb{E}_t\left[e^{-\int_t^T \ell_u\,du}\right] \quad (19.12)$$

and this can be computed in closed form whenever we choose processes for which the bond price formulas are known. Also, in case where no liquidity premium is present, the survival probability $\mathbb{Q}(\tau > T)$ appearing, for example, in formula (19.7) is computed as:

$$\mathbb{Q}(\tau > T) = \mathbb{E}_0\left[e^{-\int_0^T h_u \, du}\right] \qquad (19.13)$$

and again this is known in closed form, so that the CDS fair premium rate can be computed in closed form with the model.

The cases of affine or quadratic models are typical to have this tractability. However, when we correlate h and ℓ, the decomposition no longer occurs and the only case where calculations are still easy in the correlated case is when the two processes $[h_t, \ell_t]$ are jointly Gaussian. This is not a viable assumption for us, however, since h needs to be positive, being a time-scaled probability.

In order to avoid numerical methods, most authors assume independence between credit risk (h_t) and liquidity risk (ℓ_t) in order to be able to apply formula (19.12) and the like.

It is worth highlighting at this point that this assumption is unrealistic, as we will discuss further in Section 19.4.1. In particular, see Figure 19.2.

19.2.4   Chen, Fabozzi, and Sverdlove (2008) (CFS)

In the CFS paper, the authors study liquidity and its impact on single-name CDS prices for corporations. From a first examination of the data they notice that the bid-ask spreads are very wide, especially for the high-yield corporate names in their study. While this is precrisis data, they noticed that the liquidity in the CDS market has improved in time, while still maintaining a larger bid-ask spread than typical bid-ask spreads in the equity market.

After the preliminary analysis, the authors employ a two-factor Cox-Ingersoll-Ross model for the liquidity and hazard rates and estimate their dynamics using maximum likelihood estimation (MLE).

In the formalism, this means they made two particular choices for the processes (19.11) to be of the type:

$$
\begin{aligned}
dh_t &= [k^h\theta^h - (k^h + m^h)h_t]dt + v^h\sqrt{h_t}dW_t^h, \\
d\ell_t &= [k^\ell\theta^\ell - (k^\ell + m^\ell)\ell_t]dt + v^\ell\sqrt{\ell_t}dW_t^\ell
\end{aligned}
\qquad (19.14)
$$

for positive constants k^h, θ^h, v^h, h_0, m^h and k^ℓ, θ^ℓ, v^ℓ, ℓ_0, m^ℓ. The two processes are assumed, somewhat unrealistically (see also the discussion in Section 19.4.1), to be independent.

These are the dynamics under the risk-neutral or pricing probability measure that are used in valuation to compute risk-neutral expectations and prices. The dynamic under the physical measure related to historical estimation and MLE is:

$$dh_t = k^h(\theta^h - h_t)dt + v^h\sqrt{h_t}d\widetilde{W}_t^h, \quad d\ell_t = k^\ell(\theta^\ell - \ell_t)dt + v^\ell\sqrt{\ell_t}d\widetilde{W}_t^\ell \quad (19.15)$$

where now $\widetilde{W}$ are Brownian motions under the physical measure. In equation (19.15) the θ's are mean-reversion levels, the k's are speed of mean-reversion parameters, and the v's are instantaneous volatilities parameters. The m parameters are market prices of risk, parametrizing the change of measure from the physical probability measure to the risk-neutral one. See, for example, Brigo and Mercurio (2006). Brigo and Hanzon (1998) hint at the possible application of filtering algorithms and quasi-maximum likelihood to a similar context for interest rate models.

The advantages of the Cox-Ingersoll-Ross (CIR) model are that the processes are nonnegative, in that $h_t \geq 0$ and $\ell_t \geq 0$ (and one has strict positivity with some restrictions on the parameters), and there is a closed-form formula in terms of $k^h, \theta^h, v^h, h_0, m^h$ and $k^\ell, \theta^\ell, v^\ell, \ell_0, m^\ell$ for:

$$\mathbb{E}_0\left[e^{-\int_0^T (h_u+\ell_u)\,du}\right] = \mathbb{E}_0\left[e^{-\int_0^T h_u\,du}\right]\mathbb{E}_0\left[e^{-\int_0^T \ell_u\,du}\right] \tag{19.16}$$

and related quantities that are needed to compute the CDS prices. Indeed, through formula (19.7) combined with formula (19.13) that is known in closed form for CIR, we have the CDS premium rate in closed form for our model.

Adding the liquidity discount term, $L(t,s) = e^{-\int_t^s \ell_u du}$, to the CDS premium rate formula (19.3), we obtain:

$$S_{a,b}^*(t) = \frac{\mathbb{E}_t[\text{L}_{\text{GD}}\,\mathbf{1}_{\{T_a<\tau\leq T_b\}}L(t,\tau)D(t,\tau)]}{\mathbb{E}_t[D(t,\tau)(\tau-T_{\beta(\tau)-1})\mathbf{1}_{\{T_a<\tau<T_b\}} + \sum_{i=a+1}^b D(t,T_i)\alpha_i\mathbf{1}_{\{\tau\geq T_i\}}]}$$

$$\tag{19.17}$$

Notice that we added the additional (il)liquidity discount term only in the numerator. This is the strategy followed by CFS, who argue that the annuity should not be adjusted by liquidity. As observed earlier, this is debatable, since even the premium leg of the CDS is part of a traded product, and indeed, for example, BT06 and BT08 follow a different strategy.

Formula (19.17) can be further explicited in terms of the processes r, h, ℓ via iterated expectations with respect to the sigma field $\mathcal{F}_t$. For the special case of $t = T_a = 0$ one obtains:

$$S_{0,b}^*(0) = \frac{\mathbb{E}_0\left[\text{L}_{\text{GD}}\int_0^{T_b} h_u \exp(-\int_0^u (r_s+h_s+\ell_s)ds)du\right]}{\text{Accrual}_{0,b} + \sum_{i=a+1}^b \alpha_i \mathbb{E}_0[\exp(-\int_0^{T_i}(r_s+h_s)ds)]}$$

$$\tag{19.18}$$

$$\text{Accrual}_{0,b} = \int_0^{T_b} \mathbb{E}_0\left[h_u \exp\left(-\int_0^u (r_s+h_s)ds\right)(u-T_{\beta(u)-1})\right]du$$

This holds for general dynamics for r, h, ℓ, not necessarily of square root type, and does not require independence assumptions.

In any case, if one sticks to equation (19.17), the CDS fair premium rate formula with deterministic interest rates and hazard rates independent of liquidity spreads reads:

$$S_{0,b}^*(0) = \frac{-\mathrm{L_{GD}} \int_0^{T_b} P(0, t) A(0, t) d_t \mathbb{Q}(\tau \geq t)}{-\int_0^{T_b} P(0, t)(t - T_{\beta(t)-1}) d_t \mathbb{Q}(\tau \geq t) + \sum_{i=1}^{b} P(0, T_i)\alpha_i \mathbb{Q}(\tau \geq T_i)} \qquad (19.19)$$

where

$$A(0, T) = \mathbb{E}_0[e^{-\int_0^T \ell_s ds}] = P^{CIR}(0, T; \ell_0, k^\ell, \theta^\ell, v^\ell, m^\ell) \qquad (19.20)$$

$$\mathbb{Q}(\tau \geq T) = \mathbb{E}_0[e^{-\int_0^T h_s ds}] = P^{CIR}(0, T; h_0, k^h, \theta^h, v^h, m^h) \qquad (19.21)$$

where P^{CIR} is the bond price formula in a CIR model having ℓ or h, respectively, as short rates. For example,

$$P^{CIR}(0, T; h_0, k^h, \theta^h, v^h, m^h) = \phi(T - 0) \exp(-\psi(T - 0)h_0),$$

$$\phi(T) = \left[\frac{2\sqrt{z} \, \exp\{(k^h + m^h + \sqrt{z}) T/2\}}{2\sqrt{z} + (k^h + m^h + \sqrt{z})(\exp\{T\sqrt{z}\} - 1)} \right]^{2k^h \theta^h / (v^h)^2}$$

$$\psi(T) = \frac{2(\exp\{T\sqrt{z}\} - 1)}{2\sqrt{z} + (k^h + m^h + \sqrt{z})(\exp\{T\sqrt{z}\} - 1)}$$

$$z = (k^h + m^h)^2 + 2(v^h)^2$$

Notice that we have all the terms in closed form to compute formula (19.19) thanks to the CIR bond price formula and the independence assumption.

Then equation (19.19) combined with equations (19.20) and (19.21) provides a formula for CDS premium rates with liquidity as a function of h_0, ℓ_0, and the model parameters k^h, θ^h, v^h, m^h and $k^\ell, \theta^\ell, v^\ell, m^\ell$. Similarly, formula (19.3) coupled with equation (19.21) provides a formula for CDS premium rates without liquidity as a function of h_0 and the model parameters k^h, θ^h, v^h, m^h.

These formulas can also be applied at a time t later than 0. Indeed, while taking care of adjusting year fractions and intervals of integration, one applies the same formula at time t.

Let us denote the at-the-money liquidity-adjusted CDS rate, and the at-the-money CDS rate, at time t by:

$$S_{t, T_b+t}^*(t; h_t, \ell_t; k^h, \theta^h, v^h, m^h; k^\ell, \theta^\ell, v^\ell, m^\ell), \quad S_{t, T_b+t}(t; h_t; k^h, \theta^h, v^h, m^h)$$

respectively.

A maximum likelihood estimation would then be used ideally, trying to obtain the transition density for $S^*_{t+\Delta t, T_b+t+\Delta t}(t + \Delta t; h_{t+\Delta t}, \ell_{t+\Delta t}; k^h, \theta^h, v^h, m^h; k^\ell, \theta^\ell, v^\ell, m^\ell)$ given $S^*_{t, T_b+t}(t; h_t, \ell_t; k^h, \theta^h, v^h, m^h; k^\ell, \theta^\ell, v^\ell, m^\ell)$ from the noncentral (independent) chi-squared transition densities for $h_{t+\Delta t}$ given h_t and $\ell_{t+\Delta t}$ given ℓ_t. One would then maximize the likelihood over the sample period by using such transition densities as key tools, to obtain the estimated model parameters. Notice that this would be possible only when h and ℓ are independent, since the joint distribution of two correlated CIR processes is not known in closed form.

Similarly, the transition density for $S_{t+\Delta t, T_b+t+\Delta t}(t + \Delta t; h_{t+\Delta t}; k^h, \theta^h, v^h, m^h)$ given $S_{t, T_b+t}(t; h_t; k^h, \theta^h, v^h, m^h)$ would be obtained from the chi-squared transition density for $h_{t+\Delta t}$ given h_t.

CFS adopt a maximum likelihood estimation method based on the earlier work by Chen and Scott (1993). This maximum likelihood method allows CFS to compute:

- The credit parameters $k^h, \theta^h, v^h, h_0, m^h$ from a time series of ask premium rates $S_{0,b}(0)$.
- The liquidity parameters $k^\ell, \theta^\ell, v^\ell, \ell_0, m^\ell$ from a time series of mid CDS premium rates $S^*_{0,b}(0)$.

CFS find that the parameters of the hazard rate factor h are more sensitive to credit ratings and those for the liquidity component ℓ are more sensitive to market capitalization and number of quotes, two proxies for liquidity.

CFS also refer to earlier studies where CDS premiums had been used as a pure measure of the price of credit risk. CFS argue, through a simulation analysis, that small errors in the CDS credit premium rate can lead to substantially larger errors in the corporate bond credit spread for the same reference entity. Empirically, they use the CDS estimated hazard rate model to reprice bonds, with (h_t and ℓ_t) and without (just h_t) taking CDS liquidity into account.

When using these hazard rates to calculate bond spreads, CFS find that incorporating the CDS liquidity factor results in improved estimates of the liquidity spreads for the bonds in their sample.

CFS thus argue that while CDS premiums can be used in the analysis of corporate bond spreads, one must be careful to take into account the presence of a liquidity effect in the CDS market.

Results reported in the earlier literature before 2006 stated that bond credit spreads were substantially wider than CDS premiums. This has been contradicted by many observations during the crisis, but already CFS show that, since a small CDS liquidity premium can translate into a large liquidity discount in a bond's price, mostly due to the principal repayment at final maturity, they can successfully reconcile CDS premiums and bond credit spreads by incorporating liquidity into their model. However, the relevance of this analysis for data in-crisis remains to be proven. Finally, it is worth noticing that in CFS work the (il)liquidity premium is earned by the CDS protection buyer. Indeed, adding a positive (il)liquidity discount rate to the model (and to the default leg only) lowers the fair CDS premium rate with respect to the case with no illiquidity. This means that the protection buyer will pay a lower premium for the same protection in a universe where illiquidity is taken into account (i.e., the liquidity premium is earned by the protection buyer).

19.2.5   Chen, Cheng, and Wu (2005) (CCW)

CCW propose a general reduced-form framework similar to CFS. They, too, assume independence between default and liquidity. However, their study differs in several ways from CFS. First, they assume stochastic interest rates that are correlated with hazard rates governing defaults, but independent from liquidity. Second, liquidity appears as a stochastic discount rate in addition to the hazard rate and it enters both in the default leg and the premium leg of the mid CDS premium rate formula analogous to (19.18) but with both continuous payments (simplification) and a liquidity discount in the denominator:

$$S_{0,b}^*(0) = \frac{\mathbb{E}_0\left[\text{L}_{\text{GD}}\int_0^{T_b} h_t \exp(-\int_0^t (r_u + h_u + \ell_u)du)dt\right]}{\mathbb{E}_0[\int_0^{T_b} \exp(-\int_0^t (r_u + h_u + \ell_u)du)dt]}$$

A third major difference from CFS is the assumption that the interest rate, the hazard rate, and the liquidity discount rate are affine functions of underlying latent factors following Gaussian mean-reverting processes. Particularly, they assume a two-factor interest rate model:

$$r_t = a_r + b_r^T X_t$$

$$dX_t = [\theta_x - k_x X_t]dt + dW_t^X$$

where X is a two-dimensional column vector, and k_x is a 2×2 matrix. Here W^X is a two-dimensional standard Brownian motion. All state variables in their model are normalized to have an identity instantaneous covariance matrix. Additionally, k_x is constrained to be a lower triangular matrix with positive eigenvalues to preserve stationarity.

The hazard rate is assumed to be an affine function of three or four latent factors, two of which are the interest rate factors. This allows them to capture correlation between interest rates and credit spreads:

$$h_t = a_h + b_h^T X_t + c_h^T Y_t$$

$$dY_t = [\theta_y - k_{xy} X_t - k_y Y_t]dt + dW_t^Y$$

where Y_t is either scalar or a two-dimensional column vector. W^Y is independent of W^X. Similarly as for the interest rate factors, in the two-dimensional case k_y is assumed to be a 2×2 lower triangular matrix with positive eigenvalues.

Finally, the illiquidity spread is modeled as an affine function of one latent factor ξ, which is independent of all interest rate and hazard rate factors:

$$\ell_t = a_l + c_l \xi_t$$

$$d\xi_t = [\theta_l - k_l \xi_t] dt + d W_t^\xi$$

Brownian motions W^X, W^Y, and W^ξ are mutually independent. The model is estimated using a maximum likelihood estimator, with log-likelihood function constructed using the extended Kalman filtering. In the first step, interest rate dynamics are estimated with LIBOR and swap rates for different maturities. In the second step, the hazard rate dynamics are estimated using the average CDS premium rates for the high-liquidity names further grouped by industry and credit rating, under the assumption that liquidity discount is zero for the high-liquidity names.[2] In the third step, they identify the liquidity-risk factor using the average CDS premium rates in the low-liquidity group. In this step they also estimate an additional credit risk factor, independent of all other factors and which is assumed to drive the premium rates of the illiquid group. The estimation is done only at the portfolio level, where portfolios are formed by industry, rating, and quote frequency.

Surprisingly CCW find that within the same industry and rating class, the high-liquidity portfolios have larger CDS premium rates than the low-liquidity ones. The extra spread is driven by both credit risk and liquidity risk differences between the two groups. Results suggest that the liquidity premium is earned by the CDS protection buyer.

19.2.6 Buhler and Trapp (2006, 2008) (BT06, BT08)

BT06 make a different choice, and assume that the CDS liquidity discount appears in the premium leg of the CDS and, furthermore, that there is a bond liquidity discount for the recovery part of the default leg. Suppose, for example, that the protection payment in case of default is agreed to be done through physical settlement. In such a case the protection buyer could deliver the bond of the defaulted entity to the protection seller and obtain from the protection seller the insured notional. If we assumed the insured notional to be 1 and the residual value of the bond after default to be the recovery R, then without accounting for liquidity the protection payment would be $1 - R$. However, in computing the value of the bond under the default scenario liquidity may enter the picture, so that the residual value R of the bond after default needs to be adjusted by a liquidity factor.

This approach may look debatable as well, although it is further motivated by BT06 as follows:

> A common solution to this problem both in empirical studies and theoretical models
> ... is to assume that the CDS mid premium is perfectly liquid and thus identi-
> cal to the transaction premium. We believe that this assumption, however, is not

appropriate. From a theoretical point-of-view, the assumption suggests that transaction costs, here the bid-ask-spread, are equally divided between the protection buyer and the protection seller. This fiction neglects the possibility of asymmetric market frictions which lead to asymmetric transaction costs. The empirical evidence that CDS transaction premia tend to fluctuate around mid premia, see Buhler and Trapp (2005), adds weight to these theoretical concerns. In order to reconcile the theoretical arbitrage considerations to a model of CDS illiquidity, we assume that the mid CDS premium contains an illiquidity component.

BT06 assume that all the bonds and the CDSs for the same issuer have identical default intensity (h_t) but different liquidity intensities: ℓ_t^b for all bonds of one issuer and ℓ_t^c for that issuer's CDSs. They also assume independence among default-free rates, default intensity, and liquidity intensities. Using a similar notation as in the previous sections for simplicity, although in their actual work BT06 use discrete time payments in the default leg, the model implied CDS premium rate is equal to:

$$S_{0,b}(0) = \frac{-\int_0^T (1 - R\, A^b(0, t))\, P(0, t)\, d_t \mathbb{Q}(\tau \geq t)}{-\int_0^T P(0, t) A^c(0, t)(t - T_{\beta(t)-1}) d_t \mathbb{Q}(\tau \geq t) + \sum_{i=1}^b A^c(0, T_i) P(0, T_i) \alpha_i \mathbb{Q}(\tau \geq T_i)}$$

(19.22)

where

$$A^b(0, t) = \mathbb{E}_0[L^b(0, t)], \quad L^b(0, t) = e^{-\int_0^t \ell_s^b ds},$$

$$A^c(0, t) = \mathbb{E}_0[L^c(0, t)], \quad L^c(0, t) = e^{-\int_0^t \ell_s^c ds}$$

are the liquidity discount factors for the bond and the CDS payment leg, respectively.

The default intensity h_t is assumed to follow a mean-reverting square root process as in equation (19.14). Liquidity intensities are assumed to follow arithmetic Brownian motions with constant drift and diffusion coefficients:

$$d\ell_t^j = \mu^j dt + \eta^j dW_t^{\ell^j}, \quad j \in \{b, c\}$$

(19.23)

Notation is self-evident. Notice that the (il)liquidity premium will be negative in some scenarios, due to the left tail of the Gaussian distribution for ℓ. This is a major difference from CFS, where the illiquidity premium is always positive. These assumptions allow for analytical solutions for bonds and CDS premium rates and for calibration to observed bond spreads and CDS premium rates.

BT06 perform an empirical calibration of the model using bonds and CDSs for 10 telecommunications companies over the time period 2001–2005. They find that while the credit risk components in CDS and bond credit spreads are almost identical, the liquidity premiums differ significantly. The illiquidity premium component of bond credit spreads is always positive and is positively correlated with the default risk premium. In times of increased default risk, bonds become less liquid. The CDS illiquidity premium can take positive or negative values, but is generally very small in absolute value. Contrary to the bonds case, CDS liquidity improves when default risk increases. Thus BT06's framework can explain both positive and negative values for the CDS bond basis through variations in the CDS and bond liquidity. Given the very small sample size in their study, it is not clear whether these results are representative of the whole market. Also, they too use only precrisis data. Finally, this approach suffers again from the independence assumption, which is rather unrealistic (see once more the discussion in Section 19.4.1).

The correlation issue is addressed in BT08, which extends the previous model in BT06 to a reduced-form model now incorporating correlation between bond liquidity and CDS liquidity and between default and bond/CDS liquidity. Additionally, they assume different liquidity intensities associated with the ask ($\ell_t^{c,ask}$) and bid CDS ($\ell_t^{c,bid}$).

In the BT08 model the stochastic default intensity (h_t) and the illiquidity intensities (ℓ_t^b, $\ell_t^{c,ask}$, $\ell_t^{c,bid}$) are all driven by four independent latent factors X_t, Y_t^b, $Y_t^{c,ask}$, $Y_t^{c,bid}$ as follows:

$$\begin{pmatrix} dh_t \\ d\ell_t^b \\ d\ell_t^{c,ask} \\ d\ell_t^{c,bid} \end{pmatrix} = \begin{pmatrix} 1 & g_b & g_{ask} & g_{bid} \\ f_b & 1 & \omega_{b,ask} & \omega_{b,bid} \\ f_{ask} & \omega_{b,ask} & 1 & \omega_{ask,bid} \\ f_{bid} & \omega_{b,bid} & \omega_{ask,bid} & 1 \end{pmatrix} \begin{pmatrix} dX_t \\ dY_t^b \\ dY_t^{c,ask} \\ dY_t^{c,bid} \end{pmatrix} \quad (19.24)$$

where X_t is modeled as a mean-reverting square root process as in equation (19.14) and Y_t^b, $Y_t^{c,ask}$, $Y_t^{c,bid}$ as arithmetic Brownian motions as in equation (19.23). Again, notation is self-evident. Note that in this model f and g shape the correlations between the default intensity and the liquidity intensities, while ω shape the liquidity spillover effects between bonds and CDSs, which are assumed to be symmetrical. Notice that the system of equations in (19.24) does not guarantee $L^{c,ask}(0, t) < L^{c,bid}(0, t)$, thus not excluding the case $S_{0,b}^{bid}(0) > S_{0,b}^{ask}(0)$. However, in their empirical study, they find that this never occurs.

It is further assumed that risk-free interest rates are independent of the default and liquidity intensities.

Valuing bonds and CDSs in the BT08 framework mainly involves the computation of the expectation of the risk-free discount factor and the expectation of the product of the default and liquidity discount factors. The latter expectation is not a product of expectations as before, given the assumed dependence between default and liquidity, so that the analogous approach of formula (19.16) cannot be applied.

The bid CDS premium rate formula becomes:

$$S_{0,b}^{bid}(0) = \frac{\int_0^{T_b} P(0, t) \mathbb{E}_0[(1 - Re^{-\int_0^t \ell_s^b ds}) h_t e^{-\int_0^t h_s ds}] dt}{\sum_{i=1}^b P(0, T_i) \alpha_i \mathbb{E}_0[e^{-\int_0^{T_i} \ell_s^{c,bid} ds} e^{-\int_0^{T_i} h_s ds}] + \text{Accrual}} \quad (19.25)$$

$$\text{Accrual} = \int_0^{T_b} P(0, t)(t - T_{\beta(t)-1}) \mathbb{E}_0[e^{-\int_0^t \ell_s^{c,bid} ds} h_t e^{-\int_0^t h_s ds}] dt$$

The ask CDS premium rate formula is similar with $\ell_t^{c,ask}$ instead of $\ell_t^{c,bid}$. Note that the ask illiquidity discount rate $\ell_t^{c,ask}$ appears in the payment leg and captures the fact that part of the ask CDS premium rate may not be due to default risk but reflects an additional premium for illiquidity demanded by the protection seller. However, $\ell_t^{c,bid}$ would capture the illiquidity premium demanded by the protection buyers. Different illiquidity ask and bid spreads reflect asymmetric transaction costs, which are driven by the general observed asymmetric market imbalances.

The assumed factor structure of the model and the independence between the latent factors imply an affine term structure model with analytical formulas for both bonds and CDSs. For example, expectations in equation (19.25) can be computed in closed form.

Data on bond yields and CDS premium rates on 155 European firms for the time period covering 2001 to 2007 is then used to estimate the model parameters. The estimation procedure generates firm-level estimates for the parameters of the latent variables processes, sensitivities of the different intensities to the latent factors ($f's$, $g's$, $w's$), and the values for the credit and liquidity intensities at each point in time (h_t, ℓ_t^b, $\ell_t^{c,ask}$, $\ell_t^{c,bid}$).

The empirical estimation in BT08 implies several interesting findings. First, their results suggest that credit risk has an impact on both bond and CDS liquidity. As credit risk increases, liquidity dries up for bonds and for the CDS ask premium rates (f_b, f_{ask} are positive and significant). However, the impact of increased credit risk on CDS bid liquidity spreads is mixed across different companies, but on average higher credit risk results in lower CDS bid liquidity intensity (f_{bid} is on average negative and significant). Second, their results suggest that while the impact of bond or CDS liquidity on credit risk is negligible (g_b, g_{ask}, g_{bid} are not statistically significant), the spillover effects between bond and CDS market liquidities are significant ($w_{b,ask}$, $w_{ask,bid}$ are negative and significant; $w_{b,bid}$ is positive and significant). They explain the signs of $w_{b,ask}$, $w_{b,bid}$ as a substitution effect between bonds and CDSs: as bond liquidity dries up (bond illiquidity intensity ℓ_t^b goes up), bond prices go down, thus taking on credit risk using bonds becomes more attractive. If a trader intends to be long credit risk by selling protection through CDSs, she will need to drop the ask price (CDS ask liquidity intensity ℓ_t^{ask} goes down) compared to the case of high bond liquidity. At the same time, lower bond prices in case of lower bond liquidity (higher ℓ_t^b) makes shorting credit risk via bonds more costly, which then drives bid quotes in the CDS market higher (higher ℓ_t^{bid}).

Additionally, BT use the empirical parameter and intensity estimates to decompose the bond spreads and CDS premium rates into three separate components: the pure credit risk premium, the pure liquidity risk premium, and the rest, the credit-liquidity correlation premium. In particular they estimate the pure CDS credit risk premium ($s\,d$) as the theoretical CDS premium rate implied by the model when the liquidity intensities ℓ_t^{bid}, ℓ_t^{ask} are switched off to zero. The pure CDS liquidity premium ($s\,l$) is subsequently computed as the difference between the average theoretical mid CDS premium rate for uncorrelated credit and liquidity intensities ($f's$ and $g's$ are zero) and the pure CDS credit risk premium $s\,d$. Finally, the correlation premium is calculated as the difference between the observed market CDS premium rate and the sum of the pure credit and pure liquidity premiums.

On average BT08 find that, for CDSs, the credit risk component accounts for 95 percent of the observed mid premium, liquidity accounts for 4 percent, and correlation accounts for 1 percent. They proceed in similar fashion for the bond spread decomposition and find that overall 60 percent of the bond spread is due to credit risk, 35 percent is due to liquidity, and 5 percent is due to correlation between credit risk and liquidity.

Cross-sectionally, all credit, illiquidity, and correlation premiums for bonds and CDSs increase monotonically as the credit rating worsens from AAA to B, and then drops for the CCC category. These findings are in contrast to the Predescu et al. (2009) (PTGLKR) findings discussed in Section 19.4.1 and in Figure 19.2 in particular.

BT08 also examine the time-series dynamics of the different components. They find that, while generally similar behavior can be observed for the credit risk premium for both investment-grade (IG) and high-yield (HY) firms, the same is not true for the liquidity premium. During a period with high credit spreads (2001–2002, around Enron and WorldCom defaults) the bond liquidity premium for IG is very volatile and then flattens out at a higher level about mid-2003. In contrast, bond liquidity premium for HY firms reaches the highest level after the WorldCom default and decreases to a lower level for the rest of the time period. In the CDS market, the CDS liquidity premium for the IG firms is close to 0 for most of time, while for HY it is very volatile and becomes negative when credit risk is high. A negative CDS liquidity premium is consistent with more bid-initiated transactions in the market.

The bond premium dynamics tend to comove over time with the credit risk premium dynamics. Interestingly, the correlation premium is larger than the liquidity premium when credit spreads are high and smaller when credit spreads are low. BT interpret this finding as being consistent with the flight to quality/liquidity hypothesis. In other words, in times of stress, investors will try to move away from assets whose liquidity would decrease as credit risk increases and instead acquire liquid assets that can be easily traded. High correlation between illiquidity and credit will thus command a high spread premium component.

All the empirical results with respect to the difference between IG and HY should, in our view, be considered carefully since BT's sample is highly biased toward investment-grade firms. Also, as before, no data in-crisis has been used.

19.3 Liquidity through the CAPM Framework

19.3.1 Acharya and Pedersen (2005) (AP)

There is a fourth work by Bongaerts, De Jong, and Driessen (2009) (BDD), who use CAPM-like arguments to quantify the impact of liquidity on CDS returns. They construct an asset pricing model for CDS contracts inspired by the work of Acharya and Pedersen (2005) (AP) that allows for expected liquidity and liquidity risk. Since their approach is heavily based on AP, it is worth recalling AP's general result.

AP start from the fundamental question: "How does liquidity risk affect asset prices in equilibrium?" This question is answered by proposing an equilibrium asset pricing model with liquidity risk. Their model assumes a dynamic overlapping-generations economy where risk-averse agents trade securities (equities) whose liquidity changes randomly over time. Agents are assumed to have constant absolute risk-aversion utility functions and live for just one period. They trade securities at times t and $t + 1$ and derive utility from consumption at time $t + 1$. They can buy a security at a price P_t but must sell at $P_t - C_t$, thus incurring a liquidity cost. Liquidity risk in this model is born from the uncertainty about illiquidity costs C_t. Under further assumptions such as no short selling, the autoregressive model of order 1, or AR(1), processes with i.i.d. normal innovations for the dividends, and illiquidity costs, AP derive the liquidity-adjusted conditional CAPM:

$$\underbrace{\mathbb{E}_t^P [R_{t+1}]}_{Expected\ Asset\ Gross\ Return} = \underbrace{R^f}_{Risk\text{-}Free\ Rate} + \underbrace{\mathbb{E}_t^P [c_{t+1}]}_{Expected\ Illiquidity\ Cost}$$

$$+ \underbrace{\pi_t}_{Risk\ Premium} \underbrace{\frac{Cov_t\left(R_{t+1}, R_{t+1}^M\right)}{Var_t\left(R_{t+1}^M - c_{t+1}^M\right)}}_{\beta_{Mkt,t}} + \pi_t \underbrace{\frac{Cov_t\left(c_{t+1}, c_{t+1}^M\right)}{Var_t\left(R_{t+1}^M - c_{t+1}^M\right)}}_{\beta_{2,t}}$$

$$- \pi_t \underbrace{\frac{Cov_t\left(R_{t+1}, c_{t+1}^M\right)}{Var_t\left(R_{t+1}^M - c_{t+1}^M\right)}}_{\beta_{3,t}} - \pi_t \underbrace{\frac{Cov_t\left(c_{t+1}, R_{t+1}^M\right)}{Var_t\left(R_{t+1}^M - c_{t+1}^M\right)}}_{\beta_{4,t}}$$

where $\pi_t = \mathbb{E}_t^P \left(R_{t+1}^M - c_{t+1}^M - R^f\right)$ is the conditional market risk premium, with the expectation taken under the physical measure. The remaining notation is self-evident.

The liquidity-adjusted conditional CAPM thus implies that the asset's required conditional excess return depends on its conditional expected illiquidity cost and on the conditional covariance of the asset return and asset illiquidity cost with the market return and the market illiquidity cost. The systematic market and liquidity risks are captured by four conditional betas. The first beta ($\beta_{Mkt,t}$) is the traditional CAPM β that measures the covariation of individual security's return with the market return. The second beta ($\beta_{2,t}$) measures the covariance between the asset's illiquidity and the market illiquidity. The third beta ($\beta_{3,t}$) measures the covariance between the asset's return and the market illiquidity. This term negatively affects the required return. Investors will accept a lower return on securities that have high return in times of high market illiquidity. The fourth beta ($\beta_{4,t}$) measures the covariance between the asset's illiquidity and the market return. The effect of this is also negative. Investors will accept a lower return on securities that are liquid in times of market downturns.

In order to estimate the model empirically, the unconditional version of the model is derived under the assumption of constant conditional covariances between illiquidity and returns innovations. The unconditional liquidity adjusted CAPM can be written as:

$$\mathbb{E}^P\left[R_t - R^f\right] = \mathbb{E}^P\left[c_t\right] + \pi\beta_{Mkt} + \pi\beta_2 - \pi\beta_3 - \pi\beta_4 \qquad (19.26)$$

where $\pi = \mathbb{E}^P[\pi_t]$ is the unconditional market risk premium.

AP perform the empirical estimation of the model using daily return and volume data on the New York Stock Exchange (NYSE) and the American Stock Exchange (AMEX) stocks over the period 1962–1999. The illiquidity measure for a stock is the monthly average of the daily absolute return-to-volume ratio proposed by Amihud (2002). Illiquid stocks will have higher ratios, as a small volume will have a high impact on price. The Amihud illiquidity measure ratio addresses only one component of liquidity costs, namely the market impact of traded volume. Other components include broker fees, bid-ask spreads, and search costs.

Using portfolios sorted along different dimensions, AP find that the liquidity-adjusted CAPM performs better than the traditional CAPM in explaining cross-sectional variations in returns, especially for the liquidity-sorted portfolios. Liquidity risk and expected liquidity premiums are found to be economically significant. On average, the premium for expected liquidity—that is, the empirical estimate for the unconditional expected illiquidity cost $E(c_t)$—is equal to 3.5 percent. The liquidity risk premium, calculated as $\pi\beta_2 - \pi\beta_3 - \pi\beta_4$, is estimated to be 1.1 percent. About 80 percent of the liquidity risk premium is due to the third component, $\pi\beta_4$, which is driven by the covariation of individual illiquidity cost with the market return.

19.3.2 Bongaerts, De Jong, and Driessen (2009) (BDD)

BDD extend the model proposed by AP to an asset pricing model for both assets in positive net supply (like equities) and derivatives in zero net supply. Differently from the AP framework where short selling is not allowed, in the BDD model some of the agents are exposed to nontraded risk factors and in equilibrium they hold short positions in some assets to hedge these risk factors. Specifically, there are two types of assets in the model: basic or nonhedge assets (e.g., equities), on which agents hold long positions in equilibrium, and hedge assets, which can be held long or short by different agents in equilibrium. Hedge assets are sold short by some agents to hedge their exposures to nontraded risks. Examples of such risks are nontraded bank loans or illiquid corporate bonds held by some financial institutions such as commercial banks. These institutions can hedge the risks with CDS contracts. Other agents such as hedge funds or insurance companies may not have such exposures and may sell CDSs to commercial banks to earn the spread.

The BDD model implies that the equilibrium expected returns on the hedge assets can be decomposed in several components: priced exposure to the nonhedge asset returns, hedging demand effects, an expected illiquidity component, liquidity risk premiums, and hedge transaction costs. Unlike the AP model, where higher illiquidity leads to lower prices and higher expected returns, the impact of the liquidity on expected returns in BDD model is more complex. The liquidity risk impact depends on several factors such as heterogeneity in investors' nontraded risk exposure, risk aversion, horizon, and agent's wealth. Additionally, the BDD model implies that, for assets in zero net supply like CDSs, sensitivity of individual liquidity to market liquidity (β_2) is not priced.

BDD perform an empirical test of the model on CDS portfolio returns over the 2004–2008 period. The CDS sample captures 46 percent of the corporate bond market in terms of amount issued. The estimation procedure is a two-step procedure. In the first step, expected CDS returns, liquidity measures (proxied by the bid-ask spread), nontraded risk factor returns, nonhedge asset returns, and different betas with respect to market returns and market liquidity are estimated. The nonhedge asset returns are proxied by the S&P 500 equity index returns. Such estimates represent the explanatory variables of the asset pricing model, where the response variable is the expected excess return on the hedge asset. In the second step, the generalized method of moments is used to estimate the coefficients of the different explanatory variables in the model. Their results imply a statistically and economically significant expected liquidity premium priced in the expected CDS returns. On average this is 0.175 percent per quarter and it is earned by the protection seller, contrary to CCW and CFS. BDD also find that the liquidity risk premium is statistically significant, but economically very small, -0.005 percent. Somewhat questionably, the equity and credit risk premiums together account for only 0.060 percent per quarter.

19.4 Regression-Based Approaches for Measuring CDS Liquidity

19.4.1 Predescu et al. (2009) (PTGLKR)

Predescu et al. (2009) have built a statistical model that associates an ordinal liquidity score with each CDS reference entity.[3] This provides a comparison of relative liquidity of over 2,400 reference entities in the CDS market globally, mainly concentrated in North America, Europe, and Asia. The model estimation and the model-generated liquidity scores are based on the Fitch CDS Pricing Services database, which includes single-name CDS quotes on over 3,000 entities, corporates and sovereigns, across about two dozen broker-dealers back to 2000.

The liquidity score is built using well-known liquidity indicators like the bid-ask spread as well as other less accessible predictors of market liquidity such as number of active dealers quoting a reference entity, staleness of quotes of individual dealers, and dispersion in midquotes across market dealers. The bid-ask spread is essentially an indicator of market breadth; the existence of orders on both sides of the trading book typically corresponds to tighter bid-asks. The other measures are novel measures of liquidity that appear to be significant model predictors for the OTC CDS market. Dispersion of mid quotes across dealers is a measure of price uncertainty about the actual CDS price. Less liquid names are generally associated with more price

FIGURE 19.2 Liquidity Smile Illustrating the Correlation between Credit Quality and Liquidity

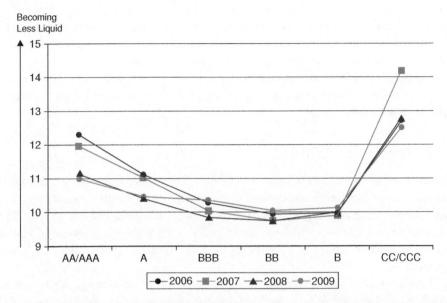

The vertical axis displays the aggregated values of liquidity scores per rating class. The higher the score, the less liquid the name is.

uncertainty and thus large dispersion. The third liquidity measure aggregates the number of active dealers and the individual dealers' quote staleness into an (in)activity measure, which is meant to be a proxy for CDS market depth. Illiquidity increases if any of the liquidity predictors increases, keeping everything else constant. Therefore liquid names are associated with smaller liquidity scores, and less liquid names with larger liquidity scores.

The liquidity scores add insight into the liquidity risk of the credit default swap (CDS) market, including understanding the difference between liquidity and credit risk, how market liquidity changes over time, what happens to liquidity in times of stress, and what impact certain credit events have on the liquidity of individual assets. For example, it reveals a U-shaped relationship between liquidity and credit with names in BB and B categories being the most liquid and names at the two ends of credit quality (AAA and CCC/C) being less liquid. (See Figure 19.2.) The U-shaped relationship between liquidity and credit is quite intuitive, as one would expect a larger-order imbalance between buy and sell orders for names with a very high or a very low credit rating than for names with ratings in the middle range. In particular, it is reasonable to expect more buying pressure for CCC names and more selling pressure for AAA names. Most of the trading will take place in the middle categories (BBB, BB, and B). The extent of the illiquidity at the two extremes also changes over time. This is particularly more pronounced for C-rated entities, which were relatively less liquid in 2007.

Additionally, Predescu et al. (2009) find that the liquidity score distribution shifts significantly over the credit/liquidity crisis, having fatter tails (i.e., more names in the very liquid and very illiquid groups) than before the crisis. The score allows for the construction of liquidity indexes at the aggregate market, region, or sector levels and, therefore, is very useful for studying market trends in liquidity.

This study produces an operational measure of liquidity for each CDS reference entity name on a daily basis, and has been extensively validated against external indicators of liquidity.

19.4.2   Tang and Yan (2007)(TY)

After the ordinal model by Predescu et al. (2009), we go back to works that decompose CDS premium rate levels or changes into liquidity and credit components. One such study is Tang and Yan (2007) (TY), which also includes bid-ask spread (BAS) information among other variables chosen as liquidity measures: volatility to volume (V2V), number of contracts outstanding (NOC), trade-to-quote ratio (T2Q), and volume.

V2V is meant to proxy for market depth, measuring price sensitivity to volume traded. As CDS volumes at name level are not easily available, they compute V2V as the ratio of CDS premium rate volatility to the number of quotes and trades for each reference entity. NOC is the number of outstanding contracts for each reference entity and is included as a proxy for the interdealers' inventory level. T2Q is built as a measure of matching intensity in an OTC search-based market. A higher T2Q should indicate faster trades and thus smaller search costs.

The authors separate liquidity from credit by including other credit control variables in the regression.[4]

The liquidity variables are generally statistically significant; however, their impacts on premium rates differ. While larger-volume V2V and NOC are associated with larger CDS premium rates, the effects of BAS and T2Q on premium rates are opposite for different subsets. The authors compare their results with the implications from some theoretical models proposed in the literature. They interpret the positive relationship between volume and CDS premium rates as being consistent with the Johnson (2008) model. In this model, volume is related to liquidity risk because volume is driven by the time-varying flux of entering and exiting agents and captures the risk of shocks to demand and supply balance. If volume is indeed a proxy for liquidity risk or liquidity variance, then TY results suggest that it is the protection sellers that receive a premium for bearing the liquidity risk.

Similarly, TY explain the positive relationship between NOC and CDS premium rates as being consistent with the model of Brunnermeier and Pedersen (2007) in which a larger number of contracts outstanding may indicate larger inventories and thus a higher probability of reaching funding limits on the dealers' side. The univariate effect of BAS and T2Q on premium rates is somewhat mixed cross-sectionally, with the more quoted names showing a negative relationship between T2Q and premium rates and a positive relationship between BAS and premium rates, and the less quoted ones showing the opposite effects.

19.5 Discussion, Conclusions, and Further Research

This chapter has reviewed different theoretical and empirical approaches for measuring the impact of liquidity on CDS prices. We started by investigating a reduced-form approach that incorporates liquidity as an additional discount yield. The different studies (Chen, Fabozzi, and Sverdlove 2008; Chen, Cheng, and Wu 2005; Buhler and Trapp 2006, 2008) that use a reduced-form model make different assumptions about how liquidity intensity enters the CDS premium rate formula, about the dynamics of the liquidity intensity process and about the credit-liquidity correlation. Among these studies BT08 provides the most general and realistic reduced-form framework by incorporating correlation between liquidity and credit, liquidity spillover effects between bonds and CDS contracts, and asymmetric liquidity effects on the bid and ask CDS premium rates. However, the empirical testing of their model can be significantly improved by using a larger, more representative sample over a longer time period including the recent credit crisis.

We then discussed the Bongaerts, De Jong, and Driessen (2009) study, which derives an equilibrium asset pricing model with liquidity effects. They test the model using CDS data and find that both expected liquidity and liquidity risk have a statistically significant impact on expected CDS returns. However, only compensation for expected liquidity is economically significant with higher expected liquidity being associated with higher expected returns for the protection sellers. This finding is contrary to Chen, Cheng, and Wu (2005) and Chen, Fabozzi, and Sverdlove (2008), which found protection buyers to earn the liquidity premium.

We approached the end of our review with a discussion of Predescu et al. (2009), which provides the only operational measure of CDS liquidity that is currently available in the market. They propose a statistical model that associates an ordinal liquidity score with each CDS reference entity and allows one to compare liquidity of over 2,400 reference entities. After the ordinal model by Predescu et al. (2009), we concluded by going back to works that decompose CDS premiums into liquidity and credit components, and more specifically to Tang and Yan (2007), which also includes bid-ask information, among other variables chosen as liquidity measures: volatility to volume, number of contracts outstanding, trade-to-quote ratio, and volume.

Despite their methodological differences, all of these studies point to one common conclusion: that CDS premium rates should not be assumed to be only pure measures of credit risk. CDS liquidity varies cross-sectionally and over time. More importantly, CDS expected liquidity and liquidity risk premiums are priced in CDS expected returns and premium rates. Nevertheless, further research is needed to test and validate the CDS liquidity premiums and the separation between credit and liquidity premiums at the CDS contract level.

Acknowledgments

We are grateful to Rutang Thanawalla, Greg Gupton, Wei Liu, Ahmet Kocagil, and Alexander Reyngold, who worked with us on the methodology of the Fitch Solutions liquidity project, contributing to our insight in this challenging field. This work expresses the opinion of its authors and is in no way representing the opinion of the institutions the authors work for.

Notes

1. See, for example, Beumee et al. (2009) for a discussion on the up-front features and on the running–up-front conversion.
2. The liquidity is proxied by the number of days with nonzero changes in the CDS premium rates. Names are then grouped in two groups: high-liquidity and low-liquidity groups based on a cutoff level for the number of nonzero daily changes.
3. Regular commentaries on liquidity scores are available from www.fitchsolutions.com under Pricing and Valuation Services.
4. The control variables included are: leverage, option-implied volatility, option-implied jumps, credit rating, number of bonds outstanding, firm size, and book-to-market and accounting transparency.

References

Acerbi, C., and G. Scandolo. 2008. Liquidity risk theory and coherent measures of risk. *Quantitative Finance* 8 (7): 681–692.

Acharya, V. V., and L. H. Pedersen. 2005. Asset pricing with liquidity risk. *Journal of Financial Economics* 77 (2): 375–410.

Amihud, Y. 2002. Illiquidity and stock returns: Cross-section and time-series effects. *Journal of Financial Markets* 5:31–56.

Amihud, Y., H. Mendelson, and L. H. Pedersen. 2005. Illiquidity and stock returns: Liquidity and asset pricing. *Foundation and Trends in Finance* 1:269–364.

Angelidis, T., and A. Benos. 2005. Liquidity adjusted value-at-risk based on the components of the bid-ask spread. Working paper, available at http://ssrn.com/abstract=661281.

Bangia, A., F. X. Diebold, T. Schuermann, and J. D. Stroughair. 1999. Modeling liquidity risk with implications for traditional market risk measurement and management. Working paper, Financial Institutions Center at the Wharton School.

Bank for International Settlements. 2008. Principles for sound liquidity risk management and supervision. Available at www.bis.org/publ/bcbs144.htm.

Beumee, J., D. Brigo, D. Schiemert, and G. Stoyle. 2009. Charting a course through the CDS Big Bang. Fitch solutions research report, available at www.defaultrisk.com/pp_crdrv176.htm.

Bielecki, T., and M. Rutkowski. 2001. *Credit risk: modelling, valuation and hedging.* New York: Springer.

Bongaerts, D., F. De Jong, and J. Driessen. 2009. Derivative pricing with liquidity risk: Theory and evidence from the credit default swap market. Forthcoming in *Journal of Finance.*

Brigo, D., and A. Alfonsi. 2005. Credit default swaps calibration and derivatives pricing with the SSRD stochastic intensity model. *Finance and Stochastics* 9 (1): 29–42.

Brigo, D., and A. Capponi. 2008. Bilateral counterparty risk valuation with stochastic dynamical models and application to credit default swaps. Available at http://papers.ssrn.com/sol3/papers.cfm?abstract_id=1318024.

Brigo, D., and K. Chourdakis. 2009. Counterparty risk for credit default swaps: Impact of spread volatility and default correlation. *International Journal of Theoretical and Applied Finance* 12 (7): 1007–1026.

Brigo, D., and N. El-Bachir. 2008. An exact formula for default swaptions' pricing in the SSRJD stochastic intensity model. Accepted for publication in *Mathematical Finance.*

Brigo, D., and B. Hanzon. 1998. On some filtering problems arising in mathematical finance. *Insurance: Mathematics and Economics* 22 (1): 53–64.

Brigo, D., and F. Mercurio. 2006. Interest rate models: Theory and practice—with smile, inflation and credit. 2nd ed. Springer-Verlag.

Brunnermeier, M., and L. H. Pedersen. 2007. Market liquidity and funding liquidity. *Review of Financial Studies* 22 (6): 2201–2238.

Buhler, W., and M. Trapp. 2005. A comparative analysis of liquidity in bonds and CDS markets. Working paper.

Buhler, W., and M. Trapp. 2006. Credit and liquidity risk in bond and CDS market. Working paper.

Buhler, W., and M. Trapp. 2008. Time-varying credit risk and liquidity premia in bond and CDS markets. Working paper.

Cetin, U., R. Jarrow, and P. Protter. 2004. Liquidity risk and arbitrage pricing theory. *Finance and Stochastics* 8 (3): 311–341.

Cetin, U., R. Jarrow, P. Protter, and M. Warachka. 2005. Pricing options in an extended Black-Scholes economy with illiquidity: Theory and empirical evidence. *Review of Financial Studies* 19 (2): 439–529.

Chen, R., R., X. Cheng, and L. Wu. 2005. Dynamic interactions between interest rate, credit, and liquidity risks: Theory and evidence from the term structure of credit default swaps. Working paper, available at http://papers.ssrn.com/sol3/papers.cfm?abstract_id=779445.

Chen, R. R, F. Fabozzi, and R. Sverdlove. 2008. Corporate CDS liquidity and its implications for corporate bond spreads. Working paper, available at http://business.rutgers.edu/files/cfs20080907.pdf.

Chen, R. R., and L. Scott. 1993. Maximum likelihood estimation of a multi-factor equilibrium model of the term structure of interest rates. *Journal of Fixed Income* 3 (3): 14–32.

Duffie, D., and K. Singleton. 1999. Modeling term structures of defaultable bonds. *Review of Financial Studies* 12 (4): 197–226.

Earnst, C., S. Stange, and C. Kaserer. 2009. Accounting for non-normality in liquidity risk. Available at http://ssrn.com/abstract=1316769.

Financial Services Authority. 2009. Strengthening liquidity standards. Available at www.fsa.gov.uk/pubs/policy/ps09_16.pdf.

Garleanu, N., L. H. Pedersen, and A. M. Poteshman. 2009. Demand-based option pricing. *Review of Financial Studies* 22 (10): 4259–4299.

Jarrow, R., and P. Protter. 2005. Liquidity risk and risk measure computation. Working paper, Cornell University.

Jarrow, R., and A. Subramanian. 1997. Mopping up liquidity. *Risk* 10 (10): 170–173.

Johnson, T. C. 2008. Volume, liquidity, and liquidity risk. *Journal of Financial Economics* 87 (2): 388–417.

Longstaff, F. A., S. Mithal, and E. Neis. 2005. Corporate yield spreads: Default risk or liquidity? New evidence from the credit default swap market. *Journal of Finance* 60 (5): 2213–2253.

Morini, M. 2009. Solving the puzzle in the interest rate market. Working paper, available at http://papers.ssrn.com/sol3/papers.cfm?abstract_id=1506046.

O'Hara, M. 1995. Market microstructure theory. Cambridge, MA: Blackwell Publishers.

Predescu, M., R. Thanawalla, G. Gupton, W. Liu, A. Kocagil, and A. Reyngold. 2009. Measuring CDS liquidity. Fitch Solutions presentation at the Bowles Symposium, Georgia State University, February 12. Available at www.pfp.gsu.edu/bowles/Bowles2009/Liu-LiquidityMeasure_MethodologyResults.pdf.

Stange, S., and C. Kaserer. 2008. Why and how to integrate liquidity risk into a VaR-framework. CEFS Working Paper 2008 No. 10, available at http://ssrn.com/abstract=1292289.

Szegö, G. 2009. The crash sonata in D major. *Journal of Risk Management in Financial Institutions* 3 (1): 31–45.

Tang, D.Y., and H. Yan. 2007. Liquidity and credit default swap spreads. Working paper, available at http://papers.ssrn.com/sol3/papers.cfm?abstract_id=891263&rec=1&srcabs=676420.

CHAPTER 20

Stressing Rating Criteria Allowing for Default Clustering: The CPDO Case

Roberto Torresetti

Quaestio Capital Management, Milano

Andrea Pallavicini

Banca Leonardo, Financial Engineering

After a brief review of the literature on rating arbitrage for corporate and structured finance, we introduce the standard criteria adopted by rating agencies to assess the riskiness of constant proportion debt obligations (CPDOs). Then, we propose a new rating model in order to incorporate a more realistic loss distribution showing a multimodal shape, which, in turn, is linked to default possibilities for clusters (possibly sectors) of names in the economy. In this framework, we show that the riskiness of CPDOs is substantially increased, leading to a decrease in their rating; in particular, we find that the expected payout of the gap-risk option, embedded in CPDOs, is notably increased.

20.1 Introduction

Constant proportion debt obligations (CPDOs) were first created by ABN Amro in 2006 but rapidly spread to the rest of the market. It has been estimated that banks globally created at least $4 billion worth of CPDOs: structures typically with a 10-year maturity, promising an annual interest of as much as two percentage points above money market rates, generated by a dynamic leveraged strategy, which were usually granted AAA rating.

It seems like the dynamic trading strategy embedded in CPDOs was delivering, almost without risk, a return of two percentage points above the risk-free rate with a very high likelihood, more than 99.3 percent probability according to the 10-year minimum survival rate that Standard & Poor's (S&P) assigns to a AAA rating and 10-year maturity. As it turned out, markets might not be as efficient as argued by some economists but nevertheless they are far from being that inefficient. As it has been pointed out by Linden et al. (2007), the rating criteria assigned to these structures were bearing a significant model risk. Put differently, not all the rating criteria used by agencies were bulletproof.

Before analyzing in detail the rating criteria of CPDOs, we will see, through a brief review of the literature, how the scope for rating arbitrage already exists for corporate bond ratings: the bread and butter of the rating agencies' business.

With time, agencies moved on to assign a rating to securitizations like residential mortgage-backed securities (RMBSs), subprime RMBSs, commercial mortgage-backed securities (CMBSs), and collateralized debt obligations (CDOs). When assigning a rating to the securitizations just mentioned, agencies have to assess the likelihood of default of different parts of the capital structure of a portfolio of credit references. This can still be considered a closely related business to their original core business of assessing the default risk of single credit references.

More recently, during the past 10 years, agencies started to assess the remoteness of the risk of structures whose payoffs depend on risks associated with the mark-to-market dynamics of underlying credit portfolios—an area, namely the modeling of the mark-to-market risk of a pool of credits, not so related to their original core business.

In particular we will focus our attention on CPDO rating criteria. We enlarge the set of criteria stresses performed in Linden et al. (2007) to include the possibility of clusters of defaults occurring to the pool of underlying names. To do so we change the pool default simulation engine from a multifactor Gaussian copula to the generalized Poisson loss model as in Brigo, Pallavicini, and Torresetti (2007a).

We will see how when allowing for clusters of defaults hitting the pool of credit references the risk of an investor holding a CPDO structure increases dramatically, or equivalently the CPDO rating worsens. From the point of view of a bank arranging a CPDO, we will also see how the gap-option reserve provision increases dramatically when allowing for clusters of defaults impacting on the pool of credit references.

20.2 Ratings

Ratings were initially thought of as an investment guideline for unsophisticated corporate bond investors. With time their scope has enlarged, as regulators set investment limits based on ratings, as some investors are constrained to investment-grade securities, or as they are used in covenants for financial contracts; for example, a company might agree with its creditors to maintain its rating above a certain level.

To assign a rating to a corporate bond, agencies rely on a series of quantitative variables, such as balance sheet leverage and profitability, and qualitative variables, such as management quality. The outcome is the rating: a letter grade ranging from AAA (highest quality) to C. The more remote the risk for an investor of not receiving in full the due interest and principal, the closer the corporate bond rating will be to AAA.

Cantor and Packer (1994) review the rating industry history and analyze the differences in the rating scales across agencies and across types of issues (corporate bonds vs. structured finance). In their review of the historical evolution of the industry, the authors point out how initially ratings were issued free of charge and agencies' revenues were linked to the sales of hard copies of research material. With the introduction of cheap photocopying and pressures from corporates during the 1970 recession seeking ratings to reassure investors, the rating industry started charging issuers a fee for the rating.

The apparent conflict of interest of agencies to assign a higher rating to please issuers at the expense of unsophisticated investors has until recently been limited by the agencies' opposite incentive to maintain an untarnished reputation. Recent events have damaged that reputation at a particularly unfortunate time. In fact, the use of ratings was expected to increase considerably with the advent of Basel II. During the recent crisis this prospective role has been questioned at times.

Instead of addressing this conflict of interest the rating industry is facing, the Financial Stability Forum has proposed an overhaul of the rating industry, publishing a set of best practices, requesting from agencies more disclosure about rating criteria and reducing their potential conflict of interest.[1]

The authors also compared the ratings assigned by different agencies on a sample of issues that received a rating from multiple agencies. Issuers that received a near investment grade or a split rating (investment grade from one agency and speculative grade from another) are statistically more prone to seek a third rating. This evidence goes in the direction of rating arbitrage activity on the part of the issuers. Despite the rating process being lengthy and time-consuming for both the issuer and the rating agency, an issuer might have an incentive to shop around in view of a group of agencies with a systematically higher rating scale.

Finally, the authors review the evolution of the structured finance rating for mortgage-backed securities (MBSs) and asset-backed securities (ABSs). In particular, they correlate the evolution of the market shares of each agency for MBS and ABS. The authors show how credit enhancements for MBS have gradually declined, and also point out how in a few instances agencies appeared to modify rating criteria as a response to declining market share.

In a later contribution, Cantor and Packer (1997) investigate further the equivalence of the rating scale across agencies. The higher rating assigned by agencies other than Moody's or S&P could in fact be due to self-selection bias. The practice of Moody's and S&P is to assign a rating to any U.S. corporate bond public issue. Other agencies instead assign only solicited ratings. An issuer that has grounds to believe that a third agency will not assign a better rating than Moody's and S&P will not ask for it. This induces a self-selection bias that could explain the average lower rating of the two major agencies: Moody's or S&P. However, the results of their analysis is that self-selection bias does not explain by itself the systematically higher ratings given by third agencies.

More recently Becker and Milbourne (2008) analyze the effects of competition in the rating industry. They do so investigating the reactions of the two incumbents, Moody's and S&P, to the increased market share gained by Fitch.

The outcome of an increased competition in the rating industry is not clear ex ante. On one hand, the increased competition makes the reputational downside risk more real: the loss of reputation resulting in a loss of business. On the other hand, reputation is a valuable asset only if it produces future revenues: An increase in competition reduces future revenues, thus reducing the incentive of maintaining a reputation.[2]

The authors measure the reaction of the two incumbents, Moody's and S&P, in the face of the increased market share by Fitch. They put forward three pieces of evidence that point to the increased competition actually reducing the quality of ratings.

1. *Positive correlation between Moody's and S&P ratings and Fitch market share.* Moody's and S&P have reacted to increased competition by issuing higher ratings on average.
2. *Ratings and bond yields have become less correlated.* In a regression of bond yields versus a set of bond characteristics including rating, the coefficient linking the bond yield and rating gets smaller when Fitch market share increases. Thus ratings are seen as less informative of an issuer default risk when competition between rating agencies is high.
3. *Equity prices have reacted more strongly to downgrades when Fitch market share increased.* Thus when ratings are less informative and more lenient, the equity market reaction to a downgrade, and in particular a downgrade to speculative grade, becomes stronger. In other words, when the quality of rating deteriorates in that rating agencies become more generous and awarding on average higher ratings, the reaction to a downgrade becomes stronger.

20.2.1 Structured Finance Ratings

A comprehensive classification of all kinds of structured finance transactions is well beyond the scope of this chapter. Here we present a broad classification of collateralized debt obligations (CDOs): the most popular structured finance transactions rated by agencies. CDOs are securities whose payments are collateralized by a pool of risky exposures. As such they can be classified by the type of the underlying exposures: Mortgages, credit cards, receivables, bonds, loans, or credit derivatives. So, for example, a cash-flow CDO would take as collateral a pool of bonds. A synthetic CDO would instead reference a basket of credit default swaps.

A defining feature of the securitization technology is the transformation of the original pool of assets into a new set of assets via different credit enhancements given to different investors. The new assets created by the securitization will correspond to the CDO tranches. So, for example, a pool of two bonds can be decomposed into two tranches: one where the investor bears the risk of the first default in the pool (junior investor) and another where the investor bears the risk of the second default in the pool (senior investor).

In a cash-flow CDO this decomposition is usually handled via a waterfall definition where the flows of the pool of assets are distributed to the junior and senior investors depending on an ex ante definition of the riskiness of the CDO. So, for example, in a market-value CDO the payments to the junior investors are discontinued in case the cumulative pool losses reach a critical level or the market value of the pool of assets falls below a certain threshold.

Another possible distinction of a CDO has to do with the purpose of the securitization. In a balance-sheet CDO a bank sells senior tranches on a collateral pool that is already owned by the bank, usually to obtain regulatory capital relief. In an arbitrage CDO, instead the originator buys in the market assets to be used as collateral in a securitization to profit from the discrepancy between the price of the assets and the price of the CDO tranches sold to the investors.

As already mentioned, structured finance deals can take a huge variety of shapes and forms. Here, we will point to only two basic features that are relevant for the scope of this article.

1. When rating most structured finance deals, as is the case for example in arbitrage CDOs, agencies have to assess the default risk of a tranche of a portfolio. Tranches are characterized by attachment and detachment points. The owner of a tranche will keep on receiving the interest and will receive principal at maturity in full unless the portfolio losses reach the attachment point.
2. In some instances, as is the case for CPDOs, rating agencies also need to assess the mark-to-market risk of a pool of credits.

For each kind of structured finance deal rating criteria were published to communicate to the public the mechanics of the rating process. In doing so investors transparently received the maximum possible disclosure of the rating process. From the underlying credit quality through a series of assumptions pinpointed to historical evidence as much as possible, eventually the structured finance deal would receive a rating.

In doing so, however, rating agencies would take some model risk to the extent that the assumptions were not conservative enough or did not have enough historical data to back them. Weaknesses in the rating criteria or more in general a misalignment between the perception of the rated risk between the agencies and the market could be reverse engineered, and possibly leveraged as for CPDOs, to provide investors with the highest possible spread for a given rating.

Skreta and Veldkamp (2008) have been investigating the issue of rating arbitrage in CDO markets. They test the null hypothesis that rating model arbitrage does not exist, testing for homogeneity of CDO characteristics across rating agencies and across rating methodologies: If S&P and Fitch assign a rating based on the probability that the interest or principal of a tranche are missed, Moody's assigns a rating focusing on the expected loss of a tranche.

Based on the significance of the mean equality test, a set of multivariate discriminant analysis is performed. The conclusion is that there appears to be rating arbitrage in the sense that some CDO characteristics (in particular currency, maturity, and capital structure composition) appear to have a significant discriminatory power. If rating arbitrage did not exist, then the CDOs rated by the various agencies should not show any particular pattern.

20.2.2   Rating Arbitrage for Arbitrage CDO Rating

In a benign credit environment with steadily decreasing default rates and tightening credit spreads, investors started to push the envelope seeking the highest possible spread within their investment guidelines limits. To this end the CDO technology became instrumental. An investor wishing to take exposure to a particular tranche of a pool of credit references with minimum requirements of diversification across sectors and rating classes will select the pool of names with the widest spread within each sector and rating category. Given the different risk assessment between the market, as measured by the CDS spread, and the rating agencies, as measured by the average historical default rate for each rating category, this strategy would provide the investor with the widest spread for the tranche.

Tejwani et al. (2007) present evidence that between 2004 and 2007 the constituents of the CDX series turned out to experience a faster than average rating downgrade. In their analysis the authors compare the number of rating upgrades and downgrades of the CDX.NA.IG S2 to S7 to their expectations as computed from the rating transition matrices. Across all CDX series from March 2004 to March 2007 the rating action as measured by the total downgrade notches minus the total upgrade notches is much above what would have been expected from the transition matrices.

One explanation of this excess of rating downgrade compared to the historical average could be the time inhomogeneity of transition matrices. There is quite some evidence that transition matrices are not time homogeneous: There is evidence of rating momentum (see Altman and Kao 1992; Lucas and Lonski 1992) and evidence that rating transitions differ depending on the credit cycle (see Nickell, Perraudin, and Varotto 2000; Bangia et al. 2002). Nevertheless, the period the authors considered, March 2004 to March 2007, was a period of expansion: thus the quicker than expected downgrades could hardly be explained along these lines.

An alternative explanation could be the focus of arbitrage CDO issuance activity on the names with the widest credit spread within each rating category. Names affected by substantial negative news flow would see their CDS spreads widening instantly, while rating action being more sticky will leave room for CDO issuers to pick these names to maximize the CDO tranche spread.

20.2.3   Senior Investor Protection: Cash-Flow CDOs versus Market-Value CDOs

A bank that originates a pool of loans and keeps them in the balance sheet would need to allocate economic capital until the loans' maturity. To free economic capital the bank could securitize the pool of loans via a cash-flow CDO and keep only some parts of the capital structure.

In a cash-flow CDO there is a waterfall in place that directs the flows generated by the pool of credit references toward the most senior part of the capital structure in case a set of overcollateralization (OC) tests and/or interest coverage (IC) tests are not passed. This is intended to give senior investors assurances about the safety of their investments.

From the point of view of senior investors there remains the risk that even though currently both OC and IC tests are passed, news might have arrived to the market regarding a disastrous expected performance of the pool of credit. In a cash-flow CDO senior investors will have to wait until the OC and/or IC tests are not passed before seeing the cash flows of the collateral being directed to serve their notes first.

In a market-value CDO instead when the market value of the collateral pool reaches some triggers, the pool cash flows are directed to senior investors without having to wait for the OC and/or IC tests to fail.

When rating market-value CDOs, agencies also had to include in their criteria assumptions regarding the market value dynamics of the collateral.

Market-value CDOs were first introduced in the late 1990s but never gained prominence in the securitization scene. Moreover, in 2001 they suffered a major drawback due to the CDO crisis. Since then they basically have disappeared and have never made a significant comeback, not even at the peak of the securitization activity in 2006.

20.2.4 Leveraged Super-Senior Rating

A CDO issuer often had the problem of placing the super-senior part of the capital structure. The remoteness of its risk and the consequent meager credit spread attached to it made super-senior tranches particularly unattractive to yield-seeking investors.

Leveraged super-senior tranches appeared in the structured credit market to make the tranche spread attractive to investors. Being a leveraged structure, the arrangers typically designed a set of triggers that depended on both the cumulative credit enhancement lost by the super-senior tranche and the market spread for the underlying super-senior tranche.

When triggers are reached, the leveraged super-senior exposure is unwound and the remaining proceeds are returned to the investor. A super-senior investor will receive the principal back at maturity if the collateral pool loss rate does not reach the super-senior attachment point. A leveraged super-senior investor also needs to worry about the mark-to-market of the underlying super-senior tranche. In fact, when the mark-to-market triggers are reached, the proceeds the investor will receive will be below par.

In order to buy the leveraged super-senior structure, investors needed reassurances that the triggers were indeed remote. To accomplish this, rating agencies started to give ratings also to the leveraged super-senior triggers. They would give an AAA rating to the super-senior tranche, thus certifying the remoteness of the risk that the pool loss would reach the super-senior attachment. Then they would give an AAA rating to the leveraged super-senior triggers, thus certifying the remoteness of the risk that the mark-to-market triggers of the leveraged super-senior tranche would be reached.

20.2.5   Rating CPDOs

One can see the usefulness for unsophisticated investors of CDO ratings given the extensive data sets of default history available to agencies in order to assess the riskiness of different parts of the capital structure. An issuer wishing to sell in the market part of the capital structure of the issuer's pool of credits asks a rating agency for an independent risk assessment.

If ratings have as their main users unsophisticated investors, one can also see the need to rate market-value CDOs. Indeed, the main purpose of rating a market-value CDO is to give senior investors more comfort that the mark-to-market trigger activation represents a remote risk.

In the case of a leveraged super-senior tranche, an issuer wishing to sell a bigger portion of the pool capital structure lures investors with attractive spreads based on the remoteness of the default risk of the underlying pool of credits and also based on the remoteness of the market value triggers. An investor should be quite sophisticated to assess these two different types of risk—default and mark-to-market risk—and their interaction as summarized in the trigger matrix. For this reason the arrangers turned to rating agencies to help them reassure investors of the remoteness of the mark-to-market risk embedded in the triggers.

CPDOs can be considered the latest and most extravagant of the structured credit products that arrived at the end of a prolonged boom in the credit markets. The anecdotical justification of their existence is to allow institutional investors to take advantage of the mean-reverting nature of credit spreads through a mechanical trading strategy. It might be argued that it would be strange for an institutional investor to take a leveraged long exposure to credit at the peak of the credit market.

The appearance in the market of CPDOs could have an alternative explanation: maximize the spread paid by the notes targeting an AAA rating, reverse engineering the criteria adopted by agencies to handle the mark-to-market risk as evidenced by the rating criteria of other structured deals (market-value CDO and leveraged super-senior).

20.3   CPDO

As in constant proportion portfolio insurance securities (CPPIs), in CPDOs investors are dynamically selling protection by leveraging the risk premium contained in credit spreads (see Hull, Predescu, and White 2005), but with a different strategy. Indeed, in the case of CPDOs if the spread widens we increase the leverage whereas in the case of CPPIs we decrease the leverage. In this way CPDOs try to exploit the mean-reverting behavior that corporate spreads have historically displayed.

Rating agencies have introduced stylized criteria to rate CPDO structures. We briefly review in Section 20.4 the standard assumptions, as can be found also in Linden et al. (2007). Then, in Section 20.5, we consider a different choice for the loss dynamics by introducing the general Poisson cluster loss model (GPCL).

The GPCL model, which we present in Section 20.5.3, is based on the possibility of the joint default of clusters of names within the simulated pool, leading to a multimodal risk-neutral loss distribution, where the modes (we often refer to them in the following simply as "bumps") are in correspondence with the size of the defaulting economic sectors.

One might argue that the bumps, arising in the right tail of the risk-neutral loss distribution, are there as a remuneration to bear the highly skewed risk of senior tranches. The evidence presented in Torresetti, Brigo, and Pallavicini (2009) points to the presence of a nonnegligible probability mass associated with a cluster of defaults. These bumps turn out to be necessary if one wishes to price standardized CDO tranches within the bid-ask spread. We hint at the evidence found in literature that these bumps might also be there in the objective measure.

Our main point will be to show how the rating of a specific CPDO structure changes by introducing a loss distribution with bumps. Also, we will see how the gap option does indeed have a nonnegligible premium as well in the objective measure when modeling the loss with the GPCL model.

CPDOs are sold to investors via so-called special purpose vehicles (SPVs). The SPV will buy gap options to be protected in the event of negative unwinding proceeds in case of a cash-out. The expected payout for the gap option seller, typically the structure issuer, is the negative part of the structure's net asset value (NAV) at the end of the unwinding procedure. During the unwinding procedure, all risky exposure is closed in the market and the proceeds, if any, are returned to the investor. Thus in the case of negative proceeds at the end of the unwinding procedure, the final balance of the structure will be zero thanks to the gap-option seller payout.

20.3.1   Payoff of a Hypothetical CPDO Structure

Quite suspiciously, CPDOs' defining characteristics, such as the dynamic leverage rule, maturity, and coupons, were quite similar across different issues. This was suspicious because institutional investors, the main investors in these structures, usually demand tailor-made solutions to better fit their investment views.

We present the details of a hypothetical CPDO structure that is extremely similar in its main characteristics to most of the CPDOs that were sold in the market: interest paid, dynamic leverage rule, fees paid, maturity, and roll of the leveraged exposure on the five-year on-the-run series of the Globoxx.[3]

A CPDO is a note bond paying the investor an interest until the earliest of:

- *Maturity.* Usually 10 years to give enough time to the structure to profit via the dynamic strategy from the mean-reverting properties of the underlying credit derivatives index spread.

- *Cash-in* as defined in a later section. In case the profit of the dynamic strategy is enough to guarantee the payment of the remaining fees, interest plus spread, and the principal at maturity, then the leveraged credit exposure is unwound and the proceeds are invested in a basket of risk-free bonds.
- *Cash-out*. In case the cumulative loss of the dynamic strategy reaches 90 percent, the leveraged credit exposure is unwound and the proceeds, if any, are given back to the investor.

The interest paid is equal to LIBOR plus a spread I_t varying depending on the leverage β_t at time t. Our hypothetical CPDO structure pays the following annualized spread over LIBOR:

$$
I_t = \begin{cases}
1.25\% & \text{if} & \beta_t \leq 7.5 \\
1.5\% & \text{if} & \beta_t = 10 \\
1.75\% & \text{if} & \beta_t = 12.5 \\
2\% & \text{if} & \beta_t = 15
\end{cases}
\tag{20.1}
$$

An investor will buy the CPDO notes at par. The structure will initially sell leveraged unfunded protection on the on-the-run series of the underlying credit derivative index and will invest the cash in short-term money market instruments.

Subsequently, the leverage will be updated according to the dynamic leverage rule, and every six months the leveraged position will be rolled in the on-the-run five-year Globoxx series. This strategy allows the structure to always execute the leverage adjustments in the most liquid index series, the on-the-run, and, at maturity, the five-year.

20.3.1.1   Dynamic Leverage Rule

The leverage β_t increases with the maximum level reached by the spread of an underlying credit derivatives index S_t up to time t, unless the value of the assets of the structure V_t falls below 40 percent, in which case the leverage is linearly reduced to 0 when V_t equals 10 percent.

$$
\beta_t = \begin{cases}
7.5 & \text{if} & \max_{s \in [0,t]} S_s < 0.40\% \text{ and} & V_t > 0.4 \\
10 & \text{if} & 0.40\% \leq \max_{s \in [0,t]} S_s < 0.50\% \text{ and} & V_t > 0.4 \\
12.5 & \text{if} & 0.50\% \leq \max_{s \in [0,t]} S_s < 0.60\% \text{ and} & V_t > 0.4 \\
15 & \text{if} & 0.60\% \leq \max_{s \in [0,t]} S_s \text{ and} & V_t > 0.4 \\
7.5(V_t - 0.1)/0.3 & \text{if} & V_t \leq 0.4
\end{cases}
\tag{20.2}
$$

where for the sake of our simulations $S_0 = 0.0035$, the prevalent Globoxx index spread at the time CPDOs were launched in the market.

Note that the structure leverage can increase only as long as the strategy asset value is above 0.4. This hypothetical structure has a much simpler leverage than the majority of CPDOs that were launched in the market where the dynamic leverage rule would decrease the leverage when the credit index spread tightened.

In the case that V_t goes below 40 percent, the structure begins reducing the leverage. The reason for this is to reduce the cost of the gap option. If the strategy does not reduce the leverage as the NAV decreases below a level deemed critical, 40 percent in our hypothetical CPDO structure, then the risk of a few defaults or the risk of a significant widening in the credit spread hitting the structure would increase. In turn the chances that the unwinding proceeds turn out to be negative increase, and this ultimately is translated into a higher cost for the gap option.

20.3.1.2   Fees

The fees X_t of the structure are of three kinds: (1) Management fees of $X_t^{MF} = 0.2\%$ per annum on the notional of the notes until the earliest of maturity and the cash-out date as a running remuneration for the arranger of the structure; (2) gap fees of $X_t^{GP} = 0.035\%$ per annum per unit of leverage until the earliest of maturity, the cash-in date, and the cash-out date, as a compensation for the gap option the structure needs to buy; and (3) up-front fees of $X^{UF} = 1\%$ as an up-front remuneration for the arranger of the structure.

$$X_t = \left(X_t^{MF} + \beta_t X_t^{GP} \right) + 1_{\{t=0\}} X^{UF} \qquad (20.3)$$

20.3.1.3   Cash-In

If the cumulative profit of the dynamic strategy reaches the bond ceiling B_t the leveraged credit exposure is unwound and the proceeds are invested in a basket of risk-free bonds that will guarantee the payment of the remaining fees X_s, interest plus spread and the principal at maturity.

$$B_t = 1 + \int_t^{T_I^{40}} (X_s + I_s) D(t, s) ds \qquad (20.4)$$

where $D(t, s)$ is the risk-free discount rate at time s evaluated[4] at time t. The quarterly interest payment dates over the 10 years of the life of the product are denoted as $\{ T_I^1, T_I^2, \ldots, T_I^{40} \}$. Notice that in the calculation of B_t we consider that the leverage remains constant from time t up to maturity T_I^{40}.

From the definition of the payoff it is clear that the CPDO structure will not be able to pay the principal at maturity in full unless the profits of the dynamic strategy reach the bond ceiling B_t before maturity.

20.3.2   Evolution in Time of the NAV of the CPDO Structure

Having in mind the specific CPDO structure outlined in Section 20.3.1, we will now recap the obligations of the CPDO structure and introduce the equation for the variation of its NAV. At inception these are the events following the investors' subscription of the CPDO notes originated by a vehicle for a given notional of, let us say, 1 euro.

- The arranger typically takes an amount in the form of up-front fee X^{UF} from the initial investment.
- The vehicle puts the notional minus the up-front fee, $1 - X^{\text{UF}}$, in a short-term deposit, thus earning the risk-free short-term rate: r_t.
- The vehicle sells protection[5] on the five-year Globoxx index for a notional equal to the notional of the CPDO notes times the initial leverage: $\beta_0 = 7.5$ given the assumed initial five-year Globoxx spread of 35 bps.

On any subsequent date the vehicle will:

- Receive LIBOR on the cash invested.
- Pay LIBOR plus spread on the notes notional to the investor.
- Pay the loss given default (LGD) times the leverage for any name defaulted in the underlying credit index to the protection buyer.
- Receive the protection premium times the leverage from the protection buyer.
- Pay the fees (management and gap risk) to the arranger.

On the roll dates all short protection positions are rolled into the new on-the-run series. Thus the net present value (NPV) accrued since the last roll, or increase in leverage, will have to be liquidated in cash.

Given the initial condition at inception of the NAV, $V_0 = 1 - X^{\text{UF}}$, and the Globoxx five-year CDS spread, $S_0 = 35$ bps, after inception the NAV process V_t is characterized by the following equation:

$$dV_t = V_t r_t dt - (F_t + I_t)dt - \beta_t dL_t + K_t dt - X_t dt + dNPV_t^{T_R^i} \qquad (20.5)$$

with

$$K_t = S_{T_R^i} \beta_{T_R^i} + \int_{T_R^i}^{t} S_s \, d\beta_s$$

where F_t and r_t are respectively the last fixing of the three-month LIBOR rate and the overnight rate,[6] I_t is the spread over LIBOR paid by the notes, β_t is the leverage of the protection sold, X_t is the fee contributions, and NPV_t is the residual (from t to index maturity) net present value (NPV) of the leveraged protection sold.

Finally, K_t is the average spread on the protection sold times the leverage at time t. On the last roll date T_R^i the strategy will sell protection for $\beta_{T_R^i}$ times the CPDO notional at a spread of $S_{T_R^i}$. On any subsequent date s where the strategy increases the leverage, the total leverage times spread will increase by $S_s\, d\beta_s$.

We also consider the recovery rate (R) to be constant in time and equal to 35 percent, which is a typical level for senior unsecured corporates, so that the number of defaults C_t and the pool loss L_t processes are linked by the usual relationship $L_t = (1 - R)C_t$. In our simulations, defaults will arrive every six months, just an instant before the next roll date. In this way the outstanding notional of the index will always be 1.

Let us call T_R^i the last roll date of the underlying credit index. The net present value $NPV_t^{T_R^i}$ of the protection sold since the last roll date T_R^i is:

$$NPV_t^{T_R^i} = K_t DV01_t^{T_R^i} + \beta_t DFLT_t^{T_R^i}$$

In computing the basis point value of the premium leg $DV01_t^{T_R^i}$ and the default leg NPV $DFLT_t^{T_R^i}$, we assume continuous premium payments and a flat CDS term structure while keeping in mind that on the roll date the new index has a maturity of five years and three months:

$$DV01_t^{T_R^i} = \int_0^{T_R^i + 5.25 - t} e^{-s(r+\lambda)}\, ds\,,$$

$$DFLT_t^T = (1 - R)\int_0^{T_R^i + 5.25 - t} \lambda e^{-s(r+\lambda)}\, dt, \quad \lambda = S_t/(1 - R)$$

20.4 Rating Criteria: Base Case and Stressed Case

From equation (20.5) we see that to simulate the NAV of a CPDO structure we need to simulate the evolution of interest rates, Globoxx index spread, and Globoxx index losses.

- *Interest rates.* Given the low sensitivity of the CPDO structure NAV to interest rates we assume that the spot zero coupon curve will move along the forward curve as time goes on.
- *Protection premium.* We model the Globoxx five-year CDS spread as an exponential Vasicek (see Section 20.4.1). In line with Linden et al. (2007) we take as the base case the mean parameter estimate and as the stressed case the mean parameter estimates marked adversely up or down, depending on the rating sensitivity, by a quarter of the standard deviation.
- *Pool losses.* Following the standard assumptions of rating agencies we model the number of defaulted names in the underlying pool with a multifactor Gaussian

copula (see Section 20.4.2). As an alternative we model the pool loss with the GPCL as in Brigo, Pallavicini, and Torresetti (2007b), thus allowing for a cluster of defaults.

When assigning a rating, agencies have to assess the likelihood that the structure can pay in full both interest and principal. In doing this they rely on quantitative criteria, as summarized by the rating criteria, as well as on qualitative assessment. The rating is delivered by a committee where different areas of expertise each contribute their unique perspective on the transaction at hand.

When the committee is debating whether to assign the highest possible rating, AAA, the quantitative criteria are usually calibrated versus a stressed historical evolution: For example, in the case of structured finance related to mortgages the AAA tranche needs to withstand some extreme (by historical standards) recessionary scenarios in terms of unemployment and housing price decline.

As we will see in the case of CPDOs, this did not seem to be the case. Agencies seemed to adopt criteria more in line with the base case rather than with the stressed case.

Also, the CPDO is quite exposed to a positive correlation between pool losses and credit spreads, whereas rating criteria do not model this joint dependency. As we will see, there will be no interaction between pool losses, sampled from a distribution that does not change and whose mean is calibrated to historical default rates, and the simulated index spread path.

20.4.1   Credit Index Spread

Following Fitch's approach described in Linden et al. (2007), we model the on-the-run five-year Globoxx index spread (S_t) as an exponential Vasicek process.

$$dS_t = \alpha S_t(\theta - \ln S_t)dt + \sigma S_t dW_t \qquad (20.6)$$

Fitch has overcome the limited history available for the iTraxx and CDX indexes by backfilling the sample with a proxy. In this way it can move back the sample start date to January 1998 even though iTtraxx and CDX indexes have only been available since July 2004. This proxy was built from cash bond indexes to match the duration, rating, and geographical composition of the Globoxx index. The parameters' estimates, and their standard deviations, reported in Linden et al. (2007) are:

$$\alpha = 0.556 \pm 0.056, \quad \theta = 0.0080 \pm 0.0025, \quad \sigma = 0.400 \pm 0.013$$

These authors point out how the standard deviation of the estimators for the mean-reversion speed and long-term mean are quite large. They also point out how CPDO ratings turn out to be quite sensitive to these parameters.

In line with their work, here we not only simulate the index spread using the mean estimates of the parameters (hereafter the mean parameter set), but we also stress contemporaneously the parameters in a conservative direction by a quarter of

TABLE 20.1 iTraxx and CDX Compositions at Inception of the Series by Whole-Letter Ratings for the Four Index Series

	iTraxx				CDX			
	S5	S6	S7	S8	S6	S7	S8	S9
AAA	00.8%	00.0%	00.0%	00.0%	03.3%	03.3%	03.2%	03.2%
AA	09.3%	13.1%	11.7%	16.9%	02.5%	02.5%	02.4%	02.4%
A	40.7%	36.9%	40.0%	36.3%	34.2%	35.8%	36.0%	38.4%
BBB	49.2%	50.0%	48.3%	46.8%	60.0%	58.3%	58.4%	56.0%

the standard deviation of the estimates: increasing the long-term mean θ by 0.0025, decreasing the mean-reversion speed α by 0.056, and increasing the instantaneous volatility σ by 0.013 (hereafter the stressed parameter set).

20.4.2 Pool Loss Simulation

The rating agencies' simulation engines for loss-dependent products are based on a multifactor Gaussian copula (see Li 2000), as can be found, for example, in S&P's CDO Evaluator[7] and Fitch's Vector Model. These are the same tool kits used to rate synthetic CDOs.

The probabilities of default of the index constituents are derived assuming that the index composition of the Globoxx throughout the 19 rolls during the 10 years of each simulation path is equal to the average rating distribution of the last four series of the iTraxx and CDX as summarized in Table 20.1. Recovery rates will be assumed to be deterministic and equal to 35 percent.

The pairwise correlation between the latent factors in the Gaussian copula is derived according to the sector and region of each pair of credit references as in Table 20.2, in line with the assumptions of S&P that could be found in the CDO Evaluator user guide at the time CPDOs were rated.

Given the rating composition, for each rating category we can look up the average historical default rates for a one-year horizon in the default rate tables provided by rating agencies. Given that a maturity shorter than one year is not available in these tables, how do we calculate the six-month average default rate we need in order to measure the average riskiness of the Globoxx in between any two roll dates?

If we consider the rating composition at inception and the Moody's rating transitions for the Globoxx, we can assume a constant default intensity for the first year given by

$$\lambda_{1y} := -\log(1 - PD_{1y}), \quad PD_{1y} := 0.0011 \tag{20.7}$$

so that we get a six-month default rate of

$$PD_{6m} = 1 - \exp(-0.5\lambda_{1y}) = 0.0005$$

TABLE 20.2 Correlation Assumptions of S&P's CDO Evaluator

	Between Sectors	Within Sectors	Sector Type
Within countries	0.05	0.15	local
		0.15	regional
		0.15	global
Within regions	0.05	0.05	local
		0.15	regional
		0.15	global
Between regions	0.00	0.00	local
		0.00	regional
		0.15	global

For example, if two entities are in the same sector but in different regions, the correlation will be higher (15 percent rather than 0 percent) only if the sector is global (technology) rather than local (regulated utilities) or regional.
Source: www.standardandpoors.com.

Assuming a constant default intensity could be quite an overestimation. Lando and Skodeberg (2002) use continous data to estimate the generator of the transition matrix, and with this we estimated the six-month transition matrix. Given the assumed Globoxx rating distribution at inception of Table 20.1 and the generator consistent with the one-year rating transition they report, this would result in a six-month default rate of 0.00016. If we were instead to assume a constant default intensity over one year, always using their transition matrix, we would obtain 0.00027: a difference of more than 60 percent between the two estimates.

These are apparently small numbers and it is debatable which is the appropriate six-month default rate to use. Nevertheless, given the highly leveraged strategy in a CPDO, which of the two different estimates to use turns out to make quite a difference, as pointed out in Linden et al. (2007).

Another issue arises with the adverse selection of Globoxx constituents. How correct is it to compute the average six-month default rate of the Globoxx given its initial rating composition? We have already highlighted the evidence presented in Tejwani et al. (2007) suggesting that the CDX pool of names on average experience a faster rating deterioration than expected given its initial rating composition.

Tejwani et al. (2007) show how adjusting for the adverse selection of the Globoxx constituents can result in a five-year cumulative loss rate much higher than the equivalent unadjusted rate. Thus one would need to stress somewhat the default rate as obtained from the Globoxx rating composition.

It is difficult to assess the relative importance of the two effects on the six-month default-rate assumption: overestimation due to the assumption of constant default rate intensity in contrast with the evidence of Lando and Skodeberg (2002); underestimation because of the adverse selection due to arbitrage CDO activity as documented in Tejwani et al. (2007).

FIGURE 20.1   Default Intensity for A-Rated (*left chart*) and Ca-Rated (*right chart*) Corporate Credit References

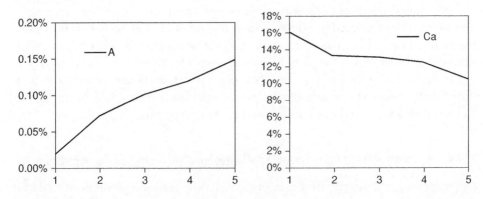

For this reason we assumed the two effects cancel out and we computed the six-month default rate from the average of the last four series of the Globoxx rating distribution as reported in Table 20.1, assuming a constant default intensity for the first year.

20.4.3   Roll-Down Benefit

The roll-down benefit (RDB) is the difference between the five-year, three months maturity Globoxx index spread at index inception and the four year, nine months maturity Globoxx index spread on the next index roll date. If this difference is assumed to be positive on average, as agencies did when rating CPDOs, then the structure will benefit when rolling the Globoxx leveraged short protection exposure.

The rationale of this assumption is that investment-grade curves are positively sloped most of the time and the iTraxx and CDX indexes are indeed refreshed every six months to include only investment-grade names.

One problem with this argument is the rating deterioration that the Globoxx might have suffered during the six months. In Figure 20.1 we report the different slope of the default intensities of A- and Ca-rated companies by Moody's for increasing time horizons.

The positive slope of investment-grade curves can be explained by the option held by the management to change the capital structure of the company; also, time-adverse and unforeseen changes can occur to the sector to which the company belongs.

Conversely, the default intensity derived from the default rate of low-rated companies is usually inverted, as these companies face a "fly or die" situation. If the overhaul of the company is successful and the adverse contingency is passed, the likelihood of a default decreases substantially.

It is true that during their short histories the iTraxx and CDX indexes have always displayed positively sloped curves. Nevertheless, as pointed out in Linden et al. (2007), the same was not true for the back-filled Globoxx index, where there were periods when the proxied Globoxx curve was negatively sloped.

We argue that part of the positive slope of investment-grade curves is a remuneration for the risk of rating downgrade. Thus only part of the roll-down benefit is a risk premium and could be recognized in the CPDO rating criteria. This risk premium turns out to be quite difficult to estimate and is outside the scope of this chapter.

In the following we will consider as base case a roll-down benefit of only 3 percent, substantially below the assumption of rating agencies, which could be as high as 7 percent, and as stressed case a roll-down benefit of 0 percent.

20.4.4   Summary of Credit Index Spread, Pool Losses Simulation, and Roll-Down Benefit

Before looking at the details of the simulations, let's do some rough numbers to detect the rating criteria assumptions contributing the most to the astonishing performance of the structure: Despite the leveraged exposure to the default risk of an underlying credit index and paying 2 percent on top of LIBOR, the simulated NAV of the strategy almost always touches the bond ceiling.

Let's consider equation (20.5) describing the NAV of the CPDO strategy V_t. Let's assume the Globoxx index spread goes from 35 bps to 80 bps, the long-term mean estimate of Section 20.4.1, immediately after inception and stays constant thereafter. The structure will thus pay a spread of 2 percent on top of the short-term rate and the leverage will be equal to 15 from then on.

The structure will accrue the short-term rate on the cash account: $V_t r_t dt$. Yet it will have to pay the notes interest $(F_t + I_t)dt$ and the management and gap fees. Assuming for the sake of these rough numbers that $V_t r_t dt = F_t dt$, the net carry of these first elements will be equal to: $-2.725\% = -2\% - 0.2\% - 0.00035 \cdot 15$.

The structure will have to pay the leveraged losses to the credit index protection buyer. In Section 20.4.2 we have introduced the assumption for simulating the pool losses: annualized default rate of 0.0011 and constant deterministic recovery of 35 percent. This translates into a $0.0107 = 0.0011(1 - 0.35)15$ average leveraged loss per annum: the term $\beta_t dL_t$ in equation (20.5).

The structure will be cashing the accrual of the leveraged protection sold, the term $\left(S_{T_R^i} \beta_{T_R^i} + \int_{T_R^i}^t S_s d\beta_s \right) dt$. Given the long-term mean estimate of 0.0080 for the Globoxx index, this makes 12 percent, assuming maximum leverage of 15. Net of the average pool losses, this makes a positive carry of $10.93\% = 12\% - 1.07\%$ per annum.

Finally, the structure will receive a roll-down benefit through the final term in equation (20.5), $dNP V_t^{T_R^i}$. In case the index tightens between any two roll dates by 3 percent of the credit index spread, then the gain resulting from the roll-down benefit is $3.38\% = 2 \cdot 15 \cdot 0.0080 \cdot 3\% \cdot 4.7$, where we assumed an index basis point value of 4.7.[8]

Via this simple accounting we can see that the biggest source of income for the structure is the leveraged default premium of 10.93 percent contained in credit spreads (see Hull, Predescu, and White 2005) (i.e., the difference between the market credit spreads and average default rates).

When closing in six months' time a leveraged short protection position on the index, we run two risks: (1) the credit index spread has widened; (2) the credit index spread curve has inverted, thus making our purchase of protection more expensive. The second risk is not modeled: To model this risk we would need to model the correlated dynamic of two maturities in the credit spread curve instead of a constant five-year maturity. Nevertheless it is contributing an impressive 3.38 percent per annum.

So the net average carry of the structure is quite impressive: $11.585\% = -2.725\% + 12\% - 1.07\% + 3.38\%$. The default risk of the structure is that the mark-to-market losses due to a spread widening or bigger than expected defaults are not recuperated before the note maturity.

In this sense a higher spread volatility, smaller mean reversion, higher long-term mean spread, and modeling the pool loss admitting the possibility of cluster of defaults can all be considered stressed assumptions.

20.5 Modification of the Standard Assumptions

So far we have introduced the standard criteria adopted by rating agencies to simulate the NAV of a CPDO structure. The standard criteria are to model independently the spread and the pool loss. The spread is modeled with a mean-reverting process, whereas the pool loss is modeled with a multifactor Gaussian copula.

Here we want to introduce a crucial modification to the standard assumptions: We will change the simulation engine for the loss of the pool of names underlying the credit index from the multifactor Gaussian copula generally adopted by rating agencies to a simulation engine that allows many defaults at the same time instant: the generalized Poisson cluster loss (GPCL) model.

20.5.1 Bumps in the Multifactor Gaussian Copula

The average correlation used by rating agencies are so low that they do not produce loss distributions with bumps in the right tail.[9]

To show this we imagine 250 homogeneous entities with the same 10-year default probability of 5 percent. In Figure 20.2 we plot the 10-year default count distribution, where the default times of the single entities are correlated through a one-factor Gaussian copula with the flat correlation parameter equal to 20 percent and 90 percent.

Both distributions have the same expected loss (5 percent), but the shapes, in particular the tails, are quite different. Even with a Gaussian copula we can obtain a bump for the extreme loss scenario (loss close to 100 percent) but with a very high flat correlation parameter.

Conversely, right-tail bumps arise naturally in many static and dynamic loss models. Among others, multimodal loss distributions are predicted in Albanese, Chen,

FIGURE 20.2   Ten-Year Loss Distribution Obtained Correlating the Default Times of 250 Homogeneous Reference Entities with Default Probability of 5 Percent with a One-Factor Gaussian Copula Assuming 0 Percent Recovery with Flat Correlation Equal to 20 Percent (*left panel*) and to 90 Percent (*right panel*)

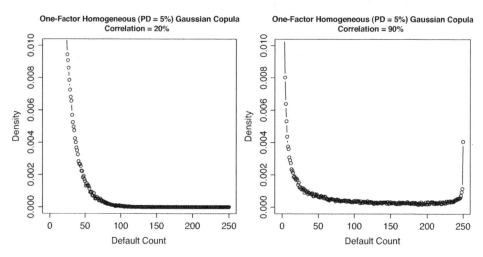

The y-axis is limited to the [0; 1%] range.

and D'Alessandro (2005); in Hull and White (2006) or Torresetti et al. (2009); in Longstaff and Rajan (2008); and in the GPL and GPCL models by Brigo et al. (2007a, 2007b).

20.5.2   Bumps in the GPCL

How reasonable is it to assume a loss distribution in the objective measure with bumps? Historical observations of default clusters are rare events even though recently we have seen a sequence of defaulted names belonging to the same sectors in a relatively short amount of time: airlines in 2001–2002 and more recently autos and financials.

For example, from September 7, 2008, to October 8, 2008, a time window of one month, we witnessed seven credit events occurring to major financial entities: Fannie Mae, Freddie Mac, Lehman Brothers, Washington Mutual, Landsbanki, Glitnir, and Kaupthing. Fannie Mae and Freedie Mac conservatorships were announced on the same date (September 7, 2008), and the appointment of a receivership committee for the three Icelandic banks (Landsbanki, Glitnir, Kaupthing) was announced between the 7th and the 8th of October.

Moreover, the changes recently proposed by S&P to the rating criteria of CDOs require that the AAA attachment should be able to withstand the default, with recovery 0 percent, of the sector in the CDO pool with the highest weight.[10]

This scenario is presented also by Longstaff and Rajan (2008). These authors, by means of a principal component analysis on the panel of daily absolute variations of the CDS spread of the CDX constituents, find that the first component is a shock affecting all CDSs (systematic shock); the remaining significant components can be interpreted as shocks affecting only one sector at a time (industry shock). This would seem to suggest that the industry shock has an economic meaning, as can be seen from the news flow priced in the CDS spread of the CDX constituents. Thus, the bumps that can be found in the loss distribution, implied from CDO quotes, could be attributed not just to the risk premium investors ask as a remuneration for bearing the skewed risk of senior tranches, see also Torresetti et al. (2009).

We think that this evidence might be relevant enough to point in the direction of bumps being present also in the objective measure. Accordingly, in the following we consider the loss distribution coming from the GPCL model, and we check the impact of bumps in the CPDO rating.

20.5.3 The GPCL Model at Work

The works of Brigo et al. (2007a, 2007b) show calibrations of the GPL and GPCL dynamic loss models against iTraxx and CDX tranche and index quotes on several market observation dates. In the GPL and GPCL models the default counting process is modeled by means of a summation of many independent Poisson processes whose intensity depends, in turn, on the number of defaults. In particular the GPCL model is built by taking into account the consistency with single-name dynamics.

Our goal is to use the GPCL model to estimate the probability distribution in the objective measure preserving the multimodal features that the model predicts for the probability distribution in the risk-neutral measure. Thus, we follow a calibration strategy rather different from the one proposed in Brigo et al. (2007b) and rather similar to the one proposed by Longstaff and Rajan (2008). The dynamics of the pool loss process L_t and of the default counting process C_t are:

$$dL_t = (1 - R)dC_t, \quad C_t = \sum_{j=1}^{M} j \, Z_j(t), \, dZ_j(t) \sim \text{Poisson}\left(\binom{M - C_{t^-}}{j}\widetilde{\lambda}_j(t)dt\right)$$

(20.8)

where M is the number of credit references in the pool. Further, we consider that at the time of inception there are no losses.

We have designed a calibration for the tranches of the last five iTraxx and CDX five-year series. For the CDX we have considered all series from S4 to S8, while for the iTraxx we have considered all series from S3 to S7. First, we fixed the jump sizes in order to evenly space the logarithmic default rate from 1/125 to 125/125. The intensities $\widetilde{\lambda}_j$ with $j \notin J := \{1, 2, 5, 11, 25, 56, 125\}$ are set to zero; namely, the

TABLE 20.3   Average Absolute-Standardized Mispricings for iTraxx Series

Series	Roll Date	0%–3%	3%–6%	6%–9%	9%–12%	12%–22%
iTraxx S1	Mar. 20, 2004	1.7	0.8	1.9	1.1	0.8
iTraxx S2	Sept. 20, 2004	0.4	0.5	0.8	2.0	1.1
iTraxx S3	Mar. 20, 2005	5.2	6.0	1.9	1.4	1.1
iTraxx S4	Sept. 20, 2005	1.6	1.6	1.5	0.8	0.9
iTraxx S5	Mar. 20, 2006	3.0	3.2	1.6	1.4	0.6
iTraxx S6	Sept. 20, 2006	1.3	1.9	1.9	1.8	0.6
iTraxx S7	Mar. 20, 2007	3.2	3.1	3.6	3.8	1.5

The averages are calculated on all weekly market data when the series were on-the-run.

counting process can jump only with an amplitude that is listed in J. Then, for each series we consider the weekly market quotes for dates when the series are on-the-run (a six-month period). We perform a different calibration for each quote set; namely, we calibrate every week. Let us call each calibration date s. We model the intensities $\bar{\lambda}_j(t)$ for each calibration date s as a piecewise constant in the time $t - s$. Further, we allow that they depend also on calibration date s via a common multiplicative factor $\varphi(s)$:

$$\bar{\lambda}_j(t;s) = \varphi(s)\psi_j(t-s)$$

where we set $\varphi(T_R^{i-1}) = 1$ and T_R^{i-1} is the last roll date (i.e., the first trading date of the new on-the-run series). Notice that we explicitly indicate the argument s to express the fact that different intensities are used on different calibration dates.

We have on average 120 market quotes for each series (six months times four weeks times five tranches), but we calibrate only $30 = 7 + 6 \cdot 4 - 1$ parameters for each series (seven jump intensities plus 23 scaling factors: one for each weekly date in the sample minus one). The target function in the calibration is the sum of squares of the standardized mispricing: theoretical spread minus market spread divided by half the bid-ask spread. Calibration results are listed in Table 20.3.

Further, it is interesting to show the probability distributions for the number of defaults both in the risk-neutral and in the objective measure for the iTraxx[11] (Figure 20.3). Notice that the distribution in the objective measure is simply computed starting from the intensities calibrated to the five-year tranches, and rescaled to match the probability of default of the underlying pool of names in between roll dates, which is 0.11 percent according to equation (20.7).

Notice that we will crudely average across the 10 iTraxx distributions throughout the five series to get the six-month loss distribution in the objective measure for the Globoxx. In the CPDO structure NAV simulations under the GPCL assumption, the pool losses will be sampled from the averaged distribution on each roll date (i.e., every six months).

FIGURE 20.3   Risk-Neutral (*upper panels*) and Objective (*lower panels*) Distributions of the Number of Defaults over a Six-Month Horizon for the iTraxx Pool Calibrated to the Five-Year iTraxx Tranches

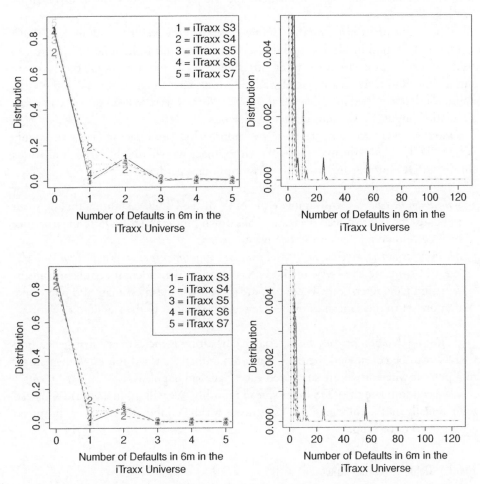

On the right panel we zoom in on the right tail of the distribution.

20.6   Numerical Results

So far we have introduced the payoff of a hypothetical CPDO structure. Then we analyzed the details of the risk factors affecting the evolution of the NAV of the structure, thus identifying the critical variables that need to be simulated when assigning a rating to CPDO structures: the Globoxx credit spread and the Globoxx loss rate.

For both credit spread and credit loss simulations we have identified a set of base case and stressed case assumptions. The stressed case assumptions are a set of conservative assumptions across both the credit spread and the credit loss parametrization: the sort of assumptions an investor would expect from a rating agency when assigning an AAA rating. The parametrization of the credit spread simulation in turn can be stressed across both the roll-down benefit and the parametrization of the exponential Vasicek.

The results of the stress on the parametrization of the credit spread on the CPDO rating can be found in Linden et al. (2007). Here we want to highlight the increased riskiness of CPDO structures when stressing the parametrization of the loss rate simulation. Rating agencies generally adopt a multifactor Gaussian copula, the same approach that was used in Linden et al. (2007). We advocate instead the GPCL: a loss simulation engine that admits clusters of defaults.

Here we want to compare these two approaches (multifactor Gaussian copula versus GPCL). Under the hypothesis of each approach we will run the NAV simulations for the CPDO intersecting two sets of assumptions regarding:

- *Roll-down benefit.* We will simulate the NAV of the CDPO assuming that between roll dates the index spread decreases (rolls down on the index CDS term structure) by 0 percent and 3 percent, respectively.
- *Mean-reversion parameters for the process of the credit index spread (exponential Vasicek).* We will simulate the NAV of the CPDO under two different settings of mean-reversion parameters: one where they are set to their mean estimate and one where they are set to their mean estimate stressed by a quarter of the standard deviation.

The case that best proxies the criteria used by rating agencies to rate first-generation CPDOs can be considered the case of mean parameter set and roll-down benefit set to 3 percent where losses are simulated via a Gaussian copula.

We will simulate the CDS index spread monthly. We will simulate the loss instead semiannually on the roll dates. Bid-ask spreads for the Globoxx five-year credit spread are assumed to be 1 bp.

20.6.1   Default and Loss Rate

The default and loss rates of the CPDO structure simulated under the various assumptions of roll-down benefit and mean-reversion parameters are presented in Figure 20.4 for the multifactor Gaussian copula and GPCL loss simulation engines, respectively.

The plots on the left side of the figure are the simulation results assuming a roll-down benefit of 3 percent; the ones on the right side assume a benefit of 0 percent. Starting from the top of the figures, the first four plots are the simulation results using the mean parameter set, followed by those with the stressed parameter set. At the bottom of each chart can be found the probability of default (PD) and average loss (Exp loss) of the CPDO structure. The histograms in the charts are the distributions of the cash-in times. A path where the structure has not cashed in before maturity (thus including the paths where a cash-out has occurred) will count as a default of the CPDO structure. Thus, the percentage of paths falling in the last rectangle of each histogram in Figure 20.4, the rectangle corresponding to the CPDO maturity, tells us the percentage of simulation paths that resulted in a CPDO default.

FIGURE 20.4 Distribution in the Cash-In Times under the Multifactor Gaussian Copula (*four upper panels*) and the GPCL (*four lower panels*) Approaches

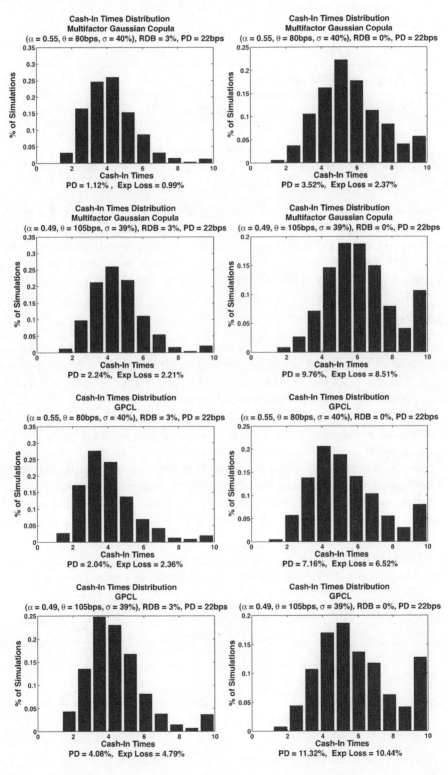

TABLE 20.4   CPDO Average Default Rate and Loss Rate under the Various Assumptions in Terms of Roll-Down Benefit (RDB) and Mean-Reversion Parameters Governing the Dynamic of the Index Spread

		Copula		GPCL	
	RDB	3%	0%	3%	0%
Default rate	Mean parameter set	1.12%	3.52%	2.36%	7.16%
	Stressed parameter set	2.24%	9.76%	4.79%	11.32%
Loss rate	Mean parameter set	0.99%	2.37%	2.04%	6.52%
	Stressed parameter set	2.21%	8.51%	4.08%	10.44%

Mean parameter set is $\{\alpha = 0.55\, , \ \theta = 0.80\, , \ \sigma = 40.0\}$, while stressed parameter set is $\{\alpha = 0.49\, , \ \theta = 1.05\, , \ \sigma = 38.7\}$.

The results contained in Figure 20.4 are summarized in Table 20.4. We see that introducing a loss distribution with bumps worsens considerably the default rate of the structure and thus reduces the rating substantially. This is particularly true in the base case for both the roll-down benefit and the mean parameter set where the structure had a very low probability of default in the multifactor Gaussian copula case.

20.6.2   Rating

When assessing the rating of a structured finance issue, S&P and Fitch take into consideration the default rate of the structure simulated under a set of scenarios, whereas Moody's takes into consideration the loss rate. Rating agencies will look up the rating from the average simulated default or loss rate table.

In Table 20.5 we report the CPDO rating based on the CPDO default rates of Table 20.4 according to the default rates assigned by S&P for 10-year maturity structured finance deals. For both the copula and the GPCL case we note that stressing the roll-down benefit assumption has a much greater impact (a difference of two notches) than stressing the parametrization of the credit spread simulation.

When stressing both the parametrization of the credit spread simulation and the roll-down benefit assumption, both the copula and the GPCL cases give the same

TABLE 20.5   CPDO Rating Based on the CPDO Default Rate of Table 20.4 According to the Probability of Default Estimated by S&P for Structured Finance Deals under the Various Assumptions in Terms of Roll-Down Benefit (RDB) and Mean-Reversion Parameters Governing the Dynamic of the Index Spread

		Copula		GPCL	
	RDB	3%	0%	3%	0%
CPDO rating	Mean parameter set	AA	A−	A+	BBB−
	Stressed parameter set	A+	BBB−	BBB+	BBB−

Parameter sets are given in Table 20.4.

TABLE 20.6 CPDO Average Gap-Risk Fee in Basis Points and Average Leverage at Cash-Out Times under the Various Assumptions in Terms of Roll-Down Benefit (RDB) and Mean-Reversion Parameters Governing the Dynamic of the Index Spread

	RDB	Copula		GPCL	
		3%	0%	3%	0%
Gap risk	Mean parameter set	0.02 bps	0.08 bps	4.32 bps	1.63 bps
	Stressed parameter set	0.12 bps	0.35 bps	2.51 bps	2.08 bps
Average leverage	Mean parameter set	5.45	5.18	11.30	13.2
	Stressed parameter set	3.8	4.5	7.9	7.37

Parameter sets are given in Table 20.4.

rating (BBB-). Instead when using the base case for both scenarios, simulating the loss with the GPCL worsens the rating of the CPDO by two notches with respect to the multifactor Gaussian copula (A+ instead of AA).

We see that in both cases, Gaussian copula and GPCL, when moving from the base case to the stressed case for both the roll-down benefit and the credit spread process parametrization, we get on the verge of the investment-grade scale.

20.6.3 Gap Risk

The specific CPDO structure we have analyzed here pays a substantial fee for the gap risk option: 3.5 bps per leverage per annum. In case the leverage goes to its maximum, 15 times the notes notional, the structure would pay 52.5 bps per annum (15 times 3.5 bps) as a gap-risk fee. Thus, the market pays quite a considerable premium for the risk that when unwinding all positions the structure might need a cash injection.

In Table 20.6 we report the average gap option fee (bps per unit of leverage per annum) across simulations: We divide the simulated gap protection payments (the absolute value of the average NAV when negative or zero otherwise at cash-out) by the average leverage to the earliest between maturity, cash-in or cash-out.

Note that when stressing the parameter of the mean-reversion process in the GPCL framework we actually reduce the average gap-risk fee. This happens because the average leverage is actually reduced and thus the expected loss we suffer when a cluster of defaults arrives is considerably reduced, as can be seen in the lower part of Table 20.6 where we report the average leverage at cash-out under the various assumptions of roll-down benefit (RDB) and mean-reversion parameters. When we stress the mean-reversion parameters, we make it more likely that a cluster of defaults arrives at a time when the NAV is already deeply depressed due to an adverse movement in spreads and thus we reduce the impact of the cluster of defaults.

Finally, we want to point out how the results of our simulation provide an insight also with respect to the reserves that the bank selling the gap option will need to book. Indeed, the bank selling the gap option would have to make a provision for the expected loss and allocate capital for the unexpected loss. The bank provision for the expected loss could be calculated as the base case with the Gaussian copula: 0.02 bps out of 3.5 bps. The capital allocated to sustain the unexpected loss could instead be calculated with the GPCL with the stressed parameters set and RBD = 0: 2.08 bps out of 3.5 bps.

20.7 Conclusion

We have introduced the details of a specific CPDO transaction. We have then reviewed the standard criteria generally adopted by rating agencies to rate first-generation CPDO transactions. We have highlighted the importance of the roll-down benefit hypothesis and the difficulty in measuring it historically.

We have then introduced one important modification to the standard criteria: namely, the adoption of the GPCL framework when simulating the index pool loss. We have then performed a batch calibration to both the iTraxx and CDX series. In this way we obtained for each series of each index an average estimate of the importance of the bumps in the right tail of the loss distribution.

The risk-neutral loss distributions thus obtained were mapped to the objective measure, rescaling the cluster default intensities in such a way as to obtain the target average default rate in the objective measure.

In the same spirit as Linden et al. (2007) we run our simulations under a set of assumptions regarding the roll-down benefit and the mean-reversion parameters. For each set of assumptions we consider both loss simulations frameworks: multifactor Gaussian copula and GPCL.

We show the increase in riskiness and decrease in rating of the CPDO when simulating the loss with the GPCL framework instead of the multifactor Gaussian copula.

Finally, we hint at the dramatic increase of the fair gap-risk fee under the objective measure in the GPCL framework with respect to the multifactor Gaussian copula.

Acknowledgment

We are grateful to Damiano Brigo, Paula Lenahan, Borja Salazar, Massimo Morini, and Matthias Neugebauer for helpful discussions.

Notes

1. The conflict of interest rating agencies are facing a serious issue as some analysts estimated that Moody's earned $884 million in 2006, or 43 percent of total revenue, from rating structured notes. See "Moody's, S&P Lose Credibility on CPDOs They Rated," Bloomberg News, August 14, 2007.

2. The Securities and Exchange Commission (SEC) since 1975 has limited competition in the rating industry to designated Nationally Recognized Statistical Rating Organizations (NRSROs). This designation was intended to put a limit on rating inflationary pressure in view of increased regulatory rating uses. The unintended consequence was to put a limit to competition creating an oligopoly. The U.S. Congress, concerned with this limitation of competition, enacted the Credit Rating Agency Reform Act in 2006 to improve rating quality for the protection of investors and in the public interest by fostering accountability, transparency, and competition in the credit rating agency industry. In particular the Credit Rating Agency Reform Act set forth objective criteria to obtain NRSRO recognition.

3. The Globoxx is a credit derivative index whose constituents are the union of the constituents of the iTraxx and CDX, the two most popular credit derivative indexes.

4. If for simplicity we assume rates to deterministically evolve along the forward curve, then the present value of the LIBOR interest plus the principal at maturity is always equal to par.

5. For the sake of simplicity and given the negligible impact, we will not consider the actual credit index trading conventions but will assume instead the same trading conventions as for single-name CDSs.

6. We have preferred not to consider explicitly the cash account. The only difference is the accrual between roll dates due to the unrealized mark-to-market, NPV_t, that differentiate the NAV from the cash account.

7. See www.sp.cdointerface.com site.

8. The index basis point value is obtained assuming 3 percent interest rate and five years and three months to index maturity.

9. For instance, in the case of S&P's CDO Evaluator we considered in Table 20.2 the maximum correlation was 15 percent.

10. See "Request for Comment: Update to Global Methodologies and Assumptions for Corporate Cash Flow CDO and Synthetic CDO Ratings," Standard & Poor's, March 18, 2009.

11. CDX's probability distributions in both the risk-neutral and the objective measure are available upon request.

References

Albanese, C., O. Chen, A. D'Alessandro, and A. Vidlec. 2005. Dynamic credit correlation modeling. Available at www.defaultrisk.com.

Altman, E. I., and D. L. Kao. 1992. The implications of corporate bond ratings drift. *Financial Analysts Journal*, 48:64–67.

Bangia, A., F. Diebold, A. Kronimus, C. Schagen, and T. Schuermann. 2002. Ratings migration and the business cycle, with applications to credit portfolio stress testing. *Journal of Banking and Finance* 26:445–474.

Becker, B., and T. Milbourn. 2008. Reputation and competition: Evidence from the credit rating industry. Working Paper 09-51, Harvard Business School.

Brigo, D., A. Pallavicini, and R. Torresetti. 2007a. Calibration of CDO tranches with the dynamical generalized-Poisson loss model. *Risk* (May).

Brigo, D., A. Pallavicini, and R. Torresetti. 2007b. Cluster-based extension of the generalized Poisson loss dynamics and consistency with single names. *International Journal of Theoritical and Applied Finance* 10: 607.

Cantor, R., and F. Packer. 1994. The credit rating industry. *Quarterly Review, Federal Reserve Bank of New York* (Summer):1–26.

Cantor, R., and F. Packer. 1997. Differences of opinion and selection bias in the credit rating industry. *Journal of Banking and Finance* 21 (10): 1395–1417.

Hull, J., M. Predescu, and A. White. 2005. Bond prices, default probabilities and risk premiums. *Journal of Credit Risk* 1 (2): 53–60.

Hull, J., and A. White. 2006. The perfect copula. *Journal of Derivatives* 14 (2) (Winter): 8–28.

Lando, D., and T. M. Skodeberg. 2002. Analyzing rating transitions and rating drift with continuous observations. *Journal of Banking and Finance* 26:423–444.

Li, D. X. 2000. On default correlation: A copula approach. *Journal of Fixed Income* 9 (March): 43–54.

Linden, A., M. Neugebauer, S. Bund, J. Schiavetta, J. Zelter, and R. Hardee. 2007. First generation CPDO: Case study on performance and ratings. Available at www.defaultrisk.com.

Longstaff, F. A., and A. Rajan. 2008. An empirical analysis of the pricing of collateralized debt obligations. *Journal of Finance* 63 (2) (April): 529–563.

Lucas, D., and J. Lonski. 1992. Changes in corporate credit quality 1970–1990. *Journal of Fixed Income* 1:7–14.

Nickell, P., W. Perraudin, and S. Varotto. 2000. Stability of transition matrices. *Journal of Banking and Finance* 24:203–227.

Skreta, V., and L. Veldkamp. 2008. Ratings shopping and asset complexity: A theory of ratings inflation. Working Paper 08-28, New York University, Leonard N. Stern School of Business, Department of Economics.

Tejwani, G., S. Hamid, S. Varma, A. Jha, and H. Manappatil. 2007. Selection bias in CDS portfolios. *Fixed Income Research*, Lehman Brothers.

Torresetti, R., D. Brigo, and A. Pallavicini. 2009. Risk neutral versus objective loss distribution and CDO tranches valuation. *Journal of Risk Management in Financial Institutions* 2 (2): 175–192.

CHAPTER 21

Interacting Path Systems for Credit Risk

Pierre Del Moral

Centre INRIA Bordeaux Sud-Ouest and Institut de Mathématiques de Bordeaux

Frédéric Patras

Université de Nice and Zeliade Systems

Interacting particle systems provide one of the most efficient ways to perform variance reduction in Monte Carlo approaches to rare events analysis. This chapter is meant as a general introduction to the theory with a particular emphasis toward applications to credit risk. We survey the main techniques and results, illustrate them with recent findings, and propose a new class of algorithms (referred to as interacting path systems) suited to the analysis of multiple defaults in credit portfolios.

21.1 Introduction

Let us consider one of the simplest possible probabilistic computations in multiname credit risk, say the probability that two companies with CDS spreads of 20 bps both suffer a default event during the next year. Assume, for simplicity, zero recovery rates and that the two default events are independent. The risk-neutral probability of this double default is roughly $p = 4 \times 10^{-6}$. A brute-force Monte Carlo (MC) estimate of this probability with a sample of size m has a variance $\sigma^2 \approx \frac{p(1-p)}{m} \approx \frac{p}{m}$. This implies that the (not very satisfactory) goal of achieving by a brute-force MC simulation a standard deviation less than 10 percent of the joint default event probability requires at least a sample size of around 2.5×10^7.

This simple example illustrates the shortcomings of classical MC techniques when it comes to multiname credit events. In other terms, variance reduction techniques are necessary. Several are available, and their choice certainly depends on the circumstances (a particular problem, a given model, etc.). Classical variance reduction techniques based on the knowledge of probability densities can lead to efficient algorithms but are usually difficult to implement. For complex and very large portfolios a practically useful solution is the use of reduced models as a control variate. Another strategy, the splitting technique, was developed by Glasserman et al. (1999) in the late 1990s for the estimation of rare event probabilities. The technique was not based on any kind of physical process evolution in a critical regime; the underlying idea (shared by various similar algorithms) can be thought of as a way to multiply the number of interesting paths. Concretely, when the rare event is associated to a path crossing a given threshold, one creates a series of intermediate thresholds and reinforces promising paths at the intermediate thresholds by splitting them into subpaths, which then evolve independently. The method obviously dedicates a greater part of the computational effort in the right direction. The main drawback of their approach is that the probability transitions between the levels were assumed to be known. However, the method also raises several questions—in particular regarding the optimal choice of the intermediate thresholds or the optimal degree of splitting.

In the present chapter we focus on still another strategy that gains momentum, namely interacting particle systems (IPS). The strategy can be understood as a subtle refinement of the splitting technique, in that it multiplies the interesting paths. More importantly, it learns on-the-fly the probability transitions between the up-crossing levels. Besides, as we shall see, IPS can be coupled with the original Glasserman et al. multilevel splitting technique. From the technical point of view, a key property of IPS is that (contrary to usual importance sampling) its implementation does not require the knowledge of the changed sampling measure, nor the knowledge of the probability transitions between the levels. In fact, the IPS method can be thought of as a sophisticated stochastic tool for sampling a sequence of optimal twisted measures with increasing level of complexity. The two properties just discussed might be essential when the asset dynamic is complex and when its modeling relies on intricated algorithms—think of the pricing algorithms for home equity loans (HELs), residential mortgage-backed securities (RMBSs), credit cards, and other asset-backed securities (ABSs)! This is a major practical advantage of IPS in applications to credit risk valuation.

Interacting particle systems and the associated MC algorithms have a long history that goes back to the pioneering work by Feynman and Kac in high-energy physics in the 1950s. The systematic development of the theory is more recent, most of the theorems on the fine convergence properties of IPS algorithms dating from the past decade. We refer to Del Moral (2004) for a systematic approach, a description of the various application fields, and references to the classical litterature. The appearance of these algorithms in the credit literature is even more recent (Carmona and Crépey forthcoming; Carmona, Fouque, and Vestal 2009).

The purpose of the present chapter is accordingly twofold. First, we introduce and survey the leading ideas and techniques of IPS. The main application field we consider is rare events analysis, with a particular emphasis on multiname credit risk. We do not aim at being fully comprehensive, and we do not discuss some important topics such as the use of IPS for nonlinear filtering, and fixed parameter estimation in hidden Markov chain models, although these questions are certainly relevant for credit risk where most models rely on unobservable quantities (asset value, default thresholds, stochastic volatilities, default correlations, etc.) that have to be implied from market prices or historical data.

Second, we introduce a new IPS technique for the analysis of defaults in credit portfolios. The method is based on a suitable path-space approach to multiple defaults—we refer to it as the interacting path systems (IPaS) approach, to distinguish it from classical IPS. This technique is inspired by a general strategy (the multilevel approach to Feynman-Kac formulas) introduced by the first author in (Del Moral (2004), to which we will refer for theoretical convergence results. The mathematical foundations of the new method and its varous possible applications in the field of credit risk (as well as some refinements that we do not consider here) will be explored further in future works.

21.2 Interacting Particle Systems

We start by surveying briefly the general methods and ideas underlying IPS. The algorithms are presented in their full generality, but we have tried to emphasize, at each step, the concrete meaning of the assumptions in view of the applications we have in mind. This survey is based on Del Moral (2004), to which we refer for further details and various possible variants of the algorithms.

21.2.1 Introduction to Genetic-Type Algorithms

Many ideas underlying IPS stem originally from two fields: particle systems in high-energy physics and population genetics. In both cases, the particles or individuals evolve according to stochastic transitions modeling either the dynamics of the particles or the reproduction patterns of the individuals. Simultaneously, some particles are absorbed by the surrounding medium (or submitted to an extrapotential) and some individuals die. We will use from now on the physics terminology and call "particles" the elements of a given sample.

The general evolution scheme of an interacting particle system decomposes accordingly (for each time step) into two substeps: First some particles are selected (selection step); then the system evolves according to the prescribed dynamics (mutation step in the langage of population genetics; this terminology has now been adopted for arbitrary IPS). In credit risk, the meaning of the algorithm is the following: We are mostly interested in rare event analysis (we want to measure joint default probabilities in credit portfolios, and these probabilities are most often very small quantities). We will therefore add to the risk-neutral dynamics of the processes modeling the time evolution of the portfolio selection steps in such a way as to increase the number of trajectories where several defaults show up. That is, we use the selection step to multiply the number of trajectories where credit events occur. Still in other terms, we force the system to move toward risky configurations. This is nothing but an importance sampling strategy for rare events, with, however, a particular feature. Namely, we do not change the process modeling the time evolution of the system and simply add an extra-prescription to select and multiply the most interesting trajectories and particles so as to explore at best the rare events we are interested in.

Intuitively, this is the basic idea. The key issue is to implement it consistently and make sure it does lead to the correct quantities. Let us start by fixing the notations. For a given sequence of state spaces E_n, we start with a sequence of Markov transitions $M_{n+1}(x, dy)$ from E_n to E_{n+1}. When all the state spaces are equal, we write simply E for E_n. The integer N will stand for the number of particles (the sample size) of the IPS simulations, whereas n should be understood as the index of the time step. The set of the N particles at time step n is written $\xi_n = (\xi_n^i)_{1 \le i \le N}$. Let us mention that contineous-time IPS algorithms exist (see, e.g., Del Moral, Patras, and Rubenthaler 2009); however, discrete ones seem much better suited to most of the problems we are interested in presently.

The state space can be any one of the usual state spaces for credit risk valuation. For example, in a structural approach to credit risk (see, e.g., Blanchet-Scalliet and Patras in the present volume or Section 21.3.2 of this chapter), the Markov transitions may describe the evolution of a sequence of firms asset values (corresponding to the components of the credit portfolio). In a ratings-based approach, they may describe the transitions of assets in the portfolio between the various ratings classes, and so on. To fix the ideas we will assume that the state spaces are of the form $\mathbb{Z}^d$ or $\mathbb{R}^d$ (with $d \in \mathbb{N} - \{0\}$ typically denoting in the forthcoming applications the number of assets in a credit portfolio).

21.2.2   Selection and Mutations

As we mentioned, the key idea of the application of IPS methods to credit risk is to add to the risk-neutral dynamics of the assets in a portfolio selection steps that increase the number of risky trajectories. The selection/mutation pattern of the corresponding scheme is denoted by:

$$\xi_n = (\xi_n^i)_{1 \le i \le N} \xrightarrow{\text{selection}} \widehat{\xi}_n = (\widehat{\xi}_n^i)_{1 \le i \le N} \xrightarrow{\text{mutation}} \xi_{n+1} = (\xi_{n+1}^i)_{1 \le i \le N}$$

The selection step is the crucial one and is specific to IPS with respect to other sampling and variance-reduction techniques. Notice that we want to select the most interesting trajectories in a suitable probabilistic way, so that the main properties of MC simulations are preserved; for example, we expect the law of large numbers and central limit theorems to hold (see Del Moral 2004, Chapters 7–9).

To model the selection $\xi_n \leadsto \widehat{\xi}_n$, we choose a $[0, 1]$-valued a sequence G_n, $n = 1, \ldots, T$ of potential functions on the E_n. For each $i = 1, \ldots, N$, we set then:

$$\widehat{\xi}_n^i = \begin{cases} \xi_n^i & \text{with probability} \quad G_n(\xi_n^i) \\ \bar{\xi}_n^i & \text{with probability} \quad 1 - G_n(\xi_n^i) \end{cases}$$

where $\bar{\xi}_n^i$ stands for a random variable with law $\sum_{j=1}^{N} \frac{G_n(\xi_n^j)}{\sum_{k=1}^{N} G_n(\xi_n^k)} \delta_{\xi_n^j}$.

Since we want to multiply the most interesting trajectories, we will choose the values of G_n to be high on these trajectories and comparatively low on the less interesting ones. As we will see, there are various ways to construct these potential functions. In some cases (for example in Bayesian analysis), the choice of the potential function is dictated by the conditional law of the trajectories (relatively to the set of observations). In other cases, the potential function has to be chosen. This choice is rarely obvious. It has to be fine-tuned to the problem, and from its choice will depend the efficiency of the algorithm; for practical purposes, IPS is an art almost as much as a science.

During the mutation phase, the particles explore the state space independently (the interactions between the various particles being created by the selection steps) according to the Markov transitions $M_{n+1}(x, dy)$. In other terms, we have:

$$\widehat{\xi}_n^i \leadsto \xi_{n+1}^i$$

where ξ_{n+1}^i stands for a random variable with the law $M_{n+1}(\widehat{\xi}_n^i, \cdot)$. Equivalently,

$$\mathbb{P}(\xi_{n+1}^i \in dy | \widehat{\xi}_n^i = x) = M_{n+1}(x, dy)$$

Notice that the algorithm fails (and has to be stopped) if $\sum_{k=1}^{N} G_n(\xi_n^k) = 0$; this may occur in practice, for example if the sample size is too small and if G_n vanishes on many trajectories. This problem (well-understood from the theoretical point of view; see (Del Moral 2004, Theorems 7.4.2, 7.4.3) has to be dealt with specifically during the numerical implementation. A simple way to avoid the problem would be to assume that the potential functions are strictly positive (or even strictly positively bounded from below). This hypothesis simplifies greatly many proofs and, for that reason, occurs frequently in the IPS literature. However, for rare event analysis, allowing zero-valued potential functions is often very convenient and efficient. We focus on that particular issue in Section 21.2.6.

Another important observation concerns the genealogical tree structure of the previously defined genetic particle model: If we interpret the selection transition as a birth and death process, then arises the important notion of the ancestral line of a current individual. More precisely, when a particle $\widehat{\xi}_{n-1}^i \longrightarrow \xi_n^i$ evolves to a new location ξ_n^i, we can interpret $\widehat{\xi}_{n-1}^i$ as the parent of ξ_n^i. Looking backwards in time and recalling that the particle $\widehat{\xi}_{n-1}^i$ has selected a site ξ_{n-1}^j in the configuration at time $(n-1)$, we can interpret this site ξ_{n-1}^{j} as the parent of $\widehat{\xi}_{n-1}^{i}$ and therefore as the ancestor denoted $\xi_{n-1,n}^{i}$ at level $(n-1)$ of ξ_{n}^{i}. Running backwards in time we may trace the whole ancestral line:

$$\xi_{0,n}^{i} \longleftarrow \xi_{1,n}^{i} \longleftarrow \cdots \longleftarrow \xi_{n-1,n}^{i} \longleftarrow \xi_{n,n}^{i} = \xi_{n}^{i} \tag{21.1}$$

This genetic type interpretation is summarized in the following synthetic picture that corresponds to the case $(N, n) = (3, 4)$:

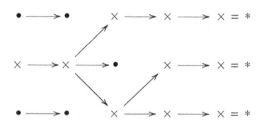

The current population (and the corresponding empirical measure) is represented by the ∗ symbols, the corresponding genealogical tree by the lines linking the × symbols, and finally the complete genealogy (where we consider also the stopped ancestral lines) is represented by all the ancestral lines of the branching process.

Concretely, the diagram should be interpreted as follows: During the first selection step, the three particles are selected but none multiplies. During the second selection step, the two outer particles die. Only the middle particle is selected and mutates (or gives birth) to three particles. So, at time 2, there are again three particles. The middle one is not selected and dies. The two other ones are selected, but only the bottom ones multiplies. So, at time 3, there are three particles again. During the last step, they are all selected but none multiplies and we end up once again with three particles.

21.2.3   Feynman-Kac Measures

Let us assume from now on that the initial values $\xi_0 = (\xi_0^i)_{1 \le i \le N} \in E_0^N$ form a sequence of independent and identically distributed (i.i.d.) random variables with common law η_0. One can then prove that, at each time step n, the random variables $(\xi_n^1, \ldots, \xi_n^N)$ are still approximately independent and follow a common law η_n. This property is referred to as "propagation of chaos," which means that the independence property is preserved asymptotically in terms of the sample size, in spite of the interactions (Del Moral 2004, chap. 8; Del Moral, Patras, and Rubenthaler 2009). The limit measure η_n is often called the Feynman-Kac measure of the system. A law of large numbers holds:

$$\eta_n^N = \frac{1}{N} \sum_{i=1}^{N} \delta_{\xi_n^i} \longrightarrow \eta_n \tag{21.2}$$

in the sense that

$$\eta_n^N(f) := \frac{1}{N} \sum_{i=1}^{N} f(\xi_n^i) \longrightarrow \eta_n(f) := \int f(x) \, \eta_n(dx)$$

for any regular function f, when the sample size $N \uparrow \infty$, and for all time steps $n \in \mathbb{N}^*$. The first rigorous proof of convergence was obtained in Del Moral (1996). For futher mathematical details, we refer to the series of volumes (Bartoli and Del Moral 2001; Del Moral 2004; Del Moral and Miclo 2000). To give a flavor of these results, we provide a recent exponential deviation result that allows us to calibrate the performance of IPS algorithms with a precision degree that does not depend on the time horizon. Under some strong regularity properties, for any time horizon $n \geq 0$, any function f with oscillations bounded by 1 ($|f(x) - f(y)| \leq 1, \forall x, y \in E_n$), and any precision parameter $x \geq 0$, the probability of the event

$$|\eta_n^N(f) - \eta_n(f)| \leq c \left(\frac{1+x}{N} + \sqrt{\frac{x}{N}} \right) \tag{21.3}$$

is greater than $1 - e^{-x}$. In this formula, c stands for some finite constant $c < \infty$ whose values can be made more explicit in terms of the stochastic model, but they do not depend on the time horizon, nor on the size of the systems N (see Del Moral and Rio forthcoming, corollary 3.7).

All these convergence properties (including central limit theorems) are basically the reason why IPS can be considered as a particular Monte Carlo scheme and computes in the end correct probabilities (a property that is not so obvious intuitively when one first encounters these algorithms).

Let us consider till the end of this first part of the chapter a simple toy model to illustrate these phenomena and better explain the underlying ideas. Let us assume that we have to deal with a stock (or any other asset) with a lognormal behavior and initial value $S_0 = S$, so that for a given choice of time steps, we have the Markovian transitions:

$$S_{n+1} - S_n = S_n(r\Delta t + \sigma\sqrt{\Delta t} B_n)$$

where r and σ are constant drift and volatility parameter and B_n a sequence of independent standard normal variables. Assume further that we are interested in the pricing of a path-dependent barrier option with time-dependent strikes K_i, $0 \leq i \leq T$, so that we need, for example, to compute the distribution of S_T conditionally to the hypothesis $S_i < K_i$, $0 \leq i < T$.

To this end, let us introduce the potential functions $G_i(x) := 1$ if $x < K_i$, $G_i(x) := 0$ else. In practice, this amounts to discarding the trajectories that hit the barrier and replacing them by sampling in the population of surviving trajectories. Then, at the time step T, the empirical measure η_T^N associated to the interacting particle system determined by the series of potential functions G_i and the lognormal Markov transitions driving S_i converges to the Feynman-Kac measure:

$$\eta_T(dx) = \mathbb{P}(S_T \in dx | S_i < K_i, \ 0 \leq i < T)$$

For further use, it is also useful to introduce the so-called updated Feynman-Kac measure:

$$\hat{\eta}_T(dx) = \mathbb{P}(S_T \in dx | S_i < K_i, \ 0 \leq i \leq T)$$

to which similar results apply. Notice that, even in such a simple example, the rigorous proof of the convergence would require some care, due to the interactions between the particles and trajectories that are created by the samplings in the populations of surviving trajectories.

Besides, what if we are interested in the unconditional law $\mathbb{P}(S_T \in dx, \ S_i < K_i, \ 0 \leq i < T)$ or on the whole path sequence conditional (or unconditional) measures $\mathbb{P}(S_i \in dx_i, \ 0 \leq i < T | S_i < K_i, \ 0 \leq i < T)$? The next section answers this question—of the utmost interest for rare event analysis.

21.2.4 Unconditional versus Feynman-Kac Measures

Let us rewrite $\mathbb{P}(S_T \in [a, b], \ S_i < K_i, \ 0 \leq i < T)$ using the potential functions:

$$\mathbb{P}(S_T \in [a, b], \ S_i < K_i, \ 0 \leq i < T) = \mathbb{E}\left(1_{[a,b]}(S_T) \prod_{p=0}^{T-1} G_p(S_p) \right)$$

This suggests the introduction for an arbitrary IPS of the unconditional—or unnormalized, the latter more common and rigorous terminology due to equation 21.4)—signed measures γ_n defined by:

$$\gamma_n(f) = \int f(x) \, \gamma_n(dx) = \mathbb{E}\left(f(X_n) \prod_{p=0}^{n-1} G_p(X_p) \right)$$

where f runs over bounded functions on the state space E_n and X_n stands for a Markov chain with initial law η_0, state spaces E_n and Markov kernels M_n. The interpretation of η_n as a conditional probability that we noticed when describing our toy model translates into the general formula (that holds for an arbitrary IPS):

$$\eta_n(f) = \frac{\gamma_n(f)}{\gamma_n(1)} = \frac{\mathbb{E}\left(f(X_n) \prod_{p=0}^{n-1} G_p(X_p) \right)}{\mathbb{E}\left(\prod_{p=0}^{n-1} G_p(X_p) \right)} \tag{21.4}$$

Of course, this makes sense only when the normalization constant is nonzero:

$$\gamma_n(1) = \mathbb{E}\left(\prod_{p=0}^{n-1} G_p(X_p)\right) > 0$$

Similarly, we have, for the updated measures: $\hat{\eta}_n(f) = \frac{\hat{\gamma}_n(f)}{\hat{\gamma}_n(1)}$ where $\hat{\gamma}_n(f) := \gamma_n(fG_n)$.

The formula (21.4) allows us to compute η_n out of the knowledge of γ_n. However, this is of little use in practice since the output of the IPS algorithm η_n^N is an approximation of η_n and not of γ_n. Fortunately, the unconditional signed measure γ_n can be deduced from the knowledge of the η_i, $i \leq n$. This is, together with the existence of a law of large numbers for IPS, the key to our forthcoming applications to rare event analysis and multiname credit portfolios.

The expression of γ_n in terms of the η_i reads as follows; notice first that

$$\gamma_n(1) = \gamma_{n-1}(G_{n-1}) = \frac{\gamma_{n-1}(G_{n-1})}{\gamma_{n-1}(1)} \times \gamma_{n-1}(1) = \eta_{n-1}(G_{n-1}) \times \gamma_{n-1}(1)$$

from which we deduce

$$\gamma_n(1) = \mathbb{E}\left(\prod_{p=0}^{n-1} G_p(X_p)\right) = \prod_{p=0}^{n-1} \eta_p(G_p)$$

or, equivalently,

$$\gamma_n(f) = \eta_n(f) \times \prod_{p=0}^{n-1} \eta_p(G_p)$$

We get therefore unbiased estimators γ_n^N of γ_n by replacing the measures η_n by their approximations η_n^N:

$$\gamma_n^N(f) = \eta_n^N(f) \times \prod_{p=0}^{n-1} \eta_p^N(G_p)$$

with the expected convergence property:

$$\gamma_n^N \longrightarrow \gamma_n$$

when the sample size $N \uparrow \infty$, and for all time steps $n \in \mathbb{N}^*$. This convergence may take various forms, from almost sure convergence results to precise asymptotic estimates. We refer, besides Del Moral (2004), to Del Moral and Garnier (2005) for the specific situation of rare event analysis and recall here two convergence results. The first one (Del Moral and Garnier 2005 lemma 2.1) is (assuming that the potential functions G_n satisfy $0 < \varepsilon_n \leq G_n \leq 1$ for some sequence $\varepsilon_1, \ldots, \varepsilon_n, \ldots$) that for any $p \geq 1$ and any bounded function f on E_n with $\|f\| \leq 1$ we have:

$$\sup_{N \geq 1} \sqrt{N} \mathbb{E}(|\gamma_n^N(f) - \gamma_n(f)|^p)^{\frac{1}{p}} \leq c_p(n)$$

for some constant $c_p(n)$ whose value does not depend on f.

To give another flavor of this convergence, we also quote without proof a recent non asymptotic variance estimate for the normalizing constants. Under some strong regularity properties, for any time horizon $n \geq 0$, we have:

$$\mathbb{E}(\gamma_n^N(1)) = \gamma_n(1) \quad \text{and} \quad \mathbb{E}([\gamma_n^N(1) - \gamma_n(1)]^2) \leq c \, \frac{n}{N} \, \gamma_n(1)^2$$

for some finite constant $c < \infty$ whose values can be made more explicit in terms of the stochastic model, but they do not depend on the time horizon, nor on the size of the systems N (see Cérou, Del Moral, and Guyader forthcoming).

In our context, these normalizing constants, $\gamma_n(1)$, coincide with the rare event probabilities. For example, in the toy model we considered, this means (by the very definition of γ_n) that we are able to compute on-the-fly the flow of unconditional probabilities $\mathbb{P}(S_n \in dx, S_i < K_i, \ 0 \leq i < n)$ using the IPS algorithm. We will see, in the next sections, how these ideas can be applied to more involved computations.

21.2.5   Path Space Measures and Genealogical Tree Models

Let us rewrite $\mathbb{P}(S_i \in [a_i, b_i], \ 0 \leq i \leq T; \ S_i < K_i, \ 0 \leq i < T)$ using the potential functions:

$$\mathbb{P}(S_i \in [a_i, b_i], \ 0 \leq i \leq T; \ S_i < K_i, \ 0 \leq i < T)$$
$$= \mathbb{E}\left(1_{[a_0, b_0] \times \ldots \times [a_T, b_T]}(S_0, \ldots, S_T) \times \prod_{p=0}^{T-1} G_p(S_p)\right)$$

As before, this suggests the introduction for an arbitrary IPS on path space of the unconditional signed measures γ_n defined by:

$$\gamma_n(f_n) = \int f_n(x) \, \gamma_n(dx) \doteq \mathbb{E}\left(f_n(X_n) \prod_{p=0}^{n-1} G_p(X_p)\right)$$

where f_n runs over bounded functions on the path space $E_n = \mathbb{R}^{n+1}$ and $X_n = (S_0, \ldots, S_n)$ stands for a Markov chain on path space with initial law η_0, state spaces E_n, and Markov kernels M_n. In the display, we assume that the potential functions on the path spaces $G_p(S_0, \ldots, S_p)$ only depend on the terminal value of the path of the assets and use therefore the slightly abusive notation $G_p(S_p) := G_p(S_0, \ldots, S_p)$. In the literature on branching processes, $X_n = (S_0, \ldots, S_n)$ is called the historical process of the Markov chain S_n.

Notice that the sampling of a transition M_n from $X_{n-1} = (S_0, \ldots, S_{n-1})$ to $X_n = ((S_0, \ldots, S_{n-1}), S_n)$ simply amounts to extending the path with an elementary transition $S_{n-1} \rightsquigarrow S_n$. The interpretation of the corresponding normalized measures η_n on path space $E_n = \mathbb{R}^{n+1}$ as a conditional probability of the whole path translates into the following general formula that holds for an arbitrary IPS on path spaces:

$$\eta_n(f_n) = \gamma_n(f_n)/\gamma_n(1) \quad \text{with} \quad \gamma_n(f_n) = \mathbb{E}\left(f_n(S_0, \ldots, S_n) \prod_{p=0}^{n-1} G_p(S_p) \right) \quad (21.5)$$

Arguing as before, the formula (21.5) allows us to compute η_n and γ_n using the IPS algorithm η_n^N and γ_n^N, with path space particles introduced in the end of Section 21.2.1:

$$\xi_n^i := \left(\xi_{0,n}^i, \xi_{1,n}^i, \ldots, \xi_{n,n}^i \right) \in E_n := \mathbb{R}^{n+1}$$

These path particles can be interpreted as the ancestral lines of the IPS algorithm with mutation transitions $S_{n-1} \rightsquigarrow S_n$ and selection potential function $G_n(S_n)$. The occupation measure η_n^N of the corresponding N-genealogical tree model converges as $N \to \infty$ to the conditional distribution η_n on path space

$$\eta_n^N := \frac{1}{N} \sum_{i=1}^{N} \delta_{(\xi_{0,n}^i, \xi_{1,n}^i, \ldots, \xi_{n,n}^i)} \longrightarrow \eta_n \quad (21.6)$$

when the sample size $N \uparrow \infty$, and for all time steps $n \in \mathbb{N}^*$. If we consider in equation (21.5) the potential functions $G_i(x) := 1$ if $x < K_i$, $G_i(x) := 0$ else, and the lognormal Markov transitions driving S_i, then the flow of empirical measures η_n^N of the genealogical tree converges to the Feynman-Kac measure:

$$\eta_n(dx_0, \ldots, dx_n) = \mathbb{P}(S_0 \in dx_0, \ldots, S_n \in dx_n \mid S_i < K_i, \ 0 \le i < n)$$

For instance the exponential deviation estimates stated in equation (21.3) are satisfied, for some finite constant c that is proportional to the final time horizon n. We emphasize that these tree-based approximations can be used to analyze on-the-fly the evolution of typical stock trajectories under critical conditioning events.

We end this section with an alternative genealogical tree-based algorithm for computing conditional distributions of the whole path sequences $(S_0, \ldots, S_n)$ with respect to some critical rare event represented by some collection of potential functions G_n. This recent particle model has been developed in Del Moral, Doucet, and Singh

(2009). In contrast with the genealogical tree–based IPS algorithm described earlier, it is now based on the complete ancestral trees. We will see that its precision is much higher but its computational cost is now of the order N^2. To describe this model with some precision, it is convenient to introduce another round of notation. First, we observe that the path space measures defined in equation (21.5) can be rewritten in terms of the measure $\mathbb{Q}_n$:

$$\mathbb{Q}_n(dx_0, \ldots, dx_n) := \frac{1}{\gamma_n(1)} \left\{ \prod_{0 \leq p < n} G_p(x_p) \right\} \mathbb{P}(S_0 \in dx_0, \ldots, S_n \in dx_n)$$

$$(21.7)$$

Also observe that the nth time marginals η_n of the measure $\mathbb{Q}_n$ defined before have the same form as the Feynman-Kac measures defined in equation (21.4) by replacing X_n by S_n. In connection with this, we recall that the flow of empirical measures $(\eta_n^N)_{n \geq 0}$ of the IPS algorithm defined in equation (21.2) can be used to approximate on-the-fly the flow of measures $(\eta_n)_{n \geq 0}$. As seen in the end of Section 21.2.2, the measures η_n^N represent the current population of the particle model at time n, so that $(\eta_p^N)_{0 \leq p \leq n}$ can be interpreted as the complete genealogical tree associated with the IPS from the origin $p = 0$, up to the current time n.

We further assume that the Markov transitions M_n of the reference Markov chain S_n have the following form:

$$M_n(x_{n-1}, dx_n) = H_n(x_{n-1}, x_n) \, \lambda_n(dx_n)$$

for some reference signed measures λ_n. Under this condition, which is met in most of the situations encountered in practice, we can prove the following backward representation:

$$\mathbb{Q}_n(d(x_0, \ldots, x_n)) = \eta_n(dx_n) \, K_{n,\eta_{n-1}}(x_n, dx_{n-1}) \ldots K_{1,\eta_0}(x_1, dx_0)$$

with the backward Markov transitions:

$$K_{p+1,\eta_p}(x, dx') := \frac{G_p(x') \, H_{p+1}(x', x) \, \eta_p(dx')}{\eta_p(G_p H_{p+1}(\cdot, x))}$$

In this situation, the complete genealogical tree $(\eta_p^N)_{0 \leq p \leq n}$ can be used to approximate the measures $\mathbb{Q}_n$ using the following particle measures:

$$\mathbb{Q}_n^N(d(x_0, \ldots, x_n)) = \eta_n^N(dx_n) \, K_{n,\eta_{n-1}^N}(x_n, dx_{n-1}) \ldots K_{1,\eta_0^N}(x_1, dx_0)$$

Notice that all the integrations with respect to the measure $\mathbb{Q}_n^N$ are simple finite summations with respect to the empirical measures $(\eta_p^N)_{0 \leq p \leq n}$. We refer to Del Moral, Doucet, and Singh (2009) for a detailed discussion on the performance of these IPS models and their applications. For instance, let us suppose that we are interested in computing conditional time-averaged quantities of a stochastic process evolving in some critical regime, such as the proportion of time spent in some region of the state, or the time deviation of the process from some typical tendency, and others. These problems can be solved by integrating with respect to the particle measure $\mathbb{Q}_n^N$ functions of the following form:

$$F_n(x_0, \ldots, x_n) := \frac{1}{n+1} \sum_{p=0}^{n} f_p(x_p)$$

for some regular functions f_n. In this situation, under some appropriate regularity properties, for functions f_n with oscillations bounded by 1, we have the following uniform and nonasymptotic bias and variance estimates:

$$\sup_{n \geq 0} \left| \mathbb{E} \left(\mathbb{Q}_n^N(F_n) \right) - \mathbb{Q}_n(F_n) \right| \leq \frac{c}{N}$$

and for any $n \geq 0$

$$\mathbb{E} \left(\left[\mathbb{Q}_n^N(F_n) - \mathbb{Q}_n(F_n) \right]^2 \right) \leq \frac{c}{N} \left(\frac{1}{n+1} + \frac{1}{N} \right)$$

with some finite constant $c < \infty$ that does not depend on the time parameter n.

21.2.6 Degenerate Potentials

As we already mentioned (and did put to use in our toy model), the use of degenerate potential functions (that is, allowing the value 0 for the potential functions) is very convenient for rare event analysis. However, proving convergence results with degenerate potentials may be trickier and require a much finer analysis of the IPS than in the nondegenerate case (see, e.g., Del Moral 2004, sect. 7.4.1). It is not our purpose in the present chapter to present a full mathematical analysis of the problems raised by degenerate potentials; we will therefore limit our presentation to a survey of the existing references and methods—and explain why, for the particular Markov chains we consider, the use of degenerate potentials should not raise specific technical problems.

Let us start with an elementary but powerful observation. The IPSs with degenerate potentials we will be mostly interested in have the particular property that the potential functions take only the values 0 and 1. The idea is that we stop the trajectories when the value of the potential becomes 0 (usually this corresponds to the surpassing of a threshold). Numerically, this choice of the potential functions values 0 and 1 is optimal since we simply kill the useless trajectories and optimize the number of meaningful ones. However, the algorithm would still behave correctly if we replace 0 (the killing of the useless trajectories) by a small but fixed value ε. We would then simply allow a small percentage of the useless trajectories to survive. However, doing so, we would ensure that the mathematical statements on the convergence of IPS schemes do hold in the various credit risk examples we consider. To state it differently: In the credit risk examples with degenerate potentials that we will consider, if we accept to pay the computational price of slowing the IPS algorithm by bounding (strictly positively from below) the potential functions, then the general convergence algorithms for IPS with bounded (above and strictly positively from below) potentials will hold mathematically (with available proofs in the literature).

However, if we insist on using the 0/1-valued potentials, some mathematical analysis has to be conducted to establish the convergence. There are actually theoretical conditions on the potential functions ensuring that the algorithms behave correctly (Del Moral 2004, sects. 2.4, 2.5). The first observation is that we should have $\eta_n(G_n) \neq 0$ for $n \leq T$. Else, in the examples we are interested in, the trajectories of the IPS have a zero probability to reach the rare event set!

This condition is satisfied in particular if *any* trajectory can reach the rare event set. Fortunately, this is what happens almost always in credit risk: In any reasonable model, whether structural or reduced-form, conditionally to the knowledge of a (nontrivial) credit portfolio at time $t < T$, we can never be certain that the portfolio will not experience defaults between t and T (this is actually the very definition of a credit portfolio!). Mathematically, this condition (encoded by "condition $\mathcal{A}$" in Del Moral 2004) can be made explicit as follows. Let us set $\hat{E}_i = \{x \in E_i, G_i(x) > 0\}$; then we say that the accessibility conditions are satisfied by the IPS if and only if, for any $x \in \hat{E}_i$, $M_{i+1}(x, \hat{E}_{i+1}) > 0$.

On the technical side, the condition allows us to translate the study of an IPS with a degenerate potential into the study of an IPS with a nondegenerate potential in the following way. Recall that the Markov operator $M_{n+1}(x, dy)$ maps functions f on E_{n+1} to functions on E_n by: $M_{n+1}(f)(x) := \int f(y) M_{n+1}(x, dy)$, $x \in E_n$. When the condition $\mathcal{A}$ is satisfied, $M_n(G_n)(x)$ is nonzero for an arbitrary $x \in \hat{E}_{n-1}$, and it follows that the integral operators

$$\hat{M}_n(x, dy) := \frac{M_n(x, dy) G_n(y)}{M_n(G_n)(x)}$$

are well-defined Markov kernels from $\hat{E}_{n-1}$ to $\hat{E}_n$. Let us also write for $x \in \hat{E}_n$, $\hat{G}_n(x) := M_{n+1}(G_{n+1})(x)$. The pair $(\hat{M}_n, \hat{G}_n)$ can then be viewed as defining an IPS on the state spaces $\hat{E}_i$ with initial distribution $\hat{\eta}_0$.

One can then show (Del Moral 2004, prop. 2.4.2) that the updated Feynman-Kac measures $\hat{\eta}_n$ associated to the IPS defined by the triple (M_n, G_n, η_0) coincide with the Feynman-Kac measures associated with the IPS defined by the triple $(\hat{M}_n, \hat{G}_n, \hat{\eta}_0)$.

In particular, results can be transferred between Feynman-Kac measures for IPS with nondegenerate potential and updated Feynman-Kac measures for IPS with degenerate potentials, provided the condition $\mathcal{A}$ is satisfied.

21.3　IPS for Rare Event Analysis

The simulation of multiple credit events is a key issue for regulatory and risk management purposes, as well as for the pricing of credit derivatives. The problem amounts often to the estimation of the probability of occurrence of the rare event, say for example the occurrence of at least 10 defaults in a portfolio of 125 CDSs. The method we discuss now would, however, also be meaningful for more general purposes (e.g., for the analysis of the series of events leading to the rare event, in order to exhibit the typical physical path that the system uses to reach the rare event set under consideration).

Standard Monte Carlo (MC) simulations fail usually, because too few simulations attain the rare event set. The classic way to handle the problem is to use importance sampling (IS): The probabilities are twisted so as to make the rare event more likely. The tricky part of these strategies, familiar to practitioners, is to guess correctly the twisted distribution. Two problems arise: make a reasonable guess, and make sure that the algorithm performs correctly. Most of the time these problems are quite challenging and for complex credit derivatives are out of reach from a systematical mathematical point of view, so one has to rely on some more or less convincing approximations and huge computation times.

From this point of view, IPS techniques are very attractive. Although requiring some knowledge of the art of MC computations and some intuition of the behavior of the models, they do not require the exact knowledge of the probability distributions of the assets or trajectories. Moreover, the IPS analog of the renormalization of probability densities occurring in IS is built in mechanically to the IPS algorithm—as we already know from the simple toy model studied previously. In practice, these features of the IPS algorithm make it extremely useful, since it can be used as a black box not requiring any change of the probability measure under which the simulation is performed. This is particularly important when these probabilities are obtained from sophisticated simulation engines (e.g., when dealing with cash-flow CDOs or similar products).

The purpose of the present section is accordingly twofold. We start by surveying briefly how the general ideas exposed previously on IPS can be adapted to multiname credit derivatives. This exposition is mostly based on the Del Moral–Garnier (2005) approach to rare events analysis; we follow largely their presentation and refer to their article for further details, mathematical proofs, and deeper insights on the behavior of IPS from the point of view of large deviations, asymptotic analysis, and similar issues. In the last subsection, we move to particular structural models for CDSs, CDOs, and tranche pricing, relying mostly on the recent seminal work by Carmona-Fouque-Vestal (2009) to illustrate how IPS can be implemented concretely.

21.3.1　IPS for Multiname Credit Derivatives

Let us choose a particular example for the forthcoming discussion. The discussion is quite general (and would apply to a great variety of situations), but the choice of a given example will help to make the meaning of the algorithms precise.

So, let us consider a portfolio of N CDSs. Several problems arise in practice: compute the market VaR at a given confidence level assuming a given dynamics for the spreads; compute the probability that the portfolio will experience more than k defaults, $0 \le k \le N$ at a given time horizon T; and so on.

The standard way to deal with these problems is to model the dynamics of each asset using a family of N correlated processes, S_n^i, $i = 1 \ldots N$, $n = 0, \ldots, T$ (in a bottom-up approach, that is, analyzing the joint behavior of the N assets—the use of IPS in a top-down reduced-form model approach can be dealt with in a similar way; the problem has been studied in a recent seminal article by Carmona and Crépey (forthcoming), to which we refer for details). Here, S_n^i may stand for the price at time step n of the ith CDS, for the asset value of the ith firm in a Merton or Black-Cox type of approach to CDS pricing (see [Chapter 13 in this volume] or the next subsection), for the default indicator associated to the ith CDS in an intensity model approach to CDS pricing, the rating of the ith firm, or more general models (e.g., the vector-valued process associated to a Black-Cox model with stochastic volatility).

We write $X_n := (S_n^1, \ldots, S_n^N)$ for the process modeling the whole portfolio. The state space of X_n (whatever it is) is written F_n. We make the standard assumption that X_n is a (strong) Markov chain; this is usually the case when it is built out of Gaussian and Poisson variables. The rare event we are interested in reads typically $\{V_T(X_T) > K\}$ or $\{V_T(X_0, \ldots, X_T) > K\}$, where $V_i, i \le T$ is a suitable function on the state space F_i or on the path space $E_i := F_0 \times \ldots \times F_i$. For example, V_i may compute the number of defaults in the portfolio or may be a more complex measure of risk, for example the notional-weighted sum of the CDS prices—that is, the market value at time T of the portfolio (for the protection buyer, so that the portfolio price rises when risks increase).

The key ingredient to use IPS to tackle the problem is the construction of a suitable series of potential functions. Naively, one would choose this series of functions as a series of functions on the state spaces $F_n, n = 1 \ldots N$. However, this is usually not a good choice, for reasons that are discussed in Del Moral and Garnier (2005) and are closely related to the problem of choosing a good strategy to multiply the good paths in the splitting technique of Glasserman et al. (1999). Very roughly, the idea is that, at a given time step n, the potential function should not depend so much on the vicinity of a given trajectory to the rare event set as on the progression in the direction of the rare event set between $n - 1$ and n. For that reason, it is usually a better choice to consider the pair (X_{i-1}, X_i) or more generally the full path process $Y_i := (X_0, \ldots, X_i)$ as the Markov chain underlying the IPS.

The potential functions G_i have then to be chosen on the path spaces E_i. Some choices of potential functions related to the V_i are discussed in Del Moral and Garnier (2005). For example, assuming that the V_i are uniformly bounded, a possible choice could be:

$$G_i(x_0, \ldots, x_i) = \mu e^{\lambda(V_i(x_0, \ldots, x_i) - V_{i-1}(x_0, \ldots, x_{i-1}))}$$

where μ is chosen so that $G_i \le 1$ (if one insists on dealing with potential functions bounded from above by 1, a condition that can be relaxed) and λ can be fine-tuned to the given rare event set. This particular form for the potential functions is used, for example, for a reduced-form top-down model in Carmona and Crépey (forthcoming). We should point out, however, that there is no universal recipe since the precise potential functions have to be fine-tuned to the problem and the rare event set; this should not be a surprise—capturing the third default in a CDO does not require the same strategy as capturing the 100th! These questions are discussed further for the pricing of CDOs in Carmona, Fouque, and Vestal (2009); we will return to that article in the next subsection. Still, notice that the general question of choosing good potential functions for IPS remains largely open; this is an important area of future academic research, meaningful for the industry.

Assume now that we have constructed a set of *strictly positive* potential functions; then the IPS algorithm looks as follows. By definition, the unconditional measures γ_n are given by:

$$\gamma_n(f) = \mathbb{E}[f(Y_n) \prod_{1 \leq i < n} G_i(Y_i)]$$

for f a bounded function on the path space E_n, whereas the Feynman-Kac measures are given by:

$$\eta_n(f) = \gamma_n(f)/\gamma_n(1) \quad \text{with} \quad \gamma_n(f) = \mathbb{E}[f(Y_n) \prod_{1 \leq i < n} G_i(Y_i)]$$

Let us write A for the rare event set we are interested in; the problem amounts finally to the computation of:

$$\mathbb{E}[1_A(Y_T)] = [(1_A(Y_T) \prod_{1 \leq i < T} G_i^{-1}(Y_i)) \prod_{1 \leq i < T} G_i(Y_i)] = \gamma_T(1)\eta_T(\xi_A)$$

where

$$\xi_A(x_0, \ldots, x_T) := 1_A(x_0, \ldots, x_T) \prod_{1 \leq i < T} G_i^{-1}(x_0, \ldots, x_i), (x_0, \ldots, x_T) \in E_T$$

The general discussion of the previous section shows that these quantities can be approximated efficiently by interacting particle systems.

We discuss now briefly the example of the processes S_i^n showing up in the structural approach to the pricing of CDOs and the corresponding choice of potential functions. We will consider the same example when introducing IPaS later on.

21.3.2 Structural Models

Recall briefly that, in structural models, the default of a firm is triggered by its assets value $V(t)$ falling behind a threshold $v(t)$ (closely related to the oustanding debt of the firm). We refer to Chapter 13 in this volume for further details and a more detailed discussion. The assets value process $V(t)$ is typically driven by a lognormal dynamics, or a variant thereof.

A nice general (and almost generic) example of such a dynamics is given by the Lipton-Sepp (2009) model that combines the classical lognormal dynamics with a jump process (that allows the calibration of short-term-maturities CDSs, a classic issue for structural models):

$$\frac{dV_t}{V_t} = (r(t) - d(t) - \lambda(t)\kappa) + \sigma(t)dW_t + (e^j - 1)dN_t$$

where $r(t)$ is the interest rate, $d(t)$ the dividend rate, $\lambda(t)$ the jump arrival intensity, j the random jump amplitude (with a fixed law), $\kappa = \mathbb{E}[e^j - 1]$ the jump compensator, W_t a standard Brownian motion, and N_t an independent Poisson process. The volatility $\sigma(t)$ may be deterministic (as in the original Lipton-Sepp model) or stochastic (to allow Heston-type dynamics to fit into this general framework).

Some assumptions are usually made on the structure of the barrier. First, one can always assume without restriction the barrier to be deterministic since one can always replace the pair (V_t, v_t) by $(V_t - v_t, 0)$ or, if $v_t > 0$ by $(\frac{V_t}{v_t}, 1)$; see, for example, Credit-Grades (2002) for a concrete example of the use of this trick. Accordingly, we will assume from now on the barrier to be deterministic. For example, Lipton-Sepp assume that

$$v(t) = v(0)exp(\int_0^t r(t') - d(t') - \frac{1}{2}\sigma^2(t'))dt'$$

A simpler tractable classical assumption is the Black-Cox type barrier $v(t) = v(0)e^{\gamma t}$. These assumptions are necessary to obtain closed formulas or, at least, tractable analytic algorithms. They are not necessary in the IPS framework, where the efficiency of the algorithm is essentialy independent of the form of the barrier, which can therefore be arbitrary.

For credit portfolios, the dynamics of the various assets values $V_i(t)$, $i = 1, \ldots, N$ associated to the entities $i = 1, \ldots, N$ in the portfolio are correlated by correlating the Brownian motions. The jump components may be correlated using a Marshall-Olkin approach—that is, allowing for collective jumps (Lipton and Sepp 2009).

To apply IPS, one chooses a suitable discretization of time: $t_0 = 0, \ldots, t_K = T$ and of the stochastic differential equation driving the asset value. The example treated by Carmona-Fouque-Vestal (2009), which we use as a benchmark, is the one where the asset values are lognormal with stochastic volatility driven by a mean-reverting square-root diffusion. In that case, with our previous notations, S_n^i is the pair $(V_i(t_n), \sigma_i(t_n))$ with $F_i = (\mathbb{R}^+)^2$. A very nice idea behind the IPS constructed in Carmona, Fouque, and Vestal (2009) is the choice of the potential functions that departs from the one used in Del Moral and Garnier (2005). For our present purposes, their construction illustrates the flexibility of the IPS algorithm regarding the crucial point of choice of the potential functions. They choose indeed the potential functions:

$$G_i(Y_i) := exp \left(-\alpha \sum_{j=1}^{N} \log \frac{\min\limits_{0 \le m \le i} V_j(t_m)}{\min\limits_{0 \le m \le i-1} V_j(t_m)} \right)$$

where the parameter α has to be fine-tuned to the rare event set (in that case, an attachment point in the CDO structure).

Notice that the image of the functions G_i is not necessarily included in $[0, 1]$, a condition that we have chosen to introduce to define IPS. In fact, as we already implied, the condition $0 \le G_i \le 1$, although often convenient, is not necessary to define the IPS algorithm: One can simply replace the definition of the selection step, and set instead the alternative rule: For $i = 1, \ldots, N$ $\tilde{\xi}_n^i$ stands for a random variable with law $\sum_{j=1}^{N} \frac{G_n(\xi_n^j)}{\sum_{k=1}^{N} G_n(\xi_n^k)} \delta_{\xi_n^j}$.

The efficiency of these potential functions is striking and discussed in Carmona, Fouque, and Vestal (2009). The idea underlying this choice is that the extreme (minimal) value of the asset value process $V_j(t_n)$ is a good approximation of the riskiness of a trajectory for the jth asset, so that one should multiply the number of trajectories according to the lowest asset value processes. This particular choice is not related to the particular features of the dynamics chosen in Carmona, Fouque, and Vestal (2009) (lognormality and stochastic volatility) and may be expected to behave similarly for different choices of the dynamics. However, to the best of our knowledge, there is at the moment no criterion allowing us to assert that this family of potential functions is optimal or simply close to optimal. Once again, our feeling is that there is still a vast unexplored domain in the field of IPS algorithms regarding the choice of the potential functions.

21.4 IPaS for Multiname Credit Risk

We turn now to a new approach to multiname credit risk that we term "interacting path systems" (IPaS). The method has several advantages when dealing with multiple defaults:

- The method is not devised specifically for a given loss level (so that, for example, it may be expected to behave correctly simultaneously on all the tranches of a CDO).
- For the same reason, the parameters of the method do not need to be fine-tuned to a given rare event set (and recalibrated when one moves from one attachment point to another).
- The method combines the power of IPS with ideas coming from the Glasserman et al. (1999) splitting technique.

- Due to the choice of the potential functions (that are 0/1-valued), the implementation is particularly simple. The algorithms run faster than usual IPS (when dealing with arbitrary potential functions, the computation is slightly trickier to deal with since the sampling is not uniform among the surviving particles).

21.4.1   IPaS

We start with a general description of the algorithm—also applicable to other situations than multiname credit portfolios. Let X_n, $T \geq n \geq 0$ be as usual a Markov chain on a sequence of state spaces F_n and Y_n (resp. $E_n = F_0 \times \cdots \times F_n$) the corresponding path space Markov chain (resp. sequence of state spaces). We assume that a sequence of subsets $U_1, \ldots, U_T, U_i \subset E_i$ is fixed and are typically interested in the probability $1 - \mathbb{P}(Y_1 \notin U_1, \ldots, Y_T \notin U_T)$ that the trajectory does enter at least one of these subsets.

It is not our purpose here to enter the mathematical analysis of the algorithm in full generality, but we should mention that (quite similarly to IPS), technical conditions are required to ensure that the IPaS algorithm converges properly. These conditions will hold for the vanilla structural models of CDOs that we consider in the next section (basically because each trajectory can ultimately reach the rare event set—condition $\mathcal{A}$—which ensures the convergence of Monte Carlo methods but might not hold for a totally arbitrary Markov chain and rare event set).

Although a large variety of industrial and technological applications involve the algorithm, the reader should keep in mind the particular case of a portfolio of 125 CDSs, with X_n modeling the defaults of the CDSs in a bottom-up approach and U_i corresponding to the event that at least k (for a fixed k) CDSs have experienced a default event before the ith time step.

The key idea of the multilevel splitting approach (Del Moral 2004, chap. 12) is to introduce a series of intermediate events interpolating between the series of the full state spaces $E_1, \ldots, E_T$ of the path space and the target rare event series $U_1, \ldots, U_T$. Let us assume therefore that such a (finite) series is given:

$$\forall i \leq T, \; U_i = U_i^{(k)} \subset U_i^{(k-1)} \subset \ldots \subset U_i^{(1)} \subset U_i^{(0)} = E_i$$

The next step consists in the introduction of a new Markov chain (with constant state space $\mathbf{S} := E_0 \cup \ldots \cup E_T \cup \{c\}$, where $\{c\}$ stands for a cemetery space state). Roughly, the cemetery state is associated to the particles that do not reach some of the intermediate rare event sets; these trajectories will be killed at some point of the recursion of the IPaS algorithm, and the precise meaning of these rather vague explanations will become clear as soon as the IPaS algorithm is made explicit. We write $\mathbf{S}^{(j)}$ for $U_1^{(j)} \cup \ldots \cup U_T^{(j)}$.

Let us define the series of stopping times:

$$\tau_i := (T + 1) \wedge \inf\{j, \, Y_j \in U_j^{(i)}\}$$

We set: $Y_{T+1} := c$. Then, from the strong Markov properties of discrete Markov chains (see e.g., Del Moral 2004, sect. 2.2.3), $Z_0 := Y_0, Z_1 := Y_{\tau_1}, \ldots, Z_k := Y_{\tau_k}$ is a Markov chain on **S**.

We introduce now the potential functions:

$$G_i(x) = 1 - 1_{\{c\}}(x)$$

From our general discussion of IPS, it follows that, at each step of the recursion, these potential functions kill the trajectories that have ended up in the cemetery state and replace them by randomly and uniformly selected surviving particles (i.e., those that did not end up in the cemetery state). Assuming that the IPS scheme convergence properties hold for the Markov chain Z_i and the potential functions G_i (e.g., if condition $\mathcal{A}$ is satisfied), we get:

Theorem 21.4.1 (Convergence of the IPaS scheme) *The IPS algorithm run with the Markov chain $Z_0, \ldots, Z_k$ and the potential functions $G_1, \ldots, G_k$ is such that, for an arbitrary $0 < j \le k$:*

$$\eta_j(1_{\mathbf{S}^{(j)}}) = \mathbb{P}(Z_j \in \mathbf{S}^{(j)} | \forall m \le j - 1, \ Z_m \in \mathbf{S}^{(m)})$$
$$\gamma_j(1_{\mathbf{S}^{(j)}}) = \mathbb{P}(\forall m \le j, \ Z_m \in \mathbf{S}^{(m)})$$

In other terms, the IPaS algorithm computes, at each step $j \le T$, the conditional and unconditional probabilities that the Markov chain Z_i, $i \le T$ has reached all the intermediate subsets.

21.4.2 IPaS for Credit Portfolios

Let us consider a portfolio of k CDSs. We consider a structural model (notations are as stated earlier) and wish to compute the probabilities that at least $l \le k$ entities in the portfolio will experience a credit event before the end of the contract. We assume that the V_i are real-valued; this is a purely notational convenience; a two-dimensional structural model (e.g., with the firm's asset value and volatility as the two components of the underlying Markov chain) could be treated along exactly the same lines. Notice that we have therefore $F_i = \mathbb{R}^k$ and $E_i = (\mathbb{R}^k)^{i+1}$.

For each entity, $m = 1, \ldots, k$, a default has occured between the time step 0 and the time step $n \le T$ if and only if $\exists j \le n$, $V_m(j) \le v_m(j)$. We introduce accordingly the series of subspaces of the state spaces E_n:

Definition 21.4.1 *The i-default subset $U_n^{(i)}$ of E_n is defined by:*

$$U_n^{(i)} = \{(\mathbf{x}_0, \ldots, \mathbf{x}_n) = ((x_1^0, \ldots, x_k^0), \ldots, (x_1^n, \ldots, x_k^n)) \in (\mathbb{R}^k)^{n+1} |$$
$$\exists 0 < a_1 < \ldots < a_i \le k, \forall j \le i, \exists l \le n, \ x_{a_j}^l \le v_{a_j}(l)\}$$

In practice, $U_n^{(i)}$ is a subset of E_n constructed so that $\mathbb{P}(Y_n \in U_n^{(i)})$ is exactly the probability that the portfolio has experienced at least i defaults during the first n time steps. The sequence $U_n := U_n^{(k)} \subset U_n^{(k-1)} \subset \ldots \subset U_n^{(0)} = E_n$ satisfies the conditions required for the application of the IPaS algorithm. We write as usual Z_i and G_i for the corresponding Markov chain and potential functions. Assume further that the conditions required for the application of the IPaS algorithm are satisfied by the pair (Z_i, G_i), we get:

Theorem 21.4.2 *When the IPS algorithm is run with the Markov chain $Z_0, \ldots, Z_k$ and the potential functions $G_1, \ldots, G_k$ associated to a credit portfolio of k names to compute $\eta_j(1_{S^{(j)}})$ and $\gamma_j(1_{S^{(j)}})$ for an arbitrary $j \leq k$, it computes respectively the probability that at least j defaults have occured before termination of the contract, conditionally to the occurrence of $j - 1$ defaults, and the unconditional probability that at least j defaults have occured in the portfolio.*

21.4.3   Examples

In this final section, we compare the performances of the IPaS algorithm with a naive Monte Carlo algorithm in two typical credit risk computations—that is, for a nth default (with a underlying CDS portfolio of six names) and for a CDO (with a typical underlying CDS portfolio of 125 names).

The model we choose for the dynamics of the underlyings is a stylized Black-Cox model. The model is not claimed to be meaningful to describe correctly the dynamics of defaults or credit spreads (a simple lognormal model, possibly with jumps such as the Lipton-Sepp model, would behave better). However, our scope here is not to compute the correct price of a given credit derivative, but to show at best the numerical behavior of IPaS.

For this purpose a simple toy model for which the computations are straightforward to reproduce does seem better suited than a more abstract one. From the numerical point of view, it is a perfect illustration of the properties of IPaS, since the model is disentangled of all the parameters (drift, stochastic volatility, random correlations, and so on) that are necessary for the correct pricing and risk valuation of CDOs but do not really change the very nature of the computational challenge. Alternatively, one may understand the computation as a naive dynamic version of the Gaussian copula approach to the pricing of CDOs. For further simplicity we assume that the portfolio is homogeneous (this makes the programming burden slightly lighter but does not modify the performance of the IPaS algorithm).

So, let us assume that the Markov chains V_i, $i = 1 \ldots 6$ are defined by: $V_i(0) = a_0$ (initial firm's value), $V_i(j + 1) := V_i(j) + \sigma B_i(j)$, $j < T$, where the $B_i(j)$ are standard normal variables with $cor(B_i(j), B_l(k)) = 0$ if $i \neq l$ and $= \rho$ if $i = l$, $j \neq k$. The thresholds are calibrated as usual by a bootstrop algorithm from the CDS spreads. We assume constant spreads, but once again this hypothesis does not change the performance of the algorithm; we insist on this since most often the homogeneity assumptions are related to the numerical tractability, whereas here this is almost the

TABLE 21.1 Default Probabilities (n-to-Default on Six Underlyings)

	0	1	2	3	4	5	6
DP	$7.6 \cdot 10^{-1}$	$1.95 \cdot 10^{-1}$	$3.7 \cdot 10^{-2}$	$6.1 \cdot 10^{-3}$	$8.2 \cdot 10^{-4}$	$8.2 \cdot 10^{-5}$	$4.2 \cdot 10^{-6}$
MC1;3	1.7%	6.1%	17%	38%	104%	300%	NS
IP1;3	1.6%	5.3%	10%	20%	37%	65%	134%
MC5;3	0.73%	2.6%	7%	20%	47%	170%	NS
IP5;3	0.8%	2.7%	4.6%	8%	16%	30%	60%
MC1;4	0.6%	2%	5%	12%	32%	106%	NS
IP1;4	0.6%	1.9%	3.4%	5.5%	12%	21%	54%

opposite: Since inhomogeneity is irrelevant to the nature and performance of the algorithm, it wouldn't make sense, for illustrative purposes, to choose an inhomogeneous portfolio!

We obtain the following results. In the first example, we consider a portfolio of six CDSs with flat spreads at 100 bp (on a quarterly basis). The recovery rate is 40 percent, $\sigma = 0.4$, $\rho = 0.4$. The maturity is three years.

In Table 21.1, numbers $i = 0 \ldots 6$ on the second line stand for the number of entities undergoing a credit event. The line starting with DP indicates the corresponding probabilities that (exactly) i entities suffer a credit event. The line starting with MC or IP indicate the empirical standard deviation of the algorithm normalized by the corresponding probability (and therefore expressed in percent). For example, "MC1; 4" means that we compute the result of a naive MC scheme with a sample size 10^4, "IP5;3" means that we run the IPaS algorithm with a sample size $5 \cdot 10^3$, and so on. The empirical variance is computed by running each algorithm 100 times. Values above 300 percent are reported as nonsignificative (NS).

In the second example (Table 21.2) we consider two portfolios of 125 CDSs with flat spreads at 80 bp (on a quarterly basis). The recovery rate is 40 percent, $\sigma = 0.4$. The first portfolio has a correlation parameter $\rho^2 = 0.4$, whereas the second is such that $\rho = 0.4$. The maturity is three years.

From the rare event point of view, a lower correlation means that the most senior tranches are less likely to experience defaults. We expect therefore the IPaS algorithm to be more useful and efficient in the second case. This indeed happens to be so.

The portfolio losses are tranched; we compute the probabilities that 0, 1 to 6, 7 to 12, 13 to 18, 19 to 24, 25 to 45, and more than 45 losses occur. In the table, the second line indicates the number of entities undergoing a credit event, so that, for example, 7–12 means that 7 to 12 entities in the portfolio may undergo a credit event. Other notations are as in Table 21.1. "MC1;3" means that we compute the result of a naive MC scheme with a sample size 10^3, "IP5;3" means that we run the IPaS algorithm with a sample size $5 \cdot 10^3$, and so on. The empirical variance is computed by running each algorithm 100 times.

Various conclusions arise from these examples. First, whereas of limited interest for events that can be dealt with correctly with classical techniques (corresponding to a

TABLE 21.2 Default Probabilities

Default Probabilities: $\rho^2 = 0.4$						
	0	1–6	7–12	13–18	19–24	25–45	45–125
DP	$3.3 \cdot 10^{-1}$	$4.5 \cdot 10^{-1}$	$1.1 \cdot 10^{-1}$	$4.8 \cdot 10^{-2}$	$2.5 \cdot 10^{-2}$	$3.1 \cdot 10^{-2}$	$8.5 \cdot 10^{-3}$
MC1;3	3.8%	3.2%	8.8%	15%	17%	16%	36%
IP1;3	4.5%	3.4%	5.6%	7.8%	8.8%	9.5%	17%
MC5;3	2%	1.6%	3.5%	7%	9.8%	7.3%	16%
IP5;3	2%	1.4%	2.9%	3.5%	4.6%	4.9%	7.5%
Default Probabilities: $\rho = 0.4$						
DP	$1.1 \cdot 10^{-1}$	$6.2 \cdot 10^{-1}$	$1.9 \cdot 10^{-1}$	$5.2 \cdot 10^{-2}$	$1.5 \cdot 10^{-2}$	$7 \cdot 10^{-3}$	$1.5 \cdot 10^{-4}$
MC1;3	9%	2.1%	6.1%	13%	24%	39%	215%
IP1;3	8.5%	2.2%	5.2%	9.2%	13.4%	20%	50%
MC5;3	3.7%	1%	2.8%	5.8%	12%	17%	115%
IP5;3	3.9%	1%	2.5%	4%	6.8%	9.7%	23%
MC5;4	1.2%	0.36%	0.97%	2%	3.6%	5.2%	33%

VaR level of 99 percent), IPaS provides a meaningful variance reduction for rare events (roughly at a 99.9 percent level and below). Second, the computational cost of running the IPaS algorithm is limited (basically, one has to draw from a uniform distribution every time a particle is killed). The algorithm is therefore particularly useful when dealing with credit derivatives or portfolios thereof where the computational cost of the simulation of a given trajectory is large.

At last, whereas it is likely that IPaS is not the final algorithmic solution to the computation of rare events in portfolio credit risk, we feel that it could certainly become an important element in the Monte Carlo toolbox of the domain, to be possibly combined with other variance-reduction techniques. Allowing more general path-dependent potential functions fine-tuned to a particular credit derivative or to a given family of time-dependent credit events could, for example, most probably improve the efficiency of the algorithm. These questions are open and left for further research.

References

Bartoli, N., and P. Del Moral. 2001. *Simulation and stochastic algorithms: An introduction with applications.* Toulouse: Cepadues Editions.

Blanchet-Scalliet, C., and F. Patras. Structural counterparty risk valuation for credit default swaps. Chapter 13 in this volume.

Carmona, R., and S. Crépey. Forthcoming. Importance sampling and interacting particle systems for the estimation of Markovian credit portfolio loss distribution. Forthcoming in *International Journal of Theoretical and Applied Finance.*

Carmona, R., J.-P. Fouque, and D. Vestal. 2009. Interacting particle systems for the computation of rare credit portfolio losses. *Finance and Stochastics* 13 (4): 613–633.

Cérou, F., P. Del Moral, and A. Guyader. Forthcoming. A nonasymptotic variance theorem for unnormalized Feynman-Kac particle models. Forthcoming in *Annales de l'Institut H. Poincaré.*

CreditGrades™. 2002. Technical document.

Del Moral, P. 1996. Non linear filtering: Interacting particle solution. Markov Processes and Related Fields **2**(4): 555–580.

Del Moral, P. 2004. *Probability and its applications.* New York: Springer-Verlag.

Del Moral, P., A. Doucet, and S. Singh. 2009. A backward particle interpretation of Feynman-Kac formulae. Research Report RR-7019, INRIA.

Del Moral, P., and J. Garnier. 2005. Genealogical particle analysis of rare events. *Annals of Applied Probability* 15:2496–2534.

Del Moral, P., and L. Miclo. 2000. Branching and interacting particle systems approximations of Feynman-Kac formulae with applications to non-linear filtering, *Seminaire de Probabilities XXXIV,* ed. J. Azema, M. Emery, M. Ledoux, and M. Yor. *Lecture Notes in Mathematics* 1729. Berlin: Springer-Verlag.

Del Moral, P., F. Patras, and S. Rubenthaler. 2009. Convergence of U-statistics for interacting particle systems. Research Report INRIA-00397366.

Del Moral, P., F. Patras, and S. Rubenthaler. 2009. Tree based functional expansions for Feynman-Kac particle models. *Annals of Applied Probabilities.* 19 (no. 2): 778–825.

Del Moral, P., and E. Rio. Forthcoming. Concentration inequalities for mean field particle models. *Annals of Applied Probabilities.*

Glasserman, P., P. Heidelberg, P. Shahabuddin, and T. Zajic. 1999. Multilevel splitting for estimating rare event probabilities. Operational Research 47 (4): 585–600.

Lipton, A., and A. Sepp. 2009. Credit value ajustment for credit default swaps via the structural model. *Journal of Credit Risk* 5 (2): 123–146.

CHAPTER 22

Credit Risk Contributions

Dan Rosen

R² Financial Technologies and The Fields Institute

David Saunders

University of Waterloo, Canada

Once the risk of a portfolio is calculated, a natural question to ask is: Where does the risk come from and what are the main contributors? *We present a survey of the theory and the practical uses of risk contributions in credit risk management. Applications presented include the computation of portfolio credit risk and the contributions of systematic and idiosyncratic risk; instrument contributions to economic capital and other risk measures; instrument contributions to the credit valuation adjustment (CVA) of a counterparty portfolio; instrument and subportfolio contributions to expected losses of tranches of collateralized debt obligations (CDOs); and contributions of risk factors to credit portfolio risk, based on approximations and orthogonal decompositions of nonlinear functions.*

22.1 Introduction

The current credit crisis has highlighted the need for transparent and robust methods for valuing, hedging, and measuring the risk of credit portfolios. An effective valuation and credit risk management framework must help portfolio managers and traders:

- Understand the sources of their exposures, and identify the major risk contributors.
- Assess how changes of various external risk factors affect a portfolio's risk.
- Attribute the performance of a portfolio, adjusted for the risk taken.
- Hedge unwanted exposures and optimally trade off risk and reward.

Once the risk of a portfolio is captured, a natural question to ask is: *Where does the risk come from and what are the main contributors?* Several applications in credit risk include:

675

- *Portfolio credit risk and economic capital allocation.* Credit portfolio managers require *economic capital* (EC) measures, which effectively capture all the risks associated with obligor credit events such as default, credit migrations (downgrades or upgrades), and credit spreads. Once the amount of capital at the portfolio level has been determined, it must be *allocated* equitably among the various components (e.g., obligors, individual transactions, sectors, strategies, portfolios, risk factors, etc.). Capital allocation is an important management decision support and business planning tool, required for pricing, profitability assessment and limits, building optimal risk-return portfolios and strategies, performance measurement, and risk-based compensation.

- *Valuing and hedging counterparty credit risk.* The value of a portfolio of over-the-counter (OTC) derivatives must incorporate the possibility of losses due to counterparty default. The *credit valuation adjustment* (CVA) is essentially the market value of counterparty credit risk (i.e., the difference between the risk-free portfolio value and the true portfolio value that takes into account the counterparty's potential to default). In addition to calculating the CVA for a portfolio of transactions with a given counterparty, it is also important to determine the incremental contribution of a new trade, as well as to understand the contributions of all individual trades to the counterparty-level CVA. In addition, the use of CVA contributions is not limited to a single counterparty. Once they have been calculated for each counterparty, one can also price the counterparty credit risk of any collection of trades (e.g., by a certain business unit or product type).

- *Valuing and hedging structured credit products.* Credit portfolio models are required to price and measure the risk of more complex credit instruments such as mortgage-backed securities (MBSs) and collateralized debt obligations (CDOs). Market participants require reliable models to mark-to-market these instruments, hedge the risk of unwanted exposures, and understand credit concentrations. This requires the ability to calculate the risk contributions of given names or subportfolios of obligations. The optionality embedded in the tranching of these products further distorts the impact that each position may have on the overall instrument's risk profile.

The risk of a portfolio can be allocated in different ways and to various components. Most commonly, risk managers calculate *risk contributions of positions*, such as individual instruments, obligors, or subportfolios of trades. Just as important for risk management is the measurement of *contributions of risk factors* to portfolio risk. Risk factors include systematic factors representing macroeconomic variables, indexes, financial variables (market factors), or idiosyncratic factors. For example, the current credit crisis has highlighted the need for tools that help us understand better the role of systematic risk factors in credit risk. Understanding the contribution to EC and pricing of various systematic factors, which are at the heart of a credit model, can lead to more effective management of concentration risk as well as hedging of credit portfolios. Risk factor contributions further allow us to understand better the risk of complex portfolios with many instruments, where individual instrument contributions may not be too enlightening, or of more complex securities (e.g., CDOs).

In this chapter, we provide a unified presentation of risk contribution techniques applied to credit portfolios and provide various examples. While the focus of the chapter is on credit risk, risk contribution methodologies are general and can be applied to other financial problems (market risk, operational risk, enterprise risk, etc.). We cover three dimensions of the problem. First, we discuss various risk contribution measures and capital allocation methodologies. There is no unique method to measure risk contributions and allocate EC; each methodology has its advantages and disadvantages, and might be appropriate for a given managerial application. In particular, *marginal risk contributions* yield an additive decomposition of risk that accounts for the effects of diversification within a portfolio. Second, we cover various practical applications, including credit capital allocation, credit valuation adjustment, and structured credit portfolios, as discussed earlier. Third, we present in a consistent way the methodologies for credit risk contributions of both positions and risk factors (systematic and idiosyncratic).

When the risk measure is homogeneous (e.g., mean, standard deviation, value at risk [VaR], and conditional value at risk [CVaR]) and the portfolio losses can be written as the sum of individual losses, there is an established theory for additive *marginal risk contributions*, sometimes referred to as *Euler allocation*. This is applicable to measure positions' contributions (instruments, counterparties, subportfolios) to portfolio credit risk, as well as CVA contributions when there is no margin agreement. Position risk contributions in general, and the Euler allocation in particular, have received much attention in the literature. Koyluoglu and Stoker (2002) and Mausser and Rosen (2008) survey different contribution measures, with the latter reference focusing on applications to portfolio credit risk management. Kalkbrener (2005) proposes an axiomatic approach for capital allocation, and demonstrates that the axioms are only satisfied by the Euler allocation. Denault (2001) relates the Euler allocation to cooperative game theory and notions of fairness in allocation, and Tasche (1999) gives an interpretation in terms of optimization and performance measurement. Several authors have also considered computational issues arising in the calculation of position risk contributions (e.g., Emmer and Tasche 2005; Glasserman 2005; Glasserman and Li 2005; Huang, Oosterlee, and Mesters 2007; Kalkbrener, Lotter, and Overbeck 2004; Mausser and Rosen 2008; Merino and Nyfeler 2004; Tchistiakov, de Smit, and Hoogbruin 2004).

The Euler allocation cannot be applied directly when the risk function is not a homogeneous function of the positions or factors. This is the case when calculating contributions for portfolios with structured credit instruments, such as CDOs, CVA contributions with a margin agreement, and contributions of risk factors to portfolio credit risk. We further discuss how the Euler allocation principle can be extended to deal with these cases, and provide some additional tools such as the Hoeffding decomposition and optimization/hedging of systematic risk with linear portfolios of factors. Several recent papers consider the problem of measuring risk contributions in these more complex cases. For example, Tasche (2008) calculates contributions of individual names to CDO tranche losses and proposes measures for the impact of risk factors in the nonlinear case. Pykhtin and Rosen (2009) demonstrate the application of the Euler allocation principle for CVA contributions in counterparty portfolios without collateral and extend it to the case where there is a margin agreement; Cherny and Madan (2007) study position contributions of conditional losses given the risk factors; Rosen and Saunders (2009a) study the best hedge (in a quadratic sense) among linear combinations of the systematic factors and apply it to credit portfolios as well as CDO tranches; Cherny, Douady, and Molchanov (2010) consider the best approximation to portfolio losses by a sum of nonlinear functions of the individual factors; Bonti et al. (2006) conceptualize the risk of credit concentrations as the impact of stress in one or more systematic risk factors on the loss distribution of a credit portfolio; and Rosen and Saunders (2010) extend the Euler allocation to nonlinear functions of a set of risk factors, based on an orthogonal decomposition of portfolio losses.

The rest of the chapter is organized as follows. Section 22.2 briefly presents the credit portfolio model, which we use as a basis for the examples in the chapter. Section 22.3 introduces the basic concepts and general theory of risk contributions and capital allocation. We discuss various contribution methods, as well as the main issues regarding position and risk factor contributions. Section 22.4 presents the basic principle and interpretation of marginal contributions (Euler allocation) for homogeneous risk measures applied to losses defined as a linear function of the risk contributors, and applies it to marginal capital allocation for credit portfolios and CVA contributions without margin agreements. Section 22.5 presents extensions of the marginal contribution methodology in the case where risk may be viewed as being calculated by applying a nonhomogeneous risk measure to the sum of the risk contributors, and studies applications to expected losses of CDO tranches and CVA allocation with margin agreements. Section 22.6 discusses nonlinear risk contributions, with applications to measuring contributions of risk factors to portfolio credit risk. Specifically, we focus on the application of the linear factor hedging and orthogonal decompositions. Finally, Section 22.7 presents some concluding remarks.

22.2 Credit Risk Model

In this section, we briefly introduce the credit risk models employed in the examples in this chapter. We focus on factor models of portfolio credit risk in general, and the Gaussian copula model in particular. The appendix briefly discusses other credit models that share the factor structure and many of the mathematical properties of the Gaussian copula model. Note that the risk contributions given in the later sections are general, and can be applied to other credit risk models, and to financial models in other contexts.

Consider a credit universe of I names, with default times denoted by $\tau_i (i = 1, \ldots, I)$. Let F_i be the cumulative probability distribution function of τ_i:

$$F_i(t) = P(\tau_i \leq t) \tag{22.1}$$

Depending on the context, we are interested in either the risk-neutral or the real-world probability distribution of the default times τ_i. Pricing applications generally require the use of a risk-neutral default distribution. In this case, F_i can be obtained by calibrating $F_i(t_j)$ to credit default swap (CDS) market prices for a fixed set of times t_j and then interpolating to get $F_i(t)$ for an arbitrary t. In contrast, risk and portfolio management applications use real-world probabilities, generally estimated using statistical models on historical data, or an institution's internal credit rating system.

For each name $i = 1, \ldots, I$, we define a creditworthiness index:

$$CWI_i = \sum_{k=1}^{K} \beta_{ik} X_k + \sqrt{1 - \sum_{k=1}^{K} \beta_{ik}^2} \cdot \varepsilon_i \qquad (22.2)$$

where the random variables X_k and ε_i have standard normal distributions and are mutually independent.

More generally, the factors can have any distribution (e.g., Rosen and Saunders 2009b) and may be defined in a dynamic setting.

The X_k are referred to as *systematic factors*, and the coefficients β_{ik} are the *factor loadings*. When $K = 1$, we say that equation (22.2) is a single-factor model, while $K > 1$ corresponds to a multifactor model. Since CWI_i is standard normal, one can ensure that every name has the correct marginal default distribution $F_i(t)$ by setting

$$\tau_i = F_i^{-1}(\Phi(CWI_i)) \qquad (22.3)$$

where Φ is the cumulative distribution function of a standard normal random variable.

The cumulative portfolio default loss at time t is:

$$L_t = \sum_{i=1}^{I} w_i 1_{\{CWI_i \leq \Phi^{-1}(F_i(t))\}} \qquad (22.4)$$

where w_i is the (loss-given-default-adjusted) exposure to name i.[1]

The systematic losses at time t are defined to be:

$$L_{t,s} = E[L_t | X] \qquad (22.5)$$

Conditional on the systematic factors $X = (X_1, \ldots, X_K)$, obligor defaults are independent and the conditional default probabilities for each name are given by:

$$F_i(t|X) = \Phi \left(\frac{\Phi^{-1}(F_i(t)) - \sum_{k=1}^{K} \beta_{ik} X_k}{\sqrt{1 - \sum_{k=1}^{K} \beta_{ik}^2}} \right) \qquad (22.6)$$

More generally, conditional on the factors X_k for k in some subset A of $\{1, \ldots, K\}$, the conditional default probabilities are:

$$F_i(t|A) = \Phi \left(\frac{\Phi^{-1}(F_i(t) - \sum\limits_{k \in A} X_k}{\sqrt{1 - \sum\limits_{k \in 1}^{K} \beta_{ik}^2}} \right) \tag{22.7}$$

The mean and variance of both the total default losses L_t and the systematic losses $L_{t,S}$ are easy to compute analytically:

$$E[L_t] = E[L_{t,S}] = \sum_{i=1}^{I} w_i F_i(t) \tag{22.8}$$

$$\sigma^2(L_t) = \sum_{i=1}^{I} w_i^2 F_i(t)(1 - F_i(t))$$

$$+ 2 \sum_{i<j} w_i w_j \left(\Phi_2 \left(\Phi^{-1}(F_i(t)), \Phi^{-1}(F_j(t)); \sum_{k=1}^{K} \beta_{ik}\beta_{jk} \right) - F_i(t)F_j(t) \right) \tag{22.9}$$

$$\sigma^2(L_t^S) = \sum_{i=1}^{I} \sum_{j=1}^{I} w_i w_j \Phi_2 \left(\Phi^{-1}(F_i(t)), \Phi^{-1}(F_j(t)); \sum_{k=1}^{K} \beta_{ik}\beta_{jk} \right) - \left(\sum_{i=1}^{I} w_i F_i(t) \right)^2 \tag{22.10}$$

where Φ_2 is the bivariate cumulative normal distribution function:

$$\Phi_2(z_1, z_2; \rho) = \int_{-\infty}^{z_1} \int_{-\infty}^{z_2} \exp \left(-\frac{(w_1^2 - 2\rho w_1 w_2 + w_2^2)}{2(1 - \rho^2)} \right) \frac{dw_1 dw_2}{2\pi \sqrt{1 - \rho^2}} \tag{22.11}$$

For notational convenience, in the case when we are only interested in portfolio losses over a single default horizon T, we write L for L_T, L_S for $L_{T,S}$ and PD_i for $F_i(T)$.

Under a general multifactor credit model, the computation of the entire loss distribution or other statistics such as value at risk (VaR) or conditional value at risk (CVaR) (or expected shortfall) is generally performed using Monte Carlo techniques, although some semianalytical methods are also available (e.g., Pykhtin 2004; Garcia Cespedes et al. 2006). In the specific case of a single-factor credit model, there is an analytical solution for VaR and CVaR (Gordy 2003; Vasicek 2002). In this case, provided that all (loss-given-default-adjusted) exposures are positive constants, the systematic portfolio loss is a monotone decreasing function of the single systematic credit risk factor X.

$$L_S = \sum_{i=1}^{I} w_i \cdot \Phi \left(\frac{\Phi^{-1}(PD_i) - \beta_i X}{\sqrt{1 - \beta_i^2}} \right) = G(X), \quad G'(x) < 0 \qquad (22.12)$$

This yields closed-form expressions for VaR and CVaR at a given confidence level α^2:

$$\text{VaR}_\alpha(L_S) = G(X_{1-\alpha}) = \sum_{i=1}^{I} w_i \Phi \left(\frac{\Phi^{-1}(PD_i) - \beta_i X_{1-\alpha}}{\sqrt{1 - \beta_i^2}} \right) \qquad (22.13)$$

$$\text{CVaR}_\alpha(L_S) = \frac{1}{1-\alpha} \sum_{i=1}^{I} w_i \cdot \Phi_2(\Phi^{-1}(PD_i), \Phi^{-1}(1-\alpha), \beta_i) \qquad (22.14)$$

where $X_{1-\alpha} = \Phi^{-1}(1-\alpha)$.

Equation (22.13) forms the basis for the credit risk regulatory capital charge in the Basel II Capital Accord (BCBS 2006). As capital is defined as the 99.9 percent quantile of the loss distribution minus expected losses, the Basel formula for default risk is given by:[3]

$$\text{Capital}_{99.9\%} = \sum_{i=1}^{I} w_i \cdot \left(\Phi \left(\frac{\Phi^{-1}(PD_i) - \beta_i \Phi^{-1}(0.001)}{\sqrt{1 - \beta_i^2}} \right) - PD_i \right) \qquad (22.15)$$

In the Basel Accord, the factor loading β_i is prescribed as a function of the default probability. For example, for corporate exposures, it is given by

$$\beta_j^2 = 0.12 \cdot \left(\frac{1 - \exp(-50 \cdot PD_j)}{1 - \exp(-50)} \right) + 0.24 \cdot \left(1 - \frac{1 - \exp(-50 \cdot PD_j)}{1 - \exp(-50)} \right) \qquad (22.16)$$

There is no closed-form formula available for the VaR or the CVaR of the total credit loss L (which includes idiosyncratic risk). However, there is an elegant approximation for VaR and CVaR based on the so-called *granularity adjustment*. This is further described in Section 22.3.4.

22.3 Risk Contributions and Capital Allocation

In this section, we define the general problem of calculating contributions to portfolio credit risk, and discuss several special cases.

22.3.1   Basic Concepts and Definitions

Let us represent the portfolio losses by a random variable L, which is a function of a collection of random variables X_m, $m = 1, \ldots, M$.[4]

$$L = f(X_1, \ldots, X_M) \tag{22.17}$$

We refer to the random variables X_m as the *factors* in the model; they represent the drivers of portfolio losses whose contributions to risk we seek to calculate. Depending on the context, they may represent different sources of financial risk.

The most common situation in applications occurs when the factors represent the losses of different positions (instruments or subportfolios) of an institution's portfolio. In other situations, X_m may represent the losses of different collateral instruments in a structured credit product, or losses of large complex financial institutions in a systemic tax scheme.[5] In each of these cases, the portfolio loss can be written as the sum of the factor losses. Thus, we refer to the loss model as *linear* if:

$$f(X) = f(X_1, \ldots, X_M) = \sum_{m=1}^{M} X_m \tag{22.18}$$

so that the portfolio loss is simply the sum of the factors.

Other applications do not satisfy this criterion. For example, the X_m may represent positions in a portfolio for which a credit valuation adjustment must be calculated (see Sections 22.4.4 and 22.5.3), or they may represent different systematic factors (e.g., GDP growth, interest rates, inflation) and idiosyncratic risk factors (such as the systematic factors Z and idiosyncratic factors ε in the Gaussian copula model from Section 22.2).

Portfolio risk is evaluated using a prescribed risk measure ρ, such as standard deviation, VaR, economic capital (defined as VaR less expected loss), and CVaR:

$$\rho(L) = \rho\left(f(X_1, \ldots, X_M)\right) \tag{22.19}$$

The goal is to calculate, for each random variable X_m, its *risk contribution*, denoted by C_m, which is a measure of the degree to which it influences the overall portfolio risk $\rho(L)$. Based on the preceding discussion, we see that from a general perspective three aspects of the portfolio loss model influence risk contributions:

1. The joint probability distribution of the factors $X_1, \ldots, X_M$.
2. The function f that links the factors X and the portfolio loss L.
3. The choice of the risk measure ρ.

More explicitly, we write:

$$C = (C_1, \ldots, C_M) = C(X_1, \ldots, X_M; f, \rho) \tag{22.20}$$

We say that the problem is *homogeneous*, or that we are considering the homogeneous case, if the risk measure ρ is positive homogeneous:

$$\rho(\lambda \cdot L) = \lambda \cdot \rho(L), \lambda > 0 \tag{22.21}$$

Risk measures satisfying this property include VaR, conditional value at risk (CVaR), expected loss, standard deviation, and economic capital. There is a large literature on risk measures and their mathematical properties. We focus on the risk measures most commonly used in practice, and discuss specific axioms or properties only when their relevance to the calculation of risk contributions arises.

Finally, we say that risk contributions are *additive* if the contributions of the factors sum to the total portfolio risk, that is, in the case that:

$$\rho(L) = \sum_{m=1}^{M} C_m \tag{22.22}$$

22.3.2 Types of Risk Contribution

From an economic perspective, we broadly classify contributions that are considered in practice into three types:

1. *Stand-alone contributions.* The mth stand-alone contribution assesses portfolio risk as if it were only exposed to factor m. For instance, if m indexes the subportfolios corresponding to different trading desks of a financial institution, then the mth stand-alone contribution is the total risk of the mth trading desk regarded as an isolated portfolio. Stand-alone contributions ignore portfolio diversification effects, and are generally not additive. They can be employed as a benchmark against which to compare other contribution measures, as well as a tool in developing measures of portfolio concentration and diversification (see Section 22.4.3).

2. *Incremental contributions.* The mth incremental contribution is the difference between the risk of the portfolio when it is exposed to the mth factor and the portfolio risk when its exposure to the mth factor is removed or ignored. In the case where the factors represent the losses of different trading desks of an institution, the mth incremental contribution is the total risk of the institution's portfolio (calculated including the losses of desk m) less the risk of the institution's portfolio with desk m removed. The incremental risk contribution is a particularly useful measure when it is possible to add or remove the risk associated with a given factor from the portfolio in total (rather than in small parts). For example, if an institution is considering selling off a particular business line, then it may look at the incremental

risk contribution of the business line in order to understand how its risk position will be changed by the sale.

3. *Marginal contributions*. The marginal contribution of the mth risk factor measures the impact when exposure to risk factor m is increased by a small amount. When assessing the contributions of different trading desks to the total risk of an institution, this may be interpreted as the change in the institution's overall risk when an additional dollar is given to desk m.

22.3.3 Position-Level Contributions

The most common situation arises when the factors X_m are the positions (instruments, subportfolios) in a given portfolio, which sum to the total portfolio loss. This case is particularly attractive from a mathematical perspective, since the loss model is linear [equation (22.18)] and the risk measure is homogeneous [equation (22.19)], and is developed further in Section 22.4.

The *stand-alone contribution* of factor m is the risk of the mth position, considered as a portfolio in isolation. When portfolio losses are the sum of the losses on individual positions, the stand-alone contribution of the mth position to the risk measure ρ is thus:

$$C_m^S = \rho(X_m) \tag{22.23}$$

When ρ is a *subadditive* risk measure (i.e., $\rho(Y + Z) \leq \rho(Y) + \rho(Z)$ for all random variables Y, Z), the total portfolio risk is bounded above by the sum of the stand-alone contributions:

$$\rho(L) = \rho \left(\sum_{m=1}^{M} X_m \right) \leq \sum_{m=1}^{M} \rho \left(X_m \right) = \sum_{m=1}^{M} C_m^S \tag{22.24}$$

This is a reflection of the fact that diversification reduces risk. It also shows that stand-alone contributions are not additive, unless equality holds in equation (22.24) (a very special case). Recall that while standard deviation and CVaR are subadditive risk measures, VaR and economic capital are not (see, e.g., McNeil, Frey, and Embrechts 2005).

The *incremental risk contribution* of a given position is the portfolio risk calculated including that position less the portfolio risk calculated without the position.

$$C_m^I = \rho \left(\sum_{j=1}^{M} X_j \right) - \rho \left(\sum_{j \neq m} X_j \right) \tag{22.25}$$

This gives the total change in risk resulting from the inclusion of position *m* in the institution's portfolio. As mentioned earlier, this is of particular importance when the position as a whole must be included in or excluded from the portfolio (e.g., acquisition or sale of a business).

The *marginal risk contribution* computes the impact of investing a small additional amount of capital in instrument *m*. Mathematically, it is defined as a partial derivative. For the purposes of exposition, we consider the loss variable L to be embedded in a family of random variables corresponding to assigning different portfolio weights to the factors X_m. Specifically, we set $L = L_1$, where 1 is a vector with M components all equal to one, and

$$L_w = w_1 X_1 + w_2 X_2 + \cdots + w_M X_M \tag{22.26}$$

Thus, the marginal risk contribution (referred to also as the *Euler* allocation) of the *m*th position can be written as:

$$C_m^{EA} = w_m \frac{\partial}{\partial w_m} \rho(L_w)\bigg|_{w=1}$$

$$= \lim_{\varepsilon \to 0} \frac{\rho\left(X_1 + \cdots + (1+\varepsilon)X_m + \cdots + X_M\right) - \rho\left(X_1 + \cdots + X_m + \cdots + X_M\right)}{\varepsilon} \tag{22.27}$$

Incremental risk contribution can be also regarded as a finite difference approximation of the marginal risk contribution, with $\varepsilon = -1$.

22.3.4 Risk Factor Contributions

In addition to determining the risk contributions of individual positions to the overall portfolio, it is important to determine the contributions of different risk factors. Risk factors may refer to market variables, such as interest or exchange rates, volatilities, and equity prices, which are relevant when determining the market risk of a large portfolio. They may also be systematic and idiosyncratic factors in a portfolio credit risk model or a factor model for an equity portfolio. Risk factor contributions help us understand better the sources of risk; this is especially important for complex portfolios with a large number of instruments, where individual instrument risk contributions may not be too enlightening, as well as for complex securities (e.g., portfolio credit derivatives).

When each position depends (perhaps in a nonlinear way) on only one independent risk factor (or a small subset of risk factors), the problem can be addressed effectively by computing position contributions and transforming them to factor contributions. This is further discussed in Section 22.6.1. However, additional mathematical difficulties arise when the portfolio loss is not a linear function of the risk factors. There are many practical financial problems where this occurs, for example:

- Portfolio credit risk with multifactor credit models.
- Portfolios with equity options (where equities are modeled using a multifactor model), foreign exchange options, or quanto options.
- Fixed income and interest rate derivatives portfolios.
- Collateralized debt obligations and asset-backed securities.

In these situations, the standard theory for position contributions does not apply directly, and alternative methods and extensions are required (see Section 22.6).

22.3.4.1   Systematic and Idiosyncratic Factor Contributions

Credit models, such as the Gaussian copula, are generally driven by a set of *systematic factors*, X, and *idiosyncratic factors*, ε; see equation (22.2). Understanding the contributions of the systematic factors requires analyzing the systematic losses, L_S [equation (22.5)]. The contribution of the idiosyncratic factors can be assessed in an incremental way by looking at the difference between the total and the systematic losses, $L - L_S$.

Risk measures can be naturally decomposed into their systematic and idiosyncratic contributions. For example, it is well known that the variance of portfolio losses can be written as the sum of the variance of the conditional expected losses and the expected conditional variance of losses:[6]

$$V[L] = V[E[L|X]] + E[V[L|X]] \qquad (22.28)$$

The first term is the systematic risk contribution, and the second is the idiosyncratic risk, which vanishes (as a percentage of the total risk) as the number of positions goes to infinity (and the idiosyncratic risk is diversified away). In a moderately large portfolio, the systematic component may be much larger than the idiosyncratic risk, but the latter may still be too significant to be neglected.

VaR and CVaR can be decomposed in a similar manner, although their idiosyncratic components do not have general closed-form expressions. When the conditional variance of losses is small, we can obtain analytical approximations of VaR and CVaR for nongranular portfolios as small adjustments to the infinitely granular portfolio. This methodology is generally referred to as the *granularity adjustment*, and can be used effectively to understand the contributions of idiosyncratic factors (see Gordy 2003).

Recall that in the Gaussian copula model, obligor losses are conditionally independent given the systematic factor X. Thus, if no individual instrument represents a large component of the overall portfolio, we have a law of large numbers result, such that:[7]

$$\lim_{I \to \infty} \{L - L_S\} = 0 \tag{22.29}$$

The basic strategy behind the granularity adjustment is to write the total portfolio loss as the sum of the systematic loss (conditional expectation of losses given the systematic factors) and a remainder term:

$$L = L_S + (L - L_S) = L_S + U \tag{22.30}$$

To approximate the total portfolio risk $\rho(L)$, it is useful to embed the loss variable in a family of models, parameterized by $\varepsilon > 0$.

$$L_\varepsilon = L_S + \varepsilon \cdot U \tag{22.31}$$

where the loss distribution of the true portfolio corresponds to $\varepsilon = 1$. Then, approximate ρ by its second-order Taylor expansion:

$$\rho(L_\varepsilon) = \rho(L_S + \varepsilon \cdot U) \approx \rho(L_S) + \varepsilon \cdot \left(\frac{d}{d\varepsilon} \rho(L_S + \varepsilon \cdot U) \right) \Bigg]_{\varepsilon=0}$$
$$+ \frac{1}{2} \varepsilon^2 \left(\frac{d^2}{d\varepsilon^2} \rho(L_S + \varepsilon \cdot U) \right) \Bigg]_{\varepsilon=0} \tag{22.32}$$

From the results of Gourieroux, Laurent, and Scaillet (2000) for the case where $\rho = \text{VaR}_\alpha$, for example, we have that:[8]

$$\frac{d}{d\varepsilon} \text{VaR}_\alpha(L_S + \varepsilon \cdot U)_{\varepsilon=0} = E[U|L_S = \text{VaR}_\alpha(L_S)] \tag{22.33}$$

Based on a simple calculation, the first-order term in the Taylor expansion of VaR_α is zero:

$$E[U|L_S = \text{VaR}_\alpha(L_S)] = E[L|L_S = \text{VaR}_\alpha(L_S)] - \text{VaR}_\alpha(L_S) = 0 \tag{22.34}$$

The second-order term in the expansion is:[9]

$$GA = \frac{1}{2} \left(\frac{d^2}{d\varepsilon^2} \rho(L_S + \varepsilon \cdot U) \right) \Bigg]_{\varepsilon=0} = -\frac{1}{2\varphi(\Phi^{-1}(\alpha))} \cdot \frac{d}{dx} \left(\frac{\sigma^2(x)\varphi(x)}{\mu(x)} \right) \Bigg|_{x=\Phi^{-1}(\alpha)} \tag{22.35}$$

where φ is the standard normal probability density function, and:

$$\mu(x) = E[L|X = x], \quad \sigma^2(x) = \text{var}(L|X = x) \tag{22.36}$$

Explicit formulas for the granularity adjustment (GA) [equation (22.35)] and the individual name contributions are available in the Gaussian copula model (e.g., Tasche 1999), as well as for other risk measures such as CVaR (e.g., Tasche 1999) and for other factor models (e.g., Gordy and Lütkebohmert 2007 for the case of the CreditRisk+ model). More thorough discussions of granularity adjustments and their applications to portfolio credit risk management are included in Gordy (2004) and Lütkebohmert (2009).

22.4 Marginal Contributions in the Linear, Homogeneous Case

In this section, we study marginal contributions to risk measures when:

- Losses are equal to the sum of the factors: $L = \sum_{m=1}^{M} X_m$
- The risk measure is positive homogeneous: $\rho(\lambda \cdot L) = \lambda \cdot \rho(L), \quad \lambda > 0$

Commonly referred to as *Euler allocation*, this is the most common case, and it includes the calculation of VaR and CVaR, and volatility contributions of positions in a portfolio. As we will further see, it yields marginal risk contributions that are additive.

We begin with a short review of the derivation and theoretical properties of the Euler allocation, as well as its justification in different contexts. We discuss its application to two different credit risk problems: credit capital allocation in a portfolio (under both a single-factor and a multifactor credit model) and computing contributions of individual instruments to a counterparty portfolio's credit valuation adjustment (CVA). In each case, we illustrate the risk contribution methodologies with an example.

22.4.1 Basic Principle and Interpretation

Under the Euler allocation, marginal risk contributions [equation (22.27)] are additive [equation (22.22)]. This follows from the fact that the risk function is homogeneous (of degree one) in the portfolio weights w and the application of Euler's theorem for homogeneous functions.

A real function $f(x)$ of a vector $\text{x} = (x_1, \ldots, x_N)$ is said to be homogeneous of degree β if for all $c > 0$, $f(c\text{x}) = c^\beta f(\text{x})$. If the function $f(\cdot)$ is piecewise differentiable, then Euler's theorem for homogeneous functions states that:

$$\beta \cdot f(\text{x}) = \sum_{i=1}^{N} \frac{\partial f(\text{x})}{\partial x_i} \cdot x_i \tag{22.37}$$

TABLE 22.1 Marginal Risk Contributions for Common Risk Measures

Name	Definition	Marginal Contributions
Standard deviation	$\sigma(L) = \sqrt{E\left[(L - E[L])^2\right]}$	$C_m^{EA} = \dfrac{\mathrm{cov}(X_m, L)}{\sigma(L)}$
VaR	$\mathrm{VaR}_\alpha(L) = \min\{V \mid P[L \geq V] \leq 1 - \alpha\}$	$C_m^{EA} = E[X_m \mid L = \mathrm{VaR}_\alpha(L)]$
CVaR	$\mathrm{CVaR}_\alpha(L) = E[L \mid L \geq \mathrm{VaR}_\alpha(L)]$	$C_m^{EA} = E[X_m \mid L \geq \mathrm{VaR}_\alpha(L)]$

The risk measures most commonly used, such as standard deviation, VaR and CVaR, are homogeneous functions of degree one ($\beta = 1$) in the portfolio positions. Thus, Euler's theorem for homogeneous functions is applied to allocate capital and compute risk contributions across portfolios, since it implies:

$$\rho(L) = \sum_{m=1}^{M} C_m^{EA} \tag{22.38}$$

Table 22.1 presents the expressions for marginal risk contributions to standard deviation, VaR and CVaR. While the expression for standard deviation contributions is classical, the marginal contributions to VaR and CVaR follow from the relationships between partial derivatives and conditional expectations first derived by Gourieroux et al. (2000) and Tasche (1999). These expressions assume that the portfolio loss L has a continuous distribution, with cumulative distribution function F_L. Technical assumptions on the differentiability of the risk measure are required for the formulas for VaR and CVaR to hold, for which we refer readers to the original references.

The Euler allocation rule has important relations to the axiomatization of contribution measures, performance measurement, and fairness in risk allocation arising from notions of cooperative game theory.

22.4.1.1 Marginal Contributions and Axiomatic Capital Allocation

Kalkbrener (2005) considers the axioms that characterize appropriate risk contribution measures for portfolio positions. He proves that the Euler allocation is the only allocation rule that satisfies the following three axioms:

K1: *Linear aggregation*. Total portfolio risk is the sum of the position contributions:

$$\rho(L) = \rho\left(\sum_{m=1}^{M} X_m\right) = \sum_{m=1}^{M} C_m \tag{22.39}$$

K2: *Diversification*. The risk contribution of a position does not exceed its stand-alone risk:

$$C_m \leq \rho(X_m) \tag{22.40}$$

K3: *Continuity.* Risk contributions are continuous. Specifically, given the definition of the loss variable L_w [equation (22.26)], this implies that the C_m are continuous functions of w.

22.4.1.2 Marginal Contributions and Performance Measurement

Tasche (1999, 2008) further studies the relationship of the Euler allocation to performance measures. In particular, with $\mu_m = -E[X_m]$ denoting the expected profit on position m, the total portfolio risk-adjusted return on capital (RAROC) is defined as:

$$RAROC(L) = \frac{-E[L]}{\rho(L)} = \frac{\sum_{m=1}^M \mu_m}{\rho(L)} \qquad (22.41)$$

The portfolio-related RAROC for the mth instrument is defined to be:

$$RAROC(X_m|L) = \frac{\mu_m}{C_m} \qquad (22.42)$$

Risk contributions are said to be *RAROC compatible* if there exist $\varepsilon_m > 0$, $m = 1, \ldots, M$ such that:

$$RAROC(X_m|L) > RAROC(L) \Rightarrow RAROC(L + hX_m) > RAROC(L) \qquad (22.43)$$

for all $0 < h < \varepsilon_m$. This implies that if the portfolio-related RAROC of the mth instrument is greater than the total portfolio RAROC, then portfolio RAROC can be improved (at the margin) by investing more in that instrument. Under technical differentiability conditions, one can prove that the Euler allocation is the only rule that is consistent with RAROC compatibility.

22.4.1.3 Marginal Contributions and Game Theory

Finally, there has been a significant amount of work relating risk contributions to cost allocation in cooperative game theory. In this context, positions (or subportfolio managers) are regarded as participating in a game, where the total cost (i.e., total portfolio risk) is allocated to each of the players. Players are allowed to withdraw from the game, and thus costs must be allocated fairly in order that they continue playing (the financial analogy would be that the risk allocation system be fair so that portfolio managers are fairly compensated and do not leave the firm). Based on axioms for what constitutes a fair cost allocation (measure of risk contribution), possible allocation mechanisms are derived. Denault (2001) shows that, under technical conditions, this results in the Euler allocation rule. For more details, see Denault (2001) and Koyluoglu and Stoker (2002).

22.4.2   Marginal Capital Allocation for Credit Portfolios

Credit portfolio managers require economic capital measures that effectively capture the risks associated with obligor credit events, such as defaults, credit downgrades, and spread changes. Credit capital is commonly defined in terms of a high quantile (e.g., in Basel II it is defined at the 99.9 percent level). The Euler allocation can be effectively applied to determine the capital contributions of instruments and subportfolios to overall portfolio credit risk within the context of a factor model for credit risk, such as the one reviewed in Section 22.2.

In practice, Monte Carlo simulation techniques are required to compute the portfolio loss distributions and calculate risk contributions when the underlying credit model presents a rich codependence structure with multiple systematic factors; when the portfolio contains name concentrations (i.e., it is not granular); when credit losses account for migration and spread risk; or when exposures and losses given defaults (LGDs) are stochastic and correlated (see, for example, Mausser and Rosen 2008 and the references cited therein). There are, however, some cases that allow for analytical or semianalytical solutions to the computation of capital and its allocation across positions. In this section, we discuss the analytical solution for the asymptotic single-factor credit model underlying the Basel II credit capital requirements (BCBS 2006), as well as the (semianalytical) diversification factor model of Garcia Cespedes et al. (2006) for a multifactor credit model.

22.4.2.1   Capital Allocation in the Asymptotic Single-Factor Credit Model

In the presence of diversification, the marginal capital required for an obligor or a position may depend on the overall portfolio composition. If capital charges are based on marginal portfolio contributions, these charges are not, in general, *portfolio-invariant*, and are different from their stand-alone capital. For a portfolio of long positions, Gordy (2003) shows that two conditions are necessary and sufficient to guarantee portfolio-invariant VaR contributions, which are also equal to the stand-alone capital contributions:

- The portfolio must be asymptotically fine-grained; that is, no single exposure can account for more than an arbitrarily small share of total portfolio exposure.
- There must be only a single systematic risk factor.

This asymptotic single-factor credit portfolio model was briefly discussed in Section 22.2, and is at the heart of the Basel II regulation. The economic capital for a portfolio covers systematic credit risk and is given in closed form by equation (22.15), with the 99.9 percent capital contribution (marginal and stand-alone) for the mth instrument given by:

$$C_m^S = C_m^{EA} = w_m \cdot \left[\Phi \left(\frac{\Phi^{-1}(PD_m) - \beta_m \Phi^{-1}(0.001)}{\sqrt{1 - \beta_m^2}} \right) - PD_m \right] \quad (22.44)$$

When idiosyncratic risk arises in nongranular portfolios, marginal capital contributions are now dependent on the portfolio composition (specifically, the level of name concentration risk in the portfolio). In this case, marginal contributions for each position can be computed further through simulation or the application of the granularity adjustment discussed in Subsection 22.3.4.1 (e.g., Emmer and Tasche 2005).

22.4.2.2 Semianalytical Methods for Credit Capital Allocation (Diversification Factor)

Portfolio-invariant capital contributions in the asymptotic single-factor model are useful for regulatory purposes and management transparency. However, the single-factor model does not fully recognize *systematic diversification* and may not be useful for capital allocation. We thus require also tools to understand and measure diversification in a multifactor portfolio setting. Pykhtin (2004) obtains an elegant, analytical multifactor adjustment to the Basel II single-factor model. This method can also be used to compute capital contributions numerically, but the closed-form expressions for capital contributions are quite intricate. Garcia Cespedes et al. (2006) present an alternative multifactor approach, which introduces the concept of a *diversification factor* at the portfolio level and also at the obligor or subportfolio level to account for diversification contributions to the portfolio.[10] In this section, we briefly introduce the application of the Euler allocation principle in the context of the diversification factor model of Garcia Cespedes et al. and discuss the interpretation of the allocation of diversification benefits across positions.

Recall that a risk measure ρ is said to be *subadditive* if the risk of the overall portfolio is less or equal to the sum of the stand-alone risks [equation (22.24)]. For two positions or subportfolios, this can be expressed as:

$$\rho(X_1 + X_2) \le \rho(X_1) + \rho(X_2)$$

The difference between the two sides of the preceding inequality represents the reduction in risk due to diversification. This risk reduction can be expressed in relative terms as a *diversification factor* (Tasche 2006; Garcia Cespedes et al. 2006):

$$DF = \frac{\rho\left(\sum_{m=1}^{M} X_m\right)}{\sum_{m=1}^{M} \rho(X_m)} \tag{22.45}$$

The numerator in equation (22.45) represents the total risk of the portfolio, and the denominator is the sum of the stand-alone risks of all positions. Similarly, applying the Euler allocation principle, we can construct the *marginal diversification factor* for each position, by substituting equation (22.30) in the numerator of equation (22.45):

$$DF = \sum_{m=1}^{M} CDF_m, \quad CDF_n = \frac{C_n}{\sum_{m=1}^{m} \rho(X_m)} \tag{22.46}$$

where the term CDF_m is the marginal contribution of the mth instrument or sub-portfolio to the portfolio diversification factor DF.

Garcia Cespedes et al. (2006) use the properties of the diversification factor to derive a semianalytical approximation to economic capital for systematic risk as well as to position and sector contributions in a multifactor Gaussian copula model. To illustrate the model, consider a portfolio with K sectors. For each obligor in a given sector k, the credit losses are driven by a single systematic factor. While the Basel II model uses the same systematic factor for all obligors, in this case we assume that the sector factors are different. Thus, the creditworthiness index of obligor i in sector k can be written as:[11]

$$CWI_i = \beta_i Y_k + \sqrt{1 - \beta_i^2} \cdot \varepsilon_i \qquad (22.47)$$

where Y_k and ε_i are standard normal random variables, representing the systematic risk factor for sector k and the idiosyncratic risk of name i, respectively ($k = 1, \ldots, K$, $i = 1, \ldots, I$). The idiosyncratic factors ε_i are independent of each other, and of the systematic factors Y_k. The systematic factors Y_k may represent different industries, geographic regions, or sectors of the economy, and have a multivariate Gaussian distribution with correlation matrix Q.

If we focus on the 99.9 percent economic capital over a one-year risk horizon (as prescribed in the Basel II Capital Accord),[12] the diversification factor [equation (22.51)] can be written as:

$$DF = \frac{EC^{mf}}{EC^{sf}} = \frac{EC^{mf}}{\sum_{k=1}^{K} EC_k} \qquad (22.48)$$

where EC^{mf} is the economic capital from the full multifactor model (for systematic losses), EC^{sf} is the economic capital computed assuming that there is only a single systematic factor. The latter is given by the sum of the stand-alone economic capital of each sector, EC_k, which can be calculated using equation (22.44). Note that the single-factor model essentially assumes that all sector factors are perfectly correlated (a correlation matrix consisting entirely of ones replacing Q).

The basic idea to make the model operational is to approximate DF by a scalar function of a small number of parameters, which leads to a reasonable approximation of the true, multifactor, economic credit capital. We can think of diversification basically being a result of two sources. The first source is the relative size of various sector portfolios (a portfolio with one very large sector results in high concentration risk and limited diversification). Hence, we seek a parameter representing essentially an effective number of sectors. The second source is the sector correlations. A natural choice for a parameter is some form of average cross-sector correlation. Thus, the Garcia Cespedes et al. (2006) model considers the ansatz:

$$DF \approx DF(CDI, \bar{\beta}) \qquad (22.49)$$

where *CDI* is called the *capital diversification index*, and is defined to be the Herfindahl index of the stand-alone sector economic capitals:

$$CDI = \frac{\sum_{k=1}^{K} EC_k^2}{\left(\sum_{k=1}^{K} EC_k\right)^2} \tag{22.50}$$

and $\bar{\beta}$ is the *average sector correlation* with respect to the economic capital weights, defined so that:

$$w^T B w = w^T Q w \tag{22.51}$$

where w is the vector with kth component $w_k = EC_k$, and B is a correlation matrix with all off-diagonal elements equal to $\bar{\beta}$. It is easy to solve for the average sector correlation explicitly:

$$\bar{\beta} = \frac{w^T(Q - I)w}{w^T(1 - I)w} \tag{22.52}$$

where I is the K-dimensional identity matrix, and 1 is a $K \times K$ matrix of ones.

The model requires one to choose a reasonable functional form for the diversification factor [equation (22.49)], and calibrate it numerically using Monte Carlo simulation methods. As an example, Garcia Cespedes et al. (2006) obtain the following approximation (for the specific case they consider):

$$DF(CDI, \bar{\beta}) = 1 + a_{1,1}(1 - \bar{\beta})(1 - CDI) + a_{2,1}(1 - \bar{\beta})^2(1 - CDI) \\ + a_{2,2}(1 - \bar{\beta})^2(1 - CDI)^2 \tag{22.53}$$

with $a_{1,1} = -0.852$, $a_{2,1} = 0.426$, $a_{2,2} = -0.481$.

Finally, to obtain capital contributions, observe that with this specification:

$$EC^{mf} \approx DF(CDI, \bar{\beta}) \cdot \sum_{k=1}^{K} EC_k = f(EC_1, \ldots, EC_K) \tag{22.54}$$

where f is a homogeneous function of degree one. This implies that Euler's theorem for homogeneous functions can be applied to obtain:[13]

$$EC^{mf} = \sum_{k=1}^{K} DF_k \cdot EC_k, \quad DF_k = \frac{\partial EC^{mf}}{\partial EC_k} \tag{22.55}$$

Using the chain rule, and the preceding definitions, the marginal sector diversification factors DF_k may be computed explicitly:

$$DF_k = \frac{\partial EC^{mf}}{\partial EC_k} = DF(CDI, \bar{\beta}) \cdot \frac{\partial EC^{cf}}{\partial EC_k} + EC^{cf} \cdot \frac{\partial DF}{\partial CDI} \cdot \frac{\partial CDI}{\partial EC_k}$$

$$+ EC^{cf} \cdot \frac{\partial DF}{\partial \beta} \cdot \frac{\partial \beta}{\partial EC_k} = DF + 2\frac{\partial DF}{\partial CDI} \cdot \left[\frac{EC_k}{EC^{cf}} - CDI \right]$$

$$+ 2\frac{\partial DF}{\partial \bar{\beta}} \cdot \frac{1 - (EC_k/EC^{cf})}{1 - CDI} \cdot (\bar{Q}_k - \bar{\beta}) \tag{22.56}$$

where

$$\bar{Q}_k = \frac{\sum_{j \neq k} Q_{kf} EC_j}{\sum_{j \neq k} EC_j} \tag{22.57}$$

Equation (22.56) gives an explicit formula for the marginal diversification factors, which provides a further, intuitive breakdown of the contribution of each position to the overall portfolio diversification. Note that DF_k is given by the sum of three components:

$$DF_k = DF + \Delta DF_{size} + \Delta DF_{corr}$$

The first term is the overall portfolio diversification factor. The second term adjusts for the relative size of the sector, and the final term adjusts for the sector's correlation to the remainder of the portfolio.

22.4.2.3 Example: Capital Allocation for a Credit Portfolio

In this section, we illustrate the Euler allocation on a credit portfolio based on the CDX investment-grade index (CDX.NA.IG), and compute the contributions of the index constituents to the overall portfolio risk. We first consider the allocation in the case of a single-factor credit model and then extend the example to the multifactor case.

The CDX.NA.IG index is composed of 125 equally weighted credit default swaps (CDSs) written on investment-grade corporations, which are relatively liquid. There is an active market in CDSs and synthetic CDO tranches on the index. Table 22.2 presents the breakdown of the current index (version 13) in terms of sectors and ratings. Annual PDs for each rating are based on historical default frequencies (Standard & Poor's 2009), with unrated names assumed to have a BB default probability. Factor

TABLE 22.2   CDX.IG.NA (Version 13) Constituents: Breakdown by Sector and Rating Class

	AA	A	BBB	BB	B	Not Rated	Total
PD (%)	0.03	0.08	0.24	0.99	4.51	N/A	
Sector/Rating							
Consumer Goods	0	2	9	1	1	1	14
Oil & Gas	1	1	7	1	0	0	10
Financials	2	6	9	3	0	1	21
Consumer Services	0	6	16	5	2	1	30
Health Care	0	3	5	1	0	0	9
Utilities	0	3	3	0	0	0	6
Industrials	0	8	7	2	0	1	18
Technology	0	2	3	2	0	0	7
Basic Materials	1	1	4	0	0	0	6
Telecommunications	0	2	1	1	0	0	4
Total	4	34	64	16	3	4	125

loadings are defined using the Basel correlations [equation (22.16)], and recovery rates are assumed to be 40 percent.

Table 22.3 presents various VaR and CVaR measures at different confidence levels for the portfolio under the single-factor model (all expressed as basis points of a unit notional). Results for systematic risk are calculated using the analytical formula, and for total losses using the granularity adjustment (GA) as well as a Monte Carlo simulation with one million scenarios.[14] The GA approximations are reasonably accurate, particularly for higher confidence levels. Since total losses converge to systematic losses as the number of instruments in the portfolio grows, the GA performs even better for larger credit portfolios that arise in practice (the CDX.IG portfolio has only 125 names).

Tables 22.4 and 22.5 show the contributions by rating class to systematic risk for VaR and CVaR, at various confidence levels. Contributions are expressed for the

TABLE 22.3   Risk Measures for the CDX Portfolio (bps)

	VaR			CVaR		
Confidence Level	Systematic	Systematic + GA	MC	Systematic	Systematic + GA	MC
0.9	59	82	96	114	148	146
0.95	90	121	96	157	198	196
0.99	192	239	240	286	343	341
0.995	250	303	288	355	418	418
0.999	415	483	480	547	624	622

TABLE 22.4 CDX Systematic VaR Contributions (Italics Indicate Contributions per Instrument)

	AA	A	BBB	BB	B	Not Rated	Total
Notional	4	34	64	16	3	4	125
VaR(0.9)	0.11	3.00	18.38	18.88	13.50	4.77	58.67
	0.00	*0.00*	*0.22*	*1.11*	*4.55*	*1.11*	
VaR(0.95)	0.22	5.77	31.53	28.25	17.25	7.00	90.06
	0.00	*0.11*	*0.44*	*1.77*	*5.77*	*1.77*	
VaR(0.99)	0.88	16.66	79.00	55.85	26.13	13.96	192.43
	0.22	*0.44*	*1.22*	*3.44*	*8.77*	*3.44*	
VaR(0.995)	1.22	23.87	107.30	69.99	30.00	17.50	249.88
	0.33	*0.77*	*1.66*	*4.33*	*10.00*	*4.33*	
VaR(0.999)	2.66	47.43	191.84	107.21	38.96	26.80	414.90
	0.66	*1.44*	*3.00*	*6.77*	*12.99*	*6.77*	

overall rating class as well as per instrument in each class (in italics). As expected, instruments of lower credit quality contribute more to risk at all confidence levels. However, this effect is more pronounced for lower confidence levels than for higher confidence levels, and more pronounced for VaR than for CVaR. This reflects the fact that in order for large losses to occur, both high-quality and low-quality names must default (in order to have sufficiently many defaults).[15] This effect is explained in more detail in Mausser and Rosen (2008).

Consider now the multifactor case. Assume that each sector in Table 22.2 is driven by a single systematic factor and that the factor loading for each name to its sector factor is the same as before. Also, for illustration purposes, assume that any two systematic sector factors corresponding to different sectors have correlation 0.5.

TABLE 22.5 CDX Systematic CVaR Contributions (Italics Indicate Contributions per Instrument)

	AA	A	BBB	BB	B	Not Rated	Total
Notional	4	34	64	16	3	4	125
CVaR(0.9)	0.44	8.77	43.45	34.37	18.96	8.55	114.49
	0.11	*0.22*	*0.66*	*2.11*	*6.33*	*2.11*	
CVaR(0.95)	0.66	13.26	63.03	45.84	22.76	11.46	157.01
	0.11	*0.33*	*0.99*	*2.88*	*7.55*	*2.88*	
CVaR(0.99)	1.55	29.53	126.38	77.70	31.70	19.42	286.31
	0.44	*0.88*	*1.99*	*4.88*	*10.57*	*4.88*	
CVaR(0.995)	2.11	39.34	161.64	93.39	35.55	23.35	355.44
	0.55	*1.11*	*2.55*	*5.88*	*11.85*	*5.88*	
CVaR(0.999)	4.11	69.46	261.86	133.49	44.41	33.37	546.70
	1.00	*2.00*	*4.00*	*8.33*	*14.80*	*8.33*	

FIGURE 22.1   Stand-Alone Capital by Sector

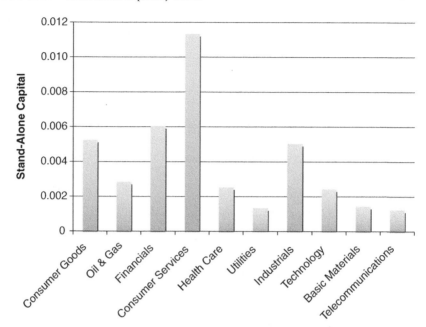

Figure 22.1 presents the stand-alone EC (99.9 percent) by sector. The stand-alone capitals sum to the single-factor EC, $EC^{sf} = 0.039$. The capital diversification index is $CDI = 0.158$, which translates into 6.3 effective sectors (inverse of the CDI). The average sector correlation is 0.5, since all intersector factor correlations are equal. Furthermore, it can be easily shown that the second term (ΔDF_{corr}) in the expression for DF_k is equal to zero for all k. Using the semianalytical approximation, we obtain a value of the diversification factor of $DF = 0.65$, which translates into an approximate multifactor economic capital of $EC^{mf} = 0.025$.

The marginal sector diversification factors DF_k and approximate sector economic capital contributions $DF_k \cdot EC_k / EC^{mf}$ are presented in Figures 22.2 and 22.3. Note for example that while the DF is 65 percent, the marginal DF for utilities is just over 50 percent (contributing less to risk) while that of consumer services is almost 80 percent, representing a more concentrated position which contributes more to risk at the margin.

The results of the diversification factor approximation are compared with a Monte Carlo simulation.[16] Sector capital contributions, evaluated by summing the contributions of all instruments belonging to a given sector, are provided in Figure 22.4. Marginal contribution estimates from a standard Monte Carlo simulation are difficult to compute accurately and can present nontrivial numerical errors (see, for example, Mausser and Rosen 2008). However, in this case, sector capital contributions (Figures 22.3 and 22.4) are very similar.

FIGURE 22.2 Marginal Sector Diversification Factors (DF_k).

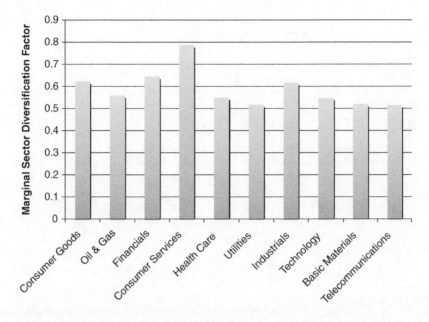

22.4.3 CVA Contributions without Collateral or Margins

The valuation of a portfolio of over-the-counter (OTC) derivatives must take into account the possibility of losses due to counterparty default. The *credit valuation adjustment* (CVA) is the difference between the value of the portfolio when counterparties are assumed to be risk-free and the true portfolio value. Essentially, it is the market value of the counterparty credit risk in a portfolio. There are two approaches

FIGURE 22.3 Percent Contributions to Multifactor Economic Capital and Stand-Alone Capital by Sector

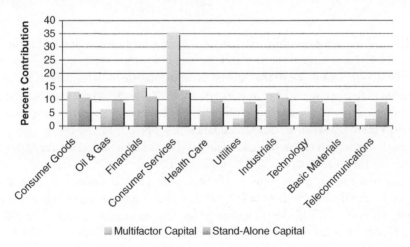

■ Multifactor Capital ■ Stand-Alone Capital

FIGURE 22.4   Sector Percentage Contributions to Multifactor Economic Capital Calculated Using Monte Carlo Simulation and the Diversification Factor Approximation

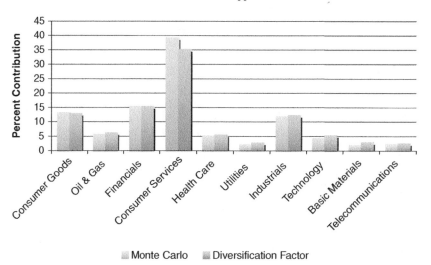

to measuring CVA: unilateral and bilateral. Unilateral CVA captures the market value of future losses due exclusively to the other counterparty's potential default (the counterparty that does the analysis is assumed default-free). In contrast, bilateral CVA takes into account the possibility of both counterparties defaulting. For exposition purposes, we focus the rest of the discussion on unilateral CVA, although the main concepts and results can be applied and extended to the bilateral case.

Consider the set of outstanding contracts with a given counterparty. Denote the (counterparty credit risk-free) value of the mth contract at time t by $V_m(t)$, $m = 1, \ldots, M$, so that the total (risk-free) value of the portfolio at time t is:

$$V(t) = \sum_{m=1}^{M} V_m(t) \tag{22.58}$$

The counterparty exposure $E(t)$ at time t is the economic value lost if the counterparty defaults at time t, and cannot be negative. This exposure depends on the values of all outstanding contracts, as well as on the nature of the collateral and netting arrangement in place with the counterparty. Table 22.6 presents the formulae for exposures in the cases when no netting is allowed, when there is a single netting agreement, and when there is also an amount of collateral $C(t)$ placed by the counterparty. For a detailed discussion on collateral agreements and their influence on counterparty credit risk, see De Prisco and Rosen (2005) or Picoult (2005).

Assume a fixed recovery rate R. If the counterparty defaults at time t, the loss incurred by the institution is $L = (1 - R)E(t)$. CVA is the present value of the risk-neutral expectation of this loss. Denoting the discount factor at time t by $D(t)$, the (risk-neutral) probability distribution of the counterparty's default time τ by $F(t)$ and

TABLE 22.6 Counterparty Exposure Formulas for Various Netting Assumptions

Collateral/Netting Arrangement	Exposure
No netting	$E(t) = \sum\limits_{m=1}^{M} \max(V_m(t), 0) = \sum\limits_{m=1}^{M} E_m(t)$
Single netting agreement No collateral	$E(t) = \max\left(\sum\limits_{m=1}^{M} V_m(t), 0 \right)$
Single netting agreement Collateral amount C(t)	$E(t) = \max\left(\sum\limits_{m=1}^{M} V_m(t) - C(t), 0 \right)$

the longest maturity of any instrument in the counterparty portfolio by T, the credit valuation adjustment is given by:

$$CVA = (1 - R) \int_0^T \bar{e}(t) dF(t) \tag{22.59}$$

where $\bar{e}(t)$ is the risk-neutral discounted *expected exposure*[17] (*EE*) at time t, *conditional* on the counterparty's default at time t:

$$\bar{e}(t) = E[D(t)E(t)|\tau = t] \tag{22.60}$$

Pykhtin and Rosen (2009) study the problem of attributing CVA to the individual instruments in a portfolio. The goal is to determine the contribution CVA_m of the mth instrument to the overall CVA. If these contributions are additive, then we must have:

$$CVA = \sum_{m=1}^{M} CVA_m \tag{22.61}$$

First note that this is accomplished if we can calculate additive contributions to the EE:

$$\bar{e}(t) = \sum_{m=1}^{M} \bar{e}_m(t) \tag{22.62}$$

Note first that, without a netting agreement, the allocation of the counterparty-level EE across the trades is trivial because the counterparty-level exposure is the sum of the stand-alone exposures (see Table 22.6) and expectation is a linear operator. Hence the CVAs for each trade are additive. CVA allocation for the case of netting without collateral can be done using the Euler allocation principle, since CVA can be seen as a positive homogeneous risk measure. Thus, we can take:

$$X_m = V_m(t), \quad L = \sum_{m=1}^{M} X_m$$

$$\rho(L) = \bar{e}(t) = E[D(t) \cdot \max(L, 0) | \tau = t] \tag{22.63}$$

The marginal EE contribution for the mth trade can be shown to be:

$$\bar{e}_m(t) = E[D(t) \cdot V_m(t) \cdot 1_{V(t)>0} | \tau = t] \tag{22.64}$$

It is essentially the expectation of the discounted values of the trade on all scenarios where the total counterparty portfolio value is positive, or zero otherwise. Pykhtin and Rosen (2009) further derive analytic expressions for contributions in the case when trade values are normally distributed. Finally, note that when there is a collateral or margin agreement, the CVA function is no longer homogeneous in the trades, and hence the Euler allocation cannot be applied directly. This case is further discussed in Section 22.5.

We illustrate the calculation of CVA contributions with a simple example. Consider a counterparty portfolio with 12 instruments, and a single time horizon t. The value of instrument m at time t is normally distributed with mean μ_m and standard deviation σ_m

$$V_m(t) = \mu_m + \sigma_m \bar{V}_m(t), \quad \bar{V}_m(t) \sim N(0, 1) \tag{22.65}$$

Instrument values are given a simple correlation structure, with their codependence driven by a single global factor:

$$\bar{V}_m(t) = \sqrt{\rho_m} \cdot Z + \sqrt{1 - \rho_m} \cdot \varepsilon_m \tag{22.66}$$

where Z, ε_m are i.i.d. standard normal random variables. We further assume, for simplicity, independence of market and credit risk.

The 12 instruments in the portfolio are chosen from the combinations of three mean returns $\mu_m = (-100, 0, 100)$; two standard deviations: $\sigma_m = (100, 200)$; and two correlation parameters $\rho_m = (0.5, 0)$. Table 22.7 presents the expected exposure contributions (equivalently, CVA contributions assuming zero interest rates and a single default horizon t), assuming no netting as well as a single netting agreement without collateral.

We make several observations from Table 22.7:

- Note the substantial reduction in CVA due to netting. CVA without netting is 830.9, while it is 316.7 with netting, which translates into a 62 percent reduction.
- In the no-netting case, contributions are always nonnegative and correlations do not affect the contributions. This is intuitively clear, since the total CVA for the

TABLE 22.7 CVA Contributions for Example Portfolio

| Asset | Mean | Std. Dev. | Correlation | Contributions | | | |
				No Netting	(%)	Netting	(%)
1	−100	100	0	8.3	1.0%	−45.0	−14.2%
2	−100	100	0.5	8.3	1.0%	−24.9	−7.9%
3	−100	200	0	39.6	4.8%	−30.0	−9.4%
4	−100	200	0.5	39.6	4.8%	5.3	1.7%
5	0	100	0	39.9	4.8%	5.0	1.6%
6	0	100	0.5	39.9	4.8%	25.1	7.9%
7	0	200	0	79.8	9.6%	20.1	6.3%
8	0	200	0.5	79.8	9.6%	55.3	17.5%
9	100	100	0	108.3	13.0%	55.0	17.4%
10	100	100	0.5	108.3	13.0%	75.1	23.7%
11	100	200	0	139.6	16.8%	70.1	22.1%
12	100	200	0.5	139.6	16.8%	105.3	33.3%
Total				830.9	100%	316.7	100%

counterparty portfolio is simply a sum of the individual instruments' (nonnegative) CVA. Everything else being equal, instruments with higher means and/or higher volatilities have greater contributions.

- The properties of the CVA allocation are very different in the case of a netting agreement. First, negative expected exposure contributions are possible, since some instruments can have negative expected values, which can counteract the contributions of other instruments with positive expected values. Negative contributions can also arise from instruments with values that are negatively correlated to other instruments in the portfolio. Also, notice that a negative expected value is not sufficient to ensure a negative contribution (e.g., Asset 4 has a mean value of −100, but still has a positive contribution, owing to its high volatility and correlation with the other instruments). As in the no-netting case, contributions are increasing functions of the mean and standard deviation of the instrument's value. Furthermore, a higher correlation leads to a higher CVA contribution. Generally, expected exposure contributions for instruments with $\rho_m = 0.5$, $\sigma_m = 100$, are quite close to the contributions for the instruments with the same mean and $\rho_m = 0$, $\sigma_m = 200$.

22.5 Marginal Contributions for Linear, Nonhomogeneous Functions

In many situations of importance in credit risk management, the Euler allocation cannot be applied directly, since the portfolio risk function cannot be written in the form $\rho = \rho(L_w)$ with ρ a positive homogeneous risk measure and L_w a homogeneous function of the portfolio weights. In this section we study the special case when the risk depends on an additional parameter c, so that $\rho = \rho(L_w; c)$. If c is chosen to vary in a meaningful way, then homogeneity may be recovered. We focus on two specific credit risk applications.

First, we consider the problem of computing instrument contributions to the expected losses of CDO tranches. In this case, c is the detachment point of the tranche under consideration. Tasche (2008) suggests taking $c = c(w)$, in such a way that $\rho(L_w; c(w))$ is a positive homogeneous function of w. The Euler allocation can then be directly applied.

The second problem is the calculation of counterparty CVA under margin agreements. In this case, c is the margin threshold, and ρ is a positive homogeneous function in the variables (w, c). As pointed out in Pykhtin and Rosen (2009), risk contributions may be calculated for (w, c), and then the contribution of c reallocated back to the components of w in a meaningful way.

22.5.1   Risk Contributions for CDO Tranches

Consider a CDO with several tranches on a credit portfolio. Let the factors X_m represent the instrument losses. The total portfolio expected losses may be written as:

$$E[L] = \sum_{m=1}^{M} E[X_m] \tag{22.67}$$

The total portfolio losses may also be written as the sum of the losses corresponding to each level in the capital structure of the CDO. In particular, if losses on the nth tranche are denoted by Y_n, then (ignoring timing effects):

$$L = \sum_{n=1}^{N} Y_n, \; Y_n = \min(L, c_n) - \min(L, c_{n-1}) \tag{22.68}$$

where $0 = c_0 < c_1 < \cdots < c_{N-1} < c_N = 1$.

We would like to derive a decomposition of the portfolio expected losses into components E_{mn} such that:

$$E[X_m] = \sum_{n=1}^{N} E_{mn}, \; \text{and} \; E[Y_n] = \sum_{m=1}^{M} E_{mn} \tag{22.69}$$

The problem is solved by decomposing the expected losses of the tranches Y_n into instrument contributions E_{mn}. Due to linearity, it is sufficient to derive instrument contributions to expected losses of the form:

$$E[\min(L, c)] = E\left[\min\left(\sum_{m=1}^{M} X_m, c\right)\right] \tag{22.70}$$

This function is not positive homogeneous in the portfolio weights. In order to resolve this difficulty, we can allow c to be a function of the portfolio weights w (recall the convention that $L = L_1$ where $L_w = \sum_{m=1}^{M} w_m X_m$). This leads to the specification:

$$\rho(L_w) = E[\min(L_w, c(w))] \tag{22.71}$$

If $c(w)$ is a positive homogeneous function of the portfolio weights, then ρ is also positive homogeneous in the portfolio weights, and the standard Euler allocation can be applied to derive tranche expected loss contributions. Two specifications of c are useful in practice:

1. Percentile of the loss function: $c(w) = F_{L_w}^{-1}(\alpha)$.
2. Fixed multiple of the expected loss: $c(w) = b \sum_{m=1}^{M} w_m E[X_m]$.

In each case the parameter (α or b) must be set so that $c(1)$ is equal to the attachment/detachment point under consideration.

For the choice $c(w) = F_{L_w}^{-1}(\alpha)$, the expectation [equation (22.71)] can be computed analytically for systematic losses ($L = L_S$) in the single-factor Gaussian copula model at a given horizon:

$$E[\min(L_s, c(w))] = \sum_{n=1}^{N} w_n \left((1-\alpha)\Phi\left(\frac{\Phi^{-1}(PD_n) - \beta_n \Phi^{-1}(1-\alpha)}{\sqrt{1-\beta_n^2}} \right) \right.$$
$$\left. + \Phi_2(\Phi^{-1}(PD_n), \Phi^{-1}(\alpha); -\beta_n) \right) \tag{22.72}$$

where α is the solution of the one-dimensional nonlinear equation:

$$\sum_{n=1}^{N} w_n \Phi\left(\frac{\Phi^{-1}(PD_n) - \beta_n \Phi^{-1}(1-\alpha)}{\sqrt{1-\beta_n^2}} \right) = c \tag{22.73}$$

We now illustrate this case with an example using the CDX.IG portfolio from Section 22.4. We calculate instrument contributions to (one-year) tranche losses at standard attachment and detachment points, assuming a single-factor Gaussian copula model and only systematic losses. Table 22.8 presents the marginal contributions for each sector, aggregated from those of the individual instruments.

Observe that sector contributions are relatively stable over the capital structure. The largest contributors at all levels are Consumer Goods, Consumer Services, Financials, and Industrials, which reflects the composition of the index (see Table 22.2). As we move up the capital structure, the contribution of Consumer Goods and Consumer

TABLE 22.8　Sector Contributions to Tranche Expected Losses

Sector/Tranche	0−3%	3−7%	7−10%	10−15%	0−100% (EL)
Consumer Goods	17.16%	12.54%	12.04%	11.72%	17.10%
Oil & Gas	5.36%	7.72%	7.96%	8.06%	5.39%
Financials	12.89%	15.86%	16.10%	16.28%	12.92%
Consumer Services	37.55%	27.05%	25.70%	24.92%	37.42%
Health Care	4.69%	6.75%	7.03%	7.17%	4.72%
Utilities	1.84%	3.77%	4.21%	4.46%	1.86%
Industrials	10.22%	13.30%	13.72%	13.99%	10.27%
Technology	5.54%	6.03%	5.88%	5.80%	5.55%
Basic Materials	2.05%	3.93%	4.30%	4.49%	2.08%
Telecommunications	2.69%	3.05%	3.07%	3.10%	2.70%

Services declines, while the contributions of Financials, Industrials, and the remaining sectors increase. The most pronounced difference in the contribution levels occurs when moving from the equity (0−3%) tranche to the first mezzanine (3−7%) tranche. Note that expected tranche loss contributions are very similar to equity tranche contributions. This reflects the fact that names with high default probabilities contribute the most to both overall portfolio expected losses and losses of the equity tranche (which they are likely to be the first to hit). Names with higher credit quality will have relatively larger contributions to more senior tranches in the collateral structure (which are likely only to be hit when some high credit quality names default as well).

22.5.2　CVA Contributions with a Margin Agreement

The problem of computing instrument contributions to CVA without a margin agreement was treated in Section 22.4.4 as a straightforward application of the Euler allocation. When collateral is included within a netting agreement, the conditional expected discounted exposure (EE) is now given by:

$$\bar{e}(t) = E\left[D(t) \max\left(\sum_{m=1}^{M} V_m(t) - C(t), 0 \right) \Bigg| \tau = t \right] \qquad (22.74)$$

where $\bar{e}(t)$ is the expected discounted exposure at time t, conditional on default occurring at t, $D(t)$ is the discount factor, $V_m(t)$ is the value of the mth instrument in the counterparty portfolio covered by the netting agreement, and $C(t)$ is the amount of collateral posted at time t.

Note that the EE, equation (22.74), is not a positive homogeneous risk function applied to the sum of the instrument values. However, the Euler allocation can still be employed *if collateral itself is considered to be a factor whose contribution is to be measured.* This leads to the following choice of factors and risk measure, to which the standard contribution theory may be applied:

$$X_m(t) = V_m(t), \, X_C = -C(t), \, L = \sum_{m=1}^{M} X_m + X_C \qquad (22.75)$$

$$\bar{e}(t) = \rho(L) = E[D(t) \cdot \max(L, 0) | \tau = t] \qquad (22.76)$$

For simplicity, now assume that the counterparty instantaneously posts collateral when the value of the contract to the institution rises above a threshold level H. Furthermore, the full value of the contract beyond the threshold level H is posted.[18] This leads to the following equation for the amount of collateral posted by the counterparty at time t:

$$C(t) = \max(V(t) - H, 0) \qquad (22.77)$$

The EE is thus given by:

$$\bar{e}(t) = E\left[D(t) \left(V(t) \cdot 1_{\{0 < V(t) < H\}} + H \cdot 1_{\{V(t) \geq H\}} \right) \Big| \tau = t \right] \qquad (22.78)$$

In addition to calculating CVA contributions of the collateral, one may also calculate the contribution of the threshold term in equation (22.78). Thus, we can write the Euler allocation of EE as:

$$\bar{e}(t) = \sum_{m=1}^{M} \bar{e}_{m,H}(t) + \bar{e}_H(t) \qquad (22.79)$$

where one can show that the instrument and threshold contributions are given respectively by:

$$\bar{e}_{m,H}(t) = E\left\lfloor D(t) \cdot V_m(t) \cdot 1_{\{0 < V(t) < H\}} \right\rfloor \qquad (22.80)$$

$$\bar{e}_H(t) = H \cdot E\left\lfloor D(t) \cdot 1_{\{V(t) \geq H\}} \right\rfloor \qquad (22.81)$$

Note that, when the threshold goes to infinity, the last term vanishes and we recover the uncollateralized contributions.

Obviously, when there is a nonzero contribution from the collateral threshold [equation (22.79)], the instrument contributions do not add up to the total CVA. As a final step, we can allocate back the threshold contribution to the individual trades, in order to restore the additivity of the instrument contributions. There are several possibilities for allocating the amount $\bar{e}_H(t)$ in meaningful proportions to each trade. For example, we can obtain additive instrument contributions of the form:

$$\hat{e}_m(t) = \bar{e}_{m,H}(t) + w_m(t) \cdot \bar{e}_H(t), \, m = 1, \ldots, M \qquad (22.82)$$

FIGURE 22.5   Expected Exposure for Different Collateral Thresholds

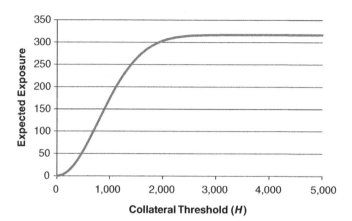

with the weights $w_m(t)$ summing to one. Given that the adjustment of the trade contributions occurs only when the portfolio value exceeds the threshold, a meaningful weighting scheme is given by the ratio of the individual instrument's expected discounted value when the threshold is crossed to the total counterparty discounted value when this occurs:

$$w_m(t) = \frac{E[D(t)V_m(t) \cdot 1_{\{V(t) \geq H\}}]}{E[D(t)V(t) \cdot 1_{\{V(t) \geq H\}}]} \tag{22.83}$$

An alternative allocation scheme is obtained by bringing the weighting scheme of the threshold contribution inside the expectation operator.[19]

We further illustrate the allocation of CVA under a margin agreement by extending the example in Section 22.4.3 to include margining. Figure 22.5 displays the EE as a function of the margin threshold H. As expected, the uncollateralized EE is recovered as the threshold H becomes large. The portfolio value is normally distributed, with a mean of zero and a standard deviation approximately equal to 794, and the effect of the threshold is minimal beyond three standard deviations.

The CVA contributions for the counterparty portfolio instruments, as well as the threshold [equation (22.79)] are presented in Table 22.9 for different levels of the threshold H. For comparison, the results with netting but no collateral (corresponding to $H = \infty$) are also presented.

We can make several observations from Table 22.9:

- In accordance with intuition, the contribution of the threshold term is highest for low threshold levels (where it is highly likely that, when exposure exceeds zero, it will be equal to the threshold), and declines dramatically for higher threshold levels.
- The negative contributions to expected exposure of instruments with negative mean values remain relatively constant (in percent terms) as a function of H. This is not true of the contributions of instruments with high means and/or volatilities and correlations, which tend to increase with the decline in the contribution of H.

TABLE 22.9 EE Contributions (%) for Instruments and the Collateral Threshold for Different Threshold Levels H

	$H = \infty$	$H = 2,000$	$H = 1,000$	$H = 500$	$H = 300$	$H = 100$	$H = 50$
A1	−14.20%	−14.15%	−13.29%	−11.98%	−11.27%	−10.47%	−10.26%
A2	−7.85%	−8.04%	−9.32%	−10.07%	−10.18%	−10.14%	−10.10%
A3	−9.44%	−9.57%	−10.31%	−10.54%	−10.45%	−10.22%	−10.14%
A4	1.67%	1.13%	−3.36%	−7.20%	−8.55%	−9.64%	−9.85%
A5	1.59%	1.53%	0.99%	0.48%	0.27%	0.08%	0.04%
A6	7.94%	7.64%	4.96%	2.39%	1.36%	0.42%	0.20%
A7	6.35%	6.11%	3.97%	1.91%	1.09%	0.33%	0.16%
A8	17.46%	16.81%	10.92%	5.26%	2.99%	0.92%	0.45%
A9	17.38%	17.21%	15.28%	12.93%	11.81%	10.64%	10.35%
A10	23.73%	23.32%	19.25%	14.85%	12.89%	10.97%	10.51%
A11	22.14%	21.79%	18.26%	14.37%	12.62%	10.89%	10.47%
A12	33.25%	32.49%	25.21%	17.72%	14.52%	11.48%	10.75%
H	0.00%	3.73%	37.45%	69.88%	82.90%	94.73%	97.42%

- As in the uncollateralized case, contributions are increasing functions of the mean value, standard deviation, and correlation. However, one particularly interesting asset is A4. This asset has a low mean value, a high standard deviation, and a high correlation. For low values of H, it acts as a hedge to counterparty credit risk, with a negative contribution to EE. Since the exposure is capped at H, the hedging effect of the low mean value dominates, and is not offset by the large standard deviation and correlation (which may lead to large portfolio exposures under some scenarios, and in particular will tend to increase the thickness of the tail). In contrast, it has a positive EE contribution for high levels of H (and for netting without collateral). In these cases, the potential contribution from large portfolio values plays a more significant role.

Table 22.10 presents instrument contributions using equation (22.82) to allocate the contribution of the threshold H back to the instruments.

In Table 22.10, we see that in this example the adjusted instrument (percent) contributions, using equation (22.83), tend to vary linearly with H. In particular, for instruments with negative mean values (A1–A4) the slope of the linear relation tends to be negative, while for instruments with zero mean value (A5–A8) the percent contributions are constant, and for instruments with positive mean values (A9–A12) the slope of the relationship is positive. For further discussion on the impact of margins on CVA allocations, see Pykhtin and Rosen (2009).

22.6 Marginal Contributions for Nonlinear Risk Functions

In this section, we discuss methods for determining risk factor contributions when losses are nonlinear functions of the factors. The standard Euler allocation cannot

TABLE 22.10 Adjusted EE Contributions (%) for Instruments (with Collateral Contribution Allocated Back)

	$H = \infty$	$H = 2{,}000$	$H = 1{,}000$	$H = 500$	$H = 300$	$H = 100$	$H = 50$
A1	−14.20%	−14.26%	−15.41%	−17.98%	−19.87%	−22.53%	−23.36%
A2	−7.85%	−7.91%	−9.06%	−11.63%	−13.52%	−16.18%	−17.01%
A3	−9.44%	−9.50%	−10.65%	−13.22%	−15.11%	−17.77%	−18.60%
A4	1.67%	1.62%	0.46%	−2.11%	−4.00%	−6.66%	−7.48%
A5	1.59%	1.59%	1.59%	1.59%	1.59%	1.59%	1.59%
A6	7.94%	7.94%	7.94%	7.94%	7.94%	7.94%	7.94%
A7	6.35%	6.35%	6.35%	6.35%	6.35%	6.35%	6.35%
A8	17.46%	17.46%	17.46%	17.46%	17.46%	17.46%	17.46%
A9	17.38%	17.43%	18.59%	21.16%	23.04%	25.71%	26.53%
A10	23.73%	23.78%	24.94%	27.51%	29.39%	32.06%	32.88%
A11	22.14%	22.19%	23.35%	25.92%	27.80%	30.47%	31.29%
A12	33.25%	33.30%	34.46%	37.03%	38.92%	41.58%	42.40%

be applied directly in this case. We begin by examining the case where the portfolio loss naturally decomposes into a sum of nonlinear functions of the individual risk factors. Second, we examine methods that use a linear approximation of the portfolio loss function. Finally, we discuss an orthogonal decomposition of the portfolio loss, which leads to expressions for the joint contributions of all possible collections of risk factors.

22.6.1   Linear Combinations of Nonlinear Functions of Factors

The simplest case where the portfolio loss, L, is a nonlinear function of the risk factors $X_1, \ldots, X_M$ occurs when it can be written in the form:

$$L = f_1(X_1) + \cdots + f_M(X_M) \tag{22.84}$$

for some functions $f_1, \ldots, f_M$. In this case, contributions of the factors X_m may be computed by defining a set of transformed factors $Y_m = f_m(X_m)$. For a positive homogeneous risk measure ρ, the marginal risk contributions of the factors Y_m are calculated using the standard Euler allocation. The marginal contribution of Y_m can then be regarded as a measure of the contribution of the factor X_m. Indeed, this method has already essentially been applied earlier in the tables where sector contributions to the CDX.IG index were calculated by summing the contributions of all individual instruments in a given sector. In the event that portfolio losses do not exactly decompose into a sum of nonlinear functions of the risk factors, it may still be possible to approximate portfolio losses by such a sum. For example, Cherny and Madan (2007) consider the case where the portfolio can nearly be decomposed into terms depending on the individual factor risks, and then consider the approximation:

$$L = f(X_1, \ldots, X_M) \approx \sum_{m=1}^{M} E[L|X_m] = \sum_{m=1}^{M} f_m(X_m) \qquad (22.85)$$

Cherny et al. (2010) consider the optimal approximation of the form (22.85) to portfolio losses, and provide an explicit solution when the factors X_m have a Gaussian copula.

22.6.2 Linear Factor Approximations

Suppose that the credit loss function can be expressed as a nonlinear function f of a set of relevant economic factors:

$$L = f(X_1, \ldots, X_M) \qquad (22.86)$$

We seek a sensible method for determining the contributions C_m to portfolio credit risk $\rho(L)$. Furthermore, we want to preserve the additive property of marginal contributions as in the linear-homogeneous case. A straightforward way to do this is to approximate the function f by one that restores linearity to the problem, and then apply the standard Euler allocation rule.

Rosen and Saunders (2009a) consider the problem of determining the linear function of the factors that best approximates portfolio losses:

$$\min_{a,b} d\left(f(X_1, \ldots, X_M), a + \sum_{m=1}^{M} b_m \cdot X_m \right) \qquad (22.87)$$

where d is a measure of distance between the random variables. Once this optimization problem has been solved, then the contributions (or relative contributions) of the factors to the risk of the linear approximation can be used as estimates of the contributions of the factors to the portfolio risk. If we take a quadratic distance d,

$$d(Y, Z) = E[(Y - Z)^2] \qquad (22.88)$$

then the solution of problem is well known, and expressions for the optimal coefficients are available based on projection arguments (see, for example, Luenberger 1969). When the factors are independent random variables, with mean zero and variance 1, the coefficients for the optimal solution are:

$$a = E[L], \, b_m = E[LX_m] \qquad (22.89)$$

Rosen and Saunders (2009a) further present closed-form expressions for these coefficients in the Gaussian copula model, as well as for losses on CDOs sensitive only to systematic risk (e.g., based on large retail credit portfolios). In particular, the optimal linear hedging coefficients for a Gaussian copula model with independent systematic factors [equation (22.2)] are given by:

$$a_m = \sum_{i=1}^{I} w_i P D_i, \quad b_m = - \sum_{i=1}^{I} \beta_{im} \varphi(\Phi^{-1}(P D_i)) \tag{22.90}$$

where φ is the standard normal probability density function.

We illustrate this method with an example on the CDX.IG portfolio. Recall from Section 22.4.2.3 that intersector factor correlations are equal to a constant, β, while individual name correlations to systematic risk in the creditworthiness indicators are given by the Basel correlations. Thus, the creditworthiness indicator of name i can be written as:

$$CWI_i = \sqrt{\beta \rho_i} \cdot X_G + \sqrt{\rho_i(1 - \beta)} \cdot X_{k(i)} + \sqrt{1 - \rho_i} \cdot \varepsilon_i \tag{22.91}$$

where $\beta = 0.5$, is the constant intersector factor correlation; the systematic correlations ρ_i for each name are given by the Basel correlations; $k(i)$ is the sector of name i; and $X_G, X_{k(i)}, \varepsilon_i$ are i.i.d. standard normal random variables. The factors in the model are:

- X_G—a global factor that influences all names in the portfolio.
- $X_{k(i)}$—sector factors, representing the components of systematic risk in each of the sectors that are not correlated to X_G.
- ε_i—the idiosyncratic risk of each of the names.

Contributions of the systematic factors X_G, X_k to the 99.9 percent systematic EC calculated using the linear factor approximation are given in Figure 22.6 and Table 22.11.

FIGURE 22.6   Systematic Factor Contributions to EC Calculated Using Linear Approximation

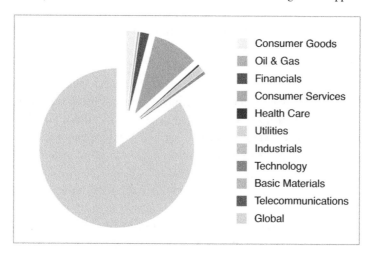

TABLE 22.11 Systemic Factor
Contributions to EC Calculated Using
Linear Approximation

Factor	Percent Contribution
Consumer Goods	1.95
Oil & Gas	0.33
Financials	1.73
Consumer Services	9.42
Health Care	0.25
Utilities	0.05
Industrials	1.12
Technology	0.30
Basic Materials	0.06
Telecommunications	0.07
Global	84.71

As expected, the global factor is the principal contributor, with nearly 85 percent of the total risk. Significant contributions are also made by the largest sectors, particularly Consumer Services (9.4 percent). Note that the results in this section are not directly comparable to the sectors' contributions calculated using the diversification factor in Section 22.4.3. The sector factors are now independent *residual* factors (it is also possible to employ the linear approximation to calculate contributions for the sector factors themselves). The independent factor decomposition above indicates that a hedge portfolio dependent on a single global credit factor can be used to reduce portfolio risk substantially. Residual risk can be hedged using instruments that are sensitive to the individual sector factors (while preserving, for example, the delta with respect to the global factor so as not to eliminate the efficacy of the global factor hedge).

22.6.3 Orthogonal Decompositions

Recall from the discussion of the granularity adjustment (Subsection 22.3.3.1) that it is sometimes useful to regard the total loss as a perturbation of the systematic losses $L = L_S + (L - L_S) = L_S + U$. Aside from providing an effective technique for deriving analytical approximations, this decomposition also has an intuitive interpretation, which helps us generalize the marginal risk contributions to nonlinear functions. First, observe that $L_S + U$ is the orthogonal decomposition of the loss variable L into its projection on the space of variables that are functions of the systematic factors, and its orthogonal complement.[20] This mathematical fact carries with it an important financial interpretation. The term L_S minimizes the variance of the random variable $L - L_S$ among all random variables that are functions of the systematic credit factors. Thus, L_S is the best hedge, in the quadratic sense, among all *possible* securities based on these systematic factors. Also note that L is the sum of the two terms L_S and U, and therefore the standard Euler allocation for linear functions described in Section 22.4 can be applied to derive the contributions (to a positive homogeneous risk measure ρ)

of systematic and idiosyncratic risk (i.e., the contributions of L_S and U respectively; see Martin and Tasche 2007).

The decomposition into systematic and idiosyncratic components can be generalized to calculate contributions of an arbitrary number of factors. Rosen and Saunders (2010) demonstrate how to decompose the risk of an arbitrary function of a set of risk factors using the Euler allocation combined with a tool from statistics called the Hoeffding decomposition. To understand the general method, it is best first to consider a simple case. Suppose that the loss variable is a function of only two factors $L = L(X_1, X_2)$. Then we may write:

$$L = E[L] + (E[L|X_1] - E[L]) + (E[L|X_2] - E[L])$$
$$+ (L - E[L|X_1] - E[L|X_2] + E[L]) \quad (22.92)$$

While this equation may seem a mere tautology, it has important mathematical properties and a financial interpretation that parallel our discussion of the decomposition into systematic and idiosyncratic risk contributions. If the factors are independent, then the terms in the above decomposition are orthogonal. Furthermore, each term in the sum represents an optimal hedge (in the quadratic sense) of the portfolio loss L with instruments of increasing complexity. More explicitly, $E[L]$ represents the best hedge of portfolio losses by investing only in the risk-free bond. The first-order terms $E[L|X_1] - E[L]$ and $E[L|X_2] - E[L]$ give the best hedges of the residual risk (i.e., after the hedging using the risk-free bond) that may be constructed using only securities whose payoffs depend on X_1 and X_2, respectively. The final term gives the residual risk, which may only be hedged with securities that depend on the joint behavior of (i.e., the interaction between) X_1 and X_2. Since L is the sum of the terms in the decomposition, the standard Euler allocation can be applied to calculate the risk contribution of each term. This yields risk contributions for a risk-free bond, the residual risk of each of the individual factors X_1 and X_2, and the impact of joint movements in these factors.

The preceding discussion may be generalized to an arbitrary number M of factors. This yields a decomposition of the loss random variable $L = L(X_1, \ldots, X_M)$, called the Hoeffding decomposition, which has many applications in statistics. The general decomposition has the form:

$$L = \sum_{B \subseteq \{1, \ldots, M\}} g_B(X_m; m \in B)$$
$$= \sum_{B \subseteq \{1, \ldots, M\}} \sum_{B' \subseteq B} (-1)^{|B| - |B'|} \cdot E[L|X_m, m \in B'] \quad (22.93)$$

The sum runs over all possible subsets of the index set $\{1, \ldots, M\}$, which implies that there are 2^M terms in the decomposition.[21] If the factors are independent, then the terms in the sum are orthogonal. The financial interpretation of a general term in the decomposition is that it gives the best hedge (in the quadratic sense) of the loss L that can be constructed using the factors in the set B, but not with any proper subset of those factors. Thus the terms in the decomposition correspond to the incremental hedges as we allow increasingly complex hedging instruments. Risk contributions of each of the terms cover the risk derived from the interaction of all the factors in B, which is not encompassed by the contributions of any subset of the factors (i.e., the risk that depends on the interaction of *all* of the factors of B, and not any proper subset of them). For more information on the mathematics of the Hoeffding decomposition, see van der Vaart (1998). For more on the application of the Hoeffding decomposition in finance, and in particular its use for the calculation of nonlinear risk contributions, see Rosen and Saunders (2010).

We illustrate this methodology by continuing the CDX example with the single global risk factor X_G and K residual sector factors X_k. We compute the risk contributions to systematic EC of each collection of factors using the Hoeffding decomposition and the Euler allocation. With this specification, the contribution of the expected loss term is zero, and only the first- and second-order terms of the decomposition (corresponding to conditional expectations with respect to one or two systematic factors) are nonzero. The resulting contributions are given in Table 22.12.

Again, the global factor has by far the most significant impact on portfolio credit risk. Interestingly, given recent events, the interaction between the global factor and

TABLE 22.12 Risk Contributions of Sets of Factors Computed Using the Hoeffding Decomposition and Euler Allocation

Factor Set	Hoeffding Percent Contribution
Consumer Goods	1.17%
Oil & Gas	0.55%
Financials	1.14%
Consumer Services	7.36%
Health Care	0.39%
Utilities	0.14%
Industrials	1.35%
Technology	0.38%
Basic Materials	0.18%
Telecommunications	0.18%
G	69.50%
G + Consumer Goods	0.69%
G + Oil & Gas	1.30%
G + Financials	12.54%
G + Consumer Services	0.56%
G + Health Care	−0.05%
G + Utilities	1.84%
G + Industrials	0.27%
G + Technology	0.30%
G + Basic Materials	0.20%
G + Telecommunications	0

the financial sector also has a significant impact on the risk of the CDX.IG. As is to be expected based on the size of the sectors in the CDX.IG index (Table 22.2), Consumer Services is the sector whose individual sector factor has the most significant contribution to portfolio risk (although note that in this case the additional contribution of the interaction between the global factor and the residual sector factor is negligible).

22.7 Conclusion

This chapter has provided a survey of the theory and practice of risk contributions, with a focus on marginal risk contributions applied to portfolio credit risk. We have given various numerical examples that illustrate the techniques in each case. Among the applications considered are the computation of portfolio credit risk and the contributions of systematic and idiosyncratic risk; instrument contributions to economic capital and other risk measures; instrument contributions to the CVA of a counterparty portfolio with and without netting and collateral; instrument and subportfolio contributions to expected losses of tranches of CDOs; and contributions of risk factors to nonlinear functions, using approximations and orthogonal decompositions (including applications to determining sector contributions to portfolio credit risk).

Appendix: Factor Models of Credit Risk

In this section, we briefly describe other credit risk models that share the factor structure and many of the mathematical properties of the Gaussian copula model reviewed in this chapter. For further discussion of factor models for credit risk, see McNeil et al. (2005).

Consider a set of systematic factors denoted by $X^t = (X_1^t, \ldots, X_K^t)$, which can in general be time-varying and with arbitrary distributions. For each obligor i, denote its creditworthiness indicator variable for time t by CWI_{it}. Also given is a set of parameters with constant terms a_{it}, and factor loadings for each obligor:

$$b_i^t = (b_{i1}^t, \ldots, b_{iK}^t)$$

Finally, we are given a probability distribution characterized by its mean, and a link function h, such that, conditional on X^t, U_{it} has the given distribution, with mean:

$$E[U_{it}|X^t] = h\left(a_{it} + \sum_{k=1}^{K} b_{ik}^t X_k^t\right) \qquad (22.94)$$

where the variables U_{*t} are conditionally independent given X^t.

Losses on a credit portfolio at time t are then defined as

$$L_t = \sum_{i=1}^{N} w_i U_{it} \tag{22.95}$$

where w_i is the (loss-given-default-adjusted) exposure to obligor i.

The Gaussian copula model presented earlier is an example of a model that fits into this framework. In this case, the conditional expectation in equation (22.11) is the conditional default probability of obligor i given the systematic factor X^t

$$F_i(t|X^t) = E[U_{it}|X^t] = h\left(a_{it} + \sum_{k=1}^{K} b_{ik}^t X_k^t\right) \tag{22.96}$$

In the standard Gaussian copula model, the variables U_i are conditionally Bernoulli, and the factor vector and the coefficient vector b are further defined to be time homogeneous ($b^t = b$, $X^t = X$). Thus, the link function is given by equation (22.12) with,

$$h = \Phi, a_{it} = \frac{\Phi^{-1}(F_i(t))}{\sqrt{1 - \sum_{k=1}^{K} \beta_k^2}}, b_{ik} = \frac{\beta_k}{\sqrt{1 - \sum_{k=1}^{K} \beta_k^2}} \tag{22.97}$$

A LOGIT model is obtained with the choice of the link function:

$$h(x) = \frac{1}{(1 + \exp(-x))} \tag{22.98}$$

The CreditRisk+ model is a single period model, where the factors X_k are independent random variables with the gamma distribution. Conditional on X, the U_i are independent and have the Poisson distribution, with parameter:

$$\lambda_i(X) = E[U_i|X] = c_i \sum_{k=1}^{K} \beta_{ik} X_k \tag{22.99}$$

where $c_i > 0$ and

$$\sum_{k=1}^{K} \beta_{ik} = 1, \beta_{ik} \geq 0 \tag{22.100}$$

This specification clearly fits the general form with a linear link function h. We have the conditional default probability:

$$PD_i(X) = P[U_i > 1|X] = 1 - \exp(-\lambda_i(X)) = 1 - \exp\left(-c_i \sum_{k=1}^{K} \beta_{ik} X_k\right) \tag{22.101}$$

Acknowledgments

Thanks to Benoit Fleury, Philippe Rouanet, and Virgile Rostand for many helpful comments and suggestions. The authors gratefully acknowledge financial support from The Fields Institute (DR), and the Natural Sciences and Engineering Research Council of Canada (NSERC) (DS).

Notes

1. For simplicity, we focus on default credit losses. The model can be easily extended to cover more general mark-to-market credit losses arising from credit migrations and spread changes. See, for example, the CreditMetrics technical document (Gupton, Finger, and Bhatia 1997).
2. See Table 22.1 for the definitions of these risk measures.
3. For simplicity, we have ignored the maturity factor.
4. The Gaussian copula model of Section 22.2 fits into this framework, with the systematic factors $X_1, \ldots, X_K$, and idiosyncratic factors $X_{K+i} = \varepsilon_i, i = 1, \ldots, I$.
5. A method for charging a "systemic risk tax" based on risk contributions of large, complex financial institutions to overall systemic risk is proposed in Acharya et al. (2009).
6. This equation follows since:

$$V[L] = E[(L - E[L])^2]$$
$$= E[(L - E[L|X])^2] + E[(E[L|X] - E[L])^2]$$
$$+ 2E[(L - E[L|X])(E[L|X] - E[L])]$$
$$= E[E[(L - E[L|X])^2|X]] + E[(E[L|X] - E[L])^2]$$
$$= E[V[L|X]] + V[E[L|X]]$$

7. Technically, for this convergence to be true, we must consider losses as a percentage of the total portfolio notional, which implies that the portfolio weights change with N. The result of practical relevance is that the percentage contribution of idiosyncratic risk to overall portfolio risk tends to zero as the size of the portfolio grows, so long as individual exposures remain small compared to the total portfolio notional. For formal statements and proofs, see Frey and McNeil (2003) and Gordy (2003).
8. See Table 22.1 for the definition of VaR_α.
9. See Gourieroux et al. (2000), Martin and Wilde (2002), and Wilde (2001).
10. See also Tasche (2006) for a mathematical foundation for the diversification factor.
11. While we focus the discussion on a Gaussian copula model for default losses, the methodology is quite general and can be used with other credit models; it can also incorporate losses due to credit migration.
12. While the model is calibrated for the prescribed risk measure, confidence level, and time horizon, the method for generating a semianalytical approximation is general.
13. We replace the approximation sign by equality for ease of notation.
14. A kernel estimator with equal weights was used to estimate value at risk.
15. Note that, for inhomogeneous portfolios, it is also more likely that names with large (loss-given-default-adjusted) exposures will have defaulted, conditional on having a large

portfolio loss; this effect can counteract differences in risk contribution owing to credit quality. See Mausser and Rosen (2008) for further details.

16. The simulation is based on one million scenarios. Kernel estimators with equal weights are used to estimate economic capital and instrument contributions.

17. We note that financial institutions define expected exposure in different ways in different contexts. Our use of the term here is consistent with that used in De Prisco and Rosen (2005), and is the standard definition in CVA computations.

18. For a discussion of more realistic and complicated collateral models, see Pykhtin and Rosen (2009).

19. Pykhtin and Rosen (2009) further derive closed-form formulas for EE allocation with margin agreements for the case when instrument values are normally distributed.

20. This is a direct consequence of the interpretation of conditional expectation as a projection.

21. This limits the decomposition as stated to being applied in situations where the number of factors is small, or where higher-order terms in the decomposition may be ignored. We note that in practice the decomposition may also be applied to disjoint groups of factors, with a corresponding reduction in the number of terms in the sum.

References

Acharya, V. V., L. H. Pedersen, T. Philippon, and M. Richardson. 2009. Regulating systemic risk. In *Restoring financial stability: How to repair a failed system*, ed. V. V. Acharya and M. Richardson. Hoboken, NJ: John Wiley & Sons.

Basel Committee on Banking Supervision (BCBS). 2006. International convergence of capital measurement and capital standards: A revised framework (comprehensive version). (June). Available at www.bis.org.

Bonti, G., M. Kalkbrener, C. Lotz, and G. Stahl. 2006. Credit risk concentrations under stress. *Journal of Credit Risk* 2:115–136.

Cherny, A. S., R. Douady, and S. A. Molchanov A. 2010. On measuring risk with scarce observations. *Finance and Stochastics* 14 (3): 375–395.

Cherny, A., and D. Madan. 2007. Coherent measurement of factor risks. Working paper, Moscow State University.

Denault, M. 2001. Coherent allocation of risk capital. *Journal of Risk* 4:7–21.

De Prisco, B., and D. Rosen. 2005. Modelling stochastic counterparty credit exposures for derivatives portfolios. In *Counterparty credit risk modelling*, ed. M. Pykhtin. London: Risk Books.

Emmer, S., and D. Tasche. 2005. Calculating credit risk capital charges with the one-factor model. *Journal of Risk* 7:85–101.

Frey, R., and A. McNeil. 2003. Dependent defaults in models of portfolio credit risk. *Journal of Risk* 6 (1): 59–92.

Garcia Cespedes, J. C., J. A. de Juan Herrero, A. Kreinin, and D. Rosen. 2006. A simple multifactor "factor adjustment" for the treatment of credit capital diversification. *Journal of Credit Risk* 2, no. 3.

Glasserman, P. 2005. Measuring marginal risk contributions in credit portfolios. *Journal of Computational Finance* 9:1–41.

Glasserman, P., and J. Li. 2005. Importance sampling for credit portfolios. *Management Science* 51:1643–1656.

Gordy, M. 2003. A risk-factor model foundation for ratings-based bank capital rules. *Journal of Financial Intermediation* 12 (3): 199–232.

Gordy, M. 2004. Granularity adjustment in portfolio credit risk measurement. In *Risk measures for the 21st century*, ed. G. Szegö. Hoboken, NJ: John Wiley & Sons.

Gordy, M., and E. Lütkebohmert. 2007. Granularity adjustment for Basel II. Discussion Paper Series 2 Banking and Financial Studies, 2007-02-09, Deutsche Bundesbank.

Gourieroux, C., J. Laurent, and O. Scaillet. 2000. Sensitivity analysis of values at risk. *Journal of Empirical Finance* 7:225–245.

Gupton, G., C. Finger, and M. Bhatia. 1997. CreditMetrics technical document. J.P. Morgan, available at www.defaultrisk.com.

Huang, X., C. Oosterlee, and M. Mesters. 2007. Computation of VaR and VaR contribution in the Vasicek portfolio credit loss model: A comparative study. *Journal of Credit Risk* 3:75–96.

Kalkbrener, M. 2005. An axiomatic approach to capital allocation. *Mathematical Finance* 15:425–437.

Kalkbrener, M., H. Lotter, and L. Overbeck. 2004. Sensible and efficient capital allocation for credit portfolios. *Risk* (September): 19–24.

Koyluoglu, U., and J. Stoker. 2002. Honour your contribution. *Risk* 15, no. 4 (April): 90–94.

Luenberger, D. 1969. *Optimization by vector space methods.* New York: John Wiley & Sons.

Lütkebohmert, E. 2009. Concentration risk in credit portfolios. New York: Springer.

Martin, R., and D. Tasche. 2007. Shortfall: A tail of two parts. *Risk* (February): 84–89.

Martin, R., and T. Wilde. 2002. Unsystematic credit risk. *Risk* (November): 123–128.

Mausser, H., and D. Rosen. 2008. Economic credit capital allocation and risk contributions. In *Handbooks in Operations Research and Management Science: Financial Engineering, Volume 15*, ed. J. Birge and V. Linetsky. Amsterdam: North-Holland.

McNeil, A., G. Frey, and P. Embrechts. 2005. *Quantitative risk management.* Princeton, NJ: Princeton University Press.

Merino, S., and M. Nyfeler. 2004. Applying importance sampling for estimating coherent credit risk contributions. *Quantitative Finance* 4:199–207.

Picoult, E. 2005. Calculating and hedging exposure, credit value adjustment and economic capital for counterparty credit risk. In *Counterparty credit risk modelling*, ed. M. Pykhtin. London: Risk Books.

Pykhtin, M. 2004. Multi-factor adjustment. *Risk* (March): 85–90.

Pykhtin, M., and D. Rosen. 2009. Pricing counterparty risk at the trade level and CVA allocations. Working paper.

Rosen, D., and D. Saunders. 2009a. Analytic methods for hedging systematic credit risk with linear factor portfolios. *Journal of Economic Dynamics and Control* 33 (1): 37–52.

Rosen, D., and D. Saunders. 2009b. Valuing CDOs of bespoke portfolios with implied factor models. *Journal of Credit Risk* 5 (3): 3–36.

Rosen, D., and D. Saunders. 2010. Risk factor contributions in portfolio credit risk models. *Journal of Banking and Finance* 34:336–349.

Standard & Poor's. 2009. Default, transition, and recovery: 2008 annual global corporate default study and rating transitions. Available at www.standardandpoors.com/.

Tasche, D. 1999. Risk contributions and performance measurement. Working paper, Technische Universität München.

Tasche, D. 2006. Measuring diversification in an asymptotic multifactor framework. *Journal of Credit Risk* 2 (3): 33–55.

Tasche, D. 2008. Capital allocation to business units and sub-portfolios: The Euler principle. In *Pillar II in the New Basel Accord: The challenge of economic capital*, ed. A. Resti. London: Risk Books.

Tchistiakov, V., J. de Smit, and P.-P. Hoogbruin. 2004. A credit loss control variable. *Risk* (July): 81–85.

van der Vaart, A. W. 1998. *Asymptotic statistics.* New York: Cambridge University Press.

Vasicek, O. 2002. The distribution of loan portfolio value. *Risk* (December): 160–162.

Wilde, T. 2001. Probing granularity. *Risk* (August): 103–106.

Conclusion

This book was conceived just after financial markets had experienced one of the most severe shocks ever. Credit risk and credit derivatives were at the center of the crisis. It is generally agreed that the subprime crisis originated largely with very classical phenomena, including market bubbles (especially in real estate); general underpricing of risk, partly due to macroeconomic choices (such as low risk-free rates); and fraudulent behaviors in the issuance of mortgages and weaknesses in the originate-to-distribute system, to give some examples. Besides this, it has become very clear that there are serious problems in general with credit risk modeling and credit derivatives in particular: their pricing, their conception, and their management. In short, both the theory and the practice of credit risk and credit derivatives have serious flaws.

Still, treasuring difficulties and failures as important lessons for progress and improvement of science and technology is paramount. While this is the case even for hard sciences, this is particularly poignant for social sciences. In the present case, the positive side is that the crisis is allowing us to improve our understanding of many fundamental issues. It is hoped that this will make future credit crises less likely and enhance the resilience of financial institutions.

The chapters in the present volume aim, accordingly, at presenting a renewed picture of the field, taking precisely into account the lessons of the past to push forward new models, new ideas, and new methods—and to analyze the past errors in light of these lessons.

Let us survey very briefly some of the issues that have been addressed and their respective contributions to credit risk.

Models, first. Mathematical models were largely blamed for being at the origin of inaccurate measurement of risk, mispricings, and mishedgings. Even in nonspecialist articles and accounts such as Salmon (2009), Lohr (2009), and Jones (2009), to give a few examples, the Gaussian copula model and more generally mathematics are blamed for the crisis. This is partly shared by Turner (2009). Even when ignoring the general causes of the crisis beyond mathematics, this is only a very partial account of reality. In fact, nobody ever claimed seriously that the Gaussian copula model reflected correctly the behavior of dependence and contagion risk and of multiname credit derivatives. Indeed, correlation skews make it very clear that the model is flawed. A number of precrisis studies criticized the Gaussian copula and the related use and inconsistencies of base correlation, some of which are available in Lipton and Rennie (2007), and others summarized in Brigo, Pallavicini, and Torresetti (2010), again to give just two examples.

However, advanced uses of this simplistic model were certainly responsible for serious problems in the valuation and rating of assets. In the valuation space, one may mention here the problem of pricing bespoke tranches using the market data available from standard ones (typically index quotes and implied correlations). It is certainly a coincidence that two of the best-known references to such mapping methods come from Bear Stearns (Reyfman, Ushakova, and Kong 2004) and Lehman Brothers (Baheti and Morgan, 2007), two of the institutions that were hardest hit by the crisis, but the fact that such methods were widespread is of some importance. In the risk space, this manifested in the Basel II credit portfolios VaR measurements (that certainly contributed to an overall underestimation of risks in the banking industry). We know now with certainty that better models are needed. But, importantly, these models should be tractable and robust. Efficient numerical schemes should make it possible to avoid making abusive simplifying assumptions. Solutions that are proposed in the present volume include mixed reduced-form/structural modeling, stochastic volatility models, dynamical models, analytical formulas, and numerical schemes for advanced models.

Products. It seems difficult now to understand how many products—collateralized debt obligations (CDOs) of mezzanine ABS tranches, CDOs on commodities and funds, CDOs of CDOs, and CPDOs, to name a few—that were created in the early 2000s could have been devised without creating at least some suspicion regarding their potential for creating uncontrollable risks. Taking into account tail phenomena shows, for example, that risks on constant proportion debt obligations (CPDOs) were largely underestimated. However, even relatively simple products such as cash-flow CDOs, collateralized loan obligations (CLOs), and residential mortgage-backed securities (RMBSs) prove in the end to be very difficult to understand quantitatively, due to the complexity of their cash flows and due to the strong links between the behavior of their underlyings and complex macroeconomic parameters, such as long-term interest rates. Here, some standardization of the contracts is necessary and has to come with more academic contributions. The present volume offers insights into these various issues—from the mathematical modeling of the framework to handle cash flows to the modeling of the various parameters that govern RMBSs.

Counterparty risk pricing and management, and credit valuation adjustment (CVA). These are hot topics in today's markets. The fact that even the top financial institutions do not have negligible risk of default is a lesson of one century of repeated crises and bank failures. Systematic risk lessens to a large extent the risk-mitigating effects of diversification—and this is another important lesson, especially when the economy becomes global. We learn from the contributions in the volume that, in this regard, sophisticated models have to come with a renewed understanding of the legal and regulatory frameworks, such as the ones associated to netting or margin calls.

In the book there are many other well-identified challenges. *Liquidity risk* was a key driver of the crisis and hit institutions with insufficient reserves to avoid spiraling fire sales, leading even to defaults. *Equity-to-credit valuation* is still insufficiently understood. It is well known that, in the present state of the art, credit markets do not properly take into account liquidity or equity information—or simply do not address the issue.

We hope that the present volume will serve as an inspiration for working out new ways of thinking about modeling and managing credit risk and credit derivatives, and that it will contribute to the emergence of new standards in this regard.

References

Baheti, P., and S. Morgan. 2007. Base correlation mapping. *Lehman Brothers, QCR Quarterly* (Q1).

Brigo, D., A. Pallavicini, and R. Torresetti. 2010. Credit models and the crisis: A journey into CDOs, copulas, correlations and dynamic models. Chichester, UK: John Wiley & Sons.

Jones, S. 2009. Of couples and copulas: The formula that felled Wall St. *Financial Times*, April 24.

Lipton, A., and A. Rennie, eds. 2007. *Credit correlation—Life after copulas.* Singapore: World Scientific.

Lohr, S. 2009. Wall Street's math wizards forgot a few variables. *New York Times*, September 12.

Reyfman, A., K. Ushakova, and W. Kong. 2004. How to value bespoke tranches consistently with standard ones. Bear Stearns educational report.

Salmon, F. 2009. Recipe for disaster: The formula that killed Wall Street. *Wired*, 17.03.

Turner, J. A. 2009. The Turner Review. Financial Services Authority, UK (March). Available at www.fsa.gov.uk/pubs/other/turner_review.pdf.

Further Reading

Balakrishna, B. S. "A Semi-Analytical Parametric Model for Credit Defaults." (2006). Available at www.defaultrisk.com.

Balakrishna, B. S. "Delayed Default Dependency and Default Contagion." (2007). Available at http://ssrn.com.

Baxter, M. "Levy Simple Structural Models." In *Credit Correlation—Life after Copulas*, edited by A. Lipton and A. Rennie. Singapore: World Scientific, 2007.

Bennani, N. "The Forward Loss Model: A Dynamic Term Structure Approach for the Pricing of Portfolio Credit Derivatives." (2005). Available at www.defaultrisk.com.

Berd, A. M., R. F. Engle, and A. B. Voronov. "The Underlying Dynamics of Credit Correlations." (2007). Available at http://ssrn.com.

Bielecki, T., S. Crépey, and A. Herbertsson. "Markov Chain Models of Portfolio Credit Risk." Working paper. (2009). Available at ww.defaultrisk.com.

Bielecki, T., S. Crépey, M. Jeanblanc, and M. Rutkowski. "Convertible Bonds in a Defaultable Diffusion Model." (2009). Available at www.defaultrisk.com.

Bielecki, T., S. Crépey, M. Jeanblanc, and M. Rutkowski. "Defaultable Options in a Markovian Intensity Model of Credit Risk." (2009). Available at www.defaultrisk.com.

Bielecki, T., M. Jeanblanc, and M. Rutkowski. "Hedging of Credit Default Swaptions in a Hazard Process Model." (Working paper, 2008).

Bielecki, T., A. Vidozzi, and L. Vidozzi. "Pricing and Hedging of Basket Default Swaps and Related Derivatives." (Preprint, 2006).

Brigo, D., A. Pallavicini, and R. Torresetti. "The Dynamical Generalized-Poisson Loss Model, Part One: Introduction and CDO Calibration." Short version in *Risk* (June 2007); extended version available at http://ssrn.com.

Brigo, D., A. Pallavicini, and R. Torresetti. "The Dynamical Generalized-Poisson Loss Model, Part Two: Calibration Stability and Spread Dynamics Extensions." (2006). Available at http://ssrn.com.

Duan, J. C. "Clustered Defaults." (2009). Available at http://ssrn.com.

Donnelly, C., and P. Embrechts. "The Devil Is in the Tails: Actuarial Mathematics and the Subprime Mortgage Crisis." (2009). Accepted for publication in the *ASTIN Bulletin*; preliminary version available at www.math.ethz.ch/\%7Ebaltes/ftp/donnemb.pdf.

Eberlein, E., R. Frey, and E. A. von Hammerstein. "Advanced Credit Portfolio Modeling and CDO Pricing." In *Mathematics—Key Technology for the Future*, edited by W. Jäger and H.-J. Krebs. New York: Springer-Verlag, 2008.

El Namaki, M. S. S. "The Credit Crisis: Leaders Who Have Failed the Drucker Test." (Working paper, 2009).

El Namaki, M. S. S. "The Credit Crisis: The Morning After." (Working paper, 2009).

Elouerkhaoui, Y. "Pricing and Hedging in a Dynamic Credit Model." (Citigroup working paper, 2006). Presented at the conference "Credit Correlation: Life after Copulas," London, September 29.

Errais, E., K. Giesecke, and L. Goldberg. "Affine Point Processes and Portfolio Credit Risk." (2006). Available at www.stanford.edu/dept/MSandE/cgi-bin/people/faculty/giesecke/pdfs/indexes.pdf.

Fermanian, J. D. "A Top-Down Approach for Asset-Backed-Securities: A Consistent Way of Managing Prepayment, Default and Interest Rate Risks." (Preprint, 2010).

Jaeckel, P. "The Gamma Loss and Prepayment Model." *Risk* (September 2008).

Joshi, M. S., and A. M. Stacey. "Intensity Gamma: A New Approach to Pricing Portfolio Credit Derivatives." (2006). Available at http://ssrn.com.

Lardy, J. P., F. Patras, and F. X. Vialard. "Correlation, CDOs of ABS and the Subprime Crisis." In *Financial Risks: New Developments in Structured Product and Credit Derivatives*, edited by C. Gourieroux and M. Jeanblanc. Paris: *Economica*, 2010.

Li, D. X., and M. Hong Liang. "CDO Squared Pricing Using Gaussian Mixture Model with Transformation of Loss Distribution." (2005). Available at www.defaultrisk.com.

Livesey, M., and L. Schlogl. "Recovery Rate Assumptions and No-Arbitrage in Tranche Markets." Lehman Brothers, London. Presented at the Summer School on Financial Derivatives, Imperial College, London. (2006).

Meng, C., and A. N. Sengupta. "CDO Tranche Sensitivities in the Gaussian Copula Model." (2008). Available at www.defaultrisk.com.

Morini, M., and D. Brigo. "No-Armageddon Arbitrage-Free Equivalent Measure for Index Options in a Credit Crisis." (2007). Accepted for publication in *Mathematical Finance*; extended version available at http://ssrn.com.

Prampolini, A., and M. Dinnis. "CDO Mapping with Stochastic Recovery." (2009). Available at http://ssrn.com.

Shreve, S. "Don't Blame the Quants." *Forbes Commentary*, October 7, 2008. Available at www.forbes.com/2008/10/07/securities-quants-models-oped-cx_ss_1008shreve.html.

Vasicek, O. A. "Probability of Loss on Loan Portfolio." (Mimeo, KMV Corporation, 1987).

Vasicek, O. A. "Limiting Loan Loss Probability Distribution." (Mimeo, KMV Corporation, 1991).

Vrins, F. D. "Double t Copula Pricing of Structured Credit Products: Practical Aspects of a Trustworthy Implementation." (2009). Available at www.defaultrisk.com.

Vrins, F. D. "On the Consistency of 'European Proxy' of Structural Models for Credit Derivatives." (Preprint, 2010).

About the Contributors

Aurélien Alfonsi, Université Paris-Est, CERMICS

Samson Assefa, Équipe Analyse et Probabilité, Université d'Évry Val d'Essonne, and CRIS Consortium

Alexander L. Belikoff, Bloomberg LP

Tomasz R. Bielecki, Professor of Applied Mathematics, Illinois Institute of Technology

Christophette Blanchet-Scalliet, Université de Lyon

Damiano Brigo, Gilbart Professor of Financial Mathematics, King's College, London

Agostino Capponi, School of Industrial Engineering, Purdue University

Areski Cousin, Université de Lyon, Université Lyon 1, ISFA

Stéphane Crépey, Université d'Évry Val d'Essonne and CRIS Consortium

Pierre Del Moral, Centre INRIA Bordeaux Sud-Ouest and Institut de Mathematiques de Bordeaux

Rüdiger Frey, Department of Mathematics, Universität Leipzig

Igor Halperin, Quantitative Research, JPMorgan

Benjamin Herzog, Société Générale

Monique Jeanblanc, Université d'Évry Val d'Essonne, Europlace Institute of Finance, and CRIS Consortium

Jean-Pierre Lardy, JPLC

Jean-Paul Laurent, Université Paris 1 Panthéon-Sorbonne and BNP Paribas

Kin Pong Lee, Bloomberg LP

Kirill Levin, Bloomberg LP

Vadim Linetsky, McCormick School of Engineering and Applied Sciences, Northwestern University

Andrei V. Lopatin, Numerix LLC

Rafael Mendoza-Arriaga, McCombs School of Business, University of Texas at Austin

Massimo Morini, Bocconi University and Banca IMI

Jovan Nedeljkovic, R^2 Financial Technologies

Andrea Pallavicini, Banca Leonardo, Financial Engineering

Philippos Papadopoulos, ABN Amro Bank

Frédéric Patras, Université de Nice and Zeliade Systems

Mirela Predescu, BNP Paribas, London

Michael Pykhtin, Federal Reserve Board

Dan Rosen, R^2 Financial Technologies and The Fields Institute
Marek Rutkowski, School of Mathematics and Statistics, University of Sydney
David Saunders, University of Waterloo, Canada
Thorsten Schmidt, TU Chemnitz
Harvey J. Stein, Bloomberg LP
Marco Tarenghi, Mediobanca
Xusheng Tian, Bloomberg LP
Roberto Torresetti, Quaestio Capital Management, Milano
Julien Turc, Société Générale

Index

Printed and bound by CPI Group (UK) Ltd, Croydon, CR0 4YY
28/03/2022
03118059-0003